Give your students choices.

Pearson's History titles are available in numerous formats to give you and your students more choices.

CourseSmart eTextbooks

offer the same content as the printed text in a convenient online format—with highlighting, online search, and printing capabilities. *60% off the list price of the traditional book.* www.coursesmart.com

MyHistoryLab is a dynamic website that provides a wealth of resources geared to meet the specific teaching and learning needs of every instructor and student. **MyHistoryLab** includes an interactive eText—identical in content and design to the printed text—so students have access to their text wherever and whenever they need it. It also features unabridged audio files of the entire text, which enable students to learn and review in a new way. **MyHistoryLab** may be packaged with a printed text for no additional charge or purchased as a standalone eText. *35% off the net price of the traditional book.* www.myhistorylab.com

Books à la Carte editions

feature the exact same text in a convenient, three-hole-punched, loose-leaf version at a discounted price—allowing students to take only what they need to class. **Books à la Carte editions** are available both with and without access to **MyHistoryLab**. *35% off the net price of the traditional book.*

The Pearson Custom Library lets you create a

textbook that meets the specific needs of your course. Combine chapters from several best-selling Pearson textbooks and/or topical reading units in the sequence you want. www.pearsonlearningsolutions.com

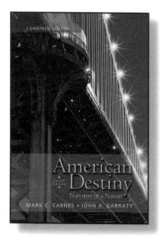

American Destiny
Fourth Edition

©2012

Mark C. Carnes
John A. Garraty

CourseSmart eText
❏ Volume 1: 9780205004348
❏ Volume 2: 9780205004331

New MyHistoryLab with eText access card
❏ Combined Volume: 9780205014026
❏ Volume 1: 9780205014095
❏ Volume 2: 9780205021376

Traditional printed text plus New MyHistoryLab
❏ Combined Volume: 9780205216550
❏ Volume 1: 9780205216536
❏ Volume 2: 9780205216543

Traditional printed text
❏ Combined Volume: 9780205790418
❏ Volume 1: 9780205790395
❏ Volume 2: 9780205790401

Pearson Custom Library
Available Now

For more information, please visit
www.pearsonhighered.com/gomakehistory

20TH CENTURY U.S. HISTORY (1945–PRESENT)

Brands America Since 1945 *
©2011, 9780205568482 / 0205568483
(Penguin Academic Series)

Opdycke Jane Addams and Her Vision of America *
©2012, 9780205598403 / 0205598404
(Part of the Library of American Biography Series) 20th Century U.S. History (1945–present)

COLONIAL AMERICAN HISTORY (1492–1776)

Kicza & Horn Resilient Cultures, 2/e
©2012, 9780205693580 / 020569358X

HISTORY OF AFRICAN AMERICANS

Carson, Lapsansky-Werner & Nash
TheStruggle for Freedom: A History of African Americans, 2/e,
Combined Volume
©2011, 9780205832408 / 0205832407
Also available in Volumes I & II
(Penguin Academic Series)

Hine, Hine & Harrold
The African-American Odyssey, 5/e,
Combined Volume
©2011, 9780205728817 / 0205728812
Also available in Volumes I & II

Hine, Hine & Harrold
The African-American Odyssey, 4/e,
Combined Volume *
©2012, 9780205806270 / 0205806279
Also available in Volumes I & II

HISTORY OF NATIVE AMERICANS

Nicholas Sources in the Native American Past, Combined Volume *
©2012, 9780205742516 / 0205742513
Also available in Volumes I & II

Townsend & Nicholas First Americans: A History of Native Peoples
©2012, 9780132069489 / 0132069482
Also available in Volumes I & II

HISTORY OF WOMEN IN AMERICA

Skinner Women and the National Experience: Sources in American History, 3/e, Combined Volume
©2011, 9780205743155 / 0205743153
Also available in Volumes I & II

U.S. HISTORY SURVEY

Primary Source Readers
Gorn, Roberts & Bilhartz Constructing the American Past: A Source Book of a People's History, 7/e
©2011, Vol. I: 9780205773640 / 0205773648
Vol. II: 9780205773633 / 020577363X

Merrell & Podair American Conversations *
©2012, Vol. I: 9780132446839 / 0132446839
Vol. II: 9780131582613 / 0131582615

Secondary Source Readers
Youngs American Realities, 8/e
©2011, Vol. I: 9780205764129 / 0205764126
Vol. II: 9780205764136 / 0205764134

THE VIETNAM WAR

Hearden The Tragedy of Vietnam, 4/e
©2012, 9780205744275 / 0205744273

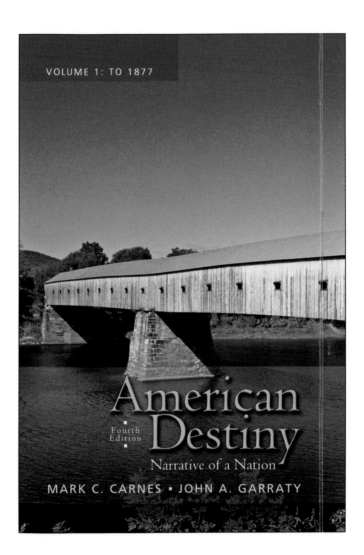

VOLUME 1: TO 1877

Americ̣an
Destiny

Fourth
Edition

Narrative of a Nation

MARK C. CARNES · JOHN A. GARRATY

To order, please request
Volume 1: Chapters 1-15
ISBN-10: 0-205-79039-9 | ISBN-13: 978-0-205-79039-5

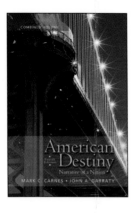

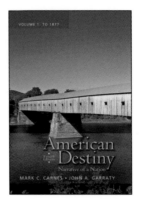

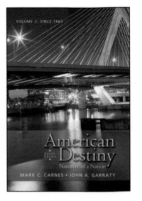

COMBINED EDITION
Chapters 1-32
ISBN-10: 0-205-79041-0
ISBN-13: 978-0-205-79041-8

VOLUME 1: TO 1877
Chapters 1-15
ISBN-10: 0-205-79039-9
ISBN-13: 978-0-205-79039-5

VOLUME 2: SINCE 1865
Chapters 15-32
ISBN-10: 0-205-79040-2
ISBN-13: 978-0-205-79040-1

Why Do You Need This New Edition?

Six good reasons why you should buy this new Fourth Edition of *American Destiny*!

1. This edition is tied more closely than ever to the innovative website, MyHistoryLab, which helps you save time and improve results as you study history (www.myhistorylab.com). MyHistoryLab icons now appear throughout the textbook, connecting the main narrative of each chapter to a powerful array of MyHistoryLab resources, including primary source documents, analytical video segments, interactive maps, and more. Also tied to each chapter of the textbook, a powerful and personalized Study Plan is available on MyHistoryLab that will help you build a deeper and more critical understanding of the subject.

2. The new edition strengthens the guiding principle of the textbook—to survey American history in a way that bridges the present and the past, showing the relevance of history to contemporary readers. For example, the essays that open each chapter connect a major topic of the chapter to experiences that pertain to many readers. For the Fourth Edition these essays are either entirely new or have been thoroughly updated; nearly all pertain to events or developments since 2008.

3. Other elements designed to bridge the present and the past, such as the *American Lives* and *Re-Viewing the Past* essays, have also been thoroughly revised. Most of these essays are entirely new to the Fourth Edition.

4. The maps and graphs in this book have been completely reworked to convey new ideas and to enhance comprehension. Many entirely new maps have been created to illuminate important themes, including a stronger global emphasis.

5. Each chapter has been revised to reflect new scholarship, to offer important new perspectives, and to streamline and sharpen the writing. For instance, the Prologue and first few chapters reflect new insights concerning the "pre-historic" period. These chapters also feature a more detailed comparison of the civilizations of the Americas with those of the "Old World"—Europe, Africa, and Asia. An almost entirely new chapter, "From Boomers to Millennials" (Chapter 31), draws an explicit comparison between the social and cultural foundations of young modern Americans and their parents; it especially explores the culture of consumption and the impact of the Internet.

6. To facilitate study and review, each chapter now ends with a set of review questions, and a list of key terms that are defined in a new glossary.

PEARSON

AMERICAN DESTINY
NARRATIVE OF A NATION

FOURTH EDITION

MARK C. CARNES
Ann Whitney Olin Professor of History
Barnard College, Columbia University

JOHN A. GARRATY
Gouverneur Morris Professor of History, Emeritus
Columbia University

PEARSON

Boston Columbus Indianapolis New York San Francisco Upper Saddle River
Amsterdam Cape Town Dubai London Madrid Milan Munich Paris Montréal Toronto
Delhi Mexico City São Paulo Sydney Hong Kong Seoul Singapore Taipei Tokyo

Editorial Director: Craig Campanella
Editor in Chief: Dickson Musslewhite
Executive Editor: Ed Parsons
Editorial Assistants: Alex Rabinowitz,
   Emily Tamburri
Director of Marketing: Brandy Dawson
Senior Marketing Manager: Maureen E. Prado
   Roberts
Marketing Assistant: Samantha Bennett
Senior Managing Editor: Ann Marie McCarthy
Senior Project Manager: Debra A. Wechsler
AV Project Manager: Mirella Signoretto
Operations Specialist: Christina Amato
Senior Art Director: Maria Lange

Text Designer: GEX Publishing Services
Cover Designer: Art-Tronic Design
Cover Art: Manhattan Bridge, Night. © 2010
   Adam Garelick/Getty Images
Director of Media and Assessment: Brian Hyland
Media Editor: Andrea Messineo
Media Project Manager: Tina Rudowski
Full-Service Project Management: GEX Publishing
   Services
Composition: GEX Publishing Services
Printer/Binder: Courier/Kendallville
Cover Printer: Lehigh-Phoenix Color /
   Hagerstown
Text Font: 10/12 Minion Pro

Credits and acknowledgments borrowed from other sources and reproduced, with permission, in this textbook appear on appropriate page within text (or starting on page C-1).

Library of Congress Cataloging-in-Publication Data
Carnes, Mark C. (Mark Christopher), 1950-
   American destiny : narrative of a nation / Mark C. Carnes, John A. Garraty. — 4th ed.
      p. cm.
   Includes bibliographical references and index.
   ISBN-13: 978-0-205-79041-8
   ISBN-10: 0-205-79041-0
   ISBN-13: 978-0-205-79039-5 (v. 1)
   ISBN-10: 0-205-79039-9 (v. 1)
   [etc.]
   1. United States—History. I. Garraty, John A. (John Arthur), 1920-2007. II. Title.

E178.6.C33 2012
973—dc22
                              2011015068
10 9 8 7 6 5 4 3 2 1

Combined Volume
ISBN 10: 0-205-79041-0
ISBN 13: 978-0-205-79041-8
Examination Copy
ISBN 10: 0-205-00149-1
ISBN 13: 978-0-205-00149-1
Volume 1
ISBN 10: 0-205-79039-9
ISBN 13: 978-0-205-79039-5
Volume 2
ISBN 10: 0-205-79040-2
ISBN 13: 978-0-205-79040-1

PROLOGUE   Beginnings 1

CHAPTER 1   Alien Encounters: Europe in the Americas 14

CHAPTER 2   American Society in the Making 48

CHAPTER 3   America in the British Empire 79

Maps and Graphs

GRAPHS   PAGE

Features

Preface

"A New American Destiny begins"—so trumpeted a liberal newspaper after the election of Barack Obama as president in 2008. Shortly after his inauguration a conservative newsletter asked, "What is Barack Obama making of our American destiny?" Its reply was brusque: "a hash."

Despite their divergent views on the merits of the new president, both publications assumed that the United States **had** a "destiny." The term "destiny" refers to an inevitable course of events. The liberal newspaper believed that the United States was predestined to embrace diversity while the conservative paper regarded the nation as foreordained to promote traditional religious values. Some contend, by contrast, that history moves in no preset direction.

This book takes no stand on these issues. But it does agree that Americans have long **assumed** a national destiny, such as John Louis O'Sullivan's 1845 editorial proclaiming it "our manifest destiny" for Americans to spread throughout North America; or Daniel Webster's terse repudiation of the looming sectional crisis: "One country, one constitution, one destiny"; or Walt Whitman's celebration, after that crisis had erupted in civil war, of "one common indivisible destiny for ALL"; or Franklin D. Roosevelt's reference during the Great Depression to his generation's "rendezvous with destiny"; or the letter from a Birmingham jail by African American leader Martin Luther King, Jr. in which he declared that "our destiny is tied up with America's destiny."

But if Americans have commonly accepted the concept of a national purpose, they have endlessly debated where the nation was headed and the nature of the force impelling it there. Some have discerned the hand of God lifting the nation up—or perhaps hurling it down. Others have claimed that the nation's destiny was dictated by accident of geography or economics, by the "laws" of social evolution or the "spirit" of democratic liberalism, by the "patterns" of demography or "processes" of modernity, and so on.

This book maintains that no single model explains the complexity of American history. Because historians are poor prophets, we make no attempt to peer into the future. For us, the concept of an American destiny refers to a vague notion that has long exerted a hold on the American imagination.

The subtitle—"Narrative of a Nation"—may also strike readers as provocative. Some contend that the diverse peoples of the United States cannot be encompassed within the analytical boundaries of a single nation. Thus we have not attempted to write a history of "the American people": No book can possibly do justice to all its infinite variations of identity—racial, gender-related, and cultural. Rather, we describe how the voices and actions of its many peoples have produced a particular political structure—the United States—and how that nation has influenced the lives of everyone.

"Relevant History"

This narrative seeks to speak directly to students. Each of the features serves to connect past and present, a bridge to help students relate the people and events of history to their own lives.

Chapter Openers

To that end, every chapter opens with questions that pertain to many readers: Chapter 6—on Jeffersonian Democracy—begins: "Do you have too much debt?" The essay that follows examines the problem of credit card debt among college students today and shows how similar concerns occupied Jefferson and his followers. Chapter 18, on society and culture during the late nineteenth century, opens with: "Have you ever been kicked out of a mall?" The succeeding paragraphs show how much more of our lives are played out in public spaces compared to a century ago. Such questions bridge present and past; they connect our lives to those of our forebears.

Re-Viewing the Past

Because movies on historical themes often figure prominently in how we think about the past, ten of the chapters include *Re-Viewing the Past* essays, which contrast Hollywood's rendering of history with what really happened. The selected movies range from those with obvious "historical" themes, such as *The Alamo* and *Saving Private Ryan*, to popular movies whose historical themes are less well known, such as *Chicago*, a musical based on the actual story of women who murdered their lovers.

American Lives

Ten of the chapters include *American Lives* essays, ranging from Sojourner Truth, a slave who became a preacher and reformer, to contemporary figures such as Bill Gates and Barack Obama. These essays focus on the young adulthood of such figures; we hope that readers of the same age will in this way find it easier to relate to them.

New to This Edition

- Each chapter has been revised to reflect new scholarship, offer new perspectives, and streamline and sharpen the prose. An almost entirely new chapter, "From Boomers to Millennials" (Chapter 31), draws an explicit comparison between the social and cultural foundations of young modern Americans and their parents; it especially explores the culture of consumption and the impact of the Internet.
- The essays that introduce each chapter are either entirely new or have been updated; nearly all pertain to events or developments since 2008.
- The Prologue and first few chapters reflect new insights unearthed (literally) by archaeologists and anthropologists concerning the "pre-historic" period. These chapters also feature a more detailed comparison of the civilizations of the Americas with those of the "Old World"—Europe, Africa, and Asia.
- This edition includes several new *American Lives*: Davy Crockett—perhaps the first person who became famous for being famous; Charlotte Perkins Gilman, a visionary who perceived that women's legal and political emancipation was largely dependent on their gaining paid work; civil rights leader Martin Luther King, Jr.; Barack Obama, the first African American to be elected president; and three randomly selected heroes who were killed in the recent wars in Afghanistan and Iraq.

- This edition also includes three new *Re-Viewing the Past* essays. *Black Robe* thoughtfully explores the interaction of Indians and colonists in the seventeenth century. Two versions of *The Alamo*: The first, released in 1960, stars John Wayne; the second (2004) tells a different story with Billy Bob Thornton as Davy Crockett. The widely acclaimed *There Will Be Blood* presents Daniel Day Lewis's searing performance as an unscrupulous wildcatting oilman loosely based on the life of Edward Doheny, who opened up the major oil fields of California and Mexico early in the twentieth century.

- The maps in this book have been completely reworked to convey new ideas and to enhance comprehension.

- Nearly every chapter now includes at least one "conceptual" table illuminating key themes and topics.

- To encourage and facilitate study and review, each chapter now ends with a set of review questions, and a list of key terms that are defined in a new glossary.

Supplements for
Instructors and Students

Supplements for Qualified College Adopters	Supplements for Students
MyHistoryLab **MyHistoryLab** (www.myhistorylab.com) **Save Time. Improve Results.** MyHistoryLab is a dynamic website that provides a wealth of resources geared to meet the diverse teaching and learning needs of today's instructors and students. MyHistoryLab's many accessible tools will encourage students to read their text and help them improve their grade in their course.	MyHistoryLab **MyHistoryLab** (www.myhistorylab.com) **Save Time. Improve Results.** MyHistoryLab is a dynamic website that provides a wealth of resources geared to meet the diverse teaching and learning needs of today's instructors and students. MyHistoryLab's many accessible tools will encourage you to read your text and help you improve your grade in your course.
Instructor's Resource Manual with Test Bank Available at the Instructor's Resource Center, at **www.pearsonhighered.com/irc**, the Instructor's Resource Manual with Test Bank contains chapter outlines, summaries, key points and vital concepts, and information on audio-visual resources that can be used in developing and preparing lecture presentations. The Test Bank includes multiple-choice questions and essay questions and is text-specific.	**CourseSmart www.coursesmart.com** CourseSmart eTextbooks offer the same content as the printed text in a convenient online format—with highlighting, online search, and printing capabilities. You **save 60% over the list price** of the traditional book.
PowerPoint Presentation Available at the Instructor's Resource Center, at **www.pearsonhighered.com/irc**, the PowerPoints contain chapter outlines and full-color images of maps and art. They are text-specific and available for download.	**Library of American Biography Series** www.pearsonhighered.com/educator/series/Library-of-American-Biography/10493.page Pearson's renowned series of biographies spotlighting figures who had a significant impact on American history. Included in the series are Edmund Morgan's *The Puritan Dilemma: The Story of John Winthrop*, B. Davis Edmund's *Tecumseh and the Quest for Indian Leadership*, J. William T. Young's *Eleanor Roosevelt: A Personal and Public Life*, John R. M. Wilson's *Jackie Robinson and the American Dilemma*, and Sandra Opdycke's *Jane Addams and Her Vision For America*.
MyTest Available at **www.pearsonmytest.com,** MyTest is a powerful assessment generation program that helps instructors easily create and print quizzes and exams. Questions and tests can be authored online, allowing instructors ultimate flexibility and the ability to efficiently manage assessments anytime, anywhere! Instructors can easily access existing questions and edit, create, and store using simple drag-and-drop and Word-like controls.	**Penguin Valuepacks** www.pearsonhighered.com/penguin A variety of Penguin-Putnam texts is available at discounted prices when bundled with *The American Nation, 14/e*. Texts include Benjamin Franklin's *Autobiography and Other Writings*, Nathaniel Hawthorne's *The Scarlet Letter*, Thomas Jefferson's *Notes on the State of Virginia*, and George Orwell's *1984*.

Supplements for Qualified College Adopters	Supplements for Students
Retreiving the American Past Available through the Pearson Custom Library (**www.pearsoncustom.com, keyword search | rtap**), the *Retrieving the American Past* (RTAP) program lets you create a textbook or reader that meets your needs and the needs of your course. RTAP gives you the freedom and flexibility to add chapters from several best-selling Pearson textbooks, in addition to *The American Nation, 14/e,* and/or 100 topical reading units written by the History Department of The Ohio State University, all under one cover. Choose the content you want to teach in depth, in the sequence you want, at the price you want your students to pay.	**A Short Guide to Writing About History, 7/e** Written by Richard Marius, late of Harvard University, and Melvin E. Page, East Tennessee State University, this engaging and practical text helps students get beyond merely compiling dates and facts. Covering both brief essays and the documented resource paper, the text explores the writing and researching processes, identifies different modes of historical writing, including argument, and concludes with guidelines for improving style. **ISBN-10: 0205673708; ISBN-13: 9780205673704**
	Longman American History Atlas This full-color historical atlas designed especially for college students is a valuable reference tool and visual guide to American history. This atlas includes maps covering the scope of American history from the lives of the Native Americans to the 1990s. Produced by a renowned cartographic firm and a team of respected historians, the *Longman American History Atlas* will enhance any American history survey course. **ISBN: 0321004868; ISBN-13: 9780321004864**
	Study Card for American History This timeline of major events in American social, political, and cultural history distills course information to the basics, helping you quickly master the fundamentals and prepare for exams. **ISBN: 0321292324; ISBN-13: 9780321292322**

MyHistoryLab

The Moment You Know

Educators know it. Students know it. It's that inspired moment when something that was difficult to understand suddenly makes perfect sense. MyHistoryLab has been designed and refined with a single purpose in mind: to help history teachers create that moment of understanding with their students.

Features of MyHistoryLab

MyHistoryLab provides **engaging experiences** that personalize, stimulate, and measure learning for each student.

- *Closer Look tours*—walk students through a variety of images, maps, and primary sources in detail, helping them to uncover their meaning and understand their context.
- **A History Bookshelf**—enables students to read, download, or print up to 100 of the most commonly assigned history works, like Thomas Paine's, *Common Sense*, Booker T. Washington's, *Up From Slavery*, and Andrew Carnegie's *Autobiography*.
- The **Pearson eText**—lets students access their textbook anytime, anywhere, and any way they want—including listening online or downloading to their iPad.
- A **personalized study plan** for each student, based on a chapter Pre-Test, arranges content from less complex thinking—like remembering basic facts—to more complex critical thinking—like understanding connections and analyzing the past. This layered approach promotes better critical-thinking skills, and helps students succeed in the course and beyond.
- **Assessment** tied to every chapter enables both instructors and students to track progress and get immediate feedback. With results flowing into a powerful gradebook, the assessment program helps instructors identify student challenges early—and find the best resources with which to help students.
- An **assignment calendar** allows instructors to assign graded activities, with specific deadlines, and measure student progress.
- *ClassPrep* collects the very best class presentation resources in one convenient online destination, so instructors can keep students engaged throughout every class.
- **Audio Files**—Full audio of the entire text is included to suit the varied learning styles of today's students. In addition there are audio clips of speeches, readings, and music that provide another engaging way to experience history.
- **Text and Visual Documents**—Over 1,500 primary source documents, images, and maps are available organized by chapter in the text. Primary source documents are also available in the MyHistoryLibrary and can be searched by author, title, theme, and topic. Many of these documents include critical thinking questions.
- **Lecture and Archival Videos**—Lectures by leading scholars on provocative topics give students a critical look at key points in history. Videos of speeches, news footage,

key historical events, and other archival video take students back to the moment in history.

- **MySearchLab**—This website provides students access to a number of reliable sources for online research, as well as clear guidance on the research and writing process.
- **Gradebook**—Students can follow their own progress and instructors can monitor the work of the entire class. Automated grading of quizzes and assignments helps both instructors and students save time and monitor their results throughout the course.

NEW In-text References to MyHistoryLab Resources

Read, View, See, Watch, Hear, Study, and Review Icons integrated in the text connect resources on MyHistoryLab to specific topics within the chapters. The icons are not exhaustive; many more resources are available than those highlighted in the book, but the icons draw attention to some of the most high-interest resources available on MyHistoryLab.

Read the Document

Points students to primary and secondary source documents related to the chapter.

View the Image

Identifies primary and secondary source images, including photographs, fine art, and artifacts to provide students with a visual perspective on history.

See the Map

Directs students to atlas and interactive maps; these present both broad overviews and detailed examinations of historical developments.

Watch the Video

Notes pertinent archival videos and videos of Pearson History authors that probe various topics.

Hear the Audio

Marks audio clips from historically significant songs and speeches that enrich students' engagement with history.

Study and Review

Alerts students to study resources for each chapter of the textbook available online through www.myhistorylab.com. These resources include practice tests and flashcards.

Acknowledgments

I THANK THE MANY FRIENDS, colleagues, and students who have helped me in writing this edition of *American Destiny*. My debt to John A. Garraty—teacher, colleague, co-author—warrants many paragraphs of acknowledgment. But his scorn for wordiness obliges me to acknowledge that he taught me the art of writing.

Mary Elin Korchinsky has lived this book (and nearly everything else) with me. My journey with her is a joy. For this edition, our particular challenge has been to relate the American nation's past to college students today. Much of the creativity in the chapters that follow—"Do you vote for *American Idol*?" "Do you illegally download?" "Do you space out during political debates?"—was a product of her special genius.

I especially thank E. Ward Smith for guidance through the murky depths of modern banking and finance. And I thank Prakhar Sharma for similarly leading me through the shrouded landscape of contemporary Iraq and Afghanistan.

Modern publishing, too, is a world of labyrinthine complexity. I thank the expert team at Pearson for sharing their mastery of its many arcane and demanding arts: Yolanda de Rooy, Roberta Meyer, Craig Campanella, Ed Parsons, Debra Wechsler, Mirella Signoretto, Maria Lange, Marisa Taylor, Brandy Dawson, Maureen Prado Roberts, and Alex Rabinowitz. Although they left me plenty of thread to find my way out, they also showed good sense in sometimes getting behind me and pushing. For that, and everything else, I am grateful.

I also thank:

Armando C. Alonzo, Texas A & M University
Andrew Bagley, Phillips Community College
Mary E. Barnes, Blinn College
Mack Bean, Blinn College
Thomas Born, Blinn College
Robert Brooks, Tyler Junior College
Dale Carnagey, Blinn College
Carrie Coston, Blinn College
Shannon Cross, Tyler Junior College
Alan Harazin, Holyoke Community College
Billy Hathorn, Laredo Community College
Peter Jones, Tyler Junior College
Gene Kirkpatrick, Tyler Junior College
Martha Kline, Blinn College
Alan Lehman, Blinn College
Jan McCauley, Tyler Junior College

Nora McMillan, San Antonio College
Horacio Salinas, Jr., Laredo Community College
Malcolum Saunders, University of the South Pacific
Kenneth McCullough, Blinn College
Dennis M. Nilsen, Molloy College
Jeff Owens, Tyler Junior College
Kahne Parsons, Tyler Junior College
Madeleine Ross, Tyler Junior College
James R. Sisson, Central Texas College
Herbert Sloan, Barnard College
Isaac Solis, Navarro College
Brian Steele, University of Alabama at Birmingham
Tracy Teslow, University of Cincinnati
Hubert P. van Tuyll, Augusta State University
Larry Watson, Blinn College
Stan Watson, Tyler Junior College
Don Whatley, Blinn College
Geoffrey Willbanks, Tyler Junior College

I thank the families of the American heroes, featured in Chapter 32, for sharing the stories of their children who served and died in the wars in Afghanistan and Iraq.

My daughter, Stephanie, read the book carefully and critically, and her comments have proven invaluable. My goal of connecting with younger readers was surely influenced by her own immense capacity for sharing love with her parents. This book is dedicated to her—in acknowledgment of that special gift and so many others.

Mark C. Carnes

Barnard College, Columbia University

About the Authors

MARK C. CARNES received his undergraduate degree from Harvard and his PhD in history from Columbia University. He has chaired both the history and American studies departments at Barnard College, Columbia University, where he serves as the Ann Whitney Olin Professor of History. Carnes and Garraty were General Editors of the 26-volume *American National Biography*, for which they were awarded the Waldo Leland Prize of the American Historical Association. Carnes has published numerous books on American social and cultural history, including *Secret Ritual and Manhood in Victorian America* (1989), *Past Imperfect: History According to the Movies* (1995), *Novel History: Historians and Novelists Confront America's Past* (2001), and *Invisible Giants: 50 Americans That Shaped the Nation but Missed the History Books* (2002). Carnes also pioneered the *Reacting to the Past* pedagogy, winner of the Theodore Hesburgh Award, sponsored by TIAA-CREF, as the outstanding pedagogical innovation in the nation (2004). In *Reacting to the Past*, college students play elaborate games, set in the past, their roles informed by classic texts. (For more on *Reacting*, see: www.barnard.edu/reacting.) In 2005 the American Historical Association named Carnes the recipient of the William Gilbert Prize for the best article on teaching history.

The late John A. Garraty, formerly Gouverneur Morris Professor Emeritus of History at Columbia University, received his PhD from Columbia University and an LHD from Michigan State University. He authored and edited scores of books, among them biographies of Silas Wright, Henry Cabot Lodge, Woodrow Wilson, George W. Perkins, and Theodore Roosevelt. Garraty's *The New Commonwealth*, included in the new *American Nation* series, challenged earlier dismissals of what was commonly known as "the Gilded Age." His *The Great Depression* argued that political leaders throughout the world happened upon "solutions" much like those proposed by Franklin D. Roosevelt. Garraty was co-General Editor with Mark Carnes of the *American National Biography*.

PROLOGUE: Beginnings

((•—[Hear the Audio Prologue at myhistorylab.com

Were ancient peoples different from you?

SOME 400 YEARS BEFORE COLUMBUS WAS BORN, INDIANS LIVING NEAR what is now Peebles, Ohio, built the Great Serpent Mound. The mound is shaped like a snake, tail coiled and mouth open—perhaps in the act of devouring an egg or spitting it out. Why the Indians built the mound remains a mystery, especially since the effigy is so huge—a quarter of a mile long—that it can only be identified as a snake from high in the sky.

Perhaps the snake functioned as a territorial marker, rather like the graffiti urban gangs use to scare rivals. Perhaps it was a religious symbol; snakes figured prominently in the beliefs of later Indians. Perhaps the serpent conveyed astronomical meanings: Its shape mirrors the constellation *Draco*; and on June 21st, the longest day of the year in the Northern Hemisphere, the snake's head points exactly at the spot where the sun sets. (Was the serpent gobbling up the sun?) Perhaps the mound is some type of memorial to the dead; skeletons dating from the period are found in nearby mounds.

Why begin a book on the American nation with a discussion of peoples who lived many generations before George Washington, especially when the historical record of their lives is so incomplete? The simplest answer is that the early peoples of the Americas proved peculiarly susceptible to a calamity none of them could have foreseen: the sudden appearance of strange, bellicose peoples. Possessing formidable weapons, riding terrifying animals, and endowed with an unfathomable power to wreak sickness and death on entire villages, these invaders swiftly seized much of the Western Hemisphere. The American nation was one product of these developments.

But first things first.

First Peoples

The first human beings emerged over 3 million years ago, probably in Africa. Some eventually devised stone tools, thus inaugurating the **Paleolithic revolution**, a life based on hunting and gathering nuts, berries, and edible plants. About 40,000 years ago human beings of a different sort—people similar to us in their aptitude for tools and language—appeared in Africa, Europe, and Asia displacing those humans who had preceded them.

1

The earth was colder than it is now, and the northward advance of these Eurasian hunters was halted by immense sheets of ice, some as broad as Australia and over 10,000-feet thick—the height of ten Empire State buildings. These ice slabs, which had been expanding for tens of thousands of years, gouged deep holes in the earth's crust.

Paleolitic hunters in Asia pushed deeper into the arctic tundra, pursuing big game—especially woolly mammoths. Weighing nearly 16,000 pounds, about as much as a large elephant, a single mammoth provided enough meat to feed two dozen hunters nearly all winter. Its fur could be worn as clothing and its fat could be burned for heat. Its bones, when stretched with fur, functioned as simple tents. A woolly mammoth was a kind of movable mall, and Paleolithic hunters regarded it with the avidity of shoppers at a clearance sale.

Some Paleolithic hunters eventually crossed into what is now Alaska. What occurred next is a matter of conjecture. Eventually these Paleo-Indians, moving south, happened upon lush grasslands, on which grazed vast herds of large mammals: mammoths and equally enormous mastodons, with massive legs and stout feet; giant beavers the size of bears; 20-foot-long ground sloths weighing over 6,000 pounds; strange monsters such as glyptodonts, which resembled armadillos but weighed over a ton; and also countless camels, horses, cheetahs, caribou, and deer.

The Demise of the Big Mammals

Loosed upon herds of unwary animals, Paleo-Indians (hereafter, simply Indians) slaughtered them or stampeded them over cliffs. They chiseled long stone blades especially designed to penetrate thick hides. Archaeologists have named these hunters after their ingenious blades, first found at Clovis, New Mexico. Archaeologists have found Clovis blades in nearly every state of the United States and even at the southern tip of South America.

View the Image

Clovis Points at **myhistorylab.com**

But around 12,000 years ago, the big mammals were disappearing from the Western Hemisphere. Thirty-three species became extinct, including mammoths, mastodons, saber-toothed cats, giant beavers, horses, and camels. Perhaps the hunters killed off the big mammals; or perhaps the heavily furred animals were ill-suited to a warming trend.

The disappearance of these mammals nearly coincided with the closing of the route from Beringia to the Americas, as melting ice worldwide raised ocean levels hundreds of feet, flooding the low-lying land that had joined Asia and Alaska. No more big mammals could make their way into the Americas.

These two factors profoundly influenced the course of human development in the Americas: The absence of big mammals deprived Indian peoples of ready sources of food and draft animals, and the geographical isolation of the Americas meant that the Indians would not be exposed to the waves of biological diversity—plants, animals, bacteria, and viruses—that repeatedly washed over Europe, Asia, and Africa.

The Archaic Period: Surviving without Big Mammals

With the big mammals gone, Indians struggled to find alternative sources of food. Prolonged droughts or severe winters resulted in starvation. North of Mexico, in what is now the United States, population likely remained stagnant: The garbage pits

A woolly mammoth consumed about 400 pounds of grass a day. This mammoth skeleton is thirteen feet high.

from archaeological sites show that diets lacked sufficient fats and proteins to promote fertility.

But over time, these Indians—termed Archaic—adapted to conditions of scarcity. They migrated according to a seasonal schedule, often returning to the same campsites year after year. In woodland areas east of the Mississippi River, they learned to hunt small animals, like rabbits and beaver, that had previously not been worth the bother; or they learned to find stealthy animals like bear and caribou or to sneak up on skittish ones like elk and deer. On the Great Plains, Indians thrived on bison, among the few large mammals that had not become extinct.

Some Archaic peoples discovered rich habitats that could sustain them throughout the year. Indians living along the coast and rivers of the Pacific Northwest and Alaska found fish to be so plentiful that they could be scooped up in baskets. These people made nets and fishhooks. Eventually they built boats out of bark and animal skins. Those living along the New England coast discovered a seemingly inexhaustible supply of shellfish. But for even these people, survival was a full-time job: it takes 83,000 clams to provide as much fat as a single deer.

As tribes remained longer in one area, they began to regard it as their own. They built more substantial habitations, developed pottery to carry water and cook food, and buried the dead with distinctive rituals in special places, often marked with mounds.

One of the earliest sedentary communities was located at what is now Poverty Point, on the Mississippi River floodplains north of Delhi, Louisiana. It was founded 3,500 years ago. Poverty Point peoples filled countless grass baskets with earth and dumped them onto enormous mounds. One mound, shaped like an octagon, had six terraced levels on which were built some 400 to 600 houses. Another was more than 700 feet long and 70 feet high. Viewed from above, it resembled a hawk. In all, the mounds consisted of over a million cubic yards of dirt.

The enormity of their construction projects reveals much about Poverty Point peoples. They could not have diverted so much time and energy to construction if they were not proficient at acquiring food. Moreover, while most Archaic bands were egalitarian, with little differentiation in status, the social structure of Poverty Point was hierarchical. Leaders conceived the plans and directed the labor to build the earthworks.

After about a thousand years, Poverty Point was abandoned. No one knows why. Several hundred years later, scores of smaller mound communities, known as Adena, sprouted in the Ohio and Mississippi River valleys. The inhabitants of these communities were also hunters and foragers who cultivated plants in their spare time. The Adena communities lasted several hundred years.

Around 2200 BP, another cluster of mound builders, known as Hopewell, flourished in Ohio and Illinois. Hopewell mounds were often shaped into squares, circles, and cones; some, viewed from above, resembled birds or serpents. Around AD 400, the Hopewell sites were abandoned.

The impermanence of these communities serves as a reminder that the transition from a nomadic existence of hunting and foraging to a settled life based on agriculture was slow and uneven. For the Indians living north of the Rio Grande, this was about to change. For people living in what is now Central America, it already had.

The Maize Revolution

Maize did not exist 7,000 years ago. But around that time, perhaps far earlier, Indians in southern Mexico interbred various species of grasses, exploiting subtle changes and perhaps significant mutations. Eventually they created maize. A geneticist writing in *Science* in 2003 declared this to be "arguably man's first, and perhaps his greatest, feat of genetic engineering." The original ears were too small to provide much food, but within several thousand years farmers in Central America had developed maize that resembled modern corn.

The **Neolithic revolution**—the transition from hunting and gathering to farming—had come to Central America. Soon most valleys in central Mexico bristled with cornstalks. Population grew and cities emerged. By AD 100 Teotihuacan, forty miles north of what is now Mexico City, had a population approaching 100,000 and featured miles of paved streets and a pyramid as large as those of Egypt. Mesoamerica was approaching its classical period, which would culminate in the great corn-growing civilizations of the Mayans and Aztecs.[1]

Eventually corn cultivation leapfrogged the deserts of northern Mexico and was adopted by the Indians of the Southwest: the Hohokam and Mogollon of Arizona and New Mexico, and the Anasazi of the Colorado Plateau. Abandoning their nomadic life, these Indians settled near rivers, built trenches and canals to channel water to the crops, dammed gullies to capture runoff from flash floods, and constructed homes near the cornfields.

Their culture revolved around corn. Sun and water became the focus of their religious beliefs, symbols of life and rebirth. Priest-astronomers carefully observed changes of the seasons. If corn was planted too early, it might shrivel before the late summer

---

[1]Less relevant to the development of the peoples of North America was the remarkable potato-cultivating Incan civilization that took root in Peru and other highland regions of South America.

Some scientists believe that thousands of years ago Indian farmers genetically engineered the transformation of teosinte, a wild grass with tiny seeds (left), to evolve into maize.

A statue of a corn goddess of the Moche peoples of coastal Peru, around 400 BP. Within several centuries, corn would spread into North America.

rains; if planted too late, it might be destroyed by frost. Corn Mother symbolism, suggesting a relationship between the fertility of the earth and of women, dominated religious practices. Control of the corn surplus was a key to political power.

Despite the arid heat of the Southwest, the corn-cultivating peoples increased in number after AD 800. The Chaco Canyon, a twenty-two-mile-long gorge in western New Mexico, witnessed the development of a most improbable human habitat. The Anasazi carved entire villages into the sandstone and shale cliffs. As population increased, they built dozens of towns and villages that were linked by an elaborate system of roads. The largest of these cliff towns, Pueblo Bonito, had buildings more than five stories tall. The Hohokam constructed an irrigation canal system that spanned hundreds of miles and contained an intricate network of dams, sluices, and headgates. Snaketown, a Hohokam village near modern Phoenix, had a population of several thousand.

View the Image

Pueblo Bonito at **myhistorylab.com**

These communities were far less populous than those of their mightier neighbors to the south. But the triumph of the corn-growing Anasazi, Hohokam, and Mogollon is measured not by wealth and population figures, but by the magnitude of the environmental challenges they overcame.

The Diffusion of Corn

Corn cultivation spread east and north. By AD 200, cornfields dotted the southern Mississippi River valley. Thereafter, the advance of corn slowed. Farther north, early cold snaps killed existing varieties of the plant. Corn cultivation in forested regions required unremitting labor, and few Indians were eager to subject themselves to its incessant demands. Fields had to be cleared, usually by burning away the undergrowth. Then the soil was hoed using flat stones, clamshells, or the shoulder blades of large animals. After planting, the fields required constant weeding. Compared to the thrill of the hunt, the taste of game, and the varied tasks associated with hunting and gathering, farming held little appeal. Males regarded it as a subsidiary activity, a task best relegated to women.

But over time many Indians learned that the alternative to agricultural labor was starvation. Fields farther north and east were cleared and planted with corn, beans, and squash. Old skeletons provide a precise means of tracking corn's advance. When corn is chewed, enzymes in the mouth convert its carbohydrates to sugar, a major cause of dental cavities. Radiocarbon dating of skeletons from the vicinity of what is now St. Louis first shows dental cavities around AD 700 and those from southern Wisconsin, around AD 900. By AD 1000 dental cavities can be found in skeletons throughout the Midwest and the East. Corn had become king.

Population Growth after AD 800

Corn stimulated population growth. An acre of woodlands fed two or three hunters or foragers; that same acre, planted in corn, provided for as many as 200 people. Hunting and foraging Indians usually found enough to eat in summer and fall, but in winter, food sources might disappear. But dried corn, stored in glazed pots or sealed in underground pits, could sustain many people over a period. Corn cultivators may not have had a particularly nutritious diet, but they were more likely to survive a long, hard winter.

◉ See the Map

Pre-Columbian Societies of the Americas at **myhistorylab.com**

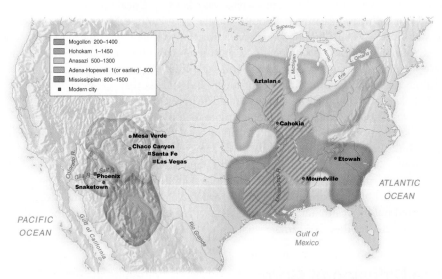

Major Indian Cultures, AD 1–1500 Thousands of Indian tribes existed in North America before 1500. Little is known about most of them, but five farming civilizations left a deep imprint on the historical record: the Mogollon and Hohokam of the desert Southwest; the Anasazi of the cliff regions and high plateaus farther north; the Adena–Hopewell mound builders of the Mississippi and Ohio valleys; and the Mississippian civilization, the successor of the Adena–Hopewell peoples, who inhabited much of what would eventually be the eastern United States. Each civilization mastered agriculture, ceramics, textiles, and metalworking, although each did so in different ways. Their surviving artifacts provide the clues to their distinctive cultures.

A sedentary lifestyle promoted population growth in other ways. Infants and toddlers were a nuisance on the trail; some hunting and foraging Indians practiced abortion or even infanticide to ensure mobility and reduce the number of mouths to feed. But farming Indians nearly always could make use of additional hands, even young ones, to help with plowing, hoeing, weeding, and harvesting. Because farmers rarely moved, they built more permanent homes and more successfully sheltered infants from inclement weather and physical dangers.

As in the Southwest, the corn-cultivating peoples of the Mississippi Valley responded to increasing population by clearing more woodland and planting more corn. At first, corn cultivators and hunting-foraging peoples successfully cohabited within the same ecosystem: Hunters traded for corn, essential for survival during winter, and corn cultivators traded for game, a source of complex protein. But over time the two groups often came into conflict, and when they did, the more numerous corn cultivators prevailed.

The corn-cultivating societies expanded west into Dakota, east through the Carolinas, south into Florida, and north into Wisconsin. Their villages consisted of clusters of homes, surrounded by cornfields. They shared a constellation of beliefs and ritual practices known as the Mississippian cultural complex. Like the Hopewell, they built burial mounds, but those of the corn cultivators were much larger. Some villages became towns and even small cities. Large temples and granaries and the homes of the governing elite were located on top of the mounds.

The most important and populous of these communities was located in the vicinity of St. Louis. Archaeologists call it Cahokia.

Cahokia: The Hub of Mississippian Culture

By AD 1000, Cahokia was a major center of trade, shops and crafts, and religious and political activities. It was the first true urban center in what is now the United States. By 1150, at the height of its development, it covered six square miles and had more than 15,000 inhabitants.

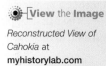

View the Image
Reconstructed View of Cahokia at **myhistorylab.com**

The earthworks at Cahokia included some twenty huge mounds around a downtown plaza, with another 100 large mounds in the outlying areas. The largest mound was 110 feet high, covered fourteen acres, and contained 20 million cubic yards of earth. It was probably the largest earthen structure in the Americas. Atop the mound was a fifty-foot-high wood-framed temple.

Cahokian society was characterized by sharp class divisions. The elite lived in larger homes and consumed a better and more varied diet (their garbage pits included bones from the best cuts of meat). The corpse of one chieftain was buried upon a bed of 20,000 beaded shells; nearby was a long piece of shaped copper from Lake Superior, several bushels of bird and animal sculptures made of mica, and over 1,000 arrows, many with beautiful quartz or obsidian points. Near the chieftain's bones were the skeletons of fifty women ranging from eighteen to twenty-three years old, likely sacrifices to the gods. Their bones were genetically different from the Cahokian skeletons, suggesting that the young women were captives in war or tribute sent by vassal states.

That the Cahokia had enemies is confirmed by the existence of a three-mile-long wooden palisade surrounding the central core of the city. It consisted of 20,000 enormous

An artist's rendering shows downtown Cahokia, around 1150 CE. Cahokia was surrounded by a palisade, made of enormous tree trunks (far left). On the great mounds within, the elite built homes and performed the ceremonial tasks of Mississippian culture. The open space in the center was probably filled with the stalls of craftspeople.

tree trunks, pounded deep into the ground, interspersed with several dozen watchtowers from which defenders could unloose arrows upon besiegers.

Cahokia dominated a region of several hundred miles. Smaller mound-building communities emerged throughout the eastern woodlands and the Southeast. Two of the largest were Moundville, Alabama, and Etowah, Georgia. Cahokia also established (or perhaps inspired) distant satellite communities. Around AD 800, Mississippian Indians moved into southern Wisconsin and built Aztalan (in what is now Jefferson County), with similar corn storage depots and large ceremonial mounds surrounding a central plaza.

Like Cahokia, Aztalan erected a massive tree-trunk palisade with watchtowers. Archaeologists have found burned and butchered body parts throughout the ruins, evidence of warfare. Some speculate that the corn-growing Mississippians encroached on the Oneota, a hunting and gathering people, and that the communities long remained hostile.

The Mississippian elites did more than supervise construction of their own massive earthen tombs. They also solved complicated problems of political and social organization.

The Collapse of Urban Centers

Yet Cahokia and Aztalan soon declined. By AD 1200, Cahokia's population had been reduced to several thousand people; by AD 1350, it was deserted. Etowah and Moundville went into decline somewhat later.

The major towns and villages of the Southwest civilizations faded as well. By AD 1200, the inhabitants of Chaco Canyon had vanished and nearly all of the pueblos of the Anasazi had been abandoned. Snaketown and dozens of towns of the Hohokam had become empty ruins, their canals choked with weeds.

What caused the collapse of these communities has long been a source of debate. Some scholars cite protracted droughts during the 1200s and 1300s. Others note that population growth harmed the environment. Slash-and-burn wood clearance thinned the eastern forests, and corn cultivation exhausted the soil. The palisade at Cahokia consisted of thousands of the trunks of fully grown trees, and it was repeatedly rebuilt. Denuded of big trees, the watershed around Cahokia became susceptible to erosion and flooding, further depleting exhausted topsoils.

Crop yields declined as the demand for food in towns and villages increased. Studies of human skeletons in Mississippian burial mounds show higher incidences of disease and malnutrition after AD 1250. What happened next is unclear. Some archaeologists believe that many Mississippian Indians abandoned the cities and villages and quietly reverted to the hunting and foraging life of their Archaic forebears. Others argue that the end was calamitous. Late Mississippian skeletons were smaller and more likely to show signs of disease; they also had more broken bones; often arms, feet, and hands were dismembered. Recurrent famines and disease may have undermined the credibility of elites and the cultural system they supervised, weakening their control of poor urban people as well as chieftains in the hinterlands. The towering log palisades of the Mississippians and the impenetrable cliff dwellings of the Anasazi were manifestations of this collective insecurity.

Warfare became endemic among the corn-growing tribes of the Northeast. By AD 1300, the Iroquoian peoples of New York and Pennsylvania were building forts with defensive earthworks and palisades. Some tribes joined together to form military alliances. Soil exhaustion, perhaps aggravated by the droughts that had parched the cornfields of the Southwest, may have forced tribes to compete for land and resources. Some scholars propose that gender tensions may have exacerbated these conflicts. Men performed most of the hunting and foraging tasks, while women did most of the work in the cornfields. As corn supplanted game and fish as staples of the diet, women acquired more status and power. To reassert male dominance, men embarked on raids and warfare.

By AD 1500, nearly all of the large towns had been abandoned. New generations of Indians puzzled over who had inhabited the ruins, or who had erected the massive earthen mounds. The Navajo Indian word for their predecessors—"Anasazi"—means the "Ancient Ones."

The collapse of the cities disrupted trade networks. Some goods continued to move many, many miles, being passed from one tribe to another; but the flow of trade goods slowed to a trickle. Moreover, if the rise of powerful urban communities had forced earlier groups to band together, the demise of the urban communities precipitated the breakup of large groups and tribes. Hundreds, perhaps thousands of small bands lived in relative isolation.

See the **Map**

Location of Major Indian Groups and Cultural Areas in the 1600s at **myhistorylab.com**

To them, the great Aztec city of Tenochtitlán, beyond the Mexican desert, was only a rumor. Of Europe, Africa, and Asia, they knew nothing. That was about to change.

Eurasia and Africa

If the Neolithic revolution had made but fitful progress north of Mexico by 1500, its advance through Eurasia and Africa was nearly complete. Wheat, first domesticated in Southwest Asia well over 10,000 years ago, spread through the Nile Valley and the Mediterranean and eastward to India and China. Rice, domesticated in China much later, diffused throughout Eurasia. These lead crops were followed by others—oats, peas, olives, grapes, almonds, barley, oranges, lentils, and millet. Several thousand years later, farmers in Africa domesticated sorghum, palm oil, and yams.

The animals of Eurasia were as diverse as its crops. While few large mammals in the Americas survived the Clovis era, the ancient peoples of Eurasia learned how to

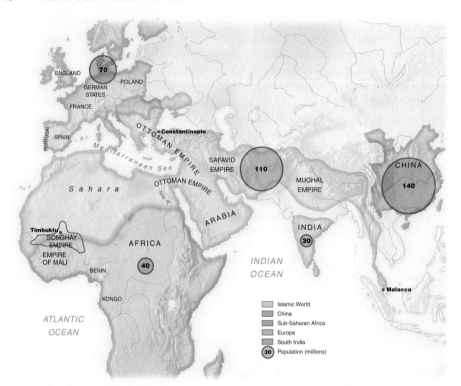

Population of Major Civilizations of Europe, Asia, and Africa, AD 1500 In 1500, most of the people of the "Old World"—Europe, Asia, and Africa—belonged to one of five major civilizations. Of these, the most populous was China under the Ming Dynasty, with about 140 million people, and then the Islamic world, with over 100 million. The fractious nations of western Europe, though less populous, had mastered formidable new technologies of warfare.

domesticate horses, pigs, cows, goats, sheep, and oxen. In addition to protein-rich meat, cows and goats provided milk and dairy products such as cheese that could be stored for winter; horses and oxen dragged trees and boulders from fields, pulled ploughs through tough sod, and contributed manure for fertilizer. Because of the diversity and nutritional value of its food sources, the Eurasian population increased rapidly.

To accommodate the growing demand for food, Eurasian farmers cut down forests, filled in marshlands, and terraced hillsides. Monarchs joined with merchants and bankers to build port facilities, canals, and fleets of ships to ensure the food supply to urban centers.

Cereal crops and animals dispersed throughout the vast Eurasian landmass, but so did new diseases. New strains of viruses and bacteria appeared in cows, pigs, goats, and sheep and readily spread to the humans who kept them. Diseases also proliferated in cities, whose sanitation facilities were poor. Recurrent plagues swept across Eurasia. But those who survived acquired biological resistance.

West Africa evolved differently. The grassy savannah just south of the Sahara became the home for mostly herding peoples. Cities emerged in response to the growth of trans-Sahara trade: Finished goods, including cloth from North Africa, were traded for gold, salt, kola (a caffeine rich nut), and slaves. Warlords command-ing horse-mounted troops vied for the control of the trade routes, and eventually

This depicts a scene of a city on the Yellow River in northern China around 1500. Chinese cities were generally cleaner, with better water supplies and sewage disposal, than their European counterparts.

founded the great kingdoms of Mali and Songhay. By AD 1500, Timbuktu had become a major city, home to an important Islamic university and library.

Seldom did pastoral and trading empires penetrate far into the tropical regions farther south. The religion of Islam, which had spread through the grasslands south of the Sahara, also made less progress among Africans on the tropical coast. There the tsetse fly, carrier of sleeping sickness, decimated horse and cattle herds. Malaria, too, discouraged potential invaders.

The village was the main unit of social organization of sub-Saharan Africa. Some villages merged into far-flung kinship networks and even small kingdoms, such as Benin and Congo. Relatively insulated from the imperial struggles farther north, these Africans mostly kept to themselves, growing crops and harvesting the lush vegetation of the forest. By 1500, the lives of these people, too, were about to change.

By 1500 China, with a population of 100–150 million people, had literally walled itself away from "barbarians" elsewhere in Asia; its own kingdom was effectively ruled by a highly-educated class of bureaucrats steeped in the principles of Confucianism. The Islamic world was nearly as populous, but stretched across three continents, ranging from the North Africa and eastern Europe through Arabia, Persia, and northern India with outposts in Southeast Asia. Unlike China, it was divided into many different empires.

Europe in Ferment

Christendom, the predominant civilization of Europe, was less consequential; its total population—perhaps 70 million—was far less than China or the Islamic World; its main cities and institutions of learning were less well-developed. But in 1500, Europe was in dynamic ferment. During the 1400s, after a period of severe plagues, Europe's population had increased by nearly a third; by 1500, population pressure was acute.

When harvests were poor or grain shipments failed to arrive in towns, hunger riots destabilized the political order. Genoa, Italy, for example, was convulsed by fourteen revolutions from 1413 to 1453. Overpopulation was one reason why Jews, a vulnerable minority, were expelled from Spain and Portugal in 1492, and from Sicily in 1493.

Scarcity shook many peasants from the land and drove the urban poor from one city to another. Christoforo Colombo—or Columbus, as we call him—was among the restless youths who left home and took to the sea in search of a better life.

New ideas also unsettled European society. Movable type, which made the printing of books profitable, was perfected during the 1440s. By 1500, over 100 cities in Europe had at least one printing press and as many as 20 million volumes had been published. Books advanced new ideas and weakened the hold of traditional ones. Within a few decades, the treatises of Martin Luther and John Calvin initiated the Protestant Reformation. Books also excited the imagination and gave tangible expression to all manner of dreams and longings. (Columbus's restless curiosity had been stimulated by books on geography and navigation, especially Marco Polo's account of his journey to China.)

Incessant squabbles over land resulted in nearly constant warfare. The military arts advanced accordingly. Improvements in metallurgy made it possible to cast bronze and iron cannon capable of containing charges of gunpowder sufficient to hurl heavy balls great distances. Mighty stone fortresses that had stood for centuries were reduced to rubble by these cannon in a few hours. By the early 1500s cannons weighing a ton or more were mounted in sailing ships or upon carriages pulled by teams of horses. Warfare of this nature was expensive; constructing fleets, equipping armies, and building massive fortifications required the resources of entire nations.

A restless hunger for land, a population made resistant to biological pathogens, an explosion in communication and knowledge, a new technology and organization of warfare, and the emergence of powerful and contentious nation-states all imparted a fateful dynamism to late fifteenth-century European society. Plainly, these Europeans had not solved pressing social problems: Population growth exceeded available food sources, poverty undermined political stability, and war loomed larger and more ominous.

Equally plainly, the people of North America had failed to solve basic social problems: Nomadic Indians who practiced a hunting-gathering lifestyle were vulnerable to starvation as well as to encroachments by the more numerous peoples of the corn-farming tribes. Farming Indians, on the other hand, found it difficult to sustain even small urban communities over a long period. The absence of writing systems made it more difficult to undertake complex administrative tasks over large distances. None of the Indians possessed military technologies comparable to the Europeans. And, more fatal still, the peoples of the Americas lacked the immunity from infectious diseases that so many Europeans had acquired.

Separating these worlds was the impenetrable void of the Atlantic Ocean. Five hundred years earlier a Norseman, Leif Eriksson, had sailed along the coast of Greenland to the shores of Labrador, but little came of his expeditions. But toward the close of the fifteenth century, European sailors of a different type, adept at navigating through the open sea and willing to sail far from land, were about to venture across the expanses of the Atlantic. In so doing they would transform it into a bridge that would join these worlds, and the West African coast as well, bringing all three into fateful collision.

Milestones

c. 14,000 BP (perhaps earlier)	Humans from Asia cross Beringia to Alaska	**c. 3700 BP**	First sedentary North American community is founded at today's Poverty Point, Louisiana
c. 14,000– 10,000 BP	Humans diffuse throughout Americas		
	Many species of large mammals become extinct in Western Hemisphere	**c. 300 BP**	Corn cultivation begins in the Southwest
		c. AD 200	Corn cultivation begins in the lower Mississippi Valley
	Clovis era ends	**c. AD 900**	Corn cultivation begins in Wisconsin
	Eurasians domesticate wheat	**c. AD 1150**	Cahokia is at its peak
c. 6300 BP	Mesoamerican peoples cultivate corn and initiate Neolithic revolution	**c. 1200s– 1300s**	Protracted droughts in North America disrupt food supply; urban areas are abandoned
c. 4500 BP	Peoples of midwestern North America domesticate sunflowers and sumpweed		

✓•⫿Study and **Review** at www.myhistorylab.com

Review Questions

1. How and when did the first peoples come to the Americas from Asia?
2. Why had most of the large mammals of the Americas become extinct by 8000 BP? Why *didn't* horses, cattle, camel, and other large mammals become extinct in Europe, Asia, and Africa?
3. Why does the onset of the Neolithic revolution—especially corn cultivation—result in the rapid increase of population in the Americas?
4. What explanations have been proposed to explain the pre-1500 collapse of the urban centers of the major Indian civilizations in what is now the United States?
5. In what ways did the major civilizations of the "Old World"—Europe, Asia, and Africa—differ from those of North America in AD 1500?

Key Terms

Neolithic
  revolution   *4*

Paleolithic
  revolution   *1*

1 Alien Encounters: Europe in the Americas

((•─[Hear the Audio Chapter 1 at myhistorylab.com

How do you rate your college's food?

SOME STUDENTS CHOOSE A COLLEGE FOR ITS FOOD, A REASON WHY the Princeton Review now publishes a "Best Campus Food" list. In 2008 Wheaton College topped the list after its food manager, who previously worked at the Ritz-Carlton in Boston, created menus with lavender-infused pork chops and cumin-lime chicken with avocado cream sauce. The next year Virginia Tech climbed over Wheaton, chiefly because of the freshness of its herbs and spices, grown by the school's horticulture department. In 2009 Sodexo, a food management company that tracks trends in student tastes, noted that college students craved spicy foods such as garlic-ginger chicken wings, Vietnamese pho (a peppery soup), green tea, pomegranate smoothies, crab cakes, and samosas. The lesson for college food services was simple: Make it spicy!

If students choose a college because of the tastiness of its fare, imagine how early modern Europeans (whose diet chiefly consisted of bread, porridge, boiled meats, and salted fish) reacted when they first tasted pepper, cinnamon, ginger, nutmeg, cloves, and other spicy foods from South Asia and the Pacific. Beyond titillating the palate, spices disguised the taste of spoiled meats in regions that had little ice. Europeans also prized such tropical foods as rice, figs, and oranges, as well as perfumes (often used as a substitute for soap), silk and cotton, rugs, textiles such as muslin and damask, dyestuffs, fine steel products, precious stones, and various drugs.

But the cost of transporting such goods from East Asia and the Pacific was exorbitant. The combined routes through central Asia were long and complicated—across strange seas, through deserts, over high mountain passes—with pirates or highwaymen as a constant threat. If the produce of eastern Asia could be carried to Europe by sea, the trip would be both cheaper and more comfortable. Christopher Columbus imagined that by sailing west, he would find an all-water route to the spicy riches of India and East Asia. By providing a cheap means of satisfying the European craving for spices, he would find a path to fame and fortune. He was half right.

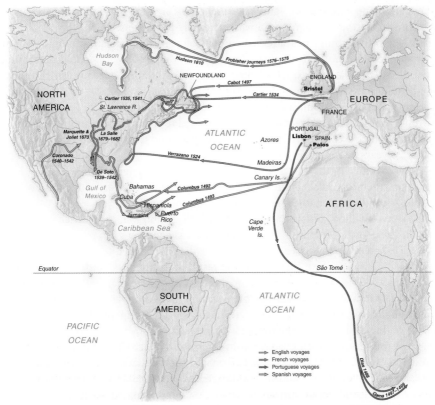

European Voyages of Discovery Before 1500, European sailors seldom ventured far across open water. They preferred to hug the coastline, like Vasco da Gama's journey around Africa in 1497–1499. Columbus's 1492 voyage across the Atlantic was extraordinarily daring. But his successful example inspired others to try alternative routes westward: Cabot, in 1497, sailed across the North Atlantic to Newfoundland; Verrazano, in 1524, sailed due west from the Azores to the Carolinas and the east coast of what is now the United States; Hudson, in 1610, took a far northern route, skirting the ice floes of the Arctic, and "discovered" Hudson Bay. Such men were the superstars of their age; and like superstars of all ages, they became free agents, selling their services to the highest bidder. Thus Columbus, an Italian, claimed Hispaniola for his employer, the Spanish monarchs; and Hudson, an Englishman, claimed the Hudson River for the Dutch East India Company.

Columbus's Great Triumph—and Error

Columbus was an intelligent and skillful mariner. Having read carefully Marco Polo's account of his adventures in the service of Kublai Khan, Columbus had decided that these rich lands could be reached by sailing directly west from Europe. The idea was not original, but while others merely talked about it, Columbus pursued it with dogged persistence.

For much of the fifteenth century, European sailors had been venturing far beyond familiar shores. The great figure in the transformation was Prince Henry the Navigator, third son of John I, king of Portugal. After distinguishing himself in 1415 in the capture of Ceuta, on the African side of the Strait of Gibraltar, he became interested

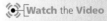

Watch the Video

So Why Did Columbus Sail Across the Atlantic Anyway? at **myhistorylab.com**

in navigation and exploration. Sailing a vessel out of sight of land was still, in Henry's day, more an art than a science and was extremely hazardous. Ships were small and clumsy. Primitive compasses and instruments for reckoning latitude existed, but under shipboard conditions they were very inaccurate. Navigators could determine longitude only by keeping track of direction and estimating speed; even the most skilled could place little faith in their estimates.

Henry attempted to improve and codify navigational knowledge. Searching for a new route to Asia, Henry's captains sailed westward to the Madeiras and the Canaries and south along the coast of Africa, seeking a way around that continent.

For 20 years after Henry's death in 1460, the Portuguese concentrated on exploiting his discoveries. In the 1480s King John II undertook systematic new explorations focused on reaching India. Gradually his caravels probed southward along the sweltering coast—to the equator, to the region of Angola, and beyond.

Into this bustling, prosperous, expectant little country in the corner of Europe came Christopher Columbus in 1476. Columbus was a weaver's son from Genoa, born in 1451. He had taken to the sea early, ranging widely in the Mediterranean. His arrival in Portugal was unplanned, since it was the result of losing his ship in a battle off the coast. For a time he worked as a chart maker in Lisbon. He married a local woman. Then he was again at sea. He cruised northward, perhaps as far as Iceland, south to the equator, and westward in the Atlantic to the Azores. Had his interest lain in that direction, he might well have been the first person to reach Asia by way of Africa.

But by this time Columbus had committed himself to reach China by sailing west into the Atlantic. How far west no one knew. Columbus believed that the earth's circumference was 18,000 miles. Because the known world stretched about 14,000 miles from the Canary Islands in the Atlantic Ocean eastward to Japan, Columbus assumed that he would have to sail west 4,000 miles across the Atlantic to reach Japan and the East Indies. A voyage of this length across open sea would be challenging but not impossible. There were doubters. Ancient Greek astronomers had estimated the earth's circumference at 24,000 miles. If they were right, a ship sailing from the Canary Islands westward across the Atlantic would have to travel 10,000 miles before reaching Asia, an impossibility because no ship of that time was large enough to carry sufficient provisions for such a voyage.

When King John II refused to finance him, Columbus turned to the Spanish court, where, after many disappointments, he persuaded Queen Isabella to equip his expedition. He also persuaded Isabella to grant him the title Admiral of the Ocean Sea, political control over all the lands he might discover, and 10 percent of the profits of the trade that would follow in the wake of his expedition. In August 1492 he set out from the port of Palos with his tiny fleet: the *Santa Maria*, the *Pinta*, and the *Niña*.

●●●ー Read the Document

The Journal of Christopher Columbus at
myhistorylab.com

At about two o'clock on the morning of October 12, 1492, a sailor named Roderigo de Triana saw a gleam of white on the moonlit horizon and shouted *"Tierra! Tierra!"* The land he had spied was an island in the West Indies called Guanahani by its inhabitants, a place distinguished neither for beauty nor size. Nevertheless, when Columbus went ashore bearing the flag of Spain, he named it San Salvador, or Holy Savior. Columbus selected this imposing name for the island out of gratitude and wonder at having found it: He had sailed with three frail vessels for thirty-three days without sighting land. According to his estimates, he was nearly on course, having traveled nearly 4,000 miles. But he was nowhere near Japan or China.

The ancient Greek astronomers were right and Columbus was wrong. He had greatly underestimated the size of the earth.

Now the combination of zeal and tenacity that had gotten Columbus across the Atlantic cost him dearly. He refused to accept the plain evidence, which everywhere confronted him, that this was an entirely new world. The copper-colored people who paddled out to inspect his fleet could no more follow the Arabic widely understood in Asia than they could Spanish. Yet Columbus, consulting his charts, convinced himself that he had reached the Indies. That is why he called the natives Indians, a misnomer that became nearly universal, and was increasingly used even by the native peoples themselves.

Searching for treasure, Columbus pushed on to Cuba. When he heard the native word *Cubanocan*, meaning "middle of Cuba," he mistook it for *El Gran Can* (Marco Polo's "Grand Khan") and sent emissaries on a fruitless search through the tropical jungle for the khan's palace. He finally returned to Spain relatively empty-handed, but certain that he had explored the edge of Asia. Three later voyages failed to shake his conviction.

Spain's American Empire

Columbus died in 1506. By that time other captains had taken up the work, most of them more willing than he to accept what Europeans called the New World on its own terms. As early as 1493, Pope Alexander VI had divided the non-Christian world between Spain and Portugal. The next year, in the **Treaty of Tordesillas**, these powers negotiated an agreement about exploiting the new discoveries. In effect, Portugal continued to concentrate on Africa, leaving the New World, except for what eventually became Brazil, to the Spanish. Thereafter, from their base on Hispaniola (Santo Domingo), founded by Columbus, the Spaniards quickly fanned out through the Caribbean and then over large parts of the two continents that bordered it.

Watch the **Video**

Achievement of Columbus at **myhistorylab.com**

In 1513 Vasco Nuñez de Balboa crossed the Isthmus of Panama and "discovered" the Pacific Ocean. In 1519 Hernán Cortés landed an army in Mexico and overran the empire of the Aztecs, rich in gold and silver. That same year Ferdinand Magellan set out on his epic three-year voyage around the world. By discovering the strait at the southern tip of South America that bears his name, he gave the Spanish a clear idea of the size of the continent. In the 1530s Francisco Pizarro subdued the Inca empire in Peru, providing the Spaniards with still more treasure, drawn chiefly from the silver mines of Potosí.

The *conquistadores* were brave and imaginative men. But they wrenched their empire from innocent hands; in an important sense, the settlement of the New World ranks among the most flagrant examples of unprovoked aggression in human history. When Columbus landed on San Salvador he planted a cross, "as a sign," he explained to Ferdinand and Isabella, "that your Highnesses held this land as your own." Of the Lucayans, the native inhabitants of San Salvador, Columbus wrote, "The people of this island . . . are

View the **Image**

Cabeza de Vaca, "Indians of the Rio Grande" at **myhistorylab.com**

artless and generous with what they have, to such a degree as no one would believe. . . . If it be asked for, they never say no, but rather invite the person to accept it, and show as much lovingness as though they would give their hearts."

Columbus and his compatriots tricked and cheated the Indians at every turn. Before entering a new area, Spanish generals customarily read a *Requerimiento* (requirement) to the inhabitants. This long-winded document recited a Spanish version of the history of the human race from the Creation to the division of the non-Christian world by Pope Alexander VI, and then called on the Indians to recognize the sovereignty of the reigning Spanish monarch: "If you do so . . . we shall receive you in all love and charity." If this demand was rejected, the Spanish promised, "We shall powerfully enter into your country, and . . . shall take you, your wives, and your children, and shall make slaves of them. . . . The death and losses which shall accrue from this are your fault." This arrogant harangue was read in Spanish and often out of earshot of the Indians. When they responded by fighting, the Spaniards decimated them, drove them from their lands, and held the broken survivors in contempt.

From the outset of the Europeans' invasion of the New World, sensitive observers had been appalled by their barbarity. Bartolomé de Las Casas, a Dominican missionary who arrived in Hispaniola nearly a decade after Columbus, compiled a passionate and grisly indictment:

> *It was the general rule among Spaniards to be cruel; not just cruel, but extraordinarily cruel so that harsh and bitter treatment would prevent Indians from daring to think of themselves as human beings or having a minute to think at all. So they would cut an Indian's hands and leave them dangling by a shred of skin and they would send him on saying "Go now, spread the news to your chiefs." They would test their swords and their manly strength on captured Indians and place bets on the slicing off of heads or the cutting of bodies in half with one blow.*

After stealing all the gold and silver they could find, the *conquistadores* sought alternatives sources of wealth. They soon learned that land was worthless without labor to cultivate crops or extract precious metals. They therefore imposed the **encomienda system**, a kind of feudalism granting the first Spanish colonists control of conquered lands and obliging the Indians to provide forced labor and a fixed portion of their harvests. Because the conquerors' income was proportionate to the number of villagers under their authority, *conquistadores* subjugated the heavily populated regions of Mexico—that is, those with the most extensive fields of maize. Cortés, for example, received payments from 23,000 families in the fertile Oaxaca valley; their labor made him the wealthiest man in Spain.

Much of the work of implanting Spanish civilization was undertaken by Catholic missionaries. Like the *conquistadores*, Spanish friars built their first missions in the largest Indian villages and towns. In an effort to "love their neighbor," as Christ enjoined, they sought to save as many Indian souls as possible. But when some Indians held tight to their own gods and beliefs, missionaries destroyed *kivas* and temples, banned Indian dances and games, and outlawed polygamy. When Indians resisted, the friars called on Spanish soldiers to arrest the rebels.

By the 1570s the Spanish had founded some 200 cities and towns, each with a central plaza that included a town hall and church and precisely rectilinear street plans. They had also set up printing presses and published pamphlets and books, and

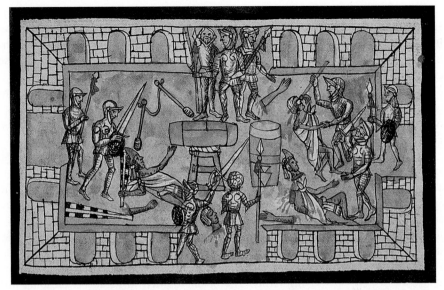

European soldiers, clad in armor and wielding iron weapons, were nearly invincible in close fighting—all the more so when their foes were unarmed, as in this drawing. Here Cortés and his men slash through Montezuma's Aztec court.

established universities in Mexico City and Lima. With the help of Indian artisans, they constructed and decorated lavishly a large number of impressive cathedrals.

Extending Spain's Empire to the North

By the early 1600s, Spanish explorers had reached Virginia, and in Florida a single Spanish military garrison remained at San Augustin—today's Saint Augustine. Years later the governor of Cuba, having failed to promote Spanish settlement of San Augustin, explained that "only hoodlums and the mischievous go there."

More consequential was the attempt to extend the Spanish empire beyond the Rio Grande into New Mexico. By the close of the sixteenth century, the Spaniards had learned that it was more profitable to acquire the crops and labor of Indian farmers than to search for rumored cities of gold. In 1598, the viceroy of New Spain charged Don Juan de Oñate with the task of conquering the Indians of New Mexico and founding a colony in their midst. Oñate led an expedition of 500 Spanish colonists and soldiers and a handful of Catholic missionaries across the Rio Grande into the territory of the Pueblo Indians, a farming people.

But the Pueblo were poor and their settlements meager; a Spanish soldier described New Mexico as "at the ends of the earth—remote beyond compare." When Oñate extorted maize, seized farmlands, and allowed cattle and pigs to plunder the fields, the Indians seethed. Eventually they ambushed and killed a Spanish patrol. Oñate retaliated by butchering 800 Pueblo, including women and children, and arresting another 500. The captured males over twenty-five years of age were sold into slavery; to prevent them from running away, one of each of their feet was chopped off. Oñate's brutality generated no profits; in 1614 he was dismissed.

Franciscan missionaries were given the task of Christianizing the Pueblo. The friars were, for the most part, dedicated men. They baptized thousands of mission Indians and instructed them in the rudiments of the Catholic faith. They also taught Indians to use European tools; to grow wheat and other European crops; and to raise chickens, pigs, and other barnyard animals.

The friars exacted a heavy price in labor from the people they presumed to enlighten and civilize. The Indians built and maintained the missions, tilled the surrounding fields, and served the every need of the friars and other Spanish colonists. For this they were paid little or nothing.

By the 1670s, after years of drought, the Pueblo became restive with these arrangements. They especially resented being coerced to take part in slave raids. Their shamans, too, increasingly called for a revival of the traditional religion. In 1675 the Spanish arrested forty-seven shamans; three were hanged and the remainder whipped as witches.

One of the latter, named Popé, secretly organized a rebellion. Without warning, some 17,000 Pueblo rose against the Spaniards, driving them out of towns and missions, destroying churches and killing priests, and plundering farms. The Spaniards fled to Santa Fe, escaping just before the Indians razed the town. The Pueblo drove the survivors all the way back to El Paso. Of the 1,000 Spanish in New Mexico, over 200 were killed.

•●•⌐Read the Document

Legal Statement by Pedro Hidalgo, soldier, Santa Fe 1680 at myhistorylab.com

In the mid-1690s the Spaniards regained control of most of the upper Rio Grande. Thereafter they maintained power with little difficulty. This was partly because they had learned to deal less harshly with the Pueblo people. The Spanish also recruited the nomadic Indians of the region to capture more distant Indians and sell them to the Spaniards as slaves.

By the early 1700s Spain had become master of a huge American empire covering all of South America except Brazil, and also all of Central America as well as a region extending from California east to Florida. New Spain was ten times larger than Spain itself. The Spanish monarch ruled three times more Indian subjects than Spaniards.

But while Spain had founded a vast empire, one major and literally fatal problem remained: The Indian population was declining rapidly, and had done so from the start. Almost as soon as Europeans set foot on American soil, Indians began to die.

Disease and Population Losses

Of all the weapons the Europeans brought to the Americas, the most potent was one they could not see and of which they were mostly unaware: microorganisms that carried diseases such as smallpox, measles, bubonic plague, diphtheria, influenza, malaria, yellow fever, and typhoid. For centuries, these diseases had ravaged Asia, Europe, and Africa. By the 1500s Eurasian and African populations had acquired some resistance to such diseases. An outbreak of smallpox or diphtheria might take a severe toll on infants and the elderly, but no longer would it decimate entire populations.

But American Indians had evolved over hundreds of generations without contact with these diseases. They lacked the requisite biological defenses. When these diseases first struck, many Indian villages were nearly wiped out. In 1585, for example, Sir Francis Drake, preparing for a raid against the Spanish, stopped at the Cape Verde

Islands. While there some of his men contracted a fever—probably typhus—but sailed for Florida undaunted by their discomfort. When they landed at St. Augustine, the disease spread to the Indians who, according to Drake, "died verie fast and said amongst themselves, it was the Englisshe God that made them die so faste."

Indian losses from diseases were incalculable, although the lowest estimates begin in the millions. Scholars agree on only one fact concerning the population history of the North American Indians following the arrival of Columbus: The number of Indians declined precipitously.

◉ See the **Map**

Native American Population Loss, 1500–1700 at **myhistorylab.com**

Ecological Imperialism

Another reason why so many Indians succumbed to disease was that they suffered from malnutrition. This was because European plants and animals had disrupted the Indian ecosystem. Pigs and cattle, brought in the first Spanish ships, were commonly set loose in the Americas. Unchallenged by the predators and microbes that had thinned their populations in Europe and Asia, pigs reproduced rapidly and ate their way through fields of maize, beans, and squash. Rats, stowaways on most European ships, also proliferated in the Americas, infesting Indian crops. Europeans also brought plants to the New World, and in the process unknowingly introduced the seeds of hardy European weeds. Like the kudzu vines from Japan that have overrun much of the southeastern United States during the twentieth century, dandelions and other weeds from Europe choked Indian crops in the sixteenth century.

The ships that brought Europeans to the Americas

Horses (blindfolded) were loaded onto Spanish warships for shipment to the Americas. Native peoples had never seen horses (which had been extinct in the Americas for over 10,000 years). Nor had they seen enormous wooden warships, powered by sails and carrying heavy cannons, or warriors, seated on horses and encased in armor.

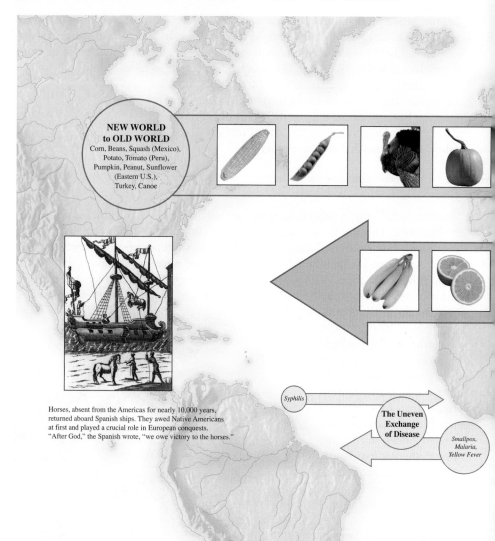

NEW WORLD to OLD WORLD
Corn, Beans, Squash (Mexico), Potato, Tomato (Peru), Pumpkin, Peanut, Sunflower (Eastern U.S.), Turkey, Canoe

Horses, absent from the Americas for nearly 10,000 years, returned aboard Spanish ships. They awed Native Americans at first and played a crucial role in European conquests. "After God," the Spanish wrote, "we owe victory to the horses."

Syphilis

The Uneven Exchange of Disease

Smallpox, Malaria, Yellow Fever

Columbian Exchange The Western Hemisphere—the Americas—has for many thousands of years been separated from the rest of the world by two great oceans. This has meant that its plants, animals, and even bacteria and viruses evolved differently. Columbus's voyage thus inaugurated an exchange, as plants and animals native to the Americas (such as corn and turkeys) were transmitted to the "Old World," and those from Europe, Africa, or Asia (bananas and horses) found their way to the Americas. The intersection of two worlds also resulted in an exchange of technologies and diseases.

returned carrying more than gold and silver. European ships also brought back maize and potato plants. These American crops yielded 50 percent more calories per acre than wheat, barley, and oats, the major European grains. Hungry European peasants swiftly shifted to maize and potato cultivation; the population of Europe rose sharply. Manioc (cassava), another Indian plant with a high caloric yield, did not grow in the colder climate of Europe, but it transformed tropical Africa. Population levels soared. As declining Indian populations proved insufficient to exploit the seemingly inexhaustible lands

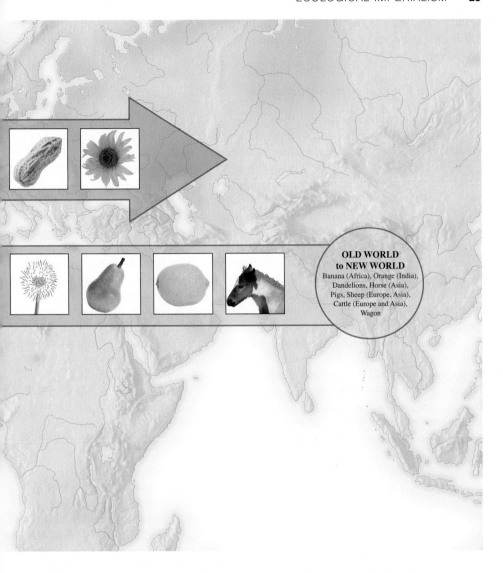

OLD WORLD
to NEW WORLD
Banana (Africa), Orange (India),
Dandelions, Horse (Asia),
Pigs, Sheep (Europe, Asia),
Cattle (Europe and Asia),
Wagon

of the Western Hemisphere, European conquerors imported African slaves to do more of the work.

Indians nevertheless benefited from some aspects of the ecological transformation of the Western Hemisphere. Horses were among the many big mammals that became extinct in the Americas over 10,000 years ago. When Spanish *conquistadors* brought horses back to the Americas, the Indians were terrified by the strange beasts. The horses, however, thrived in the vast grasslands of North America. Plains Indians used horses to hunt buffalo and harass Europeans. Farming Indians such as the Navajo profited from sheep cultivation by learning to weave fine woolen cloth.

The **Columbian Exchange** of plants and animals went both ways, yet it remained unequal. American Indians usually fared far worse than Europeans. The best indicator is the shift in population: During the 300 years after Columbus, Europe's share of the world's population nearly doubled, increasing from about 11 percent to 20 percent. During the same period, the American Indian's share declined from about 7 percent to 1 percent.

Spain's European Rivals

At first, Spain's rivals did little to oppose Spanish colonization of the New World. In 1497 and 1498 King Henry VII of England sent Captain John Cabot to explore the New World. Cabot visited Newfoundland and the northeastern coast of the continent. His explorations formed the basis for later British claims in North America, but they were not followed up for many decades. In 1524 Giovanni da Verrazano made a similar voyage for France, coasting the continent from Carolina to Nova Scotia. Some ten years later the Frenchman Jacques Cartier explored the St. Lawrence River as far inland as present-day Montréal. During the sixteenth century, fishermen from France, Spain, Portugal, and England exploited the limitless supplies of cod and other fish they found in the cold waters off Newfoundland. They landed at many points along the mainland coast from Nova Scotia to Labrador to collect water and wood and to dry their catches, but they made no permanent settlements until the next century.

●●◆─┤**Read** the **Document**

Letters of Patent Granted to
John Cabot at
myhistorylab.com

There were many reasons for this delay, the most important probably being the fact that Spain had achieved a large measure of internal tranquility by the sixteenth century, while France and England were still torn by serious religious and political conflicts. The Spanish also profited from having seized on those areas in America best suited to producing quick returns. Furthermore, in the first half of the sixteenth century, Spain, under Charles V, dominated Europe as well as America. Reinforced by the treasure of the Aztecs and the Incas, Spain seemed too mighty to be challenged in either the New World or the Old World.

Under Philip II, who succeeded Charles in 1556, Spanish strength seemed at its peak, especially after Philip added Portugal to his domain in 1580. But beneath the pomp and splendor (so well-captured by such painters as Velázquez and El Greco) the great empire was in trouble. The corruption of the Spanish court had much to do with this. So did the ever-increasing dependence of Spain on the gold and silver of its colonies, which tended to undermine the local Spanish economy. Even more important was the disruption of the Catholic Church throughout Europe by the Protestant Reformation.

The Protestant Reformation

Many factors contributed to the **Protestant Reformation**. The spiritual lethargy and bureaucratic corruption besetting the Roman Catholic Church in the early sixteenth century made it a fit target for reform. The thriving business in the sale of indulgences, payments to the church to help release dead relatives from purgatory, was a public scandal; while the luxurious lifestyle of the popes and the papal court in Rome was another. Yet countless earlier religious reform movements had generated little or no change. The fact that the movement launched by Martin Luther in 1517 and carried forward by men like John Calvin addressed genuine shortcomings in the Roman Catholic Church does not entirely explain why it led so directly to the rupture of Christendom.

The charismatic leadership of Luther and the compelling brilliance of Calvin made their protests more effective than earlier efforts at reform. Probably more important, so did the political possibilities let loose by their challenge to Rome's spiritual authority. German princes seized on Luther's campaign against the sale of indulgences to stop all payments to Rome and to confiscate church property within their domains. Swiss cities like Geneva, where Calvin took up residence in 1536, and Zurich joined the Protestant revolt for spiritual reasons, but also to establish their political independence from Catholic kings.

The decision of Henry VIII of England in 1534 to break with Rome was at bottom a political one. The refusal of Pope Clement VII to agree to an annulment of Henry's marriage of twenty years to Catherine of Aragon, the daughter of Ferdinand and Isabella, provided the occasion. Catherine had given birth to six children, but only a daughter, Mary, survived childhood; Henry was without a male heir. By repudiating the pope's spiritual authority and declaring himself head of the English (Anglican) church, Henry freed himself to divorce Catherine and to marry whomever—and however often—he saw fit. By the time of his death, five wives and thirteen years later, England had become a Protestant nation. More important for our story, the English colonies in America were mostly Protestant.

As the commercial classes rose to positions of influence, England, France, and the United Provinces of the Netherlands experienced a flowering of trade and industry. The Dutch built the largest merchant fleet in the world. Dutch traders captured most of the Far Eastern business once monopolized by the Portuguese, and they infiltrated Spain's Caribbean stronghold. A number of English merchant companies, soon to play a vital role as colonizers, sprang up in the last half of the sixteenth century. These **joint-stock companies**, ancestors of the modern corporation, enabled groups of investors to pool their capital and limit their individual responsibilities to the sums actually invested—a very important protection in such risky enterprises. The Muscovy Company, the Levant Company, and the East India Company were the most important of these ventures.

English Beginnings in America

English merchants took part in many kinds of international activity. The Muscovy Company spent large sums searching for a passage to China around Scandinavia and dispatched six overland expeditions in an effort to reach East Asia by way of Russia and Persia. In the 1570s Martin Frobisher made three voyages across the Atlantic, hoping to discover a northwest passage to East Asia or new gold-bearing lands.

Such projects, particularly in the area of North America, received strong but concealed support from the Crown. Queen Elizabeth I (1558–1603) invested heavily in Frobisher's expeditions. England was still too weak to challenge Spain openly, but Elizabeth hoped to break the Spanish overseas monopoly just the same. When Captain Francis Drake was about to set sail on his fabulous round-the-world voyage in 1577, the queen said to him, "Drake . . . I would gladly be revenged on the King of

Spain for divers injuries that I have received." Drake took her at her word. He sailed through the Strait of Magellan and terrorized the west coast of South America. After exploring the coast of California, which he claimed for England, Drake crossed the Pacific and went on to circumnavigate the globe, returning home in triumph in 1580. Although Elizabeth took pains to deny it to the Spanish ambassador, Drake's voyage was officially sponsored.

When schemes to place settlers in the New World began to mature at about this time, the queen again became involved. The first English effort was led by Sir Humphrey Gilbert, an Oxford-educated soldier and courtier. Elizabeth authorized him to explore and colonize "heathen lands not actually possessed by any Christian prince."

We know almost nothing about Gilbert's first attempt except that it occurred in 1578 and 1579; in 1583 he set sail again with five ships and over 200 settlers. He landed them on Newfoundland, then evidently decided to seek a more congenial site farther south. However, no colony was established, and on his way back to England his ship went down in a storm off the Azores.

Gilbert's half brother, Sir Walter Raleigh, took up the work. Handsome, ambitious, and impulsive, Raleigh was a great favorite of Elizabeth. He sent a number of expeditions to explore the east coast of North America, a land he named Virginia in honor of his unmarried sovereign. In 1585 he settled about a hundred men on Roanoke Island, off the North Carolina coast, but these settlers returned home the next year. In 1587 Raleigh sent another group to Roanoke, including a number of women and children. Unfortunately, the supply ships sent to the colony in 1588 failed to arrive; when help did get there in 1590, not a soul could be found. The fate of the settlers has never been determined.

One reason for the delay in getting aid to the Roanoke colonists was the attack of the Spanish Armada on England in 1588. Angered by English raids on his shipping and by the assistance Elizabeth was giving to the rebels in the Netherlands, King Philip II decided to invade England. His motives were religious as well as political and economic, for England now seemed committed to Protestantism. His great fleet of some 130 ships bore huge crosses on the sails as if on another crusade. The Armada carried 30,000 men and 2,400 guns, the largest naval force ever assembled up to that time. However, the English fleet of 197 ships shattered this armada, and a series of storms completed its destruction. Thereafter, although the war continued and Spanish sea power remained formidable, Spain could no longer block English penetration of the New World.

Experience had shown that the cost of planting settlements in a wilderness 3,000 miles from England was more than any individual purse could bear. (Raleigh lost about £40,000 in his overseas ventures; early in the game he began to advocate government support of colonization.) As early as 1584 Richard Hakluyt, England's foremost authority on the Americas and a talented propagandist for colonization, made a convincing case for royal aid. In his *Discourse on Western Planting*, Hakluyt stressed the military advantages of building "two or three strong fortes" along the Atlantic coast of North America. Ships operating from such bases would make life uncomfortable for "King Phillipe" by intercepting his treasure fleets—a matter, Hakluyt added coolly, "that toucheth him indeede to the quicke." Colonies in America would also spread the Protestant religion and enrich the parent country by expanding the market for English woolens, bringing in valuable tax revenues, and

Queen Elizabeth's right hand rests comfortably upon the globe, while in the distance the British navy destroys the Spanish Armada. This 1588 painting said it all: Elizabeth ruled the world. Such presumption helped build an empire—and eventually lose it.
Source: George Gower (1540–96), *Elizabeth I, Armada Portrait,* c.1588 (oil on panel), Gower, George (1540–96) (attr. to)/Woburn Abbey, Bedfordshire, UK/The Bridgeman Art Library.

providing employment for the swarms of "lustie youthes that be turned to no provitable use" at home. From the great American forests would come the timber and naval stores needed to build a bigger navy and merchant marine.

Queen Elizabeth read Hakluyt's essay, but she was too cautious to act on his suggestions. Only after her death in 1603 did full-scale efforts to found English colonies in America begin, and even then the organizing force came from merchant capitalists, not from the Crown.

The Settlement of Virginia

In September 1605 two groups of English merchants petitioned the new king, James I, for a license to colonize Virginia, as the whole area claimed by England was then named. This was granted the following April, and two joint-stock companies were organized: one controlled by London merchants, the other by a group from the area around Plymouth and Bristol.[1] Both were under the control of a royal council for Virginia, but James appointed prominent stockholders to the council, which meant that the companies had considerable independence.

This first charter revealed the commercial motivation of both king and company in the plainest terms. Although it spoke of spreading Christianity and bringing "the Infidels and Savages, living in those Parts, to human Civility," it stressed the right "to dig, mine, and search for all Manner of Mines of Gold, Silver, and Copper." On December 20, 1606, the London Company dispatched about 100 settlers aboard the *Susan Constant*, *Discovery*, and *Godspeed*. This little band reached the Chesapeake Bay area in May 1607 and founded Jamestown, the first permanent English colony in the New World.

From the start everything went wrong. The immigrants established themselves in what was a mosquito-infested swamp simply because it appeared easily defensible against Indian attack. They failed to get a crop in the ground because of the lateness of the season and were soon almost without food. The settlers lacked the skills of pioneers. More than a third of them were "gentlemen" unused to manual labor, and

---

[1]The London Company was to colonize southern Virginia, while the Plymouth Company (the Plymouth–Bristol group of merchants) was granted northern Virginia.

many of the rest were the gentlemen's servants, almost equally unequipped for the task of colony building. During the first winter more than half of the settlers died.

The situation demanded people skilled in agriculture. But all the land belonged to the company, and aside from the gentlemen and their retainers, most of the settlers were only hired laborers who had contracted to work for it for seven years. They had little stake in establishing permanent farms. The merchant directors of the London Company, knowing little or nothing about Virginia, made matters worse. Instead of stressing farming and public improvements, they directed the energies of the colonists into such futile labors as searching for gold, glassblowing, silk raising, winemaking, and exploring the local rivers in hopes of finding a water route to the Pacific. Although the directors set up a council of settlers, they kept all real power in their own hands.

One colonist, Captain John Smith, tried to stop some of this foolishness. Smith had come to Virginia after a fantastic career as a soldier of fortune in eastern Europe, where he had fought many battles, been enslaved by a Turkish pasha, and triumphed in a variety of adventures (military and amorous). He quickly realized that building houses and raising food were essential to survival, and he soon became an expert forager and Indian trader. Smith was as eager as any seventeenth-century European to take advantage of the Indians, and he had few compunctions about the methods employed in doing so. But he recognized both the limits of the colonists' power and the vast differences between Indian customs and values and his own. It was necessary, he insisted, to dominate the "proud Savages" yet to avoid bloodshed.

••─┤Read the Document

John Smith, *The Starving Time* at **myhistorylab.com**

Smith pleaded with company officials in London to send over more people accustomed to working with their hands, such as farmers, fishermen, carpenters, masons, "diggers up of trees," and fewer gentlemen and "Tuftaffety humorists."[2] His request was for "a plaine soldier who can use a pickaxe and a spade is better than five knights."

Lacking intelligent leaders and faced with appalling hardships, the Jamestown colonists failed to develop a sufficient sense of common purpose. Each year they died in wholesale lots from disease, starvation (there were even some cases of cannibalism among the desperate survivors), Indian attack, and, above all, ignorance and folly.

What saved the colonists was the gradual realization that they must produce their own food—cattle raising was especially important—and the cultivation of tobacco, which flourished there and could be sold profitably in England. Once the settlers discovered tobacco, no amount of company pressure could keep them at wasteful tasks like looking for gold. The "restraint of plantinge Tobacco," one company official commented, "is a thinge so distastefull to them that they will with no patience indure to heare of it."

John Rolfe introduced West Indian tobacco—much milder than the local "weed" and thus more valuable—in 1612. With money earned from the sale of tobacco, the colonists could buy the manufactured articles they could not produce in a raw new country; this freed them from dependence on outside subsidies. It did not mean profit for the London Company, however, for by the time tobacco caught on, the surviving original colonists had served their seven years and were no longer hired hands. To attract more settlers, the company had permitted first tenancy and then outright ownership of farms. Thus the profits of tobacco went largely to the planters, not to the "adventurers" who had organized the colony.

---

[2]Smith was referring to the gold tassels worn by titled students at Oxford and Cambridge at that time.

This 1616 portrait depicts Pocahontas, daughter of Powhatan, the foremost chief of coastal Virginia. The colonists, in a dispute with Powhatan, took her hostage in 1613 and kept her in Jamestown. The next year she converted to Anglicanism, took the name "Lady Rebecca," and married John Rolfe, an alliance that helped defuse tensions between colonists and Indians. In 1616 the couple came to England with their infant son, where "Lady Rebecca" was received by King James I. She became celebrated as the "belle sauvage." She was the most prominent exemplar of those "intermediaries" who readily crossed the porous boundaries between colonist and Indian cultures.

Ætatis suæ 21. Aᵒ. 1616.

The colonists erred grievously in mistreating the Powhatan Indians. It is quite likely that the settlement would not have survived if the Powhatan Indians had not given the colonists food in the first hard winters, taught them the ways of the forest, introduced them to valuable new crops such as corn and yams, and showed them how to clear dense timber by girdling the trees and burning them down after they were dead. The settlers accepted Indian aid, then took whatever else they wanted by force. English barbarities rivaled those of the Spaniards.

In 1610, for example, George Percy (an English officer), when ordered to punish a Powhatan chief for insolence, proudly described how his men marched into an Indian town, seized some of the natives, "putt some fiftene or sixtene to the Sworde" and cut off their heads. Then he ordered his men to burn the houses and crops. When the expedition returned to its boats, his men complained that Percy had spared an Indian "quene and her Children." Percy relented, and threw the children overboard "shoteinge owtt their Braynes in the water." His men insisted that he burn the queen alive, but Percy, less cruel, stabbed her to death.

The Indians did not submit meekly to such treatment. They proved brave, skillful, and ferocious fighters once they understood that their very existence was at stake. When Powhatan Chief Openchancanough concluded that the English lust for land was inexhaustible, he made plans to wipe them out. To put the Virginians at ease, he sent presents of food to Jamestown. The next day his warriors attacked, killing 347 colonists. Most of the survivors fled to the fort. They remained there for months, neglecting the crops. When winter struck, hundreds more died of hunger.

Between 1606 and 1622 the London Company invested more than £160,000 in Virginia and sent over about 6,000 settlers. Yet no dividends were ever earned, and of this group, fewer than 1,500 were still alive in 1624.

That year King James revoked the company's charter. Now a royal colony, Virginia was subject to direct control by the royal bureaucracy in London.

"Purifying" the Church of England

Although the prospect of a better material life brought most English settlers to America, for some, economic opportunity was not the only reason they abandoned what their contemporary William Shakespeare called "dear mother England." A profound unease with England's spiritual state—and therefore with their own while they remained there—explains why many colonists embarked on their "errand into the wilderness."

Despite the attempt of Henry VIII's older daughter, Queen Mary, to reinstate Catholicism during her brief reign (1553–1558), the Anglican Church became once and for all the official Church of England during the long reign of Elizabeth I (1558–1603). Like her father, Elizabeth took more interest in politics than in religion. So long as England had its own church, with her at its head, and with English rather than Latin as its official language, she was content. Aside from these changes, the Anglican Church under Elizabeth closely resembled the Catholic Church it had replaced.

This middle way satisfied most, but not all, of Elizabeth's subjects. Steadfast Catholics could not accept it. Some left England; the rest practiced their faith in private. At the other extreme, more radical Protestants, including a large percentage of England's university-trained clergy, insisted that Elizabeth had not gone far enough. The Anglican Church was still too much like the Church of Rome, they claimed. They insisted that emphasis should be put on reading the Bible and analyzing the meaning of the scriptures in order to encourage ordinary worshipers to understand their faith. Since they wanted to "purify" Anglicanism, these critics were called **puritans**.

Puritans objected to the way Elizabeth's bishops interpreted the Protestant doctrine of **predestination**. Their reading of the Book of Genesis convinced them that all human beings were properly damned by Adam's original sin and that what they did on Earth had no effect on their fate after death. To believe otherwise was to limit God's power, which was precisely what the Catholic Church did in stressing its ability to forgive sins by granting indulgences. The Anglicans implied that while God had already decided whether or not a person was saved, an individual's efforts to lead a good life could somehow cause God to change His mind. The Anglican clergy did not come right out and say that good works could win a person admission to Heaven—that heresy was called **Arminianism**. But they encouraged people to hope that good works were something more than ends in themselves. Puritans differed as to whether or not the ideal church should have any structure beyond the local congregation. Some—later called Congregationalists—favored a completely decentralized arrangement with the members of each church and their chosen minister beholden only to one another. Others, called Presbyterians, favored some organization above the local level, but one controlled by elected laymen, not by the clergy.

Puritans were also of two minds as to whether reform could be accomplished within the Anglican Church. During Elizabeth's reign most hoped that it could. Whatever they did in their local churches, the puritans remained professed Anglicans. After James I succeeded Elizabeth I in 1603, however, their fears that the royal court might be backsliding into its old "popish" ways mounted. James was married to a Catholic, and the fact that he favored toleration for Catholics gave further substance to the rumor that he was himself a secret member of that church. This rumor proved to be false, but in his twenty-two-year reign (1603–1625) James did little to advance the Protestant cause. His one contribution, which had a significance far beyond what he or anyone else anticipated, was to authorize a new translation of the Bible. The King James Version (1611) was both a monumental scholarly achievement and a literary masterpiece.

Bradford and Plymouth Colony

In 1606, worried about the future of their faith, members of the church in Scrooby, Nottinghamshire, "separated" from the Anglican Church, declaring it hopelessly corrupt. In seventeenth-century England, Separatists had to go either underground or into exile. Since only the latter would permit them to practice their religious faith openly, exile was it. In 1608 some 125 members of the group departed England for the Low Countries. They were led by their pastor, John Robinson; church elder William Brewster; and a sixteen-year-old youth, William Bradford. After a brief stay in Amsterdam, the group settled in the town of Leyden. In 1619, however, disheartened by the difficulties they had encountered in making a living, disappointed by the failure of others in England to join them, and distressed because their children were being "subjected to the great licentiousness of the youth" in Holland, these "Pilgrims" decided to move again—to seek "a place where they might have liberty and live comfortably."

The Pilgrims approached the Virginia Company about establishing a settlement near the mouth of the Hudson River on the northern boundary of the company's grant. The London Company, though unsympathetic to the religious views of the Pilgrims, agreed with their request. Since the Pilgrims were short of money, they formed a joint-stock company with other prospective emigrants and some optimistic investors who agreed to pay the expenses of the group in return for half the profits of the venture. In September 1620, about 100 strong—only thirty-five of them Pilgrims from Leyden—they set out from Plymouth, England, on the *Mayflower*.

Had the *Mayflower* reached the passengers' intended destination, the Pilgrims might have been soon forgotten. Instead their ship touched America slightly to the north on Cape Cod Bay. Unwilling to remain longer at the mercy of storm-tossed December seas, they decided to settle where they were. Since they were outside the jurisdiction of the London Company, some members of the group claimed to be free of all governmental control. Therefore, before going ashore, the Pilgrims drew up the **Mayflower Compact**. "We whose names are underwritten," the compact ran, "do by these Presents, solemnly and mutually in the presence of God and one another covenant and combine ourselves under into a civil Body Politick . . . and by Virtue hereof do enact . . . such just and equal laws . . . as shall be thought most meet and convenient for the general Good of the Colony."

Thus early in American history the idea was advanced that a society should be based on a set of rules chosen by its members. The Pilgrims chose William Bradford as their first governor. In this simple manner, ordinary people created a government that they hoped would enable them to cope with the unknown wilderness confronting them.

Bradford prided himself on treating the Indians fairly. We "did not possess one foot of land in this Colony but what was fairly obtained by honest purchase of the Indian proprietors," Bradford boasted. But the Indians yielded the land

●●—Read the Document
Bradford, *History of Plymouth Plantation* at
myhistorylab.com

The story of the first thirty years of pilgrim life in Plymouth, Massachusetts, is preserved in Governor William Bradford's *Of Plymouth Plantation*. A glimpse of the first colony is shown in this reconstruction.

readily because so many had died of smallpox, likely brought by settlers. And the Pilgrims, after hearing of the Powhatan attack on Jamestown in 1622, ambushed a band of Massachusetts Indians, killing seven, and put the leader's head atop a post at the Plymouth fort.

Yet by 1650 there were still fewer than 1,000 settlers, most of them living beyond the reach of the original church.

Winthrop and Massachusetts Bay Colony

The Pilgrims were not the first English colonists to inhabit the northern regions. The Plymouth Company had settled a group on the Kennebec River in 1607. These colonists gave up after a few months, but fishermen and traders continued to visit the area, which was christened New England by Captain John Smith after an expedition there in 1614.

In 1620 the Plymouth Company was reorganized as the Council for New England, which had among its principal stockholders Sir Ferdinando Gorges and his friend John Mason, former governor of an English settlement on Newfoundland. Their particular domain included a considerable part of what is now Maine and New Hampshire. More interested in real estate deals than in colonizing, the council disposed of a number of tracts in the area north of Cape Cod. The most significant of these grants was a small one made to a group of puritans from Dorchester, who established a settlement at Salem in 1629.

Later that year these Dorchester puritans organized the Massachusetts Bay Company and obtained a royal grant to the area between the Charles and Merrimack rivers. The

Massachusetts Bay Company was organized like any other commercial venture, but the puritans, acting with single-minded determination, made it a way of obtaining religious refuge in America.

Unlike the Separatists in Plymouth, most puritans had managed to satisfy both Crown and conscience while James I was king. The England of his son Charles I, who succeeded to the throne in 1625, posed a more serious challenge. Whereas James had been content to keep puritans at bay, Charles and his favorite Anglican cleric, William Laud, intended to bring them to heel. With the king's support, Laud proceeded to embellish the already elaborate Anglican ritual and to tighten the central control that the puritans found so distasteful. He removed ministers with puritan leanings from their pulpits and threatened church elders who harbored such ministers with imprisonment.

No longer able to remain within the Anglican fold in good conscience and now facing prison if they tried to worship in the way they believed right, many puritans decided to migrate to America. In the summer of 1630 nearly a thousand of them set out from England, carrying the charter of the Massachusetts Bay Company with them. By fall, they had founded Boston and several other towns.

The early settlements struggled. The tasks of founding a new society in a strange land were more difficult than anyone had anticipated. Of the 1,000 English settlers who arrived in Massachusetts in the summer of 1630, 200 died during their first New England winter. Governor Winthrop himself lost eleven family servants. When ships arrived the following spring, they returned to England nearly filled with immigrants who had given up.

But they were replaced many times over. Continuing bad times in England and the persecution of puritans there led to the Great Migration of the 1630s. Within a decade, over 10,000 puritans had arrived in Massachusetts. This infusion of industrious, well-educated, and often prosperous colonists swiftly created a complex and distinct culture on the edge of what one of the pessimists among them called "a hideous and desolate wilderness, full of wild beasts and wild men."

The directors of the Massachusetts Bay Company believed their enterprise to be divinely inspired. Before leaving England, they elected John Winthrop, a twenty-nine-year-old Oxford-trained attorney, as governor of the colony. Throughout his twenty years of almost continuous service as governor, Winthrop spoke for the solid and sensible core of the puritans and their high-minded experiment. His lay sermon, "A Modelle of Christian Charity," delivered mid-Atlantic on the deck of the *Arbella* in 1630, made clear his sense of the momentousness of that experiment:

> •●─[Read the Document
> Winthrop, *A Model of Christian Charity* at **myhistorylab.com**

Wee must Consider that wee shall be as a Citty upon a Hill, the eies of all people are upon us; soe that if wee shall deale falsely with our god in this worke wee have undertaken and soe cause him to withdrawe his present help from us, wee shall be made a story and a by-word through the world, wee shall open the mouthes of enemies to speake evill of the wayes of god and all professours for Gods sake.

The colonists created an elected legislature, the General Court. Their system was not democratic in the modern sense because the right to vote and hold office was limited to male church members, but this did not mean that the government was run by clergymen or that it was not sensitive to the popular will. Clergymen were influential, but since they were not allowed to hold public office, their authority was indirect and based on the respect of their parishioners, not on law or force. At least until the mid-1640s, most families included at least one adult male church member. Since these "freemen" soon secured the right to choose the governor and elect the representatives ("deputies") to the General Court, a kind of practical democracy existed.

The puritans had a clear sense of what their churches should be like. After getting permission from the General Court, a group of colonists who wished to form a new church could select a minister and conduct their spiritual affairs as they saw fit. Membership was restricted to those who could present satisfactory evidence of their having experienced "saving grace," such as by a compelling recounting of some extraordinary emotional experience, some mystical sign of intimate contact with God. This meant that full membership in the churches of early Massachusetts was reserved for "visible saints." During the 1630s, however, few applicants were denied membership.

Troublemakers: Roger Williams and Anne Hutchinson

As John Winthrop had on more than one occasion to lament, most of the colony's early troublemakers came not from those of doubtful spiritual condition but from its certified saints. The "godly and zealous" Roger Williams was a prime example. The Pilgrim leader William Bradford described Williams as possessed of "many precious parts, but very unsettled in judgment." Even by Plymouth's standards Williams was an extreme separatist. He was ready to bring down the wrath of Charles I on New England rather than accept the charters signed by him or his father, even if these documents provided the only legal basis for the governments of Plymouth and Massachusetts Bay.

Williams had arrived in Massachusetts in 1631. Following a short stay in Plymouth, he joined the church in Salem, which elected him minister in 1635. Well before then, however, his opposition to the alliance of church and civil government turned both ministers and magistrates against him. Part of his contrariness stemmed from his religious libertarianism. Magistrates should have no voice in spiritual matters, he insisted: "forced religion stinks in God's nostrils." He also offended property owners (which meant nearly everyone) by advancing the radical idea that it was "a Nationale sinne" for anyone, including the king, to take possession of land without buying it from the Indians.

As long as Williams enjoyed the support of his Salem church, there was little the magistrates could do to silence him. But his refusal to heed those who counseled moderation—"all truths are not seasonable at all times," Governor Winthrop reminded him—swiftly eroded that support. In the fall of 1635, economic pressure put on the town of Salem by the General Court turned his congregation against him. The General Court then ordered him to leave the colony within six weeks.

Williams departed Massachusetts in January 1636, traveling south to the head of Narragansett Bay. There he worked out mutually acceptable arrangements with the local Indians and founded the town of Providence. In 1644, after obtaining a charter in England from Parliament, he established the colony of Rhode Island and Providence Plantations. The government was relatively democratic, all religions were tolerated, and church and state were rigidly separated. Whatever Williams's temperamental excesses, he was more than ready to practice what he preached when given the opportunity.

Anne Hutchinson, who arrived in Boston in 1631, was another "visible saint" who, in the judgment of the puritan establishment, went too far. Hutchinson was not to be taken lightly. According to Governor Winthrop, her husband William was "a man of mild temper and weak parts, wholly guided by his wife." (He was not so weak as to be unable to father Anne's fifteen children.) Duties as a midwife brought her into the homes of other Boston women, with whom she discussed and more than occasionally criticized the sermons of their minister.

The issue in dispute was whether God's saints could be confident of having truly received His gift of eternal life. Wilson and most of the ministers of the colony thought not. God's saints should ceaselessly monitor their thoughts and behavior. But Hutchinson thought this emphasis on behavior was similar to the Catholic belief that an individual's good deeds and penitence could bring God's salvation. Ministers should not demean God, Hutchinson declared, by suggesting that He would be impressed by human actions. She insisted that God's saints knew who they were; those presumed "saints" who had doubts on the matter were likely destined for eternal hell.

Hutchinson suggested that those possessed of God's grace were exempt from the rules of good behavior and even from the laws of the commonwealth. As her detractors pointed out, this was the conclusion some of the earliest German Protestants had reached, for which they were judged guilty of the heresy of **antinomianism** ("against the law") and burned at the stake.

In 1636 the General Court charged Hutchinson with defaming the clergy and brought her to trial. When her accusers quoted the Bible ("Honor thy father and thy mother") to make their case, she announced that even the Ten Commandments must yield to one's own insights if these were directly inspired by God. When pressed for details, she acknowledged that she was a regular recipient of divine insights, communicated, as they were to Abraham, "by the voice of His own spirit in my soul." The General Court, on hearing this claim, banished her.

Hutchinson, together with her large family and a group of supporters, left Massachusetts in the spring of 1637 for Rhode Island, thereby adding to the reputation of that colony as the "sink" of New England. After her husband died in 1642, she and six of her children moved to the Dutch colony of New Netherland, where, the following year, she and all but her youngest daughter were killed by Indians.

The banishment of dissenters like Roger Williams and Anne Hutchinson did not endear the Massachusetts puritans to posterity. In both cases outspoken individualists seem to have been done in by frightened politicians and self-serving ministers. Yet Williams and Hutchinson posed genuine threats to the puritan community. Massachusetts was truly a social experiment. Could it accommodate such uncooperative spirits and remain intact? When forced to choose between the peace of the commonwealth and sending dissenters packing, Winthrop, the magistrates, and the ministers did not hesitate.

Other New England Colonies

Beginning in 1635, a number of Massachusetts congregations had pushed southwestward into the fertile valley of the Connecticut River. A group headed by the Reverend Thomas Hooker founded Hartford in 1636. Hooker was influential in the drafting of the Fundamental Orders, a sort of constitution creating a government for the valley towns, in 1639. The Fundamental Orders resembled the Massachusetts system, except that they did not limit voting to church members. Other groups of puritans came directly from England to settle towns in and around New Haven in the 1630s. These were incorporated into Connecticut shortly after the Hooker colony obtained a royal charter in 1662.

Pequot War and King Philip's War

New England colonists repeatedly exploited disunity among Indians, who identified more with their hunting group, headed by a sachem, than with a particular tribe. Savvy English settlers could often turn one group against another. In both of the major Indian uprisings in New England during the seventeenth century, the colonists prevailed in part because they were assisted by Indian allies.

In the 1630s the Pequot Indians grew alarmed at the steady stream of English settlers to southeastern Connecticut. After several clashes in 1636, the colonists demanded that the Pequots surrender tribe members responsible for the attacks and pay tribute in wampum. When the Pequots refused, the governments of Massachusetts, Connecticut, and Plymouth declared war. In 1637 the New England armies, bolstered by warriors of the Narragansett and Mohegan tribes, traditional foes of the Pequots, attacked a Pequot village enclosed by a wooden palisade. When Pequots attempted to flee, the English set fire to the village, trapping the Indians and killing nearly all 400 inhabitants.

The Narragansett and Mohegan Indians were aghast. They had intended to replace their own deceased relatives by adopting captured foes, especially women and children. The English way of fighting, they complained, was "too furious and slays too many people." Bradford, too, commented on the "fearful sight" of the trapped Pequots "thus frying in the fire," but he remembered to praise God for "so speedy a victory." The Pequots were crushed.

In the 1670s Metacom, a Wampanoag sachem, concluded that the only way to resist the English incursion was to drive them out by force of arms. By then, many Wampanoags had acquired flintlock muskets and learned to use them; warfare had become far more lethal. In 1675, after Plymouth colony had convicted and executed three Wampanoags, Metacom ignited an uprising that ravaged much of New England. Scores of sachems led attacks on more than half of the ninety puritan towns in New England, destroying twelve. About 1,000 puritans were massacred; many more abandoned their farms.

The next year the colonists went on the offensive, bolstered by Mohawk allies. The New England militias destroyed Wampanoag villages and exhausted the Wampanoag's gunpowder. The Mohawks ambushed and killed Metacom, presenting his severed head to puritan authorities in Boston. The Wampanoag retreated into the Great Swamp in Rhode Island and built a large fort. The colonists surrounded and burned the fort, massacred 300 Indians, and destroyed the winter stores. In all, about 4,000 Wampanoags and their allies died in what was called "King Philip's" war—King Philip being the colonist's derisive name for Metacom.

Maryland and the Carolinas

The Virginia and New England colonies were essentially corporate ventures. Most of the other English colonies in America were founded by individuals or by a handful of partners who obtained charters from the ruling sovereign. It was becoming easier to establish settlements in America, for experience had taught the English a great deal about the colonization process. Settlers knew better what to bring with them and what to do after they arrived.

Many influential Englishmen were eager to try their luck as colonizers. The grants they received made them "proprietors" of great estates, which were, at least in theory, their personal property. By granting land to settlers in return for a small annual rent, they hoped to obtain a steadily increasing income while holding a valuable speculative interest in all undeveloped land. At the same time, their political power, guaranteed by charter, would become increasingly important as their colonies expanded. In practice, however, the realities of life in America limited their freedom of action and their profits.

One of the first proprietary colonies was Maryland, granted by Charles I to George Calvert, Lord Baltimore. Calvert had a deep interest in America, being a member both of the London Company and of the Council for New England. He hoped to profit financially from Maryland, but, since he was a Catholic, he also intended the colony to be a haven for his co-religionists.

Calvert died shortly before Charles approved his charter, so the grant went to his son Cecilius. The first settlers arrived in 1634, founding St. Mary's, just north of the Potomac. The presence of the now well-established Virginia colony nearby greatly aided the Marylanders; they had little difficulty in getting started and in developing an economy based, like Virginia's, on tobacco. According to the Maryland charter, Lord Baltimore had the right to establish feudal manors, hold people in serfdom, make laws, and set up his own courts. He soon discovered, however, that to attract settlers he had to allow them to own their farms, and that to maintain any political influence at all he had to give the settlers considerable say in local affairs. Other wise concessions marked his handling of the religious question. He would have preferred an exclusively Catholic colony, but while Catholics did go to Maryland, Protestants greatly outnumbered them. Baltimore dealt with this problem by agreeing to a Toleration Act (1649) that guaranteed freedom of religion to anyone "professing to believe in Jesus Christ." Though religious disputes persisted, Calvert's compromise enabled them to make a fortune and maintain an influence in Maryland until the Revolution.

The Carolina charter, like that of Maryland, accorded the proprietors wide authority. With the help of the political philosopher John Locke, they drafted a grandiose plan of government called the Fundamental Constitutions, which created a hereditary nobility and provided for huge paper land grants to a hierarchy headed by the proprietors and lesser "landgraves" and "caciques." The human effort to support the feudal society was to be supplied by peasants.

This complicated system proved unworkable. The landgraves and caciques got grants, but they could not find peasants willing to toil on their domains. Probably the purpose of all this elaborate feudal nonsense was promotional; the proprietor hoped to convince investors that they could make fortunes in Carolina rivaling those of English lords. Life followed a more mundane pattern similar to what was going on in Virginia and Maryland, with property relatively easy to obtain.

The first settlers arrived in 1670, most of them from the sugar plantations of Barbados, where slave labor was driving out small independent farmers. Charles Town (now Charleston) was founded in 1680. Another center of population sprang up in the Albemarle district, just south of Virginia, settled largely by individuals from that colony. Two quite different societies grew up in these areas. The Charleston colony, with an economy based on a thriving trade in furs and on the export of foodstuffs to the West Indies, was prosperous and cosmopolitan. The Albemarle settlement, where the soil was less fertile, was poorer and more primitive. Eventually, in 1712, the two were formally separated, becoming North and South Carolina.

French and Dutch Settlements

While the English were settling Virginia and New England, other Europeans were challenging Spain's monopoly elsewhere in the New World. Jacques Cartier attempted to found a French colony at Québec in the 1530s. Spain, initially alarmed by the French incursion, considered intervening; but the Spanish emperor thought the northern region too cold and not worth the bother. Cartier soon concurred, as his settlement quickly succumbed to brutal winters, scurvy, and Indian attacks.

Not until the end of the century was another attempt made to colonize the region. Then some intrepid French traders traded with Indians for fur, which had become valuable in Europe.

Unlike the English, who occupied the Indian's land, or the Spanish, who subjugated Indians and exploited their labor, French traders viewed the Indians as essential trading partners. A handful of French traders, carrying their goods in canoes and small boats, made their way to Indian settlements along the St. Lawrence River and the shores of Lake Ontario and Lake Erie. But by 1650, there were only 700 French colonists in New France.

By then, France had perceived both the economic and military potential of North America and the vulnerability of France's thinly populated string of settlements. To protect its toehold in North America, the French government built forts on key northern waterways and sent soldiers to protect the traders. French military expenditures helped sustain the fledgling colony. By 1700, about 15,000 French colonists lived in scattered settlements along an arc ranging from the mouth of the St. Lawrence in the northeast, through the Great Lakes, and down the Mississippi to the Gulf of Mexico.

By contrast, nearly a quarter of a million English settlers (and 34,000 Africans, most brought as slaves) had occupied the English colonies. As the English filled up the Atlantic seaboard and pushed steadily westward, the French recruited the Algonquian Indians as military allies. The Algonquians were linguistically similar tribes who had been driven from the Atlantic seaboard into territory occupied by the Iroquois, a confederation of powerful tribes. English settlers commonly entered into treaties with the Iroquois.

Warfare ensued, usually French–Algonquian against English–Iroquois. But now that the Indians had guns and ammunition, warfare became bloodier, and all frontier settlements—Indian and colonist alike—became more vulnerable.

Complicating matters further was the Dutch settlement of New Netherland in the Hudson Valley. The settlers based their claim to the region on the explorations of Henry

Hudson in 1609. As early as 1624 they established an outpost, Fort Orange, on the site of present-day Albany. Two years later they founded New Amsterdam at the mouth of the Hudson River, and Peter Minuit, the director general of the West India Company, purchased Manhattan Island from the Indians for trading goods worth about sixty guilders.

The Dutch traded with the Indians for furs and plundered Spanish colonial commerce enthusiastically. Through the Charter of Privileges of Patroons, which authorized large grants of land to individuals who would bring over fifty settlers, they tried to encourage large-scale agriculture. Only one such estate—Rensselaerswyck, on the Hudson south of Fort Orange, owned by the rich Amsterdam merchant Kiliaen Van Rensselaer—was successful. Peter Minuit was removed from his post in New Amsterdam in 1631, but he organized a group of Swedish settlers several years later and founded the colony of New Sweden on the lower reaches of the Delaware River. New Sweden was in constant conflict with the Dutch, who finally overran it in 1655.

The Middle Colonies

Gradually it became clear that the English would dominate the entire coast between the St. Lawrence Valley and Florida. After 1660 only the Dutch challenged their monopoly. The two nations, once allies against Spain, had fallen out because of the fierce competition of their textile manufacturers and merchants. England's efforts to bar Dutch merchant vessels from its colonial trade also brought the two countries into conflict in America. Charles II precipitated a showdown by granting his brother James, Duke of York, the entire area between Connecticut and Maryland. This was tantamount to declaring war. In 1664 English forces captured New Amsterdam without a fight—there were only 1,500 people in the town—and soon the rest of the Dutch settlements capitulated. New Amsterdam became New York. The duke did not interfere much with the way of life of the Dutch settlers, and they were quickly reconciled to English rule.

In 1664, even before the capture of New Amsterdam, the Duke of York gave New Jersey, the region between the Hudson and the Delaware, to John, Lord Berkeley, and Sir George Carteret. To attract settlers, these proprietors offered land on easy terms and established freedom of religion and a democratic system of local government. A considerable number of puritans from New England and Long Island moved to the new province.

In 1674 Berkeley sold his interest in New Jersey to two **Quakers**. Quakers believed that they could communicate directly with their Maker; their religion required neither ritual nor ministers. Originally a sect emotional to the point of fanaticism, by the 1670s the Quakers had come to stress the doctrine of the Inner Light—the direct, mystical experience of religious truth—which they believed possible for all persons. They distrusted the intellect in religious matters and, while ardent proselytizers of their own beliefs, they tolerated those of others cheerfully. When faced with opposition, they resorted to passive resistance, a tactic that embroiled them in grave difficulties in England and in most of the American colonies. In Massachusetts Bay, for example, four Quakers were executed when they refused either to conform to puritan ideas or to leave the colony.

The acquisition of New Jersey gave the Quakers a place where they could practice their religion in peace. The proprietors, in keeping with their principles, drafted an extremely liberal constitution for the colony, the Concessions and Agreements of 1677, which created an autonomous legislature and guaranteed settlers freedom of conscience, the right of trial by jury, and other civil rights.

The main Quaker effort at colonization came in the region immediately west of New Jersey, a fertile area belonging to William Penn, the son of a wealthy English admiral. Penn had early rejected a life of ease and had become a Quaker missionary. As a result, he was twice jailed. Yet he possessed qualities that enabled him to hold the respect and friendship of people who found his religious ideas abhorrent. From his father, Penn had inherited a claim to £16,000 that the admiral had lent Charles II. The king, reluctant to part with that much cash, paid off the debt in 1681 by giving Penn the region north of Maryland and west of the Delaware River, insisting only that it be named Pennsylvania, in honor of the admiral. In 1682 Penn founded Philadelphia. The Duke of York then added Delaware, the region between Maryland and the Delaware Bay, to Penn's holdings.

William Penn considered his colony a "Holy Experiment." He treated the Indians fairly, buying title to their lands and trying to protect them in their dealings with settlers and traders. Anyone who believed in "one Almighty and Eternal God" was entitled to freedom of worship. Penn's political ideas were paternalistic rather than democratic; the assembly he established could only approve or reject laws proposed by the governor and council. But individual rights were as well protected in Pennsylvania as in New Jersey.

Penn's altruism, however, did not prevent him from taking excellent care of his own interests. He sold both large and small tracts of land to settlers on easy terms but reserved huge tracts for himself. He promoted Pennsylvania tirelessly, writing glowing, although perfectly honest, descriptions of the colony, which were circulated widely in England and, in translation, in Europe. These attracted many settlers, including large numbers of Germans—the Pennsylvania "Dutch" (a corruption of *Deutsch,* meaning "German").

William Penn was neither a doctrinaire nor an ivory tower philosopher. He came to Pennsylvania himself when trouble developed between settlers and his representatives and agreed to adjustments in his first Frame of Government when he realized that local conditions demonstrated the need for change. His combination of toughness, liberality, and good salesmanship helped the colony to prosper and grow rapidly. By 1685 there were almost 9,000 settlers in Pennsylvania, and by 1700 twice that number, a heartening contrast to the early history of Virginia and Plymouth. Pennsylvania produced wheat, corn, rye, and other crops in abundance and found a ready market for its surpluses on the sugar plantations of the West Indies.

Cultural Collisions

Since the Indians did not worship the Christian God, the Europeans dismissed them as contemptible heathens. Some insisted that the Indians were servants of Satan. Other Europeans, such as the Spanish friars, did try to convert the Indians, and with considerable success; but as late as 1569, when Spain introduced the Inquisition into its colonies, the natives were exempted from its control on the ground that they were incapable of rational judgment and thus not responsible for their "heretical" religious beliefs.

Indians who depended on hunting and fishing had little use for personal property that was not easily portable. They saw no reason to amass possessions as individuals or as tribes. Even the Aztecs, with their treasures of gold and silver, valued the metals for

Historian James Merrell notes several errors in Benjamin West's famous 1771 painting, *William Penn's Treaty with the Indians*. In 1682, when the treaty was negotiated, Penn (in brown coat) was not yet so fat; the colonists' clothing and brick buildings resemble a scene in Philadelphia in the 1750s, not the 1680s; and the Indians are implausibly posed like Greek and Roman statues. Most important, the painting includes no translator, the one indispensable figure in the proceedings. All Indian and settler exchanges required "go-betweens" or "negotiators" to help each group explain itself to the other.

their durability and the beautiful things that could be made with them rather than as objects of commerce.

Indians were puzzled that European men worked so hard in the fields. In many Indian societies, crop cultivation was women's work. Moreover, the bounty of the earth was such that no one needed to work all the time. The Europeans' ceaseless drudgery and relentless pursuit of material goods struck the Indians as perverse. In many Indian societies, sachems acquired power by giving away their goods. The Narragansett Indians even had a ritual in which they collected "almost all the riches they have to their gods"— kettles, hatchets, beads, knives—and burned them in a great fire.

This lack of concern for material things led Europeans to conclude that the native people of America were lazy and childlike. "[Indians] do but run over the grass, as do also foxes and wild beasts," an English settler wrote in 1622, "so it is lawful now to take a land, which none useth, and make use of it." In the sense that the Indians continuously interacted with nature, the first part of this statement contained a grain of truth, although of course the second did not follow from it logically.

That the Indians allowed their environment to remain pristine is a myth. Long before contact with the Europeans, Indians cleared fields, burned the underbrush of forests, diverted rivers and streams, built roads and settlements, and deposited immense quantities of earth upon mounds.

But Europeans left a deeper imprint on the land. Their iron-tipped ploughs dug into the earth and made more of it accessible to cultivation, and their iron axes and saws enabled them to clear vast forests with relative ease. Pigs and cattle, too, ate their way through fields. Indians resented the intensity of English cultivation. After capturing several

Black Robe

In 1493 Pope Alexander VI praised Christopher Columbus, "our beloved son," for having discovered "certain very remote islands and even mainlands" whose inhabitants "seem sufficiently disposed to embrace the Catholic faith." In order to save their souls, Alexander continued, such "barbaric" peoples must be "humbled." In 1629 the church dispatched to New France its most effective missionaries, the Jesuits, a militant evangelical order founded by Ignatius Loyola in 1540. The Indians, fascinated by the Jesuits' austere cassocks, called them Black Robes.

Black Robe, directed by Bruce Beresford, tells the story of Father Laforgue: a young French Jesuit who arrives in Québec in 1634. Laforgue's superiors charge him with reviving a faltering mission to the Huron Indians in the upper Great Lakes. Samuel Champlain, Governor of New France, persuades a band of Algonquin Indians to escort Laforgue on this 1,500-mile journey.

The movie is partly an adventure story that chronicles the group's voyage to the interior of the continent: paddling through ice-choked rivers, hauling canoes along snowy portages, and enduring capture and torture by Iroquois. But the movie also explores the deep cultural chasm between Indians and Europeans. When the Algonquin chief tells a story, Laforgue writes it down and takes the chief to another European, not present for the conversation, shows him the paper, and asks him to read it aloud. As he does, the chief's face falls in horror: What manner of sorcery resides in those squiggly lines? The Europeans, by contrast, were plagued with illiteracy of the arboreal kind. After losing his way in a forest, Laforgue embraces his Indian rescuers. "I was lost," he tells them, tears streaming down his face. "How was that?" the Indians ask. "Did you forget to look at the trees, Black Robe?"

When Laforgue finally arrives at the mission, he finds all but one of the missionaries have been butchered; the last, just before dying, explains that the Huron had been decimated by disease and blamed the Jesuits. As Laforgue buries him, a shattered remnant of the Huron watch in silence, their blank faces symbolizing the mutual incomprehension of Indians and Jesuits. Laforgue raises his head to the heavens, sunshine framing the church's cross. "Spare them," he intones. "Spare them, Oh Lord." The movie ends with a notice that, by 1650, the Iroquois had crushed the Hurons and the Jesuits had abandoned the mission.

Is *Black Robe* a plausible account of the relationship between Indians and Jesuit missionaries? No definitive answer is possible because our knowledge is almost entirely based on the missionaries' letters to their superiors. Sometimes the movie departs from these accounts. For example, no Indian of New France would have agreed to a 1,500-mile expedition in the middle of winter. As one missionary explained, his Indians seldom strayed from their camp during the winter "on account of the great masses of ice which are continually floating about, and which would crush not only a small boat but even a great ship."

On the other hand, the movie scrupulously depicts the physical world described by the missionaries. Viewers may complain that the interior scenes are obscured by smoke, but this reflects the historical reality. Laforgue was based in part on Paul Le Jeune, a Jesuit missionary who wrote in 1634 that the bitter cold required the Indians to build large fires indoors. The smoke from the fires was a form of "martyrdom" that

> made me weep continually. . . it caused us to place our mouths against the earth in order to breathe.

The director painstakingly reconstructed Indian villages, used Indians (who spoke Cree) as actors, and clothed them in seemingly random layers of textiles and animal skills. This, too, accorded with the accounts of missionaries, one of whom was surprised that the Indians used the same

Father Laforgue, played by Lothaire Bluteau, walks along the shores of Lake Huron, a grim and solitary figure.

Father Paul Le Jeune, the Jesuit missionary on which "Father Laforgue" was largely based, doubtless visited St. Eustache Cathedral in Paris (above), completed in the 1630s. His letters to his superiors explain his difficult adjustment to worship in the wilds of North America.

clothing for men and women. "They care only to stay warm," he sniffed. Doubtless the northern Indians were puzzled that anyone would dress for any other purpose.

The sharpest criticism of the movie has come from controversialist Ward Churchill. Churchill, who claims to be part-Indian, asserted that the movie vilified the Indians and justified their extermination.

It is tempting to dismiss Churchill's argument because of the reputation of its author, who made provocative remarks after the 9/11 attack on the World Trade Center in New York City. Whether the Jesuits undermined Indian belief systems cannot be determined from the letters of the missionaries. But there can be little doubt that many Jesuits were motivated by a desire to do what they regarded as God's work. Nothing else explains their willingness to endure the sufferings chronicled in their letters.

What the Indians thought of the Jesuits is much harder to determine. Neither side—as the movie shows—understood the other. But the movie advances a secondary hypothesis, conveyed by the haunting musical score and panoramic shots of endless forests, clad in snow and shadowed in a fading winter light. This all suggested that the Indians, consigned to live in a solitary and harsh environment, were a grim and stoical people, "noble savages," who endured unimaginable privations. This stereotype remains a staple of popular culture to this day.

But it may be wrong. Consider the account of Le Jeune, the actual missionary who was tormented by an Indian shaman named Mestigoit. Le Jeune described his relationship with the "Sorcerer" as one of "open warfare"; he expected Mestigoit to murder him at any time. But a closer reading of Le Jeune's account suggests that Mestigoit's purposes were more comedic than homicidal.

Le Jeune wrote that Mestigoit

> tried to make me the laughingstock. . .
> [His followers] continually heaped
> upon me a thousand taunts and insults.
> They were saying to me at every turn
> *sasegau*, "He looks like a Dog;"
> *attimonai oukhimau*, "He is Captain of
> the Dogs;" *cou oucousimas ouchtigonan*,
> "He has a head like a pumpkin;"
> *matchiriniou*, "He is deformed, he is
> ugly;" *khichcouebeon*, "He is drunk."

Le Jeune, alone and alienated, likely projected his own sentiments onto the Indians. An alternative reading of this and similar missionary accounts suggests that the Indians did not regard their world as harsh and difficult, nor their lives as grim and solitary. While preparing to leave for a difficult winter hunt, Le Jeune's Indians offered him encouragement: "Let thy soul be strong to endure suffering and hardship; keep thyself from being sad, otherwise thou wilt be sick; see how we do not cease to laugh, although we have little to eat?" Indeed, nothing surprised the Indians more than the joylessness of the Jesuits. How, the Indians asked, could the Black Robes speak of heaven if they had never slept with a woman?

Questions for Discussion

- Whose religious beliefs were more difficult to understand, those of the Algonquins or the Jesuit missionaries?
- Do all human beings share a similar sense of humor?

English farmers, some Algonquians buried them alive, all the while taunting: "You English have grown exceedingly above the Ground. Let us now see how you will grow when planted into the ground."

The Europeans' inability to grasp the communal nature of land tenure among Indians also led to innumerable quarrels. Traditional tribal boundaries were neither spelled out in deeds or treaties nor marked by fences or any other sign of occupation. Often corn grown by a number of families was stored in a common bin and drawn on by all as needed. Such practices were utterly alien to the European mind.

Nowhere was the cultural chasm between Indians and Europeans more evident than in warfare. Indians did not seek to possess land, so they sought not to destroy an enemy but to display their valor, avenge an insult or perceived wrong, or acquire captives who could take the place of deceased family members. The Indians preferred to ambush an opponent and seize the stragglers; when confronted by a superior force, they usually melted into the woods. The Europeans preferred to fight in heavily armed masses in order to obliterate the enemy.

Colonists denounced Indian perfidy for burning houses and towns; but they saw no inconsistency in burning Indian "nests," "wigwams," and "camps." Conversely, the Indians thought it within their rights to slaughter the cattle that devoured their crops and spoiled their hunting grounds. But when the Indians tortured the beasts in fury, the colonists regarded them as savages.

Cultural Fusions

Increase Mather, a puritan leader, worried that "Christians in this Land have become too like unto the Indians." Little wonder, he observed, that God had "afflicted us by them" through disease and other trials. Yet Mather's comments suggested that interaction between European settlers and the native peoples was characteristic of life in all the colonies. *Interaction* is the key word in this sentence. The so-called Columbian Exchange between Indian and European was a two-way street. The colonists learned a great deal about how to live in the American forest from the Indians: the names of plants and animals (hickory, pecan, raccoon, skunk, moose); what to eat in their new home and how to catch or grow it; what to wear (leather leggings and especially moccasins); how best to get from one place to another; how to fight; and in some respects how to think.

The colonists learned from the Indians how best to use many plants and animals for food and clothing, but they would probably have discovered most of these if the continent had been devoid of human life when they arrived. Corn, however, the staple of the diet of agricultural tribes, was something the Indians had domesticated. Its contribution to the success of English colonization was enormous.

The fur trade illustrates the pervasiveness of Indian–European interaction. It was in some ways a perfect business arrangement. Both groups profited. The colonists got "valuable" furs for "cheap" European products, while the Indians got "priceless" tools, knives, and other trade goods in exchange for "cheap" beaver pelts and deerskins. The demand for furs caused the Indians to become more efficient hunters and trappers and even to absorb some of the settlers' ideas about private property and capitalist accumulation. Hunting parties became larger. Farming tribes shifted their villages in order to be nearer trade routes and waterways. In some cases tribal organization was altered: Small groups combined into confederations in order to control more territory when their hunting reduced the supplies

 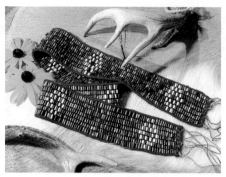

Indians were befuddled by the Europeans' craving for gold, such as these Spanish coins (left). Europeans were similarly baffled by the Indians' attraction to wampum, seashells that were drilled, placed on a string, and formed into belts, such as this eighteenth-century Oneida belt (right). No negotiations or trade with many Indian tribes could commence without gifts of wampum. The gold coins are imprinted with the Christian cross; purple beads, the most valuable, were also suffused with spiritual import among Indians.

of furs nearer home. Early in the seventeenth century, Huron Indians in the Great Lakes region, who had probably never seen a Frenchman, owned French products obtained from eastern tribes in exchange for Huron corn.

Europeans and Indians became interdependent. The colonists relied on Indian labor and products. Indians relied on European guns and metal tools. Some Indians became so enamored of European knives and metal tools that they forgot the stone-working skills of their Paleo-Indian ancestors. They now depended on Europeans for those products, much as the colonists themselves depended on Indian corn, potatoes, and other crops.

Although the colonists learned much from the Indians and adopted certain elements of Indian culture and technology eagerly, their objective was not to be like the Indians, whom they considered the epitome of savagery and barbarism. The constant conflicts with Indians forced the colonists to band together and in time gave them a sense of having shared a common history. Later, when colonists broke away from Great Britain, they used the image of the Indian to symbolize the freedom and independence they sought for themselves.

In sum, during the first 200-odd years that followed Columbus's first landfall in the Caribbean, a complex development had taken place in the Americas. Sometimes these alien encounters were amiable, as Indians and colonists exchanged ideas, skills, and goods; while sometimes the encounters were hostile and bloody, with unimaginable cruelties inflicted by and on both sides. But the coming together of Indians and European settlers was mostly characterized by ambiguity and confusion, as markedly different peoples drew from their own traditions to make sense of a new world that little resembled what they knew. In time, their world would become our own.

Christopher Columbus's fateful voyage brought alien worlds together, an encounter characterized by mutual incomprehension. In consequence, millions of American Indians perished, millions of Europeans immigrated to the Americas, and millions of Africans were sent there as slaves. The cultures of all peoples—food and diet, religious beliefs and practices, and modes of sustenance and social organization—changed in fundamental ways. During that fateful first century, American Indians, Europeans, and Africans interacted continuously—negotiating, fighting, trading, and intermarrying—without really understanding one another.

Milestones

EXPLORATION

c. 1000	Leif Eriksson reaches Newfoundland
1445–1488	Portuguese sailors explore west coast of Africa
1492	First voyage of Christopher Columbus
1497	John Cabot explores east coast of North America
1498	Vasco da Gama sails around Africa to India
1513	Ponce de Leon explores Florida
1519–1521	Hernán Cortés conquers Mexico
1519–1522	Ferdinand Magellan's crew circumnavigates globe
1539–1542	Hernando de Soto explores lower Mississippi River Valley
1540–1542	Francisco Vasquez de Coronado explores Southwest
1579	Francis Drake explores coast of California
1609	Henry Hudson discovers Hudson River

SETTLEMENT

1493	Columbus founds La Navidad, Hispaniola
1494	Treaty of Tordesillas divides New World between Spain and Portugal
1576	Spanish settle St. Augustine
1587	English found "Lost Colony" of Roanoke Island
1607	English settle Jamestown
1608	French found Québec
1612	John Rolfe introduces tobacco cultivation in Virginia
1620	Pilgrims settle Plymouth, sign Mayflower Compact
1624	Dutch settle New Amsterdam
1630	English puritans settle Massachusetts Bay
1630–1640	Waves of English come to America during the Great Migratio
1634	George Calvert, Lord Baltimore, founds Maryland as Catholic haven
1636	Roger Williams founds Rhode Island
	General Court of Massachusetts Bay Colony banishes Anne Hutchinson
1639	Thomas Hooker founds Connecticut
1642	French found Montréal
1664	English conquer Dutch New Amsterdam
1670	First settlers arrive in Carolina
1680	Charles Town (now Charleston, South Carolina) is settled
1682	William Penn founds Philadelphia

✓●─[Study and Review at www.myhistorylab.com

Review Questions

1. Why did Columbus choose to embark on his 1492 voyage and what was his "great error"?
2. What factors accounted for the ease with which Spain imposed its will upon the Indians of south and central America?
3. What accounted for the Indian susceptibility to European diseases? Why do scholarly estimates of Indian population losses vary so greatly?

4. What reasons prompted English peoples to come to the Americas? How did they choose different settlements on the Atlantic coast?
5. Why did Europeans so often treat Indians with such brutality? In what ways did Europeans and Indians interact positively?

Key Terms

antinomianism   *35*
Arminianism   *30*
Columbian
  Exchange   *23*
conquistadores   *17*
encomienda
  system   *18*

joint-stock
  companies   *25*
Mayflower
  Compact   *31*
predestination   *30*
Protestant
  Reformation   *24*

puritans   *30*
Quakers   *39*
Treaty of
  Tordesillas   *17*

2 American Society in the Making

Do you take risks?

THE UNITED STATES IS A NATION OF MIGRATORY PEOPLES: PALEO-INDIANS who ventured from Siberia tens of thousands of years ago, Europeans who explored and settled the "new" world in the sixteenth and seventeenth centuries, millions of immigrants who have arrived from other parts of the world ever since.

Alexis de Tocqueville, a French writer who visited the United States in 1831, was struck by the "restless curiosity" of Americans as they "travel up and down the vast territories" of their nation. A "feverish ardor" similarly characterized their pursuit of wealth: "They have been told that fortune is to be found somewhere toward the west, and they hasten to find it." Americans approached life "like a game of chance."

Does a uniquely American character exist and is it inspired by a migratory impulse? Some scientists think so, and their explanation is rooted in a gene that influences the release of chemicals in the brain that promote risk-taking.[1] A 2009 psychology study at Harvard found that college students with this gene bet larger sums when gambling than those without it.

Scientists speculate that people with the "risk-taking" gene are more likely to migrate to distant lands. Support for this hypothesis rests in the fact that the gene is far more common among nomadic tribes in Africa than sedentary ones, and is more common among South American Indians who migrated from East Asia tens of thousands of years ago than East Asians.

But even if this speculation is true, other factors have influenced the development of a distinctively American character. Sometimes migrants came to the Americas because staying put was riskier than moving. Land in the Americas seemed limitless and, by European standards, nearly uninhabited. Because the labor to farm it and extract its wealth was scarce, immigrants could reasonably bet that wages would be higher. Immigrants quickly discovered that the social and cultural institutions of their home country were often ill-adapted to American conditions, necessitating innovation and further risk taking: The widely spaced pattern of large American farms, for example, discouraged the residential clumping of European villages. Religious enthusiasts and educational reformers also learned that they had a broader canvas on which to realize ambitious visions.

---

[1]The "risk-taking" gene is a variant of the D4 gene that influences the release of dopamine, a neurotransmitter. It is also associated with hyperactivity and ADD.

Factors as material as the landscape, as quantifiable as population patterns, and as elusive as chance and calculation, all shaped colonial social developments. Their cumulative impact did not at first produce anything like a uniform society. The "Americans" who evolved in what is now the United States were in many ways as different from each other as they were from their foreign cousins. The process by which these identities merged into an American nation remained incomplete. It was—and is—ongoing.

Settlement of New France

After 1700 France's colonial enterprise in North America stagnated. The main problem, as before, was the difficulty in persuading French people to occupy isolated settlements in remote American frontiers. But some did come. The French government built and occupied forts along the shores of the Great Lakes and at strategic positions overlooking the Mississippi, Illinois, and other rivers. Solitary French traders ventured deep into the wilderness in search of increasingly scarce animal pelts. Jesuit missionaries endeavored to plant Christianity among the Indians. Missionaries founded Detroit in 1701, Kaskaskia (south of Cahokia) in 1703, and Fort de Chartres in 1720.

Attempts to anchor New France with a colony at the mouth of the Mississippi were frustrated by the region's maze of swamps, marshes, and meandering waterways which, though ideal for pirates, discouraged settlement. One French missionary, unable to locate the mouth of the Mississippi, complained that the "coast changes shape at every moment." In 1712 France chartered a private company to build a colony in the region. It laid out a town called New Orleans at the site of a short portage between the Mississippi River and Lake Pontchartrain. The company granted tracts of land to settlers and transported several thousand of them to Louisiana. Some established farms, planting indigo, tobacco, rice, and cotton; others acquired forest products, such as lumber, tar, and resin; and still others traded for furs. The company established more settlements in the region, including one at Natchez, on a bluff above the Mississippi. But in 1729 the Natchez Indians wiped out the settlement. The company went bankrupt.

In 1731 the French government took control of Louisiana, with New Orleans as its administrative capital. Settlement lagged. The region was unsuited for farming, bemoaned one French official: "Now there is too much drought, now too much rain." By 1750 no more than 10,000 Europeans had colonized the region.

As beaver and other game became scarce, traders ventured farther west. Eventually they came upon tribes that had been driven from Pennsylvania and New York by the mighty Iroquois confederation. These Indians, fearful of the Iroquois, sought guns and ammunition. The traders complied, though not without misgivings. This escalation in armaments ensured that warfare would be more deadly, and that the isolated outposts of New France would be more vulnerable.

Society in New Mexico, Texas, and California

Once the Indians of the upper Mississippi acquired guns from French traders, the new weaponry quickly spread to the Indians of the Great Plains. Far earlier, the Apache and Comanche had become experts at riding European horses, which proliferated on the

Architectural historians regard the Mission of San José de Laguna, completed between 1699 and 1701, as illustrative of an "architecture of permanence." This was hopeful: The previous mission church had been destroyed during the revolt of the Pueblo Indians ten years earlier.

vast grasslands in the heart of the continent. Now armed with light muskets, the Plains Indians became formidable foes; the Comanche were nearly invincible. Spanish raiders who had formerly seized Plains Indians for the slave trade now preyed upon less fearsome nomadic tribes, such as the Ute, who lived in the foothills of the Rockies.

The Comanche, always adept buffalo hunters, were even better with guns. As the number and size of their hunting bands increased, the Comanche encroached on Apache territory. Soon Comanche warriors, occasionally assisted by French traders and soldiers, raided remote Spanish and Pueblo settlements in New Mexico and Texas. "We do not have a single gun," declared one Spanish missionary in 1719, "while we see the French giving hundreds of arms to Indians."

This new threat prompted the Spanish to strengthen the *presidio*—fortified bases—at Santa Fe and San Antonio and to build new missions in east Texas. In an effort to preempt future attacks, the Spanish also dispatched a military expedition into Nebraska. But Pawnee Indians and the French ambushed and routed the invaders; from now on, Spanish garrisons and their Pueblo allies rarely ventured beyond their towns and missions.

The ascendancy of the Plains Indians endangered all of the new frontier missions and discouraged further settlement. In 1759 a Spanish commander of a

Spain's North American Frontier, c. 1750 This map of Spanish settlement is somewhat deceptive: It shows a broad swath of land "under Spanish control" extending far north of New Spain, to Santa Fe, and to San Antonio. In fact, Spanish colonization in the northern regions was patchy, consisting of scattered religious missions and military garrisons. By 1750, Spanish colonists, Indian natives, and slaves had intermarried, changing the cultures of all.

presidio complained that the Comanche were "so superior in firearms as well as in numbers that our destruction seems probable." San Antonio, the largest town, had only 600 Hispanic settlers.

The Indian slave trade remained an enduring aspect of life along the sparsely populated northern rim of New Spain. Catholic missionaries usually prevented Spanish traders from enslaving Pueblo Indians, many of whom lived in mission towns and knew the rudiments of Catholicism. But no such arguments could protect the "wild" Indians such as the Ute of the foothills of the Rockies.

Because adult males resisted capture and incorporation into colonial society, most Indian slaves were women and children. In 1761 Father Pedro Serrano reported that at one New Mexican trade fair Indian women over the age of ten were raped "in the sight of innumerable assemblies of barbarians and Catholics" before they were sold.

Indian slaves often had children by Hispanic fathers, who rarely acknowledged these offspring. Known as *genizaros*, these children occupied the bottom rung of a social system largely based on the status of fathers. *Genizaros* learned Spanish and received training in Catholicism. In some towns, they comprised a third of the population. Females usually worked as household servants, and males, as indentured servants on ranches. Spanish officials, eager to increase the numbers of Spanish colonists, granted *genizaros* the right to own property. Many became ranchers and herders.

While the Comanche terrorized the frontier of New Mexico and Texas, Spanish officials learned of a new threat in the 1760s: Britain and Russia were attempting to colonize the Northwest, the region that now comprises Oregon and Washington. This threatened Spain's claims to California, a remote wilderness inhabited by some 300,000 Indians. As in New Mexico, Spain failed to attract Hispanic settlers; so it invited Franciscan missionaries to *create* "Spanish" settlers by converting the Indians to Catholicism and Hispanicizing their language and culture. This did not prove easy. The Indians of California belonged to over 300 tribes that spoke nearly 100 different languages.

In 1769 several score Franciscans and a detachment of Spanish soldiers established a *presidio* and mission in San Diego. Other missions followed at Monterey, Santa Barbara, and San Francisco; within several decades some twenty missions had been established in California.

The Franciscans monitored Indian life closely. They segregated all unmarried girls over the age of seven so as to prevent them from indulging in freer Indian sexual mores and to protect them from lustful European men. The friars also inculcated the discipline of work; the digging of irrigation ditches; the cultivation of crops; the tending of livestock; the manufacture of handicrafts; and the construction of churches, forts, and homes. The Indians received no wages, but instead were fed and cared for by the priests, whose first obligation was to God and the church. Because the California settlements were distant from New Spain, the missions survived chiefly by provisioning Spanish military garrisons.

Whatever success the Franciscans had in establishing the missions, however, was undone by disease. As had happened throughout the Western Hemisphere, the introduction of European pathogens among formerly isolated Indian populations resulted in catastrophic losses. European diseases hit all California Indians, not just those in the missions. By the close of the eighteenth century, Spain had failed in its effort to establish a strong Hispanic colony in California.

The English Prevail on the Atlantic Seaboard

By the mid-eighteenth century, England had successfully addressed the chief problem that bedeviled the French and Spanish colonial efforts: a dearth of colonists. By then, European settlers, most of them English, had taken possession of much of the Atlantic seaboard. But this basic fact overlooks the important differences among the colonies. Each of the Middle Colonies had distinctive histories and settlement patterns. Even the New England colonies, though originally founded for similar religious purposes, soon diverged.

The southern parts of English North America comprised three regions: the Chesapeake Bay, consisting of "tidewater" Virginia and Maryland; the "low country" of the Carolinas (and eventually Georgia); and the "back country," a vast territory that extended from the "fall line" in the foothills of the Appalachians (where falls and rapids put an end to navigation on the tidal rivers) to the farthest point of western settlement. Not until well into the eighteenth century would the emergence of common features— export-oriented agricultural economies, a labor force in which black slaves figured prominently, and the absence of towns of any size—prompt people to think of the "South" as a single region.

The Chesapeake Colonies

When the English philosopher Thomas Hobbes wrote in 1651 that human life tended to be "nasty, brutish, and short," he might well have had in mind the royal colony of Virginia. Although the colony grew from about 1,300 to nearly 5,000 in the decade after the Crown took it over in 1624, the death rate remained appalling. Since more than 9,000 immigrants had entered the colony, nearly half the population died during that decade.

English Colonies on the Atlantic Seaboard The boundaries of English colonies were partially determined by geographical factors—usually the Atlantic Ocean to the east and the Appalachian mountains in the west, beyond which few colonists settled prior to 1750. Most colonial charters set the north/south borders of a colony according to a particular line of latitude—that is to say, the distance a place is located in relation to the equator.

The climate was largely to blame. Almost without exception newcomers underwent "seasoning," a period of illness that in its mildest form consisted of "two or three fits of a feaver and ague." The relatively dry summers were the chief cause of the high death rate. During the summer the slower flow of the James River allowed relatively dense salt water to penetrate inland. This blocked the flow of polluted river water, which the colonists drank. The result was dysentery, the "bloody flux." If they survived the flux, and a great many did not, settlers still ran the seasonal risk of contracting a particularly virulent strain of malaria, which, though seldom fatal in itself, could so debilitate its victims that they often died of typhoid fever and other ailments.

Long after food shortages and Indian warfare had ceased to be serious problems, life in the Chesapeake colonies remained precarious. Well into the 1700s a white male of twenty in Middlesex County, Virginia, could look forward only to about twenty-five more years of life. Across Chesapeake Bay, in Charles County, Maryland, life expectancy was even lower. The high death rate had important effects on family structure. Because relatively few people lived beyond their forties, more often than not children lost at least one of their parents— and in many instances both—before they reached maturity.

All Chesapeake settlers felt the psychological effects of their precarious and frustrating existence. Random mayhem and calculated violence posed a continuous threat. Life was coarse at best and often as "brutish" as Hobbes had claimed, even allowing for the difficulties involved in carving out a community in the wilderness.

The Lure of Land

Agriculture was the bulwark of life for the Chesapeake settlers and the rest of the colonial South; the tragic experiences of the Jamestown settlement revealed this quickly enough. Jamestown also suggested that a colony could not succeed unless its inhabitants were allowed to own their own land. The first colonists had agreed to work for seven years in return for a share of the profits. When their contracts expired there were few profits. To satisfy these settlers and to attract new capital, the London Company declared a "dividend" of land, its only asset. The surviving colonists each received 100 acres. Thereafter, as prospects continued to be poor, the company relied more and more on grants of land to attract both capital and labor. A number of wealthy Englishmen were given immense tracts, some running to several hundred thousand acres. Lesser persons willing to settle in Virginia received more modest grants. Whether dangled before a great tycoon, a country squire, or a poor farmer, the offer of land had the effect of encouraging immigration to the colony. This was a much-desired end, for without the labor to develop it the land was worthless.

Soon what was known as the **headright** system became entrenched in both Virginia and Maryland. Behind the system lay the principle that land should be parceled out according to the availability of labor to cultivate it. For each "head" entering the colony authorities issued a "right" to take any fifty acres of unoccupied land. To "seat" a claim and receive title to the property, the holder of the headright had to mark out its boundaries, plant a crop, and construct some sort of habitation. This system was adopted in all the southern colonies and in Pennsylvania and New Jersey.

The headright system encouraged landless Europeans to migrate to English America. More often than not, however, those most eager to come could not afford passage across the Atlantic. To bring such people to America, the **indentured servant** system was developed. Indenture resembled apprenticeship. In return for transportation indentured servants agreed to work for a stated period, usually about five years.

•●●—[Read the Document

Wessell Webling, *His Indenture*, *1622* at **myhistorylab.com**

During that time they were subject to strict control by the master and received no compensation beyond their keep. Servants lacked any incentive to work hard, whereas masters tended to "abuse their servantes . . . with intollerable oppression." In this clash of wills the advantage lay with the master; servants lacked full political and civil rights, and masters could administer physical punishment and otherwise abuse them. An indenture, however, was a contract; servants could and did sue when planters failed to fulfill their parts of the bargain, and surviving court records suggest that they fared reasonably well when they did so.

Servants who completed their years of labor became free. Usually the former servant was entitled to an "outfit" (a suit of clothes, some farm tools, seed, and perhaps a gun), and occasionally to a small grant of land.

Most servants eventually became landowners, but with the passage of time their lot became harder. The best land belonged to the large planters, and as more land went into cultivation, crop prices fell. Many owners of small farms, former servants especially, slipped into dire poverty. Some were forced to become "squatters" on land along the fringes of settlement that no one had yet claimed. Squatting often led to trouble; eventually, when someone turned up with a legal title to the land, the squatters demanded "squatters' rights," the privilege of buying the land from the legal owner without paying for the improvements the squatters had made upon it. This led to lawsuits and sometimes to violence.

In the 1670s conflicts between Virginians who owned choice land and former servants on the outer edge of settlement brought the colony to the brink of class warfare. The costs of meeting the region's ever-growing need for labor with indentured servants were becoming prohibitive. Some other solution was needed.

"Solving" the Labor Shortage: Slavery

Probably the first African blacks brought to English North America arrived on a Dutch ship and were sold at Jamestown in 1619. Early records are vague and incomplete, so it is not possible to say whether these Africans were treated as slaves or freed after a period of years as were indentured servants. What is certain is that by about 1640 *some* blacks were slaves (a few, with equal certainty, were free) and that by the 1660s local statutes had firmly established the institution of slavery in Virginia and Maryland.

Slavery soon spread throughout the colonies. As early as 1626 there were only a handful of slaves in New Netherland, and when the English conquered that colony in 1664 there were 700 slaves in a population of about 8,000. The Massachusetts Body of Liberties of 1641—strange title—provided that "there shall never be any bond-slavery . . . amongst us; unless it be lawful captives taken in just warrs [i.e., Indians] and such strangers as willingly sell themselves, or *are solde* to us." However, relatively few blacks were imported until late in the seventeenth century, even in the southern colonies. In 1650 there were only 300 blacks in Virginia and as late as 1670 no more than 2,000.

In 2009, President Barack Obama visited the Cape Coast Castle in Ghana, a fortress that held Africans before they were shipped to the Americas. "It is here," Obama declared, "where the journey of much of the African American experience began."

White servants were much more highly prized. The African, after all, was almost entirely unaccustomed to both the European and the American ways of life. In a country starved for capital, the cost of slaves—roughly five times that of indentured servants—was another disadvantage. In 1664 the governor of Maryland informed Lord Baltimore that local planters would use more "neigros" "if our purses would endure it." As long as white servants were available, few planters acquired slaves.

In the 1670s the flow of indentured servants slackened as the result of improving economic conditions in England and the competition of other colonies for servants. At the same time, the formation of the Royal African Company (1672) made slaves more readily available. By 1700, nearly 30,000 slaves lived in the English colonies.

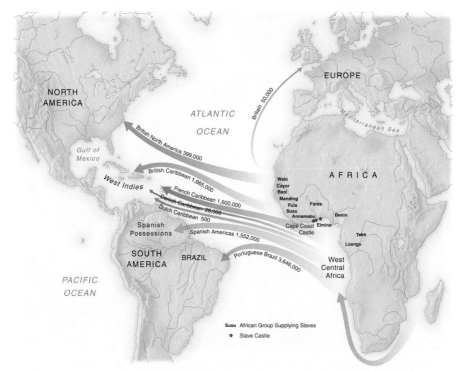

Atlantic Slave Trade, 1451–1870 From 1619, when a Dutch frigate sold several dozen slaves to English colonists at Jamestown, until 1808, when Congress abolished the African slave trade, nearly 400,000 Africans were brought against their will to what is now the United States. Approximately 8 million more were taken to the sugar or coffee plantations in Brazil and the Caribbean and to the mines and farms of Spanish America. Although most of the slaves came from western Africa and central Africa, some (not shown on this map) came from Africa's eastern coast as well.

Prosperity in a Pipe: Tobacco

Labor and land made agriculture possible, but it was necessary to find a market for American crops in the Old World if the colonists were to enjoy anything but the crudest existence. They could not begin to manufacture all the articles they required; to obtain from England such items as plows, muskets, books, and china-ware, they had to have cash crops—what their English creditors called "merchantable commodities." Here, at least, fortune favored the Chesapeake.

The founders of Virginia tried to produce all sorts of things that were needed in the old country: grapes and silk in particular, indigo, cotton, oranges, olives, sugar, and many other plants. But it was tobacco, unwanted, even strongly opposed at first, that became for farmers on both sides of Chesapeake Bay "their darling."

Tobacco was unknown in Europe until Spanish explorers brought it back from the West Indies. Since it clearly contained some habit-forming drug, many people opposed its use. King James I wrote a pamphlet attacking the weed, in which, among other things, he anticipated the findings of

Read the **Document**

James I, *A Counterblaste to Tobacco* at **myhistorylab.com**

A denunciation of the tobacco craze that swept Europe in the mid-1600s, by Abraham Teniers.
Source: Erich Lessing/Art Resource, NY.

modern cancer researchers by saying that smoking was a "vile and stinking" habit "dangerous to the Lungs." The London Company initially discouraged its colonists from growing tobacco. But English smokers and partakers of snuff ignored their king, and the Virginians ignored their company. By 1617 a pound of tobacco was worth more than 5 shillings in London. Company and Crown then changed their tune, granting the colonists a monopoly and encouraging them in every way.

Unlike wheat, which required expensive plows and oxen to clear the land and prepare the soil, tobacco plants could be set on semicleared land and cultivated with a simple hoe. Although tobacco required lots of human labor, a single laborer working two or three acres could produce as much as 1,200 pounds of cured tobacco, which, in a good year, yielded a profit of more than 200 percent. This being the case, production in America leaped from 2,500 pounds in 1616 to nearly 30 million pounds in the late seventeenth century, or roughly 400 pounds of tobacco for every man, woman, and child in the Chesapeake colonies.

The tidewater region was blessed with many navigable rivers, and the planters spread along their banks giving the Chesapeake a shabby, helter-skelter character of rough habitations and growing tobacco that was mostly planted in stump-littered fields, surrounded by fallow land and thickets interspersed with dense forest. There were no towns and almost no roads. English ships made their way up the rivers from farm to farm, gathering the tobacco at each planter's wharf. The vessels also served as general stores of a sort where planters could exchange tobacco for everything from cloth, shoes, tools, salt, and nails to such exotic items as tea, coffee, chocolate, and spices.

However, the tremendous increase in the production of tobacco caused the price to plummet in the late seventeenth century. This did not stop the expansion of the colonies, but it did alter the structure of their society. Small tobacco farmers found it more difficult to make a decent living. At the same time men with capital and individuals with political influence were amassing large tracts of land. If well-managed, a big plantation gave its owner important competitive advantages over the small farmer. Tobacco was notorious for the speed with which it exhausted the fertility of the soil. Growers with a lot of land could shift frequently to new fields within their holdings, allowing the old fields to lie fallow and thus maintain high yields; but the only option that small farmers had when their land gave out was to move to unsettled land on the frontier. To do that in the 1670s was to risk trouble with Indians. It might also violate colonial laws designed to slow westward migration and limit tobacco production. Neither was about to stop settlement.

Bacon's Rebellion

Chesapeake settlers showed little respect for constituted authority, partly because most people lived on isolated plantations and partly because the London authorities were usually ignorant of their needs. The first Virginians often disregarded directives of the London Company. The most serious challenge took place in Virginia in 1676. Planters in the outlying counties disliked the officials in Jamestown who ran the colony. The royal governor, Sir William Berkeley, and his "Green Spring" faction (the organization took its name from the governor's plantation) had ruled Virginia for more than thirty years. Outsiders resented the way Berkeley and his henchmen used their offices to line their pockets. They also resented their social pretensions, for Green Springers made no effort to conceal their opinion (which had considerable basis in fact) that western planters were a crude and vulgar lot.

Early in 1676 planters on the western edge of settlement asked Berkeley to authorize an expedition against Indians who had been attacking nearby plantations. Berkeley refused. The planters then took matters into their own hands. Their leader, Nathaniel Bacon, was (and remains today) a controversial figure. His foes described him as extremely ambitious and possessed "of a most imperious and dangerous hidden Pride of heart." But even his sharpest critics conceded that he was "of an inviting aspect and powerful elocution" and well qualified "to lead a giddy and unthinking multitude."

When Berkeley refused to authorize him to attack the Indians, Bacon promptly showed himself only too willing to lead that multitude not only against Indians but against the governor. Without permission he raised an army of 500 men, described by the Berkeley faction as a "rabble of the basest sort." Berkeley then declared him a traitor.

Several months of confusion followed during what is known as **Bacon's Rebellion**. Bacon murdered some peaceful Indians, marched on Jamestown and forced Berkeley to legitimize Bacon's command, then headed west again to kill more Indians. In September he returned to Jamestown and burned it to the ground. Berkeley fled across Chesapeake Bay to the Eastern Shore. A few weeks later, Bacon came down with a "violent flux"—probably it was a bad case of dysentery—and he died. Soon thereafter an English naval squadron arrived with enough soldiers to restore order. Bacon's Rebellion came to an end.

On the surface, the uprising changed nothing. No sudden shift in political power occurred. Indeed, Bacon had not sought to change either the political system or the social and economic structure of the colony. But if the *rebellion* did not change anything, nothing was ever again quite the same. With seeming impartiality, the Baconites had warred against Indians and against wealthy planters. But which was their real enemy? Would some future Baconite overthrow the wealthy planters? Leaders in the Chesapeake colonies increasingly looked for cheap labor that would not acquire political power.

In the quarter-century following Bacon's Rebellion, the wealthier planters increasingly bought African slaves. This intensified the differences between rich and poor tobacco growers. The few who succeeded in accumulating twenty or more slaves and enough land to keep them occupied grew richer. The majority of people either grew poorer or at best had to struggle to hold their own.

More important, however, Bacon's Rebellion sealed an implicit contract between the inhabitants of the "great houses" and those who lived in more modest lodgings: Southern whites might have differed greatly in wealth and influence, but they stood as one behind the principle that Africans must have neither. This was the basis—the price—of the harmony and prosperity achieved by those who survived "seasoning" in the Chesapeake colonies.

The Carolinas

The English and, after 1700, the Scots-Irish settlers of the tidewater parts of the Carolinas turned to agriculture as enthusiastically as had their Chesapeake neighbors. In substantial sections of what became North Carolina, tobacco flourished. In South Carolina, after two decades in which furs and cereals were the chief products, Madagascar rice was introduced in the low-lying coastal areas in 1696. It quickly proved its worth as a cash crop. By 1700 almost 100,000 pounds were being exported annually; by the eve of the Revolution rice exports from South Carolina and Georgia exceeded 65 million pounds a year.

In the 1740s another cash crop, indigo, was introduced in South Carolina by Eliza Lucas, a plantation owner. Indigo did not compete with rice either for land or labor. It prospered on high ground and needed care in seasons when the slaves were not busy in the rice paddies. The British were delighted to have a new source of indigo because the blue dye was important in their woolens industry. Parliament quickly placed a bounty—a bonus—on it to stimulate production.

Their tobacco, rice, and indigo, along with furs and forest products, meant that the southern colonies had no difficulty in obtaining manufactured articles from abroad. Planters dealt with agents in England and Scotland who managed the sale of their crops, filled their orders for manufactures, and supplied them with credit. This was a great convenience but not necessarily an advantage, for it prevented the development of a diversified economy. Throughout the colonial era, while small-scale manufacturing developed rapidly in the North, it stagnated in the South.

Slave labor predominated from the beginning on the South Carolina rice plantations, for free workers would not submit to the backbreaking and unhealthy regimen of cultivation. The first quarter of the eighteenth century saw an enormous influx of Africans into all the southern colonies. By 1730 roughly three out of every ten people south of Pennsylvania were black, and in South Carolina the blacks outnumbered the whites by two to one. "Carolina," remarked a newcomer in 1737, "looks more like a negro country than like a country settled by white people."

Given the existing race prejudice and the degrading impact of slavery, this demographic change had an enormous impact on life wherever African Americans were concentrated. In each colony regulations governing the behavior of blacks, both free and enslaved, increased in severity. The South Carolina Negro Act of 1740 denied slaves "freedom of movement, freedom of assembly, freedom to raise [their own] food, to earn money, to learn to read English." The blacks had no civil rights under any of these codes, and punishments were severe. For minor offenses whipping was common, and for serious crimes death by hanging or by being burned alive was practiced. Slaves were sometimes castrated for sexual offenses—even for lewd talk about white women—or for repeated attempts to escape.

Although organized slave rebellions were infrequent, individual assaults by blacks on whites were common enough. (Personal violence was also common among whites, then and throughout American history.) But the masters had sound reasons for fearing their slaves; the particular viciousness of the system lay in the fact that oppression bred resentment, which in turn produced still greater oppression.

Thus the "peculiar institution" was fastened on America with economic, social, and psychic barbs. Ignorance and self-interest, lust for gold and for the flesh, primitive prejudices, and complex social and legal ties all combined to convince the whites that black slavery was not so much good as a fact of life.

Home and Family in the South

Life for all but the most affluent planters was by modern standards uncomfortable. Houses were mostly one- and two-room affairs that were small, dark, and crowded. Furniture and utensils were sparse and crudely made. Chairs were rare; if a family possessed one it was reserved for the head of the house. People sat, slept, and ate on benches and planks. Toilets and plumbing of any kind were unknown; even chamber pots, which eliminated the nighttime trek to the outhouse, were beyond the reach of poorer families.

((•─[Hear the **Audio**
Lookie There! at
myhistorylab.com

White women (even indentured ones) rarely worked in the fields. Their responsibilities included tending to farm animals, making butter and cheese, pickling and preserving, spinning and sewing, and, of course, caring for children, which often involved orphans and stepchildren because of the fragility of life in the region. For exceptional women, the labor shortage created opportunities. Some managed large plantations; Eliza Lucas ran three in South Carolina for her absent father while still in her teens, and after the death of her husband, Charles Pinckney, she managed his extensive property holdings.

Southern children were not usually subjected to as strict discipline as were children in New England, but the difference was relative. Formal schooling for all but the rich

This depicts slaves on a South Carolina plantation, around 1790. Likely of Yoruba descent, they play West African instruments, such as the banjo, and also wear elaborate headgear, another Yoruba trait. But unlike their Yoruban contemporaries, who adorned faces and limbs with elaborate tattoos or scars, these slaves bear no evident body decorations. They are African, indisputably, but also American.

was nonexistent; the rural character of society made the maintenance of schools prohibitively expensive. Whatever most children learned, they got from their parents or other relatives. A large percentage of Southerners were illiterate. As in other regions, children were put to some kind of useful work at an early age.

Until the early eighteenth century only a handful of planters achieved real affluence. (The richest by far was Robert "King" Carter of Lancaster County, Virginia, who at the time of his death in 1732 owned 1,000 slaves and 300,000 acres.) Those fortunate few (masters of several plantations and many slaves) lived in solid, two-story houses of six or more rooms, furnished with English and other imported carpets, chairs, tables, wardrobes, chests, china, and silver. When the occasion warranted, the men wore fine broadcloth, the women the latest (or more likely the next-to-latest) fashions. Some even sent their children abroad for schooling. The founding of the College of William and Mary in Williamsburg, Virginia, in 1693 was an effort to provide the region with its own institution of higher learning, mainly in order to train clergymen. For decades, however, the College of William and Mary was not much more than a grammar school. Lawyers were relatively numerous, though rarely learned in the law. Doctors were so scarce that one sick planter wrote a letter to his brother in England describing his symptoms and asking him to consult a physician and let him know the diagnosis.

No matter what their station, southern families led relatively isolated lives. Churches, which might be expected to serve as centers of community life, were few and far between. By the middle of the eighteenth century the Anglican Church was the "established" religion, its ministers supported by public funds. The Virginia assembly had made attendance at Anglican services compulsory in 1619. In Maryland, Lord Baltimore's Toleration Act did not survive the settlement in the colony of large numbers of militant puritans. It was repealed in 1654, reenacted in 1657, then repealed again in 1692 when the Anglican Church was established.

Georgia and the Back Country

West of the fall line of the many rivers that irrigated tidewater Chesapeake and Carolina lay the back country. This region included the Great Valley of Virginia, the Piedmont, and what became the final English colony, Georgia, founded by a group of London philanthropists in 1733. These men were concerned over the plight of honest persons imprisoned for debt, whom they intended to settle in the New

World. (Many Europeans were still beguiled by the prospect of regenerating their society in the colonies. All told, about 50,000 British convicts were "transported" to America in the colonial period, partly to get rid of "undesirables," but partly for humane reasons.) The government, eager to create a buffer between South Carolina and the hostile Spanish in Florida, readily granted a charter (1732) to the group, whose members agreed to manage the colony without profit to themselves for a period of twenty-one years.

In 1733 their leader, James Oglethorpe, founded Savannah. Oglethorpe was a complicated person—vain and high-handed, yet idealistic. He hoped to people the colony with sober and industrious yeoman farmers. Land grants were limited to fifty acres and made nontransferable. To ensure sobriety, rum and other "Spirits and Strong Waters" were banned. To guarantee that the colonists would have to work hard, the entry of "any Black . . . Negroe" was prohibited. Trade with Indians was to be strictly regulated in the interest of fair dealing.

Oglethorpe intended that silk, wine, and olive oil would be the main products—none of which, unfortunately, could be profitably produced in Georgia. His noble intentions were in vain. The settlers swiftly found ways to circumvent all restrictions: Rum flowed, slaves were imported, large land holdings amassed. Georgia developed an economy much like South Carolina's. In 1752 the founders, disillusioned, abandoned their responsibilities. Georgia then became a royal colony.

Now settlers penetrated the rest of the southern back country. So long as cheap land remained available closer to the coast and Indians along the frontier remained a threat, only the most daring and footloose hunters or fur traders lived far inland. But once settlement began, it came with a rush. Chief among those making the trek were Scots-Irish and German immigrants. By 1770 the back country contained about 250,000 settlers, 10 percent of the population of the colonies.

This internal migration did not proceed altogether peacefully. In 1771 frontiersmen in North Carolina calling themselves "Regulators" fought a pitched battle with 1,200 troops dispatched by the Carolina assembly, which was dominated by low-country interests. The Regulators were protesting their lack of representation in the assembly. They were crushed and their leaders executed. This was neither the last nor the bloodiest sectional conflict in American history.

Puritan New England

If survival in the Chesapeake colonies required junking many European notions about social arrangements and submitting to the dictates of the wilderness, was this also true in Massachusetts and Connecticut? Ultimately it probably was, but at first puritan ideas certainly fought the New England reality to a draw.

Boston, like other early New England towns and unlike these southern ones, had a dependable water supply. The surrounding patchwork of forest, pond, dunes, and tide marsh was much more open than the malaria-infected terrain of the tidewater and low-country South. As a consequence New Englanders escaped "the agues and fevers" that beset settlers to the south, leaving them free to attend to their spiritual, economic, and social well-being. These differences alone made New England a much healthier habitat for settlers.

New England children like David, Joanna, and Abigail Mason (painted by an unknown artist around 1670) were expected to emulate adults in their chores and their appearance. Nevertheless, diaries and letters indicate that children were cherished by their parents in a way closer to modern family love than what their European contemporaries experienced.

View the Image
Colonial Families: Adult and Child Reading at **myhistorylab.com**

When it came to religion, puritans believed that church membership ought to be the joint decision of a would-be member and those already in the church. Those seeking admission would tell the congregation why they believed that they had received God's grace. Obvious sinners and those ignorant of Christian doctrine were rejected out of hand. But what of pious and God-fearing applicants who lacked compelling evidence of salvation? In the late 1630s, with the Great Migration in full swing and new arrivals clamoring for admission to the churches, such "merit-mongers" were excluded, thereby limiting church membership to the community's "visible saints." A decade later, the Great Migration over and applications down, some of the saints began to have second thoughts.

By the early 1650s fewer than half of all New England adults were church members. The examination for membership had become so exacting that most young people refused to submit themselves to it. How these growing numbers of nonmembers could be compelled to attend church services was a problem ministers could not ignore. Meanwhile, the magistrates found it harder to defend the policy of not letting taxpayers vote because they were not church members. But what really forced reconsideration of the membership policy were the concerns of nonmember parents about the souls of their children, who could not be baptized.

At first the churches permitted baptism of the children of church members. Later, some biblical purists came out against infant baptism altogether, but most puritans approved this practice, which allowed them the hope that a child who died after receiving baptism might at least be spared Hell's hottest precincts. Since most of the first generation were church members, nearly all the second-generation New Englanders were baptized, whether they became church members or not. The problem began with the third generation, the offspring of parents who had been baptized but who did not become church members. By the mid-1650s it was clear that if nothing were done, a majority of the people would soon be living in a state of original sin. If that happened, how could the churches remain the dominant force in New England life?

Fortunately, a way out was at hand. In 1657 an assembly of Massachusetts and Connecticut ministers recommended a form of intermediate church membership that would permit the baptism of people who were not visible saints. Five years later, some eighty ministers and laymen met at Boston's First Church to hammer out what came to be called the **Half-Way Covenant**. It provided limited (halfway) membership for any applicant not known to be a sinner who was willing to accept the provisions of the church covenant. They and their children could be baptized, but the sacrament of communion and a voice in church decision making were reserved for full members.

The General Court of Massachusetts endorsed the recommendations of the Half-Way Synod and urged all the churches of the Commonwealth to adopt them. Two years later it quietly extended the right to vote to halfway church members.

Opponents of the Half-Way Covenant argued that it reflected a slackening of religious fervor. Michael Wigglesworth gave poetic voice to these views in "God's Controversy with New England" and "The Day of Doom," both written in 1662. New Englanders may have lost some religious intensity, but the rise in church memberships, the continuing prestige accorded ministers, and the lessening of the intrachurch squabbling after the 1660s suggest that the secularization of New England society had a long way to go.

Democracies without Democrats

Like the southern colonies, the New England colonies derived their authority from charters granted by the Crown or Parliament. Except for rare fits of meddling by London bureaucrats, they were largely left to their own devices where matters of purely local interest were concerned. This typically involved maintaining order by regulating how people behaved.

According to puritan theory, government was both a civil covenant, entered into by all who came within its jurisdiction, and the principal mechanism for policing the institutions on which the maintenance of the social order depended. When Massachusetts and Connecticut passed laws requiring church attendance, levying taxes for the support of the clergy, and banning Quakers from practicing their faith, they were acting as "shield of the churches." When they provided the death penalty both for adultery and for blaspheming a parent, they were defending the integrity of families. When they set the price a laborer might charge for his services or even the amount of gold braid that servants might wear on their jackets, they believed they were enforcing the puritan principle that people must accept their assigned stations in life. Puritan communities were, for a time, close-knit: murder, assault, and theft were rare. Disputes were adjudicated through an active court system.

But puritan civil authorities and ministers of the puritan (Congregational) church came under sharp attack from English Anglicans, Presbyterians, and Quakers. When the Massachusetts General Court hanged four Quakers who returned after being expelled from the colony, a royal order of 1662 forbade further executions.

Laws like these have prompted historians and Americans generally to characterize New England colonial legislation as socially repressive and personally invasive. Yet many of the laws remained in force through the colonial period without rousing much local opposition. Others, particularly those upholding religious discrimination or restricting economic activity, were repealed at the insistence of Parliament.

A healthy respect for the backsliding ways of humanity obliged New Englanders not to depend too much on provincial governments, whose jurisdiction extended over several thousand square miles. Almost of necessity, the primary responsibility for maintaining "Good Order and Peace" fell to the more than 500 towns of the region. These differed greatly in size and development. By the early eighteenth century, the largest—Boston, Newport, and Portsmouth—were on their way toward becoming urban centers. This was before "frontier" towns like Amherst, Kent, and Hanover had even been founded. Nonetheless, town life gave New England the distinctiveness it has still not wholly lost.

The Dominion of New England

The most serious threat to these arrangements occurred in the 1680s. Following the execution of Charles I in 1649, England was ruled by one man, the Lord Protector, Oliver Cromwell, a puritan. Cromwell's death in 1658 led to the restoration of the Stuart monarchy in the person of Charles II (1660–1685). During his reign and the abbreviated one of his brother, James II (1685–1688), the government sought to bring the colonies under effective royal control.

Massachusetts seemed in particular need of supervision. Accordingly, in 1684 its charter was annulled and the colony, along with all those north of Pennsylvania, became part of the Dominion of New England, governed by Edmund Andros.

Andros arrived in Boston in late 1686 with orders to make the northern colonies behave like colonies, not like sovereign powers. He set out to abolish popular assemblies and to enforce religious toleration, particularly of Anglicans. Andros, being a professional soldier and administrator, scoffed at those who resisted his authority. "Knoweing no other government than their owne," he said, they "think it best, and are wedded to . . . it."

Fortunately for New Englanders so wedded, the Dominion fell victim two years later to yet another political turnabout in England, the **Glorious Revolution**. In 1688 Parliament decided it had had enough of the Catholic-leaning Stuarts and sent James II packing. In his place it installed James's daughter Mary and her resolutely Protestant Dutch husband, William of Orange. When news of these events reached Boston in the spring of 1689, a force of more than a thousand colonists led by a contingent of ministers seized Andros and lodged him in jail. Two years later Massachusetts was made a royal colony that also included Plymouth and Maine. As in all such colonies the governor was appointed by the king. The new General Court was elected by property owners; church membership was no longer a requirement for voting.

Salem Bewitched

In 1666, families living in the rural outback of the thriving town of Salem petitioned the General Court for the right to establish their own church. For political and economic reasons this was a questionable move, but in 1672 the General Court authorized the establishment of a separate parish. In so doing the Court put the 600-odd inhabitants of the village on their own politically as well.

Over the next fifteen years three preachers came and went before, in 1689, one Samuel Parris became minister. Parris had spent twenty years in the Caribbean as a merchant and had taken up preaching only three years before coming to Salem. Accompanying him were his wife; a daughter, Betty; a niece, Abigail; and the family's West Indian slave, Tituba, who told fortunes and practiced magic on the side.

Parris proved as incapable of bringing peace to the feuding factions of the Salem Village as had his predecessors. In January 1692 the church voted to dismiss him. At this point Betty and Abigail, now nine and eleven, along with Ann Putnam, a twelve-year-old, started "uttering foolish, ridiculous speeches which neither they themselves nor any others could make sense of." A doctor diagnosed the girls' ravings as the work of the "Evil Hand" and declared them bewitched.

> •••—[Read the Document
> *Ann Putnam's Deposition
> (1692)* at **myhistorylab.com**

But who had done the bewitching? The first persons accused were three women whose unsavory reputations and frightening appearances made them likely candidates. Sarah Good, a pauper with a nasty tongue; Sarah Osborne, a bedridden widow; and the slave Tituba, who had brought suspicion on herself by volunteering to bake a "witch cake," made of rye meal and the girls' urine. The cake should be fed to a dog, Tituba said. If the girls were truly afflicted, the dog would show signs of bewitchment.

The three women were brought before the local deputies to the General Court. As each was questioned, the girls went into contortions: "their arms, necks and backs

Examination of a Witch. A stern puritan patriarch adjusts his glasses to better examine a beautiful—and partially disrobed—young woman. Ostensibly, he is looking for the "witch's teats" with which she suckled "black dogs" and other creatures of the Devil. Completed in 1853 by T. H. Matteson, this painting subtly indicts puritan men as lecherous hypocrites. In fact, most accused witches were in their forties or fifties. The painting thus reveals more about the nineteenth-century reaction against puritanism than about the puritans themselves.
Source: Museum Purchase, 1978. Peabody Essex Museum, Salem, Massachussetts.

turned this way and that way ... their mouths stopped, their throats choaked, their limbs wracked and tormented." Tituba, likely impressed by the powers ascribed to her, promptly confessed to being a witch. Sarah Good and Sarah Osborne each claimed to be innocent, although Sarah Good expressed doubts about Sarah Osborne. All three were sent to jail on suspicion of practicing witchcraft.

These proceedings triggered new accusations. By the end of April 1692, twenty-four more people had been charged with practicing witchcraft. Officials in neighboring Andover, lacking their own "bewitched," called in the girls to help with their investigations. By May the hunt had extended to Maine and Boston and up the social ladder to some of the colony's most prominent citizens, including Lady Mary Phips, whose husband, William, had just been appointed governor.

By June, when Governor Phips convened a special court consisting of members of his council, more than 150 persons (Lady Phips no longer among them) stood formally charged with practicing witchcraft. In the next four months the court convicted twenty-eight of them, most of them women. Five "confessed" and were spared; the rest were condemned to death. Several others escaped. But nineteen persons were hanged. The husband of a convicted witch refused to enter a plea when charged with being a "wizard." He was executed by having stones piled on him until he suffocated.

Anyone who spoke in defense of the accused was in danger of being charged with witchcraft, but some brave souls challenged both the procedures and the findings of the court. Finally, at the urging of the leading ministers of the Commonwealth, Governor Phips adjourned the court and forbade any further executions.

No one involved in these gruesome proceedings escaped with a reputation intact, but those whose reputations suffered most were the ministers. Among the clergy only Increase Mather deserves any credit. He persuaded Phips to halt the executions, arguing that "it were better that ten witches should escape, than that one innocent person should be condemned." The behavior of his son Cotton defies apology. It was not that Cotton Mather accepted the existence of witches—at the time everyone did, which incidentally suggests that Tituba was not the only person in Salem who practiced witchcraft—or even that Mather took such pride in being the resident expert on demonology. It was rather his vindictiveness. He even stood at the foot of the gallows bullying hesitant hangmen into doing "their duty."

The episode also highlights the anxieties puritan men felt toward women. Many puritans believed that Satan worked his will especially through the allure of female sexuality. Moreover, many of the accused witches were widows of high status or older women who owned property; some of the women, like Tituba, had mastered herbal medicine and other suspiciously potent healing arts. Such women, especially those who lived apart from the daily guidance of men, potentially subverted the patriarchal authorities of church and state. (For more on this topic, see Re-Viewing the Past, *The Crucible*, pp. 74–75.)

A Merchant's World

Prior experience (and the need to eat) turned the first New Englanders to farming. They grew barley (used to make beer), rye, oats, green vegetables, and also native crops such as potatoes, pumpkins, and (most important) Indian corn, or maize. Corn was easily cultivated. In the form of corn liquor it was easy to store, to transport, and (in a pinch) to imbibe.

The colonists also had plenty of meat. They grazed cattle, sheep, and hogs on the common pastures or in the surrounding woodlands. Deer, along with turkey and other game birds, abounded. The Atlantic provided fish, especially cod, which was preserved by salting. In short, New Englanders ate an extremely nutritious diet. Abundant surpluses of firewood kept the winter cold from their doors. The combination contributed significantly to their good health and longevity.

But the shortness of the growing season, the rocky and often hilly terrain, and careless methods of cultivation, which exhausted the soil, meant that farmers did not produce large surpluses. Thus, while New Englanders could feed themselves without difficulty, they had relatively little to spare.

John Winthrop's generation of puritans accepted this economic marginality. They were to fasten their attention upon the next world rather than the one they occupied on Earth.

But later generations did not share the anticommercial bias of the early puritans. At the beginning of the eighteenth century a Boston minister told his congregation of another minister who reminded his flock that "the main end of planting this wilderness" was religion. A prominent member of the congregation could not contain his disagreement. "Sir," he cried out, "you are mistaken. You think you are preaching to the people of the Bay; our main end was to catch fish."

Fish, caught offshore from Cape Cod to Newfoundland, provided merchants with their opening into the world of transatlantic commerce. In 1643 five New England vessels set out with their holds packed with fish that they sold in Spain and the Canary Islands; they took payment in sherry and Madeira, for which a market existed in England. One of these ships also had the dubious distinction of initiating New England into the business of trafficking in human beings when its captain took payment in African slaves, whom he subsequently sold in the West Indies. This was the start of the famous **triangular trade**. Only occasionally was the pattern truly triangular; more often, intermediate legs gave it a polygonal character. So long as their ships ended up with something that could be exchanged for English goods needed at home, it did not matter what they started out with or how many things they bought and sold along the way.

So maritime trade and those who engaged in it became the driving force of the New England economy, important all out of proportion to the number of persons directly involved. Because mariners congregated in Portsmouth, Salem, Boston, Newport, and New Haven, these towns soon differed greatly from towns in the interior. They were larger and faster growing, and a smaller percentage of their inhabitants were farmers.

The largest and most thriving town was Boston, which by 1720 had become the commercial hub of the region. It had a population of more than 10,000; in the entire British Empire, only London and Bristol were larger. More than one-quarter of Boston's male adults had either invested in shipbuilding or were directly employed in maritime commerce. Ship captains and merchants held most of the public offices.

Beneath this emergent mercantile elite lived a stratum of artisans and small shopkeepers, and beneath these a substantial population of mariners, laborers, and "unattached" people with little or no property and still less political voice. By 1720 crime and poverty had become serious problems; public relief rolls frequently exceeded 200 souls, and dozens of criminals languished in the town jail. Boston bore little resemblance to what the first puritans had in mind when they planted their "Citty upon a Hill." But neither was it like any eighteenth-century European city. It stood midway between its puritan origins and its American future.

The Middle Colonies: Economic Basis

New York, New Jersey, Pennsylvania, and Delaware owe their collective name, the Middle Colonies, to geography. Sandwiched between New England and the Chesapeake region, they often receive only passing notice in accounts of colonial America. The lack of a distinctive institution, such as slavery or the town meeting, explains part of this neglect.

Actually, both institutions existed there. Black slaves made up about 10 percent of the population; indeed, one New York county in the 1740s had proportionally more blacks than large sections of Virginia. And eastern Long Island was settled by people from Connecticut who brought the town meeting system with them.

This quality of "in-betweenness" extended to other economic and social arrangements. Like colonists elsewhere, most Middle Colonists became farmers. But where northern farmers concentrated on producing crops for local consumption

This painting is presumably of Lord Cornbury, the royal governor of New York and New Jersey in the early 1700s, in a dress. Why it was painted and by whom is unknown. Some regard the painting as proof that the eighteenth century tolerated a wide range of sexual behaviors. In *The Lord Cornbury Scandal* (1998), however, Patricia Bonomi views the painting as part of a plot to unseat a brusque and high-handed governor. Some of his enemies in the colonies dispatched letters to officials in London complaining of Cornbury's penchant for wearing women's clothing in public. Bonomi doubts that the charges were true.
Source: *Portrait of an Unidentified Woman* (Formely Edward Hyde, Viscount Cornbury), 18th century. Collection of The New-York Historical Society, 1952.80.

and Southerners for export, Middle Colony farmers did both. In addition to raising foodstuffs and keeping livestock, they grew wheat, for which there existed an expanding market in the densely settled Caribbean sugar islands.

Social arrangements differed more in degree than in kind from those in other colonies. Unlike New England settlers, who clustered together in agricultural villages, families in the Hudson Valley of New York and in southeastern Pennsylvania lived on the land they cultivated, often as spatially dispersed as the tobacco planters of the Chesapeake. In contrast with Virginia and Maryland, however, substantial numbers congregated in the seaport centers of New York City and Philadelphia. They also settled interior towns like Albany, an important center of the fur trade on the upper Hudson, and Germantown, an "urban village" northwest of Philadelphia where many people were engaged in trades like weaving and tailoring and flour milling.

The Middle Colonies: An Intermingling of Peoples

The Middle Colonists also possessed traits that later would be seen as distinctly "American." Their ethnic and religious heterogeneity is a case in point. In the 1640s, when New Amsterdam was only a village, one visitor claimed to have heard eighteen languages spoken there. Traveling through Pennsylvania a century later, the Swedish botanist Peter Kalm encountered "a very mixed company of different nations and religions." In addition to "Scots, English, Dutch, Germans, and Irish," he reported, "there were Roman Catholics, Presbyterians, Quakers, Methodists, Seventh Day men, Moravians, Anabaptists, and one Jew." In New York City one embattled English resident complained, "Our chiefest unhappiness here is too great a mixture of nations, & English the least part."

Scandinavian and Dutch settlers outnumbered the English in New Jersey and Delaware even after the English took over these colonies. William Penn's first success in attracting colonists was with German Quakers and other persecuted religious sects, among them Mennonites and Moravians from the Rhine Valley. The first substantial influx of immigrants into New York after it became a royal colony consisted of French Huguenots. Immigrants more readily risked the dangers of migration when the alternative to remaining in Europe was persecution.

Early in the eighteenth century, hordes of Scots-Irish settlers from northern Ireland and Scotland descended on Pennsylvania. These colonists spoke English but felt little loyalty to the English government, which had treated them badly back home, and less to the Anglican Church, since most of them were Presbyterians. Large numbers of them followed the valleys of the Appalachians south into the back country of Virginia and the Carolinas.

Why so few English in the Middle Colonies? Here, again, timing provides the best answer. The English economy was booming. There seemed to be work for all. Migration to North America, while never drying up, slowed to a trickle. The result was colonies in which English settlers were a minority.

The intermingling of ethnic groups gave rise to many prejudices. Benjamin Franklin, though generally complimentary toward Pennsylvania's hard-working Germans, thought them clannish to a fault. The already cited French traveler Hector

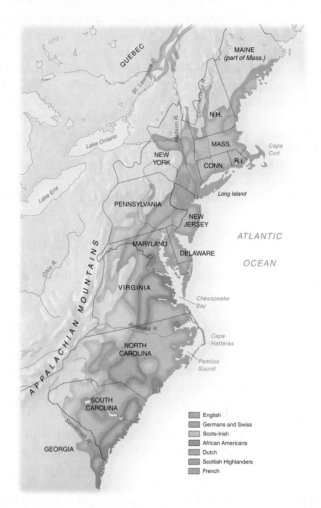

Ethnic Groups of Eastern North America, 1750 Although this chapter retains the historical convention of referring to the coastal Atlantic as "English colonies," the ethnic composition of the region was much more complicated. To be sure, people of English ancestry predominated in New England, the Chesapeake region, and the Carolinas. But the Hudson River valley remained chiefly Dutch, and southeastern Pennsylvania remained German. Much of the western frontier was populated by English-speaking people of Scottish and Irish ancestry. And in parts of Virginia and the Carolinas, slaves of African descent were in the majority.

St. John de Crèvecoeur, while marveling at the adaptive qualities of "this promiscuous breed," complained that "the Irish . . . love to drink and to quarrel; they are litigious, and soon take to the gun, which is the ruin of everything." Yet by and large the various types managed to get along with each other successfully enough. Crèvecoeur attended a wedding in Pennsylvania where the groom's grandparents were English and Dutch and one of his uncles had married a Frenchwoman. The groom and his three brothers, Crèvecoeur added with some amazement, "now have four wives of different nations."

"The Best Poor Man's Country"

Ethnic differences seldom caused conflict in the Middle Colonies because they seldom limited opportunity. The promise of prosperity had attracted all in the first place, and achieving prosperity was relatively easy, even for those who came with only a willingness to work. From its founding, Pennsylvania granted upward of 500 acres of land to families on arrival, provided they would pay the proprietor an annual fee. Similar arrangements existed in New Jersey and Delaware. Soon travelers in the Middle Colonies were being struck by "a pleasing uniformity of decent competence." Immigrants found it easier—and less risky—to abandon overcrowded Europe to till virgin fields in Pennsylvania and Delaware.

New York was something of an exception to this favorable economic situation. When the English took over New York, they extended the Dutch patroon system by creating thirty manorial estates covering about 2 million acres. But ordinary New Yorkers never lacked ways of becoming landowners. A hundred acres along the Hudson River could be bought in 1730 for what an unskilled laborer could earn in three months. Even tenants on the manorial estates could obtain long-term leases that had most of the advantages of ownership but did not require the investment of any capital.

Mixed farming offered the most commonly trod path to prosperity in the Middle Colonies, but not the only one. Inland communities offered comfortable livelihoods for artisans. Farmers always needed barrels, candles, rope, horseshoes, nails, and dozens of other articles in everyday use. Countless opportunities awaited the ambitious settler in the shops, yards, and offices of New York and Philadelphia. Unlike Boston, New York and Philadelphia profited from navigable rivers that penetrated deep into the back country. Although founded half a century after New York and Boston, Philadelphia grew more rapidly than either. In the 1750s, when its population reached 15,000, it passed Boston to become the largest city in English America.

The Politics of Diversity

Superficially the governments of the Middle Colonies closely resembled those of earlier settlements. All had popularly elected representative assemblies, and most white male adults could vote. In Pennsylvania, where Penn had insisted that there be no religious test and where fifty acres constituted a freehold, something close to white universal manhood suffrage existed. In New York even non-property-holding white male residents voted in local elections, and rural tenants with lifetime leases enjoyed full voting rights.

In Pennsylvania and most of New York, representatives were elected by counties. In this way they resembled Virginia and Maryland. But unlike the Southerners, voters did not tend to defer in politics to the landed gentry. In New York, in 1689, during the political vacuum following the abdication of King James II, Jacob Leisler, a disgruntled merchant and militia captain, seized control of the government. **Leisler's Rebellion** did not amount to much. He held power for less than two years before he was overthrown and sent to the gallows. Yet for two decades

The Crucible

Winona Ryder stars in the 1996 movie based on Arthur Miller's 1953 play, *The Crucible*, an interpretation of the Salem witch trials of 1692. Ryder plays Abigail Williams, consumed with desire for John Proctor (Daniel Day-Lewis), a married man. Proctor has broken off their affair and reconciled with his wife, Elizabeth (Joan Allen). As the movie begins, Abigail and some other girls have sneaked into the woods with Tituba, a slave who practices black magic. They ask about their future husbands, and some beg her to cast a spell on their favorites. Abigail whispers something to Tituba, who recoils in horror. Abigail's dark eyes glow with fury: She wants Elizabeth Proctor dead. Tituba slips into a trance and begins conjuring. Exhilarated by this illicit flouting of convention the girls throw off their clothes and dance wildly around a fire.

Then the minister happens onto the scene. The girls flee in terror. Some become hysterical. Later, when confronted by church elders, Abigail blurts out that Tituba was a witch who was trying to steal their souls. Tituba initially denies the charges, but after being whipped she confesses. Pressed further, she names two other women as accomplices. At the mention of their names, Abigail's face contorts with pain and she moans; taking the cue, the other girls scream and writhe upon the floor. They supply the names of more witches. Alarmed by the enormity of Satan's plot, Massachusetts authorities initiate an investigation.

After one court session, Abigail saunters over to John, standing by the side of the church. When he asks what "mischief" she has been up to, Abigail averts her eyes demurely and then gives him a wicked grin. John smiles at this prodigy in the seductive arts. She responds with a kiss. He hesitates, but then roughly pushes her away. He has reconciled with Elizabeth; he wants nothing more of Abigail. Her eyes blaze with hatred.

The girls' hysterics intensify. Eventually over 100 suspected witches, most of them women, are arrested. The Proctors themselves come under suspicion. When Abigail accuses Elizabeth of being a witch, John lashes out at the girl.

"She is a whore," he declares in court. "I have known her, sir."

"He is lying," Abigail hisses. Suddenly her eyes widen, horror-stricken, and she screams that he, too, is in league with Satan. Her flawless histrionics again prevail: He is arrested.

During the trials, the magistrates look for physical evidence of satanic possession: unnatural flaps of skin or unusual warts—witch's teats—with which Satan's minions sap human souls. Family and neighbors, too, furnish evidence. Some cite occasions when the accused lost their tempers or stole livestock. But the main evidence is the behavior of the girls, who squirm and howl, claiming that the spirits of the accused torment them. This "spectral" evidence unsettles the magistrates. Seeking stronger proof, they urge prisoners to confess. Those who do will be spared, for the act of confession signifies their break with Satan. Those who refuse must be hanged.

The Proctors are among those convicted and sentenced to death. (Because Elizabeth is pregnant, her execution is postponed.) When given the opportunity to save himself, John signs a confession. But inspired by his wife's quiet courage, he repudiates it, choosing to die with honor rather than live in shame. His noble death at the scaffold, and the deaths of others like him, cause the people of Massachusetts to end the witch hunt.

The Crucible warrants consideration apart from Ryder's remarkable performance. For one, the movie vividly recreates a puritan world inhabited by palpable spirits. Contemporary viewers may snicker at scenes of adults scanning the night sky for flying witches and evil birds, but the puritans believed in such things. They regarded comets, meteors, and lightning as signals from God. For example, when Cotton Mather lost the pages of a lecture, he concluded that "Spectres, or Agents in the invisible World, were the Robbers."

The movie's rendering of the girls' hysteria mostly corresponds with what we know from the historical record. A bewildered John Hale, a minister from Beverly, recorded that Abigail and her cousin were

> bitten and pinched by invisible agents. Their arms, necks and backs turned this way and that way, and returned back again, so as it was impossible for them to do of themselves. . . . Sometimes they were taken dumb, their mouths stopped, their throats choked, their limbs wracked and tormented so as might move an heart of stone.

This image shows actress Winona Ryder as a young puritan who accuses others of witchcraft.

The movie mostly attributes the girls' hysteria to sexual frustration, a consequence of puritan repression.

Ryder's Abigail symbolizes adolescent sexuality: Her lust for John (and hatred of Elizabeth) precipitates the witch hunt. A few historical details provide some basis for Abigail's conjectured affair with Elizabeth's husband, but others call it into question, the most telling being the gap in their ages: The real Abigail was eleven and Proctor, sixty.

Whatever the merits of playwright Arthur Miller's speculation about Abigail and John, his larger questions have long intrigued historians: Were the puritans sexually repressive? If so, did young people assent to puritan strictures or rebel against them?

Such questions cannot be answered with certainty. Few puritans left written accounts of their illicit thoughts and sexual behavior. Social historians have approached the matter from a different angle. Nearly all marriages and births in colonial New England (and most other places) were recorded. Scholars have scoured such records to determine how many brides gave birth to babies within six months of marriage; such women almost certainly had engaged in premarital intercourse.

This data for about a dozen communities in puritan New England indicate an extraordinarily low rate of premarital intercourse, far below England's at the same time or New England's a century later. This suggests that young puritan couples were watched closely. Governor William Bradford of Plymouth Colony, commenting on the relative absence of premarital pregnancy, concluded that sinners there were "more discovered and seen and made public by due search, inquisition and due punishment; for the churches look narrowly to their members, and the magistrates over all, more strictly than in other places." On the other hand, the low rate of premarital pregnancy might not signify puritan repression so much as young people's acceptance of puritan values.

When critics confronted Arthur Miller on his deviations from the historical record, and especially when they expressed skepticism over whether young Abigail Williams and the elderly John Proctor had an affair, Miller was unrepentant. "What's real?" he retorted. "We don't know what these people were like." Perhaps so, but one suspects that Winona Ryder's Abigail would have had a hard time in Salem in 1692. Could a bloom of such poisonous precocity have emerged through the stony soil of New England puritanism, and if so, could it have survived the attentive weeding of the puritans themselves?

Questions for Discussion

- What factors, apart from those mentioned in this essay, explain why puritan brides rarely had babies within six months of their marriage? Is this a good measure of premarital chastity?
- How did puritan courtship differ from modern courtship?

New York politics continued to be a struggle between the Leislerians and other self-conscious "outs" who shared Leisler's dislike of English rule, and anti-Leislerians. Each group sought the support of a succession of ineffective governors, and the group that failed to get it invariably proceeded to make that governor's tenure as miserable as possible.

New York enjoyed political tranquility during the governorship of Robert Hunter (1710–1719), but in the early 1730s conflict broke out over a claim for back salary by Governor William Cosby. When Lewis Morris, the chief justice of the supreme court, opposed Cosby's claim, the governor replaced him. Morris and his assembly allies responded by establishing the *New York Weekly Journal*. To edit the paper they hired German printer, John Peter Zenger.

Governor Cosby might have tolerated the *Weekly Journal*'s front-page lectures on the right of the people to criticize their rulers had the back pages not contained advertisements referring to his supporters as spaniels and to him as a monkey. After submitting to two months of "open and implacable malice against me," he shut down the paper, arrested Zenger, and charged him with seditious libel.

What began as a salary dispute became one of the most celebrated tests of freedom of the press in the history of journalism. At the trial Zenger's attorney, Andrew Hamilton, argued that the truth of his client's criticisms of Cosby constituted a proper defense against seditious libel. This reasoning (though contrary to English law at the time) persuaded the jury to acquit Zenger.

Politics in Pennsylvania spurred conflict between two interest groups, one clustered around the proprietor, the other around the assembly, which was controlled by a coalition of Quaker representatives from Philadelphia and the German-speaking Pennsylvania Dutch.

Neither the proprietary party nor the Quaker party qualifies as a political party in the modern sense of being organized and maintained for the purpose of winning elections. Nor can they be categorized as standing for "democratic" or "aristocratic" interests. But their existence guaranteed that the political leaders had to take popular opinion into account. Moreover, having once appealed to public opinion, they had to be prepared to defer to it. Success turned as much on knowing how to follow as on knowing how to lead.

The 1763 uprising of the "Paxton Boys" of western Pennsylvania put this policy to a full test. The uprising was triggered by eastern indifference to Indian attacks on the frontier—an indifference made possible by the fact that the east outnumbered the west in the assembly, twenty-six to ten. Fuming because it could obtain no help from Philadelphia against the Indians, a group of Scots-Irish from Lancaster county fell on a village of peaceful Conestoga Indians and murdered them. Then these Paxton Boys marched on Philadelphia, several hundred strong.

Fortunately a delegation of burghers, headed by Benjamin Franklin, talked the Paxton Boys out of attacking the town by acknowledging the legitimacy of their grievances about representation and by promising to vote a bounty on Indian scalps. It was just such fancy footwork that established Franklin, the leader of the assembly party, as Pennsylvania's consummate politician. Soon thereafter, the assembly sent Franklin to London to defend local interests against the British authorities, a situation in which he would definitely not be "with the majority."

Becoming Americans

In 1650, nearly 50,000 English settlers lived in what is now the United States. Most clung to the Atlantic coast, within easy reach of ships that could bring essential supplies, protection, and means of escape. Indians outnumbered them by about ten to one; African slaves were rare. French and Spanish colonization in what is now the United States was numerically even more inconsequential, with only about 1,000 Hispanics and even fewer Frenchmen. From the Appalachian Mountains to the Pacific, most Indians had probably never seen a European.

By 1750 the demographic situation had been transformed. Nearly a million Europeans, the great majority of English background, and perhaps a quarter of a million African slaves occupied the Atlantic seaboard. The Indians had not been entirely removed: Scores of Indian villages had been enveloped by English settlement. Tens of thousands more Indians had retreated into coastal swamplands or the foothills of the Appalachians. But English-speaking peoples had become masters of the land east of the Appalachians.

⊙ [See the **Map**
The Colonies to 1740 at
myhistorylab.com

After 1750, the immense sea of risk-taking English-speaking peoples and African slaves that had flooded into the eastern portion of the continent would spill beyond the Appalachians. By sheer force of their numbers, the English would decisively influence American identity, if only by making English the dominant language. Most of the immigrants, too, were farmers, united by a seemingly inexhaustible craving for land. But these enterprising immigrants also differed in fundamental ways. The cultures the immigrants brought with them varied according to the nationality, social status, and taste of the individual. The newcomers never lost their foreign heritage entirely, but they—and certainly their descendants—became something quite different from their relatives who remained in the Old World. They became what we call Americans.

But not right away.

Milestones

1619	First Africans are sold in Virginia	1692	Salem Village holds witchcraft trials
1636	Puritans found Boston Latin School and Harvard College	1696	Virginia colonists found College of William and Mary
1657	Half-Way Covenant leads to rise in puritan church memberships		Rice cultivation is introduced in South Carolina
1676	Western planters launch Bacon's Rebellion in Virginia	1701	Connecticut ministers found Yale College
1684–1688	Edmund Andros rules Dominion of New England	1733	George Oglethorpe leads settlement of Georgia
1689	Leisler's Rebellion in New York seizes control of government		

✓●─[Study and **Review** at **www.myhistorylab.com**

Review Questions

1. How did the strategies used by Spain, France, and England differ in peopling their colonies in North America? Why did the English prevail?

2. How did the English colonies along the Atlantic coastline differ from each other? What were the strengths and long-term weaknesses of each pattern of settlement and development?

3. Why did slavery supplant indentured servitude in the South? Why didn't slavery take hold in the northern colonies?

4. This chapter outlines the ways in which the area that now constitutes the United States was settled by people who differed in terms of nationality and religion, race and ethnic group, and even by contending classes. What did they share in common?

Key Terms

Bacon's Rebellion   *59*

Glorious Revolution   *66*

Half-Way Covenant   *65*

headright   *54*

indentured servants   *55*

Leisler's Rebellion   *73*

triangular trade   *69*

America in the British Empire

3

((•─[Hear the Audio Chapter 3 at myhistorylab.com

Do you pay too much in taxes?

IN 2009 THE AVERAGE AMERICAN PAID ABOUT ONE-THIRD OF HIS OR HER income to the federal government. Polls show that most Americans believe their taxes are too high. According to the Internal Revenue Service, about 17 percent of American taxpayers in 2008 failed to comply with the tax laws. Many say that they pay taxes only because they are forced to do so.

Yet most Americans pay, and do so voluntarily. Of the 170 million Americans who owed federal taxes in 2008, 155 million filed returns. And while the tax code includes stern punishments for cheaters, criminal prosecutions are rare. In 2008 fewer than 2,500 Americans were convicted of tax crimes, a number that has steadily declined over the past decade.

In the mid-1700s, by contrast, American colonists paid no more than one-twentieth of their income in taxes, far less than their relatives in England. Yet taxation provoked the colonists more than any other issue. John Adams, a Massachusetts lawyer whose opposition to taxes catapulted him to fame, blamed the American Revolution on England's "enormous taxes, burdensome taxes, oppressive, ruinous, intolerable taxes."

Colonial fury was partly due to a change in how London assessed and collected taxes. During the first half of the eighteenth century, most taxes were set by colonial assemblies and based on landholdings. But after 1763 the British government in London imposed new taxes on trade. When ships entered American ports, captains were required to pay taxes before the "enumerated" (taxable) cargos could be moved from the docks. Whenever Americans bought a bag of nails or a tin of tea, they were making indirect tax payments to London. Tax cheats avoided customs officials by smuggling goods. But rather than evade the "intolerable" tax burden, colonists increasingly decided to eliminate it altogether.

Resistance to taxation was only one of the sources of tumult in mid-eighteenth-century America. The taxes themselves had been necessitated by war, always a destabilizing force in human affairs. Some people, too, experienced a "great awakening" in religious faith; others looked to the European Enlightenment and its enshrinement of reason and science. Traditional ideas and institutions were being scrutinized more closely. By the 1760s and 1770s, irritation over taxes was symptomatic of a more profound societal unease.

The British Colonial System

In the earliest days of any settlement, the need to rely on home authorities was so strong that few questioned England's sovereignty. Thereafter, distance and British political inefficiency combined to allow those living in the colonies a great deal of freedom. External affairs were controlled entirely by London, and royal representatives in America tried to direct colonial policy. But in practice the Crown generally ceded control in local matters to the colonies while reserving the right to veto actions it deemed to be against national interest.

Each colony had a governor chosen by the king in the case of the royal colonies and by the proprietors of Maryland, Delaware, and Pennsylvania. The governors' powers were much like those of the king in Great Britain. They executed the local laws, appointed many minor officials, summoned and dismissed the colonial assemblies, and proposed legislation to them. They possessed the right to veto colonial laws, but in most colonies they were financially dependent on their "subjects."

Each colony also had a legislature. Except in Pennsylvania, these assemblies consisted of two houses. The lower house, chosen by qualified voters, had general legislative powers, including some control of finances. In all the royal colonies members of the upper house, or council, were appointed by the king, except in Massachusetts, where they were elected by the General Court. The councils served primarily as advisors to the governors, but they also had some judicial and legislative powers. Judges were appointed by the king and served at his pleasure. Yet both councilors and judges were normally selected from among the leaders of the local communities; London had neither the time nor the will to investigate their political beliefs. The system therefore tended to strengthen the influence of the entrenched colonials.

Most colonial legislators were practical men. Knowing their own interests, they pursued them steadily, without much regard for political theories or the desires of the royal authorities. They saw themselves as miniature Houses of Commons, steadily "nibbling" at the authority of the Crown. The king appointed governors, but governors came and went. The lawmakers remained, accumulating experience, building on precedent, and widening decade by decade their control over colonial affairs.

The official representatives of the Crown, whatever their powers or intentions, were prisoners of their surroundings. In their dealings with the assemblies they were often bound by rigid and impractical royal instructions. They had few jobs and favors to offer in their efforts to influence the legislators. Judges might interpret the law according to English precedents, but in local matters colonial juries had the final say.

Within the British government the king's Privy Council had the responsibility for formulating colonial policy. It could and did disallow (annul) specific colonial laws, but it did not proclaim constitutional principles to which all colonial legislatures must conform. It acted as a court of last appeal in colonial disputes and handled each case individually. One day the council might issue a set of instructions to the governor of Virginia, and the next day distribute a different set to the governor of South Carolina. No one person or committee thought broadly about the administration of the overseas empire.

In 1696 colonial policy was effectively determined by a new Board of Trade, which nominated colonial governors and other high officials. It reviewed all the laws passed by the colonial legislatures, recommending the disallowance of those that seemed to conflict with imperial policy. The efficiency and wisdom of the Board of Trade fluctuated over the years, but the Privy Council and the Crown nearly always accepted its recommendations.

Colonists naturally disliked having their laws disallowed, but London exercised this power with considerable restraint; only about 5 percent of the laws reviewed were rejected. Furthermore, the board served as an important intermediary for colonists seeking to influence the king and Parliament. All the colonies in the eighteenth century maintained agents in London to present the colonial point of view before board members. The most famous colonial agent was Benjamin Franklin, who represented Pennsylvania, Georgia, New Jersey, and Massachusetts at various times during his long career. In general, however, colonial agents were seldom able to exert much influence on British policy.

The British never developed an effective, centralized government for the American colonies. By and large, their American "subjects" ran their own affairs. This fact more than any other explains our present federal system and the wide areas in which the state governments are sovereign and independent.

Mercantilism

The Board of Trade was concerned with commerce as well as colonial administration. According to prevailing European opinion, colonies were important for economic reasons, chiefly as a source of raw materials. To obtain these materials, British officials developed a number of loosely related policies that later economists called **mercantilism**. The most important raw materials in the eyes of mercantilists were gold and silver, which, being universally valued and relatively rare, could be exchanged at any time or, being durable and compact, stored for future use. For these reasons, how much gold and silver a nation possessed was considered the best barometer of its prosperity and power.

Read the Document Mun, *England's Treasure by Foreign Trade* at **myhistorylab.com**

Since gold and silver could not be mined in significant amounts in western Europe, every early colonist dreamed of finding "El Dorado." The Spanish were the winners in this search; from the mines of Mexico and South America gold and silver poured into the Iberian peninsula. Failing to control the precious metals at the source, the other powers tried to obtain them by guile and warfare (witness the state-supported piracy of Francis Drake).

In the mid-seventeenth century the statesman of western Europe shifted to a less hazardous and in the long run far more profitable approach. If a country could make itself as self-sufficient as possible and also keep its citizens busy producing items sought in other lands, it could sell more goods abroad than it imported. This was known as having "a favorable balance of trade." Mercantilists regarded colonies as a means of acquiring precious metals by helping the mother country generate a favorable trade balance. Colonists thus were to supply raw materials that would otherwise have to be purchased from foreign sources or colonists were to buy substantial amounts of manufactured goods produced in the mother country.

If the possession of gold and silver signified wealth, trade was the route that led to riches, and merchants were the captains who would pilot the state to prosperity. One

Carousing in Surinam by John Greenwood, a late eighteenth-century oil painting, describes the effects of alcohol—one man guzzles his rum punch straight from the bowl, another vomits onto the floor, while a third pours his punch onto an insensate colleague. Greenwood implicitly denounces as well the trade in sugar (rum) and slaves in which these captains were engaged.

Source: John Greenwood, American, 1727–1792; *Sea Captians Carousing in Surinam*, c. 1752–58; oil on bed ticking; 37 3/4 × 75 in. (95.9 × 190.5 cm); St. Louis Art Museum, Museum Purchase 256: 1948.

must, of course, have something to sell, so internal production must be stimulated. Parliament encouraged the British people to concentrate on manufacturing by placing tariffs—taxes on trade—on foreign manufactured goods and by subsidizing British-made textiles, iron, and other products.

The Navigation Acts

The promotion of commerce was fundamental. Toward this end Parliament enacted the **Navigation Acts**. These laws, put into effect over a period of half a century and more, were designed to bring gold and silver into the Royal Treasury, to develop the imperial merchant fleet, to channel the flow of colonial raw materials into England, and to keep foreign goods and vessels out of colonial ports.

The system originated in the 1650s in response to stiff commercial competition by the Dutch. Before 1650 a large share of the produce of the English colonies in America reached Europe in Dutch vessels; the first slaves in Virginia arrived on a Dutch ship and were doubtless paid for in tobacco that was later enjoyed in the Dutch cities of Amsterdam and Rotterdam.

The Navigation Act of 1660 reserved the entire trade of the colonies to English ships and required that the captain and three-quarters of his crew be English. (Colonists, of course, were English, and their ships were treated on the same terms as those sailing out of London or Liverpool.) The act also provided that certain colonial "enumerated articles"—sugar, tobacco, cotton, ginger, and dyes like indigo (purple) and fustic (yellow)—could not be "shipped, carried, conveyed or transported" outside the empire. Three years later Parliament required that with trifling exceptions all European products destined for the colonies be brought to England before being shipped across the Atlantic. Since trade between England and the colonies was reserved to English vessels, this meant that the goods would have to be unloaded and reloaded in England.

The English looked on the empire broadly; they envisioned the colonies as part of an economic unit, not as servile dependencies to be exploited for England's selfish benefit. Growing tobacco in England was prohibited, and valuable bounties were paid to colonial producers of indigo and naval stores. The carefully planned British economic system suited the realities of life in an underdeveloped country rich in raw materials and suffering from a chronic labor shortage.

Some historians stress the significance of the restrictions that the British placed on colonial manufacturing. The Wool Act of 1699 prohibited the export (but not the manufacture for local sale) of colonial woolen cloth. A similar law regarding hats was passed in 1732, and in 1750 an Iron Act outlawed the construction of new rolling and slitting mills in America. No other restrictions on manufacturing were imposed.

At most the Wool Act stifled a potential American industry; the law was directed chiefly at Irish woolens rather than American ones. The hat industry cannot be considered a major one. Iron, however, was important; by 1775 the industry was thriving in Virginia, Maryland, New Jersey, and Pennsylvania, and America was turning out one-seventh of the world supply. Yet the Iron Act was designed to steer the American iron industry in a particular direction, not to destroy it. Eager for iron to feed English mills, Parliament eliminated all duties on colonial pig and bar iron entering England, a great stimulus to the basic industry.

The Effects of Mercantilism

Colonists increasingly complained about mercantilism, but did it harm them? The chronic colonial shortage of hard money was superficially caused by the flow of specie—gold and silver—to England to meet the "unfavorable" balance of trade. The rapidly growing colonial economy consumed far more manufactured products than it could pay for out of current production. To be "in debt" to England really meant that the English were investing capital in America, a relationship that benefited lender and borrower alike.

Important colonial products for which no market existed in England (such as fish, wheat, and corn) were never enumerated and moved freely and directly to foreign ports. Most colonial manufacturing was untouched by English law. Shipbuilding benefited from the Navigation Acts, since many English merchants bought vessels built in the colonies. Between 1769 and 1771, Massachusetts, New Hampshire, and Rhode Island yards constructed perhaps 250 ships of 100 to 400 tons for transatlantic commerce and twice that many sloops and schooners for fishermen and coastal traders.

Two forces that worked in opposite directions must be considered before arriving at any judgment about English mercantilism. While the theory presupposed a general imperial interest above that of both colony and mother country, when conflicts of interest arose the latter nearly always predominated. Whenever Parliament or the Board of Trade resolved an Anglo-American disagreement, the colonists tended to lose.

Complementary interests conspired to keep conflicts at a minimum, but in the long run, as the American economy became more complex, the colonies would have been seriously hampered and much more trouble would have occurred had the system continued to operate.

5-Year Averages (1774: 4-Year Average)

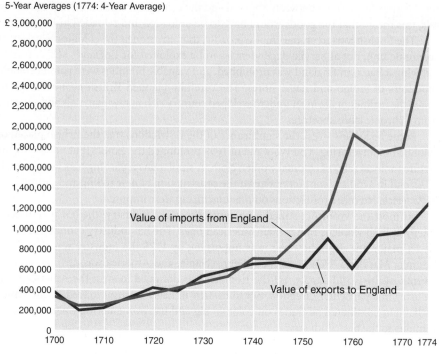

Colonial Trade with England, 1700–1774

On the other hand, the restrictions of English mercantilism were greatly lessened by inefficiency. The king and his ministers handed out government posts to win political favor or to repay political debts, regardless of the recipient's ability to perform the duties of the office.

Transported to remote America, this system scarcely functioned at all when local opinion resisted it. Smuggling became a respected profession and bribery of English officials was a standard practice. Despite a supposedly prohibitive duty of sixpence a gallon imposed by the Molasses Act of 1733, molasses from the French West Indies continued to be imported. The duty was seldom collected.

Mercantilist policies hurt some colonists such as the tobacco planters, who grew far more tobacco than British consumers could smoke. But the policies helped others, and most people proved adept at getting around those aspects of the system that threatened them.

By the same token, England profited greatly from its overseas possessions. With all its inefficiencies, mercantilism worked. Prime Minister Sir Robert Walpole's famous policy of "salutary neglect," which involved looking the other way when Americans violated the Navigation Acts, was partly a bowing to the inevitable, and partly the result of complacency. English manufactures were better and cheaper than those of other nations. This fact, together with ties of language and a common heritage, predisposed Americans toward doing business in England. All else followed naturally; the mercantilist laws merely steered the American economy in a direction it had already taken.

In this painting evangelist George Whitefield appears to be cross-eyed. This is no fault of John Wollaston, the painter. Whitefield had eye problems; his detractors called him "Dr. Squintum." The woman's rapturous gaze is unaffected by Whitefield's own curious visage.

The Great Awakening

Although a majority of the settlers were of English, Scotch, or Scots-Irish descent, and their interests generally coincided with those of their cousins in the mother country, people in the colonies were beginning to recognize their common interests and character. Their loyalties were still predominantly local, but by 1750 the word American, used to describe something characteristic of all the British possessions in North America, had entered the language. Events in one part of America were beginning to have direct effects on other regions. One of the first of these developments was the so-called **Great Awakening**.

By the early eighteenth century, religious fervor had slackened in all the colonies. Prosperity turned many colonists away from their ancestors' preoccupation with the rewards of the next world to the more tangible ones of this one. John Winthrop invested his faith in God and his own efforts in the task of creating a spiritual community; his grandsons invested in Connecticut real estate.

The proliferation of religious denominations made it impracticable to enforce laws requiring regular religious observances. Even in South Carolina, the colony that came closest to having an "Anglican Establishment," only a minority were churchgoers. Settlers in frontier districts lived beyond the reach of church or clergy. The result was a large and growing number of "persons careless of all religion."

This state of affairs came to an abrupt end with the Great Awakening of the 1740s. The Awakening began in the Middle Colonies as the result of religious developments that originated in Europe. In the late 1720s two newly arrived ministers, Theodore Frelinghuysen, a Calvinist from Westphalia, and William Tennent, an Irish-born Presbyterian, sought to instill in their sleepy Pennsylvania and New Jersey congregations the evangelical zeal and spiritual enthusiasm they had witnessed among the Pietists in Germany and the Methodist followers of John Wesley in England. Their example inspired other clergymen, including Tennent's two sons.

A more significant surge of religious enthusiasm followed the arrival in 1738 in Georgia of the Reverend George Whitefield, a young Oxford-trained Anglican minister. Whitefield was a rousing pulpit orator who played on the feelings of his audience the way a conductor directs a symphony. Whitefield undertook a series of fund-raising tours throughout the colonies. The most successful began

●●●─Read the Document

Franklin on George Whitefield (1771) at **myhistorylab.com**

in Philadelphia in 1739. Benjamin Franklin, not a very religious person and not easily moved by emotional appeals, heard one of these sermons. "I silently resolved he should get nothing from me," he later recalled.

> I had in my Pocket a Handful of Copper Money, three or four silver Dollars, and five Pistoles in Gold. As he proceeded I began to soften and concluded to give the Coppers. Another Stroke of his Oratory . . . determin'd me to give the Silver; and he finish'd so admirably that I empty'd my Pocket wholly into the Collector's Dish.

Whitefield's visit changed the "manners of our inhabitants," Franklin added.

Wherever Whitefield went he filled the churches. If no local clergyman offered his pulpit, Whitefield attracted thousands to outdoor meetings. During a three-day visit to Boston, 19,000 people (more than the population of the town) thronged to hear him. His oratorical brilliance aside, Whitefield succeeded in releasing an epidemic of religious emotionalism because his message was so well-suited to American ears. By preaching a theology that one critic said was "scaled down to the comprehension of twelve-year-olds," he spared his audiences the rigors of hard thought. Though he usually began by chastising his listeners as sinners, "half animals and half devils," he invariably took care to leave them with the hope that eternal salvation could be theirs. While not denying the doctrine of predestination, he preached a God responsive to good intentions. He disregarded sectarian differences and encouraged his listeners to do the same. "God help us to forget party names and become Christians in deed and truth," he prayed.

Of course not everyone found the Whitefield style enlightening. Some churches split into factions. Those who supported the incumbent minister were called among Congregationalists, "Old Lights," and among Presbyterians, "Old Sides," while those who favored revivalism were known as "New Lights" and "New Sides." These splits often ran along class lines. The richer, better-educated members of the church tended to support the traditional arrangements.

But many were deeply moved by the new ideas. Those chafing under the restraints of puritan authoritarianism, or feeling guilty over their preoccupation with material goods, now found release. For some the release was more than spiritual; Timothy Cutler, a conservative Anglican clergyman, complained that as a result of the Awakening "our presses are forever teeming with books and our women with bastards." Whether or not Cutler was correct, the Great Awakening helped some people to rid themselves of the idea that disobedience to authority entailed damnation. Anything that God justified, human law could not condemn. The Great Awakening did not entail opposition to British tax policies, but it did undermine traditional conceptions of authority.

Other institutions besides the churches were affected by the Great Awakening. In 1741 the president of Yale College criticized the theology of itinerant ministers who imitated Whitefield. Other revivalists called on the New Light churches of Connecticut to withdraw their support from Yale and endow a college of their own. The result was the College of New Jersey (now Princeton), founded in 1746 by New Side Presbyterians. Three other educational by-products of the Great Awakening followed: the College of Rhode Island (Brown), founded by Baptists in 1765; Queen's College (Rutgers), founded by Dutch Reformers in 1766; and Dartmouth, founded by New Light Congregationalists in 1769.

The Rise and Fall of Jonathan Edwards

Jonathan Edwards, the most famous native-born revivalist of the Great Awakening, was living proof that the evangelical temperament need not be hostile to learning. Edwards, though deeply pious, was passionately devoted to intellectual pursuits. But in 1725, four years after graduating from Yale, he was offered the position of assistant at his grandfather Solomon Stoddard's church in Northampton, Massachusetts. He accepted, and when Stoddard died two years later, Edwards became pastor.

During his six decades in Northampton, Stoddard had so dominated the ministers of the Connecticut Valley that some referred to him as "pope." His prominence came in part from the "open enrollment" admission policy he adopted for his own church. Evidence of saving grace was neither required nor expected of members: mere good behavior sufficed. As a result, the grandson inherited a congregation whose members were possessed of an "inordinate engagedness after this world." How ready they were to meet their Maker in the next world was another question.

Edwards had a talent for dramatizing what was in store for unconverted listeners. The heat of Hell's consuming fires and the stench of brimstone became palpable at his rendering. In his most famous sermon, "Sinners in the Hands of an Angry God," delivered at Enfield, Connecticut, in 1741, he pulled out all the stops, depicting a "dreadfully provoked" God holding the unconverted over the pit of Hell, "much as one holds a spider, or some loathsome insect." Later, on the off-chance that his listeners did not recognize themselves among the "insects" in God's hand, he declared that "this is the dismal case of every soul in this congregation that has not been born again, however moral and strict, sober and religious, they may otherwise be."

> **Read the Document**
> Edwards, *Sinners in the Hands of an Angry God* at **myhistorylab.com**

Unfortunately for some church members, Edwards's warnings about the state of their souls caused much anxiety. One disconsolate member, Joseph Hawley, slit his throat. Edwards took the suicide calmly. "Satan seems to be in a great rage," he declared. But for some of Edwards's most prominent parishioners, Hawley's death roused doubts.

Rather than soften his message, Edwards persisted, and in 1749 his parishioners voted unanimously to dismiss him. He became a missionary to Indians in Stockbridge, Massachusetts. In 1759 he was appointed president of Princeton, but he died of smallpox before he could take office.

By the early 1750s a reaction had set in against religious "enthusiasm" in all its forms. Except in the religion-starved South, where traveling New Side Presbyterians and Baptists continued their evangelizing efforts; the Great Awakening had run its course. Whitefield's tour of the colonies in 1754 attracted little notice.

Although it caused divisions, the Great Awakening also fostered religious tolerance. If one group claimed the right to worship in its own way, how could it deny to other Protestant churches equal freedom?

The Awakening was the first truly national event in American history. It marks the time when the previously distinct histories of New England, the Middle Colonies, and the South began to intersect. Powerful links were being forged. In 1754, not long after the Awakening, the farsighted Benjamin Franklin advanced his **Albany Plan** for a colonial union to deal with common problems, such as defense against Indian attacks on the frontier. Thirteen once-isolated colonies, expanding to the north and south as well as westward, were merging.

The Enlightenment in America

The Great Awakening pointed ahead to an America marked by religious pluralism; by the 1740s many colonists were rejecting not only the stern Calvinism of Edwards but even the easy Arminianism of Solomon Stoddard in favor of a far less forbidding theology, one more in keeping with the ideas of the European **Enlightenment**.

The Enlightenment, whose proponents enshrined reason and scientific inquiry, had an enormous impact in America. The founders of the colonies were contemporaries of the astronomer Galileo Galilei (1564–1642), the philosopher-mathematician René Descartes (1596–1650), and Sir Isaac Newton (1642–1727), who revealed to the world the workings of gravity and other laws of motion. American society developed amid the excitement generated by these great discoverers, who provided both a new understanding of the natural world and a mode of thought that implied that impersonal, scientific laws governed the behavior of all matter. Earth and the heavens, and human beings and the lower animals all seemed parts of an immense, intricate machine. God had set it all in motion and remained the master technician (the divine watchmaker) overseeing it, but he took fewer and fewer occasions to interfere with its immutable operation. If human reasoning powers and direct observation of natural phenomena rather than God's revelations provided the key to knowledge, it followed that knowledge of the laws of nature, by enabling people to understand the workings of the universe, would enable them to control their earthly destinies and to have at least a voice in their eternal destinies.

Most creative thinkers of the European Enlightenment realized that human beings were not entirely rational and that a complete understanding of the physical world was beyond their grasp. They did, however, believe that human beings were becoming more rational and would be able, by using their rational powers, to discover the laws governing the physical world. Their faith in these ideas produced the so-called Age of Reason. And while their confidence in human rationality now seems naive and the "laws" they formulated no longer appear so mechanically perfect (the universe is far less orderly than they imagined) they added immensely to knowledge.

Many churchgoing colonists, especially better educated ones, accepted the assumptions of the Age of Reason wholeheartedly. Some repudiated the doctrine of original sin and asserted the benevolence of God. Others came to doubt the divinity of Christ and

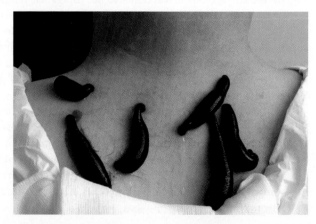

Medicinal leeches on a patient's neck. Today leeches are sometimes used in microsurgery to prevent blood from pooling or coagulating. Leeches fasten onto the skin and tap into blood vessels. Prior to the 19th century, leeches were used to draw off "excess blood," a concept that makes little medical sense.

eventually declared themselves Unitarians. Still others, among them Benjamin Franklin, embraced Deism, a faith that revered God for the marvels of his universe rather than for his power over humankind.

The impact of Enlightenment ideas went far beyond religion. The writings of John Locke and other political theorists found a receptive audience. Of special relevance to American political thinking was Locke's insistence that a person's property was a bulwark of his freedom; if a government could deprive a person of his property, it could enslave him. Also important was the work of the Scottish philosophers Francis Hutcheson and David Hume, and the French *philosophes* Montesquieu and Voltaire. Ideas generated in Europe often reached America with startling speed. No colonial political controversy really heated up in America until all involved had published pamphlets citing half a dozen European authorities. Radical ideas that in Europe were discussed only by an intellectual elite became almost commonplace in the colonies.

As the topics of learned discourse expanded, ministers lost their monopoly on intellectual life. By the 1750s, only a minority of Harvard and Yale graduates were becoming ministers. The College of Philadelphia (later the University of Pennsylvania), founded in 1751, and King's College (later Columbia), founded in New York in 1754, added two institutions to the growing ranks of American colleges, which were never primarily training grounds for clergymen.

Lawyers, who first appeared in any number in colonial towns in the 1740s, swiftly asserted their intellectual authority in public affairs. Physicians and the handful of professors of natural history declared themselves better able to make sense of the new scientific discoveries than clergymen. Yet because fields of knowledge were far less specialized than in modern times, self-educated amateurs could also make useful contributions.

Colonial Scientific Achievements

America produced no Galileo or Newton, but colonists contributed significantly to the collection of scientific knowledge. The unexplored continent provided a laboratory for the study of natural phenomena. The Philadelphia Quaker John Bartram, a "down right plain Country Man," traversed the colonies from Florida to the Great Lakes during the middle years of the eighteenth century, gathering and classifying hundreds of plants. Bartram also studied Indians closely, speculating about their origins and collecting information about their culture.

Franklin's curiosity extended to science. "No one of the present age has made more important discoveries," Thomas Jefferson declared. Franklin's studies of electricity, which he capped in 1752 with his famous kite experiment, established him as a scientist of international stature. He also invented the lightning rod, the iron Franklin stove (a far more efficient way to heat a room than an open fireplace), bifocal spectacles, and several other ingenious devices. In addition he served fourteen years (1751–1764) in the Pennsylvania assembly. He founded a circulating library and helped to get the first hospital in Philadelphia built. He came up with the idea of a lottery to raise money for public purposes. In his spare time he taught himself Latin, French, Spanish, and Italian.

Involvement at even the most marginal level in the intellectual affairs of Europe gave New Englanders, Middle Colonists, and Southerners a chance to get to know one another. Like the spread of evangelical religion, Enlightenment values created new forms of community in English America. Men who in 1750 were discussing botany, physics, and natural phenomena would soon be exchanging ideas about governance.

Repercussions of Distant Wars

The British colonies were part of a great empire that was part of a still larger world. Although Americans were seemingly isolated in their remote communities, scattered between the wide Atlantic and the trackless Appalachian forests, they were constantly affected by outside events both in the Old World and in the New. Under the spell of mercantilism, the western European nations competed fiercely for markets and colonial raw materials. War—hot and cold, declared and undeclared—was almost a permanent condition of seventeenth- and eighteenth-century life, and when the powers clashed they fought wherever they could get at one another, in America, in Europe, and elsewhere.

Although the American colonies were minor pieces in the game and were sometimes casually exchanged or sacrificed by the masterminds in London, Paris, and Madrid, the colonists quickly generated their own international animosities. Frenchmen and Spaniards clashed savagely in Florida as early as the sixteenth century. Before the Pilgrims landed, Samuel Argall of Virginia was sacking French settlements in Maine and carrying off Jesuit priests into captivity at Jamestown. Instead of fostering tranquility and generosity, the abundance of America seemed to make the settlers belligerent and greedy.

The North American fur trade became a source of trouble. The yield of the forest was easily exhausted and traders clashed while trying to control valuable hunting grounds. The French in Canada conducted their fur trading through tribes such as the Algonquin and the Huron. This brought them into conflict with the Five Nations, the powerful Iroquois confederation of central New York. As early as 1609 the Five Nations were at war with the French and their Indian allies. For decades this struggle flared sporadically, the Iroquois more than holding their own both as fighters and as traders. The Iroquois brought quantities of beaver pelts to the Dutch at Albany, some obtained by their own trappers, others taken by ambushing the fur-laden canoes of their enemies. They preyed on and ultimately destroyed the Huron in the land north of Lake Ontario and dickered with Indian trappers in far-off Michigan. When the English took over the New Amsterdam colony, they eagerly adopted the Iroquois as allies, buying their furs and supplying them with trading goods and guns.

By the last decade of the seventeenth century it had become clear that the Dutch lacked the strength to maintain a big empire and that Spain was fast declining. The future, especially in North America, belonged to England and France. In the wars of the next 125 years European alliances shifted dramatically, yet the English and what the Boston lawyer John Adams called "the turbulent Gallicks" were always on opposite sides.

Colonists played only minor parts in the first three of these conflicts. The fighting in America consisted chiefly of sneak attacks on isolated outposts. In King William's War (1689–1697), the American phase of the War of the League of Augsburg, French forces raided Schenectady in New York and frontier settlements in New England. English colonists retaliated by capturing Port Royal, Nova Scotia, only to lose that outpost in a counterattack in 1691. The Peace of Ryswick in 1697 restored all captured territory in America to the original owners.

The next struggle was the War of the Spanish Succession (1702–1713), fought to prevent the union of Spain and France under the Bourbons. The Americans named this conflict Queen Anne's War. Incited by the French, Indians razed Deerfield, Massachusetts. A party of Carolinians burned St. Augustine in Spanish Florida. The New Englanders retook Port Royal. In the Treaty of Utrecht in 1713, France yielded Nova Scotia, Newfoundland, and the Hudson Bay region to Great Britain.

If the colonies were mere pawns in these wars, battle casualties were proportionately high and the civilian population of New England (and of Canada) paid heavily because of the fighting. Many frontier settlers were killed in the raids. Hundreds of townspeople died during the campaigns in Nova Scotia. Massachusetts taxes went up sharply and the colony issued large amounts of paper currency to pay its bills, causing an inflation that ate into the living standards of wage earners.

The American phase of the third Anglo-French conflict, the War of the Austrian Succession (1740–1748), was called King George's War. The usual Indian raids were launched in both directions across the forests that separated the St. Lawrence settlements from the New York and New England frontier. A New England force captured the strategic fortress of Louisbourg on Cape Breton Island, guarding the entrance to the Gulf of St. Lawrence. The Treaty of Aix-la-Chapelle in 1748, however, required the return of Louisbourg, much to the chagrin of the New Englanders.

As this incident suggests, the colonial wars generated a certain amount of trouble between England and the colonies; matters that seemed unimportant in London might loom large in American eyes, and vice versa. But the conflicts were seldom serious. The wars did, however, increase the bad feelings between settlers north and south of the St. Lawrence. Every Indian raid was attributed to French provocateurs, although more often than not the English colonists themselves were responsible for the Indian troubles. Conflicting land claims further aggravated the situation. Massachusetts, Connecticut, and Virginia possessed overlapping claims to the Ohio Valley, and Pennsylvania and New York also had pretensions in the region. Yet the French, ranging broadly across the mid-continent, insisted that the Ohio country was exclusively theirs.

The Great War for the Empire

In this beautiful, almost untouched land, a handful of individuals determined the future of the continent. Over the years the French had established a chain of forts and trading posts running from Mackinac Island in northern Michigan to Kaskaskia on the Mississippi and Vincennes on the Wabash, and from Niagara in the east to the Bourbon River, near Lake Winnipeg, in the west. By the 1740s, however, Pennsylvania fur traders, led by George Croghan, were setting up posts north of the Ohio River and bargaining with Miami and Huron Indians, who ordinarily sold their furs to the French. In 1748 Croghan built a fort at Pickawillany, deep in the Miami country, in what is now western Ohio. That same year agents of a group of Virginia land speculators who had recently organized what they called the Ohio Company reached this area.

With trifling exceptions, an insulating band of wilderness had always separated the French and English in America. Now the two powers came into contact. The immediate result was a battle for control of North America, the "great war for the empire." Thoroughly alarmed by the presence of the English on land they had long considered

This is the first portrait of George Washington, painted by John Gadsby Chapman. Washington's right hand is inside his vest, a convention later associated with Napoleon; his left hand is behind his back. Perhaps this was to spare the painter of the trouble of rendering hands and fingers, which were always a challenge.

their own, the French struck hard. Attacking suddenly in 1752, they wiped out Croghan's post at Pickawillany and drove his traders back into Pennsylvania. Then they built a string of barrier forts south from Lake Erie along the Pennsylvania line: Fort Presque Isle, Fort Le Boeuf, and Fort Venango.

The Pennsylvania authorities chose to ignore this action, but Lieutenant Governor Robert Dinwiddie of Virginia (who was an investor in the Ohio Company) dispatched a twenty-one-year-old surveyor named George Washington to warn the French that they were trespassing on Virginia territory.

Washington, a gangling, inarticulate, and intensely ambitious young planter, made his way northwest in the fall of 1753 and delivered Dinwiddie's message to the commandant at Fort Le Boeuf. It made no impression. "[The French] told me," Washington reported, "that it was their absolute Design to take Possession of the Ohio, and by G— they would do it." Governor Dinwiddie thereupon promoted Washington to lieutenant colonel and sent him back in the spring of 1754 with 150 men to seize a strategic junction south of the new French forts, where the Allegheny and Monongahela Rivers join to form the Ohio River.

Eager but inexperienced in battle, Washington botched his assignment. As his force labored painfully through the tangled mountain country southeast of the fork of the Ohio, he received word that the French had already occupied the position and were constructing a powerful post, Fort Duquesne. Outnumbered by perhaps four to one, Washington pushed on. He surprised and routed a French reconnaissance party, and then blundered into the main body of enemy troops.

Hastily he threw up a defensive position, aptly named Fort Necessity, but the ground was ill chosen; the French easily surrounded the fort and Washington had to surrender. After tricking the young officer, who could not read French, into signing an admission that he had "assassinated" the leader of the reconnaissance party, his captors, with the gateway to the Ohio country firmly in their hands, permitted him and his men to march off. Nevertheless, Washington returned to Virginia a hero, for although still undeclared, this was war, and he had struck the first blow against the French.

In the resulting conflict, which historians call the **French and Indian War** (to the colonists it was simply "the French War"), the English outnumbered the French by about 1.5 million to 90,000. But the English were divided and disorganized, while the

Table 3.1   English Wars, 1689–1763

War	Date	Purpose in North America	Outcome
King William's War	1689–1697	Control of New England and New York frontier, St. Lawrence Valley	No change
Queen Anne's War	1702–1713	Control of northern frontier, also much of Canada	France surrenders Nova Scotia, Newfoundland, and Hudson Bay to Great Britain
King George's War	1744–1748	Control of St. Lawrence River and its Approaches	Louisbourg fortress captured by British but returned to France by treaty
Great War for the Empire	1754–1763	Control of New France	France cedes nearly all of New France to Great Britain

French were disciplined and united. The French controlled the disputed territory, and most of the Indians took their side. As a colonial official wrote, together they made formidable forest fighters, "sometimes in our Front, sometimes in our Rear, and often on all sides of us, Hussar Fashion, taking the Advantage of every Tree and Bush." With an ignorance and arrogance typical of eighteenth-century colonial administration, the British mismanaged the war and failed to make effective use of local resources. For several years they stumbled from one defeat to another.

See the **Map**

The Seven Years' War at **myhistorylab.com**

General Edward Braddock was dispatched to Virginia to take command. In June 1755 he marched against Fort Duquesne with 1,400 Redcoats and a smaller number of colonials, only to be decisively defeated by a much smaller force of French and Indians. Braddock died in battle, and only 500 of his men, led by Colonel Washington, who was serving as his aide-de-camp, made their way back to Virginia.

Elsewhere Anglo-American arms fared little better in the early years of the war. Expeditions against Fort Niagara, key to all French defenses in the West, and Crown Point, gateway to Montréal, bogged down. Meanwhile Indians, armed by the French, bathed the frontier in blood. Venting the frustration caused by 150 years of white advance, they attacked defenseless outposts with unrestrained brutality.

The most feared of the "French" Indians were the Delaware, a once-peaceful Pennsylvania tribe that had been driven from their homelands by English and Iroquois. General Braddock paid his Indian allies only £5 each for French scalps but offered £200 for the hair of Shinngass, the Delaware chieftain.

In 1756 the conflict spread to Europe to become the **Seven Years' War**. Prussia sided with Great Britain, and Austria with the French. On the world stage, too, things went badly for the British. Finally, in 1758, as defeat succeeded defeat, King George II was forced to allow William Pitt, whom he detested, to take over leadership of the war effort. Pitt, grandson of "Diamond" Pitt, a nouveau riche East India merchant, was an unstable man who spent much of his life on the verge of madness, but he was a brilliant strategist and capable of inspiring the nation in its hour of trial.

Pitt recognized, as few contemporaries did, the potential value of North America. Instead of relying on the tightfisted and shortsighted colonial assemblies for men and money, he poured regiment after regiment of British regulars and the full resources of the British treasury into the contest, mortgaging the future recklessly to ensure victory over the French. Grasping the importance of sea power in fighting a war on the other side of the Atlantic, he used the British navy to bottle up the enemy fleet and hamper French communications with Canada. He possessed a keen eye for military genius, and when he discovered it, he ignored seniority and the outraged feelings of mediocre generals and promoted talented young officers to top commands.

In the winter of 1758, as Pitt's grand strategy matured, Fort Duquesne fell. It was appropriately renamed Fort Pitt, the present Pittsburgh. The following summer Fort Niagara was overrun. General Jeffrey Amherst took Crown Point, and Wolfe sailed up the St. Lawrence to Québec. There General Louis Joseph de Montcalm had prepared formidable defenses, but after months of probing and planning, Wolfe found and exploited a chink in the city's armor and captured it. Both he and Montcalm died in the battle. In 1760 Montréal fell and the French abandoned all Canada to the British. The British also won major victories against Spanish forces in Cuba and Manila, and against the French in the West Indies and India.

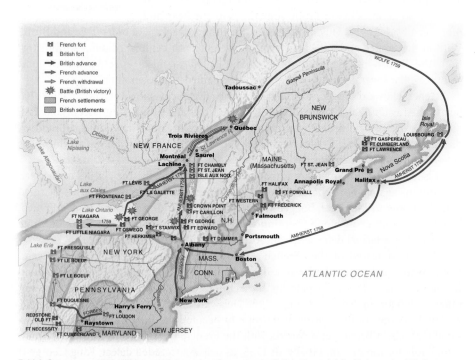

British Successes, 1758–1763 In 1758, in western Pennsylvania, British General John Forbes seized Ft. Duquesne and renamed it Ft. Pitt, in honor of William Pitt, who had orchestrated the military campaign in London. (In 1909 Forbes was posthumously honored when the Pittsburgh Pirates named their new stadium after him.) In 1759 a multipronged British expedition seized northern and western New York while another British army, commanded by James Wolfe, sailed down the St. Lawrence and captured Montréal in 1760.

Britain Victorious: The Peace of Paris

Peace was restored in 1763 by the Treaty of Paris. Its terms were moderate considering the extent of the British triumph. France abandoned all claim to North America except for two small islands near Newfoundland; Great Britain took over Canada and the eastern half of the Mississippi Valley. Spain got back both the Philippine Islands and Cuba, but in exchange ceded East and West Florida to Great Britain. In a separate treaty, Spain also got New Orleans and the huge area of North America west of the Mississippi River.

No honest American could deny that the victory had been won chiefly by British troops and with British gold. Colonial militiamen fought well in defense of their homes or when some highly prized objective seemed ripe for the plucking; they lacked discipline and determination when required to fight far from home and under commanders they did not know. As one American official admitted, it was difficult to get New Englanders to enlist "unless assurances can be given that they shall not march to the southward of certain limits."

Colonials were delighted that scarlet-clad British regulars had borne the brunt of the fighting and happier still that the Crown had shouldered most of the financial burden of the long struggle. The local assemblies contributed to the cost, but except for Massachusetts and Virginia their outlays were trivial compared with the £82 million poured into the worldwide conflict by the British.

Little wonder that great victory produced a burst of praise for king and mother country throughout America. Parades, cannonading, fireworks, banquets, the pealing of church bells were the order of the day in every colonial town. "Nothing," said Thomas Pownall, wartime governor of Massachusetts and a student of colonial administration, "can eradicate from [the colonists'] hearts their natural, almost mechanical affection to Great Britain." A young South Carolinian who had been educated in England claimed that the colonists were "more wrapped up in a king" than any people he had ever known.

Burdens of an Expanded Empire

In London peace proved a time for reassessment; it was obvious that the empire of 1763 was not the same as the empire of 1754. The new, far larger dominion would be much more expensive to maintain. Pitt had spent a huge sum winning and securing it, much of it borrowed money. Great Britain's national debt had doubled between 1754 and 1763. Now this debt must be repaid, and the strain that this would place on the economy was clear to all. Furthermore, the day-to-day cost of administering an empire that extended from the Hudson Bay to India was far larger than that which the already burdened British taxpayer could be expected to bear. Before the great war for the empire, Britain's North American possessions were administered for about £70,000 a year; after 1763 the cost was five times as much.

The American empire had also become far more complex. A system of administration that treated the colonies as a string of separate plantations struggling to exist on the edge of the forest would no longer suffice. The war had been fought for control of the Ohio Valley. Now that the prize had been secured, 10,000 hands were eager to make off

European Claims in North America after British Victory, 1763 The British victory in the French and Indian War caused nearly all of New France to be transferred to Great Britain. The Mississippi and Ohio Valleys, the Great Lakes region, and most of what is now eastern Canada were now under British rule. Only Spain now vied with Britain for control of what is now the continental United States. Russia claimed the coastline of what is now Alaska.

with it. The urge to expand was, despite the continent's enormous empty spaces, an old American drive. As early as the 1670s eastern stay-at-homes were lamenting the "insatiable desire after Land" that made people willing to "live like Heathen, only that so they might have Elbow-room enough in the world." Frontier warfare had frustrated this urge for seven long years. How best could it be satisfied now that peace had come?

Conflicting colonial claims, based on charters drafted by men who thought the Pacific lay over the next hill, threatened to make the Ohio valley a battleground once more. The Indians remained "unpacified." Rival land companies contested for charters, while fur traders strove to hold back the wave of settlement that would inevitably destroy the world of the beaver and the deer.

Apparently only Great Britain could deal with these problems and rivalries, for when Franklin had proposed a rudimentary form of colonial union—the Albany Plan of 1754—it was rejected by almost everyone. Unfortunately, the British government did not rise to the challenge. Perhaps this was to be expected. A handful of aristocrats (fewer than 150 peers were active in government affairs) dominated British politics, and they were more concerned with local offices and personal advantage than with large questions of policy. An American who spent some time in London in 1764 trying to obtain approval for a plan for the development of the West reported, "The people hear Spend thire time in Nothing but abuseing one Another and Striveing who shall be in power with a view to Serve themselves and Thire friends." King George III was not a tyrant, as once was commonly believed, but he was an inept politician and the victim of frequent bouts of illness.

This engraving depicts Pontiac confronting Colonel Henry Bouquet. Pontiac had good reason to be angry. In a letter dated July 16, 1763, Sir Jeffrey Amherst, commander of British forces in North America, advised Bouquet to infect Pontiac's Indians with smallpox: "You will do well to try to Innoculate the Indians by means of Blanketts, as well as to try Every other method that can serve to Extirpate this Execrable Race." Bouquet responded a week later: "All your directions will be observed."

Most English leaders insisted that colonials were uncouth and generally inferior beings. During the French and Indian War, British commanders repeatedly expressed contempt for colonial militiamen, whom they considered fit only for "fatigue" duties such as digging trenches, chopping wood, and other noncombat tasks. General Wolfe characterized colonial troops as the "most contemptible cowardly dogs you can conceive," and another English officer, annoyed by their unsanitary habits, complained that they "infect the air with a disagreeable stink." The British officers failed to understand that colonial soldiers were volunteers who had agreed to serve under specific conditions. Lord Loudoun, the British commander-in-chief during the French and Indian War, was flabbergasted to discover that New England troops refused to obey one of his direct orders on the ground that it violated their contracts.

Many English people resented Americans simply because the colonies were rapidly becoming rich and powerful. As Franklin predicted, the population growth rate in British America was extraordinary, increasing from 1 million to more than 2 million from 1750 to 1770. (His long-term predictions were nearly on the mark: In 1850 the population of Great Britain was 20.8 million, that of the United States 23.1 million, including some 4 million slaves and others who were not of British descent.) If the English did not say much about this possibility, they too considered it from time to time—without Franklin's complacency.

Tightening Imperial Controls

The attempt of the inefficient British government to deal with the intricate colonial problems that resulted from the great war for the empire led to the American Revolution. Trouble began when the British decided after the French and Indian War to intervene more actively in American affairs. Theoretically the colonies were entirely subordinate to Crown and Parliament; yet except for the disastrous attempt to centralize control of the

Proclamation of 1763 Although France ceded nearly all of New France to Great Britain in 1763, that same year King George III proclaimed that colonists would not be allowed to move into "British territory" west of the Appalachians. These lands were to be reserved for Indians.

colonies in the 1680s, they had been allowed a remarkable degree of freedom to manage their own affairs. They had come to expect this as their right.

Parliament had never attempted to tax American colonists. "Compelling the colonies to pay money without their consent would be rather like raising contributions in an enemy's country than taxing Englishmen for their own benefit," Benjamin Franklin wrote. Sir Robert Walpole, initiator of the policy of salutary neglect, recognized the colonial viewpoint. He responded to a suggestion that Parliament tax the colonies by saying, "I will leave that for some of my successors, who may have more courage than I have." Nevertheless, the *legality* of parliamentary taxation, or of other parliamentary intervention in colonial affairs, had not been seriously contested. During King George's War and again during the French and Indian War many British officials in America suggested that Parliament tax the colonies.

Despite the peace treaty of 1763, the American colonies continued to be a drain on the British treasury. Mostly this was due to the cost of fighting Indians. Freed of the restraint posed by French competition, Englishmen and colonists increased their pressure on the Indians. Fur traders cheated them outrageously, while callous military men hoped to exterminate them like vermin. One British officer expressed the wish that they could be hunted down with dogs.

Led by an Ottawa chief named Pontiac, the Indian tribes made one last effort to drive the whites back across the mountains. What the whites called Pontiac's "Rebellion" caused much havoc, but it failed. By 1764 most of the western tribes had accepted the peace terms offered by a royal commissioner, Sir William Johnson, one of the few whites who understood and sympathized with them. The British government then placed 15 regiments, some 6,000 soldiers, in posts along the entire arc of the frontier, as much to protect the Indians from the settlers as the settlers from the Indians. It proclaimed a new western policy: No settlers were to cross the Appalachian divide.

Originally the British had intended the Proclamation of 1763 to be temporary. With the passage of time, however, checking westward expansion seemed a good way to save money, prevent trouble with the Indians, and keep the colonies tied closely to the mother country. The proclamation line, the Board of Trade declared, was "necessary for the preservation of the colonies in due subordination."[1] Naturally this attitude caused resentment in America. To close off the West temporarily in order to pacify the Indians made some sense; to keep it closed was like trying to contain a tidal wave.

The Sugar Act

Americans disliked the new western policy but realized that the problems were complex and that no simple solution existed. Great Britain's effort to raise money in America to help support the increased cost of colonial administration caused far more vehement complaints. George Grenville, who became prime minister in 1763, was a fairly able man, although narrow in outlook. His reputation as a financial expert was based chiefly on his eagerness to reduce government spending. Under his leadership Parliament passed, in April 1764, the so-called Sugar Act. This law placed tariffs on sugar, coffee, wines, and other things imported into America in substantial amounts. At the same time, measures aimed at enforcing all the trade laws were put into effect. Those accused of violating the Sugar Act were to be tried before British naval officers in vice admiralty courts. Grenville was determined to end smuggling, corruption, and inefficiency. Soon the customs service was collecting each year 15 times as much in duties as it had before the war.

More alarming was the nature of the Sugar Act and the manner of its passage. The Navigation Act duties had been intended to regulate commerce, and the sums collected had not cut deeply into profits. Yet few Americans were willing to concede that Parliament had the right to tax them. As Englishmen they believed that no one should be deprived arbitrarily of property and that, as James Otis put it in his stirring pamphlet *The Rights of the British Colonies Asserted and Proved* (1764), everyone should be "free from all taxes but what he consents to in person, or by his representative." John Locke had made clear in his *Second Treatise on Government* (1690) that property ought never be taken from people without their consent, not because material values transcend all others, but because human liberty can never be secure when arbitrary power of any kind exists. "If our Trade may be

•◦•—Read the **Document**

Otis, *The Rights of the British Colonies Asserted and Proved* at **myhistorylab.com**

---

[1]The British were particularly concerned about preserving the colonies as markets for their manufactures. They feared that the spread of population beyond the mountains would stimulate local manufacturing because the high cost of land transportation would make British goods prohibitively expensive.

taxed why not our Lands?" the Boston town meeting asked when news of the Sugar Act reached America. "Why not the produce of our Lands and every Thing we possess or make use of?"

American Colonists Demand Rights

To most people in Great Britain the colonial protest against taxation without representation seemed a hypocritical quibble, and it is probably true that in 1764 many of the protesters had not thought the argument through. The distinction between tax laws and other types of legislation was artificial, the British reasoned. Either Parliament was sovereign in America or it was not, and only a fool or a traitor would argue that it was not. If the colonists were loyal subjects of George III, as they claimed, they should bear their fair share of the cost of governing his widespread dominions. As to representation, the colonies *were* represented in Parliament; every member of that body stood for the interests of the entire empire. If Americans had no say in the election of members of Commons, neither did most English subjects.

This concept of "virtual" representation accurately described the British system. But it made no sense in America, where from the time of the first settlements members of the colonial assemblies had represented the people of the districts in which they stood for office. The confusion between virtual and actual (geographically based) representation revealed the extent to which colonial and British political practices had diverged over the years.

The British were correct in concluding that selfish motives influenced colonial objections to the Sugar Act. The colonists denounced taxation without representation, but an offer of a reasonable number of seats in Parliament would not have satisfied them. American abundance and the simplicity of colonial life had enabled them to prosper without assuming any considerable tax burden. Now their maturing society was beginning to require communal rather than individual solutions to the problems of existence. Not many of them were prepared to face this hard truth.

Over the course of colonial history Americans had taken a narrow view of imperial concerns. They had avoided complying with the Navigation Acts whenever they could profit by doing so. Colonial militiamen had compiled a sorry record when asked to fight for Britain or even for the inhabitants of colonies other than their own. True, most Americans professed loyalty to the Crown, but not many would voluntarily open their purses except to benefit themselves.

Although the colonists were opposed in principle to taxation without representation, they failed to agree on a common plan of resistance. Many of the assemblies drafted protests, but these varied in force as well as in form. Merchant groups that tried to organize boycotts of products subject to the new taxes met with indifferent success. Then in 1765 Parliament galvanized colonial opinion by passing the Stamp Act.

The Stamp Act: The Pot Set to Boiling

View the **Image**

Stamp Act Stamps at myhistorylab.com

The Stamp Act placed stiff excise taxes on all kinds of printed matter. No one could sell newspapers or pamphlets, or convey licenses, diplomas, or legal papers without first buying special stamps and affixing them to the printed matter. Stamp duties

Outraged at the Stamp Act of 1765, which implemented a direct tax on printed matter, an angry mob burned the stamps in protest. Note the enthusiastic participation of women and a young black man; that they are not wearing shoes indicates that they were of working-class background.

were intended to be relatively painless to pay and cheap to collect; in England similar taxes brought in about £100,000 annually. Grenville hoped the Stamp Act would produce £60,000 a year in America, and the law provided that all revenue should be applied to "defraying the necessary expenses of defending, protecting, and securing, the . . . colonies."

Hardly a penny was collected. As the Boston clergyman Jonathan Mayhew explained, "Almost every British American . . . considered it as an infraction of their rights, or their dearly purchased privileges." The Sugar Act had been related to Parliament's uncontested power to control colonial trade, but the Stamp Act was a direct tax. When Parliament ignored the politely phrased petitions of the colonial assemblies, more vigorous protests swiftly followed.

Virginia took the lead. In late May 1765 Patrick Henry introduced resolutions asserting that the Burgesses possessed "the only and sole and exclusive right and power to lay taxes" on Virginians and suggesting that Parliament had no legal authority to tax the colonies at all. Henry spoke for what the royal governor called the "Young, hot and Giddy Members" of the legislature (most of whom, incidentally, had absented themselves from the meeting). The more extreme of Henry's resolutions were defeated, but the debate they occasioned attracted wide and favorable attention. On June 6 the Massachusetts assembly proposed an intercolonial **Stamp Act Congress**, which, when it met in New York City in October, passed another series of resolutions of protest. The Stamp Act and other recent acts of Parliament were "burthensome and grievous," the delegates declared. "It is unquestionably essential to the freedom of a people . . . that no taxes be imposed on them but with their own consent."

During the summer irregular organizations known as Sons of Liberty began to agitate against the act. Far more than anyone realized, this marked the start of the revolution. For the first time extralegal organized resistance was taking place, distinct from protest and argument conducted by constituted organs of government like the House of Burgesses and the Massachusetts General Court.

Although led by men of character and position, the "Liberty Boys" frequently resorted to violence to achieve their aims. In Boston they staged riots, looting and vandalizing the houses of the stamp master and his brother-in-law, Lieutenant Governor Thomas Hutchinson. In Connecticut, stamp master Jared Ingersoll, a man of great courage and dignity, faced an angry mob demanding his resignation.

The stamps were printed in England and shipped to stamp masters (all Americans) in the colonies well in advance of November 1, 1765, the date the law was to go into effect. The New York stamp master had resigned, but the stamps were stored in the city under military guard. Radicals distributed placards read-ing, "The first Man that either distributes or makes use of Stampt Paper let him take care of his House, Person, and Effects. We dare." When Major Thomas James, the British officer who had charge of the stamps, promised that "the stamps would be crammed down New Yorkers' throats," a mob responded by breaking into his house, drinking all his wine, and smashing his furniture and china.

•••⌐Read the Document

Franklin, *Testimony Against the Stamp Act* at **myhistorylab.com**

In some colonies the stamps were snatched by mobs and put to the torch amid rejoicing. Elsewhere they were locked up in secret by British officials or held on ship-board. For a time no business requiring stamped paper was transacted; then, gradually, people began to defy the law by issuing and accepting unstamped documents. Threatened by mob action should they resist, British officials stood by helplessly. The law was a dead letter.

The looting associated with this crisis alarmed many colonists, including some prominent opponents of the Stamp Act. "When the pot is set to boil," the lawyer John Adams remarked sadly, "the scum rises to the top." Another Bostonian called the van-dalizing of Thomas Hutchinson's house a "flagrant instance of to what a pitch of infat-uation an incensed populace can rise." Such people worried that the protests might be aimed at the wealthy and powerful in America as well as at British tyranny. This does not mean that they disapproved of crowd protests, or even the destruction of prop-erty during such protests, as distinct from stealing. Many such people took part in the rioting. "State-quakes," John Adams also said, this time complacently, were compara-ble to "earth-quakes" and other kinds of natural violence.

Rioters or Rebels?

That many of the poor resented the colonial elite goes without saying, as does the fact that in many instances the rioting got out of hand and took on a social as well as a polit-ical character. Times were hard, and the colonial elite, including most of the leading critics of British policy, had little compassion for the poor, whom they feared could be corrupted by anyone who offered them a square meal or a glass of rum. Once roused, laborers and artisans may well have directed their energies toward righting what they considered local wrongs. Yet the mass of the people, being owners of property and capable of influencing political decisions, were not social revolutionaries.

The British were not surprised that Americans disliked the Stamp Act. They had not anticipated, however, that Americans would react so violently and so unanimously. Americans did so for many reasons. Business continued to be poor in 1765, and at a time when 3 shillings was a day's wage for an urban laborer, the stamp tax was 2 shillings for an advertisement in a newspaper, 5 shillings for a will, and 20 shillings for a license to sell liquor. The taxes would hurt the business of lawyers, merchants, newspaper editors, and tavern keepers. The protests of such influential and articulate people had a powerful impact on public opinion.

The greatest cause of concern to the colonists was Great Britain's flat rejection of the principle of no taxation without representation. This alarmed them for two closely related reasons. First of all, *as Americans* they objected to being taxed by a legislative body they had not been involved in choosing. To buy a stamp was to surrender all claim to self-government. Secondly, as *British subjects* they valued what they called "the rights of Englishmen." They saw the Stamp Act as only the worst in a series of arbitrary invasions of these rights.

Already Parliament had passed still another measure, the Quartering Act, requiring local legislatures to house and feed new British troops sent to the colonies. Besides being a form of indirect taxation, a standing army was universally deemed to be a threat to liberty. Why were Redcoats necessary in Boston and New York where there was no foreign enemy for thousands of miles in any direction? In hard times, soldiers were particularly unwelcome because, being miserably underpaid, they took any odd jobs they could get in their off hours, thus competing with unemployed colonists. Reluctantly, many Americans were beginning to fear that the London authorities had organized a conspiracy to subvert the liberties of all British subjects.

Americans also responded to the Stamp Act by boycotting British goods. Nearly a thousand merchants signed nonimportation agreements. These struck British merchants hard in their pocketbooks, and they began to pressure Parliament for repeal. After a hot debate the hated law was repealed in March 1766. The ban on British goods was lifted and the colonists congratulated themselves on having stood fast in defense of principle.

The Declaratory Act

The great controversy over the constitutional relationship of colony to mother country was only beginning. The same day that it repealed the Stamp Act, Parliament passed a Declaratory Act stating that the colonies were "subordinate" and that Parliament could enact any law it wished "to bind the colonies and people of America."

To most Americans this bald statement of parliamentary authority seemed unconstitutional—a flagrant violation of their understanding of how the British imperial system was supposed to work. Actually the Declaratory Act highlighted the degree to which British and American views of the system had drifted apart. The English and the colonials were using the same words but giving them different meanings. Their conflicting definitions of the word *representation* was a case in point. Another involved the word *constitution*. To the British the Constitution meant the totality of laws, customs, and institutions that had developed over time and under which the nation functioned. If Parliament passed an "unconstitutional" law, the result might be rebellion, but that the law existed none would deny. In America, partly because governments were based on specific charters, the word meant a written document or contract spelling out, and thus limiting, the powers of government. If a law were unconstitutional, it simply had no force.

Even more basic were the differing meanings that English and Americans were giving to the word *sovereignty*. Eighteenth-century English political thinkers believed that sovereignty (ultimate political power) could not be divided. Government and law being based ultimately on force, some "final, unqualified, indivisible" authority had to exist if social order was to be preserved. The Glorious Revolution in England had settled the question of where sovereignty resided—in Parliament.

Given these ideas and the long tradition out of which they had sprung, one can sympathize with the British failure to follow the colonists' reasoning (which had not yet evolved into a specific proposal for constitutional reform). But most responsible British officials refused even to listen to the American argument.

The Townshend Duties

Despite the repeal of the Stamp Act, the British did not abandon the policy of taxing the colonies. If direct taxes were challenging to collect, indirect ones like the Sugar Act were not. To persuade Parliament to repeal the Stamp Act, some Americans (most notably Benjamin Franklin) had claimed that the colonists objected only to direct taxes. Therefore, in June 1767, the chancellor of the exchequer, Charles Townshend, introduced a new series of indirect taxes, this time on glass, lead, paints, paper, and tea imported into the colonies.

By this time the colonists were thoroughly on guard, and they responded quickly to the Townshend levies with a new boycott of British goods. In addition they made elaborate efforts to stimulate colonial manufacturing. By the end of 1769 imports from the mother country had been almost halved. Meanwhile, administrative measures enacted along with the Townshend duties were creating more ill will. A Board of Customs Commissioners, with headquarters in Boston, took charge of enforcing the trade laws, and new vice admiralty courts were set up at Halifax, Boston, Philadelphia, and Charleston to handle violations. These courts operated without juries, and many colonists considered the new commissioners racketeers who systematically attempted to obtain judgments against honest merchants in order to collect their share of all seizures.

The struggle forced Americans to do some deep thinking about both American and imperial political affairs. The colonies' common interests and growing economic and social interrelationships probably made some kind of union inevitable. Trouble with England speeded the process. In 1765 the Stamp Act Congress (another extralegal organization and thus a further step in the direction of revolution) had brought the delegates of nine colonies to New York. Now, in 1768, the Massachusetts General Court took the next step. It sent the legislatures of the other colonies a "Circular Letter" expressing the "humble opinion" that the Townshend Acts were "Infringements of their natural & constitutional Rights."

After the passage of the Townshend Acts, John Dickinson, a Philadelphia lawyer, published "Letters from a Farmer in Pennsylvania to the Inhabitants of the British Colonies." Dickinson considered himself a loyal British subject trying to find a solution to colonial troubles. "Let us behave like dutiful children, who have received unmerited blows from a beloved parent," he wrote. Nevertheless, he stated plainly that Parliament had no right to tax the colonies. Another moderate Philadelphian, John Raynell, put it this way: "If the Americans are to be taxed by a Parliament where they are not . . . Represented, they are no longer Englishmen but Slaves."

Some Americans were much more radical than Dickinson. Samuel Adams of Boston, a genuine revolutionary agitator, believed by 1768 that Parliament had no right at all to legislate for the colonies. If few were ready to go that far, fewer still accepted the reasoning behind the Declaratory Act.

The British ignored American thinking. The Massachusetts Circular Letter had been framed in moderate language and clearly reflected the convictions of most of the people in the Bay Colony, yet when news of it reached England, the secretary of state for the colonies, Lord Hillsborough, ordered the governor to dissolve the legislature. Two regiments of British troops were transferred from the frontier to Boston, part of the aforementioned policy of bringing the army closer to the centers of colonial unrest.

The Boston Massacre

These acts convinced more Americans that the British were conspiring to destroy their liberties. Resentment was particularly strong in Boston, where the postwar depression had come on top of two decades of economic stagnation. Crowding 4,000 tough British

This engraving of the Boston Massacre (1770) became the most reprinted depiction of the event, and probably the most inaccurate. It was done by Paul Revere, engraver, silversmith, and eventual patriot. The British soldiers did not form ranks and fire on command at the crowd. The judge at the subsequent trial of the British soldiers warned jurors not to be influenced by "the prints exhibited in our houses" that added "wings to fancy"—prints, specifically, such as this one. The jury of colonists acquitted all the British soldiers but two, who received mild punishments.

soldiers into a town of 16,000 people, many of them as capable of taking care of themselves when challenged as any Redcoat, was a formula for disorder.

How many brawls and minor riots took place in the waterfront taverns and darkened alleys of the colonial ports that winter is lost to history. In January 1770 scuffles between Liberty Boys and Redcoats in the Golden Hill section of New York City resulted in a number of injuries. Then, in Boston on March 5, 1770, real trouble erupted. Late that afternoon a crowd of idlers began tossing snowballs at a company of Redcoats guarding the Custom House. Some of the snowballs had been carefully wrapped around rocks. Gradually the crowd grew larger and angrier. The soldiers panicked and began firing their muskets. When the smoke cleared, five Bostonians lay dead or dying on the bloody ground.

This so-called **Boston Massacre** infuriated the populace. The violence played into the hands of radicals like Samuel Adams. But just as at the time of the Stamp Act riots, cooler heads prevailed. Announcing that he was "defending the rights of man and unconquerable truth," John Adams volunteered his services to make sure the soldiers got a fair trial. Most were acquitted; the rest were treated leniently by the standards of the day. In Great Britain, confrontation also gave way to adjustment. In April 1770 all the Townshend duties except a threepenny tax on tea were repealed. The tea tax was maintained as a matter of principle.

A kind of postmassacre truce settled over Boston and the rest of British America. During the next two years no crisis erupted. Imports of British goods were nearly 50 percent higher than before the nonimportation agreement. So long as the British continued to be conciliatory, the colonists seemed satisfied with their place in the empire.

The Boiling Pot Spills Over

In 1772 this informal truce ended and new troubles broke out. The first was plainly the fault of the colonists involved. Early in June the British patrol boat *Gaspee* ran aground in Narragansett Bay, south of Providence, while pursuing a suspected smuggler. The *Gaspee*'s commander, Lieutenant Dudingston, had antagonized everyone in the area with his officiousness and zeal; that night a gang of local people boarded the *Gaspee* and put it to the torch. This action was clearly criminal, but when the British attempted to bring the culprits to justice no one would testify against them. The British, frustrated and angry, were strengthened in their conviction that the colonists were utterly lawless.

Then Thomas Hutchinson, governor of Massachusetts, announced that henceforth the Crown rather than the local legislature would pay his salary. Since control over the salaries of royal officials gave the legislature a powerful hold on them, this development was disturbing. Groups of radicals formed "committees of correspondence" and stepped up communications with one another, planning joint action in case of trouble. This was another monumental step along the road to revolution; an organized colony-wide resistance movement, lacking in any "legitimate" authority but ready to consult and act in the name of the public interest, was taking shape.

The Tea Act Crisis

In the spring of 1773 an entirely unrelated event precipitated the final crisis. The British East India Company held a monopoly of all trade between India and the rest of the empire. This monopoly had yielded fabulous returns, but decades of corruption and

A noose hanging from a "Liberty Tree" reveals this artist's bias: The "tar-and-feathering" of a British official would doubtlessly culminate in greater violence. As historian Gordon Wood points out, however, the mob actions of the colonists often "grew out of folk festivals and traditional popular rites." Tarring and feathering, though painful and occasionally dangerous, was mostly a humiliation. By the early 1770s, though, the mockery was becoming tinged with violence.

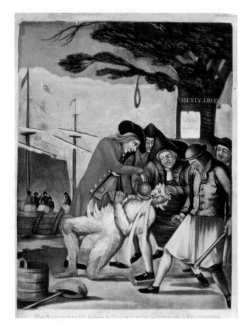

inefficiency together with heavy military expenses in recent years had weakened the company until it was almost bankrupt.

Among the assets of this venerable institution were some 17 million pounds of tea stored in English warehouses. The decline of the American market, a result first of the boycott and then of the smuggling of cheaper Dutch tea, partly accounted for the glut. Normally, East India Company tea was sold to English wholesalers. They in turn sold it to American wholesalers, who distributed it to local merchants for sale to the consumer. A substantial British tax was levied on the tea as well as the threepenny Townshend duty. Now Lord North, the new prime minister, decided to remit the British tax and to allow the company to sell directly in America through its own agents. The savings would permit a sharp reduction of the retail price and at the same time yield a nice profit to the company. The Townshend tax was retained, however, to preserve (as Lord North said when the East India Company directors suggested its repeal) the principle of Parliament's right to tax the colonies.

The company then shipped 1,700 chests of tea to colonial ports. Though the idea of high-quality tea offered at bargain prices was tempting, after a little thought nearly everyone in America appreciated the dangers involved in buying it. If Parliament could grant the East India Company a monopoly of the tea trade, it could parcel out all or any part of American commerce to whomever it pleased. More important, the act appeared utterly diabolical, a dastardly trick to trap them into paying the tea tax. The plot seemed obvious: The real price of Lord North's tea was American submission to parliamentary taxation.

Public indignation was so great in New York and Philadelphia that when the tea ships arrived, the authorities ordered them back to England without attempting to unload. The tea could be landed only "under the Protection of the Point of the Bayonet and Muzzle of the Cannon," the governor of New York reported. "Even then," he added, "I do not see how the Sales or Consumption could be effected."

The situation in Boston was different. The tea ship *Dartmouth* arrived on November 27. The radicals, marshaled by Sam Adams, were determined to prevent it from landing its cargo. Governor Hutchinson (who had managed to have two of his sons appointed to receive and sell the tea) was equally determined to collect the tax and enforce the law. For days the town seethed. Crowds milled in the streets, harangued by Adams and his friends, while the *Dartmouth* and two later arrivals swung with the tides on their moorings. Then, on the night of December 16, as Hutchinson was preparing to seize the tea for nonpayment of the duty, a band of colonists disguised as Indians rowed out to the ships and dumped the tea chests into the harbor.

The destruction of the tea was a serious crime and it was obvious that a solid majority of the people of Boston approved of it. The painted "Patriots" who jettisoned the chests were a cross-section of society, and a huge crowd gathered at wharfside and cheered them on. The British burned with indignation when news of the "Tea Party" reached London. People talked (fortunately it was only talk) of flattening Boston with heavy artillery. Nearly everyone, even such a self-described British friend of the colonists as Edmund Burke, agreed that the colonists must be taught a lesson. George III himself said, "We must master them or totally leave them to themselves."

What particularly infuriated the British was the certain knowledge that no American jury would render a judgment against the criminals. The memory of the *Gaspee* affair was fresh in everyone's mind in England, as undoubtedly it was in the minds of those Bostonians who, wearing the thinnest of disguises, brazenly destroyed the tea.

From Resistance to Revolution

Parliament responded in the spring of 1774 by passing the **Coercive Acts**. The Boston Port Act closed the harbor of Boston to all commerce until its citizens paid for the tea. The Administration of Justice Act provided for the transfer of cases to courts outside Massachusetts when the governor felt that an impartial trial could not be had within the colony. The Massachusetts Government Act revised the colony's charter drastically, strengthening the power of the governor, weakening that of the local town meetings, making the council appointive rather than elective, and changing the method by which juries were selected. These were unwise laws—they cost Great Britain an empire. All of them, and especially the Port Act, were unjust laws as well. Parliament was punishing the entire community for the crimes of individuals. Even more significant, they marked a drastic change in British policy—from legislation and strict administration to treating colonial protesters as criminals, and from attempts to persuade and conciliate to coercion and punishment.

The Americans named the Coercive Acts the Intolerable Acts. Although neither the British nor the colonists yet realized it, the American Revolution had begun.

Step by step, in the course of a single decade, a group of separate political bodies, inhabited by people who (if we put aside the slaves who were outside the political system) were loyal subjects of Great Britain, had been forced to take political power into their own hands and to unite with one another to exercise that power effectively. Ordinary working people, not just merchants, lawyers, and other well-to-do people, played increasingly more prominent roles in public life as crisis after crisis roused their indignation. This did not yet mean that most Americans wanted to be free from British rule. Nearly every colonist was willing to see Great Britain continue to control, or at least regulate, such things as foreign relations, commercial policy, and other matters of general American interest. Parliament, however—and in the last analysis George III and most supporters of the British—insisted that their authority over the colonies was unlimited.

Lord North directed the Coercive Acts at Massachusetts alone because he assumed that the other colonies, profiting from the discomfiture of Massachusetts, would not intervene, and because of the British tendency to think of the colonies as separate units connected only through London. His strategy failed because his assumption was incorrect: The colonies began at once to act in concert.

Extralegal political acts now became a matter of course. In June 1774 Massachusetts called for a meeting of delegates from all the colonies to consider common action. This **First Continental Congress** met at Philadelphia in September; only Georgia failed to send delegates. Many points of view were represented, but even the so-called conservative proposal, introduced by Joseph Galloway of Pennsylvania, called for a thorough overhaul of the empire. Galloway suggested an *American* government, consisting of a president general appointed by the king and a grand council chosen by the colonial assemblies, that would manage intercolonial affairs and possess a veto over parliamentary acts affecting the colonies.

This was not what the majority wanted. If taxation without representation was tyranny, so was all legislation. Therefore Parliament had no right to legislate in any way for the colonies. John Adams, while prepared to *allow* Parliament to regulate colonial trade, now believed that Parliament had no inherent right to control it. "The foundation . . . of all free government," he declared, "is a right in the people to participate in their legislative council." Americans "are entitled to a free and exclusive power of legislation in their several provincial legislatures."

Propelled by the reasoning of Adams and others, the Congress passed a declaration of grievances and resolves that amounted to a complete condemnation of Britain's actions since 1763. A Massachusetts proposal that the people take up arms to defend their rights was endorsed. The delegates also organized a "Continental Association" to boycott British goods and to stop all exports to the empire. To enforce this boycott, committees were appointed locally "to observe the conduct of all persons touching this association" and to expose violators to public scorn.

If the Continental Congress reflected the views of the majority—there is no reason to suspect that it did not—it is clear that the Americans had decided that drastic changes must be made. It was not merely a question of mutual defense against the threat of British power, nor was it (in Franklin's aphorism) a matter of hanging together lest they hang separately. A nation was being born.

Table 3.2 Major British Tax Policies and American Resistance, 1763–1776

Year	British Policy	Colonist Response
1763	Proclamation of 1763	Wealthy speculators, coveting Indian lands west of Appalachians, protest
1764	Sugar Act	Massachusetts legislature denounces "taxation without representation"
1765	Stamp Act	Sons of Liberty emerge and call for radical measures; boycott of British goods
1767	Townshend Duties	Widespread protests, riots in port cities, culminating in "Boston Massacre"
1773	Tea Act	Boston Tea Party
1774	Coercive Acts	First Continental Congress

Looking back many years later, one of the delegates to the First Continental Congress made just these points. He was John Adams of Massachusetts, and he said, "The revolution was complete, in the minds of the people, and the Union of the colonies, before the war commenced."

American resistance to the new taxes baffled British officials. In 1774 Lord North declared that colonial opposition betrayed a "distempered state of turbulence." Some members of Parliament declared that the Americans had gone "stark staring mad" over taxes any reasonable person would pay willingly.

But what had begun as a dispute over taxes had shifted to a struggle over sovereignty. Colonists were not against taxes in principle—and their descendants would willingly (if not happily) pay taxes that most colonists would have regarded as enslavement. The colonists insisted, however, that they also have a say in their governance. Their "madness," originally manifested in bitter opposition to trade taxes, would become a feverish commitment to war.

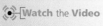
Watch the Video

The American Revolution as Different Americans Saw It at **myhistorylab.com**

Milestones

1650–1696	Parliament enacts Navigation Acts	1754–1763	British and American Colonists fight French and Indians in French and Indian War (Seven Years' War)
1689–1697	King William's War (War of the League of Augsburg)	1760	George III becomes king of England
1699–1750	Parliament enacts laws regulating colonial manufacturing	1763	George III's Proclamation forbids settlement beyond Appalachians
1702–1713	Queen Anne's War (War of the Spanish Succession): France loses Nova Scotia, Newfoundland, and Hudson Bay to Britain	1764	Sugar Act places tariffs on sugar, coffee, wines, and other imports
		1765	Stamp Act places excise taxes on all printed matter; leads to Stamp Tax Congress
1733	Molasses Act's duty leads to smuggling	1766	Stamp Act is repealed; Declaratory Act asserts parliamentary authority over colonies
1738–1742	Religious enthusiasm surges during Great Awakening		
1740–1748	King George's War (War of the Austrian Succession)	1767	Townshend Duties lead to Massachusetts Circular Letter
1743	Benjamin Franklin founds American Philosophical Society	1770	Five American colonists die in Boston Massacre
1752	Franklin discovers nature of lightning	1772	Colonists burn *Gaspee*
		1773	Tea Act leads to Boston Tea Party
1754	Albany Congress paves way for Stamp Act Congress and Continental Congress	1774	Coercive Acts lead to First Continental Congress

✓•⌐Study and Review at www.myhistorylab.com

Review Questions

1. Nowadays American manufacturers seek protection—high import taxes—on imported manufactured goods. Why did American colonists oppose such taxes in the eighteenth century?

2. The 1700s witnessed an explosion of interest in evangelical religion, and also the broader diffusion of Enlightenment ideas. What did these phenomena have in common?

3. Why did the British finally prevail in the French and Indian War in 1763 and what were the repercussions of their victory?

4. The colonists believed that the British government was depriving them of the customary liberties accorded all Englishmen; and yet many of the same colonists owned slaves. Can such opinions be reconciled, or were the slave-owning Patriots hypocrites?

5. From 1763 to 1775, the British government made many mistakes: Would different policies have long kept the American colonies within the British empire?

Key Terms

Albany Plan   *87*
Boston Massacre   *106*
Coercive Acts   *108*
Enlightenment   *88*
First Continental
    Congress   *109*

French and Indian
    War   *92*
Great Awakening   *85*
mercantilism   *81*

Navigation Acts   *82*
Seven Years' War   *93*
Stamp Act
    Congress   *101*

4 The American Revolution

((•─Hear the Audio Chapter 4 at myhistorylab.com

Do you rebel against authority?

IN 2010 THE SAMUEL ADAMS BEER COMPANY TRUMPETED BEER'S ROLE IN founding the nation. It claimed that William Bradford's Pilgrims came ashore in Plymouth, Massachusetts, only because they were "out of beer." The Boston beer company further claimed that the American Revolution originated in the taverns of New England. "The revolutionaries gathered over beer to plot their rebellion," it added, noting that George Washington and Thomas Jefferson were home brewers. Samuel Adams inherited his father's beer company, although he "clearly preferred fomenting rebellion to fermenting beer." This was true: Adams's chief claim to posterity is related to tea.

Yet the founders are so deeply embedded in our culture that their names, in addition to appearing on beer bottles, can be spotted almost everywhere. "Washington" is the name of thirty-one counties and forty-two cities. Iowa and Indiana together have nearly 100 "Washington" townships; California has twenty-eight "Washington Elementary Schools." After "Main Street," Washington is the most common street name in the United States. School children also relish his name: Since Washington's birthday was declared a national holiday in 1968, most states have chosen to honor him by closing schools.

Indeed, the founders now loom so large that it may seem that they could not have lost to the British. But their triumph was not inevitable. To understand the American Revolution, we must examine it from the perspective of the past, before the names of the founders adorned beer bottles and elementary schools, and before the United States had become a mighty nation. The simple truth is that the American Revolution was accomplished by men and women who did not know if they would succeed. At the outset, they did not even know whether they sought British concessions or independence, whether most colonists would side with them or remain loyal to His Majesty's government, whether foreign powers such as France could be enlisted to provide support, whether rebellion against political authority in London would undermine social order in America, or whether the many different peoples of the colonies could be knitted into a single nation. The revolutionaries did know, however, that if they failed they would likely face arrest, imprisonment, and even death.

As the rebellion escalated into a full-scale war for independence, the colonists confronted the challenge of creating and financing an army that could defeat the mightiest empire in the world. In the midst of fighting, and in the wake of freedom from British rule, they faced an even greater challenge—the founding of a new nation, with a new government and a new national spirit.

The Shot Heard Round the World

The actions of the First Continental Congress led the British authorities to force a showdown with their colonial offspring. "The New England governments are in a state of rebellion," George III announced. "Blows must decide whether they are to be subject to this country or independent." General Thomas Gage, veteran of Braddock's ill-fated expedition against Fort Duquesne and now commander-in-chief of all British forces in North America, had already been appointed governor of Massachusetts. Some 4,000 Redcoats were concentrated in Boston, camped on the town common—a place once peacefully reserved for the citizens' cows.

Parliament echoed with demands for a show of strength in America. After the Tea Party the general impression was that resistance to British rule was concentrated in Massachusetts. Based on the behavior of colonial militia in the French and Indian War, most British subjects did not think people in the other colonies would be inclined to fight outside their own region. General James Grant announced that with 1,000 men he "would undertake to go from one end of America to the other, and geld all the males, partly by force and partly by a little coaxing." Some opposed the idea of crushing the colonists, and others believed that it could not be easily managed, but they were a small minority. The House of Commons listened to Edmund Burke's magnificent speech on conciliating the colonies and then voted 270 to 78 against him.

The London government decided to use troops against Massachusetts in January 1775, but the order did not reach General Gage until April. In the interim both sides were active. Parliament voted new troop levies and declared Massachusetts to be in a state of rebellion. The Massachusetts Patriots, as they were now calling themselves, formed an extralegal provincial assembly, reorganized the militia, and began training "Minute Men" and other fighters. Soon companies armed with anything that would shoot were drilling on town commons throughout Massachusetts and in other colonies too.

When Gage received his orders on April 14, he acted swiftly. The Patriots had been accumulating arms at Concord, some twenty miles west of Boston. On the night of April 18, Gage dispatched 700 crack troops to seize these supplies. The Patriots were prepared. Paul Revere and other horsemen rode off to alert the countryside and warn John Hancock and Sam Adams, leaders of the provincial assembly, whose arrests had been ordered.

When the Redcoats reached Lexington early the next morning, they found the common occupied by about seventy Minute Men. After an argument, the Americans began to withdraw. Then someone fired a shot. There was a flurry of gunfire and the Minute Men fled, leaving eight of their number dead. The British then marched on to Concord, where they destroyed whatever supplies the Patriots had been unable to carry off.

But militiamen were pouring into the area from all sides. A hot skirmish at Concord's North Bridge forced the Redcoats to yield that position. Becoming alarmed, they began to march back to Boston. Soon they were being subjected to a withering fire from American irregulars along their line of march. A strange battle developed on a "field" sixteen miles

Two weeks after the battle of Lexington and Concord, Ralph Earl, a colonial militiaman from Connecticut, was ordered to make sketches and paintings of what had transpired. Earl revisited the battlefield and interviewed those who had fought. He was an accurate painter, but not a very good one. Each of the British formations, facing the officers, contains exactly twenty-five men.

long and only a few hundred yards wide. Gage was obliged to send out an additional 1,500 soldiers, and total disaster was avoided only by deploying skirmishers to root out snipers hiding in barns and farmhouses along the road to Boston. When the first day of the Revolutionary War ended, the British had sustained 273 casualties, the Americans fewer than 100. "The Rebels are not the despicable rabble too many have supposed them to be," General Gage admitted.

For a brief moment of history, tiny Massachusetts stood alone at arms against an empire that had humbled France and Spain. Yet Massachusetts assumed the offensive! The provincial government organized an expedition that captured Fort Ticonderoga and Crown Point, on Lake Champlain. The other colonies rallied quickly to the cause, sending reinforcements to Cambridge. When news of the battle reached Virginia, George Washington wrote sadly, "A brother's sword has been sheathed in a brother's breast and the once happy and peaceful plains of America are either to be drenched in blood or inhabited by a race of slaves." And then he added, "Can a virtuous man hesitate in his choice?"

●●●—[Read the Document

Warren, *Account of the Battle of Lexington* at
myhistorylab.com

The Second Continental Congress

On May 10, 1775, the day Ticonderoga fell, the **Second Continental Congress** met in Philadelphia. It was a distinguished group, more radical than the First Congress. Besides John and Sam Adams, Patrick Henry and Richard Henry Lee of Virginia, and Christopher Gadsden of South Carolina (all holdovers from the First Congress), there was Thomas Jefferson, a young planter from Virginia. Jefferson had recently published "A Summary View of the Rights of British America," an essay criticizing the institution of monarchy and warning George III that "kings are the servants, not the proprietors of the people." The Virginia convention had also sent George Washington, who knew more than any other colonist about commanding men and who wore his buff-and-blue colonel's uniform, a not-too-subtle indication of his willingness to place this knowledge at the disposal of the Congress. The renowned Benjamin Franklin was a delegate, moving rapidly to the radical position.

The Boston merchant John Hancock was chosen president of the Congress, which, like the first, had no legal authority. Yet the delegates had to make agonizing decisions under the pressure of rapidly unfolding military events, with the future of every American depending on their actions. Delicate negotiations and honeyed words might yet persuade king and Parliament to change their ways, but precipitate, bold effort was essential to save Massachusetts.

In this predicament the Congress naturally dealt first with the military crisis. It organized the forces gathering around Boston into the so-called **Continental army** and appointed George Washington commander-in-chief. After Washington and his staff left for Massachusetts on June 23, the Congress turned to the task of requisitioning men and supplies.

The Battle of Bunker Hill

Meanwhile, in Massachusetts, the first major battle of the war had been fought. The British position on the peninsula of Boston was impregnable to direct assault, but high ground north and south, at Charlestown and Dorchester Heights, could be used to

On June 17, the British tried to dislodge Continentals from fortified (and concealed) positions atop Breed's Hill in Charlestown. Note the British cannon batteries on the shore in Boston, lobbing shells into Charlestown. When colonists brought a cannon from Ticonderoga and placed it on hills commanding Boston, the British had no choice but to leave the city.

Source: Winthrop Chandler, American, *The Battle of Bunker Hill* (detail), c. 1776–1777. Oil on panel, 88.58 x 136.21 cm (34-7/8 x 53-5/8"). Museum of Fine Arts, Boston. Gift of Mr. and Mrs. Gardner Richardson, 1982.281. Photograph © 2002 Museum of Fine Arts, Boston.

pound the British positions in the city. When the Continentals seized Bunker Hill and Breed's Hill at Charlestown and set up defenses on the latter, Gage determined at once to drive them off. This was accomplished on June 17. Twice the Redcoats marched in close ranks, bayonets fixed, up Breed's Hill, and each time were driven back after suffering heavy losses. Stubbornly they came again, and this time they carried the redoubt, for the defenders had run out of ammunition.

The British then cleared the Charlestown peninsula, but the victory was really the Americans', for they had proved themselves against professional soldiers and had exacted a terrible toll. More than 1,000 Redcoats had fallen in a couple of hours, out of a force of some 2,500, while the Continentals lost only 400 men, most of them cut down by British bayonets after the hill was taken. "The day ended in glory," a British officer wrote, "but the loss was uncommon in officers for the number engaged."

The Battle of Bunker Hill greatly reduced whatever hope remained for a negotiated settlement. The British recalled General Gage, replacing him with General William Howe, a respected veteran of the French and Indian War, and George III formally proclaimed the colonies to be "in open rebellion." The Continental Congress dispatched one last plea to the king, but this was a sop to the moderates. Immediately thereafter it adopted the Declaration of the Causes and Necessity of Taking Up Arms, which condemned everything the British had done since 1763. Americans were "a people attacked by unprovoked enemies"; the time had come to choose between "submission" to "tyranny" and "resistance by force." The Congress then ordered an attack on Canada and created committees to seek foreign aid and to buy munitions abroad.

The Great Declaration

The Congress (and the bulk of the people) still hung back from a break with the Crown. To declare for independence would be to burn the last bridge, to become traitors in the eyes of the mother country. It was sobering to think of casting off everything that being English meant: love of the king, the traditions of a great nation, pride in the power of a mighty empire.

Then, too, rebellion might end in horrors worse than submission to British tyranny. The disturbances following the Stamp Act and the Tea Act had revealed an alarming fact about American society. The organizers of those protests, mostly persons of wealth and status, had thought in terms of "ordered resistance." They countenanced violence only as a means of forcing the British authorities to pay attention to their complaints. But protest meetings and mob actions had brought thousands of ordinary citizens into the struggle for local self-government. Some of the upper-class leaders among the Patriots, while eager to have the support of the lower classes, were concerned about what they would make of actual independence. Too much exalted talk about "rights" and "liberties" might well give the poor (to say nothing of the slaves) an exaggerated impression of their importance.

Finally, in a world where every country had some kind of monarch, could common people *really* govern themselves? The most ardent defender of American rights might well hesitate after considering all the implications of independence.

Yet independence was probably inevitable by the end of 1775. The belief that George III had been misled by evil or stupid advisers on both sides of the Atlantic became progressively more difficult to sustain. Mistrust of Parliament—indeed, of the whole of British society—grew apace.

Two events in January 1776 pushed the colonies a long step toward a final break. First came the news that the British were sending hired Hessian soldiers to fight against them. Colonists associated mercenaries with looting and rape and feared that the German-speaking Hessians would run amok among them. Such callousness on the part of Britain made reconciliation seem out of the question.

The second decisive event was the publication of **Common Sense**. This tract was written by Thomas Paine, a one-time English corset-maker and civil servant turned pamphleteer, who had been in America scarcely a year. *Common Sense* called for complete independence. It attacked not only George III but the idea of monarchy itself. Paine applied the uncomplicated logic of the zealot to the recent history of America and called George a "Royal Brute" and "the hardened sullen-tempered Pharaoh of England." Many Americans had wanted to control their own affairs but feared the instability of untried republican government. To them Paine said, "We have it in our power to begin the world again." "A government of our own is our natural right," he insisted. "O! ye that love mankind! Ye that dare oppose not only tyranny but the tyrant, stand forth!"

The tone of the debate changed sharply as Paine's slashing attack took effect. In March 1776 the Congress unleashed privateers against British commerce; in April it opened American ports to foreign shipping; in May it urged the Patriots who had set up extralegal provincial conventions to frame constitutions and establish state governments.

On June 7 Richard Henry Lee of Virginia introduced a resolution of the Virginia Convention:

> RESOLVED: That these United Colonies are, and of right ought to be, free and independent States, that they are absolved from all allegiance to the British Crown, and that all political connection between them and the State of Great Britain is, and ought to be, totally dissolved.

This momentous resolution was not passed until July 2; the Congress first appointed a committee consisting of Thomas Jefferson, Benjamin Franklin, John Adams, Roger Sherman, and Robert Livingston to frame a suitable justification of independence. Livingston, a member of one of the great New York landowning families, was put on the committee in an effort to push New York toward independence. Sherman, a self-educated Connecticut lawyer and merchant, was a conservative who opposed parliamentary control over colonial affairs. Franklin, the best known of all Americans and an experienced writer, was a natural choice; so was John Adams, whose devotion to the cause of independence combined with his solid conservative qualities made him perhaps the typical man of the Revolution.

Thomas Jefferson was probably placed on the committee because politics required that a Virginian be included and because of his literary skill and general intelligence. Aside from writing *A Summary View of the Rights of British America*, he had done little to attract notice. At age 33 he was the youngest member of the Continental Congress and was only marginally interested in its deliberations. He had been slow to take his seat in the fall of 1775, and arrived in Philadelphia only on May 14. Had he delayed another month, someone else would have written the Declaration of Independence.

●●●─[Read the **Document**

Jefferson, *"Rough Draft" of the Declaration of Independence* at **myhistorylab.com**

The committee asked Jefferson to prepare a draft. The result, with a few amendments made by Franklin and Adams and somewhat toned down by the whole Congress, was officially adopted by the delegates on July 4, 1776, two days after the delegates had voted for the decisive break with Great Britain.

Jefferson's Declaration of Independence consisted of two parts. The introductory section justified the abstract right of any people to revolt and described the theory on which the Americans based their creation of a new, republican government. The second section was a list of the "injuries and usurpations" of George III, a bill of indictment explaining why the colonists felt driven to exercise the rights outlined in the first part of the document. Here Jefferson stressed the monarch's interference with the functioning of representative government in America, his harsh administration of colonial affairs, his restrictions on civil rights, and his maintenance of troops in the colonies without their consent.

Jefferson sought to marshal every possible evidence of British perfidy, and he made George III, rather than Parliament, the villain because the king was the personification of the nation against which America was rebelling. He held the monarch responsible for Parliament's efforts to tax the colonies and restrict their trade, for many actions by subordinates that George III had never deliberately authorized, and for some things that never happened. He even blamed the king for the existence of slavery in the colonies, a charge the Congress cut from the document not entirely because of its concern for accuracy. The long bill of particulars was intended to convince the world that the Americans had good reasons for exercising their right to form a government of their own.

Jefferson's general statement of the right of revolution has inspired oppressed peoples all over the world for more than 200 years:

> We hold these truths to be self-evident, that all men are created equal, that they are endowed by their Creator with certain unalienable Rights, that among these are Life, Liberty and the pursuit of Happiness.—That to secure these rights, Governments are instituted among Men, deriving their just powers from the consent of the governed,—That whenever any Form of Government becomes destructive of these ends, it is the Right of the People to alter or to abolish it, and to institute new Government. . . .

The Declaration was intended to influence foreign opinion, but its proclamation had little immediate effect outside Great Britain, and there it only made people angry and determined to subdue the rebels. Why, then, has the Declaration had so much influence on modern history? Not because the thought was original with Jefferson. As John Adams later pointed out, the basic idea was commonplace among eighteenth-century liberals. "I did not consider it any part of my charge to invent new ideas," Jefferson explained, "but to place before mankind the common sense of the subject, in terms so plain and firm as to command their assent. . . . It was intended to be an expression of the American mind."

Revolution was not new, but the spectacle of a people solemnly explaining and justifying their right, in an orderly manner, to throw off their oppressors and establish a new system on their own authority was almost without precedent. Soon the French would be drawing on this example in their revolution, and rebels everywhere have since done likewise. And if Jefferson did not create the concept, he gave it a nearly perfect form.

1776: The Balance of Forces

A formal declaration of independence merely cleared the way for tackling the problems of founding a new nation. Lacking both traditions and authority based in law, the Congress had to create political institutions and a new national spirit, all in the midst of war.

Always the military situation took precedence, for a single disastrous setback might make everything else meaningless. At the start the Americans already possessed their lands (except for the few square miles occupied by British troops). Although thousands of colonists fought for George III, the British soon learned that to put down the American rebellion they would have to bring in men and supplies from bases on the other side of the Atlantic.

Certain long-run factors operated in America's favor. Although His Majesty's soldiers were brave and well disciplined, the army was as inefficient as the rest of the British government. Whereas nearly everyone in Great Britain wanted to crack down on Boston after the Tea Party, many boggled at engaging in a full-scale war against all the colonies. Aside from a reluctance to spill so much blood, there was the question of expense. Finally, the idea of dispatching the cream of the British army to America while powerful enemies on the continent still smarted from past defeats seemed risky. For all these reasons the British approached gingerly the task of subduing the rebellion. When Washington fortified Dorchester Heights overlooking Boston, General Howe withdrew his troops to Halifax rather than risk another Bunker Hill.

Awareness of Britain's problems undoubtedly spurred the Continental Congress to the bold actions of the spring of 1776. However, on July 2, 1776, the same day that Congress voted for independence, General Howe was back on American soil, landing in force on Staten Island in New York harbor in preparation for an assault on the city. Soon Howe had at hand 32,000 well-equipped troops and a powerful fleet commanded by his brother, Richard, Lord Howe. If the British controlled New York City and the Hudson River, they could, as Washington realized, "stop intercourse between the northern and southern Colonies, upon which depends the Safety of America."

Suddenly the full strength of the empire seemed to have descended on the Americans. Superior British resources (a population of 9 million to the colonies' 2.5 million, large stocks of war materials and the industrial capacity to boost them further, mastery of the seas, a well-trained and experienced army, a highly centralized and, when necessary, ruthless government) were now all too evident.

The demonstration of British might in New York harbor accentuated American military and economic weaknesses: Both money and the tools of war were continually in short supply in a predominantly agricultural country. Many of Washington's soldiers were armed with weapons no more lethal than spears and tomahawks. Few had proper uniforms. Even the most patriotic resisted conforming to the conventions of military discipline; the men hated drilling and all parade-ground formality. And all these problems were complicated by the fact that Washington had to create an army organization out of whole cloth at the same time that he was fighting a war.

See the Map

The American Revolution at **myhistorylab.com**

Loyalists

Behind the lines, the country was far from united. Whereas nearly all colonists had objected to British policies, many still hesitated to take up arms against the mother country. Even Massachusetts harbored many **Loyalists**, or Tories, as they were called; about a thousand Americans left Boston with General Howe, abandoning their homes rather than submit to the rebel army.

No one knows exactly how the colonists divided on the question of independence. John Adams's off-the-cuff estimate was that a third of the people were ardent Patriots, another third loyal to Great Britain, and the rest neutral or tending to favor whichever side seemed to be winning. Most historians think that about a fifth of the people were Loyalists and about two-fifths Patriots, but there are few hard figures to go by. What is certain is that large elements, perhaps a majority of the people, were more or less indifferent to the conflict or, in Tom Paine's famous phrase, were summer soldiers and sunshine patriots—they supported the Revolution when all was going well and lost their enthusiasm in difficult hours.

The divisions cut across geographical, social, and economic lines. A high proportion of those holding royal appointments and many Anglican clergymen remained loyal to King George, as did numbers of merchants with close connections in Britain. There were important pockets of Tory strength in rural sections of New York, in the North Carolina backcountry, and among persons of non-English origin and other minority groups who tended to count on London for protection against the local majority (see the map "Campaign in the South, 1779–1781," p. 126).

Although the differences separating Patriots and Loyalists were sometimes unclear, feelings were nonetheless bitter. Individual Loyalists were often set upon by mobs, tarred and feathered, and otherwise abused. Some were thrown into jail for no legitimate reason; others were exiled and their property confiscated. Battles between Tory units and the Continental army were often exceptionally bloody. "Neighbor was against neighbor, father against son and son against father," one Connecticut Tory reported. "He that would not thrust his own blade through his brother's heart was called an infamous villain."

The British Take New York City

General Howe's campaign against New York brought to light another American weakness—the lack of military experience. Washington, expecting Howe to attack New York, had moved south to meet the threat immediately after Howe had abandoned Boston. But both he and his men failed badly in this first major test. Late in August Howe crossed from Staten Island to Brooklyn. In the Battle of Long Island he easily outflanked and defeated Washington's army. Had he acted decisively, he probably could have ended the war on the spot, but Howe could not make up his mind whether to be a peacemaker or a conqueror. This hesitation in consolidating his gains permitted Washington to withdraw his troops to Manhattan Island.

Howe could still have trapped Washington simply by using his fleet to land troops on the northern end of Manhattan; instead he attacked New York City directly, leaving the Americans an escape route to the North. Again Patriot troops proved no match for

British regulars. Although Washington threatened to shoot cowardly Connecticut soldiers as they fled the battlefield, he could not stop the rout and had to fall back on Harlem Heights in upper Manhattan. Yet once more Howe failed to pursue his advantage promptly.

Still, Washington refused to see the peril in remaining on an island while the enemy commanded the surrounding waters. Only when Howe shifted a powerful force to Westchester, directly threatening his rear, did Washington move north to the mainland. Finally, after several narrow escapes, he crossed the Hudson River and marched south to New Jersey, where the British could not use their naval superiority against him.

The battles in and around New York City suggested that the British would win easily. Yet somehow Washington salvaged a moral victory from these ignominious defeats. He learned rapidly; seldom thereafter did he place his troops in such vulnerable positions. And his men, in spite of repeated failure, had become an army. In November and December 1776

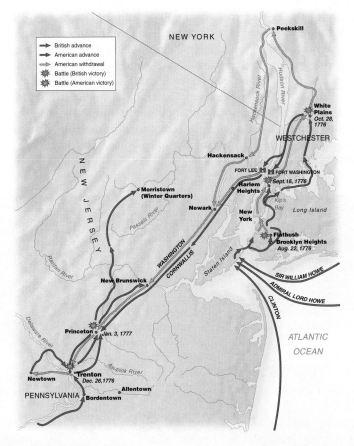

New York and New Jersey Campaigns, 1776–1777 In the summer of 1776, after abandoning Boston, several British fleets converged on New York City. After taking Staten Island, the British crossed to Brooklyn, and won a string of decisive battles in the New York region. Washington's troops retreated through New Jersey nearly to Newtown, Pennsylvania. But in the final week of 1776, Washington recrossed the Delaware River and won morale-boosting battles at Trenton and Princeton.

Emanuel Leutze's *Washington Crossing the Delaware* (1851) is riddled with historical inaccuracies, most obviously, the time of day: Washington's face shines and the ice gleams white, but the December 1776 crossing was actually made at night during a snowstorm.

they retreated across New Jersey and into Pennsylvania. General Howe then abandoned the campaign, going into winter quarters in New York but posting garrisons at Trenton, Princeton, and other strategic points.

The troops at Trenton were Hessian mercenaries, and Washington decided to attack them. He crossed the ice-clogged Delaware River with 2,400 men on Christmas night during a wild storm, and arrived at daybreak. The Hessians were taken completely by surprise. Those who could fled in disorder; the rest—900 of them—surrendered.

The Hessians were first-class professional soldiers, probably the most competent troops in Europe at that time. The victory gave a boost to American morale. A few days later Washington outmaneuvered General Cornwallis, who had rushed to Trenton with reinforcements, and won another battle at Princeton. These engagements had little strategic importance, since both armies then went into winter quarters. Without them, however, there might not have been an army to resume the war in the spring.

William Mercer, painter of *The Battle of Princeton* (1786–1790), was deaf and mute. Charles Wilson Peale, perhaps the foremost painter of the day, took Mercer on as a student in part to see if Mercer could learn the craft.

Saratoga and the French Alliance

When spring reached New Jersey in April 1777, Washington had fewer than 5,000 men under arms. Great plans—far too many and too complicated, as it turned out—were afoot in the British camp. The strategy called for General John Burgoyne to lead a large army from Canada down Lake Champlain toward Albany while a smaller force under Lieutenant Colonel Barry St. Leger pushed eastward toward Albany from Fort Oswego on Lake Ontario. General Howe was to lead a third force north up the Hudson. The Patriots would be trapped and the New England states isolated from the rest.

As a venture in coordinated military tactics, the British campaign of 1777 was a fiasco. General Howe had spent the winter in New York wining and dining his officers and prominent local Loyalists. He was less attentive to his responsibilities for the British army advancing south from Canada.

General "Gentleman Johnny" Burgoyne, a charming if somewhat bombastic character (part politician, part poet, part gambler, part ladies' man), yet also a brave soldier, had begun his march from Canada in mid-June. By early July his army, which consisted of 500 Indians, 650 Loyalists, and 6,000 regulars, had captured Fort Ticonderoga at the southern end of Lake Champlain. He quickly pushed beyond Lake George but then got bogged down. Burdened by a huge baggage train he could advance at but a snail's pace through the woods north of Saratoga. Patriot militia impeded his way by felling trees across the forest trails.

St. Leger was also slow in carrying out his part of the grand design. He did not leave Fort Oswego until July 26, and when he stopped to besiege a Patriot force at Fort Stanwix, General Benedict Arnold had time to march west with 1,000 men from the army resisting Burgoyne and drive him back to Oswego.

Meanwhile, with magnificent disregard for the agreed-on plan, Howe wasted time trying to trap Washington into exposing his army in New Jersey. This enabled Washington to send some of his best troops to buttress the militia units opposing Burgoyne. Then, just when St. Leger was setting out for Albany, Howe took the bulk of his army off by sea to attack Philadelphia, leaving only a small force commanded by General Sir Henry Clinton to aid Burgoyne.

When Washington moved south to oppose Howe, the British commander taught him a series of lessons in tactics, defeating him at the Battle of Brandywine, then feinting him out of position and moving unopposed into Philadelphia. But by that time it was late September, and disaster was about to befall General Burgoyne.

The American forces under Philip Schuyler and later under Horatio Gates and Benedict Arnold had erected formidable defenses immediately south of Saratoga. Burgoyne struck at this position twice and was thrown back both times with heavy losses. Each day more local militia swelled the American forces. Soon Burgoyne was under siege, his troops pinned down by withering fire from every direction, unable even to bury their dead. The only hope was General Clinton, who had finally started up the Hudson from New York. Clinton got as far as Kingston, about 80 miles south of Saratoga, but on October 16 he decided to return to New York for reinforcements. The next day, at Saratoga, Burgoyne surrendered. Some 5,700 British prisoners were marched off to Virginia.

This overwhelming triumph changed the course and character of the war. France would probably have entered the war in any case; the country had never reconciled itself to its losses in the Seven Years' War and for years had been building a navy capable of taking on the British. Helping the Americans was simply another way of weakening their British enemy. Spain also contributed, not out of sympathy for the Revolution, but because of its desire to injure Great Britain. When news of the victory at Saratoga reached Paris, the time seemed ripe and Louis XVI recognized the United States. Then Comte de Vergennes, France's foreign minister, and three American commissioners in Paris (Benjamin Franklin, Arthur Lee, and Silas Deane) drafted a commercial treaty and a formal treaty of alliance. The two nations agreed to make "common cause and aid each other mutually" should war "break out" between France and Great Britain. Meanwhile, France guaranteed "the sovereignty and independence absolute and unlimited" of the United States. The help of Spain and France, Washington declared, "will not fail of establishing the Independence of America in a short time."

When the news of Saratoga reached England, Lord North realized that a Franco-American alliance was almost inevitable. To forestall it, he was ready to give in on all the issues that had agitated the colonies before 1775. Both the Coercive Acts and the Tea Act would be repealed; Parliament would pledge never to tax the colonies.

Instead of implementing this proposal promptly, Parliament delayed until March 1778. Royal peace commissioners did not reach Philadelphia until June, a month after Congress had ratified the French treaty. The British proposals were rejected, and while the peace commissioners were still in Philadelphia, war broke out between France and Great Britain.

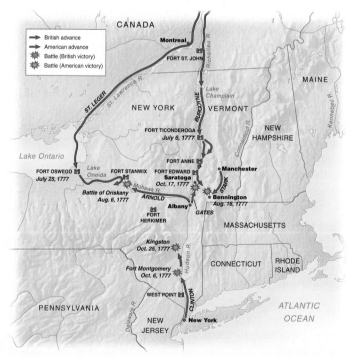

Saratoga Campaign, September 19 to October 17, 1777 In 1777 the British, who controlled New York City, decided to drive the Patriots from the rest of the colony through a three-pronged attack on Albany. All three British generals failed to achieve their objectives: St. Leger, coming from the west, failed to advance beyond Ft. Stanwix; Burgoyne, from the north, bogged down and found himself surrounded; and Clinton, from New York City, made it to Kingston, but failed to relieve Burgoyne, whose army surrendered.

The American Revolution, however, had yet to be won. After the loss of Philadelphia, Washington had settled his army for the winter at Valley Forge, 20 miles to the northwest. The army's supply system collapsed. According to the Marquis de Lafayette, one of many Europeans who volunteered to fight on the American side, "the unfortunate soldiers . . . had neither coats, nor hats, nor shirts, nor shoes; their feet and legs froze till they grew black, and it was often necessary to amputate them."

As the winter dragged on, the Continental army melted away. So many officers resigned that Washington was heard to say that he was afraid of "being left Alone with the Soldiers only." Since enlisted men could not legally resign, they deserted by the hundreds. Yet the army survived. Gradually the soldiers who remained became a tough, professional fighting force.

The War Moves South

Spring brought a revival of American hopes in the form of more supplies, new recruits, and, above all, word of the French alliance. In May 1778 the British replaced General Howe as commander with General Clinton, who decided to transfer his base back to New York. While Clinton was moving across New Jersey, Washington attacked him at Monmouth Court House. The fight was inconclusive, but the Americans held the field when the day ended and were able to claim a victory.

Thereafter British strategy changed. Fighting in the northern states degenerated into skirmishes and other small-unit clashes. Instead, relying on sea power, the supposed presence of many Tories in the South, and the possibility of obtaining the help of slaves, the British concentrated their efforts in South Carolina and Georgia. Savannah fell to them late in 1778, and most of the settled parts of Georgia were overrun during 1779. In 1780 Clinton led a massive expedition against Charleston. When the city surrendered in May, more than 3,000 soldiers were captured, the most overwhelming American defeat of the war. Leaving General Cornwallis and some 8,000 men to carry on the campaign, Clinton then sailed back to New York.

The Tories in South Carolina and Georgia came closer to meeting British expectations than in any other region, but the callous behavior of the British troops persuaded large numbers of hesitating citizens to join the Patriot cause. Guerrilla bands led by Francis Marion, the "Swamp Fox," Thomas Sumter (after whom Fort Sumter, famous in the Civil War, was named), and others like them provided a nucleus of resistance in areas that had supposedly been subdued. (For an additional perspective on this campaign, see Re-Viewing the Past at the end of this chapter about the movie, *The Patriot*.)

But the tide soon turned. In 1779 the Spanish governor of Louisiana, José de Gálvez, administered a stinging defeat to British troops in Florida, and in 1780 and 1781 he captured the British-held Gulf ports of Pensacola and Mobile. More important, in June 1780 Congress placed Horatio Gates in charge of a southern army consisting of the irregular militia units and a hard core of Continentals transferred from Washington's command. Gates encountered Cornwallis at Camden, South Carolina. Foolishly, he entrusted a key sector of his line to untrained militiamen, who panicked when the British charged with fixed bayonets. Gates suffered heavy losses and had to fall back. Congress then recalled him, permitting Washington to replace him with General Nathanael Greene, a first-rate officer.

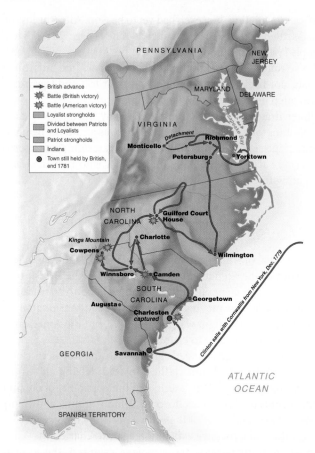

Campaign in the South, 1779–1781 In 1779 the British moved south, seeking support from Loyalist strongholds in the port cities of Savannah, Charleston, and Wilmington, as well as some interior regions. After taking Charleston, the British were harried throughout South Carolina and North Carolina, prompting their retreat northward to Virginia.

A band of militiamen had trapped a contingent of Tories at King's Mountain and forced its surrender. Greene, avoiding a major engagement with Cornwallis's superior numbers, divided his troops and staged a series of raids on scattered points. In January 1781, at the Battle of Cowpens in northwestern South Carolina, General Daniel Morgan inflicted a costly defeat on Colonel Banastre Tarleton, one of Cornwallis's most effective officers. Cornwallis pursued Morgan hotly, but the American rejoined Greene, and at Guilford Court House they again inflicted heavy losses on the British. Then Cornwallis withdrew to Wilmington, North Carolina, where he could rely on the fleet for support and reinforcements. Greene's Patriots quickly regained control of the Carolina backcountry.

Victory at Yorktown

Seeing no future in the Carolinas and unwilling to vegetate at Wilmington, Cornwallis marched north into Virginia, where he joined forces with troops under Benedict Arnold. (Disaffected by what he considered unjust criticism of his generalship, Arnold

The Yorktown Campaign, April to September 1781 Cornwallis assumed that his army at Yorktown could be provisioned and, if necessary, evacuated by the mighty British navy. But when several French admirals converged on the Chesapeake Bay in August and defeated the British fleet commanded by Admiral Graves, Cornwallis was trapped. He surrendered in October.

had sold out to the British in 1780. He intended to betray the bastion of West Point on the Hudson River. The scheme was foiled when incriminating papers were found on the person of a British spy, Major John André. Arnold fled to the British and André was hanged.) As in the Carolina campaign, the British had numerical superiority at first but lost it rapidly when local militia and Continental forces concentrated against them. Cornwallis soon discovered that Virginia Tories were of little help in such a situation. "When a Storm threatens, our friends disappear," he grumbled.

General Clinton ordered Cornwallis to establish a base at Yorktown where he could be supplied by sea. It was a terrible mistake. The British navy in American waters far outnumbered American and French vessels, but the Atlantic is wide, and in those days communication was slow. The French had a fleet in the West Indies under Admiral François de Grasse and another squadron at Newport, Rhode Island, where a French army was stationed. In the summer of 1781 Washington, de Grasse, and the Comte de Rochambeau, commander of French land forces, designed and carried out with an efficiency unparalleled in eighteenth-century warfare a complex plan to bottle up Cornwallis.

The British navy in the West Indies and at New York might have forestalled this scheme had it moved promptly and in force. But Admiral Sir George Rodney sent only part of his Indies fleet. As a result, de Grasse, after a battle with a British fleet commanded by Admiral Thomas Graves, won control of the Chesapeake and cut Cornwallis off from the sea.

The next move was up to Washington, and this was his finest hour as a commander. He desperately wanted to attack the British base at New York, but at the urging of

This painting of the surrender of Cornwallis at Yorktown on October 19, 1781 was done by John Trumbull in 1820. Trumbull's original version of the painting depicted Cornwallis in the act of surrender. But this was a serious mistake: Cornwallis, unwilling to admit defeat in person, had sent a subordinate to surrender on his behalf. Trumbull repainted the scene, changing the uniform color of the central figure from red to blue: An American officer reaches for a sword presented by Cornwallis's second-in-command.

Rochambeau he agreed instead to strike at Yorktown. After tricking Clinton into thinking he was heading for New York, he pushed boldly south. In early September he reached Yorktown and joined up with an army commanded by Lafayette and troops from de Grasse's fleet. He soon had nearly 17,000 French and American veterans in position.

Cornwallis was helpless. He held out until October 17 and then asked for terms. Two days later more than 7,000 British soldiers marched out of their lines and laid down their arms. Then the jubilant Lafayette ordered his military band to play "Yankee Doodle."

Negotiating a Favorable Peace

((•—[Hear the Audio

The Liberty Song at
myhistorylab.com

The British gave up trying to suppress the rebellion after Yorktown, but the event that confirmed the existence of the United States as an independent nation was the signing of a peace treaty with Great Britain. But the problem of peacemaking was complicated. The United States and France had pledged not to make a separate peace.

The Continental Congress appointed John Adams, Benjamin Franklin, John Jay, Thomas Jefferson, and Henry Laurens as a commission to conduct peace talks in Paris, France. Franklin and Jay did most of the actual negotiating. Congress, grateful for French aid during the Revolution, had instructed the commissioners to rely on the advice of the Comte de Vergennes. In Paris, however, the commissioners soon discovered that Vergennes was not the perfect friend of America that Congress believed him to be. He was, after all, a French official, and France had other interests far more important than concern for its American ally. Vergennes "means to keep his hand under our chin to prevent us from drowning," Adams complained, "but not to lift our head out of the water."

Franklin, whose fame as a scientist and sage had spread to Europe, was wined and dined by the cream of Paris. He did not press the American point of view as forcefully as he might have. But this was because he took the long view, which was to achieve a true reconciliation with the British, not simply to drive the hardest bargain possible. John Jay was somewhat more tough-minded. But on basic issues all the Americans were in agreement. They hinted to the British representative, Richard Oswald, that they would consider a separate peace if it were a generous one and suggested that Great Britain would be far better off with America, a nation that favored free trade, in control of the trans-Appalachian region than with a mercantilist power like Spain.

The British government reacted favorably, authorizing Oswald "to treat with the Commissioners appointed by the Colonys, under the title of Thirteen United States." Soon the Americans were deep in negotiations with Oswald. They told Vergennes what they were doing but did not discuss details.

By the end of November 1782 a preliminary treaty had been signed. "His Britannic Majesty," Article 1 began, "acknowledges the said United States . . . to be free, sovereign and independent States." Other terms were equally in line with American hopes and objectives. The boundaries of the nation were set at the Great Lakes, the Mississippi River, and 31° north latitude (roughly the northern boundary of Florida, which the British turned over to Spain).[1] Britain recognized the right of Americans to take fish on the Grand Banks off Newfoundland and, far more important, to dry and cure their catch on unsettled beaches in Labrador and Nova Scotia. The British agreed to withdraw their troops from American soil "with all convenient speed." On the touchy problem of Tory property seized during the Revolution, the Americans agreed only that Congress would "earnestly recommend" that the states "provide for the restitution of all estates, rights and properties which have been confiscated." They promised to prevent further property confiscation and prosecutions of Tories—certainly a wise as well as a humane policy—and they agreed not to impede the collection of debts owed British subjects. Vergennes was flabbergasted by the success of the Americans. "The English buy the peace more than they make it," he wrote. "Their concessions . . . exceed all that I should have thought possible."

The American commissioners obtained these favorable terms because they were shrewd diplomats and because of the rivalries that existed among the great European powers. In the last analysis, Britain preferred to have a weak nation of English-speaking people in command of the Mississippi Valley rather than France or Spain.

From their experience at the peace talks, the American leaders learned the importance of playing one power against another without committing themselves completely to any. This policy demanded constant contact with European affairs and skill at adjusting policies to changes in the European balance of power. It enabled the United States, a young and relatively feeble country, to grow and prosper.

---

[1]Much of this vast region, of course, was controlled not by the British but by various Indian tribes.

The United States under the Articles of Confederation, 1787 New York and Virginia gave up their claims to the vast area that became the Northwest Territory and thus set a precedent for trans-Appalachian land policy. By 1802 the various state claims had been ceded to the national government. The original Northwest Territory (the Old Northwest) was bounded by the Ohio and Mississippi rivers and the Great Lakes.

National Government under the Articles of Confederation

Independence was won on the battlefield and at the Paris Peace Conference, but it could not have been achieved without the work of the Continental Congress and the new state governments. The delegates recognized that the Congress was essentially a legislative body rather than a complete government and from the start they struggled to create a workable central authority. In July 1776 John Dickinson prepared a draft national constitution, but it could not command much support. The larger states objected to equal representation of all the states, and the states with large western land claims refused to cede them to the central government. It was not until November 1777 that the **Articles of Confederation** were submitted to the states for ratification. The approval of all states was required before the Articles could go into effect. All acted fairly promptly but Maryland, which did not ratify the document until 1781.

●●◀─[**Read the Document**

The Articles of Confederation
at **myhistorylab.com**

The Articles merely provided a legal basis for authority that the Continental Congress had already been exercising. Each state, regardless of size, was to have but one vote; the union it created was only a "league of friendship." Article 2 defined the limit of national power: "Each state retains its sovereignty, freedom, and independence, and every Power, jurisdiction, and right, which is not by this confederation expressly delegated to the United States, in Congress assembled." Time proved this an inadequate arrangement, chiefly because the central government lacked the authority to impose taxes and had no way of enforcing the powers it did have.

See the **Map**

Western Land Claims Ceded by the States at **myhistorylab.com**

Financing the War

In practice, Congress and the states carried on the war cooperatively. General officers were appointed by Congress, lesser ones locally. The Continental army, the backbone of Washington's force, was supported by Congress. The states raised militia chiefly for short-term service. Militiamen fought well at times but often proved unreliable, especially when asked to fight at any great distance from their homes. Washington continually fretted about their "dirty mercenary spirit" and their "intractable" nature, yet he could not have won the war without them.

The fact that Congress's requisitions of money often went unhonored by the states does not mean that the states failed to contribute heavily to the war effort. Altogether they spent about $5.8 million in hard money, and they met Congress's demands for beef, corn, rum, fodder, and other military supplies. In addition, Congress raised large sums by borrowing. Americans bought bonds worth between $7 and $8 million during the war. Foreign governments lent another $8 million, most of this furnished by France. Congress also issued more than $240 million in paper money, and the states issued over $200 million more. This currency fell rapidly in value, resulting in an inflation that caused hardship and grumbling. The people, in effect, paid much of the cost of the war through the depreciation of their savings, but it is hard to see how else the war could have been financed, given the prejudice of the populace against paying taxes to fight a war against British taxation.

State Republican Governments

However crucial the role of Congress, in an important sense the real revolution occurred when the individual colonies broke their ties with Great Britain. Using their colonial charters as a basis, the states began framing new constitutions even before the Declaration of Independence. By early 1777 all but Connecticut and Rhode Island, which continued under their colonial charters well into the nineteenth century, had taken this decisive step.

On the surface the new governments were not drastically different from those they replaced. The most significant change was the removal of outside control, which had the effect of making the governments more responsive to public opinion. Gone were the times when a governor could be appointed and maintained in office by orders from

London. The new constitutions varied in detail, but all provided for an elected legislature, an executive, and a system of courts. In general the powers of the governor and of judges were limited, the theory being that elected rulers no less than those appointed by kings were subject to the temptations of authority, that, as one Patriot put it, all men are "tyrants enough at heart." The typical governor had no voice in legislation and little in appointments. Pennsylvania went so far as to eliminate the office of governor, replacing it with an elected council of twelve.

Power was concentrated in the legislature, which the people had come to count on to defend their interests. In addition to the lawmaking authority exercised by the colonial assemblies, the state constitutions gave the legislatures the power to declare war, conduct foreign relations, control the courts, and perform many other essentially executive functions. While continuing to require that voters be property owners or tax-payers, the constitution makers remained suspicious even of the legislature.

They rejected the British concept of virtual representation. They saw legislators as representatives—that is, as agents reflecting the interests of the voters of a particular district rather than superior persons chosen to decide public issues according to their own best judgment. Where political power was involved, the common American principle was every man for himself, but also everyone for the nation, the republic. People were no longer subjects, but citizens, *parts* of government, obedient to its laws, but not blindly subordinate to governmental authority epitomized in the monarch.

A majority of the constitutions contained bills of rights (such as the one George Mason wrote for Virginia) protecting the people's civil liberties against all branches of the government. In Britain such guarantees checked only the Crown; the Americans invoked them against their elected representatives as well.

The state governments combined the best of the British system, including its respect for status, fairness, and due process with the uniquely American stress on individualism and a healthy dislike of excessive authority. The idea of drafting written frames of government—contracts between the people and their representatives that carefully spelled out the powers and duties of the latter—grew out of the experience of the colonists after 1763, when the vagueness of the unwritten British constitution had caused so much controversy, and from the compact principle, the heart of republican government as described so eloquently in the Declaration of Independence. This constitutionalism represented one of the most important innovations of the Revolutionary era: a peaceful method for altering the political system. In the midst of violence, the states changed their frames of government in an orderly, legal manner—a truly remarkable achievement that became a beacon of hope to reformers all over the world. The states' example, the Reverend Simeon Howard of Massachusetts predicted, "will encourage the friends and rouse a spirit of liberty through other nations."

Social Reform and Antislavery

Many states seized the occasion of constitution making to introduce important political and social reforms. In Pennsylvania, Virginia, North Carolina, and other states the seats in the legislature were reapportioned in order to give the western districts their fair share. Primogeniture, entail (the right of an owner of property to prevent heirs from ever selling it), and quitrents were abolished wherever they had existed. Steps toward greater freedom of religion were taken, especially in states where the Anglican Church had enjoyed a privileged position. In Virginia the movement to separate church and state was given the force of law by Jefferson's Statute of Religious Liberty, enacted in 1786. "Our civil rights have no dependence on our religious opinions, any more than our opinions in physics or geometry," the statute declared. "Truth is great and will prevail if left to herself."

A number of states moved tentatively against slavery. In attacking British policy after 1763, colonists had frequently claimed that Parliament was trying to make slaves of them. No less a personage than George Washington wrote in 1774: "We must assert our rights, or submit to every imposition, that can be heaped upon us, till custom and use shall make us tame and abject slaves." However exaggerated the language, such reasoning led to denunciations of slavery, often vague but significant in their effects on public opinion. The fact that practically every important thinker of the European Enlightenment (Montesquieu, Voltaire, Diderot, and Rousseau in France; David Hume, Samuel Johnson, and Adam Smith in England, to name the most important) had criticized slavery on moral and economic grounds also had an impact on educated opinion. Then, too, the forthright statements in the Declaration of Independence about liberty and equality seemed impossible to reconcile with slaveholding. "How is it," asked Dr. Samuel Johnson, the celebrated English writer who opposed independence, "that we hear the loudest yelps for liberty among the drivers of negroes?"

The war opened direct paths to freedom for some slaves. In November 1775 Lord Dunmore, the royal governor of Virginia, proclaimed that all slaves "able and willing to bear arms" for the British would be liberated. In fact, the British treated slaves as captured property, seizing them by the thousands in their campaigns in the South. The fate of these blacks is obscure. Some ended up in the West Indies, still slaves. Others were evacuated to Canada and liberated, and some of them settled the British colony of Sierra Leone in West Africa, founded in 1787. Probably many more escaped from bondage by running away during the confusion accompanying the British campaigns in the South.

About 5,000 blacks served in the Patriot army and navy. Most black soldiers were assigned noncombat duties, but there were some African American soldiers in every major battle from Lexington to Yorktown.

Beginning with Pennsylvania in 1780, the northern states all did away with slavery. In most cases slaves born after a certain date were to become free on reaching maturity. Since New York did not pass a gradual emancipation law until 1799 and New Jersey not until 1804, there were numbers of slaves in the so-called free states well into the nineteenth century—more than 3,500 as late as 1830. But the institution was on its way toward extinction. All the states prohibited the importation of slaves from abroad, and except for Georgia and South Carolina, the southern states passed laws removing restrictions on the right of individual owners to free their slaves. The greatest success of voluntary emancipation came in Virginia, where, between 1782 and 1790, as many as 10,000 blacks were freed.

These advances encouraged foes of slavery to hope that the institution would soon disappear. But slavery died only where it was not economically important. Except for owners whose slaves were "carried off" by the British, only in Massachusetts (where the state supreme court ruled slavery unconstitutional in 1783) were slaves taken away from their owners.

Despite the continuing subordination of blacks, the Revolution permanently changed the tone of American society. In the way they dressed, in their manner of speech, and in the way they dealt with one another in public places, Americans paid at least lip service to the idea of equality.

Little of the social and economic upheaval usually associated with revolutions occurred, before, during, or after 1776. At least part of the urban violence of the period (just how large a part is difficult to determine at this distance) had no social objective. America had its share of criminals, mischievous youths eager to flex their muscles, and other people unable to resist the temptation to break the law when it could be done without much risk of punishment.

The property of Tories was frequently seized by the state governments, but almost never with the idea of redistributing wealth or providing the poor with land. While some large Tory estates were broken up and sold to small farmers, others passed intact to wealthy individuals or to groups of speculators. The war disrupted many traditional business relationships. Some merchants were unable to cope with the changes; others adapted well and grew rich. But the changes occurred without regard for the political beliefs or social values of either those who profited or those who lost.

Finally, the new governments became more responsive to public opinion, no matter what the particular shape of their political institutions. This was true principally because *Common Sense*, the Declaration of Independence, and the experience of participating in a revolution had made people conscious of their rights in a republic and of their power to enforce those rights. Conservatives swiftly discovered that state constitutions designed to insulate legislators and officials from popular pressures were ineffective when the populace felt strongly about any issue.

Women and the Revolution

In the late eighteenth century women in the Western world were acquiring more legal rights, although the change was barely perceptible at the time. This movement was strengthened in America by the events leading up to the break with Great Britain and still more by the Declaration of Independence. When Americans began to think and talk about the rights of the individual and the evils of arbitrary rule, subtle effects on relations between the sexes followed. For example, it became somewhat easier for women to obtain divorces. In colonial times divorces were relatively rare, but easier for men to obtain than for women. After the Revolution the difference did not disappear, but it became considerably smaller. In 1791 a South Carolina judge went so far as to say that the law protecting "the absolute dominion" of husbands was "the offspring of a rude and barbarous age." The "progress of civilization," he continued, "has tended to ameliorate the condition of women, and to allow even to wives, something like personal identity."

As the tone of this "liberal" opinion indicates, the change in male attitudes that took place in America because of the Revolution was small. Courts in New York and Massachusetts refused to take action against Tory women whose husbands were Tories on the grounds that it was the duty of women to obey their husbands; and when John Adams's wife Abigail warned him in 1776 that if he and his fellow rebels did not "remember the ladies" when reforming society, the women would "foment a

In 2009, historian Woody Holton described how Abigail Adams shrewdly invested in the Continental Congress's war debts; when the new government decided to pay those debts in full, those who had invested in the debt made a killing. Because John Adams himself supported this policy, Holton suggests that she had engaged in unsavory (but not uncommon) investment practices.

Rebellion" of their own, he treated her remarks as a joke. Adams believed that voting (and as he wrote on another occasion, writing history) was "not the Province of the Ladies."[2]

However, the war effort increased the influence of women in several ways. With so many men in uniform, women took over the management of countless farms, shops, and businesses, and they became involved in the handling of other day-to-day matters that men had normally conducted. Their experiences made both them, and in many cases their fathers and husbands, more aware of their ability to take on all sorts of work previously considered exclusively masculine in character. At the same time, women wanted to contribute to the winning of independence, and their efforts to do so made them conscious of their importance. Furthermore, the rhetoric of the Revolution, with its stress on liberty and equality, affected women in the same way that it caused many whites of both sexes to question the morality of slavery.

Attitudes toward the education of women also changed because of the Revolution. According to the best estimates, at least half the white women in America could not read or write as late as the 1780s. In a land of opportunity like the United States, women seemed particularly important, not only because they themselves were citizens, but because of their role in training the next generation. "You distribute 'mental nourishment' along with physical," one orator told the women of America in 1795. "The reformation of the world is in your power. . . . The solidity and stability of your country rest with you." The idea of female education began to catch on. Schools for girls were founded, and the level of female literacy gradually rose.

Growth of a National Spirit

The growth of American **nationalism** was an important result of the Revolution. Most modern revolutions have been *caused* by nationalism and have *resulted* in independence. In the case of the American Revolution, the desire to be free antedated any intense national feeling. The colonies entered into a political union not because they felt an overwhelming desire to bring all Americans under one rule but because unity offered the only hope of winning a war against Great Britain. That they remained

---

[2]Adams's distaste for women historians may have been based on the fact that in his friend Mercy Otis Warren's *History of the Rise, Progress, and Termination of the American Revolution* (1805) Warren claimed that Adams sometimes allowed his "prejudices" to distort his judgment.

united after throwing off British rule reflects the degree to which nationalism had developed during the conflict.

By the middle of the eighteenth century the colonists had begun to think of themselves as a separate society distinct from Europe and even from Britain. Benjamin Franklin described himself not as a British subject but as "an American subject of the King," and in 1750 a Boston newspaper could urge its readers to drink "American" beer in order to free themselves from being "beholden to Foreigners" for their alcoholic beverages. Little political nationalism existed before the Revolution, however, in part because most people knew little about life outside their own colony. When a delegate to the first Continental Congress mentioned "Colonel Washington" to John Adams soon after the Congress met, Adams had to ask him who this "Colonel Washington" was. He had never heard the name before.

The new nationalism arose from a number of sources and expressed itself in different ways. Common sacrifices in war certainly played a part; the soldiers of the Continental army fought in the summer heat of the Carolinas for the same cause that had led them to brave the ice floes of the Delaware in order to surprise the Hessians. Such men lost interest in state boundary lines; they became Americans.

The war caused many people to move from place to place. Soldiers traveled as the tide of war fluctuated; so too—far more than in earlier times—did prominent leaders. Members of Congress from every state had to travel to Philadelphia; in the process they saw much of the country and the people who inhabited it. Listening to their fellows and serving with them on committees almost inevitably broadened these men, most of them highly influential in their local communities.

With its thirteen stars and thirteen stripes representing the states, the American flag symbolized national unity and reflected the common feeling that such a symbol was necessary. Yet the flag had separate stars and stripes; local interests and local loyalties remained extremely strong, and these could be divisive when conflicts of interest arose.

Certain practical problems that demanded common solutions also drew the states together. No one seriously considered having thirteen postal systems or thirteen sets of diplomatic representatives abroad. Every new diplomatic appointment, every treaty of friendship or commerce signed, committed all to a common policy and thus bound them more closely together. And economic developments had a unifying effect. Deprived of English goods, Americans manufactured more things themselves, stimulating both interstate trade and national pride.

The Great Land Ordinances

The lands west of the Appalachians, initially a source of dispute, became a force for unity once they had been ceded to the national government. Everyone realized what a priceless national asset they were, and all now understood that no one state could determine the future of the West.

The politicians argued hotly about how these lands should be developed. Some advocated selling the land in township units in the traditional New England manner to groups or companies; others favored letting individual pioneers stake out farms in the helter-skelter manner common in the colonial South. The decision was a compromise. The Land Ordinance of 1785 provided for surveying the Western Territories into six-mile-square townships before sale. Every other township was to be further subdivided into thirty-six sections of 640 acres (one square mile) each. The land was sold at auction at a minimum price of $1 an acre. The law favored speculative land-development companies, for even the 640-acre units were far too large and expensive for the typical frontier family. But the fact that the land was to be surveyed and sold by the central government was a nationalizing force. It ensured orderly development of the West and simplified the task of defending the frontier in the event of Indian attack. Congress set aside the sixteenth section of every township for the maintenance of schools, another farsighted decision.

Still more significant was the **Northwest Ordinance** of 1787, which established governments for the West. As early as 1775 settlers in frontier districts were petitioning Congress to allow them to enter the Union as independent states, and in 1780 Congress had resolved that all lands ceded to the nation by the existing states should be "formed into distinct republican States" with "the same rights of sovereignty, freedom and independence" as the original thirteen. In 1784 a committee headed by Thomas Jefferson worked out a plan for doing this, and in 1787 it was enacted into law. The area bounded by the Ohio, the Mississippi, and the Great Lakes was to be carved into not fewer than three or more

••••⎡**Read** the **Document**

Northwest Ordinance, 1787 at
myhistorylab.com

The Land Ordinance of 1785 called for surveying and dividing the Western Territories into square mile subdivisions—640 acres. These were further subdivided and sold as forty-acre tracts. Few pieces of legislation have left a more visible imprint upon the landscape. Today's Midwest, as seen from an airplane, resembles a patchwork quilt of forty-acre squares, as in the section of Kansas shown here.

The Patriot

As the opening credits roll, Benjamin Martin (Mel Gibson) pries open a wooden box. It contains yellowing papers, a few medals, and a tomahawk. He lifts the tomahawk, fingers it gingerly, and stares at the blade. "I had long feared that my sins would revisit me," a voice intones, "and the cost is more than I can bear." The viewer suspects—rightly—that Martin's sins had something to do with hacking people apart. But at the outset of *The Patriot*, Hollywood's $100-million blockbuster, Martin is more pacifist than patriot. When the South Carolina legislature votes to go to war with Great Britain, he declares that his obligation is to his family: "I will not fight."

He soon changes his mind after the British capture Charleston (1780) which brings onto the scene a villainous British cavalry officer, Colonel Tavington. Ordered by General Cornwallis to subdue the insurrection, Tavington ransacks plantations, forces slaves into the king's service, and hounds the rebel militia. He also arrests Gabriel (Heath Ledger), Martin's oldest son, and orders the boy's execution as a spy. When Gabriel's younger brother tries to intervene, Tavington shoots the boy dead. Overcome with rage, Martin races to his room, grabs the hatchet, and proceeds to bury it—repeatedly—into the chests and skulls of countless British soldiers. He takes command of the militia, recruits more Patriots, and harries the British at every turn.

Tavington responds by intensifying his campaign against the rebels. His culminating barbarity is to round up the villagers of Wakefield (including Gabriel's fiancé), herd them into a church, and set it ablaze. All perish in unimaginable (and mercifully unfilmed) agony. Martin checks his rage long enough to plot the defeat of Cornwallis's army. This occurs at the Battle of Cowpens. When Tavington leads a cavalry charge, Martin reaches for the tomahawk. Tavington dies at Martin's hands, and Cornwallis is routed, too; the latter's subsequent surrender at Yorktown is now a foregone conclusion.

Historians have found much to criticize in the movie's retelling of the war in the South. There was no such person as Benjamin Martin, though elements of his story can be found in the exploits of guerrilla leaders such as Francis Marion ("the Swamp Fox"), Thomas Sumter, Andrew Pickens, and General Daniel Morgan, who commanded the Continentals at Cowpens. The movie's version of the Battle of Cowpens featured a glorious display of fireworks, though neither army's artillery in South Carolina was capable of firing explosive shells. Cornwallis was not humiliated at Cowpens because he was not there. The most serious deviation from the historical record was the incineration of the occupied church: It didn't happen. "*The Patriot* is to history what Godzilla was to biology," declared historian David Hackett Fischer.

However, *The Patriot* raises and addresses an important historical issue: How can any society reconcile peaceable virtues—love for family, neighborliness, cooperation—with the violence of war? In *The Patriot*, the dilemma is symbolized by Martin's tomahawk. This weapon helps free his captured son and vanquish the evil Tavington; and yet it is also a manifestation of Martin's savage, even pathological, rage.

Eighteenth-century Europeans struggled to reconcile the violence of war with the need for social order. Their particular refinement of the military arts was the ordered massing of musket fire. Because muskets were highly inaccurate, a troop of soldiers, dispersed and firing on their own, were unlikely to drive an enemy from the field. But when soldiers were brought together in concentrated formations and ordered to fire simultaneously, the enemy would be decimated. The technology of warfare required intense discipline; and the new penchant for order imposed seeming coherence upon the chaos of the battlefield.

The Patriot provides a vivid rendering of this juxtaposition. Soldiers in beautifully colored uniforms march in straight columns to the steady cadence of drums while officers

William Ranney's painting, *The Battle of Cowpens* (1845) anticipated an error of the movie, *The Patriot*. General Daniel Morgan's troops are shown in green uniforms while the British cavalry are wearing red. In fact the British commander, Banastre Tarleton, on whom Tavington was based, commanded the Green Dragoons, a name reflected in their uniform color. Source: William Ranney, *The Battle of Cowpens*. Oil on canvas. Photo by Sam Holland. Courtesy South Carolina State House.

Mel Gibson as Patriot leader Benjamin Martin with Jason Isaacs as Colonel Tavington, a barbarous British officer.

bark precise commands: "Circle right. Face forward. Lift weapons . . ." Then musket fire shatters the formations, low-velocity cannon balls decapitate soldiers, and bayonets pierce their chests.

Martin concludes that the British cannot be defeated in this type of battle. And they seldom were. Martin advocates guerrilla tactics, as did many southern Patriot militiamen. The British had good reason to doubt the legitimacy of this type of warfare. When men went wild on the battlefield, or fired their weapons and then hid among civilians, they were criminals. If such behavior were condoned, warfare would become barbarity.

During a truce, Martin confers with Cornwallis, who complains that the Patriot militia targeted British officers. Such behavior was inconsistent with "civilized warfare." Officers, as gentlemen, were bound by codes of honor. If they were killed, who would prevent the regular soldiers from reverting to a frenzy of terror and rage?

The movie's debate over "civilized" warfare parallels an ongoing debate at the time. At the outset of the war, British officers took an oath affirming the British Articles of War, which protected citizens and soldiers who had surrendered. The American Congress also adopted the British Articles of War. But with the outbreak of guerrilla warfare in the South, both sides frequently ignored these rules.

"Colonel Tavington" was based on Banastre Tarleton, the actual commander of the Green Dragoons. Tarleton became notorious after his soldiers raped plantation women and killed militiamen who had surrendered. This worried Cornwallis, who sent a dispatch that, while commending Tarleton's courage and zeal, also warned: "Use your utmost endeavors to prevent the troops under your command from committing irregularities." In a subsequent engagement at Waxhaws, however, Tarleton again lost control of his men, who stabbed and slashed vanquished foes.

British and American officers sought to affirm that the war could be civilized. But such high-minded notions were repeatedly subverted during tomahawk-wielding guerrilla warfare and by excessively zealous commanders. The question then remained, as it does today, whether unchecked aggression is, among soldiers, a virtue or a vice. *The Patriot* raises these issues but does not resolve them. Martin, surely, should have kept his tomahawk in its locked box; but if he had, would the Patriots have won?

Questions for Discussion

- Does the justice of a cause warrant the use of violence to attain it?
- Was guerrilla warfare in the South morally justified?
- In general, how can filmmakers contribute to understanding the past? How are they likely to alter the past to suit cinematic purposes?

than five territories. Until the adult male population of the entire area reached 5,000, it was to be ruled by a governor and three judges, all appointed by Congress. When 5,000 men of voting age had settled in the territory, the Ordinance authorized them to elect a legislature, which could send a nonvoting delegate to Congress. Finally, when 60,000 persons had settled in any one of the political subdivisions, it was to become a state. It could draft a constitution and operate in any way it wished, save that the government had to be "republican" and that slavery was prohibited.

Seldom has a legislative body acted more wisely. That the western districts must become states everyone conceded from the start. The people had had their fill of colonialism under British rule, and the rebellious temper of frontier settlers made it impossible even to consider maintaining the West in a dependent status. But it would have been unfair to turn the territories over to the first-comers, who would have been unable to manage such large domains and would surely have taken advantage of their priority to dictate to later arrivals. A period of tutelage was necessary, a period when the "mother country" must guide and nourish its growing offspring.

Thus the intermediate territorial governments corresponded almost exactly to the governments of British royal colonies. The appointed governors could veto acts of the assemblies and could "convene, prorogue, and dissolve" them at their discretion. The territorial delegates to Congress were not unlike colonial agents. Yet it was vital that this intermediate stage end and that its end be determined in advance so that no argument could develop over when the territory was ready for statehood.

The system worked well and was applied to nearly all the regions absorbed by the nation as it advanced westward. Together with the Ordinance of 1785, which branded its checkerboard pattern on the physical shape of the West, this law gave the growing country a unity essential to the growth of a national spirit.

National Heroes

The Revolution further fostered nationalism by giving the people their first commonly revered heroes. Benjamin Franklin was widely known before the break with Great Britain through his experiments with electricity, his immensely successful *Poor Richard's Almanack*, and his invention of the Franklin stove. His staunch support of the Patriot cause, his work in the Continental Congress, and his diplomatic successes in France, where he was extravagantly admired, added to his fame. Franklin demonstrated, to Europeans and to Americans themselves, that not all Americans need be ignorant rustics.

Stern, cold, a man of few words, Washington did not seem a likely candidate for hero worship. "My countenance never yet revealed my feelings," he himself admitted. Yet he had qualities that made people name babies after him and call him "the Father of His Country" long before the war was won: his personal sacrifices in the cause of independence, his integrity, and above all, perhaps, his obvious desire to retire to his Mount Vernon estate (for many Americans feared any powerful leader and worried lest Washington seek to become a dictator).

As a general, Washington was not a brilliant strategist like Napoleon. Neither was he a tactician of the quality of Caesar or Robert E. Lee. But he was a remarkable organizer and administrator—patient, thoughtful, conciliatory. In a way, his lack of genius made his achievements all the more impressive. He held his forces together in adversity, avoiding both useless slaughter and catastrophic defeat. People of all sections, from every walk of life, looked on Washington as the embodiment of American virtues: a man of deeds rather than words; a substantial citizen accustomed to luxury yet capable of enduring great hardships stoically and as much at home in the wilderness as an Indian; a bold Patriot, quick to take arms against British tyranny, yet eminently respectable. The Revolution might have been won without Washington, but it is unlikely that the free United States would have become so easily a true nation had he not been at its call.

Milestones

1774	Thomas Jefferson writes *A Summary View of the Rights of British America*	1777	Washington's troops win Battle of Princeton
	General Thomas Gage, commander-in-chief of British army in North America, is named governor of Massachusetts		American victory at Saratoga turns the tide and leads to alliance with France
1775	Colonists fight British in Battles of Lexington and Concord		British occupy Philadelphia after the Battle of Germantown
	Second Continental Congress names George Washington commander-in-chief (of Continental army)	1777–1778	Continental army winters at Valley Forge
		1778	British capture Savannah
	Gage is replaced as British commander by General Sir William Howe after the Battle of Bunker Hill	1780	British capture Charleston
		1781	States ratify Articles of Confederation
1776	Thomas Paine publishes *Common Sense*		General Cornwallis surrenders at Yorktown
	Washington's troops occupy Boston	1783	Great Britain recognizes independence of United States by signing the Peace of Paris
	Second Continental Congress issues Declaration of Independence		
	Washington's troops are defeated in Battle of Long Island	1785	Congress passes the Land Ordinance of 1785
	Washington evacuates New York City	1787	Northwest Ordinance establishes governments for the West
	Washington's victory at Battle of Trenton boosts morale		

✓•⎰Study and Review⎱ at www.myhistorylab.com

Review Questions

1. The introduction for this chapter states that the American victory over Britain was not inevitable. Do you agree?

2. Which of the following was the most important: Washington's morale-saving crossing of the Delaware and defeat of Hessian troops in Trenton, the surrender of Burgoyne at Saratoga, or the surrender of Cornwallis at Yorktown?

3. What were the main effects of the American Revolution on women? On relations between rich and poor?

Key Terms

Articles of
  Confederation   *130*
Common Sense   *117*
Continental army   *115*

Loyalists   *120*
nationalism   *135*
Northwest
  Ordinance   *137*

Second Continental
  Congress   *114*

The Federalist Era: Nationalism Triumphant

5

((•—[Hear the Audio Chapter 5 at myhistorylab.com

Do you illegally download?

WHEN THE PHONE RANG IN THE DORM ROOM OF BRITTANY KRUGER, a first-year student at Northern Michigan University, she had no idea that the Constitution of the United States was about to crash into her life. Kruger's dean was on the line. The dean informed Kruger that the nation's record companies had charged her with copyright infringement for having downloaded Guns N' Roses' "Welcome to the Jungle," Lynyrd Skynyrd's "Free Bird," and other popular songs. Because each copyright infringement carried a $150,000 penalty, Kruger was responsible for millions of dollars in fines. If she paid $8,100 immediately, the record companies would settle the claim. Kruger, who earned $4,500 working at a Dairy Queen, called her parents.

The record companies sued Joel Tenenbaum, a Boston University physics graduate student, for $4.5 million. He had downloaded and shared thirty songs. Instead of settling, Tenenbaum was among the first to seek his day in court. In 2009 a federal jury ordered Tenenbaum to pay $625,000; he said he would declare bankruptcy.

If the Articles of Confederation had remained the law of the land, Kruger, Tenenbaum, and the other 40,000 people charged with illegally downloading songs and games would have done nothing wrong. The Articles made no mention of copyright. But James Madison reasoned that if inventors did not "own" their inventions, they would have little incentive to invent. Authors, too, could expect no profit if their books could be freely reprinted. The economy would suffer from the lack of innovation and knowledge would languish. Thomas Jefferson, on the other hand, observed that in England copyright laws allowed businesses to monopolize inventions and books. This drove prices up and restricted dissemination of ideas. He argued that ideas, once divulged, should be made available to the public swiftly and freely. Jefferson had himself evaded Britain's copyright laws by stocking his library at Monticello with pirated books, printed on the cheap in Dublin.

Eventually the framers reached a compromise that became Article 1, Section 8 of the Constitution of the United States. It empowered Congress to "promote the Progress of Science and the Useful Arts" by providing "authors and inventors" the "exclusive right" to their creations; but this right would be for a "limited" time. Once the copyright had expired, the invention or book would become public property.

Polls today show that most Americans overwhelmingly endorse the United States Constitution (although some of those charged with illegal downloads may have second thoughts). In the 1780s, many Americans were satisfied with the federal government under the Articles of Confederation. Whatever its weaknesses, the government had negotiated the treaty ending the Revolutionary War, adopted humane and farsighted land policies, and established a rudimentary bureaucracy to manage routine affairs. If, as Washington said, that government had moved "on crutches . . . tottering at every step," it moved forward nevertheless. Yet the country's evolution placed demands on the national government that its creators had not anticipated. Dissatisfaction with the Articles mounted; the Founders sought solutions that through a process of conflict and compromise would finally result in the Constitution.

Inadequacies of the Articles of Confederation

Following the American Revolution and the Peace of Paris, the United States faced new challenges. The new nation struggled to achieve control of its own territory, to define the nature of its trade relationships with Europe, and to overcome crippling economic depression and the specter of inflation. If the Articles had proved adequate in achieving victory in the war, they proved less so in addressing these new concerns.

Both Great Britain and Spain stood in the way of the United States winning control of its borders. Although the British kept their promise to withdraw their troops from American soil promptly, they refused to abandon seven military posts beyond the periphery of the original thirteen states. The inability to eject the British seemed a national disgrace. In 1784, moreover, the Spaniards had closed the lower Mississippi River to American commerce. This harmed settlers beyond the Appalachians who depended on the Mississippi and its network of tributaries to get their corn, tobacco, and other products to eastern and European markets. Many reasoned that a stronger central government might have dealt with Britain and Spain more forcefully and effectively.

Another key problem concerned trade. After hostilities had ended, British merchants, eager to regain markets closed to them during the Revolution, poured low-priced manufactured goods of all kinds into the United States. Americans, long deprived of British products, rushed to take advantage of the bargains. Soon imports of British goods were approaching the levels of the early 1770s, while exports to the empire reached no more than half their earlier volume.

The influx of British goods aggravated the situation just when the economy was suffering as a result of the ending of the war. The inability of Congress to find money to pay the nation's debts undermined public confidence. Veterans who had still not been paid, and private individuals and foreign governments that had lent the government money during the Revolution, were clamoring for their due. In some regions crop failures compounded the difficulties.

An obvious way of dealing with these problems would have been to place tariffs on British goods in order to limit British imports, but the Confederation lacked the authority to do this. When individual states erected tariff barriers, British merchants easily got around them by bringing their goods in through states that did not. That the central government lacked the power to control commerce disturbed merchants, other businessmen, and the ever-increasing number of national-minded citizens in every walk of life.

Thus a movement developed to give the Confederation the power to tax imports, and in 1781 Congress sought authority to levy a 5 percent tariff duty. This would enable Congress to pay off some of its obligations and also put pressure on the British to relax their restrictions on American trade with the West Indies. Every state but Rhode Island agreed, but the measure required the unanimous consent of the states and therefore failed.

Defeat of the tariff pointed to the need for revising the Articles of Confederation, for here was a case where a large percentage of the states were ready to increase the power of the national government yet were unable to do so. Although many individuals in every region were worried about creating a centralized monster that might gobble up the sovereignty of the states, the practical needs of the times convinced many others that this risk must be taken.

Daniel Shays's "Little Rebellion"

Especially alarming to conservatives was an outbreak of violence in Massachusetts. The Massachusetts legislature was determined to pay off the state debt and maintain a sound currency. Taxes amounting to almost £1.9 million were levied between 1780 and 1786, the burden falling most heavily on those of moderate income. The average Massachusetts farmer paid about a third of every year's income in taxes. Bad times and deflation led to many foreclosures, and the prisons were crowded with honest debtors.

In the summer of 1786 mobs in the western communities began to stop foreclosures by forcibly preventing the courts from holding their sessions. Under the leadership of Daniel Shays, a veteran of Bunker Hill, Ticonderoga, and Saratoga, the "rebels" marched on Springfield and prevented the state supreme court from meeting. When

the state government sent troops against them, the rebels attacked the Springfield arsenal. They were routed, and the uprising then collapsed. Shays fled to Vermont.

Most well-to-do Americans considered **Shays's rebellion** "Liberty run mad." "What, gracious God, is man! that there should be such inconsistency and perfidiousness in his conduct?" the usually unexcitable George Washington asked when news of the riots reached Virginia. "We are fast verging to anarchy and confusion!" During the crisis private persons had to subscribe funds to put the rebels down, and when Massachusetts had

Massachusetts militia crushing Shays's revolt in 1787.
Source: North Wind Picture Archives.

●●━[Read the Document

Military Reports on Shays's at
myhistorylab.com

appealed to Congress for help there was little Congress could legally do. The lessons seemed plain: Liberty must not become an excuse for license; greater authority must be vested in the central government.

To Philadelphia, and the Constitution

If most people wanted to increase the power of Congress, they were also afraid to shift the balance too far lest they destroy the sovereignty of the states and the rights of individuals. The machinery for change established in the Articles of Confederation, which required the unanimous consent of the states for all amendments, posed a particularly delicate problem. Experience had shown it unworkable, yet to bypass it would be revolutionary and therefore dangerous.

The first fumbling step toward reform was taken in March 1785 when representatives of Virginia and Maryland suggested a conference of all the states to discuss common problems of commerce. In January 1786 the Virginia legislature sent out a formal call for such a gathering to be held in September at Annapolis. However, the Annapolis Convention disappointed advocates of reform; delegates from only five states appeared; even Maryland, supposedly the host state, did not send a representative. Being so few the group did not feel it worthwhile to propose changes.

Among the delegates was a young New York lawyer named Alexander Hamilton, a brilliant, imaginative, and daring man who was convinced that only drastic centralization would save the nation from disintegration. Hamilton described himself as a "nationalist."

This engraving by William Russell Birch shows Congress Hall (left) which was occupied by Congress from 1790 to 1800, when Philadelphia was capital of the nation. Here, too, was the site of President Washington's second inauguration in 1793 and President John Adams's inauguration in 1797.

While the war still raged he contrasted the virtues of "a great Federal Republic" with the existing system of "petty states with the appearance only of union, jarring, jealous, and perverse." Instead of giving up, he proposed calling another convention to meet at Philadelphia to deal generally with constitutional reform.

View the Image

Alexander Hamilton-Portrait at **myhistorylab.com**

The Annapolis group approved Hamilton's suggestion, and Congress reluctantly endorsed it. This time all the states but Rhode Island sent delegates. On May 25, 1787, the convention opened its proceedings at the State House in Philadelphia and unanimously elected George Washington its president. When it adjourned four months later, it had drafted the Constitution.

The Great Convention

Collectively the delegates possessed a rare combination of talents. Most of them had considerable experience in politics, and the many lawyers among them were skilled in logic and debate. Furthermore, the times made them acutely aware of their opportunities. It was "a time when the greatest lawgivers of antiquity would have wished to live," an opportunity to "establish the wisest and happiest government that human wisdom can contrive," John Adams wrote. "We . . . decide for ever the fate of republican government," James Madison said during the deliberations.

If these remarks overstated the importance of their deliberations, they nonetheless represented the opinion of most of those present. They were boldly optimistic about their country. "We are laying the foundation of a great empire," Madison predicted. At the same time the delegates recognized the difficulties they faced. The ancient Roman republic was one model, and all knew that it had been overthrown by tyrants and eventually overrun by barbarians. The framers were familiar with Enlightenment thinkers such as John Locke, Thomas Hobbes, and Montesquieu, and also with the ideas that swirled around the great disputes between Parliament and the Stuart monarchs during the seventeenth century.

Fortunately, they were nearly all of one mind on basic questions. That there should be a federal system, with both independent state governments and a national government with limited powers to handle matters of common interest, was accepted by all but one or two of them. Republican government, drawing its authority from the people and remaining responsible to them, was a universal assumption. A measure of democracy followed inevitably from this principle, for even the most aristocratic delegates agreed that ordinary citizens should share in the process of selecting those who were to make and execute the laws.

All agreed that no group within society, no matter how numerous, should have unrestricted authority. People meant well and had limitless possibilities, the constitution makers believed, but they were selfish by nature and could not be counted on to respect the interests of others. The ordinary people—small farmers, artisans, any taxpayer—should have a say in government in order to be able to protect themselves against those who would exploit their weakness, and the majority must somehow be prevented from plundering the rich, for property must be secure or no government could be stable. Freedom, as Locke had maintained, rested on a right to property. No single state or section must be allowed to predominate, nor should the legislature be supreme over the executive or the courts. Power, in short, must be divided, and the segments must be balanced one against the other.

At the outset the delegates decided to keep the proceedings secret. That way no one was tempted to play to the gallery or seek some personal political advantage at the expense of the common good. Next they agreed to go beyond their instructions to revise the Articles of Confederation and draft an entirely new form of government. This was a bold, perhaps illegal act, but it was in no way irresponsible because nothing the convention might recommend was binding on anyone. Alexander Hamilton captured the mood of the gathering when he said, "We can only propose and recommend—the power of ratifying or rejecting is still in the States. . . . We ought not to sacrifice the public Good to narrow Scruples."

The Compromises That Produced the Constitution

The delegates voted on May 30, 1787, that "a national Government ought to be established." They then set to work hammering out a specific plan. The delegates believed that the national government should have separate executive and judicial branches as well as a legislature. But two big questions had to be answered. The first—*What powers should this national government be granted?*—occasioned relatively little discussion. The right to levy taxes and to regulate interstate and foreign commerce was assigned to the central government almost without debate, as was the power to raise and maintain an army and navy and to summon the militia of the states to enforce national laws and suppress insurrections. With equal absence of argument, the states were deprived of their rights to issue money, to make treaties, and to tax either imports or exports without the permission of Congress. Thus, in summary fashion, was brought about a massive shift of power.

The second major question—*Who shall control the national government?*—proved more difficult to answer in a manner satisfactory to all. Led by Virginia, the larger states pushed for representation in the national legislature based on population. The smaller states wished to maintain the existing system of equal representation for each state regardless of population. The large states rallied behind the **Virginia Plan**, drafted by James Madison and presented to the convention by Edmund Randolph, governor of the state. The small states supported the **New Jersey Plan**, prepared by William Paterson, a former attorney general of that state. The question was important; equal state representation would have been undemocratic, whereas a proportional system would have effectively destroyed the influence of all the states as states. But the delegates saw it in terms of combinations of large or small states, and this old-fashioned view was unrealistic: When the states combined, they did so on geographic, economic, or social grounds that seldom had anything to do with size. Nevertheless, the debate was long and heated, and for a time it threatened to disrupt the convention.

Day after day in the stifling heat of high summer, the weary delegates struggled to find a suitable compromise. July 2 was perhaps the most fateful day of the whole proceedings. "We are at full stop," said Roger Sherman of Connecticut, who had been one of the drafters of the Declaration of Independence. "If we do not concede on both sides," a North Carolina delegate warned, "our business must soon be at an end."

But the delegates did "concede on both sides," and the debates went on. Again on July 17 collapse threatened as the representatives of the larger states caucused to consider walking out of the convention. Fortunately they did not walk out, and the delegates adopted what is known as the Great Compromise. In the lower branch of the new legislature—the House of Representatives—places were to be assigned according to population and filled by popular vote. In the upper house—the Senate—each state was to have two members, elected by its legislature.

Then a complicated struggle took place between northern and southern delegates, occasioned by the institution of slavery and the differing economic interests of the regions. About one American in seven in the 1780s was a slave. Northerners contended that slaves should be counted in deciding each state's share of direct federal taxes. Southerners, of course, wanted to exclude slaves from the count. Yet Southerners wished to include slaves in determining each district's representation in the House of Representatives, although they had no intention of permitting the slaves to vote. In the **Three-Fifths Compromise** it was agreed that "three-fifths of all other Persons" should be counted for both purposes. Settlement of the knotty issue of the African slave trade was postponed by a clause making it illegal for Congress to outlaw the trade before 1808.

The final document, signed on September 17, established a legislature of two houses: an executive branch consisting of a president with wide powers and a vice president whose only function was to preside over the Senate; and a national judiciary consisting of a Supreme Court and such "inferior courts" as Congress might decide to create. The lower, popularly elected branch of the Congress—the House of Representatives—was supposed to represent especially the mass of ordinary citizens. It was given the sole right to introduce bills for raising revenue. The twenty-six-member Senate was looked on by many as a sort of advisory council similar to the upper houses of the colonial legislatures. Its consent was required before any treaty could go into effect and for major presidential appointments. The founders also intended the Senate to represent in Congress the interests not only of the separate states but of what Hamilton called "the rich and the well-born" as contrasted with "the great mass of the people."

The creation of a powerful president was the most drastic departure from past experience, and it is doubtful that the founders would have gone so far had everyone not counted on Washington, a man universally esteemed for character, wisdom, and impartiality, to be the first to occupy the office. Besides giving him general responsibility for executing the laws, the Constitution made the president commander-in-chief of the armed forces of the nation and general supervisor of its foreign relations. He was to appoint federal judges and other officials, and he might veto any law of Congress, although his veto could be overridden by a two-thirds majority of both houses. While not specifically ordered to submit a program of legislation to Congress, he was to deliver periodic reports on the "State of the Union" and recommend "such Measures as he shall judge necessary and expedient." Most modern presidents have interpreted this requirement as authorizing them to submit detailed legislative proposals and to use the full power and prestige of the office to get Congress to enact them.

Looking beyond Washington, whose choice was sure to come about under any system, the Constitution established a cumbersome method of electing presidents. Each state was to choose "electors" equal in number to its representation in Congress.

Table 5.1 Issues and Compromises that Produced the Constitution

Issue	Yes	No	Compromise
Debate 1785–1787			
Should Articles of Confederation be replaced?	Federalists	Antifederalists	Federalists win: All states but R.I. send delegates to Constitutional Convention at Philadelphia (1787)
Constitutional Convention Debates			
Should national government have broad powers?	Federalists	Antifederalists	Federalists win: National government imposes taxes, regulates trade, maintains army, issues money
Should seats in national legislature be unequal, based on a state's population?	Populous states	Small states	**Great Compromise:** Two-house legislature: In House of Representatives, delegates are apportioned by size of each state's population; in Senate, each state gets two senators

The electors, meeting separately in their own states, were to vote for two persons for president. Supposedly the procedure would prevent anyone less universally admired than Washington from getting a majority in the **Electoral College**, in which case the House of Representatives would choose the president from among the leading candidates, each state having but one vote. However, the swift rise of national political parties prevented the expected fragmentation of the electors' votes.

The national court system was set up to adjudicate disputes under the laws and treaties of the United States. No such system had existed under the Articles, a major weakness. Although the Constitution did not specifically authorize the courts to declare laws void when they conflicted with the Constitution, the courts soon exercised this right of **judicial review** in cases involving both state and federal laws.

That the Constitution reflected the commonly held beliefs of its framers is everywhere evident in the document. It greatly expanded the powers of the central government yet did not seriously threaten the independence of the states. Foes of centralization, at the time and ever since, have predicted the imminent disappearance of the states as sovereign bodies. But despite a steady trend toward centralization the states remain powerful political organizations that are sovereign in many areas of government.

The founders believed that since the new powers of government might easily be misused, each should be held within safe limits by some countervailing force. The Constitution is full of mechanisms ("checks and balances") whereby one power controls and limits another without reducing it to impotence. "Let Congress Legislate, let others execute, let others judge," John Jay suggested. This separation of legislative, executive, and judicial functions is the fundamental example of the principle. Other examples are the president's veto; Congress's power of impeachment, cleverly divided between the House and Senate; the Senate's power over treaties and appointments; and the balance between Congress's right to declare war and the president's control of the armed forces.

Ratifying the Constitution

Influenced by the widespread approval of the decision of Massachusetts to submit its state constitution of 1780 to the voters for ratification, the framers of the Constitution provided (Article VII) that their handiwork be ratified by special state conventions. This procedure gave the Constitution what Madison called "the highest source of authority"—the endorsement of the people, expressed through representatives chosen specifically to vote on it. The framers may also have been motivated by a desire to

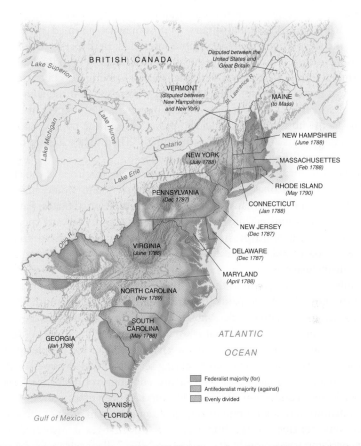

Ratification of the Federal Constitution, 1787–1790 Historian Jackson Turner Main argued that the debate over ratification of the Constitution was fundamentally a struggle between radical frontiersmen and conservative easterners. The Antifederalists were democratic populists; the Federalists sought to prevent further democratization of American society, or so Main claimed. The accompanying map showing the vote on ratification by congressional district provides support for Main's thesis. Kentucky and Tennessee were almost solidly opposed to the Constitution, along with most of the western sections of South Carolina, North Carolina, and Virginia. Western Pennsylvania and western Massachusetts were also mostly Antifederalists. Conversely, support for the Constitution was strongest in coastal regions of the Carolinas, the plantation districts of tidewater Virginia and the Chesapeake, as well as New Jersey, New York, Connecticut, and the New England coast. But such an explanation fails to explain why some districts in western Kentucky, Tennessee, Pennsylvania, and even Massachusetts, supported the Constitution. Some frontiersmen thought that a federal army could do better than state militias against Indian threats; and some sober citizens, even those living west of the Susquehanna, worried that society might devolve into anarchy if the Constitution were not approved.

bypass the state legislatures, where many members might resent the reductions being made in state authority. This was not of central importance because the legislatures could have blocked ratification by refusing to call conventions. Only Rhode Island did so, and since the Constitution was to go into operation when nine states had approved it, Rhode Island's stubbornness did no vital harm.

Such a complex and controversial document as the Constitution naturally excited argument throughout the country. Those who favored it called themselves **Federalists**, thereby avoiding the more accurate but politically unattractive label of Centralizers. Their opponents thus became the **Antifederalists**.

The Federalists tended to be substantial individuals, members of the professions, well-to-do, active in commercial affairs, and somewhat alarmed by the changes wrought by the Revolution. They were more interested, perhaps, in orderly and efficient government than in safeguarding the maximum freedom of individual choice.

The Antifederalists were more often small farmers, debtors, and persons to whom free choice was more important than power and who resented those who sought and held power. "Lawyers and men of learning and money men . . . expect to be the managers of the Const[itution], and get all the power and all the money into their own hands," a Massachusetts Antifederalist complained. "Then they will swallow up all us little folks . . . just as the whale swallowed up *Jonah*."

Many persons, including some who had been in the forefront of the struggle for independence, believed that a centralized republican system would not work in a country so large and with so many varied interests as the United States. Patrick Henry considered the Constitution "horribly frightful." It "squints toward monarchy," he added. That Congress could pass all laws "necessary and proper" to carry out the functions assigned it and legislate for the "general welfare" of the country seemed alarmingly all-inclusive.

Very little of the opposition to the Constitution grew out of economic issues. Most people wanted the national debt paid off; nearly everyone opposed an unstable currency; most favored uniform trade policies; most were ready to give the new government a chance if they could be convinced that it would not destroy the states. When backers agreed to add amendments guaranteeing the civil liberties of the people against challenge by the national government and reserving all unmentioned power to the states, much of the opposition disappeared. Sam Adams ended up voting for the Constitution in the Massachusetts convention after the additions had been promised.

The Constitution met with remarkably little opposition in most of the state ratifying conventions, considering the importance of the changes it instituted. Delaware acted first, ratifying unanimously on December 7, 1787. Pennsylvania followed a few days later, voting for the document by a 2 to 1 majority. New Jersey approved it unanimously on December 18, as did Georgia on January 2, 1788. A week later Connecticut fell in line, 128 to 40.

The Massachusetts convention provided the first close contest. Early in February, after an extensive debate, the delegates ratified by a vote of 187 to 168. In April, Maryland accepted the Constitution by nearly 6 to 1, and in May, South Carolina approved it, 149 to 73. New Hampshire came along on June 21, voting 57 to 47 for the Constitution. This was the ninth state, making the Constitution legally operative.

Before the news from New Hampshire had spread throughout the country, the Virginia convention debated the issue. Virginia, the largest state and the home of so many prestigious figures, was absolutely essential if the Constitution was to succeed. With unquestioned patriots like Richard Henry Lee and Patrick Henry opposed, the result was not easy to predict. But when the vote came on June 25, Virginia ratified, eighty-nine to seventy-nine. Aside from Rhode Island, this left only New York and North Carolina outside the Union.

New York politics presented a complex and baffling picture. Although New York was the third largest state, with a population rapidly approaching 340,000, it sided with the small states at Philadelphia, and two of its three delegates (Hamilton was the exception) walked out of the convention and took the lead in opposing ratification. A handful of great landowning and mercantile families dominated politics, but they were divided into shifting factions. In general, New York City, including most ordinary working people as well as the merchants, favored ratification and the rural areas were against it.

The Antifederalists, well-organized and competently led in New York by Governor George Clinton, won forty-six of the sixty-five seats at the ratifying convention. The New York Federalists had one great asset in the fact that so many states had already ratified and another in the person of Alexander Hamilton. Although contemptuous of the *weakness* of the Constitution, Hamilton supported it with all his ener-

●◆●⌐Read the **Document**

Madison Defends the Consti-
tutions at **myhistorylab.com**

gies as being incomparably stronger than the old government. Working with Madison and John Jay, he produced the **Federalist Papers**, a series of brilliant essays explaining and defending the new system. In his articles, Hamilton stressed the need for a strong federal executive, while Madison sought to allay fears that the new national government would have too much power by emphasizing the many checks and balances in the Constitution. The essays were published in the local press and later in book form. Although generations of judges and lawyers have treated them almost as parts of the Constitution, their impact on contemporary public opinion was probably slight. Open-minded members of the convention were undoubtedly influenced, but few delegates were open-minded.

Hamilton became a kind of one-man army in defense of the Constitution, plying hesitating delegates with dinners and drinks, facing obstinate ones with the threat that New York City would secede from the state if the Constitution were rejected. Once New Hampshire and Virginia had ratified, opposition in New York became a good deal less intransigent. In the end, by promising to support a call for a second national convention to consider amendments, the Federalists carried the day, thirty to twenty-seven. With New York in the fold, the new government was free to get under way. North Carolina finally ratified in November 1789, and Rhode Island the following year in May 1790.

Washington as President

Elections took place in the states during January and February 1789, and by early April enough congressmen had gathered in New York, the temporary national capital, to commence operation. The ballots of the presidential electors were officially counted in the Senate on April 6, Washington being the unanimous choice. John Adams, with thirty-four electoral votes, won the vice-presidency.

Washington made a firm, dignified, conscientious, but cautious president. His acute sense of responsibility led him to face the task "with feelings not unlike those of a

◉┤**View** the **Image**

Washington's Arrival in New York City, 1789 at
myhistorylab.com

culprit who is going to the place of his execution." Each presidential action must of necessity establish a precedent. "The eyes of Argus are upon me," he complained, "and no slip will pass unnoticed." Hoping to make the presidency appear respectable in the eyes of the world, he saw to it that his carriage was drawn by six cream-colored horses, and when he rode (he was a magnificent horseman), he sat upon a great white charger, with the saddle of leopard skin and the cloth edged in gold.

Washington meticulously avoided treading on the toes of Congress, for he took seriously the principle of the separation of powers. Never would he speak for or against a candidate for Congress, nor did he think that the president should push or even propose legislation. When he knew a controversial question was to be discussed in Congress, he avoided the subject in his annual message. The veto, he believed, should be employed only when the president considered a bill unconstitutional.

Washington was a strong chief executive. As Hamilton put it, he "consulted much, pondered much, resolved slowly, resolved surely." His stress on the dignity of his office suited the needs of a new country whose people tended to be perhaps too informal. Because opponents of republican government predicted it must inevitably succumb to dictatorship and tyranny, Washington took scrupulous care to avoid overstepping the bounds of presidential power. Yet Washington's devotion to duty did not always come easily. Occasionally he exploded. Thomas Jefferson has left us a graphic description of the president at a Cabinet meeting, in a rage because of some unfair criticism, swearing that "by god he had rather be on his farm than to be made emperor of the world."

George Washington arriving by boat to New York City—the nation's capital—for his First Inaugural in 1789.
Source: North Wind Picture Archives.

Congress under Way

By September 1789 Congress had created the State, Treasury, and War Departments and passed a Judiciary Act establishing thirteen federal district courts and three circuit courts of appeal. The number of Supreme Court justices was set at six, and Washington named John Jay the chief justice.

True to Federalist promises—for a large majority of both houses were friendly to the Constitution—Congress prepared a list of a dozen amendments guaranteeing what Congressman James Madison, who drafted the amendments, called the "great rights of mankind." These amendments, known as the **Bill of Rights**, provided that Congress should make no law infringing freedom of speech, the press, or religion. The right of trial by jury was reaffirmed, and the right to bear arms guaranteed. No one was to be subject to "unreasonable" searches or seizures or compelled to testify against himself or herself in a criminal case. No one was to "be deprived of life, liberty, or property, without due process of law."

Despite Washington's reluctance to interfere with the activities of Congress, he urged acceptance of these amendments so that the "rights of freemen" would be "impregnably fortified." The Bill of Rights was unique; the English Bill of Rights of 1689 was much less broad-gauged and, being an act of Parliament, was subject to repeal by Parliament at any time. The Tenth Amendment—not, strictly speaking, a part of the Bill of Rights—was designed to mollify those who feared that the states would be destroyed by the new government. It provided that powers not delegated to the United States or denied specifically to the states by the Constitution were to reside either in the states or in the people.

The Bill of Rights did much to convince doubters that the new government would not become too powerful. More complex was the task of proving that it was powerful enough to deal with those national problems that the Confederation had not been able to solve: the threat to the West posed by the British, Spaniards, and Indians, the disruption of the pattern of American foreign commerce resulting from independence, and the collapse of the financial structure of the country.

Hamilton and Financial Reform

One of the first acts of Congress in 1789 was to employ its new power to tax. The simplest means of raising money seemed to be that first attempted by the British after 1763, a tariff on foreign imports. Congress levied a 5 percent tax on all foreign products entering the United States, applying higher rates to certain products, such as hemp, glass, and nails, as a measure of protection for American producers. The Tariff Act of 1789 also placed heavy taxes on foreign-owned ships, assessed by their weight, on entering

"To confess my weakness," Hamilton wrote when he was only 14, "my ambition is prevalent." This pastel drawing by James Sharples was made about 1796.

William Russell Birch painted this view of the capitol building, under construction, in Washington, DC. The site, located at the junction of two rivers, was chosen in part because it could be easily defended; this proved to be untrue during the War of 1812, when the capitol was burned.

American ports, a mercantilist measure designed to stimulate the American merchant marine.

Raising money for current expenses was a small and relatively simple aspect of the financial problem faced by Washington's administration. But the nation's debt from the revolutionary war was large, its credit shaky, and its economic future uncertain. In October 1789 Congress deposited on the slender shoulders of Secretary of the Treasury Hamilton the task of straightening out the fiscal mess and stimulating the country's economic development.

Hamilton admired aristocracy and disparaged the abilities of the common run of mankind who, he said, "seldom judge or determine right." Although granting that Americans must be allowed to govern themselves, he was as apprehensive of the "turbulence" of the masses as a small boy passing a graveyard in the dark. "No popular government was ever without its Catilines and its Caesars," he warned—a typical example of that generation's concern about the fate of the Roman republic.

The country, Hamilton insisted, needed a strong national government. "I acknowledge," he wrote in one of the *Federalist Papers*, "my aversion to every project that is calculated to disarm the government of a single weapon, which in any possible contingency might be usefully employed for the general defense and security." He avowed that government should be "a great Federal Republic," not "a number of petty states, with the appearance only of union, jarring, jealous, perverse, without any determined direction." He wished to reduce the states to mere administrative units, like English counties.

As secretary of the treasury, Hamilton proved to be a farsighted economic planner. The United States, a "Hercules in the cradle," needed capital to develop its untapped material and resources. To persuade investors to commit their funds in America, the country would have to convince them that it would meet every obligation in full. His *Report on the Public Credit* outlined a plan for the federal government to borrow money to pay all of its debts as well as those of the states.

While most members of Congress agreed, albeit somewhat grudgingly, that the debt should be paid in full, they had misgivings as to who should get those payments. Many of the soldiers, farmers, and merchants who had been forced to accept government securities in lieu of cash for goods and services, had sold their securities for a fraction of their face value to speculators; under Hamilton's proposal, the speculators—now paid for the full value of the securities—would make a killing. To the argument for divided payment, Hamilton answered coldly: "[The speculator] paid what the commodity was worth in the market, and took the risks. . . . He . . . ought to reap the benefit of his hazard."

Hamilton was essentially correct, and in the end Congress had to go along. After all, the speculators had not caused the securities to fall in value; indeed, as a group they had favored sound money and a strong government. The best way to restore the nation's credit was to convince investors that the government would honor all obligations in full. What infuriated his contemporaries and still attracts the scorn of many historians was Hamilton's motive. He deliberately intended his plan to give a special advantage to the rich. The government would be strong, he thought, only if well-to-do Americans enthusiastically supported it. What better way to win them over than to make it worth their while financially to do so?

In part, opposition to the funding plan was sectional, for citizens of the northern states held more than four-fifths of the national debt. The scheme for assuming the state debts aggravated the controversy, since most of the southern states had already paid off much of their Revolutionary War obligations. For months Congress was deadlocked. Finally, in July 1790, Hamilton worked out a compromise with Representative James Madison and Secretary of State Jefferson. The two Virginians swung a few southern votes, and Hamilton induced some of his followers to support the southern plan for locating the permanent capital of the Union on the Potomac River.

Jefferson later claimed that Hamilton had hoodwinked him. Having only recently returned from Europe, he said, "I was really a stranger to the whole subject." Hamilton had persuaded him to "rally around" by the false tale that "our Union" was threatened with dissolution. This was nonsense; Jefferson agreed to the compromise because he expected that Virginia and the rest of the South would profit from having the capital so near at hand.

The assumption bill passed, and the entire funding plan was a great success. Soon the United States had the highest possible credit rating in the world's financial centers. Foreign capital poured into the country.

Hamilton next proposed that Congress charter a national bank. Such an institution would provide safe storage for government funds and serve as an agent for the government in the collection, movement, and expenditure of tax money. Most important, because of its substantial resources, a bank could finance new and expanding business enterprises, greatly speeding the economic growth of the nation.

Read the Document

Alexander Hamilton, *Bank* at **myhistorylab.com**

It would also be able to issue bank notes, thereby providing a vitally needed medium of exchange for the specie-starved economy. This **Bank of the United States** was to be partly owned by the government, but 80 percent of the $10 million stock issue was to be sold to private individuals.

The country had much to gain from such a bank, but again—Hamilton's cleverness was never more in evidence—the well-to-do commercial classes would gain still more. Government balances in the bank belonging to all the people would earn dividends for a handful of rich investors. Manufacturers and other capitalists would profit from the bank's credit facilities. Public funds would be invested in the bank, but control would remain in private hands, since the government would appoint only five of the twenty-five directors. Nevertheless, the bill creating the bank passed both houses of Congress with relative ease in February 1791.

President Washington, however, hesitated to sign it, for the bill's constitutionality had been questioned during the debate in Congress. Nowhere did the Constitution specifically authorize Congress to charter corporations or engage in the banking business. As was his wont when in doubt, Washington called on Jefferson and Hamilton for advice.

Hamilton defended the legality of the bank by enunciating the doctrine of "implied powers." If a logical connection existed between the purpose of the bill and powers clearly stated in the Constitution, he wrote, the bill was constitutional.

If the *end* be clearly comprehended within any of the specified powers, and if the measure have an obvious relation to that *end* . . . it may safely be deemed to come within the compass of the national authority. . . . A bank has a natural relation to the power of collecting taxes—to that of regulating trade—to that of providing for the common defence.

Jefferson disagreed. Congress could only do what the Constitution specifically authorized, he said. The "elastic clause" granting it the right to pass "all Laws which shall be necessary and proper" to carry out the specified powers must be interpreted literally or Congress would "take possession of a boundless field of power, no longer susceptible to any definition." Because a bank was obviously not necessary, it was not authorized.

Although not entirely convinced, Washington accepted Hamilton's reasoning and signed the bill. He could just as easily have followed Jefferson, for the Constitution is not clear. If one stresses *proper* in the "necessary and proper" clause in Article I, Section 8 of the Constitution, one ends up a Hamiltonian; if one stresses *necessary*, then Jefferson's view is correct. Historically politicians have nearly always adopted the "loose" Hamiltonian "implied powers" interpretation when they favored a measure and the "strict" Jeffersonian one when they do not.

In 1819 the Supreme Court officially sanctioned Hamilton's construction of the "necessary and proper" clause, and in general that interpretation has prevailed. Because the majority tends naturally toward an argument that increases its freedom of action, the pressure for this view has been continual and formidable. The Bank of the United States succeeded from the start. When its stock went on sale, investors snapped up every share in a matter of hours. People eagerly accepted its bank notes at face value. Business ventures of all kinds found it easier to raise new capital. Soon state-chartered banks entered the field. There were only three state banks in 1791; by 1801, there were thirty-two.

Hamilton had not finished. In December 1791 he submitted his *Report on Manufactures*, a bold call for economic planning. The pre-Revolutionary nonimportation agreements and wartime shortages had stimulated interest in manufacturing. Already a number of joint-stock companies had been founded to manufacture textiles, and an elaborate argument for economic diversification had been worked out by American economists such as Tench Coxe and Mathew Carey. Hamilton was familiar with these developments. In his *Report* he called for government tariffs, subsidies, and awards to encourage American manufacturing. He hoped to change an essentially agricultural nation into one with a complex, self-sufficient economy. Once again business and commercial interests in particular would benefit. They would be protected against foreign competition and otherwise subsidized, whereas the general taxpayer, particularly the farmer, would pay the bill in the form of higher taxes and higher prices on manufactured goods. Hamilton argued that in the long run every interest would profit, and he was undoubtedly sincere, being too much the nationalist to favor one section at the expense of another. A majority of the Congress, however, balked at so broad-gauged a scheme. Hamilton's *Report* was set aside, although many of the specific tariffs he recommended were enacted into law in 1792.

Nevertheless, the secretary of the treasury had managed to transform the financial structure of the country and to prepare the ground for an economic revolution. The constitutional reforms of 1787 had made this possible, and Hamilton turned possibility into reality.

The Ohio Country: A Dark and Bloody Ground

The western issues and those related to international trade proved more difficult because other nations were involved. The British showed no disposition to evacuate their posts on American soil simply because the American people had decided to strengthen their central government, nor did the western Indians suddenly agree to abandon their hunting grounds.

Trouble came swiftly when white settlers moved onto the land north of the Ohio River in large numbers. The Indians, determined to hold this country at all costs, struck hard at the invaders. In 1790 the Miami chief Little Turtle inflicted a double defeat on militia units commanded by General Josiah Harmar. The next year Little Turtle and his men defeated the forces of General Arthur St. Clair still more convincingly. Both Harmar and St. Clair resigned from the army, their careers ruined, but the defeats led Congress to authorize raising a regular army of 5,000 men.

By early 1792 the Indians had driven the whites into "beachheads" at Marietta and Cincinnati on the Ohio. Resentment of the federal government in the western counties of every state from New York to the Carolinas mounted, the people feeling that it was ignoring their interests. They were convinced that the British were inciting the Indians to attack them, yet the supposedly powerful national government seemed unable to force Great Britain to surrender its forts in the West.

Still worse, the Westerners believed, was the way the government was taxing them. In 1791, as part of his plan to take over the debts of the states, Hamilton had persuaded Congress to adopt a sales tax of 8 cents a gallon on American-made whiskey. Excise taxes were particularly disliked by most Americans. Westerners, who were heavy drinkers and who turned much of their grain into whiskey in order to cope with the high cost of transportation, were especially angered by the tax on whiskey.

But Hamilton was determined to enforce the law. To western complaints, he suggested that farmers drank too much to begin with. If they found the tax oppressive, they should cut down on their consumption. Of course this did nothing to reduce western opposition to the tax. Resistance was especially intense in western Pennsylvania, where treasury agents were forcibly prevented from collecting the tax.

Revolution in France

Momentous events in Europe influenced the situation. In 1789 the **French Revolution** erupted, and four years later war broke out between France and Great Britain and most of the rest of Europe. With France fighting Great Britain and Spain, there arose the question of America's obligations under the Alliance of 1778. That treaty required the United States to defend the French West Indies "forever against all other powers." Suppose the British attacked the French island of Martinique; must America declare war on Britain? Legally

In the summer of 1793, a yellow fever epidemic struck Philadelphia, killing nearly 4,000. Tens of thousands fled the city, including President Washington and much of the federal government. Absalom Jones, a religious leader, was among the free blacks who remained to take care of the sick and the dead. This portrait of Jones is by Raphaelle Peale.

the United States was so obligated, but no responsible American statesman urged such a policy. With the British in Canada and Spanish forces to the west and south, the nation would be in serious danger if it entered the war. Instead, in April 1793, Washington issued a proclamation of neutrality committing the United States to be "friendly and impartial" toward both sides in the war.

Meanwhile the French had sent a special representative, Edmond Charles Genet, to the United States to seek support. During its early stages, especially when France declared itself a republic in 1792, the revolution had excited much enthusiasm in the United States, for it seemed to indicate that American democratic ideas were already engulfing the world. The increasing radicalism in France tended to dampen some of the enthusiasm, yet when "Citizen" Genet landed at Charleston, South Carolina, in April 1793, the majority of Americans probably wished the revolutionaries well. As Genet, a charming, ebullient young man, made his way northward to present his credentials, cheering crowds welcomed him in every town. Quickly concluding that the proclamation of neutrality was "a harmless little pleasantry designed to throw dust in the eyes of the British," he began, in plain violation of American law, to license American vessels to operate as privateers against British shipping and to grant French military commissions to a number of Americans in order to mount expeditions against Spanish and British possessions in North America.

Washington received Genet coolly, and soon thereafter demanded that he stop his illegal activities. Genet, whose capacity for self-deception was monumental, appealed to public opinion over the president's head and continued to commission privateers. Washington then requested his recall. The incident ended on a ludicrous note. When Genet left France, he had been in the forefront of the Revolution. But events there had marched swiftly leftward, and the new leaders in Paris considered him a dangerous reactionary. His replacement arrived in America with an order for his arrest. To return might well mean the guillotine, so Genet asked the government that was expelling him for political asylum! Washington agreed, for he was not a vindictive man. A few months later the bold revolutionary married the daughter of the governor of New York and settled down as a farmer on Long Island, where he raised a large family and "moved agreeably in society."

The Genet affair was incidental to a far graver problem. Although the European war increased the foreign demand for American products, it also led to attacks on American shipping by both France and Great Britain. Each power captured American vessels headed for the other's ports whenever it could. In 1793 and 1794 about 600 United States ships were seized.

The British attacks caused far more damage, both physically and psychologically, because the British fleet was much larger than France's, and France at least professed to be America's friend and to favor freedom of trade for neutrals. In addition the British issued secret orders late in 1793 turning their navy loose on neutral ships headed for the French West Indies. Pouncing without warning, British warships captured about 250 American vessels and sent them off as prizes to British ports. The merchant marine, one American diplomat declared angrily, was being "kicked, cuffed, and plundered all over the Ocean."

The attacks roused a storm in America, reviving hatreds that had been smoldering since the Revolution. The continuing presence of British troops in the Northwest (in 1794 the British began to build a new fort in the Ohio country) and the restrictions imposed on American trade with the British West Indies raised tempers still further. To try to avoid a war, for he wisely believed that the United States should not become embroiled in the Anglo-French conflict, Washington sent Chief Justice John Jay to London to seek a settlement with the British.

Federalists and Republicans: The Rise of Political Parties

The furor over the violations of neutral rights focused attention on a new development, the formation of political parties. Why national political parties emerged after the ratification of a Constitution that made no provision for such organizations is a question that has long intrigued historians. Probably the main reason was the obvious one: By creating a strong central government the Constitution produced national issues and a focus on national discussion and settlement of these issues. Furthermore, by failing to create machinery for nominating candidates for federal offices, the Constitution left a vacuum, which informal party organizations filled. That the universally admired Washington headed the government was a force limiting partisanship, but his principal advisers, Hamilton and Jefferson, were in sharp disagreement, and they soon became the leaders around which parties coalesced.

In the spring of 1791 Jefferson and James Madison began to sound out other politicians about forming an informal political organization. Jefferson also appointed the poet Philip Freneau to a minor state department post and Freneau then began publishing a newspaper, the *National Gazette*, to disseminate the views of what became known as the Republican party. Hamilton organized his own followers in the Federalist party, the organ of which was John Fenno's *Gazette of the United States*.

The personal nature of early American political controversies goes far toward explaining why the party battles of the era were so bitter. So does the continuing anxiety that plagued partisans of both persuasions about the supposed frailty of a republican government. The United States was still very much an experiment; leaders who sincerely proclaimed their own devotion to its welfare suspected that their opponents wanted to undermine its institutions. Federalists feared that the Jeffersonians sought a dictatorship based on "mob rule," and Republicans feared that the Hamiltonians hid "under the mask of Federalism hearts devoted to monarchy."

At the start Hamilton had the ear of the president, and his allies controlled a majority in Congress. Jefferson, who disliked controversy, avoided a direct confrontation as long as he could. He went along with Hamilton's funding plan and traded the assumption of state debts for a capital on the Potomac. However, when Hamilton proposed the Bank of the United States, he dug in his heels. It seemed designed to benefit the northeastern commercial classes at the expense of southern and western farmers. He sensed a plot to milk the producing masses for the benefit of a few capitalists.

The growing controversy over the French Revolution and the resulting war between France and Great Britain widened the split between the parties. After the radicals in France executed Louis XVI and instituted the Reign of Terror, American conservatives were horrified. The Jeffersonians were also deeply shocked. However, they continued to defend the Revolution. Great southern landlords whose French counterparts were losing their estates—some their heads—extolled "the glorious successes of our Gallic brethren." In the same way the Federalists began to idealize the British, whom they considered the embodiment of the forces that were resisting French radicalism.

This created an explosive situation. Enthusiasm for a foreign country might tempt Americans to betray their own. Hamilton came to believe that Jefferson was so prejudiced in favor of France as to be unable to conduct foreign affairs rationally, and Jefferson could say contemptuously, "Hamilton is panick struck, if we refuse our breech to every kick which Great Britain may choose to give it." This, of course, was an exaggeration, but Hamilton was certainly predisposed toward England. As he put it to an English official, *we think in English.*

In fact, Jefferson never lost his sense of perspective. When the Anglo-French war erupted, he recommended neutrality. In the Genet affair, although originally sympathetic to the young envoy, Jefferson cordially approved Washington's decision to send Genet packing. Hamilton perhaps went a little too far in his friendliness to Great Britain, but the real danger was that some of Hamilton's and Jefferson's excitable followers might become so committed as to forget the true interests of the United States.

1794: Crisis and Resolution

During the summer of 1794 several superficially unrelated events brought the partisan conflicts of the period to a peak. For the better part of two years the government had been unable to collect Hamilton's whiskey tax in the West. In Pennsylvania, mobs had burned the homes of revenue agents, and several men had been killed. Late in July, 7,000 "rebels" converged on Pittsburgh, threatening to set fire to the town. They were turned away by the sight of federal artillery and the liberal dispensation of whiskey by the frightened inhabitants.

Early in August President Washington was determined "to go to every length that the Constitution and laws would permit" to enforce the law. He mustered an enormous army of nearly 13,000 militiamen. This had the desired effect; when the troops arrived in western Pennsylvania, rebels were nowhere to be seen. The expected **Whiskey Rebellion** simply did not happen. Moderates in the region (not everyone, after all, was a distiller) agreed that even unpopular laws should be obeyed.

More important, perhaps, than the militia in pacifying the Pennsylvania frontier was another event that occurred while that army was being mobilized. This was the Battle of Fallen Timbers in Ohio near present-day Toledo, where the regular army troops of Major General "Mad Anthony" Wayne won a decisive victory over the

The United States and Its Territories, 1787–1802 In 1804 Georgia's cession became part of the Mississippi Territory. The seven British forts were evacuated as a result of Jay's Treaty (1795).

Indians. Wayne's victory opened the way for the settlement of the region. Some 2,000 of the whiskey tax rebels simply pulled up stakes and headed for Ohio after the effort to avoid the excise collapsed.

Jay's Treaty

Still more significant was the outcome of President Washington's decision to send John Jay to England to seek a treaty settling the conflicts between the two nations. The British genuinely wanted to reach an accommodation with the United States—as one minister quipped, the Americans "are so much in debt to this country that we scarcely dare to quarrel with them." The British also feared that the two new republics, France and the United States, would draw together in a battle against Europe's monarchies. On the other hand, the British were riding the crest of a wave of important victories in the war in Europe and were not disposed to make concessions to the Americans simply to avoid trouble.

The treaty that Jay brought home did contain a number of concessions. The British agreed to evacuate the posts in the West. They also promised to compensate American shipowners for seizures in the West Indies and to open up their colonies in Asia to

American ships. They conceded nothing, however, to American demands that the rights of neutrals on the high seas be respected; no one really expected them to do so in wartime. A provision opening the British West Indies to American commerce was so hedged with qualifications limiting the size of American vessels and the type of goods allowed that the United States refused to accept it.

Jay's Treaty also committed the United States to paying pre-Revolutionary debts still owed British merchants, a slap in the face to many states whose courts had been impeding their collection. Yet nothing was said about the British paying for the slaves they had "abducted" during the fighting in the South.

Although Jay might have driven a harder bargain, this was a valuable treaty for the United States. But it was also a humiliating one. Most of what the United States gained already legally belonged to it, and the treaty sacrificed principles of importance to a nation dependent on foreign trade. When the terms became known, they raised a storm of popular protest. It seemed possible that President Washington would repudiate the treaty or that if he did not, the Senate would refuse to ratify it.

1795: All's Well That Ends Well

Washington did not repudiate Jay's Treaty and after long debate the Senate ratified it in June 1795. After a bitter debate, with most Republicans opposing the measure, the House passed the requisite funding resolution. The treaty marked an important step toward the regularization of Anglo-American relations, which in the long run was essential for both the economic and political security of the nation. And the evacuation of the British forts in the Northwest was of enormous immediate benefit.

Still another benefit was totally unplanned. Unexpectedly, the Jay Treaty enabled the United States to solve its problems on its southeastern frontier. During the early 1790s Spain had entered into alliances with the Cherokee, Creek, and other Indian tribes hostile to the Americans and built forts on territory ceded to the United States by Great Britain in the Treaty of Paris. In 1795, however, Spain intended to withdraw from the European war against France. Fearing a joint Anglo-American attack on Louisiana and its other American possessions, it decided to improve relations with the United States. Therefore the king's chief minister, Manuel de Godoy, known as "the Prince of Peace," offered the American envoy Thomas Pinckney a treaty that granted the United States the free navigation of the Mississippi River and the right of deposit at New Orleans that western Americans so urgently needed. This Treaty of San Lorenzo, popularly known as Pinckney's Treaty, also accepted the American version of the boundary between Spanish Florida and the United States.

The Senate ratified the Jay Treaty in June. Pinckney signed the Treaty of San Lorenzo in October that same year. These agreements put an end, at least temporarily, to European pressures in the trans-Appalachian region. Between the signings, in August 1795, as an aftermath of the Battle of Fallen Timbers, twelve tribes signed the Treaty of Greenville. The Indians surrendered huge sections of their lands, thus ending a struggle that had consumed a major portion of the government's revenues for years.

After the events of 1794 and 1795, settlers poured into the West. "I believe scarcely anything short of a Chinese Wall or a line of Troops will restrain . . . the Incroachment of Settlers, upon the Indian Territory," President Washington explained in 1796.

Kentucky had become a state in 1792; now, in 1796, Tennessee was admitted. Two years later the Mississippi Territory was organized, and at the end of the century, the Indiana Territory was organized as well. The great westward flood reached full tide.

Washington's Farewell

Settlement of western problems did not, however, put an end to partisan strife. Even the sainted Washington was neither immune to attack nor entirely above the battle. On questions of finance and foreign policy he usually sided with Hamilton and thus increasingly incurred the anger of the Jeffersonians. But he was, after all, a Virginian. Only the most rabid partisan could think him a tool of northern commercial interests. He remained as he intended himself to be, a symbol of national unity. In September 1796 he announced his retirement in a **Farewell Address** to the nation.

•••┤Read the Document

George Washington, *Farewell Addresss* at
myhistorylab.com

Washington found the acrimonious rivalry between Federalists and Republicans most disturbing. Hamilton advocated national unity, yet he seemed prepared to smash any individual or faction that disagreed with his vision of the country's future. Jefferson had risked his neck for independence, but he opposed the economic development needed to make America strong enough to defend that independence. Washington was less brilliant than either Hamilton or Jefferson, but wiser. He appreciated how important it was that the new nation should remain at peace with the rest of the world and with itself. In his farewell he deplored the "baneful effects of the spirit of party" that led honest people to use unscrupulous means to win a mean advantage over fellow Americans. He tried to show how the North benefited from the prosperity of the South, the South from that of the North, and the East and West also in reciprocal fashion.

Washington urged the people to avoid both "inveterate antipathies" and "passionate attachments" to any foreign nation. Nothing had alarmed him more than the sight of Americans dividing into "French" and "English" factions. Furthermore, France had repeatedly interfered in American domestic affairs. "Against the insidious wiles of foreign influence," Washington now warned, "the jealousy of a free people ought to be constantly awake." America should develop its foreign trade but steer clear of foreign political connections as far as possible. "Permanent alliances" should be avoided, although "temporary alliances for extraordinary emergencies" might sometimes be useful.

The Election of 1796

Washington's Farewell Address was destined to have a long and important influence on American thinking, but its immediate impact was small. He had intended it to cool political passions. Instead, in the words of Federalist congressman Fisher Ames, people took it as "a signal, like dropping a hat, for the party racers to start." By the time the 1796 presidential campaign had ended, many Federalists and Republicans were refusing to speak to one another.

Jefferson was the only Republican candidate seriously considered in 1796. The logical Federalist was Hamilton, but, as was to happen so often in American history with powerful leaders, he was not considered "available" because his controversial policies had made him many enemies. Gathering in caucus, the Federalists in Congress nominated Vice President John Adams for the top office and Thomas Pinckney of South Carolina, negotiator of the popular Spanish treaty, for vice president. In the election the Federalists were victorious.

Hamilton, hoping to run the new administration from the wings, preferred Pinckney to Adams. He arranged for some of the Federalist electors from South Carolina to vote only for Pinckney. (Pinckney, who was on the high seas at the time, did not even know he was running for vice president!) Catching wind of this, a number of New England electors retaliated by cutting Pinckney. As a result, Adams won in the electoral college, seventy-one to sixty-eight, over Jefferson, who thus became vice president. Pinckney got only fifty-nine electoral votes.

That Adams would now be obliged to work with a vice president who led the opposition seemed to presage a decline in partisanship. Adams actually preferred the Virginian to Pinckney for the vice presidency, while Jefferson said that if Adams would "relinquish his bias to an English constitution," he might make a fine chief executive. The two had in common a distaste for Hamilton—a powerful bond.

However, the closeness of the election indicated a trend toward the Republicans, who were making constant and effective use of the charge that the Federalists were "monocrats" (monarchists) determined to destroy American liberty. Without Washington to lead them, the Federalist politicians were already quarreling among themselves; honest, able, hardworking John Adams was too caustic and too scathingly frank to unite them. Everything seemed to indicate a Republican victory at the next election.

The XYZ Affair

At this point occurred one of the most remarkable reversals of public feeling in American history. French attacks on American shipping, begun out of irritation at the Jay Treaty and in order to influence the election, continued after Adams took office. Hoping to stop them, Adams appointed three commissioners to try to negotiate a settlement. They were instructed to seek a moderate settlement, to "terminate our differences . . . without referring to the merits."

Their mission was a fiasco. Talleyrand, the French foreign minister, sent an agent later spoken of as X to demand "something for the pocket," a "gratification,"—read a bribe—as the price of making a deal. Later two other Tallyrand agents, Y and Z, made the same demand. The Americans refused, more because they suspected Talleyrand's good faith than because of any particular distaste for bribery. "No, no, not a sixpence," Pinckney later told X. The talks broke up, and in April 1798 President Adams released the commissioners' reports.

They caused a sensation. Americans' sense of national honor, perhaps overly tender because the country was so young and insecure, was outraged. Pinckney's laconic refusal to pay a bribe was translated into the grandiose phrase "Millions for defense, but not one cent for tribute!" and broadcast throughout the land. John Adams, never a man with mass appeal, suddenly found himself a national hero. Federalist hotheads burned for a fight. Congress unilaterally abrogated the French Alliance, created a Navy

Department, and appropriated enough money to build forty-odd warships and triple the size of the army. Washington came out of retirement to lead the forces, with Hamilton, now a general, as second in command. On the seas American privateers began to attack French shipping.

Adams did not much like the French and he could be extremely stubborn. A declaration of war would have been immensely popular. But perhaps the famously prickly president did not want to be popular. Instead of calling for war, he contented himself with approving the buildup of the armed forces.

The Republicans, however, committed to friendship with France, did not appreciate Adams's moderation. Although angered by the **XYZ Affair**, they tried, one Federalist complained, "to clog the wheels of government" by opposing the military appropriations. John Daly Burk of the New York *Time Piece* called Adams a "mock Monarch" surrounded by a "court composed of tories and speculators," which of course was a lie. Many Federalists expected the Republicans to side with France if war broke out. Hysterical and near panic, they easily persuaded themselves that the danger of subversion was acute.

The Alien and Sedition Acts

Conservative Federalists saw in this situation a chance to smash the opposition. In June and July 1798 they pushed through Congress a series of repressive measures known as the **Alien and Sedition Acts**. The Alien Enemies Act gave the president the power to arrest or expel aliens in time of "declared war," but since the quasi-war with France was never declared, this measure had no practical importance. The Alien Act authorized the president to expel all aliens whom he thought "dangerous to the peace and safety of the United States." (Adams never invoked this law, but a number of aliens left the country out of fear that he might.)

●●–⎡Read the **Document**
The Alien and Sedition Acts at **myhistorylab.com**

Finally, there was the Sedition Act. Its first section, making it a crime "to impede the operation of any law" or to attempt to instigate a riot or insurrection, was reasonable enough; but the act also made it illegal to publish, or even to utter, any "false, scandalous and malicious" criticism of high government officials. This proviso rested, as James Madison said, on "the exploded doctrine" that government officials "are the masters and not the servants of the people."

Matthew Lyon of Vermont, holding tongs, and Roger Griswold of Connecticut, come to blows in Congress. After denouncing Adams' call for war against Spain, Lyon was convicted of violating the Alien and Sedition Acts. While serving a four-month jail sentence, he was re-elected.

The Kentucky and Virginia Resolves

While Thomas Jefferson did not object to state sedition laws, he believed that the Alien and Sedition Acts violated the First Amendment's guarantees of freedom of speech and the press and were an invasion of the rights of the states. In 1798 he and Madison decided to draw up resolutions arguing that the laws were unconstitutional. Madison's draft was presented to the Virginia legislature and Jefferson's to the legislature of Kentucky. (Although separate documents, historians refer to them collectively as the **Kentucky and Virginia Resolves**.)

●●●[Read the Document

The Virginia and Kentucky Resolutions at
myhistorylab.com

Jefferson argued that since the Constitution was a compact made by sovereign states, each state had "an equal right to judge for itself" when the compact had been violated. Thus a state could declare a law of Congress unconstitutional. Madison's Virginia Resolves took an only slightly less forthright position.

Neither Kentucky nor Virginia tried to implement these resolves or to prevent the enforcement of the Alien and Sedition Acts. Jefferson and Madison were protesting Federalist high-handedness and firing the opening salvo of Jefferson's campaign for the presidency, not advancing a new constitutional theory of extreme states' rights. "Keep away all show of force," Jefferson advised his supporters.

This was sound advice, for events were again playing into the hands of the Republicans. Talleyrand had never wanted war with the United States. When he discovered how vehemently the Americans had reacted to his little attempt to replenish his personal fortune, he let Adams know that new negotiators would be properly received.

President Adams quickly grasped the importance of the French change of heart. Other leading Federalists, however, had lost their heads. By shouting about the French danger, they had roused the country against radicalism, and they did not intend to surrender this advantage tamely. Hamilton in particular wanted war at almost any price—if not against France, then against Spain. He saw himself at the head of the new American army sweeping first across Louisiana and the Floridas, then on to the South. "We ought to squint at South America," he suggested. "Tempting objects will be within our grasp."

But the puritan John Adams was a specialist at resisting temptation. At this critical point his intelligence, his moderate political philosophy, and his stubborn integrity stood him in good stead. He would neither go to war merely to destroy the political opposition in America nor follow "the fools who were intriguing to plunge us into an alliance with England . . . and wild expeditions to South America." Instead he submitted to the Senate the name of a new minister plenipotentiary to France, and when the Federalists tried to block the appointment, he threatened to resign. This would have made Jefferson president. So the furious Federalists had to give in, although they forced Adams to send three men instead of one.

Napoleon had taken over France by the time the Americans arrived, and he drove a harder bargain than Talleyrand would have. But in the end he signed an agreement (the Convention of 1800) abrogating the Franco-American treaties of 1778. Nothing was said about the damage done to American shipping by the French, but the war scare was over.

The Kentucky and Virginia Resolves, however, had raised an issue that would loom large in the next century. If Congress passed laws that particular states thought to be unconstitutional, did states have the right to ignore those laws—or to withdraw from the Constitution altogether?

Milestones

1781	States fail to approve Congress's tariff	1791	Philip Freneau's *National Gazette* and John Fenno's *Gazette of the United States* are founded
1786	Rhode Island Supreme Court upholds state legal tender act (*Trevett v. Weeden*)	1793	French revolutionaries execute King Louis XVI
	Shays's Rebellion collapses in Springfield, Massachusetts		Washington issues Declaration of Neutrality
	Only five states send delegates to Annapolis Convention	1794	"Mad Anthony" Wayne's troops defeat Indians at Battle of Fallen Timbers
1787	Delegates meet at Philadelphia Constitutional Convention		Washington's militiamen thwart Whiskey Rebellion in Pennsylvania
1787– 1788	All states but North Carolina and Rhode Island ratify Constitution	1795	Senate ratifies humiliating Jay's Treaty
1789	President Washington is inaugurated	1796	Washington announces his retirement in Farewell Address
	Storming of Paris Bastille begins French Revolution		John Adams is elected president
1790	Hamilton issues his *Report on Public Credit*	1798	French demand bribe during XYZ Affair
1791	Hamilton issues his *Report on Manufactures*		Congress passes Alien and Sedition Acts
	First Ten Amendments (Bill of Rights) to the Constitution are ratified	1798– 1799	Jefferson presents Kentucky Resolutions
	Republican and Federalist political parties are organized		Madison presents Virginia Resolutions

✓•—[Study and Review at www.myhistorylab.com

Review Questions

1. The Articles of Confederation are famously known to have been "ineffective." What were their strengths?
2. Who were the winners and losers in the political compromises that resulted in the Constitution?
3. How did the Constitution expand the powers of the federal government?
4. The rise of the Federalists and Republicans constituted what some historians call the "First American Political Party System." What were the key points of dispute? Agreement?
5. How did the Alien and Sedition Acts exacerbate political tensions?
6. Did Washington succeed in bringing the country together, or was his toleration of division a reason for the rise of political factions?

Key Terms

Jeffersonian Democracy   6

Do you have too much debt?

DㅡuRING THEIR FIRST WEEK IN COLLEGE, FRESHMEN RECEIVE ON average eight applications for credit cards. Credit card companies target college students because they have a lifetime to acquire debt—and pay it off. The average freshman in 2008 finished the year with a credit card debt of $2,038, while graduating seniors owed $4,138— up 44 percent since 2004. Many students cope with debt by cutting expenses, taking jobs, or skipping school, while some do not cope. A 2006 documentary film described the plight of two college students in Oklahoma who, awash in credit card debt, committed suicide.

Many college students incur debt responsibly, most often to pay for college. In 2008 the average college graduate owed $23,000, mostly for college loans. But this investment usually pays off—literally: College graduates on average earned $57,200, while individuals with only a high school education earned $31,300.

Many of the founders of the nation were also entangled in personal debt. In 1798 Robert Morris, the financier who had devised the funded debt to pay and equip George Washington's army, was imprisoned for personal debt. He languished in the Prune Street debtor's prison in Philadelphia for three years. Thomas Jefferson, on paper one of the richest men in Virginia, owner of thousands of acres of land and 200 slaves, was also plagued by debt. His financial woes mounted as he built additions to Monticello, his home, and acquired more books for his library, one of the finest in the nation. Creditors harassed him. "I am miserable till I shall owe not a shilling," he wrote in 1787. When he died, he was bankrupt. His slaves were sold to pay creditors.

Jefferson's antipathy toward debt influenced his ideas about government. He opposed federal expenditures because they could lead to indebtedness. A weak government, too, was less likely to restrict individual freedoms, a doctrine that endures to this day. Few presidents have left a deeper imprint. His parsimony sometimes left the nation vulnerable to foreigners, whether high-handed European rulers or pirate states in northern Africa. On a few occasions—such as the chance to acquire the Louisiana territory—he splurged, but soon recanted. On leaving office he urged his successor to pay off the federal deficit.[1]

---

[1]After the 3,000-volume Library of Congress was destroyed by fire in 1814, Madison persuaded Congress to purchase Jefferson's 6,000-volume library for $23,950. This helped pay some of Jefferson's debts. At the time, some politicians grumbled that Jefferson's library had been overvalued. Many of his books, after all, were pirated (published by printers who had not paid copyright fees), that era's equivalent of an "illegal download."

Jefferson Elected President

Once the furor over war and subversion subsided, public attention focused on the presidential contest between Adams and Jefferson. Because of his stand for peace, Adams personally escaped the brunt of popular indignation against the Federalist party. His solid qualities had a strong appeal to conservatives, and fear that the Republicans would introduce radical "French" social reforms did not disappear when the danger of war with France ended. Many nationalist-minded voters worried that the Republicans, waving the banner of states' rights, would weaken the strong government established by the Federalists. The economic progress stimulated by Hamilton's financial reforms also seemed threatened. When the electors' votes were counted in February 1801, however, the Republicans were discovered to have won narrowly, seventy-three to sixty-five.

But which Republican was to be president? The Constitution did not distinguish between presidential and vice presidential candidates; it provided only that each elector vote for two candidates, the one with the most votes becoming president and the runner-up vice president. The development of national political parties made this system impractical. The vice presidential candidate of the Republicans was Aaron Burr of New York, a former senator and a rival of Hamilton in law and politics. But Republican party solidarity had been perfect; Jefferson and Burr received seventy-three votes each. Because of the tie, the Constitution required that the House of Representatives (voting by states) choose between them.

In the House the Republicans could control only eight of the sixteen state delegations. On the first ballot Jefferson got these eight votes, one short of election, while six states voted for Burr. Two state delegations, being evenly split, lost their votes. Through thirty-five ballots the deadlock persisted; the Federalist congressmen, fearful of Jefferson's supposed radicalism, voted solidly for Burr.

In the end, Alexander Hamilton decided who would be the next president. Although he considered Jefferson "too much in earnest in his

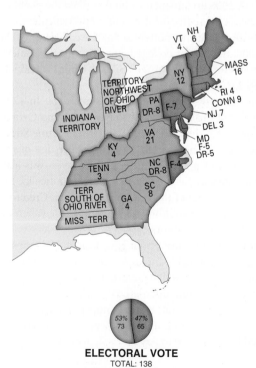

ELECTORAL VOTE
TOTAL: 138

53% 47%
73   65

Democratic-Republican (Jefferson)
Federalist (J. Adams)

The Wild Election of 1800 The election of 1800 was arguably the weirdest in the nation's history. When the electors' votes were counted in February 1801, the Republicans won New York State—and, seemingly, the election, seventy-three to sixty-five. But which Republican was to be president? The Republican electors held to the party line: Jefferson and Burr each received seventy-three votes. Because of the tie, the Constitution required that the House of Representatives (voting by states) choose between them. Jefferson ultimately prevailed.

democracy" and "not very mindful of truth," he detested Burr. He exerted his considerable influence on Federalist congressmen on Jefferson's behalf. Finally, on February 17, 1801, Jefferson was elected. Burr became vice president.

To make sure that this deadlock would never be repeated, the Twelfth Amendment was drafted, providing for separate balloting in the Electoral College for president and vice president. This change was ratified in 1804, shortly before the next election.

The Federalist Contribution

On March 4, 1801, in the new national capital on the Potomac River named in honor of George Washington, Thomas Jefferson took the presidential oath and delivered his inaugural address. His goal was to recapture the simplicity and austerity—the "pure republicanism"—that had characterized "the spirit of '76." The new president believed that a revolution as important as that heralded by his immortal Declaration of Independence had occurred, and for once most of his political enemies agreed with him.

●●●[Read the **Document**
Thomas Jefferson, *First Inaugural Address* at
myhistorylab.com

Jefferson erred, however, in calling this triumph a revolution. The real upheaval had been attempted in 1798; it was Federalist-inspired, and it failed. In 1800 the voters expressed a preference for individual freedom and limited national power. And Jefferson, despite Federalist fears that he would destroy the Constitution and establish a radical social order, presided instead over a regime that confirmed the great achievements of the Federalist era, chiefly, the creation and implementation of the Constitution itself.

What was most significant about the election of 1800 was that it was *not* a revolution. After a bitter contest, the Jeffersonians took power and proceeded to change the policy of the government. They did so peacefully. Thus American republican government passed a crucial test: Control of its machinery had changed hands in a democratic and orderly way. And only slightly less significant, the informal party system had demonstrated its usefulness. The Jeffersonians had organized popular dissatisfaction with Federalist policies, formulated a platform of reform, chosen leaders to put their plans into effect, and elected those leaders to office.

Thomas Jefferson: Political Theorist

Much as Jefferson worried that an indebted nation could become enslaved to its creditors, he feared banks because they, too, deprived debtors of true liberty. He believed *all* government a necessary evil at best, for by its nature it restricted the freedom of the individual. For this reason, he wanted the United States to remain a society of small independent farmers. Such a nation did not need much political organization.

Jefferson's main objection to Alexander Hamilton was that Hamilton wanted to commercialize and centralize the country; Hamilton embraced public debt so as to initiate public projects and promote investment. This Jefferson feared, for it would mean that financial speculators and creditors would acquire economic power. Moreover, a commercial economy would lead to the growth of cities, which would complicate society and hence require more regulation. "The mobs of great cities add just as much to the support of pure government," he said, "as sores do to the strength of the human body." Like Hamilton, he believed that city workers were easy prey for demagogues. "I consider the class of artificers as the panderers of vice, and the instruments by which the liberties of a country are usually overturned," he said. Like Hamilton, Jefferson thought human beings basically selfish. "Lions and tigers are mere lambs compared with men," he once said. Although he claimed to have some doubts about the subject, he suspected that blacks were "inferior to whites in the endowments both of body and mind." (Hamilton, who also owned slaves, stated flatly of blacks that "Their natural faculties are as good as ours.") Jefferson's pronouncements on race are yet more troubling in light of recent research, including DNA studies, that point to the likelihood that he fathered one or more children by Sally Hemings, one of his slaves.

•••—|Read the **Document**

Memoirs of a Monticello Slave at **myhistorylab.com**

Jefferson as President

The novelty of the new administration lay in its style and its moderation. Both were apparent in Jefferson's inaugural address. The new president's opening remarks showed that he was neither a demagogue nor a firebrand. "The task is above my talents," he said modestly, "and . . . I approach it with . . . anxious and awful presentiments." The people had spoken, and their voice must be heeded, but the rights of dissenters must be respected. "All . . . will bear in mind this sacred principle," he said, "that though the will of the majority is in all cases to prevail, that will to be rightful must be reasonable; that the minority possess their equal rights, which equal law must protect, and to violate would be oppression."

Jefferson spoke at some length about specific policies. He declared himself against "entangling alliances" and for economy in government, and he promised to pay off the national debt, preserve the government's credit, and stimulate both agriculture and its "handmaid" commerce. His main stress was on the cooling of partisan passions: "Every difference of opinion is not a difference of principle. We have called by different names brethren of the same principle. We are all Republicans—we are all Federalists." And he promised the country "a wise and frugal Government which shall restrain men from injuring one another" and "leave them otherwise free to regulate their own pursuits."

•••—|Read the **Document**

Reflections Upon Meeting Jefferson at **myhistorylab.com**

Jefferson quickly demonstrated the sincerity of his remarks. He saw to it that the whiskey tax and other Federalist excises were repealed, and he made sharp cuts in military and naval

This portrait of Thomas Jefferson, painted when he was thirty-seven years old, in 1800, the year before he was elected president, is considered an accurate likeness. Its artist, just twenty at the time, was the American painter, Rembrandt Peale. Rembrandt's father—the painter Charles Willson Peale—also named his other sons after painters: Rubens, Titian, Raphaelle, and Titian II.

expenditures to keep the budget in balance. The Naturalization Act of 1798 was repealed, and the old five-year residence requirement for citizenship restored. The Sedition Act and the Alien Act expired of their own accord in 1801 and 1802.

The changes were not drastic. Jefferson made no effort to tear down the fiscal structure that Hamilton had erected. "We can pay off his debt," the new president confessed, "but we cannot get rid of his financial system." Nor did the author of the Kentucky Resolves try to alter the balance of federal-state power.

Yet there was a different tone to the new regime. Jefferson had no desire to surround himself with pomp and ceremony; the excessive formality of the Washington and Adams administrations had been distasteful to him. From the moment of his election, he played down the ceremonial aspects of the presidency. He asked that he be notified of his election by mail rather than by a committee, and he would have preferred to have taken the oath at Charlottesville, near Monticello, his home, rather than at Washington. After the inauguration, he returned to his boardinghouse on foot and took dinner in his usual seat at the common table.

In the White House he often wore a frayed coat and carpet slippers, even to receive the representatives of foreign powers when they arrived. At social affairs he paid little heed to the status and seniority of his guests. During business hours congressmen, friends, foreign officials, and plain citizens coming to call took their turn in the order of their arrival. "The principle of society with us," Jefferson explained, "is the equal rights of all. . . . Nobody shall be above you, nor you above anybody, *pell-mell* is our law."

"Pell-mell" was also good politics, and Jefferson turned out to be a superb politician. He gave dozens of small stag dinner parties for congressmen, serving the food personally from a dumbwaiter connected with the White House kitchen. The guests, carefully chosen to make congenial groups, were seated at a round table to encourage general conversation, and the food and wine were first-class. These were ostensibly social occasions—shoptalk was avoided—yet they paid large political dividends. Jefferson learned to know every congressman personally, Democratic Republican and Federalist alike, and not only their political views but their strengths, their quirks, and their flaws as well. And he worked his personal magic on them, displaying the breadth of his knowledge, his charm and wit, and his lack of pomposity.

Jefferson made effective use of his close supporters in Congress and of Cabinet members as well, in persuading Congress to go along with his proposals. His state papers were models of reason, minimizing conflicts, stressing areas where all honest people must agree. After all, as he indicated in his inaugural address, nearly all Americans believed in having both a federal government and a republican system. No great principle divided them into irreconcilable camps. Jefferson set out to bring them all into *his* camp, and he succeeded so well in four years that when he ran for reelection against Charles Pinckney, he got 162 of the 176 electoral votes cast. Eventually even John Quincy Adams, son of the second president, became a Jeffersonian.

At the same time, Jefferson was anything but nonpartisan in the sense that Washington had been. His Cabinet consisted exclusively of men of his own party. He exerted almost continuous pressure on Congress to make sure that his legislative program was enacted into law. He did not remove many Federalist officeholders, and at one point he remarked ruefully that government officials seldom died and never resigned. But when he could, he used his power of appointment to reward his friends and punish his enemies.

Jefferson's Attack on the Judiciary

Although notably open-minded and tolerant, Jefferson had a few stubborn prejudices. One was against kings, another against the British system of government. A third was against judges, or rather, against entrenched judicial power. The biased behavior of Federalist judges during the trials under the Sedition Act had enormously increased this distrust, and it burst all bounds when the Federalist majority of the dying Congress rammed through the Judiciary Act of 1801.

The Judiciary Act created six new circuit courts, presided over by sixteen new federal judges and a small army of attorneys, marshals, and clerks. The expanding country needed the judges, but with the enthusiastic cooperation of President Adams, the Federalists made shameless use of the opportunity to fill all the new positions with conservative members of their own party. The new appointees were dubbed "midnight justices" because Adams had stayed up until midnight on March 3, his last day as president, feverishly signing their commissions.

The Republicans retaliated as soon as the new Congress met by repealing the Judiciary Act of 1801. But on taking office Jefferson had discovered that in the confusion of Adams's last hours, the commissions of a number of justices of the peace for the new District of Columbia had not been distributed. While these were small fry indeed, Jefferson was so angry that he ordered the commissions held up even though they had been signed by Adams.

One of the appointees, William Marbury, then petitioned the Supreme Court for a writ of mandamus (Latin for "we order") directing the new secretary of state, James Madison, to give him his commission.

The case of ***Marbury v. Madison*** (1803) placed Chief Justice John Marshall, one of Adams's "midnight" appointments, in an embarrassing position. Marbury had a strong claim; if Marshall refused to order Madison to give Marbury the job, everyone would say Marshall dared not stand up to Jefferson, and the prestige of the Court would suffer. If he ordered that Marbury be seated, however, he would place the Court in direct conflict with the President. Jefferson particularly disliked Marshall. He would probably tell Madison to ignore the order, and in the prevailing state of public opinion nothing could be done about it. This would be a still more staggering blow to the judiciary. If its decisions were ignored, would the Supreme Court have any purpose?

Marshall had studied law only briefly and had no previous judicial experience, but in this crisis he first displayed the genius that was to mark him as a great judge. By right Marbury should have his commission, Marshall announced. However, the Court could not require Madison to give it to him. Marbury's request for a court order had been based on an ambiguous clause in the Judiciary Act of 1789. That clause was unconstitutional, Marshall declared, and therefore void. Congress could not legally give the Supreme Court the right to issue such orders.

With the skill and foresight of a chess grand master, Marshall turned what had looked like a trap into a triumph. By sacrificing the pawn, Marbury, he established the power of the Supreme Court to invalidate federal laws that conflicted with the Constitution. Jefferson could not check him because Marshall had *refused* power instead of throwing an anchor ahead, as Jefferson had

●●●[Read the Document

Opinion of the Supreme Court for Marbury v. Madison at myhistorylab.com feared. Yet he had certainly grappled a "further hold for future advances of power," and the president could do nothing to stop him.

The Marbury case made Jefferson more determined to strike at the Federalist-dominated courts. He decided to press for the impeachment of some of the more partisan judges. First he had the House of Representatives bring charges against District Judge John Pickering. Pickering was clearly deranged—he had frequently delivered profane and drunken harangues from the bench—and the Senate quickly voted to remove him. Then Jefferson went after a much larger fish, Samuel Chase, associate justice of the Supreme Court.

Chase had been prominent for decades and active in the affairs of the Continental Congress. Washington had named him to the Supreme Court in 1796, and he had delivered a number of important opinions. But his handling of cases under the Sedition Act had been outrageously high-handed. Defense lawyers had become so exasperated as to throw down their briefs in disgust at some of his prejudiced rulings. However, the trial demonstrated that Chase's actions had not constituted the "high crimes and misdemeanors" required by the Constitution to remove a judge. Even Jefferson became disenchanted with the efforts of some of his more extreme followers and accepted Chase's acquittal with equanimity.

The Barbary Pirates

The North African Arab states of Morocco, Algiers, Tunis, and Tripoli had for decades made a business of piracy, seizing vessels all over the Mediterranean and holding crews and passengers for ransom. The European powers found it simpler to pay them annual protection money than to crush them. Under Washington and Adams, the United States joined in the payment of this tribute; while large, the sums were less than the increased costs of insurance for shippers when the protection was not purchased.

Such spinelessness ran against Jefferson's grain. "When this idea comes across my mind, my faculties are absolutely suspended between indignation and impatience," he said. When the pasha of Tripoli tried to raise the charges, Jefferson balked. Tripoli then declared war in May 1801, and Jefferson dispatched a squadron to the Mediterranean.

But the pirates were not overwhelmed, and a major American warship, the frigate *Philadelphia*, had to be destroyed after running aground off the Tripolitan coast. The payment of tribute continued until 1815. Just the same, America, though far removed from the pirate bases, was the only maritime nation that tried to resist the blackmail. Although the war failed to achieve Jefferson's purpose of ending the payments, the pasha agreed to a new treaty more favorable to the United States, and American sailors, led by Commodore Edward Preble, won valuable experience.

The Louisiana Purchase

The major achievements of Jefferson's first term had to do with the American West, and the greatest by far was the **Louisiana Purchase**, the acquisition of the huge area between the Mississippi River and the Rocky Mountains. In a sense the purchase of this region, called Louisiana, was fortuitous, an accidental by-product of

See the **Map**

The Louisiana Purchase at **myhistorylab.com**

UNDER MY WINGS EVERY THING PROSPERS

This depicts New Orleans in 1803, when the city was acquired—along with much of the modern United States—in the Louisiana Purchase. It was known as the Crescent City because of the way it hugged a curved section of the Mississippi River. In 1803, New Orleans's population was about 8,000, including 4,000 whites, 2,700 slaves, and about 1,300 free "persons of color."
Source: P&S-1932.0018/Creator—Boqueto de Woieseri/Chicago History Museum.

European political adjustments and the whim of Napoleon Bonaparte. Certainly Jefferson had not planned it, for in his inaugural address he had expressed the opinion that the country already had all the land it would need "for a thousand generations." It was nonetheless the perfectly logical—one might almost say inevitable—result of a long series of events in the history of the Mississippi Valley.

Along with every other American who had even a superficial interest in the West, Jefferson understood that the United States must have access to the mouth of the Mississippi and the city of New Orleans or eventually lose everything beyond the Appalachians. "There is on the globe one single spot, the possessor of which is our natural and habitual enemy," he was soon to write. "It is New Orleans." Thus when he learned shortly after his inauguration that Spain had given Louisiana back to France, he was immediately on his guard. Control of Louisiana by Spain, a "feeble" country with "pacific dispositions," could be tolerated; control by a resurgent France dominated by Napoleon, the greatest military genius of the age, was entirely different.

Deeply worried, the president instructed his minister to France, Robert R. Livingston, to seek assurances that American rights in New Orleans would be respected and to negotiate the purchase of West Florida in case that area had also been turned over to France.

Jefferson's concern was well-founded; France was indeed planning new imperial ventures in North America. Immediately after settling its difficulties with the United States through the Convention of 1800, France signed a secret treaty with Spain, which returned Louisiana to France. Napoleon hoped to use this region as a breadbasket for the French West Indian sugar plantations, just as colonies like Pennsylvania and Massachusetts had fed the British sugar islands before the Revolution.

However, the most important French island, Saint Domingue (Hispaniola), at the time occupied entirely by the nation of Haiti, had slipped from French control. During the French Revolution, the slaves of the island had revolted. In 1793 they were granted personal freedom, but they fought on under the leadership of the "Black Napoleon," a self-taught genius named Toussaint L'Ouverture, and by 1801 the island was entirely in their hands. The original Napoleon, taking advantage of the slackening of war in Europe, dispatched an army of 20,000 men under General Charles Leclerc to reconquer it.

When Jefferson learned of the Leclerc expedition, he had no trouble divining its relationship to Louisiana. His uneasiness became outright alarm. In April 1802 he again urged Minister Livingston to attempt the purchase of New Orleans and Florida or, as an alternative, to buy a tract of land near the mouth of the Mississippi where a new port could be constructed. Of necessity, the mild-mannered, idealistic president now became an aggressive realist. "The day that France takes possession of New Orleans," he warned, "we must marry ourselves to the British fleet and nation."

In October 1802 the Spanish, who had not yet actually turned Louisiana over to France, heightened the tension by declaring that American boats plying the Mississippi could no longer deposit and store their goods in warehouses in New Orleans, the first step to exporting them to Europe. We now know that the French had no hand in this action, but it was beyond reason to expect Jefferson or the American people to believe it at the time. With the West clamoring for relief, Jefferson appointed his friend and

Toussaint L'Ouverture leading a revolt of slaves against the French in Haiti—the first and only successful slave rebellion in history.

disciple James Monroe minister plenipotentiary and sent him to Paris with instructions to offer up to $10 million for New Orleans and Florida. If France refused, he and Livingston should open negotiations for a "closer connection" with the British.

The tension broke before Monroe even reached France. General Leclerc's Saint Domingue expedition ended in disaster. Although Toussaint surrendered, Haitian resistance continued. Yellow fever raged through the French army; Leclerc himself fell to the fever, which wiped out practically his entire force.

When news of this calamity reached Napoleon early in 1803, he had second thoughts about reviving French imperialism in the New World. Without Saint Domingue, the wilderness of Louisiana seemed of little value. Napoleon was preparing a new campaign in Europe. He could no longer spare troops to recapture a rebellious West Indian island or to hold Louisiana against a possible British attack, and he needed money.

For some weeks the commander of the most powerful army in the world mulled the question without consulting anyone. Then, with characteristic suddenness, he made up his mind. On April 10 he ordered Foreign Minister Talleyrand to offer not merely New Orleans but all of Louisiana to the Americans. The next day Talleyrand summoned Livingston to his office on the rue du Bac and dropped this bombshell. Livingston was almost struck speechless but quickly recovered his composure. When Talleyrand asked what the United States would give for the province, he suggested the French equivalent of about $5 million. Talleyrand pronounced the sum "too low" and urged Livingston to think about the subject for a day or two.

Livingston faced a situation that no modern diplomat would ever have to confront. His instructions said nothing about buying an area almost as large as the entire United States, and there was no time to write home for new instructions. The offer staggered the imagination. Luckily, Monroe arrived the next day to share the responsibility. The two Americans consulted, dickered with the French, and finally agreed—they could scarcely have done otherwise—to accept the proposal. Early in May they signed a treaty. For 60 million francs—about $15 million—the United States was to have all of Louisiana.

No one knew exactly how large the region was or what it contained. When Livingston asked Talleyrand about the boundaries of the purchase, he replied, "I can give you no direction. You have made a noble bargain for yourselves, and I suppose you will make the most of it." Never, as the historian Henry Adams wrote, "did the United States government get so much for so little."

Napoleon's unexpected concession caused consternation in America, though there was never real doubt that the treaty would be ratified. Jefferson did not believe that the government had the power under the Constitution to add new territory or to grant American citizenship to the 50,000 residents of Louisiana by executive act, as the treaty required. He even drafted a constitutional amendment: "The province of Louisiana is incorporated with the United States and made part thereof." But his advisers convinced him that it would be dangerous to delay approval of the treaty until an amendment could be acted on by three-fourths of the states. Jefferson then suggested that the Senate ratify the treaty and submit an amendment afterward "confirming an act which the nation had not previously authorized." This idea was so obviously illogical that he quickly dropped it. Finally, he came to believe "that the less we say about constitutional difficulties the better." Since what he called "the good sense of our country" clearly wanted Louisiana, he decided to "acquiesce with satisfaction" while Congress overlooked the "metaphysical subtleties" of the problem and ratified the treaty.

Louisiana Purchase Jefferson bought the Louisiana region from Napoleon. No payments were made to the many Indians who had no idea that the world of their ancestors was owned by distant rulers.

Some of the more partisan Federalists, who had been eager to fight Spain for New Orleans, attacked Jefferson for undermining the Constitution. One such critic described Louisiana contemptuously as a "Gallo-Hispano-Indian" collection of "savages and adventurers." Even Hamilton expressed hesitation about absorbing "this new, immense, unbounded world," though he had dreamed of seizing still larger domains himself. In the end Hamilton's nationalism reasserted itself, and he urged ratification of the treaty, as did such other important Federalists as John Adams and John Marshall. It was ironic—and a man as perceptive as Hamilton must surely have recognized the irony—that the acquisition of Louisiana ensured Jefferson's reelection and further contributed to the downfall of the Federalists. The purchase was popular even in the New England bastions of that party. While the negotiations were progressing in Paris, Jefferson had written the following of partisan political affairs: "If we can settle happily the difficulties of the Mississippi, I think we may promise ourselves smooth seas during our time." These words turned out to be no more accurate than most political predictions, but the Louisiana Purchase drove another spike into the Federalists' coffin.

Read the **Document**
The Louisiana Purchase at **myhistorylab.com**

Read the **Document**
Fisher Ames on the Louisiana Purchase at **myhistorylab.com**

The Federalists Discredited

As the election of 1804 approached, the West and South were solidly for Jefferson, and the North was rapidly succumbing to his charm. The addition of new western states would soon further reduce New England's power in national affairs.

These pistols were used in the duel between Aaron Burr and Alexander Hamilton. Before the duel Hamilton's lawyer drew up a contract specifying the terms: The duelists were to shoot at ten paces, and the barrels of the guns were to be no longer than 11 inches. Witnesses claimed that Hamilton never fired his fine pistol, but Burr took deadly aim, firing a .54-caliber ball that hit Hamilton in the chest. It ricocheted off his rib, punctured his liver, and lodged in his backbone. Hamilton died the next day.

So complete did the Republican triumph seem that a handful of diehard Federalists in New England began to think of secession. Led by former secretary of state Timothy Pickering, a group known as the Essex Junto organized in 1804 a scheme to break away from the Union and establish a "northern confederacy."

Even within the dwindling Federalist ranks the junto had little support. Nevertheless, Pickering and his friends pushed ahead, drafting a plan whereby, having captured political control of New York, they would take the entire Northeast out of the Union. Since they could not begin to win New York for anyone in their own ranks, they hit on the idea of supporting Vice President Aaron Burr, who was running against the "regular" Republican candidate for governor of New York. Although Burr did not promise to bring New York into their confederacy if elected, he encouraged them enough to win their backing. The foolishness of the plot was revealed in the April elections: Burr was overwhelmed by the regular Republican. The junto's scheme collapsed.

The incident, however, had a tragic aftermath. Hamilton had campaigned against Burr, whom he considered "an embryo Caesar." When he continued after the election to cast aspersions on Burr's character (not a very difficult assignment, since Burr, despite being a grandson of the preacher Jonathan Edwards, frequently violated both the political and sexual mores of the day), Burr challenged him to a duel. It was well known that Hamilton opposed dueling in principle, his own son having been slain in such an encounter, and he certainly had no need to prove his courage. But he believed that his honor was at stake. The two met with pistols on July 11, 1804, at Weehawken, New Jersey, across the Hudson from New York City. Hamilton made no effort to hit the challenger, but Burr took careful aim. Hamilton fell, wounded; he died the next day.

Thus a great, if enigmatic, man was cut off in his prime. His work, in a sense, had been completed, and his philosophy of government was being everywhere rejected, yet the nation's loss was large.

Lewis and Clark

While the disgruntled Federalists dreamed of secession, Jefferson was planning the exploration of Louisiana and the region beyond. He especially hoped to find a water route to connect the upper Mississippi or its tributaries with the Pacific Ocean. Early in 1803 he got $2,500 from Congress and obtained the permission of the French to send his exploring party across Louisiana. To command the expedition he appointed his private secretary, Meriwether Lewis,

●◆●─│Read the Document

Thomas Jefferson to Meriwether Lewis at **myhistorylab.com**

a young Virginian who had seen considerable service with the army in the West and who possessed, according to Jefferson, "a great mass of accurate information on all the subjects of nature." Lewis chose as his companion officer William Clark, another soldier (he had served with General Anthony Wayne at the Battle of Fallen Timbers) who had much experience in negotiating with Indians.

The country greeted the news of the explorers' return to St. Louis with delight. Besides locating several passes across the Rockies, Lewis and Clark had established friendly relations with a great many Indian tribes to whom they presented gifts, medals, American flags,

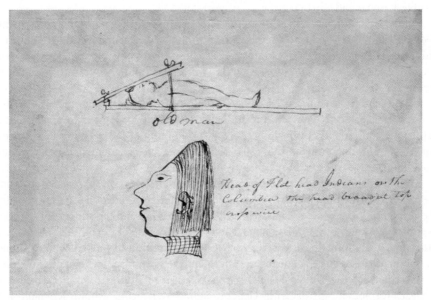

The "Flat Head" (Chinook) Indians acquired their name through shaping in infancy, as shown in a diagram from the Lewis and Clark journals. More remarkable to the explorers than the shape of the Indians' heads was the tribeswomen's open sexuality. "The young females are fond of the attention of our men and appear to meet the sincere approbation of their friends and connections for thus obtaining their favors," Captain Clark confided in his diary.

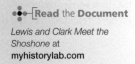

Read the **Document**

Lewis and Clark Meet the Shoshone at
myhistorylab.com

and a sales talk designed to promote peace and the fur trade. They brought back a wealth of data about the country and its resources. The journals kept by members of the group were published and, along with their accurate maps, became major sources for scientists, students, and future explorers.

The success of the **Lewis and Clark expedition** did not open the gates of Louisiana very wide. Other explorers sent out by Jefferson accomplished far less. Thomas Freeman, an Irish-born surveyor, led a small party up the Red River but ran into a powerful Spanish force near the present junction of Arkansas, Oklahoma, and Texas and was forced to retreat. Between 1805 and 1807 Lieutenant Zebulon Pike explored the upper Mississippi Valley and the Colorado region. (He discovered but failed to scale the peak south of Denver that bears his name.) Pike eventually made his way to Santa Fe and the upper reaches of the Rio Grande,

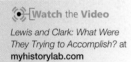

Watch the **Video**

*Lewis and Clark: What Were
They Trying to Accomplish?* at
myhistorylab.com

but he was not nearly so careful and acute an observer as Lewis and Clark were and consequently brought back much less information. By 1808 fur traders based at St. Louis were beginning to invade the Rockies, and by 1812 there were 75,000 people in the southern section of the new territory, which was admitted to the Union that year as the state of Louisiana. The northern region lay almost untouched until much later.

The Burr Conspiracy

Republican virtue seemed to have triumphed, but Jefferson soon found himself in trouble at home and abroad.

In part his difficulties arose from the extent of the Republican victory. In 1805 his Federalist opponents had no useful ideas, no intelligent leadership, and no effective numbers. They held only a quarter of the seats in Congress. As often happens in such situations, lack of opposition weakened party discipline and encouraged factionalism among the Republicans.

The Republican who caused Jefferson the most trouble was Aaron Burr, and the president was partly to blame for the difficulty. After their contest for the presidency in 1801, Jefferson pursued Burr vindictively, depriving him of federal patronage in New York and replacing him as the 1804 Republican vice presidential candidate with Governor George Clinton, Burr's chief rival in the state.

While still vice president, Burr began to flirt with treason. He approached Anthony Merry, the British minister in Washington, and offered to "effect a separation of the Western part of the United States." His price was £110,000 and the support of a British fleet off the mouth of the Mississippi. The British did not fall in with his scheme, but Burr went ahead nonetheless. Exactly what he had in mind has long been in dispute. Certainly he dreamed of acquiring a western empire for himself; whether he intended to wrest it from the United States or from Spanish territories beyond Louisiana is unclear. He joined forces with General James Wilkinson, whom Jefferson had appointed governor of the Louisiana Territory and was secretly in the pay of Spain.

The opening of the Ohio and Mississippi valleys had not totally satisfied land-hungry westerners. In 1806 Burr and Wilkinson had no difficulty raising a small force at a place called Blennerhassett Island, in the Ohio River. Some six dozen men began to move downriver toward New Orleans under Burr's command. Whether the objective was New Orleans or some part of Mexico, the scheme was clearly illegal. For some reason, however—possibly because he was incapable of loyalty to anyone[2]—Wilkinson betrayed Burr to Jefferson at the last moment. Burr tried to escape to Spanish Florida but was captured in February 1807, brought to Richmond, Virginia, under guard, and charged with high treason.

Any president will deal summarily with traitors, but Jefferson's attitude during Burr's trial reveals the depth of his hatred. He "made himself a party to the prosecution," personally sending evidence to the United States attorney who was handling the case and offering blanket pardons to associates of Burr who would agree to turn state's evidence. In stark contrast, Chief Justice Marshall, presiding at the trial in his capacity as judge of the circuit court, repeatedly showed favoritism to the prisoner.

In this contest between two great men at their worst, Jefferson as a vindictive executive and Marshall as a prejudiced judge, the victory went to the judge. Organizing "a military assemblage," Marshall declared on his charge to the jury, "was not a levying of war." To "advise or procure treason" was not in itself treason. Unless two independent witnesses testified to an overt act of treason as thus defined, the accused should be declared innocent. The jury, deliberating only twenty-five minutes, found Burr not guilty.

The Burr affair was a blow to Jefferson's prestige; it left him more embittered against Marshall and the federal judiciary, and it added nothing to his reputation as a statesman.

Napoleon and the British

Jefferson's difficulties with Burr may be traced at least in part to the purchase of Louisiana, which, empty and unknown, excited the greed of men like Burr and Wilkinson. But problems infinitely more serious were also related to Louisiana.

Napoleon had jettisoned Louisiana to clear the decks before resuming the battle for control of Europe. This war had the effect of stimulating the American economy, for the warring powers needed American goods and American vessels. Shipbuilding boomed and foreign trade, which had quintupled since 1793, nearly doubled again between 1803 and 1805. By the summer of 1807, however, the situation had changed: An unusual stalemate had developed in the war.

In October 1805 Britain's Horatio Nelson demolished the combined Spanish and French fleets in the Battle of Trafalgar, off the coast of Spain. Napoleon, now at the summit of his powers, quickly redressed the balance, smashing army after army thrown against him by Great Britain's continental allies. By 1807 he was master of Europe, while the British controlled the seas around the Continent. Neither nation could strike directly at the other.

They therefore resorted to commercial warfare, striving to disrupt each other's economy. Napoleon struck first with his Berlin Decree (November 1806), which made "all commerce and correspondence" with Great Britain illegal. The British retaliated with a series of edicts called Orders in Council, blockading most continental ports and barring from them all foreign vessels unless they first stopped at a British port and paid customs duties. Napoleon then issued his Milan Decree (December 1807), declaring any vessel that submitted to the British rules "to have become English property" and thus subject to seizure.

---

[2]John Randolph said that "Wilkinson is the only man that I ever saw who was from the bark to the very core a villain."

American traders in the exchange at a port in China.

When war first broke out between Britain and France in 1792, the colonial trade of both sides had fallen largely into American hands because the danger of capture drove many belligerent merchant vessels from the seas. This commerce had engaged Americans in some devious practices.

For example, American merchants carried sugar from the French colony of Martinique first to the United States, a legal peacetime voyage under French mercantilism. Then they reshipped it to France as American sugar. Since the United States was a neutral nation and sugar was not contraband of war, the Americans expected the British to let their ships pass with impunity. Continental products likewise reached the French West Indies by way of United States ports, and the American government encouraged the traffic in both directions by refunding customs duties on foreign products reshipped within a year.

This underhanded commerce irritated the British. Thus just when Britain and France were cracking down on direct trade by neutrals, Britain determined to halt the American reexport trade, thereby gravely threatening American prosperity.

The Impressment Controversy

More dismaying were the cruel indignities being visited on American seamen by the British practice of **impressment**. Under British law any able-bodied subject could be drafted for service in the Royal Navy in an emergency. Normally, when the commander of a warship found himself shorthanded, he put into a British port and sent a "press gang" ashore to round up the necessary men in harborside pubs. When far from home waters, he might hail any passing British merchant ship and commandeer the necessary men, though this practice was understandably unpopular in British maritime circles. He might also stop a *neutral* merchant vessel on the high seas and remove any British subject. Since the United States owned by far the largest merchant fleet among the neutrals, its vessels bore the brunt of this practice.

Many British captains made little effort to be sure they were impressing British subjects. Furthermore, there were legal questions in dispute. When did an English immigrant become an American? When he was naturalized, the United States claimed. Never, the British retorted: "once an Englishman, always an Englishman."

The Jefferson administration conceded the right of the British to impress their own subjects from American merchant ships. When naturalized Americans were impressed, however, the administration was irritated, and when native-born Americans were taken, it became incensed. Impressment, Secretary of State Madison said in 1807, was "anomalous in principle . . . grievous in practice, and . . . abominable in abuse." Between 1803 and 1812 at least 5,000 sailors were snatched from the decks of United States vessels and forced to serve in the Royal Navy. Most of them—estimates run as high as three out of every four—were Americans.

The combination of impressment, British interference with the reexport trade, and the general harassment of neutral commerce instituted by both Great Britain and France would have perplexed the most informed and hardheaded of leaders, and in dealing with these problems Jefferson was neither informed nor hardheaded. He believed it much wiser to stand up for one's rights than to compromise, yet he hated the very thought of war. Perhaps, being a Southerner, he was less sensitive than he might have been to the needs of New England commercial interests. While the American merchant fleet passed 600,000 tons and continued to grow at an annual rate of over 10 percent, Jefferson kept only a skeleton navy on active service, despite the fact that the great powers were fighting a worldwide, no-holds-barred war. Instead of building a navy that other nations would have to respect, he relied on a tiny fleet of frigates and a swarm of gunboats that were useless against the Royal Navy—"a macabre monument," in the words of one historian, "to his hasty, ill-digested ideas" about defense.[3]

The Embargo Act

The frailty of Jefferson's policy became obvious once the warring powers began to attack neutral shipping in earnest. Between 1803 and 1807 the British seized more than 500 American ships, Napoleon more than 200. The United States could do nothing.

---

[3]The gunboats had performed effectively against the Barbary pirates, but Jefferson was enamored of them mainly because they were cheap. A gunboat cost about $10,000 to build, a big frigate over $300,000.

The Ograbme ("embargo" spelled backward), a snapping turtle drawn by cartoonist Alexander Anderson, frustrates an American tobacco smuggler.
Source: Collection of The New-York Historical Society, [Neg. No. 7278].

The ultimate in frustration came on June 22, 1807, off Norfolk, Virginia. The American forty-six-gun frigate *Chesapeake* had just left port for patrol duty in the Mediterranean. Among its crew were a British sailor who had deserted from HMS *Halifax* and three Americans who had been illegally impressed by the captain of HMS *Melampus* and had later escaped. The *Chesapeake* was barely out of sight of land when HMS *Leopard* (fifty-six guns) approached and signaled it to heave to. Thinking that *Leopard* wanted to make some routine communication, Captain James Barron did so. A British officer came aboard and demanded that the four "deserters" be handed over to him. Barron refused, whereupon as soon as the officer was back on board, *Leopard* opened fire on the unsuspecting American ship, killing three sailors. Barron had to surrender. The "deserters" were seized, and then the crippled *Chesapeake* was allowed to limp back to port.

The attack was in violation of international law, for no nation claimed the right to impress sailors from warships. The British government admitted this, though it delayed making restitution for years. The American press clamored for war, but the country had nothing to fight with. Jefferson contented himself with ordering British warships out of American territorial waters. However, he was determined to put a stop to the indignities being heaped on the flag by Great Britain and France. The result was the **Embargo Act**.

The Embargo Act prohibited all exports. American vessels could not clear for any foreign port, and foreign vessels could do so only if empty. Although the law was sure to injure the American economy, Jefferson hoped that it would work in two ways to benefit the nation. By keeping U.S. merchant ships off the seas, it would end all chance of injury to them and to the national honor. By cutting off American goods and markets, it would

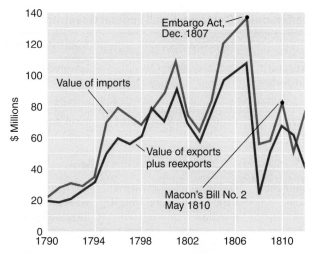

American Foreign Trade, 1790–1812 This graph shows the embargo's effects. The space between the upper (import) and the lower (export) line indicates a persistent foreign-trade deficit.

put great economic pressure on Britain and France to moderate policies toward American shipping.

Seldom has a law been so bitterly resented and resisted by a large segment of the public. It demanded of the maritime interests far greater sacrifices than they could reasonably be expected to make. Massachusetts-owned ships alone were earning over $15 million a year in freight charges by 1807, and Bay State merchants were making far larger gains from the buying and selling of goods. Foreign commerce was the most expansive force in the economy, the chief reason for the nation's prosperity. As John Randolph remarked in a typical sally, the administration was trying "to cure the corns by cutting off the toes."

The Embargo Act had catastrophic effects. Exports fell from $108 million in 1807 to $22 million in 1808, imports from $138 million to less than $57 million. Prices of farm products and manufactured goods reacted violently, seamen were thrown out of work, and merchants found their businesses disrupted.

Surely the embargo was a mistake. The United States ought either to have suffered the indignities heaped on its vessels for the sake of profits or, by constructing a powerful navy, made it dangerous for the belligerents to treat its merchant ships so roughly. Jefferson was too proud to choose the former alternative, too parsimonious to choose the latter. Instead he applied harsher and harsher regulations in a futile effort to accomplish his purpose. Jefferson refused to admit that the embargo was a fiasco and urge its repeal. Only in his last week in office did a leaderless Congress finally abolish it, substituting the Non-Intercourse Act, which forbade trade only with Great Britain and France and authorized the president to end the boycott against either power by proclamation when and if it stopped violating the rights of Americans.

Thus Jefferson's political career ended on a sour note. Several weeks after he had left office and returned to Monticello, he privately advised his successor, James Madison, to trust his own judgment to govern because the people readily succumbed to "the floating lies of the day."

Table 6.1 **Jeffersonian Doctrine: Small Federal Government**

Measure	Advantages	Disadvantages
Repealed whiskey and other taxes on imports (excise)	Reduced taxes	Lowered federal revenue
Curtailed military and naval spending	Reduction in federal debt	Weak navy: Foreign powers could "impress" American sailors and seize American ships
Embargo Act (1807): no export trade	End to humiliations at the hand of British and French warships	Collapse of foreign trade, weakening of economy, increased smuggling

Jeffersonian Democracy

Yet Jefferson completed the construction of the political institution known as the Republican party and the philosophy of government known as Jeffersonian democracy. In part his success was a matter of personality; he was perfectly in tune with the thinking of his times. The colonial American had practiced democracy without really believing in it, for example, the maintenance of property qualifications for voting in regions where nearly everyone owned property. Stimulated by the libertarian ideas of the Revolution, Americans were rapidly adjusting their beliefs to conform with their practices. However, it took Jefferson, possessed of the general prejudice in favor of the old-fashioned citizen rooted in the soil, yet deeply committed to majority rule, to oversee the transition.

Jefferson's marvelous talents as a writer help explain his success. He expounded his ideas in language that few people could resist. He had a remarkable facility for discovering practical arguments to justify his beliefs—as when he suggested that by letting everyone vote, elections would be made more honest because with large numbers going to the polls, bribery would become prohibitively expensive.

Jefferson prepared the country for democracy by proving that a democrat could establish and maintain a stable regime. The Federalist tyranny of 1798 was compounded of selfishness and stupidity, but it was also based in part on honest fears that an egalitarian regime would not protect the fabric of society from hotheads and crackpots. The impact of the French Revolution on conservative thinking in the mid-1790s cannot be overestimated. America had fought a seven-year revolution without executing a single Tory, yet during the few months that the Reign of Terror ravaged France, nearly 17,000 persons were officially put to death for political "crimes" and many thousands more were killed in civil disturbances. Worse, in the opinion of many, the French extremists had attempted to destroy Christianity, substituting for it a "cult of reason." Little wonder that many Americans feared that the Jeffersonians, lovers of France and of *liberté, égalité, fraternité*, would try to remodel American society in a similar way.

Jefferson calmed these fears. The most partisan Federalist was hard put to see a Robespierre, leader during the Reign of Terror in France, in the amiable Jefferson scratching out state papers at his desk or chatting with a Kentucky congressman at a

The storming of the Bastille in 1789. After the crowd seizes the fortification, they tear it down, stone by stone.

"republican" dinner party. Furthermore, Jefferson accepted Federalist ideas on public finance, even learning to live with Hamilton's bank. As a good democrat, he drew a nice distinction between his own opinions and the wishes of the majority, which he felt must always take priority. Even in his first inaugural address he admitted that manufacturing and commerce were, along with agriculture, the "pillars of our prosperity," and he accepted the principle that the government should protect them when necessary from "casual embarrassments." During his term the country grew and prospered, the commercial classes sharing in the bounty along with the farmers so close to Jefferson's heart.

Thus Jefferson undermined the Federalists all along the line. They had said that the country must pay a stiff price for prosperity and orderly government, and they demanded prompt payment in full, both in cash (taxes) and in the form of limitations on human liberty. Under Jefferson these much-desired goals had been achieved cheaply and without sacrificing freedom. A land whose riches could only be guessed at had been obtained without firing a shot and without burdening the people with new taxes. Order without discipline, security without a large military establishment, prosperity without regulatory legislation, freedom without license—truly the Sage of Monticello appeared to have led his fellow Americans into a golden age.

Jefferson insisted that one of his chief accomplishments had been to reduce the national debt from $83 million to $57 million. Writing from Monticello shortly after leaving office, he urged his successors to eliminate the remainder. "The discharge of the public debt," he warned Treasury Secretary Gallatin, "is vital to the destinies of our government."

Yet Jefferson had also learned the perils of an inadequately funded government. His unwillingness to build a real navy had rendered the nation vulnerable to foreign states. Conversely, he had exulted in the purchase of Louisiana, and he backed modest proposals for spending federal money on roads, canals, and other projects that, according to his political philosophy, ought to have been left to the states and private individuals. Debt, Jefferson accepted, was sometimes good policy.

Milestones

1801	Judiciary Act of 1801 allows Adams to appoint many Federalist judges	1804–1806	Lewis and Clark explore West
	Jefferson is elected president	1806	Aaron Burr schemes to take land in West during Burr Conspiracy
1801–1805	U.S. wages war against Barbary pirates in North Africa	1806–1807	Napoleon issues Berlin and Milan decrees in order to disrupt British shipping and economy
1803	Supreme Court declares part of Judiciary Act of 1789 unconstitutional (*Marbury v. Madison*)	1807	HMS *Leopard* attacks USS *Chesapeake*
	Jefferson negotiates Louisiana Purchase with France		Embargo Act prohibits all exports
1804	Aaron Burr kills Alexander Hamilton in duel	1809	Non-Intercourse Act forbids trade with Great Britain and France
	Jefferson is reelected		

✓•⌐**Study** and **Review** at **www.myhistorylab.com**

Review Questions

1. The Federalist vision of the nation largely prevailed during the 1790s. Why did it fade so rapidly during the 1800s? Was its decline caused by a failure of Federalist leadership or the successes of Jefferson?
2. What effect did the Napoleonic wars have on events in America? Why did Napoleon abandon his dreams of a French economic empire in the Americas?
3. What chief obstacle—literally—stood in the way of an all-water route across the United States connecting the Atlantic and Pacific Oceans?
4. The text asserts that the Embargo Act was "surely" a mistake, yet Jefferson was a savvy politician. How did he decide to propose it in the first place?

Key Terms

Embargo Act   *188*
impressment   *187*
Lewis and Clark expedition   *184*

Louisiana Purchase   *177*
Marbury v. Madison   *176*

National Growing Pains 7

((•—⌐Hear the Audio Chapter 7 at myhistorylab.com

Does the government help you pay for college?

THE RECESSION THAT STRUCK IN 2008 HIT YOUNG ADULTS THE HARDEST. By the end of the year, less than half (46 percent) of those aged eighteen to twenty-four had jobs—the lowest rate on record.[1] Many of those who couldn't find jobs decided to go to college. This influx produced another record in 2008: More young adults ages eighteen to twenty-four were enrolled in either two- or four-year colleges than ever before. The chief enrollment increase was in community colleges, whose costs (tuition, fees, books and expenses) averaged $7,000, compared to four-year public colleges ($10,000) and four-year private colleges ($27,000).

But how could young people pay for college during a severe recession? The federal government provided the answer—through loans for college, chiefly Pell grants. By 2010, for example, nearly 8 million students received Pell grants averaging $3,700 with a maximum grant of $5,500.

That the federal government would one day play so profound a role in the lives of its people would have astonished the founding generation. Well into the nineteenth century, the federal government failed to generate much income. In 1809 its total revenue fell short of $8 million. Of that, $7 million came from taxes on imports (the tariff); the balance came mostly from the sale of federal lands and postage stamps. Without income from the tariff, the federal government could have done little more than deliver the mail.

From 1809 to 1828, Americans repeatedly expanded the role of the federal government. Armies and navies were raised to subdue the Indians and defend the nation from European predators; highways were built to encourage trade and promote settlement of the Louisiana territories. The federal budget tripled. The nation was growing, and the federal government grew with it. The tariff inevitably increased as well. The 1828 "**Tariff of Abominations**" was the highest to that time.

But the sharp increase in the tariff, and in the role of the federal government, sent shock waves through American society. As the tariff raised the price of manufactured goods, farmers had to pay more for clothing and farm implements. Worse, Britain and

---

[1]The federal government began tracking such data in 1948.

other foreign nations retaliated against high American tariffs by setting their own high tariffs on American imports—chiefly tobacco, cotton, wheat, and other foodstuffs mostly grown in the South and West. This angered southern farmers because it made their products more expensive—and so less desirable—in foreign markets.

The tariff pitted one section of the nation against another, especially North vs. South. The years from 1809 to 1828 were marked by growth and governmental expansion; but new problems—none more important than the question of slavery—loomed ever larger and more menacing.

Madison in Power

In his inaugural address, James Madison observed that the "present situation" of the United States was "full of difficulties" and that war continued to rage among European powers. Yet he assumed the presidency, he said, "with no other discouragement than what springs from my own inadequacy." The content of the speech was as modest as its delivery; virtually no one could hear it.

●●●─ Read the Document

Madison, *First Inaugural Address* at **myhistorylab.com**

Madison was narrower in his interests than Jefferson but in many ways a deeper thinker. He was more conscientious in the performance of his duties and more consistent in adhering to his principles. Ideologically, however, they were as close as two active and intelligent people could be. Madison had no better solution to offer for the problem of the hour than had Jefferson. The Embargo Act had failed and its successor, the Non-Intercourse Act, proved difficult to enforce—once an American ship left port, there was no way to prevent the skipper from steering for England or France. The British continued to seize American vessels.

Because prudent captains remained in port, trade stagnated. Federal revenue through the tariff declined. In 1809, Secretary of the Treasury Gallatin was alarmed by the growing federal deficit. He urged Representative Nathaniel Macon of North Carolina to introduce legislation to remove all restrictions on commerce with France and Britain. Known as Macon's Bill No. 2, it authorized the president to reapply the principle of non-intercourse to either of the major powers if the other should "cease to violate the neutral commerce of the United States." This bill became law in May 1810.

The volume of U.S. commerce with the British Isles zoomed to pre-embargo levels. The mighty British fleet controlled the seas. Napoleon therefore announced that he had repealed his decrees against neutral shipping, seemingly fulfilling the provisions of Macon's Bill No. 2. Madison, seeking concessions from Britain, closed American ports to British ships and goods. Napoleon, despite his announcement to the contrary, continued to seize American ships and cargoes whenever it suited his purposes.

The British refused to modify the Orders in Council. Madison could not afford either to admit that Napoleon had deceived him or to reverse American policy still another time. Reluctantly he came to the conclusion that unless Britain repealed the Orders, the United States must declare war.

Tecumseh and Indian Resistance

There were other reasons for war with Britain besides its violations of neutral rights. The Indians were again restive, and western farmers believed that the British in Canada were egging them on. This had been true in the past but was no longer the case in 1811 and 1812.

As a young man Tecumseh was a superb hunter and warrior; his younger brother, Tenskwatawa, was awkward and inept with weapons; he accidentally gouged out his right eye with an arrow. In 1805 he had a religious vision, became known as "The Prophet," and inspired Tecumseh's warriors.

American domination of the southern Great Lakes region was no longer in question. Canadian officials had no desire to force a showdown between the Indians and the Americans, for that could have but one result. Aware of their own vulnerability, the Canadians wanted to preserve Indian strength in case war should break out between Great Britain and the United States.

●●●[Read the Document

Pennsylvania *Gazette*, "Indian hostilities" at
myhistorylab.com

American political leaders tended to believe that Indians should be encouraged to become farmers and to copy the "civilized" ways of whites. However, no government had been able to control the frontiersmen, who by bribery, trickery, and force were driving the tribes back year after year from the rich lands of the Ohio Valley. General William Henry Harrison, governor of the Indiana Territory, kept constant pressure on them. He wrested land from one tribe by promising it aid against a traditional enemy, from another as a penalty for having murdered a white man, from others by corrupting a few chiefs. Harrison justified his sordid behavior by citing the end in view—that "one of the fairest portions of the globe" be secured as "the seat of civilization, of science, and of true religion." The "wretched savages" should not be allowed to stand in the path of this worthy objective. Unless something drastic was done, Harrison's aggressiveness, together with the corroding effects of white civilization, would soon obliterate the tribes.

Tecumseh, the Shawnee chief, made a bold and imaginative effort to reverse the trend by binding all the tribes east of the Mississippi into a great confederation. Traveling from the Wisconsin country to the Floridas, he persuaded tribe after tribe to join him.

To Tecumseh's political movement his brother Tenskwatawa, known as "The Prophet," added the force of a moral crusade. Instead of aping white customs, the Prophet said that Indians must give up white ways, white clothes, and white liquor and reinvigorate their own culture. Ceding lands to the whites must stop because the Great Spirit intended that the land be used in common by all.

The Prophet saw visions and claimed to be able to control the movement of heavenly bodies. Tecumseh, however, possessed true genius. A powerful orator and a great organizer, he had deep insight into the needs of his people. Harrison himself said of Tecumseh, "He is one of those uncommon geniuses which spring up occasionally to produce revolutions and overturn the established order of things." The two brothers made a formidable team. By 1811 thousands of Indians were organizing to drive the whites off Indian land.

With about a thousand soldiers, General Harrison marched against the brothers' camp at Prophetstown in Indiana. Tecumseh was away recruiting men, and the Prophet recklessly ordered an assault on Harrison's camp outside the village on November 7, 1811. When the white soldiers held their ground despite the Prophet's magic, the Indians lost confidence and fell back. Harrison then destroyed Prophetstown.

Unwilling as usual to admit that their own excesses were the chief cause of the trouble, the settlers directed their resentment at the British in Canada. "This combination headed by the Shawanese prophet is a British scheme," a resolution adopted by the citizens of Vincennes, Indiana, proclaimed. As a result, the cry for war with Great Britain rang along the frontier.

Depression and Land Hunger

Some westerners pressed for war because they were suffering an agricultural depression. The prices they received for their wheat, tobacco, and other products in the markets of New Orleans were falling, and they attributed the decline to the loss of foreign markets and the depredations of the British. American commercial restrictions had more to do with the western depression than the British, and in any case the slow and cumbersome transportation and distribution system that western farmers were saddled with was the major cause of their difficulties. But the farmers were no more inclined to accept these explanations than they were to absolve the British from responsibility for the Indian difficulties. If only the seas were free, they reasoned, costs would go down, prices would rise, and prosperity would return.

It was primarily because of Canada, nearby and presumably vulnerable, that westerners wanted war. President Madison probably regarded an attack on Canada as a way to force the British to respect neutral rights. Still more important in Madison's mind, if the United States conquered Canada, Britain's hope of obtaining food in Canada for its West Indian sugar islands would be shattered. Then it would have to end its hateful assaults and restrictions on American merchant ships or the islands' economy would collapse.

But westerners, and many easterners too, were more patriots than imperialists or merchants in 1811 and 1812. When the **War Hawks** (their young leaders in Congress) called for war against Great Britain, they did so because they saw no other way to defend the national honor and force repeal of the Orders in Council. The choice seemed to lie between war and surrender of true independence. As Madison put it, to bow to British policy would be to "recolonize" American foreign commerce.

Opponents of War

Large numbers of people, however, thought that a war against Great Britain would be a national calamity. No shipowner could view with equanimity the idea of taking on the largest navy in the world. Such persons complained sincerely enough about impressment and the Orders in Council, but war seemed worse to them by far. Self-interest led them to urge patience.

Such a policy would have been wise, for Great Britain did not represent a real threat to the United States. British naval officers were high-handed, officials in London complacent, British diplomats in Washington second-rate and obtuse. Yet language, culture, and strong economic ties bound the two countries. Napoleon, on the other hand, represented a tremendous potential danger. He had offhandedly turned over Louisiana, but even Jefferson, the chief beneficiary of his largesse, hated everything he stood for. Jefferson called Napoleon "an unprincipled tyrant who is deluging the continent of Europe with blood."

No one understood the Napoleonic danger to America more clearly than the British; part of the stubbornness and arrogance of their maritime policy grew out of their conviction that Napoleon was a threat to all free nations. The *Times* of London declared, "The Alps and the Apennines of America are the British Navy. If ever that should be removed, a short time will suffice to establish the headquarters of a [French] Duke-Marshal at Washington." Yet by going to war with Britain, the United States was aiding Napoleon.

What made the situation even more unfortunate was the fact that by 1812 conditions had changed in England in a way that made a softening of British maritime policy likely. A depression caused chiefly by the increasing effectiveness of Napoleon's Continental System was plaguing the country. Manufacturers, blaming the slump on the loss of American markets, were urging repeal of the Orders in Council. On June 23, after a change of ministries, the new foreign secretary, Lord Castlereagh, suspended the Orders. Five days earlier, alas, the United States had declared war.

The War of 1812

In the first phase of the war, 1812–1813, the United States attempted to invade Canada near Detroit, Buffalo, and Plattsburgh (New York); it failed. In the second phase, 1814, the British invaded the Chesapeake and burned Washington, DC. The final phase of the war occurred from November 1814 to early 1815, after the Treaty of Ghent was signed. British troops landed at the mouth of the Mississippi River and were defeated by General Andrew Jackson at New Orleans.

The illogic of the War Hawks in pressing for a fight was exceeded only by their ineffectiveness in planning and managing what would become the **War of 1812**. By what possible strategy could the ostensible objective of the war be achieved? To construct a navy capable of challenging the British fleet would have been the work of many years and a more expensive proposition than the War Hawks were willing to consider. Several hundred merchant ships lashed a few cannon to their decks and sailed off as privateers to attack British commerce. The navy's seven modern frigates, built during the war scare after the XYZ Affair, put to sea. But these forces could make no pretense of disputing Britain's mastery of the Atlantic.

For a brief moment the American frigates held center stage, for they were faster, tougher, larger, and more powerfully armed than their British counterparts. Barely two months after the declaration of war, Captain Isaac Hull of the USS *Constitution* chanced upon the HMS *Guerrière* mid-Atlantic, outmaneuvered the *Guerrière* brilliantly, and gunned it into submission. In October the USS *United States* caught the HMS *Macedonian* off the Madeiras, pounded it unmercifully at long range, and forced the British

The USS *Constitution*, restored in 1997.

ship to surrender. The *Macedonian* was taken into New London as a prize; over a third of the 300-man crew were casualties, while American losses were but a dozen. Then, in December, the *Constitution*, now under Captain William Bainbridge, took on the British frigate *Java* off Brazil. "Old Ironsides" shot away *Java's* mainmast and reduced it to a hulk too battered for salvage.

These victories had little influence on the outcome of the war. The Royal Navy had thirty-four frigates, seven more powerful ships of the line, and dozens of smaller vessels. As soon as these forces could concentrate against them, the American frigates were immobilized, forced to spend the war gathering barnacles at their moorings while powerful British squadrons ranged offshore. The privateering merchantmen were more effective because they were so numerous; they captured more than 1,300 British vessels during the war. The best of them—vessels like the *America* and the *True-Blooded Yankee*—were redesigned, given more sail to increase their speed, and formidably armed. The *America* captured twenty-six prizes valued at more than a million dollars. The *True-Blooded Yankee* took twenty-seven vessels and destroyed seven more in a Scottish harbor.

Great Britain's one weak spot seemed to be Canada. The colony had but half a million inhabitants to oppose 7.5 million Americans. Only 2,257 British regulars guarded the long border from Montréal to Detroit. The Canadian militia was feeble, and many of its members, being American-born, sympathized with the "invaders." According to the War Hawk congressman Henry Clay of Kentucky, the West was one solid horde of ferocious frontiersmen, armed to the teeth and thirsting for Canadian blood. Yet such talk was mostly brag and bluster; when Congress authorized increasing the army by 25,000 men, Kentucky produced 400 enlistments.

American military leadership proved extremely disappointing. Madison showed poor judgment by relying on officers who had served with distinction in the Revolution. Instead of a concentrated strike against Canada's St. Lawrence River lifeline, which would have isolated Upper Canada, the generals planned a complicated three-pronged attack. It failed dismally. In July 1812 General William Hull, veteran of the battles of Trenton, Saratoga, and Monmouth and now governor of the Michigan Territory, marched forth with 2,200 men against the Canadian positions facing Detroit. Hoping that the Canadian militia would desert, he delayed his assault, only to find his communications threatened by hostile Indians led by Tecumseh. Hastily he retreated to Detroit, and when the Canadians, under General Isaac Brock, pursued him, he surrendered the fort without firing a shot! In October

In the heat of the Battle of Lake Erie, Perry had to abandon his flagship, the *Lawrence*, which had been shot to pieces by enemy fire. (Over three-fourths of the ship's crew were killed or wounded.) He was rowed to the *Niagara*, from which he directed the rest of the engagement.

another force attempted to invade Canada from Fort Niagara. After an initial success it was crushed by superior numbers, while a large contingent of New York militiamen watched from the east bank of the Niagara River, unwilling to fight outside their own state.

The third arm of the American "attack" was equally unsuccessful. Major General Henry Dearborn, who had fought honorably in the Revolution from Bunker Hill to Yorktown, but who had now grown so fat that he needed a specially designed cart to get from place to place, set out from Plattsburgh, New York, at the head of an army of militiamen. Their objective was Montréal, but when they reached the border, the troops refused to cross. Dearborn meekly marched them back to Plattsburgh.

Meanwhile, the British had captured Fort Michilimackinac in northern Michigan, and the Indians had taken Fort Dearborn (now Chicago), massacring eighty-five captives. Instead of sweeping triumphantly through Canada, the Americans found themselves trying desperately to keep the Canadians out of Ohio.

Stirred by these disasters, westerners rallied somewhat in 1813. General Harrison, the victor of Tippecanoe, headed an army of Kentuckians in a series of inconclusive battles against British troops and Indians led by Tecumseh. He found it impossible to recapture Detroit because a British squadron controlling Lake Erie threatened his communications. President Madison therefore assigned Captain Oliver Hazard Perry to the task of building a fleet to challenge this force. In September 1813, at Put-in-Bay near the western end of the lake, Perry destroyed the British vessels in a battle in which 85 of the 103 men on Perry's flagship were casualties. "We have met the enemy and

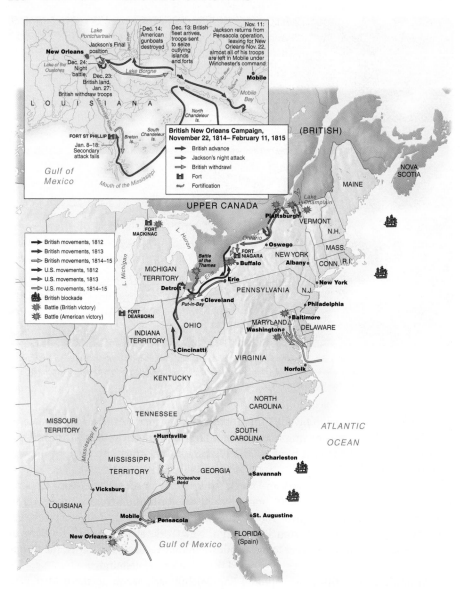

The War of 1812 In the first phase of the war, 1812–1813, the United States attempted to invade Canada near Detroit, Buffalo, and Plattsburgh (New York); it failed. In the second phase, 1814, the British invaded the Chesapeake and burned Washington, DC. The final phase of the war occurred from November 1814 to early 1815, after the Treaty of Ghent was signed. British troops landed at the mouth of the Mississippi River and were defeated by General Andrew Jackson at New Orleans.

they are ours," he reported. About a quarter of Perry's 400 men were blacks, which led him to remark that "the color of a man's skin" was no more an indication of his worth than "the cut and trimmings" of his coat. With the Americans in control of Lake Erie, Detroit became untenable for the British, and when they fell back, Harrison gave chase and defeated them at the Thames River, some 60 miles northeast of Detroit. Although little more than a skirmish, this battle had large repercussions. Tecumseh was among the dead and without him the Indians lost heart. But American attempts to win control of Lake Ontario and to invade Canada in the Niagara region were again thrown back. Late in 1813 the British captured Fort Niagara and burned the town of Buffalo. The conquest of Canada was as far from realization as ever.

The British fleet had intensified its blockade of American ports, extending its operations to New England waters previously spared to encourage the antiwar sentiments of local maritime interests. All along the coast, patrolling cruisers, contemptuous of Jefferson's puny gunboats, captured small craft, raided shore points to commandeer provisions, and collected ransom from port towns by threatening to bombard them. One captain even sent a detail ashore to dig potatoes for his ship's mess.

Britain Assumes the Offensive

Until 1814 the British put relatively little effort into the American war, being concerned primarily with the struggle against Napoleon. However, in 1812 Napoleon had invaded Russia and been thrown back; thereafter, one by one, his European satellites rose against him. Gradually he relinquished his conquests, and in April 1814 the Allies drove Napoleon from power. Then the British, free to strike hard at the United States, dispatched some 14,000 veterans to Canada.

By the spring of 1814 British strategists had devised a master plan for crushing the United States. One army, 11,000 strong, was to march from Montréal, tracing the route that General Burgoyne had followed to disaster in the Revolution. A smaller amphibious force was to make a feint at the Chesapeake Bay area, destroying coastal towns and threatening Washington and Baltimore. A third army was to assemble at Jamaica and sail to attack New Orleans and bottle up the West.

While the main British army was assembling in Canada, some 4,000 veterans under General Robert Ross sailed from Bermuda for the Chesapeake. After making a rendezvous with a fleet commanded by Vice Admiral Sir Alexander Cochrane and Rear Admiral Sir George Cockburn, which had been terrorizing the coast, they landed in Maryland at the mouth of the Patuxent River, southeast of Washington. A squadron of gunboats "protecting" the capital promptly withdrew upstream; when the British pursued, their commander ordered them blown up to keep them from being captured.

The British troops marched rapidly toward Washington. At Bladensburg, on the outskirts of the city, they came upon an army twice their number, commanded by General William H. Winder, a Baltimore lawyer who had already been captured and released by the British in the Canadian fighting. While President Madison and other officials watched, the British charged—and Winder's army turned tail almost without firing a shot. The British swarmed into the capital and put most public buildings to the torch. Before personally setting fire to the White House, Admiral Cockburn took one of the president's hats and a cushion from Dolley Madison's chair as souvenirs, and, finding the table set for dinner, derisively drank a toast to "Jemmy's health."

•◆•⌐Read the Document

Dolley Payne Madison to Lucy Payne Todd at **myhistorylab.com**

This was the sum of the British success. When they attempted to take Baltimore, they were stopped by a formidable line of defenses devised by General Samuel Smith, a militia officer. General Ross fell in the attack. The fleet then moved up the Patapsco

River and pounded Fort McHenry with its cannon, raining 1,800 shells upon it in a twenty-five-hour bombardment on September 13 and 14.

"The Star Spangled Banner"

While this attack was in progress, an American civilian, Francis Scott Key, who had been temporarily detained on one of the British ships, watched anxiously through the night. As twilight faded, Key had seen the Stars and Stripes flying proudly over the battered fort. During the night the glare of rockets and bursting of bombs proved that the defenders were holding out. Then, by the first light of the new day, Key saw again the flag, still waving over Fort McHenry. Drawing an old letter from his pocket, he dashed off the words to "The Star Spangled Banner," which, when set to music, was to become the national anthem of the United States.

To Key that dawn seemed a turning point in the war. He was roughly correct, for in those last weeks of the summer of 1814 the struggle began to move toward resolution. Unable to crack the defenses of Baltimore, the British withdrew to their ships; shortly after, they sailed to Jamaica to join the forces preparing to attack New Orleans.

The destruction of Washington had been a profound shock. Thousands came forward to enlist in the army. The new determination and spirit were strengthened by news from the northern front, where General Sir George Prevost had been leading the main British invasion force south from Montréal. At Plattsburgh, on the western shore of Lake Champlain, his 1,000 Redcoats came up against a well-designed defense line manned by 3,300 Americans under General Alexander Macomb. Prevost called up his

The Bombardment of Fort McHenry by John Bower, with the Stars and Stripes flying over the fort (center). The British fleet fired 1,800 bombs and red-glaring incendiary rockets. The fort did not return fire because the British ships were beyond the range of its cannon. Although "The Star Spangled Banner" celebrates the "home of the brave," the defenders of Fort McHenry sensibly fled the ramparts and took cover below during the bombardment; they sustained only thirty casualties.

supporting fleet of four ships and a dozen gunboats. An American fleet of roughly similar strength under Captain Thomas Macdonough came forward to oppose the British. On September 11, in a brutal battle at point-blank range, Macdonough destroyed the British ships and drove off the gunboats. With the Americans now threatening his flank, Prevost lost heart and retreated to Canada.

The Treaty of Ghent

The war might as well have ended with the battles of Plattsburgh, Washington, and Baltimore, for later military developments had no effect on the outcome. Earlier in 1814 both sides had agreed to discuss peace terms. Commissioners were appointed and negotiations begun during the summer at Ghent, in Belgium.

The talks at Ghent were drawn out and frustrating. The British were in no hurry to sign a treaty, believing that their three-pronged offensive in 1814 would swing the balance in their favor. But news of the defeat at Plattsburgh modified their ambitions, and when the Duke of Wellington advised that from a military point of view they had no case for territorial concessions so long as the United States controlled the Great Lakes, they agreed to settle for *status quo ante bellum*, to leave things as they were before the war. The other issues, everyone suddenly realized, had simply evaporated. The mighty war triggered by the French Revolution seemed finally over. The seas were free to all ships, and the Royal Navy no longer had need to snatch sailors from the vessels of the United States or of any other power. On Christmas Eve 1814 the treaty, which merely ended the state of hostilities, was signed. Although, like other members of his family, he was not noted for tact, John Quincy Adams rose to the spirit of the occasion. "I hope," he said, "it will be the last treaty of peace between Great Britain and the United States." And so it was.

●●◀─[**Read the Document**

The Treaty of Ghent at **myhistorylab.com**

The Hartford Convention

Before news of the treaty could cross the Atlantic, two events took place that had important effects but that would not have occurred had the news reached America more rapidly. The first was the **Hartford Convention**, a meeting of New England Federalists held in December 1814 and January 1815 to protest the war and to plan for a convention of the states to revise the Constitution.

Sentiment in New England had opposed the war from the beginning. The governor of Massachusetts titled his annual address in 1813 "On the Present Unhappy War," and the General Court went on record calling the conflict "impolitic, improper, and unjust." The Federalist party had been quick to employ the discontent to revive its fortunes. Federalist-controlled state administrations refused to provide militia to aid in the fight and discouraged individuals and banks from lending money to the hard-pressed national government. Trade with the enemy flourished as long as the British fleet did not crack down on New England ports, and goods flowed across the Canadian line in as great or greater volume as during Jefferson's embargo.

Their attitude toward the war made the Federalists even more unpopular with the rest of the country, and this in turn encouraged extremists to talk of seceding from the Union. After Massachusetts summoned the meeting of the Hartford Convention, the fear was widespread that the delegates would propose a New England Confederacy, thereby striking at the Union in a moment of great trial.

Luckily for the country, moderate Federalists controlled the convention. They approved a statement that in the case of "deliberate, dangerous and palpable infractions of the Constitution" a state has the right "to interpose its authority" to protect itself. This concept, similar to that expressed in the Kentucky and Virginia resolutions by the Republicans when they were in the minority, was accompanied by a list of proposed constitutional amendments designed to weaken the federal government, reduce Congress's power to restrict trade, and limit presidents to a single term.

Nothing formally proposed at Hartford was treasonable, but the proceedings were kept secret, and rumors of impending secession were rife. In this atmosphere came the news from Ghent of an honorable peace. The Federalists had been denouncing the war and predicting a British triumph; now they were discredited.

The Battle of New Orleans and the End of the War

Still more discrediting to Federalists was the second event that would not have happened had communications been more rapid: the Battle of New Orleans. During the fall of 1814 the British had gathered an army at Negril Bay in Jamaica, commanded by Major General Sir Edward Pakenham, brother-in-law of the Duke of Wellington. Late in November an armada of sixty ships set out for New Orleans with 11,000 soldiers. Instead of sailing directly up from the mouth of the Mississippi as the Americans expected, Pakenham approached the city by way of Lake Borgne, to the east. Proceeding through a maze of swamps and bayous, he advanced close to the city's gates before being detected. Early on the afternoon of December 23, three mud-spattered local planters burst into the headquarters of General Andrew Jackson, commanding the defenses of New Orleans, with the news.

For once in this war of error and incompetence the United States had the right man in the right place at the right time. After his Revolutionary War experiences, Jackson had studied law, then moved west, settling in Nashville, Tennessee. He served briefly in both houses of Congress and was active in Tennessee affairs. Jackson was a hard man and fierce-tempered, frequently involved in brawls and duels, but honest and, by western standards, a good public servant. When the war broke out, he was named major general of volunteers. Almost alone among nonprofessional troops during the conflict, his men won impressive victories, savagely crushing the Creek Indians in a series of battles in Alabama.

Following these victories, Jackson was assigned the job of defending the Gulf Coast against the expected British strike. Although he had misjudged Pakenham's destination, he was ready when the news of the British arrival reached him. "By the Eternal," he vowed, "they shall not sleep on our soil." "Gentlemen," he told his staff officers, "the British are below, we must fight them tonight."

While the British rested and awaited reinforcements, planning to take the city the next morning, Jackson rushed up men and guns. At 7:30 PM on December 23 he attacked, taking the British by surprise. But Pakenham's veterans rallied quickly, and the battle was inconclusive. With Redcoats pouring in from the fleet, Jackson fell back to a point five miles below New Orleans and dug in.

He chose his position wisely. On his right was the Mississippi, on his left an impenetrable swamp, to the front an open field. On the day before Christmas (while the commissioners in Ghent were signing the peace treaty), Jackson's army, which included a segregated unit of free black militiamen, erected an earthen parapet about ten yards behind a dry canal bed. Here the Americans would make their stand.

General Andrew Jackson, on the horse, exhorts his men to throw back the advancing British; they succeed, and Jackson becomes a war hero.

For two weeks Pakenham probed the American line. Jackson strengthened his defenses daily. At night, patrols of silent Tennesseans slipped out with knives and tomahawks to stalk British sentries. They called this grim business "going hunting." On January 8, 1815, Pakenham ordered an all-out frontal assault. The American position was formidable, but these were men who had defeated Napoleon. At dawn, through the lowland mists, the Redcoats moved forward with fixed bayonets. Pakenham assumed that the undisciplined Americans—about 4,500 strong—would run at the sight of bare steel.

The Americans did not run. Perhaps they feared the wrath of their commander more than enemy bayonets. Artillery raked the advancing British, and when the range closed to about 150 yards, the riflemen opened up. Jackson had formed his men in three ranks behind the parapet. One rank fired, then stepped down as another took its place. By the time the third had loosed its volley, the first had reloaded and was ready to fire again. Nothing could stand against this rain of lead. General Pakenham was wounded twice, then killed by a shell fragment while calling up his last reserves. During the battle a single brave British officer reached the top of the parapet. When retreat was finally sounded, the British had suffered almost 2,100 casualties, including nearly 300 killed. Thirteen Americans lost their lives, and fifty-eight more were wounded or missing.

Word of Jackson's magnificent triumph reached Washington almost simultaneously with the good news from Ghent. People found it easy to confuse the chronology and consider the war a victory won on the battlefield below New Orleans instead of the standoff it had been. Jackson became the "Hero of New Orleans"; his proud fellow citizens rated his military abilities superior to those of the Duke of Wellington. The nation rejoiced. One sour Republican complained that the Federalists of Massachusetts had fired off more powder and wounded more men celebrating the victory than they had during the whole course of the conflict. The Senate ratified the peace treaty unanimously, and the frustrations and failures of the past few years were forgotten. Moreover, American success in holding off Great Britain despite internal frictions went a long way toward convincing European nations that both the United States and its republican form of government were here to stay. The powers might accept these truths with less pleasure than the Americans, but accept them they did.

Anglo-American Rapprochement

There remained a few matters to straighten out with Great Britain, Spain, and Europe generally. Since no territory had changed hands at Ghent, neither signatory had reason to harbor a grudge. For years no serious trouble marred Anglo-American relations. The war had taught the British to respect Americans, if not to love them.

In this atmosphere the two countries worked out peaceful solutions to a number of old problems. American trade was becoming ever more important to the British, that of the sugar islands less so. In July 1815 they therefore signed a commercial convention ending discriminatory duties and making other adjustments favorable to trade. Boundary difficulties also moved toward resolution. At Ghent the diplomats had created several joint commissions to settle the disputed boundary between the United States and Canada. Many years were to pass before the line was finally drawn, but establishing the principle of defining the border by negotiation was important. In time, a line extending over 3,000 miles was agreed to without the firing of a single shot.

Immediately after the war the British reinforced their garrisons in Canada and began to rebuild their shattered Great Lakes fleet. The United States took similar steps. But both nations found the cost of rearming more than they cared to bear. When the United States suggested demilitarizing the lakes, the British agreed. The Rush-Bagot Agreement of 1817 limited each country to one 100-ton vessel armed with a single eighteen-pounder on Lake Champlain and another on Lake Ontario. The countries were to have two each for all the other Great Lakes.

Gradually, as an outgrowth of this decision, the entire border was demilitarized, a remarkable achievement. In the Convention of 1818 the two countries agreed to the forty-ninth parallel as the northern boundary of the Louisiana Territory between the Lake of the Woods and the Rockies, and to the joint control of the Oregon country for ten years. The question of the rights of Americans in the Labrador and Newfoundland fisheries, which had been much disputed during the Ghent negotiations, was settled amicably.

The Transcontinental Treaty

The acquisition of Spanish Florida and the settlement of the western boundary of Louisiana were also accomplished as an aftermath of the War of 1812, but in a far different spirit. Spain's control of the Floridas was feeble. West Florida had passed into American hands by 1813, and frontiersmen in Georgia were eyeing East Florida greedily. Indians struck frequently into Georgia from Florida, then fled to sanctuary across the line. American slaves who escaped across the border could not be recovered. In 1818 James Monroe, who had been elected president in 1816, ordered General

Andrew Jackson to clear raiding Seminole Indians from American soil and to pursue them into Florida if necessary. Seizing on these instructions, Jackson marched into Florida and easily captured two Spanish forts.

Although Jackson eventually withdrew from Florida, the impotence of the Spanish government made it obvious even in Madrid that if nothing were done, the United States would soon fill the power vacuum by seizing the territory. The Spanish minister in Washington, Luis de Onís, set out in December 1817 to negotiate a treaty with John Quincy Adams, Monroe's secretary of state. Adams pressed the minister mercilessly on the question of Louisiana's western boundary and eventually the minister agreed to accept a boundary that followed the Sabine, Red, and Arkansas Rivers to the Continental Divide and the forty-second parallel to the Pacific, thus abandoning Spain's claim to a huge area beyond the Rockies that had no connection at all with the Louisiana Purchase. The United States obtained Florida in return for a mere $5 million.

This **Transcontinental Treaty** was signed in 1819, although ratification was delayed until 1821. Most Americans at the time thought the acquisition of Florida the most important part of the treaty, but Adams, whose vision of America's future was truly continental, knew better. "The acquisition of a definite line of boundary to the [Pacific] forms a great epoch in our history," he recorded in his diary.

The Monroe Doctrine

Concern with defining the boundaries of the United States did not reflect a desire to limit expansion; rather, most Americans felt that quibbling and quarreling with foreign powers might prove a distraction from the great task of

●●─[Read the Document
Monroe Doctrine at
myhistorylab.com

national development. The classic enunciation of this point of view, the completion of America's withdrawal from Europe, was the **Monroe Doctrine**.

Two separate strands met in this pronouncement. The first led from Moscow to Alaska and down the Pacific coast to the Oregon country. Beginning with the explorations of Vitus Bering in 1741, the Russians had maintained an interest in fishing and fur trading along the northwest coast of North America. In 1821 the czar extended his claim south to the fifty-first parallel and forbade the ships of other powers to enter coastal waters north of that point. This announcement was disturbing.

The second strand ran from the courts of the European monarchs to Latin America. Between 1817 and 1822 practically all of the region from the Rio Grande to the southernmost tip of South America had won its independence. Spain, former master of all the area except Brazil, was too weak to win it back by force, but Austria, Prussia, France, and Russia decided at the Congress of Verona in 1822 to try to regain the area for Spain in the interests of "legitimacy." There was talk of sending a large French army to South America. This possibility also caused grave concern in Washington.

To the Russian threat, Monroe and Secretary of State Adams responded with a terse warning: "The American continents are no longer subjects for any new European colonial establishments." This statement did not impress the Russians, but they had no intention of colonizing the region. In 1824 they signed a treaty with the United States abandoning all claims below the present southern limit of Alaska (54°40'; north latitude) and removing their restrictions on foreign shipping.

HARBOUR of NEW ARCHANGEL in SITCA or NORFOLK SOUND.

The harbor of New Archangel in Sitka, Alaska, part of the Russian empire's expansive claims to North America.

The Latin American problem was more complex. The United States was not alone in its alarm at the prospect of a revival of French or Spanish power in that region. Great Britain, having profited greatly from the breakup of the mercantilist Spanish empire by developing a thriving commerce with the new republics, had no intention of permitting a restoration of the old order. But the British monarchy preferred not to recognize the new revolutionary South American republics, for England itself was only beginning to recover from a period of social upheaval as violent as any in its history. Bad times and high food prices had combined to cause riots, conspiracies, and angry demands for parliamentary reform.

In 1823 the British foreign minister, George Canning, suggested to the American minister in London that the United States and Britain issue a joint statement opposing any French interference in South America, pledging that they themselves would never annex any part of Spain's old empire, and saying nothing about recognition of the new republics. This proposal of joint action with the British was flattering to the United States but scarcely in its best interests. The United States had already recognized the new republics, and it had no desire to help Great Britain retain its South American trade. As Secretary Adams pointed out, to agree to the proposal would be to abandon the possibility of someday adding Cuba or any other part of Latin America to the United States. America should act independently, Adams urged.

Monroe heartily endorsed Adams's argument and decided to include a statement of American policy in his annual message to Congress in December 1823. "The American continents," he wrote, "by the free and independent condition which they have assumed and maintain, are henceforth not to be considered as subjects for future colonization by any European powers." Europe's political system was "essentially

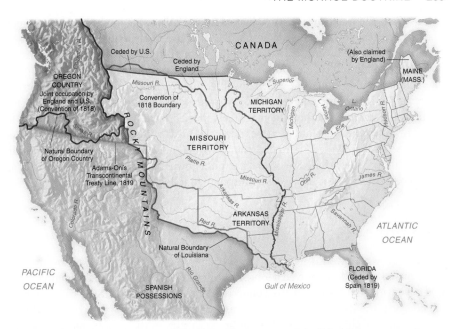

The United States, 1819 As American settlers ventured farther westward, the United States government sought to extend the nation's boundaries, negotiating with Spain for control of Florida and border sections of the Southwest, and with Britain for the Oregon Country.

different" from that developing in the New World, and the two should not be mixed. The United States would not interfere with existing European colonies in North or South America and would avoid involvement in strictly European affairs, but any attempt to extend European control to countries in the hemisphere that had already won their independence would be considered, Monroe warned, "the manifestation of an unfriendly disposition toward the United States" and consequently a threat to the nation's "peace and safety."

This policy statement—it was not dignified with the title Monroe Doctrine until decades later—attracted little notice in Europe or Latin America and not much more at home. European statesmen dismissed Monroe's message as "arrogant" and "blustering," worthy only of "the most profound contempt." Latin Americans, while appreciating the intent behind it, knew better than to count on American aid in case of attack from European powers.

Nevertheless, the principles laid down by President Monroe so perfectly expressed the wishes of the people of the United States that when the country grew powerful enough to enforce them, there was little need to alter or embellish his pronouncement. However understood at the time, the doctrine may be seen as the final stage in the evolution of American independence.

From this perspective, the famous Declaration of 1776 merely began a process of separation and self-determination. The peace treaty ending the Revolutionary War was a further step, and Washington's Declaration of Neutrality in 1793 was another, demonstrating as it did the capacity of the United States to determine its own best interests despite the treaty of alliance with France. The removal of British troops from the northwest forts, achieved by the otherwise ignominious Jay Treaty, marked the next stage. Then the Louisiana Purchase made a further advance toward true independence by ensuring that the Mississippi River could not be closed to the commerce so vital to the development of the western territories.

The standoff War of 1812 ended any lingering British hope of regaining control of America, the Latin American revolutions further weakened colonialism in the Western Hemisphere, and the Transcontinental Treaty pushed the last European power from the path of westward expansion. Monroe's "doctrine" was a kind of public announcement that the sovereign United States had completed its independence and wanted nothing better than to be left alone to concentrate on its own development. Better yet, Europe should be made to allow the entire hemisphere to follow its own path.

The Era of Good Feelings

The person who gave his name to the so-called Monroe Doctrine was an unusually lucky man. James Monroe lived a long life in good health and saw close up most of the great events in the history of the young republic. At the age of 18 he shed his blood for liberty at the Battle of Trenton. He was twice governor of Virginia, a United States senator, and a Cabinet member. He was at various times the nation's representative in Paris, Madrid, and London. Elected president in 1816, his good fortune continued. The world was finally at peace, the country united and prosperous. A person of good feeling who would keep a steady hand on the helm and hold to the present course seemed called for, and Monroe possessed exactly the qualities that the times required. "He is a man whose soul might be turned wrongside outwards, without discovering a blemish," Jefferson said, and John Quincy Adams, a harsh critic of public figures, praised Monroe's courtesy, sincerity, and sound judgment.

By 1817 the divisive issues of earlier days had vanished. Monroe dramatized their disappearance by beginning his first term with a goodwill tour of New England, heartland of the opposition. The tour was a triumph. Everywhere the president was greeted with tremendous enthusiasm. After he visited Boston, once the headquarters and now the graveyard of Federalism, a Federalist newspaper, the *Columbian Centinel*, gave the age its name. Pointing out that the celebrations attending Monroe's visit had brought together in friendly intercourse many persons "whom party politics had long severed," it dubbed the times the **Era of Good Feelings**.

The people of the period had good reasons for thinking it extraordinarily harmonious. Peace, prosperity, liberty, and progress all flourished in 1817 in the United States. The heirs of Jefferson had accepted, with a mixture of resignation and enthusiasm, most of the economic policies advocated by the Hamiltonians.

The Jeffersonian balance between individual liberty and responsible government, having survived both bad management and war, had justified itself to the opposition. The new unity was symbolized by the restored friendship of Jefferson and John Adams. Although they continued to disagree vigorously about matters of philosophy and government, the bitterness between them disappeared entirely. By Monroe's day, Jefferson was writing long letters to "my dear friend," and receiving equally warm and voluminous replies. "Whether you or I were right," Adams wrote amiably to Jefferson, "Posterity must judge."

When political divisions appeared again, as they soon did, it was not because the old balance had been shaky. Few of the new controversies challenged Republican principles or revived old issues. Instead, these controversies were children of the present and the future, products of the continuing growth of the country. From 1790 to 1820, the area of the United States doubled, but very little of the Louisiana Purchase had been settled. More significant, the population of the nation had more than doubled, from 4 million to 9.6 million. The pace of the westward movement had also quickened; by 1820 the moving edge of the frontier ran in a long, irregular curve from Michigan to Arkansas.

New Sectional Issues

The War of 1812 and the depression that struck the country in 1819 had shaped many controversies. The tariff question was affected by both. Before the War of 1812 the level of duties averaged about 12.5 percent of the value of dutiable products, but to meet the added expenses occasioned by the conflict, Congress doubled all tariffs. In 1816, when the revenue was no longer needed, a new act kept duties close to wartime levels. Infant industries that had grown up during the years of embargo, non-intercourse, and war were able to exert considerable pressure. The act especially favored textiles because the British were dumping cloth in America at bargain prices in their attempt to regain lost markets. Unemployed workers and many farmers became convinced that prosperity would return only if American industry were shielded against foreign competition.

At first every section endorsed high duties, but with the passage of time the South rejected protection almost completely. Besides increasing the cost of nearly everything they bought, Southerners exported most of their cotton and tobacco and high duties on imports would limit the foreign market for southern staples by inhibiting international exchange. As this fact became clear, the West tended to divide on the tariff question: The Northwest and much of Kentucky, which had a special interest in protecting its considerable hemp production, favored high duties; the Southwest, where cotton was the major crop, favored low duties.

National banking policy was another important political issue affected by the war and the depression. Presidents Jefferson and Madison had managed to live with the Bank of the United States despite its dubious constitutionality, but its charter was not renewed when it expired in 1811. Aside from the constitutional question, the major opposition to recharter came from state banks eager to take over the business of the Bank for themselves. The fact that English investors owned most of the Bank's stock was also used as an argument against recharter.

Many more state banks were created after 1811, and most extended credit recklessly. When the British raid on Washington and Baltimore in 1814 sent panicky depositors scurrying to convert their deposits into gold or silver, the overextended financiers could not oblige them. All banks outside New England suspended specie payments; that is, they stopped exchanging their bank notes for hard money on demand.

Table 7.1   Key Sectional Issues

Issue	West	South	North
Favorite leaders	Henry Clay (Kentucky)	John Calhoun (South Carolina), William Crawford (Georgia), Andrew Jackson (Tennessee)	John Quincy Adams (Massachusetts), Daniel Webster (Massachusetts), Martin Van Buren (New York)
Should import taxes (tariffs) be high?	Yes and no, depending on the region	No, because high tariffs increased the cost of manufactured goods and harmed export trade (cotton, tobacco)	Yes, because manufacturers and factory workers wanted protection from inexpensive foreign-made products; the exception: New England, because high tariffs harmed trade
Should federal government support construction of roads and canals?	Yes, to reduce transportation costs of products from western farms	No, because this would require more federal revenue— and thus an increase in the tariff	Yes and no, depending on the locality
Should federally owned lands be sold as cheaply as possible?	Yes, because pioneers and farmers needed cheap land	No, because income from land sales would reduce the need for tariffs to raise money; and the products of cheap western farms would compete with southern farms	No, because cheap land in the west would drain off surplus labor and increase labor costs in the East
Should slavery be allowed in the new states being created in the West?	Yes and no, but generally yes because much of the West was economically tied to the South, which supported slavery	Yes, because slaveowners were moving into western regions and were entitled to keep their "property"	No, because new "slave states" would give the South more power in the Senate and because free labor could not fairly compete with a slave system

The shaded boxes indicate the critical issue for each region.

Paper money immediately fell in value; a paper dollar was soon worth only eighty-five cents in coin in Philadelphia, less in Baltimore. Government business also suffered from the absence of a national bank. In October 1814 Secretary of the Treasury Alexander J. Dallas submitted a plan for a second Bank of the United States, and after considerable wrangling over its precise form, the institution was authorized in April 1816.

The new Bank was much larger than its predecessor, being capitalized at $35 million. However, unlike Hamilton's creation, it was badly managed at the start. Its first president, William Jones, a former secretary of the treasury, allowed his institution to join in the irresponsible creation of credit. By the summer of 1818 the Bank's eighteen branches had issued notes in excess of ten times their specie reserves, far more than was prudent, considering the Bank's responsibilities. When depression struck the country in 1819, the Bank of the United States was as hard pressed as many of the state banks. Jones resigned.

The new president, Langdon Cheves of South Carolina, was as rigid as Jones had been permissive. During the bad times, when easy credit was needed, he pursued a policy of stern curtailment. The Bank thus regained a sound position at the expense of hardship to borrowers. "The Bank was saved," the contemporary economist William Gouge wrote somewhat hyperbolically, "and the people were ruined." Indeed, the bank reached a low point in public favor. Irresponsible state banks resented it, as did the advocates of hard money.

Regional lines were less sharply drawn on the Bank issue than on the tariff. Northern congressmen voted against the Bank fifty-three to forty-four in 1816—many of them because they objected to the particular proposal, not because they were against any national bank. Those from other sections favored it, fifty-eight to thirty. The collapse occasioned by the Panic of 1819 produced further opposition to the institution in the West.

Land policy in the West also caused sectional controversy. No one wished to eliminate the system of survey and sale, but there was continuous pressure to reduce the price of public land and the minimum unit offered for sale. The Land Act of 1800 set $2 an acre as the minimum price and 320 acres (a half section) as the smallest unit. In 1804 the minimum was cut to 160 acres, which could be had for about $80 down, roughly a quarter of what the average artisan could earn in a year.

Sectional attitudes toward the public lands were fairly straightforward. The West wanted cheap land; the North and South tended to look on the national domain as an asset that should be converted into as much cash as possible. Northern manufacturers feared that cheap land in the West would drain off surplus labor and force wages up, while southern planters were concerned about the competition that would develop when the virgin lands of the Southwest were put to the plow to make cotton. The West, however, was ready to fight to the last line of defense over land policy, while the other regions would usually compromise on the issue to gain support for their own vital interests.

The most divisive sectional issue was slavery. After the compromises affecting the "peculiar institution" made at the Constitutional Convention, it caused remarkably little conflict in national politics before 1819. Although the importation of blacks rose in the 1790s, Congress abolished the African slave trade in 1808 without major incident. As the nation expanded, free and slave states were added to the Union in equal numbers with Ohio, Indiana, and Illinois being balanced by Louisiana, Mississippi, and Alabama. In 1819 there were twenty-two states, eleven slave and eleven free. The expansion of slavery occasioned by the cotton boom led Southerners to support it more aggressively, which tended to irritate many Northerners, but most persons considered slavery mainly a local issue. To the extent that it was a national question, the North opposed it and the South defended it ardently. The West leaned toward the southern point of view, for in addition to the southwestern slave states, the Northwest was sympathetic, partly because much of its produce was sold on southern plantations and partly because at least half of its early settlers came from Virginia, Kentucky, and other slave states.

New Leaders

By 1824 the giants of the Revolutionary generation had completed their work. Washington, Hamilton, Franklin, Samuel Adams, Patrick Henry, and most of their peers were dead. John Adams (88), Thomas Jefferson (81), and James Madison (73) were passing their declining years quietly on their ancestral acres, full of memories and sage advice, but no longer active in national affairs. In every section new leaders had come forward, men shaped by the past but chiefly concerned with the present. Quite suddenly, between the war and the panic, they had inherited power. They would shape the future of the United States.

In the North, John Quincy Adams was the best-known of the new political leaders. Just completing his brilliant work as secretary of state under Monroe, highlighted by his negotiation of the Transcontinental Treaty and his design of the Monroe Doctrine, he had behind him a record of public service dating to the Confederation period.

Adams was farsighted, imaginative, hardworking, and extremely intelligent, but he was inept in personal relations. He had all the virtues and most of the defects

Samuel Morse, chiefly famous for his work on the telegraph and Morse code, was also a talented painter. His *House of Representatives* (1822–1823) shows the legislators at work at night, a symbolic expression of their commitment to the nation.

Source: Samuel F.B. Morse, *The House of Representatives*. 1822–23. oil on Canvas. 86 $\frac{7}{8}$ × 130 $\frac{5}{8}$. Corcoran Gallery of Art, Museum Purchase, Gallery Fund.

Eyes like "anthracite furnaces," the Scottish historian Thomas Carlyle remarked of Daniel Webster; this is the "Black Dan" portrait by Francis Alexander (1835).
Source: Hood Museum of Art, Dartmouth College, Hanover, New Hampshire, Gift of George C. Shattuck, Class of 1803.

of the puritan, being suspicious both of others and of himself. He suffered in two ways from being his father's child: As the son of a president he was under severe pressure to live up to the Adams name, and his father expected a great deal of him. When the boy was only seven, John Adams wrote the following to his wife: "Train [the children] to virtue. Habituate them to industry, activity, and spirit. Make them consider vice as shameful and unmanly. Fire them with ambition to be useful."

Like his father, John Quincy Adams was a strong nationalist. While New England still opposed high tariffs, he was at least open-minded on the subject. Unlike most easterners, he believed that the federal government should spend freely on roads and canals in the West. To slavery he was, like most New Englanders, personally opposed. As Monroe's second term drew toward its close, Adams seemed one of the most likely candidates to succeed him, and at this period his ambition to be president was his great failing. It led him to make certain compromises with his principles, which in turn plagued his oversensitive conscience and had a corrosive effect on his peace of mind.

Daniel Webster, a congressman from Massachusetts, was recognized as one of the coming leaders of New England. He owed much of his reputation to his formidable presence and his oratorical skill. Dark, broad-chested, large-headed, and craggy of brow, he projected a remarkable appearance of heroic power and moral strength. His thunderous voice, his resourceful vocabulary, and his manner—all backed by the mastery of every oratorical trick—made him unique.

New York's man of the future was a sandy-haired politico named Martin Van Buren. The Red Fox, as he was called, was one of the most talented politicians ever to play a part in American affairs. He was clever and hardworking, but his mind and his energy were always devoted to some political purpose. From 1812 to 1820 he served in the state legislature; in 1820 he was elected United States senator.

Van Buren had great charm and immense tact. By nature affable, he never allowed partisanship to mar his personal relationships with other leaders. The members of his political machine, known as the Albany Regency, were almost fanatically loyal to him, but even his enemies could seldom dislike him as a person.

The most prominent southern leader was William H. Crawford, Monroe's secretary of the treasury. After being elected to the Senate from Georgia, he became controversial. Many of his contemporaries considered him no more than a cynical spoilsman, although his administration of the treasury department was first-rate. Yet he had many friends. His ambition was vast, his power great. Fate, however, was about to strike Crawford a crippling blow.

John C. Calhoun, the other outstanding southern leader, was born in South Carolina in 1782 and graduated from Yale in 1804. After serving in the South Carolina legislature, he was elected to Congress in 1811. He took a strong nationalist position on all the issues of the day. In 1817 Monroe made him secretary of war.

Calhoun, a well-to-do planter, was devoted to the South and its institutions, but he took the broadest possible view of political affairs. John Quincy Adams, seldom charitable in his private opinions of colleagues (he called Crawford "a worm" and Henry Clay a "gamester" with an "undigested system of ethics"), praised Calhoun's "enlarged philosophic views" and considered him "above all sectional and factional prejudices."

The outstanding western leader of the 1820s was Henry Clay of Kentucky, one of the most charming and colorful of American statesmen. On the platform he ranked with Webster; behind the political scenes he was the peer of Van Buren. In every environment he was warm and open—what a modern political scientist might call a charismatic personality. Clay loved to drink, swear, tell tales, and play poker. He was a reasonable man, skilled at arranging political compromises, but he possessed a reckless streak: Twice in his career he challenged men to duels for having insulted him. Fortunately, all concerned were poor shots.

Clay was elected to Congress in 1810. He led the War Hawks in 1811 and 1812 and was Speaker of the House from 1811 to 1820 and from 1823 to 1825.

In the early 1820s he was just developing his **American System**. In return for eastern support of a policy of federal aid in the construction of roads and canals, the West would back the protective tariff. He justified this deal on the widest national grounds. America has a "great diversity of interests," ranging from agriculture and fishing to manufacturing, shipbuilding, and commerce. "The good of each . . . and of the whole should be carefully consulted. This is the only mode by which we can preserve, in full vigor, the harmony of the whole Union." Stimulating manufacturing, for example, would increase the demand for western raw materials, while western prosperity would lead to greater consumption of eastern manufactured goods.

Although himself a slaveowner, Clay called slavery the "greatest of human evils." He favored freeing the slaves and "colonizing" them in Africa, which could, he said, be accomplished gradually and at relatively minor cost.

The Missouri Compromise

The sectional concerns of the 1820s repeatedly influenced politics. The depression of 1819–1822 increased tensions by making people feel more strongly about the issues of the day. For example, manufacturers who wanted high tariffs in 1816 were more vehemently in favor of protection in 1820 when their business fell off. Even when economic conditions improved, geographic alignments on key issues tended to solidify.

One of the first and most critical of the sectional questions concerned the admission of Missouri as a slave state. When Louisiana entered the Union in 1812, the rest of the Louisiana Purchase was organized as the Missouri Territory. Building on a nucleus of Spanish and French inhabitants, the region west and north of St. Louis grew rapidly, and in 1817 the Missourians petitioned for statehood. A large percentage of the settlers—the population exceeded 60,000 by 1818—were Southerners who had moved into the valleys of the Arkansas and Missouri rivers. Since many of them owned slaves, Missouri would become a slave state.

The admission of new states had always been a routine matter in keeping with the admirable pattern established by the Northwest Ordinance. But during the debate on the Missouri Enabling Act in February 1819, Congressman James Tallmadge of New York introduced an amendment prohibiting "the further introduction of slavery" and providing that all slaves born in Missouri after the territory became a state should be freed at age 25.

While Tallmadge was merely seeking to apply in the territory the pattern of race relations that had developed in the states immediately east of Missouri, his amendment represented, at least in spirit, something of a revolution. The Northwest Ordinance had prohibited slavery in the land between the Mississippi and the Ohio, but that area had only a handful of slaveowners in 1787 and little prospect of attracting more. Elsewhere no effort to restrict the movement of slaves into new territory had been attempted. If one assumed (as whites always had) that the slaves themselves should have no say in the matter, it appeared democratic to

●●●⌐Read the **Document**
Missouri Enabling Act at
myhistorylab.com

let the settlers of Missouri decide the slavery question for themselves. Nevertheless, the Tallmadge amendment passed the House, the vote following sectional lines closely. The Senate, however, resoundingly rejected it. The less populous southern part of Missouri was then organized separately as the Arkansas Territory, and an attempt to bar slavery there was stifled. The Missouri Enabling Act failed to pass before Congress adjourned.

When the next Congress met in December 1819, the Missouri issue came up at once. The vote on Tallmadge's amendment had shown that the rapidly growing North controlled the House of Representatives. Southerners thought it vital to preserve a balance in the Senate. Yet Northerners objected to the fact that Missouri extended hundreds of miles north of the Ohio River, which they considered slavery's natural boundary. Angry debate raged in Congress for months.

The debate did not turn on the morality of slavery or the rights of blacks. Northerners objected to adding new slave states because under the Three-Fifths Compromise these states would be overrepresented in Congress (60 percent of their slaves would be counted in determining the size of the states' delegations in the House of Representatives) and because they did not relish competing with slave labor. Since the question was political influence rather than the rights and wrongs of slavery, a compromise was worked out in 1820. Missouri entered the Union as a slave state and Maine, having been separated from Massachusetts, was admitted as a free state to preserve the balance in the Senate.

To prevent further conflict, Congress adopted the proposal of Senator Jesse B. Thomas of Illinois, that "forever prohibited" slavery in all other parts of the Louisiana Purchase north of 36°300' latitude, the westward extension of Missouri's southern boundary. Although this division would keep slavery out of most of the territory, Southerners accepted it cheerfully. The land south of the line, the present states of Arkansas and Oklahoma, seemed ideally suited for the expanded plantation economy, and most persons considered the treeless northern regions little better than a desert.

The **Missouri Compromise** did not end the crisis. When Missouri submitted its constitution for approval by Congress (the final step in the admission process), the document, besides authorizing slavery and prohibiting the emancipation of any slave without the consent of the owner, required the state legislature to pass a law barring free blacks and mulattos from entering the state "under any pretext whatever." This provision plainly violated Article IV, Section 2, of the U.S. Constitution: "The Citizens of each State shall be entitled to all Privileges and Immunities of Citizens in the several States." It did not, however, represent any more of a break with established racial patterns, North or South, than the Tallmadge amendment; many states east of Missouri barred free blacks without regard for the Constitution.

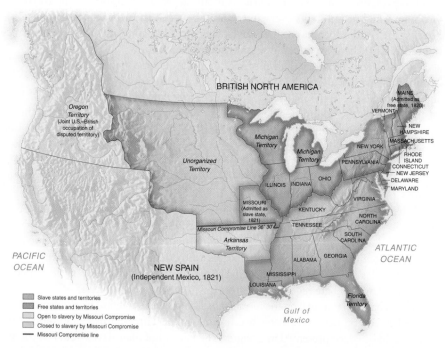

The Missouri Compromise, 1820 The Missouri Compromise admitted Missouri as a slave state, and Maine as a free state, retaining a balance in the Senate: Half of the nation's 24 states allowed slavery; half did not. The Compromise also drew an imaginary line along the 36°30' latitude (northern boundary of Arkansas): Slavery would be allowed in the lands to the south of the line.

Nevertheless, northern congressmen hypocritically refused to accept the Missouri constitution. Once more the debate raged. Again, since few Northerners cared to defend the rights of blacks, the issue was compromised. In March 1821 Henry Clay found a face-saving formula: Out of respect for the "supreme law of the land," Congress accepted the Missouri constitution with the demurrer that no law passed in conformity to it should be construed as contravening Article IV, Section 2.

Every thinking person recognized the political dynamite inherent in the Missouri controversy. The sectional lineup had been terrifyingly compact. Moreover, despite the timidity and hypocrisy of the North, everyone realized that the rights and wrongs of slavery lay at the heart of the conflict. "We have the wolf by the ears, and we can neither safely hold him, nor safely let him go," Jefferson wrote a month after Missouri became a state. The dispute, he said, "like a fire bell in the night, awakened and filled me with terror." Jefferson knew that the compromise had not quenched the flames ignited by the Missouri debates. "This is a reprieve only," he said. John Quincy Adams called it the "title page to a great tragic volume." Yet one could still hope that the fire bell was only a false alarm, that Adams's tragic volume would remain unread.

The Election of 1824

The tariff continued to divide the country. When a new, still higher tariff was enacted in 1824, the slave states voted almost unanimously against it, the North and Northwest in favor, and New England remained of two minds. Webster (after conducting a poll of business leaders before deciding how to vote) made a powerful speech against the act, but the measure passed without creating a major storm.

The presidential fight was waged on personal grounds, although the heat generated by the contest began the process of reenergizing party politics. Besides Calhoun the candidates were Andrew Jackson (hero of the battle of New Orleans), Crawford, Adams, and Clay. The maneuvering among them was complex, the infighting savage. In March 1824, Calhoun, who was young enough to wait for the White House, withdrew and declared for the vice presidency, which he won easily. Crawford, who had the support of many congressional leaders, seemed the likely winner, but he suffered a series of paralytic strokes that gravely injured his chances.

Despite the bitterness of the contest, it attracted relatively little public interest; barely a quarter of those eligible took the trouble to vote. In the Electoral College Jackson led with ninety-nine, Adams had eighty-four, Crawford forty-one, and Clay thirty-seven. Since no one had a majority, the contest was thrown into the House of Representatives, which, under the Constitution, had to choose from among the three leaders, each state delegation having one vote. By employing his great influence in the House, Clay swung the balance. Not wishing to advance the fortunes of a rival westerner like Jackson and feeling, with reason, that Crawford's health made him unavailable, Clay gave his support to Adams, who was thereupon elected.

John Quincy Adams as President

Adams, elected in 1824, hoped to use the national authority to foster all sorts of useful projects. He asked Congress for a federal program of internal improvements so vast that even Clay boggled when he realized its scope. He came out for aid to manufacturing and agriculture, for a national university, and even for a government astronomical observatory. For a nationalist of unchallengeable Jeffersonian origins like Clay or Calhoun to have pressed for so extensive a program would have been politically risky. For the son of John Adams to do so was disastrous; every doubter remembered his Federalist background and decided that he was trying to overturn the glorious "Revolution of 1800."

●●━[Read the Document

John Quincy Adams, *Inaugural Address* at **myhistorylab.com**

Adams proved to be his own worst enemy, for he was an inept politician. To persuade Americans, who were almost pathological on the subject of monarchy, to support his road building program, he cited with approval the work being done abroad by "the nations of Europe and . . . their rulers," which revived fears that all Adamses were royalists at heart. He was insensitive to the ebb and flow of public feeling; even when he wanted to move with the tide, he seldom managed to dramatize and publicize his stand effectively. Many Americans, for example, endorsed a federal bankruptcy law to protect poor debtors; Adams agreed, but instead of describing himself as a friend of debtors, he called for the "amelioration" of the "often oppressive codes relating to insolvency" and buried the recommendation at the tail end of a dull state paper.

Calhoun's *Exposition and Protest*

The tariff question added to the president's troubles. An increasingly powerful federal government required higher revenues—and higher duties—culminating in what became known as the record-high 1828 "Tariff of Abominations." This exacerbated sectional divisions.

Vice President Calhoun was especially upset; he believed that the new tariff would impoverish the South. His essay, *The South Carolina Exposition and Protest*, repudiated the nationalist philosophy he had previously championed.

The South Carolina legislature released this document to the country in December 1828, along with eight resolutions denouncing the protective tariff as unfair and unconstitutional. The theorist Calhoun, however, was not content with outlining the case against the tariff. His *Exposition* provided an ingenious defense of the right of the people of a state to reject a law of Congress. Starting with John Locke's revered concept of government as a contractual relationship, he argued that since the states had created the Union, logic dictated that they be the final arbiters of the meaning of the Constitution. If a special state convention, representing the sovereignty of the people, decided that an act of Congress violated the Constitution, it could interpose its authority and "nullify" the law within its boundaries. Calhoun did not seek to implement this theory in 1828, for he hoped that the next administration would lower the tariff and make nullification unnecessary.

The Meaning of Sectionalism

The sectional issues that occupied the energies of politicians and strained the ties between the people of the different regions were produced by powerful forces that actually bound the sections together. Growth caused differences that sometimes led to conflict, but growth itself was the product of prosperity. People were drawn to the West by the expectation that life would be better there, as more often than not it was, at least in the long run.

Another force unifying the nation was patriotism; the increasing size and prosperity of the nation made people proud to be part of a growing, dynamic society. Still another was the uniqueness of the American system of government and the people's knowledge that their immediate ancestors had created it. John Adams and Thomas Jefferson died on the same day, July 4, 1826, the fiftieth anniversary of the signing of the Declaration of Independence. People took this not as a remarkable coincidence, but as a sign from the heavens, an indication that God looked with favor on the American experiment. Many believed that patriotism and providence would transcend the intensifying sectionalism. They would be proven wrong.

John Lewis Krimmel's painting of the *Fourth of July in Centre Square Philadelphia* (1812). Note the diversity of those who've assembled to observe the festivities.

Source: Courtesy of the Pennsylvania Academy of Fine Arts, Philadelphia. Pennsylvania Academy purchase (from the estate of Paul Beck, Jr.).

Milestones

1808	James Madison is elected president
1810	Macon's Bill No. 2 removes all restrictions on commerce with Britain and France
1811	Battle of Tippecanoe shatters Indian confederation
1812	James Madison is reelected president
	Congress declares war on Great Britain
	USS *Constitution* and *United States* win naval victories
1813	Captain Oliver Hazard Perry destroys British fleet in Battle of Lake Erie
	General William Henry Harrison defeats British in Battle of the Thames
	Tecumseh dies at Battle of the Thames
1814	British burn Washington, DC
	Francis Scott Key writes "The Star Spangled Banner" during the bombardment of Fort McHenry
	New England Federalists meet at Hartford Convention
	Treaty of Ghent officially ends War of 1812
1815	General Andrew Jackson defeats British at Battle of New Orleans

1816	James Monroe is elected president
1817	Rush-Bagot Agreement limits American and British forces on Lake Champlain and Great Lakes
1819	United States signs Transcontinental Treaty with Spain
1819–1822	United States experiences economic depression
1820	James Monroe is reelected president
1820–1821	Missouri Compromise closes Missouri Territory to slavery, but opens Arkansas Territory to slavery
1820–1850	Cities and manufacturing grow rapidly
1823	Monroe Doctrine says United States will consider future European colonization in Western Hemisphere a threat to American peace and safety
1824–1825	House of Representatives decides election of 1824 in favor of John Quincy Adams, leading to claims of a "corrupt bargain" with Henry Clay
1828	Congress passes Tariff of Abominations, leading to nullification debate

✓●⦗Study and Review at www.myhistorylab.com

Review Questions

1. The period covered in this chapter saw a steady increase in federal power. During that time, the Democratic party, which opposed federal power, was dominant. What explains this seeming contradiction?

2. Before 1812, who sought war against the British and who opposed it? Why?

3. What accounted for the military reverses during the war and its one major success?

4. What factors led to the Missouri Compromise and what were its main provisions?

Key Terms

American System   *216*
Era of Good
   Feelings   *210*
Hartford
   Convention   *203*

Missouri
   Compromise   *218*
Monroe Doctrine   *207*
Tariff of
   Abominations   *193*

Transcontinental
   Treaty   *207*
War Hawks   *196*
War of 1812   *197*

8 Toward a National Economy

((•—[Hear the Audio Chapter 8 at myhistorylab.com

Are you wearing anything made in the United States?

IF YOU'RE WEARING SOCKS, THEY WERE LIKELY MADE IN DATANG, China, a small city near the Vietnamese border. Datang manufactures eight billion socks annually, about one-third of the world's output. Within Datang, companies specialize in different aspects of sock production: some buy yarn, dye it, or weave it into cloth; some sew in toes or heels; some press the socks or bind them with metal clips; some put socks into packages. Because of the huge scale and specialization, Datang manufactures a pair of socks for twenty-five cents, about half the cost of socks made in the United States.

That a single city provides socks for much of the world illustrates the global character of the modern economy. The emergence of a global economy has been going on for centuries. A global market for Asian spices was well-established at the time of Columbus, a reason for his voyage in 1492 (see the introduction to Chapter 1, p. 14).

As late as the 1700s, American farmers still produced much of what they needed—food, soap, candles, clothing, and even their socks. Farm women working in their homes spun locally produced flax, wool, and cotton into thread and yarn; knitted the yarn into fabric; and sewed the pieces into socks.

But by the early 1800s the "Age of Homespun" was waning. Manufactured products, often produced in distant factories, increasingly supplanted home-made goods. Historians still debate whether the shift from rural self-sufficiency to a specialized market economy occurred over a few pivotal decades during the early 1800s or whether it evolved slowly, over a longer period of time.

Nearly all agree, though, that after 1810 a cluster of changes imparted a new dynamism to the American economy: the growing demand for high-quality, store-bought goods; the rise of the factory system; the recruitment and training of a cheap labor force; the emergence of corporations; the revival of the Southern economy based on slavery and cotton production; the development of improved transportation that facilitated the exchange of farm and factory goods; and the creation of legal structures that promoted economic growth.

By the mid-nineteenth century, most Americans had been contributors to and consumers of an economic system that, while not yet fully global, had become national in scope. Most Americans wore socks that were manufactured in a handful of cities in Massachusetts, New York, and Pennsylvania. Thus while political tendencies tended to pull the nation apart, especially the growing dispute over the future of slavery in the territories, Americans were becoming more interdependent economically.

Gentility and the Consumer Revolution

The democratic revolution that led to the founding of the American nation was accompanied by widespread emulation of aristocratic behavior. Sometimes the most ardent American democrats proved the most susceptible to the allure of European gentility. Thus young John Adams, while lampooning "the late Refinements in modern manners," nevertheless advised his future wife, Abigail, to be more attentive to posture: "You very often hang your Head like a Bulrush, and you sit with your legs crossed to the ruin of the figure." On his trip to Paris in 1778 on behalf of the Continental Congress, he denounced the splendor of the houses, furniture, and clothing. "I cannot help suspecting that the more Elegance, the less Virtue," he concluded. Yet despite the exigencies of war, on returning to America, Adams bought a three-story mansion and furnished it with Louis XV chairs and, among other extravagances, an ornate wine cooler from Vincennes.

> Watch the Video
>
> *Coming of Age in 1833 (a great period of change/ reinvention in the world)* at **myhistorylab.com**

Among aristocratic circles in Europe, gentility was the product of ancestry and cultivated style; but in America it was largely defined by possession of material goods. By the mid-eighteenth century the "refinement of America" had touched the homes of some Southern planters and urban merchants; but a half century later porcelain plates

Americans enshrined the simple life and a homespun equality; yet they coveted the cultural markers of aristocracy, such as imported porcelain tea services. This one, made in France, was given to Alexander Hamilton. Gentility spread, historian Richard Bushman writes, "because people longed to be associated with the 'best society.'"

made by English craftsman Josiah Wedgwood and mahogany washstands by Thomas Chippendale were appearing even in frontier communities. Americans were demanding more goods than such craftsmen could turn out. Everywhere producers sought to expand their workshops, hire and train more artisans, and acquire large stocks of materials and labor-saving machines.

But first they had to locate the requisite capital, find ways to supervise large numbers of workers, and discover how to get raw materials to factories and products to customers. The solutions to these problems, taken together, constituted the "market revolution" of the early nineteenth century. The "industrial revolution" came on its heels.

Birth of the Factory

By the 1770s British manufacturers, especially those in textiles, had made astonishing progress in mechanizing their operations, bringing workers together in buildings called factories where waterpower, and later steam, supplied the force to run new spinning and weaving devices that increased productivity and reduced labor costs.

Because machine-spun cotton was cheaper and of better quality than that spun by hand, producers in other countries were eager to adopt British methods. Americans had depended on Great Britain for such products until the Revolution cut off supplies; then the new spirit of nationalism gave impetus to the development of local industry. A number of state legislatures offered bounties to anyone who would introduce the new machinery. The British, however, guarded their secrets vigilantly. It was illegal to export any of the new machines or to send their plans abroad. Workers skilled in their construction and use were forbidden to leave the country. These restrictions were effective for a time; the principles on which the new machines were based were simple enough, but to construct workable models without plans was another matter. Although a number of persons tried to do so, it was not until Samuel Slater installed his machines in Pawtucket, Rhode Island, that a successful factory was constructed.

Slater, born in England, was more than a skilled mechanic. Attracted by stories of the rewards offered in the United States, he slipped out of England in 1789. Not daring to carry any plans, he depended on his memory and his mechanical sense for the complicated specifications of the necessary machines. Moses Brown brought Slater to Rhode Island to help run his textile-manufacturing operation. Working in secrecy with a carpenter who was "under bond not to steal the patterns nor disclose the nature of the work," Slater built and installed his machinery. In December 1790 the first American factory began production.

It was a humble beginning indeed. Slater's machines made only cotton thread, which Brown's company sold in its Providence store and "put out" to individual artisans, who, working for wages, wove it into cloth in their homes. The machines were tended by a labor force of nine children, for the work was simple and the pace slow. The young operatives' pay ranged from thirty-three to sixty-seven cents a week, about what a youngster could earn in other occupations. The factory was profitable from the start. Slater soon branched out on his own, and others trained by him opened their own establishments. By 1800 seven mills possessing 2,000 spindles were in operation; by 1815, after production had been stimulated by the War of 1812, there were 130,000 spindles turning in 213 factories.

Before long the Boston Associates, a group of merchants headed by Francis Cabot Lowell, added a new dimension to factory production. Beginning at Waltham, Massachusetts, where the Charles River provided the necessary waterpower, between 1813 and 1850 they revolutionized textile production. Some early factory owners had set up hand looms in their plants, but the weavers could not keep pace with the spinning jennies. After an extensive study of British mills, Lowell smuggled the plans for an efficient power loom into America. His Boston Manufacturing Company at Waltham, capitalized at $300,000, combined machine production, large-scale operation, efficient management, and centralized marketing procedures. It concentrated on the mass production of a standardized product.

●●●┌**Read** the **Document**

The Harbinger, "Female Workers at Lowell" at **myhistorylab.com**

Lowell's cloth, though plain and rather coarse, was durable and cheap. His profits averaged almost 20 percent a year during the Era of Good Feelings. In 1823 the Boston Associates began to harness the power of the Merrimack River, setting up a new $600,000 corporation at the sleepy village of East Chelmsford, Massachusetts (population 300), where there was a fall of thirty-two feet in the river. Within three years the town, appropriately renamed Lowell, had 2,000 inhabitants.

An Industrial Proletariat?

As machines displaced skilled labor, the ability of laborers to influence working conditions declined. If skilled, they either became employers and developed entrepreneurial and managerial skills, or they descended into the mass of wage earners. Simultaneously, the changing structure of production widened the gap between owners and workers and blurred the distinction between skilled and unskilled labor.

These trends might have been expected to generate hostility between workers and employers. To some extent they did. There were strikes for higher wages and to protest work speedups throughout the 1830s and again in the 1850s. Efforts to found unions and to create political organizations dedicated to advancing the interests of workers were also undertaken. But well into the 1850s Americans displayed less evidence of the class solidarity common among European workers.

Why America did not produce a self-conscious working class is a question that has long intrigued historians. Some historians argue that the existence of the frontier siphoned off displaced and dissatisfied workers. The number of urban laborers who went west could not have been large, but the fact that the expanding economy created many opportunities for laborers to rise out of the working class was surely another reason why so few of them developed strong class feelings.

Other historians believe that ethnic and racial differences kept workers from seeing themselves as a distinct class with common needs and common enemies. The influx of needy immigrants willing to accept almost any wage was certainly resented by native-born workers. The growing number of free blacks in Northern cities—between 1800 and 1830 the number tripled in Philadelphia and quadrupled in New York—also inhibited the development of a self-identified working class.

These answers help explain the relative absence of class conflict during the early stages of the industrial revolution in America, but so does the fact that conditions in

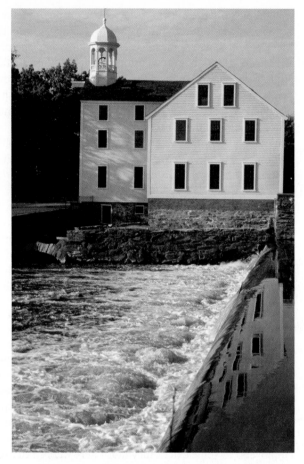

Slater's Mill, in Pawtucket, Rhode Island.
Source: N. Carter/North Wind Picture Archives.

the early shops and factories represented an improvement for the people who worked in them. This was the case with nearly all European immigrants, though less so for urban free blacks, since in the South many found work in the skilled trades.

Most workers in the early textile factories were drawn from outside the regular labor market. Relatively few artisan spinners and weavers became factory workers; indeed, some of them continued to work as they had, for it was many years before the factories could even begin to satisfy the ever-increasing demand for cloth. Nor did immigrants attend the new machines. Instead, the mill owners relied chiefly on women and children. They did so because machines lessened the need for skill and strength and because the labor shortage made it necessary to tap unexploited sources. By the early 1820s about half the cotton textile workers in the factories were under sixteen years of age.

Most people of that generation reasoned that the work was easy and that it kept youngsters busy at useful tasks while providing their families with extra income. Roxanna Foote, whose daughter, Harriet Beecher Stowe, wrote *Uncle Tom's Cabin*, came from a solid, middle-class family in Guilford, Connecticut. Nevertheless, she worked full-time before her marriage in her grandfather's small spinning mill. "This spinning-mill was a favorite spot," a relative recalled many years later. "Here the girls often received visitors, or read or chatted while they spun." Roxanna explained her daily regimen as a mill girl matter-of-factly: "I generally rise with the sun, and, after breakfast, take my wheel, which is my daily companion, and the evening is generally devoted to reading, writing, and knitting."

This seems like an idealized picture, or perhaps working for one's grandfather made a difference. Another young girl, Emily Chubbock, later a well-known writer, had a less pleasant recollection of her experience as an eleven-year-old factory hand earning

$1.25 a week: "My principal recollections . . . are of noise and filth, bleeding hands and aching feet, and a very sad heart." In any case, a society accustomed to seeing the children of fairly well-to-do farmers working full-time in the fields was not shocked by the sight of children working all day in mills. In factories where laborers were hired in family units, no member earned very much, but with a couple of adolescent daughters and perhaps a son of nine or ten helping out, a family could take home enough to live decently. For most working Americans, that was success enough.

Lowell's Waltham System: Women as Factory Workers

Instead of hiring children, the Boston Associates developed the "Waltham System" of employing young, unmarried women in their new textile mills. For a generation after the opening of the Merrimack Manufacturing Company in 1823, the thriving factory towns of Lowell, Chicopee, and Manchester provided the background for a remarkable industrial idyll. Young women came from farms all over New England to work for a year or two in the mills. They were lodged in company boardinghouses, which, like college dormitories, became centers of social life. Unlike modern college dormitories, the boardinghouses were strictly supervised; straitlaced New Englanders did not hesitate to permit their daughters to live in them. The regulations laid down by one company, for example, required that all employees "show that they are penetrated by a laudable love of temperance and virtue." "Ardent spirits" were banished from company property, and "games of hazard and cards" prohibited. A 10 PM curfew was strictly enforced.

The women earned between $2.50 and $3.25 a week, about half of which went for room and board. Some of the remainder they sent home, the rest (what there was of it) they could spend as they wished.

Most of these young women did not have to support themselves. They worked to save for a trousseau, to help educate a younger brother, or simply for the experience and excitement of meeting new people and escaping the confining environment of the farm. Anything but an industrial proletariat, they filled the windows of the factories with flowering plants, organized sewing circles, edited their own literary periodicals, and attended lectures on edifying subjects. That such activity was possible on top of a seventy-hour work week is a commentary on both the resiliency of youth and the leisurely pace of these early factories.

Life in the mills was nevertheless demanding. Although they made up 85 percent of the workforce, women were kept out of supervisory positions. In 1834 workers in several mills "turned out" to protest cuts in their wages and a hike in what they paid for board. This work stoppage did not force a reversal of management policy. Another strike two years later in response to a work speedup was somewhat more successful. But when a drop in prices in the 1840s led the owners to introduce new rules designed to increase production, workers lacked the organizational strength to block them. By then young women of the kind that had flocked to the mills in the 1820s and 1830s were beginning to find work as schoolteachers and clerks. Mill owners turned increasingly to Irish immigrants to operate their machines.

●●●─ Read the Document
Regarding Life in the Mills at
myhistorylab.com

Irish and German Immigrants

Between 1790 and 1820 the population of the United States had more than doubled to 9.6 million. The most remarkable feature of this growth was that it resulted almost entirely from natural increase. The birthrate in the early nineteenth century exceeded fifty per 1,000 population, a rate as high as that of any country in the world today. Fewer than 250,000 immigrants entered the United States between 1790 and 1820. European wars, the ending of the slave trade, and doubts about the viability of the new republic slowed the flow of humanity across the Atlantic to a trickle.

But soon after the final defeat of Napoleon in 1815, immigration picked up. In the 1820s, some 150,000 European immigrants arrived; in the 1830s, 600,000; and in the 1840s, 1.7 million. The 1850 census, the first to make the distinction, estimated that of the nation's population of 23 million, more than 10 percent were foreign-born. In the Northeast the proportion exceeded 15 percent.

Most of this human tide came from Germany and Ireland, but substantial numbers also came from Great Britain and the Scandinavian countries. As with earlier immigrants, most were drawn to America by what are called "pull" factors: the prospect of abundant land, good wages, and economic opportunity generally, or by the promise of political and religious freedom. But many came because of "push" factors: To stay where they were meant to face starvation. This was particularly true of those from Ireland, where a potato blight triggered the flight of tens of thousands. This Irish exodus continued; by the end of the century there were more people of Irish origin in America than in Ireland.

Once ashore in New York, Boston, or Philadelphia, most relatively prosperous immigrants pushed directly westward. Others found work in the new factory towns

Population Density, 1790 Then, as now, the most densely populated part of the nation was the coastal region from Virginia to Massachusetts.

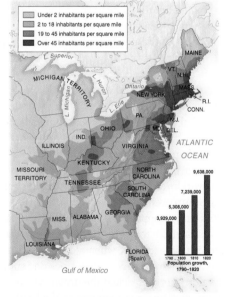

Population Density, 1820 The thirty years from 1790 to 1820 saw a sizable increase in population, especially along the Ohio and Mississippi River valleys.

along the route of the Erie Canal, in the lower Delaware Valley southeast of Philadelphia, or along the Merrimack River north of Boston. But most of the Irish immigrants, "the poorest and most wretched population that can be found in the world," one of their priests called them, lacked the means to go west. Like it or not, they had to settle in the eastern cities.

Viewed in historical perspective, this massive wave of immigration stimulated the American economy. In the short run, the influx of the 1830s and 1840s depressed living standards and strained the social fabric. For the first time the nation had acquired a culturally distinctive, citybound, and propertyless class. The poor Irish immigrants had to accept whatever wages employers offered them. By doing so they caused resentment among native workers—resentment exacerbated by the unfamiliarity of the Irish with city ways and by their Roman Catholic faith, which the Protestant majority associated with European authoritarianism and corruption.

The Persistence of the Household System

Since technology affected American industry unevenly, contemporaries found the changes difficult to evaluate. Interchangeable firing pins for rifles did not lead at once even to matching pairs of shoes. More than fifteen years passed after John Fitch built and launched the world's first regularly scheduled steamboat in 1790 before it was widely accepted. Few people in the 1820s appreciated how profound the impact of the factory system would be. The city of Lowell seemed remarkable and important but not necessarily a herald of future trends.

Yet in nearly every field apparently minor changes were being made. Beginning around 1815, small improvements in the design of waterwheels, such as the use of leather transmission belts and metal gears, made possible larger and more efficient machinery in mills and factories. Iron production advanced beyond the stage of the blacksmith's forge and the small foundry only slowly; nevertheless, by 1810 machines were stamping out nails at a third of the cost of the hand-forged type. At about this time the puddling process for refining pig iron made it possible to use coal for fuel instead of expensive charcoal.

Rise of Corporations

Mechanization required substantial capital investment, and capital was chronically in short supply. The modern method of organizing large enterprises, the corporation, was slow to develop. Between 1781 and 1801 only 326 corporations were chartered by the states, and only a few of them were engaged in manufacturing.

The general opinion was that only quasi-public projects, such as roads and waterworks, were entitled to the privilege of incorporation. Anyone interested in organizing a corporation had to obtain a special act of a state legislature. And even among businessmen there was a tendency to associate corporations with monopoly, with corruption, and with the undermining of individual enterprise. In 1820 the economist Daniel Raymond wrote, "The very object . . . of the act of incorporation is to produce inequality, either in rights, or in the division of property. Prima facie, therefore all money corporations are detrimental to national wealth. They are always created for the benefit of the rich. . . ." Such feelings help explain why as late as the 1860s most manufacturing was being done by unincorporated companies.

While the growth of industry did not suddenly revolutionize American life, it reshaped society in various ways. For a time it lessened the importance of foreign commerce. Some relative decline from the lush years immediately preceding Jefferson's embargo was no doubt inevitable, especially in the fabulously profitable reexport trade. But American industrial growth reduced the need for foreign products and thus the business of merchants. Only in the 1850s, when the wealth and population of the United States were more than three times what they had been in the first years of the century, did the value of American exports climb back to the levels of 1807. As the country moved closer to self-sufficiency (a point it never reached), nationalistic and isolationist sentiments were subtly augmented. During the embargo and the War of 1812 a great deal of capital had been transferred from commerce to industry; afterward new capital continued to prefer industry, attracted by the high profits and growing prestige of manufacturing. The rise of manufacturing affected farmers too, for as cities grew in size and number, the need to feed the populace caused commercial agriculture to flourish.

Cotton Revolutionizes the South

By far the most important indirect effect of industrialization occurred in the South, which soon began to produce cotton to supply the new textile factories of Great Britain and New England. Beginning in 1786, "sea-island" cotton was grown successfully in the mild, humid lowlands and offshore islands along the coasts of Georgia and South Carolina. This was a high-quality cotton, silky and long-fibered like the Egyptian kind. But its susceptibility to frost severely limited the area of its cultivation. Elsewhere in the South, "green-seed," or upland, cotton flourished, but this plant had little commercial value because the seeds could not be easily separated from the lint. When sea-island cotton was passed between two rollers, its shiny black seeds simply popped out; with upland cotton the seeds were pulled through with the lint and crushed, the oils and broken bits destroying the value of the fiber. To remove the seeds by hand was laborious; a slave working all day could clean scarcely a pound of the white fluff. This made it an uneconomical crop. In 1791 the usually sanguine Hamilton admitted in his *Report on Manufactures* that "the extensive cultivation of cotton can, perhaps, hardly be expected."

Early American cotton manufacturers used the sea-island variety or imported foreign fiber, in the latter case paying a duty of 3 cents a pound. However, the planters of South Carolina and Georgia, suffering from hard times after the Revolution, needed a new cash crop. Rice production was not expanding, and indigo, the other staple of the area, had ceased to be profitable when it was no longer possible to claim the British bounty. Cotton seemed an obvious answer. Farmers were experimenting hopefully with varieties of the plant and mulling the problem of how upland cotton could be more easily deseeded.

Generations of American schoolchildren—and college students—have been taught that over the course of two weeks in 1793 Eli Whitney, a Yankee who had never seen a

In 2005 historian Angela Lakwete used this print as the cover of *Inventing the Cotton Gin: Machine and Myth in Antebellum America* to show that devices similar to that "invented" by Eli Whitney in 1793 had long been in use in the South. The human details in the image are revealing as well.

cotton plant, invented a machine that instantly revolutionized the production of cotton. His cotton gin (engine) consisted of a cylinder covered with rows of wire teeth rotating in a box filled with cotton. As the cylinder turned, the teeth passed through narrow slits in a metal grating. Cotton fibers were caught by the teeth and pulled through the slits. The seeds, too thick to pass through the openings, were left behind. A second cylinder, with brushes rotating in the opposite direction to sweep the cotton from the wires, prevented matting and clogging.

In fact, as the lithograph on this page suggests, Southern cotton planters had for decades used a roller gin, which operated according to similar principles—tugging cotton through meshed teeth to pull out seeds without harming the fibers. Many regarded Whitney's design as an improvement, but it took nearly three decades before it replaced the roller gins. The expansion of cotton production did not rise sharply until the 1820s.

Upland cotton would grow wherever there were 200 consecutive days without frost and twenty-four inches of rain. The crop engulfed Georgia and South Carolina and spread north into parts of Virginia. After Andrew Jackson defeated the southeastern Indians during the War of 1812, the rich "Black Belt" area of central Alabama and northern Mississippi and the delta region along the lower Mississippi River were rapidly taken over by the fluffy white staple. In 1821 Alabama alone raised 40,000 bales. Central Tennessee also became important cotton country.

Cotton stimulated the economy of the rest of the nation as well. Most of it was exported, the sale paying for much-needed European products. The transportation,

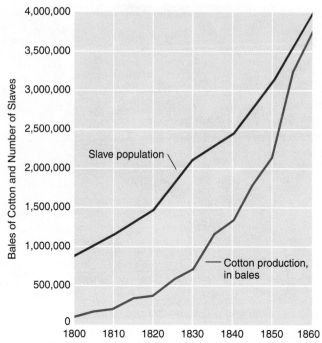

Cotton Production and Slave Population, 1800–1860 As the number of slaves increased, the production of cotton increased also.

insurance, and final disposition of the crop fell largely into the hands of Northern merchants, who profited accordingly. And the surplus corn and hogs of western farmers helped feed the slaves of the new cotton plantations. Cotton was the major force in the economy for a generation, beginning about 1815.

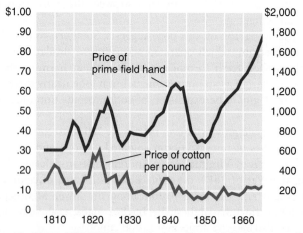

Prices for Cotton and for Slaves, 1802–1860 These prices for cotton and field slaves appear in New Orleans records. The left axis shows the price of cotton; the right, the price of a slave. The rising trend of slave prices (especially from 1850 to 1860), and a growing slave population, show the continuing profitability and viability of slavery up to 1860.

Revival of Slavery

Amid the national rejoicing over this prosperity, one aspect both sad and ominous was easily overlooked. Slavery, a declining or at worst stagnant institution in the decade of the Revolution, was revitalized in the following years.

Libertarian beliefs inspired by the Revolution ran into the roadblock of race prejudice as soon as some of the practical aspects of freedom for blacks became apparent. As disciples of John Locke, the Revolutionary generation had a deep respect for property rights; in the last analysis most white Americans placed these rights ahead of the personal liberty of black Americans. Forced abolition of slavery therefore attracted few recruits. Moreover, the rhetoric of the Revolution had raised the aspirations of blacks. Increasing signs of rebelliousness appeared among them, especially after the slave uprising in Saint Domingue, which culminated, after a great bloodbath, in the establishment of the black Republic of Haiti in 1804. This example of a successful slave revolt filled white Americans with apprehension. Their fears were irrational (Haitian blacks outnumbered whites and mulattos combined by seven to one), but nonetheless real. And fear led to repression; the exposure in 1801 of a plot to revolt in Virginia resulted in some three dozen executions even though no actual uprising had occurred.

The mood of the Revolutionary decade had led a substantial number of masters to free their slaves. Unfortunately this led many other whites to have second thoughts about ending slavery. "If the blacks see all of their color slaves, it will seem to them a disposition of Providence, and they will be content," a Virginia legislator claimed. "But if they see others like themselves free . . . they will repine." As the number of free blacks rose, restrictions on them were everywhere tightened.

In the 1780s many opponents of slavery began to think of solving the "Negro problem" by colonizing freed slaves in some distant region—in the western districts or perhaps in Africa. The colonization movement had two aspects. The first one was a manifestation of an embryonic black nationalism that reflected the disgust of black Americans with local racial attitudes and their interest in African civilization. Paul Cuffe, a Massachusetts Quaker, managed to finance the emigration of thirty-eight of his fellow blacks to British Sierra Leone in 1815, but few others followed. Most influential Northern blacks, the most conspicuous among them the Reverend Richard Allen, bishop of the African Methodist Church, opposed the idea vigorously.

The other colonization movement, led by whites, was paternalistic. Some white colonizationists genuinely abhorred slavery. Others could not stomach living with free blacks; to them colonization was merely a polite word for deportation. Most white colonizationists were conservatives who considered themselves realists.

The colonization idea became popular in Virginia in the 1790s, but nothing was achieved until after the founding of the **American Colonization Society** in 1817. The society purchased African land and established the Republic of Liberia. However, despite the cooperation of a handful of black nationalists and the patronage of many important white Southerners, including Presidents Madison and Monroe and Chief Justice Marshall, it accomplished little. Although some white colonizationists expected ex-slaves to go to Africa as Christian missionaries to convert and "civilize" the natives, few blacks wished to migrate to a land so alien to their own experience. Only about 12,000 went to Liberia, and the toll taken among them by tropical diseases was large. As late as 1850 the black American population of Liberia was only 6,000.

The cotton boom of the early nineteenth century acted as a brake on the colonization movement. As cotton production expanded, the need for labor in the South grew apace. The price of slaves doubled between 1795 and 1804. As it rose, the inclination of even the most kindhearted masters to free their slaves began to falter. Although the importation of slaves from abroad had been outlawed by all the states, perhaps 25,000 were smuggled into the country in the 1790s. In 1804 South Carolina reopened the trade, and between that date and 1808, when the constitutional prohibition of importation became effective, some 40,000 were brought in. Thereafter the miserable traffic in human beings continued clandestinely, though on a lesser scale.

The cotton boom triggered an internal trade in slaves that frequently ripped black families apart. While it had always been legal for owners to transport their own slaves to a new state if they were settling there, many states forbade, or at least severely restricted, interstate commercial transactions in human flesh. A Virginia law of 1778, for example, prohibited the importation of slaves for purposes of sale, and persons entering the state with slaves had to swear that they did not intend to sell them. Once cotton became important, these laws were either repealed or systematically evaded. There was a surplus of slaves in one part of the United States and an acute shortage in another. A migration from the upper South to the cotton lands quickly sprang up. Slaves from "free" New York and New Jersey and even from New England began to appear on the auction blocks of Savannah and Charleston. Early in the Era of Good Feelings, newspapers in New Orleans were carrying reports such as, "Jersey negroes appear to be particularly adapted to this market. . . . We have the right to calculate on large importations in the future, from the success which hitherto attended the sale."

The lot of African Americans in the Northern states was almost as bad as that of Southern free blacks. Except in New England, where there were few blacks to begin with, most were denied the vote, either directly or by extralegal pressures. They could not testify in court, intermarry with whites, obtain decent jobs or housing, or get even a rudimentary education. Most states segregated blacks in theaters, hospitals, churches, and on public transportation facilities. They were barred from hotels and restaurants patronized by whites.

Northern blacks could at least protest and try to convince the white majority of the injustice of their treatment. These rights were denied their Southern brethren. They could and did publish newspapers and pamphlets, organize for political action, and petition legislatures and Congress for redress of grievance—in short, they applied methods of peaceful persuasion in an effort to improve their position in society.

Roads to Market

Inventions and technological improvements were extremely important in the settlement of the West. On superficial examination, this may not seem to have been the case, for the hordes of settlers who struggled across the mountains immediately after the War of 1812 were no better equipped than their ancestors who had pushed up the eastern slopes in previous generations. Many plodded on foot over hundreds of miles, dragging crude carts laden with their meager possessions. More

See the Map

Expanding America and Internal Improvements at myhistorylab.com

This stagecoach has just passed over a solid road made of tree trunks, but it must now continue traveling across a dirt road. Already its wheels have sunk several inches into the mud.

Source: George Tattersall, English, 1817–1849 (active U.S. 1836), *Album of Western Sketches: Highways and Byeways of the Forest*, a Scene on "the Road", 1836. Pen and brown ink with brush and brown wash, heightened with white gouache, over graphite pencil, on gray paper. 21.0 x 29.8 cm (8 1/4 x 11 3/4 in.) Museum of Fine Arts, Boston. Gift of Maxim Karolik for the M. and M. Karolik Collection of American Watercolors and Drawings, 1800–1875, 56.400.11. Photograph © 2011 Museum of Fine Arts, Boston.

fortunate pioneers traveled on horseback or in heavy, cumbersome wagons, the best known being the canvas-topped Conestoga "covered wagons," pulled by horses or oxen.

In many cases the pioneers followed trails and roads no better than those of colonial days—quagmires in wet weather, rutted and pitted with potholes a good part of the year. When they settled down, their way of life was no more advanced than that of the Pilgrims. At first they were creatures of the forest, feeding on its abundance, building their homes and simple furniture with its wood, clothing themselves in the furs of forest animals. They usually planted the first crop in a natural glade; thereafter, year by year, they pushed back the trees with ax and saw and fire until the land was cleared. Until the population of the territory had grown large enough to support town life, settlers were as dependent on crude household manufacturers as any earlier pioneer.

The spread of settlement into the Mississippi Valley created challenges that required technological advances if they were to be met. In the social climate of that age in the United States, these advances were not slow in coming. Most were related to transportation, the major problem for westerners. Everyone recognized that an efficient transportation network would increase land values, stimulate domestic and foreign trade, and strengthen the entire economy. The Mississippi River and its tributaries provided a natural highway for western commerce and communication, but it was one that had grave disadvantages. Farm products could be floated down to New Orleans on rafts and flatboats, but the descent along the Ohio River from Pittsburgh to the Mississippi took at least a month. In any case, the natural flow of trade was between the East and West. That is why, from early in the westward movement, much attention was given to building roads linking the Mississippi Valley to the eastern seaboard.

Constructing decent roads over the rugged Appalachians was a formidable task. The steepest grades had to be reduced by cutting through hills and filling in low places, all without modern blasting and earth-moving equipment. Drainage ditches were essential if the roads were not to be washed out by the first rains, and a firm foundation of stones had to be provided if they were to stand up under the pounding of heavy wagons. The skills required for building roads of this quality had been developed in Great Britain and France, and the earliest American examples, constructed in the 1790s, were similar to good European highways. The first such road, connecting Philadelphia and Lancaster, Pennsylvania, opened to traffic in 1794.

Transportation and the Government

Most of the improved highways and many bridges were built as business ventures by private interests. Promoters charged tolls, the rates being set by the states. Tolls were collected at gates along the way; hinged poles suspended across the road were turned back by a guard after receipt of the toll. Hence these thoroughfares were known as turnpikes, or simply pikes.

The profits earned by a few early turnpikes, such as the one between Philadelphia and Lancaster, caused the boom in private road building, but even the most fortunate of the turnpike companies did not make much money. Maintenance was expensive, and traffic spotty. (Ordinary public roads paralleling turnpikes were sometimes called "shunpikes" because penny-pinching travelers used them to avoid the tolls.) Some states bought stock to bolster weak companies, and others built and operated turnpikes as public enterprises. Local governments everywhere provided considerable support, for every town was eager to develop efficient communication with its neighbors.

Despite much talk about individual self-reliance and free enterprise, local, state, and national governments contributed heavily to the development of what in the jargon of the day were called "internal improvements." They served as "primary entrepreneurs," supplying capital for risky but socially desirable enterprises with the result that a fascinating mixture of private and public energy went into the building of these institutions. At the federal level even the parsimonious Jeffersonians became deeply involved. In 1808 Secretary of the Treasury Albert Gallatin drafted a comprehensive plan for constructing much-needed roads at a cost of $16 million. This proposal was not adopted, but the government poured money in an erratic and unending stream into turnpike companies and other organizations created to improve transportation.

Logically, the major highways, especially those over the mountains, should have been built by the national government. Strategic military requirements alone would have justified such a program. One major artery, the Old National Road, running from Cumberland, Maryland, to Wheeling, in western Virginia, was constructed by the United States between 1811 and 1818. In time it was extended as far west as Vandalia, Illinois. However, further federal road building was hampered by political squabbles in Congress, usually phrased in constitutional terms but in fact based on sectional rivalries and other economic conflicts. Thus no comprehensive highway program was undertaken in the nineteenth century.

While the National Road, the New York Pike, and other, rougher trails such as the Wilderness Road into the Kentucky country were adequate for the movement of settlers, they did not begin to answer the West's need for cheap and efficient transportation.

Wagon freight rates averaged at least thirty cents a ton-mile around 1815. At such rates, to transport a ton of oats from Buffalo to New York would have cost twelve times the value of the oats! To put the problem another way, four horses could haul a ton and a half of oats about eighteen or twenty miles a day over a good road. If they could obtain half their feed by grazing, the horses would still consume about fifty pounds of oats a day. It requires little mathematics to figure out how many pounds of oats would be left in the wagon when it reached New York City, almost 400 miles away.

Until the coming of the railroad, which was just being introduced in England in 1825, the cost of shipping bulky goods by land over the great distances common in America was prohibitive. Businessmen and inventors concentrated instead on improving water transport, first by designing better boats and then by developing artificial waterways.

Development of Steamboats

Rafts and flatboats were adequate for downstream travel, but the only practical solution to upstream travel was the steamboat. After John Fitch's work around 1790, a number of others made important contributions to the development of steam navigation. One early enthusiast was John Stevens, a wealthy New Jerseyite, who designed an improved steam boiler for which he received one of the first patents issued by the United States. Stevens got his brother-in-law, Robert R. Livingston, interested in the problem, and the latter used his political influence to obtain an exclusive charter to operate steamboats on New York waters. In 1802, while in France trying to buy New Orleans from Napoleon, Livingston got to know Robert Fulton, a young American artist and engineer who was experimenting with steam navigation, and agreed to finance his work. In 1807, after returning to New York, Fulton constructed the *North River Steam Boat*, famous to history as the *Clermont*.

The *Clermont* was 142 feet long, 18 feet abeam, and drew 7 feet of water. With its towering stack belching black smoke, its side wheels could push it along at a steady five miles an hour. Nothing about it was radically new, but Fulton brought the essentials—engine, boiler, paddle wheels, and hull—into proper balance and thereby produced an efficient vessel.

No one could patent a steamboat; soon the new vessels were plying the waters of every navigable river from the Mississippi east. After 1815 steamers were making the run from New Orleans as far as Ohio. By 1820 at least sixty vessels were operating between New Orleans and Louisville, and by the end of the decade there were more than 200 steamers on the Mississippi.

The day of the steamboat had dawned, and although the following generation would experience its high noon, even in the 1820s its major effects were clear. The great Mississippi Valley, in the full tide of its development, was immensely enriched. Produce poured down to New Orleans, which soon ranked with New York and Liverpool among the world's great ports. From 1816–1817, only 80,000 tons of freight was shipped down the Mississippi to New Orleans; but by 1840–1841, that freight arriving in New Orleans had increased to 542,000 tons. Upriver traffic was affected even more spectacularly. Freight charges plummeted, in some cases to a tenth of what they had been after the War of 1812. Around 1818 coffee cost sixteen cents a pound more in Cincinnati than in

New Orleans, a decade later less than three cents more. The Northwest emerged from self-sufficiency with a rush and became part of the national market.

Steamboats were far more comfortable than any contemporary form of land transportation, and competition soon led builders to make them positively luxurious. The *General Pike*, launched in 1819 and set the fashion. Marble columns, thick carpets, mirrors, and crimson curtains adorned its cabins and public rooms. Soon the finest steamers were floating palaces where passengers could dine, drink, dance, and gamble in luxury as they sped smoothly to their destinations. Yet raft and flatboat traffic increased. Farmers, lumbermen, and others with goods from upriver floated down in the slack winter season and returned in comfort by steamer after selling their produce and their rafts as well, for lumber was in great demand in New Orleans. Every January and February New Orleans teemed with westerners and Yankee sailors, their pockets jingling, bent on a fling before going back to work. The shops displayed everything from the latest Paris fashions to teething rings made of alligator teeth mounted in silver. During the carnival season the city became one great festival, where every human pleasure could be tasted, every vice indulged.

The Canal Boom

While the steamboat was conquering western rivers, canals were being constructed that further improved the transportation network. Since the midwestern rivers all emptied into the Gulf of Mexico, they did not provide a direct link with the eastern seaboard. If an artificial waterway could be cut between the great central valley and some navigable stream flowing into the Atlantic, all sections would profit immensely.

Canals were more expensive than roads, but so long as the motive power used in overland transportation was the humble horse, they offered enormous economic advantages to shippers. Because there is less friction to overcome, a team plodding along a towpath could pull a canal barge with a 100-ton load and make better time over long distances than it could pulling a single ton in a wagon on the finest road.

Although canals were as old as Egypt, only about 100 miles of them existed in the United States as late as 1816. Construction costs aside, in a rough and mountainous country canals presented formidable engineering problems. To link the Mississippi Valley and the Atlantic meant somehow circumventing the Appalachian Mountains. Most people thought this impossible.

Mayor DeWitt Clinton of New York believed that such a project was feasible in New York State. In 1810, while serving as state canal commissioner, he traveled across central New York and convinced himself that it would be practicable to dig a canal from Buffalo, on Lake Erie, to the Hudson River. The Mohawk Valley cuts through the Appalachian chain just north of Albany, and at no point along the route to Buffalo does the land rise more than 570 feet above the level of the Hudson. Marshaling a mass of technical, financial, and commercial information and using his political influence cannily, Clinton placed his proposal before the New York legislature. In its defense he was eloquent and farsighted:

> As an organ of communication between the Hudson, the Mississippi, the
> St. Lawrence, the great lakes of the north and west, and their tributary rivers,
> [the canal] will create the greatest inland trade ever witnessed. The most fertile

and extensive regions of America will avail themselves of its facilities for a market. All their surplus . . . will concentrate in the city of New York. . . . That city will, in the course of time, become the granary of the world, the emporium of commerce, the seat of manufactures, the focus of great moneyed operations. . . . And before the revolution of a century, the whole island of Manhattan, covered with habitations and replenished with a dense population, will constitute one vast city.

The legislators were convinced, and in 1817 the state began construction along a route 363 miles long, most of it across densely forested wilderness. At the time the longest canal in the United States ran less than twenty-eight miles!

The construction of the Erie Canal, as it was called, was a remarkable accomplishment. The chief engineer, Benjamin Wright, a surveyor-politician from Rome, New York, had had almost no experience with canal building. Fortunately, Wright proved to be a good organizer and a fine judge of engineering talent. He quickly spotted young men of ability among the workers and pushed them forward. One of his finds, Canvass White, was sent to study British canals. White became an expert on the design of locks; he also discovered an American limestone that could be made into waterproof cement, a vital product in canal construction that had previously been imported at a substantial price from England. Another of Wright's protégés, John B. Jervis, began as an axman, rose in two years to resident engineer in charge of a section of the project, and went on to become perhaps the outstanding American civil engineer of his time. Workers who learned the business digging the "Big Ditch" supervised the construction of dozens of canals throughout the country in later years.

((•─[Hear the Audio

Erie Canal at
myhistorylab.com

The Erie, completed in 1825, was an immediate financial success. Together with the companion Champlain Canal, which linked Lake Champlain and the Hudson, it brought in over half a million dollars in tolls in its first year. Soon its entire $7 million cost had been recovered, and it was earning profits of about $3 million a year. The effect of this prosperity on New York State was enormous. Buffalo, Rochester, Syracuse, and half a dozen lesser towns along the canal flourished.

New York City: Emporium of the Western World

New York City had already become the largest city in the nation, thanks chiefly to its merchants who had established a reputation for their rapid and orderly way of doing business. In 1818 the Black Ball Line opened the first regularly scheduled freight and passenger service between New York and England. Previously shipments might languish in port for weeks while a skipper waited for additional cargo. Now merchants on both sides of the Atlantic could count on the Black Ball packets to move their goods between Liverpool and New York on schedule whether or not the transporting vessel had a full cargo. This improvement brought much new business to the port.

Now the canal cemented New York's position as the national metropolis. Most European-manufactured goods destined for the Mississippi Valley entered the country at New York and passed on to the West over the canal. The success of the Erie also sparked a nationwide canal-building boom. Most canals were constructed either by the states, as in the case of the Erie, or as "mixed enterprises" that combined public and private energies.

Nicolino V. Calyo's painting, *Burning of the Merchant's Exchange* (1835) in New York.
The entire block was rebuilt within a year.
Source: Museum of the City of New York.

No state profited as much from this construction as New York, for none possessed New York's geographic advantages. The rocky hills of New England discouraged all but fanatics. Canals were built connecting Worcester and Northampton, Massachusetts, with the coast, but they were financial failures. The Delaware and Hudson Canal, running from northeastern Pennsylvania across northern New Jersey and lower New York to the Hudson, was completed by private interests in 1828. It managed to earn respectable dividends by barging coal to the eastern seaboard, but it made no attempt to compete with the Erie for the western trade. Pennsylvania, desperate to keep up with New York, engaged in an orgy of construction. In 1834 it completed a complicated system, part canal and part railroad, over the mountains to Pittsburgh. This Mainline Canal cost a staggering sum for that day. With its 177 locks and cumbersome "inclined-plane railroad" it was slow and expensive to operate and never competed effectively with the Erie. Efforts in Maryland to link Baltimore with the West by water failed utterly.

Beyond the mountains there was even greater zeal for canal construction in the 1820s and still more in the 1830s. Once the Erie opened the way across New York, farmers in the Ohio country demanded that links be built between the Ohio River and the Great Lakes so that they could ship their produce by water directly to the East. Local feeder canals seemed equally necessary; with corn worth 20 cents a bushel at Columbus selling for 50 cents at Marietta, on the Ohio, the value of cheap transportation became obvious to Ohio farmers.

Even before the completion of the Erie, Ohio had begun construction of the Ohio and Erie Canal running from the Ohio River to Cleveland. Another, from Toledo to Cincinnati, was begun in 1832. Meanwhile, Indiana had undertaken the 450-mile Wabash and Erie Canal. These canals were well conceived, but the western states overextended themselves building dozens of feeder lines, trying, it sometimes seemed, to supply all farmers west of the Appalachians with water connections from their barns to the New York docks. Politics made such programs almost inevitable, for in order to win support for their pet projects, legislators had to back the schemes of their fellows. The result was frequently financial disaster. There was not enough traffic to pay for all the waterways that were dug. By 1844, $60 million in state "improvement" bonds were in default. Nevertheless, the canals benefited both western farmers and the national economy.

The Marshall Court

The most important legal advantages bestowed on business in the period were the gift of Chief Justice John Marshall. His particular combination of charm, logic, and forcefulness made the Court during his long reign remarkably submissive to his view of the Constitution. Marshall's belief in a powerful central government explains his tendency to hand down decisions favorable to manufacturing and business interests. He also thought that "the business community was the agent of order and progress" and tended to interpret the Constitution in a way that would advance its interests.

Many important cases came before the Court between 1819 and 1824, and in each one Marshall's decision was applauded by most of the business community. The cases involved two major principles: the "sanctity" of contracts and the supremacy of federal legislation over the laws of the states. Marshall shared the conviction of the Revolutionary generation that property had to be protected against arbitrary seizure if liberty was to be preserved. Contracts between private individuals and between individuals and the government must be strictly enforced, he believed, or chaos would result. He therefore gave the widest possible application to the constitutional provision that no state could pass any law "impairing the Obligation of Contracts."

•••—Read the **Document**

Martin v. Hunter's Lessee at **myhistorylab.com**

In *Dartmouth College v. Woodward* (1819), which involved an attempt by New Hampshire to alter the charter granted to Dartmouth by King George III in 1769, Marshall held that such a charter was a contract which could not be canceled or altered without the consent of both parties. The state had sought not to destroy the college but to change it from a private to a public institution, yet Marshall held that to do so would violate the contract clause.

Marshall's decisions concerning the division of power between the federal government and the states were even more important. The question of the constitutionality of a national bank, first debated by Hamilton and Jefferson, had not been submitted to the courts during the life of the first Bank of the United States. By the time of the second Bank there were many state banks, and some of them felt that their interests were threatened by the national institution. Responding to pressure from local banks, the Maryland legislature placed an annual tax of $15,000 on "foreign" banks, including the Bank of the United States! The Maryland branch of the Bank of the United States refused to pay, whereupon the state brought suit against its cashier, John W McCulloch. *McCulloch v. Maryland* was crucial to the Bank, for five other states had levied taxes on its branches, and others would surely follow suit if the Maryland law were upheld.

Marshall extinguished the threat. The Bank of the United States was constitutional, he announced in phrases taken almost verbatim from Hamilton's 1791 memorandum to Washington on the subject; its legality was implied in many of the powers specifically granted to Congress. Full "discretion" must be allowed Congress in deciding exactly how its powers "are to be carried into execution." Since the Bank was legal, the Maryland tax was unconstitutional. Marshall found a "plain repugnance" in the thought of "conferring on one government a power to control the constitutional measures of another." He put this idea in the simplest possible language: "The power to tax involves the power to destroy . . . the power to destroy may defeat and render useless the power to create." The long-range significance of the decision lay in its strengthening of the implied powers of Congress and its confirmation of the "loose" interpretation of the Constitution. By establishing the legality of the Bank, it also aided the growth of the economy.

In 1824 Marshall handed down an important decision involving the regulation of interstate commerce. This was the "steamboat case," ***Gibbons v. Ogden***. In 1815 Aaron Ogden, former U.S. senator and governor of New Jersey, had purchased the right to operate a ferry between Elizabeth Point, New Jersey, and New York City from Robert Fulton's backer, Robert R. Livingston, who held a New York monopoly of steamboat navigation on the Hudson. When Thomas Gibbons, who held a federal coasting license, set up a competing line, Ogden sued him. Ogden argued in effect that Gibbons could operate his boat on the New Jersey side of the Hudson but had no right to cross into New York waters. After complicated litigation in the lower courts, the case reached the Supreme Court on appeal. Marshall decided in favor of Gibbons, effectively destroying the New York monopoly. A state can regulate commerce that begins and ends in its own territory but not when the transaction involves crossing a state line; then the national authority takes precedence. "The act of Congress," he said, "is supreme; and the law of the state . . . must yield to it."

This decision threw open the interstate steamboat business to all comers, and since an adequate 100-ton vessel could be built for as little as $7,000, dozens of small operators were soon engaged in it. More important in the long run was the fact that in order to include the ferry business within the federal government's power to regulate interstate commerce, Marshall had given the word the widest possible meaning: "Commerce, undoubtedly, is traffic, but it is something more,—it is intercourse." By construing the "commerce" clause so broadly, he made it easy for future generations of judges to extend its coverage to include the control of interstate electric power lines and even radio and television transmission.

●●●—Read the Document

McCulloch v. Maryland at
myhistorylab.com

Many of Marshall's decisions aided the economic development of the country in specific ways, but his chief contribution lay in his broadly national view of economic affairs. When he tried consciously to favor business by making contracts inviolable, his influence was important but limited—and, as it worked out, impermanent. In the steamboat case and in *McCulloch v. Maryland*, where he was really deciding between rival property interests, his work was more truly judicial in spirit and far more lasting. In such matters his nationalism enabled him to add form and substance to Hamilton's vision of the economic future of the United States.

Marshall and his colleagues firmly established the principle of judicial limitation on the power of legislatures and made the Supreme Court a vital part of the American system of government. In an age plagued by narrow sectional jealousies, Marshall's contribution was of immense influence and significance, and on it rests his claim to greatness.

John Marshall died in 1835. Two years later, in the *Charles River Bridge* case, the court handed down another decision that aided economic development. The state of Massachusetts had built a bridge across the Charles River between Boston and Cambridge that drew traffic from an older, privately owned toll bridge nearby. Since no

Table 8.1   Supreme Court Decisions and Economic Growth

	Specific Issue	Marshall Court Ruled—	Economic Consequences
Dartmouth College v. Woodward (1819)	NH sought to revoke the charter of Dartmouth College, a private school, and turn it into a public institution	For Dartmouth College: Contracts cannot be overturned	Ensured the security and regularity of business agreements and protected property rights
McCullough v. Maryland (1819)	Maryland proposed to tax the Baltimore branch of the Bank of the United States; McCullough, cashier for the bank, refused to pay Maryland tax	For federal government: States cannot tax the federal government	Ensured the supremacy of federal government over states; also strengthened the Bank of the United States and promoted economic growth
Gibbons v. Ogden (1824)	NJ steamboat operator sought to run a ferry across the Hudson River between New Jersey and New York (City), challenging a company that had a New York monopoly on such ferries	For the competing ferry: States cannot make laws that impede interstate commerce	Encouraged interstate commerce and fully national markets
Charles River Bridge Case (1837)	Operators of a company that had a contract to run a ferry across the Charles River sued Massachusetts for building a bridge that ruined the company— thereby rendering its contract worthless	For Massachusetts: The needs of the community transcend contract rights (Note: Marshall had died by time of decision)	Promoted new economic initiatives

tolls were collected from users of the state bridge after construction costs were recovered, owners of the older bridge sued for damages on the ground that the free bridge made the stock in their company worthless. They argued that in building the bridge, Massachusetts had violated the contract clause of the Constitution.

The Court, however, now speaking through the new Chief Justice, Roger B. Taney, decided otherwise. The state had a right to place "the comfort and convenience" of the whole community over that of a particular company, Taney declared. "Improvements" that add to public "wealth and property" take precedence. Like most of the decisions of the Court that were made while Marshall was chief justice, the *Charles River Bridge* case advanced the interests of those who favored economic development. Whether they were pursuing political or economic advantage, the Americans of the early nineteenth century seemed committed to a policy of compromise and accommodation.

Milestones

1790	Samuel Slater sets up first American factory	1819	Chief Justice John Marshall asserts "sanctity" of contracts in *Dartmouth College v. Woodward*
1793	Eli Whitney is widely—but wrongly—credited for inventing the cotton gin		Chief Justice Marshall strengthens implied powers of Congress in *McCulloch v. Maryland* (Bank of United States)
1794	Philadelphia–Lancaster turnpike is built		
1807	Robert Fulton constructs the *North River Steam Boat* (the *Clermont*)		
1808	Constitutional prohibition of importation of slaves goes into effect	1824	Chief Justice Marshall defends supremacy of federal government over states in *Gibbons v. Ogden* (steamboat case)
1813	Boston Manufacturing Company opens in Waltham, Massachusetts	1825	Erie Canal is completed
1816	Second Bank of the United States is created	1837	Chief Justice Roger B. Taney rules in favor of the whole community over a particular company in *Charles River Bridge v. Warren Bridge*
1817	American Colonization Society is founded in order to establish Republic of Liberia for freed slaves		

✓●─[**Study** and **Review** at **www.myhistorylab.com**

Review Questions

1. That we live in a global economy is obvious; Americans in the early 1800s similarly perceived that their economy was undergoing substantial changes. Historians chiefly debate whether this transformation from self-sufficient farms to a market economy was sudden—revolutionary—or whether it was more gradual. What evidence can be cited in support of both positions?

2. How did cotton "revolutionize" the South?

3. How did the Marshall Court stimulate economic development?

Key Terms

American Colonization Society   *235*
Dartmouth College v. Woodward   *243*

Gibbons v. Ogden   *244*
McCulloch v. Maryland   *243*

Jacksonian Democracy 9

((•─[Hear the Audio Chapter 9 at myhistorylab.com

Do you vote?

THE 2008 OBAMA CAMPAIGN BROUGHT THE INTERNET REVOLUTION TO American politics. By election night Obama had 7 million friends on Facebook and 1 million on MySpace. Some 137,573 followed his every move on Twitter ("Traveling through PA today & asking folks to vote for change!") Obama's YouTube site logged 15 million viewer-hours. Yet this high-tech media blitz had little impact on the young voters it was supposed to mobilize. Fewer than half of the registered voters aged eighteen to twenty-four cast ballots, an increase of only 2 percent over 2004. And the young-voter turnout (49 percent) remained below the turnout for all age groups—64 percent.

By contrast, the political revolution inaugurated by Andrew Jackson in 1828 energized voters like nothing before or since. Prior to 1828, only one in four eligible voters cast ballots on average during a presidential election. But Jackson transformed his supporters—called Jacksonians—into a well-structured Democratic party, built a rudimentary bureaucracy to manage its affairs, and appealed directly—and effectively—to masses of voters. In 1828 more than 1.1 million ballots were cast by 58 percent of the eligible voters, more than doubling the turnout of previous elections.

Jackson won in a landslide. During the next few decades, his opponents had little choice but to imitate his techniques and build a rival mass party—the Whigs. A new type of politics emerged, which some historians call the "Second American Party System." Its central feature was the mass mobilization of the electorate, characterized by a consistent turnout of over half of all voters.

Almost from the start, Jackson's more inclusive politics encountered new challenges and obstacles. Victorious campaign workers clamored for government jobs. Energized voters, seeking cheap land, ignored the plight of the Indians, not to mention legal rights secured by treaties. As more people voted, too, politicians were obliged to "represent" a vast electorate, which made it difficult to broker deals. Sectional tensions became more intractable. The new politics of democratic engagement were not without costs; within several decades, these would include civil war.

"Democratizing" Politics

At 11 AM on March 4, 1829, a bright sunny day, Andrew Jackson, hatless and dressed severely in black, left his quarters at Gadsby's Hotel. Accompanied by a few close associates, he walked up Pennsylvania Avenue to the Capitol. At a few minutes after noon he emerged on the East Portico with the justices of the Supreme Court and other dignitaries. Before a throng of more than 15,000 people he delivered an almost inaudible and thoroughly commonplace inaugural address and then took the presidential oath. The first man to congratulate him was Chief Justice Marshall, who had administered the oath. The second was "Honest George" Kremer, a Pennsylvania congressman who led the cheering crowd that brushed past the barricade and scrambled up the Capitol steps to wring the new president's hand.

●●●–[**Read** the **Document**

Jackson, *First Annual Message to Congress* at **myhistorylab.com**

Jackson shouldered his way through the crush, mounted a splendid white horse, and rode off to the White House. A reception had been announced, to which "the officially and socially eligible as defined by precedent" had been invited. As Jackson rode down Pennsylvania Avenue, the crowds that had turned out to see the Hero of New Orleans followed—on horseback, in rickety wagons, and on foot. Nothing could keep them out of the executive mansion, and the result was chaos. Jackson was pressed back helplessly as men tracked mud across valuable rugs and clambered up on delicate chairs to catch a glimpse of him. The White House shook with their shouts. Glassware splintered, furniture was overturned, women fainted.

Jackson was a thin old man despite his toughness, and soon he was in danger. Fortunately, friends formed a cordon and managed to extricate him through a rear door. The new president spent his first night in office at Gadsby's Hotel.

Jackson's inauguration, and especially this celebration in the White House, symbolized the triumph of "democracy," the achievement of place and station by "the common man." Having been taught by Jefferson that all men are created equal, the Americans of Jackson's day (conveniently ignoring black males, to say nothing of women, regardless of color) found it easy to believe that every person was as competent and as politically important as his neighbor.

The difference between **Jacksonian democracy** and the Jefferson variety was more one of attitude than of practice. Jefferson had believed that ordinary citizens could be educated to determine what was right. Jackson insisted that they knew what was right by instinct. Jefferson's pell-mell encouraged the average citizen to hold up his head; by the time of Jackson, the "common man" gloried in ordinariness and made mediocrity a virtue. The slightest hint of distinctiveness or servility became suspect. While most middle-class families could still hire people to do their cooking and housework, the word *servant* itself fell out of fashion, replaced by the egalitarian *help*.

The Founders had not foreseen all the implications of political democracy for a society like the one that existed in the United States. They believed that the ordinary man should have political power in order to protect himself against the superior man, but they assumed that the latter would always lead. The people would naturally choose the best men to manage public affairs. In Washington's day and even in Jefferson's this was generally the case, but the inexorable logic of democracy gradually produced a change. The new western states, unfettered by systems created in a less democratic age, drew up constitutions that eliminated property qualifications for voting and holding office. Many more public offices were made elective rather than appointive. The eastern states revised their own frames of government to accomplish the same purposes.

Even the presidency, designed to be removed from direct public control by the Electoral College, felt the impact of the new thinking. By Jackson's time only two states, Delaware and South Carolina, still provided for the choice of presidential electors by the legislature; in all others they were selected by popular vote. The system of permitting the congressional caucus to name the candidates for the presidency came to an end before 1828. Jackson and Adams were put forward by state legislatures, and soon thereafter the still more democratic system of nomination by national party conventions was adopted.

Certain social changes reflected a new way of looking at political affairs. The final disestablishment of churches further reveals the dislike of special privilege. The beginnings of the free-school movement, the earliest glimmerings of interest in adult education, and the slow spread of secondary education all bespeak a concern for improving the knowledge and judgment of the ordinary citizen. The rapid increase in the number of newspapers, their declining prices, and their ever-greater concentration on political affairs indicate an effort to bring political news to the common man's attention.

All these changes emphasized the idea that every citizen was equally important and the conviction that all should participate in government. Officeholders began to stress the fact that they were *representatives* as well as leaders and to appeal more openly and much more intensively for votes. The public responded. At each succeeding presidential election, more people went to the polls. Eight times as many people voted in 1840 as in 1824.

As voting became more important, so did competition among candidates, and this led to changes in the role and structure of political parties. Running campaigns and getting out the vote required money, people, and organized effort. Party managers, often holders of relatively minor offices, held rallies, staged parades, dreamed up catchy slogans, and printed broadsides, party newspapers, and ballots containing the names of the party's nominees for distribution to their supporters. Parties became powerful institutions that instilled loyalty among adherents.

1828: The New Party System in Embryo

The new system could scarcely have been imagined in 1825 while John Quincy Adams ruled over the White House; Adams was not well equipped either to lead King Mob or to hold it in check. Indeed, it was the battle to succeed Adams that caused the system to develop. The campaign began almost on the day of his selection by the House of Representatives. Jackson felt that he, the man who had received the largest number of votes, had been cheated of the presidency in 1824 by "the corrupt bargain" that he believed Adams had made with Henry Clay, and he sought vindication.

Relying heavily on his military reputation and on Adams's talent for making enemies, Jackson avoided taking a stand on issues where his views might displease one or another faction. The political situation thus became chaotic, one side unable to marshal support for its policies, the other unwilling to adopt policies for fear of losing support.

Rachel Jackson, wife of Andrew Jackson. At seventeen she had married Lewis Robards, but the marriage failed and after two years she returned to her family in Natchez, Mississippi. Robards sued for divorce in Virginia. Several months later, Rachel married Jackson in Mississippi, unaware that Robards would not finalize the divorce until a year later. In defending Rachel's honor from a charge of bigamy, Jackson killed a man in a duel. During the 1824 and 1828 presidential campaigns, critics denounced their marriage as immoral. Rachel died in December 1828, several weeks before her husband was inaugurated.

The campaign was disgraced by character assassination and lies of the worst sort. Administration supporters denounced Jackson as a bloodthirsty military tyrant, a drunkard, and a gambler. His wife Rachel, ailing and shy, was dragged into the campaign by an Adams pamphleteer who branded her a "convicted adulteress."

Furious, the Jacksonians (now calling themselves Democrats) replied in kind. Discovering that Adams had purchased a chess set and a billiard table for the White House, they accused him of squandering public money on gambling devices. They translated his long and distinguished public service into the statistic that he had received over the years a sum equal to $16 for every day of his life in government pay. The great questions of the day were largely ignored.

All this was inexcusable, and both sides must share the blame. But as the politicians noticed when the votes were counted, their efforts had certainly brought out the electorate. *Each* candidate received far more votes than all four candidates had received in the preceding presidential election.

The Jacksonian Appeal

Although Jackson's supporters liked to cast him as the political heir of Jefferson, he was in many ways like the conservative Washington: a soldier first, an inveterate speculator in western lands, the owner of a fine plantation and of many slaves, a man with few intellectual interests, and only sketchily educated.

Nor was Jackson quite the rough-hewn frontier character he sometimes seemed. True, he could not spell (again, like Washington), he possessed the unsavory habits of the tobacco chewer, and he had a violent temper. But his manners and lifestyle were those of a southern planter. "I have always felt that he was a perfect savage," Grace Fletcher Webster, wife of Senator Daniel Webster, explained. "But," she added, "his manners are very mild and gentlemanly." Jackson's judgment was intuitive yet usually

1828

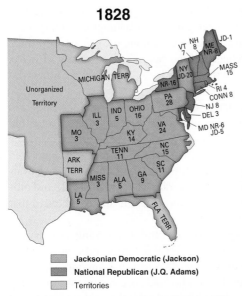

Jacksonian Democratic (Jackson)
National Republican (J.Q. Adams)
Territories

The Rise of the Second American Party System, 1828
Jackson's enormous turnout in 1828 heralded a new era in
mass political participation. In the past, Federalists tended
to take New England, and Democrats, the South. But in
1832 Jackson shattered his fragmented opposition.

Andrew Jackson as president.

sound; his frequent rages were often feigned, designed to accomplish some carefully thought-out purpose. Once, after scattering a delegation of protesters with an exhibition of wrath, he turned to an observer and said impishly, "They thought I was mad."

Whatever his personal convictions, Jackson stood as the symbol for a new, democratically oriented generation. That he was both a great hero and in many ways a most extraordinary person helps explain his mass appeal. He had defeated a mighty British army and killed many Indians, but he acted on hunches and not always consistently, put loyalty to old comrades above efficiency when making appointments, and distrusted "aristocrats" and all special privilege. Perhaps he was rich, perhaps conservative, but he was a man of the people, born in a frontier cabin, and familiar with the problems of the average citizen.

For these reasons Jackson drew support from every section and every social class: western farmers and southern planters, urban workers and bankers, and merchants. In this sense he was profoundly democratic. He believed in equality of opportunity, distrusted entrenched status of every sort, and rejected no free American because of humble origins or inadequate education.

The Spoils System

Jackson took office with the firm intention of punishing the "vile wretches" who had attacked him so viciously during the campaign. (Rachel Jackson died shortly after the election, and her devoted husband was convinced that the indignities heaped on her by

Adams partisans had hastened her decline.) The new concept of political office as a reward for victory seemed to justify a housecleaning in Washington. Henry Clay captured the fears of anti-Jackson government workers. "Among the official corps here there is the greatest solicitude and apprehension," he said. "The members of it feel something like the inhabitants of Cairo when the plague breaks out; no one knows who is next to encounter the stroke of death."

Eager for the "spoils," an army of politicians invaded Washington. Such invasions were customary, for the principle of filling offices with one's partisans was almost as old as the republic. However, the long lapse of time since the last real political shift, and the recent untypical example of John Quincy Adams, who rarely removed or appointed anyone for political reasons, made Jackson's policy appear revolutionary. His removals were not entirely unjustified, for many government workers had grown senile and others corrupt. Jackson was determined to root out the thieves. Even Adams admitted that some of those Jackson dismissed deserved their fate.

Aside from going along with the **spoils system** and eliminating crooks and incompetents, Jackson advanced another reason for turning experienced government employees out of their jobs: the principle of rotation. "No man has any more intrinsic right to official station than another," he said. Those who hold government jobs for a long time "are apt to acquire a habit of looking with indifference upon the public interests and of tolerating conduct from which an unpracticed man would revolt." By "rotating" jobholders periodically, more citizens could participate in the tasks of government, and the danger of creating an entrenched bureaucracy would be eliminated. The problem was that the constant replacing of trained workers by novices was not likely to increase the efficiency of the government. Jackson's response to this argument was typical: "The duties of all public officers are . . . so plain and simple that men of intelligence may readily qualify themselves for their performance."

Contempt for expert knowledge and the belief that ordinary Americans can do anything they set their minds to became fundamental tenets of Jacksonian democracy. To apply them to present-day government would be to court disaster, but in the early nineteenth century it was not so preposterous, because the role that government played in American life was simple and nontechnical.

President of All the People

President Jackson was not cynical about the spoils system. As a strong man who intuitively sought to increase his authority, the idea of making government workers dependent on him made excellent sense. His opponents had pictured him as a simple soldier fronting for a rapacious band of politicians, but he soon proved he would exercise his authority directly. Except for Martin Van Buren, the secretary of state, his Cabinet was not distinguished, and he did not rely on it for advice. He turned instead to an informal "Kitchen Cabinet," which consisted of the influential Van Buren and a few close friends. But these men were advisers, not directors; Jackson was clearly master of his own administration.

More than any earlier president, he conceived of himself as the direct representative of all the people and therefore the embodiment of national power. From Washington to John Quincy Adams, his predecessors together had vetoed only nine bills, all on the ground that they believed the measures unconstitutional. Jackson vetoed a dozen, some simply because he thought the legislation inexpedient. Yet he had no ambition to expand the scope of federal authority at the expense of the states. Basically he was a Jeffersonian; he favored a "frugal," constitutionally limited national government. Furthermore, he was a poor administrator, given to penny-pinching and lacking in imagination. His strong prejudices and his contempt for expert advice, even in fields such as banking where his ignorance was almost total, did him no credit and the country considerable harm.

Sectional Tensions Revived

In office Jackson had to say something about western lands, the tariff, and other issues. He tried to steer a moderate course, urging a slight reduction of the tariff and "constitutional" internal improvements. He suggested that once the rapidly disappearing federal debt had been paid off, the surplus revenues of the government might be "distributed" among the states.

So complex were the interrelations of sectional disputes that even these cautious proposals caused conflict. If the federal government turned its expected surplus over to the states, it could not afford to reduce the price of public land without going into the red. This disturbed westerners, notably Senator Thomas Hart Benton of Missouri, and western concern suggested to southern opponents of the protective tariff an alliance of South and West. The Southerners argued that a tariff levied only to raise revenue would increase the cost of foreign imports, bring more money into the treasury, and thus make it possible to reduce the price of public land.

The question came up in the Senate in December 1829, when Senator Samuel A. Foot of Connecticut suggested restricting the sale of government land. Benton promptly denounced the proposal. On January 19, 1830, Senator Robert Y. Hayne of South Carolina, a spokesman for Vice President Calhoun, supported Benton vigorously, suggesting an alliance of South and West based on cheap land and low tariffs. Daniel Webster then rose to the defense of northeastern interests, cleverly goading Hayne by accusing South Carolina of advocating disunionist policies. Responding to this attack, the South Carolinian launched into an impassioned exposition of the states' rights doctrine.

Webster then took the floor again and for two days, before galleries packed with the elite of Washington society, cut Hayne's argument to shreds. The Constitution was a compact of the American people, not merely of the states, he insisted, the Union perpetual and indissoluble. Webster made the states' rights position appear close to treason; his "second reply to Hayne" effectively prevented the formation of a West–South alliance and made Webster a presidential candidate.

Jackson: "The Bank . . . I Will Kill It!"

In the fall of 1832 Jackson was reelected president, handily defeating Henry Clay. The main issue in this election, aside from Jackson's personal popularity, was the president's determination to destroy the Second Bank of the United States. In this **Bank war**, Jackson won a complete victory, yet the effects of his triumph were anything but beneficial to the country.

After *McCulloch v. Maryland* had presumably established its legality and the conservative Langdon Cheves had gotten it on a sound footing, the Bank of the United States had flourished. In 1823 Cheves was replaced as president by Nicholas Biddle, who managed it brilliantly. A talented Philadelphian, Biddle realized that his institution could act as a rudimentary central bank, regulating the availability of credit throughout the nation by

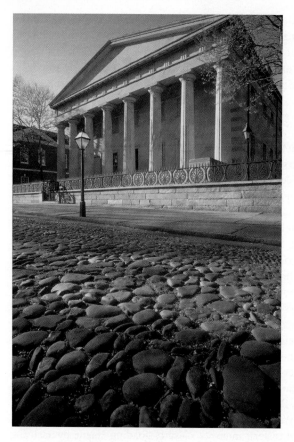

With its simple lines and perfect symmetry, the Second Bank of the United States was a symbol of Classical architecture. Jackson thought its internal workings were less simple and transparent.

controlling the lending policies of the state banks. Small banks, possessing limited amounts of gold and silver, sometimes overextended themselves in making large amounts of bank notes available to borrowers in order to earn interest. All this paper money was legally convertible into hard cash on demand, but in the ordinary run of business people seldom bothered to convert their notes so long as they thought the issuing bank was sound.

Bank notes passed freely from hand to hand and from bank to bank in every section of the country. Eventually much of the paper money of the local banks came across the counter of one or another of the twenty-two branches of the Bank of the United States. By collecting these notes and presenting them for conversion into coin, Biddle could compel the local banks to maintain adequate reserves of gold and silver—in other words, make them hold their lending policies within bounds. "The Bank of the United States," he explained, "has succeeded in keeping in check many institutions which might otherwise have been tempted into extravagant and ruinous excesses."

Biddle's policies in the 1820s were good for the Bank of the United States (which earned substantial profits), for the state banks, and probably for the country. Pressures on local bankers to make loans were enormous. The nation had an insatiable need for capital, and the general mood of the people was optimistic. Everyone wanted to borrow, and everyone expected values to rise, as in general they did. But by making liberal loans to produce merchants, for example, rural bankers indirectly stimulated farmers to expand their output beyond current demand, which eventually led to a decline in prices and an agricultural depression. In every field of economic activity, reckless lending caused inflation and greatly exaggerated the ups and downs of the business cycle. (This lesson was hammered home to Americans during the financial meltdown of 2008, when lending for home mortgages spiraled out of control and the mortgage market crashed.)

Biddle's policies acted to stabilize the economy, and many interests, including a substantial percentage of state bankers, supported them. They also provoked a great deal of opposition. In part the opposition originated in pure ignorance: Distrust of paper money did not disappear, and people who disliked all paper saw the Bank as merely the largest (and thus the worst) of many bad institutions. At the other extreme, some bankers chafed under Biddle's restraints because by discouraging them from lending freely, he was limiting their profits.

Finally, some people objected to the Bank because it was a monopoly. Distrust of chartered corporations as agents of special privilege tended to focus on the Bank, which had a monopoly of public funds but was managed by a private citizen and controlled by a handful of rich men. Biddle's wealth and social position intensified this feeling. Like many brilliant people, he sometimes appeared arrogant. He was unused to criticism and disdainful of ignorant and stupid attacks, failing to see that they were sometimes the most dangerous.

Jackson's Bank Veto

This formidable opposition to the Bank was diffuse and unorganized until Andrew Jackson brought it together. When he did, the Bank was quickly destroyed. Jackson can be included among the ignorant enemies of the institution, a hard-money man suspicious of all commercial banking. "I think it right to be perfectly frank with you," he told Biddle in 1829. "I do not dislike your Bank any more than all banks. But ever since I read the history of the South Sea Bubble I have been afraid of banks."

Jackson's attitude dismayed Biddle. It also mystified him, since the Bank was the country's best defense against a speculative mania like the eighteenth-century South Sea Bubble, in which hundreds of naive British investors had been fleeced. Bankers usually *opposed* government restraints on lending. Almost against his will, Biddle found himself gravitating toward Clay and the new National Republican party, offering advantageous loans and retainers to politicians and newspaper editors in order to build up a following. Thereafter, events moved inevitably toward a showdown, for the president's combative instincts were easily aroused. "The Bank," he told Van Buren, "is trying to kill me, *but I will kill it!*"

Henry Clay, Daniel Webster, and other prominent National Republicans hoped to use the Bank controversy against Jackson. They reasoned that the institution was so important to the country that Jackson's opposition to it would undermine his popularity. They therefore urged Biddle to ask Congress to renew the Bank's charter. The charter would not expire until 1836, but by pressing the issue before the 1832 presidential election, they could force Jackson either to approve the recharter bill or to veto it (which would give candidate Clay a lively issue in the campaign). The banker yielded to this strategy and a recharter bill passed Congress early in July 1832. Jackson promptly vetoed it.

•●• **Read** the Document

Jackson, *Veto of the Bank Bill* at **myhistorylab.com**

Jackson's message explaining why he had rejected the bill was immensely popular, but it adds nothing to his reputation as a statesman. Being a good Jeffersonian—and no friend of John Marshall—he insisted that the Bank was unconstitutional. (*McCulloch v. Maryland* he brushed aside, saying that as president he had sworn to uphold the Constitution as *he* understood it.) The Bank was inexpedient, he argued. A dangerous private monopoly that allowed a handful of rich men to accumulate "many millions" of dollars, the Bank was making "the rich richer and the potent more powerful."

Furthermore, many of its stockholders were foreigners: "If we must have a bank . . . it should be *purely American*."[1]

Buttressed by his election triumph, Jackson acted swiftly. He ordered the withdrawal of government funds from the Bank, but his own secretary of the treasury thought it unwise and refused to do so. Jackson replaced him with Attorney General Roger B. Taney, who had been advising him closely on Bank affairs. Taney carried out the order by depositing new federal receipts in seven state banks in eastern cities while continuing to meet government expenses with drafts on the Bank of the United States.

Set on winning the Bank war, Jackson lost sight of his fear of unsound paper money. Taney, however, knew exactly what he was doing. One of the state banks receiving federal funds was the Union Bank of Baltimore. Taney owned stock in this institution, and its president was his close friend. Little wonder that Jackson's enemies were soon calling the favored state banks "pet" banks.

When Taney began to remove the deposits, the government had $9,868,000 to its credit in the Bank of the United States; within three months the figure fell to about $4 million. Faced with the withdrawal of so much cash, Biddle had to contract his operations. He decided to exaggerate the contraction, pressing the state banks hard by presenting all their notes and checks that came across his counter for conversion into specie and drastically limiting his own bank's business loans. He hoped that the resulting shortage of credit would be blamed on Jackson and that it would force the president to return the deposits.

For a time the strategy appeared to be working. Paper money became scarce, specie almost unobtainable. A serious panic threatened. New York banks were soon refusing to make any loans at all. "Nobody buys; nobody can sell," a French visitor to the city observed. Petitions poured in on Congress. Worried and indignant delegations of businessmen began trooping to Washington seeking "relief." Clay, Webster, and John C. Calhoun thundered against Jackson in the Senate.

The president would not budge. "I am fixed in my course as firm as the Rockey Mountain," he wrote Vice President Van Buren. No "frail mortals" who worshiped "the golden calf" could change his mind. To others he swore he would sooner cut off his right arm and "undergo the torture of ten Spanish inquisitions" than restore the deposits. When delegations came to him, he roared, "Go to Nicholas Biddle . . . . Biddle has all the money!" And in the end—because he was right—business leaders began to take the old general's advice. Pressure on Biddle mounted swiftly, and in July 1834 he suddenly reversed his policy and began to lend money freely. The artificial crisis ended.

Jackson versus Calhoun

The Webster-Hayne debate had revived discussion of Calhoun's argument about nullification. Although southern-born, Jackson had devoted too much of his life to fighting for the entire United States to countenance disunion. Therefore, in April 1830,

---

[1]The country needed all the foreign capital it could attract. Foreigners owned only $8 million of the $35 million stock, and in any case they could not vote their shares.

when the states' rights faction invited him to a dinner to celebrate the anniversary of Jefferson's birth, he came prepared. The evening reverberated with speeches and toasts of a states' rights tenor, but when the president was called on to volunteer a toast, he raised his glass, fixed his eyes on John C. Calhoun, and said, "Our *Federal* Union: It must be preserved!" Calhoun took up the challenge at once. "The Union," he retorted, "next to our liberty, most dear!"

It is difficult to measure the importance of the animosity between Jackson and Calhoun in the crisis to which this clash was a prelude. Calhoun wanted very much to be president. He had failed to inherit the office from John Quincy Adams and had accepted the vice presidency again under Jackson in the hope of succeeding him at the end of one term, if not sooner, for Jackson's health was known to be frail. Yet Old Hickory showed no sign of passing on or retiring. Jackson also seemed to place special confidence in the shrewd Van Buren, who, as secretary of state, also had claim to the succession.

A silly social fracas in which Calhoun's wife appeared to take the lead in the systematic snubbing of Peggy Eaton, wife of the secretary of war, had estranged Jackson and Calhoun. (Peggy was supposed to have had an affair with Eaton while she was still married to another man, and Jackson, undoubtedly sympathetic because of the attacks he and Rachel had endured, stoutly defended her good name.) Then, shortly after the Jefferson Day dinner, Jackson discovered that in 1818, when he had invaded Florida, Calhoun, then secretary of war, had recommended to President Monroe that Jackson be summoned before a court of inquiry and charged with disobeying orders. Since Calhoun had repeatedly led Jackson to believe that he had supported him at the time, the revelation convinced the president that Calhoun was not a man of honor.

The personal difficulties are worth stressing because Jackson and Calhoun were not far apart ideologically except on the ultimate issue of the right of a state to overrule federal authority. Jackson was a strong president, but he did not believe that the area of national power was large or that it should be expanded. His interests in government economy, in the distribution of federal surpluses to the states, and in interpreting the powers of Congress narrowly were all similar to Calhoun's. Like most westerners, he favored internal improvements, but he preferred that local projects be left to the states.

Indian Removals

The president also took a states' rights position in the controversy that arose between the Cherokee Indians and Georgia. The Cherokee inhabited a region coveted by whites because it was suitable for growing cotton. Since most Indians preferred to maintain their tribal ways, Jackson pursued a policy of removing them from the path of white settlement. This policy seems heartless to modern critics, but since few Indians were willing to adopt the white way of life, most contemporary whites considered removal the only humane solution if the nation was to continue to expand. Jackson insisted that the Indians receive fair prices for their lands and that the government bear the expense of resettling them. He believed that moving them beyond the Mississippi would protect them from the "degradation and destruction to which they were rapidly hastening . . . in the States."

Many tribes resigned themselves to removal without argument. Between 1831 and 1833, some 15,000 Choctaw migrated from their lands in Mississippi to the region west of the Arkansas Territory.

In *Democracy in America*, the French writer Alexis de Tocqueville described "the frightful sufferings that attend these forced migrations," and he added sadly that the migrants "have no longer a country, and soon will not be a people." He vividly described a group of Choctaw crossing the Mississippi River at Memphis in the dead of winter:

> The cold was unusually severe; the snow had frozen hard upon the ground, and the river was drifting huge masses of ice. The Indians had their families with them, and they brought in their train the wounded and the sick, with children newly born and old men upon the verge of death. They possessed neither tents nor wagons, but only their arms and some provisions. I saw them embark to pass the mighty river, and never will that solemn spectacle fade from my remembrance. No cry, no sob, was heard among the assembled crowd; all were silent.

A few tribes, such as Black Hawk's Sac and Fox in Illinois and Osceola's Seminole in Florida, resisted removal and were subdued by troops. One Indian nation, the Cherokee, sought to hold on to their lands by adjusting to white ways. They took up farming and cattle raising, developed a written language, drafted a constitution, and tried to establish a state within a state in northwestern Georgia. Several treaties with the United States seemed to establish the legality of their government. But Georgia would not recognize the Cherokee Nation. It passed a law in 1828 declaring all Cherokee laws void and the region part of Georgia.

The Indians challenged this law in the Supreme Court. In *Cherokee Nation v. Georgia* (1831), Chief Justice John Marshall had ruled that the Cherokee were "not a foreign state, in the sense of the Constitution" and therefore could not sue in a U.S. court. However, in *Worcester v. Georgia* (1832), a case involving two missionaries to the Cherokee who had not procured licenses required by Georgia law, he ruled that the state could not control the Cherokee or their territory. Later, when a Cherokee named Corn Tassel, convicted in a Georgia court of the murder of another Indian, appealed on the ground that the crime had

taken place in Cherokee territory, Marshall agreed and declared the Georgia action unconstitutional.

Jackson backed Georgia's position. No independent nation could exist within the United States, he insisted. Georgia thereupon hanged Corn Tassel. In 1838, after Jackson had left the White House, the United States forced 15,000 Cherokee to leave

Osceola had led the Seminole Indians' resistance to their forced removal from Florida to lands west of the Mississippi. He was seized during a truce parlay and imprisoned at Fort Moultrie, South Carolina. George Catlin, incensed by this treatment, became friends with Osceola and then painted this picture.

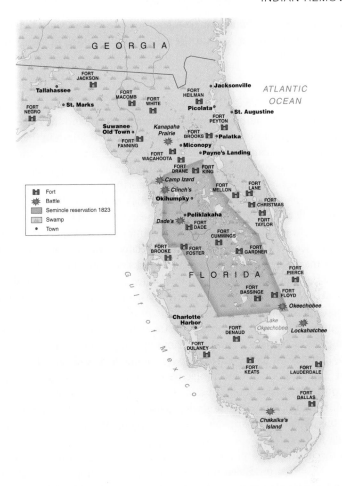

Osceola's Rebellion Osceola, a young warrior, refused to accept tribal elders' decision to cede Seminole land in Florida and move to Oklahoma. In 1835 he murdered the tribal leader who had accepted removal and spearheaded Seminole resistance. Seminole warriors, augmented by African Americans who had escaped from slavery, proved to be astute tacticians in guerrilla warfare. During the next seven years, the federal government spent $20 million, an immense sum, and lost 1,500 soldiers in the war to force the remaining Seminole from Florida. When Osceola hoisted a white flag to negotiate with federal officers, they seized him and put him in prison. He died shortly after George Catlin completed his portrait. Because of his courageous resistance and the treacherous manner of his capture, Osceola became famous after his death.

Georgia for Oklahoma. At least 4,000 of them died on the way; the route has been aptly named the **Trail of Tears**.

Jackson's willingness to allow Georgia to ignore decisions of the Supreme Court persuaded extreme southern states' righters that he would not oppose the doctrine of nullification should it be formally applied to a law of Congress. They deceived themselves egregiously. Jackson did not challenge Georgia because he approved of the state's position. He spoke of "the poor deluded . . . Cherokees" and called William Wirt, the distinguished lawyer who defended

See the Map
Native American Removal at
myhistorylab.com

their cause, a "truly wicked" man. Jackson was not one to worry about being inconsistent. When South Carolina revived the talk of nullification in 1832, he acted in quite a different manner.

The Nullification Crisis

The proposed alliance of South and West to reduce the tariff and the price of land had not materialized, partly because Webster had discredited the South in the eyes of western patriots and partly because the planters of South Carolina and Georgia, fearing the competition of fertile new cotton lands in Alabama and Mississippi, opposed the rapid exploitation of the West almost as vociferously as northern manufacturers did. When a new tariff law was passed in 1832, it lowered duties much less than the Southerners desired. At once talk of nullifying it began to be heard in South Carolina.

In addition to the economic woes of the up-country cotton planters, the great planter-aristocrats of the rice-growing Tidewater, though relatively prosperous, were troubled by northern criticisms of slavery. In the rice region, blacks outnumbered whites two to one; it was the densest concentration of blacks in the United States. Usually controlled by overseers of the worst sort, the slaves seemed to their masters like savage beasts straining to rise up against their oppressors. In 1822 the exposure in Charleston of a planned revolt organized by Denmark Vesey, who had bought his freedom with money won in a lottery, had alarmed many whites. News of a far more serious uprising in Virginia led by the slave Nat Turner in 1831, just as the tariff controversy was coming to a head, added to popular concern. Radical South Carolinians saw protective tariffs and agitation against slavery as the two sides of one coin; against both aspects of what appeared to them the tyranny of the majority, nullification seemed the logical defense. Yield on the tariff, editor Henry L. Pinckney of the influential *Charleston Mercury* warned, and "abolition will become the order of the day."

Endless discussions of Calhoun's doctrine after the publication of his *Exposition and Protest* in 1828 had produced much interesting theorizing without clarifying the issue. Plausible at first glance, it was based on false assumptions: that the Constitution was subject to definitive interpretation; that one party could be permitted to interpret a compact unilaterally without destroying it; that a minority of the nation could reassume its sovereign independence but that a minority of a state could not.

President Jackson was in this respect Calhoun's exact opposite. The South Carolinian's mental gymnastics he brushed aside; intuitively he realized the central reality: If a state could nullify a law of Congress, the Union could not exist. "Tell . . . the Nullifiers from me that they can talk and write resolutions and print threats to their hearts'

View along the East Battery, Charleston by Samuel Bernard (1831). Many whites feared a slave uprising in South Carolina where African Americans outnumbered whites.

content," he warned a South Carolina representative when Congress adjourned in July 1832. "But if one drop of blood be shed there in defiance of the laws of the United States, I will hang the first man of them I can get my hands on to the first tree I can find."

The warning was not taken seriously in South Carolina. In October the state legislature provided for the election of a special convention, which, when it met, contained a solid majority of nullifiers. On November 24, 1832, the convention passed an ordinance of **nullification** prohibiting the collection of tariff duties in the state after February 1, 1833. The legislature then authorized the raising of an army and appropriated money to supply it with weapons.

●●●—Read the **Document**

South Carolina's Ordinance of Nullification at **myhistorylab.com**

Jackson quickly began military preparations of his own, telling friends that he would have 50,000 men ready to move in a little over a month. He also made a statesmanlike effort to end the crisis peaceably. First he suggested to Congress that it lower the tariff further. On December 10 he delivered a "Proclamation to the People of South Carolina." Nullification could only lead to the destruction of the Union: "The laws of the United States must be executed. I have no discretionary power on the subject. . . . Those who told you that you might peaceably prevent their execution deceived you." Old Hickory added sternly, "Disunion by armed force is *treason*. Are you really ready to incur its guilt?" If South Carolina did not back down, the president's threat to use force would mean civil war and possibly the destruction of the Union he claimed to be defending.

Calhoun sought desperately to control the crisis. By prearrangement with Senator Hayne, he resigned as vice president and was appointed to replace Hayne in the Senate, where he led the search for a peaceful solution. Having been defeated in his campaign for the presidency, Clay was a willing ally. In addition, many who admired Jackson nonetheless, as Van Buren later wrote, "distrusted his prudence," fearing that he would "commit some rash act." They believed in dealing with the controversy by discussion and compromise.

As a result, administration leaders introduced both a new tariff bill and a Force Bill granting the president additional authority to execute the revenue laws. Jackson was perfectly willing to see the tariff reduced but insisted that he was determined to enforce the law. As the February 1 deadline approached, he claimed that he could raise 200,000 men if needed to suppress resistance. "Union men, fear not," he said. "*The Union will be preserved.*"

Jackson's determination sobered the South Carolina radicals. Their appeal for the support of other southern states fell on deaf ears: All rejected the idea of nullification. The unionist minority in South Carolina added to the radicals' difficulties by threatening civil war if federal authority were defied.

Ten days before the deadline, South Carolina postponed nullification pending the outcome of the tariff debate. Then, in March 1833, Calhoun and Clay pushed a compromise tariff through Congress. As part of the agreement Congress also passed the Force Bill, mostly as a face-saving device for the president.

The compromise reflected the willingness of the North and West to make concessions in the interest of national harmony. And so the Union weathered the storm. Having stepped to the brink of civil war, the nation had drawn hastily back. The South Carolina legislature professed to be satisfied with the new tariff (in fact it made few immediate reductions, providing for a gradual lowering of rates over a ten-year period) and repealed the Nullification Ordinance. But the radical South Carolina planters were becoming convinced that only secession would protect slavery. The nullification fiasco had proved that they could not succeed without the support of other slave states. Thereafter they devoted themselves ceaselessly to obtaining it.

Boom and Bust

During 1833 and 1834 Secretary of the Treasury Taney insisted that the pet banks maintain large reserves. But other state banks began to offer credit on easy terms, aided by a large increase in their reserves of gold and silver resulting from causes unconnected with the policies of either the government or Biddle's Bank. A decline in the Chinese demand for Mexican silver led to increased exports of the metal to the United States, and the rise of American interest rates attracted English capital into the country. Heavy English purchases of American cotton at high prices also increased the flow of specie into American banks. These developments caused bank notes in circulation to jump from $82 million in January 1835 to $120 million in December 1836. Bank deposits rose even more rapidly.

Much of the new money flowed into speculation in land; a mania to invest in property swept the country. The increased volume of currency caused prices to soar 15 percent in six months, buoying investors' spirits and making them ever more optimistic about the future. By the summer of 1835 one observer estimated that in New York City, which had about 250,000 residents, enough house lots had been laid out and sold to support a population of 2 million. Chicago at this time had only 2,000 to 3,000 inhabitants, yet most of the land for twenty-five miles around had been sold and resold in small lots by speculators anticipating the growth of the area. Throughout the West farmers borrowed money from local banks by mortgaging their land, used the money to buy more land from the government, and then borrowed still more money from the banks on the strength of their new deeds.

So long as prices rose, the process could be repeated endlessly. In 1832, while the Bank of the United States still regulated the money supply, federal income from the sale of land was $2.6 million; in 1834 it was $4.9 million; and in 1835, $14.8 million. In 1836 it rose to $24.9 million, and the government found itself totally free of debt and with a surplus of $20 million!

Finally Jackson became alarmed by the speculative mania. In the summer of 1836 he issued the **Specie Circular,** which provided that purchasers must henceforth pay for public land in gold or silver. At once the rush to buy land came to a halt. As demand slackened, prices sagged. Speculators, unable to dispose of lands mortgaged to the banks, had to abandon them to the banks, but the banks could not realize enough on the foreclosed property to recover their loans. Suddenly the public mood changed. Commodity prices tumbled 30 percent between February and May. Hordes of depositors sought to withdraw their money in the form of specie, and soon the banks exhausted their supplies. Panic swept the country in the spring of 1837 as every bank in the nation was forced to suspend specie payments. The boom was over.

Major swings in the business cycle can never be attributed to the actions of a single person, however powerful, but there is no doubt that Jackson's war against the Bank exaggerated the swings of the economic pendulum, not so much by its direct effects as by the impact of the president's ill-considered policies on popular thinking. His Specie

Circular did not prevent speculators from buying land—at most it caused purchasers to pay a premium for gold or silver. But it convinced potential buyers that the boom was going to end and led them to make decisions that in fact ended it. Old Hickory's combination of impetuousness, combativeness, arrogance, and ignorance rendered the nation he loved so dearly a serious disservice.

The Jacksonians

Jackson's personality had a large impact on the shape and tone of American politics and thus with the development of the **second party system**. When he came to office, nearly everyone professed to be a follower of Jefferson. By 1836 being a Jeffersonian no longer meant much; what mattered was how one felt about Andrew Jackson. He had ridden to power at the head of a diverse political army, but he left behind him an organization with a fairly cohesive, if not necessarily consistent, body of ideas. This Democratic party contained rich citizens and poor, easterners and westerners, abolitionists as well as slaveholders. It was not yet a close-knit national organization, but the Jacksonians agreed on certain underlying principles. These included suspicion of special privilege and large business corporations, both typified by the Bank of the United States; freedom of economic opportunity, unfettered by private or governmental restrictions; absolute political freedom, at least for white males; and the conviction that any ordinary man is capable of performing the duties of most public offices.

Jackson's ability to reconcile his belief in the supremacy of the Union with his conviction that national authority should be held within narrow limits tended to make the Democrats the party of those who believed that the powers of the states should not be diminished. Tocqueville caught this aspect of Jackson's philosophy perfectly: "Far from wishing to extend Federal power," he wrote, "the president belongs to the party that wishes to limit that power."

Although the radical Locofoco[2] wing of the party championed the idea, nearly all Jacksonians, like their leader, favored giving the small man his chance—by supporting public education, for example, and by refusing to place much weight on a person's origin, dress, or manners. "One individual is as good as another" (for accuracy we must insert the adjective *white*) was their axiom. This attitude helps explain why immigrants, Catholics, and other minority groups usually voted Democratic. However, the Jacksonians showed no tendency either to penalize the wealthy or to intervene in economic affairs to aid the underprivileged. The motto "That government is best which governs least" graced the masthead of the chief Jacksonian newspaper, the *Washington Globe*, throughout the era.

Rise of the Whigs

The opposition to Jackson was far less cohesive. Henry Clay's National Republican party provided a nucleus, but Clay never dominated that party as Jackson dominated the Democrats. Its orientation was basically anti-Jackson. It was as though the

---

[2]A locofoco was a type of friction match. The name was first applied in politics when a group of New York Jacksonians used these matches to light candles when a conservative faction tried to break up their meeting by turning off the gaslights.

American people were a great block of granite from which some sculptor had just fashioned a statue of Jackson, the chips scattered about the floor of the studio representing the opposition.

While Jackson was president, the impact of his personality delayed the formation of a true two-party system, but as soon as he surrendered power, the opposition, taking heart, began to coalesce. Many Democrats could not accept the odd logic of Jacksonian finance. As early as 1834 they (together with the Clay element, the extreme states' righters who followed Calhoun, and other dissident groups) were calling themselves **Whigs**. The name harkened back to the Revolution. It implied patriotic distaste for too-powerful executives, expressed specifically as resistance to the tyranny of "King Andrew."

This coalition possessed great resources of wealth and talent. Anyone who understood banking was almost obliged to become a Whig unless he was connected with one of Jackson's "pets." Those spiritual descendants of Hamilton who rejected the administration's refusal to approach economic problems from a broadly national perspective also joined in large numbers. Those who found the coarseness and "pushiness" of the Jacksonians offensive were another element in the new party. The anti-intellectual and antiscientific bias of the administration (Jackson rejected proposals for a national university, an observatory, and a scientific and literary institute) drove many ministers, lawyers, doctors, and other well-educated people into the Whig fold.

The philosopher Ralph Waldo Emerson was no doubt thinking of these types when he described the Whigs as "the enterprizing, intelligent, well-meaning & wealthy part of the people," but Whig arguments also appealed to ordinary voters who were predisposed to favor strong governments that would check the "excesses" of unrestricted individualism.

Table 9.1   Second American Party System: Democrats and Whigs, 1828–1850s

	Democrats	Whigs
Leaders	Andrew Jackson, Martin Van Buren, John Calhoun, James Polk	Henry Clay, Daniel Webster
Key issue	For: "the common man"	Against: "King Andrew" (Jackson)
Bank of United States	Oppose	Favor
Federal support for internal improvements (roads, canals)	Oppose	Favor
Removal of Indians	Favor	Oppose
Tariffs	Favor low	Favor high
States' rights vs. strong central government	Endorse states' rights	Endorse strong federal government

The Whigs were slow to develop effective party organization. They had too many generals and not enough troops. The issues that defined the Whigs varied from one state to another. For the most part, the sole unifying principle was opposition to Jackson. Furthermore, they stood in conflict with the major trend of the age: the glorification of the common man.

Lacking a dominant leader in 1836, the Whigs relied on "favorite sons," hoping to throw the presidential election into the House of Representatives. Daniel Webster ran in New England. For the West and South, Hugh Lawson White of Tennessee, a former friend who had broken with Jackson, was counted on to carry the fight. General William Henry Harrison was supposed to win in the Northwest and to draw support everywhere from those who liked to vote for military heroes. This sorry strategy failed; Jackson's handpicked candidate, Martin Van Buren, won a majority of both the popular and the electoral votes.

Martin Van Buren: Jacksonianism without Jackson

Van Buren's brilliance as a political manipulator—the Red Fox, the Little Magician—has tended to obscure his statesmanlike qualities and his engaging personality. He made a powerful argument, for example, that political parties were a force for unity, not for partisan bickering. In addition, high office sobered him, and improved his judgment. He fought the Bank of the United States as a monopoly, but he also opposed irresponsible state banks. New York's Safety Fund System (requiring all banks to contribute to a fund) supervised by the state (to be used to redeem the notes of any member bank that failed) was established largely through his efforts. Van Buren believed in public construction of internal improvements, but he favored state rather than national programs, and he urged a rational approach: Each project must stand on its own as a useful and profitable public utility.

Van Buren had outmaneuvered Calhoun easily in the struggle to succeed Jackson, winning the old hero's confidence and serving him well. In 1832 he was elected vice president and thereafter was conceded to be the "heir apparent." In 1835 the Democratic National Convention unanimously nominated him for president.

((•─[Hear the **Audio**

Van Buren at **myhistorylab.com**

Van Buren took office just as the Panic of 1837 struck the country. Its effects were frightening but short-lived. When the banks stopped converting paper money into gold and silver, they outraged conservatives but in effect eased the pressure on the money market: Interest rates declined and business loans again became relatively easy to obtain. In 1836, at the height of the boom in land sales, Congress had voted to "distribute" the new treasury surplus to the states, and this flow of money, which the states promptly spent, also stimulated the revival. Late in 1838 the banks resumed specie payments.

But in 1839 a bumper crop caused a sharp decline in the price of cotton. Then a number of state governments that had overextended themselves in road- and canal-building projects were forced to default on their debts. This discouraged investors, particularly foreigners. A general economic depression ensued that lasted until 1843.

Van Buren was not responsible for the panic or the depression, but his manner of dealing with economic issues was scarcely helpful. He saw his role as being concerned only with problems plaguing the government, ignoring the economy as a whole.

DAVY CROCKETT

Davy Crockett, the myth, is known better than the man, who was born David Crockett in 1786 in a cabin in hardscrabble east Tennessee. John Crockett, his father, borrowed money to buy cheap frontier land and seldom repaid his creditors. When a passing Dutchman said he needed help to drive his cattle to market in Virginia, John proposed he take on David as a "bound boy" to help out. David was twelve.

After delivering the cattle to Virginia, the driver declared that David's term of service was not over. The boy pretended to accept the arrangement, but after several weeks he sneaked away in a snowstorm; two months later he was back home in Tennessee.

The next fall his father enrolled David at a small country school. But after beating up another boy, he played hooky, fearing the wrath of the schoolmaster. When his father learned of his son's truancy, he came after the boy with a hickory stick. David hightailed it into the woods.

He was gone for over two years, wandering through Tennessee, North Carolina, Virginia, and Maryland. He moved from town to town "to see what sort of place it was, and what sort of folks lived there." He mostly did odd jobs on farms for twenty-five cents a day. When he showed up back home two years later, his father, near bankruptcy, bartered David's labor to settle the debts with various creditors.

Soon young Crockett's thoughts turned to girls, few of whom had much interest in such an uncouth boy. Crockett could not even write his name. So he broke free from his father and made his own deal with a local schoolteacher, bartering his labor for board and instruction. The arrangement lasted for six months, Crockett's only formal schooling.

Shortly afterward he attended a "stomp down"—a community-wide harvest festival with games, music, and dancing—where he met Polly Finley, "a very pretty" Irish girl. Within a few months they were married. Polly's parents gave the couple two cows. Crockett rented a nearby farm.

This 1839 engraving of Davy Crockett was based on an earlier painting.

But Crockett proved to be a poor farmer. Time and again he fell into debt, lost his farm, and moved to cheaper land farther west. "I found that I was better at increasing my family than my fortune," he observed: He and his wife had three children. In 1813 they took possession of land deep in Creek territory, near the Alabama border.

The timing was poor. By then, the War of 1812 had spread to the frontier, as Tecumseh, the Indian leader, incited Indian uprisings throughout the West. In Alabama, Creeks attacked and overran Fort Mims, killing hundreds of soldiers and settlers. In response Crockett enlisted in the Tennessee militia. He served under

Andrew Jackson, participating in the slaughter of scores of Indians. "We shot them like dogs," Crockett noted.

After returning to Tennessee, he was elected magistrate for Lawrence County, a rough frontier district. Again, his farm failed; but the woodsy region was thick with game and Crockett was accurate with a long rifle. He killed deer, wolves, panthers, alligators and, in one winter alone, 105 bear. Soon tales of Crockett's hunting prowess spread throughout the region.

In 1821 Crockett was elected to the Tennessee legislature, the first of many victories. Once, accused of telling lies about an opponent, Crockett conceded that he had. But therein lay the difference, he explained, for he truthfully admitted his lies while his opponent did not. The crowd roared. In 1826 Crockett was elected to the House of Representatives.

Newspapermen delighted in the spectacle of the rough frontiersman in the nation's capital. They reported that at a White House dinner Crockett drank from the finger bowls and accused a waiter of trying to steal his food.

In Congress, Crockett's key issue—indeed, the only one he pursued with much passion—was cheap land for frontier farmers. "The rich require but little legislation," he said. "We should, at least occasionally, legislate for the poor." Such positions aligned him with the Jacksonian Democrats.

But in 1830 Crockett broke with Jackson over the removal of Indians from the South. Although Crockett readily acknowledged that he had fought to "kill up Indians," he thought it wrong that "the poor remnants of a once powerful people" should be driven from their homes. He voted against the Indian removal bill. In the next election Jackson, furious, campaigned against Crockett, who lost.

But by then his fame had spread. Newspaper editors seized on the story of the rough-hewn, bear-killing frontiersman. An 1831 play entitled *The Lion of the West,* based on Crockett, was performed in New York and London. Publishers found an eager audience for books about Crockett: some celebrated him, others lampooned him, but all exaggerated his exploits. The *Crockett Almanacs*—the first comic books—told of how Crockett rode his pet alligator up Niagara Falls, skinned Indians "the natural way, with his teeth," and indulged in insatiable and exotic sexual appetites. Tens of thousands were sold.

After seeing others make money off his celebrity, Crockett published several books of his own. In 1833 he was reelected to Congress. There was talk of his running for president on a Whig ticket, allowing that party to steal the "common man" claims of the Jacksonians. In 1835, however, Crockett was defeated for reelection to Congress by several hundred votes. Thereafter, always on the lookout for cheaper land, he told the voters of Tennessee, "you may all go to hell and I will go to Texas."

Several months later, toting his long rifle, Crockett rode into the Alamo in Texas, then a part of Mexico. Thirteen days later history caught up with the legend of Davy Crockett—and perhaps surpassed it. (See Re-Viewing the Past, *The Alamo*, pp. 320–321.)

Questions for Discussion

- Davy Crockett was arguably the first American to become famous for his fame. What explains the appeal of Crockett to Americans in the 1830s?
- Davy Crockett symbolized the frontier as violent, savage, and uncouth. How did his life sustain that image? And how did it undermine it?

"The less government interferes with private pursuits the better for the general prosperity," he pontificated. As Daniel Webster scornfully pointed out, Van Buren was following a policy of "leaving the people to shift for themselves," one that many Whigs rejected.

Van Buren's chief goal was finding a substitute for the state banks as a place to keep federal funds. He soon settled on the idea of "divorcing" the government from all banking activities. His independent treasury bill called for the construction of government-owned vaults where federal revenues could be stored until needed. To ensure absolute safety, all payments to the government were to be made in hard cash. After a battle that lasted until the summer of 1840, the Independent Treasury Act passed both the House and the Senate.

Opposition to the Independent Treasury Act had been bitter, and not all of it was partisan. Bankers and businessmen objected to the government's withholding so much specie from the banks because they needed all the hard money they could get to support loans that were the lifeblood of economic growth. It seemed irresponsible for the federal government to turn its back on the banks, which so obviously performed a semipublic function. These criticisms made good sense, but through a lucky combination of circumstances, the system worked reasonably well for many years.

By creating suspicion in the public mind, officially stated distrust of banks acted as a damper on their tendency to overexpand. No acute shortage of specie developed because heavy agricultural exports and the investment of much European capital in American railroads beginning in the mid-1840s brought in large amounts of new gold and silver. After 1849 the discovery of gold in California added another important source of specie. The supply of money and bank credit kept pace roughly with the growth of the economy, but through no fault of the government. "Wildcat" banks proliferated. Fraud and counterfeiting were common, and the operation of everyday business affairs was inconvenienced in countless ways. The disordered state of the currency remained a grave problem until corrected by Civil War banking legislation.

The Log Cabin Campaign

It was not his financial policy that led to Van Buren's defeat in 1840. The depression naturally hurt the Democrats, and the Whigs were far better organized than in 1836. The Whigs also adopted a different strategy. The Jacksonians had come to power on the coattails of a popular general whose views on public questions they concealed or ignored. They had maintained themselves by shouting the praises of the common man. Now the Whigs seized on these techniques and carried them to their logical—or illogical—conclusion. Not even bothering to draft a program, and passing over Clay and Webster, whose views were known and therefore controversial, they nominated General William Henry Harrison for president. To "balance" the ticket, the Whigs chose a former Democrat, John Tyler of Virginia, an ardent supporter of states' rights, as their vice presidential candidate.

The Democrats used the same methods as the Whigs and were equally well organized, but they had little heart for the fight. The best they could come up with was the fact that their vice presidential candidate, Richard Mentor Johnson, had killed Tecumseh, not merely defeated him. Van Buren tried to focus public attention on issues, but his voice could not be heard above the huzzahs of the Whigs.

A huge turnout (four-fifths of the eligible voters) carried Harrison to victory by a margin of almost 150,000. The electoral vote was 234 to 60.

The Whigs continued to repeat history by rushing to gather the spoils of victory. Washington was again flooded by office seekers, the political confusion was monumental. Harrison had no ambition to be an aggressive leader. He believed that Jackson had misused the veto and professed to put as much emphasis as had Washington on the principle of the separation of legislative and executive powers. This delighted the Whig leaders in Congress, who had had their fill of the "executive usurpation" of Jackson. Either Clay or Webster seemed destined to be the real ruler of the new administration, and soon the two were squabbling over their old general like sparrows over a crust.

At the height of their squabble, less than a month after his inauguration, Harrison fell gravely ill. Pneumonia developed, and on April 4 he died. John Tyler of Virginia, honest and conscientious but doctrinaire, became president of the United States. The political climate of the country was changed dramatically. Events began to march in a new direction.

Milestones

1828	Andrew Jackson is elected president	1831–1838	Chief Justice Marshall rules in Cherokees' favor in *Worcester v. Georgia*
1829	Crowds cause chaos at Jackson's White House inaugural reception		Jackson is reelected president
	Jackson relies on his "Kitchen Cabinet"	1833	Treasury Secretary Roger B. Taney orders Treasury funds removed from Bank of the United States
1830	Daniel Webster, in his "Second Reply to Hayne," calls Union perpetual and indissoluble		Calhoun and Clay push through Compromise Tariff
	Jackson vetoes the Maysville Road Bill	1836	Jackson issues Specie Circular to control speculation
1831	Nat Turner leads slave rebellion in Virginia		Martin Van Buren is elected president
	Chief Justice Marshall denies Cherokee rights in *Cherokee Nation v. Georgia*	1837–1838	Panic sweeps nation, ending boom
1831–1838	Southern Indians are removed to Oklahoma	1838	4,000 Cherokee die on Trail of Tears to Oklahoma
	South Carolina defends states' rights in Ordinance of Nullification	1840	"Log Cabin" Campaign is first to use "hoopla"
	Force Bill grants president authority to execute revenue laws		William Henry Harrison is elected president
	Jackson vetoes Bank Recharter Bill	1841	Harrison dies one month after inauguration; John Tyler becomes president

✓●─⌐Study and Review⌐ at www.myhistorylab.com

Review Questions

1. How did the Jacksonian Democrats agree with the principles of the Jeffersonian Democrats? How did they disagree?
2. How did Jackson generate so high a turnout in the election of 1828? How did the opponents of the Jacksonian Democrats respond to Jackson's success?
3. How did the Second Bank of the United States restrain local banks from loaning too much money? Why did President Jackson seek to "kill"

the Bank of the United States? Was this policy wise?
4. Why did Jackson insist on the removal of Indians from the Southeast? Was the policy justified? Were there alternatives?
5. The Jacksonian Democrats stood for "states' rights" on many issues. Why did Jackson break so vociferously with fellow Democrat Calhoun's claim that states had the right to "nullify" federal laws with which they disagreed?

Key Terms

Bank war   *253*
Jacksonian
   democracy   *248*
nullification   *261*

second party
   system   *263*
Specie Circular   *262*
spoils system   *252*

Trail of Tears   *259*
Whigs   *264*

The Making of Middle-Class America

10

((•—[Hear the Audio Chapter 10 at myhistorylab.com

Who is your family?

FEARS ABOUT A "CRISIS" IN THE FAMILY HAVE GENERATED HEADLINES since the early 1900s, when divorce rates began to rise. Nowadays defenders of the traditional family cite a set of familiar statistics: Nearly a third of all children are born to unwed mothers; half of all marriages end in divorce; a third of all families are headed by a single parent; more than half of all single mothers with children younger than six work outside the home. Some even redefine marriage itself. By 2010 state legislatures and judges in New Hampshire, Iowa, Massachusetts, Vermont, and Connecticut allowed same sex marriages. Yet when the issue was put directly to the electorate, the voters of thirty-five states rejected it.

If ever the traditional "ideal" prevailed in America, it was among white families in the 1820s and 1830s. Divorce was rare; the overwhelming majority of families had two parents; only one woman in fifteen worked outside the home.

Whether such families were "happier" or "stronger" than now is a different matter. Divorce was rare partly because so few could obtain it. South Carolina recognized no legal grounds for divorce. Many other states granted divorce only if a spouse committed adultery. Many couples thus endured loveless, unhappy marriages.

Nevertheless the family after 1820 was perceived as a new and dynamic force in American society. Middle-class women, especially those freed from the drudgery of farm chores, were especially influential. Sarah Hale, the leading female journalist of the era, pronounced women to be "God's appointed agents of morality." Such women organized religious revivals, spearheaded efforts to improve prisons and mental asylums, and campaigned for temperance, abolition, and women's rights. Young middle-class women, too, were avid readers, and their patronage stimulated publication of countless books and magazines. These women shaped society and culture even more directly by serving as teachers in the common schools that extended public education to much of the nation.

The reformers of the era decried the pessimism of their Calvinist forebears. Romanticism in the arts and literature affirmed that Americans and their institutions could—and would—grow and change for the better.

Tocqueville: Democracy in America

On May 12, 1831, two French aristocrats, Alexis de Tocqueville and Gustave de Beaumont, arrived in New York City from Le Havre. Their official purpose was to make a study of American prisons for the French government. But they really came, as Tocqueville explained, "to see what a great republic is like."

Tocqueville and Beaumont believed that Europe was passing from its aristocratic past into a democratic future. How better to prepare for the change, they believed, than by studying the United States, where democracy was already the "enduring and normal state" of the land. The visit provided the material for Tocqueville's classic *De la Démocratie en Amérique*, published in France in 1835 and a year later in an English translation. *Democracy in America* has been the starting point for virtually all subsequent writers who have tried to describe what Tocqueville called "the creative elements" of American institutions.

The gist of *Democracy in America* is contained in the book's first sentence: "No novelty in the United States struck me more vividly during my stay there than the equality of conditions." Tocqueville meant not that Americans lived in a state of total equality, but that the inequalities that did exist among white Americans were not enforced by institutions or supported by public opinion. "In America," he concluded, "men are nearer equality than in any other country in the world."

This sweeping generalization, however comforting to Americans then and since, is an oversimplification. Few modern students of Jacksonian America would accept it without qualification. In the 1830s and 1840s a wide and growing gap existed between the rich and poor in the eastern cities. According to one study, the wealthiest 4 percent of the population of New York controlled about half the city's wealth in 1828, about two-thirds in 1845. The number of New Yorkers worth $100,000 or more tripled in that period. A similar concentration of wealth was occurring in Philadelphia and Boston. Moreover, Tocqueville failed to observe the many poor people in Jacksonian America. Particularly in the cities, bad times forced many unskilled laborers and their families into dire poverty. Tocqueville took little notice of such inequalities, in part because he was so captivated by the theme of American equality.

Despite his blind spots, Tocqueville realized that America was undergoing some fundamental social changes. These changes, he wrote, were being made by "an innumerable crowd who are . . . not exactly rich nor yet quite poor [and who] have enough property to want order and

Rural versus Urban Population, 1820–1860 As the balance of rural and urban population began to shift during the years from 1820 to 1860, the number of cities with populations over 100,000 grew from one in 1820—New York—to nine in 1870, including southern and western cities like New Orleans and San Francisco.

not enough to excite envy." In his notes he put it even more succinctly: "The whole society seems to have turned into one middle class."

The Family Recast

Tocqueville was particularly struck by the character of the family. Americans, he wrote, showed an "equal regard" for husbands and wives, but defined their roles differently. This was made possible by the growth of the market economy, which undermined the importance of home and family as the unit of economic production. More and more people did their work in shops, in offices, or on factory floors. Whether a job was skilled or unskilled, white-collar or blue-collar, or strictly professional, it took the family breadwinner out of the house during working hours six days a week. This did not mean that the family necessarily ceased to be an economic unit. But the labor of the father and any children with jobs came home in the form of cash, thus at least initially in the custody of the individual earners. The social consequences of this change were enormous for the traditional "head of the family" and for his wife and children.

Because he was away so much, the husband had to surrender to his wife some of the power in the family that he had formerly exercised, if for no other reason than the fact that she was always there. Noah Webster explained that the ideal father's authority was "like the mild dominion of a limited monarch, and not the iron rule of an austere tyrant." It certainly explains why Tocqueville concluded that "a sort of equality reigns around the domestic hearth" in America.

> **Read** the **Document**
>
> Carey, *Rules for Husbands and Wives* at **myhistorylab.com**

The new power and prestige that wives and mothers enjoyed were not obtained without cost. Since they were exercising day-to-day control over household affairs, they were expected to tend only to those affairs. Expanding their interest to other fields of human endeavor was frowned on. Where the typical wife had formerly been a partner in a family enterprise, she now left earning a living entirely to her husband. She was certainly not encouraged to have an independent career as, say, a lawyer or doctor. Time spent away from home or devoted to matters unrelated to

Lilly Martin Spencer's *Young Husband: First Marketing* (1854). Note that passersby are amused at this husband's inept attempt to do "women's work."
Source: *Young Husband: First Marketing*, 1854 by Lilly Martin Spencer. The Metropolitan Museum of Art, New York, NY, U.S.A. Image copyright © The Metropolitan Museum of Art.

the care of husband and family was, according to the new normative doctrine of "separate spheres," time misappropriated.

This trend widened the gap between the middle and lower classes. For a middle-class wife and mother to take a job or, still worse, to devote herself to any "frivolous" activity outside the home was considered a dereliction of duty. Such an attitude could not possibly develop in lower-class families where everyone had to work simply to keep food on the table.

Some women objected to the **Cult of True Womanhood**: By placing an ideal on so high a pedestal, all real women would fall short. Others escaped its more suffocating aspects by forming close friendships with other women. But most women, including such forceful proponents of women's rights as Hale and the educator Catharine Beecher, subscribed to the view that a woman's place was in the home. "The formation of the moral and intellectual character of the young is committed mainly to the female hand," Beecher wrote in *A Treatise on Domestic Economy for the Use of Young Ladies* (1841). "The mother forms the character of the future man."

●●●—[Read the **Document**

Beecher, from *A Treatise on Domestic Economy* at myhistorylab.com

Another reason for the shift in domestic influence from husbands to wives was that women began to have fewer children. People married later than in earlier periods. Long courtships and broken engagements were common, probably because prospective marriage partners were becoming more selective. On average, women began having their children two or three years later than their mothers had, and they stopped two or three years sooner. Apparently many middle-class couples made a conscious effort to limit family size, even when doing so required sexual abstinence.

As families became smaller, relations within them became more caring. Parents ceased to think of their children mostly as future workers. The earlier tendency even among loving parents to keep their children at arm's length, yet within reach of the strap, gave way to more intimate relationships. Gone was the puritan notion that children possessed "a perverse will, a love of what's forbid," and with it the belief that parents were responsible for crushing all juvenile resistance to their authority. In its place arose the view described by Lydia Maria Child in *The Mother's Book* (1831) that children "come to us from heaven, with their little souls full of innocence and peace." Mothers "should not interfere with the influence of angels," Child advised her readers.

●●●—[Read the **Document**

Mother's Magazine at myhistorylab.com

The Second Great Awakening

The basic goodness of children contradicted the Calvinist doctrine of infant damnation, to which most American Protestant churches formally subscribed. "Of all the impious doctrines which the dark imagination of man ever conceived," Bronson Alcott wrote in his journal, "the worst [is] the belief in original and certain depravity of infant nature." Alcott was far from alone in thinking infant damnation a "debased doctrine," despite its standing as one of the central tenets of orthodox Calvinism. Mothers enshrined infancy and childhood; they became increasingly active and vocal in church. They scathingly indicted the concept of infant damnation.

The inclination to set aside other Calvinist tenets, such as predestination, became more pronounced as a new wave of revivalism took shape in the 1790s. This **Second Great Awakening** began as a counteroffensive to the deistic thinking and other forms of "infidelity" that New England Congregationalists and southern Methodists alike identified with the French Revolution. Prominent New England ministers, who considered themselves traditionalists but also revivalists (men such as Yale's president, Timothy Dwight, and Dwight's student, the Reverend Lyman Beecher) placed less stress in their sermons on God's arbitrary power over mortals, and more on the promise of the salvation of sinners because of God's mercy and "disinterested benevolence." When another of Dwight's students, Horace Bushnell, declared in a sermon on "Christian nurture" in 1844 that Christian parents should prepare their children "for the skies," he meant that parents could contribute to their children's salvation.

Calvinism came under more direct assault from Charles Grandison Finney, probably the most effective of a number of charismatic Evangelists who brought the Second Great Awakening to its crest. In 1821 Finney abandoned a promising career as a lawyer and became an itinerant preacher. His most spectacular successes occurred during a series of revivals conducted in towns along the Erie Canal, a region Finney called "the burned-over district" because it had been the site of so many revivals before his own. From Utica, where his revival began in 1826, to Rochester, where it climaxed in 1831, he

•●•─|Read the Document

Finney, *What a Revival of Religion Is* at **myhistorylab.com**

exhorted his listeners to take their salvation into their own hands. He insisted that people could control their own fate. He dismissed Calvinism as a "theological fiction." Salvation was available to anyone. But the day of judgment was just around the corner; there was little time to waste.

During and after Finney's efforts in Utica, conversions increased sharply. In Rochester, church membership doubled in six months. Elsewhere in the country, churches capitalized on the efforts of other Evangelists to fill their pews. In 1831 alone, church membership grew by 100,000, an increase, according to a New England minister, "unparalleled in the history of the church." The success of the Evangelists of the Second Great Awakening stemmed from the timeliness of their assault on Calvinist doctrine and even more from their methods. Finney, for example, consciously set out to be entertaining as well as edifying. The singing of hymns and the solicitation of personal testimonies provided his meetings with emotional release and human interest. Prominent among his innovations was the "anxious bench," where leading members of the community awaited the final prompting from within before coming forward to declare themselves saved.

Economic changes and their impact on family life also contributed to the Second Awakening. The growth of industry and commerce that followed the completion of the Erie Canal in 1825, along with the disappearance of undeveloped farmland, led hundreds of young men to leave family farms to seek their fortunes in Utica and other towns along the canal. There, uprooted, uncertain, and buffeted between ambition, hope, and anxiety, they found it hard to resist the comfort promised by the revivalists to those who were saved.

Women, and especially the wives of the business leaders of the community, felt particularly responsible for the Christian education of their children, which fell within

Lily Spenser Martin's painting, *Domestic Happiness* (1844), reflects the change in attitudes toward infants. Parents such as these could not believe that God had consigned their angelic babies to eternal damnation.
Source: *Domestic Happiness*, 1849 (oil on canvas), Spencer, Lilly Martin (1827–1902)/Detroit Institute of Arts, USA/Gift of Dr. and Mrs. James Cleland Jr./The Bridgeman Art Library International.

their separate sphere. Many women had servants and thus had time and energy to devote to their own and their offsprings' salvation.

Paradoxically, this caused many of them to venture out of that sphere and in doing so they moved further out of the shadow of their husbands. They founded the Oneida County Female Missionary Society, an association that did most of the organizing and a good deal of the financing of the climactic years of the Second Awakening. The Female Missionary Society raised more than $1,000 a year (no small sum at that time) to support the revival in Utica, in its environs, and throughout the burned-over district.

Watch the Video

Evangelical Religion & Politics, Then and Now at **myhistorylab.com**

Apparently without consciously intending to do so, women challenged the authority of the paternalistic, authoritarian churches they so fervently embraced. Then, by mixtures of exhortation, example, and affection, they set out to save the souls of their loved ones, first their children and ultimately their husbands too.

The Era of Associations

Alongside the recast family and the "almost revolutionized" church, a third pillar of the emerging American middle class was the voluntary association. Unlike the other two, it had neither colonial precedents nor contemporary European equivalents. The voluntary association of early nineteenth-century America was unique. "In France," Tocqueville wrote of this phenomenon, "if you want to proclaim a truth or propagate some feeling . . . you would find the government or in England some territorial magnate." In America, however, "you are sure to find an association."

The leaders of these associations tended to be ministers, lawyers, or merchants, but the rank and file consisted of tradesmen, foremen, clerks, and especially their wives. Some of these associations were formed around a local cause that some townspeople wished to advance, such as the provision of religious instruction for orphaned children; others were affiliated with associations elsewhere for the purposes of combating some national evil, such as drunkenness. Some, such as the American Board of Commissioners of Foreign Missions, founded in Boston in 1810, quickly became large and complex enterprises. (By 1860 the board had sent 1,250 missionaries into the "heathen world" and raised $8 million to support them.) Others lasted only as long as it took to accomplish a specific good work, such as the construction of a school or a library.

In a sense the associations were assuming functions previously performed in the family, such as caring for old people and providing moral guidance to the young, but without the paternalistic discipline of the old way. They constituted a "benevolent empire," eager to make society over into their members' idea of how God wanted it to be.

Backwoods Utopias

Americans frequently belonged to several associations at the same time and more than a few made reform their life's work. The most adventuresome tested their reform theories by withdrawing from workaday American society and establishing experimental communities. The communitarian point of view aimed at "commencing a wholesale social reorganization by first establishing and demonstrating its principles completely on a small scale." The first communitarians were religious reformers. In a sense the Pilgrims fall into this category, along with a number of other groups in colonial times, but only in the nineteenth century did the idea flourish.

One of the most influential of the earlier communities were the **Shakers**, founded by an Englishwoman, Ann Lee, who came to America in 1774. Mother Ann, as she was called, saw visions that convinced her that Christ would come to earth again as a woman and that she was that woman. With a handful of followers she founded a community near Albany, New York. The group grew rapidly, and after Ann Lee's death in 1784 her movement continued to expand. By the 1830s her followers had established about twenty successful communities.

[*] Watch the Video
Religious Troublemakers of the Nineteenth Century at **myhistorylab.com**

The Shakers practiced celibacy; believing that the millennium was imminent, they saw no reason for perpetuating the human race. Each group lived in a large Family House, the sexes strictly segregated. Property was held in common but controlled by a ruling hierarchy. So much stress was placed on equality of labor and reward and on voluntary acceptance of the rules, however, that the system does not seem to have been oppressive.

The Shaker religion, joyful and fervent, was marked by much group singing and dancing, which provided the members with emotional release from their tightly controlled regimen. An industrious, skillful people, they made a special virtue of simplicity; some of their designs for buildings and, especially, furniture achieved a classic beauty seldom equaled among untutored artisans. Despite their customs, the Shakers were universally tolerated and even admired.

The most important of the religious communitarians were the Mormons. A remarkable Vermont farm boy, Joseph Smith, founded the religion in western New York in the 1820s. Smith saw visions; he claimed to have discovered and translated an ancient text, the Book of Mormon, which described the adventures of a tribe of Israelites that had populated America from biblical times until their destruction in a great war in 400 CE. With a small band of followers, Smith established a community in Ohio in 1831. The Mormons' dedication and economic efficiency attracted large numbers of converts, but their unorthodox religious views and their exclusivism, a product of their sense of being a chosen people, caused resentment among unbelievers. The Mormons were forced to move first to Missouri and then back to Illinois, where in 1839 they founded the town of Nauvoo.

In 1839 Mary Cragin, 29, became a convert to John Humphrey Noyes's "communism of love" and persuaded her husband to move with her to the commune. In 1846, after having an affair with another member of the commune, she and Noyes developed an attachment. After a meeting of the church, Noyes proposed that he and Cragin's husband share each other's wives. In an understatement, he called the arrangement a "complex marriage."

Nauvoo flourished—by 1844 it was the largest city in the state, with a population of 15,000—but once again the Mormons ran into local trouble. They quarreled among themselves, especially after Smith secretly authorized polygamy and a number of other unusual rites for members of the "Holy Order," the top leaders of the church.[1] They created a paramilitary organization, the Nauvoo Legion, headed by Smith, envisaging themselves as a semi-independent state within the Union. Smith announced that he was a candidate for president of the United States. Rumors circulated that the Mormons intended to take over the entire Northwest for their "empire." Once again local "gentiles" rose against them. Smith was arrested, then murdered by a mob.

Under a new leader, Brigham Young, the Mormons sought a haven beyond the frontier. In 1847 they marched westward, pressing through the mountains until they reached the desolate wilderness on the shores of the Great Salt Lake. There, at last, they established their Zion and began to make their truly significant impact on American history. Irrigation made the desert flourish, precious water wisely being treated as a community asset. Hard, cooperative, intelligently directed effort spelled growth and prosperity; more than 11,000 people were living in the area when it became part of the Utah Territory in 1850. In time the communal Mormon settlement broke down, but the religion has remained—known as the Church of Latter-Day Saints, a major force in the shaping of the West. The Mormon Church is still by far the most powerful single influence in Utah and is a thriving organization in many other parts of the United States and in Europe.

The religious communities had some influence on reformers who wished to experiment with social organization. When Robert Owen, a British **utopian** socialist who believed in economic as well as political equality and who considered competition debasing, decided to create an ideal community in America, he purchased the Rappite settlement at New Harmony, Indiana. Owen's advocacy of free love and "enlightened atheism" did not add to the stability of his group or to its popularity among outsiders. The colony was a costly failure.

The American followers of Charles Fourier, a French utopian socialist who proposed that society should be organized in cooperative units called phalanxes, fared

---

[1]One justification of polygamy, paradoxically, was that marriage was a sacred, eternal state. If a man remarried after his wife's death, eventually he would have two wives in heaven. Therefore why not on earth?

New England Roots of Utopian Communities The shaded section represents areas that were settled predominantly by people from New England. It suggests that communitarian sentiments were strongly influenced by New England culture.

better. Fourierism did not seek to tamper with sexual and religious mores. Its advocates included important journalists such as Horace Greeley of the *New York Tribune* and Parke Godwin of the *New York Evening Post*. In the 1840s several dozen Fourierist colonies were established in the northern and western states. Members worked at whatever tasks they wished and only as much as they wished. As might be expected, none of the communities lasted very long.

See the **Map**

Utopian Communities before the Civil War at **myhistorylab.com**

The Age of Reform

The communitarians were the most colorful of the reformers, their proposals the most spectacular. More effective, however, were the many individuals who took on themselves responsibility for caring for the physically and mentally disabled and for the rehabilitation of criminals. The work of Thomas Gallaudet in developing methods for educating deaf people reflects the spirit of the times. Gallaudet's school in Hartford, Connecticut, opened its doors in 1817; by 1851 similar schools for the deaf had been established in fourteen states.

Dr. Samuel Gridley Howe did similar work with the blind, devising means for making books with raised letters (Louis Braille's system of raised dots was not introduced until later in the century) that the blind could "read" with their fingers. Howe headed a school for the blind in Boston, the pioneering Perkins Institution, which opened in 1832. Of all that Charles Dickens observed in America, nothing so favorably impressed him as Howe's success in educating twelve-year-old Laura Bridgman, who was deaf, mute, and blind. Howe was also interested in trying to educate the mentally disabled and in other causes, including antislavery. "Every creature in human shape should command our respect," he insisted. "The strong should help the weak, so that the whole should advance as a band of brethren."

One of the most striking aspects of the reform movement was the emphasis reformers placed on establishing special institutions for dealing with social problems. In the colonial period, orphans, indigent persons, the insane, and the feebleminded were usually cared for by members of their own families or boarded in a neighboring household. They remained part of the community. Even criminals were seldom "locked away" for extended jail terms; punishment commonly consisted of whipping, being placed in stocks in the town square, or (for serious crimes) execution. But once persuaded that people were primarily shaped by their surroundings, reformers demanded that deviant and dependent members of the community be taken from their present corrupting circumstances and placed in specialized institutions where they could be trained or rehabilitated. Almshouses, orphanages, reformatories, prisons, and "lunatic asylums" sprang up throughout the United States like mushrooms in a forest after a summer rain.

Eastern State Penitentiary, opened in 1829 in Philadelphia, sought to reform prisoners by enforcing a solitary life to promote reflection.

The rationale for this movement was scientific; elaborate statistical reports attested to the benefits that such institutions would bring to both inmates and society as a whole. The motivating spirit of the founders of these asylums was humane, although many of the institutions seem anything but humane to the modern eye. The highly regarded Philadelphia prison system was based on strict solitary confinement, which was supposed to lead culprits to reflect on their sins and then reform their ways. The prison was literally a penitentiary, a place to repent. In fact, the system drove some inmates mad, and soon a rival Auburn system was introduced in New York State, which allowed for some social contact among prisoners and for work in shops and stone quarries. Absolute silence was required at all times. The prisoners were herded about in lockstep and punished by flogging for the slightest infraction of the rules. Regular "moral and religious instruction" was provided, which the authorities believed would lead inmates to reform their lives. Tocqueville and Beaumont, in their report on American prisons, concluded that the Philadelphia system produced "the deepest impression on the soul of the convict," while the Auburn system made the convict "more conformable to the habits of man in society."

The hospitals for mental patients were intended to cure inmates, not merely to confine them. The emphasis was on isolating them from the pressures of society; on order, quiet, routine; and on control—but not on punishment. The unfortunates were seen as *de*ranged; the task was to *ar*range their lives in a rational manner. In practice, shortages of trained personnel, niggardly legislative appropriations, and the inherent difficulty of managing violent and irrational patients often produced deplorable conditions in the asylums.

This situation led Dorothea Dix, a woman of almost saintlike selflessness, to devote thirty years of her life to a campaign to improve the care of the insane. She traveled to every state in the Union, and as far afield as Turkey and Japan, inspecting asylums and poorhouses. Insane persons in Massachusetts, she wrote in a memorial intended to shock state legislators into action, were being kept in cages and closets, "*chained, naked, beaten with rods, and lashed into obedience!*" Her reports led to some improvement in conditions in Massachusetts and other states, but in the long run the bright hopes of the reformers were never realized. Institutions founded to uplift the deviant and dependent all too soon became places where society's "misfits" might safely be kept out of sight.

"Demon Rum"

Women did much of the work in all antebellum reforms, but they were especially active in the **temperance movement**. The husband who squandered his earnings on booze, or who came home drunk and debauched, imperiled the family. Thus middle-class women who believed that a woman's place was in the home were obliged to take on a public role to protect the family.

Alcohol—"demon rum"—was perhaps foremost among those threats. By the 1820s Americans were consuming prodigious amounts of alcohol, more than ever before or since. Not that the colonists had been teetotalers. Liquor, mostly in the form of rum or hard apple cider, was cheap and everywhere available; taverns were an integral part of colonial society.

Watch the Video

Drinking & the Temperance Movement in Nineteenth-Century America at **myhistorylab.com**

There were alcoholics in colonial America, but because neither political nor religious leaders considered drinking dangerous, there was no alcohol "problem." Most doctors recommended the regular consumption of alcohol as healthy. John Adams, certainly the soul of propriety, drank a tankard of hard cider every day for breakfast. Dr. Benjamin Rush's *Inquiry into the Effects of Ardent Spirits* (1784), which questioned the medicinal benefits of alcohol, fell on deaf ears.

However, alcohol consumption increased markedly in the early years of the new republic, thanks primarily to the availability of cheap corn and rye whiskey distilled in the new states of Kentucky and Tennessee. In the 1820s the per capita consumption of hard liquor reached five gallons, well over twice what it is today. Since small children and many grown people did not drink that much, others obviously drank a great deal more.

The foundation of the American Temperance Union in 1826 signaled the start of a national crusade against drunkenness. Employing lectures, pamphlets, rallies, essay contests, and other techniques, the union set out to persuade people to "sign the pledge" not to drink liquor. Primitive sociological studies of the effects of drunkenness (reformers were able to show a high statistical correlation between alcohol consumption and crime) added to the effectiveness of the campaign.

●●●―[Read the Document**

Beecher, *Six Sermons on Intemperance* at myhistorylab.com

Revivalist ministers like Charles Grandison Finney argued that alcohol was one of the great barriers to conversion, which helps explain why Utica, a town of fewer than 13,000 residents in 1840, supported four separate temperance societies in that year. Employers all over the country also signed on, declaring their businesses henceforward to be "cold-water" enterprises. Soon the temperance movement claimed a million members.

The temperance people aroused bitter opposition, particularly after they moved beyond calls for restraint to demands for prohibition of all alcohol. German and Irish immigrants, for the most part Catholics, and also members of Protestant sects that used wine in their religious services, objected to being told by reformers that their drinking would have to stop. But by the early 1840s the reformers had secured legislation in many states that imposed strict licensing systems and heavy liquor taxes. Local option laws permitted towns and counties to ban the sale of alcohol altogether.

In 1851 Maine passed the first effective law prohibiting the manufacture and sale of alcoholic beverages. The leader of the campaign was Mayor Neal Dow of Portland, a businessman who became a prohibitionist after seeing the damage done by drunkenness among workers in his tannery. By 1855 a dozen other states had passed laws based on the Maine statute, and the nation's per capita consumption of alcohol had plummeted to two gallons a year.

The Abolitionist Crusade

No reform movement of this era was more significant, more ambiguous, or more provocative of later historical investigation than **abolitionism**—the drive to abolish slavery. That slavery should have been a cause of indignation to reform-minded Americans was inevitable. Humanitarians were outraged by the master's whip and by the practice of disrupting families. Democrats protested the denial of political and civil rights to slaves. Perfectionists of all stripes deplored the fact that slaves had no chance to improve themselves. However, well into the 1820s, the abolitionist cause attracted few followers because there seemed to be no way of getting rid of slavery short of revolution. While a few theorists argued that the Fifth Amendment, which provides that no one may be "deprived of life, liberty, or property, without due process of law," could be interpreted to mean that the Constitution outlawed slavery, the great majority believed that the institution was not subject to federal control.

Particularly in the wake of the Missouri Compromise, antislavery Northerners neatly compartmentalized their thinking. Slavery was wrong; they would not tolerate it in their own communities. But since the Constitution obliged them to tolerate it in states where it existed, they felt no responsibility to fight it. The issue was explosive enough even when limited to the question of the expansion of slavery into the territories. People who advocated any kind of forced abolition in states where it was legal were judged irresponsible in the extreme. Most critics of slavery therefore confined themselves to urging "colonization" or persuading slaveowners to treat their property humanely.

More provocative and less accommodating to local sensibilities were people such as William Lloyd Garrison of Massachusetts, who called for "immediate" abolition. When his extreme position made continued residence in Baltimore impossible, he returned to Boston, where in 1831 he established his own newspaper, *The Liberator*. "I am in earnest," he announced in the first issue. "I will not equivocate—I will not excuse—I will not retreat a single inch—and I will be heard."

●●●⌐ Read the Document
Garrison, First Issue of *The Liberator* at **myhistorylab.com**

Garrison's position, and that espoused by the New England Anti-Slavery Society, which he organized in 1831, was absolutely unyielding: Slaves must be freed immediately and treated as equals; compensated emancipation was unacceptable, colonization unthinkable. Because the U.S. government countenanced slavery, Garrison refused to engage in political activity to achieve his ends. Burning a copy of the Constitution—that "agreement with hell"—became a regular feature at Society-sponsored public lectures.

Few white Americans found Garrison's line of argument convincing, and many were outraged by his confrontational tactics. In 1833 a Garrison meeting in New York City was broken up by colonizationists. Two years later a mob dragged Garrison through the streets of his own Boston. That same day a mob broke up the convention of the New York Anti-Slavery Society in Utica. In 1837 Elijah Lovejoy, a Garrisonian newspaper editor in Alton, Illinois, first saw his press destroyed by fire and then was himself murdered by a mob. When the proprietors of Philadelphia's Pennsylvania Hall booked an abolitionist meeting in 1838, a mob burned the hall to the ground to prevent the meeting from taking place.

In the wake of this violence some of Garrison's backers had second thoughts about his call for an immediate end to slavery. The wealthy New York businessmen Arthur and Lewis Tappan, who had subsidized *The Liberator*, turned instead to Theodore Dwight Weld, a young minister who was part of Charles Grandison Finney's "holy band" of revivalists. Weld and his followers spoke of "immediate" emancipation "gradually" achieved, and they were willing to engage in political activity to achieve that goal.

In 1840 the Tappans and Weld broke with Garrison over the issue of involvement in politics and the participation of female abolitionists as public lecturers. Garrison, mindful of women's central role in other reforms, supported the women. "The destiny of the slaves is in the hands of American women," he declared in 1833. Weld thought women lecturers would needlessly antagonize would-be supporters. The Tappans then organized the Liberty party, which nominated as its presidential candidate James G. Birney, a Kentucky slaveholder who had been converted to evangelical Christianity and abolitionism by Weld. Running on a platform of universal emancipation to be gradually brought about through legislation, Birney received only 7,000 votes.

Many blacks were abolitionists long before the white movement began to attract attention. In 1830 some fifty black antislavery societies existed, and thereafter these groups grew in size and importance, being generally associated with the Garrisonian wing. White abolitionists eagerly sought out black speakers, especially runaway slaves, whose heartrending accounts of their experiences aroused sympathies and who, merely by speaking clearly and with conviction, stood as living proof that blacks were neither animals nor fools.

The first prominent black abolitionist was David Walker, whose powerful *Appeal to the Coloured Citizens of the World* (1829) is now considered one of the roots of the modern black nationalist movement. Walker was born free and had experienced American racism extensively in both the South and the North. He denounced white talk of democracy and freedom as pure hypocrisy and predicted that when God finally brought justice to America white "tyrants will wish they were never born!"

Frederick Douglass, a former slave who had escaped from Maryland, was one of the most remarkable Americans of his generation. While a bondsman he had received a full portion of beatings and other indignities, but he had been allowed to learn to read and write and to master a trade, opportunities denied the vast majority of slaves.

A photo of Frederick Douglass in 1847, having escaped from slavery nine years earlier. He attracted large audiences as an antislavery lecturer, though his white supporters worried that he neither looked nor sounded like a former slave. Lest audiences think him an imposter, William Lloyd Garrison counseled him to not sound too "learned." Another thought it would be better if he had "a little of the plantation in his speech." Douglass rejected such suggestions.

Settling in Boston, he became an agent of the Massachusetts Anti-Slavery Society and a featured speaker at its public meetings.

Douglass was a tall, majestically handsome man who radiated determination and indignation. Slavery, he told white audiences, "brands your republicanism as a sham, your humanity as a base pretense, your Christianity as a lie." In 1845 he published his *Narrative of the Life of Frederick Douglass,* one of the most gripping autobiographical accounts of a slave's life ever written. Douglass insisted that freedom for blacks required not merely emancipation but full equality, social and economic as well as political. Not many white Northerners accepted his reasoning, but few who heard him or read his works could afterward maintain the illusion that all blacks were dull-witted or resigned to inferior status.

•●•⌐Read the Document

Passages from *The Autobiography of Frederick Douglass* at **myhistorylab.com**

At first Douglass was, in his own words, "a faithful disciple" of Garrison, prepared to tear up the Constitution and destroy the Union to gain his ends. In the late 1840s, however, he changed his mind, deciding that the Constitution, created to "establish Justice, insure domestic Tranquility . . . and secure the Blessings of Liberty," as its preamble states, "could not well have been designed at the same time to maintain and perpetuate a system of rapine and murder like slavery." Thereafter he fought slavery and race prejudice from within the system, something Garrison was never willing to do.

Garrison's importance cannot be measured by the number of his followers, which was never large. Unlike more moderately inclined enemies of slavery, he recognized that abolitionism was a revolutionary movement, not merely one more middle-class reform. He also understood that achieving racial equality, not merely "freeing" the slaves, was the only way to reach the abolitionists' professed objective: full justice for blacks. And he saw clearly that few whites, even among abolitionists, believed that blacks were their equals.

Both Garrison's insights into the limits of northern racial egalitarianism and his blind contempt for southern whites led him to the conclusion that American society was rotten to the core. Thus he refused to make any concession to the existing establishment, religious or secular. He was hated in the North as much for his explicit denial of the idea that a constitution that supported slavery merited respect as for his implicit denial of the idea that a professed Christian who tolerated slavery for even an instant could hope for salvation. He was, in short, a perfectionist, a trafficker in moral absolutes who wanted his Kingdom of Heaven in the here and now. By contrast, most other American reformers were willing to settle for perfection on the installment plan.

Women's Rights

The question of slavery was related to another major reform movement of the era, the crusade for women's rights. Superficially, the connection can be explained in this way: Women were as likely as men to find slavery offensive and to protest against it. When they did so, they ran into even more adamant resistance: the prejudices of those who objected to abolitionists being reinforced by their feelings that women should not speak in public or participate in political affairs. Thus female abolitionists, driven by the urgencies of conscience, were almost forced to become advocates of women's rights. "We have good cause to be

⟨●⌐Watch the Video

The Women's Rights Movement in Nineteenth-Century America at **myhistorylab.com**

Single women worth at least 50 pounds were allowed to vote in New Jersey from 1775 to 1807.

grateful to the slave," the feminist Abby Kelley wrote. "In striving to strike his irons off, we found most surely, that we were manacled ourselves."

At a more profound level, the reference that abolitionists made to the Declaration of Independence to justify their attack on slavery radicalized women with regard to their own place in society. Were only all men created equal and endowed by God with unalienable rights? For many women the question was a consciousness-raising experience; they began to believe that, like African Americans, they were imprisoned from birth in a caste system, legally subordinated and assigned menial social and economic roles that prevented them from developing their full potentialities. Such women considered themselves in a sense worse off than blacks, who had at least the psychological advantage of confronting an openly hostile and repressive society rather than one concealed behind the cloying rhetoric of romantic love.

With the major exception of Margaret Fuller, whose book *Women in the Nineteenth Century* (1844) made a frontal assault on all forms of sexual discrimination, the leading advocates of equal rights for women began their public careers in the abolitionist movement. Among the first were Sarah and Angelina Grimké, South Carolinians who abandoned their native state and the domestic sphere to devote themselves to speaking out against slavery. Male objections to the Grimkés' activities soon made them advocates of women's rights. Similarly, the refusal of delegates to the World Anti-Slavery Convention held in London in 1840 to let women participate in their debates precipitated the decision of two American abolitionists, Lucretia Mott and Elizabeth Cady Stanton, to turn their attention to the women's rights movement.

As Lydia Child, a popular novelist noted, the subordination of women was as old as civilization. The attack on it came not because of any new discrimination but for the same reasons that motivated reformers against other forms of injustice: belief in progress, a sense of personal responsibility, and the conviction that institutions could be changed and that the time for changing them was limited.

When women sought to involve themselves in reform, they became aware of perhaps the most serious handicap that society imposed on them—the conflict between their roles as wives and mothers and their urge to participate in the affairs of the larger world. Elizabeth Cady Stanton has left a striking description of this dilemma. She lived in the 1840s in Seneca Falls, a small town in central New York. Her husband was frequently away on business; she had a brood of growing children and little domestic help. When, stimulated by her interest in abolition and women's rights, she sought to become active in the movements, her family responsibilities made it almost impossible even to read about them.

"I now fully understood the practical difficulties most women had to contend with," she recalled in her autobiography *Eighty Years and More* (1898):

> The general discontent I felt with woman's portion as wife, mother, housekeeper, physician, and spiritual guide, the chaotic condition into which everything fell without her constant supervision, and the wearied, anxious look of the majority of women, impressed me with the strong feeling that some active measures should be taken.

Active measures she took. Together with Lucretia Mott and a few others of like mind, she organized a meeting, the **Seneca Falls Convention** (July 1848), and drafted a Declaration of Sentiments patterned on the Declaration of Independence. "We hold these truths to be self-evident: that all men and women are created equal," it stated, and it went on to list the "injuries and usurpations" of men, just as Jefferson had outlined those of George III.

•••⊦Read the Document

Stanton, *Declaration of Sentiments* at **myhistorylab.com**

From this seed the movement grew. During the 1850s a series of national conventions was held, and more and more reformers, including William Lloyd Garrison, joined the cause. Of the recruits, Susan B. Anthony was the most influential, for she was the first to see the need for thorough organization if effective pressure was to be brought to bear on male-dominated society. Her first campaign, mounted in 1854 and 1855 in behalf of a petition to the New York legislature calling for reform of the property and divorce laws, accumulated 6,000 signatures. But the petition did not persuade the legislature to act. Indeed, the feminists achieved very few practical results during the Age of Reform. Their leaders, however, were persevering types, most of them extraordinarily long-lived. Their major efforts lay in the future.

Despite the aggressiveness of many reformers and the extremity of some of their proposals, little social conflict blighted these years. Although Americans argued about everything from prison reform to vegetarianism, from women's rights to phrenology (a pseudoscience much occupied with developing the diagnostic possibilities of measuring the bumps on people's heads), they seldom came to blows. Even the abolitionist movement might not have caused serious social strife if the territorial expansion of the late 1840s had not dragged the slavery issue back into politics. When that happened, politics again assumed center stage, public discourse grew embittered, and the first great Age of Reform came to an end.

The Romantic View of Life

The spreading belief that human institutions were improving had a profound effect on the arts and literature. In the Western world, it gave rise to **romanticism**, a revolt against the bloodless logic of the Age of Reason. It was a noticeable if unnamed point of view in Germany, France, and England as early as the 1780s and in America a generation later; by the second quarter of the nineteenth century, few intellectuals were unmarked by it. "Romantics" believed that change and growth were the essence of life, for individuals and for institutions. They valued feeling and intuition over pure thought, and they stressed the differences between individuals and societies rather than the similarities. Ardent love of country characterized the movement; individualism, optimism, ingenuousness, and emotion were its bywords. Romanticism, too, drew much from the religious sensibilities of mothers. Children were innately good; pernicious influences led to their corruption.

The romantic way of thinking found its greatest American expression in **transcendentalism**, a New England creation that is difficult to describe because it emphasized the indefinable and the unknowable. It was a mystical, intuitive way of looking at life that subordinated facts to feelings. Its literal meaning was "to go beyond the world of the senses," by which the transcendentalists meant the material and observable world. To the transcendentalists, human beings were truly divine because they were part of nature, itself the essence of divinity. Peoples' intellectual capacities

Frederic Edwin Church conveyed the romantic sensibility in *Twilight in the Wilderness* (1860). The clouds glow with religious portent, and their reflected light pervades Nature.

did not define their capabilities, for they could "transcend" reason by having faith in themselves and in the fundamental benevolence of the universe. Transcendentalists were complete individualists, seeing the social whole as no more than the sum of its parts. Organized religion, indeed all institutions, were unimportant if not counterproductive; what mattered was the single person and that people aspire, stretch *beyond* their known capabilities.

Emerson and Thoreau

The leading transcendentalist thinker was Ralph Waldo Emerson. Born in 1803 and educated at Harvard, Emerson became a minister, but in 1832 he gave up his pulpit, deciding that "the profession is antiquated." After traveling in Europe he settled in Concord, Massachusetts, where he had a long career as an essayist, lecturer, and sage.

Emerson's philosophy was at once buoyantly optimistic, rigorously intellectual, self-confident, and conscientious. In "The American Scholar," a notable address he delivered at Harvard in 1837, he urged Americans to put aside their devotion to things European and seek inspiration in their immediate surroundings. Emerson saw himself as pitting "spiritual powers" against "the mechanical powers and the mechanical philosophy of this time." The new industrial society of New England disturbed him profoundly.

Because he put so much emphasis on self-reliance, Emerson disliked powerful governments. "The less government we have the better," he said. In a sense he was the prototype of some modern alienated intellectuals, so repelled by the world as it was that he would not actively try to change it. Nevertheless he thought strong leadership essential. Emerson also had a strong practical streak. He made his living by lecturing, tracking tirelessly across the country, talking before every type of audience for fees ranging from $50 to several hundreds.

●●●[Read the Document

Emerson, *The Concord Hymn* at **myhistorylab.com**

Closely identified with Emerson was his Concord neighbor Henry David Thoreau. After graduating from Harvard in 1837, Thoreau taught school for a time and helped out in a small pencil-making business run by his family. He was a strange man, content to absorb the beauties of nature almost intuitively, yet stubborn and individualistic to the point of selfishness. The hectic scramble for wealth that Thoreau saw all about him he found disgusting and alarming, for he believed it was destroying both the natural and the human resources of the country.

Like Emerson, Thoreau objected to many of society's restrictions on the individual. "That government is best which governs not at all," he said, surpassing both Emerson and the Jeffersonians. He was perfectly prepared to see himself as a majority of one. "When were the good and the brave ever in a majority?" Thoreau asked. "If a man does not keep pace with his companions," he wrote on another occasion, "perhaps it is because he hears a different drummer."

In 1845 Thoreau decided to put to the test his theory that a person need not depend on society for a satisfying existence. He built a cabin at Walden Pond on some property owned by Emerson and lived there alone for two years. The best fruit of this period was that extraordinary book *Walden* (1854). Superficially, *Walden* is the story of Thoreau's experiment, movingly and beautifully written. It is also an indictment of the social behavior of the average American, an attack on unthinking conformity, on subordinating one's own judgment to that of the herd.

Walden Pond, where Henry David Thoreau lived from 1845 to 1847: "I went to the woods because I wished to live deliberately, to front only the essential facts of life, and see if I could not learn what it had to teach, and not, when I came to die, to discover that I had not lived."

The most graphic illustration of Thoreau's confidence in his own values occurred while he was living at Walden. At that time the Mexican War was raging. Thoreau considered the war immoral because it advanced the cause of slavery. To protest, he refused to pay his Massachusetts poll tax. For this he was arrested and lodged in jail, although only for one night because an aunt promptly paid the tax for him. His essay "Civil Disobedience," explaining his view of the proper relation between the individual and the state, resulted from this experience. Like Emerson, however, Thoreau refused to participate in practical reform movements. "I love Henry," one of his friends said, "but I cannot like him; and as for taking his arm, I should as soon think of taking the arm of an elm tree."

Edgar Allan Poe

The work of all the imaginative writers of the period reveals romantic influences, and it is possibly an indication of the affinity of the romantic approach to American conditions that a number of excellent writers of poetry and fiction first appeared in the 1830s and 1840s. Edgar Allan Poe, one of the most remarkable, seems almost a caricature of the romantic image of the tortured genius. Poe was born in Boston in 1809, the son of poor actors who died before he was three years old. He was raised by a wealthy Virginian, John Allan.

Few persons as neurotic as Poe have been able to produce first-rate work. In college he ran up debts of $2,500 in less than a year and had to withdraw. He won an appointment to West Point but was discharged after a few months for disobedience and "gross neglect of duty." He was a lifelong alcoholic and an occasional taker of drugs. He married a child of thirteen.

Poe responded strongly to the lure of romanticism. His works abound with examples of wild imagination and fascination with mystery, fright, and the occult. If he did not invent the detective story, he perfected it; his tales "The Murders in the Rue Morgue" and "The Purloined Letter" stressed the thought processes of a clever detective in solving a mystery by reasoning from evidence.

Although dissolute in his personal life, when Poe touched pen to paper, he became a disciplined craftsman. The most fantastic passages in his works are the result of careful, reasoned selection; not a word, he believed, could be removed without damage to the whole. And despite his rejection of most of the values prized

An image of Edgar Allan Poe on a cigar box. In 1845, impoverished and an alcoholic, Poe was living in the "greatest wretchedness." His young wife was dying of tuberculosis. That same year he wrote, "The Raven," a poem about an ill-omened bird that intrudes on a young man's grief over the death of his beloved. "Take thy beak from out my heart," the man screams. Quoth the raven—famously—"Nevermore."

by middle-class America, Poe was widely read in his own day. His poem "The Raven" won instantaneous popularity when it was published in 1845. Had he been a little more stable, he might have made a good living with his pen—but in that case he might not have written as he did.

Nathaniel Hawthorne

Another product of the prevailing romanticism was Nathaniel Hawthorne, born in 1804 in Salem, Massachusetts. When Hawthorne was a small child, his father died and his grief-stricken mother became a recluse. Left largely to his own devices, he grew to be a lonely, introspective person. Wandering about New England by himself in summertime, he soaked up local lore, which he drew on in writing short stories.

Hawthorne's early stories, originally published in magazines, were brought together in *Twice-Told Tales* (1837). They made excellent use of New England culture and history for background but were concerned chiefly with the struggles of individuals with sin, guilt, and especially the pride and isolation that often afflict those who place too much reliance on their own judgment. His greatest works were two novels written after the Whigs turned him out of his government job in 1849. *The Scarlet Letter* (1850), a grim yet sympathetic analysis of adultery, condemned not the woman, Hester Prynne, but the people who presumed to judge her. *The House of the Seven Gables* (1851) was a gripping account of the decay of an old New England family brought on by the guilty feelings of the current owners of the house, caused by the way their ancestors had cheated the original owners of the property.

Like Poe, Hawthorne was appreciated in his own day and widely read; unlike Poe, he made a modest amount of money from his work. Yet he was never very comfortable in the society he inhabited. He had no patience with the second-rate. And despite his success in creating word pictures of a somber, mysterious world, he considered America too prosaic a country to inspire good literature. "There is no shadow, no antiquity, no mystery, no picturesque and gloomy wrong, nor anything but a commonplace prosperity," he complained.

Herman Melville

In 1850, while Hawthorne was writing *The House of the Seven Gables*, his publisher introduced him to another writer who was in the midst of a novel. The writer was Herman Melville and the book, *Moby-Dick*. Hawthorne and Melville became good friends at once, for despite their dissimilar backgrounds, they had a great deal in common. Melville was a New Yorker, born in 1819, one of eight children of a merchant of distinguished lineage. His father, however, lost all his money and died when the boy was twelve. Melville left school at fifteen, worked briefly as a bank clerk, and in 1837 went to sea. For eighteen months, in 1841 and 1842, he was crewman on the whaler *Acushnet*. Then he jumped ship in the South Seas. For a time he lived among a tribe of cannibals in the Marquesas; later he made his way to Tahiti, where he idled away nearly a year. After another year at sea he returned to America in the fall of 1844.

Experience made Melville too aware of the evil in the world to be a transcendentalist. His dark view of human nature culminated in *Moby-Dick* (1851). This book, Melville said, was "broiled in hellfire." Against the background of a whaling voyage he dealt subtly and symbolically with the problems of good and evil, of courage and cowardice, of faith, stubbornness, and pride. In Captain Ahab, driven relentlessly to hunt down the huge white whale Moby Dick, which had destroyed his leg, Melville created one of the great figures of literature; in the book as a whole, he produced one of the finest novels written by an American, comparable to the best in any language.

As Melville's work became more profound, it lost its appeal to the average reader, and its originality and symbolic meaning escaped most of the critics. *Moby-Dick*, his masterpiece, received little attention and most of that unfavorable. He kept on writing until his death in 1891 but was virtually ignored. Only in the 1920s did the critics rediscover him and give him his merited place in the history of American literature.

Walt Whitman

Walt Whitman, whose *Leaves of Grass* (1855) was the last of the great literary works of this brief outpouring of genius, was the most romantic and by far the most distinctly American writer of his age. He was born on Long Island, outside New York City, in 1819. At thirteen he left school and worked for a printer; thereafter he held a succession of newspaper jobs in the metropolitan area.

●●●[Read the **Document**
Whitman, Preface to *Leaves of Grass* at **myhistorylab.com**

Although genuinely a "common man," thoroughly at home among tradesmen and laborers, he was surely not an ordinary man. During the early 1850s, while employed as a carpenter and composing the poems that made up *Leaves of Grass*, he regularly carried a book of Emerson in his lunch box. "I was simmering, simmering, simmering," he later recalled. "Emerson brought me to a boil." The transcendental idea that inspiration and aspiration are at the heart of all achievement captivated him. Poets could best

Some scholars regard Walt Whitman as a poet of nature, and others, a poet of the body—a reference to erotic lines such as: "Without shame the man I like knows and avows the deliciousness of his sex. Without shame the woman I like knows and avows hers." Whitman's Leaves of Grass had every leaf in nature, complained critic E. P. Whipple, except the fig leaf.

express themselves, he believed, by relying uncritically on their natural inclinations without regard for rigid metrical forms.

Leaves of Grass consisted of a preface, in which Whitman made the extraordinary statement that Americans had "probably the fullest poetical nature" of any people in history, and twelve poems in free verse: rambling, uneven, appearing to most readers shocking both in the commonplace nature of the subject matter and the coarseness of the language. Emerson, Thoreau, and a few others saw a fresh talent in these poems, but most readers and reviewers found them offensive. Indeed, the work was so undisciplined and so much of it had no obvious meaning that it was easy to miss the many passages of great beauty and originality.

Part of Whitman's difficulty arose because there was much of the charlatan in his makeup; often his writing did not ring true. He loved to use foreign words and phrases, and since he had no more than a smattering of any foreign language, he sounded pretentious and sometimes downright foolish when he did so. In reality a sensitive, gentle person, he tried to pose as a great, rough character. (Later in his career he bragged of fathering no less than six illegitimate children, which was assuredly untrue.) He never married, and his work suggests that his strongest emotional ties were with men. Thomas Carlyle once remarked shrewdly that Whitman thought he was a big man because he lived in a big country.

Whitman's work was more authentically American than that of any contemporary. His egoism—he titled one of his finest poems "Song of Myself"—was tempered by his belief that he was typical of all humanity:

> *I celebrate myself and sing myself*
> *And what I assume you shall assume,*
> *For every atom belonging to me as good belongs to you.*

Source: Walt Whitman "Song of Myself."

He had a remarkable ear for rendering common speech poetically, for employing slang, and for catching the breezy informality of Americans and their faith in themselves:

Earth! you seem to look for something at my hands,
Say, old top-knot, what do you want?
I bequeath myself to the dirt to grow from the grass I love,
If you want me again look for me under your boot-soles.

Source: Walt Whitman "Song of Myself."

Because of these qualities and because in his later work, especially during the Civil War, he occasionally struck a popular chord, Whitman was never as neglected as Melville. When he died in 1892, he was, if not entirely understood, at least widely appreciated.

Reading and the Dissemination of Culture

As the population grew and became more concentrated, and as society, especially in the North, was permeated by a middle-class point of view, popular concern for "culture" in the formal sense increased. A largely literate people, committed to the idea of education but not generally well-educated, set their hearts on being "refined" and "cultivated." Industrialization made it easier to satisfy this new demand for culture, though the new machines also tended to make the artifacts of culture more stereotyped.

Improved printing techniques reduced the cost of books, magazines, and newspapers. In the 1850s one publisher sold a fifty-volume set of Sir Walter Scott for $37.50. The first penny newspaper was the *New York Sun* (1833), but James Gordon Bennett's *New York Herald*, founded in 1835, brought the cheap new journalism to perfection. The *Boston Daily Times* and the *Philadelphia Public Ledger* soon followed. The penny newspapers depended on sensation, crime stories, and society gossip to attract readers, but they covered important national and international news too.

The desire for knowledge and culture in America is well illustrated by the success of the mutual improvement societies known as **lyceums**. The movement began in Great Britain; in the United States its prime mover was Josiah Holbrook, an itinerant lecturer and sometime schoolmaster from Connecticut. Holbrook founded the first lyceum in 1826 at Millbury, Massachusetts; within five years there were over a thousand scattered across the country. The lyceums conducted discussions, established libraries, and lobbied for better schools. Soon they began to sponsor lecture series on topics of every sort. Many of the nation's political and intellectual leaders, such as Webster, Emerson, Melville, and Lowell, regularly graced their platforms. So did other less famous lecturers who in the name of culture pronounced on subjects ranging from "Chemistry Applied to the Mechanic Arts" to a description of the tombs of the Egyptian pharaohs.

Education for Democracy

Except on the edge of the frontier and in the South, most youngsters between the ages of five and ten attended a school for at least a couple of months of the year. These schools, however, were privately run and charged fees. Attendance was not required and fell off sharply once children learned to read and do their sums well enough to get along in day-to-day life. The teachers were usually young men waiting for something better to turn up.

All this changed with the rise of the common school movement. At the heart of the movement was the belief, widely expressed in the first days of the republic, that a government based on democratic rule must provide the means, as Jefferson put it, to "diffuse knowledge throughout the mass of the people." This meant free tax-supported schools that all children were expected to attend. It also came to mean that such an educational system should be administered on a statewide basis and that teaching should become a profession that required formal training.

The two most effective leaders of the common school movement were Henry Barnard and Horace Mann. Both were New Englanders, Whigs, trained in the law, and in other ways conservative types. They shared an unquenchable faith in the improvability of the human race through education. Mann drafted the 1837 Massachusetts law creating a state school board and then became its first secretary. Over the next decade Mann's annual reports carried the case for common schools to every corner of the land. Seldom given to understatement, Mann called common schools "the greatest discovery ever made by man." He encouraged young women to become teachers while commending them to school boards by claiming that they could get along on lower salaries than men.

●**◆**●┤**Read** the **Document**

Mann, *Report of the Massachusetts Board of Education* at **myhistorylab.com**

Young women heeded the call. By 1860, women comprised 78 percent of the common school teachers in Massachusetts, a trend that prefigured developments elsewhere. The influx of young women invigorated the common schools and brought to the enterprise the zeal of a missionary. Harriet Beecher Stowe, who once taught at the Hartford Seminary, explained that men teachers lacked the "patience, the long-suffering, and gentleness necessary to superintend the formation of character."

By the 1850s every state outside the South provided free elementary schools and supported institutions for training teachers. Many extended public education to include high schools, and Michigan and Iowa even established publicly supported colleges.

Historians differ in explaining the success of the common school movement. Some stress the arguments Mann used to win support from employers by appealing to their need for trained and well-disciplined workers. Others see the schools as designed to "Americanize" the increasing numbers of non-English and non-Protestant immigrants who were flooding into the country. (Supporting this argument is the fact that Catholic bishops in New York and elsewhere opposed laws requiring Catholic children to attend these "Protestant" schools and set up their own private, parochial schools.)

Still other scholars argue that middle-class reformers favored public elementary schools on the theory that they would instill the values of hard work, punctuality, and submissiveness to authority in children of the laboring classes. All these reasons played a part in advancing the cause of the common schools. Yet it remains the case that the most compelling argument for common schools was cultural; more effectively than any other institution, they brought Americans of different economic circumstances and ethnic backgrounds into early and mutually beneficial contact with one another. They served the two roles that Mann assigned to them: "the balance wheel of the social machinery" and "the great equalizer."

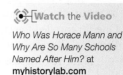

Watch the **Video**

Who Was Horace Mann and Why Are So Many Schools Named After Him? at **myhistorylab.com**

The State of the Colleges

Unlike common schools, with their democratic overtones, private colleges had at best a precarious place in Jacksonian America. For one thing, there were too many of them. Any town with pretensions of becoming a regional center felt it had to have a college. Ohio had twenty-five in the 1850s, and Tennessee sixteen. Many of these institutions were short-lived. Of the fourteen colleges founded in Kentucky between 1800 and 1850, only half were still operating in 1860.

Watch the Video

What Was the Progressive Education Movement? at **myhistorylab.com**

The problem of supply was compounded by a demand problem—too few students. Enrollment at the largest, Yale, never topped 400 until the mid-1840s. On the eve of the Civil War the largest state university, North Carolina, had fewer than 500. Higher education was beyond the means of the average family. Although most colleges charged less than half the $55 tuition required by Harvard, that was still too much for most families. So desperate was the shortage that colleges accepted applicants as young as eleven and twelve and as old as thirty.

The typical college curriculum, dominated by the study of Latin and Greek, had almost no practical relevance except for future clergymen. The Yale faculty, most of them ministers, defended the classics as admirably providing for both "the discipline and the furniture of the mind," but these subjects commended themselves to college officials chiefly because they did not require costly equipment or a faculty that knew anything else. Professors spent most of their time in and out of the classroom trying to maintain a semblance of order, "to the exclusion of any great literary undertakings to which their choice might lead them," one explained. "Our country is yet too young for old professors," a Bostonian informed a foreign visitor in the 1830s, "and, besides, they are too poorly paid to induce first rate men to devote themselves to the business of lecturing. . . . We consider professors as secondary men."

Fortunately for the future of higher education, some college officials recognized the need for a drastic overhaul of their institutions. President Francis Wayland of Brown University used his 1842 address, "On the Present Collegiate System," to call for a thorough revamping of the curriculum to make it responsive to the economic realities of American society. This meant more courses in science, economics (where Wayland's own *Elements of Political Economy* might be used), modern history, and applied mathematics; and fewer in Hebrew, biblical studies, Greek, and ancient history.

Yale established a separate school of science in 1847, which it hoped would attract serious-minded students and research-minded professors. At Harvard, which also opened a scientific school, students were allowed to choose some of their courses and were compelled to earn grades as a stimulus to study. Colleges in the West and the South began to offer mechanical and agricultural subjects relevant to their regional economies. Oberlin enrolled four female students in 1837, and the first women's college, the Georgia Female College, opened its doors in 1839.

These reforms slowed the downward spiral of colleges; they did not restore them to the honored place they had enjoyed in the Revolutionary era. Of the first six presidents of the United States, only Washington did not graduate from college. Beginning in 1829, seven of the next eleven did not. In this Presidents Jackson, Van Buren, Harrison, Taylor, Fillmore, Lincoln, and Johnson were like 98 of every 100 white males, all blacks and Indians, and all but a handful of white women in mid-nineteenth-century America. Going to college had yet, in Wayland's words, to "commend itself to the good sense and patriotism of the American people."

Milestones

1774	Mother Ann Lee founds first Shaker community	1843	Dorothea Dix exposes treatment of the insane in *Memorial to the Legislature of Massachusetts*
1784	Dr. Benjamin Rush's *Inquiry into the Effects of Ardent Spirits* questions alcohol's benefits	1844	Margaret Fuller condemns sexual discrimination in *Women in the Nineteenth Century*
1826	American Temperance Union begins campaign against drunkenness		Nauvoo mob murders Joseph Smith
1829	Black abolitionist David Walker publishes *Appeal to the Coloured Citizens of the World*	1845	Frederick Douglass describes slave life in *Narrative of the Life of Frederick Douglass*
1830s	Second Great Awakening stresses promise of salvation	1847	Brigham Young leads Mormon migration to Great Salt Lake
	Prison reformers debate Auburn versus Philadelphia system	1848	Elizabeth Cady Stanton and Lucretia Mott organize Seneca Falls Convention and draft Declaration of Sentiments
1830–1850	Utopian communities flourish		
1830	Joseph Smith shares his "vision" in *Book of Mormon*	1850	Nathaniel Hawthorne publishes *The Scarlet Letter*
1831	Abolitionist William Lloyd Garrison founds *The Liberator* and New England Anti-Slavery Society	1851	Maine bans alcoholic beverages
			Herman Melville publishes *Moby-Dick*
1831–1832	Alexis de Tocqueville and Gustave de Beaumont tour America	1854–1855	Susan B. Anthony leads petition campaign against New York property and divorce laws
1832	Perkins Institution for the Blind opens in Boston		
1837	Illinois abolitionist Elijah Lovejoy is murdered	1854	Henry David Thoreau attacks conformity in *Walden*
	Ralph Waldo Emerson delivers "The American Scholar" at Harvard	1855–1892	Walt Whitman publishes *Leaves of Grass* (various editions)
	Horace Mann and Henry Barnard call for common schools		

✔●─Study and **Review** at **www.myhistorylab.com**

Review Questions

1. The introduction to this chapter suggests that the "traditional" family was far more common in the mid-nineteenth century than nowadays. What were its strengths and limitations?
2. Many institutions were created during the years from 1820 to 1850; many remain a part of contemporary life. Prisons are an obvious example. What other institutions were established during this period that exist today? Does their persistence prove their value to society or the difficulty of eliminating outmoded institutions?
3. How did the changing attitudes toward marriage and children influence the rise of reform movements during the first half of the nineteenth century? How did the Great Awakening contribute to the social reforms of the era?
4. The campaign for women's rights and woman suffrage gained momentum during this period. Did these new ideas of women's roles in society stimulate the structural transformation of the family (fewer children, for example), or did the smaller families free women to undertake new initiatives such as reform and woman's suffrage?
5. Why did the great writers of the age—Emerson, Thoreau, Melville, Hawthorne, Whitman—fail to find large audiences?

Key Terms

abolitionism *282*
Cult of True
    Womanhood *274*
lyceums *294*
romanticism *288*

Second Great
    Awakening *275*
Seneca Falls
    Convention *287*
Shakers *277*

temperance
    movement *281*
transcendentalism *288*
utopian *278*

Westward Expansion

11

(((•—|Hear the Audio Chapter 11 at myhistorylab.com

Has your family crossed borders?

IN 2010 ADRIANA CARILLO, A MEMBER OF THE MEXICAN SENATE, DERIDED President Barack Obama's plans to strengthen the 700-mile fence between the United States and Mexico. She explained that Spanish-speaking peoples, many of them of Mexican descent, constituted a third of the population of New Mexico, California, Texas, and Arizona. No fence, she declared, should separate the southwestern United States and Mexico, a region bound by economic and cultural ties. On the other side of the fence—literally and rhetorically—U.S. Senator Lamar Smith of San Antonio, Texas, complained that Obama was not doing enough to stem the flood of illegal immigrants into the United States.

As the debate raged, few noted that the United States had built the fence to prevent Mexicans from passing into lands that had once belonged to Mexico. In 1821, when Mexico secured its independence from Spain, the American Southwest became Mexican territory. But the heavy influx of American settlers into the Mexican state of Texas prompted Mexico to restrict further American immigration. Yet the "illegal" immigrants kept coming into Texas; some talked of independence and in 1836 secured it by war. In 1845 Texas became part of the United States; California (1850), New Mexico (1912) and Arizona (1912) would follow. Mexicans who entered the region were trespassing; in time, they would become illegal immigrants.

The acquisition of the Southwest by the United States had several important (if unintended) consequences. The most important concerned slavery. The annexation of Texas as a slave state raised the question of slavery throughout the Southwest. Would the "peculiar institution" eventually span the entire continent, stretching all the way to California? And, if the federal government disallowed slavery in some of the western regions, why not all of them? A crisis of inconceivable dimensions loomed.

Tyler's Troubles

John Tyler, who became president in 1841 after the death of William Henry Harrison, was a thin, rather delicate-appearing man. Courteous, tactful, and soft-spoken, he gave the impression of being weak, an impression reinforced by his professed belief that the

299

president should defer to Congress in the formulation of policy. This was a false impression; John Tyler was stubborn and proud, and these characteristics combined with an almost total lack of imagination to make him worship consistency. He had turned away from Jackson because of the aggressive way the president had used his powers of appointment and the veto, but he also disagreed with Henry Clay and the northern Whigs about the Bank, protection, and federal internal improvements. Being a states' rights Southerner, he considered such measures unconstitutional. Nevertheless, he was prepared to cooperate with Clay as the leader of what he called the "more immediate representatives" of the people, the members of Congress. But he was not prepared to be Clay's puppet. He asked all of Harrison's Cabinet to remain in office.

Tyler and Clay did not get along, and for this Clay was chiefly to blame. He behaved in an overbearing manner that was out of keeping with his nature, probably because he resented having been passed over by the Whigs in 1840. He considered himself the real head of the Whig party and intended to exercise his leadership.

In Congress, Clay announced a comprehensive federal program that ignored Tyler's states' rights view of the Constitution. Most important was his plan to set up a new Bank of the United States. When Congress passed the new Bank bill, Tyler vetoed it. The entire Cabinet except Secretary of State Daniel Webster thereupon resigned in protest.

Abandoned by the Whigs, Tyler attempted to build a party of his own. He failed to do so, and for the remainder of his term the political squabbling in Washington was continuous.

The Webster-Ashburton Treaty

Webster's decision to remain in the Cabinet was motivated in part by his desire to settle the boundary between Maine and New Brunswick. The intent of the peace treaty of 1783 had been to award the United States all land in the area drained by rivers flowing into the Atlantic rather than into the St. Lawrence, but the wording was obscure and the old maps conflicting. In 1842 the British sent a new minister, Lord Ashburton, to the United States to try to settle all outstanding disputes. Ashburton and Webster easily worked out a compromise boundary. The British needed only a small part of the territory to build a military road connecting Halifax and Quebec. Webster, who thought any settlement desirable simply to eliminate a possible cause of war, willingly agreed.

Webster solved the problem of placating Maine and Massachusetts, both of which wanted every acre of the land in dispute, in an extraordinary manner. During the peace negotiations ending the Revolution, Franklin had marked the boundary between Maine and Canada on a map with a heavy red line, but no one could find the Franklin map. Webster obtained an old map of the area and had someone mark off in red a line that followed the British version of the boundary. He showed this document to representatives of Maine and Massachusetts, convincing them that they had better agree to his compromise before the British got wind of it and demanded the whole region! It later came out that the British had a true copy of the Franklin map, which showed that the entire area rightfully belonged to the United States.

Nevertheless, Webster's generosity made excellent sense. Lord Ashburton, gratified by having obtained the strategic territory, made concessions elsewhere along the Canadian and American border. British dependence on foreign foodstuffs was increasing; America's need for British capital was rising. War, or even unsettled affairs, would have injured vital business relations and produced no compensating gains. The **Webster-Ashburton Treaty** was regarded as a diplomatic triumph.

The Texas Question

The settlement with Great Britain won support in every section of the United States, but the same could not be said for Tyler's attempt to annex the Republic of Texas, for this involved the question of slavery. In the Transcontinental Treaty of 1819 with Spain the boundary of the United States had been drawn in such a way as to exclude Texas. This seemed unimportant at the time, yet within months of the treaty's ratification in February 1821, Americans led by Stephen F. Austin had begun to settle in the area. Almost simultaneously Mexico threw off the last vestiges of Spanish rule and secured its independence. Texas was now part of Mexico.

Cotton flourished on the fertile Texas plains, and for a time, the new Mexican authorities offered free land and something approaching local autonomy to groups of settlers from the United States. By 1830 there were some 20,000 white Americans in Texas, about 2,000 slaves, and only a few thousand Mexicans.

President John Quincy Adams had offered Mexico $1 million for Texas, and Jackson was willing to pay $5 million, but Mexico would not sell. Nevertheless, by the late 1820s, the flood of American settlers was giving the Mexican authorities second thoughts. The immigrants apparently felt no loyalty to Mexico. Most were Protestants, though Mexican law required that all immigrants be Catholics; few attempted to learn more than a few words of Spanish. When Mexico outlawed slavery in 1829, American settlers evaded the law by "freeing" their slaves and then signing them to lifetime contracts as indentured servants. In 1830 Mexico prohibited further immigration of Americans into Texas, though again the law proved impossible to enforce.

As soon as the Mexican government began to restrict them, the Texans began to seek independence. In 1835 a series of skirmishes escalated into a full-scale rebellion. The Mexican president, Antonio López de Santa Anna, marched north with over 5,000 soldiers to subdue the rebels. Late in February 1836 he reached San Antonio.

A force of 187 men under Colonel William B. Travis held the city. They took refuge behind the stout walls of a former mission called the Alamo. For nearly two weeks they held off Santa Anna's assaults, inflicting terrible casualties on the attackers. Finally, on March 6, the Mexicans breached and scaled the walls. Once inside they killed everyone, even the wounded. Among the dead were the legendary Davy Crockett and Jim Bowie, inventor of the Bowie knife. (See Re-Viewing the Past, *The Alamo*, pp. 320–321.)

●●●┤Read the Document

Travis, *Letter from the Alamo* at **myhistorylab.com**

After the Alamo and the slaughter of another garrison at Goliad, southeast of San Antonio, peaceful settlement of the dispute between Texas and Mexico was impossible. Meanwhile, on March 2, 1836, Texas had declared its independence. Sam Houston, a former congressman and governor of Tennessee and an experienced Indian fighter, was placed in charge of the rebel army. For a time Houston retreated before Santa Anna's troops, who greatly outnumbered his own. At the San Jacinto River he took a stand. On April 21, 1836, shouting "Forward! Charge! Remember the Alamo! Remember Goliad!" his troops routed the Mexican army, which soon retreated across the Rio Grande. In October, Houston was elected president of the Republic of Texas, and a month later a plebiscite revealed that an overwhelming majority favored annexation by the United States.

President Jackson hesitated. To take Texas might lead to war with Mexico. Assuredly it would stir up the slavery controversy. On his last day in office he recognized the republic, but he made no move to accept it into the Union, nor did his successor, Van Buren. Texas thereupon went its own way, which involved developing friendly ties with Great Britain. An independent Texas suited British tastes perfectly, for it could provide an alternative supply of raw cotton and a market for manufactures unfettered by tariffs.

Sam Houston—and his horse—earned this heroic tribute. At the Battle of San Jacinto, a musket ball shattered Houston's right ankle; his horse, hit by five bullets, fell dead.
Source: San Jacinto Museum of History, Houston.

These events caused alarm in the United States, especially among Southerners, who dreaded the possibility that a Texas dominated by Great Britain might abolish slavery. As a Southerner, Tyler shared these feelings; as a beleaguered politician, spurned by the Whigs and held in contempt by most Democrats, he saw in annexation a chance to revive his fortunes. When Webster resigned as secretary of state in 1843, Tyler replaced him with a fellow Virginian, Abel P. Upshur, whom he ordered to seek a treaty of annexation. The South was eager to take Texas, and in the West and even the Northeast the patriotic urge to add such a magnificent new territory to the national domain was great. Upshur negotiated a treaty in February 1844, but before he could sign it he was killed by the accidental explosion of a cannon on USS *Princeton* during a weapons demonstration.

To ensure the winning of Texas, Tyler appointed John C. Calhoun secretary of state. This was a blunder; by then Calhoun was so closely associated with the South and with slavery that his appointment alienated thousands of Northerners who might otherwise have welcomed annexation. Suddenly Texas became a hot political issue. Clay and Van Buren, who seemed assured of the 1844 Whig and Democratic presidential nominations, promptly announced that they opposed annexation, chiefly on the ground that it would probably lead to war with Mexico. With a national election in the offing, northern and western senators refused to vote for annexation, and in June the Senate rejected the treaty, 35 to 16. The Texans were angry and embarrassed, the British eager again to take advantage of the situation.

Watch the Video
The Annexation of Texas
at **myhistorylab.com**

Manifest Destiny

The Senate, Clay, and Van Buren had all misinterpreted public opinion. John C. Calhoun, whose world was so far removed from that of the average citizen, in this case anticipated the mood of the country.

After 200 years of westward expansion, Americans perceived their destined goal: *The whole continent was to be theirs!* A New York journalist, John L. O'Sullivan, captured the new mood in a sentence. Nothing must interfere, he wrote in 1845, with "the fulfillment of our *manifest destiny* to overspread the continent allotted by Providence for the free development of our yearly multiplying millions."

Read the Document
John O'Sullivan, *Annexation* at **myhistorylab.com**

The expansion, stimulated by the natural growth of the population and by a revived flood of immigration, was going on in every section and with little regard for political boundaries. New settlers rolled westward in hordes to fulfill their **manifest destiny**. The politicians did not sense the new mood in 1844; even Calhoun, who saw the acquisition of Texas as part of a broader program, was thinking of balancing sectional interests rather than of national expansion.

Life on the Trail

The romantic myths attached by later generations to this mighty human tide have obscured the adjustments forced on the pioneers and focused attention on the least significant of the dangers they faced and the hardships they endured. For example, Indians could of course be deadly enemies, but pioneers were more likely to complain that

In *American Progress* (1872), John Gast depicts a feminized (and eroticized) America moving westward, a school book in one hand, a telegraph wire in the other. Confronted with the onslaught of "civilization," the buffalo flee and the Indians cringe.

the Indians they encountered were dirty, lazy, and pitiably poor than to worry about the danger of Indian attack.

The greater dangers were accidents on the trail, particularly to children, and also unsanitary conditions and exposure to the elements. "Going west" had always been laborious, but in the 1840s the distances covered were longer by far and the comforts and conveniences of "civilization" that had to be left behind, being more extensive than those available to earlier generations, tended to be more painful to surrender.

Travel on the plains west of the Mississippi was especially taxing for women. Some assumed tasks traditionally performed by men. "I keep close to my gun and dog," a woman from Illinois wrote in her diary. But most found the experience disillusioning. Guidebooks promised them that "regular exercise, in the open air . . . gives additional vigor and strength." But the books did not prepare women for collecting dried buffalo dung for fuel, for the heat and choking dust of summer, for the monotony, the dirt, the cramped quarters. Caring for an infant or a two-year-old in a wagon could be torture week after week on the trail.

California and Oregon

By 1840 many Americans had settled far to the west in California, which was unmistakably Mexican territory, and in the Oregon country, jointly claimed by the United States and Great Britain; and it was to these distant regions that the pioneers traveled in increasing numbers as the decade progressed. California was a sparsely settled land of some 7,000 Spanish-speaking ranchers and a handful of "Anglo" settlers from the United States. Until the 1830s, when their estates were broken up by the anticlerical Mexican government, twenty-one Catholic missions, stretching north from San Diego to San Francisco, controlled more than 30,000 Indian converts, who were little better off than slaves.

Oregon, a vaguely defined area between California and Russian Alaska, proved still more alluring to Americans. Captain Robert Gray had sailed up the Columbia River in 1792, and Lewis and Clark had visited the region on their great expedition. In 1811 John Jacob Astor's Pacific Fur Company had established trading posts on the Columbia. Two decades later Methodist, Presbyterian, and Catholic missionaries began to find their way into the Willamette Valley, a green land of rich soil, mild climate, and tall forests teeming with game. Gradually a small number of settlers followed, until by 1840 there were about 500 Americans in the Willamette area.

In the early 1840s, fired by the spirit of manifest destiny, the country suddenly burned with "Oregon fever." In dozens upon dozens of towns, societies were founded to collect information and organize groups to make the march to the Pacific. Land hunger (stimulated by glowing reports from the scene) drew the new migrants most powerfully, but the patriotic concept of manifest destiny gave the trek across the 2,000 miles of wilderness separating Oregon from the western edge of American settlement in Missouri the character of a crusade. In 1843 nearly 1,000 pioneers made the long trip.

The Oregon Trail began at the western border of Missouri and followed the Kansas River and the muddy Platte past Fort Laramie to the Rockies. It crossed the Continental Divide by the relatively easy South Pass, veered south to Fort Bridger (on Mexican soil), and then ran north and west through the valley of the Snake River and

Ada McColl gathers buffalo chips, used for fuel, in western Nebraska.
Source: Kansas State Historical Society.

eventually, by way of the Columbia, to Fort Vancouver, a British post guarding the entrance to the Willamette Valley.

Over this tortuous path wound the canvas-covered caravans with their scouts and their accompanying herds. Each group became a self-governing community on the march, with regulations democratically agreed on "for the purpose of keeping good order and promoting civil and military discipline." Most of the travelers consisted of young families, some from as far away as the East Coast cities, more from towns and farms in the Ohio Valley. Few could be classified as poor because the cost of the trip for a family of four was about $600, no small sum at that time. (The faster and less fatiguing trip by ship around South America cost about $600 per person.)

●●─[Read the Document
Geer, *Oregon Trail Journal* at
myhistorylab.com

For large groups Indians posed no great threat (though constant vigilance was necessary), but the five-month trip was full of labor, discomfort, and uncertainty. "It became so monotonous after a while that I would have welcomed an Indian fight if awake," one man wrote. And at the end lay the regular tasks of pioneering. The spirit of the trailblazers is caught in an entry from the diary of James Nesmith:

> Friday, October 27.—Arrived at Oregon City at the falls of the Willamette.
> Saturday, October 28.—Went to work.

Trails West The Old Spanish Trail was the earliest of the trails west. Part of it was mapped in 1776 by a Franciscan missionary. The Santa Fe Trail came into use after 1823. The Oregon Trail was pioneered by trappers and missionaries. The Mormon Trail was first traversed in 1847, while the Oxbow Route, developed under a federal mail contract, was used from 1858 to 1861.

Behind the dreams of the Far West as an American Eden lay the commercial importance of the three major West Coast harbors: San Diego, San Francisco, and the Strait of Juan de Fuca leading into Puget Sound. Eastern merchants considered these harbors the keys to the trade of the Orient. That San Diego and San Francisco were Mexican and the Puget Sound district was claimed by Great Britain only heightened their desire to possess them. As early as 1835, Jackson tried to buy the San Francisco region. Even Calhoun called San Francisco the future New York of the Pacific and proposed buying all of California from Mexico.

The Election of 1844

In the spring of 1844 expansion did not seem likely to affect the presidential election. The Whigs nominated Clay unanimously and ignored Texas in their party platform. When the Democrats gathered in convention at Baltimore in May, Van Buren appeared to have the nomination in his pocket. He too wanted to keep Texas out of the campaign. John C. Calhoun, however, was determined to make Texas a campaign issue.

That a politician of Van Buren's caliber, controlling the party machinery, could be upset at a national convention seemed unthinkable. But upset he was, for the southern delegates rallied round the Calhoun policy of taking Texas to save it for slavery. "I can beat Clay and Van Buren put together on this issue," Calhoun boasted. "They are behind the age." James K. Polk of Tennessee, who favored expansion, swept the convention.

Polk was a good Jacksonian; his supporters called him "Young Hickory." He opposed high tariffs and was dead set against establishing another national bank. But he believed in taking Texas. The Democratic platform demanded that Texas be "rean-nexed" (implying that it had been part of the Louisiana Purchase) and that all of Oregon be "reoccupied" (suggesting repeal of the joint occupation of the region with Great Britain, which had been agreed to in the Convention of 1818).

Texas was now in the campaign. When Clay sensed the new expansionist sentiment of the voters, he tried to hedge on his opposition to annexation, but by doing so he probably lost as many votes as he gained. The election was extremely close. The campaign followed the pattern established in 1840, with stress on parades, mass meetings, and slogans. Polk carried the country by only 38,000 of 2.7 million votes. In the Electoral College the vote was 170 to 105. Polk's victory was nevertheless taken as a mandate for expansion. Tyler promptly called on Congress to take Texas by joint resolution, which was done a few days before Tyler left the White House. Under the resolution, if the new state agreed, as many as four new states might be carved from its territory. Polk accepted this arrangement, and in December 1845 Texas became a state.

Polk as President

Polk was uncommonly successful in doing what he set out to do as president. He persuaded Congress to lower the tariff of 1842 and to restore the independent treasury. He opposed federal internal improvements and managed to have his way. He made himself the spokesman of American expansion by committing himself to obtaining, in addition to Texas, both Oregon and the great Southwest. Here again, he succeeded.

Oregon was the first order of business. In his inaugural address Polk stated the American claim to the entire region in the plainest terms, but he informed the British minister in Washington, Richard Pakenham, that he would accept a boundary following the forty-ninth parallel to the Pacific. Pakenham rejected this proposal without submitting it to London, and Polk thereupon decided to insist again on the whole area. When Congress met in December 1845, he asked for authority to give the necessary one year's notice for withdrawing from the 1818 treaty of joint occupation. Following considerable discussion, Congress complied and in May 1846 Polk notified Great Britain that he intended to terminate the joint occupation.

The British then decided to compromise. Officials of the Hudson's Bay Company had become alarmed by the rapid growth of the American settlement in the Willamette Valley. By 1845 some 5,000 people had poured into the region, whereas the country north of the Columbia contained no more than 750 British subjects. The company decided to shift its base from the Columbia to Vancouver Island. And British experts outside the company reported that the Oregon country could not possibly be defended in case of war. Thus, when Polk accompanied the one-year notice with a hint that he would again consider a compromise, the British foreign secretary, Lord Aberdeen, hastily suggested Polk's earlier proposal, dividing the Oregon territory along the forty-ninth parallel. Polk agreed. The treaty followed that line from the Rockies to Puget Sound, but Vancouver Island, which extends below the line, was left entirely to the British, so that both nations retained free use of the Strait of Juan de Fuca. Although some northern Democrats accused Polk of treachery because he had failed to fight for all of Oregon, the treaty so obviously accorded with the national interest that the Senate approved it by a large majority in June 1846. Polk was then free to take up the Texas question in earnest.

War with Mexico

One reason for the popularity of the Oregon compromise was that the country was already at war with Mexico and wanted no trouble with Great Britain. The **Mexican War** had broken out in large measure because of the expansionist spirit, and the confidence born of its overwhelming advantages of size and wealth certainly encouraged the United States to bully Mexico. In addition, Mexico had defaulted on debts owed the United States, which caused some people to suggest using force to obtain the money. But Mexican pride was also involved. Texas had been independent for the better part of a decade, and Mexico had made no serious effort to reconquer it; nevertheless, Mexico never recognized its independence and promptly broke off diplomatic relations when the United States annexed the republic.

Polk then ordered General Zachary Taylor into Texas to defend the border. However, the location of that border was in dispute. Texas claimed the Rio Grande; Mexico insisted that the boundary was the Nueces River, which emptied into the Gulf of Mexico about 150 miles to the north. Taylor reached the Nueces in July 1845 with about 1,500 troops and crossed into the disputed territory. He stopped on the southern bank at Corpus Christi, not wishing to provoke the Mexicans by marching to the Rio Grande.

In November, Polk sent an envoy, John Slidell, on a secret mission to Mexico to try to obtain the disputed territory by negotiation. He authorized Slidell to

The War with Mexico, 1846–1848 The war with Mexico required considerable coordination of far-flung military and naval operations.

cancel the Mexican debt in return for recognition of the annexation of Texas and acceptance of the Rio Grande boundary. The president also empowered Slidell to offer as much as $30 million if Mexico would sell the United States all or part of New Mexico and California.

It would probably have been to Mexico's advantage, at least in the short run, to have made a deal with Slidell. The area Polk wanted, lying in the path of American expansion, was likely to be engulfed as Texas had been, without regard for the actions of the American or Mexican governments. But the Mexican government refused to receive Slidell. Amid a wave of anti-American feeling, a military coup occurred and General Mariano Paredes, the new head of state, promptly reaffirmed his country's claim to all of Texas. Slidell returned to Washington convinced that the Mexicans would not give an inch until they had been "chastised."

Polk had already ordered Taylor to advance to the Rio Grande. By late March 1846 the army, which swelled to about 4,000, had taken up positions near the Mexican town of Matamoros. The Mexicans crossed the river on April 25 and attacked an American mounted patrol. They were driven back easily, but when news of the fighting reached Washington, Polk asked Congress to declare war. He treated the matter as a *fait accompli*: "War exists," he stated flatly. Congress accepted this reasoning and without actually declaring war voted to raise and supply an additional 50,000 troops.

From the first battle, the outcome of the Mexican War was never in doubt. At Palo Alto, north of the Rio Grande, 2,300 Americans scattered a Mexican force more than twice their number. Then, 1,700 Americans routed 7,500 Mexicans at Resaca de la Palma near what is now Brownsville, Texas. Fewer than 50 U.S. soldiers lost their lives in these engagements, while Mexican losses in killed, wounded, and captured exceeded 1,000. Within a week of the outbreak of hostilities, the Mexicans had been driven across the Rio Grande and General Taylor had his troops firmly established on the southern bank.

To the Halls of Montezuma

President Polk insisted not only on directing grand strategy but on supervising hundreds of petty details, down to the purchase of mules and the promotion of enlisted men. But he allowed party considerations to control his choice of generals. This partisanship caused unnecessary turmoil in army ranks. He wanted, as Thomas Hart Benton said, "a small war, just large enough to require a treaty of peace, and not large enough to make military reputations dangerous for the presidency."

Read the **Document**

Thomas Corwin, *Against the Mexican War* at **myhistorylab.com**

Unfortunately for Polk, both Taylor and Winfield Scott, the commanding general in Washington, were Whigs. Polk, who tended to suspect the motives of anyone who disagreed with him, feared that one or the other would make political capital of his popularity as a military leader. The examples of his hero, Jackson, and of General Harrison loomed large in Polk's thinking.

Polk's attitude was narrow, almost unpatriotic, but not unrealistic. Zachary Taylor was not a brilliant soldier. He had joined the army in 1808 and made it his whole life. He cared so little for politics that he had never bothered to cast a ballot in an election. Polk believed that he lacked the "grasp of mind" necessary for high command, and

American soldiers—some of them regulars in deep blue uniforms, others in buckskin cowboy outfits—fight in the streets to drive Mexicans from a Spanish mission in Monterrey, California, in 1846.

General Scott complained of his "comfortable, laborsaving contempt for learning of every kind." But Taylor commanded the love and respect of his men, and he knew how to deploy them in the field. He had won another victory against a Mexican force three times larger than his own at Buena Vista in February 1847.

The dust had barely settled on the field of Buena Vista when Whig politicians began to pay Taylor court. "Great expectations and great consequences rest upon you," a Kentucky politician explained to him. "People everywhere begin to talk of converting you into a political leader, when the War is done."

Polk's concern was heightened because domestic opposition to the war was growing. Many Northerners feared that the war would lead to the expansion of slavery. Others—among them an obscure Illinois congressman named Abraham Lincoln—felt that Polk had misled Congress about the original outbreak of fighting and that the United States was the aggressor. The farther from the Rio Grande one went in the United States, the less popular "Mr. Polk's war" became; in New England opposition was almost as widespread as it had been to "Mr. Madison's war" in 1812.

Polk's design for prosecuting the war consisted of three parts. First, he would clear the Mexicans from Texas and occupy the northern provinces of Mexico. Second, he would take possession of California and New Mexico. Finally, he would march on Mexico City. Proceeding west from the Rio Grande, Taylor swiftly overran Mexico's northern provinces. In June 1846, American settlers in the Sacramento Valley seized Sonoma and raised the Bear Flag of the Republic of California. Another group, headed by Captain John C. Frémont, leader of an American exploring party that happened to be in the area, clashed with the Mexican authorities around Monterey, California, and then joined with the Sonoma rebels. A naval squadron under Commodore John D. Sloat captured Monterey and San Francisco in July 1846, and a squadron of cavalry joined the other American units in mopping-up operations around San Diego and Los Angeles. By February 1847 the United States had won control of nearly all of Mexico north of the capital city.

The campaign against Mexico City was the most difficult of the war. Fearful of Taylor's growing popularity and entertaining certain honest misgivings about his ability to oversee a complicated campaign, Polk put Winfield Scott in charge of the offensive.

About Scott's competence no one entertained a doubt. But he seemed even more of a threat to the Democrats than Taylor, because he had political ambitions as well as military ability. In 1840 the Whigs had considered him for president. Scion of an old Virginia family, Scott was intelligent, even-tempered, and cultivated, if somewhat pompous. After a sound but not spectacular record in the War of 1812, he had added to his reputation by helping modernize military administration and strengthen the professional training of officers. On the record, and despite the politics of the situation, Polk had little choice but to give him this command.

Scott landed his army south of Veracruz, Mexico, on March 9, 1847, laid siege to the city, and obtained its surrender in less than three weeks with the loss of only a handful of his 10,000 men. Marching westward through hostile country, he maintained effective discipline, avoiding atrocities that might have inflamed the countryside against him. Finding his way blocked by well-placed artillery and a large army at Cerro Gordo, where the National Road rose steeply toward the central highlands, Scott outflanked the Mexican position and then carried it by storm, capturing more than 3,000 prisoners and much equipment. By mid-May he had advanced to Puebla, only eighty miles southeast of Mexico City.

After delaying until August for the arrival of reinforcements, he pressed on, won two hard-fought victories at the outskirts of the capital, and on September 14 hammered his way into the city. In every engagement the American troops had been outnumbered, yet they always exacted a far heavier toll from the defenders than they themselves were forced to pay. In the fighting on the edge of Mexico City, for example, Scott's army sustained about 1,000 casualties, for the Mexicans defended their capital bravely. But 4,000 Mexicans were killed or wounded in the engagements, and 3,000 (including eight generals, two of them former presidents of the republic) were taken prisoner. No less an authority than the Duke of Wellington, the conqueror of Napoleon, called Scott's campaign the most brilliant of modern times.

The Treaty of Guadalupe Hidalgo

Following the fall of Mexico City, the Mexican government was in turmoil. Polk had authorized payment of $30 million for New Mexico, upper and lower California, and the right of transit across Mexico's narrow isthmus of Tehuantepec. Now, observing the disorganized state of Mexican affairs, he began to consider demanding more territory and paying less for it. He recalled his chief negotiator, Nicholas P. Trist, who ignored the order. Trist realized that unless a treaty was arranged soon, the Mexican government might disintegrate, leaving no one in authority to sign a treaty. He dashed off a sixty-five-page letter to the president, in effect refusing to be recalled, and continued to negotiate. Early in February the **Treaty of Guadalupe Hidalgo** was completed. By its terms Mexico accepted the Rio Grande as the boundary of Texas and ceded New Mexico and upper California to the United States. In return the United States agreed to pay Mexico $15 million and to take on the claims of American citizens against Mexico, which by that time amounted to another $3.25 million.

When he learned that Trist had ignored his orders, the president ordered that he be fired from the State Department and placed under arrest. Yet Polk had no choice but to submit the treaty to the Senate, for to have insisted on more territory would have meant more fighting, and the war had become increasingly unpopular. The relatively easy military victory made some people ashamed that their country was crushing a weaker neighbor. Abolitionists, led by William Lloyd Garrison, called it an "invasion . . . waged solely for the detestable and horrible purpose of extending and perpetuating American slavery." The Senate, subject to the same pressures as the president, ratified the agreement by a vote of thirty-eight to fourteen.

The Fruits of Victory: Further Enlargement of the United States

See the **Map**

U.S. Territorial Expansion in the 1850s at
myhistorylab.com

The Mexican War, won quickly and at relatively small cost in lives and money, brought huge territorial gains. The Pacific coast from south of San Diego to the forty-ninth parallel and all the land between the coast and the Continental Divide had become the property of the American people.

Immense amounts of labor and capital would have to be invested before this new territory could be made to yield its bounty, but the country clearly had the capacity to accomplish the job.

In this atmosphere came what seemed a sign from the heavens. In January 1848, while Scott's veterans rested on their victorious arms in Mexico City, a mechanic named James W. Marshall was building a sawmill on the American River in the Sacramento Valley east of San Francisco. One day, while supervising the deepening of the millrace, he noticed a few flecks of yellow in the bed of the stream. These he gathered up and tested. They were pure gold.

Other strikes had been made in California and been treated skeptically or as matters of local curiosity; since the days of Jamestown, too many pioneers had run fruitlessly in search of El Dorado, and too much fool's gold had been passed off as the real thing. Yet this discovery produced an international sensation. The gold was real and plentiful—$200 million of it was extracted in four years—but equally important was the fact that everyone was ready to believe the news. The **gold rush** reflected the heady confidence inspired by Guadalupe Hidalgo; it seemed the ultimate justification of manifest destiny. Surely an era of continental prosperity and harmony had dawned.

Slavery: Storm Clouds Gather

Prosperity came in full measure but harmony did not, for once again expansion brought the nation face to face with the divisive question of slavery. The future of this giant chunk of North America, most of it vacant, was soon to be determined—slave or free? The question, in one sense, seems hardly worth the national crisis it provoked. Slavery appeared to have little future in New Mexico and California, and none in Oregon. Why did the South fight so hard for the right to bring slaves into a region that seemed so poorly suited to their exploitation?

Slavery raised a moral question. Most Americans tried to avoid confronting this truth; as patriots they assumed that any sectional issue could be solved by compromise. However, while the majority of whites had little respect for blacks, slave or free, few persons, northern or southern, could look upon the ownership of one human being by another as simply an alternative form of economic organization and argue its merits as they would those of the protective tariff or a national bank. Twist the facts as they might, slavery was either right or it was wrong; being on the whole honest and moral, they could not, having faced that truth, stand by unconcerned while the question was debated.

Slavery had complicated the Texas problem from the start, and it beclouded the future of the Southwest even before the Mexican flag had been stripped from the staffs at Santa Fe and Los Angeles. The northern, Van Burenite wing of the Democratic party had become increasingly uneasy about the proslavery cast of Polk's policies, which were unpopular in that part of the country. Once it became likely that the war would bring new territory into the Union, these Northerners felt compelled to try to check the president and to assure their constituents that they would resist the admission of further slave territory. On August 8, 1846, during the debate on a bill appropriating money for the conduct of the war, Democratic Congressman David Wilmot of Pennsylvania introduced an amendment that provided "as an express and fundamental condition to the acquisition of any territory from the Republic of Mexico" that "neither slavery nor involuntary servitude shall ever exist in any part of said territory."

Southerners found the **Wilmot Proviso** particularly insulting. Nevertheless, it passed the House, where northern congressmen outnumbered southern. But it was defeated in the Senate, where Southerners held the balance. To counter the Proviso, Calhoun, once again serving as senator from South Carolina, introduced resolutions in 1846 arguing that Congress had no right to bar slavery from any territory; because territories belonged to all the states, slave and free, all should have equal rights in them. From this position it was only a step (soon taken) to demanding that Congress guarantee the right of slave owners to bring slaves into the territories and establish federal slave codes in the territories. Most Northerners considered this proposal as repulsive as Southerners found the Wilmot Proviso.

To resolve the territorial problem, two compromises were offered. One, eventually backed by President Polk, would extend the Missouri Compromise line to the Pacific. The majority of Southerners were willing to go along with this scheme, but most Northerners would no longer agree to the reservation of *any* new territory for slavery. The other possibility, advocated by Senator Lewis Cass of Michigan, called for organizing new territories without mention of slavery, thus leaving it to local settlers, through their territorial legislatures, to determine their own institutions. Cass's **popular sovereignty**, known more vulgarly as "squatter sovereignty," had the superficial merit of appearing to be democratic. Its virtue for the members of Congress, however, was that it allowed them to escape the responsibility of deciding the question themselves.

The Election of 1848

One test of strength occurred in August, before the 1848 presidential election. After six months of acrimonious debate, Congress passed a bill barring slavery from Oregon. The test, however, proved little. If it required half a year to settle the question for Oregon, how could an answer ever be found for California and New Mexico? Plainly the time had come, in a democracy, to go to the people. The coming presidential election seemed to provide an ideal opportunity.

The opportunity was missed. The politicians of the parties hedged, fearful of losing votes in one section or another. With the issues blurred, voters had no real choice. That the Whigs should behave in such a manner was perhaps to be expected. In 1848 they nominated Zachary Taylor for president, despite his lack of political sophistication and even after he had flatly refused to state his opinion on any current subject. The party offered no platform. Taylor's contribution to the campaign was so naive as to be pathetic. "I am a Whig, *but not an ultra Whig. . . .* If elected . . . I should feel bound to administer the government untrammeled by party schemes."

The Democratic party had little better to offer. All the drive and zeal characteristic of it in the Jackson period had gradually seeped away. Polk's espousal of Texas's annexation had driven many Northerners from its ranks. The party members finally nominated Lewis Cass, the father of popular sovereignty, but they did not endorse that or any other solution to the territorial question. The Van Buren wing of the Democratic party could not stomach Cass's willingness to countenance the extension of slavery into new territories. Combining with the antislavery Liberty party, they formed the **Free Soil party** and nominated Van Buren.

The Free Soil party polled nearly 300,000 votes, about 10 percent of the total, in a very dull campaign. Offered a choice between the honest ignorance of Taylor and the cynical opportunism of Cass, the voters—by a narrow margin—chose the former, Taylor receiving 1.36 million votes to Cass's 1.22 million. Taylor carried eight of the fifteen slave states and seven of the fifteen free states, proof that the sectional issue

AN AVAILABLE CANDIDATE.

According to this Democratic cartoon, the only qualification of General Zachary Taylor, the Whig candidate for president in 1848, is that he killed many Mexicans.

had been avoided. The chief significance of the election was the growing strength of the antislavery forces; in the next decade, this would bring about the collapse of the second party system.

The Gold Rush

The question of slavery in the territories could no longer be deferred. The discovery of gold had brought an army of prospectors into California. By the summer of 1848 San Francisco had become almost a ghost town, and an estimated two-thirds of the adult males of Oregon had hastened south to the gold fields. After President Polk confirmed the "extraordinary character" of the strike in his annual message of December 1848, there was no containing the gold seekers. During 1849, some 25,000 Americans made their way to California from the East by ship; more than 55,000 others crossed the continent by overland routes. About 8,000 Mexicans, 5,000 South Americans, and numbers of Europeans joined the rush.

The rough limits of the gold country had been quickly marked out. For 150 miles and more along the western slope of the Sierra stretched the great mother lode. Along the expanse any stream or canyon, or any ancient gravel bed might conceal a treasure in nuggets, flakes, or dust. Between 1849 and 1860 about 200,000 people, nearly all of them males, crossed the Rockies to California and thousands more reached California by ship via Cape Horn. Disregarding justice and reason alike, the newcomers from the East, as one observer noted, "regarded every man but a native [North] American as an interloper." They referred to people of Latin American origin as "greasers" and sought by law and by violence to keep them from mining for gold. Even the local Californians (now American citizens) were discriminated against. The few free blacks in California and the several thousand more who came in search of gold were treated no better. As for the far larger Indian population, it was almost wiped out. There were about 150,000 Indians in California in the mid-1840s but only 35,000 in 1860.

•●•⌐Read the Document

Burrum, from *Six Months in the Gold Mines* at **myhistorylab.com**

The ethnic conflict was only part of the problem. Rough, hard men, separated from women, lusted for gold in a strange, wild country where fortunes could be made in a day, gambled away in an hour, or stolen in an instant. The situation demanded the establishment of a territorial government. President Taylor appreciated this, and in his gruff, simple-hearted way he suggested an uncomplicated answer: Admit California directly as a state, letting the Californians decide for themselves about slavery. The rest of the Mexican cession could be formed into another state. No need for Congress, with its angry rivalries, to meddle at all, he believed. In this way the nation could avoid the divisive effects of sectional debate.

The Californians reacted favorably to Taylor's proposal. They were overwhelmingly opposed to slavery, though not for humanitarian reasons. On the contrary, they tended to look on blacks as they did Mexicans and feared that if slavery were permitted, white gold seekers would be disadvantaged. By October 1849 they had drawn up a constitution that outlawed slavery, and by December the new state government was functioning.

Taylor was the owner of a large plantation and more than 100 slaves; Southerners had assumed (without bothering to ask) that he would fight to keep the territories open to slavery. But being a military man, he was above all a nationalist; he disliked the divisiveness that partisan discussion of the issue was producing. Southerners were horrified by the president's reasoning. To admit California would destroy the balance between free and slave states in the Senate; to allow all the new land to become free would doom the South to wither in a corner of the country, surrounded by hostile free states. Radicals were already saying that the South would have to choose between secession and surrender. Taylor's plan played into the hands of extremists.

The Compromise of 1850

This was no longer a squabble over territorial governments. With the Union itself at stake, Henry Clay rose to save the day. He had been as angry and frustrated when the Whigs nominated Taylor as he had been when they passed him over for Harrison. Now, well beyond age seventy and in poor health, he put away his ambition and his resentment and for the last time concentrated his remarkable vision on a great, multifaceted national problem. On

●●●⎯⎤Read the **Document**
Clay, *Speech to the U.S. Senate* at **myhistorylab.com**

January 29, 1850, he laid his proposal, "founded upon mutual forbearance," before the Senate. A few days later he defended it on the floor of the Senate in the last great speech of his life.

California should be brought directly into the Union as a free state, he argued. The rest of the Southwest should be organized as a territory without mention of slavery: The Southerners would retain the right to bring slaves there, while in fact none would do so. "You have got what is worth more than a thousand Wilmot Provisos," Clay pointed out to his northern colleagues. "You have nature on your side." Empty lands in dispute along the Texas border should be assigned to the New Mexico Territory, Clay continued, but in exchange the United States should take over Texas's preannexation debts. The slave trade should be abolished in the District of Columbia (but not slavery itself), and a more effective federal fugitive slave law should be enacted and strictly enforced in the North.

Clay's proposals occasioned one of the most magnificent debates in the history of the Senate. Every important member had his say. Calhoun, perhaps even more than Clay, realized that the future of the nation was at stake and that his own days were numbered (he died four weeks later). He was so feeble that he could not deliver his speech himself. He sat impassive, wrapped in a great cloak, gripping the arms of his chair, while Senator James M. Mason of Virginia read it to the crowded Senate. Calhoun thought his plan would save the Union, but his speech was an argument for secession; he demanded that the North yield completely on every point, ceasing even to discuss the question of slavery. Clay's compromise was unsatisfactory; he himself had no other to offer. If you will not yield, he said to the northern senators, "let the States . . . agree to separate and part in peace. If you are unwilling we should part in peace, tell us so, and we shall know what to do."

Three days later, on March 7, Daniel Webster took the floor. He too had begun to fail. Years of heavy drinking and other forms of self-indulgence had taken their toll. The brilliant volubility and the thunder were gone, and when he spoke his face was bathed in sweat and there were strange pauses in his delivery. But his argument was lucid. Clay's proposals should be adopted. Since the future of all the territories had

●●●─[Read the Document

Webster, *Speech to the U.S. Senate* at **myhistorylab.com**

already been fixed by geographic and economic factors, the Wilmot Proviso was unnecessary. The North's constitutional obligation to yield fugitive slaves, he said, braving the wrath of New England abolitionists, was "binding in honor and conscience." The Union, he continued, could not be sundered without bloodshed. At the thought of that dread possibility, the old fire flared: "Peaceable secession!" Webster exclaimed, "Heaven forbid! Where is the flag of the republic to remain? Where is the eagle still to tower?" The debate did not end with the aging giants. Every possible viewpoint was presented, argued, rebutted, rehashed.

The majority clearly favored some compromise, but nothing could have been accomplished without the death of President Taylor on July 9, 1850. Obstinate, probably resentful because few people paid him half the heed they paid Clay and other prominent members of Congress, the president had insisted on his own plan to bring both California and New Mexico directly into the Union. When Vice President Millard Fillmore, who was a politician, not an ideologue, succeeded Taylor, the deadlock between the White House and Capitol Hill was broken.

In the Senate and then in the House, tangled combinations pushed through the separate measures, one by one. California became the thirty-first state. The rest of the Mexican cession was divided into two territories, New Mexico and Utah, each to be admitted to the Union when qualified, "with or without slavery as [its] constitution may prescribe." Texas received $10 million to pay off its debt in return for accepting a narrower western boundary. The slave trade in the District of Columbia was abolished as of January 1, 1851. The **Fugitive Slave Act** of 1793 was amended to provide for the appointment of federal commissioners with authority to issue warrants, summon posses, and compel citizens under pain of fine or imprisonment to assist in the capture of fugitives. Commissioners who decided that an accused person was a runaway received a larger fee than if they declared the person legally free. The accused could not testify in their own defense. They were to be returned to the South without jury trial merely on the submission of an affidavit by their "owner."

Only four senators and twenty-eight representatives voted for all these bills. The two sides did not meet somewhere in the middle as is the case with most compromises. Each

●●●─[Read the Document

The Fugitive Slave Act (1850) at **myhistorylab.com**

bill passed because those who preferred it outnumbered those opposed. In general, the Democrats gave more support to the **Compromise of 1850** than the Whigs, but party lines never held firmly. In the Senate, for example, seventeen Democrats and fifteen Whigs voted to admit California as a free state. A large number of congressmen absented themselves when parts of the settlement unpopular in their home districts came to a vote; twenty-one senators and thirty-six representatives failed to commit themselves on the new fugitive slave bill.

In this piecemeal fashion the Union was preserved. The credit belongs mostly to Clay, whose original conceptualization of the compromise enabled lesser minds to understand what they must do.

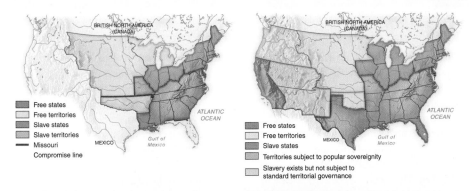

| Free states |
| Free territories |
| Slave states |
| Slave territories |
| Missouri Compromise line |

| Free states |
| Free territories |
| Slave states |
| Territories subject to popular sovereignty |
| Slavery exists but not subject to standard territorial governance |

Missouri Compromise 1820	Compromise of 1850
Missouri admitted as slave state, Maine as free state	California admitted as free state
Slavery prohibited in balance of Louisiana Purchase territory north of 36°30'.	Texas (slave state) has its borders finalized
	Status of remainder of territory acquired from Mexico left undetermined
	Congress to enact Fugitive Slave Law to capture escaped slaves

Everywhere sober and conservative citizens sighed with relief. Mass meetings throughout the country "ratified" the result. Hundreds of newspapers gave the compromise editorial approval. In Washington patriotic harmony reigned. When Congress met again in December it seemed that party discord had been buried forever. "I have determined never to make another speech on the slavery question," Senator Stephen A. Douglas of Illinois told his colleagues. "Let us cease agitating, stop the debate, and drop the subject." If this were done, he predicted, the compromise would be accepted as a "final settlement." With this bit of wishful thinking the year 1850 passed into history.

The Alamo

Alamo, Pearl Harbor, 9/11: Each of these syllables has been seared into the national consciousness. Each galvanized Americans to go to war; and each has persisted in memory.

Two movies entitled *The Alamo* have influenced how Americans remember the event: John Wayne directed the 1960 movie by that name, and also starred in it as Davy Crockett. The second was a 2004 release by director John Lee Hancock. Both movies briskly establish the historical context: Mexico secures independence from Spain in 1821, with Texas as a state within the Mexican federation. Antonio Lopez de Santa Anna, a Mexican general who regarded himself as the "Napoleon of the West," becomes dictator of Mexico. The American settlers in Texas seize several of Santa Anna's garrisons, including the Alamo, a fortified Spanish mission near San Antonio.

Neither movie explains that, up to this time, Santa Anna had been razing Zacatecas, a Mexican state that had also opposed his rule. Early in 1836, though, he marched an army of several thousand soldiers north to crush the Texas rebels. Late in February, his advance units entered San Antonio and took up positions outside the Alamo. Both movies show the Texans sending riders to get reinforcements from the fledgling Texas government at Washington-on-the-Brazos, far to the east. There Sam Houston tried but failed to find a way to relieve the beleaguered garrison.

At the Alamo, the defenders, probably fewer than 200, were divided into three sets of volunteers and a fourth group, consisting of the "regular" soldiers of the Texas government, commanded by William B. Travis, a twenty-six-year-old cavalryman. One of the volunteer groups was led by Jim Bowie, an Indian fighter known for his long-bladed knife. David Crockett, the bear-hunter-turned-Congressman-turned-celebrity led the second group of volunteer fighters. (See Chapter 9, American Lives, "Davy Crockett.") The third group of volunteers consisted of Mexicans seeking to restore the Mexican republic.

Both movies ended with the battle that began on March 6, the thirteenth day of the siege. Within an hour, resistance had been silenced. All of the defenders were dead; some 500–600 Mexicans were killed, many caught in their own crossfire as they converged upon the Alamo.

Both movies *mostly* adhere to these facts. The 1960 movie added many fanciful plot elements: John Wayne's Crockett spends his nights stealing Mexican cattle, destroying their cannon, and romancing their prettiest senorita. There is no evidence for any of this. Both movies also show Santa Anna pounding the Alamo with artillery fusillades. In fact, Santa Anna had no big cannon. Some of his generals urged him to postpone the attack until heavier cannon had arrived; they would reduce the Alamo to rubble, sparing the heavy losses of a frontal assault. (Santa Anna, eager for victory in battle, refused to wait.) The 1960 movie also contends, wrongly, that Bowie wanted to abandon the Alamo while Travis insisted on staying. In fact, both men thought it essential to hold the Alamo. Sam Houston, by contrast, thought it was unwise for the commanders to have allowed their men to be "forted up" and destroyed.

The main question—for historians and movie makers—concerns the motivations of the defenders. Why did they persist against impossible odds? Santa Anna had signaled his intention to take no prisoners—certainly reason enough to fight on—but there was an alternative. Until the final forty-eight hours or so, escape was possible. Messengers and even small groups of men slipped through Santa Anna's lines at night. Some historians contend that the defenders remained at their posts because they expected to be rescued, but the defenders of the Alamo were not fools. The impossibility of their situation was clear. Why, then, did most choose to remain and die?

John Wayne as Crockett.

Billy Bob Thornton as Crockett.

John Wayne's movie provided a simple answer. Wayne's Crockett is fighting for freedom: "Republic. I like the sound of that word. Means people can live free, talk free. Go or come, buy or sell. Republic is one of the words that makes you tight in the throat, same tightness he gets when his baby takes his first step.

Such words made sense to Wayne's audience in 1960s America, then embroiled in a "cold war" against Communism. Santa Anna, a "tyrannical ruler," was akin to Soviet Communism, and the defenders of the Alamo were freedom fighters. But this analogy makes little historical sense. Mexico had outlawed slavery while the Texas rebels drafted a constitution that legalized slavery and prohibited the immigration of free blacks. From that perspective, Mexico stood for freedom, Texas for slavery.

The 2004 movie offered an alternative explanation of the defenders' self-sacrifice, citing the words of Travis: "We will show the world what patriots are made of." This notion of a death for posthumous honor was most strikingly scripted in the character of Davy Crockett, played by Billy Bob Thornton. As the prospects for reinforcement fade, Thornton's Crockett muses about escaping:

If it was just simple old me, David, from Tennessee, I might drop over the wall some night and take my chances. But this Davy Crockett feller, they are all watching him. He's been fightin' on this wall every day of his life.

This resonates with what we know about the real Crockett. Similarly, the actual Travis, who had abandoned his wife and neglected his children, wrote a letter before the final battle hoping that he would leave his boy "the proud recollection that he is the son of a man who died for his country."

Much the same could have been said of the others at the Alamo. Most had grown up beneath the long shadow of the Revolutionary generation that had fought and died to found a great nation. As the men of the Alamo looked upon a horizon darkened by enemy troops, they perhaps realized that their deaths would assure their own immortality. The Alamo would not be forgotten, although doubtless none could have imagined the malleability of memory centuries later.

Questions for Discussion

- How was the rebellion of the Texas settlers against Santa Anna comparable to the Founders' battle against the British in 1776? How did it differ?
- Why do some events and people leave a deep imprint upon subsequent generations?

Milestones

1835	Alamo falls to Santa Anna's Mexican army	1845	John L. O'Sullivan coins the expression *manifest destiny*
1836	Sam Houston routs Santa Anna at Battle of San Jacinto	1846	United States and Britain settle Oregon boundary dispute
1837	United States recognizes Republic of Texas	1846–1848	United States wages "Mr. Polk's War" with Mexico
1840	Richard Henry Dana describes voyage to California in *Two Years Before the Mast*	1846	House of Representatives adopts Wilmot Proviso prohibiting slavery in Mexican cession, but Senate defeats it
	William Henry Harrison is elected president	1847	General Winfield Scott captures Mexico City
1841	William Henry Harrison dies; Vice President John Tyler becomes president	1848	James W. Marshall discovers gold at Sutter's Mill, California
	Preemption Act grants "squatters' rights" in West		Treaty of Guadalupe Hidalgo brings United States huge territorial gains
1842	Webster-Ashburton Treaty determines Maine boundary		Zachary Taylor is elected president
1843	Oregon Trail opens	1850	Taylor dies; Vice President Millard Fillmore becomes president
1844	James K. Polk is elected president		Henry Clay's Compromise of 1850 preserves Union
1845	United States annexes Texas		

✓• Study and Review at www.myhistorylab.com

Review Questions

1. From the Louisiana Purchase (1803) until the war with Mexico in 1845 the United States only added Florida (1819) to the national domain. But in the next three years, with the addition of Texas, California, and much of the Southwest, the nation increased in size 50 percent. What accounts for this sudden expansionism?

2. Why did the United States go to war with Mexico and what were its consequences politically?

3. How did the frontier undermine traditional gender roles? How did it reinforce those roles?

4. What was the relationship between slavery and manifest destiny?

Key Terms

Compromise of 1850 *318*
Free Soil party *315*
Fugitive Slave Act *318*
gold rush *313*

manifest destiny *303*
Mexican War *308*
popular sovereignty *314*

Treaty of Guadalupe Hidalgo *312*
Webster-Ashburton Treaty *301*
Wilmot Proviso *314*

The Sections Go
Their Own Ways

12

((•—[Hear the Audio Chapter 12 at myhistorylab.com

What do you do when someone curses at you?

YOUR RESPONSE MAY DEPEND ON WHERE YOU'RE FROM. IN 2009
Malcolm Gladwell, author of the non-fiction bestseller *The Tipping Point*, described a
psychology test in which researchers asked male students at the University of Michigan
to complete questionnaires and, one-by-one, to take them to an office down a narrow
corridor past a row of file cabinets. As each student neared the office, a researcher posing
as a clerk opened a file drawer, forcing the student to squeeze past. As he did, the "clerk"
slammed the drawer and muttered, "Asshole." The student, after delivering his question-
naire, was asked to provide a technician with a saliva sample. It turned out that the saliva of
students from the South showed heightened levels of cortisol and testosterone—chemicals
released as part of a person's fight response; but the saliva of students from northern states
showed no such elevation. Gladwell regarded this as proof that cultural legacies persist
"virtually intact" over many generations. Today's southern men, even though attending a
northern university, were behaving much as had their great-great-grandfathers 180 years
earlier. When confronted with a challenge to their honor, their psychic defenses readied
them to fight, or so Gladwell contended.

This thesis is speculative: Over the past 200 years, countless peoples have washed
over the regions of the United States; how distinctive cultural patterns could have been
continually imprinted upon such different peoples is unclear. Yet nowadays many
people still speak of distinctive regional cultures; and a glance at the political maps in
this book illustrates the persistence of regional voting patterns: Over the past forty-six
presidential elections, for example, Massachusetts and South Carolina have voted for
the same candidate only thirteen times.

If regional cultural variations have become an enduring trait in American life, this
was largely a consequence of changes that gained momentum during the three decades
after 1830. Each section of the country was shaped by distinctive economic systems and
workforces. Industrialization took hold of much of the Northeast, attracting immigrants
who found work in factories in the burgeoning cities and factory towns. To the West,
farming became more commercial and productive, attracting immigrant and other forms
of free (if lowly paid) labor. The South was characterized in large part by the production
of cash crops, especially cotton, and by its unwilling immigrants, the slaves.

But countervailing forces after 1830 also reduced the differences among regions. The Northeast and the West became economically interdependent, linked by an increasingly elaborate network of canals and railroads. The South, whose transportation infrastructure lagged, nevertheless benefited from the improvements in international transportation and trade. By the 1850s the nation remained divided—chiefly between the slave economy of the South and the nominally "free" labor of the North. But as the nation was knit together more tightly, the incompatibility of those diverse economic systems could no longer be ignored.

The South

The South was less affected than other sections by urbanization, European immigration, the transportation revolution, and industrialization. The region remained predominantly agricultural; cotton was still king, slavery the most distinctive southern institution. But important changes were occurring. Cotton continued to march westward, until by 1859 fully 1.3 million of the 4.3 million bales grown in the United States came from beyond the Mississippi. In the upper South, Virginia held its place as the leading tobacco producer, but states beyond the Appalachians were raising more than half the crop. The introduction of Bright Yellow, a mild variety of tobacco that grew best in poor soil, gave a great stimulus to production. The older sections of Maryland, Virginia, and North Carolina shifted to the kind of diversified farming usually associated with the Northeast. By 1849 the wheat crop of Virginia was worth twice as much as the tobacco crop.

The Economics of Slavery

The increased importance of cotton in the South strengthened the hold of slavery on the region. The price of slaves rose until by the 1850s a prime field hand was worth as much as $1,800, roughly three times the cost in the 1820s. While the prestige value of owning this kind of property affected prices, the rise chiefly reflected the increasing value of the South's agricultural output. "Crop value per slave" jumped from less than $15 early in the century to more than $125 in 1859.

In the cotton fields of the Deep South slaves brought several hundred dollars per head more than in the older regions; thus the tendency to sell them "down the river" continued. Mississippi took in some 10,000 slaves a year throughout the period; by 1830 the black population of the state exceeded the white. The westward shift of cotton cultivation was accompanied by the forcible transfer of more than a million African American slaves from the seaboard states to the dark, rich soil of regions watered by the Mississippi and Arkansas rivers and their tributaries. This "second great migration" of blacks far surpassed the original uprooting of blacks from Africa to the United States.

The impact of the trade on the slaves was frequently disastrous. Husbands were often separated from wives, and parents from children. This was somewhat less likely to happen on large, well-managed plantations than on small farms, but it was common enough everywhere. According to one study, one-third of all slave first "marriages" in the upper South were broken by forced separation and nearly half of all children were separated from at least one parent. Families were torn apart less frequently in the lower South, where far more slaves were bought than sold.

A woman in a net on a Congo shore. Although the importation of slaves was illegal after 1807, historians William Cooper and Thomas Terrill estimate in *The American South* (2009) that 50,000 were smuggled into the United States between 1808 and 1860.

As blacks became more expensive, the ownership of slaves became more concentrated. In 1860 only about 46,000 of the 8 million white residents of the slave states had as many as twenty slaves. When one calculates the cost of twenty slaves and the land to keep them profitably occupied, it is easy to understand why this figure is so small. The most efficient size of a plantation worked by gangs of slaves ranged between 1,000 and 2,000 acres. In every part of the South the majority of farmers cultivated no more than 200 acres, and in many sections fewer than 100 acres. On the eve of the Civil War only one white family in four in the South owned any slaves at all. A few large plantations and many small farms—this was the pattern.

There were few genuine economies of scale in southern agriculture. Small farmers grew the staple crops; and many of them owned a few slaves, often working beside them in the fields. These yeomen farmers were hardworking, self-reliant, and moderately prosperous, quite unlike the poor whites of the Appalachians who scratched a meager subsistence from substandard soils.

Well-managed plantations yielded annual profits of 10 percent and more, and, in general, money invested in southern agriculture earned at least a modest return. Considering the way the workforce was exploited, this is hardly surprising. Recent estimates indicate that after allowing for the cost of

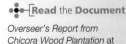

●●●─[**Read** the **Document**

Overseer's Report from Chicora Wood Plantation at **myhistorylab.com**

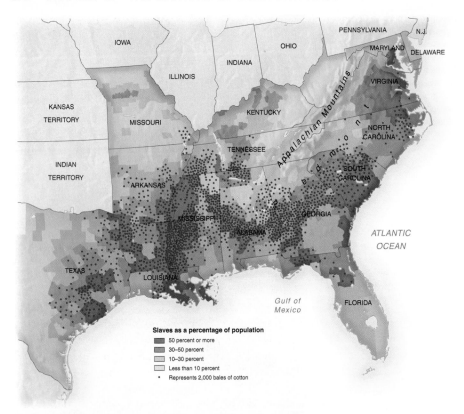

Cotton and Slaves in the South, 1860 Not surprisingly, the areas of greatest cotton production were also the areas with the highest proportion of slaves in the population. Note the concentrations of both in the Piedmont, the Alabama Black Belt, and the lower Mississippi Valley, and the relative absence of both in the Appalachian Mountains.

land and capital, the average plantation slave "earned" cotton worth $78.78 in 1859. It cost masters about $32 a year to feed, clothe, and house a slave. In other words, almost 60 percent of the product of slave labor was expropriated by the masters.

The South failed to develop locally owned marketing and transportation facilities, and for this slavery was at least partly responsible. In 1840 *Hunt's Merchant Magazine* estimated that it cost $2.85 to move a bale of cotton from the farm to a seaport and that additional charges for storage, insurance, port fees, and freight to a European port exceeded $15. Middlemen from outside the South commonly earned most of this money. New York capitalists gradually came to control much of the South's cotton from the moment it was picked, and a large percentage of the crop found its way into New York warehouses before being sold to manufacturers. The same middlemen supplied most of the foreign goods that the planters purchased with their cotton earnings.

Southerners complained about this state of affairs but did little to correct it. Capital tied up in the ownership of labor could not be invested in anything else, and social pressures in the South militated against investment in trade and commerce. Ownership of land and slaves yielded a kind of psychic income not available to any middleman. As one British visitor pointed out, the southern blacks were "a nonconsuming class." Still more depressing, under slavery the enormous reservoir of intelligence and skill that the blacks represented was almost entirely wasted. Many slave artisans worked on the plantations, and a few free blacks made their way in the South remarkably well, but the amount of talent unused, energy misdirected, and imagination smothered can only be guessed.

Foreign observers in New England frequently noted the alertness and industriousness of ordinary laborers and attributed this, justifiably, to the high level of literacy. Nearly everyone in New England could read and write. Correspondingly, the stagnation and inefficiency of southern labor could be attributed in part to the high degree of illiteracy, for over 20 percent of *white* Southerners could not read or write, another tragic squandering of human resources.

Antebellum Plantation Life

The "typical" plantation did not exist, but it is possible to describe, in a general way, what a medium-to-large operation employing twenty or more slaves was like in the two decades preceding the Civil War. Such a plantation was more like a small village than a northern-type agricultural unit, and in another way more like a self-sufficient colonial farm than a nineteenth-century commercial operation, although its major activity involved producing cotton or some other cash crop.

Slaveholding families were also quite different from northern families of similar status, in part because they were engaged in agriculture and in part because of their so-called peculiar institution. Husbands and wives did not function in separate spheres to nearly the same extent, although their individual functions were different and gender-related.

The master was in general charge and his word was law—the system was literally paternalistic. But his wife nearly always had immense responsibilities. Running the household meant supervising the servants (and sometimes punishing them, which often meant wielding a lash), nursing the sick, taking care of the vegetable and flower gardens, planning meals, and seeing to the education of her own children and the training of young slaves. It could also involve running the entire plantation on the frequent occasions when her husband was away on business. At the same time, her role entailed being a "southern lady": refined, graceful, and supposedly untroubled by worldly affairs.

The majority of the slaves of both sexes were field hands who labored on the land from dawn to dusk. Household servants and artisans, indeed any slave other than small children and the aged and infirm, might be called on for such labor when needed. Slave women were expected to cook for their own families and do other chores after working in the fields.

Children, free and slave, were cared for by slaves, the former by household servants, the latter usually by an elderly woman, perhaps with the help of a girl only a little older than the children. Infants were brought to their mothers in the fields for nursing several times a day, for after a month or two at most, slave mothers were required to go back to work. Slave children were not put to work until they were six or seven years old, and until they were about ten they were given only small tasks such as feeding the chickens or minding a smaller child. Black and white youngsters played together and were often cared for by the same nursemaid.

●●●─[Read the **Document**

Harper, *The Slave Mother* at **myhistorylab.com**

Slave cabins were simple and crude; most consisted of a single room, dark, with a fireplace for cooking and heat. Usually the flooring was raised above ground level, though some were set on the bare earth. In 1827 Basil Hall, a British naval officer, reported that in a large South Carolina plantation, 140 slaves lived in twenty-eight cottages or huts. These were "uncommonly neat and comfortable, and might have shamed those of many countries I have seen." Yet Hall dismissed the claims of whites that slaves were happier than the peasantry of England. Slavery was, above all, a "humiliation" imposed upon "the whole mass of the labouring population" of the South.

The Sociology of Slavery

It is difficult to generalize about the peculiar institution because so much depended on the individual master's behavior. Although some ex-slaves told of masters who refused to whip them, Bennet Barrow of Louisiana, a harsh master, averaged one whipping a month. "The great secret of our success," another planter recalled years later, "was the great motive power contained in that little instrument." Overseers were commonly instructed to give twenty lashes for ordinary offenses, such as shirking work or stealing, and thirty-nine for more serious offenses, such as running away. Sometimes slaves were whipped to death; by 1821, however, all southern states had passed laws allowing a master to be charged with murder if he caused a slave's death from excessive punishment. Conviction normally resulted in a fine. In 1840 a South Carolina woman convicted of killing a slave was fined $214.28.

On balance, it is significant that the United States was the only nation in the Western Hemisphere where the slave population grew by natural increase. After the

This slave burial service, painted by John Antrobus in 1860, reflects an inversion of power relations, a slave preacher leads the mourners while the white overseer and the plantation owners watch uneasily, shunted (literally) to the sides.

ending of the slave trade in 1808, the black population increased at nearly the same rate as the white. Put differently, during the entire period from the founding of Jamestown to the Civil War, only a little more than half a million slaves were imported into the country, about 5 percent of the number of Africans carried by slavers to the New World. Yet in 1860 there were about 4 million blacks in the United States.

Most owners felt responsibilities toward their slaves, and slaves were dependent on and in some ways imitative of white values. However, powerful fears and resentments, not always recognized, existed on both sides. The plantation environment forced the two races to live in close proximity. From this circumstance could arise every sort of human relationship. One planter, using the appropriate pseudonym Clod Thumper, could write, "Africans are nothing but brutes, and they will love you better for whipping, whether they deserve it or not." Another, describing a slave named Bug, could say, "No one knows but myself what feeling I have for him. Black as he is we were raised together." One southern white woman tended a dying servant with "the kindest and most unremitting attention." Another, discovered crying after the death of a slave she had repeatedly abused, is said to have explained her grief by complaining that she "didn't have nobody to whip no more."

Slaves were without rights; they developed a distinctive way of life by attempting to resist oppression and injustice while accommodating themselves to the system. Their marriages had no legal status, but their partnerships seem to have been loving and stable. Even families whose members were sold to different masters often maintained close ties over considerable distances.

Slave religion, on the surface an untutored form of Christianity tinctured with some African infusions, seemed to most slave owners a useful instrument for teaching meekness and resignation and for providing harmless emotional release, which it sometimes was and did. However, religious meetings, secret and open, provided slaves with the opportunity to organize, which led at times to rebellions and more often to less drastic ways of resisting white domination. Religion also sustained the slaves' sense of their own worth as beings made in the image of God, and it taught them, therefore, that while human beings can be enslaved in body, their spirits cannot be enslaved without their consent.

((•—Hear the **Audio**

When the Roll Is Called up Yonder at **myhistorylab.com**

•••—Read the **Document**

A Catechism for Slaves at **myhistorylab.com**

Observing that slaves often seemed happy and were only rarely overtly rebellious, whites persuaded themselves that most blacks accepted the system without resentment and indeed preferred slavery to the uncertainties of freedom. There was much talk about "loyal and faithful servants." The Civil War, when slaves flocked to the Union lines once assured of freedom and fair treatment, would disabuse them of this illusion.

As the price of slaves rose and as northern opposition to the institution grew more vocal, the system hardened perceptibly. White Southerners made much of the danger of insurrection. When a plot was uncovered or a revolt took place, instant and savage reprisals resulted. In 1811, Charles Deslondes led a rebellion of several hundred slaves, armed with tools, who burned a handful of plantations and marched toward New Orleans before being routed by the United States Army. Over fifty slaves were slaughtered immediately; a tribunal of plantation owners ordered the execution of several dozen more. In 1822, after the conspiracy of Denmark Vesey was exposed by informers, thirty-seven slaves were executed and another thirty-odd deported, although no overt act of rebellion had occurred.

The Nat Turner revolt in Virginia in 1831 was the most sensational of the slave uprisings; fifty-seven whites lost their lives before it was suppressed. White Southerners treated runaways almost as brutally as rebels, although they posed no real threat to whites. The authorities tracked down fugitives with bloodhounds and subjected captives to merciless lashings.

●●●─[Read the **Document**

Turner, *The Confessions of Nat Turner* at **myhistorylab.com**

After the Nat Turner revolt, interest in doing away with slavery vanished in the white South. The southern states made it increasingly difficult for masters to free their slaves; during 1859 only about 3,000 in a slave population of nearly 4 million were given their freedom.

Slavery did not flourish in urban settings, and cities did not flourish in societies where slavery was important. Most southern cities were small, and within them, slaves made up a small fraction of the labor force. The existence of slavery goes a long way toward explaining why the South was so rural and why it had so little industry. Slaves were much harder to supervise and control in urban settings. Individual slaves were successfully employed in southern manufacturing plants, but they made up only an insignificant fraction of the South's small industrial labor supply.

Southern whites considered the existence of free blacks undesirable, no matter where they lived. The mere fact that they could support themselves disproved the notion that African Americans were by nature childlike and shiftless, unable to work efficiently without white guidance. From the whites' point of view, free blacks set a bad example for slaves. In a petition calling for the expulsion of free blacks from the state, a group of South Carolinians noted that slaves

> continualy [sic] have before their eyes, persons of the same color . . . freed from the control of masters, working where they please, going where they please, and expending their money how they please.

Many southern states passed laws aimed at forcing free blacks to emigrate, but these laws were not well enforced. There is ample evidence that the white people of, say, Maryland, would have liked to get rid of the state's large free-black population. Free blacks were barred from occupations in which they might cause trouble—no free black could be the captain of a ship, for example—and they were required by law to find a "respectable" white person who would testify as to their "good conduct and character." But whites, who needed slave labor, did not try very hard to expel them.

Psychological Effects of Slavery

The injustice of slavery needs no proof; less obvious is the fact that it had a corrosive effect on the personalities of Southerners, slave and free alike. By "the making of a human being an animal without hope," the system bore heavily on all slaves' sense of their own worth. Some found the condition absolutely unbearable. They became the habitual runaways who collected whip scars like medals, the "loyal" servants who struck out in rage against a master knowing that the result would be certain death, and the leaders of slave revolts.

Table 12.1   Major Slave Rebellions

Rebellion	Year	Description	Backlash against slaves	Legislative response
New York Slave Revolt	1712	Several buildings burned; whites attacked	Twenty-one African Americans executed, including free blacks	Slaves prohibited from carrying firearms and free blacks from owning land; slave owners obliged to pay tax for freeing slaves
Gabriel's Rebellion	1800	Conspiracy to rebel near Richmond, Virginia	Over two dozen slaves hanged, including Gabriel	Restrictions placed on owner's right to free slaves; free blacks not allowed to congregate freely on Sundays
Deslondes' Rebellion	1811	Burned plantations near New Orleans	Nearly 100 slaves killed, including Deslondes	Restrictions on right of free blacks to congregate
Denmark Vesey's Rebellion	1822	Plot to free blacks, kill whites, flee to Haiti	Thirty-five slaves hanged, including Vesey	Municipal guard established in Charleston, South Carolina
Nat Turner's Rebellion	1831	Fifty-five whites killed in Virginia	Over 100 slaves killed, including Turner	Virginia legislature prohibited teaching literacy to blacks, slave and free alike, and required the presence of white ministers during slave religious meetings

Denmark Vesey of South Carolina, even after buying his freedom, could not stomach the subservience demanded of slaves by the system. When he saw Charleston slaves step into the gutter to make way for whites, he taunted them: "You deserve to remain slaves!" For years he preached resistance to his fellows, drawing his texts from the Declaration of Independence and the Bible and promising help from black Haiti. So vehemently did he argue that some of his followers claimed they feared Vesey more than their masters, even more than God. He planned his uprising for five years, patiently working out the details, only to see it aborted at the last moment when a few of his recruits lost their nerve and betrayed him. For Denmark Vesey, death was probably preferable to living with such rage as his soul contained.

Yet Veseys were rare. Most slaves appeared at least resigned to their fate. Many seemed even to accept the whites' evaluation of their inherent abilities and place in society. Of course in most instances it is impossible to know whether this apparent subservience was feigned in order to avoid trouble.

Slaves had strong family and group attachments and a complex culture of their own, maintained, so to speak, under the noses of their masters. By a mixture of subterfuge, accommodation, and passive resistance, they erected subtle defenses against exploitation, achieving a sense of community that helped sustain the psychic integrity of individuals. But slavery discouraged, if it did not extinguish, independent judgment and self-reliance.

SOJOURNER TRUTH

Isabella was born in 1797, or perhaps 1799, in Ulster County, New York. She was a slave. Her owner was Colonel Ardinburgh, a Dutch farmer, who grew tobacco, corn, and flax. Because he could make use of only a handful of slaves, he sold most of the slave children, including Isabella's brother and sister. When Ardinburgh died in 1807, his heirs sold his "slaves, horses, and other cattle" at auction. A local farmer of English descent bought Isabella for $100. Isabella's parents, too old to work, were freed. Destitute, they soon died.

Isabella, who spoke only Dutch, found herself at odds with her new English master and family. "If they sent me for a frying pan, not knowing what they meant, perhaps I carried them the pot hooks," she recalled. Once, for failing to obey an order she did not understand, her master whipped her with a bundle of rods, scarring her back permanently.

In 1810 she was sold to John Dumont, a farmer. Though she came to regard him "as a God," she claimed that his wife subjected her to cruel and "unnatural" treatment. What exactly transpired, she refused "from motives of delicacy" to say. In 1815 Dumont arranged for Isabella to marry another of his slaves. Isabella had no say in the matter. She had five children by him.

Isabella labored in the fields, sowing and harvesting crops. She also cooked and cleaned the house. In recognition of her diligence, Dumont promised to set her free on July 4, 1826, exactly one year prior to the date set by the New York State legislature to end slavery. But on the proposed date, Dumont reneged. Soon thereafter Isabella heard the voice of God tell her to leave. She picked up her baby and walked to the house of a neighbor. When Dumont showed up to bring her back, the neighbor paid him $25 for Isabella and the baby and set them free.

But Isabella learned that her five-year-old son, Peter, had been sold to a planter in Alabama, which had no provision for ending slavery. She angrily confronted the Dumonts, who scoffed at her concern for "a paltry nigger." "I'll have my child again," Isabella retorted. She consulted a Quaker lawyer. He filed suit in her behalf and won. In 1828 the boy was returned.

Now on her own, Isabella went to New York City, then awash in religious ferment. Isabella, whose views on religion were a complex amalgam of African folkways, spiritualism, temperance, and dietary asceticism, was attracted to various unorthodox religious leaders. The most curious of these was Robert Matthews, a bearded, thundering tyrant who claimed to be the Old Testament prophet Matthias. Matthews acquired a house in the town of Sing Sing, housed nearly a dozen converts, and ruled it with an iron hand. Isabella was among those who joined the commune. In 1834, local authorities, who had heard stories of sexual and other irregularities, arrested Matthews.

Isabella had by this time become a preacher. Tall and severe in manner, she jabbed at the air with bony fingers and demanded the obedience she had formerly given to others. She changed her name to Sojourner Truth, a messenger conveying God's true spirit, and embarked on a career of antislavery feminism.

Sojourner Truth

Questions for Discussion

- In what ways did Sojourner Truth's life likely differ from that of a slave on a plantation in the Deep South?
- How did religion contribute to Sojourner Truth's self-empowerment?

These qualities are difficult enough to develop in human beings under the best of circumstances; when every element in white society encouraged slaves to let others do their thinking for them, to avoid questioning the status quo, to lead a simple life, many did so willingly enough. Was this not slavery's greatest shame?

●●─[Read the **Document**
Runaway Slave Advertisements
at **myhistorylab.com**

Whites, too, were harmed by the slave system. Associating working for others with servility discouraged many poor whites from hiring out to earn a stake. Slavery provided the weak, the shiftless, and the unsuccessful with a scapegoat that made their own miserable state easier to bear but harder to escape.

More subtly, the patriarchal nature of the slave system reinforced the already existing tendency toward male dominance over wives and children typical of the larger society. For men of exceptional character, the responsibilities of ownership could be ennobling, but for hotheads, alcoholics, or others with psychological problems, the power could be brutalizing, with terrible effects on the whole plantation community, whites and blacks alike.

Aside from its fundamental immorality, slavery caused basically decent people to commit countless petty cruelties. "I feel badly, got very angry and whipped Lavinia," one Louisiana woman wrote in her diary. "O! for government over my temper." But for slavery, she would surely have had better self-control. The finest white Southerners were often warped by the institution. Even those who abhorred slavery sometimes let it corrupt their thinking: "I consider the labor of a breeding woman as no object, and that a child raised every 2 years is of more profit than the crop of the best laboring man." This cold calculation came from the pen of Thomas Jefferson, author of the Declaration of Independence, a man who, it now seems likely, fathered at least one child by a slave.

Manufacturing in the South

Although the temper of southern society discouraged business and commercial activities, considerable manufacturing developed.

The availability of the raw material and the abundance of waterpower along the Appalachian slopes made it possible to manufacture textiles profitably. By 1825 a thriving factory was functioning at Fayetteville, North Carolina, and soon others sprang up elsewhere in North Carolina and in adjoining states. William Gregg's factory, at Graniteville, South Carolina, established in 1846, was employing about 300 people by 1850. An able propagandist as well as a good businessman, Gregg saw the textile business not only as a source of profit but also as a device for improving the lot of the South's poor whites. He worked hard to weaken the southern prejudice against manufacturing and made his plant a model of benevolent paternalism similar to that of the early mills of Lowell, Massachusetts. As with every other industry, however, southern textile manufacturing amounted to very little when compared with that of the North. While Gregg was employing 300 textile workers in 1850, the whole state of South Carolina had fewer than 900. In 1860 Lowell, Massachusetts had more spindles turning cotton into yarn than the entire South.

Less than 15 percent of all the goods manufactured in the United States in 1860 came from the South; the region did not really develop an industrial society. Its textile manufacturers depended on the North for machinery, for skilled workers and technicians, for financing, and for insurance. When the English geologist Charles Lyell visited New Orleans in 1846, he was astounded to discover that the thriving city supported not a single book publisher. Even a local guidebook that he purchased bore a New York imprint.

The Northern Industrial Juggernaut

The most obvious change in the North in the decades before the Civil War was the rapid growth of industry. The best estimates suggest that immediately after the War of 1812 the United States was manufacturing less than $200 million worth of goods annually. In 1859 the northeastern states alone produced $1.27 billion of the national total of almost $2 billion.

Manufacturing expanded in so many directions that it is difficult to portray or to summarize its evolution. The factory system made great strides. The development of rich anthracite coal fields in Pennsylvania was particularly important in this connection. The coal could be floated cheaply on canals to convenient sites and used to produce both heat for smelting and metalworking and steam power to drive machinery. Steam permitted greater flexibility in locating factories and in organizing work within them, and since waterpower was already being used to capacity, steam was essential for the expansion of output.

American industry displayed a remarkable receptivity to technological change. The list of inventions and processes developed between 1825 and 1850, included—besides such obviously important items as the sewing machine, the vulcanization of rubber, and the cylinder press—the screw-making machine, the friction match, the lead pencil, and an apparatus for making soda water.

By 1850 the United States led the world in the manufacture of goods that required the use of precision instruments, and in certain industries the country was well on the way toward modern mass production methods. American clocks, pistols, rifles, and locks were outstanding.

Industrial growth led to a great increase in the demand for labor. The effects, however, were mixed. Skilled artisans, technicians, and toolmakers earned good wages and found it relatively easy to set themselves up first as independent craftsmen, later as small manufacturers. The expanding frontier drained off much agricultural labor that might otherwise have been attracted to industry, and the thriving new towns of the West absorbed large numbers of eastern artisans of every kind. At the same time, the pay of an unskilled worker was never enough to support a family decently, and the new machines weakened the bargaining power of artisans by making skill less important.

Many other forces acted to stimulate the growth of manufacturing. Immigration increased rapidly in the 1830s and 1840s. By 1860 Irish immigrants alone made up more than 50 percent of the labor force of the New England mills. An avalanche of strong backs, willing hands, and keen minds descended on the country from Europe. European investors poured large sums into the booming American economy, and the savings of millions of Americans and the great hoard of new California gold added to the supply of capital. Improvements in transportation, population growth, the absence of internal tariff barriers, and the relatively high per capita wealth all meant an ever expanding market for manufactured goods.

A Nation of Immigrants

Rapid industrialization influenced American life in countless ways, none more significant than its effect on the character of the workforce and consequently on the structure of society. The jobs created by industrial expansion attracted European immigrants by the tens of thousands. It is a truism that America is a nation of immigrants—recall that even the ancestors of the Indians came to the New World from Asia.

●●─┤Read the **Document**

Foreign Immigration at **myhistorylab.com**

But only with the development of nationalism, that is, with the establishment of the independent United States, did the word *immigrant*, meaning a foreign-born resident, come into existence.

The "native" population (native in this case meaning those whose ancestors had come from Europe rather than native Americans, the Indians) tended to look down on immigrants, and many of the immigrants, in turn, developed prejudices of their own. The Irish, for example, disliked blacks, with whom they often competed for work. Antiblack prejudice was less noticeable among other immigrant groups but by no means absent; most immigrants adopted the views of the local majority, which was often unfriendly to African Americans.

Social and racial rivalries aside, the infusion of unskilled immigrants into the factories of New England speeded the disintegration of the system of hiring young farm women. Already competition and technical advances in the textile industry were increasing the pace of the machines and reducing the number of skilled workers needed to run them. Fewer young farm women were willing to work under these conditions. Recent immigrants replaced the women in large numbers. By 1860 Irish immigrants alone made up more than 50 percent of the labor force in the New England mills.

How Wage Earners Lived

The influx of immigrants does not entirely explain the low standard of living of industrial workers during this period. Low wages and the crowding that resulted from the swift expansion of city populations produced slums that would make the most noisome modern ghetto seem a paradise. In New York tens of thousands of the poor lived in dark, rank cellars, those in the waterfront districts often invaded by high tides. Tenement houses rose back to back, each with many windowless rooms and often without heat or running water.

Out of doors, city life for the poor was almost equally squalid. Slum streets were littered with garbage and trash. Recreational facilities were almost nonexistent. Police and fire protection in the cities were pitifully inadequate. "Urban problems" were less critical than a century later only because they affected a smaller part of the population; for those who experienced them, they were, all too often, crushing.

In 1851 the editor Horace Greeley's *New York Tribune* published a minimum weekly budget for a family of five. The budget, which allowed nothing for savings, medical bills, recreation, or other amenities (Greeley did include 12 cents a week for newspapers), came to $10.37. Since the weekly pay of a factory hand seldom reached $5, the wives and children of most male factory workers also had to labor in the factories merely to survive. And child labor in the 1850s differed fundamentally

A girl stares blankly as the manager of an employment agency suggests her suitability as a maid or housekeeper. The lady, seated, ponders whether the girl will do. The sign on the wall reads, "Agent for Domestics: Warranted Honest." This painting is by William Henry Burr, 1849.
Source: Assession no. 1959.46 Collection of The New-York Historical Society.

from child labor in the 1820s. The pace of the machines had become much faster by then, and the working environment more debilitating.

Relatively few workers belonged to unions, but federations of craft unions sprang up in some cities, and during the boom that preceded the Panic of 1837, a National Trades Union representing a few northeastern cities managed to hold conventions. Early in the Jackson era, "workingmen's" political parties enjoyed a brief popularity, occasionally electing a few local officials. These organizations were made up mostly of skilled craftsmen, professional reformers, and even businessmen. They soon expired, destroyed by internal bickering over questions that had little or nothing to do with working conditions.

The depression of the late 1830s led to the demise of most trade unions. Nevertheless, skilled workers improved their lot somewhat in the 1840s and 1850s. The working day declined gradually from about twelve and a half hours to ten or eleven hours. Many states passed ten-hour laws and laws regulating child labor, but they were poorly enforced. Most states, however, enacted effective mechanic's lien laws, giving workers first call on the assets of bankrupt and defaulting employers, and the Massachusetts court's decision in the case of *Commonwealth v. Hunt* (1842), establishing the legality of labor unions, became a judicial landmark when other state courts followed the precedent.

The flush times of the early 1850s caused the union movement to revive. Many strikes occurred, and a few new national organizations appeared. However, most unions were local institutions, weak and with little control over their membership. The Panic of 1857 dealt the labor movement another body blow. Thus there was no trend toward the general unionization of labor between 1820 and the Civil War.

For this the workers themselves were partly responsible: Craftsmen took little interest in unskilled workers except to keep them down. Few common laborers considered themselves part of a permanent working class with different objectives from those of their employers. Although hired labor had existed throughout the colonial period, it was only with the growth of factories and other large enterprises that significant numbers of people worked for wages. To many people, wage labor seemed almost un-American, a violation of the republican values of freedom and independence that had triumphed in the Revolution. Jefferson's professed dislike of urban life was based in part on his fear that people who worked for wages would be so beholden to their employers that they could not act independently.

This republican value system, along with the fluidity of society, the influx of job-hungry immigrants, and the widespread employment of women and children in unskilled jobs made labor organization difficult. The assumption was that nearly anyone who was willing to work could eventually escape from the wage-earning class. "If any continue through life in the condition of the hired laborer," Abraham Lincoln declared in 1859, "it is . . . because of either a dependent nature which prefers it, or improvidence, folly, or singular misfortune."

Progress and Poverty

Any investigation of American society before the Civil War reveals a paradox that is obvious but difficult to resolve. The United States was a land of opportunity, a democratic society with a prosperous, expanding economy and few class distinctions. Its people had a high standard of living in comparison with the citizens of European countries. Yet within this rich, confident nation there existed a class of miserably underpaid and depressed unskilled workers, mostly immigrants, who were worse off materially than nearly any southern slave. In 1848 more than 56,000 New Yorkers, about a quarter of the population, were receiving some form of public relief. A police drive in that city in 1860 brought in nearly 500 beggars.

The middle-class majority seemed indifferent to or at best unaware of these conditions. Reformers conducted investigations, published exposés, and labored to help the victims of urbanization and industrialization. They achieved little. Great fires burned in these decades to release the incredible energies of America. The poor were the ashes, sifting down silent and unnoticed beneath the dazzle and the smoke. Industrialization produced poverty and riches (in Marxian terminology, a proletarian class and an aristocracy of capitalists).

Economic opportunities were great, and taxation was minimal. Little wonder that as the generations passed, the rich got richer. Industrialization accelerated the process and, by stimulating the immigration of masses of poor workers, skewed the social balance still further. By the mid-nineteenth century Americans were convinced that all men were equal, and indeed all *white* men had equal political rights. Socially and economically, however, the distances between top and bottom were widening. This situation endured for the rest of the century, and in some respects it still endures.

Foreign Commerce

Changes in the pattern of foreign commerce were less noticeable than those in manufacturing but were nevertheless significant. After increasing erratically during the 1820s and 1830s, both imports and exports leapt forward in the next twenty years. The nation remained primarily an exporter of raw materials and an importer of manufactured goods, and in most years it imported more than it exported. Cotton continued to be the most valuable export, in 1860 accounting for a record $191 million of total exports of $333 million. Despite America's own thriving industry, textiles still held the lead among imports, with iron products second. As in earlier days, Great Britain was both the best customer of the United States and its leading supplier.

The increase in the volume and value of trade and its concentration at larger ports had a marked effect on the construction of ships. By the 1850s the average vessel was three times the size of those built thirty years earlier. Startling improvements in design, culminating in the long, sleek, white-winged clipper ships, made possible speeds previously undreamed of. Appearing just in time to supply the need for fast transportation to the

The American clipper ship, *Red Jacket*, off Cape Horn, sails from Australia to Liverpool, England in 1854.

California gold fields, the clippers cut sailing time around Cape Horn to San Francisco from five or six months to three, the record of eighty-nine days being held jointly by *Andrew Jackson* and Donald McKay's famous *Flying Cloud*. To achieve such speeds, cargo capacity had to be sacrificed, making clippers uneconomical for carrying the bulky produce that was the mainstay of commerce. But for specialty goods, in their brief heyday the clippers were unsurpassed.

Steam Conquers the Atlantic

The reign of the clipper ship was short. Like so many other things, ocean commerce was being mechanized. Steamships conquered the high seas more slowly than the rivers because early models were unsafe in rough waters and uneconomical. A riverboat could take on fuel along its route, whereas an Atlantic steamer had to carry tons of coal across the ocean, thereby reducing its capacity for cargo. However, by the late 1840s, steamships were capturing most of the passenger traffic, mail contracts, and first-class freight. These vessels could not keep up with the clippers in a heavy breeze, but their average speed was far greater, especially on the westward voyage against the prevailing winds. Steamers were soon crossing the Atlantic in less than ten days.

The steamship, and especially the iron ship, which had greater cargo-carrying capacity and was stronger and less costly to maintain, took away the advantages that American shipbuilders had held since colonial times. American lumber was cheap, but the British excelled in iron technology. Although the United States invested about $14.5 million in subsidies for the shipping industry, the funds were not employed intelligently and did little good. In 1858 government efforts to aid shipping were abandoned.

The combination of competition, government subsidy, and technological advance drove down shipping rates from one cent to about a third of a cent. Transatlantic passengers could obtain the best accommodations on the fastest ships for under $200, good accommodations on slower packets for as little as $75.

Rates were especially low for European emigrants willing to travel to America on cargo vessels. By the 1840s at least 4,000 ships were engaged in carrying bulky American cotton and Canadian lumber to Europe. On their return trips with manufactured goods they had unoccupied space, which they converted into rough quarters for passengers. Conditions on these ships were crowded, gloomy, and foul. Frequently epidemics took a fearful toll among steerage passengers. On one crossing of the ship *Lark*, 158 of 440 passengers died of typhus.

Yet without this cheap means of transportation, thousands of poor immigrants would simply have remained at home. Bargain freight rates also help explain the clamor of American manufacturers for high tariffs, for transportation costs added relatively little to the price of European goods.

Canals and Railroads

Another dramatic change was the shift in the direction of the nation's internal commerce and its immense increase. From the time of the first settlers in the Mississippi Valley, the Great River had controlled the flow of goods from farm to market. The completion of the Erie Canal in 1825 heralded a shift. In 1830 there were 1,277 miles of canal in the United States; by 1840 there were 3,326 miles.

Each year saw more western produce moving to market through the canals. In 1845 the Erie Canal was still drawing over two-thirds of its west to east traffic from within New York, but by 1847, despite the fact that this local business held steady, more than half of its traffic came from west of Buffalo, and by 1851 more than two-thirds. The volume of western commerce over the Erie Canal in 1851 amounted to more than twenty times what it had been in 1836, while the value of western goods reaching New Orleans in this period increased only two and a half times.

The expanding traffic and New York's enormous share of it caused businessmen in other eastern cities whose canal projects had been unsuccessful to respond promptly when a new means of transport, the railroad, became available. The first railroads were built in England in the 1820s. In 1830 the first American line, the ambitiously named Baltimore and Ohio Railroad, carried 80,000 passengers over a thirteen-mile stretch of track. By 1833 Charleston, South Carolina, had a line reaching 136 miles to Hamburg, on the Savannah River. Two years later the cars began rolling on the Boston and Worcester Railroad. The Panic of 1837 slowed construction, but by 1840 the United States had 3,328 miles of track, equal to the canal mileage and nearly double the railroad mileage of all Europe.

The first railroads did not compete with the canals for intersectional traffic. The through connections needed to move goods economically over great distances materialized slowly. Of the 6,000 miles of track operating in 1848, nearly all lay east of the Appalachians, and little of it had been coordinated into railroad systems. The intention of most early builders had been to monopolize the trade of surrounding districts, not to establish connections with competing centers. Frequently, railroads used tracks of different widths deliberately to prevent other lines from tying into their tracks.

Between 1848 and 1852 railroad mileage nearly doubled. Three years later it had doubled again, and by 1860 the nation had 30,636 miles of track. During this extraordinary burst of activity, four companies drove lines of gleaming iron from the Atlantic seaboard to the great interior valley. In 1851 the Erie Railroad, the longest road in the world with 537 miles of track, linked the Hudson River north of New York City with Dunkirk on Lake Erie. Late the next year the Baltimore and Ohio reached the Ohio River at Wheeling, and in 1853 a banker named Erastus Corning consolidated eight short lines connecting Albany and Buffalo to form the New York Central Railroad. Finally, in 1858 the Pennsylvania Railroad completed a line across the mountains from Philadelphia to Pittsburgh.

In the states beyond the Appalachians, building went on at an even more feverish pace. By 1855 passengers could travel from Chicago or St. Louis to the east coast at a cost of $20 to $30, the trip taking, with luck, less than forty-eight hours. A generation earlier such a trip had required two to three weeks. Construction was slower in the South: Mississippi laid about 800 miles of track, and Alabama about 600.

Financing the Railroads

Railroad building required immense amounts of labor and capital at a time when many other demands for these resources existed. Immigrants or (in the South) slaves did most of the heavy work. Raising the necessary money proved a more complex task.

Private investors supplied about three-quarters of the money invested in railroads before 1860, more than $800 million in the 1850s alone. Much of this capital came from local merchants and businessmen and from farmers along the proposed rights-of-way. Funds were easy to raise because subscribers seldom had to lay out the full price of their stock at one time; instead they were subject to periodic "calls" for a percentage of their commitment as construction progressed. If the road made money, much of the additional mileage could be paid for out of earnings from the first sections built.

But many railroads that failed to find enough investors sought public money. Towns, counties, and the states themselves lent money to railroads and invested in their stock. Special privileges, such as exemption from taxation and the right to condemn property, were often granted, and in a few cases states built and operated roads as public corporations.

As with earlier internal improvement proposals, federal financial aid to railroads was usually blocked in Congress by a combination of eastern and southern votes. But in 1850 a scheme for granting federal lands to the states to build a line from Lake Michigan to the Gulf of Mexico passed both houses. The main beneficiary was the Illinois Central Railroad, which received a 200-foot right-of-way and alternate strips of land along the track one mile wide and six miles deep, a total of almost 2.6 million acres. By mortgaging this land and by selling portions of it to farmers, the Illinois Central raised nearly all the $23.4 million it spent on construction. The success of this operation led to additional grants of almost 20 million acres in the 1850s, benefiting more than forty railroads. Far larger federal grants were made after the Civil War, when the transcontinental lines were built.

•ᴥ•⸢Read the Document
Senate Report on the Railroads
at **myhistorylab.com**

Frequently, the capitalists who promoted railroads were more concerned with making money out of the construction of the lines than with operating them.

Others in the business were unashamedly crooked and avidly took advantage of the public passion for railroads. Some officials issued stock to themselves without paying for it and then sold the shares to gullible investors. Others manipulated the books of their corporations and set up special construction companies and paid them exorbitant returns out of railroad assets. These practices did not become widespread until after the Civil War, but all of them first sprang up in the decades preceding the war. At the same time that the country was first developing a truly national economy, it was also producing its first really big-time crooks.

Railroads and the Economy

The effects of so much railroad construction were profound. Although the main reason that farmers put more land under the plow was an increase in the price of agricultural products, the railroad helped determine just what land was used and how profitably it could be farmed. Much of the fertile prairie through which the Illinois Central ran had been available for settlement for many years before 1850, but development had been slow because it was remote from navigable waters and had no timber. In 1840 the three counties immediately northeast of Springfield had a population of about 8,500. They produced about 59,000 bushels of wheat and 690,000 bushels of corn. In the next decade the region grew slowly by the standards of that day: The three counties had about 14,000 people in 1850 and produced 71,000 bushels of wheat and 2.2 million bushels of corn. Then came the railroad and with it an agricultural revolution. By 1860 the population of the three counties had soared to over 38,000, wheat production had topped 550,000 bushels, and corn 5.7 million bushels.

Access to world markets gave the farmers of the upper Mississippi Valley an incentive to increase output. Land was plentiful and cheap, but farm labor was scarce; consequently agricultural wages rose sharply, especially after 1850. New tools and machines appeared in time to ease the labor shortage. First came the steel plowshare, invented by John Deere, a Vermont-born blacksmith who had moved to Illinois in 1837. In 1839 Deere turned out ten such plows in his little shop in Moline, Illinois. By 1857 he was selling 10,000 a year.

Still more important was the perfection of the mechanical reaper, for wheat production was limited more by the amount that farmers could handle during the brief harvest season than by the acreage they could plant and cultivate. The major figure in the development of the reaper was Cyrus Hall McCormick. McCormick's horse-drawn reaper bent the grain against the cutting knife and then deposited it neatly on a platform, whence it could easily be raked into windrows. With this machine, two workers could cut fourteen times as much wheat as with scythes.

The railroad had an equally powerful impact on American cities. The eastern seaports benefited, and so did countless intermediate centers, such as Buffalo and Cincinnati. But no city was affected more profoundly by railroads than Chicago. In 1850 not a single line had

Railroads, 1860 Major trunk lines carrying long-distance traffic crisscrossed the area east of the Mississippi. The North had a more extensive rail grid than the South; the North and West were linked, while the South was not as tightly connected to the national economy.

reached there; five years later it was terminal for 2,200 miles of track and controlled the commerce of an imperial domain. By extending half a dozen lines west to the Mississippi, it drained off nearly all the river traffic north of St. Louis. The Illinois Central sucked the expanding output of the prairies into Chicago as well. Most of this freight went eastward over the new railroads or on the Great Lakes and the Erie Canal. Nearly 350,000 tons of shipping plied the lakes by 1855.

The railroads, like the textile industry, stimulated other kinds of economic activity. They transformed agriculture; both real estate values and the buying and selling of land increased whenever the iron horse puffed into a new district. The railroads spurred regional concentration of industry and an increase in the size of business units. Their insatiable need for capital stimulated the growth of investment banking. Their massive size required the creation of complex structures and the employment of salaried managers.

Agriculture, 1860 Cotton was central to the southern economy, while tobacco was the primary crop in Virginia, Tennessee, and Kentucky. Wheat was the key crop in the upper Midwest, and corn was grown nearly everywhere.

The proliferation of trunk lines and the competition of the canal system led to a sharp decline in freight and passenger rates. Cheap transportation had a revolutionary effect on western agriculture. Farmers in Iowa could now raise grain to feed the factory workers of Lowell and even of Manchester, England. Two-thirds of the meat consumed in New York City was soon arriving by rail from beyond the Appalachians. The center of American wheat production shifted westward to Illinois, Wisconsin, and Indiana. When the Crimean War (1853–1856) and European crop failures increased foreign demand, these regions boomed. Success bred success for farmers and for the railroads. Profits earned from carrying wheat enabled the roads to build feeder lines that opened up still wider areas to commercial agriculture and made it easy to bring in lumber, farm machinery, household furnishings, and the settlers themselves at low cost.

Railroads and the Sectional Conflict

Increased production and cheap transportation boosted the western farmer's income and standard of living. The days of isolation and self-sufficiency, even for the family on the edge of the frontier, rapidly disappeared. Pioneers quickly became operators of businesses and, to a far greater extent than their forebears, consumers, buying all sorts of manufactured articles that their ancestors had made for themselves or done without. These changes had their costs. Like southern planters, they now became dependent on middlemen and lost some of their feeling of self-reliance. Overproduction became a problem. Buying a farm began to require more capital, for as profits increased, so did the price of land. Machinery was an additional expense. The proportion of farm laborers and tenants increased.

The linking of the East and West had fateful effects on politics. The increased ease of movement from section to section and the ever more complex social and economic integration of the East and West stimulated nationalism and thus became a force for the preservation of the Union. Without the railroads and canals, Illinois and Iowa would scarcely have dared to side against the South in 1861. When the Mississippi ceased to be essential to them, citizens of the upper valley could afford to be more hostile to slavery and especially to its westward extension. Economic ties with the Northeast reinforced cultural connections.

The South might have preserved its influence in the Northwest if it had pressed forward its own railroad-building program. It failed to do so. There were many southern lines but nothing like a southern system. As late as 1856 one could get from Memphis to Richmond or Charleston only by very indirect routes. As late as 1859 the land-grant road extending the Illinois Central to Mobile, Alabama, was not complete, nor did any economical connection exist between Chicago and New Orleans.

This state of affairs could be accounted for in part by the scattered population of the South, the paucity of passenger traffic, the seasonal nature of much of the freight business, and the absence of large cities. Southerners placed too much reliance on the Mississippi: The fact that traffic on the river continued to be heavy throughout the 1850s blinded them to the precipitous rate at which their relative share of the nation's trade was declining. But the fundamental cause of the South's backwardness in railroad construction was the attitude of its leaders. Southerners of means were no more interested in commerce than in industry; their capital found other outlets.

The Economy on the Eve of Civil War

Between the mid-1840s and the mid-1850s the United States experienced one of the most remarkable periods of growth in the history of the world. Every economic indicator surged forward: manufacturing, grain and cotton production, population, railroad mileage, gold production, sales of public land. The building of the railroads stimulated business, and by making transportation cheaper, the completed lines energized the nation's economy. The American System that Henry Clay had dreamed of arrived with a rush just as Clay was passing from the scene.

Inevitably, this growth caused dislocations that were aggravated by the boom psychology that once again infected the popular mind. In 1857 there was a serious collapse. The return of Russian wheat to the world market after the Crimean War caused grain prices to fall. This checked agricultural expansion, which hurt the railroads and cut down on the demand for manufactures. Unemployment increased. Frightened depositors started runs on banks, most of which had to suspend specie payments.

People called this abrupt downturn the Panic of 1857. Yet the vigor of the economy was such that the bad times did not last long. The upper Mississippi Valley suffered most, for so much new land had been opened up that supplies of farm produce greatly exceeded demand. Elsewhere conditions improved rapidly.

The South, somewhat out of the hectic rush to begin with, was affected very little by the collapse of 1857, for cotton prices continued to be high. This gave planters the false impression that their economy was immune to such violent downturns. Some began to argue that the South would be better off out of the Union.

Before a new national upward swing could become well established, however, the sectional crisis between North and South shook people's confidence in the future. Then the war came, and a new set of forces shaped economic development.

Milestones

1808	Congress bans further importation of slaves	1840–1857	Economy surges during boom in manufacturing, railroad construction, and foreign commerce
1822	Thirty-seven slaves are executed when Denmark Vesey's "conspiracy" is exposed	1842	Massachusetts declares unions legal in *Commonwealth v. Hunt*
1825	Erie Canal is completed, connecting the East and the Midwest	1846	Elias Howe invents sewing machine
1830	Baltimore and Ohio Railroad begins operation	1850	Congress grants land to aid construction of Illinois Central Railroad
1831	Nat Turner's slave uprising kills fifty-seven whites	1854	Clipper ship *Flying Cloud* sails from New York to San Francisco in eighty-nine days
1837	Cyrus Hall McCormick invents reaper to harvest wheat	1857	Brief economic depression (Panic of 1857) collapses economy
1839	John Deere begins manufacturing steel plows		

✓•─[Study and **Review** at **www.myhistorylab.com**

Review Questions

1. This chapter explores two tendencies: an increasing economic and cultural gap between the South and the rest of the country; and a tighter integration of the nation through spreading transportation systems. In 1860, was the United States breaking into different economic and cultural systems, or did politicians exaggerate the significance of regional variations?

2. The harshness of the slave system was everywhere apparent. In what ways did slaves succeed in fashioning their own culture?

3. Southerners often insisted that immigrants who toiled in northern factories were subjected to far worse conditions than southern slaves. What arguments can be used to support and reject this thesis?

4. During these decades, southern cities sought militia units and armories to help defend against slave insurrections. Northern cities sought such protections to defend against industrial worker insurrections. Which was the greater threat?

The Coming of the Civil War

13

((•─[Hear the Audio Chapter 13 at myhistorylab.com

Do you space out during political debates?

IN LATE JULY 2008 PRESIDENTIAL CANDIDATE JOHN MCCAIN, BEHIND IN the polls, ran a 30-second TV ad attacking Barack Obama. "He's the biggest celebrity in the world," the narrator declared, as the camera moved from Obama's beaming face to a crowd shouting, "Obama! Obama!" "But is he ready to lead?" the narrator intoned, with a quick cut to glamour shots of Britney Spears and Paris Hilton. Obama retaliated with an attack ad of his own: "John McCain. Same old politics. Same failed policies." By the time the 2008 campaign was over, Obama had placed 553,629 television ads, McCain 287,090. The great majority of these ads were negative.

Many pundits claimed that politics had devolved into little more than name-calling. It had been different 150 years earlier, they said, when Abraham Lincoln squared off against Stephen A. Douglas in a series of debates that framed the national discussion over slavery.

In fact, though, Lincoln and Douglas tore into each other. "Mr. Lincoln has not character enough for integrity and truth," Douglas declared in the first debate. Lincoln responded in kind: "I don't want to quarrel with him—to call him a liar—but when I come square up to him I don't know what else to call him."

If the tone of politics has changed little over the past century and a half, its substance is of an entirely different character. Each of the seven Lincoln-Douglas debates lasted three hours: For the first debate Douglas spoke for one hour. Lincoln's reply lasted ninety minutes, and Douglas concluded with another thirty minute speech. The order of speakers was reversed in subsequent debates. Such a debate nowadays is unimaginable. Most viewers would soon be reaching for the remote.

But during the 1850s audiences stood for hours to hear candidates debate the issues at the heart of this chapter: the morality of the Fugitive Slave Act; the accuracy of Harriet Beecher Stowe's description of slavery in *Uncle Tom's Cabin*; the question of whether "bleeding Kansas" should be admitted to the Union as a slave or free state; the Supreme Court's inflammatory decision in the Dred Scott case; John Brown's manic crusade to free the slaves by force. Most knew, or at least sensed, that the fate of the nation depended on the outcome of these debates. The drumbeat of words came faster and louder. The din culminated in the superheated rhetoric of the 1860 presidential campaign and the secession of the South. Soon words would be drowned out by the roar of cannon.

Slave-Catchers Come North

The political settlement between the North and South that Henry Clay designed—the Compromise of 1850—lasted only four years (see Chapter 11). Its central provisions inevitably sparked controversy. Allowing new territories to decide the question of slavery themselves ensured that the issue would resurface. Americans continued to migrate westward by the thousands, and as long as slaveholders could carry their human property into federally controlled territories, northern resentment would smolder. The Fugitive Slave Act, another part of the Compromise of 1850, imposed fines for hiding or rescuing fugitive slaves. Abolitionists fought against the law and expanded the **underground railroad**, a secret network to help escaped slaves make their way to freedom.

Watch the Video
Underground Railroad at
myhistorylab.com

When two Georgians came to Boston to reclaim William and Ellen Craft, admitted fugitives, a "vigilance committee" hounded them through the streets shouting "slave hunters, slave hunters," and forced them to return home empty-handed. The Crafts prudently—or perhaps in disgust—decided to leave the United States for

This painting by Thomas S. Noble describes the story of Margaret Garner, a slave who escaped with her family across the frozen Ohio River to Cincinnati. When apprehended by slavecatchers, she killed her daughter rather than return her to slavery. Garner's story inspired Toni Morrison's Pulitzer Prize-winning novel *Beloved* (1987).

Free Blacks in 1850 The existence of so many free blacks caused many slaves to question their own servitude and facilitated the attempts of others to escape from bondage.

England. Early in 1851 a Virginia agent captured Frederick "Shadrach" Jenkins, a waiter in a Boston coffeehouse. While Jenkins was being held for deportation, a mob of African Americans broke into the courthouse and hustled him off to Canada. That October a slave named Jerry, who had escaped from Missouri, was arrested in Syracuse, New York. Within minutes the whole town had the news. Crowds surged through the streets, and when night fell, a mob smashed into the building where Jerry was being held and spirited him away to safety in Canada.

•◄•—Read the **Document**

Drew, from *Narratives of Fugitive Slaves in Canada* at **myhistorylab.com**

Such incidents exacerbated sectional feelings. White Southerners accused the North of reneging on one of the main promises made in the Compromise of 1850, while the sight of harmless human beings being hustled off to a life of slavery disturbed many Northerners who were not abolitionists.

However, most white Northerners were not prepared to interfere with the enforcement of the Fugitive Slave Act themselves. Of the 332 blacks put on trial under the law, about 300 were returned to slavery, most without incident. Nevertheless, enforcing the law in the northern states became steadily more difficult.

Uncle Tom's Cabin

Tremendously important in increasing sectional tensions and bringing home the evils of slavery to still more people in the North was Harriet Beecher Stowe's novel *Uncle Tom's Cabin* (1852). Stowe was neither a professional writer nor an abolitionist, and she had almost no firsthand knowledge of slavery. But her conscience had been roused by the Fugitive Slave Act. In gathering material for the book, she depended heavily on abolitionist writers, many of whom she knew. *Uncle Tom's Cabin* was an enormous success: 10,000 copies were sold in a week, and 300,000 in a year. It was translated into dozens of languages. Dramatized versions were staged in countries throughout the world.

●◆●⎡Read the **Document**

Stowe, *Uncle Tom's Cabin* at **myhistorylab.com**

Harriet Beecher Stowe was hardly a distinguished writer; it was her approach to the subject that explains the book's success. Her tale of the pious, patient slave Uncle Tom, the saintly white child Eva, and the callous slave driver Simon Legree appealed to an audience far wider than that reached by the abolitionists. She avoided the self-righteous, accusatory tone of most abolitionist tracts and did not seek to convert readers to belief in racial equality. Many of her southern white characters were fine, sensitive people, while the cruel Simon Legree was a transplanted Connecticut Yankee. There were many heart-rending scenes of pain, self-sacrifice, and heroism. The story proved especially effective on the stage: The slave Eliza crossing the frozen Ohio River to freedom, the death of Eva, Eva and Tom ascending to Heaven—these scenes left audiences in tears.

⎧⊚⎫⎡Watch the **Video**

Harriet Beecher Stowe & The Making of Uncle Tom's Cabin at **myhistorylab.com**

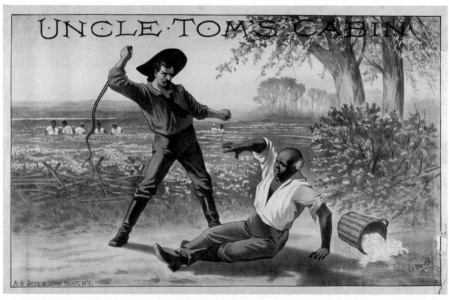

Harriet Beecher Stowe's novel, *Uncle Tom's Cabin*, became a staple of the mid-nineteenth-century theater. This poster shows Simon Legree whipping a blameless Uncle Tom.

Southern critics pointed out, correctly enough, that Stowe's picture of plantation life was distorted, her slaves atypical. They called her a "coarse, ugly, long-tongued woman" and accused her of trying to "awaken rancorous hatred and malignant jealousies" that would undermine national unity. Most Northerners, having little basis on which to judge the accuracy of the book, tended to discount southern criticism as biased. In any case, *Uncle Tom's Cabin* raised questions that transcended the issue of accuracy. Did it matter if every slave was not as kindly as Uncle Tom, as determined as George Harris? What if only one white master was as evil as Simon Legree? No earlier white American writer had looked at slaves as people.

Uncle Tom's Cabin touched the hearts of millions. Some became abolitionists; others, still hesitating to step forward, asked themselves as they put the book down, "Is slavery just?"

Diversions Abroad: The "Young America" Movement

Clearly a distraction was needed to help keep the lid on sectional troubles. Some people hoped to find one in foreign affairs. The spirit of manifest destiny explains this in large part; once the United States had reached the Pacific, expansionists began to think of transmitting the dynamic, democratic U.S. spirit to other countries by aiding local revolutionaries, opening new markets, or perhaps even annexing foreign lands. This became known as the **Young America movement**, whose adherents were confident that democracy would triumph everywhere, even if by conquest.

One of those who dreamt of conquest was an adventurer named William Walker. In 1855 Walker, backed by an American company engaged in transporting migrants to California across Central America, seized control of Nicaragua and elected himself president. He was ousted two years later but made repeated attempts to regain control until, in 1860, when he died before a Honduran firing squad. There were reasons unrelated to slavery why Central America suddenly seemed important. The rapid development of California created a need for improved communication with the West Coast. A canal across Central America would cut weeks from the sailing time between New York and San Francisco. In 1850 Secretary of State John M. Clayton and the British minister to the United States, Henry Lytton Bulwer, negotiated a treaty providing for the demilitarization and joint Anglo-American control of any canal across the isthmus.

As this area assumed strategic importance to the United States, the desire to obtain Cuba grew stronger. In 1854 President Franklin Pierce instructed his minister to Spain to offer $130 million for the island. The State Department prepared a confidential dispatch suggesting that if Spain refused to sell Cuba, "the great law of self-preservation" might justify "wresting" it from Spain by force.

News of the dispatch—known as the **Ostend Manifesto**—leaked out, and it had to be published. Northern opinion was outraged by this "slaveholders' plot" to add another slave state to the Union. Europeans claimed to be shocked by such "dishonorable" and "clandestine" diplomacy. The government had to disavow the manifesto, and any hope of obtaining Cuba or any other territory in the Caribbean vanished.

The expansionist mood of the moment also explains President Fillmore's dispatching an expedition under Commodore Matthew C. Perry to try for commercial concessions in the isolated kingdom of Japan in 1854. Perry's expedition was a great success. The Japanese, impressed by American naval power, agreed to establish diplomatic relations. In 1858 an American envoy, Townsend Harris, negotiated a commercial treaty that opened to American ships six Japanese ports heretofore closed to foreigners. President Pierce's negotiation of a Canadian reciprocity treaty with Great Britain in 1854 and an unsuccessful attempt, also made under Pierce, to annex the Hawaiian Islands are further demonstrations of the assertive foreign policy of the period.

Stephen Douglas: "The Little Giant"

The most prominent spokesman of the Young America movement was Stephen A. Douglas. The senator from Illinois was the Henry Clay of his generation. Like Clay at his best, Douglas was able to see the needs of the nation in the broadest perspective. He held a succession of state offices before being elected to Congress in 1842 at the age of twenty-nine. After only two terms in the House, he was chosen to be a United States senator.

The foundations of Douglas's politics were expansion and popular sovereignty. He had been willing to fight for all of Oregon in 1846, and he supported the Mexican War to the hilt, in sharp contrast to his one-term Illinois colleague in Congress, Abraham Lincoln. That local settlers should determine their own institutions was, to his way of thinking, axiomatic. Since he believed that arguments over the future of slavery in the territories were a foolish waste of energy and time, he was convinced that natural conditions would keep the institution out of the West.

The main thing, he insisted, was to get on with the development of the United States. Let the nation build railroads, acquire new territory, expand its trade. He believed slavery "a curse beyond computation" for both blacks and whites, but he refused to admit that any moral issue was involved. He cared not, he boasted, whether slavery was voted up or voted down. This was not really true, but the question was interfering with the rapid exploitation of the continent. Douglas wanted it settled so that the country could concentrate on more important matters.

Douglas's success in steering the Compromise of 1850 through Congress added to his reputation. In 1851, he set out to win the Democratic presidential nomination, reasoning that since he was the brightest, most imaginative, and hardest-working Democrat around, he had every right to press his claim.

This brash aggressiveness proved his undoing. He expressed open contempt for James Buchanan and said of his other chief rival, Lewis Cass, who had won considerable fame while serving as minister to France, that his "reputation was beyond the C."

At the 1852 Democratic convention Douglas had no chance. Cass and Buchanan killed each other off, and the delegates finally chose a dark horse, Franklin Pierce of New Hampshire. The Whigs, rejecting the colorless Fillmore, nominated General Winfield Scott, who was known as "Old Fuss and Feathers" because of his "punctiliousness in dress and decorum." In the campaign both sides supported the Compromise of 1850. The Democrats won an easy victory, 254 electoral votes to 42.

So handsome a triumph seemed to ensure stability, but in fact it was a prelude to political chaos. The Whig party was crumbling fast. The "Cotton" Whigs of the South, alienated by the antislavery sentiments of their northern brethren, were flocking into the Democratic fold. In the North the Whigs, divided between an antislavery wing ("conscience Whigs") and another that was undisturbed by slavery, found themselves more and more at odds with each other. Congress fell overwhelmingly into the hands of proslavery southern Democrats, a development profoundly disturbing to northern Democrats as well as to Whigs.

The Kansas-Nebraska Act

Franklin Pierce appeared a youthful forty-eight years old when he took office. He was generally well-liked by politicians. His career had included service in both houses of Congress. Alcohol had become a problem for him in Washington, however, and in 1842 he had resigned from the Senate and returned home to try to best the bottle, a struggle in which he was successful. His law practice boomed,

See the **Map**

The Compromise of 1850 and the Kansas-Nebraska Act at **myhistorylab.com**

This engraving of Franklin Pierce shows him on his horse during the Mexican War. In actuality, he did not remain there long. During one battle, Pierce was thrown from his horse and sustained pelvic and knee injuries. While leading his men the next day, he fainted. Another officer assumed that Pierce was drunk. For years, Whigs attacked Pierce's military record, calling him "hero of many a bottle."

and he added to his reputation by serving as a brigadier general during the Mexican War. Although his nomination for president came as a surprise, once made, it had appeared perfectly reasonable. Great things were expected of his administration, especially after he surrounded himself with men of all factions: To balance his appointment of a radical states' rights Mississippian, Jefferson Davis, as secretary of war, for example, he named a conservative Northerner, William L. Marcy of New York, as secretary of state.

Only a strong leader, however, can manage a ministry of all talents, and that President Pierce was not. The ship of state was soon drifting; Pierce seemed incapable of holding firm the helm.

This was the situation in January 1854 when Senator Douglas, chairman of the Committee on Territories, introduced what looked like a routine bill organizing the land west of Missouri and Iowa as the Nebraska Territory. Since settlers were beginning to trickle into the area, the time had arrived to set up a civil administration. But besides his expansionist motives, Douglas also acted because a territorial government was essential to railroad development. As a director of the Illinois Central line and as a land speculator, he hoped to make Chicago the terminus of a transcontinental railroad, but construction could not begin until the route was cleared of Indians and brought under some kind of civil control.

The railroad question aside, Nebraska would presumably become a free state, for it lay north of latitude 36°30' in a district from which slavery had been excluded by the Missouri Compromise. Under pressure from the Southerners, led by Senator David R. Atchison of Missouri, Douglas agreed first to divide the region into two territories, Kansas and Nebraska, and then—a fateful concession—to repeal the part of the Missouri Compromise that excluded slavery from land north of 36°30'. Whether the new territories should become slave or free, he argued, should be left to the decision of the settlers in accordance with the democratic principle of popular sovereignty. The fact that he might advance his presidential ambitions by making concessions to the South must have influenced Douglas too, as must the local political situation in Missouri, where slaveholders feared being "surrounded" on three sides by free states.

Douglas's miscalculation of northern sentiment was monumental. It was one thing to apply popular sovereignty to the new territories in the Southwest, but quite another to apply it to a region that had been part of the United States for half a century and free soil for thirty-four years. A group of abolitionist congressmen issued what they called their "Appeal of the Independent Democrats" (actually, all were Free Soilers and Whigs) denouncing the Kansas-Nebraska bill as "a gross violation of a sacred pledge" and calling for a campaign of letter writing, petitions, and public meetings to prevent its passage. The unanimity and force of the northern public's reaction was like nothing in America since the days of the Stamp Act and the Intolerable Acts.

But protests could not defeat the bill. Southerners in both houses backed it regardless of party. Douglas, at his best when under attack, pushed it with all his power. The authors of the "Appeal," he charged, were "the pure unadulterated representatives of Abolitionism, Free Soilism, [and] Niggerism." President Pierce added whatever force the administration could muster. As a result, the northern Democrats split and the **Kansas-Nebraska Act** was passed late in May 1854. In this manner the nation took the greatest single step in its march toward the abyss of secession and civil war.

The repeal of the Missouri Compromise struck the North like a slap in the face—at once shameful and challenging. Presumably the question of slavery in the territories had been settled forever; now, seemingly without justification, it had been reopened. On May 24, two days after the Kansas-Nebraska bill passed the House of Representatives, Anthony Burns, a slave who had escaped from Virginia by stowing away on a ship, was arrested in Boston. Massachusetts abolitionists brought suit against Burns's former master, charging false arrest. They also organized a protest meeting at which they inflamed the crowd into attacking the courthouse where Burns was being held. The mob broke into the building and a guard was killed, but federal marshals drove off the attackers.

President Pierce ordered the Boston district attorney to "incur any expense" to enforce the law. He also sent a federal ship to Boston to carry Burns back to Virginia. Thus Burns was returned to his master, but it required two companies of soldiers and 1,000 police and marines to get him aboard ship. As the grim parade marched past buildings festooned with black crepe, the crowd screamed "Kidnappers! Kidnappers!" at the soldiers. Estimates of the cost of returning this single slave to his owner ran as high as $100,000. A few months later, northern sympathizers bought Burns his freedom—for a few hundred dollars.

In previous cases Boston's conservative leaders, Whig to a man, had tended to hold back; after the Burns incident, they were thoroughly radicalized. "We went to bed one night old fashioned . . .Whigs," one of them explained, "and waked up stark mad Abolitionists."

Know-Nothings, Republicans, and the Demise of the Two-Party System

There were ninety-one free-state Democrats in the House of Representatives when the Kansas-Nebraska Act was passed, only twenty-five after the next election. With the Whig party already moribund, dissidents flocked to two new parties.

One was the American party, or **Know-Nothing party**, so called because it grew out of a secret society whose members used the password "I don't know." The Know-Nothings were primarily nativists—immigration was soaring in the early 1850s, and the influx of poor foreigners was causing genuine social problems. Crime was on the rise in the cities along with drunkenness and other "diseases of poverty."

Several emotion-charged issues related to the fact that a large percentage of the immigrants were Irish and German Catholics also troubled the Know-Nothings. Questions such as public financing of parochial schools, lay control of church policies, the prohibition of alcoholic beverages, and increasing the time before an immigrant could apply for citizenship (the Know-Nothings favored twenty-one years) were matters of major importance to them. Since these were divisive issues, the established political parties tried to avoid them—hence the development of the new party.

The American party was important in the South as well as in the North, and while most Know-Nothings disliked blacks and considered them inherently inferior beings, they tended to adopt the dominant view of slavery in whichever section they were located. In the North most opposed the Kansas-Nebraska Act.

Operating often in tacit alliance with the antislavery forces (dislike of slavery did not prevent many abolitionists from being prejudiced against Catholics and immigrants), the northern Know-Nothings won a string of local victories in 1854 and elected more than forty congressmen.

Far more significant in the long run was the formation of the Republican party, which was made up of former Free Soilers, Conscience Whigs, and "Anti-Nebraska" Democrats. The American party was a national organization, but the **Republican party** was purely sectional. It sprang up spontaneously throughout the Old Northwest and caught on with a rush in New England.

Republicans presented themselves as the party of freedom. They were not abolitionists (though most abolitionists were soon voting Republican), but they insisted that slavery be kept out of the territories. They believed that if America was to remain a land of opportunity, free white labor must have exclusive access to the West. Thus the party appealed not only to voters who disapproved of slavery, but also to those who wished to keep blacks—free or slave—out of their states. In 1854 the Republicans won more than a hundred seats in the House of Representatives and control of many state governments.

The Whig party had almost disappeared in the northern states and the Democratic party had been gravely weakened, but it was unclear how these two new parties would fare. The Know-Nothing party had the superficial advantage of being a nationwide organization, but where slavery was concerned, this was anything but advantageous. And many Northerners who disliked slavery were troubled by the harsh Know-Nothing policies toward immigrants and Catholics. If the Know-Nothings were in control, said former Whig congressman Abraham Lincoln in 1855, the Declaration of Independence would read "all men are created equal, except negroes, *and foreigners, and catholics.*"

"Bleeding Kansas"

The furor over slavery might have died down if settlement of the new territories had proceeded in an orderly manner. Almost none of the settlers who flocked to Kansas owned slaves and relatively few of them were primarily interested in the slavery question. Most had a low opinion of blacks. Like nearly all frontier settlers, they wanted land and local political office, lucrative government contracts, and other business opportunities.

When Congress opened the gates to settlement in May 1854, none of the land in the territory was available for sale. Treaties extinguishing Indian titles had yet to be ratified, and public lands had not been surveyed. In July Congress authorized squatters to occupy unsurveyed federal lands, but much of this property was far to the west of the frontier and practically inaccessible. The situation led to confusion over property boundaries, to graft and speculation, and to general uncertainty, thereby exacerbating the difficulty of establishing an orderly government.

The legal status of slavery in Kansas became the focus of all these conflicts. Both northern abolitionists and southern defenders of slavery were determined to have Kansas. They made of the territory first a testing ground and then a battlefield, thus exposing the fatal flaw in the Kansas-Nebraska Act and the idea of popular sovereignty. The law said that the people of Kansas were "perfectly free" to decide the slavery question. But the citizens of territories were not entirely free because territories were not sovereign political units. The Act had created a political vacuum, which its vague statement that the settlers must establish their domestic institutions "subject. . . to the Constitution" did not begin to fill. The virtues of the time-tested system of congressional control established by the Northwest Ordinance became fully apparent only when the system was discarded.

In November 1854 an election was held in Kansas to pick a territorial delegate to Congress. A large band of Missourians crossed over specifically to vote for a proslavery candidate and elected him easily. In March 1855 some 5,000 "border ruffians" again descended on Kansas and elected a territorial legislature. A census had recorded 2,905 eligible voters, but 6,307 votes were cast. The legislature promptly enacted a slave code and laws prohibiting abolitionist agitation. Antislavery settlers refused to recognize this regime and held elections of their own. By January 1856 two governments existed in Kansas: one based on fraud, the other extralegal.

"Bleeding Kansas" In the late 1850s, one Kansas government (located in Topeka) abolished slavery; the other (located in Lecompton) legalized slavery. As proslavery settlers poured into Kansas from Missouri, and antislavery settlers from the North, clashes were inevitable.

By denouncing the free-state government located at Topeka, President Pierce encouraged the proslavery settlers to assume the offensive. In May, 800 of them sacked the antislavery town of Lawrence. An extremist named John Brown then took the law into his own hands in retaliation. By his reckoning, five Free Soilers had been killed by proslavery forces. In May 1856, together with six companions (four of them his sons), Brown stole into a settlement on Pottawatomie Creek in the dead of night. They dragged five unsuspecting men from their cabins and murdered them. This slaughter brought men on both sides to arms by the hundreds. Marauding bands came to blows and terrorized homesteads, first attempting to ascertain the inhabitants' position on slavery.

Brown and his followers escaped capture and were never indicted for the murders, but pressure from federal troops eventually forced him to go into hiding. He finally left Kansas in October 1856. By that time some 200 persons had lost their lives.

A certain amount of violence was normal in any frontier community, but it suited the political interests of the Republicans to make the situation in Kansas seem worse than it was. Exaggerated accounts of "bleeding Kansas" filled the pages of northern newspapers. The Democrats were also partly to blame, for although residents of nearby states often tried to influence elections in new territories, the actions of the border ruffians made a mockery of the democratic process.

However, the main responsibility for the Kansas tragedy must be borne by the Pierce administration. Under popular sovereignty the national government was supposed to see that elections were orderly and honest. Instead, the president acted as a partisan. When the first governor of the territory objected to the manner in which the proslavery legislature had been elected, Pierce replaced him with a man who backed the southern group without question.

Senator Sumner Becomes a Martyr for Abolitionism

As counterpoint to the fighting in Kansas there arose an almost continuous clamor in the halls of Congress. Epithets like "liar" were freely tossed about. Prominent in these angry outbursts was a new senator, Charles Sumner of Massachusetts. Brilliant, learned, and articulate, Sumner had made a name for himself in New England as a reformer interested in the peace movement, prison reform, and the abolition of slavery. His unyielding devotion to his principles was less praiseworthy than it seemed on casual examination, for it resulted from his complete lack of respect for the principles of others. Reform movements evidently provided him with a kind of emotional release; he became combative and totally lacking in objectivity when espousing a cause.

In the Kansas debates Sumner displayed an icy disdain for his foes. Colleagues threatened him with assassination, called him a "filthy reptile" and a "leper." He was impervious to such hostility. In the spring of 1856 he loosed a dreadful blast titled "The Crime Against Kansas." Characterizing administration policy as tyrannical, imbecilic, absurd, and infamous, he demanded that Kansas be admitted to the Union at once as a free state. Then he began a long and intemperate attack on both Douglas and the elderly Senator Andrew P. Butler of South Carolina, who was not present to defend himself.

SOUTHERN CHIVALRY — ARGUMENT versus **CLUB'S.**

In this cartoon Charles Sumner of Massachusetts is caned on the floor of the Senate by Preston Brooks of South Carolina.

Source: J. L. Magee, *Southern Chivalry-Argument Versus Clubs*, 1856. Lithograph. Weitenkampf Collection #745, Prints Collection: Miriam and Ira D. Wallach Division of Art, Prints and Photographs, The New York Public Library, Astor, Lenox, and Tilden Foundations.

Sumner described Butler as a "Don Quixote" who had taken "the harlot, slavery" as his mistress, and he spoke scornfully of "the loose expectoration" of Butler's speech. This was an inexcusable reference to the uncontrollable drooling to which the elderly senator was subject. While he was still talking, Douglas, who shrugged off most political name-calling as part of the game, was heard to mutter, "That damn fool will get himself killed by some other damn fool."

Such a "fool" quickly materialized in the person of Congressman Preston S. Brooks of South Carolina, a nephew of Senator Butler. Since Butler was absent from Washington, Brooks, who was probably as mentally unbalanced as Sumner, assumed the responsibility of defending his kinsman's honor. A southern romantic par excellence, he decided that caning Sumner would reflect his contempt more effectively than challenging him to a duel. Two days after the speech, Brooks entered the Senate as it adjourned. Sumner remained at his desk writing. Waiting until a talkative woman in the lobby had left so that she would be spared the sight of violence, Brooks then walked up to Sumner and rained blows on his head with a cane until Sumner fell, unconscious and bloody, to the floor. "I. . . gave him about 30 first-rate stripes," Brooks later boasted. "Towards the last he bellowed like a calf. I wore my cane out completely but saved the head which is gold." The physical damage suffered by Sumner was not life-threatening, but the incident so affected him psychologically that he was unable to return to his seat in Congress until 1859.

Both sides made much of this disgraceful incident. When the House censured him, Brooks resigned, returned to his home district, and was triumphantly reelected. A number of well-wishers sent him souvenir canes. Northerners viewed the affair as illustrating the brutalizing effect of slavery on southern whites and made a hero of Sumner.

Buchanan Tries His Hand

Such was the atmosphere surrounding the 1856 presidential election. The Republican party now dominated much of the North. It nominated John C. Frémont, "the Pathfinder," one of the heroes of the conquest of California during the war with Mexico. Frémont fit the Whig tradition of presidential candidates: a popular military man with almost no political experience. Unlike Taylor and Scott, however, he was articulate on the issue of slavery in the territories. Although citizens of diverse interests had joined the party, Republicans expressed their objectives in one simple slogan: "Free soil, free speech, and Frémont."

The Democrats cast aside the ineffectual Pierce, but they did not dare nominate Douglas because he had raised such a storm in the North. They settled on James Buchanan, chiefly because he had been out of the country serving as minister to Great Britain during the long debate over Kansas! The American party nominated former president Millard Fillmore, a choice the remnants of the Whigs endorsed.

In the campaign, the Democrats concentrated on denouncing the Republicans as a sectional party that threatened to destroy the Union. On this issue they carried the day. Buchanan won only a minority of the popular vote, but he had strength in every section. He got 174 electoral votes to Frémont's 114 and Fillmore's 8. The significant contest took place in the populous states just north of slave territory—Pennsylvania, Ohio, Indiana, and Illinois. Of these, Buchanan carried all but Ohio, although by narrow margins.

No one could say that James Buchanan lacked political experience. Elected to the Pennsylvania legislature in 1815 when he was only twenty-four years old, he served for well over twenty years in Congress and had served as minister to Russia, as secretary of state, and as minister to Great Britain.

Personally, Buchanan was a bundle of contradictions. Dignified in bearing and by nature cautious, he could consume enormous amounts of liquor without showing the slightest sign of inebriation. He wore a very high collar to conceal a scarred neck, and because of an eye defect he habitually carried his head to one side and slightly forward, which gave him, as his biographer says, "a perpetual attitude of courteous deference and attentive interest" that sometimes led individuals to believe they had won a greater share of his attention and support than was actually the case. In fact he was extremely stubborn and sometimes vindictive.

The Dred Scott Decision

Before Buchanan could fairly take the Kansas problem in hand, an event occurred that drove another deep wedge between North and South. Back in 1834 Dr. John Emerson of St. Louis joined the army as a surgeon and was assigned to duty at Rock Island, Illinois. Later he was transferred to Fort Snelling, in the Wisconsin Territory. In 1838 he returned to Missouri. Accompanying him on these travels was his body servant, Dred Scott, a slave. In 1846, after Emerson's death, Scott and his wife Harriet, whom he had married while in Wisconsin, brought suit in the Missouri courts for their liberty with the help of a friendly lawyer. They claimed that residence in Illinois, where slavery was barred under the Northwest Ordinance, and in the Wisconsin Territory, where the Missouri Compromise outlawed it, had made them free.

The future of Dred and Harriet Scott mattered not at all to the country or the courts; at issue was the question of whether Congress or the local legislatures had the power to outlaw slavery in the territories. After many years of litigation, the case reached the Supreme Court of the United States. On March 6, 1857, two days after Buchanan's inauguration, the high tribunal acted, issuing what is known as the **Dred Scott decision**. Free or slave, the Court declared, blacks were not citizens; therefore, Scott could not sue in a federal court. This was dubious legal logic because many blacks were accepted as citizens in some states when the Constitution was drafted and ratified, and Article IV, Section 2, says that "the citizens of each state shall be entitled to all privileges and immunities of citizens in the several states." But the decision settled Scott's fate.

However, the Court went further. Since the plaintiff had returned to Missouri, the laws of Illinois no longer applied to him. His residence in the Wisconsin Territory—this was the most controversial part of the decision—did not make him free because the Missouri Compromise was unconstitutional. According to the Bill of Rights (the Fifth Amendment), the federal government cannot deprive any person of life, liberty, or property without due process of law.[1] Therefore, Chief Justice Roger B. Taney reasoned, "an Act of Congress which deprives a person . . . of his liberty or property merely because he

Watch the **Video**

Dred Scott & The Crises that led to the Civil War at **myhistorylab.com**

---

[1] Some state constitutions had similar provisions, but the slave states obviously did not.

Dred Scott and his wife and children are featured on the cover of *Frank Leslie's Illustrated Newspaper*. Historian Joshua Brown argues in *Beyond the Lines* (2002) that this publication was the precursor to today's popular newsmagazines. Its plentiful pictures were made possible by the new technology of mass-produced wood engraving.

came himself or brought his property into a particular Territory. . . could hardly be dignified with the name of due process of law." The Missouri Compromise had deprived Dr. Emerson of his "property"—his slaves—and thus was unconstitutional!

In addition to invalidating the already repealed Missouri Compromise, the decision threatened Douglas's principle of popular sovereignty, for if Congress could not exclude slaves from a territory, how could a mere territorial legislature do so? Until statehood was granted, slavery seemed as inviolate as freedom of religion or speech or any other civil liberty guaranteed by the Constitution. Where formerly freedom (as guaranteed in the Bill of Rights) was a national institution and slavery a local one, now, according to the Court, slavery was nationwide, excluded only where states had specifically abolished it.

Read the Document

Opinion of the Supreme Court for Dred Scott v. Sanford at **myhistorylab.com**

The irony of employing the Bill of Rights to keep blacks in chains did not escape northern critics. Now slaves could be brought into the Minnesota Territory, even into Oregon. In his inaugural address Buchanan had urged the people to accept the forthcoming ruling, "whatever this may be," as a final settlement. Many assumed (indeed, it was true) that he had put pressure on the Court to act as it did and that he knew in advance of his speech what the decision would be. The Dred Scott decision convinced thousands that the South was engaged in an aggressive attempt to extend the peculiar institution so far that it could no longer be considered peculiar.

The Proslavery Lecompton Constitution

Kansas soon provided a test for northern suspicions. The proslavery leaders in Kansas had managed to convene a constitutional convention at Lecompton, but the Free Soil forces had boycotted the election of delegates. When this rump body drafted a proslavery constitution and then refused to submit it to a fair vote of all the settlers, Kansas governor Robert J. Walker denounced its work and hurried back to Washington to explain the situation to Buchanan.

The president refused to face reality. His prosouthern advisers were clamoring for him to "save" Kansas. Instead of rejecting the **Lecompton constitution**, he asked Congress to admit Kansas to the Union with this document as its frame of government.

Buchanan's decision brought him head-on against Stephen A. Douglas, and the repercussions of their clash shattered the Democratic party. Principle and self-interest forced Douglas to oppose the leader of his party. If he stood aside while Congress admitted Kansas, he not only would be abandoning popular sovereignty, but he would be committing political suicide as well. He was up for reelection to the Senate in 1858. All but one of the fifty-six newspapers in Illinois had declared editorially against the Lecompton constitution; if Douglas supported it, his defeat was certain. In a dramatic confrontation at the White House, he and Buchanan argued the question at length, tempers rising. Finally, the president tried to force him into line. "Mr. Douglas," he said, "I desire you to remember that no Democrat ever yet differed from an Administration of his own choice without being crushed." "Mr. President," Douglas replied contemptuously, "I wish you to remember that General Jackson is dead!" And he stalked out of the room.

Buchanan then compounded his error by putting tremendous political pressure on Douglas, cutting off his Illinois patronage on the eve of his reelection campaign. Of course Douglas persisted, openly joining the Republicans in the fight. Congress rejected the Lecompton bill.

Meanwhile, the extent of the fraud perpetrated at Lecompton became clear. In October 1857 a new legislature had been chosen in Kansas, antislavery voters participating in the balloting. It ordered a referendum on the Lecompton constitution in January 1858. This time the proslavery settlers boycotted the vote and the constitution was overwhelmingly rejected. When Buchanan persisted in pressing Congress to admit Kansas under the Lecompton constitution, Congress ordered another referendum. To slant the case in favor of approval, the legislators stipulated that if the constitution were voted down, Kansas could not be admitted into the Union until it had a population of 90,000. Nevertheless, the Kansans rejected it by a ratio of six to one.

The Emergence of Lincoln

Dissolution threatened the Union. To many Americans, Stephen A. Douglas seemed to offer the best hope of preserving it. For this reason unusual attention was focused on his campaign for reelection to the Senate in 1858. The importance of the contest and Douglas's national prestige put great pressure on the Republicans of Illinois to nominate someone who would make a good showing against him. The man they chose was Abraham Lincoln.

After a towering figure has passed from the stage, it is always difficult to discover what he was like before his rise to prominence. This is especially true of Lincoln, who changed greatly when power, responsibility, and fame came to him. Lincoln was not unknown in 1858, but his public career had not been distinguished. He was born in Kentucky in 1809, and the story of his early life can be condensed, as he once said himself, into a single line from Gray's *Elegy*: "The short and simple annals of the poor." His illiterate father, Thomas Lincoln, was a typical frontier wanderer. When Abraham was seven years old, the family moved to Indiana. In 1830 they pushed west again into southern Illinois. The boy received almost no formal schooling.

However, Lincoln had a good mind, and he was extremely ambitious.[2] In 1834, when barely twenty-five, he won a seat in the Illinois legislature as a Whig. Meanwhile, he studied law and was admitted to the bar in 1836.

Lincoln remained in the legislature until 1842, displaying a perfect willingness to adopt the Whig position on all issues. In 1846 he was elected to Congress. After one term in Congress, marked by his partisan opposition to Polk's Mexican policy, his political career petered out. He seemed fated to pass his remaining years as a small-town lawyer.

Even during this period Lincoln's personality was extraordinarily complex. His bawdy sense of humor and his endless fund of stories and tall tales made him a legend first in Illinois and then in Washington. He was thoroughly at home with toughs like the "Clary's Grove Boys" of New Salem and in the convivial atmosphere of a party caucus. But in a society where most men drank heavily, he never touched liquor. And he was subject to periods of profound melancholy. He wrote of himself in the early 1840s, "I am now the most miserable man living. If what I felt were equally distributed to the whole human family, there would not be one cheerful face on earth."

The revival of the slavery controversy in 1854 stirred Lincoln deeply. No abolitionist, he had tried to take a "realistic" view of the problem. The Kansas-Nebraska bill led him to see the moral issue more clearly. "If slavery is not wrong, nothing is wrong," he stated with the directness and simplicity of expression for which he later became famous. Yet unlike most Free Soilers, he did not blame the Southerners for slavery. "They are just what we would be in their situation," he confessed.

Thus Lincoln was at once compassionate toward the slave owner and stern toward the institution. "A house divided against itself cannot stand," he warned. "I believe this government cannot endure permanently half slave and half free." Without minimizing the difficulties or urging a hasty or ill-considered solution, Lincoln demanded that the people look toward a day, however remote, when not only Kansas but the entire country would be free.

---

[2]His law partner, William Herndon, said that Lincoln's ambition was "a little engine that knows no rest."

The Lincoln-Douglas Debates

As Lincoln developed these ideas his reputation grew. In 1855 he almost won the Whig nomination for senator. He became a Republican shortly thereafter, and in June 1856, at the first Republican National Convention, he received 110 votes for the vice-presidential nomination. He seemed the logical man to pit against Douglas in 1858. The Lincoln-Douglas debates were well-attended and widely reported, for the idea of a direct confrontation between candidates for an important office captured the popular imagination.

The choice of the next senator lay, of course, in the hands of the Illinois legislature. Technically, Douglas and Lincoln were campaigning for candidates for the legislature who were pledged to support them for the Senate seat. The two employed different political styles, each calculated to project a particular image. Douglas epitomized efficiency and success. Ordinarily he arrived in town in a private railroad car, to be met by a brass band, then to ride at the head of a parade to the appointed place.

Lincoln appeared before the voters as a man of the people. He wore ill-fitting black suits and a stovepipe hat that exaggerated his great height. He presented a worn and rumpled appearance, partly because he traveled from place to place on day coaches, accompanied by only a few advisers. When local supporters came to meet him at the station, he preferred to walk with them through the streets to the scene of the debate.

●●●─[Read the Document

Douglas, *Debate at Galesburg, Illinois* at **myhistorylab.com**

Lincoln and Douglas maintained a high intellectual level in their speeches, but these were political debates. Both tailored their arguments to appeal to local audiences—more antislavery in the northern counties, more proslavery in the southern. They also tended to exaggerate their differences,

Abraham Lincoln speaks as Stephen Douglas gazes at the audience—mostly standing—during the debate in Charleston, Illinois in 1858, as painted by Robert Root.

which were not in fact enormous. Neither wanted to see slavery in the territories or thought it economically efficient, and neither sought to abolish it by political action or by force. Both believed blacks congenitally inferior to whites, although Douglas took more pleasure in expounding on supposed racial differences than Lincoln did.

Douglas's strategy was to make Lincoln look like an abolitionist. He accused the Republicans of favoring racial equality and refusing to abide by the decision of the Supreme Court in the Dred Scott case. Himself he pictured as a heroic champion of democracy, attacked on one side by the "black" Republicans and on the other by Buchanan supporters, yet ready to fight to his last breath for popular sovereignty.

Lincoln tried to picture Douglas as proslavery and a defender of the Dred Scott decision. "Slavery is an unqualified evil to the negro, to the white man, to the soil, and to the State," he said. "Judge Douglas," he also said, "is blowing out the moral lights around us, when he contends that whoever wants slaves has a right to hold them."

However, Lincoln often weakened the impact of his arguments, being perhaps too eager to demonstrate his conservatism. "All men are created equal," he would say on the authority of the Declaration of Independence, only to add, "I am not, nor ever have been, in favor of bringing about in any way the social and political equality of the white and black races." He opposed allowing blacks to vote, to sit on juries, to marry whites, even to be citizens. He predicted the "ultimate extinction" of slavery, but when pressed he predicted that it would not occur "in less than a hundred years at the least."

In the debate at Freeport, a town northwest of Chicago near the Wisconsin line, Lincoln asked Douglas if, considering the Dred Scott decision, the people of a territory could exclude slavery before the territory became a state. Unhesitatingly Douglas replied that they could, simply by not passing the local laws essential for holding blacks in bondage. "It matters not what way the Supreme Court may hereafter decide as to the abstract question," Douglas said. "The people have the lawful means to introduce or exclude it as they please, for the reason that slavery cannot exist. . . unless it is supported by local police regulations."

This argument saved Douglas in Illinois. The Democrats carried the legislature by a narrow margin, whereas it is almost certain that if Douglas had accepted the Dred Scott decision outright, the balance would have swung to the Republicans. But the so-called Freeport Doctrine cost him heavily two years later when he made his bid for the Democratic presidential nomination. "It matters not what way the Supreme Court may hereafter decide"—southern extremists would not accept a man who suggested that the Dred Scott decision could be circumvented, although in fact Douglas had only stated the obvious.

Probably Lincoln had not thought beyond the senatorial election when he asked the question; he was merely hoping to keep Douglas on the defensive and perhaps injure him in southern Illinois, where considerable proslavery sentiment existed. In any case, defeat did Lincoln no harm politically. He had more than held his own against one of the most formidable debaters in politics, and his distinctive personality and point of view had impressed themselves on thousands of minds. Indeed, the defeat revitalized his political career.

The campaign of 1858 marked Douglas's last triumph, Lincoln's last defeat. Elsewhere the elections in the North went heavily to the Republicans. When the old Congress reconvened in December, northern-sponsored economic measures (a higher tariff, the transcontinental railroad, river and harbor improvements, a free homestead bill) were all blocked by southern votes.

Whether the South could continue to prevent the passage of this legislation in the new Congress was problematical. In early 1859 even many moderate Southerners were uneasy about the future. The radicals, made panicky by Republican victories and their own failure to win in Kansas, spoke openly of secession if a Republican were elected president in 1860. Lincoln's "house divided" speech was quoted out of context, while Douglas's Freeport Doctrine added to southern woes. When Senator William H. Seward of New York spoke of an "irrepressible conflict" between freedom and slavery, white Southerners became still more alarmed.

John Brown's Raid

In October 1859, John Brown, the scourge of Kansas, made his second contribution to the unfolding sectional drama. Gathering a group of eighteen followers, white and black, he staged an attack on Harpers Ferry, Virginia, a town on the Potomac River upstream from Washington. Having boned up on guerrilla tactics, he planned to seize the federal arsenal there; arm the slaves, whom he thought would flock to his side; and then establish a black republic in the mountains of Virginia.

Simply by overpowering a few night watchmen, Brown and his men occupied the arsenal and a nearby rifle factory. They captured several hostages, one of them Colonel Lewis Washington, a great-grandnephew of George Washington. But no slaves came forward to join them. Federal troops commanded by Robert E. Lee soon trapped Brown's men in an engine house of the Baltimore and Ohio Railroad. After a two-day siege in which the attackers picked off ten of his men, Brown was captured.

After John Brown's capture, Emerson called him "a martyr" who would "make the gallows as glorious as the cross." Brown's principled radicalism found favor during the Depression decade of the 1930s. John Stewart Curry's mural, completed in 1943, depicted the demented John Brown in the pose of Christ on the cross. The image offended the Kansas legislature, which had commissioned Curry to portray Kansas history in a "sane and sensible manner."
Source: Kansas State Historical Society, Copy and Reuse Restrictions apply.

No incident so well illustrates the role of emotion and irrationality in the sectional crisis as does John Brown's raid. Over the years before his Kansas escapade, Brown had been a drifter, horse thief, a swindler, and several times a bankrupt, a failure in everything he attempted. After his ghastly Pottawatomie murders it should have been obvious to anyone that he was both a fanatic and mentally unstable: Some of the victims were hacked to bits with a broadsword. Yet numbers of high-minded Northerners, including Emerson and Thoreau, had supported Brown and his antislavery "work" after 1856. White Southerners reacted to Harpers Ferry with equal irrationality, some with a rage similar to Brown's. Dozens of hapless Northerners in the southern states were arrested, beaten, or driven off. One, falsely suspected of being an accomplice of Brown, was lynched.

Brown's fate lay in the hands of the Virginia authorities. Ignoring his obvious derangement, they charged him with treason, conspiracy, and murder. He was speedily convicted and sentenced to death by hanging.

Yet "Old Brown" had still one more contribution to make to the developing sectional tragedy. Despite the furor he had created, cool heads everywhere called for calm and denounced his attack. Most Republican politicians repudiated him. Even execution would probably not have made a martyr of Brown had he behaved like a madman after his capture. Instead, an enormous dignity descended on him as he lay in his Virginia jail awaiting death. Whatever his faults, he truly believed in racial equality. He addressed blacks who worked for him as "Mister" and arranged for them to eat at his table and sit with his family in church.

This conviction served him well in his last days. "If it is deemed necessary that I should forfeit my life for the furtherance of the ends of justice, and mingle my blood further with the blood of. . . millions in this slave country whose rights are disregarded by wicked, cruel, and unjust enactments," he said before the judge pronounced sentence, "I say, let it be done."

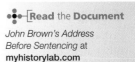

Read the Document

John Brown's Address Before Sentencing at **myhistorylab.com**

This John Brown, with his patriarchal beard and sad eyes, so apparently incompatible with the bloody terrorist of Pottawatomie and Harpers Ferry, led thousands in the North to ignore his past and treat him almost as a saint.

And so Brown, hanged on December 2, 1859, became to the North a hero and to the South a symbol of northern ruthlessness. Soon, as the popular song had it, Brown's body lay "a-mouldering in the grave," and the memory of his bloody act did indeed go "marching on."

The Election of 1860

By 1860 the nation was teetering on the brink of disunion. Radicals in the North and South were heedlessly provoking one another.

Extremism was more evident in the South, and to any casual observer that section must have seemed the aggressor in the crisis. Yet even in demanding the reopening of the African slave trade, southern radicals believed that they were defending themselves against attack. They felt surrounded by hostility. The North was growing at a much faster rate; if nothing was done, they feared, a flood of new free states would soon be able to amend the Constitution and emancipate the slaves. John Brown's raid, with its threat of an insurrection like Nat Turner's, reduced them to a state of panic.

THE UNDECIDED POLITICAL PRIZE FIGHT.

That politics was always a rough business is shown in this cartoon, which shows Lincoln, assisted by an African American (who carries a basket of liquor bottles) while Douglas is backed by some Irish pols, who have a basket overflowing with cash. John Breckinridge thumbs his nose at the combatants as he hustles up the hill toward the White House.

When legislatures in state after state in the South cracked down on freedom of expression, made the manumission of slaves illegal, banished free blacks, and took other steps that Northerners considered blatantly provocative, the advocates of these policies believed that they were only defending the status quo. Perhaps, by seceding from the Union, the South could raise a dike against the tide of abolitionism. Secession also provided an emotional release, a way of dissipating tension by striking back at criticism.

Stephen A. Douglas was probably the last hope of avoiding a rupture between North and South. But when the Democrats met at Charleston, South Carolina, in April 1860 to choose a presidential candidate, the southern delegates would not support him unless he promised not to disturb slavery in the territories. Indeed, they went further in their demands. The North, William L. Yancey of Alabama insisted, must accept the proposition that slavery was not merely tolerable but right. When southern proposals were voted down, most of the delegates from the Deep South walked out and the convention adjourned without naming a candidate.

In June the Democrats reconvened at Baltimore. Again they failed to reach agreement. The two wings then met separately, the Northerners nominating Douglas, the Southerners John C. Breckenridge of Kentucky, Buchanan's vice president. On the question of slavery in the territories, the Northerners promised to "abide by the decision of the Supreme Court," which meant, in effect, that they stood for Douglas's Freeport Doctrine. The Southerners announced their belief that neither Congress nor any territorial government could prevent citizens from settling "with their property" in any territory.

Meanwhile, the Republicans, who met in Chicago in mid-May, had drafted a platform attractive to all classes and all sections of the northern and western states.

Presidential Election, 1860 This map shows clearly the North-South electoral divide, and the fracturing of the Democratic party.

For manufacturers they proposed a high tariff, for farmers a homestead law providing free land for settlers. Internal improvements "of a National character," notably a railroad to the Pacific, should receive federal aid. No restrictions should be placed on immigration. As to slavery in the territories, the Republicans did not equivocate: "The normal condition of all the territory of the United States is that of freedom." Neither Congress nor a local legislature could "give legal existence to Slavery in any Territory."

In choosing a presidential candidate the Republicans displayed equally shrewd political judgment. Senator Seward was the front-runner, but he had taken too extreme a stand and appeared unlikely to carry the crucial states of Pennsylvania, Indiana, and Illinois. He led on the first ballot but could not get a majority. Then the delegates began to look closely at Abraham Lincoln. His thoughtful and moderate views on the main issue of the times and his formidable debating skills attracted many, and so did his political personality. "Honest Abe," the "Railsplitter," a man of humble origins (born in a log cabin), self-educated, self-made, a common man but by no means an ordinary man— the combination seemed unbeatable.

On the second ballot Lincoln drew shoulder to shoulder with Seward, on the third he was within two votes of victory. Before the roll could be called again, delegates began to switch their votes, and in a landslide, soon made unanimous, Lincoln was nominated.

A few days earlier the remnants of the American and Whig parties had formed the Constitutional Union party and nominated John Bell of Tennessee for president. "It is both the part of patriotism and of duty," they resolved, "to recognize no political principle

Table 13.1 Descent into War: The 1850s

Harriet Beecher Stowe's, *Uncle Tom's Cabin*	1852	Best-selling novel fuels abolitionist sentiment and enrages Southerners.
Kansas-Nebraska Act	1854	Opens Kansas and Nebraska Territories for settlement and repeals Missouri Compromise of 1820 by allowing residents to determine whether the new states would be slave or free.
Lecompton Constitution	1857	Proslavery constitution drafted by proslavery "government" of Kansas: It is accepted by President James Buchanan but rejected by Congress.
Dred Scott Case	1857	Supreme Court rules that Congress lacked the authority to ban slavery from the territories; slavery is legal everywhere unless states prohibit it.
John Brown's Raid at Harpers Ferry, Virginia	1859	Brown attacks federal arsenal in order to initiate slave rebellion; Brown's execution angers abolitionists; the martyrdom of Brown infuriates Southerners.
Election of 1860	1860	The Democrats, divided over slavery, disintegrate. Lincoln wins presidency but receives no electoral votes from South.

other than the Constitution of the country, the union of the states, and the enforcement of the laws." Ostrichlike, the Constitutional Unionists ignored the conflicts rending the nation. Only in the border states, where the consequences of disunion were sure to be most tragic, did they have any following.

With four candidates in the field, no one could win a popular majority, but it soon became clear that Lincoln was going to be elected. Breckenridge had most of the slave states in his pocket and Bell would run strong in the border regions, but the populous northern and western states had a majority of the electoral votes, and there the choice lay between the Republicans and the Douglas Democrats. In such a contest the Republicans, with their attractive economic program and their strong stand against slavery in the territories, were sure to come out on top.

Lincoln avoided campaigning and made no public statements. Douglas, recognizing the certainty of Lincoln's victory, accepted his fate and for the first time in his career rose above ambition. "We must try to save the Union," he said. "I will go South." In the heart of the Cotton Kingdom, he appealed to the voters to stand by the Union regardless of who was elected. He was the only candidate to do so; the others refused to remind the people that their election might result in secession and civil war.

When the votes were counted, Lincoln had 1.866 million, almost a million fewer than the combined total of his three opponents, but he swept the North and West, which gave him 180 electoral votes and the presidency. Douglas received 1.383 million votes, so distributed that he carried only Missouri and part of New Jersey. Breckenridge, with 848,000 popular votes, won most of the South; Bell, with 593,000, carried Virginia,

Tennessee, and Kentucky. Lincoln was thus a minority president, but his title to the office was unquestionable. Even if his opponents could have combined their popular votes in each state, Lincoln would have won.

The Secession Crisis

Only days after Lincoln's victory, the South Carolina legislature ordered an election of delegates to a convention to decide the state's future course. On December 20 the convention voted unanimously to secede, basing its action on the logic of Calhoun. "The State of South Carolina has resumed her position among the nations of the world," the delegates announced. By February 1, 1861, the six other states of the lower South had followed suit. A week later, at

•••—Read the Document

South Carolina Declaration of the Causes of Secession at **myhistorylab.com**

Montgomery, Alabama, a provisional government of the Confederate States of America was established. Virginia, Tennessee, North Carolina, and Arkansas did not leave the Union but announced that if the federal government attempted to use force against the Confederacy, they too would secede.

Why were white Southerners willing to wreck the Union their forebears had put together with so much love and labor? No simple explanation is possible. Lincoln had assured them that he would respect slavery where it existed. The Democrats had retained control of Congress in the election; the Supreme Court was firmly in their hands as well. If the North did try to destroy slavery, secession would perhaps be a logical tactic, but why not wait until the threat materialized? To leave the Union meant abandoning the very objectives for which the South had been contending for over a decade: a share of the federal territories and an enforceable fugitive slave law.

One reason why the South rejected this line of thinking was the tremendous economic energy generated in the North, which seemed to threaten the South's independence.

Secession, white Southerners argued, would "liberate" the South and produce the kind of balanced economy that was proving so successful in the North. Moreover, the mere possibility of emancipation was a powerful force for secession. "We must either submit to degradation, and to the loss of property worth four billions," the Mississippi convention declared, "or we must secede."

Although states' rights provided the rationale for leaving the Union, and Southerners expounded the strict constructionist interpretation of the Constitution with great ingenuity, the economic and emotional factors were far more basic. The lower South decided to go ahead with secession regardless of the cost. "Let the consequences be what they may," an Atlanta newspaper proclaimed. "Whether the Potomac is crimsoned in human gore, and Pennsylvania Avenue is paved ten fathoms in depth with mangled bodies . . . the South will never submit."

Not every slave owner could contemplate secession with such bloodthirsty equanimity. Some believed that the risks of war and slave insurrection were too great. Others retained a profound loyalty to the United States. Many accepted secession only after the deepest examination of conscience. Lieutenant Colonel Robert E. Lee of Virginia was typical of thousands. "I see only that a fearful calamity is upon us," he wrote during the secession crisis. "There is no sacrifice I am not ready to

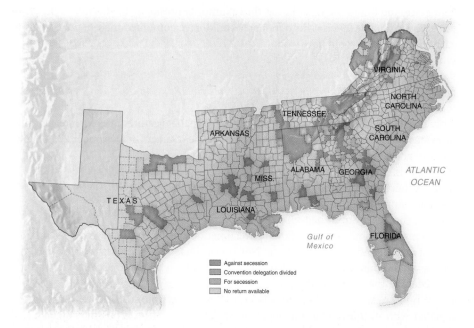

Secession of the South, 1860–1861 A comparison of this map with the one on page 326 shows the minimal support for secession in the nonslave mountain areas of the Appalachians. The strong antisecession sentiment in the mountainous areas of Virginia eventually led several counties there to break from Virginia in 1863 and form the new state of West Virginia.

make for the preservation of the Union save that of honour. If a disruption takes place, I shall go back in sorrow to my people & share the misery of my native state."

In the North there was a foolish but understandable reluctance to believe that the South really intended to break away. President-elect Lincoln was inclined to write off secession as a bluff designed to win concessions he was determined not to make. He also showed lamentable political caution in refusing to announce his plans or to cooperate with the outgoing Democratic administration before his inauguration.

In the South there was an equally unrealistic expectation that the North would not resist secession forcibly. The "Yankees" were timid materialists who would neither bear the cost nor risk their lives to prevent secession. President Buchanan recognized the seriousness of the situation but professed himself powerless. Secession, he said, was illegal, but the federal government had no legal way to prevent it. He urged making concessions to the South yet lacked the forcefulness to take the situation in hand.

Of course he faced unprecedented difficulties. His term was about to run out— Lincoln's inauguration day was March 4—and since he could not commit to his successor, his influence was minuscule. Yet a bolder president would have denounced secession in uncompromising terms. Instead Buchanan vacillated between compromise and aimless drift.

Appeasers, well-meaning believers in compromise, and those prepared to fight to preserve the Union were alike—incapable of effective action. A group of moderates headed by Henry Clay's disciple, Senator John J. Crittenden of Kentucky, proposed a constitutional amendment in which slavery would be "recognized as existing" in all territories south of latitude 36°30'. Crittenden had a special reason for seeking to avoid a conflict. His oldest son was about to become a southern general, another son a northern general. His amendment also promised that no future amendment would tamper with the institution in the slave states and offered other guarantees to the South. But Lincoln refused to consider any arrangement that would open new territory to slavery. "On the territorial question," he wrote, "I am inflexible." The **Crittenden Compromise** got nowhere.

The new southern Confederacy set vigorously to work drafting a constitution, choosing Jefferson Davis as provisional president, seizing arsenals and other federal property within its boundaries, and preparing to dispatch diplomatic representatives to enlist the support of foreign powers. Buchanan bumbled helplessly in Washington. And out in Illinois, Abraham Lincoln juggled Cabinet posts and grew a beard.

Watch the Video
What Caused the Civil War? at **myhistorylab.com**

Milestones

1850	Compromise of 1850 preserves Union; United States and Great Britain sign Clayton-Bulwer Treaty on interoceanic canal	**1856**	John Brown and followers murder five proslavery men in Pottawatomie Massacre
1851–1860	Northerners resist enforcement of Fugitive Slave Act		South Carolina's Preston Brooks canes Senator Charles Sumner of Massachusetts on Senate floor
1852	Harriet Beecher Stowe publishes *Uncle Tom's Cabin*, a novel depicting slavery		James Buchanan is elected president
		1857	U.S. Supreme Court issues decision in Dred Scott case, declaring slaves are not citizens
	Franklin Pierce is elected president		
1854	United States disavows secret Ostend Manifesto on Cuba		Panic of 1857 collapses economy
	Kansas-Nebraska Act repeals Missouri Compromise	**1858**	Abraham Lincoln loses Senate race to Stephen Douglas after Lincoln-Douglas Debates, but wins national attention
	Commodore Matthew Perry forces Japan to open its ports to U.S. trade	**1859**	John Brown raids Harpers Ferry, Virginia, arsenal
	Senate ratifies Gadsden Purchase of Mexican territory	**1860**	Abraham Lincoln is elected president
			South Carolina secedes from Union
1855	William Walker seizes power in Nicaragua	**1861**	Seven southern states establish Confederate States of America
1856–1858	Proslavery forces oppose Free Soilers in "Bleeding Kansas" Territory		Lincoln rejects Crittenden Compromise, last peaceful attempt to save Union

✓●─[Study and **Review** at www.myhistorylab.com

Review Questions

1. The introduction to this chapter claims that Americans in the 1850s paid close attention to the issues that culminated in the election of Lincoln and the secession of the South. If political agitation can precipitate such anger and even war, is it always a good thing? Can there be such a thing as too much democracy—too much "popular sovereignty"? Should leaders refrain from raising questions that will elicit passionate responses?

2. What events during the 1850s reduced the prospects of finding a political compromise between North and South?

3. Were the economic divisions—free vs. slave labor—more consequential than the moral ones—freedom vs. slavery?

4. The 1858 Lincoln-Douglas debate largely turned on Lincoln's assertion that the United States could not endure half-slave and half-free. But for over seventy years, Douglas replied, the United States under the Constitution had done just that; compromise remained a possibility. Who was right?

Key Terms

Crittenden Compromise *373*

Dred Scott decision *360*

Kansas-Nebraska Act *354*

Know-Nothing party *355*

Lecompton constitution *362*

Ostend Manifesto *351*

Republican party *356*

underground railroad *348*

Young America movement *351*

The War to Save the Union

14

((•—[Hear the Audio Chapter 14 at myhistorylab.com

Are you a Northerner or a Southerner?

ON FEBRUARY 22, 2006, SUNNI MUSLIMS OVERWHELMED THE CARETAKER and staff of the Mosque of the Golden Dome in Samarra, sixty miles north of Baghdad, Iraq. The mosque was among the most revered Shiite shrines in the Middle East, visited by more than a million Muslims each year. Sunni and Shiite Muslims differed in their interpretation of Islam. Sunni insurgents placed explosives at the base of the dome and left the building. Moments later, an explosion collapsed the dome, shattering its 72,000 golden tiles. By sunset, Shiite militiamen had destroyed twenty-seven Sunni mosques and killed three imams—Islamic holy men. Over the next twelve months, the violence escalated, resulting in the deaths of over 34,000 Iraqi civilians. "The gates of hell are open in Iraq," declared Amr Moussa, head of the Arab League.

In 2009 President Barack Obama visited Iraq after a spate of bombings had destroyed another Shiite shrine and killed scores of Muslims. Obama called on Iraqis to end "this senseless violence."

But no civil war makes much sense, as Americans learned in 1861. Then, brother fought brother; men intent on destroying each other prayed to the same God. The horrors of the war eclipsed any good that might attend victory, or so it seemed.

The U.S. Civil War moved forward, impelled by its own terrible momentum. The first inconclusive battle led to others. More men were called to arms, often against their will. Farms and factories were diverted to the war effort. Lincoln emancipated some slaves to weaken the South. The strains of the war fractured the political consensus. When the guns at last fell silent, a half million men lay dead, and millions more were casualties. While touring a hospital ward after another gruesome battle, President Lincoln despaired at the horror of it all. "If there is a place worse than hell, I am in it."

Lincoln's Cabinet

The nomination of Lincoln had succeeded brilliantly for the Republicans, but was his election a good thing for the country? Honest Abe was a clever politician who had spoken well about the central issue of the times, but would he act decisively in this crisis? People remembered uneasily that he had never held executive office, that his congressional career had been short and undistinguished. When he finally uprooted himself from Springfield in February 1861, his occasional speeches en route to Washington were vague, almost flippant. Some people thought it downright cowardly that he let himself be spirited in the dead of night through Baltimore, where feeling against him ran high.

Everyone waited tensely to see whether Lincoln would oppose secession with force, but Lincoln seemed concerned only with organizing his Cabinet. The final slate was not ready until the morning of inauguration day, March 4, and shrewd observers found it alarming, for the new president had chosen to construct a "balanced" Cabinet representing a wide range of opinion instead of putting together a group of harmonious advisers who could help him face the crisis.

William H. Seward, the secretary of state, was the ablest and best known of the appointees. Despite his reputation for radicalism, Seward hoped to conciliate the South and was thus in bad odor with the radical wing of the Republican party. In time Seward proved himself Lincoln's strong right arm, but at the start he underestimated the president and expected to dominate him. Senator Salmon P. Chase, an antislavery leader from Ohio whom Lincoln named secretary of the treasury, represented the radicals. Chase was humorless and vain but able; he detested Seward. Many of the president's other selections worried thoughtful people.

Lincoln's inaugural address was conciliatory but firm. Southern institutions were in no danger from his administration. Secession, however, was illegal, and the Union "perpetual." "A husband and wife may be divorced," Lincoln said, "but the different parts of our country cannot." His tone was calm and warm. His concluding words catch the spirit of the inaugural perfectly:

•●•[Read the Document
Lincoln, *First Inaugural
Address* at **myhistorylab.com**

> I am loath to close. We are not enemies, but friends. We must not be enemies. Though passion may have strained, it must not break, our bonds of affection. The mystic chords of memory, stretching from every battlefield and patriot grave to every living heart . . . will yet swell the chorus of the Union when again touched, as surely they will be, by the better angels of our nature.

Fort Sumter: The First Shot

While denying the legality of secession, Lincoln had not decided what to do next. The Confederates had seized most federal property in the Deep South. Lincoln admitted frankly that he would not attempt to reclaim this property. However, two strongholds, Fort Sumter, on an island in Charleston harbor, and Fort Pickens, at Pensacola, Florida, were still in loyal Union hands. Most Republicans did not want to surrender them without a show of resistance. To do so, one wrote, would be to convert the American eagle into a "debilitated chicken."

Yet to reinforce the forts might mean bloodshed that would make reconciliation impossible. After weeks of indecision, Lincoln took the moderate step of sending a naval expedition to supply the beleaguered Sumter garrison with food. Unwilling to permit this, the Confederates opened fire on the fort on April 12 before the supply ships arrived. After holding out for thirty-four hours, Major Robert Anderson and his men surrendered.

This lithograph by Currier and Ives gives an erroneous impression of the "battle." Major Robert Anderson, commander of Ft. Sumter, did not want to expose his men to the looping mortar shells and artillery of the Confederates, so he manned only the cannon on the lowest floor, just above the water. The top two levels of guns were seldom fired.

The attack precipitated an outburst of patriotic indignation in the North. Lincoln issued a call for 75,000 volunteers; his request prompted Virginia, North Carolina, Arkansas, and Tennessee to secede. After years of crises and compromises, the nation chose to settle the great quarrel between the sections by force of arms.

Lincoln took the position that secession was a rejection of democracy. If the South could refuse to abide by the result of an election in which it had freely participated, then everything that monarchists and other conservatives had said about the instability of republican governments would be proved true. "The central idea of secession is the essence of anarchy," he said. The United States must "demonstrate to the world" that "when ballots have been fairly and constitutionally decided, there can be no successful appeal except to ballots themselves, at succeeding elections."

This was the proper ground to take. A war against slavery would not have been supported by a majority of Northerners. Slavery was the root cause of secession but not of the North's determination to resist secession, which resulted from the people's commitment to the Union. Although abolition was to be one of the major results of the Civil War, the war was fought for nationalistic reasons, not to destroy slavery. Lincoln made this plain when he wrote in response to an editorial by Horace Greeley urging immediate emancipation: "I would save the Union. . . . If I could save the Union without freeing any slave, I would do it; and if I could save it by freeing all the slaves, I would do it; and if I could do it by freeing some and leaving others alone, I would also do that." He added, however, "I intend no modification of my oft-expressed personal wish that all men, everywhere, could be free."

The Blue and the Gray

In any test between the United States and the Confederacy, the former possessed tremendous advantages. There were more than 20 million people in the northern states (excluding Kentucky and Missouri, where opinion was divided) but only 9 million in the South, including 3.5 million slaves whom the whites hesitated to trust with arms. The North's economic capacity to wage war was even more preponderant. It was manufacturing nine times as much as the Confederacy (including 97 percent of the nation's firearms) and had a far larger and more efficient railroad system than the South. Northern control of the merchant marine and the navy made possible a blockade of the Confederacy, a particularly potent threat to a region so dependent on foreign markets.

The Confederates discounted these advantages. Many doubted that public opinion in the North would sustain Lincoln if he attempted to meet secession with force. Northern manufacturers needed southern markets, and merchants depended heavily on southern business. Many western farmers still sent their produce down the Mississippi. War would threaten the prosperity of all these groups, Southerners maintained. Should the North try to cut Europe off from southern cotton, the European powers, particularly Great Britain, would descend on the land in their might, force open southern ports, and provide the Confederacy with the means of defending itself forever. Moreover, the South provided nearly three-fourths of the world's cotton, essential for most textile mills. "You do not dare to make war on cotton," Senator Hammond of South Carolina had taunted his northern colleagues in 1858. "No power on earth dares to make war upon it. Cotton is king."

The Confederacy also counted on certain military advantages. The new nation need only hold what it had; it could fight a defensive war, less costly in men and material and of great importance in maintaining morale and winning outside sympathy. Southerners would be defending not only their social institutions but also their homes and families.

Luck played a part too; the Confederacy quickly found a great commander, while many of the northern generals in the early stages of the war proved either bungling or indecisive. In battle after battle

Why did these young volunteers of the First Virginia Militia join the Confederate army in 1861? "It is better to spend our all in defending our country than to be subjugated and have it taken away from us," one explained, a sentiment that appeared often in the letters of Confederate soldiers. Soldiers on both sides believed that their cause was righteous.

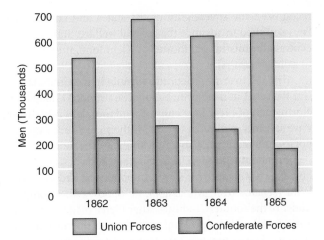

Men Present for Service during the Civil War From 1862 to 1864, the North had twice as many soldiers as the South; by 1865, the North had over three times more than the South.

Union armies were defeated by forces of equal or smaller size. There was little to distinguish the enlisted men of the two sides. Both, conscious of their forefathers of 1776, fought for liberty, though they interpreted the concept in different ways.

Both sides faced massive difficulties in organizing for a war long feared but never properly anticipated. After southern defections, the regular Union army consisted of only 13,000 officers and enlisted men, far too few to absorb the 186,000 who had joined the colors by early summer, much less the additional 450,000 who had volunteered by the end of the year. Recruiting was left to the states, each being assigned a quota; there was little central organization. Unlike later conflicts in which men from all parts of the country were mixed in each regiment, Civil War units were recruited locally. Few knew even the rudiments of soldiering. The hastily composed high command, headed by the elderly Winfield Scott, debated grand strategy endlessly while regimental commanders lacked decent maps of Virginia.

Lincoln's strength lay in his ability to think problems through. When he did, he acted unflinchingly. Anything but a tyrant by nature, he boldly exceeded the conventional limits of presidential power in the emergency: expanding the army without congressional authorization, suspending the writ of habeas corpus (which entitles those seized by the government to go before a court to see if their arrest were warranted), even emancipating the slaves when he thought military necessity demanded that action. Yet he also displayed remarkable patience and depth of character: He would willingly accept snubs and insults in order to advance the cause.

Gradually Lincoln's stock rose—first with men like Seward, who saw him close up and experienced both his steel and his gentleness, and then with the people at large, who sensed his compassion, his humility, and his wisdom. He was only fifty-two when he became president, and already people were calling him Old Abe. Before long they would call him Father Abraham.

The Confederacy faced far greater problems than the North, for it had to create an entire administration under pressure of war with the additional handicap of the states' rights philosophy to which it was committed. The Confederate constitution explicitly

Read the Document

Davis, *Address to the Provisional Congress* at **myhistorylab.com** recognized the sovereignty of the states and contained no broad authorization for laws designed to advance the general welfare. State governments repeatedly defied the central administration, located at Richmond after Virginia seceded, even with regard to military affairs.

The call to arms produced a turnout in the Confederacy perhaps even more impressive than that in the North; by July 1861 about 112,000 men were under arms. As in the North, men of every type enlisted, and morale was high. Some wealthy recruits brought slave servants with them to care for their needs in camp, cavalrymen supplied their own horses, and many men arrived with their own shotguns and hunting rifles.

President Jefferson Davis represented the best type of southern planter, noted for his humane treatment of his slaves. In politics he had pursued a somewhat unusual course. While senator from Mississippi, he opposed the Compromise of 1850 and became a leader of the southern radicals. After Pierce made him secretary of war, however, he took a more nationalistic position, one close to that of Douglas. After the 1860 election he supported secession only reluctantly, preferring to give Lincoln a chance to prove that he meant the South no harm.

Davis was courageous, industrious, and intelligent, but he was too reserved and opinionated to make either a good politician or a popular leader. As president he devoted too much time to details, failed to delegate authority, and (unlike Lincoln) was impatient with garrulous and dull-witted people, types political leaders frequently have to deal with. Being a graduate of West Point, he fancied himself a military expert, but he was a mediocre military thinker. Unlike Lincoln, he quarreled frequently with his subordinates, held grudges, and allowed personal feelings to distort his judgment.

The Test of Battle: Bull Run

"Forward to Richmond!" "On to Washington!" Such shouts propelled the armies into battle long before either was properly trained. On July 21 at Manassas Junction, Virginia, some

⊙ **See the Map**

The Civil War, Part I: 1861–1862
at **myhistorylab.com**

twenty miles below Washington, on a branch of the Potomac called Bull Run, 30,000 Union soldiers under General Irvin McDowell attacked a roughly equal force of Confederates commanded by the "Napoleon of the South," Pierre G. T. Beauregard. McDowell swept back the Confederate left flank. Victory seemed sure. Then a Virginia brigade under Thomas J. Jackson rushed to the field by rail from the Shenandoah Valley in the nick of time and checked the advance.

The Southerners then counterattacked, driving the Union soldiers back. As often happens with green troops, retreat quickly turned to rout. McDowell's men fled toward the defenses of Washington, abandoning their weapons, stumbling through lines of supply wagons, trampling foolish sightseers who had come out to watch the battle. Panic engulfed Washington. Richmond exulted. Both sides expected the northern capital to fall within hours.

The inexperienced southern troops were too disorganized to follow up their victory. Casualties on both sides were light, and the battle had little direct effect on anything but morale. Southern confidence soared, while the North began to realize how immense the task of subduing the Confederacy would be.

Eighteen-year-olds were the largest age group in the first year of the war in both armies. Soldiers were universally called "the boys"; and officers, even in their thirties, were called "old men." One of the most popular war songs was "Just Before the Battle, Mother."

After Bull Run, Lincoln devised a broader, more systematic strategy for winning the war. The navy would clamp a tight blockade on all southern ports. In the West Union generals made plans to gain control of the Mississippi. (This was part of General Scott's **Anaconda Plan**, designed to starve the South into submission.) More important, a new army would be mustered at Washington to invade Virginia. Congress promptly authorized the enlistment of 500,000 three-year volunteers. To lead this army and—after General Scott's retirement in November—to command the Union forces, Lincoln appointed a thirty-four-year-old major general, George B. McClellan.

McClellan was the North's first military hero. After graduating from West Point second in his class in 1846, he had served in the Mexican War. During the Crimean War he spent a year in the field, talking with British officers and studying fortifications. He was a talented administrator and organizer. He liked to concoct bold plans and dreamed of striking swiftly at the heart of the Confederacy to capture Richmond, Nashville, even New Orleans. Yet he was sensible enough to insist on massive logistic support, thorough training for the troops, iron discipline, and meticulous staff work before making a move.

Paying for the War

After Bull Run, this policy was exactly right. By the fall of 1861 a real army was taking shape along the Potomac: disciplined, confident, adequately supplied. Northern shops and factories were producing guns, ammunition, wagons, uniforms, shoes, and the countless other supplies needed to fight a great war. Most manufacturers operated on a small scale, but with the armed forces soon wearing out 3 million pairs of shoes and 1.5 million uniforms a year and with men leaving their jobs by the hundreds of thousands to fight, the tendency of industry to mechanize and to increase the size of the average manufacturing unit became ever more pronounced.

At the beginning of the war Secretary of the Treasury Salmon P. Chase underestimated how much it would cost. He learned quickly. In August 1861 Congress passed an income tax law and assessed a direct tax on the states. Loans amounting to $140 million were authorized. As the war dragged on and expenses mounted, new excise taxes on every imaginable product and service were passed, and still further borrowing was necessary. In 1863 the banking system was overhauled.

During the war the federal government borrowed a total of $2.2 billion and collected $667 million in taxes, slightly over 20 percent of its total expenditures. These unprecedented large sums proved inadequate. Some debts were repaid by printing paper money unredeemable in coin. About $431 million in **greenbacks**—the term distinguished this fiat money from the redeemable yellowback bills—were issued during the conflict. Public confidence in all paper money vacillated with each change in the fortunes of the Union armies, but by the end of the war the cost of living in the North had doubled.

Politics as Usual

Partisan politics was altered by the war but not suspended. The secession of the southern states left the Republicans with large majorities in both houses of Congress. Most Democrats supported measures necessary for the conduct of the war but objected to the way the Lincoln administration was conducting it. The sharpest conflicts came when slavery and race relations were under discussion. The Democrats adopted a conservative stance, as reflected in the slogan "The Constitution as it is; the Union as it was; the Negroes where they are." The Republicans divided into Moderate and Radical wings. Political divisions on economic issues such as tariffs and land policy tended to cut across party lines and, so far as the Republicans were concerned, to bear little relation to slavery and race. As the war progressed, the Radical faction became increasingly influential.

In 1861 the most prominent Radical senator was Charles Sumner, finally recovered from his caning by Preston Brooks and brimful of hatred for slaveholders. In the House, Thaddeus Stevens of Pennsylvania was the rising power. Sumner and Stevens were uncompromising on all questions relating to slaves; they insisted not merely on abolition but on granting full political and civil rights to blacks. Moderate Republicans objected vehemently to treating blacks as equals and opposed making abolition a war aim, and even many of the so-called **Radical Republicans** disagreed with Sumner and Stevens on race relations. Senator Benjamin Wade of Ohio, for example, was a lifelong opponent of slavery, yet he disliked blacks (whom he called by a racial slur). But prejudice, he maintained, gave no one the right "to do injustice to anybody"; he insisted that blacks were at least as intelligent as whites and were entitled not merely to freedom but to full political equality.

At the other end of the political spectrum stood the so-called Peace Democrats. These **Copperheads** (apparently a reference to a time when some hard-money Democrats wore copper pennies around their necks) opposed all measures in support of the war. They hoped to win control of Congress and force a negotiated peace. Few were actually disloyal, but their activities at a time when thousands of men were risking their lives in battle infuriated many Northerners.

The most notorious domestic foe of the administration was the Peace Democrat Congressman Clement L. Vallandigham of Ohio, who was sent to prison by a military court. There were two rebellions in progress, Vallandigham claimed, "the Secessionist Rebellion" and "the Abolitionist Rebellion." "I am against both," he added. But Lincoln ordered him released and banished to the Confederacy. Once at liberty Vallandigham moved to Canada, from which refuge he ran unsuccessfully for governor of Ohio.

"Perish offices," he once said, "perish life itself, but do the thing that is right." In 1864 he returned to Ohio. Although he campaigned against Lincoln in the presidential election, he was not arrested. Lincoln was no dictator.

Behind Confederate Lines

The South also revised its strategy after Bull Run. Although it might have been wiser to risk everything on a bold invasion of the North, President Davis relied primarily on a strong defense to wear down the Union's will to fight. In 1862 the Confederate Congress passed a conscription act that permitted the hiring of substitutes and exempted many classes of people (including college professors, druggists, and mail carriers) whose work could hardly have been deemed essential. A provision deferring one slave owner or overseer for every plantation of twenty or more slaves led many to grumble about "a rich man's war and a poor man's fight."

Finance was the Confederacy's most vexing problem. The blockade made it impossible to raise much money through tariffs. The Confederate Congress passed an income tax together with many excise taxes but all told they covered only 2 percent of its needs by taxation. The most effective levy was a tax in kind, amounting to one-tenth of each farmer's production. The South borrowed as much as it could ($712 million), even mortgaging cotton undeliverable because of the blockade, in order to gain European credits. But it relied mainly on printing paper currency; over $1.5 billion poured from the presses during the war. Considering the amount issued, this currency held its value well until late in the war, when the military fortunes of the Confederacy began to decline. Then the bottom fell out, and by early 1865 the Confederate dollar was worth less than 2 cents in gold.

Outfitting the army strained southern resources to the limit. Large supplies of small arms (some 600,000 weapons during the entire war) came from Europe through the blockade, along with other valuable military supplies. As the blockade became more efficient, however, it became increasingly difficult to obtain European goods. The Confederates did manage to build a number of munitions plants, and they captured huge amounts of northern arms. No battle was lost because of a lack of guns or other military equipment, although shortages of shoes and uniforms handicapped the Confederate forces on some occasions.

Foreign policy loomed large in Confederate thinking, for the "cotton is king" theory presupposed that the great powers would break any northern blockade to get cotton for their textile mills. Southern expectations were not realized, however. The European nations would have been delighted to see the United States broken up, but none was prepared to support the Confederacy directly. The attitude of Great Britain was decisive.

The cutting off of cotton did not hit the British as hard as the South had hoped. They had a large supply on hand when the war broke out, and when that was exhausted, alternative sources in India and Egypt took up part of the slack. Furthermore, British crop failures necessitated the importation of large amounts of northern wheat, providing a powerful reason for not antagonizing the United States. The fact that most ordinary people in Great Britain favored the North also influenced British policy.

War in the West: Shiloh

After Bull Run no battles were fought until early 1862. Then, while McClellan continued his deliberate preparations to attack Richmond, important fighting occurred far to the west. Most of the Plains Indians sided with the Confederacy, principally because of their resentment of the federal government's policies toward them. White settlers from Colorado to California were mostly Unionists. In March 1862 a Texas army advancing beyond Santa Fe clashed with a Union force in the Battle of Glorieta Pass. The battle was indecisive, but a Union unit destroyed the Texans' supply train. The Texans felt compelled to retreat to the Rio Grande, thus ending the Confederate threat to the Far West.

Meanwhile, far larger Union forces, led by a shabby, cigar-smoking West Pointer named Ulysses S. Grant, had invaded Tennessee from a base at Cairo, Illinois. Making effective use of armored gunboats, Grant captured Fort Henry and Fort Donelson, strongholds on the Tennessee and Cumberland rivers, taking 14,000 prisoners. Next he marched toward Corinth, Mississippi, an important railroad junction.

To check Grant's advance, the Confederates massed 40,000 men under Albert Sidney Johnston. On April 6, while Grant slowly concentrated his forces, Johnston struck suddenly at Shiloh, twenty miles north of Corinth. Some Union soldiers were caught half-dressed, others in the midst of brewing their morning coffee. A few died in their blankets. "We were more than surprised," one Illinois officer later admitted. "We were astonished." However, Grant's men stood their ground. At the end of a day of ghastly carnage the Confederates held the advantage, but fresh Union troops poured in during the night, and on the second day of battle the tide turned. The Confederates fell back toward Corinth, exhausted and demoralized.

Grant, shaken by the unexpected attack and appalled by his losses, allowed the enemy to escape. This cost him the fine reputation he had won in capturing Fort Henry and Fort Donelson. He was relieved of his command. Although Corinth eventually fell and New Orleans was captured by a naval force under the command of Captain David Farragut, Vicksburg, key to control of the Mississippi, remained firmly in Confederate hands. A great opportunity had been lost.

Shiloh had other results. The staggering casualties shook the confidence of both belligerents. More Americans fell there in two days than in all the battles of the Revolution, the War of 1812, and the Mexican War combined. Union losses exceeded 13,000 out of 63,000 engaged; the Confederates lost 10,699, including General Johnston. Technology in the shape of more accurate guns that could be fired far more rapidly than the muskets of earlier times and more powerful artillery were responsible for the carnage. Gradually the generals began to reconsider their tactics and to experiment with field fortifications and other defensive measures. And the people, North and South, stopped thinking of the war as a romantic test of courage and military guile.

Battles in the West The Anaconda Plan called for the North to gain control of the Mississippi River. To that end, in the spring of 1862 Grant seized western Kentucky and Tennessee and won a major battle at Shiloh, just north of Corinth. Farragut, attacking by sea from the Gulf of Mexico, moved up the mouth of the Mississippi, seizing New Orleans and Baton Rouge. But the South retained Vicksburg: The Confederacy had not been sliced in two.

McClellan: The Reluctant Warrior

In Virginia, General McClellan, after unaccountable delays, was finally moving against Richmond. Instead of trying to advance across the difficult terrain of northern Virginia, he transported his army by water to the tip of the peninsula formed by the York and James rivers in order to attack Richmond from the southeast. After the famous battle on March 9, 1862, between the USS *Monitor* and the Confederate *Merrimack*, the first fight in history between armored warships, control of these waters was securely in northern hands.

While McClellan's plan alarmed many congressmen because it seemed to leave Washington relatively unprotected, it simplified the problem of keeping the army supplied in hostile country. But McClellan now displayed the weaknesses that eventually ruined his career. His problems were both intellectual and psychological. Basically he approached tactical questions in the manner of a typical eighteenth-century general. He considered war a kind of gentlemanly contest in which maneuver, guile, and position determined victory. He believed it more important to capture Richmond than to destroy the army protecting it. With their capital in northern hands, surely the Southerners would acknowledge defeat and agree to return to the Union. The idea of crushing the South seemed to him wrongheaded and uncivilized.

McClellan began the Peninsular campaign in mid-March. Proceeding deliberately, he floated an army of 112,000 men down the Potomac. Landing near Yorktown, he prepared to besiege the Confederates, much as Washington had done against Cornwallis in 1781. But in early May the Confederate army slipped away and McClellan pursued them nearly to Richmond. A swift thrust might have ended the war quickly, but McClellan delayed, despite the fact that he had 80,000 men in striking position and large reserves. As he pushed forward slowly, the Confederates caught part of his force separated from the main body by the rain-swollen Chickahominy River and attacked. The Battle of Seven Pines was indecisive yet resulted in more than 10,000 casualties.

At Seven Pines, General Joseph E. Johnston, the Confederate commander, was severely wounded; leadership of the Army of Northern Virginia then passed to Robert E. Lee. Although a reluctant supporter of secession, Lee was a superb soldier. During the Mexican War his gallantry under fire inspired General Scott to call him the bravest man in the army. He also had displayed an almost instinctive mastery of tactics. Admiral Raphael Semmes, who accompanied Scott's army on the march to Mexico City, recalled in 1851 that Lee "seemed to receive impressions intuitively, which it cost other men much labor to acquire."

Lee was McClellan's antithesis. McClellan seemed almost deliberately to avoid understanding his foes, acting as though every southern general was a genius. Lee, a master psychologist on the battlefield, took the measure of each Union general and devised his tactics accordingly. Where McClellan was complex, egotistical, perhaps even unbalanced, Lee was courtly, tactful, and entirely without McClellan's vainglorious belief that he was a man of destiny. Yet on the battlefield Lee's boldness skirted the edge of foolhardiness.

To relieve the pressure on Richmond, Lee sent General "Stonewall" Jackson, soon to be his most trusted lieutenant, on a diversionary raid in the Shenandoah Valley, west of Richmond and Washington. Jackson struck swiftly at scattered Union forces in the region, winning a number of battles and capturing vast stores of equipment. Lincoln dispatched 20,000 reserves to the Shenandoah to check him—to the dismay of McClellan, who wanted the troops to attack Richmond from the north. But after Seven Pines, Lee ordered Jackson back to Richmond. While Union armies streamed toward the valley, Jackson slipped stealthily between them. On June 25 he reached Ashland, directly north of the Confederate capital.

Before that date McClellan had possessed clear numerical superiority yet had only inched ahead; now the advantage lay with Lee, and the very next day he attacked. From

Read the Document

McClellan to Abraham Lincoln (July 7, 1862) at myhistorylab.com

June 25 to July 1 (the Seven Days' Battles) Lee repeatedly struck different parts of McClellan's lines. The full weight of his force never hit the northern army at any one time. Nevertheless, the shock was formidable. McClellan, who excelled in defense, fell back, his lines intact, exacting a fearful toll. Under difficult conditions he managed to transfer his troops to a new base on the James River at Harrison's Landing, where the guns of the navy could shield his position. Again the loss of life was terrible: Northern casualties totaled 15,800, and those of the South nearly 20,000 in the Seven Days' Battle for Richmond.

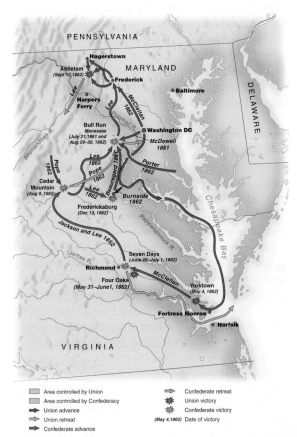

War in the East, 1861–1862 In the spring of 1862, McClellan seized Yorktown on the Virginia Peninsula (Peninsular Campaign). But he failed to take Richmond and his army was recalled to the Potomac. That fall, McClellan halted Lee's northern advance into Maryland at Antietam. By the end of 1862, the situation in the East was much as it had been a year earlier, except for the nearly 100,000 casualties.

Lee Counterattacks: Antietam

McClellan was still within striking distance of Richmond, in an impregnable position with secure supply lines and 86,000 soldiers ready to resume battle. Lee had absorbed heavy losses without winning any significant advantage. Yet Lincoln was exasperated with McClellan for having surrendered the initiative and, after much deliberation, reduced his authority by placing him under General Henry W. Halleck. Halleck called off the Peninsular campaign and ordered McClellan to move his army from the James to the Potomac, near Washington. He was to join General John Pope, who was gathering a new army between Washington and Richmond.

If McClellan had persisted and captured Richmond, the war might have ended and the Union been restored without the abolition of slavery, since at that point the North was still fighting for union, not for freedom for the slaves. By prolonging the war, Lee inadvertently enabled it to destroy slavery along with the Confederacy, though no one at the time looked at the matter this way.

For the president to have lost confidence in McClellan was understandable. Nevertheless, to allow Halleck to pull back the troops was a bad mistake. When they withdrew, Lee seized the initiative. With typical decisiveness and daring, he marched rapidly north. Late in August his Confederates drove General Pope's confused troops from the same ground, Bull Run, where the first major engagement of the war had been fought.

While McClellan was regrouping the shaken Union Army, Lee once again took the offensive. He realized that no number of individual southern triumphs could destroy the enormous material advantages of the North. Unless some dramatic blow, delivered on northern soil, persuaded the people of the United States that military victory was impossible, the South would surely be crushed in the long run. Lee therefore marched rapidly northwest around the defenses of Washington.

Acting with even more than his usual boldness, Lee divided his army of 60,000 into a number of units. One, under Jackson, descended on weakly defended Harpers Ferry, capturing more than 11,000 prisoners. Another pressed as far north as Hagerstown, Maryland, nearly to the Pennsylvania line. McClellan pursued with his usual deliberation until a captured dispatch revealed to him Lee's dispositions. Then he moved a bit more swiftly, forcing Lee to stand and fight on September 17 at Sharpsburg, Maryland, between the Potomac and Antietam Creek. On a field that offered Lee no room to maneuver, 70,000 Union soldiers clashed with 40,000 Confederates. When darkness fell, more than 22,000 lay dead or wounded on the bloody field.

Although casualties were evenly divided and the Confederate lines remained intact, Lee's position was perilous. His men were exhausted. McClellan had not yet thrown in his reserves, and new federal units were arriving hourly. A bold northern general would have continued the fight without respite through the night. One of ordinary aggressiveness would have waited for first light and then struck with every soldier who could hold a rifle, for with the Potomac at his back, Lee could not retreat under fire without inviting disaster. McClellan, however, did nothing. For an entire day, while Lee scanned the field in futile search of some weakness in the Union lines, he held his fire. That night the Confederates slipped back across the Potomac into Virginia.

Lee's invasion had failed; his army had been badly mauled; the gravest threat to the Union in the war had been checked. But McClellan had let victory slip through his fingers. Soon Lee was back behind the defenses of Richmond, rebuilding his army.

Once again, this time finally, Lincoln dismissed McClellan from his command.

The Emancipation Proclamation

Antietam, though hardly the victory he had hoped for, gave Lincoln the excuse he needed to take a step that changed the character of the war decisively. When the fighting started, fear of alienating the border states was reason enough for not making emancipation of the slaves a war aim. Lincoln even insisted on enforcing the Fugitive Slave Act for this reason. However, pressures to act against the South's "peculiar institution" mounted steadily. Slavery had divided the nation; now it was driving Northerners to war within themselves. Love of country led them to fight to save the

Union, but fighting aroused hatreds and caused many to desire to smash the enemy. Sacrifice, pain, and grief made abolitionists of many who had no love for blacks—they sought to free the slave only to injure the master.

To make abolition an object of the war might encourage the slaves to revolt, but Lincoln disclaimed this objective. Nevertheless, the possibility existed. Already the slaves seemed to be looking to the North for freedom: Whenever Union troops invaded Confederate territory, slaves flocked into their lines.

As the war progressed, the Radical faction in Congress gradually chipped away at slavery. In April 1862 the Radicals pushed through a bill abolishing slavery in the District of Columbia; two months later another measure outlawed it in the territories; in July the Confiscation Act "freed" all slaves owned by persons in rebellion against the United States. In fighting for these measures and in urging general emancipation, some Radicals made statements harshly critical of Lincoln; but while he carefully avoided being identified with them or with any other faction, the president was never very far from their position. He resisted emancipation because he feared it would divide the country and injure the war effort, not because he personally disapproved. Indeed, he frequently cited Radical pressure as an excuse for doing what he wished to do on his own.

When Union troops pushed toward Richmond in June of 1862, these slaves crossed the Rappahonnock River heading north toward freedom. But McClellan's offensive failed and the Union army withdrew to Washington. Whether these slaves made it to Maryland in time is unknown.

Lincoln would have preferred to see slavery done away with by state law, with compensation for slave owners and federal aid for former slaves willing to leave the United States. He tried repeatedly to persuade the loyal slave states to adopt this pol-icy, but without success. By the summer of 1862 he was convinced that for military reasons and to win the support of liberal opinion in Europe, the government should make abolition a war aim. "We must free the slaves or be our-selves subdued," he explained to a member of his Cabinet. He delayed temporarily, fearing that a statement in the face of military reverses would be taken as a sign of weakness. The "victory" at Antietam Creek gave him his opportunity, and on September 22 he made public the **Emancipation Proclamation**. After January 1, 1863, it said, all slaves in areas in rebellion against the United States "shall be then, thenceforward, and forever free."

•●•⎯[Read the **Document**

The Emancipation Proclamation
at **myhistorylab.com**

No single slave was freed directly by Lincoln's announcement, which did not apply to the border states or to those sections of the Confederacy, like New Orleans and Norfolk, Virginia, already controlled by federal troops. The proclamation differed in philosophy, however, from the Confiscation Act in striking at the institution, not at the property of rebels. Henceforth every Union victory would speed the destruction of slavery without regard for the attitudes of individual masters.

Southerners considered the Emancipation Proclamation an incitement to slave rebellion—as one of them put it, an "infamous attempt to . . . convert the quiet, ignorant, and dependent black son of toil into a savage incendiary and brutal murderer." Most antislavery groups thought it did not go far enough. Lincoln "is only stopping on the edge of Niagara, to pick up a few chips," one abolitionist declared. "He and they will go over together." Foreign opinion was mixed: Liberals tended to applaud, conservatives to react with alarm or contempt.

As Lincoln anticipated, the proclamation had a subtle but continuing impact in the North. Its immediate effect was to aggravate racial prejudices. Millions of whites disapproved of slavery yet abhorred the idea of equality for blacks. David Wilmot, for example, insisted that his famous proviso was designed to preserve the territories for whites rather than to weaken slavery, and as late as 1857 the people of Iowa had rejected black suffrage by a vote of 49,000 to 8,000.

The Democrats spared no effort to make political capital of these fears and prejudices even before Lincoln's Emancipation Proclamation, and they made large gains in the 1862 election, especially in the Northwest. So strong was antiblack feeling that most of the Republican politicians who defended emancipation did so with racist arguments. Far from encouraging southern blacks to move north, they claimed, the ending of slavery would lead to a mass migration of northern blacks to the South.

When the Emancipation Proclamation began actually to free slaves, the govern-ment pursued a policy of "containment," that is, of keeping the former slaves in the South. Panicky fears of an inundation of blacks subsided in the North. Nevertheless, emancipation remained a cause of social discontent. In March 1863, volunteering having fallen off, Congress passed the Conscription Act. The law applied to all men between ages twenty and forty-five, but it allowed draftees to hire substitutes and even to buy exemption for $300, provisions that were patently unfair to the poor. During the remainder of the war 46,000 men were actually drafted, whereas 118,000 hired substitutes, and another 161,000 "failed to report." Conscription represented an enormous expansion of national authority, since in effect it gave the government the power of life and death over individual citizens.

The Draft Riots

After the passage of the Conscription Act, draft riots erupted in a number of cities. By far the most serious disturbance occurred in New York City in July 1863. Many workers resented conscription in principle and were embittered by the $300 exemption fee (which represented a year's wages). The idea of being forced to risk their lives to free slaves who would then, they believed, compete with them for jobs infuriated them. On July 13 a mob attacked the office where the names of conscripts were being drawn. For four days the city was an inferno. Public buildings, shops, and private residences were put to the torch. What began as a protest against the draft became an assault on blacks and the well-to-do. It took federal troops and the temporary suspension of the draft in the city to put an end to the rioting. By the time order was restored more than a hundred people had lost their lives.

Most white Northerners did not surrender their comforting belief in black inferiority, and Lincoln was no exception. Yet Lincoln was evolving. He talked about deporting freed slaves to the tropics, but he did not send any there. And he began to receive black leaders in the White House and to allow black groups to hold meetings on the grounds.

Many other Americans were changing too. The brutality of the New York riots horrified many white citizens. Over $40,000 was swiftly raised to aid the victims, and some conservatives were so appalled by the Irish rioters that they began to talk of giving blacks the vote.

SACKING BROOKS'S CLOTHING STORE.

This lithograph of the New York draft riots, 1863, shows that although the rioters mainly targeted blacks, they also attacked homes and businesses of prominent Republicans: Brooks Brothers, Horace Greeley's newspaper, and the *Times*.

The Emancipated People

To blacks, both slave and free, the Emancipation Proclamation served as a beacon. Even if it failed immediately to liberate one slave or to lift the burdens of prejudice from one black back, it stood as a promise of future improvement. "I took the proclamation for a little more than it purported," Frederick Douglass recalled in his autobiography, "and saw in its spirit a life and power far beyond its letter." Lincoln was by modern standards a racist, but his most militant black contemporaries respected him deeply. Douglass said of him, "Lincoln was not . . . either our man or our model. In his interests, in his association, in his habits of thought and in his prejudices, he was a white man." Nevertheless, Douglass described Lincoln as "one whom I could love, honor, and trust without reserve or doubt."

As for the slaves of the South, after January 1, 1863, whenever the "Army of Freedom" approached, they laid down their plows and hoes and flocked to the Union lines in droves. Such behavior came as a shock to the owners. "[The slaves] who loved us best—as we thought—were the first to leave us," one planter mourned. Talk of slave "ingratitude" increased. Instead of referring to their workers as "servants" or "my black family," many owners began to describe them as "slaves" or "niggers."

African American Soldiers

A revolutionary shift occurred in white thinking about using black men as soldiers. Although they had fought in the Revolution and in the Battle of New Orleans during the War of 1812, a law of 1792 barred blacks from the army. During the early stages of the rebellion, despite the eagerness of thousands of free blacks to enlist, the prohibition remained in force. By 1862, however, the need for manpower was creating pressure for change. In August Secretary of War Edwin M. Stanton authorized the military government of the captured South Carolina sea islands to enlist slaves in the area. After the Emancipation Proclamation specifically authorized the enlistment of blacks, the governor of Massachusetts moved to organize a black regiment, the famous Massachusetts 54th. (See Re-Viewing the Past, *Glory*, pp. 404–405.) Swiftly thereafter, other states began to recruit black soldiers, and in May 1863 the federal government established a Bureau of Colored Troops to supervise their enlistment. By the end of the war one soldier in eight in the Union army was black.

Enlisting so many black soldiers changed the war from a struggle to save the Union to a kind of revolution. "Let the black man . . . get an eagle on his button and a musket on his shoulder," wrote Frederick Douglass, "and there is no power on earth which can deny that he has won the right to citizenship."

At first black soldiers received only $7 a month, about half what white soldiers were paid. But they soon proved themselves in battle; of the 178,000 who served in the Union army, 37,000 were killed, a rate of loss about 40 percent higher than that among white troops. The Congressional Medal of Honor was awarded to twenty-one blacks.

The higher death rates among black soldiers were partly due to the fury of Confederate soldiers. Many black captives were killed on the spot. After overrunning the garrison of Fort Pillow on the Mississippi River, the Confederates massacred several dozen black soldiers, along with their white commander. Lincoln was tempted to order reprisals, but he and his advisers realized that to do so would have been both morally wrong (two wrongs never make a right) and likely to lead to still more atrocities. "Blood can not restore blood," Lincoln said in his usual direct way.

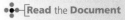

•ᐧ•─⸢Read the **Document**

Letter from a Free Black Volunteer to the *Christian Recorder* (1864) at **myhistorylab.com**

Antietam to Gettysburg

It was well that Lincoln seized on Antietam to release his proclamation; had he waited for a more impressive victory, he would have waited nearly a year. To replace McClellan, he chose General Ambrose E. Burnside, best known to history for his magnificent side-whiskers (originally called burnsides, later, at first jokingly, sideburns). Burnside was a good corps commander, but he lacked the self-confidence essential to anyone who takes responsibility for major deci-

◉─⸢See the **Map**

The Civil War, Part II: 1863–1865 at **myhistorylab.com**

sions. He knew his limitations and tried to avoid high command, but patriotism and his sense of duty compelled him, when pressed, to accept leadership of the Army of the Potomac. He prepared to march on Richmond.

Unlike McClellan, Burnside was aggressive—too aggressive. He planned to ford the Rappahannock River at Fredericksburg. Supply problems and bad weather delayed him until mid-December, giving Lee time to concentrate his army in impregnable positions behind the town. Although he had more than 120,000 men against Lee's 75,000, Burnside should have called off the attack when he saw Lee's advantage; instead he ordered the troops forward. Crossing the river over pontoon bridges, his divisions occupied Fredericksburg. Then, in wave after wave, they charged the Confederate defense line while Lee's artillery riddled them from nearby Marye's Heights.

On December 14, the day following this futile assault, General Burnside, tears streaming down his cheeks, ordered the evacuation of Fredericksburg. Shortly thereafter General Joseph Hooker replaced him.

Unlike Burnside, "Fighting Joe" Hooker was ill-tempered, vindictive, and devious. He proved no better than his predecessor, but his failings were more like McClellan's than Burnside's. By the spring of 1863 he had 125,000 men ready for action. Late in April he forded the Rappahannock and quickly concentrated at Chancellorsville, about ten miles west of Fredericksburg. His army outnumbered the Confederates by more than two to one; he should have forced a battle at once. Instead he delayed, and while he did, Lee sent Jackson's corps of 28,000 men across tangled countryside to a position directly athwart Hooker's unsuspecting flank. At 6 PM on May 2, Jackson attacked.

Completely surprised, the Union right crumbled, brigade after brigade overrun before it could wheel to meet Jackson's charge. At the first sound of firing, Lee had struck along the entire front to impede Union troop movements. If the battle had begun earlier in the day, the Confederates might have won a decisive victory; as it happened, nightfall brought a lull, and the next day the Union troops rallied and held their ground. Heavy fighting continued until May 5, when Hooker abandoned the field and retreated in good order behind the Rappahannock.

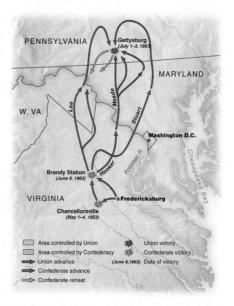

Gettysburg Campaign, 1863 As Lee's main army advanced north, Meade paralleled his movements to the east, preventing Lee from attacking Baltimore or Philadelphia. When the armies converged at Gettysburg, Lee was for the first time soundly defeated. Jeb Stuart, Lee's calvalry commander, had been marauding to the east and missed the decisive engagement.

Chancellorsville cost the Confederates dearly, for their losses, in excess of 12,000, were almost as heavy as the North's and harder to replace. They also lost Stonewall Jackson, struck down by the bullets of his own men while returning from a reconnaissance. Nevertheless, the Union army had suffered another fearful blow to its morale.

Lee knew that time was still on the side of the North; to defend Richmond was not enough. Already federal troops in the West were closing in on Vicksburg, threatening to cut Confederate communications with Arkansas and Texas. Now was the time to strike, while the morale of the North was at low ebb. With 75,000 soldiers he crossed the Potomac again, a larger Union force dogging his right flank. By late June his army had fanned out across southern Pennsylvania in a fifty-mile arc from Chambersburg to the Susquehanna. Gray-clad soldiers ranged fifty miles *northwest* of Baltimore, within ten miles of Harrisburg, Pennsylvania.

As Union soldiers had been doing in Virginia, Lee's men destroyed property and commandeered food, horses, and clothing wherever they could find them. They even seized a number of blacks and sent them south to be sold as slaves. On July 1 a Confederate division looking for shoes in the town of Gettysburg clashed with two brigades of Union cavalry northwest of the town. Both sides sent out calls for reinforcements. Like iron filings drawn to a magnet, the two armies converged. The Confederates won control of the town, but the Union army, now commanded by General George G. Meade, took a strong position on Cemetery Ridge, a hook-shaped stretch of high ground just to the south. Lee's men occupied Seminary Ridge, a parallel position.

On this field the fate of the Union was probably decided. For two days the Confederates attacked Cemetery Ridge, pounding it with the heaviest artillery barrage ever seen in America and sweeping bravely up its flanks in repeated assaults. During General George E. Pickett's famous charge, a handful of his men actually reached the Union lines, but reserves drove them back. By nightfall on July 3 the Confederate army was spent, the Union lines unbroken.

The following day was the Fourth of July. The two weary forces rested on their arms. Had the Union army attacked in force, the Confederates might have been crushed, but just as McClellan had hesitated after Antietam, Meade let opportunity pass. On July 5 Lee retreated to safety. For the first time he had been clearly bested on the field of battle.

Lincoln Finds His General: Grant at Vicksburg

On Independence Day, a day after Gettysburg, federal troops won another great victory far to the west. When General Halleck was called east in July 1862, Ulysses S. Grant resumed command of the Union troops. Grant was one of the most controversial officers in the army. During the Mexican War he served well, but when he was later assigned to a lonely post in the West, he took to drink and was forced to resign his commission. Thereafter he was by turns a farmer, a real estate agent, and a clerk in a leather goods store. In 1861, approaching age forty, he seemed well into a life of frustration and mediocrity.

The war gave him a second chance. Back in service, however, his reputation as a ne'er-do-well and his unmilitary bearing worked against him, as did the heavy casualties suffered by his troops at Shiloh. Yet the fact that he knew how to manage a large army and win battles did not escape Lincoln. According to tradition, when a gossip tried to poison the president against Grant by referring to his drinking, Lincoln retorted that if he knew what brand Grant favored, he would send a barrel of it to some of his other generals.

Grant's major aim was to capture Vicksburg, a city of tremendous strategic importance. Together with Port Hudson, a bastion north of Baton Rouge, Louisiana, it guarded a 150-mile stretch of the Mississippi. The river between these points was inaccessible to federal gunboats. So long as Vicksburg remained in southern hands, the trans-Mississippi region could send men and supplies to the rest of the Confederacy.

Vicksburg sits on a bluff overlooking a sharp bend in the river. When it proved unapproachable from either the west or the north, Grant devised an audacious scheme for getting at it from the east. He descended the Mississippi from Memphis to a point a few miles north of the city. Then, leaving part of his force behind to create the impression that he planned to attack from the north, he crossed the west bank and slipped quickly southward. Recrossing the river below Vicksburg, he abandoned his communications and supply lines and struck at Jackson, the capital of Mississippi. In a series of swift engagements his troops captured Jackson, cutting off the army of General John C. Pemberton, defending Vicksburg, from other Confederate units. Turning next on Pemberton, Grant defeated him in two decisive battles, Champion's Hill and Big Black River, and drove him inside the Vicksburg fortifications. By mid-May the city was under siege. Grant applied relentless pressure, and on July 4 Pemberton surrendered. With Vicksburg in Union hands, federal gunboats could range the entire length of the Mississippi. Texas and Arkansas were for all practical purposes lost to the Confederacy.

Vicksburg Campaign Unable to seize Vicksburg by direct assualt, Grant swept to the south, crossed the Mississippi near Port Gibson, and then took Vicksburg from the east.

Lincoln had disliked Grant's plan for capturing Vicksburg. Now he generously confessed his error and placed Grant in command of all federal troops west of the Appalachians. Grant promptly took charge of the fighting around Chattanooga, Tennessee, where Confederate advances, beginning with the Battle of Chickamauga (September 19–20), were threatening to develop into a major disaster for the North. Shifting corps commanders and bringing up fresh units, he won another decisive victory at Chattanooga in a series of battles ending on November 25, 1863. This cleared the way for an invasion of Georgia. Suddenly this unkempt man emerged as the military leader the North had been so desperately seeking. In March 1864 Lincoln summoned him to Washington, named him lieutenant general, and gave him supreme command of the armies of the United States.

Economic and Social Effects, North and South

Although much blood would yet be spilled, by the end of 1863 the Confederacy was on the road to defeat. Northern military pressure, gradually increasing, was eroding the South's most precious resource: manpower. An ever-tightening naval blockade was reducing its economic strength. Shortages developed that, combined with the flood of currency pouring from the presses, led to drastic inflation. By 1864 an officer's coat cost $2,000 in Confederate money, cigars sold for $10 each, butter was $25 a pound, and flour went for $275 a barrel. Wages rose too, but not nearly as rapidly.

The southern railroad network was gradually wearing out, the major lines maintaining operations only by cannibalizing less vital roads. Imported products such as coffee disappeared; even salt became scarce. Efforts to increase manufacturing were only moderately successful because of the shortage of labor, capital, and technical knowledge. In general, southern prejudice against centralized authority prevented the Confederacy from making effective use of its scarce resources.

In the North, after a brief depression in 1861 caused by the uncertainties of the situation and the loss of southern business, the economy flourished: Government purchases greatly stimulated certain lines of manufacturing, the railroads operated at close to capacity and with increasing efficiency, the farm machinery business boomed because so many farmers left their fields to serve in the army, and bad harvests in Europe boosted agricultural prices.

Congress passed a number of economic measures long desired but held up in the past by southern opposition. The **Homestead Act (1862)** gave 160 acres to any settler who would farm the land for five years. The Morrill Land Grant Act of the same year provided the states with land at the rate of 30,000 acres for each member of Congress to support state agricultural colleges. Various tariff acts raised the duties on manufactured goods to an average rate of 47 percent in order to protect domestic manufacturers from foreign competition. The Pacific Railway Act (1862) authorized subsidies in land and money for the construction of a transcontinental railroad. And the National Banking Act of 1863 gave the country, at last, a uniform currency.

Although the economy grew, it did so more slowly during the 1860s than in the decades preceding and following. Prices soared beginning in 1862, averaging about 80 percent over the 1860 level by the end of the war. As in the South, wages did not keep pace. This did not make for a healthy economy. As the war dragged on and the continuing inflation eroded purchasing power, resentment on the part of workers deepened. During the 1850s iron molders, cigar makers, and some other skilled workers had formed national unions. This trend continued through the war years. There were many strikes. Inflation and shortages encouraged speculation and fostered a selfish, materialistic attitude toward life. Many contractors took advantage of wartime confusion to sell the government shoddy goods. By 1864 cotton was worth $1.90 a pound in New England. It could be had for twenty cents a pound in the South. Although it was illegal to traffic in the staple across the lines, unscrupulous operators did so and made huge profits.

Yet the war undoubtedly hastened industrialization and laid the basis for many other aspects of modern civilization. It posed problems of organization and planning, both military and civilian, that challenged the talents of creative persons and thus led to a more complex and efficient economy. The mechanization of production, the growth of large corporations, the creation of a better banking system, and the emergence of business leaders attuned to these conditions would surely have occurred in any case, for industrialization was under way long before the South seceded. Nevertheless, the war greatly speeded all these changes.

Civilian participation in the war effort was far greater than in earlier conflicts. Some churches split over the question of emancipation, but in North and South, church directors took the lead in recruitment drives and in charitable activities aimed at supporting the armed forces. In the North a Christian Commission raised the money and coordinated the personnel needed to provide Union soldiers with half a million Bibles, several million religious tracts, and other books, along with fruit, coffee, and spare clothing.

Women in Wartime

Many southern women took over the management of farms and small plantations when their menfolk went off to war. Others became volunteer nurses, and after an initial period of resistance, the Confederate army began to enlist women in the medical corps. At least two female nurses, Captain Sally Tompkins and Kate Cumming, left records of their experiences that throw much light on how the wounded were treated during the war. Other southern women worked as clerks in newly organized government departments.

Southern "ladyhood" more generally was yet another casualty of the war. The absence or death of husbands or other male relations changed attitudes toward gender roles. When her husband obeyed a military order to abandon Atlanta to the advancing Union armies, Julia Davidson, about to give birth, denounced the "men of Atlanta" for having "run and left Atlanta" and their homes. Such women learned to fend for themselves. "Necessity," Davidson later wrote her husband, would "make a different woman of me."

Large numbers of women also contributed to the northern war effort. As in the South, farm women went out into fields to plant and harvest crops, aided in many instances by new farm machinery. Many others took jobs in textile factories; in establishments making shoes, uniforms, and other supplies for the army; and in government agencies. But as was usually the case, the low wages traditionally paid women acted as a brake on wage increases for their male colleagues.

Besides working in factories and shops and on farms, northern women, again like their southern counterparts, aided the war effort more directly. Elizabeth Blackwell, the

Sarah Rosetta Wakeman, a.k.a. Private Lyons Wakeman of the 153rd Regiment of New York, and Janeta Velasquez, a.k.a. Lt. Harry T. Buford of the Confederate army, disguised themselves as men to fight.

first American woman doctor of medicine, had already founded the New York Infirmary for Women and Children. After war broke out she helped set up what became the U.S. **Sanitary Commission**, an organization of women similar to the Christian Commission dedicated to improving sanitary conditions at army camps, supplying hospitals with volunteer nurses, and raising money for medical supplies. Many thousands of women volunteers took part in Sanitary Commission and related programs.

An additional 3,000-odd women served as regular army nurses during the conflict. At the start the high command of both armies resisted the efforts of women to help, but

Read the Document

Barton, *Memoirs About Medical Life at the Battlefield* at myhistorylab.com

necessity and a grudging recognition of the competence of these women gradually brought the generals around. Clara Barton, a schoolteacher and government clerk, was among the first women to dress wounds at forward stations on the battlefield. After she ran out of bandages at Antietam, she dressed wounds with green corn leaves. The chief surgeon declared her to be "the angel of the battlefield." The "proper sphere" of American women was expanding, another illustration of the modernizing effect of the war.

Grant in the Wilderness

Grant's strategy as supreme commander was simple, logical, and ruthless. He would attack Lee and try to capture Richmond, Virginia. General William Tecumseh Sherman would drive from Chattanooga toward Atlanta, Georgia. Like a lobster's claw,

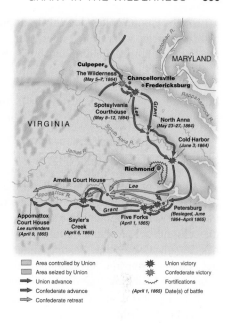

Toward Lee's Surrender in Virginia, 1864–1865
During the final year of the war in the East, Grant kept driving toward Richmond, and Lee kept blocking his way, like two whirling wrestlers locked in a hold. His army battered and bloodied, Lee surrendered at Appomattox Courthouse on April 9, 1865.

the two armies could then close to crush all resistance. Early in May 1864 Grant and Sherman commenced operations, each with more than 100,000 men.

Grant marched the Army of the Potomac directly into the tangled wilderness area south of the Rappahannock, where Hooker had been routed a year earlier. Lee, having only 60,000 men, forced the battle in the roughest possible country, where Grant found it difficult to make efficient use of his larger force. For two days (May 5–6) the Battle of the Wilderness raged. When it was over, the North had sustained another 18,000 casualties, far more than the Confederates. But unlike his predecessors, Grant did not fall back after being checked, nor did he expose his army to the kind of devastating counterattack at which Lee was so expert. Instead he shifted his troops to the southeast, attempting to outflank the Confederates. Divining his intent, Lee rushed his divisions southeastward and disposed them behind hastily erected earthworks in well-placed positions around Spotsylvania Court House. Grant attacked. After five more days, at a cost to the Union army of another 12,000 men, the Confederate lines were still intact.

Grant had grasped the fundamental truth that the war could be won only by grinding the South down beneath the weight of numbers. His own losses of men and equipment could be replaced; Lee's could not. When critics complained of the cost, he replied doggedly that he intended to fight on in the same manner if it took all summer. Once more he pressed southeastward in an effort to outflank the enemy. At Cold Harbor, nine miles from Richmond, he found the Confederates once more in strong defenses. He attacked. It was a battle as foolish and nearly as one-sided as General Pakenham's assault on Jackson's line outside New Orleans in 1815. "At Cold Harbor," the forthright Grant confessed in his memoirs, "no advantage whatever was gained to compensate for the heavy losses we sustained."

Sixty thousand casualties in less than a month! The news sent a wave of dismay through the North. There were demands that "Butcher" Grant be removed from command. Lincoln, however, stood firm. Although the price was fearfully high, Grant was gaining his objective. At Cold Harbor, Lee had to fight without a single regiment in general reserve while Grant's army was larger than at the start of the offensive. When Grant next swung around his flank, striking south of the James River toward Petersburg, Lee had to rush his troops to that city to hold him.

As the Confederates dug in, Grant put Petersburg under siege. Soon both armies had constructed complicated lines of breastworks and trenches, running for miles in a great arc south of Petersburg, much like the fortifications that would be used in France in World War I. Methodically the Union forces extended their lines, seeking to weaken the Confederates and cut the rail connections supplying Lee's troops and the city of Richmond. Grant could not overwhelm him, but by late June, Lee was pinned to earth. Moving again would mean having to abandon Richmond.

Sherman in Georgia

The summer of 1864 saw the North submerged in pessimism. The Army of the Potomac held Lee at bay but appeared powerless to defeat him. In Georgia, General Sherman inched forward methodically against the wily Joseph E. Johnston, but when he tried a direct assault at Kennesaw Mountain on June 27, he was thrown back with heavy casualties. In July Confederate raiders under General Jubal Early dashed suddenly across the Potomac from the Shenandoah Valley to within five miles of Washington before being turned back. A draft call for 500,000 additional men did not improve the public temper. Huge losses and the absence of a decisive victory were taxing the northern will to continue the fight.

In June, Lincoln had been renominated on a National Union ticket, with the Tennessee Unionist Andrew Johnson, a former Democrat, as his running mate. He was under attack not only from the Democrats, who nominated General McClellan and came out for a policy that might almost be characterized as peace at any price, but also from the Radical Republicans, many of whom had wished to dump him in favor of Secretary of the Treasury Chase.

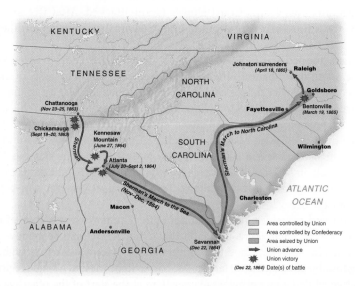

Sherman Pierces the Heart of the South, 1864–1865 After slogging through tenacious Confederate resistance in the Appalachians, Sherman finally broke through and seized Atlanta in September, 1864; he then marched "to the sea" to Savannah and in 1865 drove north through South Carolina and into North Carolina.

Table 14.1   Turning Points in the War

Pivotal Battles	Date	Outcome	Consequence
Ft. Sumter	April, 1861	Confederates fire on Ft. Sumter; Union garrison surrenders	Civil War commences
First Bull Run	July, 1861	Confederate victory	Northerners sobered, Southerners exhilarated; no swift ending to war likely
Shiloh	April, 1862	Tactical Union victory	23,000 casualties stagger everyone: Was the war worth such a high cost?
Antietam	September, 1862	Lee's advance northward halted	Lincoln, confidence regained, issues Emancipation Proclamation freeing slaves in rebel areas
Chancellorsville	May, 1863	Lee defeats Union army that had crossed into Virginia	Emboldened by victory, Lee invades North in search of decisive victory
Gettysburg	July, 1863	Confederate defeat; Lee retreats to Virginia	Confederate hopes dashed
Vicksburg	July, 1863	Grant seizes control of lower Mississippi River	Texas and Arkansas cut off from the Confederacy
Wilderness and Cold Harbor	May and June, 1864	Lee inflicts staggering losses on Union troops	Though criticized as a butcher, Grant perseveres, backed by Lincoln: War becomes battle of attrition
Sherman's March	November, 1864 through March, 1865	Sherman drives through Georgia and South Carolina	Demoralizes South
Siege of Petersburg	June 1864 through April 1865	Lee's defenses exhausted	South surrenders

Then, almost overnight, the whole atmosphere changed. On September 2, General Sherman's army fought its way into Atlanta. When the Confederates countered with an offensive northward toward Tennessee, Sherman did not follow. Instead he abandoned his communications with Chattanooga and marched unopposed through Georgia, "from Atlanta to the sea."

Sherman was in some ways like Grant. He was a West Pointer who resigned his commission only to fare poorly in civilian occupations. Back in the army in 1861, he suffered a brief nervous breakdown. After recovering he fought well under Grant at Shiloh and the two became close friends. "He stood by me when I was crazy," Sherman later recalled, "and I stood by him when he was drunk." Far more completely than most military men of his generation, Sherman believed in total war—in appropriating or destroying everything that might help the enemy continue the fight.

The march through Georgia had many objectives besides conquering territory. One obvious one was economic, the destruction of southern resources. "[We] must make old and young, rich and poor feel the hard hand of war," Sherman said.

Another object of Sherman's march was psychological. "If the North can march an army right through the South," he told General Grant, Southerners will take it "as proof positive that the North can prevail." This was certainly true of Georgia's blacks, who flocked to the invaders by the thousands, women and children as well as men, all cheering mightily when the soldiers put their former masters' homes to the torch. "They pray and shout and mix up my name with Moses," Sherman explained.

Sherman's victories staggered the Confederacy and the anti-Lincoln forces in the North. In November the president was easily reelected, 212 electoral votes to 21. The country was determined to carry on the struggle.

At last the South's will to resist began to crack. Sherman entered Savannah on December 22, having denuded a strip of Georgia sixty miles wide. Early in January 1865 he marched northward, leaving behind "a broad black streak of ruin and desolation—the fences all gone; lonesome smoke-stacks, surrounded by dark heaps of ashes and cinders, marking the spots where human habitations had stood." In February his troops captured Columbia, South Carolina. Soon they were in North Carolina, advancing relentlessly. In Virginia, Grant's vise grew tighter day by day while the Confederate lines became thinner and more ragged.

●◆●⊣Read the Document

Sherman, *The March Through Georgia* at **myhistorylab.com**

These photos are of Lincoln, when he became president, and shortly before he was assassinated.
Source: (left) ICHi-20265/Photo by Alexander Hesler/Chicago Historical Society.

To Appomattox Court House

On March 4 Lincoln took the presidential oath and delivered his second inaugural address. Photographs taken at about this time show how four years of war had marked him. Somehow he had become both gentle and steel-tough, both haggard and inwardly calm. With victory sure, he spoke for tolerance, mercy, and reconstruction. "Let us judge not," he said after stating again his personal dislike of slavery, "that we be not judged." He urged all Americans to turn without malice to the task of mending the damage and to make a just and lasting peace between the sections.

Now the Confederate troops around Petersburg could no longer withstand the federal pressure. Desperately Lee tried to pull his forces back to the Richmond and Danville Railroad at Lynchburg, but the swift wings of Grant's army enveloped them. Richmond fell on April 3. With fewer than 30,000 men to oppose Grant's 115,000, Lee recognized the futility of further resistance. On April 9 he and Grant met by prearrangement at Appomattox Court House.

It was a scene at once pathetic and inspiring. Lee was noble in defeat; Grant, despite his rough-hewn exterior, was sensitive and magnanimous in victory. "I met you once before, General Lee, while we were serving in Mexico," Grant said after they had shaken hands. "I have always remembered your appearance, and I think I should have recognized you anywhere." They talked briefly of that earlier war, and then, acting on Lincoln's instructions, Grant outlined his terms. All that would be required was that the Confederate soldiers lay down their arms. They could return to their homes in peace. When Lee hinted that his men would profit greatly if allowed to retain possession of their horses, Grant agreed to let them do so.

Winners, Losers, and the Future

And so the war ended in 1865. It had cost the nation more than 600,000 lives, nearly as many as in all other American wars combined. The story of one of the lost thousands must stand for all, Union and Confederate. Jones Budbury, a tall, nineteen-year-old redhead, was working in a Pennsylvania textile mill when the war broke out, and he enlisted at once. His regiment first saw action at Bull Run. He took part in McClellan's Peninsular campaign. He fought at Second Bull Run, at Chancellorsville, and at Gettysburg. A few months after Gettysburg he was wounded in the foot and spent some time in an army hospital. By the spring of 1864 he had risen through the ranks to first sergeant and his hair had turned gray. In June he was captured and sent to Andersonville military prison, near Macon, Georgia, but he fell ill and the Confederates released him. In March 1865 he was back with his regiment in the lines besieging Richmond. On April 6, three days before Lee's surrender, Jones Budbury was killed while pursuing Confederate units near Sayler's Creek, Virginia.

The war also caused enormous property losses, especially in the Confederacy. All the human and material destruction explains the corrosive hatred and bitterness that the war implanted in millions of hearts. The corruption, the gross materialism, and the selfishness generated by wartime conditions were other disagreeable by-products of the conflict. Such sores fester in any society, but the Civil War bred conditions that inflamed and multiplied them. The war produced many examples of

Glory

Glory (1989) tells the story of the 54th Massachusetts Volunteer Infantry, a black regiment, from its establishment in the fall of 1862 through its attack on Fort Wagner, South Carolina, on July 18, 1863.

"Historical accuracy," director Edward Zwick declared, was "the goal of everyone involved in the production." Filmmakers commonly make such assertions, but Zwick proved that he had attended to the historical record. The peak of Shaw's cap was dyed the exact shade of medium green used by officers of the Massachusetts 54th; and when shoes were distributed to the recruits, there were no "lefts" or "rights": Shoes were to shape themselves to either foot from wear.

Zwick's evident commitment to history makes his deviations all the more interesting. The movie begins with a panoramic shot of rolling hills, dotted with tents. Fog blankets the valley and softens the morning light. Then the quiet is shattered by explosions: Soldiers hasten to form ranks, trot toward a battlefield, and charge across it, a young officer in the vanguard. (He is Captain Robert Gould Shaw, played by Matthew Broderick.) The attackers are decimated. Shaw is hit and loses consciousness.

Shaw is sent home to Boston to convalesce. At a reception, Governor Andrew offers the young officer command of the Massachusetts 54th, a black regiment being raised in Boston. Shaw hesitates for a moment. Then he confers privately with another officer, who is appalled.

"I knew how much you'd like to be a colonel, but a colored regiment?"

"I'm gonna do it," Shaw replies.

"You're not serious."

"Yeah."

These scenes contain truths without being entirely truthful. Governor Andrew did offer the commission and Shaw accepted it. But at the time Shaw was in Virginia. Andrew, in Boston, conveyed it through Shaw's father and young Shaw initially refused. Zwick has compressed the story chronologically, squeezing weeks into minutes; and he has rearranged it geographically to enable Andrew and young Shaw to meet. Such modifications are common in "reel history," and these do not impair historical understanding.

But *Glory* deviates from the historical record in more significant ways. It suggests, for example, that the Massachusetts 54th was composed mostly of former slaves. In fact, most of its volunteers were from northern states and had never been slaves.

The fiction that they had been slaves, however, made it possible for Zwick to examine a larger truth. Of the 178,000 blacks who served in the Union army, fewer than one-fifth were from the North; the great majority *were* former slaves. Nearly 100,000 were recruited from Louisiana, Mississippi, or Tennessee, among the first states occupied by the Union army. *Glory* thus merges the story of the free blacks of the Massachusetts 54th with that of former slaves who were recruited from the Deep South.

Zwick exploited the dramatic potential of the latter groups. How did slaves respond when, having just received their freedom, they were placed under the absolute power of white officers?

Glory develops the question chiefly through the character of Trip (Denzel Washington), a former slave who hates all whites, including Shaw. Shaw illuminates the other side of the question. An abolitionist, he reluctantly decides that former slaves must be whipped (literally) into shape. When Trip sneaks off one night and is captured for desertion, Shaw orders him flogged. When Trip's back is bared, Shaw sees that it is laced with scars from whippings by slave masters. During the flogging, Trip fixes Shaw with a hateful stare, a powerful scene that underscores the movie's central irony: To end slavery, Shaw has become Trip's master while Trip has again become a slave.

Whatever its dramatic merits, the scene is ahistorical. In 1861 Congress had outlawed flogging in the military. Disobedient soldiers were tied in a crouched position, or they were

Matthew Broderick as Robert Gould Shaw, and Denzel Washington as the former slave recruit Trip, in the movie *Glory*.

suspended by their thumbs, toes just touching the ground.

Physical punishment was, in fact, one of the chief sources of contention between ex-slave soldiers and white officers. "I am no slave to be driven," one black recruit informed a brutish commander. When an officer of the 38th Colored Infantry tied a black recruit up by the thumbs, his friends cut him down and forced the officers back with bayonets: "No white son of a bitch can tie a man up here," they declared. The blacks were charged with mutiny and several were executed, an incident that shows that former slaves did not willingly submit to army discipline tainted with racism. Though African Americans constituted only 8 percent of the Union army, 80 percent of those executed for mutiny were black. Many white officers, as the movie suggests, did assert that former slaves must be treated as slaves.

Could such soldiers—black recruits and white officers alike—have been good ones? The movie answers the question by recreating the actual attack on Fort Wagner, the first step in the offensive on Charleston. It shows the blacks of the Massachusetts 54th marching to the front of the line, and forming up along a narrow beach. On Shaw's command, they charge forward. Unlike the white troops in the opening scene, the blacks follow him to the ramparts; when he falls, they continue onward until they are wiped out.

Were the actual soldiers of the Massachusetts 54th as courageous as those in the movie? Shortly after the battle, Lieutenant Iredell Jones, a Confederate officer, reported,

"The negroes fought gallantly, and were headed by as brave a colonel as ever lived." Of the 600 members of the 54th Massachusetts, 40 percent were casualties on that day, an extraordinarily high ratio. But did ex-slaves fight as courageously as the free blacks of the 54th? The answer to this question came not at Fort Wagner, but at other, less publicized battles. A few weeks earlier, for example, several companies of the Louisiana (Colored) Infantry, composed of former slaves who had been in the army only for several weeks, fought off a furious Confederate assault at Milliken's Bend near Vicksburg. The Confederate general was astonished when whites in the Union army fled but the blacks held their ground despite sustaining staggering casualties—45 percent— the highest of any single battle in the war.

Thus while *Glory* is a fictional composite— of free black and ex-slave recruits, and of the assault on Fort Wagner and Milliken's Bend—it conveys a broader truth about black soldiers. Howell Cobb, a Confederate senator from Georgia, declared, "If the black can make a good soldier, our whole system of government is wrong." *Glory* shows that although white officers and black recruits did not form a harmonious team, they together proved that slavery was doomed.

Questions for Discussion
- Was conscription during the Civil War a form of slavery?
- Would free blacks or former slaves more likely have been the better soldiers?

Casualities of the Civil War The Union death rate was 23 percent, the Confederate 24 percent. Twice as many soldiers were killed by disease as were killed by bullets.

Union Troops

Total: 1,566,678

Wounded: 275,175

Died of Wounds: 110,070

Died of Disease: 249,458

Confederate Troops

Total: 1,082,119

Wounded: 100,000

Died of Wounds: 94,000

Died of Disease: 164,000

charity, self-sacrifice, and devotion to duty as well, yet if the general moral atmosphere of the postwar generation can be said to have resulted from the experiences of 1861 to 1865, the effect overall was bad.

What had been obtained at this price? Slavery was dead. Paradoxically, while the war had been fought to preserve the Union, after 1865 the people tended to see the United States not as a union of states but as a nation. After Appomattox, secession was almost literally inconceivable. In a strictly political sense, as Lincoln had predicted from the start, the northern victory heartened friends of republican government and democracy throughout the world. A better-integrated society and a more technically advanced and productive economic system also resulted from the war.

The Americans of 1865 estimated the balance between cost and profit according to their individual fortunes and prejudices. Only the wisest realized that no final accounting could be made until the people had decided what to do with the fruits of victory. That the physical damage would be repaired no one could reasonably doubt; that even the loss of human resources would be restored in short order was equally apparent. But would the nation make good use of the opportunities the war had made available? What would the former slaves do with freedom? How would whites, northern and southern, react to emancipation? To what end would the new technology and social efficiency be directed? Would the people be able to forget the recent past and fulfill the hopes for which so many brave soldiers had given their "last full measure of devotion"?

[◉] Watch the Video

The Meaning of the Civil War for Americans at myhistorylab.com

Milestones

1861	Confederates attack Fort Sumter; Lincoln calls for 75,000 volunteers	1862	Lincoln's Emancipation Proclamation frees slaves in "areas of rebellion"
	First Battle of Bull Run (Virginia) boosts Confederate morale		Congress passes Homestead, Morrill Land Grant, and Pacific Railway acts
	Lincoln appoints George B. McClellan Union commander	1863	Congress passes Conscription and National Banking acts
	Supreme Court rules against Lincoln's suspension of habeas corpus in *Ex parte Merryman*		Federal troops subdue draft riots in New York City
1862	Confederate Congress passes Conscription Act		Union army defeats Confederates at turning point Battle of Gettysburg, Pennsylvania
	USS *Monitor* defeats Confederate *Merrimack* in first battle between ironclads		Union siege and capture of Vicksburg, Mississippi, gives Union control of entire Mississippi River
	Battle of Shiloh, Tennessee, leaves 23,000 dead, wounded, or missing	1864	Grant pushes deep into Virginia in costly Battles of the Wilderness, Spotsylvania Court House, and Cold Harbor
	Robert E. Lee assumes command of Confederate Army of Northern Virginia		Sherman captures Atlanta, Georgia; marches to sea; captures Savannah
	Lee and Stonewall Jackson defeat huge Union army at Seven Days' Battle for Richmond		Lincoln is reelected president
	Lee and Jackson defeat Union army at Second Battle of Bull Run	1864–1865	Grant takes Petersburg, Virginia, after ten-month siege
	Lee's northern advance is stopped at Battle of Antietam; 22,000 casualties	1865	Sherman captures Columbia, South Carolina
			Lee surrenders to Grant at Appomattox Court House, Virginia

 **Study** and **Review** at www.myhistorylab.com

Review Questions

1. The introduction to this chapter notes that civil wars, in retrospect, often seem senseless. If the American people had known in advance the terrible cost of its civil war, would it have been fought? Why did each side think it could win?

2. Dwight D. Eisenhower, U.S. general during World War II and subsequently President, once declared that "every war is going to astonish you in the way it occurred and the way it is carried out." What were the astonishing aspects of the Civil War?

3. How did Lincoln's war aims evolve? What were the reasons for and consequences of Lincoln's Emancipation Proclamation?

4. What factors on the home front influenced the course of war?

5. The table on page 401 summarizes the "turning points" during the Civil War. Which one was the most important?

6. How did the Civil War strengthen the American nation? Was the nation stronger after the war than before?

Key Terms

Anaconda Plan   *381*
Copperheads   *382*
Emancipation Proclamation   *390*
greenbacks   *382*

Homestead Act (1862)   *396*
Radical Republicans   *382*
Sanitary Commission   *398*

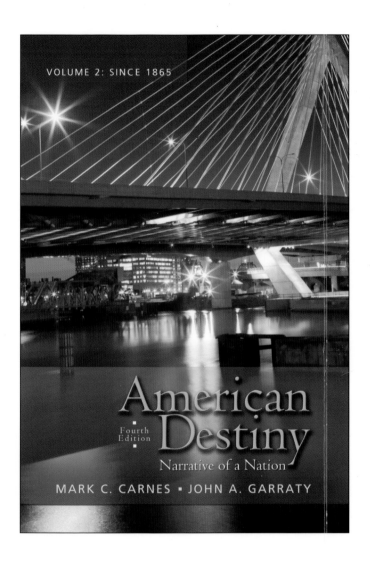

VOLUME 2: SINCE 1865

American
Fourth Edition
Destiny
Narrative of a Nation

MARK C. CARNES · JOHN A. GARRATY

To order, please request
Volume 2: Chapters 15-32
ISBN-10: 0-205-79040-2 | ISBN-13: 978-0-205-79040-1

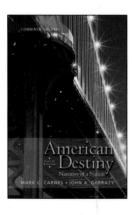
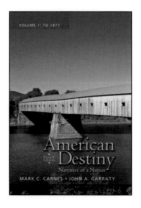
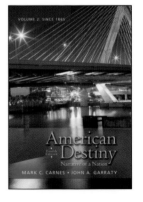

COMBINED EDITION
Chapters 1-32
ISBN-10: 0-205-79041-0
ISBN-13: 978-0-205-79041-8

VOLUME 1: TO 1877
Chapters 1-15
ISBN-10: 0-205-79039-9
ISBN-13: 978-0-205-79039-5

VOLUME 2: SINCE 1865
Chapters 15-32
ISBN-10: 0-205-79040-2
ISBN-13: 978-0-205-79040-1

Has your family overcome adversity?

WITH NEARLY $3 BILLION IN ASSETS, OPRAH WINFREY IS THE RICHEST self-made woman in America. Her great-great-grandfather, Constantine Winfrey, was an illiterate slave in Sanford, Mississippi. On gaining his freedom in 1865, he owned little more than a strong back and a knowledge of cotton farming. But within fifteen years, he had learned to read and write and was owner of several farms and over 100 acres of land.

Whoopi Goldberg, another prominent black woman TV host and actress, is the great-great-granddaughter of William Washington and Elsa Tucker, slaves who were living in Alachua County, Florida when Lee surrendered at Appomattox. Over the next decade, the couple fulfilled the demanding provisions of the Southern Homestead Act, passed by the Republican-dominated Congress in 1866.

Chris Rock, comedian and actor, is the great-great-grandson of Julius Caesar Tingman, a slave in South Carolina. In March 1865, a few weeks after Sherman had marched through South Carolina, Tingman joined the U.S. Colored Troops in the Union army. Three years later, at the age of twenty-four, he was elected to the "reconstructed" South Carolina legislature.

Such accounts add another dimension to the usual narrative of the Reconstruction era (1865–1877). The period began with the liberal readmission of southern states to the Union as proposed by Lincoln and his successor, Andrew Johnson. Once readmitted, southern states restricted the rights of former slaves through a series of "**Black Codes**." A furious Republican Congress overturned white southern rule through a series of laws and constitutional amendments that empowered former slaves—and their Republican allies. A white backlash, often violent, followed Republican rule. Ultimately, white political power was restored, and a corrupt bargain secured the presidency for the Republican, Hayes. When Hayes removed Union troops from the South in 1877, Reconstruction was over.

•••—Read the Document

The Mississippi Black Code, at **myhistorylab.com**

Deprived of federal assistance, former slaves were obliged to make do on their own. Many failed. Only 10 percent of freed slaves acquired farms. But the ancestors of Oprah Winfrey, Whoopi Goldberg, Chris Rock, and many others prove that *some* former slaves succeeded, almost entirely through their own efforts. Harvard historian Louis Henry parlors into the texts, ultimately changing the official narrative of American history itself." This chapter describes the era's bitter wrangles and recriminations, its political failures and disappointments, but it also shows that many survived and even flourished during these difficult years.

The Assassination of Lincoln

On April 5, 1865, Abraham Lincoln visited Richmond. The fallen capital lay in ruins, sections blackened by fire, but the president was able to walk the streets unmolested and almost unattended. Everywhere African Americans crowded around him worshipfully; some fell to their knees as he passed, crying "Glory, Hallelujah," hailing him as a messiah. Even white townspeople seemed to have accepted defeat without resentment.

A few days later, in Washington, Lincoln delivered an important speech on Reconstruction, urging compassion and open-mindedness. On April 14 he held a Cabinet meeting at which postwar readjustment was considered at length. That evening, while Lincoln was watching a performance of the play *Our American Cousin* at Ford's Theater, an actor, John Wilkes Booth, slipped into his box and shot him in the back of the head with a small pistol. Early the next morning, without having regained consciousness, Lincoln died.

Richmond, Virginia lies in ruins in April, 1865 at the time of Lincoln's visit—and a few days before his assassination.

The murder was part of a complicated plot organized by die-hard pro-Southerners. One of Booth's accomplices went to the home of Secretary of State William Seward and stabbed him—Seward recovered from his wounds. A third conspirator, assigned to kill Vice President Andrew Johnson, changed his mind and fled Washington. Seldom have fanatics displayed so little understanding of their own interests, for with Lincoln perished the South's best hope for a mild peace. After his body had been taken home to Illinois, the national mood hardened; apparently the awesome drama was still unfolding—retribution and a final humbling of the South were inevitable.

Presidential Reconstruction

Despite its bloodiness, the Civil War had caused less intersectional hatred than might have been expected. The legal questions related to bringing the defeated states back into the Union, however, were extremely complex. Since Southerners believed that secession was legal, logic should have compelled them to argue that they were out of the Union and would thus have to be formally readmitted. Northerners should have taken the contrary position, for they had fought to prove that secession was illegal. Yet the people of both sections did just the opposite. Senator Charles Sumner and Congressman Thaddeus Stevens, who in 1861 had been uncompromising expounders of the theory that the Union was indissoluble, now insisted that the Confederate states had "committed suicide" and should be treated like "conquered provinces."

The process of readmission began in 1862, when Lincoln reappointed provisional governors for those parts of the South that had been occupied by federal troops. On December 8, 1863, he issued a proclamation setting forth a general policy. With the exception of high Confederate officials and a few other special groups, all Southerners could reinstate themselves as United States citizens by taking a simple loyalty oath. When, in any state, a number equal to 10 percent of those voting in the 1860 election had taken this oath, they could set up a state government. Under this **Ten Percent Plan**, such governments had to be republican in form, must recognize the "perma- nent freedom" of the slaves, and must provide for black education. The plan, however, did not require that blacks be given the right to vote.

President Andrew Johnson poses regally with carefully manicured fingernails. Although Johnson hated southern aristocrats, he sometimes craved their approval.

The Ten Percent Plan reflected Lincoln's lack of vindictiveness and his political wisdom. He realized that any government based on such a small minority of the population would be, as he put it, merely "a tangible nucleus which the remainder . . . may rally around as fast as it can," a sort of puppet regime, like the paper government established in those sections of Virginia under federal control.[1] The regimes established under this plan in Tennessee, Louisiana, and Arkansas bore, in the president's mind, the same relation to finally reconstructed states that an egg bears to a chicken. "We shall sooner have the fowl by hatching it than by smashing it," he remarked. He knew that eventually representatives of the southern states would again be sitting in Congress, and he wished to lay the groundwork for a strong Republican party in the section. Yet he realized that Congress had no intention of seating representatives from the "10 percent" states at once.

The Radicals in Congress disliked the Ten Percent Plan, partly because of its moderation and partly because it enabled Lincoln to determine Union policy toward the recaptured regions. In July 1864 they passed the **Wade-Davis Bill**, which provided for constitutional conventions only after a majority of the others in a southern state had taken a loyalty oath. Confederate officials and anyone who had "voluntarily borne arms against the United States" were barred from voting in the election or serving at the convention. Besides prohibiting slavery, the new state constitutions would have to repudiate Confederate debts. Lincoln disposed of the Wade-Davis Bill with a pocket veto and that's where matters stood when Andrew Johnson became president following the assassination.

Lincoln had picked Johnson for a running mate in 1864 because he was a border-state Unionist Democrat and something of a hero as a result of his courageous service as military governor of Tennessee. His political strength came from the poor whites and yeomen farmers of eastern Tennessee, and he was fond of extolling the common man and attacking "stuck-up aristocrats."

Johnson was a Democrat, but because of his record and his reassuring penchant for excoriating southern aristocrats, the Republicans in Congress were ready to cooperate with him. "Johnson, we have faith in you," said Senator Ben Wade, author of the Wade-Davis Bill, the day after Lincoln's death. "By the gods, there will be no trouble now in running the government!"

Johnson's reply, "Treason must be made infamous," delighted the Radicals, but the president proved temperamentally unable to work with them. Like Randolph of Roanoke, his antithesis intellectually and socially, opposition was his specialty; he soon alienated every powerful Republican in Washington.

Radical Republicans listened to Johnson's diatribes against secessionists and the great planters and assumed that he was anti-southern. Nothing could have been further from the truth. He had great respect for states' rights and he shared most of his poor white Tennessee constituents' contempt of blacks. "Damn the negroes, I am fighting these traitorous aristocrats, their masters," he told a friend during the war. "I wish to God," he said on another occasion, "every head of a family in the United States had one slave to take the drudgery and menial service off his family."

The new president did not want to injure or humiliate all white Southerners. He issued an amnesty proclamation only slightly more rigorous than Lincoln's. It assumed, correctly

---

[1] By approving the separation of the western counties that had refused to secede, this government had provided a legal pretext for the creation of West Virginia in 1863.

enough, that with the war over most southern voters would freely take the loyalty oath; thus it contained no 10 percent clause. More classes of Confederates, including those who owned taxable property in excess of $20,000, were excluded from the general pardon. By the time Congress convened in December 1865, all the southern states had organized governments, ratified the **Thirteenth Amendment** abolishing slavery, and elected senators and representatives. Johnson promptly recommended these new governments to the attention of Congress.

Republican Radicals

Peace found the Republicans in Congress no more united than they had been during the war. A small group of "ultra" Radicals were demanding immediate and absolute civil and political equality for blacks; they should be given, for example, the vote, a plot of land, and access to a decent education. Senator Sumner led this faction. A second group of Radicals, headed by Thaddeus Stevens in the House and Ben Wade in the Senate, agreed with the ultras' objectives but were prepared to accept half a loaf if necessary to win the support of less radical colleagues.

Nearly all Radicals distinguished between the "natural" God-given rights described in the Declaration of Independence, and social equality. The moderate Republicans wanted to protect the former slaves from exploitation and guarantee their basic rights but were unprepared to push for full political equality. A handful of Republicans sided with the Democrats in support of Johnson's approach, but all the rest insisted at least on the minimal demands of the moderates. Thus Johnsonian Reconstruction was doomed.

Johnson's proposal had no chance in Congress for reasons having little to do with black rights. The Thirteenth Amendment had the effect of increasing the representation of the southern states in Congress because it made the Three-fifths Compromise meaningless (see Chapter 5). Henceforth those who had been slaves would be counted as whole persons in apportioning seats in the House of Representatives. If Congress seated the Southerners, the balance of power might swing to the Democrats. To expect the Republicans to surrender power in such a fashion was unrealistic. Former Copperheads gushing with extravagant praise for Johnson put them instantly on guard.

Congress Rejects Johnsonian Reconstruction

The Republicans in Congress rejected Johnsonian Reconstruction. Quickly they created a joint committee on Reconstruction, headed by Senator William P. Fessenden of Maine, a moderate, to study the question of readmitting the southern states.

The committee held public hearings that produced much evidence of the mistreatment of blacks. Colonel George A. Custer, stationed in Texas, testified: "It is of weekly, if not of daily occurrence that Freedmen are murdered." The nurse Clara Barton told a gruesome tale about a pregnant woman who had been brutally whipped. Others described the intimidation of blacks by poor whites. The hearings strengthened the Radicals, who had been claiming all along that the South was perpetuating slavery under another name.

President Johnson's attitude speeded the swing toward the Radical position. While the hearings were in progress, Congress passed a bill expanding and extending the **Freedmen's Bureau**, which had been established in March 1865 to care for refugees. The bureau, a branch of the war department, was already exercising considerable coercive and supervisory power in the South. Now Congress sought to add to its authority in order to protect the black population. Although the bill had wide support, Johnson vetoed it, arguing that it was an unconstitutional extension of military authority in peacetime. Congress then passed a Civil Rights Act that, besides declaring specifically that blacks were citizens of the United States, denied the states the power to restrict their rights to testify in court, to make contracts for their labor, and to hold property. In other words, it put teeth in the Thirteenth Amendment.

Once again the president refused to go along, although his veto was sure to drive more moderates into the arms of the Radicals. On April 9, 1866, Congress repassed the Civil Rights Act by a two-thirds majority, the first time in American history that a major piece of legislation became law over the veto of a president. This event marked a revolution in the history of Reconstruction. Thereafter Congress, not President Johnson, had the upper hand.

In the clash between the president and Congress, Johnson was his own worst enemy. His language was often intemperate, his handling of opponents inept, his analysis of southern conditions incorrect. He had assumed that the small southern farmers who made up the majority in the Confederacy shared his prejudices against the planter class. They did not, as their choices in the postwar elections demonstrated.

●●●—Read the Document

Southern Skepticism of the Freedmen's Bureau at
myhistorylab.com

The president also misread northern opinion. He believed that Congress had no right to pass laws affecting the South before southern representatives had been readmitted to Congress. However, in the light of the refusal of most southern whites to grant any real power or responsibility to the freedmen (an attitude that Johnson did not condemn), the public would not accept this point of view. Johnson placed his own judgment over that of the overwhelming majority of northern voters, and this was a great error, morally and tactically. By encouraging white Southerners to resist efforts to improve the lot of blacks, Johnson played into the hands of the Radicals.

The Radicals encountered grave problems in fighting for their program. Northerners might object to the Black Codes and to seating "rebels" in Congress, but few believed in racial equality. Between 1865 and 1868, Wisconsin, Minnesota, Connecticut, Nebraska, New Jersey, Ohio, Michigan, and Pennsylvania all rejected bills granting blacks the vote.

The Radicals were in effect demanding not merely equal rights for freedmen but extra rights; not merely the vote but special protection of that right against the pressure that southern whites would surely apply to undermine it. This idea flew in the face of conventional American beliefs in equality before the law and individual self-reliance. Such protection would involve interference by the federal government in local affairs, a concept at variance with American practice. Events were to show that the Radicals were correct—that what amounted to a political revolution in state–federal relations was essential if blacks were to achieve real equality. But in the climate of that day their proposals encountered bitter resistance, and not only from white Southerners.

Thus, while the Radicals sought partisan advantage in their battle with Johnson and sometimes played on war-bred passions in achieving their ends, they were taking large political risks in defense of genuinely held principles.

The Fourteenth Amendment

In June 1866 Congress submitted to the states a new amendment to the Constitution. The **Fourteenth Amendment** was, in the context of the times, a truly radical measure. Never before had newly freed slaves been granted significant political rights. For example, in the British Caribbean sugar islands, where slavery had been abolished in the 1830s, stiff property qualifications and poll taxes kept freedmen from voting. The Fourteenth Amendment was also a milestone along the road to the centralization of political power in the United States because it reduced the power of all the states. In this sense it confirmed the great change wrought by the Civil War: the growth of a more complex, more closely integrated social and economic structure requiring closer national supervision. Few people understood this aspect of the amendment at the time.

●●●─Read the Document

13th, 14th, and 15th Amendments at **myhistorylab.com**

First the amendment supplied a broad definition of American citizenship: "All persons born or naturalized in the United States, and subject to the jurisdiction thereof, are citizens of the United States and of the State wherein they reside." Obviously this included blacks. Then it struck at discriminatory legislation like the Black Codes: "No State shall make or enforce any law which shall abridge the privileges or immunities of citizens of the United States; nor shall any State deprive any person of life, liberty, or property, without due process of law." The next section attempted to force the southern states to permit blacks to vote. If a state denied the vote to any class of its adult male citizens, its representation was to be reduced proportionately. Under another clause, former federal officials who had served the Confederacy were barred from holding either state or federal office unless specifically pardoned by a two-thirds vote of Congress. Finally, the Confederate debt was repudiated.

While the amendment did not specifically outlaw segregation or prevent a state from disenfranchising blacks, the southern states would have none of it. Without them the necessary three-fourths majority of the states could not be obtained.

President Johnson vowed to make the choice between the Fourteenth Amendment and his own policy the main issue of the 1866 congressional elections. He embarked on "a swing around the circle" to rally the public to his cause. He failed dismally. Northern women objected to the implication in the amendment that black men were more fitted to vote than white women, but a large majority of northern voters was determined that African Americans must have at least formal legal equality. The Republicans won better than two-thirds of the seats in both houses, together with control of all the northern state governments. Johnson emerged from the campaign discredited, the Radicals stronger and determined to have their way. The southern states, Congressman James A. Garfield of Ohio said in February 1867, have "flung back into our teeth the magnanimous offer of a generous nation. It is now our turn to act."

The Reconstruction Acts

Had the southern states been willing to accept the Fourteenth Amendment, coercive measures might have been avoided. Their recalcitrance and continuing indications that local authorities were persecuting blacks finally led to the passage, on March 2, 1867, of the First Reconstruction Act. This law divided the former Confederacy—exclusive of Tennessee, which had ratified the Fourteenth Amendment—into five military districts, each controlled by a major general. It gave these officers almost dictatorial power to protect the civil rights of "all persons," maintain order, and supervise the administration of justice. To rid themselves of military rule, the former states were required to adopt new state constitutions guaranteeing blacks the right to vote and disenfranchising broad classes of ex-Confederates. If the new constitutions proved satisfactory to Congress, and if the new governments ratified the Fourteenth Amendment, their representatives would be admitted to Congress and military rule ended. Johnson's veto of the act was easily overridden.

Although drastic, the Reconstruction Act was so vague that it proved unworkable. Military control was easily established. But in deference to moderate Republican views, the law had not spelled out the process by which the new

⊙ See the Map
Reconstruction at
myhistorylab.com

constitutions were to be drawn up. Southern whites preferred the status quo, even under army control, to enfranchising blacks and retiring their own respected leaders. They made no effort to follow the steps laid down in the law. Congress therefore passed a second act, requiring the military authorities to register voters and supervise the election of delegates to constitutional conventions. A third act further clarified procedures.

Still white Southerners resisted. The laws required that the constitutions be approved by a majority of the registered voters. Simply by staying away from the polls, whites prevented ratification in state after state. At last, in March 1868, a full year after the First Reconstruction Act, Congress changed the rules again. The constitutions were to be ratified by a majority of the voters. In June 1868 Arkansas, having fulfilled the requirements, was readmitted to the Union, and by July a sufficient number of states had ratified the Fourteenth Amendment to make it part of the Constitution. But it was not until July 1870 that the last southern state, Georgia, qualified to the satisfaction of Congress.

Congress Supreme

To carry out this program in the face of determined southern resistance required a degree of single-mindedness over a long period seldom demonstrated by an American legislature. The persistence resulted in part from the suffering and frustrations of the war years. The refusal of the South to accept the spirit of even the mild reconstruction designed by Johnson goaded the North to ever more overbearing efforts to bring the ex-Confederates to heel. President Johnson's stubbornness also influenced the Republicans. They became obsessed with the need to defeat him. The unsettled times and the large Republican majorities, always threatened by the possibility of a Democratic resurgence if "unreconstructed" southern congressmen were readmitted, sustained their determination.

These considerations led Republicans to attempt a kind of grand revision of the federal government, one that almost destroyed the balance between judicial, executive, and legislative power established in 1789. A series of measures passed between 1866 and 1868 increased the authority of Congress over the army, over the process of amending the Constitution, and over Cabinet members and lesser appointive officers. Even the Supreme Court was affected. Its size was reduced and its jurisdiction over civil rights cases limited. Finally, in a showdown caused by emotion more than by practical considerations, the Republicans attempted to remove President Johnson from office.

The chief issue was the Tenure of Office Act of 1867, which prohibited the president from removing officials who had been appointed with the consent of the Senate without first obtaining Senate approval. In February 1868 Johnson "violated" this act by dismissing Secretary of War Edwin M. Stanton, who had been openly in sympathy with the Radicals for some time. The House, acting under the procedure set up in the Constitution for removing the president, promptly impeached him before the bar of the Senate, Chief Justice Salmon P. Chase presiding.

In the trial, Johnson's lawyers easily established that he had removed Stanton only in an effort to prove the Tenure of Office Act unconstitutional. They demonstrated that the act did not protect Stanton to begin with, since it gave Cabinet members tenure "during the term of the President by whom they may have been appointed," and Stanton had been appointed in 1862, during Lincoln's first term!

Nevertheless the Radicals pressed the charges (eleven separate articles) relentlessly. Tremendous pressure was applied to the handful of Republican senators who were unwilling to disregard the evidence.

Seven of them resisted to the end, and the Senate failed by a single vote to convict Johnson. This was probably fortunate. The trial weakened the presidency, but if Johnson had been forced from office on such flimsy grounds, the independence of the executive might have been permanently undermined. Then the legislative branch would have become supreme.

The Fifteenth Amendment

The failure of the impeachment did not affect the course of Reconstruction. The president was acquitted on May 16, 1868. A few days later, the Republican National Convention nominated General Ulysses S. Grant for the presidency. At the Democratic convention Johnson had considerable support, but the delegates nominated Horatio Seymour, a former governor of New York. In November Grant won an easy victory in the Electoral College, 214 to 80, but the popular vote was close: 3 million to 2.7 million. Although he would probably have carried the Electoral College in any case, Grant's margin in the popular vote was supplied by southern blacks enfranchised under the Reconstruction acts, about 450,000 of whom supported him. A majority of white voters probably preferred Seymour. Since many citizens undoubtedly voted Republican because of personal admiration for General Grant, the election statistics suggest that a substantial white majority opposed the policies of the Radicals.

The Reconstruction acts and the ratification of the Fourteenth Amendment achieved the purpose of enabling black Southerners to vote. The Radicals, however, were

Thomas Waterman Wood, a Northerner, painted this hopeful interpretation of Reconstruction, *His First Vote* (1868).

not satisfied; despite the unpopularity of the idea in the North, they wished to guarantee the right of blacks to vote in every state. Another amendment seemed the only way to accomplish this objective, but passage of such an amendment appeared impossible. The Republican platform in the 1868 election had smugly distinguished between blacks voting in the South.

However, after the election had demonstrated how important the black vote could be, Republican strategy shifted. Grant had carried Indiana by fewer than 10,000 votes and lost New York by a similar number. If blacks in these and other closely divided states had voted, Republican strength would have been greatly enhanced.

Suddenly Congress blossomed with suffrage amendments. After considerable bickering over details, the **Fifteenth Amendment** was sent to the states for ratification in February 1869. It forbade all the states to deny the vote to anyone "on account of race, color, or previous condition of servitude." Once again nothing was said about denial of the vote on the basis of sex, which caused feminists, such as Elizabeth Cady Stanton, to be even more outraged than they had been by the Fourteenth Amendment.

Most southern states, still under federal pressure, ratified the amendment swiftly. The same was true in most of New England and in some western states. Bitter battles were waged in Connecticut, New York, Pennsylvania, and the states immediately north of the Ohio River, but by March 1870 most of them had ratified the amendment and it became part of the Constitution.

When the Fifteenth Amendment went into effect, President Grant called it "the greatest civil change and . . . the most important event that has occurred since the nation came to life." The American Anti-Slavery Society formally dissolved itself, its work apparently completed. "The Fifteenth Amendment confers upon the African race the care of its own destiny," Radical Congressman James A. Garfield wrote proudly after the amendment was ratified.

"Black Republican" Reconstruction: Scalawags and Carpetbaggers

The Radicals had at last succeeded in imposing their will on the South. Throughout the region former slaves had real political influence; they voted, held office, and exercised the "privileges" and enjoyed the "immunities" guaranteed them by the Fourteenth Amendment. Nearly all voted Republican.

The spectacle of blacks not five years removed from slavery in positions of power and responsibility attracted much attention. But the real rulers of the "black Republican" governments were white: the **scalawags**—Southerners willing to cooperate with the Republicans because they accepted the results of the war and wished to advance their own interests—and the **carpetbaggers**—Northerners who went to the South as idealists to help the freed slaves as employees of the federal government, or more commonly as settlers hoping to improve themselves.

Although scalawags were by far the more numerous, the carpetbaggers were a particularly varied lot. Most had mixed motives for coming south and personal gain was certainly among them. But so were opposition to slavery and the belief that blacks deserved to be treated decently and given a chance to get ahead in the world.

Many northern blacks became carpetbaggers: former Union soldiers, missionaries from northern black churches, and also teachers, lawyers, and other members of the small northern black professional class. Many of these became officeholders, but like southern black politicians their influence was limited.

That blacks should fail to dominate southern governments is certainly understandable. They lacked experience in politics and were mostly poor and uneducated. They were nearly everywhere a minority. Those blacks who held office during Reconstruction tended to be better educated and more prosperous than most southern blacks.

In South Carolina and elsewhere, blacks proved in the main to be able and conscientious public servants. Even at the local level, where the quality of officials was usually poor, there was little difference in the degree of competence displayed by white and black officeholders. In power, the blacks were not vindictive; by and large they did not seek to restrict the rights of ex-Confederates.

Not all black legislators and administrators were paragons of virtue. In South Carolina, despite their control of the legislature, they broke up into factions repeatedly and failed to press for laws that would improve the lot of poor black farm workers. Waste and corruption were common during Reconstruction governments. Half the budget of Louisiana in some years went for salaries and "mileage" for representatives and their staffs. A South Carolina legislator was voted an additional $1,000 in salary after he lost that sum betting on a horse race.

However, the corruption must be seen in perspective. The big thieves were nearly always white; blacks got mostly crumbs. Furthermore, graft and callous disregard of the public interest characterized government in every section and at every level during the decade after Appomattox. Big-city bosses in the North embezzled sums that dwarfed the most brazen southern frauds. The New York City Tweed Ring probably made off with more money than all the southern thieves, black and white, combined. While the

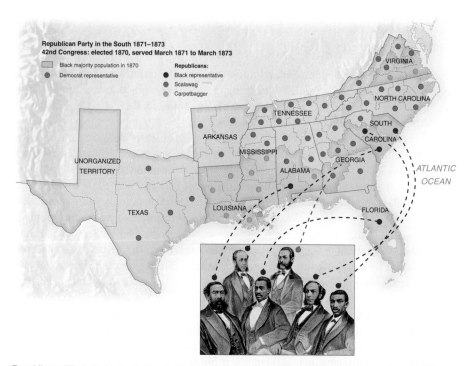

Republicans Win in Deep South The six black members of the House of Representatives in 1871 are from left to right: Benjamin Turner, Robert De Large, Josiah Wells, Jefferson Long, Joseph Rainey, Robert Brown Elliott. Each is linked to his district; the member in the blue coat—center—is not connected to a "black" dot. A special Republican primary replaced him with a scalawag.

evidence does not justify the southern corruption, it suggests that the unique features of Reconstruction politics—black suffrage, military supervision, and carpetbagger and scalawag influence—do not explain it.

In fact, the Radical southern governments accomplished a great deal. They spent money freely but not entirely wastefully. Tax rates zoomed, but the money financed the repair and expansion of the South's dilapidated railroad network, rebuilt crumbling levees, and expanded social services. Before the Civil War, southern planters possessed a disproportionate share of political as well as economic power, and they spent relatively little public money on education and public services of all kinds.

During Reconstruction an enormous gap had to be filled, and it took money to fill it. The Freedmen's Bureau made a major contribution. Northern religious and philanthropic organizations also did important work. Eventually, however, the state governments established and supported hospitals, asylums, and systems of free public education that, while segregated, greatly benefited everyone, whites as well as blacks. Much state money was also spent on economic development: land reclamation, repairing and expanding the war-ravaged railroads, maintaining levees.

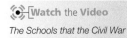

Watch the Video

The Schools that the Civil War & Reconstruction created at **myhistorylab.com**

The Ravaged Land

The South's grave economic problems complicated the rebuilding of its political system. The section had never been as prosperous as the North, and wartime destruction left it desperately poor by any standard. In the long run the abolition of slavery released immeasurable quantities of human energy previously stifled, but the immediate effect was to create confusion. Freedom to move without a pass, to "see the world," was one of the former slaves' most cherished benefits of emancipation. Understandably, many at first equated legal freedom with freedom from having to earn a living, a tendency reinforced for a time by the willingness of the Freedmen's Bureau to provide rations and other forms of relief in war-devastated areas. Most, however, soon accepted the fact that they must earn a living; a small plot of land of their own ("40 acres and a mule") would complete their independence.

This objective was forcefully supported by the relentless Congressman Thaddeus Stevens, whose hatred of the planter class was pathological. "The property of the chief rebels should be seized," he stated. If the lands of the richest "70,000 proud, bloated and defiant rebels" were confiscated, the federal government would obtain 394 million acres. Every adult male ex-slave could easily be supplied with 40 acres. The beauty of his scheme, Stevens insisted, was that "nine-tenths of the [southern] people would remain untouched." Dispossessing the great planters would make the South "a safe republic," its lands cultivated by "the free labor of intelligent citizens." If the plan drove the planters into exile, "all the better."

Although Stevens's figures were faulty, many Radicals agreed with him. "We must see that the freedmen are established on the soil," Senator Sumner declared. "The great plantations, which have been so many nurseries of the rebellion, must be broken up, and the freedmen must have the pieces." Stevens, Sumner, and others who wanted to give land to the freedmen weakened their case by associating it with the idea of punishing the former rebels; the average American had too much respect for property rights to support a policy of confiscation.

The former slaves had either to agree to work for their former owners or strike out on their own. White planters, influenced by the precipitous decline of sugar production in Jamaica and other Caribbean islands that had followed the abolition of slavery there, expected freed blacks to be incapable of self-directed effort. If allowed to become independent farmers, they would either starve to death or descend into barbarism. Of course the blacks did neither. True, the output of cotton and other southern staples declined precipitously after slavery was abolished. Observers soon came to the conclusion that a free black produced much less than a slave had produced. "You can't get only about two-thirds as much out of 'em now as you could when they were slaves," an Arkansas planter complained.

View the Image

Five Generations of a Slave Family at **myhistorylab.com**

However, the decline in productivity was not caused by the inability of free blacks to work independently. They simply chose no longer to work like slaves. They let their children play instead of forcing them into the fields. Mothers devoted more time to childcare and housework, less to farm labor. Elderly blacks worked less.

Noting these changes, white critics spoke scornfully of black laziness and shiftlessness. "You cannot make the negro work without physical compulsion," was the common view. Even General Oliver O. Howard, head of the Freedmen's Bureau, used the phrase "wholesome compulsion" in describing the policy of forcing blacks to sign exploitive labor contracts. Moreover, studies show that emancipated blacks earned almost 30 percent more than the value of the subsistence provided by their former masters.

Sharecropping and the Crop-Lien System

Before the passage of the Reconstruction acts, plantation owners tried to farm their land with gang labor, the same system as before, only now paying wages to the former slaves. But blacks did not like working for wages because it kept them under the direction of whites and thus reminded them of slavery. They wanted to be independent, to manage not merely their free time but their entire lives for themselves.

Quite swiftly, a new agricultural system known as **sharecropping** emerged. Instead of cultivating the land by gang labor as in antebellum times, planters broke up their estates into small units and established on each a black family. The

Read the Document

A Sharecrop Contract at **myhistorylab.com**

planter provided housing, agricultural implements, draft animals, seed, and other supplies, and the family provided labor. The crop was divided between them, usually on a fifty-fifty basis. If the landlord supplied only land and housing, the laborer got a larger share. This was called share tenancy.

Sharecropping gave blacks the day-to-day control of their lives that they craved and the hope of earning enough to buy a small farm. Many former slaves succeeded, as evidenced by the accounts narrated at the outset of this chapter. Oprah Winfrey's great-great-grandfather bought several plots of land and eventually moved a schoolhouse to his property so that black children in Sanford, Mississippi, could get an education. But not all managed to climb the first rungs into the middle class. As late as 1880 blacks owned less than 10 percent of the agricultural land in the South, although they made up more than half of the region's farm population.

Many white farmers in the South were also trapped by the sharecropping system and by white efforts to keep blacks in a subordinate position. New fencing laws kept them from grazing livestock on undeveloped land, a practice common before the Civil War. But the main cause of southern rural poverty for whites as well as for blacks was the lack of enough capital to finance the sharecropping system. Like their colonial ancestors, the landowners had to borrow against October's harvest to pay for April's seed. Thus the **crop-lien system** developed.

Under the crop-lien system, both landowner and sharecropper depended on credit supplied by local bankers, merchants, and storekeepers for everything from seed, tools, and fertilizer to overalls, coffee, and salt. Crossroads stores proliferated, and a new class of small merchants appeared. The prices of goods sold on credit were high, adding to the burden borne by the rural population. The small southern merchants were almost equally victimized by the system, for they also lacked capital, bought goods on credit, and had to pay high interest rates.

Seen in broad perspective, the situation is not difficult to understand. The South, drained of every resource by the war, was competing for funds with the North and West, both vigorous and expanding and therefore voracious consumers of capital. Reconstruction, in the literal sense of the word, was accomplished chiefly at the expense of the standard of living of the producing classes. The crop-lien system and the small

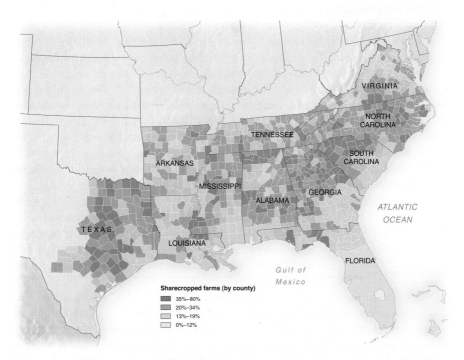

Sharecropped farms (by county)
- 35%–80%
- 20%–34%
- 13%–19%
- 0%–12%

Sharecropping, 1880 Sharecropping became especially common in areas outside of the cotton belt—eastern Texas, upland Alabama, and North Carolina.

storekeeper were only agents of an economic process dictated by national, perhaps even worldwide, conditions.

Compared with the rest of the country, progress was slow. Just before the Civil War cotton harvests averaged about 4 million bales. During the conflict, output fell to about half a million, and the former Confederate states did not enjoy a 4-million-bale year again until 1870. In contrast, national wheat production in 1859 was 175 million bushels and in 1878, 449 million. About 7,000 miles of railroad were built in the South between 1865 and 1879; in the rest of the nation nearly 45,000 miles of track were laid.

But in the late 1870s, cotton production revived. It soon regained, and thereafter long retained, its title as "king" of the southern economy. This was true in large measure because of the crop-lien system.

The White Backlash

Radical southern governments could sustain themselves only as long as they had the support of a significant proportion of the white population, for except in South Carolina and Louisiana, the blacks were not numerous enough to win elections alone. The key to survival lay in the hands of the wealthy merchants and planters, mostly former Whigs. People of this sort had nothing to fear from black economic competition. Taking a broad view, they could see that improving the lot of the former slaves would benefit all classes.

Southern white Republicans used the Union League of America, a patriotic club founded during the war, to control the black vote. Employing secret rituals, exotic symbols, and other paraphernalia calculated to impress unsophisticated people, they enrolled the freedmen in droves and marched them to the polls en masse.

Powerless to check the League by open methods, dissident Southerners established a number of secret terrorist societies, bearing such names as the **Ku Klux Klan**, the Knights of the White Camelia, and the Pale Faces. The most notorious of these organizations was the Klan, which originated in Tennessee in 1866. At first it was purely a social club, but by 1868 it had been taken over by vigilante types dedicated to driving blacks out of politics, and it was spreading rapidly across the South. Sheet-clad nightriders roamed the countryside, frightening the impressionable and chastising the defiant. Klansmen, using a weird mumbo jumbo and claiming to be the ghosts of Confederate soldiers, spread horrendous rumors and published broadsides designed to persuade the freedmen that it was unhealthy for them to participate in politics.

When intimidation failed, the Klansmen resorted to force. After being whipped by one group in Tennessee, a recently elected justice of the peace reported, "They said they had nothing particular against me . . . but they did not intend any nigger to hold office." In hundreds of cases the KKK murdered their opponents, often in the most gruesome manner.

●●─[Read the Document
Accounts from Victims of the Ku Klux Klan at
myhistorylab.com

Congress struck at the Klan with three **Force Acts** (1870–1871), which placed elections under federal jurisdiction and imposed fines and prison sentences on persons convicted of interfering with any citizen's exercise of the franchise. Troops were dispatched to areas where the Klan was strong, and by 1872 the federal authorities had arrested enough Klansmen to break up the organization.

Nevertheless the Klan contributed substantially to the destruction of Radical regimes in the South. Its depredations weakened the will of white Republicans (few of whom really believed in racial equality), and it intimidated many blacks. The fact that the army had to be called in to suppress it was a glaring illustration of the weakness of the Reconstruction governments.

Gradually it became respectable to intimidate black voters. Beginning in Mississippi in 1874, terrorism spread through the South. Instead of hiding behind masks and operating in the dark, these terrorists donned red shirts, organized into military companies, and paraded openly. Mississippi redshirts seized militant blacks and whipped them publicly. Killings were frequent. When blacks dared to fight back, heavily armed whites put them to rout. In other states similar results followed.

Before long the blacks learned to stay home on election day. One by one, "Conservative" parties—Democratic in national affairs—took over southern state governments. Intimidation was only a partial explanation of this development. The increasing solidarity of whites, northern and southern, was equally significant.

The North had subjected the South to control from Washington while preserving state sovereignty in the North itself. In the long run this discrimination proved unworkable. Many Northerners had supported the Radical policy only out of irritation with President Johnson. After his retirement their enthusiasm waned. The war was fading into the past and with it the worst of the anger it had generated.

Northern voters could still be stirred by references to the sacrifices Republicans had made to save the Union and by reminders that the Democratic party was the organization of rebels, Copperheads, and the Ku Klux Klan. "If the Devil himself were at the helm of the ship of state," wrote the novelist Lydia Maria Child in 1872, "my conscience would not allow me to aid in removing him to make room for the Democratic party." Yet emotional appeals could not convince Northerners that it was still necessary to maintain a large army in the South. In 1869 the occupying forces were down to 11,000 men. After Klan disruption and intimidation had made a farce of the 1874 elections in Mississippi, Governor Ames appealed to Washington for help. President Grant's attorney general, Edwards Pierrepont, refused to act. "The whole public are tired out with these autumnal outbreaks in the South," he told Ames. "Preserve the peace by the forces of your own state."

Nationalism was reasserting itself. Had not Washington and Jefferson been Virginians? Was not Andrew Jackson Carolina-born? Since most Northerners had little real love or respect for African Americans, their interest in racial equality flagged once they felt reasonably certain that blacks would not be re-enslaved if left to their own devices in the South.

Another, much subtler force was also at work. The prewar Republican party had stressed the common interest of workers, manufacturers, and farmers in a free and mobile society, a land of equal opportunity where all could work in harmony. Southern whites had insisted that laborers must be disciplined if large enterprises were to be run efficiently. By the 1870s, as large industrial enterprises developed in the northern states, the thinking of business leaders changed—the southern argument began to make sense to them, and they became more sympathetic to the southern demand for more control over "their" labor force.

An 1872 Grant campaign poster of "Our Three Great Presidents" at best got it about two-thirds right.

Grant as President

Other matters occupied the attention of northern voters. The expansion of industry and the rapid development of the West, stimulated by a new wave of railroad building, loomed more important to many than the fortunes of the former slaves. Beginning in 1873, when a stock market panic struck at public confidence, economic difficulties plagued the country and provoked another debate over the tariff.

Grant's most serious weakness as president was his failure to deal effectively with economic and social problems, what injured him and the Republicans most was his inability to cope with government corruption. The worst of the scandals did not become public knowledge during Grant's first term. However, in 1872 Republican reformers, alarmed by rumors of corruption and disappointed by Grant's failure to press for civil service reform, organized the Liberal Republican party and nominated Horace Greeley, the able but eccentric editor of the *New York Tribune*, for president.

The Liberal Republicans were mostly well-educated, socially prominent types— editors, college presidents, economists, along with a sprinkling of businessmen and politicians. Their liberalism was of the laissez-faire variety; they were for low tariffs and sound money, and against what they called "class legislation," meaning measures benefiting particular groups, whether labor unions or railroad companies or farm organizations. Nearly all had supported Reconstruction at the start, but by the early 1870s most were including southern blacks among the special interests that ought to be left to their own devices. Their observation of urban corruption and of unrestricted immigration led them to disparage universal suffrage, which, one of them said, "can only mean in plain English the government of ignorance and vice."

The Democrats also nominated Greeley in 1872, although he had devoted his political life to flailing the Democratic party in the *Tribune*. That surrender to expediency, together with Greeley's temperamental unsuitability for the presidency, made the campaign a fiasco for the reformers. Grant triumphed easily, with a popular majority of nearly 800,000.

Nevertheless, the defection of the Liberal Republicans hurt the Republican party in Congress. In the 1874 elections, no longer hampered as in the presidential contest by Greeley's notoriety and Grant's fame, the Democrats carried the House of Representatives. It was clear that the days of military rule in the South were ending. By the end of 1875 only three southern states—South Carolina, Florida, and Louisiana—were still under Republican control.

The Republican party in the South was "dead as a doornail," a reporter noted. He reflected the opinion of thousands when he added, "We ought to have a sound sensible republican . . . for the next President as a measure of safety; but only on the condition of absolute noninterference in Southern local affairs, for which there is no further need or excuse."

The Disputed Election of 1876

Against this background the presidential election of 1876 took place. Since corruption in government was the most widely discussed issue, the Republicans passed over their most attractive political personality, the dynamic James G. Blaine, Speaker of the House of Representatives, who had been connected with some chicanery involving railroad securities. Instead they nominated Governor Rutherford B. Hayes of Ohio, a former general with an untarnished reputation. The Democrats picked Governor Samuel J. Tilden of New York, a wealthy lawyer who had attracted national attention for his part in breaking up the Tweed Ring in New York City.

In November early returns indicated that Tilden had carried New York, New Jersey, Connecticut, Indiana, and all the southern states, including Louisiana, South Carolina, and Florida, where Republican regimes were still in control. This seemed to give him 203 electoral votes to Hayes's 165, and a popular plurality in the neighborhood of 250,000 out of more than 8 million votes cast. However, Republican leaders had anticipated the possible loss of Florida, South Carolina, and Louisiana and were prepared to use their control of the election machinery in those states to throw out sufficient Democratic ballots to alter the results if doing so would change the national outcome. Realizing that the electoral votes of those states were exactly enough to elect their man, they telegraphed their henchmen on the scene, ordering them to go into action. The local Republicans then invalidated Democratic ballots in wholesale lots and filed returns showing Hayes the winner. Naturally the local Democrats protested vigorously and filed their own returns.

The Constitution provides (Article II, Section 1) that presidential electors must meet in their respective states to vote and forward the results to "the Seat of the Government." There, it adds, "the President of the Senate shall, in the Presence of the Senate and House of Representatives, open all the Certificates, and the Votes shall then be counted." But who was to do the counting? The House was Democratic, the Senate Republican; neither would agree to allow the other to do the job. On January 29, 1877, scarcely a month before inauguration day, Congress created an electoral commission to decide the disputed cases. The commission consisted of five senators (three Republicans and two Democrats), five representatives (three Democrats and two Republicans), and five justices of the Supreme Court (two Democrats, two Republicans, and one "independent" judge, David Davis).

Since it was a foregone conclusion that the others would vote for their party no matter what the evidence, Davis would presumably swing the balance in the interest of fairness.

But before the commission met, the Illinois legislature elected Davis senator. He had to resign from the Court and the commission. Since independents were rare even on the Supreme Court, no neutral justice was available to replace him. The vacancy went to Associate Justice Joseph P. Bradley of New Jersey, a Republican.

Evidence presented before the commission revealed a disgraceful picture of corruption. On the one hand, in all three disputed states Democrats had clearly cast a majority of the votes; on the other, it was unquestionable that many blacks had been forcibly prevented from voting.

In truth, both sides were shamefully corrupt. The governor of Louisiana was reported

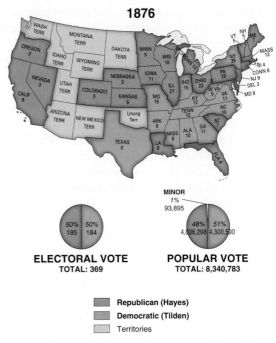

1876

ELECTORAL VOTE
TOTAL: 369

50% 185 | 50% 184

POPULAR VOTE
TOTAL: 8,340,783

48% 4,036,298 | 51% 4,300,590

MINOR 1% 93,895

- Republican (Hayes)
- Democratic (Tilden)
- Territories

The Republicans Gain the Presidency, the White South Loses the Union Army, 1877 By 1876 white Democrats had regained political control in much of the South, giving Tilden 203 electoral votes to the Republican Hayes's 185. But Republican election officials in South Carolina, Florida, and Louisiana invalidated thousands of Democratic votes, which seemingly gave the election to Tilden. In 1877 a congressional commission finalized a deal giving the presidency to Hayes, who would withdraw the Union army from the South.

willing to sell his state's electoral votes for $200,000. The Florida election board was supposed to have offered itself to Tilden for the same price. "That seems to be the standard figure," Tilden remarked ruefully.

The Democrats had some hopes that Justice Bradley would be sympathetic to their case, for he was known to be opposed to harsh Reconstruction policies. On the eve of the commission's decision in the Florida controversy, he was apparently ready to vote in favor of Tilden. But the Republicans subjected him to tremendous political pressure. When he read his opinion on February 8, it was for Hayes. Thus, by a vote of eight to seven, the commission awarded Florida's electoral votes to the Republicans.

Grant, a Republican and a Union war hero, won easily in 1868 and 1872 because ex-Confederates, many of whom had voted Democratic, were barred from the polls. By 1876, however, white Democrats had regained political control in much of the South, creating the electoral stalemate that led to the Compromise of 1877.

The rest of the proceedings was routine. The commission assigned all the disputed electoral votes (including one in Oregon where the Democratic governor had seized on a technicality to replace a single Republican elector with a Democrat) to Hayes.

Democratic institutions, shaken by the South's refusal to go along with the majority in 1860 and by the suppression of civil rights during the rebellion, and further weakened by military intervention and the intimidation of blacks in the South during Reconstruction, seemed now a farce. According to Tilden's campaign manager, angry Democrats in fifteen states, chiefly war veterans, were readying themselves to march on Washington to force the inauguration of Tilden. Tempers flared in Congress, where some spoke ominously of a filibuster that would prevent the recording of the electoral vote and leave the country, on March 4, with no president at all.

The Compromise of 1877

Forces for compromise had been at work behind the scenes in Washington for some time. Although northern Democrats threatened to fight to the last ditch, many southern Democrats were willing to accept Hayes if he would promise to remove the troops and allow the southern states to manage their internal affairs by themselves. Ex-Whig planters and merchants who had reluctantly abandoned the carpetbag governments and who sympathized with Republican economic policies hoped that by supporting Hayes they might contribute to the restoration of the two-party system that had been destroyed in the South during the 1850s.

Tradition has it that a great compromise between the sections was worked out during a dramatic meeting at the Wormley Hotel[2] in Washington on February 26. Actually the negotiations were drawn out and informal, and the Wormley conference was but one of many. With the tacit support of many Democrats, the electoral vote was counted by the president of the Senate on March 2, and Hayes was declared elected, 185 votes to 184.

Like all compromises, the **Compromise of 1877** was not entirely satisfactory; like most, it was not honored in every detail. Hayes recalled the last troops from South Carolina and Louisiana in April. He appointed a former Confederate general, David M. Key of Tennessee, postmaster general and delegated to him the congenial task of finding Southerners willing to serve their country as officials of a Republican administration. But the alliance of ex-Whigs and northern Republicans did not flourish; the South remained solidly Democratic. The major significance of the compromise, one of the great intersectional political accommodations of American history, was that it ended Reconstruction and inaugurated a new political order in the South. More than the Constitutional amendments and federal statutes, this new regime would shape the destinies of the four million freedmen.

For many former slaves, this future was to be bleak. Forgotten in the North, manipulated and then callously rejected by the South, rebuffed by the Supreme Court, voiceless in national affairs, they and their descendants were condemned in the interests of sectional harmony to lives of poverty, indignity, and little hope. But many other former slaves managed to thrive during the last third of the nineteenth century. Their hard work, discipline, and financial savvy elevated them into a property-owning middle class whose existence—more than Union armies—marked the end of slavery.

Watch the Video

The Promise and Failure of Reconstruction at
myhistorylab.com

---

[2]Ironically, the hotel was owned by James Wormley, reputedly the wealthiest black person in Washington.

Table 15.1 Two Phases of Reconstruction: 1863–1877

Phase	Measure	Consequence
1. Presidential Reconstruction: Accommodation with white South		
	Lincoln's Ten-Percent Plan (1863)	Re-admits Southern states when 10 percent of 1860 voters profess loyalty to Union
	Lincoln vetoes Wade-Davis Bill (1864)	Retains 10 percent "easy-admission" policy
	Andrew Johnson pardons many Confederates and recommends admission of all former Confederate states	By 1866, all southern states are readmitted
	Southern states pass Black Codes (1864–1865) sharply restricting rights of former slaves	Outrages Republicans
2. Radical Reconstruction: Republicans gain power in Congress		
	Thirteenth Amendment (1865)	Ends Slavery
	Freedmen's Bureau (1865) established as branch of war department	Promotes education and economic opportunities for former slaves and destitute whites
	Congress passes Civil Rights Act over Johnson's veto (1866)	Republicans in Congress dominate federal government Washington
	Reconstruction Act of 1867	Divides South into five military districts, each under command of Union general
	Tenure of Office Act (1867)	Prohibits president from removing high officials
	Johnson impeached for firing Secretary of State Stanton	Johnson is tried but not removed from office

Table 15.1   Two Phases of Reconstruction: 1863–1877 (Continued)

	Fourteenth Amendment (passed 1866, ratified 1868)	Requires that all citizens have "equal protection" of laws
	Republican Grant elected president (1868)	Further increases Republican domination
	Fifteenth Amendment (passed 1869, ratified 1870)	Prohibits voting restrictions on basis of race
	Force Acts (1870-1871)	Federal control of elections in South

Milestones

1863	Lincoln announces "Ten Percent Plan" for Reconstruction
1865	Federal government sets up Freedmen's Bureau to ease transition from slavery to freedom
	General Lee surrenders at Appomattox Court House
	Abraham Lincoln is assassinated
	Andrew Johnson becomes president
	Johnson issues amnesty proclamation
	States ratify Thirteenth Amendment abolishing slavery
1865–1866	Southern states enact Black Codes
1866	Civil Rights Act passes over Johnson's veto
	Johnson campaigns for his Reconstruction policy
1867	First Reconstruction Act puts former Confederacy under military rule
	Tenure of Office Act protects Senate appointees
1868	House of Representatives impeaches Johnson

1868	Fourth Reconstruction Act requires a majority of Southern voters to ratify state constitutions
	Senate acquits Johnson
	States ratify Fourteenth Amendment extending rights to freed slaves
	Ulysses S. Grant is elected president
	Ku Klux Klan uses intimidation and force throughout South
1870	States ratify Fifteenth Amendment granting black suffrage
1870–1871	Force Act destroys Ku Klux Klan
1872	Liberal Republican party nominates Horace Greeley for president
	Grant is reelected president
1876	Rutherford B. Hayes runs against Samuel Tilden in disputed presidential election
1877	Electoral Commission awards disputed votes to Rutherford B. Hayes who becomes president
	Hayes agrees to Compromise of 1877 ending Reconstruction

✓•⌐Study and **Review** at **www.myhistorylab.com**

Review Questions

1. The introduction to this chapter—which cites the success of some randomly-chosen figures during Reconstruction—can be easily dismissed: Extraordinary people can prevail against any odds. What gains did most former slaves achieve during Reconstruction? Which federal policies and actions promoted their prospects?

2. What strategies did white Southerners use to control slaves after the Thirteenth Amendment had ended slavery?

3. Why did the Republicans in Congress disagree with Lincoln? With Andrew Johnson? In what sense did the Republican Congress come to "dominate" the political process?

4. What were the economic consequences of Reconstruction?

5. How did Reconstruction come to an end?

Key Terms

Black Codes   *409*
carpetbaggers   *419*
Compromise
   of 1877   *429*
crop-lien system   *423*
Fifteenth
   Amendment   *419*
Force Acts   *424*

Fourteenth
   Amendment   *415*
Freedmen's
   Bureau   *414*
Ku Klux Klan   *424*
Radical
   Republicans   *412*
scalawags   *419*

sharecropping   *422*
Ten Percent Plan   *411*
Thirteenth
   Amendment   *413*
Wade-Davis Bill   *412*

((•─[Hear the Audio Chapter 16 at myhistorylab.com

Do you live on land stolen from Indians?

IN 2010 THE CENSUS BUREAU REPORTED THAT BUFFALO COUNTY, South Dakota was the poorest in the nation, with well over half its residents below the poverty level. Buffalo County contains the Crow Creek Indian reservation. Six of the other ten poorest counties in the nation also consist of Indian reservations. Nationwide, nearly a quarter of all Indians live in poverty, twice the national average.

In 1988 Congress proposed to alleviate the plight of Native Americans with the Indian Gaming Regulatory Act. It allowed tribes to own casinos and other gambling operations. Within two decades, over 200 tribes had built 360 casinos and gaming establishments. By 2009, annual revenue from Indian casinos exceeded $25 billion, twice as much as the combined income of the National Football League (NFL) and Major League Baseball.

But little of the casino revenue has flowed to the poorest reservations. Foxwoods in Connecticut, the largest casino in the United States, generates about $1 billion annually, a windfall for the tiny Mashantucket Pequot tribe. But the Little Big Horn Casino, located in southeastern Montana near the battlefield where Custer lost his scalp, yielded a profit of only $100 a month during its first year of operation. Half of all reservation Indians live in Montana, Nevada, North and South Dakota, and Oklahoma, far from potential throngs of gamblers; those Indians remain mired in poverty.

Events that transformed the West after 1865 determined the plight of most Indians today. Ranchers and farmers acquired more Indian land. Railroad construction destabilized the habitat that sustained Indian life, especially the grazing lands of the buffalo, and brought still more settlers. The discovery of new deposits of gold, silver, and other valuable minerals caused miners and prospectors to swarm over and onto Indian lands. The federal government pushed Indians onto reservations, often on land unsuitable for cultivation, and sent troops to harass those who refused to abandon nomadic life. The new civilization that emerged in the West was increasingly controlled and organized by large-scale business enterprises.

By the turn of the twentieth century, the economic foundations of tribal life had been destroyed; relief, when it finally arrived many decades later, came in the form of slot machines. That so many Native Americans overcame the legacy of this past is testimony to their own initiative, and to traditional cultures characterized by both perseverance and adaptation.

The West after the Civil War

Although the image of the West as the land of great open spaces is accurate enough, after the Civil War the region contained several bustling cities. San Francisco, with a population approaching 250,000 in the late 1870s, had long outgrown its role as a rickety boomtown where the forty-niners bought supplies and squandered whatever wealth they had sifted from the streams of the Sierras. Though still an important warehouse and supply center, it had become the commercial and financial heart of the Pacific Coast and a center of light manufacturing, food processing, and machine shops. Denver, San Antonio, and Salt Lake City were far smaller, but growing rapidly and equally "urban."

Beginning in the mid-1850s a steady flow of Chinese migrated to the United States, most of them to the West Coast. About four or five thousand a year came, until the negotiation of the Burlingame Treaty of 1868, the purpose of which was to provide cheap labor for railroad construction crews. Thereafter the annual influx more than doubled, although before 1882 it exceeded 20,000 only twice. When the railroads were completed and the Chinese began to compete with native workers, a great cry of resentment went up on the west coast. Riots broke out in San Francisco in 1877. Chinese workers were called "groveling worms," "more slavish and brutish than the beasts that roam the fields." The California constitution of 1879 denied the right to vote to any "native of China" along with idiots, the insane, and persons convicted of "any infamous crime."

When Chinese immigration increased in 1882 to nearly 40,000, the protests reached such a peak that Congress passed the **Chinese Exclusion Act**, prohibiting all Chinese immigration for ten years. Later legislation extended the ban indefinitely.

Nevertheless, many parts of the West had as large a percentage of foreign-born residents as the populous eastern states—nearly a third of all Californians were foreign-born, as were more than 40 percent of Nevadans and more than half the residents of Idaho and Arizona. There were, of course, large populations of Spanish-speaking Americans of Mexican origin all over the Southwest. Chinese and Irish laborers were pouring into California by the thousands, and there were substantial numbers of Germans in Texas. Germans, Scandinavians, and other Europeans were also numerous on the High Plains east of the Rockies.

The Plains Indians

For 250 years the Indians had been driven back steadily, yet on the eve of the Civil War they still inhabited roughly half the United States. By the time of Hayes's inauguration, however, the Indians had been shattered as independent peoples, and in another decade the survivors were penned up on reservations, the government committed to a policy of extinguishing their way of life.

In 1860 the survivors of most of the eastern tribes were living peacefully in Indian Territory, what is now Oklahoma. In California the forty-niners had made short work of many of the local tribes. Elsewhere in the West—in the deserts of the Great Basin between the Sierras and the Rockies, in the mountains themselves, and on the semiarid, grass-covered plains between the Rockies and the edge of white civilization in eastern Kansas and Nebraska—nearly a quarter of a million Indians dominated the land.

In Charles Russell's
Trail of the Iron Horse
(1910) the steel rails
stretch nearly to the
sun, while wispy
brushstrokes depict
the Indians almost
as ghosts.

By far the most important lived on the High Plains. From the Blackfoot of southwestern Canada and the Sioux of Minnesota and the Dakotas to the Cheyenne of Colorado and Wyoming and the Comanche of northern Texas, the plains tribes possessed a generally uniform culture. All lived by hunting the hulking American bison, or buffalo, which ranged over the plains by the millions.

Although they seemed the epitome of freedom, pride, and self-reliance, the Plains Indians had begun to fall under the sway of white power. They eagerly adopted the products of the more technically advanced culture—cloth, metal tools, weapons, and cheap decorations. However, the most important thing the whites gave them had nothing to do with technology: It was the horse.

Horses thrived on the plains and so did their masters. Mounted Indians could run down buffalo instead of stalking them on foot. They could move more easily over the country and fight more effectively too. They could acquire and transport more possessions and increase the size of their tepees, for horses could drag heavy loads.

The Indians also adopted modern weapons: the cavalry sword, which they particularly admired, and the rifle. Both added to their effectiveness as hunters and fighters. However, like the whites' liquor and diseases, horses and guns caused problems. The buffalo herds began to diminish, and warfare became bloodier and more frequent.

After the start of the gold rush the need to link the East with California meant that the tribes were pushed aside. Deliberately the government in Washington prepared the way. In 1851 Thomas Fitzpatrick—an experienced mountain man, a founder of the Rocky Mountain Fur Company, scout for the first large group of settlers to Oregon in 1841 and for American soldiers in California during the Mexican War, and now an Indian agent—summoned a great "council" of the tribes. About 10,000 Indians, representing nearly all the plains tribes, gathered that September at Horse Creek, thirty-seven miles east of Fort Laramie, in what is now Wyoming.

In the Fort Laramie Treaty of 1851, Fitzpatrick persuaded each tribe to accept definite limits to its hunting grounds. In return the Indians were promised gifts and annual payments. This policy, known as "concentration," was designed to cut down on intertribal warfare and—far more important—to enable the government to negotiate separately with each tribe. It was the classic strategy of divide and conquer.

Although it made a mockery of diplomacy to treat Indian tribes as though they were European powers, the United States maintained that each tribe was a sovereign nation, to be dealt with as an equal in solemn treaties. Both sides knew that this was not the case. When Indians agreed to meet in council, they were tacitly admitting defeat. They seldom drove hard bargains or broke off negotiations. Moreover, tribal chiefs had only limited power; young braves frequently refused to respect agreements made by their elders.

Indian Wars

The government showed little interest in honoring agreements with Indians. No sooner had the Kansas-Nebraska bill become law than the Kansas, Omaha, Pawnee, and Yankton Sioux tribes began to feel pressure for further concessions of territory. A gold rush into Colorado in 1859 sent thousands of greedy prospectors across the plains to drive the Cheyenne and Arapaho from land guaranteed them in 1851. By 1860 most of Kansas and Nebraska had been cleared. Thus it happened that in 1862, after federal troops had been pulled out of the West for service against the Confederacy, most of the Plains Indians rose up against the whites. For five years intermittent but bloody clashes kept the entire area in a state of alarm.

This was guerrilla warfare, with all its horror and treachery. In 1864 a party of Colorado militia under the command of Colonel J. M. Chivington fell on an unsuspecting Cheyenne community at Sand Creek and killed several hundred Indians. General Nelson A. Miles called this "Chivington massacre" the "foulest and most unjustifiable crime in the annals of America."

Robert Lindneux's *The Battle of Sand Creek*, 1864. Lindneux, born in 1871, did not witness what transpired at Sand Creek, Colorado. But although he used "battle" in the title of his painting, he depicted a massacre. "Kill and scalp all, big and little," Colonel J. M. Chivington, a minister in private life, told his men. The American flag (center right) was doubtless included as irony.

In turn the Indians slaughtered dozens of isolated white families, ambushed small parties, and fought many successful skirmishes against troops and militia. They achieved their most notable triumph in December 1866, when the Oglala

•••⌐Read the Document
Red Cloud's Speech at
myhistorylab.com

Sioux, under their great chief Red Cloud, wiped out a party of eighty-two soldiers under Captain W. J. Fetterman. Red Cloud fought ruthlessly, but only when goaded by the construction of the Bozeman Trail, a road through the heart of the Sioux hunting grounds in southern Montana.[1]

In 1867 the government tried a new strategy. The "concentration" policy had evidently not gone far enough. All the Plains Indians would be confined to two small reservations, one in the Black Hills of the Dakota Territory, the other in Oklahoma, and forced to become farmers. At two great conclaves held in 1867 and 1868 at Medicine Lodge Creek and Fort Laramie, the principal chiefs yielded to the government's demands and signed the 1868 Treaty of Fort Laramie.

Many Indians refused to abide by these agreements. With their whole way of life at stake, they raged across the plains like a prairie fire—and were almost as destructive.

That a relative handful of "savages," without central leadership, could hold off the cream of the army, battle-hardened in the Civil War, can be explained by the fact that the U.S. Army, usually with fewer than 20,000 soldiers, had to operate over a million square miles. Few Indian leaders were capable of organizing a campaign or following up an advantage. But the Indians made superb guerrillas. Every observer called them the best cavalry soldiers in the world. Armed with stubby, powerful bows capable of driving an arrow clear through a bull buffalo, they were a fair match for troops equipped with carbines and Colt revolvers.

If one concedes that no one could reverse the direction of history or stop the invasion of Indian lands, then some version of the "small reservation" policy would probably have been best for the Indians. Had they been guaranteed a reasonable amount of land and adequate subsidies and allowed to maintain their way of life, they might have accepted the situation and ceased to harass the whites.

Whatever chance that policy had was weakened by the government's poor administration of Indian affairs. In dealing with Indians, nineteenth-century Americans displayed a grave insensitivity. After 1849 the Department of the Interior supposedly had charge of tribal affairs. Most of its agents systematically cheated the Indians. "No branch of the national government is so spotted with fraud, so tainted with corruption . . . as this Indian Bureau," Congressman Garfield charged in 1869.

At about this time a Yale paleontologist, Othniel C. Marsh, who wished to dig for fossils on the Sioux reservation, asked Red Cloud for permission to enter his domain. The chief agreed on condition that Marsh, whom the Indians called Big Bone Chief, take back with him samples of the moldy flour and beef that government agents were supplying to his people. Appalled by what he saw on the reservation, Professor Marsh took the rotten supplies directly to President Grant and prepared a list of charges against the agents.

In 1874 gold was discovered in the Black Hills Indian reservation. By the next winter thousands of miners had invaded the reserved area. Already alarmed by the

---

[1]Fetterman had boasted that with eighty cavalrymen he could ride the entire length of the Bozeman Trail. When he tried, however, he blundered into an ambush.

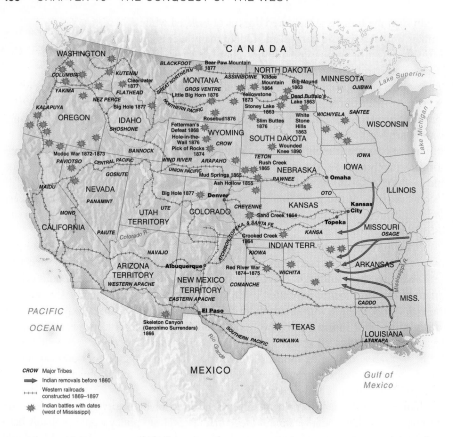

Indian Wars, 1860–1890 The frequent battles, involving nearly all tribes, show that the Indians did not cede their lands: The lands were taken in battle.

approach of crews building the Northern Pacific Railroad, the Sioux once again went on the warpath. Joining with nontreaty tribes to the west, they concentrated in the region of the Bighorn River, in southern Montana Territory.

The summer of 1876 saw three columns of troops in the field against them. The commander of one column, General Alfred H. Terry, sent ahead a small detachment of the Seventh Cavalry under Colonel George A. Custer with orders to locate the Indians' camp and then block their escape route into the inaccessible Bighorn Mountains. Grossly underestimating the number of the Indians, Custer decided to attack directly with his tiny force of 264 men. At the Little Bighorn late in June he found himself surrounded by 2,500 Sioux under Rain-in-the-Face, Crazy Horse, and Sitting Bull. He and all his men died on the field.

Because it was so one-sided, "Custer's Last Stand" was not a typical battle, although it may be taken as symbolic of the Indian warfare of the period in the sense that it was characterized by bravery, foolhardiness, and a tragic waste of life. The battle greatly heartened the Indians, but it did not gain them their cause. That autumn, short of rations and hard-pressed by overwhelming numbers of soldiers, they surrendered and returned to the reservation.

The Destruction of Tribal Life

Thereafter, the fighting slackened. For this the building of transcontinental railroads and the destruction of the buffalo were chiefly responsible. Thousands of buffalo were butchered to feed the gangs of laborers engaged in building the Union Pacific Railroad. Thousands more fell before the guns of sportsmen. Buffalo hunting became a fad, and a brisk demand developed for buffalo rugs and mounted buffalo heads. Railroads made the Army a far more efficient force. Troops and supplies could be moved swiftly when trouble with the tribes erupted. The lines also contributed to the decimation of the buffalo by running excursion trains for hunters.

The discovery in 1871 of a way to make commercial use of buffalo hides completed the tragedy. In the next three years about 9 million head were killed; after another decade the animals were almost extinct. No more efficient way could have been found for destroying the Plains Indians. The disappearance of the bison left them starving and homeless.

By the 1880s, the advance of whites into the plains had become, in the words of one congressman, as irresistible "as that of Sherman's to the sea." Greed for land lay behind the pressure, but large numbers of disinterested people, including most of those who deplored the way the Indians had been treated in the past, believed that the only practical way to solve the "Indian problem" was to persuade the Indians to abandon their tribal culture and live on family farms. The "wild" Indian must be changed into a "civilized" member of "American" society.

To accomplish this goal Congress passed the **Dawes Severalty Act of 1887**. Tribal lands were to be split up into individual allotments. To keep speculators from wresting the allotments from the Indians while they were adjusting to their new way of life, the land could not be disposed of for twenty-five years. Funds were to be appropriated for educating and training the Indians, and those who accepted allotments—took up residence "separate from any tribe," and "adopted the habits of civilized life"— were to be granted U.S. citizenship.

•••⊣Read the Document

Secretary of the Interior's Report on Indian Affairs at **myhistorylab.com**

A mound of buffalo skulls. In 1870 an estimated 30 million buffalo roamed the plains; by 1900, there were fewer than 1,000. During an eight-month period between 1867 and 1868, William F. Cody (Buffalo Bill) killed 4,280 buffalo, which fed construction crews for the Union Pacific railroad. Tourists also took up buffalo hunting, often shooting them from trains. The depletion of the buffalo, which provided the Plains Indians with meat and hides, was a major source of conflict with whites.

The sponsors of the Severalty Act thought they were effecting a fine humanitarian reform. "We must throw some protection over [the Indian]," Senator Henry L. Dawes declared. "We must hold up his hand." But no one expected all the Indians to accept allotments at once, and for some years little pressure was put on any to do so.

The Dawes Act had disastrous results in the long run. It assumed that Indians could be transformed into small agricultural capitalists by an act of Congress. It shattered what was left of the Indians' culture without enabling them to adapt to white ways. Moreover, unscrupulous white men tricked many Indians into leasing their allotments for a pittance, and local authorities often taxed Indian lands at excessive rates. In 1934, the government returned to a policy of encouraging tribal ownership of Indian lands.

The story of U.S.–Indian relations in the nineteenth century concludes, predictably, with a sad coda. In 1890 the Teton Sioux, suffering from cold and hunger, took heart from the words of Wovoka, a prophet, who had said that the whites would disappear if the Sioux performed their "ghost dance" rituals. When the Ghost Dance movement spread, federal military authorities resolved to stamp it out. On December 14 they attempted to arrest Chief Sitting Bull, a legendary Sioux warrior. When he resisted, shots rang out and Sitting Bull was killed. His people left the reservation at Pine Ridge and fled into the Badlands. The soldiers pursued them and the Indians surrendered. As they were

Table 16.1 Key Federal Policies Affecting Indians

Policy	Year	Provisions	Consequences
Indian Removal Bill	1830	Indians surrender land east of Mississippi to settle in Oklahoma and elsewhere	Forcible removal of Indians from South
Treaty of Fort Laramie	1851	Indian tribes establish tribal boundaries over shared hunting grounds and ensure safe passage of westward-bound settlers through Indian territory	Discourages concerted action among Indian tribes; settlers encroach on Indian lands
Railroad land grants	1850–1871	Gives railroads lands to lay track throughout the West	Promotes settlement and further encroachment; hastens demise of buffalo
Treaty of Fort Laramie	1868	Concentrates Indians in reservations in the Dakotas and Oklahoma	Dissident Indians commence open warfare against U.S. government
Dawes Severalty Act	1887	Breaks Indian lands into small plots for Indian families or sale to whites	Weakens tribal authority; causes loss of Indian land
Indian Reorganization Act	1934	Rescinds Dawes	Increases tribal authority
Indian Gaming Regulatory Act	1988	Allows tribes to run federally regulated casinos and gambling operations	Generates huge revenue for a handful of eastern tribes, and little for the rest

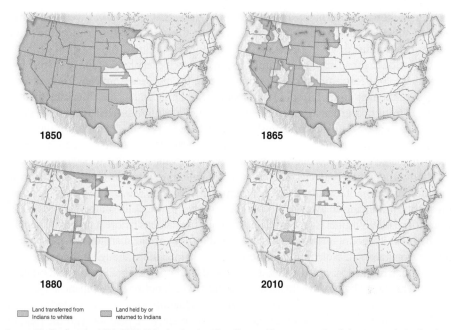

Loss of Indian Lands, 1850–2010 This chapter describes the specific government policies, economic tendencies, and specific treaties that wrested land from the Indians. But the simplest explanation is that an aggressive, acquisitive, and militarily powerful people craved the West and they took it.

being disarmed, however, a scuffle broke out and the troops opened fire. Some 150 Sioux were killed, including many women and children. Thirty federal soldiers also died during the fighting at Wounded Knee.

The Lure of Gold and Silver in the West

The natural resources of the nation were exploited in these decades even more ruthlessly and thoughtlessly than were its human resources. From the mid-1850s to the mid-1870s thousands of gold-crazed prospectors fanned out through the Rockies, panning every stream and hacking furiously at every likely outcropping from the Fraser River country of British Columbia to Tucson in southern Arizona, from the eastern slopes of the Sierras to the Great Plains.

Gold and silver were scattered throughout the area, though usually too thinly to make mining profitable. Whenever anyone made a "strike," prospectors, the vast majority utterly without previous experience but driven by what a mining journal of the period called an "unhealthy desire" for sudden wealth, flocked to the site. For a few months the area teemed with activity. Then, usually, expectations faded in the light of reality: high prices, low yields, hardship, violence, and deception. A few found significant wealth, the rest only backbreaking labor and disappointment—that is, until tales of another strike sent them dashing feverishly across the land on another golden chase.

In June 1859 came the finds in Nevada, where the famous **Comstock Lode** yielded ores worth nearly $4,000 a ton. In 1861, while men in the settled areas were laying down their tools to take up arms, the miners were racing to the Idaho panhandle, hoping to become millionaires overnight. The next year the rush was to the Snake River valley, then in 1863 and 1864 to Montana. In 1874 to 1876 the Black Hills in the heart of the Sioux lands were inundated.

The sudden prosperity of the mining towns attracted every kind of shady character—according to one forty-niner "rascals from Oregon, pickpockets from New York, accomplished gentlemen from Europe, interlopers from Lima and Chile, Mexican thieves, gamblers from no particular spot, and assassins manufactured in Hell." Gambling dens, dance halls, saloons, and brothels mushroomed wherever precious metal was found.

Law enforcement was a constant problem. Storekeepers charged outrageous prices; claim holders "salted" worthless properties with nuggets in order to swindle gullible investors. Ostentation characterized the successful, mere swagger those who failed. During the administration of President Grant, Virginia City, Nevada, was at the peak of its vulgar prosperity, producing an average of $12 million a year in ore. Built on the richness of the Comstock Lode, Virginia City, Nevada had twenty-five saloons before it had 4,000 people. By the 1870s its mountainside site was disfigured by ugly, ornate mansions where successful mine operators ate from fine china and swilled champagne as though it were water.

Though marked by violence, fraud, greed, and lost hopes, the gold rushes had valuable results. The most obvious was the new metal itself, which bolstered the financial position of the United States during and after the Civil War. Quantities of European goods needed for the war effort and for postwar economic development were paid for with the yield of the new mines. Gold and silver also caused a great increase of interest in the West. A valuable literature appeared, part imaginative, part reportorial, describing the mining camps and the life of the prospectors. These works fascinated contemporaries. Mark Twain's *Roughing It* (1872), based in part on his experiences in the Nevada mining country, is the most famous example of this literature.

The mines also speeded the political organization of the West. Colorado and Nevada became territories in 1861, Arizona and Idaho in 1863, and Montana in 1864. Although Nevada was admitted before it had 60,000 residents, most of these territories did not become states for decades. But because of the miners, the framework for future development was early established.

Farmers Struggle to Keep Up

While miners were extracting the mineral wealth of the West, others were snapping up the region's choice farmland. Presumably the Homestead Act of 1862 was supposed to make it easier for poor families to acquire farms, thereby ending the reign of the speculator and the large landholder. The West, land reformers had assumed, would soon be dotted with 160-acre family farms.

They were doomed to disappointment. Most landless Americans were too poor to become farmers even when they could obtain land without cost. The expense of moving a family to the ever-receding frontier exceeded the means of many. As for the industrial workers for whom the free land was supposed to provide a "safety valve," they had neither the skills nor the inclination to become farmers. Homesteaders usually came from districts not far removed from frontier conditions.

The first settlers in western Kansas, Nebraska, and the Dakotas took up land along the rivers and creeks, where they found enough timber for home building, fuel, and fencing. Later arrivals had to build houses of the tough prairie sod and depend on hay, sunflower stalks, and buffalo dung for fuel.

Frontier farm families had always had to work hard and endure the hazards of storm, drought, and insect plagues, along with isolation and loneliness. But all these burdens were magnified on the prairies and the High Plains. Life was particularly hard for farm women, who, in addition to childcare and housework, performed endless farm chores.

Farming as Big Business

Immediately after the Civil War, Congress reserved 47.7 million acres of public land in the South for homesteaders, stopping all cash sales in the region. But in 1876 this policy was reversed and the land thrown open. Speculators flocked to the feast in such numbers that the Illinois Central Railroad ran special trains from Chicago to Mississippi and Louisiana.

The flat immensity of the land, combined with newly available farm machinery and the development of rail connections with the East, encouraged the growth of enormous corporation-controlled "bonanza" farms.

Bonanza farmers could buy supplies wholesale and obtain concessions from railroads and processors, but even the biggest organizations could not cope with prolonged drought, and most of the bonanza outfits failed in the dry years of the late 1880s. Those wise farmers who diversified their crops and cultivated their land intensively fared better in the long run, although even they could not hope to earn a profit in really dry years.

Despite the hazards of plains agriculture, the region became the breadbasket of America in the decades following the Civil War. By 1889 Minnesota topped the nation in wheat production, and ten years later four of the five leading wheat states lay west of the Mississippi. The plains also accounted for heavy percentages of the nation's other cereal crops, together with immense quantities of beef, pork, and mutton.

Like other exploiters of the nation's resources, farmers took whatever they could from the soil with little heed for preserving its fertility and preventing erosion. The consequent national loss was less apparent because it was diffuse and slow to assume drastic proportions, but it was nonetheless real.

Western Railroad Building

Further exploitation of land resources by private interests resulted from the government's policy of subsidizing western railroads. Here was a clear illustration of the conflict between the idea of the West as a national heritage to be disposed of to deserving citizens and the concept of the region as a cornucopia pouring forth riches to be gathered up and carted off. When it came to a choice between giving a particular tract to railroads or to homesteaders, the homesteaders nearly always lost out. On the other hand, the swift development of western railroads was essential if farmers, miners, and cattle ranchers were to prosper.

Unless the government had been willing to build the transcontinental lines itself—and this was unthinkable in an age dominated by belief in individual exploitation—some system of subsidy was essential. Private investors would not hazard the huge sums needed to lay tracks across hundreds of miles of rugged, empty country when traffic over the road could not possibly profit for many years. Most voters were wary of entrusting the dispensing of large sums to politicians. Grants of land seemed a sensible way of financing construction. The method avoided direct outlays of public funds, for the companies could pledge the land as security for bond issues or sell it directly for cash.

Federal land grants to railroads began in 1850 with those allotted to the Illinois Central. Over the next two decades about 49 million acres were given to various lines

Chinese work on a railway in the Far West. "Without them," Leland Stanford, president of the Central Pacific Railroad said, "it would be impossible to complete the western portion of this great national highway." Some Chinese were drawn from the gold fields farther north, and others were imported from China, under five-year contracts with the railroads, which paid them $10 or $12 a month.

indirectly in the form of grants to the states, but the most lavish gifts of the public domain were those made directly to builders of intersectional trunk lines. These roads received more than 155 million acres, although about 25 million acres reverted to the government because some companies failed to lay the required miles of track. About 75 percent of this land went to aid the construction of four transcontinental railroads: the Union Pacific–Central Pacific line, running from Nebraska to San Francisco, completed in 1869; the Atchison, Topeka, and Santa Fe, running from Kansas City to Los Angeles by way of Santa Fe and Albuquerque, completed in 1883; the Southern Pacific, running from San Francisco to New Orleans by way of Yuma and El Paso, completed in 1883; and the Northern Pacific, running from Duluth, Minnesota, to Portland, Oregon, completed in 1883.

The Pacific Railway Act of 1862 established the pattern for these grants. It gave the builders of the Union Pacific and Central Pacific railroads five square miles of public land on each side of their right-of-way for each mile of track laid. The land was allotted in alternate sections, forming a pattern like a checkerboard: the squares of one color representing railroad property, the other government property. Presumably this arrangement benefited the entire nation since half the land close to the railroad remained in public hands.

However, whenever grants were made to railroads, the adjacent government lands were not opened to homesteaders—on the theory that free land in the immediate vicinity of a line would prevent the road from disposing of its properties at good prices. In addition to the land granted the railroads, a wide zone of "indemnity" lands was reserved to allow the roads to choose alternative sites to make up for lands that settlers had already taken up within the checkerboard. Thus, homesteading was in fact prohibited near land-grant railroads. More than twenty years after receiving its immense grant, the Northern Pacific was still attempting to keep homesteaders from filing in the indemnity zone. President Cleveland finally put a stop to this in 1887, saying that he could find "no evidence" that "this vast tract is necessary for the fulfillment of the grant."

Historians have argued at length about the fairness of the land-grant system. Land-grant lines encouraged the growth of the West by advertising their property widely and by providing cheap transportation for prospective settlers and efficient shipping services for farmers. They were required by law to carry troops and handle government business free or at reduced rates, which saved the government millions over the years. At the same time the system imposed no effective restraints on how the railroads used the funds raised with federal aid. Being able to lay track with money obtained from land grants, the operators tended to be extravagant and often downright corrupt.

The construction of the Central Pacific in the 1860s illustrates how the system encouraged extravagance. The line was controlled by four businessmen: Collis P. Huntington, Leland Stanford, Mark Hopkins, and Charles Crocker. The Central Pacific and the Union Pacific were given, in addition to their land grants, loans in the form of government bonds—from $16,000 to $48,000 for each mile of track laid, depending on the difficulty of the terrain. The two competed with each other for the subsidies, the Central Pacific building eastward from Sacramento, the Union Pacific westward from Nebraska. They put huge crews to work grading and laying track, bringing up supplies over the already completed road. The Union Pacific employed Civil War veterans and Irish immigrants, while the Central employed Chinese immigrants.

This plan favored the Union Pacific. While the Central Pacific was inching up the gorges and granite of the mighty Sierras, the Union Pacific was racing across the level plains laying 540 miles of track between 1865 and 1867. Once beyond the Sierras, the Central Pacific would have easy going across the Nevada–Utah plateau country, but by then it might be too late to prevent the Union Pacific from making off with most of the government aid.

Crocker managed the Central Pacific construction crews. He wasted huge sums by working through the winter in the High Sierras. In 1866, over the most difficult terrain, he laid twenty-eight miles of track, at a cost of more than $280,000 a mile. Experts later estimated that 70 percent of this sum could have been saved had speed not been a factor.

Crocker's Herculean efforts paid off. The mountains were conquered, and then the crews raced across the Great Basin to Salt Lake City and beyond. The meeting of the rails—the occasion of a national celebration—took place at Promontory, north of Ogden, Utah, on May 10, 1869. Leland Stanford drove the final ceremonial golden spike with a silver hammer.[2] The Union Pacific had built 1,086 miles of track, the Central 689 miles.

In the long run the wasteful way in which the Central Pacific was built hurt the road severely. It was ill-constructed, over grades too steep and around curves too sharp, and burdened with debts that were too large. Such was the fate of nearly all the railroads constructed with the help of government subsidies.

The only transcontinental railroad built without land grants was the Great Northern, running from St. Paul, Minnesota, to the Pacific. Spending private capital, its guiding genius, James J. Hill, was compelled to build economically and to plan carefully. As a result, his was the only transcontinental line to weather the depression of the 1890s without going into bankruptcy.

---

[2] A mysterious "San Francisco jeweler" passed among the onlookers, taking orders for souvenir watch chains that he proposed to make from the spike at $5 each.

NAT LOVE

Nat Love, a slave, was born on a plantation in Davidson County, Tennessee sometime in 1854. Nat's father was a foreman on the plantation; his mother milked cows, cooked, and operated a loom.

After the Civil War, Love's father rented twenty acres from his former master. Nat spent Sundays at a horse farm, where he learned how to ride. Soon he was earning ten cents for every colt he "broke."

When Nat's father died, the family's circumstances became dire. He and his siblings went shoeless and their clothes were in tatters. Nat longed to escape from it all and see the world. His opportunity came when he won a horse in a raffle. In February 1869, he set out for the frontier. He was fifteen years old.

Months later, he arrived in Dodge City, Kansas, "a typical frontier city, with a great many saloons, dance halls, and gambling houses, and very little of anything else." At a camp outside of town, he asked a group of cowboys for a job. Eager to have some fun with the black "tenderfoot," they agreed if he could prove he could ride; then they put him on the wildest horse in camp. Love clung to the bucking bronco, much to everyone's astonishment. The boss hired him at $30 a month. He also gave Nat a saddle, a Colt 45 pistol and a new name—"Love" being unsuitable for a cowboy. Nat was now "Red River Dick."

Three days after the cowboys left Dodge, they were attacked by mounted Indians. "When I saw them coming after us and heard their blood curdling yell, I was too badly scared to run," Love recalled. Before the Indians were driven away by gunfire, they had killed one cowboy and made off with most of the horses and provisions. Love and the others walked to Texas.

Love then served with outfits that drove cattle to grazing ranges and markets throughout the West. Every spring and fall the ranchers staged a great roundup, driving in all the cattle to a central place, separating them by the brands, and culling steers for shipment to market. Love specialized as a brand reader. He "cut out" those belonging to his employer and drove them back to that herd.

Love's life was filled with adventure. In 1876, while Love was driving 500 steers from the Rio Grande to a ranch in the Shoshone mountains of Wyoming, Indians attacked and stampeded the cattle. The battle raged through the night. By morning, several score Indians were dead, most of them trampled by cattle. Another time, Love broke up a robbery of a Union Pacific railroad station. After he won a roping and riding competition in Deadwood, South Dakota, "Red River Dick" became known as "Deadwood Dick." Shortly afterward he was shot by Indians and captured. When he recovered, the chief offered him his daughter in marriage along with 100 ponies. Dick pretended to go along with the marriage, but then stole a horse and escaped.

By the late 1880s, the heyday of the cowboy had ended. Now railroads hauled cattle from the grazing ranges to slaughterhouses in Kansas City, Omaha, Chicago, and St. Louis. In 1889, Dick went to Denver and got married. The following year he found a job as a porter on the Pullman Railroad cars. He died in 1921.

Question for Discussion
■ Which factors perhaps promoted racial equality among ranch hands?

Nat Love, posed here with the requisite implements, claimed to have been the "Deadwood Dick" on whom a series of novels was based.

The Cattle Kingdom

While miners were digging out the mineral wealth of the West and railroaders were taking possession of much of its land, another group was exploiting endless acres of its grass. For twenty years after the Civil War cattlemen and sheep raisers dominated huge areas of the High Plains, making millions of dollars by grazing their herds on lands they did not own.

> **Watch the Video**
> *Cowboys and Cattle* at **myhistorylab.com**

The lack of markets and transportation explains why cattle, which existed in southern Texas by the millions, were lightly regarded. But conditions were changing. Industrial growth in the East was causing an increase in the urban population and a consequent rise in the demand for food. At the same time, the expansion of the railroad network made it possible to move cattle cheaply over long distances. As the iron rails inched across the plains, astute cattlemen began to do some elementary figuring. Longhorns could be had locally for $3 and $4 a head. In the northern cities they would bring ten times that much, perhaps even more. Why not round them up and herd them northward to the railroads, allowing them to feed along the way on the abundant grasses of the plains? The land was unoccupied and owned by the federal government. Anyone could drive cattle across it without paying a fee or asking anyone's permission.

In 1867 the drovers, inspired by a clever young Illinois cattle dealer named Joseph G. McCoy and other entrepreneurs, led their herds across unsettled grasslands to the Kansas Pacific line at Abilene, Kansas. They earned excellent profits, and during the next five years about 1.5 million head made the "long drive" over the Chisholm Trail to Abilene, where they were sold to ranchers, feedlot operators, and the agents of eastern meatpackers. Other shipping points sprang up as the railroads pushed westward. According to the best estimates 10 million head were driven north before the practice ended in the mid-1880s. (For the story of one cowboy, see the American Lives essay on "Nat Love," p. 446.)

> **Read the Document**
> *Chisholm Trail* at **myhistorylab.com**

Open-Range Ranching

Soon cattlemen discovered that the hardy Texas stock could survive the winters of the northern plains. Attracted by the apparently limitless forage, they began to bring up herds to stock the vast regions where the buffalo had so recently roamed. By 1880 some 4.5 million head had spread across the sea of grass that ran from Kansas to Montana and west to the Rockies.

The prairie grasses offered ranchers a bonanza almost as valuable as the gold mines. Open-range ranching required actual ownership of no more than a few acres along some watercourse. In this semiarid region, control of water enabled a rancher to dominate all the surrounding area back to the divide separating his range from the next stream without investing a cent in the purchase of land. His cattle, wandering freely on the public domain, fattened on grass owned by all the people, were to be turned into beefsteak and leather for the profit of the rancher.

Theoretically, anyone could pasture stock on the open range, but without access to water it was impossible to do so. "I have 2 miles of running water," a cattleman said in testifying before the Public Land Commission. "That accounts for my ranch being where it is. The next water from me in one direction is 23 miles; now no man can have a ranch between these two places. I have control of the grass, the same as though I owned it." In the late 1870s one Colorado cattle baron controlled an area roughly the size of Connecticut and Rhode Island even though he owned only 105 small parcels that totaled about 15,500 acres.

With the demand for meat rising and transportation cheap, princely fortunes could be made in a few years. Capitalists from the East and from Europe began to pour funds into the business. Soon large outfits such as the Nebraska Land and Cattle Company, controlled by British investors, and the Union Cattle Company of Wyoming, a $3 million corporation, dominated the business, just as large companies had taken over most of the important gold and silver mines.

Unlike other exploiters of the West's resources, cattle ranchers did not at first injure or reduce any public resource. Grass eaten by their stock annually renewed itself; droppings from the animals enriched the soil. Furthermore, ranchers poached on the public domain because there was no reasonable way for them to obtain legal possession of the large areas necessary to raise cattle on the plains. Federal land laws made no allowance for the special conditions of the semiarid West.

A system to take account for those conditions was soon devised by Major John Wesley Powell, later the director of the United States Geological Survey. His *Report on the Lands of the Arid Region of the United States* (1879) suggested that western lands be divided into three classes: irrigable lands, timber lands, and "pasturage" lands. On the pasturage lands the "farm unit" ought to be at least 2,560 acres (four sections), Powell urged. Groups of these units should be organized into "pasturage districts" in which the ranchers "should have the right to make their own regulations for the division of lands, the use of the water . . . and for the pasturage of lands in common or in severalty."

Barbed-Wire Warfare

Congress refused to change the land laws in any basic way, and this had two harmful effects. First, it encouraged fraud: Those who could not get title to enough land honestly turned to subterfuge. The Desert Land Act (1877) allowed anyone to obtain 640 acres in the arid states for $1.25 an acre provided the owner irrigated part of it within three years. Since the original claimant could transfer the holding, the ranchers set their cowboys and other hands to filing claims, which were then signed over to them. Over 2.6 million acres were taken up under the act, and according to the best estimate, 95 percent of the claims were fraudulent—no sincere effort was made to irrigate the land.

Second, overcrowding became a problem that led to serious conflicts, even killings, because no one had uncontestable title to the land. The leading ranchers banded together in cattlemen's associations to deal with overcrowding and with such problems as quarantine regulations, water rights, and thievery. In most cases these associations devised effective and sensible rules, but their functions would better have been performed by the government.

To keep other ranchers' cattle from those sections of the public domain they considered their own, the associations and many individuals began to fence huge areas. This was possible only because of the invention in 1874 of barbed wire by Joseph F. Glidden, an

Illinois farmer. By the 1880s thousands of miles of the new fencing had been strung across the plains, often across roads and in a few cases around entire communities. "Barbed-wire wars" resulted, fought by rancher against rancher, cattleman against sheepman, herder against farmer. Posted signs gave dire warnings to trespassers. "The Son of a Bitch who opens this fence had better look out for his scalp," one such sign announced, another fine statement of the philosophy of the age.

By stringing so much wire the cattlemen were unwittingly destroying their own way of doing business. On a truly open range, cattle could fend for themselves, instinctively finding water during droughts, drifting safely downwind before blizzards. Barbed wire prevented their free movement. During winter storms these slender strands became as lethal as high-tension wires: the drifting cattle piled up against them and died by the thousands.

The boom times were ending. Overproduction was driving down the price of beef; expenses were on the rise; many sections of the range were badly overgrazed. The dry summer of 1886 left the stock in such poor condition as winter approached that the *Rocky Mountain Husbandman* urged its readers to sell their cattle despite the prevailing low prices rather than "endanger the whole herd by having the range overstocked."

Some ranchers took this advice; those who did not made a fatal error. Winter that year arrived early and with unparalleled fury. Blizzards raged and temperatures plummeted far below zero. Cattle crowded into low places only to be engulfed in giant snowdrifts; barbed wire took a fearful toll. When spring finally came, the streams were choked with rotting carcasses. Between 80 and 90 percent of all cattle on the range were dead.

That cruel winter finished open-range cattle-raising. The large companies were bankrupt; many independent operators became discouraged and sold out. When the industry revived, it was on a smaller, more efficiently organized scale. The fencing movement continued, but now ranchers enclosed only the land they actually owned. It then became possible to bring in pedigreed bulls to improve the breed. Cattle-raising, like mining before it, ceased to be an adventure in rollicking individualism and became a business.

By the late 1880s the bonanza days of the West were over. No previous frontier had caught the imagination of Americans so completely as the Great West, with its heroic size, its awesome emptiness, its massive, sculptured beauty. Most of what Walter Prescott Webb, author of the classic study *The Great Plains* (1931) called the "primary windfalls" of the region—the furs, the precious metals, the forests, the cattle, and the grass—had been snatched up by first comers and by individuals already wealthy. Big companies were taking over all the West's resources. The frontier was no more.

But the frontier never existed except as an intellectual construction among white settlers and those who wrote about them. To the Indians, the land was simply home. The "conquest of the frontier" was thus an appealing evasion: It transformed the harmful actions and policies of the nation into an expression of human progress, the march westward of "civilization."

See the **Map**

Resources and Conflict in the West at **myhistorylab.com**

"Civilization," though, was changing. The nation was becoming more powerful, richer, and larger, and its economic structure more complex and diversified as the West yielded its treasures. But the East, and especially eastern industrialists and financiers, were increasingly dominating the economy of the entire nation.

Milestones

1859	Discovery of the Comstock Lode lures miners west	1877	U.S. troops capture Chief Joseph of Nez Percé after 1,000-mile retreat
1864	Chivington massacre of Cheyenne	1878	Timber and Stone Act favors lumber companies
1869	Union Pacific Railroad completed	1879	Major Powell's *Report on the Lands of the Arid Region* suggests division of West
	Board of Indian Commissioners established		
1873	Timber Culture Act encourages western forestation	1882	Chinese Exclusion Act bans Chinese immigrant workers for ten years
1876	Sioux slaughter Custer's cavalry at Battle of Little Bighorn	1886–1887	Blizzards end open-range ranching
1877	Desert Land Act favors ranchers	1887	Dawes Severalty Act splits tribal lands

✓•─Study and Review at www.myhistorylab.com

Review Questions

1. The text suggests that if federal policy had been more tolerant, there would have been no need to drive Indians from so much of their land. What alternative policies might have succeeded and how?

2. In The *Comanche Empire* (2009), historian Pekka Hamalainen insists that the Comanche themselves managed to forge a mighty empire. Maps showing the steady loss of Indian lands (such as that on p. 441) deprive the Indians of their "agency" in history. In what ways did Indians leave their own imprint upon this period?

3. How did the treatment of African Americans during the last third of the nineteenth century compare with that of Indians?

4. The West has exerted a powerful hold on the American imagination. What explains the popularity of western themes in American life? How does the history compare with the popular image?

Key Terms

Chinese Exclusion Act   *434*
Comstock Lode   *441*

Dawes Severalty Act of 1887   *439*

An Industrial Giant Emerges

17

((•─┤Hear the Audio Chapter 17 at myhistorylab.com

Do you save money at big box stores?

IN 2010 WALMART, WITH 2.1 MILLION EMPLOYEES, WAS THE LARGEST corporation in the history of the world. Its revenues of $405 billion exceeded the gross domestic product of Sweden and Saudi Arabia. The company's clout made it a frequent target of popular satire. A 2008 episode of *The Simpsons* was set at "Sprawl-Mart," where Homer was offered a job as Executive Greeter. "Is there a chance for advancement?" he asks. "No," the manager says. "You get to work overtime without us paying you extra."

Real-world critics of Walmart leveled similar charges. A labor union website described Walmart as a "death star" that "destroys all other economic activity in its path." Others complained that many Walmart employees qualified for public assistance.

In 2009 Walmart, whose motto is "Save Money Live Better," claimed that it saved $3,100 per American household. Former CEO Lee Scott credited Walmart with having "democratized consumption" in the United States by enabling "working-class families to buy former luxuries like inexpensive flat-screen televisions, down comforters and porterhouse steaks." A retailer helps society best by lowering prices, or so the company contended.

The debate over the human costs of corporate efficiencies echoes the one that accompanied the rise of powerful industrial combinations during the last third of the nineteenth century. Then, the power of the railroads enabled them to bring substantial benefits to thousands of communities; but this power also enabled the railroads to ruin those who opposed their will. Industrial corporations followed suit, especially in steel, iron, oil, and electricity, providing millions with new and improved products at lower prices. But the industrial behemoths also controlled political processes and often exploited workers. Reformers and labor leaders denounced this concentration of wealth and power. Some advocated regulation; others called for revolution. Then as now, defenders of big business pointed out its benefits: new technology, better products, lower prices.

The question remains: Does the efficiency generated by economic concentration justify its threat to smaller businesses and communities—and to democratic institutions?

Essentials of Industrial Growth

When the Civil War began, the country's industrial output, while important and increasing, did not approach that of major European powers. By the end of the century the United States had become far and away the colossus among world manufacturers, dwarfing the production of Great Britain and Germany. The world had never seen such a remarkable example of rapid economic growth. The value of American manufactured products rose from $1.8 billion in 1859 to over $13 billion in 1899.

American manufacturing flourished for many reasons. New natural resources were discovered and exploited steadily, thereby increasing opportunities. These opportunities, in turn, attracted the brightest and most energetic of a vigorous and expanding population. The growth of the country added constantly to the size of the national market, and protective tariffs shielded that market from foreign competition. Foreign capital, however, entered the market freely, in part because tariffs kept out so many foreign goods.

The dominant spirit of the time encouraged businessmen to maximum effort by emphasizing progress, yet it also produced a generation of Robber Barons. The energetic search for wealth led to corrupt business practices such as stock manipulation, bribery, and cutthroat competition and ultimately to "combinations in restraint of trade," a kind of American euphemism for monopoly.

The period witnessed rapid advances in basic science, and technicians created a bountiful harvest of new machines, processes, and power sources that increased productivity in many industries and created new industries as well. Agriculture was transformed by improved harvesters and binding machines, and combines capable of threshing and bagging 450 pounds of grain a minute. An 1886 report of the Illinois Bureau of Labor Statistics claimed that "new machinery has displaced fully 50 percent of the muscular labor formerly required to do a given amount of work in the manufacture of agricultural implements." Of course that also meant that many farm families were "displaced" from their homes and livelihoods, and it made farmers dependent on the vagaries of distant markets and powerful economic forces they could not control.

As a result of improvements in the milling of grain, packaged cereals appeared on the American breakfast table. The commercial canning of food, spurred by the "automatic line" canning factory, expanded so rapidly that by 1887 a writer in *Good Housekeeping* could say, "Housekeeping is getting to be ready made, as well as clothing." The Bonsack cigarette-rolling machine created a new industry that changed the habits of millions. George B. Eastman created still another with his development of mass-produced, roll photographic film and the simple but efficient Kodak camera. The perfection of the typewriter by the Remington company in the 1880s revolutionized office work. But even some of these inventions were mixed blessings. The harm done by cigarettes, for example, needs no explanation.

Railroads: The First Big Business

In 1866, returning from his honeymoon in Europe, thirty-year-old Charles Francis Adams Jr., (great-grandson of John Adams and grandson of John Quincy Adams), full of ambition and ready, as he put it, to confront the world "face to face," looked about in search of a career. "Surveying the whole field," he later explained, "I fixed on the railroad system as the most developing force and the largest field of the day, and determined to attach myself to it." Adams's judgment was acute: For the next twenty-five years the

The Union Railroad Station in Montgomery, Alabama, was designed by Henry Hobson Richardson, the nation's foremost architect in the late nineteenth century. Richardson borrowed ideas from the past, including arches that evoked ancient Rome. The building's massiveness and horizontal lines suggested the power and reach of the railroads: the American empire as built on steel rails.

railroads were probably the most significant element in American economic development, railroad executives the most powerful people in the country.

Railroads were important first as an industry in themselves. Fewer than 35,000 miles of track existed when Lee laid down his sword at Appomattox. In 1875 railroad mileage exceeded 74,000 and the skeleton of the network was complete. Over the next two decades the skeleton was fleshed out. In 1890 the mature but still-growing system took in over $1 billion in passenger and freight revenues. (The federal government's income in 1890 was only $403 million.) The value of railroad properties and equipment was more than $8.7 billion. The national railroad debt of $5.1 billion was almost five times the national debt of $1.1 billion. By 1900 the nation had 193,000 miles of track.

The emphasis in railroad construction after 1865 was on organizing integrated systems. The lines had high fixed costs: taxes, interest on their bonds, maintenance of track and rolling stock, and salaries of office personnel. A short train with half-empty cars required almost as many workers and as much fuel to operate as a long one jammed with freight or passengers. To earn profits the railroads had to carry as much traffic as possible. They therefore spread out feeder lines to draw business to their main lines the way the root network of a tree draws water into its trunk.

Before the Civil War, passengers and freight could travel by rail from beyond Chicago and St. Louis to the Atlantic coast, but only after the war did true interregional trunk lines appear. In 1867 the New York Central passed into the hands of "Commodore" Cornelius Vanderbilt, who had made a large fortune in the shipping business. Vanderbilt already controlled lines running from Albany to New York City; now he merged these properties with the New York Central. In 1873 he integrated the Lake Shore and Michigan

Southern into his empire and two years later the Michigan Central. At his death in 1877 the New York Central operated a network of over 4,500 miles of track between New York City and most of the principal cities of the Midwest.

While Vanderbilt was putting together the New York Central complex, Thomas A. Scott was fusing roads to Cincinnati, Indianapolis, St. Louis, and Chicago to his Pennsylvania Railroad, which linked Pittsburgh and Philadelphia. In 1871 the Pennsylvania line obtained access to New York; soon it reached Baltimore and Washington. By 1869 another important system, the Erie, extended from New York to Cleveland, Cincinnati, and St. Louis. Soon thereafter it too tapped the markets of Chicago and other cities. In 1874 the Baltimore and Ohio rail line also obtained access to Chicago.

The Civil War had highlighted the need for thorough railroad connections in the South. Shortly after the conflict the Chesapeake and Ohio opened a direct line from Norfolk, Virginia, to Cincinnati, Ohio. By the late 1880s, the Richmond and West Point Terminal Company controlled an 8,558-mile network. Like other southern trunk lines such as the Louisville and Nashville and the Atlantic Coast Line, this system was controlled by northern capitalists.

The trunk lines interconnected and thus had to standardize many of their activities. This in turn led to the standardization of other aspects of life. The present system of time zones was developed in 1883 by the railroads. The standard track gauge (four feet eight and one-half inches) was established in 1886. Standardized car coupling and braking mechanisms, standard signal systems, even standard methods of accounting were essential to the effective functioning of the network.

The lines sought to work out fixed rates for carrying different types of freight, charge more for valuable manufactured goods than for bulky products like coal or wheat, and they agreed to permit rate concessions to shippers when necessary to avoid hauling empty cars. In other words, they charged what the traffic would bear. However, by the 1880s the men who ran the railroads had come to recognize the advantages of cooperating with one another to avoid "senseless" competition. Railroad management was becoming a kind of profession, with certain standard ways of doing things, its own professional journals, and with regional organizations such as the Eastern Trunk Line Association and the Western Traffic Association.

To speed the settlement of new regions, the land-grant railroads sold land cheaply and on easy terms, for sales meant future business as well as current income. They offered reduced rates to travelers interested in buying farms and set up "bureaus of immigration" that distributed brochures describing the wonders of the new country. Their agents greeted immigrants at the eastern ports and tried to steer them to railroad property. They sent agents who were usually themselves immigrants—often ministers—all over Europe to recruit prospective settlers.

See the **Map**

Railroads & New Transportation Systems at **myhistorylab.com**

Iron, Oil, and Electricity

The transformation of iron manufacturing affected the nation almost as much as railroad development. Output rose from 920,000 tons in 1860 to 10.3 million tons in 1900, but the big change came in the development of ways to mass-produce steel. In its pure form (wrought iron) the metal is tough but relatively pliable: It bends under great stresses.

Ordinary cast iron, which contains large amounts of carbon and other impurities, is hard but brittle. Steel, which contains 1 or 2 percent carbon, combines the hardness of cast iron with the toughness of wrought iron. For nearly every purpose—structural girders for bridges and buildings, railroad track, machine tools, boiler plate, barbed wire—steel is immensely superior to other kinds of iron.

But steel was so expensive that it could not be used for bulky products until the invention in the 1850s of the Bessemer process, perfected independently by Henry Bessemer, an Englishman, and William Kelly of Kentucky. Bessemer and Kelly discovered that a stream of air directed into a mass of molten iron caused the carbon and other impurities to combine with oxygen and burn off. When measured amounts of carbon, silicon, and manganese were then added, the brew became steel. What had been a rare metal could now be produced by the hundreds and thousands of tons. In 1870, 77,000 tons of steel were manufactured; by 1890, that had expanded to nearly 5 million tons. Such growth would have been impossible without the huge supplies of iron ore in the United States and the coal necessary to fire the furnaces that refined it.

Pittsburgh, surrounded by vast coal deposits, became the iron and steel capital of the country, the Minnesota ores reaching it by way of steamers on the Great Lakes and rail lines from Cleveland. Other cities in Pennsylvania and Ohio were important producers, and a separate complex, centering on Birmingham, Alabama, developed to exploit local iron and coal fields.

The petroleum industry expanded even more spectacularly than iron and steel. Edwin L. Drake drilled the first successful well in Pennsylvania in 1859. During the Civil War,

This 1900 photograph of steel factories at night in Duquesne, near Pittsburgh, was tinted by hand.
Source: North Wind Picture Archives.

production ranged between 2 million and 3 million barrels a year. By 1890 the figure had leaped to about 50 million barrels.

Before the invention of the gasoline engine and the automobile, the most important petroleum product was kerosene, which was burned in lamps. Refiners heated crude oil in large kettles and, after the volatile elements had escaped, condensed the kerosene in coils cooled by water. The heavier petroleum tars were discarded.

Technological advances came rapidly. By the early 1870s, refiners had learned how to "crack" petroleum by applying high temperatures to the crude oil in order to rearrange its molecular structure, thereby increasing the percentage of kerosene yielded. By-products such as naphtha, gasoline (used in vaporized form as an illuminating gas), rhigolene (a local anesthetic), cymogene (a coolant for refrigerating machines), and many lubricants and waxes began to appear on the market. At the same time a great increase in the supply of crude oil drove prices down.

These circumstances put a premium on refining efficiency. Larger plants using expensive machinery and employing skilled technicians became more important. In the mid-1860s only three refineries in the country could process 2,000 barrels of crude oil a week; a decade later plants capable of handling 1,000 barrels a day were common.

Two other important new industries were the telephone and electric light businesses. Both were typical of the period, being products of technical advances and intimately related to the growth of a high-speed, urban civilization that put great stress on communication. The telephone was invented in 1876 by Alexander Graham Bell, who had been led to the study of acoustics through his interest in the education of the deaf. The invention soon proved its value. By 1900 there were almost 800,000 telephones in the country, twice the total for all Europe. The American Telephone and Telegraph Company, a consolidation of over 100 local systems, dominated the business.

When the Western Union Telegraph Company realized the importance of the telephone, it tried for a time to compete with Bell by developing a machine of its own. The man it commissioned to devise this machine was Thomas A. Edison, but Bell's patents proved unassailable. Edison had already made a number of contributions toward solving what he called the "mysteries of electrical force," including a multiplex telegraph capable of sending four messages over a single wire at the same time. At Menlo Park, New Jersey, he built the prototype of the modern research laboratory, where specific problems could be attacked on a mass scale by a team of trained specialists. During his lifetime he took out more than 1,000 patents dealing with machines as varied as the phonograph, the motion-picture projector, the storage battery, and the mimeograph.

Edison's most significant achievement was the incandescent lamp, or electric lightbulb. Others before him had experimented with the idea of producing light by passing electricity through a filament in a vacuum. Always, however, the filaments quickly burned out.

•••⊢Read the Document

Edison, *The Success of the Electric Light* at
myhistorylab.com

Edison tried hundreds of fibers before producing, in 1879, a carbonized filament that would glow brightly in a vacuum tube for as long as 170 hours without crumbling. At Christmastime he decorated the grounds about his laboratory with a few dozen of the new lights. People flocked by the thousands to see this miracle of the "Wizard of Menlo Park." The inventor boasted that soon he would be able to illuminate entire towns, even great cities like New York.

He was true to his promise. In 1882 his Edison Illuminating Company opened a power station in New York City and began to supply current for lighting to eighty-five consumers, including the *New York Times* and the banking house of J.P. Morgan and Company. Soon central stations were springing up everywhere until, by 1898, there were about 3,000 in the country.

The substitution of electric for steam power in factories was as liberating as that of steam for waterpower before the Civil War. Small, safe electric motors replaced dangerous and cumbersome mazes of belts and wheels. The electric power industry expanded rapidly. By the early years of the twentieth century almost 6 billion kilowatt-hours of electricity were being produced annually. Yet this was only the beginning.

Competition and Monopoly: The Railroads

During the post–Civil War era, expansion in industry went hand in hand with concentration. The principal cause of this trend, aside from the obvious economies resulting from large-scale production and the growing importance of expensive machinery, was the downward trend of prices after 1873. The deflation, which resulted mainly from the failure of the money supply to keep pace with the rapid increase in the volume of goods produced, affected agricultural goods as well as manufactures, and it lasted until 1896 or 1897.

Contemporaries believed that they were living through a "great depression." That label is misleading, for output expanded almost continuously, and at a rapid rate, until 1893, when production slumped and a true depression struck the country. Falling prices, however, kept a steady pressure on profit margins, and this led to increased production and thus to intense competition for markets.

According to the classical economists, competition advanced the public interest by keeping prices low and ensuring the most efficient producer the largest profit. Up to a point it accomplished these purposes in the years after 1865, but it also caused side effects that injured both the economy and society as a whole. Railroad managers, for instance, found it impossible to enforce "official" rate schedules and maintain their regional associations once competitive pressures mounted. In 1865 it had cost from ninety-six cents to $2.15 per 100 pounds, depending on the class of freight, to ship goods from New York to Chicago. In 1888 rates ranged from thirty-five cents to seventy-five cents.

Competition cut deeply into railroad profits, causing the lines to seek desperately to increase volume. It did so chiefly by reducing rates still more, on a selective basis. The competition gave rebates (secret reductions below the published rates) to large shippers in order to capture their business. Giving discounts to those who shipped in volume made economic sense: It was easier to handle freight in carload lots than in smaller units. So intense was the battle for business, however, that the railroads often made concessions to big customers far beyond what the economics of bulk shipment justified.

Railroad officials disliked rebating but found no way to avoid the practice. In extreme cases the railroads even gave large shippers drawbacks, which were rebates on the business of the shippers' competitors. Besides rebating, railroads issued passes to favored shippers, built sidings at the plants of important companies without charge, and gave freely of their landholdings to attract businesses to their territory.

To make up for losses forced on them by competitive pressures, railroads charged higher rates at waypoints along their tracks where no competition existed. Frequently it cost more to ship a product a short distance than a longer one. Rochester, New York, was served only by the New York Central. In the 1870s it cost thrity cents to transport a barrel of flour from Rochester to New York City, a distance of 350 miles. At the same time flour could be shipped from Minneapolis to New York, a distance of well over 1,000 miles, for only twenty cents a barrel.

Although cheap transportation stimulated the economy, few people benefited from cutthroat competition. Small shippers—and all businessmen in cities and towns with limited rail outlets—suffered; railroad discrimination speeded the concentration of industry in large corporations located in major centers. The instability of rates even troubled interests like the midwestern flour millers who benefited from the competitive situation, for it hampered planning. Nor could manufacturers who received rebates be entirely happy, since few could be sure that some other producer was not getting a larger reduction.

Probably the worst sufferers were the railroads themselves. The loss of revenue resulting from rate cutting, combined with inflated debts, put most of them in grave difficulty when faced with a downturn in the business cycle. In 1876 two-fifths of all railroad bonds were in default; three years later sixty-five lines were bankrupt.

Since the public would not countenance bankrupt railroads going out of business, these companies were placed in the hands of court-appointed receivers. The receivers, however, seldom provided efficient management and had no funds at their disposal for new equipment.

During the 1880s the major railroads responded to these pressures by building or buying lines in order to create interregional systems. These were the first giant corporations, capitalized in the hundreds of millions of dollars. Their enormous cost led to another wave of bankruptcies when a true depression struck in the 1890s.

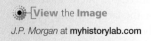
View the Image
J.P. Morgan at **myhistorylab.com**

The consequent reorganizations brought most of the big systems under the control of financiers, notably J. Pierpont Morgan and such other private bankers as Kuhn, Loeb of New York and Lee, Higginson of Boston.

Critics called the reorganizations "Morganizations." Representatives of the bankers sat on the board of every line they saved and their influence was predominant. They consistently opposed rate wars, rebating, and other competitive practices. In effect, control of the railroad network became centralized, even though the companies maintained their separate existences and operated in a seemingly independent manner. When Morgan died in 1913, "Morgan men" dominated the boards of the New York Central; the Erie; the New York, New Haven, and Hartford; the Southern; the Pere Marquette; the Atchison, Topeka, and Santa Fe; and many other lines.

Competition and Monopoly: Steel

The iron and steel industry was also intensely competitive. Despite the trend toward higher production, demand varied erratically from year to year, even from month to month. In good times producers built new facilities, only to suffer heavy losses when demand declined. The forward rush of technology put a tremendous emphasis on efficiency; expensive plants quickly became obsolete. Improved transportation facilities allowed manufacturers in widely separated places to compete with one another.

The kingpin of the industry was Andrew Carnegie. Carnegie was born in Scotland and came to the United States in 1848 at the age of twelve. His first job, as a bobbin boy

This early 1900 photograph shows how steel mills spread along the riverfront of Pittsburgh, Pennsylvania.

in a cotton mill, brought him $1.20 a week, but his talents perfectly fitted the times and he rose rapidly: to Western Union messenger boy, to telegrapher, to private secretary, to railroad manager. He saved his money, made some shrewd investments, and by 1868 had an income of $50,000 a year.

At about this time he decided to specialize in the iron business. Carnegie possessed great talent as a salesman, boundless faith in the future of the country, an uncanny knack of choosing topflight subordinates, and enough ruthlessness to survive in the iron and steel jungle. Where other steel men built new plants in good times, he preferred to expand in bad times, when it cost far less to do so.

Carnegie grasped the importance of technological improvements. Slightly skeptical of the Bessemer process at first, once he became convinced of its practicality he adopted it enthusiastically. In 1875 he built the J. Edgar Thomson Steel Works, named after a president of the Pennsylvania Railroad, his biggest customer. He employed chemists and other specialists and was soon making steel from iron oxides that other manufacturers had discarded as waste. He was a merciless competitor. Carnegie sold rails by paying "commissions" to railroad purchasing agents, and he was not above reneging on a contract if he thought it profitable and safe to do so.

By 1890 the Carnegie Steel Company dominated the industry, and its output increased nearly tenfold during the next decade. Profits soared. Alarmed by his increasing control of the industry, the makers of finished steel products such as barbed wire and tubing considered pooling their resources and making steel themselves. Carnegie, his competitive temper aroused, threatened to manufacture wire, pipes, and other finished products. A colossal steel war seemed imminent.

However, Carnegie longed to retire in order to devote himself to philanthropic work. He believed that great wealth entailed social responsibilities and that it was a disgrace to die rich. When J.P. Morgan approached him through an intermediary with an offer to buy him out, he assented readily. In 1901 Morgan put together United States Steel, the "world's first billion-dollar corporation." This combination included all the Carnegie properties, the Federal Steel Company (Carnegie's largest competitor), and such important fabricators of finished products as the American Steel and Wire Company, the American Tin Plate Company, and the National Tube Company. Vast reserves of Minnesota iron ore and a fleet of Great Lakes ore steamers were also included. U.S. Steel was capitalized at $1.4 billion, about twice the value of its component properties but not necessarily an overestimation of its profit-earning capacity. The owners of Carnegie Steel received $492 million, of which $250 million went to Carnegie himself.

●●●─┤Read the Document

Carnegie, *Wealth* at
myhistorylab.com

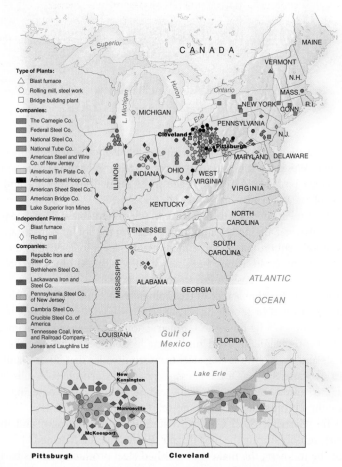

Firms Incorporated into U.S. Steel J.P. Morgan's consolidation that created U.S. Steel.

Competition and Monopoly: Oil

The pattern of fierce competition leading to combination and monopoly is well illustrated by the history of the petroleum industry. Irresistible pressures pushed the refiners into a brutal struggle to dominate the business. Production of crude oil, subject to the uncertainties of prospecting and drilling, fluctuated constantly and without regard for need. In general, output surged far ahead of demand.

By the 1870s the chief oil-refining centers were Cleveland, Pittsburgh, Baltimore, and the New York City area. Of these Cleveland was the fastest growing, chiefly because the New York Central and Erie railroads competed fiercely for its oil trade and the Erie Canal offered an alternative route.

The Standard Oil Company of Cleveland, founded in 1870 by a thirty-one-year-old merchant named John D. Rockefeller, emerged as the giant among the refiners. Rockefeller exploited every possible technical advance and employed fair means and foul to persuade competitors either to sell out or to join forces. By 1879 he controlled 90 percent of the nation's oil-refining capacity along with a network of oil pipelines and large reserves of petroleum in the ground.

Standard Oil emerged victorious from the competitive wars because Rockefeller and his associates were the toughest and most imaginative fighters as well as the most efficient refiners in the business. In addition to obtaining from the railroads a 10 percent rebate and drawbacks on its competitors' shipments, Standard Oil cut prices locally to force small independents to sell out or face ruin. Since kerosene was sold in grocery stores, Standard supplied its own outlets with meat, sugar, and other products at artificially low prices to help crush the stores that handled other brands of kerosene. The company employed spies to track down the customers of independents and offer them oil at bargain prices. Bribery was also a Standard practice; the reformer Henry Demarest Lloyd quipped that the company had done everything to the Pennsylvania legislature except refine it.

Although a bold planner and a daring taker of necessary risks, Rockefeller was far too orderly and astute to enjoy the free-swinging battles that plagued his industry. Born in an upstate New York village in 1839, he settled in Cleveland in 1855 and became a produce merchant. During the Civil War he invested in a local refinery and by 1865 was engaged full time in the oil business.

Having achieved his monopoly, Rockefeller stabilized and structured it by creating a new type of business organization, the trust. Standard Oil was an Ohio corporation, prohibited by local law from owning plants in other states or holding stock in out-of-state corporations. As Rockefeller and his associates took over dozens of companies with facilities scattered across the country, serious legal and managerial difficulties arose. How could these many organizations be integrated with Standard Oil of Ohio?

A Pennsylvania lawyer named Samuel C. T. Dodd came up with an answer to this question in 1879.[1] The stock of Standard of Ohio and of all the other companies that the Rockefeller interests had swallowed up was turned over to nine trustees, who were empowered to "exercise general supervision" over all the properties. In exchange, stockholders received trust certificates, on which dividends were paid. This seemingly simple device brought order to the petroleum business. Competition almost

---

[1]The trust formula was not "perfected" until 1882.

disappeared, prices steadied, and profits skyrocketed. By 1892 John D. Rockefeller was worth over $800 million.

The Standard Oil Trust was not a corporation. It had no charter, indeed no legal existence at all. For many years few people outside the organization knew that it existed. The form they chose persuaded Rockefeller and other Standard Oil officials that without violating their consciences, they could deny under oath that Standard Oil of Ohio owned or controlled other corporations "directly or indirectly through its officers or agents." The trustees controlled these organizations—and Standard of Ohio too!

After Standard Oil's duplicity was revealed during a New York investigation in 1888, the word *trust*, formerly signifying a fiduciary arrangement for the protection of the interests of individuals incompetent or unwilling to guard them themselves, became a synonym for monopoly. However, from the company's point of view, monopoly was not the purpose of the trust—that had been achieved before the device was invented. Centralization of the management of diverse and far-flung operations in the interest of efficiency was its chief function.

Competition and Monopoly: Retailing and Utilities

That utilities such as the telephone and electric lighting industries tended to form monopolies is not difficult to explain, for in such fields competition involved costly duplication of equipment and, particularly in the case of the telephone, loss of service efficiency. However, competitive pressures were strong in the early stages of their development. Since these industries depended on patents, Bell and Edison had to fight mighty battles in the courts with rivals seeking to infringe on their rights. A patent, Edison said bitterly, was "simply an invitation to a lawsuit."

The pattern of competition leading to dominance by a few great companies was repeated in many businesses. In life insurance an immense expansion took place after the Civil War. High-pressure salesmanship prevailed; agents gave rebates to customers by shaving their own commissions; companies stole crack agents from their rivals and raided new territories. They sometimes invested as much as 96 percent of the first year's premiums in obtaining new business. By 1900, after three decades of fierce competition, three giants dominated the industry—Equitable, New York Life, and Mutual Life, each with approximately $1 billion of insurance in force.

[●]Watch the Video
Rural Free Delivery Mail at myhistorylab.com

American Ambivalence to Big Business

The expansion of industry and its concentration in fewer and fewer hands changed the way many people felt about the role of government in economic and social affairs. On the one hand, they professed to believe strongly in a government policy of noninterference, or **laissez-faire**. " 'Things regulate themselves' . . . means, of course, that God regulates them by his general laws," Professor Francis Bowen of Harvard wrote in his *American Political Economy* (1870).

Certain intellectual currents encouraged this type of thinking. Charles Darwin's *The Origin of Species* was published in 1859, and by the 1870s his theory of evolution was beginning to influence opinion in the United States. That nature had ordained a kind of inevitable progress, governed by the natural selection of those individual organisms best

A sneeze is captured on film—the first copyrighted movie (1894). In 1889 Thomas A. Edison conceived of a machine that would do for the eye what the phonograph did for the ear. Over the next two years, Edison invented two separate devices—a camera to take a rapid sequence of pictures and a machine to view them, called a kinetoscope. In 1893 he developed reliable film for his camera. The motion picture industry was born.

adapted to survive in a particular environment, seemed eminently reasonable to most Americans, for it fitted well with their own experiences. "Let the buyer beware; that covers the whole business," the sugar magnate Henry O. Havemeyer explained to an investigating committee. "You cannot wet-nurse people from the time they are born until the time they die. They have to wade and get stuck, and that is the way men are educated."

This reasoning was similar to that of the classical economists and was thus at least as old as Adam Smith's *Wealth of Nations* (1776). But it appeared to supply a hard scientific substitute for Smith's "invisible hand" as an explanation of why free competition advanced the common good.

Yale professor William Graham Sumner sometimes used the survival-of-the-fittest analogy in teaching undergraduates. "Professor," one student asked Sumner, "don't you believe in any government aid to industries?" "No!" Sumner replied, "It's root, hog, or die." The student persisted: "Suppose some professor of political science came along and took your job away from you. Wouldn't you be sore?" "Any other professor is welcome to try," Sumner answered promptly. "If he gets my job, it is my fault. My business is to teach the subject so well that no one can take the job away from me." Sumner's argument described what came to be known as **social Darwinism,** the belief that the activities of people, that is, their business and social relationships, were governed by the Darwinian principle that "the fittest" will always "survive" if allowed to exercise their capacities without restriction.

But the fact that Americans disliked powerful governments in general and strict regulation of the economy in particular had never meant that they objected to all government activity in the economic sphere. Banking laws, tariffs, internal-improvement legislation, and the granting of public land to railroads are only the most obvious of the economic regulations enforced in the nineteenth century by both the federal government and the states. Americans saw no contradiction between government activities of this type and the free enterprise philosophy.

The growth of huge industrial and financial organizations and the increasing complexity of economic relations frightened people yet made them at the same time greedy for more of the goods and services the new society was turning out. To many, the great new corporations and trusts resembled Frankenstein's monster—marvelous and powerful but a grave threat to society.

To some extent public fear of the industrial giants reflected concern about monopoly—much as some people today worry that Walmart may drive other retailers out of business. If Standard Oil dominated oil refining, it might raise prices inordinately at vast cost to consumers.

Far more important in causing resentment was the fear that the monopolists were destroying economic opportunity and threatening democratic institutions. It was not the wealth of tycoons like Carnegie and Rockefeller and Morgan so much as their influence that worried people. "The belief is common," wrote Charles Francis Adams's brother Henry as early as 1870, "that the day is at hand when corporations . . . will ultimately succeed in directing government itself."

Table 17.1   Defenders of Economic Consolidation

Defenders	Occupation	Argument
J. Pierpont Morgan	Wall Street financier	Excessive competition was wasteful and unstable; stable growth and efficiency required large business combinations
William Graham Sumner	Yale professor	Large corporations were those that were "fittest"—best-suited to prevail in the Darwinian world of capitalism
Andrew Carnegie	Steel manufacturer	Large corporations generated wealth, which could be channeled into charitable and other worthy causes

As criticism mounted, business leaders rose to their own defense. Rockefeller described in graphic terms the chaotic conditions that plagued the oil industry before the rise of Standard Oil: "It seemed absolutely necessary to extend the market for oil . . . and also greatly improve the process of refining so that oil could be made and sold cheaply, yet with a profit. We proceeded to buy the largest and best refining concerns and centralized the administration of them with a view to securing greater economy and efficiency." Carnegie, in an essay published in 1889, insisted that the concentration of wealth was necessary if humanity was to progress, softening this "Gospel of Wealth" by insisting that the rich must use their money "in the manner which . . . is best calculated to produce the most beneficial results for the community."

The voices of the critics were louder if not necessarily more influential. Many clergymen denounced unrestrained competition, which they considered un-Christian. The new class of professional economists tended to repudiate laissez-faire. State aid, Richard T. Ely of Johns Hopkins University wrote, "is an indispensable condition of human progress."

Reformers: George, Bellamy, Lloyd

The popularity of a number of radical theorists reflects public feeling in the period. In 1879 Henry George, a California journalist, published *Progress and Poverty*, a forthright attack on the uneven distribution of wealth in the United States. George argued that labor was the true and only source of capital. Observing the speculative fever of the West, which enabled landowners to reap profits merely by holding property while population increased, George proposed a property tax that would confiscate this "unearned increment." George's "single tax," as others called it, would bring in so much money that no other taxes would be necessary, and the government would have plenty of funds to establish badly needed social and cultural services. Single tax clubs sprang up throughout the nation, and *Progress and Poverty* became a best-seller.

Even more spectacular was the reception afforded *Looking Backward, 2000–1887*, a utopian novel written in 1888 by Edward Bellamy. This book, which sold over a million copies in its first few years, described a future America that was completely socialized, all economic activity carefully planned. Bellamy compared nineteenth-century

Edward Bellamy, author of the utopian novel *Looking Backward* (1888). Bellamy's socialism worried many. *The Household Encyclopedia* (1892) included this photograph of Bellamy in a section on phrenology, the "science" of ascertaining a person's character and intellectual traits from the shape of his or her cranium. Referring to Bellamy's, it concluded, "Large perceptive faculties; defective reasoning powers."

●●◦─Read the Document

Bellamy, from *Looking Backward*
at myhistorylab.com

society to a lumbering stagecoach upon which the favored few rode in comfort while the mass of the people hauled them along life's route. The trend toward consolidation would continue, he predicted, until one monster trust controlled all economic activity. At this point everyone would realize that nationalization was essential.

A third influential attack on monopoly was that of Henry Demarest Lloyd, whose *Wealth Against Commonwealth* appeared in 1894. Lloyd, a journalist of independent means, devoted years to preparing a denunciation of the Standard Oil Company. Marshaling masses of facts and vivid examples of Standard's evildoing, he assaulted the trust at every point. In his zeal, Lloyd sometimes distorted and exaggerated the evidence; his forceful but uncomplicated arguments and his copious references to official documents made *Wealth Against Commonwealth* utterly convincing to thousands. The book was more than an attack on Standard Oil. Lloyd denounced the application of Darwin's concept of survival of the fittest to economic and social affairs, and he condemned laissez-faire policies as leading directly to monopoly.

The popularity of these books indicates that the trend toward monopoly in the United States worried many. But despite the drastic changes suggested in their pages, none of these writers questioned the underlying values of the middle-class majority. They insisted that reform could be accomplished without serious inconvenience to any individual or class.

Most of their millions of readers did not seriously consider trying to apply the reformers' ideas. Henry George ran for mayor of New York City in 1886 and lost narrowly to Abram S. Hewitt, a wealthy iron manufacturer, but even if he had won, he would have been powerless to apply the single tax to metropolitan property. The national discontent was apparently not as profound as the popularity of these works might suggest.

Reformers: The Marxists

By the 1870s the ideas of European socialists were beginning to penetrate the United States, and in 1877 a Socialist Labor party was founded. The first serious attempt to explain the ideas of German political philosopher Karl Marx to Americans was Laurence Gronlund's *The Cooperative Commonwealth*, which was published in 1884, two years before Marx's *Das Kapital* was translated into English.

Capitalism, Gronlund claimed, contained the seeds of its own destruction. The state ought to own all the means of production. Competition was "Established Anarchy," middlemen were "parasites," speculators "vampires." Yet like other harsh critics of that day, Gronlund expected the millennium to arrive in a peaceful, indeed orderly manner. The movement could accommodate "representatives of all classes," even "thoughtful" middlemen parasites.

The leading voice of the Socialist Labor party, Daniel De Leon, editor of the party's weekly publication, *The People*, was a different type. He was born in the West Indies, son of a Dutch army doctor stationed in Curaçao, and educated in Europe. He emigrated to the United States in the 1870s, where he was progressively attracted by the ideas of Henry George, then Edward Bellamy and the Knights of Labor, and finally Marx. While personally mild-mannered and kindly, when he put pen to paper he became a doctrinaire revolutionary. He excoriated American labor unions in *The People*, insisting that industrial workers could improve their lot only by adopting socialism and joining the

Table 17.2   Reformers Oppose Economic Consolidation

Reformers	Publication	Argument
Henry George	Author, *Progress and Poverty* (1879)	Labor was the source of wealth; but investors made money from *capital and property*. Governments should tax property, to help redistribute the unearned income of the wealthy.
Edward Bellamy	Author, *Looking Backward* (1888)	The trend toward industrial concentration would culminate in the government owning everything: an era of prosperity, stability, and cooperative planning would ensue.
Henry Demarest Lloyd	Author, *Wealth Against Commonwealth* (1894)	Concentration of power in corporations inevitably led to monopoly; the government must step in to prevent corporations from becoming behemoths.
Laurence Gronlund	Author, *The Cooperative Commonwealth* (1884)	Capitalism, including corporations, was doomed, as Marx had predicted; but the collapse of capitalism would not require a violent revolution.
Daniel De Leon	Editor, Socialist Labor, *The Weekly*	Capitalism, though doomed, would not fall without a fight; violent revolution was inevitable.

Socialist Labor party. He paid scant attention, however, to the practical needs or even to the opinions of rank-and-file working people. In 1891 he was the Socialist Labor party's candidate for governor of New York.

The Government Reacts to Big Business: Railroad Regulation

Political action related to the growth of big business came first on the state level and dealt chiefly with the regulation of railroads. Even before the Civil War, a number of New England states established railroad commissions to supervise lines within their borders; by the end of the century, twenty-eight states had such boards.

Strict regulation was largely the result of agitation by the **National Grange of the Patrons of Husbandry**. The Grange, founded in 1867 by Oliver H. Kelley, was created to provide social and cultural benefits for isolated rural communities. As it spread and grew in influence—fourteen states had Granges by 1872 and membership reached 800,000 in 1874—the movement became political too. "Granger" candidates won control of a number of state legislatures in the West and South. Granger-controlled legislatures established "reasonable" maximum rates and outlawed "unjust" discrimination. The legislature also set up a commission to enforce the laws and punish violators.

The railroads protested, insisting that they were being deprived of property without due process of law. In *Munn v. Illinois* (1877), a case that involved a grain elevator whose owner had refused to comply with a state warehouse act, the Supreme Court upheld the constitutionality of this kind of act. Any business that served a public interest, such as a railroad or a grain warehouse, was subject to state control, the justices ruled. Legislatures might fix maximum charges; if the charges seemed unreasonable to the parties concerned, they should direct their complaints to the legislatures or to the voters, not to the courts.

Regulation of the railroad network by the individual states was inefficient, and in some cases the commissions were incompetent and even corrupt. When the Supreme Court, in the case of *Wabash, St. Louis & Pacific Railroad v. Illinois* (1886), declared unconstitutional an Illinois regulation outlawing the long-and-short-haul evil, federal action became necessary. The railroad had charged twenty-five cents per 100 pounds for shipping goods from Gilman, Illinois, to New York City but only fifteen cents to ship goods from Peoria, which was eighty-six miles farther from New York. Illinois judges had held this to be illegal, but the Supreme Court decided that Illinois could not regulate interstate shipments.

Congress filled the gap created by the *Wabash* decision in 1887 by passing the **Interstate Commerce Act**. All charges made by railroads "shall be reasonable and just," the act stated. Rebates, drawbacks, the long-and-short-haul evil, and other competitive practices were declared unlawful, and so were their monopolistic counterparts—pools and traffic-sharing agreements. Railroads were required to publish

•●•—⌐Read the **Document**

Interstate Commerce Act at
myhistorylab.com

A farmer with a pitchfork, wearing a hat identifying him as a Granger, warns of an oncoming railroad train. But the American people— one reads a newspaper, another smokes a cigar, but most doze—are oblivious of the danger that will soon crush them.

schedules of rates and forbidden to change them without due public notice. Most important, the law established an Interstate Commerce Commission (ICC), the first federal regulatory board, to supervise the affairs of railroads, investigate complaints, and issue cease and desist orders when the roads acted illegally.

The new commission had less power than the law seemed to give it. It could not fix rates; it could only bring the roads to court when it considered rates unreasonably high. Such cases could be extremely complicated; applying the law "was like cutting a path through a jungle." With the truth so hard to determine and the burden of proof on the commission, the courts in nearly every instance decided in favor of the railroads.

Nevertheless, by describing so clearly the right of Congress to regulate private corporations engaged in interstate commerce, the Interstate Commerce Act challenged the philosophy of laissez-faire. Later legislation made the commission more effective. The commission also served as the model for a host of similar federal administrative authorities, such as the Federal Communications Commission (1934).

The Government Reacts to Big Business: The Sherman Antitrust Act

As with railroad legislation, the first antitrust laws originated in the states, but they were southern and western states with relatively little industry, and most of the statutes were vaguely worded and ill-enforced. Federal action came in 1890 with the passage of the **Sherman Antitrust Act**. Any combination "in the form of trust or otherwise" that was "in restraint of trade or commerce among the several states, or with foreign nations" was declared illegal. Persons forming such combinations were subject to fines of $5,000 and a year in jail. Individuals and businesses suffering losses because of actions that violated the law were authorized to sue in the federal courts for triple damages.

Where the Interstate Commerce Act sought to outlaw the excesses of competition, the Sherman Act was supposed to restore competition. If businessmen joined together to "restrain" (monopolize) trade in a particular field, they should be punished and their deeds undone. "The great thing this bill does," Senator George Frisbie Hoar of Massachusetts explained, "is to extend the common-law principle . . . to international and interstate commerce." This was important because the states ran into legal difficulties when they tried to use the common law to restrict corporations engaged in interstate activities.

The Supreme Court quickly emasculated the Sherman Act. In *United States v. E. C. Knight Company* (1895) it held that the American Sugar Refining Company had not violated the law by taking over a number of important competitors. Although the Sugar Trust now controlled about 98 percent of all sugar refining in the United States, it was not restraining trade. "Doubtless the power to control the manufacture of a given thing involves in a certain sense the control of its disposition," the Court said in one of the greatest feats of judicial understatement of all time. "Although the exercise of that power may result in bringing the operation of commerce into play, it does not control it, and affects it only incidentally and indirectly."

If the creation of the Sugar Trust did not violate the Sherman Act, it seemed unlikely that any other combination of manufacturers could be convicted under the law. However, in several cases in 1898 and 1899 the Supreme Court ruled that agreements to fix prices or divide markets did violate the Sherman Act. These decisions precipitated a wave of

Table 17.3   Major Congressional and Supreme Court Decisions Concerning Corporations

Case/Act	Year	Decision/Action	Consequence
Munn v. Illinois	1877	State legislatures can regulate economic enterprises	Expansion of state powers against powerful corporations and trusts
Wabash, St. Louis & Pacific Railroad v. Illinois	1886	State legislatures can NOT regulate interstate economic activity; only federal government can do that	Congress passes Interstate Commerce Act 1887, regulating railroad behavior
Interstate Commerce Act	1887	Federal government can regulate railroad rates and practices	Sets precedent for federal intervention in national economic matters
Sherman Antitrust Act	1890	The federal government can break up economic enterprises that are so big and powerful that they have a monopoly	Originally used to weaken labor unions; eventually allows government to break up large corporations
United States v. E. C. Knight	1895	Huge corporations that dominated markets can not be broken up if they do not also behave badly	Weakens Sherman Antitrust Act

outright mergers in which a handful of large companies swallowed up hundreds of smaller ones. Presumably mergers were not illegal. When, some years after his retirement, Andrew Carnegie was asked by a committee of the House of Representatives to explain how he had dared participate in the formation of the U.S. Steel Corporation, he replied, "Nobody ever mentioned the Sherman Act to me that I remember."

The Labor Union Movement

At the time of the Civil War only a small percentage of the American workforce was organized, and most union members were cigarmakers, printers, carpenters, and other skilled artisans, not factory hands. Aside from ironworkers, railroad workers, and miners, few industrial laborers belonged to unions. Nevertheless the union was the workers' response to the big corporation: a combination designed to eliminate competition for jobs and to provide efficient organization for labor.

After 1865 the growth of national craft unions, which had been stimulated by labor dissatisfaction during the Civil War, quickened perceptibly. In 1866 a federation of these organizations, the National Labor Union, was founded and by the early 1870s many new trades, notably in railroading, had been unionized.

Most of the leaders of these unions were visionaries who were out of touch with the practical needs and aspirations of workers. They opposed the wage system, strikes, and anything that increased the laborers' sense of being members of the working class. A major objective was the formation of worker-owned cooperatives.

Far more remarkable was the **Knights of Labor,** a curious organization founded in 1869 by a group of Philadelphia garment workers headed by Uriah S. Stephens. Like so many labor organizers of the period, Stephens was a reformer of wide interests rather than a man dedicated to the specific problems of industrial workers. He, his successor Terence V. Powderly, and many other leaders of the Knights would have been thoroughly at home in the labor organizations of the Jacksonian era. Like the Jacksonians, they supported political objectives that had no direct connection with working conditions, such as currency reform and the curbing of land speculation. They rejected the idea that workers must resign themselves to remaining wage earners. By pooling their resources, working people could advance up the economic ladder and enter the capitalist class. The leading Knights saw no contradiction between their denunciation of "soulless" monopolies and "drones" like bankers and lawyers and their talk of "combining all branches of trade in one common brotherhood." Such muddled thinking led the Knights to attack the wage system and to frown on strikes as "acts of private warfare."

View the Image

Terence Powderly at Knights of Labor Convention at **myhistorylab.com**

If the Knights had one foot in the past, they also had one foot in the future. They supported some startlingly advanced ideas. Rejecting the traditional grouping of workers by crafts, they developed a concept closely resembling modern industrial unionism. They welcomed blacks, women, and immigrants, and they accepted unskilled workers as well as artisans. The eight-hour day was one of their basic demands, their argument being that increased leisure would give workers time to develop more cultivated tastes and higher aspirations. Higher pay would inevitably follow.

Between 1882 and 1886 successful strikes by local "assemblies" against western railroads, including one against the hated Jay Gould's Missouri Pacific, brought recruits by the thousands. The membership passed 42,000 in 1882, 110,000 in 1885, and in 1886 it soared beyond the 700,000 mark. Alas, sudden prosperity was too much for the Knights. Its national leadership was unable to control local groups. A number of poorly planned strikes failed dismally, and the public was alienated by sporadic acts of violence and intimidation. Disillusioned recruits began to drift away.

Circumstances largely fortuitous caused the collapse of the organization. By 1886 the movement for the eight-hour day had gained wide support among workers, including many who did not belong to unions. Several hundred thousand were on strike in various parts of the country by May of that year. In Chicago, a center of the eight-hour movement, about 80,000 workers were involved, and a small group of anarchists was trying to take advantage of the excitement to win support.

When a striker was killed in a fracas at the McCormick Harvesting Machine Company, the anarchists called a protest meeting on May 4, at Haymarket Square. Police intervened to break up the meeting, and someone—his identity was never established—hurled a bomb into their ranks. Seven policemen were killed and many others injured.

The American Federation of Labor

Although the anarchists were the immediate victims of the resulting public indignation and hysteria, organized labor, especially the Knights, suffered heavily. No tie between the Knights and the bombing could be established, but the union had been closely connected with the eight-hour agitation, and the public tended to associate it with violence and radicalism. Its membership declined as suddenly as it had risen, and soon it ceased to exist as a force in the labor movement.

The Knights' place was taken by the **American Federation of Labor (AFL)**, a combination of national craft unions established in 1886. In a sense the AFL was a reactionary organization. Its principal leaders, Adolph Strasser and Samuel Gompers of the Cigarmakers Union, were, like the founders of the Knights of Labor, originally interested in utopian social reforms. They even toyed with the idea of forming a workers' political party. Experience, however, soon led them to concentrate on organizing skilled workers and fighting for "bread-and-butter" issues such as higher wages and shorter hours.

Strasser and Gompers paid great attention to building a strong organization of dues-paying members committed to unionism as a way of improving their lot. Rank-and-file AFL members were naturally eager to win wage increases and other benefits, but most also valued their unions for the companionship they provided, the sense of belonging to a group. Unions were a kind of club as well as a means of defending and advancing their members' material interests.

The chief weapon of the federation was the strike, which it used to win concessions from employers and to attract recruits. Gompers, president of the AFL almost continuously from 1886 until his death in 1924, encouraged workers to make "intelligent use of the ballot" in order to advance their interests. The federation avoided direct involvement in politics. "I have my own philosophy and my own dreams," Gompers once told a left-wing French politician, "but first and foremost I want to increase the workingman's welfare year by year. . . . The French workers waste their economic force by their political divisions."

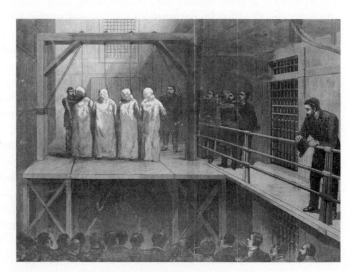

On November 11, 1887, four anarchists were hanged in Chicago on charges they had thrown a bomb that had killed policemen at the Haymarket demonstration. The *Chicago Tribune* reported that after nooses were placed around the men's necks, and white hoods over their heads, "for a moment or two the men stood like ghosts." "Long live anarchy" one shouted.

Gompers's approach to labor problems produced solid, if unspectacular, growth for the AFL. Unions with a total of about 150,000 members formed the federation in 1886. By 1892 the membership had reached 250,000, and in 1901 it passed the million mark.

Labor Militancy Rebuffed

The stress of the AFL on the strike weapon reflected rather than caused the increasing militancy of labor. Workers felt themselves threatened from all sides: the growing size and power of their corporate employers; the substitution of machines for human skills; the invasion of foreign workers willing to accept substandard wages. At the same time they had tasted some of the material benefits of industrialization and had learned the advantages of concerted action.

The average employer behaved like a tyrant when dealing with his workers: He discharged them arbitrarily when they tried to organize unions; he hired scabs to replace strikers; he frequently failed to provide the most rudimentary protection against injury on the job. Some employers, Carnegie for example, professed to approve of unions, but almost none would bargain with labor collectively. To do so, they argued, would be to deprive workers of their freedom to contract for their own labor in any way they saw fit.

The industrialists of the period were not all ogres; they were as alarmed by the rapid changes of the times as their workers, and since they had more at stake materially, they were probably more frightened by the uncertainties. Deflation, technological change, and intense competition kept even the most successful under constant pressure.

The thinking of most employers was remarkably confused. They considered workers who joined unions "disloyal," and at the same time they treated labor as a commodity to be purchased as cheaply as possible. When labor was scarce, employers resisted demands for higher wages by arguing that the price of labor was controlled by its productivity; when it was plentiful, they justified reducing wages by referring to the law of supply and demand.

Thus capital and labor were often spoiling for a fight, frequently without fully understanding why. When labor troubles developed, they tended to be bitter, even violent. In 1877 a great railroad strike convulsed much of the nation. It began on the Baltimore and Ohio system in response to a wage cut and spread to other eastern lines and then throughout the West until about two-thirds of the railroad mileage of the country had been shut down. Violence broke out, rail yards were put to the torch, and dismayed and frightened businessmen formed militia companies to patrol the streets of Chicago and other cities. Eventually President Hayes sent federal troops to the trouble spots to restore order, and the strike collapsed. There had been no real danger of revolution, but the violence and destruction of the strike had been without precedent in America.

The disturbances of 1877 were a response to a business slump, those of the next decade a response to good times. Twice as many strikes occurred in 1886 as in any previous year. Even before the Haymarket bombing centered the country's attention on labor problems, the situation had become so disturbing that President Grover Cleveland, in the first presidential message devoted to labor problems, had urged Congress to create a voluntary arbitration board to aid in settling labor disputes— a remarkable suggestion for a man of Cleveland's conservative, laissez-faire approach to economic issues.

In 1892 a violent strike broke out among silver miners at Coeur d'Alene, Idaho, and a far more important clash shook Andrew Carnegie's Homestead steel plant near Pittsburgh when strikers attacked 300 private guards brought in to protect strikebreakers. Seven guards were killed at Homestead and the rest forced to "surrender" and march off ignominiously. The Homestead affair was part of a struggle between capital and labor in the steel industry. Steel producers insisted that the workers were holding back progress by resisting technological advances, while the workers believed that the company was refusing to share the fruits of more efficient operation fairly. The strike was precipitated by the decision of company officials to crush the union at all costs. The final defeat, after a five-month walkout, of the 24,000-member Amalgamated Association of Iron and Steel Workers, one of the most important elements in the AFL, destroyed unionism as an effective force in the steel industry and set back the progress of organized labor all over the country.

As in the case of the Haymarket bombing, the activities of radicals on the fringe of the dispute turned the public against the steelworkers. The boss of Homestead was Henry Clay Frick, a tough-minded foe of unions who was determined to "teach our employees a lesson." Frick made the decision to bring in strikebreakers and to employ Pinkerton detectives to protect them. During the course of the strike, Alexander Berkman, an anarchist, burst into Frick's office and attempted to assassinate him. Frick was only slightly wounded, but the attack brought him much sympathy and unjustly discredited the strikers.

The most important strike of the period took place in 1894. It began when the workers at George Pullman's Palace Car factory outside Chicago walked out in protest against wage cuts. Some Pullman workers belonged to the American Railway Union, headed by Eugene V. Debs. After the strike had dragged along for weeks, the union voted to refuse to handle trains with Pullman sleeper cars. The union was perfectly willing to handle mail trains, but the owners refused to run trains unless they were made up of a full complement of cars.

When Pullman cars were added to mail trains, the workers refused to move them. The resulting railroad strike tied up trunk lines running in and out of Chicago. The railroad owners appealed to President Cleveland to send troops to preserve order. On the pretext that the soldiers were needed to ensure the movement of the mails, Cleveland agreed. When Debs defied a federal injunction to end the walkout, he was jailed for contempt and the strike was broken.

Whither America, Whither Democracy?

Each year more of the nation's wealth and power seemed to fall into fewer hands. As with the railroads, other industries were being influenced, if not completely dominated, by bankers. The firm of J.P. Morgan and Company controlled many railroads; the largest steel, electrical, agricultural machinery, rubber, and shipping companies; two life insurance companies; and a number of banks. By 1913 Morgan and the Rockefeller National City Bank group between them could name 341 directors to 112 corporations worth over $22.2 billion. The "Money Trust," a loose but potent fraternity of financiers, seemed fated to become the ultimate monopoly.

Centralization unquestionably increased efficiency, at least in industries that used a great deal of expensive machinery to turn out goods for the mass market, and in those where close coordination of output, distribution, and sales was important. The public benefited immensely from the productive efficiency of the new empires. Living standards rose.

The crushing of the Pullman strike demonstrated the power of the courts to break strikes by issuing injunctions. And the courts seemed only concerned with protecting the interests of the rich and powerful. Particularly ominous for organized labor was the fact that the federal government based its request for the injunction that broke the strike on the Sherman Antitrust Act, arguing that the American Railway Union was a combination in restraint of trade. An indirect result of the Pullman strike was that while serving his sentence for contempt, Eugene Debs was visited by a number of prominent socialists who sought to convert him to their cause. One gave him a copy of Karl Marx's *Capital*, which he found too dull to finish, but he did read *Looking Backward* and *Wealth Against Commonwealth*. In 1897 he became a socialist.

Milestones

1859	First oil well is drilled in Pennsylvania	1886	Craft unions found American Federation of Labor (AFL)
	Charles Darwin publishes *The Origin of Species*	1887	Interstate Commerce Act regulates railroads
1868	Carnegie Steel Company is formed		
1869	George Westinghouse invents air brake	1888	Edward Bellamy publishes utopian *Looking Backward*
	Garment workers found Knights of Labor	1889	Philanthropist Andrew Carnegie publishes "Gospel of Wealth"
1870–1890	Railroad trunk lines are completed	1890	Sherman Antitrust Act outlaws monopolies
1876	Alexander Graham Bell invents telephone	1892	Seven Pinkerton guards are killed in Homestead steel strike
1877	Great railroad strike convulses nation		General Electric Company is formed
	Munn v. Illinois upholds state regulatory laws	1894	Eugene V. Debs leads American Railway Union in Pullman strike
1879	Thomas Edison invents electric light bulb		Henry Demarest Lloyd condemns laissez-faire in *Wealth Against the Commonwealth*
	Reformer Henry George publishes *Progress and Poverty*		
1884	Marxist Laurence Gronlund publishes *The Cooperative Commonwealth*	1895	*U.S. v. E.C. Knight Company* weakens Sherman Act
1886	Anarchists clash with police in Chicago's Haymarket bombing	1901	J.P. Morgan forms U.S. Steel, "world's first billion-dollar corporation"

✓●─[Study and **Review** at www.myhistorylab.com

Review Questions

1. The introduction asked whether the benefits of economic concentration outweighed its social and political costs. List the benefits and costs: Which argument is stronger?

2. What factors contributed to the nation's extraordinarily rapid industrial growth during the last third of the nineteenth century?

3. What technological developments had the greatest economic impact? Greatest social impact?

4. Who were the major critics of economic concentration in the late nineteenth century and how did they differ?

5. How did Congress respond to critics of monopoly? How did the Supreme Court respond to attempts to regulate the economy?

Key Terms

American Federation of Labor (AFL) *472*
Interstate Commerce Act *468*
Knights of Labor *471*

laissez-faire *462*
National Grange of the Patrons of Husbandry *467*

Sherman Antitrust Act *469*
social Darwinism *464*

American Society in the Industrial Age

18

Have you been kicked out of a mall?

THE MALL OF AMERICA OUTSIDE MINNEAPOLIS, MINNESOTA, IS THE largest enclosed mall in the United States. It is also the nation's most popular tourist destination, visited by 42.5 million people in 2009.

This mall, like many others, was also once a popular hangout for young people. On Friday and Saturday nights, as many as 10,000 teenagers would gather there. But this practice ended in 1996, when the Mall of America instituted a 6:00 PM weekend curfew for teenagers under sixteen unless accompanied by an adult. Since then, hundreds of malls have adopted similar curfews.

Teenagers, who in 2009 bought $170 billion in merchandise, spend much of their free time in malls—over fifty minutes a day on the average. Many resent the curfews. Malls insist that as privately owned enterprises, they are exempt from First Amendment protections, such as freedom of speech and the right to assemble. Malls are not public property.

Yet recent malls have been designed to evoke the public spaces of the nineteenth-century city. The Mall of America includes an exhibition gallery, amusement park, wedding chapel, assembly hall, school, medical clinic, and a central "Rotunda" for staging "public events" ranging from gardening shows to Hulk Hogan wrestling matches.

In the late nineteenth century, city life was played out in spaces that really were public. Factory workers walked to work along crowded streets or jammed into streetcars or subways. Courting couples strolled through shopping districts or public parks. Children played in streets. "Little Italy" or "Chinatown" provided exotic attractions for all. Amusement parks and sporting events drew huge throngs.

But city life was not for all. In 1900, 50 percent more Americans lived in rural areas than in urban areas—even when "urban" was generously defined as holding more than 2,500 people. Why, asked sociologist Henry Fletcher in 1895, do "large masses of people, apparently against their own interests," abandon the nation's healthful and sociable rural areas and crowd into the nation's disease-ridden, anonymous cities?

Nineteenth-century cities, though noisy, chaotic, and often ill-governed, exerted a peculiar fascination. In cities, workers, even immigrants and young women, could more easily find jobs. Housing was cheap. Urban problems were daunting, but the immense aggregation of peoples and their resources constituted a limitless potential for uplift and reform.

Middle-Class Life

"This middle-class country had got a middle-class president, at last," Ralph Waldo Emerson had noted with satisfaction when Lincoln took office in 1861. Lincoln, in contrast to the presidents who had been wealthy planters or businessmen or high-ranking military men, was a self-made man who embraced middle-class values. Middle-class culture took the best aspects of romanticism—the enshrinement of human potential, the restless striving for personal betterment, the zest for competition and excitement—and tempered them with a passion for self-control and regularity.

But the Civil War sapped middle-class culture of its reforming zeal. The vital energy that invigorated antebellum reforms and had impelled the North to war became dissipated by that war. Afterwards, middle-class Americans focused their energies on building

The Breakfast (1911), by William McGregor Paxton, shows a middle-class husband, absorbed in the newspaper and in the world beyond the home. His wife, in a gorgeous dress, sits—very much a "bird in a gilded cage," the title of a popular song in 1900. The servant girl, face unseen, cleans up the cage.

Source: *The Breakfast*, William McGregor Paxton, American, 1911 The Metropolitan Museum of Art, New York, NY, U.S.A. Image copyright ©The Metropolitan Museum of Art.

institutions. American society and culture underwent a process of "incorporation," as the predominant form of the business world seeped deep into the American consciousness.

No institution was more central to middle-class life than the family. After the Civil War, it lost some of its moral fervor but gained a new substantiality. Increasingly family life was defined in terms of tangible goods. Modern scholars have often indicted this "culture of consumption" for its superficiality, a criticism commonly aired by patrician elites at the time. But no attack on middle-class culture and its conspicuous consumption surpassed the venom of Thorstein Veblen's *Theory of the Leisure Class* (1899). Veblen contended that consumers derived little real pleasure from their big homes and gaudy purchases; they were simply showing off their wealth. No one was ever satisfied with their wealth because everyone else was scrambling to get ahead of them. Everyone wanted more.

Middle-class people regarded the matter differently. They conceived of the family as a refuge from the increasingly chaotic and unsavory aspects of urban life: A beautiful house that was filled with books, paintings, and musical instruments would inculcate the finer sensibilities and elevate the minds of its occupants. Better for children to find stimulation at home than to visit the vice districts or unsupervised amusements downtown. The abundant material culture of the "Victorian age" reflected not its superficiality but its solidity.

Skilled and Unskilled Workers

Wage earners, too, were drawn to urban areas. They felt the full force of the industrial tide, being affected in countless ways—some beneficial, others unfortunate. As manufacturing became more important, the number of manufacturing workers increased nearly ten-fold, from around 600,000 in 1860 to nearly 5 million in 1890. While workers lacked much sense of solidarity, they exerted a far larger influence on society at the turn of the century than they had in the years before the Civil War.

More efficient methods of production enabled them to increase their output, making possible a rise in their standard of living. The working day still tended to approximate the hours of daylight, but it was shortening perceptibly by the 1880s, at least in many occupations. In 1860 the average had been eleven hours, but by 1880 only one worker in four labored more than ten hours and radicals were beginning to talk about eight hours as a fair day's work.

Industrialization created problems for workers beyond the obvious one of earning enough money to support themselves. By and large, skilled workers improved their positions relatively, despite the increased use of machinery. Furthermore, when machines took the place of human skills, jobs became monotonous. Mechanization undermined both the artisans' pride and their bargaining power with employers. As expensive machinery became more important, the worker seemed of necessity less important. Machines controlled the pace of work and its duration. The time clock regulated the labor force more rigidly than the most exacting foreman. The length of the workday may have declined, but the pace of work and the danger involved in working around heavy, high-speed machinery increased accordingly.

Another problem for workers was that industrialization tended to accentuate swings of the business cycle. On the upswing something approaching full employment

This girl ran four spinning machines in a cotton mill in Whitnel, North Carolina. Only four feet, three inches tall, she earned forty-eight cents a day. Photographer Lewis Hine hoped that pictures such as this one (1908) would generate public support for child labor laws.

existed, but in periods of depression unemployment became a problem that affected workers without regard for their individual abilities. It is significant that the word *unemployment* (though not, of course, the condition itself) was a late-nineteenth-century invention.

Working Women

Women continued to supply a significant part of the industrial working force. But now many more of them were working outside their homes; the factory had almost completely replaced the household as the seat of manufacturing.[1] Such women had no choice but to leave the "domestic sphere" to make a living. Textile mills and "the sewing trades" absorbed a large percentage of women, but in all fields women were paid substantially lower wages than men.

●●●─[**Read** the **Document**

Massachusett Bureau of Statistics of Labor at **myhistorylab.com**

Women found many new types of work in these years. They made up the over-whelming majority of salespersons and cashiers in the big new department stores. Store managers considered women more polite, easier to control, and more honest than male workers, all qualities especially valuable in the huge emporiums.

Educated, middle-class women also dominated the new profession of nursing that developed alongside the expanding medical profession and the establishment of large urban hospitals. To nearly all doctors, to most men, and indeed to many women of that day, nursing seemed the perfect female profession since it required the same character-istics that women were thought to have by nature: selflessness, cleanliness, kindliness, tact, sensitivity, and submissiveness to male control. Typical was this remark of a con-temporary authority: "Since God could not care for all the sick, he made women to nurse." Why it had not occurred to God to make more women physicians, or for that matter members of other prestigious professions like law and the clergy, this man did not explain, probably because it had not occurred to him either.

Middle-class women did replace men as teachers in most of the nation's grade schools, and they also replaced men as clerks and secretaries and operators of the new typewriters in government departments and in business offices. Most men with

---

[1]However, at least half of all working women were domestic servants.

the knowledge of spelling and grammar that these positions required had better opportunities and were uninterested in office work, so women high school graduates, of whom there was an increasing number, filled the gap.

Working-Class Family Life

Early social workers who visited the homes of industrial laborers in this period reported enormous differences in the standard of living of people engaged in the same line of work, differences related to such variables as health, intelligence, the wife's ability as a homemaker, the degree of the family's commitment to middle-class values, and pure luck. Some families spent most of their income on food; others saved substantial sums even when earning no more than $400 or $500 a year. Family incomes varied greatly among workers who received similar hourly wages, depending on the steadiness of employment and on the number of family members holding jobs.

Consider the cases of two families headed by railroad brakemen. One man brought home only $360 to house and feed a wife and eight children. Here is the report of a state official who interviewed the family: "Clothes ragged, children half-dressed and dirty. They all sleep in one room regardless of sex. . . . The entire concern is as wretched as could be imagined. Father is shiftless. . . . Wife is without ambition or industry."

The other brakeman and his wife had only two children, and he earned $484 in 1883. They owned a well-furnished house, kept a cow, and raised vegetables for home consumption. Although they were far from rich, they managed to put aside enough for insurance, reading matter, and a few small luxuries.

Working-Class Attitudes

Social workers and government officials made many efforts in the 1880s and 1890s to find out how working people felt about all sorts of matters connected with their jobs. Their reports reveal a wide spectrum of opinion. To the question, asked of two Wisconsin carpenters, "What new laws, in your opinion, ought to be enacted?" one replied, "Keep down strikes and rioters. Let every man attend to his own business." But the other answered, "Complete nationalization of land and all ways of transportation. Burn all government bonds. A graduated income tax. . . . Abolish child labor and [pass] any other act that capitalists say is wrong."

Every variation of opinion between these extremes was expressed by working people in many sections and in many kinds of work. In 1881 a female textile worker in Lawrence, Massachusetts, said to an interviewer, "If you will stand by the mill, and see the people coming out, you will be surprised to see the happy, contented look they all have."

Despite such remarks and the general improvement in living standards, it is clear, if only from the large number of bitter strikes of the period, that there was a considerable dissatisfaction among industrial workers. Writing in 1885, the labor leader Terence V. Powderly reported that "a deep-rooted feeling of discontent pervades the masses."

The discontent had many causes. For some, poverty was still the chief problem, but for others, rising aspirations triggered discontent. Workers were confused about their destiny; the tradition that no one of ability need remain a hired hand died hard. They wanted to believe their bosses and the politicians when those worthies voiced the old slogans about a classless society and the community of interest of capital and labor. The rich were growing richer and more people were growing rich, but ordinary workers were better off too. However, the gap between the very rich and the ordinary citizen was widening. "The tendency . . . is toward centralization and aggregation," the Illinois Bureau of Labor Statistics reported in 1886. "This involves a separation of the people into classes, and the permanently subordinate status of large numbers of them."

Working Your Way Up

Americans in the late nineteenth century believed their society offered great opportunities for individual advancement, and to prove it they pointed to men like Andrew Carnegie and to other poor boys who accumulated large fortunes. How general was the rise from rags to riches (or even to modest comfort) is another question.

Americans had been on the move, mostly, of course, in a westward direction, since the colonial period, but studies of census records show that there was considerable geographic mobility in urban areas throughout the last half of the nineteenth century and into the twentieth. Most investigations reveal that only about half the people recorded in one census were still in the same place ten years later. The nation had a vast reservoir of rootless people. For many, the way to move up in the world was to move on.

In most of the cities studied, mobility was accompanied by some economic and social improvement. On the average, about a quarter of the manual laborers traced rose to middle-class status during their lifetimes, and the sons of manual laborers were still more likely to improve their place in society. In New York City about a third of the Italian and Jewish immigrants of the 1890s had risen from unskilled to skilled jobs a decade later.

Such progress was primarily the result of the economic growth the nation was experiencing and of the energy and ambition of the people, native-born and immigrant alike, who were pouring into the cities in such numbers. The public education system gave an additional boost to the upwardly mobile.

The history of American education after about 1870 reflects the impact of social and economic change. Although Horace Mann, Henry Barnard, and others had laid the foundations for state-supported school systems in the 1840s and 1850s (see Chapter 10), most of these systems became compulsory only after the Civil War, when the growth of cities provided the concentration of population and financial resources necessary for economical mass education. In the 1860s about half the children in the country were getting some formal education, but this did not mean that half the children were attending school at any one time. Sessions were short, especially in rural areas, and many teachers were poorly trained. President Calvin Coolidge noted in his autobiography that the one-room school he attended in rural Vermont in the 1880s was open only in slack seasons when the twenty-odd students were not needed in the fields. "Few, if any, of my teachers reached the standard now required," he wrote, adding that his own younger sister had obtained a teaching certificate and actually taught a class when she was only twelve.

Jacob Riis's photograph of a class on the Lower East Side of New York City. At Riis's death, Theodore Roosevelt called him "the staunchest, most efficient, friend the children of New York City have ever had."

Thereafter, steady growth and improvement took place. Attendance in the public schools increased from 6.8 million in 1870 to 15.5 million in 1900, a remarkable expansion even when allowance is made for the growth of the population. More remarkable still, during a time when prices were declining steadily, public expenditures for education nearly quadrupled. A typical elementary school graduate, at least in the cities, could count on having studied, besides the traditional "Three Rs," history, geography, a bit of science, drawing, and physical training.

Secondary education was still assumed to be only for those with special abilities and youths whose families did not require that they immediately become breadwinners. As late as 1890 fewer than 300,000 of the 14.3 million children attending public and private schools had progressed beyond the eighth grade and nearly a third of these were attending private institutions.

Education certainly helped young people to rise in the world, but progress from rags to real riches was far from common. Carnegies were rare. A study of the family backgrounds of 200 late-nineteenth-century business leaders revealed that nearly all of them grew up in well-to-do middle-class families. They were far better educated than the general run, and most were members of one or another Protestant church.

The unrealistic expectations inspired by the rags-to-riches myth more than the absence of real opportunity probably explains why so many workers, even when expressing dissatisfaction with life as it was, continued to subscribe to such middle-class values as hard work and thrift—that is, they continued to hope.

The "New" Immigration

Industrial expansion increased the need for labor, and this in turn powerfully stimulated immigration. Between 1866 and 1915 about 25 million foreigners entered the United States. Industrial growth alone does not explain the influx. The launching in 1858 of the English liner *Great Eastern*, which was nearly 700 feet from stem to stern and weighed about 19,000 tons, opened a new era in transatlantic travel. Although most immigrants traveled in steerage, which was cramped and almost totally lacking in anything that could be considered an amenity, the Atlantic crossing, once so hazardous, became safe and speedy with the perfection of the steamship. Competition between the great packet lines such as Cunard, North German Lloyd, and Holland-America drove down the cost of the passage, and advertising by the lines further stimulated traffic.

"Push" pressures as well as these "pull" factors had much to do with the new patterns of immigration. Improvements in transportation produced unexpected and disruptive changes in the economies of many European countries. Cheap wheat from the United States, Russia, and other parts of the world poured into Europe, bringing disaster to farmers throughout Europe. The spreading industrial revolution and the increased use of farm machinery led to the collapse of the peasant economy of central and southern Europe. For rural inhabitants this meant the loss of self-sufficiency, the fragmentation of landholdings, unemployment, and for many the decision to make a new start in the New World.

While immigrants continued to people the farms of America, industry absorbed an ever-increasing number of the newcomers. In 1870 one industrial worker in three was foreign-born. When congressional investigators examined twenty-one major industries

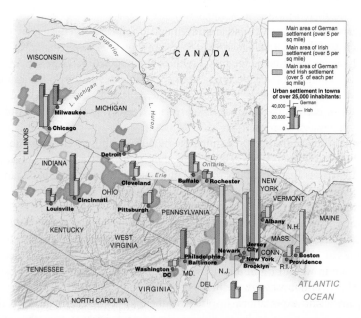

German and Irish Settlement in the Northeastern United States, 1870 In 1870, New York was the greatest immigrant city; its Irish population dwarfed that of Philadelphia or Boston. Its German population, too, greatly exceeded that of "German" cities such as Milwaukee and Chicago.

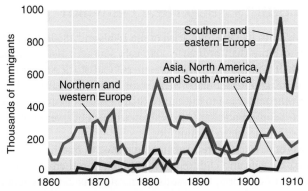

Immigration, 1860–1910 In this graph, Germany is counted as a part of northern and western Europe. Note the new immigration from southern and eastern Europe in the early 1900s.

early in the new century, they discovered that well over half of the labor force had not been born in the United States.

Before 1882, when—in addition to the Chinese—criminals, and persons adjudged mentally defective or liable to become public charges were excluded, entry into the United States was almost unrestricted. Indeed, until 1891 the Atlantic coast states, not the federal government, exercised whatever controls were imposed on newcomers. Even when federally imposed, medical inspection was perfunctory. Public health officials boasted that with "one glance" at each arrival, the inspectors could "take in six details, namely the scalp, face, neck, hands, gait and general condition, both mental and physical." Only those who failed this "test" were examined more closely. On average, only one immigrant in fifty was ultimately rejected.

Watch the Video

Ellis Island Immigrants, 1903
at **myhistorylab.com**

View the Image

Health Check at Ellis Island
at **myhistorylab.com**

Private agencies, philanthropic and commercial, served as a link between the new arrivals and employers looking for labor. Until the Foran Act of 1885 outlawed the practice, a few companies brought in skilled workers under contract, advancing them passage money and collecting it in installments from their paychecks, a system somewhat like the indentured servitude of colonial times. Numerous nationality groups assisted (and sometimes exploited) their compatriots by organizing "immigrant banks" that recruited labor in the old country, arranged transportation, and then housed the newcomers in boardinghouses in the United States while finding them jobs.

Beginning in the 1880s, the spreading effects of industrialization in Europe caused a shift in the sources of American immigration from northern and western to southern and eastern sections of the continent. In 1882, 789,000 immigrants entered the United States; more than 350,000 came from Great Britain and Germany, only 32,000 from Italy, and fewer than 17,000 from Russia. In 1907—the all-time peak year, with 1,285,000 immigrants—Great Britain and Germany supplied fewer than half as

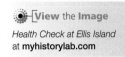

See the Map

Foreign-Born Population, 1890
at **myhistorylab.com**

many as they had twenty-five years earlier, while the **new immigration** from southern and eastern Europe was supplying eleven times as many as then. Up to 1880, only about 200,000 southern and eastern Europeans had migrated to America. Between 1880 and 1910, approximately 8.4 million arrived.

New Immigrants Face New Nativism

The "new" immigrants, like the "old" Irish of the 1840s and 1850s, were mostly peasants. They also seemed more than ordinarily clannish; southern Italians typically called all people outside their families *forestieri*, "foreigners." Old-stock Americans thought them harder to assimilate, and in fact many were. Some Italian immigrants, for example, were unmarried men who had come to the United States to earn enough money to buy a farm back home. Such people made hard and willing workers but were not much concerned with being part of an American community.

These "birds of passage" were a substantial minority, but the immigrant who saved in order to bring his wife and children or his younger brothers and sisters to America was more typical. In addition, thousands of immigrants came as family groups and intended to remain. Some, like the eastern European Jewish migrants, were refugees who were almost desperately eager to become Americans, although of course they retained and nurtured much of their traditional culture.

Many "older" Americans concluded, wrongly but understandably, that the new immigrants were incapable of becoming good citizens and should be kept out. During the 1880s, large numbers of social workers, economists, and church leaders, worried by the problems that arose when so many poor immigrants flocked into cities already bursting at the seams, began to believe that some restriction should be placed on the incoming human tide.

Social Darwinists and people obsessed with pseudoscientific ideas about "racial purity" also found the new immigration alarming. Misunderstanding the findings of the new science of genetics, they attributed the social problems associated with mass immigration to supposed physiological characteristics of the newcomers. Forgetting that earlier Americans had accused pre–Civil War Irish and German immigrants of similar deficiencies, they decided that the peoples of southern and eastern Europe were racially inferior to "Nordic" and "Anglo-Saxon" types and ought to be kept out.

Workers, fearing the competition of people with low living standards and no bargaining power, spoke out against the "enticing of penniless and unapprised immigrants . . . to undermine our wages and social welfare." In 1883 the president of the Amalgamated Iron and Steel Workers told a Senate committee that Hungarian, Polish, Italian, and other immigrants "can live where I think a decent man would die; they can live on . . . food that other men would not touch." A Wisconsin iron worker put it this way: "Immigrants work for almost nothing and seem to be able to live on wind—something I can not do."

◉ View the Image

Looking Backward at Immigrant Origins at **myhistorylab.com**

Employers were not disturbed by the influx of people with strong backs willing to work hard for low wages. Nevertheless, by the late 1880s many employers were alarmed about the supposed radicalism of the immigrants. The Haymarket bombing focused attention on the handful of foreign-born extremists in the country and loosed a flood of unjustified charges that "anarchists and communists" were dominating the labor movement. **Nativism**, which had grown in the 1850s under the Know-Nothing banner and faded during the Civil War, now flared up again, and for similar reasons. Denunciations of "longhaired, wild-eyed, bad-smelling, atheistic, reckless foreign wretches," of "Europe's human and inhuman rubbish" crowded the pages of the nation's press.

These nativists, again like the pre–Civil War variety, disliked Catholics and other minority groups more than immigrants as such. The largest nativist organization of the period, the American Protective Association, founded in 1887, existed primarily to resist what its members called "the Catholic menace." The Protestant majority treated "new" immigrants as underlings, tried to keep them out of the best jobs, and discouraged their efforts to climb the social ladder. This prejudice functioned only at the social and economic level. But nowhere in America did prejudice lead to interference with religious freedom in the narrow sense. And neither labor leaders nor important industrialists, despite their misgivings about immigration, took a broadly antiforeigner position.

After the Exclusion Act of 1882 and the almost meaningless 1885 ban on importing contract labor, no further restrictions were imposed on immigration until the twentieth century. Strong support for a literacy test for admission developed in the 1890s, pushed by a new organization, the Immigration Restriction League. Since there was much more illiteracy in the southeastern quarter of Europe than in the northwestern, such a test would discriminate without seeming to do so on national or racial grounds. A literacy test bill passed both houses of Congress in 1897, but President Cleveland vetoed it. Such a "radical departure" from the "generous and free-handed policy" of the past, Cleveland said, was unjustified. He added, perhaps with tongue in cheek, that a literacy requirement would not keep out "unruly agitators," who were only too adept at reading and writing.

The Expanding City and Its Problems

Industrialization does not entirely explain the growth of nineteenth-century cities. All the large American cities began as commercial centers, and the development of huge metropolises like New York and Chicago would have been impossible without the national transportation network. But by the final decades of the century, the expansion of industry had become the chief cause of city growth. Thus the urban concentration continued; in 1890 one person in three lived in a city, by 1910 nearly one in two.

A steadily increasing proportion of the urban population was made up of immigrants. In 1890 the foreign-born population of Chicago almost equaled the total population of Chicago in 1880; a third of all Bostonians and a quarter of all Philadelphians were immigrants; and four out of five residents of New York City were either foreign-born or the children of immigrants.

After 1890 the immigrant concentration became even more dense. The migrants from eastern and southern Europe lacked the resources to travel to the agriculturally developing regions. As the concentration progressed it fed upon itself, for all the eastern cities developed many ethnic neighborhoods, in each of which immigrants of one nationality congregated. Lonely, confused, often unable to speak English, the Italians, the Greeks, the Polish and Russian Jews, and other immigrants tended to settle where their predecessors had settled.

Although ethnic neighborhoods were crowded, unhealthy, and crime-ridden, and many of the residents were desperately poor, they were not ghettos in the European sense, for those who lived there were not compelled by law to remain. Thousands "escaped" yearly to better districts. American ghettos were places where hopes and ambitions were fulfilled, where people worked hard and endured hardships in order to improve their own and their children's lot.

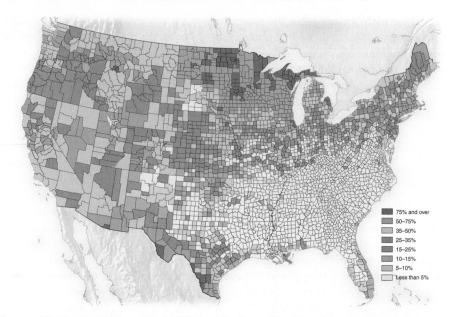

Legend:
- 75% and over
- 50–75%
- 35–50%
- 25–35%
- 15–25%
- 10–15%
- 5–10%
- Less than 5%

Percent of Foreign-Born Whites and Native Whites of Foreign or Mixed Parentage in Total Population, by Counties, 1910 In 1910, the South had the lowest proportion of immigrants; in Minnesota, Wisconsin, North Dakota, Massachusetts, Connecticut, Rhode Island, in the regions bordering Mexico, and in parts of the Rocky Mountains, over half of the population was immigrant.

Observing the immigrants' attachment to "foreign" values and institutions, numbers of "natives" accused the newcomers of resisting Americanization and blamed them for urban problems. The immigrants were involved in these problems, but the rapidity of urban expansion explains the troubles associated with city life far more fully than the high percentage of foreigners.

Teeming Tenements

The cities were suffering from growing pains. Sewer and water facilities frequently could not keep pace with skyrocketing needs. By the 1890s the tremendous growth of Chicago had put such a strain on its sanitation system that the Chicago River had become virtually an open sewer, and the city's drinking water contained such a high concentration of germ-killing chemicals that it tasted like creosote. In the 1880s all the sewers of Baltimore emptied into the sluggish Back Basin, and according to the journalist H. L. Mencken, every summer the city smelled "like a billion polecats." Fire protection became less and less adequate, garbage piled up in the streets faster than it could be carted away, and the streets themselves crumbled beneath the pounding of heavy traffic. Urban growth proceeded with such speed that new streets were laid out more rapidly than they could be paved. Chicago had more than 1,400 miles of dirt streets in 1890.

Substandard living quarters aggravated other evils such as disease and the disintegration of family life, with its attendant mental anguish, crime, and juvenile delinquency. The bloody New York City riots of 1863, though sparked by dislike of the Civil War draft

Impoverished immigrant families, like the one in this 1889 Jacob Riis photograph, often lived in tiny windowless rooms in crowded tenement districts. Riis devised a "flash bulb" for indoor photographs in poorly illuminated rooms like this one.
Source: Jacob A. Riis, *In Poverty Gap: An English Coal-Heaver's Home.* Courtesy of Museum of the City of New York.

and of blacks, reflected the bitterness and frustration of thousands jammed together amid filth and threatened by disease. A citizens' committee seeking to discover the causes of the riots expressed its amazement after visiting the slums "that so much misery, disease, and wretchedness can be huddled together and hidden . . . unvisited and unthought of, so near our own abodes."

New York City created a Metropolitan Health Board in 1866, and a state tenement house law the following year made a feeble beginning at regulating city housing. The magazine *Plumber and Sanitary Engineer* sponsored a contest to pick the best design for a **tenement**. The winner of the competition was James E. Ware, whose plan for a "dumbbell" apartment house managed to crowd from twenty-four to thirty-two four-room apartments on a plot of ground only 25 by 100 feet.

The unhealthiness of the tenements was notorious. No one knows exactly, but as late as 1900 about three-quarters of the residents of New York City's Lower East Side lacked indoor toilets and had to use backyard outhouses to relieve themselves.

View the Image
New York City Tenements
at **myhistorylab.com**

One noxious corner became known as the "lung block" because of the prevalence of tuberculosis among its inhabitants. In 1900 three out of five babies born in one poor district of Chicago died before their first birthday.

Slums bred criminals—the wonder was that they did not breed more. They also drove well-to-do residents into exclusive sections and to the suburbs. From Boston's

Beacon Hill and Back Bay to San Francisco's Nob Hill, the rich retired into their cluttered mansions and ignored conditions in the poorer parts of town.

The Cities Modernize

Gradually the basic facilities of urban living were improved. Streets were paved, first with cobblestones and wood blocks and then with smoother, quieter asphalt. Gaslight, then electric arc lights, and finally Edison's incandescent lamps brightened the cities after dark, making law enforcement easier, stimulating night life, and permitting factories and shops to operate after sunset.

Urban transportation underwent enormous changes. Until the 1880s, horse-drawn cars running on tracks set flush with the street were the main means of urban public transportation. In 1860 New York City's horsecars were carrying about 100,000 passengers a day. But horsecars had serious drawbacks. Enormous numbers of horses were needed, and feeding and stabling the animals was costly. Their droppings (ten pounds per day per horse) became a major source of urban pollution. That is why the invention of the electric trolley car in the 1880s put an end to horsecar transportation. Trolleys were cheaper and less unsightly than horsecars and quieter than steam-powered trains.

A retired naval officer, Frank J. Sprague, installed the first practical electric trolley line in Richmond, Virginia, in 1887–1888. At once other cities seized on the trolley. Lines soon radiated outward from the city centers, bringing commuters and shoppers from the residential districts to the business district. Without them the big-city department stores could not have flourished as they did. By 1895 some 850 lines were busily hauling city dwellers over 10,000 miles of track, and mileage tripled in the following decade. As with other new enterprises, ownership of street railways quickly became centralized until a few big operators controlled the trolleys of more than 100 eastern cities and towns.

Streetcars changed the character of big-city life. Before their introduction urban communities were limited by the distances people could conveniently walk to work. The "walking city" could not easily extend more than twenty-one-and-a-half miles from its center. Streetcars increased this radius to six miles or more, which meant that the area of the city expanded enormously. Dramatic population shifts resulted as the better-off moved away from the center in search of air and space, abandoning the crumbling, jam-packed older neighborhoods to the poor. Thus economic segregation speeded the growth of ghettos. Older peripheral towns that had maintained some of the self-contained qualities of village life were swallowed up, becoming metropolitan centers.

As time passed, each new area, originally peopled by rising economic groups, tended to become crowded and then deteriorated. By extending their tracks beyond the developed areas, the streetcar companies further speeded suburban growth because they assured developers, bankers, builders, and middle-class home buyers of efficient transport to the center of town. By keeping fares low (five cents a ride was standard) the lines enabled poor people to "escape" to the countryside on holidays.

Leisure Activities: More Fun and Games

By bringing together large numbers of people, cities made possible many kinds of social activity difficult or impossible to maintain in rural areas. Cities remained unsurpassed as centers of artistic and intellectual life. New York was the outstanding example, as seen in its many theaters and in the founding of the American Museum of Natural History (1870), the Metropolitan Museum of Art (1870), and the Metropolitan Opera (1883), but other cities were equally hospitable to such endeavors. Boston's Museum of Fine Arts, for example, was founded in 1870 and the Boston Symphony in 1881.

•●•⌐Read the Document

Fox, from *Coney Island Frolics* at **myhistorylab.com**

Of course less sophisticated forms of recreation also flourished in the urban environment. From 1865 to 1885 the number of breweries in Massachusetts quadrupled. It is only a slight exaggeration to say that in crowded urban centers there was a saloon on every corner; during the last third of the century the number of saloons in the country tripled. Saloons were strictly male working-class institutions, usually decorated with pictures and other mementos of sports heroes, the bar perhaps under the charge of a retired pugilist.

Calvinist-inspired opposition to sports as a frivolous waste of valuable time was steadily evaporating, replaced among the upper and middle classes by the realization that games like golf and tennis were "healthy occupation[s] for mind and body." Bicycling became a fad, both as a means of getting from place to place in the ever-expanding cities and as a form of exercise and recreation.

The postwar era also saw the first important development of spectator sports, again because cities provided the concentrations of population necessary to support them. Curious relationships developed between upper- and working-class interests and between competitive sports as pure enjoyment for players and spectators and sports as something to bet on. Horse racing had strictly upper-class origins, but racetracks attracted huge crowds of ordinary people more intent on picking a winner than on improving the breed.

Professional boxing offers an even better example. It was in a sense a hobby of the rich, who sponsored favorite gladiators, offered prizes, and often wagered large sums on the matches. But the audiences were made up overwhelmingly of young working-class males, from whose ranks most of the fighters emerged. The gambling and also the brutality of the bloody, bare-knuckle character of the fights caused many communities to outlaw boxing, a fact that added to the appeal of the sport for some.

Three major team games—baseball, football, and basketball—developed in something approaching their modern form during the last quarter of the century. Various forms of what became baseball were played long before that time. Organized teams, in most cases made up of upper-class amateurs, first emerged in the 1840s, but the game only became truly popular during the Civil War, when it was a major form of camp recreation for the troops.

After the war professional teams began to appear (the first, the Cincinnati Red Stockings, paid players between $800 and $1,400 for the season), and in 1876 teams in eight cities formed the National League. The American League followed in 1901. After a brief period of rivalry, the two leagues made peace in 1903, the year of the first World Series.

Organized play led to codification of the rules and improvements in technique and strategy: for example, the development of "minor" leagues; impartial umpires calling balls and strikes and ruling on close plays; the use of catcher's masks and padded gloves; the invention of various kinds of curves and other erratic pitches (often enhanced by "doctoring" the ball). As early as the 1870s, baseball was being called "the national game" and losing all upper-class connotations. Important games

Luna Park at Coney Island was a vast living theater in which the strollers were both spectators and actors. At night, a quarter of a million electric lights turned Luna Park into what its designer, Frederic Thompson, called "a different world—a dream world, perhaps a nightmare world—where all is bizarre and fantastic."

attracted crowds in the tens of thousands; betting became a problem. Despite its urban origins, its broad green fields and dusty base paths gave the game a rural character that only recently has begun to fade away.

Nobody "invented" baseball, but both football and basketball owe their present form to individuals. James Naismith's invention of basketball is undisputed. In 1891, while a student at a YMCA school, he attached peach baskets to the edge of an elevated running track in the gymnasium and drew up what are still the basic rules of the game. The first basketball was a soccer ball. The game was popular from the start, but because it was played indoors it was not an important spectator sport until much later.

Football was not created by one person in the way that basketball was; it evolved out of English rugby. For many decades it remained almost entirely a college sport (and thus played almost entirely by upper- and middle-class types). Organized collegiate sports dated back to before the Civil War; the first intercollegiate matches were rowing races between Harvard and Yale students. The first intercollegiate football game occurred when Rutgers defeated Princeton in 1869, and by the 1880s college football had become extremely popular.

Much of the game's modern character, however, was the work of Walter Camp, the athletic director and football coach of Yale. Camp cut the size of teams from fifteen to eleven, and he invented the scrimmage line, the four-down system, and the key position of quarterback. He publicized the game in a series of books, ranging from *How to Coach a Team* (1886) to *Jack Hall at Yale* (1909). Camp's prestige was such that when he named his first All-American team after the 1889 season, no one challenged his judgment. Well into the twentieth century, the players that Camp selected were the All-Americans.

A football game pits Yale and Princeton in 1879. The field was not lined or bounded, and play consisted mostly of disorganized scrums.

Spectator sports had little appeal to women at this time and indeed for decades thereafter. And few women participated in organized athletics. Sports were "manly" activities; a woman might ride a bicycle, play croquet, and perhaps play a little tennis, but to display any concentrated interest in excelling in a sport was considered unfeminine.

Christianity's Conscience and the Social Gospel

The modernization of the great cities was not solving most of the social problems of the slums. As this fact became clear, a number of urban religious leaders began to take a hard look at the situation. Traditionally, American churchmen had insisted that where sin was concerned there were no extenuating circumstances. To the well-to-do they preached the virtues of thrift and hard work; to the poor they extended the possibility of a better existence in the next world; to all they stressed one's responsibility for one's own behavior—and thus for one's own salvation. Such a point of view brought meager comfort to residents of slums. Consequently, the churches lost influence in the poorer sections. Furthermore, as better-off citizens followed the streetcar lines out from the city centers, their church leaders followed them.

In New York, seventeen Protestant congregations abandoned the depressed areas of Lower Manhattan between 1868 and 1888. Catering thereafter almost entirely to middle-class and upper-class worshippers, the pastors tended to become even more conservative. No more strident defender of reactionary ideas existed than the pastor of Brooklyn's fashionable Plymouth Congregational Church, Henry Ward Beecher. Beecher, a younger brother of Harriet Beecher Stowe, the author of *Uncle Tom's Cabin*, attributed poverty to the improvidence of laborers who, he claimed, squandered their wages on liquor and tobacco. "No man in this land suffers from poverty," he said, "unless it be more than his fault—unless it be his sin." The best check on labor unrest was a plentiful supply of cheap immigrant labor, he told President Hayes. Unions were "the worst form of despotism and tyranny in the history of Christendom."

An increasing proportion of the residents of the blighted districts were Catholics, and the Roman church devoted much effort to distributing alms, maintaining homes for orphans and old people, and other forms of social welfare. But church leaders seemed unconcerned with the social causes of the blight; they were deeply committed to the idea that sin and vice were personal, while poverty was an act of God. They deplored the rising tide of crime, disease, and destitution among their coreligionists, yet they failed to see the connection between these evils and the squalor of the slums. "Intemperance is the great evil we have to overcome," wrote the president of the leading Catholic charitable organization, the Society of St. Vincent de Paul. "It is the source of the misery for at least three-fourths of the families we are called upon to visit and relieve."

The conservatism of most Protestant and Catholic clergymen did not prevent some earnest preachers from working directly to improve the lot of the city poor. Some followed the path blazed by Dwight L. Moody, a lay evangelist who became famous throughout America and Great Britain in the 1870s. A gargantuan figure weighing nearly 300 pounds, Moody conducted a vigorous campaign to persuade the denizens of the slums to cast aside their sinful ways. He went among them full of enthusiasm and God's love and made an impact no less powerful than that of George Whitefield during the Great Awakening of the eighteenth century or Charles Grandison Finney in the first part of the nineteenth. The evangelists founded mission schools in the slums and tried to provide spiritual and recreational facilities for the unfortunate. They were prominent in the establishment of American branches of the YMCA (1851) and the Salvation Army (1880).

However, many evangelists paid little heed to the causes of urban poverty and vice, believing that faith in God would enable the poor to transcend the material difficulties of

Dwight L. Moody, a lay preacher, saw the church he had built destroyed by the Chicago fire of 1871. But the fire also intensified his faith. His conversational manner appealed to working people, and his adherence to the literal word of the Bible provided them with an anchor in a sea of change.

life. For a number of Protestant clergymen who had become familiar with the slums, a different approach seemed called for. Slum conditions caused the sins and crimes of the cities; the wretched human beings who committed them could not be blamed, these ministers argued. They began to preach a **Social Gospel** that focused on improving living conditions rather than on saving souls. If people were to lead pure lives, they must have enough to eat, decent homes, and opportunities to develop their talents. Social Gospelers advocated civil service reform, child labor legislation, regulation of big corporations, and heavy taxes on incomes and inheritances.

The most influential preacher of the Social Gospel was probably Washington Gladden. At first, Gladden, who was raised on a Massachusetts farm, had opposed all government interference in social and economic affairs, but his experiences as a minister in Springfield, Massachusetts, and Columbus, Ohio, exposed him to the realities of life in industrial cities, and his views changed. In *Applied Christianity* (1886) and in other works he defended laborers' right to organize and strike and denounced the idea that supply and demand should control wage rates. He favored factory inspection laws, strict regulation of public utilities, and other reforms.

Nothing so well reveals the receptivity of the public to the Social Gospel as the popularity of Charles M. Sheldon's novel *In His Steps* (1896), one of America's all-time best-sellers. Sheldon, a minister in Topeka, Kansas, described what happened in the mythical city of Raymond when a group of leading citizens decided to live truly Christian lives, asking themselves "What would Jesus do?" before adopting any course of action. Naturally the tone of Raymond's society was immensely improved, but basic social reforms followed quickly. The Rectangle, a terrible slum area, "too dirty, too coarse, too sinful, too awful for close contact," became the center of a great reform effort. One of Raymond's "leading society heiresses" undertook a slum clearance project, and a concerted attack was made on drunkenness and immorality. The moral regeneration of the entire community was soon accomplished.

The Settlement Houses

Although millions read *In His Steps*, its effect, and that of other Social Gospel literature, was merely inspirational. On the practical level, a number of earnest souls began to grapple with slum problems by organizing what were known as **settlement houses**. These were community centers located in poor districts that provided guidance and services to all who would use them. The settlement workers, most of them idealistic, well-to-do young people, lived in the houses and were active in neighborhood affairs.

The prototype of the settlement house was London's Toynbee Hall, founded in the early 1880s; the first American example was the Neighborhood Guild, opened on the Lower East Side of New York in 1886 by Dr. Stanton Coit. By the turn of the century 100 had been established, the most famous being Jane Addams's Hull House in Chicago (1889), Robert A. Woods's South End House in Boston (1892), and Lillian Wald's Henry Street Settlement in New York (1893).

The settlement workers tried to interpret American ways to the new immigrants and to create a community spirit in order to teach, in the words of one of them, "right living through social relations." Unlike most charity workers, who acted out of a sense of upper-class responsibility toward the unfortunate, they expected to benefit morally

Table 18.1 Reformers and the Urban Poor

Person	Occupation	Action	Consequences
Jacob Riis, Lewis Hine	Photojournalists	Increased public awareness of poor immigrants' living conditions	Stimulated reform movements
Horace Mann	Educator	Favored state laws that supported public education	Increased proportion of young people in school
Dwight L. Moody	Lay evangelist	Encouraged people to consult the Bible for moral guidance and refrain from vice	Promoted spread of YMCA (1850) and Salvation Army (1880) in immigrant districts
Washington Gladden	Congregationalist minister	Persuaded people that they are obliged as Christians to improve conditions in the slums	Advanced the "social gospel"
Jane Addams, Robert Woods, and Lillian Wald	Settlement house organizers	Showed immigrants and impoverished people how to cope with urban conditions	Constructed playgrounds and provided social clubs, day-care centers, and schools

and intellectually themselves by experiencing a way of life far different from their own and by obtaining "the first-hand knowledge the college classroom cannot give."

Settlement workers soon discovered that practical problems absorbed most of their energies. They agitated for tenement house laws, the regulation of the labor of women and children, and better schools. They employed private resources to establish playgrounds in the slums, along with libraries, classes in everything from child nutrition and home management to literature and arts and crafts, social clubs, and day-care centers. When they observed that many poor families were so occupied with the struggle to survive that they were neglecting or even abandoning their children, they tried to place the children in foster homes in the country.

In Boston Robert A. Woods organized clubs to get the youngsters of the South End off the streets, helped establish a restaurant where a meal could be had for five cents, acted as an arbitrator in labor disputes, and lobbied for laws tightening up the franchises of public utility companies. In Chicago Jane Addams developed an outstanding cultural program that included classes in music and art and an excellent "little theater" group. Hull House soon boasted a gymnasium, a day nursery, and several social clubs. Addams also worked tirelessly and effectively for improved public services and for social legislation of all kinds. She even got herself appointed garbage inspector in her ward and hounded local landlords and the garbage contractor until something approaching decent service was established.

A few critics considered the settlement houses mere devices to socialize the unruly poor by teaching them the "punctilios of upper-class propriety," but almost everyone appreciated their virtues. By the end of the century the Catholics, laggard in entering the arena of practical social reform, were joining the movement, partly because they were losing many communicants to socially minded Protestant churches. The first Catholic-run settlement house was founded in 1898 in an Italian district of New York. Two years later Brownson House in Los Angeles, catering chiefly to Mexican immigrants, threw open its doors.

With all their accomplishments, the settlement houses seemed to be fighting a losing battle. "Private beneficence," Jane Addams wrote of Hull House, "is totally inadequate to deal with the vast numbers of the city's disinherited." Much as a tropical forest grows faster than a handful of men armed with machetes can cut it down, so the slums, fed by an annual influx of hundreds of thousands, blighted new areas more rapidly than settlement house workers could clean up old ones. It became increasingly apparent that the wealth and authority of the state must be brought to bear in order to keep abreast of the problem.

Civilization and Its Discontents

As the nineteenth century died, the majority of the American people, especially those comfortably well-off, the residents of small towns, the shopkeepers, and some farmers and skilled workers, remained confirmed optimists and uncritical admirers of their civilization. However, blacks, immigrants, and others who failed to share equitably in the good things of life, along with a growing number of humanitarian reformers, found little to cheer about and much to lament in their increasingly industrialized society. Giant monopolies flourished despite federal restrictions. The gap between rich and poor appeared to be widening while the slum spread its poison and the materially successful made a god of their success. Human values seemed in grave danger of being crushed by impersonal forces typified by the great corporations.

In 1871 Walt Whitman, usually so full of extravagant praise for everything American, had called his fellow countrymen the "most materialistic and money-making people ever known":

> I say we had best look our times and lands searchingly in the face, like a physician diagnosing some deep disease. Never was there, perhaps, more hollowness of heart than at present, and here in the United States.

By the late 1880s a well-known journalist could write to a friend, "The wheel of progress is to be run over the whole human race and smash us all." Others noted an alarming jump in the national divorce rate and an increasing taste for all kinds of luxury. "People are made slaves by a desperate struggle to keep up appearances," a Massachusetts commentator declared, and the economist David A. Wells expressed concern over statistics showing that heart disease and mental illness were on the rise. These "diseases of civilization," Wells explained, were "one result of the continuous mental and nervous activity which modern high-tension methods of business have necessitated."

Wells was a prominent liberal, but pessimism was no monopoly of liberals. A little later, Senator Henry Cabot Lodge of Massachusetts, himself a millionaire, complained of the "lawlessness" of "the modern and recent plutocrat" and his "disregard of the rights of others." Lodge spoke of "the enormous contrast between the sanguine mental attitude prevalent in my youth and that, perhaps wiser, but certainly darker view, so general today." His one-time Harvard professor, Henry Adams, was still more critical of the way his contemporaries had become moneygrubbers. "All one's friends," he complained, along with church and university leaders and other educated people, "had joined the banks to force submission to capitalism."

Of course intellectuals often tend to be critical of the world they live in, whatever its nature; Thoreau denounced materialism and the worship of progress in the 1840s as vigorously as any late-nineteenth-century prophet of gloom. But the voices of the dissatisfied were rising. Despite the many benefits that industrialization had made possible, it was by no means clear around 1900 that the American people were really better off under the new dispensation.

That the United States was fast becoming a modern nation no one disputed. Physician George M. Beard contended that "modern civilization" overloaded the human nervous system the way burning too many of Thomas Edison's lightbulbs overloaded an electrical circuit. On the other hand, Edward Bellamy saw the future as a "paradise of order, equity, and felicity." Most took a more balanced view, believing that the modern world encompassed new possibilities as well as perils. The future beckoned, and yet it also menaced.

Milestones

1858	English launch transatlantic liner *Great Eastern*	1885	Foran Act outlaws importing contract skilled labor
1870	Metropolitan Museum of Art and American Museum of Natural History open in New York City	1887	Nativists found American Protective Association
1876	Eight teams form National Baseball League	1888	Richmond, Virginia, opens first urban electric streetcar system
1880	American branch of Salvation Army is founded	1889	Jane Addams founds Hull House
			Yale's Walter Camp names first All-American football team
1880s	New immigration begins	1890s	Louis Sullivan's skyscrapers rise
1882	John L. Sullivan wins heavyweight boxing championship	1890	Jacob Riis publishes *How the Other Half Lives*
	Exclusion Act bans Chinese immigrants	1896	Charles M. Sheldon asks "What would Jesus do?" in best-selling *In His Steps*
1883	Roebling completes Brooklyn Bridge	1897	Cleveland vetoes Congress's literacy test bill

✓●—[Study and **Review** at **www.myhistorylab.com**

Review Questions

1. The introduction to this chapter contrasts the appeal of cities in the late nineteenth century with their failures and limitations. Did people move into cities because they had no choice or because they wanted to do so? Were their lives better or worse in doing so?

2. What is the relationship between the rise of industry and economic consolidation, described in Chapter 17, to the rapid growth of cities described in this chapter?

3. How did the influx of immigrants into the cities affect relations among ethnic groups? Between immigrants and "natives"—nonimmigrant Americans?

4. How did the new forms of amusement and leisure differ from those in earlier, predominantly rural settings?

5. Which urban problems were most acute and what different solutions were proposed by the leading religious figures and social reformers?

Key Terms

nativism   *486*
new immigration   *485*
settlement houses   *495*

Social Gospel   *495*
tenement   *489*

19 Intellectual and Cultural Trends in the Late Nineteenth Century

((•—[Hear the Audio Chapter 19 at myhistorylab.com

Is winning everything?

IN 2010 THE STATE OF CALIFORNIA CUT FUNDING FOR THE UNIVERSITY of California at Berkeley by several hundred million dollars, raised student fees 10 percent, and forced faculty and staff to take unpaid furloughs. Despite this, the university covered the nearly $6.4 million deficit generated by its intercollegiate athletics program. Campus supporters of the football program noted that two-thirds of the top NCAA football teams ran even larger deficits; the average was about $8 million.

Although some of Berkeley's faculty endorsed an "Academics First" petition, others applauded the chancellor's decision to pursue "competitive excellence" in all aspects of campus life. Berkeley's football team was mandated to compete "at the top levels of the Pacific Ten conference and in postseason and national championship play." To that end, Berkeley paid its head coach $1.5 million, about average for a Division I head coach.

This insistence on winning intercollegiate football originated in the late nineteenth century. At that time, a few colleges decided to pay coaches, recruited star prep school athletes, and charged spectators to watch the games. The game became faster and rougher. Soon the spectacle attracted huge audiences. Action often got out of hand and, lacking satisfactory protective equipment, many football players sustained serious injuries; each year, some were killed.

In 1892, William Rainey Harper, president of the University of Chicago, defended the high cost of winning football. "If the world can afford to sacrifice lives for commercial gain"—a reference to the victims of industrial accidents—"it can more easily afford to make similar sacrifices on the altar of vigorous and unsullied manhood." In 1896 Massachusetts Senator Henry Cabot Lodge told Harvard students that "the injuries incurred on the playing-field are part of the price which the English-speaking race has paid for being world-conquerors."

The rise of football in the 1890s symbolized a profound transformation in cultural and intellectual life. The religious sensibilities and gentlemanly precepts of an earlier age were yielding to a tougher, "more manly" mind-set. Life was a struggle, Darwin had proclaimed, in which the fittest prevailed and the losers vanished. In this "competition" for survival, power trounced sentiment. Ideas were valuable not because they espoused truths or evinced beauty, but because they left an imprint on the world. Art and literature functioned not to transcend life or prettify it but to lay bare its grim reality. This stern ethos unsettled many but also invigorated those who yearned to confront the world as it was.

Colleges and Universities

Industrialization altered the way Americans thought at the same time that it transformed their ways of making a living. Technological advances revolutionized the communication of ideas more drastically than they did the transportation of goods or the manufacture of steel. The materialism that permeated American attitudes toward business also affected contemporary education and literature, while Charles Darwin's theory of evolution influenced American philosophers, lawyers, and historians profoundly. This was especially true of the nation's institutions of higher education.

Between 1878 and 1898, the number of colleges and universities increased from about 350 to 500, and the student body roughly tripled. Despite this growth, less than 2 percent of the college-age population attended college, but the aspirations of the nation's youth were rising, and more and more parents had the financial means necessary for fulfilling them.

More significant than the expansion of the colleges were the alterations in their curricula and in the atmosphere permeating the average campus. In 1870 most colleges remained what they had been in the 1830s: small, limited in their offerings, and intellectually stagnant. Thereafter, change came like a flood tide: State universities proliferated; the federal government's land-grant program in support of training in "agriculture and the mechanic arts," established under the Morrill Act of 1862, came into its own; wealthy philanthropists poured fortunes into old institutions and founded new ones; educators introduced new courses and adopted new teaching methods; professional schools of law, medicine, education, business, journalism, and other specialties increased in number.

●●●⌐Read the Document
The Morrill Act at
myhistorylab.com

In the forefront of reform was Harvard, the oldest and most prestigious college in the country. In the 1860s it possessed an excellent faculty, but teaching methods were antiquated and the curriculum had remained almost unchanged since the colonial period. In 1869, however, a dynamic president, the chemist Charles W. Eliot, undertook a transformation of the college. Eliot introduced the elective system, gradually eliminating required courses and expanding offerings in such areas as modern languages, economics, and the laboratory sciences.

An even more important development in higher education was the founding of Johns Hopkins in 1876. This university was one of many established in the period by wealthy industrialists; its benefactor, the Baltimore merchant Johns Hopkins, had made his fortune in the Baltimore and Ohio Railroad. Its distinctiveness, however, was due to the vision of Daniel Coit Gilman, its first president.

Gilman modeled Johns Hopkins on the German universities, where meticulous research and freedom of inquiry were the guiding principles. In staffing the institution, he sought scholars of the highest reputation, scouring Europe as well as America in his search for talent and offering outstanding men high salaries for that time—up to $5,000 for a

●●⌐Read the Document
Frederick Jackson Turner, *The Significance of the Frontier in American History (1893)* at
myhistorylab.com

A physics lecture, circa 1890, at the University of Michigan. Note that women are segregated from men; but in the men's section white and black men are sitting together. Many of the Morrill Act universities admitted women.

professor, roughly ten times the income of a skilled artisan. Johns Hopkins specialized in graduate education. In the generation after its founding, it churned out a remarkable percentage of the most important scholars in the nation, including Woodrow Wilson in political science, John Dewey in philosophy, Frederick Jackson Turner in history, and John R. Commons in economics.

State and federal aid to higher education expanded rapidly. The Morrill Act, granting land to each state at a rate of 30,000 acres for each senator and representative, provided the endowments that gave many important modern universities, such as Illinois, Michigan State, and Ohio State, their start. While the federal assistance was earmarked for specific subjects, the land-grant colleges offered a full range of courses, and all received additional state funds. The land-grant universities adopted new ideas quickly. They were coeducational from the start, and most developed professional schools and experimented with extension work and summer programs.

Typical of the better state institutions was the University of Michigan, which reached the top rank among the nation's universities during the presidency of James B. Angell (1871–1909). Like Eliot at Harvard, Angell expanded the undergraduate curriculum and strengthened the law and medical schools. He encouraged graduate studies, seeking to make Michigan "part of the great world of scholars," and sought ways in which the university could serve the general community.

Important advances were made in women's higher education. Beginning with Vassar College, which opened its doors to 300 women students in 1865, the opportunity for young women to pursue serious academic work gradually expanded. Wellesley and Smith, both founded in 1875, completed the so-called Big Three women's colleges. Together with the already established Mount Holyoke (1837), and with Bryn Mawr (1885), Barnard (1889), and Radcliffe (1893), they became known as the Seven Sisters.

Not all the changes in higher education were beneficial. The elective system led to superficiality; students gained a smattering of knowledge of many subjects and mastered none. For example, 55 percent of the Harvard class of 1898 took elementary courses and no others during their four years of study. Intensive graduate work often produced narrowness of outlook and research monographs on trivial subjects. Attempts to apply the scientific method in fields such as history and economics often enticed students into making smug (and preposterous) claims to objectivity and definitiveness.

The gifts of rich industrialists sometimes came with strings, and college boards of trustees tended to be dominated by businessmen who sometimes attempted to impose their own social and economic beliefs on faculty members. Although few professors lost their positions because their views offended trustees, at many institutions trustees exerted constant nagging pressures that limited academic freedom and scholarly objectivity. At state colleges, politicians often interfered in academic affairs, even treating professorships as part of the patronage system.

As the number of college graduates increased, and as colleges ceased being primarily training institutions for clergymen, the influence of alumni on educational policies began to make itself felt, not always happily. Campus social activities became more important. Fraternities proliferated. Interest in organized sports first appeared as a laudable outgrowth of the general expansion of the curriculum, but soon athletic contests were playing a role all out of proportion to their significance. After football evolved as the leading intercollegiate sport (over 50,000 attended the Yale-Princeton game in 1893), it became a source of revenue that many colleges dared not neglect. Since students, alumni, and the public demanded winning teams, college administrators stooped to subsidizing student athletes, in extreme cases employing players who were not students at all. One exasperated college president quipped that the BA degree was coming to mean Bachelor of Athletics.

Watch the **Video**
College Football (1903) at
myhistorylab.com

Thus higher education reflected American values, with all their strengths and weaknesses. A complex society required a more professional and specialized education for its youth; the coarseness and the rampant materialism and competitiveness of the era inevitably found expression in the colleges and universities.

Revolution in the Social Sciences

In the social sciences a close connection existed between the practical issues of the age and the achievements of the leading thinkers. The application of the theory of evolution to every aspect of human relations, the impact of industrialization on society—such topics were of intense concern to American economists, sociologists, and historians. An understanding of Darwin increased the already strong interest in studying the development of institutions and their interactions with one another. Controversies over trusts, slum conditions, and other problems drew scholars out of their towers and into practical affairs.

Among the economists something approaching a revolution took place in the 1880s. The classical school, which maintained that immutable natural laws governed all human behavior and which used the insights of Darwin only to justify unrestrained competition and laissez-faire, was challenged by a group of young economists who argued that as times changed, economic theories and laws must be modified in order to remain relevant. Richard T. Ely, another of the scholars who made Johns Hopkins a font of new ideas in the 1880s, summarized the thinking of this group in 1885. "The state [is] an educational and ethical agency whose positive aid is an indispensable condition of human progress," Ely proclaimed. Laissez-faire was outmoded and dangerous. Economic problems were basically moral problems; their solution required "the united efforts of Church, state and science." The proper way to study these problems was by analyzing actual conditions, not by applying abstract laws or principles.

This approach produced the so-called institutionalist school of economics, whose members made detailed, on-the-spot investigations of labor unions, sweatshops, factories, and mines. The study of institutions would lead both to theoretical insights and to practical social reform, they believed. John R. Commons, one of Ely's students at Johns Hopkins and later professor of economics at the University of Wisconsin, was the outstanding member of this school. His ten-volume *Documentary History of American Industrial Society* (1910–1911) reveals the institutionalist approach at its best.

A similar revolution struck sociology in the mid-1880s. Prevailing opinion up to that time rejected the idea of government interference with the organization of society. The influence of the English social Darwinist, Herbert Spencer, who objected even to public schools and the postal system, was immense. Spencer and his American disciples, among them Edward L. Youmans, editor of *Popular Science Monthly*, twisted the ideas of Darwin to mean that society could be changed only by the force of evolution, which moved with cosmic slowness. "You and I can do nothing at all," Youmans told the reformer Henry George. "It's all a matter of evolution. Perhaps in four or five thousand years evolution may have carried men beyond this state of things."

••⊸⎰Read the Document

Herbert Spencer, Social Darwinism at
myhistorylab.com

Progressive Education

Traditionally, American teachers had emphasized the three Rs and relied on strict discipline. Yet new ideas were attracting attention. According to a German educator, Johann Friedrich Herbart, teachers could best arouse the interest of their students by relating new information to what they already knew; good teaching called for professional training, psychological insight, enthusiasm, and imagination, not merely facts and a birch rod. At the same time, evolutionists were pressing for a kind of education that would help children to "survive" by adapting to the demands of their rapidly changing urban environment.

Forward-looking educators seized on these ideas because dynamic social changes were making the old system increasingly inadequate. Settlement house workers discovered that slum children needed training in handicrafts, citizenship, and personal hygiene as much as in reading and writing. They were appalled by the local schools, which suffered from the same diseases—filth, overcrowding, rickety construction—that plagued the tenements, and by school systems that were controlled by machine politicians who doled out teaching positions to party hacks and other untrained persons. They argued that school playgrounds, nurseries, kindergartens, and adult education programs were essential in communities where most women worked and many people lacked much formal education. The philosopher who summarized and gave direction to these forces was John Dewey, a professor at the University of Chicago. Dewey was concerned with the implications of evolution—indeed, of all science—for education.

"Education," Dewey insisted in *The School and Society* (1899), was "the fundamental method of social progress and reform." To seek to improve conditions merely by passing laws was "futile." Moreover, in an industrial society the family no longer performed many of the educational functions it had carried out in an agrarian society. Farm children learn about nature, about work, about human character in countless ways denied to children in cities. The school can fill the gap by becoming "an embryonic community . . . with types of occupations that reflect the life of the larger society." At the same time, education should center on the child, and new information should be related to what the child already knows. Finally, the school should become an instrument for social reform.

The School and Society created a stir, and Dewey immediately assumed leadership of what in the next generation was called progressive education. Although the gains made in public education before 1900 were more quantitative than qualitative and the philosophy dominant in most schools was not very different at the end of the century from that prevailing in Horace Mann's day, change was in the air. The best educators of the period were full of optimism, convinced that the future was theirs.

Law and History

Even jurisprudence, by its nature conservative and rooted in tradition, felt the pressure of evolutionary thought. In 1881 Oliver Wendell Holmes Jr. published *The Common Law.* Rejecting the ideas that judges should limit themselves to the mechanical explication of statutes and that law consisted only of what was written in law books, Holmes argued that "the felt necessities of the time" rather than precedent should determine the rules by which people are governed. "The life of the law has not been logic; it has been experience," he wrote.

Holmes went on to a long and brilliant judicial career, during which he repeatedly stressed the right of the people, through their elected representatives, to deal with contemporary problems in any reasonable way, unfettered by outmoded conceptions of the proper limits of government authority. Like the societies they regulated, laws should evolve as times and conditions changed, he said.

The new approach to knowledge did not always advance the cause of liberal reform. Historians in the graduate schools became intensely interested in studying the origins and evolution of political institutions. They concluded, after much "scientific" study of old charters and law codes, that the roots of democracy were to be found in the customs of the ancient tribes of northern Europe. This theory of the "Teutonic origins" of democracy, which has since been thoroughly discredited, fitted well with the prejudices of people of British stock, and it provided ammunition for those who favored restricting immigration and for those who argued that blacks were inferior beings.

Out of this work, however, came an essentially democratic concept, the frontier thesis of Frederick Jackson Turner, still another scholar trained at Johns Hopkins. Turner's essay "The Significance of the Frontier in American History" (1893) argued that the frontier experience, through which every section of the country had passed, had affected the thinking of the people and the shape of American institutions. The isolation of the frontier and the need during each successive westward advance to create civilization anew, Turner wrote, account for the individualism of Americans and the democratic character of their society. Nearly everything unique in our culture could be traced to the existence of the frontier, he claimed.

Turner, and still more his many disciples, made too much of his basic insights. Life on the frontier was not as democratic as Turner believed, and it certainly does not "explain" American development as completely as he said it did. Nevertheless, his work showed how important it was to investigate the evolution of institutions, and it encouraged historians to study social and economic, as well as purely political, subjects. If the

CHARLOTTE PERKINS GILMAN

In 1885, severe depression gripped twenty-five-year-old Charlotte Perkins Stetson. "Every morning the same helpless waking," she confided in her journal. "Retreat impossible, escape impossible." She had married the previous year and had just given birth to a daughter. But the infant gave her no pleasure. "I would hold her close—that lovely child!—and instead of love and happiness, feel only pain. The tears ran down my breast." Over the next few years, her depression worsened. She feared she was approaching "the edge of insanity."

Charlotte's life had not been easy. Shortly after she was born, her father abandoned the family. He visited every couple of years, and occasionally sent a check, but Charlotte, her brother, and her mother lacked regular income and lived with relatives, moving frequently. "What I do know is that my childhood had no father," she wrote. Charlotte's relationship with her mother was not much better. Shattered by her husband's abandonment, she refused to cuddle Charlotte as an infant lest the child become dependent on affection. They never were close. When she was an adolescent, Charlotte and her mother lived in a cooperative run by a spiritualist, a woman who claimed to communicate with spirits. One day Charlotte saw her taking grapes that were meant for the whole group. The woman accused Charlotte of thinking evil thoughts about her.

Charlotte's mother insisted that Charlotte apologize for her thoughts; Charlotte refused. "And what are you going to do about it?" she taunted. Her mother hit her. At that moment, "I was born," Charlotte recalled. "Neither she, nor any one, could *make* me do anything."

Charlotte devised a stern regimen to ensure her future independence. Every day she ran a mile and educated herself by drawing, reading, and writing. Never would she depend on anyone— especially a man. "I am not domestic and I don't want to be," she told a female confidante.

Her resolve weakened when she was courted by an aspiring young writer. They married and the baby soon followed. Charlotte's bouts of depression became more frequent and incapacitating. Finally she agreed to consult with neurologist S. Weir Mitchell,

Charlotte Perkins Stetson, shortly after her marriage, wrote, "You were called to serve humanity, and you cannot serve yourself. No good as a wife, no good as a mother, no good at anything. And you did it yourself!"

the nation's foremost expert on neurasthenia, a disease that especially afflicted well-to-do young women. Its chief symptoms were depression, listlessness, and invalidism.

Mitchell believed that women's nervous systems were attuned to childbearing and childrearing. Women who pursued education and careers would exhaust their nervous energy and become neurasthenic. Charlotte's condition, Mitchell assured her, resulted from her intellectual labors. His prescription was simple:

> Live as domestic a life as possible. Have your child with you all the time. Lie down an hour after each meal. Have but two hours' intellectual life a day. And never touch pen, brush, or pencil as long as you live.

For a time, Charlotte accepted his regimen. "I went home, followed those directions rigidly for months, and came perilously close to losing my mind," she noted. Then she decided to "cast off Dr. Mitchell bodily" and "do exactly as I pleased."

She separated from her husband, took her child to Pasadena, California, and wrote essays, editorials, and fiction.

In 1890 she finished "The Yellow Wallpaper," a story about a young wife who, suffering from depression, was confined by her doctor-husband to bed in an upstairs room, with servants tending to her every need. As she endlessly stared at her surroundings, the designs on the wallpaper changed shape; a figure appeared and wandered in and out of her consciousness. The wallpaper then grew bars that locked her into the room. Unable to escape through the bars, the woman chewed at the bed, fleeing ultimately into madness. The story was well-received as a literary horror story reminiscent of Edgar Allan Poe.

Having at last purged Mitchell from her psyche, Charlotte wrote incessantly and supported herself by giving lectures. She developed close and even intimate relationships with several women. When she sent her daughter to live with her father, newspapers denounced her for neglecting woman's proper function. Then she fell in love with Houghton Gilman, who accepted her refusal to embrace domesticity. "I *must not* focus on 'home duties' and entangle myself with them," she told him. They married in 1900.

Charlotte's first book, *Women and Economics* (1898), was a work of extraordinary creativity. A thoroughgoing Social Darwinist, Charlotte explained that marriage was founded on women's economic subjugation. Marx was wrong: Gender, not class, was the fundamental social distinction. The most important revolution would promote women's independence by allowing them to work outside the home.

In this and subsequent books and articles, Charlotte Perkins Gilman insisted that the domestic ideal had deprived society of women's creativity and ideas. Her own life was a case in point. With only four years of education, none after the age of fifteen, she achieved economic independence through her own heroic effort. Lacking alternative child-care arrangements, she sent her young child to live with her father so that she could pursue her life and work as an intellectual. The decision would psychologically scar both her and her daughter, but her work anticipated many of the themes of modern feminism.

claims of the new historians to objectivity and definitiveness were absurdly overstated, their emphasis on thoroughness, exactitude, and impartiality did much to raise standards in the profession.

Realism in Literature

When what Mark Twain called the Gilded Age began, American literature was dominated by the romantic mood. All the important writers of the 1840s and 1850s, except Hawthorne, Thoreau, and Poe, were still living. Longfellow stood at the height of his fame, and the lachrymose Susan Warner—"tears on almost every page"—continued to turn out stories in the style of her popular *The Wide, Wide World*. Romanticism, however, had lost its creative force; much of the popular writing in the decade after 1865 was sentimental trash pandering to the preconceptions of middle-class readers. Magazines like the *Atlantic Monthly* overflowed with stories about fair ladies worshiped from afar by stainless heroes, women coping selflessly with drunken husbands, and poor but honest youths rising through various combinations of virtue and diligence to positions of wealth and influence. Most writers of fiction tended to ignore the eternal conflicts inherent in human nature and the social problems of the age; polite entertainment and pious moralizing appeared to be their only objectives.

The patent unreality, even dishonesty, of contemporary fiction eventually caused a reaction. The most important forces giving rise to the Age of Realism were those that were transforming every other aspect of American life: industrialism, with its associated complexities and social problems; the theory of evolution, which made people more aware of the force of the environment and the basic conflicts of existence; the new science, which taught dispassionate, empirical observation. Novelists undertook the examination of social problems such as slum life, the conflict between capital and labor, and political corruption. They created multidimensional characters, depicted persons of every social class, used dialect and slang to capture the flavor of particular types, and fashioned painstaking descriptions of the surroundings into which they placed their subjects. The romantic novel did not disappear. General Lew Wallace's *Ben Hur* (1880) and Frances Hodgson Burnett's *Little Lord Fauntleroy* (1886) were best-sellers. But by 1880 realism was the point of view of the finest literary talents in the country.

Mark Twain

While it was easy to romanticize the West, that region lent itself to the realistic approach. Almost of necessity, novelists writing about the West described coarse characters from the lower levels of society and dealt with crime and violence. The outstanding figure of western literature, the first great American realist, was Mark Twain.

●●●―[Read the Document

Mark Twain, *Incident in the Philippines (1924)* at **myhistorylab.com**

Twain, whose real name was Samuel L. Clemens, was born in 1835. He grew up in Hannibal, Missouri, on the banks of the Mississippi. After mastering the printer's trade and working as a riverboat pilot, he went west to Nevada in 1861. The wild, rough life of Virginia City fascinated him, but prospecting got him nowhere, and he became a reporter for the *Territorial Enterprise*. Soon he was publishing humorous stories about the local life under the nom de plume Mark Twain. In 1865, while working in California, he wrote "The Celebrated Jumping Frog of Calaveras County," a story that brought him national recognition. A tour of Europe and the Holy Land in 1867 to 1868 led to *The Innocents Abroad* (1869), which made him famous.

Twain's greatness stemmed from his keen reportorial eye and ear, his eagerness to live life to the full, his marvelous sense of humor, and his ability to be at once in society and outside it, and to love humanity yet be repelled by human vanity and perversity. He epitomized the zest and adaptability of his age and also its materialism. No contemporary pursued the almighty dollar more zealously. An inveterate speculator, he made a fortune with his pen and lost it in foolish business ventures.

> ••⊢Read the Document
> Mark Twain, from *The Gilded Age* at **myhistorylab.com**

He was equally at home and equally successful on the Great River of his childhood, in the mining camps, and in the eastern bourgeois society of his mature years. But every prize slipped through his fingers. Twain died a dark pessimist, surrounded by adulation yet alone, an alien and a stranger in the land he loved and knew so well.

Whether directly, as in *The Innocents Abroad* and in his fascinating account of the world of the river pilot, *Life on the Mississippi* (1883), or when transformed by his imagination in works of fiction such as *Tom Sawyer* (1876) and *A Connecticut Yankee in King Arthur's Court* (1889), Mark Twain always put much of his own experience and feeling into his work. A story, he told a fellow author, "must be written with the blood out of a man's heart." His innermost confusions, the clash between his recognition of the pretentiousness and meanness of human beings and his wish to be accepted by society, added depths and overtones to his writing that together with his comic genius give it last-

> ••⊢Read the Document
> Mark Twain, *To the Person Sitting in Darkness (1901)* at **myhistorylab.com**

ing appeal. He could not rise above the sentimentality and prudery of his generation entirely, for these qualities were part of his nature. He never dealt effectively with sexual love, for example, and often—even in *Huckleberry Finn*—contrived to end his tales on absurdly optimistic notes that ring false after so many brilliant pages portraying life as it is. On balance Twain's achievement was magnificent. Rough and uneven like the man himself, his works catch more of the spirit of the age he named than those of any other writer.

William Dean Howells

Twain's realism was far less self-conscious than that of his longtime friend William Dean Howells. Like Twain, Howells, who was born in Ohio in 1837, had little formal education. He learned the printer's trade from his father and became a reporter for the *Ohio State Journal*. After the Civil War he worked briefly for *The Nation* in New York and then moved to Boston, where he became editor of the *Atlantic Monthly*. In 1886 he returned to New York as editor of *Harper's*.

A long series of novels and much literary criticism poured from Howells's pen over the next thirty years. While he insisted on treating his material honestly, he was not at first a critic of society, being content to write about what he called "the smiling aspects" of life. Realism to Howells meant concern for the complexities of

In 1891 William Dean Howells championed the poetry of Emily Dickinson: "This poetry is as characteristic of our life as our business enterprise, our political turmoil, our demagogism, or our millionaires." Yet few of her poems appeared during her lifetime; arguably the most important poet of her age was unknown to that age.

individual personalities and faithful description of the genteel, middle-class world he knew best.

Besides a sharp eye and an open mind, Howells had a real social conscience. Gradually he became aware of the problems that industrialization had created. In 1885, in *The Rise of Silas Lapham*, he dealt with some of the ethical conflicts faced by businessmen in a competitive society. The harsh public reaction to the Haymarket bombing in 1886 stirred him, and he threw himself into a futile campaign to prevent the execution of the anarchist suspects. Thereafter he moved rapidly toward the left. In *A Hazard of New Fortunes* (1890), he attempted to portray the whole range of metropolitan life, weaving the destinies of a dozen interesting personalities from diverse sections and social classes.

His own works were widely read, and Howells was also the most influential critic of his time. He encouraged many important young American novelists, among them Stephen Crane, Theodore Dreiser, Frank Norris, and Hamlin Garland.

Some of these writers went far beyond Howells's realism to what they called naturalism. Many, like Twain and Howells, began as newspaper reporters. Working for a big-city daily in the 1890s was sure to teach anyone a great deal about the dark side of life. Naturalist writers believed that the human being was essentially an animal, a helpless creature whose fate was determined by environment. Their world was Darwin's world—mindless, without mercy or justice. They wrote chiefly about the most primitive emotions—lust, hate, and greed. In *Maggie, A Girl of the Streets* (1893), Stephen Crane described the seduction, degradation, and eventual suicide of a young woman, all set against the background of a sordid slum; in *The Red Badge of Courage* (1895), he captured the pain and humor of war. In *McTeague* (1899), Frank Norris told the story of a brutal, dull-witted dentist who murdered his greed-crazed wife with his bare fists.

Such stuff was too strong for Howells, yet he recognized its importance and befriended the younger writers in many ways. He found a publisher for *Maggie* after it had been rejected several times, and he wrote appreciative reviews of the work of Garland and Norris. Even Theodore Dreiser, who was contemptuous of Howells's writings and considered him hopelessly middle-class in point of view, appreciated his aid and praised his influence on American literature. Dreiser's first novel, *Sister Carrie* (1900), treated sex so forthrightly that it was withdrawn after publication.

Henry James

Henry James was very different in spirit and background from the tempestuous naturalists. Born to wealth, reared in a cosmopolitan atmosphere, twisted in some strange way while still a child and unable to achieve satisfactory relationships with women, James spent most of his mature life in Europe, writing novels, short stories, plays, and volumes of criticism. He was preeminently a realist, determined, as he once said, "to leave a multitude of pictures of my time" for the future to contemplate.

James dealt with social issues such as feminism and the difficulties faced by artists in the modern world, but he subordinated them to his interest in his subjects as individuals. *The American* (1877) told the story of the love of a wealthy American in Paris for a French noblewoman who rejected him because her family disapproved of his commercial background. *The Portrait of a Lady* (1881) described the disillusionment of an intelligent woman married to a charming but morally bankrupt man and her eventual decision to remain with him nonetheless. *The Bostonians* (1886) was a complicated and psychologically sensitive study of the varieties of female behavior in a seemingly uniform social situation.

James's reputation, greater today than in his lifetime, rests more on his highly refined accounts of the interactions of individuals and their environment and his masterful commentaries on the novel as a literary form than on his ability as a storyteller. Few major writers have been more long-winded, more prone to circumlocution. Yet few have been so dedicated to their art, possessed of such psychological penetration, or so successful in producing a large body of important work.

Realism in Art

American painters responded to the times as writers did, but with this difference: Despite the new concern for realism, the romantic tradition retained its vitality. Preeminent among the realists was Thomas Eakins, who was born in Philadelphia in 1844. Eakins studied in Europe in the late 1860s and was influenced by the great realists of the seventeenth century, Velasquez and Rembrandt. Returning to America in 1870, he passed the remainder of his life teaching and painting in Philadelphia.

The scientific spirit of the age suited Eakins perfectly. He mastered human anatomy; some of his finest paintings, such as *The Gross Clinic* (1875), are graphic illustrations of surgical operations. He was an early experimenter with motion pictures, using the camera to capture exactly the attitudes of human beings and animals in action. Like his friend Walt Whitman, whose portrait is one of his greatest achievements, Eakins gloried in the ordinary. But he had none of Whitman's weakness for self-delusion. His portraits are monuments to his integrity and craftsmanship: Never would he touch up a likeness to please his sitter.

Winslow Homer, a Boston-born painter best known for his brilliant watercolors, was also influenced by realist ideas. Homer was a lithographer as well as a master of the watercolor medium, yet he had had almost no formal training. During the Civil War, he worked as an artist-reporter for *Harper's Weekly*, and he continued to do magazine illustrations for some years thereafter. He roamed America, painting

Thomas Eakins's interest in science was as great as his interest in art. In the early 1880s he collaborated with photographer Eadweard Muybridge in serial-action photographic experiments and later devised a special camera for his anatomical studies. The accompanying picture (top) was taken with the Marey wheel. The impact of Eakins's photographic experiments is evident in *The Swimming Hole* (bottom), painted in 1883. At that time Eakins was director of the art school at the Pennsylvania Academy of the Fine Arts.
Source: (top) Philadelpia Museum of Art. Gift of Charles Bregler.

scenes of southern farm life, Adirondack campers, and, after about 1880, magnificent seascapes and studies of fishermen and sailors.

The careers of Eakins and Homer show that the late-nineteenth-century American environment was not uncongenial to first-rate artists. Nevertheless, at least two major American painters abandoned native shores for Europe. One was James A. McNeill Whistler, whose portrait of his mother, which he called *Arrangement in Grey and Black,* is probably the most famous canvas ever painted by an American. Whistler left the United States in 1855 when he was twenty-one and spent most of his life in Paris and London. "I shall come to America," he announced grandly, "when the duty on works of art is abolished!"

Whistler made a profession of eccentricity, but he was a talented and versatile artist. Spare and muted in tone, his paintings are more interesting as precise arrangements of color and space than as images of particular objects; they had considerable influence on the course of modern art.

The second important expatriate artist was Mary Cassatt, daughter of a wealthy Pittsburgh banker and sister of Alexander J. Cassatt, who was president of the Pennsylvania Railroad around the turn of the century. She went to Paris as a tourist and dabbled in art like many conventional young socialites, then was caught up in the impressionist movement and decided to become a serious painter. Her work is more French than American and was little appreciated in the United States before World War I.

The Pragmatic Approach

The theory of evolution posed an immediate challenge to religion: If Darwin was correct, the biblical account of the creation was apparently untrue and the idea that the human race had been formed in God's image was highly unlikely. A bitter controversy erupted, described by President Andrew D. White of Cornell in *The Warfare of Science with Theology in Christendom* (1896). While millions continued to believe in the literal truth of the Bible, among intellectuals, lay and clerical, victory went to the evolutionists because, in addition to the arguments of the geologists and the biologists, scholars were throwing light on the historical origins of the Bible, showing that its words were of human rather than divine inspiration.

If the account of the creation in Genesis could not be taken literally, the Bible remained a repository of wisdom and inspiration. Such books as John Fiske's *The Outlines of Cosmic Philosophy* (1874) provided religious persons with the comforting thesis that evolution, while true, was merely God's way of ordering the universe—as the liberal preacher Washington Gladden put it, "a most impressive demonstration of the presence of God in the world."

The effects of Darwinism on philosophy were less dramatic but in the end more significant. Fixed systems and eternal truths were difficult to justify in a world that was constantly evolving. By the early 1870s a few philosophers had begun to reason that ideas and theories mattered little except when applied to specifics.

"Nothing justifies the development of abstract principles but their utility in enlarging our concrete knowledge of nature," wrote Chauncey Wright, secretary of the American Academy of Arts and Sciences. This startling philosophy, known as **pragmatism**, was further developed by William James, brother of the novelist. James was one of the most remarkable persons of his generation. His *Principles of Psychology* (1890) may be said to have established that discipline as a modern science. His *Varieties of Religious Experience* (1902), which treated the subject from both psychological and philosophical points of view, helped thousands of readers

Table 19.1 Key Figures and Intellectual Currents

Intellectual	Chief Accomplishment	Major Ideas
Charles W. Eliot	Elective system at Harvard	Encouraged development of college majors and hiring of specialized faculty
Daniel Coit Gilman	Graduate education at Johns Hopkins	Brought German standards of research to the United States
Richard Ely	Founded "institutional school of economics"	Challenged theorists who focused on markets and advocated laissez-faire governmental policy
John Dewey	*The School and Society* (1899)	Insisted that meaningful social change was impossible without educational change
Oliver Wendell Holmes, Jr.	*The Common Law* (1881)	Demonstrated that law was not founded on historical precedent; legal principles evolved with society
Frederick Jackson Turner	"The Significance of the Frontier in American History" (1893)	Frontier conditions explained the individualism and democracy that characterized American society
Mark Twain	*Huckleberry Finn* (1884)	Lampooned the sentimentality and hypocrisy of Victorian culture
Charlotte Perkins Gilman	*Women and Economics* (1898)	Maintained that society was unjustly built upon women's economic dependence on men; social change depended on women finding meaningful paid work
William Dean Howells	*A Hazard of New Fortunes* (1890)	Promoted a realistic, nonsentimental look at society
Henry James	*The Portrait of a Lady* (1881)	Showed how literature could probe the depths and complexities of human relationships
Thomas Eakins	*The Gross Clinic* (1875)	Applied realistic perspectives to art
William James	*The Principles of Psychology* (1890)	Contended that the will, as influenced by psychological factors, was an independent force in human affairs

reconcile their religious faith with their increasing knowledge of psychology and the physical universe.

James's wide range and his verve and imagination as a writer made him by far the most influential philosopher of his time. He rejected the deterministic interpretation of Darwinism and all other one-idea explanations of existence. Belief in free will was one of his axioms; environment might influence survival, but so did the *desire* to survive, which existed independent of surrounding circumstances. Even truth was relative; it did not exist in the abstract but *happened* under particular circumstances. What a person thought helped to make thought occur, or come true. The mind, James wrote in a typically vivid phrase, has "a vote" in determining truth. Religion was true, for example, because people were religious.

Pragmatism brought Americans face-to-face with somber problems. While relativism made them optimistic, it also bred insecurity, for there could be no certainty, no comforting reliance on any eternal value in the absence of absolute truth. Pragmatism also seemed to suggest that the end justified the means, that what worked was more important than what ought to be. At the time of James's death in 1910, the *Commercial and Financial Chronicle* pointed out that the pragmatic philosophy was helpful to businessmen in making decisions. By emphasizing practice at the expense of theory, the new philosophy encouraged materialism, anti-intellectualism, and other unlovely aspects of the American character. And what place had conventional morality in such a system? Perhaps pragmatism placed too much reliance on the free will of human beings, ignoring their capacity for selfishness and self-delusion.

The people of the new century found pragmatism a heady wine. They would quaff it freely and enthusiastically—down to the bitter dregs.

The Knowledge Revolution

Improvements in public education and the needs of an increasingly complex society for every type of intellectual skill caused a veritable revolution in how knowledge was discovered, disseminated, and put to use. Nothing so well illustrates the desire for new information as the rise of the Chautauqua movement, founded by John H. Vincent, a Methodist minister, and Lewis Miller, an Ohio manufacturer of farm machinery. Vincent had charge of Sunday schools for the Methodist church. In 1874 he and Miller organized a two-week summer course for Sunday school teachers on the shores of Lake Chautauqua in New York. Besides instruction, they offered good meals, evening songfests around the campfire, and a relaxing atmosphere—all for $6 for the two weeks.

The forty young teachers who attended were delighted with the program, and soon the leafy shore of Lake Chautauqua became a city of tents each summer as thousands poured into the region from all over the country. The founders expanded their offerings to include instruction in literature, science, government, and economics. Famous authorities, including, over the years, six presidents of the United States, came to lecture to open-air audiences on every subject imaginable. Eventually Chautauqua supplied speakers to reading circles throughout the country; it even offered correspondence courses leading over a four-year period to a diploma, the program designed, in Vincent's words, to give "the college outlook" to persons who had not had the opportunity to obtain a higher education. Books were written specifically for the program, and a monthly magazine, the *Chautauquan*, was published.

Still larger numbers profited from the proliferation of public libraries. By the end of the century nearly all the states supported libraries. Private donors, led by the steel industrialist Andrew Carnegie, contributed millions to the cause. In 1900 over 1,700 libraries in the

The first commercially successful typewriter, manufactured in quantity beginning in 1874. It used the QWERTY keyboard found on later typewriters—and eventually found on computer keyboards.

United States had collections of more than 5,000 volumes.

Publishers tended to be conservative, but reaching the masses meant lowering intellectual and cultural standards, appealing to emotions, and adopting popular, sometimes radical, causes. Cheap, mass-circulation papers had first appeared in the 1830s and 1840s, the most successful being the *Sun*, the *Herald*, and the *Tribune* in New York; the *Philadelphia Public Ledger*; and the *Baltimore Sun*. None of them much exceeded a circulation of 50,000 before the Civil War. The first publisher to reach a truly massive audience was Joseph Pulitzer, a Hungarian-born immigrant who made a first-rate paper of the *St. Louis Post-Dispatch*. In 1883 Pulitzer bought the *New York World*, a sheet with a circulation of perhaps 20,000. Within a year he was selling 100,000 copies daily, and by the late 1890s the *World*'s circulation regularly exceeded 1 million.

Growth and ferment also characterized the magazine world. In 1865 there were about 700 magazines in the country, and by the turn of the century more than 5,000. Until the mid-1880s, few of the new magazines were in any way unusual. A handful of serious periodicals, such as the *Atlantic Monthly*, *Harper's*, and the *Century*, dominated the field. They were staid in tone and conservative in politics. Although they had great influence, none approached mass circulation because of the limited size of the upper-middle-class audience they aimed at.

Popular magazines rarely discussed the great issues that preoccupied intellectuals—the impact of Darwinism on law, sociology, and anthropology; the theories of John Dewey and the progressive educators; the import of realism in literature and art; the implications of pragmatism to psychology, philosophy, and theology. But some phenomena—such as the mania for college football—pressed forward because they represented so powerful a convergence of popular culture and intellectual trends.

Milestones

1862	Morrill Act establishes land-grant colleges	1886	William Dean Howells becomes editor of *Harper's*
1865	Vassar College is founded for women	1889	Edward W. Bok becomes editor of the *Ladies' Home Journal*
1869	Charles W. Eliot becomes Harvard's president	1890	William James publishes *Principles of Psychology*
1874	Chautauqua movement begins	1893	Frederick Jackson Turner publishes "Significance of the Frontier in American History"
1876	Johns Hopkins University is founded to specialize in graduate education		
1881	Oliver Wendell Holmes Jr. publishes *The Common Law*	1895	William Randolph Hearst purchases the *New York Journal*
	Henry James publishes *The Portrait of a Lady*	1898	Charlotte Perkins Gilman publishes *Women and Economics*
1883	Joseph Pulitzer purchases *New York World*	1899	John Dewey publishes *The School and Society*
1884	Mark Twain publishes *Huckleberry Finn*		
1886	Ottmar Mergenthaler invents linotype machine		

✓•[**Study** and **Review** at www.myhistorylab.com

Review Questions

1. The introductory essay argues that football was embraced by colleges and universities in the late nineteenth century because it reflected hard-nosed Darwinian concepts. What other aspects of late-nineteenth-century intellectual and cultural life were influenced by Darwinism? What intellectual trends and movements rejected social Darwinism?

2. What institutional developments transformed higher education during the last third of the nineteenth century?

3. How was popular culture at odds with intellectual trends in literature and the arts?

4. How did pragmatism—the belief that ideas must be judged by their consequences—challenge earlier outlooks on philosophy and morality?

Key Terms

pragmatism   *513*

20 From Smoke-Filled Rooms to Prairie Wildfire: 1877–1896

((•—[Hear the Audio Chapter 20 at myhistorylab.com

Did you vote for an American Idol?

ON MAY 20, 2009, TWENTY-THREE-YEAR-OLD GUITAR-STRUMMING Kris Allen captivated the audience of *American Idol* with his rendition of Keith Urban's "Kiss a Girl" and Bill Withers's "Ain't No Sunshine." By receiving a majority of the nearly 100 million "votes"—by telephone and text message—Allen became the *American Idol* for 2009.

Although pundits had for years grumbled that Americans cared more about pop stars on *American Idol* than about their president, this may not have been true in 2009. The producers of the show did not release the exact number of votes for Allen, but they did say the vote was close; probably he received no more than 55 million. Six months earlier, presidential candidates Barack Obama and John McCain received more votes than Allen, with 69 million and 60 million respectively.

A better comparison is of voter turnout for presidential elections nowadays and during the late nineteenth century. Since 1946, fewer than half of the eligible voters have on the average voted in presidential elections. By contrast, over three-fourths of eligible voters did so in presidential campaigns from 1876 to 1896—the highest rates in the nation's history.

This puzzles scholars, because the issues of that time seem inconsequential: Civil War soldiers' pensions, the tariff, paper money vs. gold and silver coins, and civil service reform. Perhaps the most volatile issue—the plight of former slaves—never attracted much notice because most politicians looked the other way. The other key issue—the minimal role of the federal government in the nation's industrial ascent—went without saying and, being unsaid, generated little controversy.

Why, then, did so many people vote? Local issues seem to have loomed large in most people's thinking. Public health, municipal services, and corruption all dominated the headlines. Then, during the 1890s, a nationwide industrial depression crushed many local manufacturing firms, just as an agricultural crisis was sweeping through the midsection of the nation.

Because the nation had become more tightly integrated, these economic upheavals jolted nearly every community. National policy and local issues converged, culminating in the extraordinary election of 1896, which brought over 80 percent of the electorate to the polls. In these years, politics had become the greatest show around.

Congress Ascendant

A succession of weak presidents occupied the White House during the last quarter of the nineteenth century. Although the impeachment proceedings against Andrew Johnson had failed, Congress dominated the government. Within Congress, the Senate generally overshadowed the House of Representatives. Critics called the Senate a "rich man's club," and it did contain many millionaires. However, the true sources of the Senate's influence lay in the long tenure of many of its members (which enabled them to master the craft of politics), in the fact that it was small enough to encourage real debate, and in its long-established reputation for wisdom, intelligence, and statesmanship.

The House of Representatives, on the other hand, was one of the most disorderly and inefficient legislative bodies in the world.

Desks slammed; members held private conversations, hailed pages, shuffled from place to place, clamored for the attention of the Speaker—and all the while some poor orator tried to discuss the question of the moment. Speaking in the House, one writer said, was like trying to address the crowd on a passing Broadway bus from the curb in front of the Astor House in New York. On one occasion in 1878 the adjournment of the House was held up for more than twelve hours because most of the members of an important committee were too drunk to prepare a vital appropriations bill for final passage.

The fundamental division between Democrats and Republicans was sectional, a result of the Civil War. The South, after the political rights of blacks had been drastically circumscribed, became heavily Democratic. Most of New England was solidly Republican. Elsewhere the two parties stood in fair balance, although the Republicans tended to have the advantage. A preponderance of the well-to-do, cultured Northerners were Republicans. Perhaps in reaction to this concentration, immigrants, Catholics, and other minority groups—except for blacks—tended to vote Democratic. But the

An 1887 cartoon indicting the Senate for closely attending to the Big (read, fat) Trusts rather than to the needs of the public (whose "entrance" to the Senate is "closed"). Drawn by Joseph Keppler, a caricaturist who was born and trained in Germany, this type of grotesque satire greatly influenced late-nineteenth-century American comic arts.

numerous exceptions weakened the applicability of these generalizations. German and Scandinavian immigrants usually voted Republican; many powerful business leaders supported the Democrats.

The bulk of the people—farmers, laborers, shopkeepers, white-collar workers— distributed their ballots fairly evenly between the two parties in most elections; the balance of political power after 1876 was almost perfect. Between 1856 and 1912 the Democrats elected a president only twice (1884 and 1892), but most contests were extremely close. Majorities in both the Senate and the House fluctuated continually. Between 1876 and 1896 the "dominant" Republican party controlled both houses of Congress and the presidency at the same time for only a single two-year period.

Recurrent Issues

Four questions obsessed politicians in these years. One was the "bloody shirt." The term, which became part of the language after a Massachusetts congressman dramatically displayed to his colleagues in the House the bloodstained shirt of an Ohio carpetbagger who had been flogged by terrorists in Mississippi, referred to the tactic of reminding the electorate of the northern states that the men who had precipitated the Civil War had been Democrats. Should Democrats regain power, former rebels would run the government and undo all the work accomplished at such sacrifice during the war. "Every man that endeavored to tear down the old flag," a Republican orator proclaimed in 1876, "was a Democrat. Every man that tried to destroy this nation was a Democrat. . . . The man that assassinated Abraham Lincoln was a Democrat. . . . Soldiers, every scar you have on your heroic bodies was given you by a Democrat." And every scoundrel or incompetent who sought office under the Republican banner waved the bloody shirt in order to divert the attention of northern voters from his own shortcomings. The technique worked so well that many decent candidates could not resist the temptation to employ it in close races.

Waving the bloody shirt was related intimately to the issue of the rights of African Americans. Throughout this period Republicans vacillated between trying to build up their organization in the South by appealing to black voters—which required them to make sure that blacks in the South could vote—and trying to win conservative white support by stressing economic issues such as the tariff.

The tariff was another perennial issue in post–Civil War politics. Despite considerable loose talk about free trade, almost no one in the United States except for a handful of professional economists, believed in eliminating duties on imports. Manufacturers desired protective tariffs to keep out competing products, and a majority of their workers were convinced that wage levels would fall if goods produced by cheap foreign labor entered the United States untaxed. Congressman William McKinley of Ohio stated the majority opinion in the clearest terms: high tariffs foster the growth of industry and thus create jobs. "Reduce the tariff and labor is the first to suffer," he said.

The tariff could have been a real political issue because American technology was advancing so rapidly that many industries no longer required protection from foreign competitors. The Democrats professed to believe in moderation, yet whenever party leaders tried to revise the tariff downward, Democratic congressmen from Pennsylvania, New York, and other industrial states sided with the Republicans. Many Republicans endorsed tariff reform in principle, but when particular schedules came up for discussion, most of them demanded the highest rates for industries in their own districts and traded votes shamelessly with colleagues representing other interests in order to get what they wanted. Every new tariff bill became an occasion for logrolling, lobbying, and outrageous politicking rather than for sane discussion and careful evaluation of the public interest.

A third political question in this period was currency reform. During the Civil War, the government, faced with obligations it could not meet by taxing or borrowing, suspended specie payments and issued about $450 million in paper money, originally printed in green ink. This currency, called greenbacks, did not command the full confidence of a people accustomed to money readily convertible into gold or silver. Greenbacks seemed to encourage inflation, for how could one trust the government not to print them in wholesale lots to avoid passing unpopular tax laws? Thus, when the war ended, strong sentiment developed for withdrawing the greenbacks from circulation and returning to a bullion standard—to coining money from silver and gold.

In fact, beginning during Reconstruction, prices declined sharply. The deflation increased the real income of bondholders and other creditors but injured debtors. Farmers were particularly hard-hit, for many of them had borrowed heavily during the wartime boom to finance expansion.

Many groups supported some kind of currency inflation. However, the major parties refused to confront each other over the currency question. While Republicans professed to be the party of sound money, most western Republicans favored expansion of the currency. Conservative Democrats favored deflation as much as Republicans did. Under various administrations steps were taken to increase or decrease the amount of money in circulation, but the net effect on the economy was not significant.

The final major political issue of these years was civil service reform. As American society grew larger and more complex, the government necessarily took on more functions. The need for professional administration increased. Corruption flourished; waste and inefficiency were the normal state of affairs.

Every honest observer could see the need for reform, but the politicians refused to surrender the power of dispensing government jobs to their lieutenants without regard for their qualifications. They argued that patronage was the lifeblood of politics, that parties could not function without armies of loyal political workers, and that the workers expected and deserved the rewards of office when their efforts were crowned with victory at the polls. When reformers suggested establishing the most modest kind of professional, nonpartisan civil service, politicians of both parties subjected them to every kind of insult and ridicule even though both the Democratic and Republican parties regularly wrote civil service reform planks into their platforms.

Party Politics: Sidestepping the Issues

With the Democrats invincible in the South and the Republicans predominant in New England and most of the states beyond the Mississippi, the outcome of presidential elections was usually determined in a handful of populous states: New York (together with its satellites, New Jersey and Connecticut), Ohio, Indiana, and Illinois. In every presidential election, Democrats and Republicans concentrated their heaviest guns on these states. Of the eighteen Democrats and Republicans nominated for president in the nine elections between 1868 and 1900, only three were not from New York, Ohio, Indiana, or Illinois, and all three lost.

With so much depending on so few, the level of political morality was abysmal. Mudslinging, character assassination, and plain lying were standard practice; bribery was routine. Drifters and other dissolute citizens were paid in cash—or more often in free drinks—to vote the party ticket. The names of persons long dead were solemnly inscribed in voting registers, their suffrages exercised by impostors.

Lackluster Presidents: From Hayes to Harrison

The leading statesmen of the period were disinterested in important contemporary questions, powerless to influence them, or content with things the way they were. Consider the presidents.

Rutherford B. Hayes, president from 1877 to 1881, came to office with a distinguished record. He attended Kenyon College and Harvard Law School before settling down to practice in Cincinnati. Although he had a family to support, he volunteered for service in the Union army within weeks after the first shell fell on Fort Sumter. "A just and necessary war," he called it in his diary. "I would prefer to go into it if I knew I was to die . . . than to live through and after it without taking any part."

In 1864 he was elected to Congress; four years later he became governor of Ohio, serving three terms altogether. The Republicans nominated him for president in 1876 because of his reputation for honesty and moderation, and his election, made possible by the Compromise of 1877, seemed to presage an era of sectional harmony and political probity.

Outwardly Hayes had a sunny disposition; inwardly, in his own words, he was sometimes "nervous to the point of disaster." Despite his geniality, he was utterly without political glamour. He played down the tariff issue. On the money question he was conservative. He approved the resumption of gold payments in 1879 and vetoed bills to expand the currency. He accounted himself a civil service reformer, being opposed to the collection of political contributions from federal officeholders.

Hayes complained about the South's failure to treat blacks decently after the withdrawal of federal troops, but he took no action. He worked harder for civil service reform, yet failed to achieve the "thorough, rapid, and complete" change he had promised. In most matters, he was content to "let the record show that he had made the requests."

Hayes's successor, James A. Garfield, fought at Shiloh and later at Chickamauga. In 1863 he won a seat in Congress, where his oratorical and managerial skills brought him to prominence in the affairs of the Republican party.

Garfield had been a compromise choice at the 1880 Republican convention. His election precipitated a great battle over patronage, the new president standing in a sort of no-man's land between contending factions within the party. In July 1881 an unbalanced office-seeker named Charles J. Guiteau shot Garfield in the Washington railroad station. The president died on September 19.

The assassination of Garfield elevated Chester A. Arthur to the presidency. A New York lawyer and abolitionist, Arthur became an early convert to the Republican party and rose rapidly in its local councils. In 1871 Grant gave him the juiciest political plum in the country, the collectorship of the Port of New York, which he held until removed by Hayes in 1878 for refusing to keep his hands out of party politics.

The vice presidency was the only elective position that Arthur had ever held. Before Garfield's death, he had paid little attention to questions like the tariff and

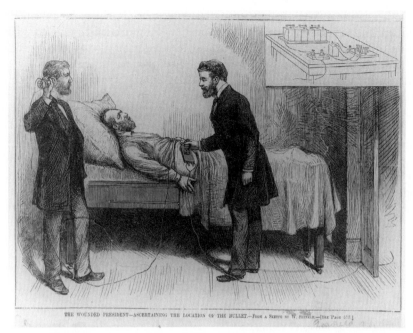

THE WOUNDED PRESIDENT—ASCERTAINING THE LOCATION OF THE BULLET.—FROM A SKETCH BY W. PRINDLE.—[SEE PAGE 555.]

James A. Garfield lies mortally wounded. After failing to locate the bullet, surgeons called in Alexander Graham Bell, the famous inventor. Bell conceived of a device, pictured here, that anticipated the mine detector. Bell's machine failed to locate the bullet, however, perhaps because the metal bed springs interfered with its operation. Garfield died, either from the bullet or the surgeon's unsuccessful attempts to extricate it.

monetary policy, being content to take in fees ranging upward of $50,000 a year as collector of the port and to oversee the operations of the New York customs office, with its hordes of clerks and laborers. Of course, Arthur was an unblushing defender of the spoils system, though in fairness it must be said that he was personally honest and an excellent administrator.

The tragic circumstances of his elevation to the presidency sobered Arthur. Although he was a genial, convivial man, perhaps overly fond of good food and flashy clothes, he comported himself with dignity as president. He handled patronage matters with restraint, and he gave at least nominal support to the movement for civil service reform, which had been strengthened by the public's indignation at the assas-

•••[Read the Document
Pendleton Civil Service Act at
myhistorylab.com

sination of Garfield. In 1883 Congress passed the **Pendleton Act**, "classifying" about 10 percent of all government jobs and creating the bipartisan Civil Service Commission to administer competitive examinations for these positions. The law made it illegal to force officeholders to make political contributions and empowered the president to expand the list of classified positions at his discretion.

The election of 1884 brought the Democrat Grover Cleveland to the White House. Cleveland grew up in western New York. After studying law, he settled in Buffalo. Although somewhat lacking in the social graces and in intellectual pretensions, he had a basic integrity that everyone recognized; when a group of reformers sought a candidate for mayor in 1881, he was a natural choice. His success in Buffalo led to his election as governor of New York in 1882.

In the governor's chair his no-nonsense attitude toward public administration endeared him to civil service reformers at the same time that his basic conservatism pleased businessmen. When he vetoed a popular bill to force a reduction of the fares charged by the New York City elevated railway on the ground that it was an unconstitutional violation of the company's franchise, his reputation soared. Here was a man who cared more for principle than for the adulation of the multitude, a man who was courageous, honest, hardworking, and eminently sound. The Democrats nominated him for president in 1884.

The election revolved around personal issues, for the platforms of the parties were almost identical. On the one hand, the Republican candidate, the dynamic James G. Blaine, had an immense following, but his reputation had been soiled by the publication of the "Mulligan letters," which connected him with the corrupt granting of congressional favors to the Little Rock and Fort Smith Railroad. On the other hand, it came out during the campaign that Cleveland, a bachelor, had fathered an illegitimate child. Instead of debating public issues, the Republicans chanted the ditty,

Ma! Ma! Where's my pa?
Gone to the White House,
Ha! Ha! Ha!

to which the Democrats countered,

Blaine, Blaine, James G. Blaine,
The continental liar from the State of Maine.

Blaine lost more heavily in the mudslinging than Cleveland, whose quiet courage in saying "Tell the truth" when his past was brought to light contrasted favorably with Blaine's glib and unconvincing denials. A significant group of eastern Republicans, known as **mugwumps,** campaigned for the Democrats.[1] However, Blaine ran a strong race against a general pro-Democratic trend; Cleveland won the election by fewer than 25,000 votes. The change of 600 ballots in New York would have given that state, and the presidency, to his opponent.

Cleveland had little imagination and too narrow a conception of his powers and duties to be a dynamic president. He could defend a position against heavy odds, yet he lacked flexibility. He took a fairly broad view of the powers of the federal government, but he thought it unseemly to put pressure on Congress, believing in "the entire independence of the executive and legislative branches."

Toward the end of his term Cleveland bestirred himself and tried to provide constructive leadership on the tariff question. The government was embarrassed by a large revenue surplus, which Cleveland hoped to reduce by cutting the duties on necessities and on raw materials used in manufacturing. He devoted his entire annual message of December 1887 to the tariff, thereby focusing public attention on the subject. When worried Democrats reminded him that an election was coming up and that the tariff might cause a rift in the organization, he replied simply, "What is the use of being elected or re-elected, unless you stand for something?"

In that contest, Cleveland obtained a plurality of the popular vote, but his opponent, Benjamin Harrison, grandson of President William Henry Harrison, carried most of

---

[1]The mugwumps considered themselves reformers, but on social and economic questions nearly all of them were very conservative. They were sound-money proponents and advocates of laissez-faire. Reform to them consisted almost entirely of doing away with corruption and making the government more efficient.

President Grover Cleveland and Frances Folsom in 1888. The couple had married two years earlier; he was 48, and she, 21, the youngest First Lady. Her popularity blunted criticisms that Cleveland, a bachelor, had earlier fathered an illegitimate child. When he lost the 1888 election, his wife predicted that she would return as First Lady. Four years later, she did.

the key northeastern industrial states by narrow margins, thereby obtaining a comfortable majority in the electoral college, 233 to 168.

Although intelligent and able, Harrison was too reserved to make a good politician. During the Civil War he fought under Sherman at Atlanta and won a reputation as a stern, effective disciplinarian. In 1876 he ran unsuccessfully for governor of Indiana, but in 1881 was elected to the Senate.

Harrison believed ardently in protective tariffs. His approach to fiscal policy was conservative, though he was freehanded in the matter of veterans' pensions. Harrison professed to favor civil service reform, but fashioned an unimpressive record on the question. He appointed the vigorous young reformer Theodore Roosevelt to the Civil Service Commission and then proceeded to undercut him systematically. Before long the frustrated Roosevelt was calling the president a "cold blooded, narrow minded, prejudiced, obstinate, timid old psalm singing Indianapolis politician."

View the Image

Harrison and Morton Campaign Ad at myhistorylab.com

Under Harrison, Congress distinguished itself by expending, for the first time in a period of peace, more than $1 billion in a single session. It raised the tariff to an all-time high. The Sherman Antitrust Act was also passed.

Harrison had little to do with the fate of any of these measures. The Republicans lost control of Congress in 1890, and two years later Grover Cleveland swept back into power, defeating Harrison by more than 350,000 votes.

African Americans in the South after Reconstruction

Perhaps the most important issue of the last quarter of the nineteenth century was the fate of the former slaves after the withdrawal of federal troops from the South. Shortly after his inauguration in 1877, President Hayes made a goodwill tour of the South and he urged blacks to trust southern whites. That same year Governor Wade Hampton of South Carolina proposed to "secure to every citizen, the lowest as well as the highest, black as well as white, full and equal protection in the enjoyment of all his rights under the Constitution."

But the pledge was not kept. By December, Hayes was sadly disillusioned. "By state legislation, by frauds, by intimidation, and by violence of the most atrocious character, colored citizens have been deprived of the right of suffrage," he wrote in his diary. However, he did nothing to remedy the situation. Frederick Douglass called Hayes's policy "sickly conciliation."

Hayes's successors in the 1880s did no better. "Time is the only cure," President Garfield said, thereby confessing that he had no policy at all. President Arthur gave federal patronage to antiblack groups in an effort to split the Democratic South. In 1887 President Cleveland explained to a correspondent why he opposed "mixed [integrated] schools." Expert opinion, the president said, believed "that separate schools were of much more benefit for the colored people." Hayes, Garfield, and Arthur were Republicans, and Cleveland a Democrat; party made little difference. Both parties subscribed to hypocritical statements about equality and constitutional rights, and neither did anything to implement them.

For a time blacks were not totally disenfranchised in the South. Rival white factions tried to manipulate them, and corruption flourished as widely as in the machine-dominated wards of the northern cities. In the 1890s, however, the southern states, led by Mississippi, began to deprive blacks of the vote despite the Fifteenth Amendment. Poll taxes raised a formidable economic barrier, one that also disenfranchised many poor whites. Literacy tests completed the work; a number of states provided a loophole for illiterate whites by including an "understanding" clause whereby an illiterate person could qualify by demonstrating an ability to explain the meaning of a section of the state constitution when an election official read it to him. Blacks who attempted to take the test were uniformly declared to have failed it.

In Louisiana, 130,000 blacks voted in the election of 1896. Then the law was changed. In 1900 only 5,000 votes were cast by blacks. "We take away the Negroes' votes," a Louisiana politician explained, "to protect them just as we would protect a little child and prevent it from injuring itself with sharp-edged tools." Almost every Supreme Court decision after 1877 that affected blacks somehow nullified or curtailed their rights. The **civil rights cases** (1883) declared the Civil Rights Act of 1875 unconstitutional. Blacks who were refused equal accommodations or privileges by hotels, theaters, and other privately owned facilities had no recourse at law, the Court announced. The Fourteenth Amendment guaranteed their civil rights against invasion by the states, not by individuals.

Finally, in ***Plessy v. Ferguson*** (1896), the Court ruled that even in places of public accommodation, such as railroads and, by implication, schools, segregation was legal as long as facilities of equal quality were provided: "If one race be inferior to the other socially, the Constitution of the United States cannot put them upon the same plane." In a noble dissent in the Plessy case, Justice John Marshall Harlan protested this line of argument. "Our Constitution is color-blind," he said. "The two races in this country are indissolubly linked together, and the interests of both require that the common government of all shall not permit the seeds of race hatred to be planted under the sanction of law."

⊙⊢[View the Image

Plessy v. Ferguson, 1896
at myhistorylab.com

Most Northerners supported the government and the Court. Newspapers presented a stereotyped, derogatory picture of blacks, no matter what the circumstances. Northern magazines, even high-quality publications such as *Harper's*, *Scribner's*, and the *Century*, repeatedly made blacks the butt of crude jokes.

A cartoon from *Judge* magazine in 1892 depicts Ku Klux Klansmen barring a black voter from the polls.

The restoration of white rule abruptly halted the progress in public education for blacks that the Reconstruction governments had made. Church groups and private foundations such as the Peabody Fund and the Slater Fund, financed chiefly by northern philanthropists, supported black schools after 1877. Among them were two important experiments in vocational training, Hampton Institute and Tuskegee Institute.

These schools had to overcome considerable resistance and suspicion in the white community; they survived only because they taught a docile philosophy, preparing students to accept second-class citizenship and become farmers and craftsmen. Since proficiency in academic subjects might have given the lie to the southern belief that blacks were intellectually inferior to whites, such subjects were avoided.

Booker T. Washington: A "Reasonable" Champion for African Americans

Since nearly all contemporary biologists, physicians, and other supposed experts on race were convinced that African Americans were inferior, white Americans generally accepted black inferiority as fact. By denying blacks decent educational opportunities and good jobs, the dominant race could use the blacks' resultant ignorance and poverty to justify the inferior facilities offered them.

Southern blacks reacted to this deplorable situation in a variety of ways. Some sought redress in racial pride and what would later be called black nationalism. Some became so disaffected that they tried to revive the African colonization movement. "Africa is our home," insisted Bishop Henry M. Turner, a huge, plainspoken man who had served as an army chaplain during the war and as a member of the Georgia legislature during Reconstruction. Another militant, T. Thomas Fortune, editor of the New York *Age* and founder of the Afro-American League (1887), called on blacks to demand full civil rights, better schools, and fair wages and to fight against discrimination of every sort. "Let us stand up like men in our own organization," he urged. "If others use . . . violence to combat our peaceful arguments, it is not for us to run away from violence."

For a time, militancy and black separatism won few adherents among southern blacks. For one thing, life was better than it had been under slavery. Segregation actually helped southern blacks who became barbers, undertakers, restaurateurs, and shopkeepers because whites were reluctant to supply such services to blacks. According to the most conservative estimates, the living standard of the average southern black more than doubled between 1865 and 1900. But this only made many southern whites more vindictive.

This helps explain the tactics of Booker T. Washington, one of the most extraordinary Americans of that generation. Washington had been born a slave in Virginia in 1856. Laboriously he obtained an education, supporting himself while a student by working as a janitor. In 1881, with the financial help of northern philanthropists, he founded Tuskegee Institute in Alabama. His experiences convinced Washington that blacks must lift themselves up by their own bootstraps but that they must also accommodate themselves to white prejudices. A persuasive speaker and a brilliant fund-raiser, he soon developed a national reputation as a "reasonable" champion of his race.

In 1895 Washington made a now-famous speech to a mixed audience at the Cotton States International Exposition in Atlanta. To the blacks he said, "Cast down your bucket where you are," by which he meant stop fighting segregation and second-class citizenship and concentrate on learning useful skills. Progress up the social and economic ladder would come not from "artificial forcing" but from self-improvement.

Booker T. Washington in his office at Tuskegee Institute, 1900. Washington chose a policy of accommodation. Washington did not urge blacks to accept inferiority and racial slurs but to ignore them. His own behavior was indeed subtle, even devious. In public he minimized the importance of civil and political rights. Behind the scenes he lobbied against restrictive measures, marshaled large sums of money to fight test cases in the courts, and worked hard in northern states to organize the black vote and make sure that black political leaders got a share of the spoils of office.

Washington asked the whites of what he called "our beloved South" to lend the blacks a hand in their efforts to advance themselves. If you will do so, he promised, you will be "surrounded by the most patient, faithful, law-abiding, and unresentful people that the world has seen."

This **Atlanta Compromise** delighted white Southerners and won Washington financial support in every section of the country. He became one of the most powerful men in the United States, consulted by presidents, in close touch with business and philanthropic leaders, and capable of influencing in countless unobtrusive ways the fate of millions of blacks.

Blacks responded to the compromise with mixed feelings. Accepting Washington's approach might relieve them of many burdens and dangers. But Washington was asking them to give up specific rights in return for vague promises of future help. The cost was high in surrendered personal dignity and lost hopes of obtaining real justice.

Washington's career illustrates the dilemma that American blacks have always faced: the choice between confrontation and accommodation. This choice was particularly difficult in the late nineteenth century.

City Bosses

Outside of the South, the main issue concerned municipal government.

The immigrants who flocked into American cities in the 1880s and early 1890s were largely of peasant stock, and having come from societies unacquainted with democracy, they had no experience with representative government. The tendency of urban workers to move frequently in search of better jobs further lessened the likelihood that they would develop political influence independently.

Furthermore, the difficulties of life in the slums bewildered and often overwhelmed newcomers, both native- and foreign-born. Hopeful, but passive and naive, they could hardly be expected to take a broad view of social problems when so beset by personal ones. This enabled shrewd urban politicians to take command of the city masses and march them in obedient phalanxes to the polls.

Most city machines were loose-knit neighborhood organizations headed by ward bosses, not tightly geared hierarchical bureaucracies ruled by a single leader. "Big Tim" Sullivan of New York's Lower East Side and "Hinky Dink" Kenna of Chicago were typical of the breed. Sullivan, Kenna, and others like them performed many useful services for people they liked to think of as their constituents. They found jobs for new arrivals and distributed food and other help to all in bad times. Anyone in trouble with the law could obtain at least a hearing from the ward boss, and often, if the crime was minor or due to ignorance, the difficulty was quietly "fixed" and the culprit was sent off with a word of caution. Informally, probably without consciously intending to do so, the bosses educated the immigrants in the complexities of American civilization, helping them to leap the gulf between the almost medieval society of their origins and the modern industrial world.

The price of such aid was unquestioning political support, which the bosses converted into cash. In New York, Sullivan levied tribute on gambling, had a hand in the liquor business, and controlled the issuance of peddlers' licenses. When he died in 1913, he was reputedly worth $1 million. Yet he and others like him were immensely popular; 25,000 grieving constituents followed Big Tim's coffin on its way to the grave.

The more visible and better-known city bosses played even less socially justifiable roles than the ward bosses. Their principal technique for extracting money from the public till was the kickback. To get city contracts, suppliers were made to pad their bills and, when paid for their work with funds from the city treasury, turn over the excess to the politicians. Similarly, operators of streetcar lines, gas and electricity companies, and other public utilities were compelled to pay huge bribes to obtain favorable franchises.

The most notorious of the nineteenth-century city bosses was William Marcy Tweed, whose "Tweed Ring" extracted tens of millions of dollars from New York City during the brief period of 1869–1871. He was swiftly jailed!

Despite their welfare work and their popularity, most bosses were essentially thieves. Efforts to romanticize them as the Robin Hoods of industrial society grossly distort the facts. However, the system developed and survived because too many middle-class city dwellers were indifferent to the fate of the poor. Except during occasional reform waves, few tried to check the rapaciousness of the politicos.

Many substantial citizens shared at least indirectly in the corruption. The owners of tenements were interested in crowding as many rent payers as possible into their buildings. Utility companies seeking franchises preferred a system that enabled them to buy favors. Honest citizens who had no selfish stake in the system and who were repelled by the sordidness of city government were seldom sufficiently concerned to do anything about it.

Many so-called urban reformers resented the boss system mainly because it gave political power to people who were not "gentlemen" or, as one reformer put it, to a "proletarian mob" of "illiterate peasants, freshly raked from Irish bogs, or Bohemian mines, or Italian robber nests."

Crops and Complaints

The vacuity of American politics may well have stemmed from the complacency of the middle-class majority. The country was growing; no foreign enemy threatened it; the poor were mostly recent immigrants, blacks, and others with little influence, who were easily ignored by those in comfortable circumstances. However, one important group in society suffered increasingly as the years rolled by: the farmers. Out of their travail came the force that finally, in the 1890s, brought American politics face to face with the problems of the age.

After the Civil War most farmers did well, but in the 1890s disaster struck. First came a succession of dry years and poor harvests. Then farmers in Australia, Canada, Russia, and Argentina took advantage of improvements in transportation to sell their produce in European markets that had relied on American foodstuffs. The price of wheat fell to about sixty cents a bushel. Cotton, the great southern staple, which sold for more than thirty cents a pound in 1866 and fifteen cents in the early 1870s, at times in the 1890s fell below six cents.

The tariff on manufactured goods appeared to aggravate the farmers' predicament, and so did the domestic marketing system, which enabled a multitude of middlemen to gobble up a large share of the profits of agriculture. The shortage of credit, particularly in the South, was an additional burden.

The downward swing of the business cycle in the early 1890s completed the devastation. Settlers who had paid more for their lands than they were worth and borrowed money at high interest rates to do so found themselves squeezed relentlessly. Thousands lost their farms and returned eastward, penniless and dispirited.

The Populist Movement

The agricultural depression triggered a new outburst of farm radicalism, the Alliance movement. Alliances were organizations of farmers' clubs, most of which had sprung up during the bad times of the late 1870s. The first Knights of Reliance group was founded in 1877 in Lampasas County, Texas. As the Farmers' Alliance, this organization gradually expanded in northeastern Texas, and after 1885 it spread rapidly throughout the cotton states. Alliance leaders stressed cooperation. Their co-ops bought fertilizer and other supplies in bulk and sold them at fair prices to members. They sought to market their crops cooperatively but could not raise the necessary capital from banks, with the result that some of them began to question the workings of the American financial and monetary system. They became economic and social radicals in the process.

Although the state alliances of the Dakotas and Kansas joined the Southern Alliance in 1889, for a time local prejudices and conflicting interests prevented the formation of a single national organization. But the farm groups emerged as a potent force in the 1890 elections.

In the South, Alliance-sponsored gubernatorial candidates won in Georgia, Tennessee, South Carolina, and Texas; eight southern legislatures fell under Alliance control, and forty-four representatives and three senators committed to Alliance objectives were sent to Washington. In the West, Alliance candidates swept Kansas, captured a majority in the Nebraska legislature, and accumulated enough seats in Minnesota and South Dakota to hold the balance of power between the major parties.

Such success, coupled with the reluctance of the Republicans and Democrats to make concessions to their demands, encouraged Alliance leaders to create a new national party. By uniting southern and western farmers, they succeeded in breaking the sectional barrier erected by the Civil War. If they could recruit industrial workers, perhaps a real political revolution could be accomplished. In February 1892, farm leaders, representatives of the Knights of Labor, and various professional reformers met at St. Louis. They organized the **People's (Populist) party**, and issued a call for a national convention to meet at Omaha in July.

That convention nominated General James B. Weaver of Iowa for president and drafted a platform that called for a graduated income tax and national ownership of railroads, the telegraph, and telephone systems. It also advocated a "subtreasury" plan that would permit farmers to keep nonperishable crops off the market when prices were low. Under this proposal the government would make loans in the form of greenbacks to farmers, secured by crops held in storage in federal ware-

●●●[Read the Document

The People's Party Platform
at **myhistorylab.com**

houses. When prices rose, the farmers could sell their crops and repay the loans. To combat deflation further, the platform demanded the unlimited coinage of silver and an increase in the money supply "to no less than $50 per capita."

To make the government more responsive to public opinion, the Populists urged the adoption of the initiative and referendum procedures and the election of U.S. senators by popular vote. To win the support of industrial workers, their platform denounced the use of Pinkerton detectives in labor disputes and backed the eight-hour day and the restriction of "undesirable" immigration.

The Populists saw themselves not as a persecuted minority but as a victimized majority betrayed by what would a century later be called the establishment. They were at most ambivalent about the free enterprise system, and they tended to attribute social and

In Kansas in 1893 a Populist governor and a Populist-controlled Senate invalidated the election of some Republicans in the Kansas House of Representatives, giving the Populists control of that body, too. The displaced Republicans, denied seats, smashed their way into the capitol building with this sledgehammer and ousted the Populists, who decided to meet in a separate building. Each proclaimed itself to be the true legislature and passed its own laws. Eventually the Kansas Supreme Court decided in favor of the Republican legislature and disbanded the Populist gathering.
Source: Kansas State Historical Society.

economic injustices not to built-in inequities in the system but to nefarious conspiracies organized by selfish interests in order to subvert the system.

The appearance of the new party was the most exciting and significant aspect of the presidential campaign of 1892, which saw Harrison and Cleveland refighting the election of 1888. The Populists put forth a host of colorful spellbinders: Tom Watson, a Georgia congressman whose temper was such that on one occasion he administered a beating to a local planter with the man's own riding crop; William A. Peffer, a senator from Kansas whose long beard and grave demeanor gave him the look of a Hebrew prophet; "Sockless Jerry" Simpson of Kansas, unlettered but full of grassroots shrewdness and wit, a former Greenbacker, and an admirer of the single tax doctrine of Henry George; and Ignatius Donnelly, the "Minnesota Sage," who claimed to be an authority on science, economics, and Shakespeare.

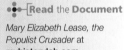

●●●─Read the Document

Mary Elizabeth Lease, the Populist Crusader at **myhistorylab.com**

In the one-party South, Populist strategists sought to wean black farmers away from the ruling Democratic organization. Southern black farmers had their own Colored Farmers' Alliance, and even before 1892 their leaders had worked closely with the white alliances. Of course, the blacks would be useless to the party if they could not vote; therefore, white Populist leaders opposed the southern trend toward disfranchising African Americans and called for full civil rights for all.

The results proved disappointing. Tom Watson lost his seat in Congress, and Donnelly ran a poor third in the Minnesota gubernatorial race. The Populists did sweep Kansas. They elected numbers of local officials in other western states and cast over a million votes for General Weaver. But the effort to unite white and black farmers in the South failed miserably. Conservative Democrats, while continuing with considerable success to attract black voters, played on racial fears, insisting that the Populists sought to undermine white supremacy. Since most white Populists saw the alliance with blacks as at best a marriage of convenience, this argument had a deadly effect. Elsewhere, even in the old centers of the Granger movement, the party made no significant impression.

Mary Elizabeth Lease was a prominent Populist, noted for her rallying cry to "raise less corn and more hell."
Source: Kansas State Historical Society.

By standing firmly for conservative financial policies, Cleveland attracted considerable Republican support and won a solid victory over Harrison in the electoral college, 277 to 145. Weaver received twenty-two electoral votes.

Showdown on Silver

One conclusion that politicians reached after analyzing the 1892 election was that the money question, particularly the controversy over the coinage of silver, was of paramount interest to the voters. Despite the wide-ranging appeal of the Populist platform, most of Weaver's strength came from the silver-mining states.

In truth, the issue of gold versus silver was superficial; the important question was what, if anything, should be done to check the deflationary spiral. The declining price level benefited people with fixed incomes and injured most others. Industrial workers profited from deflation except when depression caused unemployment.

By the early 1890s, discussion of federal monetary policy revolved around the coinage of silver. Traditionally, the United States had been on a bimetallic standard. Both gold and silver were coined, the number of grains of each in the dollar being adjusted periodically to reflect the commercial value of the two metals. The discovery of numerous gold mines in

California in the 1840s and 1850s depressed the price of gold relative to silver. By 1861, a silver dollar could be melted down and sold for $1.03. No miner took silver to the mint to be stamped into coin. In a short time, silver dollars were withdrawn and only gold dollars circulated. However, an avalanche of silver from the mines of Nevada and Colorado gradually depressed the price until, around 1874, it again became profitable for miners to coin their bullion. Alas, when they tried to do so, they discovered that the Coinage Act of 1873, taking account of the fact that no silver had been presented to the mint in years, had demonetized the metal.

Silver miners denounced this as the "Crime of '73." Inflationists joined them in demanding a return to bimetallism. They knew that if more dollars were put into circulation, the value of each dollar would decline; that is, prices and wages would rise. Conservatives, still fighting the battle against inflationary greenback paper money, resisted strongly. The result was a series of compromises. In 1878 the **Bland-Allison Silver Purchase Act** authorized the buying of between $2 million and $4 million of silver a month at the market price, but this had little inflationary effect because the government consistently purchased the minimum amount. The commercial price of silver continued to fall. In 1890 the **Sherman Silver Purchase Act** required the government to buy 4.5 million *ounces* of silver monthly, but in the face of increasing supplies the price of silver fell still further. By 1894, a silver coin weighed thirty-two times more than a gold one.

L. Frank Baum, author of *The Wonderful Wizard of Oz* (1900) and a fan of William Jennings Bryan, perhaps wrote his story as an allegory of the 1896 election. Dorothy, wearing "silver" slippers (in the original), follows a "yellow brick road" (gold) on a crusade to free the Munchkins (the oppressed little people) from the Wicked Witch of the East (the rapacious corporations and financiers). Liberation is to come in Emerald City (greenbacks) through the intervention of a kindly, but ultimately ineffective wizard (Bryan). Only the entire people—Dorothy and entourage—can prevail against wickedness. Judy Garland starred as Dorothy in the film version of *The Wizard of Oz* (1939).

The compromises satisfied no one. Silver miners grumbled because their bullion brought in only half what it had in the early 1870s. Debtors noted angrily that because of the general decline in prices, the dollars they used to meet their obligations were worth more than twice as much as in 1865. Advocates of the gold standard feared that unlimited silver coinage would be authorized, "destroying the value of the dollar."

The Depression of 1893

Both the silverites and "gold bugs" warned of economic disaster if their policies were not followed. Then, in 1893, after the London banking house of Baring Brothers collapsed, a financial panic precipitated a worldwide industrial depression. In the United States hundreds of cotton mills and iron foundries closed, never to reopen. During the harsh winter of 1893–1894, millions were without jobs.

President Cleveland believed that the controversy over silver had caused the depression by shaking the confidence of the business community and that all would be well if the country returned to a single gold standard. He summoned a special session of Congress, and by exerting immense political pressure he obtained the repeal of the Sherman Silver Purchase Act in October 1893. All that this accomplished was to split the Democratic party, its southern and western wings deserting him almost to a man.

During 1894 and 1895, while the nation floundered in the worst depression it had ever experienced, a series of events further undermined public confidence. In the spring of 1894 several "armies" of the unemployed, the most imposing led by Jacob S. Coxey, an eccentric Ohio businessman, marched on Washington to demand relief. Coxey wanted the government to undertake a program of federal public works and other projects to hire unemployed workers to build roads.

When Coxey's group of demonstrators, perhaps 500 in all, reached Washington, he and two other leaders were arrested for trespassing on the grounds of the Capitol. Their followers were dispersed by club-wielding policemen. This callous treatment convinced many Americans that the government had little interest in the suffering of the people, an opinion strengthened when Cleveland, in July 1894, used federal troops to crush the Pullman strike.

The next year the Supreme Court handed down several reactionary decisions. In *United States v. E. C. Knight Company* it refused to employ the Sherman Antitrust Act to break up the Sugar Trust. The Court also denied a writ of habeas corpus to Eugene V. Debs of the American Railway Union, who was languishing in prison for disobeying a federal injunction during the Pullman strike.

On top of these indications of official conservatism came a desperate financial crisis. Throughout 1894 the Treasury's supply of gold dwindled as worried citizens exchanged greenbacks (now convertible into gold) for hard money and foreign investors cashed in large amounts of American securities. The government tried to sell bonds for gold to bolster the reserve, but the gold reserve continued to melt away. Early in 1895 it touched a low point of $41 million.

At this juncture a syndicate of bankers headed by J. P. Morgan turned the tide by underwriting a $62 million bond issue, guaranteeing that half the gold would come from Europe. This caused a great public outcry; the spectacle of the nation being saved from bankruptcy by a private banker infuriated millions.

As the presidential election of 1896 approached, the major parties found it impossible to continue straddling the money question. The Populist vote had increased by 42 percent

Table 20.1 The Supreme Court Supports Racial Segregation and Corporate Power

Civil Rights Cases	1883	Overturned Civil Rights Act of 1875	Limited Fourteenth Amendment to protecting blacks from deprivation of rights by *states*; allowed individuals to do so
Plessy v. Ferguson	1896	Upheld principle of "separate but equal" in public accommodations	Allowed southern states and municipalities to pass laws enforcing separation of whites and blacks
U.S. v. E. C. Knight Co.	1895	Refused to break up the Sugar Trust for being a monopoly	Rendered the Sherman Antitrust Act of 1890 nearly meaningless
In Re Debs	1895	Refused to free Eugene V. Debs, president of the American Railway Union who had been jailed for leading a strike	Enabled the government to use injunctions to stop strikes, thereby depriving union leaders of the chance to plead their case in court

in the 1894 congressional elections. Southern and western Democratic leaders feared that they would lose their following unless Cleveland was repudiated. Western Republicans, led by Senator Henry M. Teller of Colorado, were threatening to bolt to the Populists unless their party came out for silver coinage. After a generation of political equivocation, the major parties had to face an important issue squarely.

The Republicans, meeting to choose a candidate at St. Louis in June 1896, announced for the gold standard. "We are unalterably opposed to every measure calculated to debase our currency or impair the credit of our country," the platform declared. "We are therefore opposed to the free coinage of silver. . . . The existing gold standard must be maintained." The party then nominated Ohio's William McKinley for president. McKinley, best known for his staunch advocacy of the protective tariff yet highly regarded by labor, was expected to run strongly in the Midwest and the East.

The Democratic convention met in July in Chicago. The pro-gold Cleveland element made a hard fight, but the silverites swept them aside. The high point came when a youthful Nebraskan named William Jennings Bryan spoke for silver against gold, for western farmers against the industrial East.

"Burn down your cities and leave our farms," he said, "and your cities will spring up again as if by magic; but destroy our farms and the grass will grow in the streets of every city in the country." He ended with a marvelous figure of speech that set the tone for the coming campaign. "You shall not press down upon the brow of labor this crown of thorns," he warned, bringing his hands down suggestively to his temples. "You shall not crucify mankind upon a cross of gold!" Dramatically, he extended his arms to the side, the very figure of the crucified Christ.

The convention promptly adopted a platform calling for "the free and unlimited coinage of both silver and gold at the present legal ratio of 16 to 1" and went on to nominate Bryan, who was barely thirty-six, for president.

This action put tremendous pressure on the Populists. If they supported the Democrat Bryan, they risked losing their party identity; if they nominated another candidate, they would ensure McKinley's election. In part because the delegates could not find a person of stature willing to become a candidate against Bryan, the Populist convention nominated him, seeking to preserve the party identity by substituting Watson for the Democratic vice-presidential nominee, Arthur Sewall of Maine.

The Election of 1896

Never did a presidential campaign raise such intense emotions. The Republicans from the silver-mining states swung solidly behind Bryan. But many solid-money Democrats, especially in the Northeast, refused to accept the decision of the Chicago convention. Many others adopted the policy of Governor David B. Hill of New York, who said, "I am a Democrat still—very still." The extreme gold bugs, calling themselves National Democrats, nominated their own candidate, seventy-nine-year-old Senator John M. Palmer of Illinois. Palmer ran only to injure Bryan. "Fellow Democrats," he announced, "I will not consider it any great fault if you decide to cast your vote for William McKinley."

At the start the Republicans seemed to have everything in their favor. Bryan's youth and relative lack of political experience—two terms in the House—contrasted unfavorably with McKinley's distinguished war record, his long service in Congress and as governor of Ohio, and his reputation for honesty and good judgment. The severe depression operated in favor of the party out of power, although by repudiating Cleveland the Democrats escaped much of the burden of explaining away his errors. The newspapers came out almost unanimously for the Republicans. The Democrats had very little money and few well-known speakers to fight the campaign.

Bryan vs. McKinley, 1896 Democrat/Populist Bryan carried much of the South and West, and most of the farming regions of the plains. But he failed to win over enough industrial workers to take states in the North.

But Bryan proved a formidable opponent. Casting aside tradition, he took to the stump personally, traveling 18,000 miles and making over 600 speeches. He was one of the greatest of orators, projecting an image of absolute sincerity without appearing fanatical or argumentative. At every major stop on his tour, huge crowds assembled. His energy was amazing, and his charm and good humor were unfailing. Everywhere he hammered away at the money question. Yet he did not totally neglect other issues. He was defending, he said, "all the people who suffer from the operations of trusts, syndicates, and combines."

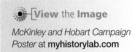

●◆─[Read the Document

William Jennings Bryan, *Cross of Gold* Speech at **myhistorylab.com**

◉─[View the Image

McKinley and Hobart Campaign Poster at **myhistorylab.com**

McKinley's campaign was managed by a new type of politician, Marcus "Mark" Alonzo Hanna, an Ohio businessman. In a sense Hanna was a product of the Pendleton Civil Service Act. When deprived of the contributions of officeholders, the parties turned to business for funds, and Hanna was one of the first leaders with a foot in both camps. Politics fascinated him, and despite his wealth and wide interests, he was willing to labor endlessly at the routine work of political organization.

Before most Republicans realized how effective Bryan was on the stump, Hanna perceived the danger and sprang into action.

Certain that money was the key to political power, he raised an enormous campaign fund. When businessmen hesitated to contribute, he pried open their purses by a combination of persuasiveness and intimidation. Banks and insurance companies were "assessed" a percentage of their assets, big corporations a share of their receipts, until some $3.5 million had been collected.

Hanna disbursed these funds with efficiency and imagination. He sent 1,500 speakers into the doubtful districts and blanketed the land with 250 million pieces of campaign literature, printed in a dozen languages. "He has advertised McKinley as if he were a patent medicine," Theodore Roosevelt, never at a loss for words, exclaimed.

Incapable of competing with Bryan as a swayer of mass audiences, McKinley conducted a "front-porch campaign." This technique dated from the first Harrison-Cleveland election, when Harrison regularly delivered off-the-cuff speeches to groups of visitors representing special interests or regions in his hometown of Indianapolis. The system conserved the candidate's energies and enabled him to avoid the appearance of seeking the presidency too openly—which was still considered bad form—and at the same time allowed him to make headlines throughout the country.

Guided by the masterful Hanna, McKinley brought the front-porch method to perfection. Superficially the proceedings were delightfully informal. From every corner of the land, groups representing various regions, occupations, and interests descended on McKinley's unpretentious frame house in Canton, Ohio. Gathering on the lawn—the grass was soon reduced to mud, the fence stripped of pickets by souvenir hunters—the visitors paid their compliments to the candidate and heard him deliver a brief speech, while beside him on the porch his aged mother and adoring invalid wife listened with rapt attention. Then there was a small reception, during which the delegates were given an opportunity to shake their host's hand.

Despite the air of informality, these performances were carefully staged. The delegations arrived on a tightly coordinated schedule worked out by McKinley's staff and the railroads, which operated cut-rate excursion trains to Canton from all over the nation.

William Jennings Bryan's "Cross of Gold" speech inspired this cartoonist's caricature of it as "plagiarized from the Bible." Bryan's speech in favor of bimetallism was, in fact, studded with religious references. He described the unlimited coinage of silver and gold as a "holy cause" supported by those who built churches "where they praise their Creator."

THE SACRILEGIOUS CANDIDATE.
No man who drags into the dust the most sacred symbols of the Christian world is fit to be president of the United States.

McKinley was fully briefed on the special interests and attitudes of each group, and the speeches of delegation leaders were submitted in advance. Often his secretary amended these remarks, and on occasion McKinley wrote the visitors' speeches himself. His own talks were carefully prepared, each calculated to make a particular point. All were reported fully in the newspapers. Thus without moving from his doorstep, McKinley met thousands of people from every section of the country.

These tactics worked admirably. On election day McKinley collected 271 electoral votes to Bryan's 176, the popular vote being 7,036,000 to 6,468,000.

The Meaning of the Election

During the campaign, some frightened Republicans had laid plans for fleeing the country if Bryan were elected, and belligerent ones, such as Theodore Roosevelt, then police commissioner of New York City, readied themselves to meet the "social revolutionaries" on the battlefield. Victory sent such people into transports of joy. Most conservatives concluded that the way of life they so fervently admired had been saved for all time.

However heartfelt, such sentiments were not founded on fact. With workers standing beside capitalists and with the farm vote split, it cannot be said that the election divided the nation class against class or that McKinley's victory saved the country from revolution.

Far from representing a triumph for the status quo, the election marked the coming of age of modern America. The battle between gold and silver, which everyone had considered so vital, had little real significance. The inflationists seemed to have been beaten, but new discoveries of gold in Alaska and South Africa and improved methods of extracting gold from low-grade ores soon led to a great expansion of the money supply. In any case, within two decades the system of basing the volume of currency on bullion had been abandoned. Bryan and the "political" Populists who supported him, supposedly the advance agents of revolution, were oriented more toward the past than the future; their ideal was the rural America of Jefferson and Jackson.

McKinley, for all his innate conservatism, was capable of looking ahead toward the new century. His approach was national where Bryan's was basically parochial. Though never daring and seldom imaginative, McKinley was able to deal pragmatically with current problems. Before long, as the United States became increasingly an exporter of manufactures, he would even modify his position on the tariff. And no one better reflected the spirit of the age than Mark Hanna, the outstanding political realist of his generation. Far from preventing change, the outcome of the election of 1896 made possible still greater changes as the United States moved into the twentieth century.

Milestones

1872	Ulysses Grant is reelected president	1890	Sherman Silver Purchase Act requires government silver purchase
1873	Congress suspends the coining of silver ("Crime of '73")	1890–1900	Blacks are deprived of the vote in the South
1876	Rutherford B. Hayes is elected president	1892	People's (Populist) party is founded
1877	Farmers' Alliance movement is founded		Cleveland is elected president a second time
1878	Bland-Allison Act authorizes government silver purchases	1893	Sherman Silver Purchase Act is repealed
1879	Specie payments resume	1893	Panic of 1893 causes industrial depression
1880	James Garfield is elected president		
1881	Garfield is assassinated; Grover Cleveland becomes president	1894	Coxey's Army marches to Washington to demand relief
1881	Booker T. Washington founds Tuskegee Institute for blacks	1895	Supreme Court declares federal income tax unconstitutional (*Pollock v. Farmers' Loan and Trust Company*)
1883	Pendleton Act creates Civil Service Commission		
	Supreme Court Overturns Civil Rights Act of 1875 in the civil rights cases		Booker T. Washington urges self-improvement in Atlanta Compromise Speech
1884	Republicans support Democrats during Mugwump Movement		J. P. Morgan raises $62 million in gold for the U.S. Treasury
	Grover Cleveland is elected president	1896	William Jennings Bryan delivers "Cross of Gold" speech
1887	Interstate Commerce Act regulates railroad rates		William McKinley is elected president
	Cleveland delivers tariff message		Supreme Court upholds "separate but equal" in *Plessy v. Ferguson*
1888	Benjamin Harrison is elected president		
	Englishman James Bryce analyzes American politics in *The American Commonwealth*		

✓•⎯Study and Review at www.myhistorylab.com

Review Questions

1. The introduction to this chapter suggests that Americans from 1877 to 1896 were as enthralled with politics as Americans are today with *American Idol*. And yet the chapter contends that the major parties took similar positions on the major issues. What explains the high voter turnouts of the era?

2. How did the urban bosses respond to the challenges confronting the cities?

3. How did the decisions of the Supreme Court aggravate race relations and give rise to political protest? What strategies did African American leaders consider in response to increased segregation?

4. Why did such a seemingly dull issue as currency reform generate such passion, culminating in William Jennings Bryan's crusade against "a cross of gold" in 1896? Why did the Populists fail to win the support of northern labor, and thus the election?

5. How has populism fared among historians? How is populism regarded by politicians today? Why?

Key Terms

Atlanta Compromise *529*

Bland-Allison Silver Purchase Act *534*

civil rights cases *526*

mugwumps *524*

Pendleton Act *523*

People's (Populist) party *531*

Plessy v. Ferguson *526*

Sherman Silver Purchase Act *534*

21 The Age of Reform

((•—[Hear the Audio Chapter 21 at myhistorylab.com

Are college students apathetic?

SOME THINK SO. IN 2007 *NEW YORK TIMES* COLUMNIST THOMAS Friedman proposed that they be known as Generation Q—for Quiet. That generation, he reported, was "too quiet, too online, for its own good, and for the country's own good."

In 2010 Gabrielle Grow, a senior at the University of California at Davis, offered an explanation in the *Huffington Post*: "From those who deem us apathetic, we have not only inherited a country up to its neck in debt but a society and lifestyle in which we are constantly expected to outperform each other. . . [An] intense course load combined with little free time leaves little room for political inquiry or investigation."

Other students challenged Friedman's stereotype through civic engagement of the old-fashioned sort, by rolling up their sleeves and helping out. In a 2009 UCLA survey, two-thirds of college seniors reported that they "occasionally" or "frequently" performed volunteer work. Over three-fourths said that they voted in the 2008 presidential election. In 2009 AmeriCorps, a federally sponsored public-service plan, received twice as many applications from college graduates as the previous year. That same year, more than 168,000 college students worked for Habitat for Humanity, far more than a decade earlier.

Today's college-age volunteers in many ways resemble their counterparts during the "age of reform" a century ago. Then, large numbers of young adults worked to improve society in various ways. They investigated tenements, factories, schools, municipal governments, and consumer goods. They promoted legislation to protect children from exploitative employers and to secure voting rights for women. They advocated conservation of natural resources. They swelled the ranks of the Socialist party, the Progressive party, and of more radical movements. In response to this sea change among younger voters, the Republican and Democratic parties embraced reforms that earlier generations had regarded as wild-eyed radicalism.

Roots of Progressivism

The progressives were never a single group seeking a single objective. The movement sprang from many sources. One was the fight against corruption and inefficiency in government, which began with the Liberal Republicans of the Grant era and was

Orchard Street, a tenement in lower Manhattan in New York City. The unpaved street, ankle-deep in mud, is lined with garbage. But while reformers deplored life in such slums, many who lived there enjoyed the sociability of the congested streets.

continued by the mugwumps of the 1880s. The struggle for civil service reform was only the first skirmish in this battle; the continuing power of corrupt political machines and the growing influence of large corporations and their lobbyists on municipal and state governments outraged thousands of citizens and led them to seek ways to make the machinery of government at all levels responsive to the majority rather than to special-interest groups.

Progressivism also had roots in the effort to regulate and control big business, which characterized the Granger and Populist agitation of the 1870s and 1890s. The failure of the Interstate Commerce Act to end railroad abuses and of the Sherman Antitrust Act to check the growth of large corporations became increasingly apparent after 1900. The return of prosperity after the depression of the 1890s encouraged reformers by removing the fear, so influential in the 1896 presidential campaign, that an assault on the industrial giants might lead to the collapse of the economy.

Between 1897 and 1904 the trend toward concentration in industry accelerated. Such new giants as Amalgamated Copper (1899), U.S. Steel (1901), and International Harvester (1902) attracted most of the attention, but even more alarming were the overall statistics. In a single year (1899) more than 1,200 firms were absorbed in mergers, the resulting combinations being capitalized at $2.2 billion. By 1904 there were 318 industrial combinations in the country with an aggregate capital of $7.5 billion. People who considered bigness inherently evil demanded that the huge new "trusts" be broken up or at least strictly controlled.

America was becoming more urban, more industrial, more mechanized, more centralized—in short, more complex. This trend put a premium on efficiency and cooperation. It seemed obvious to the progressives that people must become more socially minded, and the economy more carefully organized.

By attracting additional thousands of sympathizers to the general cause of reform, the return of prosperity after 1896 fueled the progressive movement. Good times made people more tolerant and generous. As long as profits were on the rise, the average employer did not object if labor improved its position too. Middle-class Americans who had been prepared to go to the barricades in the event of a Bryan victory in 1896 became conscience-stricken when they compared their own comfortable circumstances with those of the "huddled masses" of immigrants and native-born poor.

Giant industrial and commercial corporations undermined not so much the economic well-being as the ambitions and sense of importance of the middle class. The growth of large labor organizations worried such types. In general, character and moral values seemed less influential; organizations—cold, impersonal, heartless—were coming to control business, politics, and too many other aspects of life.

The middle classes could support reform measures without feeling that they were being very radical because they were resisting change and because the intellectual currents of the time harmonized with their ideas of social improvement and the welfare state. The new doctrines of the social scientists, the Social Gospel religious leaders, and the philosophers of pragmatism provided a salubrious climate for progressivism. Many of the thinkers who had formulated these doctrines in the 1880s and 1890s turned to the task of putting them into practice in the new century. Their number included the economist Richard T. Ely, the philosopher John Dewey, and the Baptist clergyman Walter Rauschenbusch, a civic reformer who wrote many books extolling the Social Gospel.

The Muckrakers

As the diffuse progressive army gradually formed its battalions, a new journalistic fad brought the movement into focus. For many years magazines had been publishing articles discussing current political, social, and economic problems. In the fall of 1902, *McClure's* began two particularly hard-hitting series of articles, one on Standard Oil by Ida Tarbell, the other on big-city political machines by Lincoln Steffens. When the editor, S. S. McClure, decided to include in the January 1903 issue an attack on labor gangsterism in the coal fields along with installments of the Tarbell and Steffens series, he called attention to the circumstance in a striking editorial.

Something was radically wrong with the "American character," McClure wrote. These articles showed that large numbers of American employers, workers, and politicians were fundamentally immoral. Lawyers were becoming tools of big business, judges were permitting evildoers to escape justice, the churches were materialistic, and educators seemed incapable of understanding what was happening.

McClure's editorial caused a sensation. The issue sold out quickly. Thousands of readers found their own vague apprehensions brought into focus. Some became active in progressive movements; still more lent passive support.

Other editors jumped to adopt the McClure formula. A small army of professional writers soon flooded the periodical press with denunciations of the insurance business, the drug business, college athletics, prostitution, sweatshop labor, political corruption, and dozens of other subjects. This type of article inspired Theodore Roosevelt, with his gift for vivid language, to compare the journalists to "the Man with the Muck-Rake" in John Bunyan's *Pilgrim's Progress*, whose attention was so fixed on the filth at his feet that he could not notice the "celestial crown" that was offered him in exchange. Roosevelt's characterization grossly misrepresented the literature of exposure, but the label *muckraking* was thereafter affixed to the type. Despite its literal connotations, **muckraker** became a term of honor.

The Progressive Mind

Unlike many earlier reformers, progressives believed that the source of society's evils lay in the structure of its institutions, not in the weaknesses or sinfulness of individuals. Therefore local, state, and national government must be made more responsive to the will of citizens who stood for the traditional virtues. In the South, many people who considered themselves progressives even argued that poll taxes and other measures designed to deny blacks the vote were reforms because they discouraged a class of people they considered unthinking and shiftless from voting.

When government had been thus reformed, then it must act; whatever its virtues, laissez-faire was obsolete. Businessmen, especially big businessmen, must be compelled to behave fairly, their acquisitive drives curbed in the interests of justice and equal opportunity for all. The weaker elements in society—women, children, the poor, the infirm—must be protected against unscrupulous power.

Despite its fervor and democratic rhetoric, progressivism was paternalistic, moderate, and often softheaded. Typical reformers of the period oversimplified complicated issues and treated their personal values as absolute standards of truth and morality. Thus progressives often acted at cross-purposes; at times some were even at war with themselves. This accounts for the diffuseness of the movement.

The progressives never challenged the fundamental principles of capitalism, nor did they attempt a basic reorganization of society. They would have little to do with the socialist brand of reform. Many progressives were anti-immigrant, and only a handful had anything to offer blacks, surely the most exploited group in American society.

A good example of the relatively limited radicalism of most progressives is offered by the experiences of progressive artists. Early in the century a number of painters, including Robert Henri, John Sloan, and George Luks, tried to develop a distinctively American style. They turned to city streets and the people of the slums for their models, and they depended more on inspiration and inner conviction than on careful craftsmanship to achieve their effects.

These artists of the **Ashcan School** were individualists, yet they supported political and social reform and were caught up in the progressive movement. Sloan was a socialist; Henri claimed to be an anarchist. Most saw themselves as rebels. But artistically the Ashcan painters were not very advanced. Their idols were long-dead European masters such as Hogarth, Goya, and Daumier. They were uninfluenced by the outburst of post-impressionist activity then taking place in Europe. To their dismay, when they included canvases by Matisse, Picasso, and other European artists in a show of their own works at the Sixty-Ninth Regiment Armory in New York City in 1913, the "advanced" Europeans got all the attention.

In 1900, Ashcan artist George Luks portrayed corporate monopolies and franchises as a monster preying on New York City.

"Radical" Progressives: The Wave of the Future

The hard times of the 1890s and the callous reactions of conservatives to the victims of that depression pushed many toward Marxian socialism. In 1900 the labor leader Eugene V. Debs ran for president on the Socialist ticket. He polled fewer than 100,000 votes. When he ran again in 1904 he got more than 400,000, and in later elections still more. Labor leaders hoping to organize unskilled workers in heavy industry were increasingly frustrated by the craft orientation of the American Federation of Labor, and some saw in socialism a way to win rank-and-file backing.

In 1905 Debs, William "Big Bill" Haywood of the Western Federation of Miners, Mary Harris "Mother" Jones (a former organizer for the United Mine Workers), Daniel De Leon of the Socialist Labor party, and a few others organized a new union: the **Industrial Workers of the World (IWW)**. The IWW was openly anticapitalist. The preamble to its constitution began: "The working class and the employing class have nothing in common."

But the IWW never attracted many ordinary workers. Haywood, its most prominent leader, was usually a general in search of an army. His forte was attracting attention to spontaneous strikes by unorganized workers, not the patient recruiting of workers and the pursuit of practical goals. In 1912 he was closely involved in a bitter and, at times, bloody strike of textile workers in Lawrence, Massachusetts, which was settled with some benefit to the strikers; he was also involved in a failed strike the following winter and spring by silk workers in Paterson, New Jersey.

Other "advanced" European ideas affected the thinking and behavior of some important progressive intellectuals. Sigmund Freud's psychoanalytical theories attracted numbers of Americans. Many picked up enough of the vocabulary of psychoanalysis to discourse impressively about the significance of slips of the tongue, sublimation, and infant sexuality.

Some saw in Freud's ideas reason to effect a "revolution of manners and morals" that would have shocked (or at least embarrassed) Freud, who was personally quite conventional. They advocated easy divorce, trial marriage, and doing away with the double standard in all matters relating to sex. They rejected Victorian reticence and what they incorrectly identified as "puritan" morality out of hand, and they called for programs of sex education, especially the dissemination of information about methods of birth control.

Most large cities boasted groups of these "bohemian" thinkers, by far the most famous being the one centered in New York City's Greenwich Village. The dancer Isadora Duncan, the photographer Alfred Stieglitz, the novelist Floyd Dell, several of the Ashcan artists, and the playwright Eugene O'Neill rubbed shoulders with Big Bill Haywood of the IWW, the anarchist Emma Goldman, the psychoanalyst A. A. Brill, the militant feminist advocate of birth control Margaret Sanger, Max Eastman, and John Reed, a young Harvard graduate who was soon to become famous for his eyewitness account of the Russian Revolution in *Ten Days That Shook the World.*

Goldman, Haywood, Sanger, and a few others in this group were genuine radicals who sought basic changes in bourgeois society, but most of the Greenwich Village intellectuals were as much concerned with aesthetic as social issues. Nearly all of them came from middle-class backgrounds. They found the far-different world of the Italian and Jewish immigrants of the Village and its surrounding neighborhoods charming. But they did not become involved in the immigrants' lives the way the settlement house workers did. Their influence on their own times, therefore, was limited. They are historically important, however, because many of them were genuinely creative people and because many of the ideas and practices they advocated were adopted by later generations.

The creative writers of the era, applying the spirit of progressivism to the realism they had inherited from Howells and the naturalists, tended to adopt an optimistic tone. The poet Ezra Pound, for example, at this time talked grandly of an American renaissance and fashioned a new kind of poetry called imagism, which, while not appearing to be realistic, rejected all abstract generalizations and concentrated on concrete word pictures to convey meaning. "Little" magazines and experimental theatrical companies sprang to life by the dozen, each convinced that it would revolutionize its art. The poet Carl Sandburg, the best-known representative of the Chicago school, denounced the local plutocrats but sang the praises of the city they had made: "Hog Butcher for the World," "City of the Big Shoulders."

Most writers eagerly adopted Freudian psychology without understanding it. Freud's teachings seemed only to mean that they should cast off the restrictions of Victorian prudery; they ignored his essentially dark view of human nature. Theirs was an "innocent rebellion," exuberant and rather muddleheaded.

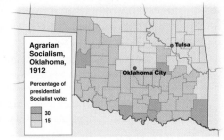

Rural Socialism Socialist strength extended far beyond the cities. Socialists in rural areas called for tenants to be allowed to work on state-owned plots of land. In 1912, Socialist candidates received nearly half the vote in southern Oklahoma.

Agrarian
Socialism,
Oklahoma,
1912

Percentage of
presidential
Socialist vote:

30
15

EMMA GOLDMAN

In January 1886 a sixteen-year-old Jewish girl named Emma Goldman arrived in New York City from St. Petersburg, Russia, where her parents ran a grocery store. As soon as immigration officials had approved her entry into the United States, she hurried on to Rochester, New York, where her half-sister lived. Like most immigrants she expected the United States to be a kind of paradise on earth.

After moving in with her half-sister's family, Emma got a job in a factory sewing coats and earning $2.50 a week. She paid her sister $1.50 a week for room and board and spent sixty cents a week to get to her job. But when she asked her employer for more money he told her to "look for work elsewhere. " She found a job at another factory that paid $4 a week.

In 1887 she married Jacob Kirshner, another Russian immigrant, but they soon divorced. In 1889 she took up with a group of radicals, most of them either socialists or anarchists. By this time Goldman was herself an ardent anarchist, convinced by her experiences that *all* governments repressed individual freedom and should be abolished.

In New York Emma fell in love with another Russian-born radical, Alexander Berkman. They started a kind of commune. Emma worked at home sewing shirts. Alexander found a job making cigars. They never married.

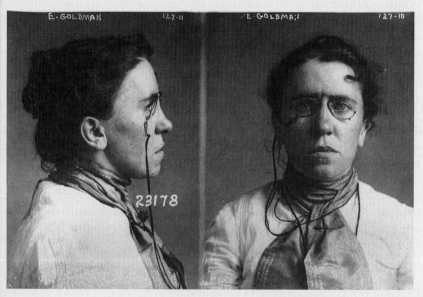

A "mug shot" of Emma Goldman, 1901. She was arrested so often that she took to carrying a book with her everywhere so that she would have something to read in jail if she were arrested.

The couple moved to New Haven, where Emma started a cooperative dressmaking shop. Then they moved to Springfield, Massachusetts, where, with Berkman's cousin, an artist, they opened a photography studio. When this business failed, they opened an ice cream parlor.

Nearly all immigrants of that period retained their faith in the promise of American life even after they discovered that the streets were not paved with gold. But Emma was so disappointed that she became a radical.

In 1892 when she and Berkman learned of the bloody battle between Pinkertons and strikers during the Homestead steel strike, they closed the ice cream parlor and plotted to assassinate Henry Clay Frick, the archvillain of the Homestead drama. Berkman went to Pittsburgh, where, posing as a representative of an agency that provided strikebreakers, he got into Frick's office. Pulling a pistol, Berkman aimed for Frick's head but the shot went wide and hit Frick in the shoulder. Berkman then stabbed Frick, but still the Homestead boss survived. Convicted of the attempt on Frick's life, Berkman was imprisoned for fourteen years.

The next year Goldman was herself arrested and sentenced to a year in jail for making an "incendiary" speech urging unemployed workers to distrust politicians. Upon her release, Goldman went to Vienna, where she trained as a nurse. When she returned to America, she worked as a midwife among the New York poor, an experience that made her an outspoken advocate of birth control. She also helped organize a theatrical group, managed a touring group of Russian actors, and lectured on theatrical topics. In 1901, Goldman was arrested on charges of inspiring Leon Czolgosz to assassinate President McKinley. Czolgosz had attended one of Goldman's lectures, but there was no direct connection between the two, and the charges against her were dropped.

In 1906 Goldman founded *Mother Earth*, an anarchist journal. When Alexander Berkman was released from prison later that year, she made him its editor. *Mother Earth* denounced governments, organized religion, and private property. By this time Goldman had become a celebrity. "She was considered a monster, an exponent of free love and bombs," recalled Margaret Anderson, editor of a literary magazine.

Now Goldman campaigned for freedom of speech and lectured in support of birth control. In 1915, after Margaret Sanger was arrested for disseminating information on birth control, Goldman did the same in public speeches. She was arrested and spent two weeks in jail.

Goldman regarded the Great War—and especially American entry in it—as a calamity beyond measure. In 1917 Goldman and Berkman were convicted of conspiring to persuade men not to register for the draft. They served two years in federal prison. In 1919 they were deported to Russia. Two years later, disillusioned with the Bolsheviks, Goldman left the Soviet Union.

"Red Emma" Goldman was not a typical American, but she was in many ways a typical American immigrant. She learned English and quickly became familiar with American ways. She worked hard and developed valuable skills. Gradually she moved up the economic ladder. And while she was critical of the United States, she was a typical immigrant also in insisting that she was an American patriot. "The kind of patriotism we represent," she said during her trial in 1917, "is the kind of patriotism which loves America with open eyes."

Questions for Discussion

- Why did most immigrants, on learning of the gap between the promise of America and its reality, not become radicals?
- Was Goldman a radical by birth or by acculturation?

Political Reform: Cities First

To most "ordinary" progressives, political corruption and inefficiency lay at the root of the evils plaguing American society, nowhere more obvious than in the nation's cities. Urban life's anonymity and complexity help explain why slavery did not flourish in cities, but also why the previously named vices did flourish. As the cities grew, their antiquated and boss-ridden administrations became more and more disgraceful.

City reformers could seldom destroy the machines without changing urban political institutions. Some cities obtained "home rule" charters that gave them greater freedom from state control in dealing with local matters. Many created research bureaus that investigated government problems in a scientific and nonpartisan manner. A number of middle-sized communities (Galveston, Texas, was the prototype) experimented with a system that integrated executive and legislative powers in the hands of a small elected commission, thereby concentrating responsibility and making it easier to coordinate complex activities. Out of this experiment came the city manager system, under which the commissioners appointed a professional manager to administer city affairs on a nonpartisan basis. Dayton, Ohio, which adopted the plan after a flood devastated the town in 1913, offers the best illustration of the city manager system in the Progressive Era.

Once the political system had been made responsive to the desires of the people, the progressives hoped to use it to improve society itself. Many cities experimented with "gas and water socialism," taking over public utility companies and operating them as departments of the municipal government. Under "Golden Rule" Jones, Toledo established a minimum wage for city employees, built playgrounds and golf courses, and moderated its harsh penal code. Mayor Seth Low improved New York's public transportation system and obtained passage of the tenement house law of 1901. Mayor Tom Johnson forced a fare cut to three cents on the Cleveland street railways.

Political Reform: The States

To carry out this kind of change required the support of state legislatures since all municipal government depends on the authority of a sovereign state. Such approval was often difficult to obtain—local bosses were usually entrenched in powerful state machines, and rural majorities insensitive to urban needs controlled most legislatures. Therefore the progressives had to strike at inefficiency and corruption at the state level too.

During the first decade of the new century, Robert M. La Follette, one of the most remarkable figures of the age, transformed Wisconsin. He had served three terms as a Republican congressman (1885–1891) and developed a reputation as an uncompromising foe of corruption before being elected governor in 1900. That the people would always do the right thing if properly informed and inspired was the fundamental article of his political faith. "Machine control is based upon misrepresentation and ignorance," La Follette said. "Democracy is based upon knowledge."

Despite the opposition of railroad and lumbering interests, Governor La Follette obtained a direct primary system for nominating candidates, a corrupt practices act, and laws limiting campaign expenditures and lobbying activities. In power he became something of a boss himself. He made ruthless use of patronage, demanded absolute loyalty of his subordinates, and often stretched, or at least oversimplified, the truth when presenting complex issues to the voters.

La Follette was a consummate showman who never rose entirely above rural prejudices. He was prone to see a nefarious "conspiracy" organized by "the interests" behind even the mildest opposition to his proposals. But he was devoted to the cause of honest government. Realizing that some state functions called for specialized technical knowledge, he used commissions and agencies to handle such matters as railroad regulation, tax assessment, conservation, and highway construction. Wisconsin established a legislative reference library to assist lawmakers in drafting bills. For work of this kind, La Follette called on the faculty of the University of Wisconsin, enticing top-notch economists and political scientists into the public service and drawing freely on the advice of such outstanding social scientists as Richard T. Ely, John R. Commons, and E. A. Ross.

The success of these policies, which became known as the Wisconsin Idea, led other states to adopt similar programs. Reform administrations swept into office in Iowa and Arkansas (1901); Oregon (1902); Minnesota, Kansas, and Mississippi (1904); New York and Georgia (1906); Nebraska (1909); and New Jersey and Colorado (1910). In some cases the reformers were Republicans, in others Democrats, but in all the example of Wisconsin was influential. By 1910, fifteen states had established legislative reference services, most of them staffed by personnel trained in Wisconsin. The direct primary system, in which candidates were selected by voters rather than party bosses, became almost universal.

Some states went beyond Wisconsin in striving to make their governments responsive to the popular will. In 1902 Oregon began to experiment with the initiative, a system by which a bill could be forced on the attention of the legislature by popular petition, and the referendum, a method for allowing the electorate to approve measures rejected by their representatives and to repeal measures that the legislature had passed. Eleven states, most of them in the West, legalized these devices by 1914.

State Social Legislation

The first state laws aimed at social problems long preceded the Progressive Era, but most were either so imprecise as to be unenforceable or, like the Georgia law "limiting" textile workers to eleven hours a day, so weak as to be ineffective. In 1874 Massachusetts restricted the working hours of women and children to ten per day, and by the 1890s many other states, mostly in the East and Midwest, had followed suit. Illinois passed an eight-hour law for women workers in 1893.

As part of this trend, some states established special rules for workers in hazardous industries. In the 1890s several states limited the hours of railroad workers on the grounds that fatigue sometimes caused railroad accidents. Utah restricted miners to eight hours in 1896. In 1901 New York finally enacted an effective tenement house law, greatly increasing the area of open space on building lots and requiring toilets for each apartment, better ventilation systems, and more adequate fireproofing.

Before 1900 the collective impact of such legislation was not impressive. Powerful manufacturers and landlords often succeeded in defeating the bills or rendering them innocuous. The federal system further complicated the task of obtaining effective legislation.

The Fourteenth Amendment to the Constitution, although enacted to protect the civil rights of blacks, imposed a revolutionary restriction on the states by forbidding them to "deprive any person of life, liberty, or property without due process of law." Since much state social legislation represented new uses of coercive power that conservative judges considered dangerous and unwise, the Fourteenth Amendment gave such judges

On March 25, 1911, as scores of young factory girls leaped to their deaths from the eighth, ninth, and tenth stories of the Triangle Shirtwaist Factory in New York City, eighteen-year-old Victor Gatto watched in horror. Thirty-three years later he painted this rendering of his nightmare, the bodies of the dead girls placed in order at the base of the building. Source: Victor Joseph Gatto (1893–1965), *Triangle Fire: March 25, 1911*. c. 1944 (depicting 1911), oil on canvas, 19 × 28", Gift of Mrs. Henry L. Moses, 54.75. The Museum of the City of New York.

an excuse to overturn the laws that deprived employers of the "liberty" to choose how long their employees should work or the conditions of the workplace.

As stricter and more far-reaching laws were enacted, many judges, fearing a trend toward socialism and regimentation, adopted an increasingly narrow interpretation of state authority to regulate business. In 1905 the U.S. Supreme Court declared in the case of *Lochner v. New York* that a New York ten-hour act for bakers deprived the bakers of the liberty of working as long as they wished and thus violated the Fourteenth Amendment. Justice Oliver Wendell Holmes, Jr., wrote a famous dissenting opinion in this case. If the people of New York believed that the public health was endangered by bakers working long hours, he reasoned, it was not the Court's job to overrule them.

Nevertheless, the progressives continued to battle for legislation to use state power against business. Women played a particularly important part in these struggles. Sparked by the National Child Labor Committee, organized in 1904, reformers over the next ten years obtained laws in nearly every state banning the employment of young children and limiting the hours of older ones. Many of these laws were poorly enforced, yet when Congress passed a federal child labor law in 1916, the Supreme Court, in *Hammer v. Dagenhart* (1918), declared it unconstitutional.[1]

●ﬂView the Image

Little Spinner in Globe Cotton Mill at **myhistorylab.com**

---

[1]A second child labor law, passed in 1919, was also thrown out by the Court, and a child labor amendment, submitted in 1924, failed to achieve ratification by the necessary three-quarters of the states.

By 1917 nearly all the states had placed limitations on the hours of women indus-trial workers, and about ten had set minimum wage standards for women. But once again federal action that would have extended such regulation to the entire country did not materialize. A minimum wage law for women in the District of Columbia was overturned by the Court in *Adkins v. Children's Hospital* (1923).

The passage of so much state social legislation sent conservatives scurrying to the Supreme Court for redress. Such persons believed that no government had the power to deprive either workers or employers of the right to negotiate any kind of labor contract they wished. The decision of the Supreme Court in *Lochner v. New York* seemed to indi-cate that the justices would adopt this point of view. When an Oregon law limiting women laundry workers to ten hours a day was challenged in *Muller v. Oregon* (1908), Florence Kelley and Josephine Goldmark of the Consumers' League persuaded Louis D. Brandeis to defend the statute before the Court.

The Consumers' League, whose slogan was "investigate, agitate, legislate," was probably the most effective of the many women's reform organizations of the period. With the aid of league researchers, Brandeis prepared a remarkable brief stuffed with economic and sociological evidence indicating that long hours dam-aged both the health of individual women and the health of society. This nonlegal evidence greatly impressed the justices, who upheld the constitutionality of the Oregon law.

Political Reform: The Woman Suffrage Movement

On the national level the Progressive Era saw the culmination of the struggle for **woman suffrage**. The shock occasioned by the failure of the Fourteenth and Fifteenth Amendments to give women the vote after the Civil War continued to embitter most-leaders of the movement. But it resulted in a split among feminists.

One group, the American Woman Suffrage Association (AWSA), focused on the vote question alone. The more radical National Woman Suffrage Association (NWSA), led by Elizabeth Cady Stanton and Susan B. Anthony, concerned itself with many issues of importance to women as well as suffrage. The NWSA put the immediate interests of women ahead of everything else. It was deeply involved in efforts to unionize women workers, yet it did not hesitate to urge women to be strikebreakers if they could get better jobs by doing so.

See the Map
Woman Suffrage Before the 19th Century at myhistorylab.com

Aside from their lack of unity, feminists were handicapped in the late nineteenth century by widely held Victorian ideals: Sex was a taboo topic, and women were to be "pure" guardians of home and family. Even under the best of circumstances, dislike of male-dominated society is hard enough to separate from dislike of men. Most feminists, for example, opposed contraception, insisting that birth control by any means other than continence would encourage what they called masculine lust.

These ideas and prejudices enticed feminists into a logical trap. If women were morally superior to men—a tempting conclusion—giving women the vote would improve the character of the electorate. Society would benefit because politics would become less corrupt, war a thing of the past. "City housekeeping has failed," said

Another argument in support of woman suffrage claimed that women were intrinsically *better* than men. Note that this woman in the turn-of-the-century poster, crowned by a halo, has her clothes arranged in the shape of a cross.

Jane Addams of Hull House in arguing for the reform of municipal government, "partly because women, the traditional housekeepers, have not been consulted."

By the early twentieth century there were signs of progress. In 1890 the two major women's groups combined as the **National American Woman Suffrage Association (NAWSA)**. Stanton and Anthony were the first two presidents of the association, but new leaders were emerging, the most notable being Carrie Chapman Catt, a woman who combined superb organizing abilities and political skills with commitment to broad social reform. The NAWSA made winning the right to vote its main objective and concentrated on a state-by-state approach. Wyoming gave women the vote in 1869, and Utah, Colorado, and Idaho had been won over to woman suffrage by 1896.

The burgeoning of the progressive movement helped as middle-class recruits of both sexes adopted the suffrage cause. The 1911 referendum in California was crucial. Fifteen years earlier, California voters had rejected the measure. But in 1911, despite determined opposition from saloonkeepers, the proposal barely passed. Within three years, most other Western states fell into line. For the first time, large numbers of working-class women began to agitate for the vote. In 1917, bosses at New York City's Tammany Hall, who had engineered the defeat of woman suffrage in that state two years earlier, concluded that passage was inevitable and threw their support to the measure, which passed. The suffragists then shifted the campaign back to the national level, the lead taken by a new organization, the Congressional Union, headed by Alice Paul and the wealthy reformer Alva Belmont. When President Wilson refused to support the idea of a constitutional amendment granting women the vote, militant women picketed the White House. A number of them were arrested and sentenced to sixty days in the workhouse. This roused a storm of criticism, and Wilson quickly pardoned the picketers. After some hesitation the NAWSA stopped concentrating on the state-by-state approach and began to campaign for a constitutional amendment. Pressure on Congress mounted steadily. The amendment finally won congressional approval in 1919. By 1920 the necessary three-quarters of the states had ratified the Nineteenth Amendment; the long fight was over.

Woman Suffrage, 1896–1914

- States that adopted full woman suffrage, 1869–1896
- States that adopted full woman suffrage, 1910–1914
- States that had not adopted full woman suffrage by 1914

Woman Suffrage Resolution May 21, 1919, House of Representatives

- Yes
- No
- Not voting
- Unsettled

- Boston
- New York City
- Philidelphia
- Baltimore
- Detroit

The Advance of Woman Suffrage In 1869 Wyoming, still a territory, voted to give women the vote. The next year, after Mormon leader Brigham Young endorsed woman suffrage, Utah followed. Then came Colorado (1893) and Idaho (1896), frontier states that sought to attract women settlers. In 1911, by a margin of 3,587 votes, California endorsed woman suffrage, and within three years the remainder of the western states had done so, too. World War I stimulated support for the Woman Suffrage (Nineteenth) Amendment. The May 21, 1919, vote in the House of Representatives shows that most of the opposing votes came from southern congressmen who believed that woman suffrage would be the first step toward securing the vote for blacks.

Theodore Roosevelt: Cowboy in the White House

On September 6, 1901, an anarchist named Leon Czolgosz shot President McKinley during a public reception at the Pan-American Exposition at Buffalo, New York. Eight days later McKinley died and Theodore Roosevelt became president of the United States. His ascension to the presidency marked the beginning of a new era in national politics.

Although only forty-two, by far the youngest president in the nation's history up to that time, Roosevelt brought solid qualifications to the office. Son of a well-to-do New York merchant, he had graduated from Harvard in 1880 and studied law briefly at Columbia, though he did not obtain a degree. In addition to political experience that included three terms in the New York assembly, six years on the U.S. Civil Service Commission, two years as police commissioner of New York City, another as assistant secretary of the navy, and a term as governor of New York, he had been a rancher in the Dakota Territory and a soldier in the Spanish-American War. Politically, he had always been a loyal Republican. He rejected the mugwump heresy in 1884, and during the tempestuous 1890s he vigorously denounced populism, Bryanism, and "labor agitators."

Nevertheless, Roosevelt's elevation to the presidency alarmed many conservatives, and not without reason. He did not fit their conception, based on a composite image of the chief executives from Hayes to McKinley, of a president. He seemed too undignified, too energetic, too outspoken, too unconventional. It was one thing to have operated a cattle ranch, another to have captured a gang of rustlers at gunpoint; one thing to have run a metropolitan police force, another to have roamed New York slums in the small hours to catch patrolmen fraternizing with thieves and prostitutes; and one thing to have commanded a regiment, another to have killed a Spaniard personally.

Roosevelt worshiped aggressiveness and was extremely sensitive to any threat to his honor as a gentleman. When another young man showed some slight interest in Roosevelt's fiancée, he sent for a set of French dueling pistols. His teachers found him an interesting student, for he was intelligent and imaginative, if annoyingly argumentative.

Few individuals have rationalized or sublimated their feelings of inferiority as effectively as Roosevelt and to such good purpose. And few have been more genuinely warmhearted, more full of spontaneity, more committed to the ideals of public service and national greatness. As a political leader he was energetic and hard-driving. Conservatives and timid souls, sensing his aggressiveness even

Theodore Roosevelt addressing a crowd in Evanston, Illinois, in the early 1900s.

when he held it in check, distrusted Roosevelt's judgment. In fact his judgment was nearly always sound; responsibility usually tempered his aggressiveness.

When Roosevelt was first mentioned as a running mate for McKinley in 1900, he wrote, "The Vice Presidency is a most honorable office, but for a young man there is not much to do." As president it would have been unthinkable for him to preside over a caretaker administration devoted to maintaining the status quo. However, the reigning Republican politicos, basking in the sunshine of the prosperity that had contributed so much to their victory in 1900, distrusted anything suggestive of change.

Had Roosevelt been the impetuous hothead that conservatives feared, he would have plunged ahead without regard for their feelings and influence. Instead he moved slowly and often got what he wanted by using his executive power rather than by persuading Congress to pass new laws. His domestic program included some measure of control of big corporations, more power for the Interstate Commerce Commission (ICC), and the conservation of natural resources. By consulting congressional leaders and following their advice not to bring up controversial matters like the tariff and currency reform, he obtained a modest budget of new laws.

The Newlands Act (1902) funneled the proceeds from land sales in the West into federal irrigation projects. The Department of Commerce and Labor, which was to include a Bureau of Corporations with authority to investigate industrial combines and issue reports, was established. The Elkins Railroad Act of 1903 strengthened the ICC's hand against the railroads by making the receiving as well as the granting of rebates illegal and by forbidding the roads to deviate in any way from their published rates.

Roosevelt and Big Business

Roosevelt soon became known as a trustbuster, and in the sense that he considered the monopoly problem the most pressing issue of the times, this was accurate to an extent. But he did not believe in breaking up big corporations indiscriminately. Regulation seemed the best way to deal with large corporations because, he said, industrial giantism "could not be eliminated unless we were willing to turn back the wheels of modern progress."

With Congress unwilling to pass a stiff regulatory law, Roosevelt resorted to the Sherman Act to get at the problem. Although the Supreme Court decision in the Sugar Trust case (*E.C. Knight* [1895], see p. 469) seemed to have emasculated that law, in 1902 he ordered the Justice Department to bring suit against the Northern Securities Company.

He chose his target wisely. The Northern Securities Company controlled the Great Northern, the Northern Pacific, the Chicago, the Burlington, and the Quincy railroads. It had been created in 1901 after a titanic battle on the New York Stock Exchange between the forces of J. P. Morgan and James J. Hill and those of E. H. Harriman, who was associated with the Rockefeller interests. In their efforts to obtain control of the Northern Pacific, the rivals had forced its stock up to $1,000 a share, ruining many speculators and threatening to cause a panic.

Neither side could win a clear-cut victory, so they decided to put the stock of all three railroads in a holding company owned by the two groups. Since Harriman already controlled the Union Pacific and the Southern Pacific, the plan resulted in a virtual monopoly of western railroads. The public had been alarmed, for the merger seemed to typify the rapaciousness of the tycoons.

The announcement of the suit caused consternation in the business world. Morgan rushed to the White House. "If we have done anything wrong," he said to the president, "send your man to my man and they can fix it up." Roosevelt was not fundamentally opposed to this sort of agreement, but it was too late to compromise in this instance. Attorney General Philander C. Knox pressed the case vigorously, and in 1904 the Supreme Court ordered the dissolution of the Northern Securities Company.

Roosevelt then ordered suits against the meat packers, the Standard Oil Trust, and the American Tobacco Company. His stock among progressives rose, yet he had not embarrassed the conservatives in Congress by demanding new antitrust legislation.

The president went out of his way to assure cooperative corporation magnates that he was not against size per se. At a White House conference in 1905, Roosevelt and Elbert H. Gary, chairman of the board of U.S. Steel, reached a "gentlemen's agreement" whereby Gary promised "to cooperate with the Government in every possible way." The Bureau of Corporations would conduct an investigation of U.S. Steel, Gary allowing it full access to company records. Roosevelt in turn promised that if the investigation revealed any corporate malpractices, he would allow Gary to set matters right voluntarily, thereby avoiding an antitrust suit. He reached a similar agreement with the International Harvester Company two years later.

There were limits to the effectiveness of such arrangements. Standard Oil agreed to a similar détente and then reneged, refusing to turn over vital records to the bureau. The Justice Department brought suit against the company under the Sherman Act, and eventually the company was broken up at the order of the Supreme Court. Roosevelt would have preferred a more binding kind of regulation, but when he asked for laws giving the government supervisory authority over big combinations, Congress refused to act.

Roosevelt and the Coal Strike

Roosevelt made remarkable use of his executive power during the anthracite coal strike of 1902. In June the United Mine Workers (UMW), led by John Mitchell, laid down their picks and demanded higher wages, an eight-hour day, and recognition of the union. Most of the anthracite mines were owned by railroads. Two years earlier the miners had won a 10 percent wage increase in a similar strike, chiefly because the owners feared that labor unrest might endanger the election of McKinley. Now the coal companies were dead set against further concessions; when the men walked out, they shut down the mines and prepared to starve the strikers into submission.

The strike dragged on through summer and early fall. The miners conducted themselves with great restraint, avoiding violence and offering to submit their claims to arbitration. As the price of anthracite soared with the approach of winter, sentiment in their behalf mounted.

Roosevelt shared the public's sympathy for the miners, and the threat of a coal shortage alarmed him. Early in October he summoned both sides to a conference in Washington and urged them as patriotic Americans to sacrifice any "personal consideration" for the "general good." His action enraged the coal owners, for they believed he was trying to force them to recognize the union. They refused even to speak to the UMW representatives at the conference and demanded that Roosevelt end the strike by force and bring suit against the union under the Sherman Act. Mitchell, aware of the immense prestige that Roosevelt had conferred on the union by calling the conference, cooperated fully with the president.

Table 21.1   Major Supreme Court Rulings during the Progressive Era

Northern Securities Case	1904	Upheld antitrust ruling against railroad conglomerate
Lochner v. New York	1905	Overturned (progressive) New York law restricting the hours bakers could work; invoked the Fourteenth Amendment to protect bakers' "right" to work as long as they wished
Muller v. Oregon	1908	Affirmed the right of Oregon to limit the hours worked by women in laundries

The attitudes of management and of the union further strengthened public support for the miners. Even former president Grover Cleveland, who had used federal troops to break the Pullman strike, said that he was "disturbed and vexed by the tone and substance of the operators' deliverances." Encouraged by this state of affairs, Roosevelt took a bold step: He announced that unless a settlement was reached promptly, he would order federal troops into the anthracite regions, not to break the strike but to seize and operate the mines.

The threat of government intervention brought the owners to terms. A Cabinet member, Elihu Root, worked out the details with J. P. Morgan, whose firm had major interests in the Reading and other railroads. The miners would return to the pits and all issues between them and the coal companies would be submitted for settlement to a commission appointed by Roosevelt. Both sides accepted the arrangement, and the men went back to work. In March 1903 the commission granted the miners a 10 percent wage increase and a nine-hour workday.

To the public the incident seemed a perfect illustration of the progressive spirit—in Roosevelt's words, everyone had received a **Square Deal**. In fact the results were by no means so clear-cut. The miners gained relatively little and the companies lost still less. The president was the main winner. The public acclaimed him as a fearless, imaginative, public-spirited leader. Without calling on Congress for support, he had expanded his own authority and hence that of the federal government. His action marked a major forward step in the evolution of the modern presidency.

TR's Triumphs

By reviving the Sherman Act, settling the coal strike, and pushing moderate reforms through Congress, Roosevelt ensured that he would be reelected president in 1904. Despite his resentment at Roosevelt's attack on the Northern Securities Company, J. P. Morgan contributed $150,000 to the Republican campaign. Other tycoons gave with equal generosity. Roosevelt swept the country, carrying even the normally Democratic border states of Maryland and Missouri.

Encouraged by the landslide and the increasing militancy of progressives, Roosevelt pressed for more reform legislation. His most imaginative proposal was a plan to make the District of Columbia a model progressive community. He suggested child labor and factory inspection laws and a slum clearance program, but Congress refused to act. Likewise, his request for a minimum wage for railroad workers was rejected.

Early in the twentieth century, when malnutrition was common, companies such as this one advertised that its pills could make people fatter. The Pure Food and Drug Act of 1906 fined manufacturers who made false claims for their products. A century later, in 2010, the *Seattle Post Intelligencer*, under the headline "Too Fat to Fight," reported that over a fourth of eighteen to twenty-four-year-old potential army recruits were rejected as unfit.

With progressive state governors demanding federal action and farmers and manufacturers, especially in the Midwest, clamoring for relief against discriminatory rates, Roosevelt was ready by 1905 to make railroad legislation his major objective. The ICC should be empowered to fix rates, not merely to challenge unreasonable ones. It should have the right to inspect the private records of the railroads since fair rates could not be determined unless the true financial condition of the roads were known.

Because these proposals struck at rights that businessmen considered sacrosanct, many congressmen balked. But Roosevelt applied presidential pressure, and in June 1906 the Hepburn bill became law. It gave the commission the power to inspect the books of railroad companies, to set maximum rates (once a complaint had been filed by a shipper), and to control sleeping car companies, owners of oil pipelines, and other firms engaged in transportation. Railroads could no longer issue passes freely—an important check on their political influence. In all, the **Hepburn Act** made the ICC a more powerful and more active body. Congress also passed meat inspection and pure food and drug legislation. In 1906 Upton Sinclair published *The Jungle*, a devastating exposé of the filthy conditions in the Chicago slaughterhouses. Sinclair was more interested in writing a socialist tract than he was in meat inspection, but his book, a best seller, raised a storm against the packers. After Roosevelt read *The Jungle* he sent two officials to Chicago to investigate. Their report was so shocking, he said, that its publication would "be well-nigh ruinous to our export trade in meat." He threatened to release the report unless Congress acted. After a fight, the meat inspection bill passed. The Pure Food and Drug Act, forbidding the manufacture and sale of adulterated and fraudulently labeled products, rode through Congress on the coattails of this measure.

••• Read the Document

"Inside the Packinghouse"
from Upton Sinclair's *The Jungle* at **myhistorylab.com**

To advanced liberals Roosevelt's achievements seemed limited when placed beside his professed objectives and his smug evaluations of what he had done. How could he be a reformer and a defender of established interests at the same time? Roosevelt found no difficulty in holding such a position. As one historian has said, "He stood close to the center and bared his teeth at the conservatives of the right and the liberals of the extreme left."

Roosevelt Tilts Left

As the progressive movement advanced, Roosevelt advanced with it. He never accepted all the ideas of what he called its "lunatic fringe," but he took steadily more liberal positions. He always insisted that he was not hostile to business interests, but when those interests sought to exploit the national domain, they had no more implacable foe. **Conservation** of natural resources was dear to his heart and probably his most significant achievement as president. He placed some 150 million acres of forest lands in federal reserves, and he strictly enforced the laws governing grazing, mining, and lumbering.

As Roosevelt became more liberal, conservative Republicans began to balk at following his lead. The sudden panic that struck the financial world in October 1907 speeded the trend. Government policies had no direct bearing on the panic, which began with a run on several important New York trust companies and spread to the Stock Exchange when speculators found themselves unable to borrow money to meet their obligations. In the emergency Roosevelt authorized the deposit of large amounts of government cash in New York banks. He informally agreed to the acquisition of the Tennessee Coal and Iron Company by U.S. Steel when the bankers told him that the purchase was necessary to end the panic. In spite of his efforts, conservatives insisted on referring to the financial collapse as "Roosevelt's panic," and they blamed the president for the depression that followed on its heels.

Roosevelt, however, turned left rather than right. In 1908 he came out in favor of federal income and inheritance taxes, stricter regulation of interstate corporations, and reforms designed to help industrial workers. He denounced "the speculative folly and the flagrant dishonesty" of "malefactors of great wealth," further alienating conservative, or Old Guard, Republicans. When the president began criticizing the courts, the last bastion of conservatism, he lost all chance of obtaining further reform legislation. As he said himself, during his last months in office "stagnation continued to rage with uninterrupted violence."

William Howard Taft: The Listless Progressive, or More Is Less

But Roosevelt remained popular and politically powerful; before his term ended, he chose William Howard Taft, his secretary of war, to succeed him and easily obtained Taft's nomination. William Jennings Bryan was again the Democratic candidate. Campaigning on Roosevelt's record, Taft carried the country by well over a million votes, defeating Bryan 321 to 162 in the Electoral College.

Taft was intelligent, experienced, and public spirited; he seemed ideally suited to carry out Roosevelt's policies. Born in Cincinnati in 1857, educated at Yale, he had served as an Ohio judge, as solicitor general of the United States under Benjamin Harrison, and

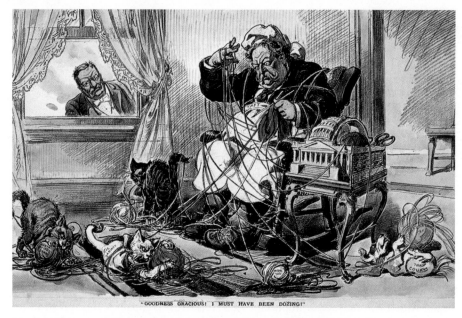

"GOODNESS GRACIOUS! I MUST HAVE BEEN DOZING!"

A hapless Taft is entangled in governmental yarn, while a disapproving Roosevelt looks on. "Goodness gracious! I must have been dozing," reads the caption, a reference to Taft's penchant for naps.

then as a federal circuit court judge before accepting McKinley's assignment to head the Philippine Commission in 1900. His success as civil governor of the Philippines led Roosevelt to make him secretary of war in 1904.

Taft supported the Square Deal loyally. This, together with his mentor's ardent endorsement, won him the backing of most progressive Republicans. Yet the Old Guard liked him too; although outgoing, he had none of the Roosevelt impetuosity and aggressiveness. His genial personality and his obvious desire to avoid conflict appealed to moderates.

However, Taft lacked the physical and mental stamina required of a modern chief executive. Although not lazy, he weighed over 300 pounds and needed to rest this vast bulk more than the job allowed. Campaigning bored him; speech making seemed a useless chore. The judicial life was his real love; intense partisanship dismayed and confused him. He was too reasonable to control a coalition and not ambitious enough to impose his will on others. He supported many progressive measures, but he never absorbed the progressive spirit.

Taft honestly wanted to carry out most of Roosevelt's policies. He enforced the Sherman Act vigorously and continued to expand the national forest reserves. He signed the Mann-Elkins Act of 1910, which empowered the ICC to suspend rate increases without waiting for a shipper to complain and established the Commerce Court to speed the settlement of railroad rate cases. An eight-hour day for all persons engaged in work on government contracts, mine safety legislation, and several other reform measures received his approval. He even summoned Congress into special session specifically to reduce tariff duties—something that Roosevelt had not dared to attempt.

But Taft had been disturbed by Roosevelt's sweeping use of executive power. "We have got to work out our problems on the basis of law," he insisted. Whereas Roosevelt had excelled at maneuvering around congressional opposition and at finding ways to accomplish his objectives without waiting for Congress to act, Taft adamantly refused to use such tactics. His restraint was in many ways admirable, but it reduced his effectiveness.

In 1910 Taft got into difficulty with the conservationists. Although he believed in husbanding natural resources carefully, he did not like the way Roosevelt had circumvented Congress in adding to the forest reserves. He demanded, and eventually obtained, specific legislation to accomplish this purpose. The issue that aroused the conservationists concerned the integrity of his secretary of the interior, Richard A. Ballinger. A less than ardent conservationist, Ballinger returned to the public domain certain waterpower sites that the Roosevelt administration had withdrawn on the legally questionable ground that they were to become ranger stations. Ballinger's action alarmed Chief Forester Gifford Pinchot, the darling of the conservationists. When Pinchot learned that Ballinger intended to validate the shaky claim of mining interests to a large tract of coal-rich land in Alaska, he launched an intemperate attack on the secretary.

In the Ballinger-Pinchot controversy Taft felt obliged to support his own man. The coal lands dispute was complex, and Pinchot's charges were exaggerated. It was certainly unfair to call Ballinger "the most effective opponent the conservation policies have yet had." When Pinchot, whose own motives were partly political, persisted in criticizing Ballinger, Taft dismissed him. He had no choice under the circumstances, but a more adept politician might have found some way of avoiding a showdown.

Breakup of the Republican Party

One ominous aspect of the Ballinger-Pinchot affair was that Pinchot was a close friend of Theodore Roosevelt. After Taft's inauguration, Roosevelt had gone off to hunt big game in Africa, bearing in his baggage an autographed photograph of his protégé and a touching letter of appreciation, in which the new president said, "I can never forget that the power I now exercise was a voluntary transfer from you to me." As soon as he emerged from the wilderness in March 1910, bearing more than 3,000 trophies, including nine lions, five elephants, and thirteen rhinos, he was caught up in the squabble between the progressive members of his party and its titular head. Pinchot met him in Italy, laden with injured innocence and a packet of angry letters from various progressives. TR's intimate friend Senator Henry Cabot Lodge, essentially a conservative, barraged him with messages, the gist of which was that Taft was lazy and inept and that Roosevelt should prepare to become the "Moses" who would guide the party "out of the wilderness of doubt and discontent" into which Taft had led it.

Roosevelt hoped to steer a middle course, but Pinchot's complaints impressed him. Taft had decided to strike out on his own, he concluded. Taft sensed the former president's coolness and was offended. He was egged on by his ambitious wife, who wanted him to stand clear of Roosevelt's shadow and establish his own reputation.

Perhaps the resulting rupture was inevitable. The Republican party was dividing into two factions, the progressives and the Old Guard. Forced to choose between them, Taft threw in his lot with the Old Guard. Roosevelt backed the progressives. Speaking at Osawatomie, Kansas, in August 1910 he came out for a comprehensive program of social legislation, which he called the **New Nationalism**. Besides attacking "special privilege" and the "unfair money-getting"

••⬤─⎡Read the **Document**

Roosevelt, *The New Nationalism* at myhistorylab.com

practices of "lawbreakers of great wealth," he called for a broad expansion of federal power. "The betterment we seek must be accomplished," he said, "mainly through the National Government."

The final break came in October 1911 when Taft ordered an antitrust suit against U.S. Steel. He was prepared to enforce the Sherman Act "or die in the attempt." But this initiative angered Roosevelt because the lawsuit focused on U.S. Steel's absorption of the Tennessee Coal and Iron Company, which Roosevelt had unofficially authorized during the panic of 1907. The government's antitrust brief made Roosevelt appear to have been either a proponent of the monopoly or, far worse, a fool who had been duped by the steel corporation. Early in 1912 he declared himself a candidate for the Republican presidential nomination.

Roosevelt plunged into the preconvention campaign with typical energy. He was almost uniformly victorious in states that held presidential primaries, carrying even Ohio, Taft's home state. However, the president controlled the party machinery and entered the national convention with a small majority of the delegates. Since some Taft delegates had been chosen under questionable circumstances, the Roosevelt forces challenged the right of 254 of them to their seats. The Taft-controlled credentials committee, paying little attention to the evidence, gave all but a few of the disputed seats to the president, who then won the nomination on the first ballot.

Roosevelt was understandably outraged by the ruthless manner in which the Taft "steamroller" had overridden his forces. When his leading supporters urged him to organize a third party, and when two of them, George W. Perkins, formerly a partner of the banker J. P. Morgan, and the publisher Frank Munsey, offered to finance the campaign, Roosevelt agreed to make the race.

In August, amid scenes of hysterical enthusiasm, the first convention of the Progressive party met at Chicago and nominated him for president. Announcing that he felt "as strong as a bull moose," Roosevelt delivered a stirring "confession of faith," calling for strict regulation of corporations, a tariff commission, national presidential primaries, minimum wage and workers' compensation laws, the elimination of child labor, and many other reforms.

Watch the Video
Bull Moose Campaign Speech
at **myhistorylab.com**

The Election of 1912

The Democrats made the most of the opportunity offered by the Republican schism. Had they nominated a conservative or allowed Bryan a fourth chance, they would probably have ensured Roosevelt's election. Instead, they nominated Woodrow Wilson, who had achieved a remarkable liberal record as governor of New Jersey.

Although as a political scientist Wilson had criticized the status quo and taken a pragmatic approach to the idea of government regulation of the economy, he had objected strongly to Bryan's brand of politics. In 1896 he voted for the Gold Democratic party candidate instead of Bryan. But by 1912, influenced partly by ambition and partly by the spirit of the times, he had been converted to progressivism. He called his brand of reform the **New Freedom**.

The federal government could best advance the cause of social justice, Wilson reasoned, by eradicating the special privileges that enabled the "interests" to flourish. Where

1912: Divided Republicans, Democratic Victory In 1912, when Theodore Roosevelt chose to run as a Progressive, he took away millions of votes from the Republican Taft. This ensured Democrat Woodrow Wilson's landslide election.

1912

Democratic (Wilson)
Progressive (T. Roosevelt)
Republican (Taft)

Roosevelt had lost faith in competition as a way of protecting the public against monopolies, Wilson insisted that competition could be restored. The government must break up the great trusts, establish fair rules for doing business, and subject violators to stiff punishments. Thereafter, the free enterprise system would protect the public from exploitation without destroying individual initiative and opportunity.

Roosevelt's reasoning was perhaps theoretically more sound. He called for a New Nationalism. Laissez-faire made less sense than it had in earlier times. The complexities of the modern world seemed to call for a positive approach, a plan, the close application of human intelligence to social and economic problems.

But being more in line with American experience than the New Nationalism, Wilson's New Freedom had much to recommend it. The danger that selfish individuals would use the power of the state for their own ends had certainly not disappeared, despite the efforts of progressives to make government more responsive to popular opinion. Any considerable expansion of national power, as Roosevelt proposed, would increase the danger and probably create new difficulties. Managing so complicated an enterprise as an industrialized nation was sure to be a formidable task for the federal government. Furthermore, individual freedom of opportunity merited the toleration of a certain amount of inefficiency.

To choose between the New Nationalism and the New Freedom, between the dynamic Roosevelt and the idealistic Wilson, was indeed difficult. Taft got the hard-core Republican vote but lost the progressive wing of the GOP to Roosevelt. Wilson had the solid support of both conservative and liberal Democrats. As a result, Wilson won an easy victory in the Electoral College, receiving 435 votes to Roosevelt's 88 and Taft's 8. The popular vote was Wilson, 6,286,000; Roosevelt, 4,126,000; and Taft, 3,484,000.

If partisan politics had determined the winner, the election was nonetheless an overwhelming endorsement of progressivism. The temper of the times was shown by the 897,000 votes for Eugene Debs, who was again the Socialist candidate. Altogether, professed liberals amassed over 11 million of the 15 million ballots cast. Wilson was a minority president, but he took office with a clear mandate to press forward with further reforms.

Wilson: The New Freedom

No one ever rose more suddenly or spectacularly in American politics than Woodrow Wilson. In the spring of 1910 he was president of Princeton University; he had never held or even run for public office. In the fall of 1912 he was president-elect of the United States. Yet if his rise was meteoric, in a very real sense he had devoted his life to preparing for it. As a student he became interested in political theory, dreaming of representing his state in the Senate. He studied law solely because he thought it the best avenue to public office, and when he discovered that he did not like legal work, he took a doctorate at Johns Hopkins in political science.

For years Wilson's political ambitions appeared doomed to frustration. He taught at Bryn Mawr, then at Wesleyan, and finally at his alma mater, Princeton. He wrote several influential books, among them *Congressional Government* and *The State*, and achieved an outstanding reputation as a teacher and lecturer. In 1902 he was chosen president of Princeton and soon won a place among the nation's leading educators. In time Wilson's educational ideas and his overbearing manner of applying them got him in trouble with some of Princeton's alumni and trustees. Although his university career was wrecked, the controversies, in which he appeared to be championing democracy and progress in the face of reactionary opponents, brought him at last to the attention of the politicians. Then, in a great rush, came power and fame.

Wilson was an immediate success as president. Since Roosevelt's last year in office, Congress had been almost continually at war with the executive branch and with itself. Legislative achievements had been few. Now a small avalanche of important measures received the approval of the lawmakers. In October 1913 the **Underwood Tariff** brought the first significant reduction of duties since before the Civil War. To compensate for the expected loss of revenue, the act provided for a graduated tax on personal incomes.

Two months later the **Federal Reserve Act** gave the country a central banking system for the first time since Jackson destroyed the Bank of the United States. The measure divided the nation into twelve banking districts, each under the supervision of a Federal Reserve bank, a sort of bank for bankers. All national banks in each district and any state banks that wished to participate had to invest 6 percent of their capital and surplus in the reserve bank, which was empowered to exchange paper money, called Federal Reserve notes, for the commercial and agricultural paper that member banks took in as security from borrowers. The volume of currency was no longer at the mercy of the supply of gold or any other particular commodity.

The nerve center of the system was the Federal Reserve Board in Washington, which appointed a majority of the directors of the Federal Reserve banks and had some control over rediscount rates. The board provided a modicum of public control over the banks, but the effort to weaken the power of the great New York banks by decentralizing the system proved ineffective. Nevertheless, a true central banking system was created.

When inflation threatened, the reserve banks could raise the rediscount rate, discouraging borrowing and thus reducing the amount of money in circulation. In bad times it could lower the rate, making it easier to borrow and injecting new dollars into the economy. Much remained to be learned about the proper management of the money supply, but the nation finally had a flexible yet safe currency.

In 1914 Congress passed two important laws affecting corporations. One created the Federal Trade Commission (FTC) to replace Roosevelt's Bureau of Corporations. In addition to investigating corporations and publishing reports, this nonpartisan board could issue cease-and-desist orders against "unfair" trade practices brought to light through its research. The law did not define the term *unfair*, and the commission's rulings could be taken on appeal to the federal courts, but the FTC was nonetheless a powerful instrument for protecting the public against the trusts.

The second measure, the **Clayton Antitrust Act**, made certain specific business practices illegal, including price discrimination that tended to foster monopolies; "tying" agreements, which forbade retailers from handling the products of a firm's competitors; and the creation of interlocking directorates as a means of controlling competing companies. The act exempted labor unions and agricultural organizations from the antitrust laws and curtailed the use of injunctions in labor disputes. The officers of corporations could be held individually responsible if their companies violated the antitrust laws.

The Democrats controlled both houses of Congress for the first time since 1890 and were eager to make a good record, but Wilson's imaginative and aggressive use of presidential power was decisive. He called the legislators into special session in April 1913 and appeared before them to lay out his program; he was the first president to address Congress in person since John Adams. Then he followed the course of administration bills closely. Administration representatives haunted the cloakrooms and lobbies of both houses. Cooperative congressmen began to receive notes of praise and encouragement, whereas recalcitrant ones received stern demands for support, often pecked out on the president's own portable typewriter.

Wilson explained his success by saying, only half humorously, that running the government was child's play for anyone who had managed the faculty of a university. Responsible party government was his objective; he expected individual Democrats to support the decisions of the party majority, and his idealism never prevented him from awarding the spoils of office to city bosses and conservative congressmen, as long as they supported his program. Nor did his career as a political theorist make him rigid and doctrinaire. In practice the differences between his New Freedom and Roosevelt's New Nationalism tended to disappear. The FTC and the Federal Reserve system represented steps toward the kind of regulated economy that Roosevelt advocated.

Table 21.2 Progressive Legislation (Federal)

Newlands Act	1902	Funneled revenues from sale of public lands to irrigation projects
Elkins Act	1903	Strengthened the ICC by making it illegal for railroads to deviate from published rates, such as by granting rebates
Hepburn Act	1906	Gave ICC the power to fix rates of railroads and other corporations involved in interstate commerce (such as corporations operating oil pipelines)
Pure Food and Durg Act	1906	Prohibited the fraudulent advertising, manufacturing, and selling of impure foods and drugs
Mann-Elkins Act	1910	Empowered ICC to suspend rate increases for railroads or telephone companies
Underwood Tariff	1913	Lowered tariff rates; introduced graduated tax on personal incomes
Federal Reserve Act	1913	Established federal supervision of banking system
Sixteenth Amendment	1913	Authorized federal income tax
Clayton Antitrust Act	1914	Exempted labor unions from antitrust laws and curtailed injunctions against labor leaders
Nineteenth Amendment	1920	Established woman suffrage

There were limits to Wilson's progressivism. He objected as strenuously to laws granting special favors to farmers and workers as to those benefiting the tycoons. When a bill was introduced in 1914 making low-interest loans available to farmers, he refused to support it. He considered the provision exempting unions from the antitrust laws equally unsound. Nor would he push for a federal law prohibiting child labor; such a measure would be unconstitutional, he believed. He also refused to back the constitutional amendment giving the vote to women.

By the end of 1914 Wilson's record, on balance, was positive but distinctly limited. The president believed that the major progressive goals had been achieved; he had no plans for further reform. Many other progressives thought that a great deal more remained to be done.

The Progressives and Minority Rights

On one important issue, race relations, Wilson was distinctly reactionary. With a mere handful of exceptions, the progressives exhibited strong prejudices against nonwhite people and against certain categories of whites as well. Many were as unsympathetic to immigrants from Asia and eastern and southern Europe as any of the "conservative" opponents of immigration in the 1880s and 1890s.

American Indians were also affected by the progressives' racial attitudes. Where the sponsors of the Dawes Act (1887) had assumed that Indians were inherently capable of adopting the ways of "civilized" people, in the progressive period the tendency was to write Indians off as fundamentally inferior and to assume that they would make second-class citizens at best. Francis Leupp, Theodore Roosevelt's commissioner of Indian affairs, put it this way in a 1905 report: "If nature has set a different physical stamp upon different races of men it is fair to assume that the variation . . . is manifested in mental and moral traits as well. . . . Nothing is gained by trying to undo nature's work." A leading muckraker, Ray Stannard Baker, who was far more sympathetic to blacks than most progressives, dismissed Indians as pathetic beings, "eating, sleeping, idling, with no more thought of the future than a white man's child."

In 1902 Congress passed the Dead Indian Land Act, which made it easier for Indians to sell allotments that they had inherited, and in 1906 another law further relaxed restrictions on land sales. Efforts to improve the education of Indian children continued, but most progressives assumed that only vocational training would help them. Theodore Roosevelt knew from his experiences as a rancher in the Dakota Territory that Indians could be as energetic and capable as whites, but he considered these "exceptional." As for the rest, it would be many generations before they could be expected to "move forward" enough to become "ordinary citizens," Roosevelt believed.

To say that African Americans did not fare well at the hands of progressives would be a gross understatement. White southerners, furious at Populist efforts to unite white and black farmers, imposed increasingly repressive measures after 1896. Segregation became more rigid, white opposition to black voting more monolithic. In 1900 the body of a Mississippi black was dug up by order of the state legislature and reburied in a segregated cemetery; in Virginia in 1902 the daughter of Robert E. Lee was arrested for riding in the black section of a railroad car.

On May 15, 1916, after deliberating for one hour, an all-white jury in Waco, Texas, found seventeen-year-old Jesse Washington guilty of bludgeoning a white woman to death. A mob rushed him out of the courtroom, chained him to a tree, and burned him to death. The story was chronicled by Patricia Bernstein in *The First Waco Horror* (2005).

Many progressive women, still smarting from the insult to their sex entailed in the Fourteenth and Fifteenth Amendments and eager to attract southern support for their campaign for the vote, adopted racist arguments. They contrasted the supposed corruption and incompetence of black voters with their own "purity" and intelligence. Southern progressives of both sexes argued that disfranchising blacks would reduce corruption by removing from unscrupulous white politicians the temptation to purchase black votes!

The typical southern attitude toward the education of blacks was summed up in a folk proverb: "When you educate a Negro, you spoil a good field hand." In 1910 only about 8,000 black children in the entire South were attending high schools. Despite the almost total suppression of black rights, lynchings persisted; between 1900 and 1914 more than 1,100 blacks were murdered by mobs, most (but not all) in the southern states. In the rare cases in which local prosecutors brought the lynchers to trial, juries almost without exception brought in verdicts of not guilty.

●●━[Read the **Document**

"Events in Paris, Texas," from Ida B. Wells, *A Red Record* at **myhistorylab.com**

Booker T. Washington was shaken by this trend, but he could find no way to combat it. The times were passing him by. He appealed to his white southern "friends" for help but got nowhere. Increasingly he talked about the virtues of rural life, the evils of big cities, and the uselessness of higher education for black people. By the turn of the century a number of young, well-educated blacks, most of them Northerners, were breaking away from his accommodationist leadership.

Black Militancy

William E. B. Du Bois was the most prominent of the militants. Du Bois was born in Great Barrington, Massachusetts, in 1868. His father, a restless wanderer of Negro and French Huguenot stock, abandoned the family, and young William grew up on the edge of poverty. Neither accepted nor openly rejected by the overwhelmingly white community, he devoted himself to his studies, showing such brilliance that his future education was ensured by scholarships: to Fisk University, then to Harvard, and then to the University of Berlin. In 1895 Du Bois became the first American black to earn a PhD in history from Harvard; his dissertation, *The Suppression of the African Slave Trade* (1896), remains a standard reference.

Like Washington, Du Bois wanted blacks to lift themselves up by their own bootstraps. They must establish their own businesses, run their own newspapers and colleges, and write their own literature; they must preserve their identity rather than seek to amalgamate themselves into a society that offered them only crumbs and contempt. At first he cooperated with Washington, but in 1903, in the essay "Of Mr. Booker T. Washington and Others," he subjected Washington's "attitude of adjustment and submission" to polite but searching criticism. Washington had asked blacks to give up political power, civil rights, and the hope of higher education, not realizing that "voting is necessary to modern manhood, that . . . discrimination is barbarism, and that black boys need education as well as white boys." Washington "apologizes for injustice," Du Bois charged. "He belittles the emasculating effects of caste distinctions, and opposes the higher training and ambitions of our brightest minds." Du Bois deemed this totally wrong: "The way for a people to gain their reasonable rights is not by voluntarily throwing them away."

Du Bois was not an uncritical admirer of the ordinary American black. He believed that "immorality, crime, and laziness" were common vices. He blamed the weaknesses of blacks on the treatment afforded them by whites, but his approach to the solution of racial problems was frankly elitist. "The Negro race," he wrote, "is going to be saved by its exceptional men," what he called the "talented tenth" of the black population. Whatever his prejudices, Du Bois exposed both the weaknesses of Washington's strategy and the callousness of white American attitudes. Accommodation was not working. Washington was praised, even lionized by prominent southern whites, yet when Theodore Roosevelt invited him to a meal at the White House they exploded with indignation, and Roosevelt, although not personally prejudiced, meekly backtracked, never repeating his "mistake." He defended his record by saying, "I have stood as valiantly for the rights of the negro as any president since Lincoln." That, sad to relate, was true enough.

Watch the Video

The conflict between Booker T. Washington & W.E.B Du Bois at **myhistorylab.com**

Not mere impatience but despair led Du Bois and a few like-minded blacks to meet at Niagara Falls in July 1905 and to issue a stirring list of demands: the unrestricted right to vote, an end to every kind of segregation, equality of economic opportunity, higher education for the talented, equal justice in the courts, and an end to trade-union discrimination. This **Niagara movement** did not attract mass support, but it did stir the consciences of some whites, many of them the descendants of abolitionists, who were also becoming disenchanted by the failure of accommodation to provide blacks with real opportunity.

In 1909, the centennial of the birth of Abraham Lincoln, a group of these liberals, including the newspaperman Oswald Garrison Villard (grandson of William Lloyd Garrison), the social worker Jane Addams, the philosopher John Dewey, and the novelist William Dean Howells, founded the **National Association for the Advancement of Colored People (NAACP).** The organization was dedicated to the eradication of racial discrimination. Its leadership was predominantly white in the early years, but Du Bois became a national officer and the editor of its journal, *The Crisis.*

A turning point had been reached. After 1909 virtually every important leader, white and black alike, rejected the Washington approach. More and more, blacks turned to the study of their past in an effort to stimulate pride in their heritage. In 1915 Carter G. Woodson founded the Association for the Study of Negro Life and History; the following year he began editing the *Journal of Negro History,* which became the major publishing organ for scholarly studies on the subject.

This militancy produced few results in the Progressive Era. Theodore Roosevelt behaved no differently than earlier Republican presidents; he courted blacks when he thought it advantageous, and turned his back when he did not. When he ran for president on the Progressive ticket in 1912, he pursued a "lily-white" policy, hoping to break the Democrats' monopoly in the South. By trusting in "[white] men of justice and of vision," Roosevelt argued in the face of decades of experience to the contrary, "the colored men of the South will ultimately get justice."

The southern-born Wilson was actively hostile to blacks. During the 1912 campaign he appealed to them for support and promised to "assist in advancing the interest of their race" in every possible way. Once elected, he refused even to appoint a privately financed commission to study the race problem. Southerners dominated his administration and Congress; as a result, blacks were further degraded.

These actions stirred such a storm that Wilson backtracked a little, but he never abandoned his belief that segregation was in the best interests of both races. "Wilson . . . promised a 'new freedom,'" one newspaperman complained. "On the contrary we are given a stone instead of a loaf of bread." Even Booker T. Washington admitted that his people were more "discouraged and bitter" than at any time in his memory.

Du Bois, who had supported Wilson in 1912, attacked administration policy in *The Crisis.* In November 1914 the militant editor of the *Boston Guardian,* William Monroe Trotter, a classmate of Du Bois at Harvard and a far more caustic critic of the Washington approach, led a delegation to the White House to protest the segregation policy of the government. When Wilson accused him of blackmail, Trotter lost his temper, and an ugly confrontation resulted. The mood of black leaders had changed completely.

By this time the Great War had broken out in Europe. Soon every American would feel its effects, blacks perhaps more than any other group. In November 1915, a year almost to the day after Trotter's clash with Wilson, Booker T. Washington died. One era had ended; a new one was beginning.

Many of the young Americans who had participated in the various crusades of the "age of reform" would soon embark on another crusade—but one of a very different character.

Milestones

1890	National American Woman Suffrage Association is founded	1908	*Muller v. Oregon* upholds law limiting women's work hours
1900	Robert La Follette is elected governor of Wisconsin		William Howard Taft is elected president
	McKinley is reelected president	1909	NAACP is founded
1901	McKinley is assassinated; Theodore Roosevelt becomes president	1910	Ballinger-Pinchot Affair deepens Roosevelt–Taft rift
1902	Roosevelt helps settle anthracite coal strike	1911	Roosevelt gives New Nationalism speech
	Oregon adopts initiative system for proposing legislation	1912	Roosevelt runs for president on Progressive ticket
1904	Northern Securities case revives Sherman Antitrust Act		Woodrow Wilson is elected president
	National Child Labor Committee is established	1913	Sixteenth Amendment authorizes federal income taxes
	Theodore Roosevelt is elected president		Seventeenth Amendment provides for direct election of U.S. senators
1905	Anticapitalist Industrial Workers of the World (IWW) is founded		Underwood Tariff Act reduces duties and imposes personal income tax
1906	Hepburn Act strengthens Interstate Commerce Commission		Federal Reserve Act gives the United States a central banking system again
	Upton Sinclair exposes Chicago slaughterhouses in *The Jungle*	1914	Federal Trade Commission is created to protect against trusts
1907	U.S. Steel absorbs Tennessee Coal and Iron Company		Clayton Antitrust Act regulates business
1908	Theodore Roosevelt convenes National Conservation Conference	1920	Nineteenth Amendment guarantees women the right to vote

✓•⸢Study and Review at www.myhistorylab.com

Review Questions

1. The introduction to this chapter compares volunteers today to young reformers early in the twentieth century. What were the similarities and differences?

2. List the ideas of the various progressive-thinking leaders and their movements. What attitudes and values did they share? Were these sufficiently coherent to constitute a "Progressive movement"?

3. How did the attitudes of the reformers and political activists compare with those of the people whose lives they meant to improve? How did immigrants, Native Americans, and workers respond to Progressive reforms?

4. In what ways was the Progressive Era especially challenging for African Americans?

5. How did the relationship between business and government change during the presidencies of Roosevelt, Taft, and Wilson? Did business oppose government regulation or favor it as a means of controlling competition and weakening radicalism?

Key Terms

Ashcan School *545*
Clayton Antitrust
 Act *566*
Conservation *561*
Federal Reserve Act *566*
Hepburn Act *560*
Industrial Workers of the
 World (IWW) *546*

muckraker *545*
National American Woman
 Suffrage Association
 (NAWSA) *554*
National Association for
 the Advancement of
 Colored People
 (NAACP) *571*

New Freedom *564*
New Nationalism *563*
Niagara movement *570*
Progressivism *543*
Square Deal *559*
Underwood Tariff *566*
woman suffrage *553*

22 From Isolation to Empire

((•─[Hear the Audio Chapter 22 at myhistorylab.com

Can you find Afghanistan on a map?

DURING THE PRESIDENTIAL CAMPAIGN OF 2000, REPUBLICAN CANDIDATE George W. Bush chastised the Clinton administration for sending troops to Haiti and the Balkans. "If we don't stop extending our troops all around the world in nation-building missions," Bush declared, "then we're going to have a serious problem coming down the road."

Few could have imagined that within two years, following the 9/11 attacks on the World Trade Center and the Pentagon, thousands of American troops would be patrolling the high mountains of the Hindu Kush, fighting enemies at places named Tora Bora and Mazar-e Sharif, and working to install a new government in Afghanistan. A National Geographic Society survey found that nearly half of Americans aged 18 to 24 knew that the fictional island for the *Survivor* TV series was located in the South Pacific, but five in six could not find Afghanistan on a map.

Yet by the summer of 2010, President Barack Obama had increased American troops in Afghanistan to nearly 100,000. "If I thought for a minute that America's vital interests were not at stake here in Afghanistan," he told American soldiers, "I would order all of you home right away." These vital interests in many ways originated during the late nineteenth and early twentieth centuries.

Until then, Americans had given little thought to foreign affairs. In 1888 Benjamin Harrison articulated a widely held belief when he said that the United States was "an apart nation" and should remain so.

But sentiment was shifting. Intellectuals and many others cited "Darwinian" principles, such as "survival of the fittest," to justify American expansion abroad. Missionaries called on Americans to help impoverished and ill-educated peoples elsewhere in the world. American businessmen, increasingly confident of their own powers, craved access to foreign resources and markets. Such factors converged in Cuba, prompting the United States to go to war with Spain.

In 1898 tens of thousands of American troops were dispatched to Cuba and, within a year, to the Philippines. For years thereafter, Americans at home would struggle to locate on globes and in atlases battle sites in places such as Balangiga, Pulang Lupa, and Kandahar. They still do.

Isolation or Imperialism?

If Americans had little concern for what was going on far beyond the seas, their economic interest in Latin America was great and growing, and in East Asia only somewhat less so. Whether one sees isolation or expansion as the hallmark of American foreign policy after 1865 depends on what part of the world one looks at.

The disdain of the people of the United States for Europe rested on several historical foundations. Faith in the unique character of American civilization—and the converse of that belief, suspicion of Europe's supposedly aristocratic and decadent society—formed the chief basis of this **isolationism**. Bitter memories of indignities suffered during the Revolution and the Napoleonic Wars and anger at the hostile attitude of the great powers toward the United States during the Civil War strengthened it. In an era before airplanes, the United States was virtually invulnerable to European attack and at the same time incapable of mounting an offensive against any European power. In turning their backs on Europe, Americans were taking no risk and passing up few opportunities.

Origins of the Large Policy: Coveting Colonies

The nation's interests elsewhere in the world gradually increased. During the Civil War, France had established a protectorate over Mexico, installing the Archduke Maximilian of Austria as emperor. In 1866 Secretary of State William H. Seward demanded that the French withdraw, and the United States moved 50,000 soldiers to the Rio Grande. While fear of American intervention was only one of many reasons for their action, the French pulled their troops out of Mexico during the winter of 1866–1867. Mexican nationalists promptly seized and executed Maximilian. In 1867, at the instigation of

Midway Island, an inhospitable atoll acquired in 1867, was valuable as a military base located midway between Pearl Harbor, another naval station, and East Asia. The acquisition of a Pacific empire during these years was a reason why Pearl Harbor and Midway became pivotal during the war in the Pacific in World War II.

Seward, the United States purchased Alaska from Russia for $7.2 million, ridding the continent of another foreign power.

In 1867 Seward acquired the Midway Islands in the western Pacific. He also made overtures toward annexing the Hawaiian Islands, and he looked longingly at Cuba. In 1870 President Grant submitted to the Senate a treaty annexing the Dominican Republic. He applied tremendous pressure in an effort to obtain ratification, thus forcing a "great debate" on extracontinental expansion. The distance of the Dominican Republic from the continent and its population of what one congressman called "semi-civilized, semi-barbarous men who cannot speak our language" made annexation unattractive. The treaty was rejected.

The internal growth that preoccupied Americans eventually led them to look outward. By the late 1880s the country was exporting a steadily increasing share of its agricultural and industrial output. Exports, only $450 million in 1870, passed the billion-dollar mark early in the 1890s. Imports increased at a rate only slightly less spectacular.

The character of foreign trade was also changing: Manufactures loomed ever more important among exports until in 1898 the country shipped abroad more manufactured goods than it imported. By this time American steelmakers could compete with producers anywhere in the world. When American industrialists became conscious of their ability to compete with Europeans in far-off markets, they took more interest in world affairs, particularly during periods of depression.

Shifting intellectual currents further altered the attitudes of Americans. Darwin's theories, applicable by analogy to international relations, gave the concept of manifest destiny a new plausibility. Darwinists like the historian John Fiske argued that the American democratic system of government was so clearly the world's "fittest" that it was destined to spread peacefully over "every land on the earth's surface." In *Our Country* (1885) Josiah Strong found racist and religious justifications for American expansionism, again based on the theory of evolution. The Anglo-Saxon race, centered now in the United States, possessed "an instinct or genius for colonization," Strong claimed.

The completion of the conquest of the American West encouraged Americans to consider expansion beyond the seas. "For nearly 300 years the dominant fact in American life has been expansion," declared Frederick Jackson Turner, propounder of the frontier thesis. "That these energies of expansion will no longer operate would be a rash prediction." Turner and writers who advanced other expansionist arguments were much influenced by foreign thinking. European liberals had tended to disapprove of colonial ventures, but in the 1870s and 1880s many of them were changing their minds. English liberals in particular began to talk and write about the "superiority" of English culture, to describe the virtues of the "Anglo-Saxon race," to stress a "duty" to spread Christianity among the heathen, and to advance economic arguments for overseas expansion.

European ideas were reinforced for Americans by their observation of the imperialist activities of the European powers in what would today be called underdeveloped areas. "While the great powers of Europe are steadily enlarging their colonial domination in Asia and Africa," James G. Blaine said in 1884, "it is the especial province of this country to improve and expand its trade with the nations of America." While Blaine emphasized commerce, the excitement and adventure of overseas enterprises appealed to many people even more than the economic possibilities or any sense of obligation to fulfill a supposed national, religious, or racial destiny.

Finally, military and strategic arguments were advanced to justify adopting a "large" policy. The powerful Union army had been demobilized rapidly after Appomattox; in the 1880s only about 25,000 men were under arms, their chief occupation fighting Indians in the West.

Half the navy, too, had been scrapped after the war, and the remaining ships were obsolete. While other nations were building steam-powered iron warships, the United States still depended on wooden sailing vessels. In 1867 a British naval publication accurately described the American fleet as "hapless, broken-down, tattered [and] forlorn."

Although no foreign power menaced the country, the decrepit state of the navy vexed many of its officers and led one of them, Captain Alfred Thayer Mahan, to develop a startling theory about the importance of sea power. According to him, history proved that a nation with a powerful navy and the overseas bases necessary to maintain it would be invulnerable in war and prosperous in time of peace. Applied to the current American situation, this meant that in addition to building a modern fleet, the United States should obtain a string of coaling stations and bases in the Caribbean, annex the Hawaiian Islands, and cut a canal across Central America. A more extensive colonial empire might follow, but these bases and the canal they would protect were essential first steps to ensure America's future as a great power.

Mahan attracted many influential disciples. One was Congressman Henry Cabot Lodge of Massachusetts, a prominent member of the Naval Affairs Committee. Lodge had married into a navy family and was close with the head of the new Naval War College, Commodore Stephen B. Luce. In 1883 he helped push through Congress an act authorizing the construction of three steel warships, and he consistently advocated expanding and modernizing the fleet. Elevated to the Senate in 1893, Lodge pressed for expansionist policies, basing his arguments on the

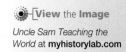

View the **Image**

Uncle Sam Teaching the World at **myhistorylab.com**

strategic concepts of Mahan. Lodge's friend Theodore Roosevelt was another ardent supporter of the "large" policy, but he had little influence until McKinley appointed him assistant secretary of the navy in 1897.

Toward an Empire in the Pacific

The interest of the United States in the Pacific and East Asia began in the late eighteenth century, when the first American merchant ship dropped anchor in Canton harbor. After the Treaty of Wanghia (1844), American merchants in China enjoyed many privileges and trade expanded rapidly.

The Hawaiian Islands were an important way station on the route to China, and by 1820 merchants and missionaries were making contacts there. As early as 1854 a movement to annex the islands existed, although it foundered because Hawaii insisted on being admitted to the Union as a state. Commodore Perry's expedition to Japan led to the signing of a commercial treaty (1858) that opened several Japanese ports to American traders.

American influence in Hawaii increased steadily; the descendants of missionary families, most of them engaged in raising sugar, dominated the Hawaiian monarchy. While they made no overt effort to make the islands an American colony, all the expansionist ideas of the era—manifest destiny, Darwinism, Josiah Strong's racist and religious assumptions, and the relentless force of American commercial interests—pointed them in that direction. In 1875 a reciprocity treaty admitted Hawaiian sugar to the United

The Course of Empire, 1867–1901 China was the focus of American imperial visions: Missionaries, most of them women, flocked into China, and American manufacturers craved access to the huge China market.

States free of duty in return for a promise to yield no territory to a foreign power. When this treaty was renewed in 1887, the United States obtained the right to establish a naval base at Pearl Harbor. In addition to occupying Midway, America obtained a foothold in the Samoan Islands in the South Pacific.

During the 1890s American interest in the Pacific area steadily intensified as a result of the situation in Hawaii. The McKinley Tariff Act of 1890, discontinuing the duty on raw sugar and compensating American producers of cane and beet sugar by granting them a bounty of two cents a pound, struck Hawaiian sugar growers hard, for it destroyed the advantage they had gained in the reciprocity treaty.

The following year the death of King Kalakaua brought Queen Liliuokalani, a determined nationalist, to the throne. Placing herself at the head of a "Hawaii for the Hawaiians" movement, she abolished the existing constitution under which the white minority had pretty much controlled the islands and attempted to rule as an absolute monarch. The resident Americans then staged a coup. In January 1893, with the connivance of the U.S. minister, John L. Stevens, who ordered 150 marines into Honolulu, they deposed Queen Liliuokalani and set up a provisional government.

View the Image

Iolani Palace, Hawaii at
myhistorylab.com

Stevens recognized their regime at once, and the new government sent a delegation to Washington to seek a treaty of annexation.

In the closing days of the Harrison administration such a treaty was negotiated and sent to the Senate, but when Cleveland took office in March, he withdrew it.

The new president disapproved of the way American troops had been used to over-throw the monarchy and attempted to restore Queen Liluokalani. But by now the new regime, backed by American businessmen, was firmly entrenched. Cleveland found himself unable to do anything.

Finally, in July 1898, after the outbreak of the Spanish-American War, Congress annexed the islands by joint resolution, a procedure requiring only a simple majority vote.

Toward an Empire in Latin America

Most of the arguments for extending American influence in the Pacific applied more strongly to Central and South America, where the United States had much larger eco-nomic interests and where the strategic importance of the region was clear.

As early as 1869 President Grant had come out for an American-owned canal across the isthmus of Panama, in spite of the fact that the United States had agreed in the Clayton-Bulwer Treaty with Great Britain (1850) that neither nation would "obtain or maintain for itself any exclusive control" over an inter-oceanic canal. In 1880, when the French engineer Ferdinand de Lesseps organized a company to build a canal across the isthmus, President Hayes announced that the United States would not permit a European power to control such a waterway.

When Cleveland returned to power in 1893, the possibility of trouble in Latin America seemed remote, for he had always opposed imperialistic ventures. Yet scarcely two years later the United States was again on the verge of war in South America as a result of a crisis in Venezuela, and before this issue was settled Cleveland had made the most powerful claim to American hegemony in the hemisphere ever uttered. The tangled borderland between Venezuela and British Guiana had long been in dispute, Venezuela demanding more of the region than it was entitled to and Great Britain making exaggerated claims and refusing to submit the question to arbitration. What made a crisis of the controversy was the political situation in the United States. With his party rapidly deserting him because of his stand on the silver question, and with the election of 1896 approaching, President Cleveland desperately needed a popular issue.

There was considerable anti-British feeling in the United States. By taking the Venezuelan side in the boundary dispute, Cleveland would be defending a weak neighbor against a great power, a position certain to evoke a popular response.

In July 1895 he ordered Secretary of State Richard Olney to send a near ultimatum to the British. By occupying the disputed territory, Olney insisted, Great Britain was invading Venezuela and violating the Monroe Doctrine. Unless Great Britain responded promptly by agreeing to arbitration, the president would call the question to the attention of Congress.

The note threatened war, but the British ignored it for months. They did not take the United States seriously as a world power. The American navy, although expanding, could not hope to stand up against the British, who had fifty battleships, twenty-five armored cruisers, and many smaller vessels. When Lord Salisbury, the prime minister and foreign secretary, finally replied, he rejected outright the argu-ment that the Monroe Doctrine had any status under international law and refused to arbitrate what he called the "exaggerated pretensions" of the Venezuelans.

Cleveland was furious. On December 17, 1895, he asked Congress for authority to appoint an American commission to determine the correct line between British Guiana and Venezuela. When that had been done, he added, the United States should "resist by every means in its power" the appropriation by Great Britain of any territory "we have determined of right belongs to Venezuela." Congress responded at once, unanimously appropriating $100,000 for the boundary commission. Popular approval was almost universal.

In Great Britain government and people suddenly awoke to the seriousness of the situation. No one wanted a war with the United States over a remote patch of tropical real estate. In Europe, Britain was concerned about German economic competition and the increased military power of that nation. The immense potential strength of the United States could no longer be ignored. Why make an enemy of a nation of 70 million, already the richest industrial power in the world?

Great Britain agreed to arbitrate the boundary, and the war scare subsided. When the boundary tribunal awarded nearly all the disputed region to Great Britain, whatever ill feeling the surrender may have occasioned in that country faded away. Instead of leading to war, the affair marked the beginning of an era of Anglo-American friendship. It had the unfortunate effect, however, of adding to the long-held American conviction that the nation could get what it wanted in international affairs by threat and bluster—a dangerous illusion.

The Cuban Revolution

On February 10, 1896, scarcely a week after Venezuela and Great Britain had signed the treaty ending their dispute, General Valeriano Weyler arrived in Havana from Spain to take up his duties as governor of Cuba. His assignment to this post was occasioned by the guerrilla warfare that Cuban nationalist rebels had been waging for almost a year. Weyler, a tough and ruthless soldier, began herding the rural population into wretched **"reconcentration" camps** to deprive the rebels of food and recruits. Resistance in Cuba hardened.

The United States had been interested in Cuba since the time of John Quincy Adams and, were it not for Northern opposition to adding more slave territory, might well have obtained the island one way or another before 1860. When the Cubans revolted against Spain in 1868, considerable support for intervening on their behalf developed. Hamilton Fish, Grant's secretary of state, resisted this sentiment, and Spain managed to pacify the rebels in 1878 by promising reforms. But change was slow in coming—slavery was not abolished until 1886. The worldwide depression of the 1890s hit the Cuban economy hard, and when an American tariff act in 1894 jacked up the rate on Cuban sugar by 40 percent, thus cutting off Cuban growers from the American market, the resulting distress precipitated another revolt.

Public sympathy in the United States went to the Cubans, who seemed to be fighting for liberty and democracy against an autocratic Old World power. Most newspapers supported the rebels; labor unions, veterans' organizations, many Protestant clergymen, a great majority of American blacks, and important politicians in both major parties demanded that the United States aid their cause. Rapidly increasing American investments in Cuban sugar plantations, now approaching $50 million, were endangered by the fighting and by the social chaos sweeping across the island.

In April 1896 Congress adopted a resolution suggesting that the revolutionaries be granted the rights of belligerents. Since this would have been akin to formal recognition, Cleveland would not go that far, but he did exert diplomatic pressure on Spain to remove the causes of the rebels' complaints, and he offered the services of his government as mediator. The Spanish rejected the suggestion. For a time the issue subsided. The election of 1896 deflected American attention from Cuba, and then McKinley refused to take any action that might disturb Spanish-American relations. In Cuba General Weyler made some progress toward stifling rebel resistance.

American expansionists, however, continued to demand intervention, and the press kept resentment alive with tales of Spanish atrocities. McKinley remained adamant. Although he warned Spain that Cuba must be pacified, his tone was friendly and he issued no ultimatum. A new government in Spain relieved the situation by recalling Weyler and promising partial self-government to the Cubans. In a message to Congress in December 1897, McKinley urged that Spain be given "a reasonable chance to realize her expectations" in the island.

His hopes were doomed. The fighting in Cuba continued. When riots broke out in Havana in January 1898, McKinley ordered the battleship *Maine* to Havana harbor to protect American citizens.

Shortly thereafter Hearst's *New York Journal* printed a letter written to a friend in Cuba by the Spanish minister in Washington, Dupuy de Lôme. The letter had been stolen by a spy. De Lôme, an experienced but arrogant diplomat, failed to appreciate McKinley's efforts to avoid intervening in Cuba. In the letter he characterized the president as a *politicastro*, or "small-time politician," which was a gross error, and a "bidder for the admiration of the crowd," which was equally insulting though somewhat closer to the truth. Americans were outraged, and de Lôme's hasty resignation did little to soothe their feelings.

Then, on February 15, the *Maine* exploded and sank in Havana harbor, 260 of the crew perishing in the disaster. Interventionists in the United States accused Spain of having destroyed the ship and clamored for war. The willingness of Americans to blame Spain indicates the extent of anti-Spanish opinion in the United States by 1898. No one has ever discovered what actually happened. A naval court of inquiry decided that the vessel had been sunk by a submarine mine, but it now seems

Watch the Video
Burial of the *Maine* Victims at **myhistorylab.com**

more likely that an internal explosion destroyed the *Maine*. The Spanish government could hardly have been foolish enough to commit an act that would probably bring American troops into Cuba.

With admirable courage, McKinley refused to panic; but he could not resist the wishes of millions of citizens that something be done to stop the fighting and allow the Cubans to determine their own fate. Spanish pride and Cuban patriotism had taken the issue of peace or war out of the president's hands. Spain could not put down the rebellion, and it would not yield to the nationalists' increasingly extreme demands. The Cubans, sensing that the continuing bloodshed aided their cause, refused to give the Spanish regime room to maneuver. After the *Maine* disaster, Spain might have agreed to an armistice had the rebels asked for one, and in the resulting negotiations it might well have given up the island. The rebels refused to make the first move. The fighting continued, bringing the United States every day closer to intervention.

The president faced a dilemma. Most of the business interests of the country, to which he was particularly sensitive, opposed intervention. Congress, however, seemed

The explosion of the *Maine* in Havana harbor, killing 260 men, caused much speculation in the newspapers and across the nation. Many Americans accused Spain of destroying the ship, a reaction that typified American sentiment toward the Spanish in 1898. What really caused the explosion remains unknown.
Source: ICHi-08428/Kurz & Allison/Chicago History Museum.

determined to act. When he submitted a restrained report on the sinking of the *Maine*, the Democrats in Congress, even most of those who had supported Cleveland's policies, accused him of timidity. Vice President Garret A. Hobart warned him that the Senate could not be held in check for long; should Congress declare war on its own, the administration would be discredited.

Finally, early in April, the president drafted a message asking for authority to use the armed forces "to secure a full and final termination of hostilities" in Cuba.

At the last moment the Spanish government seemed to yield; it ordered its troops in Cuba to cease hostilities. McKinley passed this information on to Congress along with his war message, but he gave it no emphasis and did not try to check the march toward war. To seek further delay would have been courageous but not necessarily wiser. Merely to stop fighting was not enough. The Cuban nationalists now insisted on full independence, and the Spanish politicians were unprepared to abandon the last remnant of their once-great American empire. If the United States took Cuba by force, the Spanish leaders might save their political skins; if they meekly surrendered the island, they were done for.

The "Splendid Little" Spanish-American War

On April 20, 1898, Congress, by joint resolution, recognized the independence of Cuba and authorized the use of the armed forces to drive out the Spanish. An amendment proposed by Senator Henry M. Teller disclaiming any intention of adding Cuban territory to the United States passed without opposition. Four days after passage of the **Teller Amendment**, Spain declared war on the United States.

Sailors on the USS *Oregon* watch the destruction of the Spanish cruiser, *Cristobal Colon*, during the Battle of Santiago, Cuba, July 3, 1898.

The Spanish-American War was fought to free Cuba, but the first action took place on the other side of the globe, in the Philippine Islands. Weeks earlier, Theodore Roosevelt, at the time assistant secretary of the navy, had alerted Commodore George Dewey, who was in command of the United States Asiatic Squadron located at Hong Kong, to move against the Spanish base at Manila if war came. Dewey had acted promptly, drilling his gun crews, taking on supplies, giving his gleaming white ships a coat of battle-gray paint, and establishing secret contacts with the Filipino nationalist leader, Emilio Aguinaldo. When word of the declaration of war reached him, Dewey steamed from Hong Kong across the South China Sea with four cruisers and two gun-boats. On the night of April 30 he entered Manila Bay, and at daybreak he opened fire on the Spanish fleet at 5,000 yards. His squadron made five passes, each time reducing the range; when the smoke had cleared, all ten of Admiral Montojo's ships had been destroyed. Not a single American was killed in the engagement.

Dewey immediately asked for troops to take and hold Manila, for now that war had been declared, he could not return to Hong Kong or any other neutral port. McKinley took the fateful step of dispatching some 11,000 soldiers and additional naval support. On August 13 these forces, assisted by Filipino irregulars under Aguinaldo, captured Manila.

▶ Watch the Video
Roosevelt's Rough Riders
at **myhistorylab.com**

Meanwhile, in Cuba, the United States had won a total victory. When the war began, the U.S. regular army consisted of about 28,000 men. This tiny force was bolstered by 200,000 hastily enlisted volunteers. Aggressive units like the regiment of "Rough Riders" raised by Theodore Roosevelt, who had resigned his Navy Department post to become a lieutenant colonel of volunteers, scrambled for space and supplies, shouldering aside other units to get what they needed.

Since a Spanish fleet under Admiral Pascual Cervera was known to be in Caribbean waters, no invading army could safely embark until the fleet could be located. On May 29 American ships found Cervera at Santiago harbor, on the eastern end of Cuba, and established a blockade. In June a 17,000-man expeditionary force landed at Daiquirí, east of Santiago, and pressed quickly toward the city. The Americans sweated through Cuba's torrid summer in heavy wool winter uniforms, ate "embalmed beef" out of cans, and fought mostly with old-fashioned rifles using black powder cartridges that marked the position of each soldier with a puff of smoke whenever he pulled the trigger. On July 1 they broke through undermanned Spanish defenses and stormed San Juan Hill, the intrepid Roosevelt in the van.

With Santiago harbor in range of American artillery, Admiral Cervera had to run the blockade. On July 3 his black-hulled ships, flags proudly flying, steamed forth from the harbor and fled westward along the coast. Five American battleships and two cruisers, commanded by Rear Admiral William T. Sampson and Commodore Winfield Scott Schley, ran them down. In four hours the entire Spanish force was destroyed. Damage to the American ships was superficial; only one American seaman lost his life in the engagement.

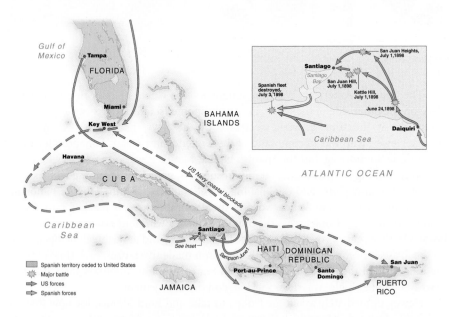

Spanish-American War: Caribbean Theater, 1898 After boarding in Tampa, American soldiers landed near Santiago, Cuba. They swiftly overran Spanish fortifications on the heights to the east of the city. When U.S. troops came within artillery range of Santiago Bay, the Spanish fleet fled. Soon the Spanish ships were intercepted and destroyed by the American navy.

The end then came abruptly. Santiago surrendered on July 17. A few days later, other U.S. troops completed the occupation of Puerto Rico. On August 12, one day before the fall of Manila, Spain agreed to get out of Cuba and to cede Puerto Rico and an island in the Marianas (Guam) to the United States. The future of the Philippines was to be settled at a formal peace conference, convening in Paris on October 1.

Developing a Colonial Policy

Although the Spanish resisted surrendering the Philippines at Paris, they had been so thoroughly defeated that they had no choice. The decision hung rather on the outcome of a conflict over policy within the United States. The war, won at so little cost militarily, produced problems far larger than those it solved.[1] The nation had become a great power in the world's eyes. European leaders had been impressed by the forcefulness of Cleveland's diplomacy in the Venezuela boundary dispute and by the efficiency displayed by the navy in the war. The annexation of Hawaii and other overseas bases intensified their conviction that the United States was determined to become a major force in international affairs.

But were the American people determined to exercise that force? The debate over taking the Philippine Islands throws much light on their attitudes. It was titillating for Americans to think of a world map liberally sprinkled with American flags and of the economic benefits that colonies might bring, but most citizens were not prepared to join in a worldwide struggle for power and influence. They entered blithely on adventures in far-off regions without facing the implications of their decision.

Since the United States had abjured any claim to Cuba, even though the island had long been desired by expansionists, logic dictated that a similar policy be applied to the Philippines. But expansionists were eager to annex the entire archipelago. Even before he had learned to spell the name, Senator Lodge was saying that "the Phillipines [sic] mean a vast future trade and wealth and power," offering the nation a greater opportunity "than anything that has happened . . . since the annexation of Louisiana."

President McKinley adopted a more cautious stance, but he too favored "the general principle of holding on to what we can get." A speaking tour of the Midwest in October 1898, during which he experimented with varying degrees of commitment to expansionism, convinced him that the public wanted the islands. Business opinion had shifted dramatically during the war. Business leaders were now calling the Philippines the gateway to the markets of East Asia.

The Anti-Imperialists

The war had produced a wave of unifying patriotic feeling. It greatly furthered reconciliation between the North and the South. But victory raised new divisive questions. An important minority objected strongly to the U.S. acquisition of overseas possessions.

The anti-imperialists insisted that since no one would consider statehood for the Philippines, it would be unconstitutional to annex them. It was a violation of the spirit of

---

[1] More than 5,000 Americans died as a result of the conflict, but fewer than 400 fell in combat. The others were mostly victims of yellow fever, typhoid, and other diseases.

While the good children (the states) sit at their seats, with the Indian off to the side, the unruly blacks—"Cuba," "Puerto Rico," "Hawaii," and "Philippines"—are lectured by Uncle Sam. Racist anti-imperialists argued, as did this cartoon in *Puck* in 1899, that the inclusion of other peoples would weaken the American nation.

the Declaration of Independence to govern a foreign territory without the consent of its inhabitants, Senator George Frisbie Hoar of Massachusetts argued; by taking over "vassal states" in "barbarous archipelagoes" the United States was "trampling . . . on our own great Charter, which recognizes alike the liberty and the dignity of individual manhood."

McKinley was not insensitive to this appeal to idealism and tradition, which was the fundamental element in the anti-imperialist argument. But he rejected it for several reasons.

Public opinion would not sanction restoring Spanish authority in the Philippines or allowing some other power to have them. That the Filipinos were sufficiently advanced and united socially to form a stable government if granted independence seemed unlikely. Senator Hoar believed that "for years and for generations, and perhaps for centuries, there would have been turbulence, disorder and revolution" in the islands if they were left to their own devices.

The president searched the depths of his soul and could find no solution but annexation. The state of public feeling made the decision easier, and he probably found the idea of presiding over an empire appealing. Certainly the commercial possibilities did not escape him. In the end it was with a heavy sense of responsibility that he ordered the American peace commissioners to insist on acquiring the Philippines. To salve the feelings of the Spanish the United States agreed to pay $20 million for the archipelago, but it was a forced sale, accepted by Spain under duress.

The peace treaty faced a hard battle in the U.S. Senate, where a combination of partisan politics and anticolonialism made it difficult to amass the two-thirds majority necessary for ratification. McKinley had shrewdly appointed three senators, including one

Democrat, to the peace commission. This predisposed many members of the upper house to approve the treaty, but the vote was close. William Jennings Bryan, titular head of the Democratic party, could probably have prevented ratification had he urged his supporters to vote nay. Although he was opposed to taking the Philippines, he did not do so. To reject the treaty would leave the United States technically at war with Spain and the fate of the Philippines undetermined; better to accept the islands and then grant them independence. The question should be decided, Bryan said, "not by a minority of the Senate but by a majority of the people" at the next presidential election. Perplexed by Bryan's stand, a number of Democrats allowed themselves to be persuaded by the expansionists' arguments and by McKinley's judicious use of patronage; the treaty was ratified in February 1899 by a vote of fifty-seven to twenty-seven.

The Philippine Insurrection

The national referendum that Bryan had hoped for never materialized. Bryan himself confused the issue in 1900 by making free silver a major plank in his platform, thereby driving conservative anti-imperialists into McKinley's arms. Moreover, early in 1899 the Filipino nationalists under Aguinaldo, furious because the United States would not withdraw, took up arms. A savage guerrilla war resulted, one that cost far more in lives and money than the "splendid little" Spanish-American conflict.

Neither side displayed much regard for the "rules" of war. Goaded by sneak attacks and instances of cruelty to captives, American soldiers, most of whom had little respect for Filipinos to begin with, responded in kind. (See American Lives, "Frederick Funston," pp. 590–591.) Civilians were rounded up, prisoners tortured, and property destroyed. Horrifying tales of rape, arson, and murder by U.S. troops filtered into the country, providing ammunition for the anti-imperialists. In fact, far more than 8,000 Filipinos lost their lives during the conflict, which raged for three years. More than 70,000 American soldiers had to be sent to the islands before the resistance was crushed, and about as many of them lost their lives as had perished in the Cuban conflict.

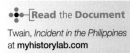

Read the Document

Twain, *Incident in the Philippines* at **myhistorylab.com**

View the Image

Filipino Guerrillas at **myhistorylab.com**

In 1900 McKinley sent a commission headed by William Howard Taft, a federal judge, to establish a government. Taft took an instant liking to the

Emilio Aguinaldo, shown here with his young son, commanded Filipino insurgents who worked with Commodore Dewey to help overthrow Spanish rule of the Philippines in 1898. He later took up arms against the United States in a brutal three-year struggle when President McKinley opposed granting independence to the islands.

Filipinos, and his policy of encouraging them to participate in the territorial government attracted many converts. In July 1901 he became the first civilian governor of the Philippines.

Actually, the reelection of McKinley in 1900 settled the Philippine question so far as most Americans were concerned. Anti-imperialists still claimed that it was unconstitutional to take over territories without the consent of the local population. Their reasoning, while certainly not unsound, was unhistorical. No American government had seriously considered the wishes of the American Indians, the French and Spanish settlers in Louisiana, the Eskimos of Alaska, or the people of Hawaii when it had seemed in the national interest to annex new lands.

Cuba and the United States

Nevertheless, grave constitutional questions arose as a result of the acquisitions that followed the Spanish-American War. McKinley acted with remarkable independence in handling the problems involved in expansion. He set up military governments in Cuba, Puerto Rico, and the Philippines without specific congressional authority. The Supreme Court, in what became known as the "insular cases," granted Congress permission to act toward the colonies much as it pleased.

While the most heated arguments raged over Philippine policy, the most difficult colonial problems concerned the relationship between the United States and Cuba. Despite the desire of most Americans to get out of Cuba, an independent government could not easily be created.

The insurgent government was feeble, corrupt, and oligarchic, the Cuban economy in a state of collapse, and life was chaotic. The first Americans entering Havana found the streets littered with garbage and the corpses of horses and dogs. All public services were at a standstill; it seemed essential for the United States, as McKinley said, to give "aid and direction" until "tranquillity" could be restored.

The problems were indeed knotty, for no strong local leader capable of uniting Cuba appeared. Even Senator Teller, father of the Teller Amendment, expressed concern lest "unstable and unsafe" elements gain control of the country. European leaders expected that the United States would eventually annex Cuba; and many Americans, including General Leonard Wood, who became military governor in December 1899, considered this the best solution. The desperate state of the people, the heavy economic stake of Americans in the region, and its strategic importance militated against withdrawal.

In the end the United States did withdraw, after doing a great deal to modernize sugar production, improve sanitary conditions, establish schools, and restore orderly administration. In November 1900 a Cuban constitutional convention met at Havana and proceeded without substantial American interference or direction to draft a frame of government. The chief restrictions imposed by this document on Cuba's freedom concerned foreign relations; at the insistence of the United States, it authorized American intervention whenever necessary "for the preservation of Cuban independence" and "the maintenance of a government adequate for the protection of life, property, and individual liberty." Cuba had to promise to make no treaty with a foreign power compromising its independence and to grant naval bases on its soil to the United States.

The Cubans, after some grumbling, accepted this arrangement, known as the **Platt Amendment**. It had the support of most American opponents of imperialism. The amendment was a true compromise: It safeguarded

●●●─┤Read the Document

The Platt Amendment at
myhistorylab.com

American interests while granting to the Cubans real self-government on internal matters. In May 1902 the United States turned over the reins of government to the new republic. The next year the two countries signed a reciprocity treaty tightening the economic bonds between them.

True friendship did not result. Although American troops occupied Cuba only once more, in 1906, and then at the specific request of Cuban authorities, the United States repeatedly used the threat of intervention to coerce the Cuban government. American economic penetration proceeded rapidly and without regard for the well-being of the Cuban peasants, many of whom lived in a state of peonage on great sugar plantations. Nor did the Americans' good intentions make up for their tendency to consider themselves innately superior to the Cubans and to overlook the fact that Cubans did not always wish to adopt American customs and culture.

The United States in the Caribbean and Central America

If the purpose of the Spanish-American War had been to bring peace and order to Cuba, the Platt Amendment was a logical step. The same purpose soon necessitated a further extension of the principle, for once the United States accepted the role of protector and stabilizer in parts of the Caribbean and Central America, it seemed desirable to supervise the entire region.

The Caribbean and Central American countries were economically underdeveloped, politically unstable, and desperately poor. Most of the people were uneducated peasants, many of whom were little better off than slaves. Rival cliques of wealthy families struggled for power, force being the usual method of effecting a change in government. Most of the meager income of the average Caribbean state was swallowed up by the military or diverted into the pockets of the current rulers.

Cynicism and fraud poisoned the relations of most of these nations with the great powers. European merchants and bankers systematically cheated their Latin American customers, who in turn frequently refused to honor their obligations. Foreign bankers floated bond issues on outrageous terms, while revolutionary governments in the region annulled concessions and repudiated debts with equal disdain for honest business dealing.

In 1902, shortly after the United States had pulled out of Cuba, trouble erupted in Venezuela, where a dictator, Cipriano Castro, was refusing to honor debts owed the citizens of European nations. To force Castro to pay up, Germany and Great Britain established a blockade of Venezuelan ports and destroyed a number of Venezuelan gunboats and harbor defenses. Under American pressure the Europeans agreed to arbitrate the dispute. For the first time, European powers had accepted the broad implications of the Monroe Doctrine. By this time Theodore Roosevelt had become president of the United States, and he quickly capitalized on the new

FREDERICK FUNSTON

On the night of March 22, 1901, as rain battered his campsite in the deep jungles of Luzon Island in the Philippines, Frederick Funston pondered what awaited him the next day. Ten miles to the north lay his prey, Emilio Aguinaldo, President of the Philippine Republic. For two years, the American army had been trying to capture Aguinaldo. But repeatedly Aguinaldo had slipped away. This time Funston was close. His ruse was working.

It had been a wild idea, something out of a boy's adventure story. He conceived it after capturing a Filipino messenger carrying coded documents. Funston's interrogation of the courier had been successful. The courier confirmed that Aguinaldo's secret headquarters was located in a remote area of Luzon.

Funston had chosen eighty Filipino scouts from the Macabebes, a tribe hostile to Aguinaldo. He outfitted them in the uniforms of Aguinaldo's army and trained them to pretend to be Filipino nationalists. These "nationalists" would escort five American "prisoners" (including Funston) for presentation to Aguinaldo.

Funston longed to be a hero. Ever since he was a child, he worried that he failed to measure up to his father. Edward "Foghorn" Funston had been an artillery officer during the Civil War and a fiery Republican congressman afterward. At six feet two and 200 pounds, he was regarded by all as an exemplar of nineteenth-century manhood. But Frederick, born in 1864, was only five feet four and slightly built. He compensated with bravado displays of martial manliness. He craved a military career, but though his father was a congressman, West Point rejected him: His grades were mediocre, and he was too small.

In 1886 he enrolled at the University of Kansas but didn't fit in. He devoted himself to the pursuit of the most desirable women on campus, all of whom spurned him. Increasingly he retreated from social situations, preferring to drink alone in his room, periodically bursting out in a drunken rage.

He dropped out of college. First, he explored an unmapped section of Death Valley in California. Then he volunteered to gather botanical samples in Alaska for the Department of Agriculture. When the department proposed that he command an entire expedition for the purpose, he flatly turned them down. Alone, he trekked into the frigid wastes of northern Alaska and remained there for the better part of a year. When he ran out of food he ate his sled dogs.

During those long, silent nights, Funston realized that he could hardly prove that he measured up if no one were around to take the measurements. He decided to become a soldier, not caring much against whom he fought. In 1895 he contacted a recruiter for the cause of Cuban independence and accepted a commission as an artillery officer in the rebel army.

In Cuba he was given command of a Hotchkiss cannon; he made up for his lack of gunnery skill by sneaking his cannon absurdly close to Spanish fortifications at night, often within 400 yards. As the sun rose, the Spaniards, aghast at what was sitting on their doorstep, fired everything they had at Funston's cannon. Funston calmly adjusted the sights, pulled the lanyard, and climbed upon the parapet, shouting

Frederick Funston: hero or antihero?

"Viva Cuba libre!" He was repeatedly wounded; once, a bullet pierced his lungs. When a severe hip wound became infected, he returned to the United States for medical assistance.

But he was not done with war. In 1898 Funston was given command of the Kansas regiments that had volunteered against Spain. To his dismay, they were sent to the Philippines, where the Spaniards had already ceased fighting. But after President McKinley decided to annex the Philippines, war broke out between the Americans and the Filipino nationalists. Funston finally got what he craved: sweeping charges, glorious victories, and newspaper feature stories. Yet the jokes persisted. Behind his back, his men called him the "Bantam General." The *New York Times,* in its coverage of a battle in which he won a Congressional Medal of Honor, ran the headline: "Daring Little Colonel Funston." The opening paragraph attributed Funston's courage to the fact that he was too small to hit.

But now, if he captured Aguinaldo, Funston, the little man, would become a great one.

On March 23, 1901, Funston's Macabebes and their five American "prisoners" met up with a contingent of Aguinaldo's army. Deceived, Aguinaldo's troops escorted Funston's band into the town of Palanan. Aguinaldo watched from a window above. When shots rang out, thinking the troops were firing a salute, he shouted, "Stop that foolishness. Don't waste ammunition!"

Then Funston burst into Aguinaldo's compound: "I am General Funston. You are a prisoner of war of the Army of the United States of America."

Dazed, Aguinaldo replied, "Is this not some joke?" Funston seized Aguinaldo, dragged him through the jungle to the coast, where the USS *Vicksburg* was waiting. It took them to American headquarters in Manila.

After being subjected to intense pressure by American officials, Aguinaldo renounced the Filipino revolution, swore allegiance to the United States, and called on his followers to do likewise. The Philippine-American conflict was virtually over. Frederick Funston had almost single-handedly won the war.

For a time, Funston was a sensation. He was promoted to brigadier general. Newspaper editors and politicians championed him for governor of Kansas or for vice president on a ticket headed by Theodore Roosevelt in 1904. But within a few years Funston all but vanished. Anti-imperialists pointed out that Funston's men had surrendered and then fired their weapons, and that the Macabebes had been wearing enemy uniforms; both actions violated international law. Worse, several reporters and some of his soldiers claimed that Funston had ordered the execution of Filipino prisoners. He was ordered to an inconsequential command in San Francisco.

One hundred years after Funston's capture of Aguinaldo, U.S. troops would again be tracking a rebel fugitive: Osama bin Laden, mastermind of the September 11, 2001, attacks on the World Trade Center and Pentagon. That virtually no one recalled Funston's single-handed pursuit and capture of Aguinaldo was one measure of how completely he had slipped from view.

But Funston's name resurfaced in 2010, after major earthquakes had triggered widespread looting in Haiti and Chile. The *New York Times* observed that when the 1906 earthquake destroyed much of San Francisco, General Frederick Funston had immediately marched his troops into the city and taken charge; sometimes, the *Times* noted, leaders must act decisively.

Question for Discussion

■ To catch Aguinaldo, Funston employed tactics of doubtful legality. A century later Americans have been accused of using torture and other unsavory methods to win "the war on terror." Are such techniques morally or legally wrong? Why or why not?

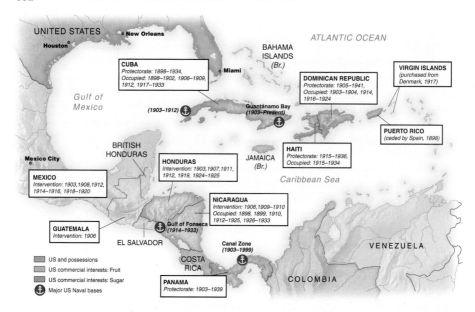

The United States in the Caribbean and Central America Puerto Rico was ceded by Spain to the United States after the Spanish-American War; the Virgin Islands were bought from Denmark; the Canal Zone was leased from Panama. The ranges of dates shown for Cuba, the Dominican Republic, Haiti, Nicaragua, and Panama cover those years during which the United States either had troops in occupation or in some other way (such as financial) had a protectorate relationship with that country.

European attitude. In 1903 the Dominican Republic defaulted on bonds totaling some $40 million. When European investors urged their governments to intervene, Roosevelt announced that under the Monroe Doctrine the United States could not permit foreign nations to intervene in Latin America. But, he added, Latin American nations should not be allowed to escape their obligations.

The president did not want to make a colony of the Dominican Republic. He therefore arranged for the United States to take charge of the Dominican customs service—the one reliable source of revenue in that poverty-stricken country. Fifty-five percent of the customs duties would be devoted to debt payment, the remainder turned over to the Dominican government to care for its internal needs. Roosevelt defined his policy, known as the Roosevelt Corollary to the Monroe Doctrine, in a message to Congress in December 1904. "Chronic wrongdoing" in Latin America, he stated with his typical disregard for the subtleties of complex affairs, might require outside intervention. Since, under the Monroe Doctrine, no other nation could step in, the United States must "exercise . . . an international police power."

In the short run this policy worked. Dominican customs were honestly collected for the first time and the country's finances put in order. The presence of American warships in the area provided a needed measure of political stability. In the long run, however, the Roosevelt Corollary caused a great deal of resentment in Latin America.

⊙ See the Map

Activities of the United States in the Caribbean at **myhistorylab.com**

The Open Door Policy in China

The insular cases, the Platt Amendment, and the Roosevelt Corollary established the framework for American policy both in Latin America and in East Asia. Coincidental with the Cuban rebellion of the 1890s, a far greater upheaval had convulsed the ancient empire of China. In 1894–1895 Japan easily defeated China in a war over Korea. Alarmed by Japan's aggressiveness, the European powers hastened to carve out for themselves new spheres of influence along China's coast. After the annexation of the Philippines, McKinley's secretary of state, John Hay, urged on by business leaders fearful of losing out in the scramble to exploit the Chinese market, tried to prevent the further absorption of China by the great powers.

For the United States to join in the dismemberment of China was politically impossible because of anti-imperialist feeling, so Hay sought to protect American interests by clever diplomacy. In a series of "Open Door" notes (1899) he asked the powers to agree to respect the trading rights of all countries and to impose no discriminatory duties within their spheres of influence.

The replies to the Open Door notes were at best noncommittal, yet Hay blandly announced in March 1900 that the powers had "accepted" his suggestions! Thus he could claim to have prevented the breakup of the empire and protected the right of Americans to do business freely in its territories. In reality nothing had been accomplished; the imperialist nations did not extend their political control of China only because they feared that by doing so they might precipitate a major war among themselves. Nevertheless, Hay's action marked a revolutionary departure from the traditional American policy of isolation, a bold advance into the complicated and dangerous world of international power politics.

Within a few months of Hay's announcement the **Open Door policy** was put to the test. Chinese nationalists, angered by the spreading influence of foreign governments, launched the so-called Boxer Rebellion. They swarmed into Peking and drove foreigners behind the walls of their legations, which were placed under siege. For weeks, until an international rescue expedition (which included 2,500 American soldiers) broke through to free them, the fate of the foreigners was unknown. Fearing that the Europeans would use the rebellion as a pretext for further expropriations, Hay sent off another round of Open Door notes announcing that the United States believed in the preservation of "Chinese territorial and administrative entity" and in "the principle of equal and impartial trade with all parts of the Chinese Empire." This broadened the Open Door policy to include all China, not merely the European spheres of influence.

Hay's diplomacy was superficially successful. But once again European jealousies and fears rather than American cleverness were responsible. When the Japanese, mistrusting Russian intentions in Manchuria, asked Hay how he intended to implement his policy, he replied meekly that the United States was "not prepared . . . to enforce these views." The United States was being caught up in the power struggle in East Asia without having faced the implications of its actions.

In time the country would pay a heavy price for this unrealistic attitude, but in the decade following 1900 its policy of diplomatic meddling worked fairly well. Japan attacked Russia in a quarrel over Manchuria, smashing the Russian fleet in 1905 and winning a series of battles on the mainland. Japan was not prepared for a long war,

Grace Service, a YMCA missionary, explained that these porters worked at the base of Mount Omei in Szechwan, China, a favorite site for Buddhist pilgrims. Upper-class Chinese women's feet were bound to keep them small. The deformities that resulted limited the distance they could walk, so they hired men such as these to carry them to the summit.

however, and suggested to President Roosevelt that an American offer to mediate would be favorably received.

Eager to preserve the balance of power in East Asia, which enabled the United States to exert influence without any significant commitment of force, Roosevelt accepted the hint. In June 1905 he invited the belligerents to a conference at Portsmouth, New Hampshire. At the conference the Japanese won title to Russia's sphere around Port Arthur and a free hand in Korea, but when they demanded Sakhalin Island and a large money indemnity, the Russians balked. Unwilling to resume the war, the Japanese settled for half of Sakhalin and no money.

The Treaty of Portsmouth was unpopular in Japan, and the government managed to place the blame on Roosevelt, who had supported the compromise. Ill feeling against Americans increased in 1906 when the San Francisco school board, responding to local opposition to the influx of cheap labor from Japan, instituted a policy of segregating Asian children in a special school. Japan protested, and President Roosevelt persuaded the San Franciscans to abandon segregation in exchange for his pledge to cut off further Japanese immigration. He accomplished this through a "Gentlemen's Agreement" (1907) in which the Japanese promised not to issue passports to laborers seeking to come to America. Discriminatory legislation based specifically on race was thus avoided. However, the atmosphere between the two countries remained charged. Japanese resentment at American racial prejudice was great; many Americans talked fearfully of the "yellow peril."

Roosevelt did not appreciably increase American naval and military strength in East Asia, nor did he stop trying to influence the course of events in the area, and he took no step toward withdrawing from the Philippines. He sent the fleet on a world cruise to demonstrate its might to Japan but knew well that this was mere bluff. "The 'Open Door' policy," he advised his successor, "completely disappears as soon as a powerful nation determines to disregard it." Nevertheless he allowed the belief to persist in the United States that the nation could influence the course of East Asian history without risk or real involvement.

The Panama Canal

In the Caribbean region American policy centered on building an interoceanic canal across Central America. The first step was to get rid of the old Clayton-Bulwer Treaty with Great Britain, which barred the United States from building a canal on its own. In 1901 Lord Pauncefote, the British ambassador, and Secretary of State John Hay negotiated an agreement abrogating the Clayton-Bulwer pact and giving the United States the right to build and defend a canal connecting the Pacific Ocean with the Caribbean Sea.

One possible canal route lay across the Colombian province of Panama, where the French-controlled New Panama Canal Company had taken over the franchise of the old De Lesseps company. Only fifty miles separated the oceans in Panama. The terrain, however, was rugged and unhealthy. While the French company had sunk much money into the project, it had little to show for its efforts aside from some rough excavations. A second possible route ran across Nicaragua. This route was about 200 miles long but was relatively easy since much of it traversed Lake Nicaragua and other natural waterways.

President McKinley appointed a commission to study the alternatives. It reported that the Panamanian route was technically superior, but recommended building in

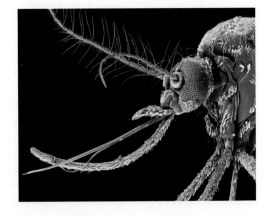

An electron microscopic photo of a mosquito that carried yellow fever. Major Walter Reed of the U.S. army proved that yellow fever was not spread directly among humans, but from the bites of infected mosquitoes. The virus then multiplied in the human bloodstream. Headache, backache, fever, and vomiting ensued. Liver cells were destroyed, resulting in jaundice—thus the name "yellow fever." American surgeon William Crawford Gorgas worked to eliminate yellow fever by destroying the breeding grounds of these mosquitoes. The last yellow fever outbreak in the United States struck New Orleans and parts of the South in 1905.

The U.S. Panama Canal Following many
negotiations, construction of the Panama Canal
began in 1904. After many delays and hardships, it
was completed in 1914.

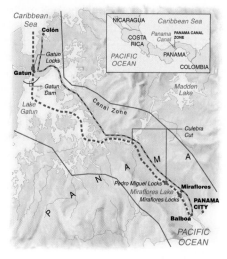

Nicaragua because the New Panama
Canal Company was asking $109 million
for its assets, which the commission valued at only $40 million. Lacking another
potential purchaser, the French company
lowered its price to $40 million, and after
a great deal of clever propagandizing by
Philippe Bunau-Varilla, a French engineer with heavy investments in the company, President Roosevelt settled on the
Panamanian route.

In January 1903 Secretary of State
Hay negotiated a treaty with Colombia. In return for a ninety-nine-year lease on a zone
across Panama six miles wide, the United States agreed to pay Colombia $10 million
and an annual rent of $250,000. The Colombian senate, however, unanimously rejected
this treaty. It demanded $15 million directly from the United States, plus one-fourth of
the $40 million U.S. payment to the New Panama Canal Company.

A little more patience might have produced a mutually satisfactory settlement, but
Roosevelt looked on the Colombians as highwaymen who were "mad to get hold of the
$40,000,000 of the Frenchmen." When Panamanians, egged on by the French company,
staged a revolution against Colombia in November 1903, he ordered the cruiser
Nashville to Panama. Colombian government forces found themselves looking down
the barrels of the guns of the *Nashville* and shortly thereafter eight other American
warships. The revolution succeeded.

Roosevelt instantly recognized the new Republic of Panama. Secretary Hay and
the new "Panamanian" minister, Bunau-Varilla, then negotiated a treaty granting
the United States a zone ten miles wide in perpetuity, on the same terms as those
rejected by Colombia. Within the Canal Zone the United States could act as "the
sovereign of the territory . . . to the entire exclusion of . . . the Republic of Panama."
The United States guaranteed the independence of the republic. The New Panama
Canal Company then received its $40 million, including a substantial share for
Bunau-Varilla.

Historians have condemned Roosevelt for his actions, and with good reason. It
was not that he fomented the Panamanian revolution, for he did not. Separated from
the government at Bogotá by an impenetrable jungle, the people of Panama province
had long wanted to be free of Colombian rule. He sinned, rather, in his disregard of
Latin American sensibilities. He referred to the Colombians as "dagoes" and insisted
that he was defending "the interests of collective civilization" when he overrode their
opposition to his plans.

If uncharitable, Roosevelt's analysis was not entirely inaccurate, yet it did not justify his haste in taking Panama under his wing. Throughout Latin America, especially
as nationalist sentiments grew stronger, Roosevelt's intolerance and aggressiveness in
the canal incident bred resentment and fear.

Table 22.1 Path to Empire, 1885–1901

Josiah Strong, *Our Country*	1885	Applied social Darwinism—"survival of the fittest"—to justify American expansion
A. T. Mahan, *The Influence of Seapower upon History*	1890	Endorsed naval power to ensure prosperity and national security
United States helped sugar planters depose Queen Liliuokalani	1893	Major step toward annexation of Hawaii
United States intervened in British dispute with Venezuela over land claims	1895	Reaffirmed the Monroe Doctrine claim to American supervision of Latin America
USS *Maine* exploded in Havana harbor	1898	Generated public pressure for war against Spain
Defeat of Spain	1898	Opened former Spanish colonies to U.S. annexation and economic penetration
U.S. annexation of Philippines	1899	United States became formal empire
"Open Door" Policy	1899	United States asserted trading rights in China
Roosevelt intervened on behalf of Panamanian independence	1903	Advanced expansive rights in Central America
Roosevelt Corollary	1904	Asserted U.S. right to military intervention in Latin America
Taft's Dollar Diplomacy	1909–1913	Encouraged U.S. government-supported investment abroad
Panama Canal opened	1914	Allowed U.S. warships to travel swiftly between Atlantic and Pacific

The first vessels passed through the canal in 1914—and American hegemony in the Caribbean expanded. Yet even in that strategically vital area there was more show than substance to American strength. The navy ruled Caribbean waters largely by default, for it lacked adequate bases in the region. In 1903, as authorized by the Cuban constitution, the United States obtained an excellent site for a base at Guantanamo Bay, but before 1914 Congress appropriated only $89,000 to develop it.

The tendency was to try to influence outlying areas without actually controlling them. Roosevelt's successor, William Howard Taft, called this policy **dollar diplomacy**, his reasoning being that economic penetration would bring stability to underdeveloped areas and power and profit to the United States without the government's having to commit troops or spend public funds.

Under Taft the State Department won a place for American bankers in an international syndicate engaged in financing railroads in Manchuria. When Nicaragua defaulted on its foreign debt in 1911, the department arranged for American bankers to reorganize Nicaraguan finances and manage the customs service. Although the government truthfully insisted that it did not "covet an inch of territory south of the Rio Grande," dollar diplomacy provoked further apprehension in Latin America. Efforts to establish similar arrangements in Honduras, Costa Rica, and Guatemala all failed. In Nicaragua orderly administration of the finances did not bring internal peace. In 1912, 2,500 American marines and sailors had to be landed to put down a revolution.

Economic penetration proceeded briskly. American investments in Cuba reached $500 million by 1920, and smaller but significant investments were made in the Dominican Republic and in Haiti. In Central America the United Fruit Company accumulated large holdings in banana plantations, railroads, and other ventures. Other firms plunged heavily into Mexico's rich mineral resources.

Imperialism without Colonies

If one defines imperialism narrowly as a policy of occupying and governing foreign lands, American imperialism lasted for an extremely short time. With trivial exceptions, all the American colonies—Hawaii, the Philippines, Guam, Puerto Rico, the Guantanamo base, and the Canal Zone—were obtained between 1898 and 1903. In retrospect it seems clear that the urge to own colonies was only fleeting; the legitimate questions raised by the anti-imperialists and the headaches connected with the management of overseas possessions soon produced a change of policy.

The objections of protectionists to the lowering of tariff barriers, the shock of the Philippine insurrection, and a growing conviction that the costs of colonial administration outweighed the profits affected American thinking. Hay's Open Door notes marked the beginning of the retreat from imperialism as thus defined, while the Roosevelt Corollary and dollar diplomacy signaled the consolidation of a new policy. Elihu Root summarized this policy as it applied to the Caribbean nations in 1905: "We do not want to take them for ourselves. We do not want any foreign nations to take them for themselves. We want to help them."

Yet imperialism can be given a broader definition. Although the United States did not seek colonies, it pursued a course that promoted American economic penetration of underdeveloped areas without the trouble of owning and controlling them. American statesmen regarded American expansion as beneficial to all concerned. They genuinely believed that they were exporting democracy along with capitalism and industrialization.

Dollar diplomacy had two main objectives, the avoidance of violence and the economic development of Latin America; it paid small heed to how peace was maintained and how the fruits of development were distributed. The policy was self-defeating, for in the long run stability depended on the support of local people, and this was seldom forthcoming.

By the eve of World War I the United States had become a world power and had assumed what it saw as a duty to guide the development of many countries with traditions far different from its own. The national psychology, if such a term has any meaning, remained fundamentally isolationist. Americans understood that their wealth and numbers made their nation strong and that geography made it virtually invulnerable. Thus they proceeded to do what they wanted to do in foreign affairs, limited more by their humanly flexible consciences than by any rational analysis of the probable consequences. This policy seemed safe enough—in 1914.

⦿ See the **Map**

World Colonial Empires, 1900
at **myhistorylab.com**

Milestones

1850	Britain and United States sign Clayton-Bulwer Treaty concerning interoceanic canal	1898	Theodore Roosevelt leads Rough Riders at Battle of San Juan Hill
			United States annexes Hawaii
1858	Commercial treaty with Japan opens several ports to American trade	1899	Hay's Open Door policy safeguards United States' access to China trade
1867	United States buys Alaska from Russia		United States annexes Philippines and becomes an empire
1871	Treaty of Washington settles *Alabama* claims	1900	Platt Amendment gives United States naval stations and right to intervene in Cuba
1875	Reciprocity treaty increases U.S. influence in Hawaii	1901	Hay-Pauncefote Treaty gives United States rights to build interoceanic canal
1885	Josiah Strong justifies expansionism in *Our Country*		
1890	A. T. Mahan fuels American imperialism in *The Influence of Sea Power*		Supreme Court's insular cases give Congress free reign over colonies
1893	United States helps sugar planters depose Queen Liliuokalani of Hawaii	1902	Europeans accept Monroe Doctrine during Venezuela bond dispute
1895	United States supports Venezuela in European border dispute over British Guiana	1904	Roosevelt Corollary to Monroe Doctrine gives United States "international police power"
1898	*Maine* explodes in Havana harbor	1907	"Gentlemen's Agreement" curtails Japanese immigration
	Spanish-American war breaks out		
	Dewey defeats Spanish fleet at Manila Bay	1914	Panama Canal opens

✓●—⌐Study and **Review** at **www.myhistorylab.com**

Review Questions

1. The introduction to this chapter holds that American soldiers are fighting in Afghanistan in part because of American imperialism after 1890. Could Americans then have avoided imperial expansion? What factors impelled them to support imperialism?

2. On what issues did the anti-imperialists and the imperialists agree? And how did they differ?

3. How did American involvement in the Caribbean differ from the United States' approach to China and East Asia?

4. Why did McKinley choose to annex the Philippines? Was his decision a wise one?

5. How did the Roosevelt Corollary modify the Monroe Doctrine? How did Taft's policies differ from those of Roosevelt?

6. Was American imperialism from 1890–1910 chiefly beneficial or harmful to other nations? To the United States?

Key Terms

dollar diplomacy *597*
isolationism *575*
Open Door policy *593*

Platt Amendment *589*
"reconcentration"
    camps *580*

Teller Amendment *582*

Woodrow Wilson and the Great War

23

((•—Hear the Audio Chapter 23 at myhistorylab.com

Do you know someone with TBI?

IN 2008 TOGGLE, A CHARACTER IN GARY TRUDEAU'S *DOONESBURY* comic strip, was driving a Humvee in Iraq when it was blown up by an improvised explosive device (IED). Toggle was hospitalized with traumatic brain injury (TBI), a buffeting of the brain caused by the shock waves of an explosion. By 2010 over 5,000 service members had been diagnosed with TBI, about a quarter of all combat casualties. "The Iraq war," the *Washington Post* observed, "has brought back one of the worst afflictions of World War I trench warfare: shell shock."

During World War I millions of men hunkered down in trenches surrounded by thickets of barbed wire. Before a major offensive, attacking armies hurled millions of artillery shells to pulverize such defenses. The casualties were staggering; many of the wounded suffered from shell shock—some 80,000 in the British army alone. Most never returned to active duty.

Just as American soldiers at the outset of the twenty-first century could not have imagined that they would be the victims of powerful explosions in Afghanistan and Iraq, few Americans in the early twentieth century thought it possible that they would get caught up in a war in Europe. To be sure, in the early 1900s Americans heard ominous rumblings from across the Atlantic Ocean. But even as European rivals spoke of war, none of it had much to do with American imperial interests in the Pacific and the Caribbean. But history unfolds in unpredictable ways.

In 1914 a spark ignited the powder keg of ethnic tensions in the Balkans. Soon, much of Europe was in flames. As the armies of the major powers became bogged down in a bloody stalemate, nonbelligerent nations were drawn into the conflagration. Woodrow Wilson, who had campaigned as a peace candidate, later called on the United States to go to war. Eventually he embraced it with an almost religious zeal. He recruited workers, farmers, financiers, manufacturers, minorities, and women to help in the war effort. He stamped out dissent. He also sought to take advantage of the transformations wrought by the war to promote various reforms—including the creation of an international body to mediate future conflicts. The tragedy of the Wilson years was that none of it turned out quite as he had imagined.

Wilson's "Moral" Diplomacy

Wilson did not lead the nation to war; both he and the nation stumbled into it without meaning to. Part of the reason was that Wilson's foreign relations, though well-intentioned, were often confused. He knew that the United States had no wish to injure any foreign state and assumed that all nations would recognize this fact and cooperate. Like nineteenth-century Christian missionaries, he wanted to spread the gospel of American democracy, to lift and enlighten the unfortunate and the ignorant—but in his own way.

Wilson set out to raise the moral tone of American foreign policy by denouncing dollar diplomacy. To seek special economic concessions in Latin America was "unfair" and "degrading." The United States would deal with Latin American nations "upon terms of equality and honor."

Yet Wilson sometimes failed to live up to his promises. Because of the strategic importance of the Panama Canal, he was unwilling to tolerate "unrest" anywhere in the Caribbean. Within months of his inauguration he was pursuing the same tactics employed by Roosevelt and Taft. The Bryan-Chamorro Treaty of 1914, which gave the United States an option to build a canal across Nicaragua, made that country virtually an American protectorate and served to maintain in power an unpopular dictator, Adolfo Díaz.

A much more serious example of missionary diplomacy occurred in Mexico. In 1911 a liberal coalition overthrew the dictator Porfirio Díaz, who had been exploiting the resources and people of Mexico for the benefit of a small class of wealthy landowners, clerics, and military men since the 1870s. Francisco Madero became president.

Perhaps inspired by progressive reforms in the United States, Madero proposed a liberal constitution for Mexico. But British oil magnates, who controlled most of Mexico's chief export, conspired with Victoriano Huerta, a general in Madero's army. In 1913 Huerta assassinated Madero and seized power. Britain promptly recognized Huerta's government.

The American ambassador urged Wilson to do so too, but he refused. His sympathies were with the government of Madero, whose murder had horrified him. "I will not recognize a government of butchers," he said. Wilson instead brought enormous pressure to bear against Huerta. He demanded that Huerta hold free elections as the price of American mediation in the continuing civil war. Huerta refused. The tense situation exploded in April 1914, when a small party of American sailors was arrested in the port of Tampico, Mexico. Wilson used the affair as an excuse to send troops into Mexico.

The invasion took place at Veracruz, where Winfield Scott had launched the

In 1911, Francisco Madero overthrew Mexican dictator Porfirio Diaz and established a constitutional government.

assault on Mexico City in 1847. Instead of surrendering the city, the Mexicans resisted, suffering 400 casualties before falling back. This bloodshed caused dismay throughout Latin America. Huerta, hard-pressed by Mexican opponents, fled from power.

Wilson now made a monumental blunder. He threw his support to Francisco "Pancho" Villa, one of Huerta's generals. But Villa was little more than an ambitious bandit whose only objective was personal power. In October 1915, realizing his error, Wilson abandoned Villa and backed another Mexican rebel, who drove Villa to the northern border of Mexico. In 1916 Villa stopped a train in northern Mexico and killed sixteen American passengers in cold blood. Then he crossed into New Mexico and burned the town of Columbus, killing nineteen.

Having learned the perils of intervening in Mexican politics, Wilson would have preferred to bear even this assault in silence; but public opinion forced him to send American troops under General John J. Pershing across the border in pursuit of Villa.

Villa proved impossible to catch. Cleverly he drew Pershing deeper and deeper into Mexico, which challenged Mexican sovereignty. Several clashes occurred between Pershing's men and Mexican regulars, and for a brief period in June 1916 war seemed imminent. Wilson now acted bravely and wisely. Early in 1917 he recalled Pershing's force, leaving the Mexicans to work out their own destiny.

Missionary diplomacy in Mexico had produced mixed, but in the long run beneficial, results. His bungling bred anti-Americanism in Mexico; but his opposition to Huerta strengthened the real revolutionaries, enabling the constitutionalists to consolidate power.

Europe Explodes in War

On June 28, 1914, in the Austro-Hungarian provincial capital of Sarajevo, Gavrilo Princip, a young student, assassinated the Archduke Franz Ferdinand, heir to the imperial throne. Princip was a member of the Black Hand, a Serbian terrorist organization. He was seeking to further the cause of Serbian nationalism. Instead his rash act precipitated a general European war. Within little more than a month, following a complex series of diplomatic challenges and responses, two great coalitions, the **Central Powers** (chiefly Germany, Austria-Hungary, and Ottoman Turkey) and the **Allied Powers** (chiefly Great Britain, France, and Russia), were locked in a brutal struggle that brought one era in world history to a close and inaugurated another.

Watch the Video
The outbreak of WWI at myhistorylab.com

The outbreak of this Great War caught Americans psychologically unprepared; few understood its significance. President Wilson promptly issued a proclamation of neutrality and asked the nation to be "impartial in thought." The almost unanimous reaction of Americans, aside from dismay, was that the conflict did not concern them.

Although most Americans hoped to keep out of the war, nearly everyone was partial to one side or the other. People of German or Austrian descent, about 8 million in number, and the nation's 4.5 million Irish Americans, motivated chiefly by hatred of the British, sympathized with the Central Powers. The majority of the people, however, influenced by bonds of language and culture, preferred an Allied victory, and when the Germans launched a mighty assault across neutral Belgium in an effort to outflank the French armies, many Americans were outraged.

As the war progressed, the Allies—especially Britain—cleverly exploited American prejudices by publishing exaggerated tales of German atrocities against Belgian civilians. A supposedly impartial study of these charges by the widely respected James Bryce, author of *The American Commonwealth*, portrayed the Germans as ruthless barbarians. The Germans also conducted a propaganda campaign in the United States, but they labored under severe handicaps and won few converts.

Freedom of the Seas

Propaganda did not basically alter American attitudes; far more important were questions arising out of trade and commerce. Under international law, neutrals could trade freely with any belligerent. Americans were prepared to do so, but because the British fleet dominated the North Atlantic, they could not. The situation was similar to the one that had prevailed during the Napoleonic Wars. The British declared nearly all commodities, even foodstuffs, to be contraband of war. They forced neutral merchant ships into British or French ports in order to search them for goods headed for the enemy. Many cargoes were confiscated, often without payment. American firms that traded with the Central Powers were "blacklisted," which meant that no British subject could deal with them. When Americans protested, the British answered that in a battle for survival, they dared not adhere to old-fashioned rules of international law.

Had the United States insisted that Great Britain abandon these "illegal" practices, as the Germans demanded, no doubt it could have had its way. The British foreign secretary, Sir Edward Grey, later admitted, "The ill-will of the United States meant certain defeat. The object of diplomacy, therefore, was to secure the maximum of blockade that could be enforced without a rupture with the United States." It is ironic that an embargo, which failed so ignominiously in Jefferson's day, would have been almost instantly effective if applied at any time after 1914, for American supplies were vital to the Allies.

Wilson faced a dilemma. To allow the British to make the rules meant siding against the Central Powers. Yet to insist on the old rules meant siding against the Allies because that would have deprived them of much of the value of their naval superiority. *Nothing* the United States might do would be truly impartial.

The immense expansion of American trade with the Allies made an embargo unthinkable. While commerce with the Central Powers fell to a trickle, that with the Allies soared from $825 million in 1914 to over $3.2 billion in 1916. An attempt to limit this commerce would have raised a storm; to have eliminated it would have caused a catastrophe. Munitions makers and other businessmen did not want the United States to enter the war. Neutrality suited their purposes admirably.

Britain and France soon exhausted their ready cash, and by early 1917 they had borrowed well over $2 billion. Although these loans violated no principle of international law, they fastened the United States more closely to the Allies' cause.

During the first months of the Great War, the Germans were not especially concerned about neutral trade or American goods because they expected to crush the Allied armies quickly. When their first swift thrust into France was blunted along the Marne River, only twenty miles from Paris, and the war became a bloody stalemate, they began to challenge the Allies' control of the seas. Unwilling to risk their battleships and cruisers against the much larger British fleet, they resorted to a new weapon, the submarine, commonly known as the U-boat (for *Unterseeboot*). German submarines played a role in World War I not unlike that of American privateers in the Revolution and the War of 1812: They ranged the seas stealthily in search of merchant ships. However, submarines could not operate under the ordinary rules of war, which required that a raider stop its prey, examine its papers and cargo, and give the crew

and passengers time to get off in lifeboats before sending it to the bottom. U-boats when surfaced were vulnerable to the deck guns that many merchant ships carried; they could even be sunk by ramming, once they had stopped and put out a boarding party. Therefore, they commonly launched their torpedoes from below the surface without warning, often resulting in a heavy loss of life.

In February 1915 the Germans declared the waters surrounding the British Isles a zone of war and announced that they would sink without warning all enemy merchant ships encountered in the area. Since Allied vessels sometimes flew neutral flags to disguise their identity, neutral ships entering the zone would do so at their own risk. This statement was largely bluff, for the Germans had only a handful of submarines at sea; but they were feverishly building more.

Wilson—perhaps too hurriedly, considering the importance of the question—warned the Germans that he would hold them to "strict accountability" for any loss of American life or property resulting from violations of "acknowledged [neutral] rights on the high seas." He did not distinguish clearly between losses incurred through the destruction of *American* ships and those resulting from the sinking of other vessels. If he meant to hold the Germans responsible for injuries to Americans on *belligerent* vessels, he was changing international law as arbitrarily as the Germans were. Secretary of State Bryan, who opposed Wilson vigorously on this point, stood on sound legal ground when he said, "A ship carrying contraband should not rely upon passengers to protect her from attack—it would be like putting women and children in front of an army."

Correct or not, Wilson's position reflected the attitude of most Americans. It seemed barbaric to them that defenseless civilians should be killed without warning; Americans refused to surrender their "rights" as neutrals to cross the North Atlantic on any ship they wished. The depth of their feeling was demonstrated when, on May 7, 1915, the submarine *U–20* sank the British liner *Lusitania* off the Irish coast. This caused a profound and emotional reaction in the United States. The sinking of the *Lusitania* evoked the sinking of HMS *Titanic* three years earlier, after it had struck an iceberg in

NOTICE!

TRAVELLERS intending to embark on the Atlantic voyage are reminded that a state of war exists between Germany and her allies and Great Britain and her allies; that the zone of war includes the waters adjacent to the British Isles; that, in accordance with formal notice given by the Imperial German Government, vessels flying the flag of Great Britain, or of any of her allies, are liable to destruction in those waters and that travellers sailing in the war zone on ships of Great Britain or her allies do so at their own risk.

IMPERIAL GERMAN EMBASSY
WASHINGTON, D. C., APRIL 22, 1915.

Three weeks before the *Lusitania* was torpedoed, this notice appeared in the classified sections of Washington newspapers.

Titanic

James Cameron's *Titanic* (1997) was a block-buster. He made audiences feel what it was like to be on the ship. What sent a shiver down the spine was the knowledge that real people had experienced what was being depicted on the screen.

Cameron well understood the audience's craving to relive a true story. The movie opens with footage of the actual HMS *Titanic* on the floor of the Atlantic, fish gliding silently through its barnacle-encrusted wreckage. Cameron also spent scores of millions of dollars devising computer-enhanced techniques to ensure that his *Titanic* looked like the one that went down in the North Atlantic on the night of April 14–15, 1912.

But Cameron's *Titanic* was more than a disaster movie. It was also the story of two young people who fall in love. The romance begins when Jack (Leonardo DiCaprio), a struggling artist, spots Rose (Kate Winslet), a wealthy socialite, climbing over the railing and peering despondently into the water below. Obliged to marry a contemptuous (and contemptible) snob, she is miserable. Jack, from a lower deck, scrambles up and persuades her to forgo the plunge.

As a reward for saving Rose, Jack is invited to dine with Rose's table. At dinner, Rose appraises Jack more carefully—and is impressed. He looks good in a tuxedo, displays plenty of moxie, and possesses artistic talent ("Jack, you see things!").

When the ship has its close encounter of the icy kind, Jack—young, vital, alive—perishes in the frigid waters. But he has imparted to Rose a gift of love, and thus of life. This tale of young lovers, held apart by society, is a nautical "Romeo and Juliet," a brief, pure instant of love, tragically ended by death.

If Cameron's *Titanic* is a love story for the ages, it was also frozen in a particular place and in a particular time. Much as Cameron spent millions to show the ship as it really was, he took similar pains to give a convincing rendering of New York society, especially its clothing, silverware, and social conventions.

Of the latter, the most significant for the story are the elaborate rituals of Victorian courtship. Rose seeks to break free from her impending marriage partly because she despises her fiancé, but also because marriage to him constitutes the final, irreversible step into the gilded cage of a society lady. Jack's presence at dinner with the "best" of society underscores the shallow materialism of this upper crust and its preoccupation with wealth, its absurd rules of etiquette, and its repressive attitudes toward sexuality. Viewers of the movie, looking through Rose's eyes, may wonder how such rituals ever came to be.

Some had existed for centuries. The idealization of courtly love and pure womanhood was a commonplace of medieval literature. In the early nineteenth century novelist Jane Austen described the subtle interplay of money and romance in England. But the rituals of New York society in the Gilded Age were characterized by sumptuous and public displays of wealth—glittering balls and extravagant "Grand Tours" of Europe.

This new mode of courtship was largely the creation of Mrs. John Jacob Astor, wife of one of New York's wealthiest business-men, and her friends. After the Civil War, industrialization and urbanization were generating new wealth and destroying the old at a dizzying pace. While prominent businessmen and investment bankers were devising institutions to impose order on this creative industrial chaos, their wives were regulating its social elite. They endeavored to determine who should be admitted to New York's "best" families—and who should not. They concluded that it was not enough to be rich; the elite of the nation must also adhere to high standards of etiquette and decorum. Society women possessed immense power.

Leonardo DiCaprio and Kate Winslet as lovers on the *Titanic*.

Although the system was created and supervised by mature women, it demanded the compliance of adolescent girls. The process began when a wealthy mother took her daughter on a round of visits to society women, to whom they would present their "calling cards." If mother and daughter were judged suitable, they would be invited in for tea; if the girl behaved with decorum (and if her father's assets proved sound), she would be invited to balls and other formal events. At or near her sixteenth birthday, her parents would hold a ball in her honor—in New York the event usually took place at Delmonico's restaurant—marking her "debut" into society. She wore a white gown symbolizing her virginity. A male relative presented her formally to the prominent women. Now she could accept male suitors from "society."

This highly stylized—almost tribal—ritual brought young women to the threshold of womanhood. Marriage awaited beyond the door. Many eagerly anticipated the acquisition of adult status and the social power it entailed. Others regarded this rite with terror. (Novelist Edith Wharton remembered her debut as a "long cold agony of shyness.") In the early twentieth century, some young women began to rebel. Elsie Clews, daughter of a Wall Street banker, refused to wear corsets. When her mother wasn't looking, she took off her veil and white gloves. She subsequently scandalized Newport—the fashionable Rhode Island summer resort for society's wealthy—by going swimming with a young man without a chaperone (but not without a bathing suit).

To her mother's dismay, Clews delayed marriage and went to Barnard College; eventually she became a respected anthropologist (Elsie Clews Parsons).

Kate Winslet's "Rose" was, like Elsie Clews, a prematurely "modern" woman. But Clews dispensed with the rituals of courtship, not its substance. Even in the waning years of the Victorian era, few wealthy young women succumbed to impoverished men, however earnest and appealing.

Victorian courtship was necessarily protracted. Young women did not unburden themselves to strangers; and even to friends, especially of the opposite sex, the process of revealing one's inner feelings unfolded slowly, often after a series of tests and trials. One person's tentative disclosure invited a reciprocal response. Letters and diaries show that, over time, these personal revelations often led to sexual intimacies. Nowadays many people regard Victorian marriages as unfeeling and stiff, but many Victorians maintained that their personal intimacies were the more delicious for having been long delayed.

Cameron's *Titanic* looks like the past; but the heart of the movie is Jack and Rose's whirlwind romance. While Rose's story addresses some of the anxieties of young society women, it more closely resembles the courtship patterns of Hollywood today than the experiences of young people at the beginning of the last century.

Questions for Discussion
- Jack and Rose "hooked up," to use modern slang. Why was such behavior improbable among young women of wealthy families in the late nineteenth century?
- What other behaviors in the film seem anachronistic?

The *Titanic* carried only twenty lifeboats, a reason why so many perished in 1912. The *Lusitania* (above) carried forty-eight lifeboats, but it sank so quickly that many went unused.

the northern Atlantic; first-person accounts rendered the tragedy all the more vivid to Americans. When it was learned that nearly 1,200 persons, including 128 Americans, lost their lives when the *Lusitania* went down (nearly as many as had perished on the *Titanic*), Americans were outraged. (For more on the *Titanic*, see Re-Viewing the Past, pp. 606–607.)

Wilson demanded that Germany disavow the sinking, indemnify the victims, and promise to stop attacking passenger vessels. When the Germans quibbled about these points, he responded with further diplomatic correspondence rather than with an ultimatum.

In one sense this was sound policy. The Germans pointed out that they had published warnings in American newspapers saying they considered the *Lusitania* subject to attack, that the liner was carrying munitions, and that on past voyages it had flown the American flag to deceive German U-boat captains. However, after dragging the controversy out for nearly a year, Germany apologized and agreed to pay an indemnity. After the torpedoing of the French channel steamer *Sussex* in March 1916 had produced another stiff American protest, the Germans at last promised, in the *Sussex* pledge, to stop sinking merchant ships without warning.

Theodore Roosevelt urged Wilson to commit the United States to war with Germany; Wilson's refusal to do so incensed him. In November 1915 Wilson, in a belated nod to such criticisms, pressed for increased military and naval expenditures.

The Election of 1916

Wilson had won the presidency in 1912 only because the Republican party had split in two. In late 1915 he sought to broaden his support by winning over the progressives. In January 1916 he appointed Louis D. Brandeis to the Supreme Court. In addition to being an advanced progressive, Brandeis was the first Jewish Justice appointed to the Court. Wilson's action won him many friends among people who favored fair treatment for minority groups. In July Wilson bid for the farm vote by signing the Farm Loan Act to provide low-cost loans based on agricultural credit. Shortly thereafter, he approved the Keating-Owen Child Labor Act barring goods manufactured by the labor of children under 16 from interstate commerce, and a workers' compensation act for federal employees. He persuaded Congress to pass the Adamson Act, establishing an eight-hour day for railroad workers, and he modified his position on the tariff by approving the creation of a tariff commission.

Each of these actions represented a sharp reversal. In 1913 Wilson had considered Brandeis too radical even for a Cabinet post. The new farm, labor, and tariff laws were all examples of the kind of "class legislation" he had refused to countenance in 1913 and 1914. Wilson was putting into effect much of the progressive platform of 1912. Although the progressive convention came out for the Republican nominee, Associate Justice Charles Evans Hughes, who had compiled a record as a progressive governor of New York, many other progressives supported Wilson.

The key issue in the campaign was American policy toward the warring powers. Wilson intended to stress preparedness, which he was now wholeheartedly supporting. However, during the Democratic convention, the delegates shook the hall with cheers whenever orators referred to the president's success in keeping the country out of the war. "He Kept Us Out of War" became the Democratic slogan.

The combination of progressivism and the peace issue placed the Democrats on substantially equal terms with the Republicans. In the end, personal factors probably tipped the balance. Hughes was very stiff and an ineffective speaker; he offended a number of important politicians, especially in crucial California, where he inadvertently snubbed the popular progressive governor, Hiram Johnson; and he equivocated on a number of issues. Nevertheless, on election night he appeared to have won, having carried nearly all the East and Midwest. Late returns gave Wilson California, however, and with it victory by the narrow margin of 277 to 254 in the Electoral College. He led Hughes in the popular vote, 9.1 million to 8.5 million.

The Road to War

Wilson's own feelings were more genuinely neutral than at any other time during the war, for the Germans had stopped sinking merchant ships without warning and the British had irritated him repeatedly by their arbitrary restrictions on neutral trade. He drafted a note to the belligerents asking them to state the terms on which they would agree to lay down their arms. Unless the fighting ended soon, he warned, neutrals and belligerents alike would be so ruined that peace would be meaningless.

When neither side responded encouragingly, Wilson, on January 22, 1917, delivered a moving speech aimed at "the people of the countries now at war" more than at their governments. Any settlement imposed by a victor, he declared, would breed hatred and more wars. There must be "peace without victory," based on the principles that all nations were equal and that every nationality should determine its own form of government. He mentioned, albeit vaguely, disarmament and freedom of the seas, and he suggested the creation of some kind of international organization to preserve world peace. This noble appeal met a tragic fate. The Germans had already decided to renounce the Sussex pledge and unleash their submarines against all vessels headed for Allied ports. After February 1, any ship in the war zone would be attacked without warning. Possessed now of more than 100 U-boats, the German military leaders had convinced themselves that they could starve the British people into submission and reduce the Allied armies to impotence by cutting off the flow of American supplies. The United States would probably declare war, but the Germans believed that they could overwhelm the Allies before the Americans could get to the battlefields in force. In 1917, after the German military leaders had made this decision, events moved relentlessly, almost uninfluenced by the actors who presumably controlled the fate of the world:

Watch the Video

American entry into WWI at **myhistorylab.com**

> *February 3: Housatonic* is torpedoed. Wilson announces to Congress that he has severed diplomatic relations with Germany.
>
> *February 24:* Walter Hines Page, United States ambassador to Great Britain, transmits to the State Department an intercepted German dispatch (the "Zimmermann telegram") revealing that Germany has proposed a secret alliance with Mexico; Mexico will receive, in the event of war with the United States, "the lost territory in Texas, New Mexico, and Arizona."
>
> *February 25:* Cunard liner *Laconia* is torpedoed; two American women perish.
>
> *February 26:* Wilson asks Congress for authority to arm American merchant ships.
>
> *March 1:* Zimmermann telegram is released to the press.
>
> *March 4:* President Wilson takes oath of office, beginning his second term.
>
> *March 9:* Wilson, acting under his executive powers, orders the arming of American merchantmen.
>
> *March 12:* Revolutionary provisional government is established in Russia. *Algonquin* is torpedoed.
>
> *March 15:* Czar Nicholas II of Russia abdicates.
>
> *March 16:* City of Memphis, *Illinois*, and *Vigilancia* are torpedoed.
>
> *March 21: New York World*, a leading Democratic newspaper, calls for declaration of war on Germany. Wilson summons Congress to convene in a special session on April 2.
>
> *March 25:* Wilson calls up the National Guard.
>
> *April 2:* Wilson asks Congress to declare war. Germany is guilty of "throwing to the winds all scruples of humanity," he says. America must fight, not to conquer, but for "peace and justice. . . . The world must be made safe for democracy."
>
> *April 4, 6:* Congress declares war—the vote, 82–6 in the Senate, 373–50 in the House.

Read the Document

United States Declaration of War (1917) at **myhistorylab.com**

Read the Document

President Wilson's War Message to Congress (1917) at **myhistorylab.com**

The bare record conceals Wilson's agonizing search for an honorable alternative to war. To admit that Germany posed a threat to the United States meant confessing that interventionists had been right all along. To go to war meant, besides sending innocent Americans to their deaths, allowing "the spirit of ruthless brutality [to] enter into the very fibre of our national life."

The president's Presbyterian conscience tortured him. He lost sleep, appeared gray and drawn. In the end Wilson could salve his conscience only by giving intervention an idealistic purpose: the war had become a threat to humanity. Unless the United States threw its weight into the balance, Western civilization itself might be destroyed.

Mobilizing the Economy

America's entry into the Great War determined its outcome. The Allies were running out of money and supplies; their troops, decimated by nearly three years in the trenches, were exhausted, disheartened, and rebellious. In February and March 1917, U-boats sent over a million tons of Allied shipping to the bottom of the Atlantic. The outbreak of the Russian Revolution in March 1917, at first lifting the spirits of the Western democracies, led to the Bolshevik takeover under Lenin. The Russian armies collapsed; by December 1917 Russia was out of the war and the Germans were moving masses of men and equipment from the eastern front to France. Without the aid of the United States, the Allies would likely have sued for peace according to terms dictated from Berlin. Instead American men and supplies helped contain the Germans' last drives and then push them back to final defeat.

It was a close thing, for the United States entered the war little better prepared to fight than it had been in 1898. The conversion of American industry to war production had to be carried out without prearrangement. Confusion and waste resulted. The hurriedly designed shipbuilding program was an almost total fiasco. The gigantic Hog Island yard in Maine, which employed at its peak over 34,000 workers, completed its first vessel only after the war ended. Airplane, tank, and artillery construction programs developed too slowly to affect the war. The big guns that backed up American soldiers in 1918 were made in France and Great Britain; of the 8.8 million rounds of artillery ammunition fired by American troops, a mere 8,000 were manufactured in the United States. Congress authorized the manufacture of 20,000 airplanes, but only a handful, mostly British-designed planes made in America, got to France.

The problem of mobilization was complicated. It took Congress six weeks of hot debate merely to decide on conscription. Only in September 1917, nearly six months after the declaration of war, did the first draftees reach the training camps, and it is hard to see how Wilson could have speeded this process. He wisely supported the professional soldiers, who insisted that he resist the appeals of politicians who wanted to raise volunteer units, even rejecting, at considerable political cost, Theodore Roosevelt's offer to raise an entire army division.

"Enlist"—a poster by Fred Spear, published in June 1915 by the Boston Committee of Public Safety— evoked the drowning deaths of women and children on the *Lusitania*.

Wilson was a forceful and inspiring war leader once he grasped what needed to be done. He displayed both determination and unfailing patience in the face of frustration and criticism. Raising an army was only a small part of the job. The Allies had to be supplied with food and munitions, and immense amounts of money had to be collected.

After several false starts, Wilson placed the task in the hands of the **War Industries Board (WIB)**. The board was given almost dictatorial power to allocate scarce materials, standardize production, fix prices, and coordinate American and Allied purchasing. Evaluating the mobilization effort raises interesting historical questions. The antitrust laws were suspended and producers were encouraged, even compelled, to cooperate with one another. Government regulation went far beyond what the New Nationalists had envisaged in 1912.

As for the New Freedom variety of laissez-faire, it had no place in a wartime economy. The nation's railroads, strained by immensely increased traffic, became progressively less efficient. A monumental tie-up in December and January 1917–1918 finally persuaded Wilson to appoint Secretary of the Treasury William G. McAdoo director-general of the railroads, with power to run the roads as a single system. McAdoo's Railroad Administration pooled all railroad equipment, centralized purchasing, standardized accounting practices, and raised wages and passenger rates.

Wilson accepted the kind of government-industry agreement that he had denounced in 1912. Prices were set by the WIB at levels that allowed large profits—U.S. Steel, for example, despite high taxes, cleared over half a billion dollars in two years. It is at least arguable that producers would have turned out just as much even if compelled to charge lower prices.

Mobilization required close cooperation between business and the military. However, the army, suspicious of civilian institutions, resisted cooperating with them. Wilson finally compelled the War Department to place officers on WIB committees, laying the foundation for what was later to be known as the "industrial-military complex," an alliance between business and military leaders.

The history of industrial mobilization was the history of the entire home-front effort in microcosm: Marvels were performed, but the task was so gigantic and unprecedented that a full year passed before an efficient system had been devised, and many unforeseen results occurred.

The problem of mobilizing agricultural resources was solved more quickly, and this was fortunate because in April 1917 the British had on hand only a six-week supply of food Wilson appointed as food administrator Herbert Hoover; Hoover, a mining engineer, had headed the Belgian Relief Commission earlier in the war. Acting under powers granted by the Lever Act of 1917, Hoover set the price of wheat at $2.20 a bushel in order to encourage production. He established a government corporation to purchase the entire American and Cuban sugar crops, which he then doled out to American and British refiners. To avoid rationing he organized a campaign to persuade consumers to conserve food voluntarily. One slogan ran "If U fast U beat U boats"; another, "Serve beans by all means."

Without subjecting its own citizens to serious inconvenience, the United States increased food exports from 12.3 million tons to 18.6 million tons. Farmers, of course, profited greatly. Their real income went up nearly 30 percent between 1915 and 1918.

Workers in Wartime

With the army siphoning so many men from the labor market and with immigration reduced to a trickle, unemployment disappeared and wages rose. Although the cost of living soared, imposing hardships on people with fixed incomes, the boom produced unprecedented opportunities.

Americans, always a mobile people, pulled up their roots in record numbers. Disadvantaged groups, especially African Americans, were particularly attracted by jobs in big-city factories. Early in the conflict, the government began regulating the wages and hours of workers building army camps and manufacturing uniforms. In April 1918 Wilson created the National War Labor Board, headed by former president Taft and Frank P. Walsh, a prominent lawyer, to settle labor disputes. The board considered more than 1,200 cases and prevented many strikes. The War Labor Policies Board, chaired by Felix Frankfurter of the Harvard Law School, set wages-and-hours standards for each major war industry. Since these were determined in consultation with employers and representatives of labor, they speeded the unionization of workers by compelling management, even in antiunion industries like steel, to deal with labor leaders. Union membership rose by 2.3 million during the war.

However, the wartime emergency roused the public against strikers. While he opposed strikes that impeded the war effort, Wilson set great store in preserving the individual worker's freedom of action. It would be "most unfortunate . . . to relax the laws by which safeguards have been thrown about labor," he said. "We must accomplish the results we desire by organized effort rather than compulsion."

Paying for the War

Wilson managed the task of financing the war effectively. The struggle cost the United States about $33.5 billion, not counting pensions and other postwar expenses. About $7 billion of this was lent to the Allies,[1] but since this money was spent largely in America, it contributed to the national prosperity.

Over two-thirds of the cost of the war was met by borrowing. Five Liberty and Victory Loan drives, spurred by advertising, parades, and other appeals to patriotism, persuaded people to open their purses. Industrialists, eager to instill in their employees a sense of personal involvement in the war effort, conducted campaigns in their plants. In addition to borrowing, the government collected about $10.5 billion in taxes during the war. A steeply graduated income tax took more than 75 percent of the incomes of the wealthiest citizens. A 65 percent excess-profits tax and a 25 percent inheritance tax were also enacted. Thus although many individuals made fortunes from the war, its cost was distributed far more equitably than during the Civil War.

Americans also contributed generously to philanthropic agencies engaged in war work. Most notable, perhaps, was the great 1918 drive of the United War Work Council, an interfaith religious group, which raised over $200 million mainly to finance recreational programs for the troops overseas.

---

[1]In 1914 Americans owed foreigners about $3.8 billion. By 1919 Americans were owed $12.5 billion by Europeans alone.

Propaganda and Civil Liberties

Wilson was preeminently a teacher and preacher, a specialist in the transmission of ideas and ideals. He excelled at mobilizing public opinion and inspiring Americans to work for the better world he hoped would emerge from the war. In April 1917 he created the Committee on Public Information (CPI), headed by the journalist George Creel. Soon 75,000 speakers were deluging the country with propaganda prepared by hundreds of CPI writers. They pictured the war as a crusade for freedom and democracy, the Germans as a bestial people bent on world domination.

A large majority of the nation supported the war enthusiastically. But thousands of persons—German Americans and Irish Americans, for example; people of pacifist leanings such as Jane Addams, the founder of Hull House; and some who thought both sides in the war were wrong—still opposed American involvement. Creel's committee and a number of unofficial "patriotic" groups allowed their enthusiasm for the conversion of the hesitant to become suppression of dissent. People who refused to buy war bonds were often exposed to public ridicule and even assault. Those with German names were persecuted without regard for their views; some school boards outlawed the teaching of the German language; sauerkraut was renamed "liberty cabbage." A cartoonist pictured Senator Robert La Follette, who had opposed entering the war, receiving an Iron Cross from the German militarists, and the faculty of his own University of Wisconsin voted to censure him.

◆◆◆—Read the Document

Buffington, *Friendly Words to the Foreign Born* at myhistorylab.com

Although Wilson spoke in defense of free speech, his actions opposed it. He signed the **Espionage Act** of 1917, which imposed fines of up to $10,000 and jail sentences ranging to twenty years on persons convicted of aiding the enemy or obstructing recruiting, and he authorized the postmaster general to ban from the mails any material that seemed treasonable or seditious.

In May 1918, again with Wilson's approval, Congress passed the **Sedition Act,** which made "saying anything" to discourage the purchase of war bonds a crime, with the proviso that investment counselors could still offer "bona fide and not disloyal advice" to clients. The law also made it illegal to "utter, print, write, or publish any disloyal, profane, scurrilous, or abusive language" about the government, the Constitution, or the uniform of the army or navy. Socialist periodicals such as The Masses were suppressed, and Eugene V. Debs, formerly a candidate for president, was sentenced to ten years in prison for making an anti-war speech. Ricardo Flores Magón, an anarchist, was sentenced to twenty

Eugene V. Debs ("Convict #9653") was imprisoned for speaking against the war. In 1920 he ran as the Socialist candidate for president from the Atlanta federal prison, receiving nearly a million votes.

Table 23.1   Suppression of Liberties during World War I

Federal Action	Year	Consequence
Espionage Act	1917	Prohibited words or actions that would aid the enemy or obstruct recruiting efforts
Sedition Act	1918	Prohibited people from "saying anything" that might discourage purchase of war bonds or otherwise undermine the federal government or the Constitution
Schenck v. United States	1919	Supreme Court upheld limitations on free speech during times of "clear and present danger" to the nation

years in jail for publishing a statement criticizing Wilson's Mexican policy, an issue that had nothing to do with the war.

These laws went far beyond what was necessary to protect the national interest. Citizens were jailed for suggesting that the draft law was unconstitutional and for criticizing private organizations like the Red Cross and the YMCA.

The Supreme Court upheld the constitutionality of the Espionage Act in *Schenck v. United States* (1919), a case involving a man who had mailed circulars to draftees urging them to refuse to report for induction into the army. Free speech has its limits, Justice Oliver Wendell Holmes, Jr., explained. When there is a "clear and present danger" that a particular statement would threaten the national interest, it can be repressed by law. In peacetime Schenck's circulars would be permissible, but not in time of war.

The "clear and present danger" doctrine did not prevent judges and juries from interpreting the espionage and sedition acts broadly, and although in many instances higher courts overturned their decisions, this usually did not occur until after the war. The wartime repression far exceeded anything that happened in Great Britain and France. In 1916 the French novelist Henri Barbusse published *Le Feu (Under Fire)*, a graphic account of the horrors and purposelessness of trench warfare. In one chapter Barbusse described a pilot flying over the trenches on a Sunday, observing French and German soldiers at Mass in the open fields, each worshiping the same God. Yet *Le Feu* circulated freely in France and even won the coveted Prix Goncourt.

Wartime Reforms

The American mobilization experience was part and product of the Progressive Era. Many progressives believed that the war was creating the sense of common purpose that would stimulate the people to act unselfishly to benefit the poor and to eradicate social evils. Patriotism and public service seemed at last united. Secretary of War Newton D. Baker, a prewar urban reformer, expressed this attitude in supporting a federal child labor law: "We cannot afford, when we are losing boys in France, to lose children in the United States."

Men and women of this sort worked for a dozen causes only remotely related to the war effort. The women's suffrage movement was brought to fruition, as was the campaign against alcohol. Both the Eighteenth Amendment, outlawing alcoholic beverages, and the Nineteenth, giving women the vote, were adopted at least in part because of the war. Reformers began to talk about health insurance. The progressive campaign against prostitution and venereal disease gained strength, winning the enthusiastic support both of persons worried about inexperienced local girls being seduced by the soldiers and of those concerned lest prostitutes lead innocent soldiers astray. One of the latter type claimed to have persuaded "over 1,000 fallen women" to promise not to go near any army camps.

The effort to wipe out prostitution around military installations was a cause of some misunderstanding with the Allies, who provided licensed facilities for their troops as a matter of course. When the premier of France offered to supply prostitutes for American units in his country, Secretary Baker is said to have remarked, "For God's sake . . . don't show this to the President or he'll stop the war." Apparently Baker had a rather peculiar sense of humor. After a tour of the front in France, he assured an American women's group that life in the trenches was "far less uncomfortable" than he had thought and that not a single American doughboy was "living a life which he would not be willing to have [his] mother see him live."

Women and Blacks in Wartime

Although a number of prominent feminists were pacifists, most supported the war enthusiastically, moved by patriotism and the belief that opposition to the war would doom their hopes of gaining the vote. They also expected that the war would open up many kinds of high-paying jobs to women. To some extent it did; about a million women replaced men in uniform, but the numbers actually engaged in war industries

were small (about 6,000 found jobs making airplanes, for example), and the gains were fleeting. When the war ended, most women who were engaged in industrial work either left their jobs voluntarily or were fired to make room for returning veterans. Some women went overseas as nurses, and a few served as ambulance drivers and YMCA workers.

Most unions were unsympathetic to the idea of enrolling women, and the government did little to encourage women to do more for the war effort than prepare bandages, knit warm clothing for soldiers, participate in food conservation programs, and encourage people to buy war bonds. The final report of another wartime agency, issued in 1919, admitted that

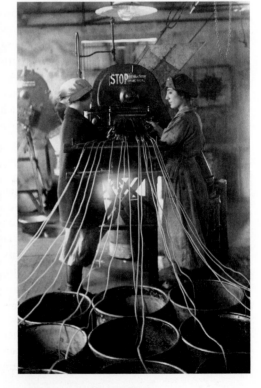

Women workers at the Dupont factory in Old Hickory, Tennessee, in 1917, form smokeless gunpowder into long strips, which will then be cut for use in artillery shells and other armaments.

few women war workers had been paid as much as men and that women had been promoted more slowly than men, were not accepted by unions, and were discharged promptly when the war ended.

The wartime "great migration" of southern blacks to northern cities where jobs were available brought them important economic benefits. Between 1870 and 1890 only about 80,000 blacks moved to northern cities. Compared with the influx from Europe and from northern farms, this number was inconsequential. The black proportion of the population of New York City, for example, fell from over 10 percent in 1800 to under 2 percent in 1900.

Watch the Video
The Great Migration at myhistorylab.com

Around the turn of the century, as the first postslavery generation reached maturity and as southern repression increased, the northward movement quickened—about 200,000 blacks migrated between 1890 and 1910. Then, after 1914, the war boom drew blacks north in a flood. Agents of northern manufacturers flocked into the cotton belt to recruit them in wholesale lots. Half a million made the move between 1914 and 1919. The African American population of New York City rose from 92,000 to 152,000; that of Chicago from 44,000 to 109,000; and that of Detroit from 5,700 to 41,000.

Life for the newcomers was difficult; many whites resented them; workers feared them as potential strikebreakers yet refused to admit them into their unions. In East St. Louis, Illinois, where employers had brought in large numbers of blacks in an attempt to discourage local unions from striking for higher wages, a bloody riot erupted during the summer of 1917 in which nine whites and an undetermined number of blacks were killed. As in peacetime, the Wilson administration was at worst antagonistic and at best indifferent to blacks' needs and aspirations.

Nevertheless, the blacks who moved north during the war were, as a group, infinitely better off than those they left behind. Many earned good wages and were accorded at least some human rights. They were not treated by the whites as equals, or even in most cases entirely fairly, but they could vote, send their children to decent schools, and within reasonable limits do and say what they pleased without fear of humiliation or physical attack.

There were two black regiments in the regular army and a number of black national guard units when the war began, and once these outfits were brought up to combat strength, no more volunteers were accepted. At first no blacks were conscripted; Southerners in particular found the thought of giving large numbers of guns to blacks and teaching them how to use them most disturbing. However, blacks were soon drafted, and once they were, a larger proportion of them were taken than whites. One Georgia draft board exempted more than 500 of 815 white registrants and only 6 of the 202 blacks in its jurisdiction before its members were relieved of their duties. After a riot in Texas in which black soldiers killed seventeen white civilians, black recruits were dispersed among many camps for training to lessen the possibility of trouble.

In the military service, all blacks were placed in segregated units. Only a handful were commissioned as officers. Despite the valor displayed by black soldiers in the Civil War and the large role they played in the Spanish-American War, where five blacks had won the Congressional Medal of Honor, most even those sent overseas, were assigned to labor battalions working as stevedores and common laborers. But many fought and died for their country. Altogether about 200,000 served overseas.

W. E. B. Du Bois supported the war wholeheartedly. He praised Wilson for making, at last, a strong statement against lynching, which had increased to a shocking extent during the previous decade. He even went along with the fact that the handful of black officer candidates were trained in a segregated camp. "Let us," he wrote in the Crisis, "while the war lasts, forget our special grievances and close ranks shoulder to shoulder with our fellow citizens and the allied nations that are fighting for democracy."

Many blacks condemned Du Bois's accommodationism, but most saw the war as an opportunity to demonstrate their patriotism and prove their worth. For the moment the prevailing mood was one of optimism. If winning the war would make the world safe for democracy, surely blacks in the United States would be better off when it was won. Whether or not this turned out to be so was (and still is) a matter of opinion.

Americans: To the Trenches and Over the Top

All activity on the home front had one ultimate objective: defeating the Central Powers on the battlefield. This was accomplished. The navy performed with special distinction. In April 1917, German submarines sank more than 870,000 tons of Allied shipping; after April 1918, monthly losses never reached 300,000 tons. The decision to send merchant ships across the Atlantic in convoys screened by destroyers made the reduction possible. Checking the U-boats was essential because of the need to transport American troops to Europe. Slightly more than 2 million soldiers made the voyage safely. Those who crossed on fast ocean liners were in little danger as long as the vessel maintained high speed and followed a zigzag course, a lesson learned from the *Lusitania*, whose

The Western Front, 1918 The Germans launched their great offensive in the spring and summer of 1918 with the goal of taking Paris. American troops helped hold the line at Château-Thierry and Belleau Woods. Several months later, a half million American soldiers participated in the counteroffensive that drove the Germans back to the Meuse River.

captain had neglected both precautions. Those who traveled on slower troop transports benefited from the protection of destroyers and also from the fact that the Germans concentrated on attacking supply ships. They continued to believe that inexperienced American soldiers would not be a major factor in the war.

The first units of the American Expeditionary Force (AEF), elements of the regular army commanded by General John J. Pershing, reached Paris on Independence Day, 1917. They took up positions on the front near Verdun in October. Not until the spring of 1918, however, did the "doughboys" play a significant role in the fighting, though their mere presence boosted French and British morale.

In March 1918 the Germans launched a great spring offensive, their armies strengthened by thousands of veterans who had been freed from the eastern front by the collapse of Russia. By late May they had reached a point on the Marne River near the town of Château-Thierry, only fifty miles from Paris. Early in June the AEF fought its first major engagements, driving the Germans back from Château-Thierry and Belleau Wood.

In this fighting only about 27,500 Americans saw action, and they suffered appalling losses. Nevertheless, when the Germans advanced again in the direction of the Marne in mid-July, 85,000 Americans were in the lines that withstood their charge. Then, in the major turning point of the war, the Allied armies counterattacked. Some 270,000 Americans participated, helping to flatten the German bulge between Reims and Soissons. By late August the American First Army, 500,000 strong, was poised before the Saint-Mihiel bulge, a deep extension of the German lines southeast of Verdun. On September 12 this army, buttressed by French troops, struck and in two days wiped out the salient.

Late in September began the greatest American engagement of the war. No fewer than 1.2 million doughboys plunged into the Argonne Forest. For over a month of indescribable horror they inched ahead through the tangle of the Argonne and the formidable defenses of the Hindenburg line, while to the west, French and British armies staged similar drives. In this one offensive the AEF suffered 120,000 casualties. Finally, on November 1, they broke the German center and raced toward the vital Sedan-Mézières railroad. On November 11, with Allied armies advancing on all fronts, the Germans signed the armistice, ending the fighting.

Preparing for Peace

The fighting ended on November 11, 1918, but the shape of the postwar world remained to be determined. European society had been shaken to its foundations. Confusion reigned. People wanted peace yet burned for revenge. Millions faced starvation. Other millions were disillusioned by the seemingly purposeless sacrifices of four years of horrible war. Communism—to some an idealistic promise of human betterment, to others a commitment to rational economic and social planning, to still others a danger to individual freedom, toleration, and democracy—having conquered Russia, threatened to envelop Germany and much of the defunct Austro-Hungarian Empire, perhaps even the victorious Allies. How could stability be restored? How could victory be made worth its enormous cost?

Woodrow Wilson had grasped the significance of the war while most statesmen still thought that triumph on the battlefield would settle everything automatically. As early as January 1917 he had realized that victory would be wasted if the winners permitted themselves the luxury of vengeance. Such a policy would disrupt the balance of power and lead to economic and social chaos. The victors must build a better society, not punish those they believed had destroyed the old one.

In a speech to Congress on January 8, 1918, Wilson outlined a plan, known as the **Fourteen Points**, designed to make the world "fit and safe to live in." The peace treaty should be negotiated in full view of world opinion, not in secret. It should guarantee the freedom of the seas to all nations, in war as in peacetime. It should tear down barriers to international trade, provide for a drastic reduction of armaments, and establish a colonial system that would take proper account of the interests of the native peoples concerned. European boundaries should be redrawn so that no substantial group would have to live under a government not of its own choosing.

More specifically, captured Russian territory should be restored, Belgium evacuated, Alsace-Lorraine returned to France, the heterogeneous nationalities of Austria-Hungary accorded autonomy. Italy's frontiers should be adjusted "along clearly recognizable lines of nationality," the Balkans made free, Turkey divested of its subject peoples, and an independent Polish state (with access to the Baltic Sea) created. To oversee the new system, Wilson insisted, "a general association of nations must be formed under specific covenants for the purpose of affording mutual guarantees of political independence and territorial integrity to great and small states alike."

Wilson's Fourteen Points for a fair peace lifted the hopes of people everywhere. After the guns fell silent, however, the vagueness and inconsistencies in his list became apparent. Complete national self-determination was impossible in Europe; there were too many regions of mixed population for every group to be satisfied. Self-determination, like the war itself, also fostered the spirit of nationalism that Wilson's dream of international organization, a league of nations, was designed to de-emphasize. Furthermore, the Allies had made territorial commitments to one another in secret treaties that ran counter to the principle of self-determination, and they were not ready to give up all claims to Germany's colonies. Freedom of the seas in wartime posed another problem; the British flatly refused to accept the idea. In every Allied country, millions rejected the idea of a peace without indemnities. They expected to make the enemy pay for the war.

Wilson assumed that the practical benefits of his program would compel opponents to fall in line. He had the immense advantage of seeking nothing for his own country and the additional strength of being leader of the one important nation to emerge from the war richer and more powerful than it had been in 1914.

Yet this combination of altruism, idealism, and power was his undoing; it intensified his tendency to be overbearing and undermined his judgment. He had never found it easy to compromise. Now, believing that the fate of humanity hung on his actions, he was unyielding. Always a preacher, he became in his own mind a prophet—almost, one fears, a kind of god.

In the last weeks of the war Wilson proved to be a brilliant diplomat, first dangling the Fourteen Points before the German people to encourage them to overthrow Kaiser Wilhelm II and sue for an armistice, then sending Colonel House to Paris to persuade Allied leaders to accept the Fourteen Points as the basis for the peace. When the Allies raised objections, House made small concessions, but by hinting that the United States might make a separate peace with Germany, he forced them to agree. Under the armistice, Germany had to withdraw behind the Rhine River and surrender its submarines, together with quantities of munitions and other materials. In return it received the assurance of the Allies that the Wilsonian principles would prevail at the Paris peace conference.

Wilson then came to a daring decision: He would personally attend the conference as a member of the United States Peace Commission. This was a precedent-shattering step, for no president had ever left American territory while in office.

Wilson probably erred in going to Paris, but not because of the novelty or possible illegality of the act. By going, he was turning his back on obvious domestic problems. Western farmers believed that they had been discriminated against during the war, since wheat prices had been controlled while southern cotton had been allowed to rise unchecked from seven cents a pound in 1914 to thirty-five cents in 1919. The administration's drastic tax program had angered many businessmen. Labor, despite its gains, was restive in the face of reconversion to peacetime conditions.

Wilson had increased his political difficulties by making a partisan appeal for the election of a Democratic Congress in 1918. Republicans, who had in many instances supported his war program more loyally than the Democrats, considered the action a gross affront. The appeal failed; the Republicans won majorities in both houses. Wilson appeared to have been repudiated at home at the very moment that he set forth to represent the nation abroad. Most important, Wilson intended to break with the isolationist tradition and bring the United States into a league of nations. Such a revolutionary change would require explanation; he should have undertaken a major campaign to convince the American people of the wisdom of this step.

The Paris Peace Conference and the Versailles Treaty

Wilson arrived in Europe a world hero. When the conference settled down to its work, control quickly fell into the hands of the so-called Big Four: Wilson, Prime Minister David Lloyd George of Great Britain, Premier Georges Clemenceau of France, and Prime Minister Vittorio Orlando of Italy. Wilson stood out in this group but did not dominate it. His principal advantage in the negotiations was his untiring industry. He alone of the leaders tried to master all the complex details of the task.

The seventy-eight-year-old Clemenceau cared only for one thing: French security. He viewed Wilson cynically, saying that since mankind had been unable to keep God's Ten Commandments, it was unlikely to do better with Wilson's Fourteen Points. Lloyd George's approach was pragmatic and almost cavalier.

Europe before the Great War In 1914, five countries dominated Europe: the German Empire, France, Great Britain, Austria-Hungary, and Russia.

Europe after the Great War The Versailles Treaty and other postwar settlements punished the losers, especially Germany and Austria-Hungary, transferring their lands to newly-created nations in eastern Europe, such as Poland, Czechoslovakia, and Yugoslavia.

He sympathized with much that Wilson was trying to accomplish but found the president's frequent sermonettes about "right being more important than might, and justice being more eternal than force" incomprehensible. "If you want to succeed in politics," Lloyd George advised a British statesman, "you must keep your conscience well under control." Orlando, clever, cultured, a believer in international cooperation but inflexible where Italian national interests were concerned, was not the equal of his three colleagues in influence. He left the conference in a huff when they failed to meet all his demands.

The conference labored from January to May 1919 and finally brought forth the Versailles Treaty. American liberals whose hopes had soared at the thought of a peace based on the Fourteen Points found the document abysmally disappointing.

The peace settlements failed to carry out the principle of self-determination completely. They gave Italy a large section of the Austrian Tyrol, though the area contained 200,000 people who considered themselves Austrians. Other German-speaking groups were incorporated into the new states of Poland and Czechoslovakia.

The victors forced Germany to accept responsibility for having caused the war—an act of senseless vindictiveness as well as a gross oversimplification—and to sign a "blank check," agreeing to pay for all damage to civilian properties and even future pensions and other indirect war costs. This reparations bill, as finally determined, amounted to $33 billion. Instead of attacking imperialism, the treaty attacked German imperialism; instead of seeking a new international social order based on liberty and democracy, it created a great-power entente designed to crush Germany and to exclude Bolshevik Russia from the family of nations.

Wilson himself backtracked on his pledge to honor the right of self-determination. For centuries, most Arabs had lived under the Turkish rulers of the Ottoman Empire. When the Ottoman Empire joined Germany and Austria-Hungary in World War I, Arab nationalists looked to the Allies and eventually worked out a deal with Britain. In return for Arab military support against the Ottoman Empire and the Germans, Britain would endorse Arab independence after the war. Wilson seemingly concurred, for Point Twelve of his Fourteen Points called for the "autonomous development" of Arab peoples. But in 1917 the British issued the Balfour Declaration in support of "a national home" for the Jewish people in Palestine, land mostly occupied by Palestinian Arabs. How could Palestinian Arabs be granted independence if Palestine was to become the home of Jewish settlers?

In the postwar negotiations, Britain retreated from its earlier promise to the Arabs. Wilson, too, had second thoughts about granting the Arab peoples self-determination.

Ottoman Empire and the Arab World, 1914 In 1914, the Ottoman Empire, also known as Turkey, controlled much of the Arab world, stretching from the Persian Gulf to the Red Sea.

Secretary of State Lansing worried about the "danger of putting such ideas into the minds of certain races," particularly the "Mohammedans [Muslims] of Syria and Palestine." Wilson reluctantly deleted explicit references to self-determination from the postwar settlements. Rather than grant the Arab peoples independence, Britain and France themselves seized Arab lands that had been ruled by the Turks. This land grab was "legalized" through the device of a mandate to rule the region issued by the League of Nations.

Similarly, Ho Chi Minh, a young Vietnamese nationalist, was embittered by the failure at Versailles to deliver his people from French colonial rule. He decided to become a communist revolutionary. The repercussions of Arab and Vietnamese discontent, though far removed from American interests at the time, would be felt in full force much later.

To those who had taken Wilson's "peace without victory" speech and the Fourteen Points literally, the Versailles Treaty seemed an abomination. The complaints of the critics were individually reasonable, yet their conclusions were not entirely fair. The new map of Europe left fewer people on "foreign" soil than in any earlier period of history. Although the Allies seized the German colonies, they were required, under the mandate system, to render the **League of Nations** annual accounts of their stewardship and to prepare the inhabitants for eventual independence. Above all, Wilson had persuaded the powers to incorporate the League of Nations in the treaty.

Wilson expected the League of Nations to make up for all the inadequacies of the Versailles Treaty. Once the League had begun to function, problems like freedom of the seas and disarmament would solve themselves, he argued, and the relaxation of trade barriers would surely follow. The League would arbitrate international disputes, act as a central body for registering treaties, and employ military and economic sanctions against aggressor nations. Each member promised (Article 10) to protect the "territorial integrity" and "political independence" of all other members. No nation could be made

Dismantling the Ottoman Empire, 1919–1920 The Ottoman Empire was the biggest loser at Versailles: It lost everything apart from Turkey itself; but the Arab nationalists lost as well, because Britain and France, through League-appointed mandates, took control of Syria, Transjordan, Palestine, and Mesopotamia (Iraq).

to go to war against its will, but Wilson emphasized that all were morally obligated to carry out League decisions. By any standard, Wilson had achieved a remarkably moderate peace, one full of hope for the future. Except for the war guilt clause and the heavy reparations imposed on Germany, he could be justly proud of his work.

The Senate Rejects the League of Nations

When Wilson returned from France, he finally directed his attention to the task of winning public approval of his handiwork. A large majority of the people probably favored the League of Nations in principle, though few understood all its implications or were entirely happy with every detail. Wilson had persuaded the Allies to accept certain changes in the original draft to mollify American opposition. No nation could be forced to accept a colonial mandate, and "domestic questions" such as tariffs, the control of immigration, and the Monroe Doctrine were excluded from League control.

Many senators found these modifications insufficient. Even before the peace conference ended, thirty-seven Republican senators signed a manifesto, devised by Henry Cabot Lodge of Massachusetts, opposing Wilson's League and demanding that the question of an international organization be put off until "the urgent business of negotiating peace terms with Germany" had been completed. Wilson rejected this suggestion icily. Further alterations were out of the question. Thus the stage was set for a monumental test of strength between the president and the Republican majority in the Senate.

Partisanship, principle, and prejudice clashed mightily in this contest. A presidential election loomed. Should the League prove a success, the Republicans wanted to be able to claim a share of the credit, but Wilson had refused to allow them to participate

Despite Wilson's serving as mother hen, the League of Nations never hatched.

in drafting the document. This predisposed all of them to favor changes. Politics aside, genuine alarm at the possible sacrifice of American sovereignty to an international authority led many Republicans to urge modification of the League covenant, or constitution. Yet the noble purpose of the League made many reluctant to reject it entirely. The intense desire of the people to have an end to the long war made Republican leaders hesitate before voting down the Versailles Treaty, and they could not reject the League without rejecting the treaty.

Wilson could count on the Democratic senators almost to a man, but he had to win over many Republicans to obtain the two-thirds majority necessary for ratification. Republican opinion divided roughly into three segments. At one extreme were some dozen "irreconcilables," led by the shaggy-browed William E. Borah of Idaho, an able and kindly person of progressive leanings but an uncompromising isolationist. Borah claimed that he would vote against the League even if Jesus Christ returned to earth to argue in its behalf, and most of his followers were equally inflexible. At the other extreme stood another dozen "mild" reservationists who were in favor of the League but who hoped to alter it in minor ways, chiefly for political purposes. In the middle were the "strong" reservationists, senators willing to go along with the League only if American sovereignty were fully protected and if it were made clear that their party had played a major role in fashioning the final document.

Senator Lodge, the leader of the Republican opposition, was an intensely partisan individual. He possessed a keen intelligence, a mastery of parliamentary procedure, and, as chairman of the Senate Foreign Relations Committee, a great deal of power. Although not an isolationist, he had little faith in the League. He also had a profound distrust of Democrats, especially Wilson, whom he considered a hypocrite and a coward. While perfectly ready to see the country participate actively in world affairs, Lodge insisted that its right to determine its own best interests in every situation be preserved. When a Democratic president tried to ram the Versailles Treaty down the Senate's throat, he fought him with every weapon he could muster.

Lodge belonged to the strong reservationist faction. His own proposals, known as the Lodge Reservations, fourteen in number to match Wilson's Fourteen Points, limited U.S. obligations to the League and stated in unmistakable terms the right of Congress to decide when to honor these obligations. Some of the reservations were mere quibbles. Others, such as the provision that the United States would not endorse Japan's seizure of Chinese territory, were included mainly to embarrass Wilson by pointing out compromises he had made at Versailles. The most important reservation applied to Article Ten of the League

●●●─[Read the **Document**

Henry Cabot Lodge's Objections to the Treaty of Versailles at **myhistorylab.com**

covenant, which committed signatories to protect the political independence and territorial integrity of all member nations. Wilson had rightly called Article Ten "the heart of the Covenant." One of Lodge's reservations made it inoperable so far as the United States was concerned "unless in any particular case the Congress . . . shall by act or joint resolution so provide."

Lodge performed brilliantly, if somewhat unscrupulously, in uniting the three Republican factions behind his reservations. He got the irreconcilables to agree to them by conceding their right to vote against the final version in any event, and he held the mild reservationists in line by modifying some of his demands and stressing the importance of party unity. Reservations—as distinct from amendments—would not have to win the formal approval of other League members. In addition, the Lodge proposals dealt forthrightly with the problem of reconciling traditional concepts of national sovereignty with the new idea of world cooperation. Supporters of the League could accept them without sacrifice of principle. Wilson, however, refused to agree.

This foolish intransigence seems almost incomprehensible in a man of Wilson's intelligence and political experience. In part his hatred of Lodge accounts for it, in part his faith in his League. His physical condition in 1919 also played a role. At Paris he had suffered a violent attack of indigestion that was probably a symptom of a minor stroke. Thereafter, many observers noted small changes in his personality, particularly increased stubbornness and a loss of good judgment. Instead of making concessions, the president set out early in September on a nationwide speaking crusade to rally support for the League. In three weeks, Wilson traveled some 10,000 miles by train and gave forty speeches, some of them brilliant. On September 25, after an address in Pueblo, Colorado, he collapsed. A few days later, in Washington, he suffered a severe stroke that partially paralyzed his left side.

For nearly two months the president was almost totally cut off from affairs of state, leaving supporters of the League leaderless while Lodge maneuvered the reservations through the Senate. Gradually, popular attitudes toward the League shifted. The arguments of the irreconcilables persuaded many citizens that Wilson had made too sharp a break with America's isolationist past and that the Lodge Reservations were therefore necessary. Other issues connected with the reconversion of society to a peacetime basis increasingly occupied the public mind.

A coalition of Democratic and moderate Republican senators could easily have carried the treaty. That no such coalition was organized was Wilson's fault. Lodge obtained the simple majority necessary to add his reservations to the treaty merely by keeping his own party united. When the time came for the final roll call on November 19, Wilson, bitter and emotionally distraught, urged the Democrats to vote for rejection. "Better a thousand times to go down fighting than to dip your colors to dishonorable compromise," he explained to his wife. Thus the amended treaty failed, thirty-five to fifty-five, the irreconcilables and the Democrats voting against it. Lodge then allowed the original draft without his reservations to come to a vote. Again the result was defeat, thirty-eight to fifty-three. Only one Republican cast a ballot for ratification.

Dismayed but not yet crushed, friends of the League in both parties forced reconsideration of the treaty early in 1920. Neither Lodge nor Wilson would yield an inch. Lodge, who had little confidence in the effectiveness of any league of nations, was under no compulsion to compromise. Wilson, who believed that the League was the world's best hope, did have such a compulsion. Yet he would not compromise either, and this ensured the treaty's defeat.

Wilson's behavior is further evidence of his physical and mental decline. Had he died or stepped down, the treaty, with reservations, would almost certainly have been ratified. When the Senate balloted again in March, half the Democrats voted for the treaty with the Lodge Reservations. The others, mostly southern party regulars, joined the irreconcilables. Together they mustered thirty-five votes, seven more than the one-third that meant defeat.

The Red Scare

Business boomed in 1919 as consumers spent wartime savings on cars, homes, and other goods that had been in short supply during the conflict. But temporary shortages caused inflation; by 1920 the cost of living stood at more than twice the level of 1913. Workers demanded that their wages be increased as well. The unions, grown strong during the war, struck for wage increases. Over four million workers, one in five in the labor force, were on strike at some time during 1919.

The activities of radicals in the labor movement led millions of citizens to associate unionism and strikes with the new threat of communist world revolution. Although there were only a relative handful of communists in the United States, Russia's experience persuaded many that a tiny minority of ruthless revolutionaries could take over a nation of millions if conditions were right. Communists appointed themselves the champions of workers; labor unrest attracted them magnetically. When strikes broke out, some accompanied by violence, many people interpreted them as communist-inspired preludes to revolution.

But organized labor in America had seldom been truly radical. The Industrial Workers of the World (IWW) had made little impression in most industries. But some labor leaders had been attracted to socialism, and many Americans failed to distinguish between the common ends sought by communists and socialists and the entirely different methods by which they proposed to achieve those ends. When a general strike paralyzed Seattle in February 1919, the fact that a procommunist had helped organize it sent shivers down countless conservative spines. When the radical William Z. Foster began a drive to organize the steel industry at about this time, the fears became more intense. In September 1919 a total of 343,000 steelworkers walked off their jobs, and in the same month the Boston police went on strike. Violence marked the steel strike, and the suspension of police protection in Boston led to looting and fighting that ended only when Governor Calvin Coolidge called out the National Guard.

During the same period a handful of terrorists caused widespread alarm by attempting to murder various prominent persons, including John D. Rockefeller, Justice Oliver Wendell Holmes Jr., and Attorney General A. Mitchell Palmer. Although the terrorists were anarchists and anarchism had little in common with communism, many citizens lumped all extremists together and associated them with a monstrous assault on society.

What aroused the public even more was the fact that most radicals were not American citizens. Wartime fear of alien saboteurs easily transformed itself into peacetime terror of foreign radicals. In place of Germany, the enemy became the lowly immigrant, usually an Italian or a Jew or a Slav and usually an industrial worker. In this muddled way, radicalism, unionism, and questions of racial and national origins combined to make many Americans believe that their way of life was in imminent danger. That few immigrants were radicals, that most workers had no interest in communism, and that the extremists themselves were faction-ridden and irresolute did not affect conservative thinking. From all over the country came demands that radicals be ruthlessly suppressed. Thus the **"red scare"** was born.

Attorney General Palmer was the key figure in the resulting purge. He had been a typical progressive, a supporter of the League of Nations and such reforms as woman suffrage and child labor legislation. But pressure from Congress and his growing conviction that the communists really were a menace led him to join the "red hunt." Soon he was saying of the radicals, "Out of the sly and crafty eyes of many of them leap cupidity, cruelty, insanity, and crime; from their lopsided faces, sloping brows, and misshapen features may be recognized the unmistakable criminal type."

In August 1919, Palmer established within the Department of Justice the General Intelligence Division, headed by J. Edgar Hoover, to collect information about clandestine radical activities. In November, Justice Department agents in a dozen cities swooped down on the meeting places of an anarchist organization known as the Union of Russian Workers. More than 650 persons, many of them unconnected with the union, were arrested but in only forty-three cases could evidence be found to justify deportation.

Nevertheless, the public reacted so favorably that Palmer, thinking now of winning the 1920 Democratic presidential nomination, planned an immense roundup of communists. He obtained 3,000 warrants, and on January 2, 1920, his agents, reinforced by local police and self-appointed vigilantes, struck simultaneously in thirty-three cities.

About 6,000 persons were taken into custody, many of them citizens and therefore not subject to the deportation laws, many others unconnected with any radical cause. Some were held incommunicado for weeks while the authorities searched for evidence against them. In a number of cases, individuals who went to visit prisoners were themselves thrown behind bars on the theory that they too must be communists. Hundreds of suspects were jammed into filthy "bullpens," beaten, and forced to sign "confessions."

The public tolerated these wholesale violations of civil liberties because of the supposed menace of communism. Gradually, however, protests began to be heard, first from lawyers and liberal magazines, then from a wider segment of the population. No revolutionary outbreak had taken place. Of 6,000 seized in the Palmer raids, only 556 proved liable to deportation. The widespread ransacking of communists' homes and meeting places produced mountains of inflammatory literature but only three pistols.

Palmer, attempting to maintain the crusade, announced that the radicals planned a gigantic terrorist demonstration for May Day, 1920. In New York and other cities thousands of police were placed on round-the-clock duty; federal troops stood by anxiously. But the day passed without even a rowdy meeting. Suddenly Palmer appeared ridiculous. The red scare swiftly subsided.

The Election of 1920

Wilson still hoped for vindication at the polls in the presidential election, which he sought to make a "great and solemn referendum" on the League. He would have liked to run for a third term, but in his enfeebled condition he attracted no support among Democratic leaders. The party nominated James M. Cox of Ohio.

Cox favored joining the League, but the election did not produce the referendum on the new organization that Wilson desired. The Republicans, whose candidate was another Ohioan, Senator Warren G. Harding, equivocated shamelessly on the issue.

The election turned on other matters, largely emotional. Disillusioned by the results of the war, many Americans had their fill of idealism. They wanted, apparently, to end the long period of moral uplift and reform agitation that had begun under Theodore Roosevelt and return to what Harding called "normalcy."

To the extent that the voters were expressing opinions on Wilson's League, their response was overwhelmingly negative. Senator Harding, a strong reservationist, swept the country, winning over 16.1 million votes to Cox's 9.1 million. In July 1921, Congress formally ended the war with the Central Powers by passing a joint resolution.

The defeat of the League was a tragedy both for Wilson, whose crusade for a world order based on peace and justice ended in failure, and for the world, which was condemned to endure another, still more horrible and costly war. Perhaps this dreadful outcome could not have been avoided. Had Wilson compromised and Lodge behaved like a statesman instead of a politician, the United States would have joined the League, but it might well have failed to respond when called on to meet its obligations. As events soon demonstrated, the League powers acted timidly and even dishonorably when challenged by aggressor nations.

Yet it might have been different had the Senate ratified the Versailles Treaty. What was lost when the treaty failed was not peace but the possibility of peace, a tragic loss indeed.

Milestones

1914	United States invades Veracruz, Mexico	1918	Sedition Act limits freedom of speech
	Great War begins in Europe		Wilson announces Fourteen Points
1915	German U-boat torpedoes *Lusitania*		Republicans gain control of both houses of Congress
1916	Wilson appoints Louis D. Brandeis to Supreme Court		Armistice ends the Great War
	Adamson Act gives railroad workers eight-hour day	1918–1919	Flu epidemic kills 600,000 Americans
	"Pancho" Villa burns Columbus, New Mexico	1919	Steel workers strike
	Wilson is reelected president		Red scare culminates in Palmer raids
1917	Germany resumes unrestricted submarine warfare		Big Four meet at Paris Peace Conference
	Russian Revolution begins		Senate rejects Versailles Treaty and League of Nations
	United States declares war on Central Powers		Wilson wins Nobel Peace Prize, suffers massive stroke
	Bernard Baruch heads War Industries Board	1920	Senate again rejects Versailles Treaty and League of Nations
	Former President Taft heads War Labor Board		Warren Harding is elected president

✓●─[**Study** and **Review** at **www.myhistorylab.com**

Review Questions

1. The chapter's introduction draws a parallel between the American efforts to fight terrorism in Afghanistan and Iraq and Woodrow Wilson's crusade to make the world "safe for democracy." Does the history of American involvement in World War I teach any "lessons" about foreign wars?

2. Why did Woodrow Wilson recommend neutrality at the outset of the European war and why did he change his mind?

3. Did progressivism play a role in leading the United States into World War I? Did it shape how the war was waged?

4. What problems did the United States encounter in mobilizing for war? How did the war effort contribute to the growth of the American state?

5. How did the war affect minorities and women? How did it restrict dissent and labor?

6. What were the arguments for and against American ratification of the League of Nations?

Key Terms

Allied Powers *603*
Central Powers *603*
Espionage Act *614*

Fourteen Points *620*
League of Nations *623*
"red scare" *628*

Sedition Act *614*
War Industries Board
   (WIB) *612*

Culture: Change and Adjustment

24

((•–Hear the Audio** Chapter 24 at myhistorylab.com

Do you drink too much?

MANY COLLEGE STUDENTS DRINK—A LOT. IN 2008 THE NATIONAL CENTER on Addiction and Substance Abuse (CASA) at Columbia University found that 44 percent of college students were binge-drinkers and that nearly one in four fulfilled the medical criteria for substance abuse. In 2010 the National Institute on Alcohol Abuse and Alcoholism reported that alcohol annually caused nearly 100,000 sexual assaults and date rapes and 1,700 deaths of college students.

"It's time to get the 'high' out of higher education," declared Joseph A. Califano, president of CASA and former U.S. secretary of health, education, and welfare. He blamed college administrators for condoning a "college culture of abuse." Campaigns to promote responsible drinking accomplished little, he noted. The only effective strategy was campus-wide prohibition.

But such words caused many to bristle. In 2010, after Iowa City banned those under twenty-one from bars, the *Daily Iowan* at the University of Iowa claimed that "harsh restrictions on alcohol drive the behavior underground, pushing young people to use more hard liquor in unsupervised private house parties." "Let's not repackage the Prohibition Era of the 1920s," the article concluded. When the University of Hawaii considered banning alcohol at the football stadium, another professor cited the nation's experience with Prohibition eighty years earlier. "You cannot root out the drinking of alcohol by outlawing it," he added.

The Prohibition Era was in many ways a response to unsettling social changes. The flood of immigration during the early 1900s had strained the nation's social fabric, especially in cities. Young women were challenging traditional gender roles. African Americans were leaving the South in droves and demanding rights that had been long deferred. Gays were becoming visible—at least to each other. Movies and radio, and even artists and writers, stimulated a rebellious youth culture. Advertising encouraged people to lose themselves in the delights of consumption.

These transformations also elicited opposition. The federal government curtailed immigration and cracked down on foreign-born radicals. The Ku Klux Klan reemerged to intimidate immigrants and blacks. Traditionalists inveighed against the enticements of popular culture and decline in faith. Prohibition was only the most visible expression of a reaction against social and cultural change.

631

Closing the Gates to New Immigrants

In 1921 Congress, reflecting a widespread prejudice against a huge influx of eastern and southern European immigrants, passed an emergency act establishing a quota system. Each year 3 percent of the number of foreign-born residents of the United States in 1910 (about 350,000 persons) might enter the country. Each country's quota was based on the number of its nationals in the United States in 1910. This meant that only a relative handful of the total would be from southern and eastern Europe. In 1924 the quota was reduced to 2 percent and the base year shifted to 1890, thereby lowering further the proportion of southern and eastern Europeans admitted.

In 1929 Congress established a system that allowed only 150,000 immigrants a year to enter the country. Each national quota was based on the supposed origins of the entire white population of the United States in 1920, not merely on the foreign-born.

The system was complicated and unscientific, for no one could determine with accuracy the "origins" of millions of citizens. More seriously, it ignored America's long history of constantly changing ethnic diversity. The motto *E Pluribus Unum*—Out of Many, One—conceived to represent the unity of the original thirteen states, applied even more appropriately to the blending of different cultures into one nationality. The new law sought to freeze the mix.

The law reduced actual immigration to far below 150,000 a year. Between 1931 and 1939, for example, only 23,000 British immigrants came to the United States, far below Britain's annual quota of 65,000. Meanwhile, hundreds of thousands of southern and eastern Europeans waited for admission.

The United States had closed the gates. The **National Origins Act** caused the foreign-born percentage of the population to fall from about 13 percent in 1920 to 4.7 percent in 1970. Instead of an open, cosmopolitan society eager to accept, in Emma Lazarus's stirring line, the "huddled masses yearning to breathe free," America now became committed to preserving a homogeneous, "Anglo-Saxon" population.

Distaste for the "new" immigrants from eastern Europe, many of whom were Jewish, expanded into a more general anti-Semitism in the 1920s. American Jews, whether foreign-born or native, were subjected to increasing discrimination, not because they were slow in adopting

"Give me your tired, your poor, your huddled masses yearning to breathe free, the wretched refuse of your teeming shore"—these words of Emma Lazarus, inscribed at the base of the Statue of Liberty, tell only part of the story. Most immigrants were young and hopeful, like this family at Ellis Island; many were resolute and ambitious. The restriction of immigration during the 1920s, conceived to exclude misfits, also deprived the nation of people such as these.

American ways but because many of them were getting ahead in the world somewhat more rapidly than expected. Prestigious colleges like Harvard, Yale, and Columbia that had in the past admitted Jews based on their academic records now imposed unofficial but effective quotas. Medical schools also established quotas, and no matter how talented, most young Jewish lawyers and bankers could find places only in so-called "Jewish" firms.

New Urban Social Patterns

The census of 1920 revealed that for the first time a majority of Americans (54 million in a population of 106 million) lived in "urban" rather than "rural" places. These figures are somewhat misleading because the census classified anyone in a community of 2,500 or more as urban. Of the 54 million "urban" residents in 1920, over 16 million lived in villages and towns of fewer than 25,000 persons and the evidence suggests strongly that a large majority of them held ideas and values more like those of rural citizens than like those of city dwellers. But the truly urban Americans, the one person in four who lived in a city of 100,000 or more, were increasing steadily in number and influence. More than 19 million persons moved from farms to cities in the 1920s, and the population living in centers of 100,000 or more increased by about a third.

The urban environment transformed family structure, educational opportunities, and dozens of other aspects of human existence. Indeed, since most of the changes in the relations of husbands, wives, and children that had occurred in the nineteenth century were related to the fact that people were leaving farms to work in towns and cities, these trends continued and were intensified in the early twentieth century as more and more people settled in urban centers.

Earlier differences between working-class and middle-class family structures persisted. In 1920 about a quarter of the American women who were working were married, but less than 10 percent of all married women were working. Middle-class married women who worked were nearly all either childless or highly paid professionals who were able to employ servants. Most male skilled workers now earned enough to support a family in

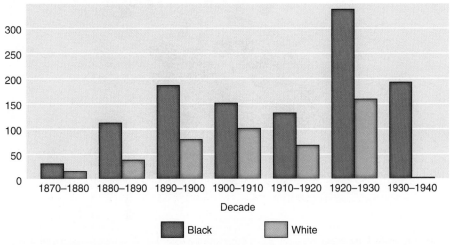

Black and White Out-Migration from Virginia and North and South Carolina, 1870–1940

modest comfort so long as they could work steadily, but an unskilled laborer still could not. Wives in most such families helped out, usually by taking in laundry or sewing.

By the 1920s the idea of intrafamily democracy had emerged. In such families, husbands and wives would deal with each other as equals; given existing conditions, this meant sharing housework and childcare, downplaying male authority, and stressing mutual satisfaction in sexual and other matters. On the one hand, they should be friends and lovers, not merely housekeepers, earners of money, and producers of children. On the other hand, advocates of these companionate relationships believed that there was nothing particularly sacred about marriage; divorce should be made easier for couples that did not get along, provided they did not have children.

Much attention was given to "scientific" child-rearing. Childcare experts agreed that routine medical examinations and good nutrition were of central importance, but they were divided about how the socialization and psychological development of the young should be handled. One school stressed rigid training. Children could be "spoiled" by indulgence; toilet training should begin early in infancy; thumb sucking should be suppressed; too much kissing could turn male youngsters into "mama's boys." Another school favored a more permissive approach. Toilet training could wait; parents should pay attention to their children's expressed needs, not impose a generalized set of rules on them.

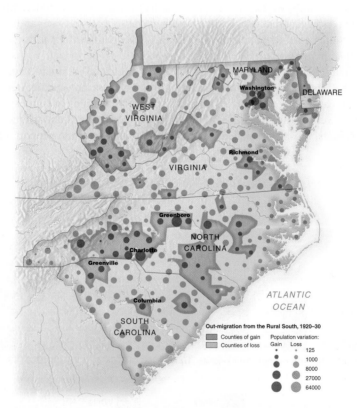

Population Losses in the South The graph shows that whites and especially blacks were leaving the South in large numbers, especially during the 1920s. The map shows that while many urban areas in the South gained population, most rural areas lost population.

The growth of large cities further loosened social constraints on sexuality. Amidst the sea of people that surged down the streets or into the subways, the solitary individual acquired a freedom derived from anonymity. (For further perspective on urban life, see Re-Viewing the Past, *Chicago*, pp. 638–639.) Homosexuals, in particular, developed a set of identifying signals and fashioned a distinctive culture in parks, cafeterias, nightclubs, and rooming houses of big cities.

The Younger Generation

The 1920s has been described as the Jazz Age, the era of "flaming youth," when young people danced to syncopated "African" rhythms, careened about the countryside in automobiles in search of pleasure and forgetfulness, and made gods of movie stars and professional athletes. This view of the period bears a superficial resemblance to reality. "Younger people," one observer noted in 1922, were attempting "to create a way of life free from the bondage of an authority that has lost all meaning." But if they differed from their parents and grandparents, it was primarily because young people were adjusting to more profound and more rapid changes in their world than their grandparents could have imagined.

Trends that were barely perceptible during the Progressive Era now reached avalanche proportions. This was particularly noticeable in relationships between the sexes. Courtship, for example, was transformed. In the late nineteenth century, a typical young man "paid a call" on a female friend. He met and conversed with her parents, perhaps over coffee and cookies. The couple remained at home, the parents nearby if not actually participating in what was essentially a social event held in a private place.

By the 1920s paying calls was being replaced by *dating*; the young man called only to "pick up" his "date," to go off, free of parental supervision, to whatever diversion they wished. There is no question that for young people of the 1920s, relations between the sexes were becoming more relaxed and uninhibited. Respectable young women smoked cigarettes, something previously done in public only by prostitutes and bohemian types. They cast off heavy corsets, wore lipstick and "exotic" perfumes, and shortened both their hair and their skirts, the latter rising steadily from instep to ankle to calf to knee and beyond as the decade progressed. For decades female dressmakers and beauty salon proprietors had sold their own beauty products. By 1920, however, new cosmetic corporations, managed primarily by men, appropriated the products and marketing strategies of local women entrepreneurs and catered to national mass markets.

Freudian psychology and the more accessible ideas of the British "sexologist" Havelock Ellis reached steadily deeper into the popular psyche. Since sex was "the central function of life," Ellis argued, it must be "simple and natural and pure and good." Bombarded by these exciting ideas, to say nothing of their own inclinations, young people found casting off their inhibitions more and more tempting.

Conservatives bemoaned what they described as the breakdown of moral standards, the fragmentation of the family, and the decline of parental authority—all with some reason. Nevertheless, society was not collapsing. Much of the rebelliousness of the young, like their particular style of dress, was faddish in nature, in a sense a kind of youthful conformity. This was particularly true of college students. Elaborate rituals governed every aspect of their extracurricular life, which was consuming a steadily larger share of most students' time and energy. Fraternity and sorority initiations, "proms," attendance at Saturday afternoon football games, styles of dress, and college slang, seemingly aspects of independence and free choice, were nearly everywhere shaped and controlled by peer pressure.

But young people's new ways of relating to one another, while influenced by the desire to conform, were not mere fads and were not confined to people under thirty. This can be seen most clearly in the birth control movement, the drive to legalize the use of contraceptives.

The "New" Woman

The young people of the 1920s were more open about sex and perhaps more sexually precocious than the young had been before the war. This does not mean that most of them engaged in sexual intercourse before marriage or that they tended to marry earlier. Single young people might "believe in" birth control, but relatively few (at least by modern standards) had occasion to practice it. Contraception was a concern of married people, and particularly of married women.

The leading American proponent of birth control in the 1920s, actually the person who coined the term, was Margaret Sanger. Before the war she was a political radical, a friend of Eugene Debs, "Big Bill" Haywood, and the anarchist Emma Goldman. Gradually, however, her attention focused on the plight of the poor women she encountered while working as a nurse; many of these women, burdened by large numbers of children, knew nothing about contraception. Sanger began to write articles and pamphlets designed to enlighten them, but when she did so she ran afoul of the Comstock Act of 1873, an anti-obscenity law that banned the distribution of information about contraception from the mail. She was frequently in trouble with the law, but she was persistent to the edge of fanaticism. In 1921 she founded the American Birth Control League and two years later a research center. (Not until the 1960s, however, did the Supreme Court determine that the right to use contraceptives was guaranteed by the Constitution.)

●◆●[Read the **Document**

Margaret Sanger, *Happiness in Marriage* at **myhistorylab.com**

Other gender-based restrictions and limitations of particular importance to women also seemed to be breaking down. The divorce laws had been modified in most states. More women were taking jobs, attracted by the expanding demand for clerks, typists, salespeople, receptionists, telephone operators, and similar service-oriented occupations. Over 10.6 million women were working by the end of the decade, in contrast with 8.4 million in 1920. The Department of Labor's Women's Bureau, outgrowth of a wartime agency, was founded in 1920 and was soon conducting investigations of the working conditions women faced in different industries and how various laws affected them.

But most of these gains were illusory. Relaxation of the strict standards of sexual morality did not eliminate the double standard. More women worked, but most of the jobs they held were still menial or of a kind that few men wanted: domestic service, elementary school teaching, clerical work, selling behind a counter. When they competed for jobs with men, women usually received much lower wages. Women's Bureau studies demonstrated this repeatedly; yet when the head of the bureau, Mary Anderson, tried to get employers to raise women's wages, most of them first claimed that the men had families to support, and when she reminded them that many female employees also had family responsibilities, they told her that there was a "tacit understanding" that women were to make less than men.

More women graduated from college, but the colleges placed more emphasis on subjects like home economics that seemed designed to make them better housewives rather than professional nutritionists or business executives. As one Vassar College

This photograph of Margaret Sanger was taken during her trial in January 1917. Having opened the nation's first birth control clinic in Brooklyn, New York, she was convicted of disseminating information on contraception and served thirty days in prison. Friends had advised Sanger to dress conservatively and affect a persona of motherhood. Despite her demure clothing, her eyes express her characteristic assertiveness.

administrator (a woman!) said, colleges should provide "education for women along the lines of their chief interests and responsibilities, motherhood and the home."

The 1920s proved disillusioning to feminists, who now paid a price for their single-minded pursuit of the right to vote in the Progressive Era. After the ratification of the Nineteenth Amendment, many activists, assuming the battle won, lost interest in agitating for change. They believed that the suffrage amendment had given them the one weapon needed to achieve whatever women still lacked. In fact, it soon became apparent that women did not vote as a bloc. Many married women voted for the candidates their husbands supported.

When radical feminists discovered that voting did not automatically bring true equality, they founded the National Woman's Party (NWP) and began campaigning for an equal rights amendment. Their dynamic leader, Alice Paul, disdained specific goals such as disarmament, ending child labor, and liberalized birth control. Total equality for women was the one objective. The party considered protective legislation governing the hours and working conditions of women discriminatory. This caused the so-called social feminists, who believed that children and working women needed the protection provided by such laws, to break away.

The NWP never attracted a wide following, but only partly because of the split with the social feminists. Many of the younger radical women were primarily concerned with their personal freedom to behave as they wished; politics did not interest them. But a more important reason was that nearly all the radicals failed to see that questions of gender—the attitudes that men and women *were taught* to take toward each other—stood in the way of sexual equality. Many more women joined the more moderate League of Women Voters, which attempted to mobilize support for a broad spectrum of reforms, some of which had no specific connection to the interests of women as such. The entire women's movement lost momentum. The battle for the equal rights amendment persisted through the 1930s, but it was lost. By the end of that decade the movement was moribund.

Popular Culture: Movies and Radio

The postwar decade saw immense changes in popular culture. Unlike the literary flowering of the era (see pp. 646–648), these changes seemed in tune with the times, not a reaction against them. This was true in part because they were products as much of technology as of human imagination.

Chicago

Chicago (2003) is a tale of illicit sex, booze, and "all that jazz." The characters played by Renée Zellweger and Catherine Zeta-Jones aspire to cabaret stardom. Each is married, each is jilted, and each shoots her wayward lover because "he had it coming." The newspapers gleefully promote the stories. From prison, while awaiting trial for murder, the women compete to garner the most headlines, courting the fame that will boost their careers. Richard Gere, who plays their celebrity lawyer, "razzle dazzles" all Chicago (including the juries) and gets the women acquitted. *Chicago* is a musical. It does not claim to be history. The movie, however, is based on a true story; and both the movie and the story illuminate important aspects of the Roaring Twenties.

On March 11, 1924, Walter Law, an automobile salesman, was found dead from a gunshot wound to the head. A pistol and an empty bottle of gin were on the floor. The car was registered to Belva Gaertner, a twice-divorced cabaret singer known as Belle Brown. Police hurried to her rooming house and peppered her with questions.

"We went driving, Mr. Law and I," she told them. She explained that they had stopped at the Bingham "café," bought a bottle of gin (illegally, since this was during Prohibition), and drove around town. "I don't know what happened next," she declared. During the interrogation Gaertner paced nervously, perhaps for good reason: Her clothes were soaked with blood. The police charged her with murder.

On April 3, police received a phone call from Beulah Annan, a young married woman who worked in a laundry. She said that a man had attempted to rape her and that she had shot him. Police raced to her apartment, where they found Harry Kalstedt dead from a gunshot wound. Annan insisted that she had acted in self-defense, and her husband supported her story. But police hammered away at the fact that Kalstedt had

worked at the same laundry as Annan, and that he had been shot in the back. Annan eventually confessed that the two had been having an affair. When he threatened to dump her, she shot him. For two hours, as he lay dying, she drank cocktails and listened to a recording of "Hula Lou," a foxtrot about a Hawaiian girl "with more sweeties than a dog has fleas."

Maurine Watkins, a young reporter, covered both stories for the Chicago *Tribune*. Murder had long been a staple of local journalism, but Watkins recognized the extraordinary appeal of this story: jazz, booze, and two comely "lady murderesses," as Watkins termed them. While awaiting trial in prison, the women provided Watkins with delicious quotes.

Gaertner told Watkins that she was innocent. "No woman can love a man enough to kill him," she explained. "There are always plenty more. " When the grand jury ruled that she could be tried for murder, Gaertner was irritated. "That was bum," she snapped. She called the jurors "narrow-minded old birds—bet they never heard a jazz band in their lives. Now, if I'm tried, I want worldly men, broad-minded men, men who know what it is to get out a bit. Why, no one like that would convict me!"

Watkins described Gaertner as "stylish" and "classy" but called Annan the "prettiest woman ever accused of murder in Chicago"—"young, slender, with bobbed auburn hair; wide set, appealing blue eyes, upturned nose; translucent skin, faintly, very faintly, rouged, an ingenuous smile. Refined features, intelligent expression—an 'awfully nice girl.'" This account appeared on the front page.

During the trial, Annan's attorney pointed to "this frail little girl, struggling with a drunken brute." On May 25, after deliberating less than two hours, the all-male jury acquitted her of the crime. Two weeks after Annan's trial, Gaertner was also found not

Catherine Zeta-Jones and Renée Zellweger from the movie *Chicago*.

Beulah Annan, "lady murderess."
Source: DN-0076798/*Chicago Daily News*/Chicago Historical Society.

guilty. "Another pretty woman gone free," muttered the prosecutor.

Unlike the movie's "lady murderesses," Annan and Gaertner did not team up in a cabaret act. Annan had a nervous breakdown, was institutionalized, and died in 1928. Of Gaertner's subsequent life, little is known. Watkins abandoned journalism and entered Yale drama school. In 1926 she wrote *Chicago*, a comedy derived from the Gaertner and Annan trials, and it ran on Broadway for 172 performances. The next year Cecil B. De Mille adapted the play as a silent movie. In 1975 director Bob Fosse bought the rights to *Chicago* and created the Broadway musical on which the 2003 movie was based.

The "lady murderesses" became part of the lore of the Roaring Twenties; the story seemed to confirm the fears of traditionalists. One minister warned about jazz's "wriggling movement and sensuous stimulation" of the body's "sensory center." Silk stockings, skirts that exposed knees, and straight dresses that de-emphasized the waist further suggested that women's bodies were not meant solely for childbirth. The movie makes all of these points with suitable salaciousness.

The movie also reiterates widespread concerns about city life. Several months after the acquittal of Gaertner and Annan, *Literary Digest* warned "country girls" of the moral dangers of large cities. Such fears echoed the judgments of sociologists, especially those of "the Chicago school" of urban sociology, headed by Robert Park of the University of Chicago. The Chicago sociologists contended that large cities disrupted traditional bonds of family and community and fostered crime and deviance. In *The Gold Coast and the Slum* (1929), sociologist Harvey Zorbaugh maintained that life in much of downtown Chicago was "the direct antithesis of all we are accustomed to think of as normal in society." Big-city life was characterized by a "laxity of conventional standards, and of personal and social disorganization."

Scholars now recognize that the portrait of urban city life as propounded by "the Chicago school"—and by movies such as *Chicago*—was overdrawn. Urbanization did not shatter family and ethnic ties. Neighborliness and community persisted even in blighted tenement districts. Few people cast off social conventions, much less succumbed to murderous impulses. In short, Belva Gaertner and Beulah Annan were good copy, and stories such as theirs helped make that celebrated decade roar, but most folks painted the town less vividly, if at all.

Questions for Discussion

- Compare the photograph of Beulah Annan with those of actresses Catherine Zeta-Jones and Renée Zellweger. What are the similarities and differences and what do they suggest about Hollywood's rendering of the past?
- Why would Hollywood take pains to depict the visual aspects of the past accurately?

The first motion pictures were made around 1900, but the medium only came into its own after the Great War. The early films, such as the eight-minute epic *The Great Train Robbery* (1903), were brief, action-packed, and unpretentious. Professional actors and most educated people viewed them with amused contempt. But their success was instantaneous with recent immigrants and many other slum dwellers. In 1912 there were nearly 13,000 movie houses in the United States, more than 500 in New York City alone.

By the mid-1920s the industry, centered in Hollywood, California, was the fourth largest in the nation in capital investment. Movie "palaces" seating several thousand people sprang up in the major cities. Daily ticket sales averaged more than 10 million. With the introduction of talking movies, *The Jazz Singer* (1927) being the first of significance, and color films a few years later, the motion picture reached technological maturity. Costs and profits mounted; by the 1930s million-dollar productions were common.

Many movies were still tasteless trash catering to the prejudices of the multitude. Sex, crime, war, romantic adventure, broad comedy, and luxurious living were the main themes, endlessly repeated in predictable patterns. Critics charged that the movies were destroying the legitimate stage (which underwent a sharp decline), corrupting the morals of youth, and glorifying the materialistic aspects of life.

Nevertheless the motion picture made positive contributions to American culture. Beginning with D. W. Griffith's *Birth of a Nation* (1915), filmmakers created an entirely new theatrical art. Movies enabled dozens of established actors to reach wider audiences and developed many first-rate new ones. As the medium matured, it produced many dramatic works of high quality. At its best the motion picture offered a breadth and power of impact superior to anything on the traditional stage.

Charlie Chaplin was the greatest film star of the era. His characterization of the sad-eyed little tramp with his toothbrush moustache and cane, tight coat, and baggy trousers became famous throughout the world. Chaplin's films were superficially unpretentious. But his work proved both universally popular and enduring; he was perhaps the greatest comic artist of all time. The animated cartoon, perfected by Walt Disney in the 1930s, was a lesser but significant cinematic achievement; Mickey Mouse, Donald Duck, and other Disney cartoon characters gave endless delight to millions of children.

Even more pervasive than the movies in its effects on the American people was radio. Wireless transmission of sound was developed in the late nineteenth century by many scientists in Europe and the United States. During the war radio was put to important military uses and was strictly controlled, but immediately thereafter the airwaves were thrown open.

Radio was briefly the domain of hobbyists, thousands of "hams" broadcasting in indiscriminate fashion. Even under these conditions, the manufacture of radio equipment became a big business. In 1920 the first commercial station (KDKA in Pittsburgh) began broadcasting, and by the end of 1922 over 500 stations were in operation. In 1926 the National Broadcasting Company, the first continent-wide network, was created.

It took little time for broadcasters to discover the power of the new medium. When one pioneer interrupted a music program to ask listeners to phone in requests, the station received 3,000 calls in an hour. The immediacy of radio explained its tremendous impact. As a means of communicating the latest news, it had no peer; beginning with the broadcast of the 1924 presidential nominating conventions, all major public events were covered live. Advertisers seized on radio too; it proved to be as effective a way to sell soap as to transmit news.

In 1927 Congress limited the number of stations and parceled out wavelengths to prevent interference. Further legislation in 1934 established the Federal Communications Commission (FCC), with power to revoke the licenses of stations that failed to operate in the public interest. But the FCC placed no effective controls on programming or on advertising practices.

The Golden Age of Sports

The extraordinary popularity of sports in the postwar period can be explained in a number of ways. People had more money to spend and more free time to fill. Radio was bringing suspenseful, play-by-play accounts of sports contests into millions of homes, thus encouraging tens of thousands to want to see similar events. New means of persuasion developed by advertisers to sell lipstick, breakfast cereal, and refrigerators were applied with equal success to sporting events and to the athletes who participated in them.

There had been great athletes before; indeed probably the greatest all-around athlete of the twentieth century was Jim Thorpe, a Sac and Fox Indian who won both the pentathlon and the decathlon at the 1912 Olympic Games, made Walter Camp's All-American football team in 1912 and 1913, then played major league baseball for several years before becoming a pioneer founder and player in the National Football League. But what truly made the 1920s a golden age was a coincidence—the emergence in a few short years of a remarkable collection of what today would be called superstars.

In football there was the University of Illinois's Harold "Red" Grange, who averaged over ten yards a carry during his college career and who in one incredible quarter during the 1924 game between Illinois and Michigan carried the ball four times and scored a touchdown each time, gaining in the process 263 yards.

During the same years William "Big Bill" Tilden dominated tennis, winning the national singles title every year from 1920 to 1925 along with nearly every other tournament he entered. Beginning in 1923, Robert T. "Bobby" Jones ruled over the world of golf with equal authority, his climactic achievement being his capture of the amateur and open championships of both the United States and Great Britain in 1930.

A few women athletes dominated their sports during this golden age in similar fashion. In tennis Helen Wills was three times United States singles champion and the winner of the women's singles at Wimbledon eight times in the late 1920s and early 1930s. The swimmer Gertrude Ederle, holder of eighteen world records by the time she was seventeen, swam the English Channel on her second attempt, in 1926. She was not only the first woman to do so, but she did it faster than any of the four men who had previously made it across.

However, the sports star among stars was "the Sultan of Swat," baseball's Babe Ruth. Ruth not only dominated baseball, he changed it from a game ruled by pitchers and low scores to one in which hitting was more greatly admired. Originally himself a brilliant pitcher, his incredible hitting ability made him more valuable in the outfield, where he could play every day. Before Ruth, John "Home Run" Baker was the most famous slugger; his greatest annual home run total was 12, achieved shortly before the Great War. Ruth hit twenty-nine in 1919 and fifty-four in 1920, his first year with the New York Yankees. By 1923 he was so feared that pitchers intentionally walked him more than half the times he appeared at the plate.

Newly built Yankee Stadium on opening day of the 1923 baseball season. Babe Ruth hit his first home run and soon Yankee Stadium was dubbed "the House that Ruth Built." That year, perhaps his best, Ruth hit forty-one home runs, batted .393, and drew 170 walks. He got on base more than half the times he appeared at the plate. Ruth's feats matched the colossal appearance of Yankee Stadium, whose arches evoked the imperial grandeur of ancient Rome.

The achievements of these and other outstanding athletes had a cumulative effect. New stadiums were built, and they were filled by "the largest crowds that ever witnessed athletic sports since the fall of Rome."

Urban–Rural Conflicts: Fundamentalism

These were buoyant times for people in tune with the times. However, the tensions and hostilities of the 1920s exaggerated an older rift in American society—the conflict between urban and rural ways of life. To many among the scattered millions who tilled the soil and among the millions who lived in towns and small cities, the new city-oriented culture seemed sinful, overly materialistic, and unhealthy.

Yet there was no denying its fascination. Made even more aware of the appeal of the city by radio and the automobile, farmers and townspeople coveted the comfort and excitement of city life at the same time that they condemned its vices. Rural society proclaimed the superiority of its ways at least in part to protect itself from temptation. Change, omnipresent in the postwar world, must be resisted even at the cost of individualism and freedom.

One expression of this resistance was a resurgence of religious fundamentalism. Although it was especially prevalent among Baptists and Methodists, fundamentalism was primarily an attitude of mind, profoundly conservative, rather than a religious idea. Fundamentalists rejected the theory of evolution as well as advanced hypotheses on the origins of the universe.

What made crusaders of the fundamentalists was their resentment of modern urban culture. The teaching of evolution must be prohibited, they insisted. Throughout the 1920s they campaigned vigorously for laws banning discussion of Darwin's theory in textbooks and classrooms. By 1929 five southern states had passed laws prohibiting the teaching of evolution in the public schools.

Their greatest asset in this crusade was William Jennings Bryan. After leaving Wilson's Cabinet in 1915 he devoted much time to religious and moral issues, but without applying himself conscientiously to the study of these difficult questions. He went about the country charging that "they"—meaning the mass of educated Americans— had "taken the Lord away from the schools." He denounced the use of public money to undermine Christian principles, and he offered $100 to anyone who would admit to being descended from an ape. His immense popularity in rural areas assured him a wide audience, and no one came forward to take his money.

The fundamentalists won a minor victory in 1925, when Tennessee passed a law forbidding instructors in the state's schools and colleges to teach "any theory that denies the story of the Divine Creation of man as taught in the Bible." The bill passed both houses by big majorities; few legislators wished to expose themselves to charges that they did not believe the Bible.

On learning of the passage of this act, the American Civil Liberties Union announced that it would finance a test case challenging its constitutionality if a Tennessee teacher would deliberately violate the statute. Urged on by friends, John T. Scopes, a young biology teacher in Dayton, reluctantly agreed to do so. He was arrested. A battery of nationally known lawyers came forward to defend him, and the state obtained the services of Bryan himself. The **Scopes trial**, also known as the "Monkey Trial," became an overnight sensation.

Clarence Darrow, chief counsel for the defendant, stated the issue clearly. "Scopes isn't on trial," he said, "civilization is on trial. No man's belief will be safe if they win." The comic aspects of the trial obscured this issue. Scopes's conviction was a foregone conclusion; after the jury rendered its verdict, the judge fined him $100.

Nevertheless, the trial exposed the danger of the fundamentalist position. The high point came when Bryan agreed to testify as an expert witness on the Bible. In a sweltering courtroom, the lanky, rough-hewn Darrow cross-examined the aging champion of fundamentalism, exposing his childlike faith and his disdain for the science of the day. "I believe in a God that can make a whale and can make a man and make both do what He pleases," Bryan explained.

The Monkey Trial ended badly for nearly everyone concerned. Scopes moved away from Dayton; the judge,

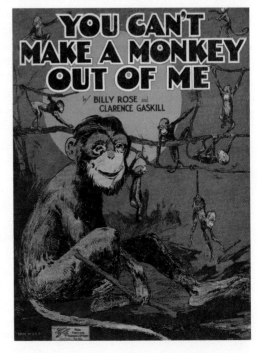

The Scopes trial was a media sensation; it even gave rise to popular songs, such as this one by Billy Rose.

John Raulston, was defeated when he sought reelection; Bryan died in his sleep a few days after the trial. But fundamentalism continued to flourish, not only in the nation's backwaters but also in many cities, brought there by rural people in search of work. In retrospect, even the heroes of the Scopes trial—science and freedom of thought—seem somewhat less stainless than they did to liberals at the time. The account of evolution in the textbook used by Scopes was hopelessly deficient and laced with bigotry, yet it was advanced as unassailable fact. In a section on the "Races of Man," for example, it described Caucasians as "the highest type of all . . . represented by the civilized white inhabitants of Europe and America."

Urban–Rural Conflicts: Prohibition

The conflict between the countryside and the city was fought on many fronts, and in one sector the rural forces achieved a quick victory. This was the Eighteenth Amendment, ratified in 1919, which prohibited the manufacture, transportation, and sale of alcoholic beverages. Although there were some big-city advocates of prohibition, the Eighteenth Amendment, in the words of one historian, marked a triumph of the "Corn Belt over the conveyor belt."

The temperance movement had been important since the age of Jackson; it was a major issue in many states during the Gilded Age, and by the Progressive Era powerful organizations like the Anti-Saloon League and the Women's Christian Temperance Union were seeking to have drinking outlawed entirely. Indeed, prohibition was a typical progressive reform, moralistic, backed by the middle class, and aimed at frustrating "the interests"—in this case the distillers.

World War I aided the prohibitionists by increasing the need for food. The Lever Act of 1917 outlawed the use of grain in the manufacture of alcoholic beverages, primarily as a conservation measure. The prevailing dislike of foreigners helped the dry cause still more: Beer drinking was associated with Germans. State and local laws had made a large part of the country dry by 1917. National prohibition became official in January 1920.

This "experiment noble in purpose," as Herbert Hoover called it, achieved a number of socially desirable results. It reduced the annual national consumption of alcohol from 2.6 gallons per capita in the period just before the war to less than 1 gallon in the early 1930s. Arrests for drunkenness fell off sharply, as did deaths from alcoholism. Fewer workers squandered their wages on drink. If the drys had been willing to legalize beer and wine, the experiment might have worked. Instead, by insisting on total abstinence, they drove thousands of moderates to violate the law. Strict enforcement became impossible, especially in the cities.

In areas where sentiment favored prohibition strongly, liquor remained difficult to find. Elsewhere, anyone with sufficient money could obtain it easily. Smuggling became a major business, *bootlegger* a household word. Private individuals busied themselves learning how to manufacture "bathtub gin." Many druggists issued prescriptions for alcohol with a free hand. The manufacture of wine for religious ceremonies was legal, and consumption of sacramental wine jumped by 800,000 gallons during the first two years of prohibition. The saloon disappeared, replaced by the speakeasy, a supposedly secret bar or club operating under the benevolent eye of the local police.

That the law was often violated does not mean that it was ineffective any more than violations of laws against theft and murder mean that those laws are ineffective.

Although gangsters such as Alphonse "Scarface Al" Capone of Chicago were engaged in the liquor traffic, their "organizations" existed before the passage of the Eighteenth Amendment. But prohibition widened already serious rifts in the social fabric of the country. Organized crime became more powerful. Besides undermining public morality by encouraging hypocrisy, prohibition almost destroyed the Democratic party as a national organization. Democratic immigrants in the cities hated it, but southern Democrats sang its praises, often while continuing to drink (the humorist Will Rogers quipped that Mississippi would vote dry "as long as the voters could stagger to the polls").

The hypocrisy of prohibition had a particularly deleterious effect on politicians, a class seldom famous for candor. Members of Congress catered to the demands of the powerful lobby of the Anti-Saloon League yet failed to grant adequate funds to the Prohibition Bureau. Nearly all the prominent leaders, Democrat and Republican, from Wilson and La Follette to Hoover and Franklin D. Roosevelt, equivocated shamelessly on the liquor question. By the end of the decade almost every competent observer recognized that prohibition at least needed to be overhauled, but the well-organized and powerful dry forces rejected all proposals for modifying it.

((•—[Hear the **Audio**

Prohibition is a Failure at **myhistorylab.com**

The Ku Klux Klan

The most horrible manifestation of the social malaise of the 1920s was the revival of the Ku Klux Klan. This new Klan, founded in 1915 by William J. Simmons, a former preacher, admitted only native-born white Protestants. The distrust of foreigners, blacks, Catholics, and Jews implicit in this regulation explains why it flourished in the social climate that spawned religious fundamentalism, immigration restriction, and prohibition. In a little over a year the Klan enrolled 100,000 recruits, and by 1923 they claimed the astonishing total of 5 million.

A Ku Klux Klan initiation ceremony photographed in Kansas in the 1920s. During its peak influence at mid-decade, Klan endorsement was essential to political candidates in many areas of the West and Midwest. Campaigning for reelection in 1934, an Indiana congressman testified, "I was told to join the Klan, or else."
Source: Kansas State Historical Society.

Simmons gave his society trappings and mystery calculated to attract gullible and bigoted people who yearned to express their frustrations and hostilities without personal risk. Klansmen masked themselves in white robes and hoods and enjoyed a childish mumbo jumbo of magnificent-sounding titles and dogmas. They burned crosses in the night, organized mass demonstrations to intimidate people they disliked, and put pressure on businessmen to fire black workers from better-paying jobs.

The Klan had relatively little appeal in the Northeast or in metropolitan centers in other parts of the country, but it found many members in mid-sized cities and in the small towns and villages of midwestern and western states. The rationale was an urge to return to an older, supposedly finer America and to stamp out all varieties of noncon-formity. Klansmen persecuted gamblers, "loose" women, violators of the prohibition laws, and anyone who happened to differ from them on religious questions or who belonged to a "foreign race."

The very success of the Klan led to its undoing. Factionalism sprang up, and rival leaders squabbled over the large sums that had been collected from the membership. The cruel and outrageous behavior of the organization roused both liberals and conser-vatives in every part of the country. And of course its victims joined forces against their tormentors. When the powerful leader of the Indiana Klan, a middle-aged repro-bate named David C. Stephenson, was convicted of assault-ing and causing the death of a young woman, the rank and file abandoned the organization in droves. The Klan remained influential for a number of years, but it ceased to be a dynamic force after 1924. By 1930 it had only some 9,000 members.

•◦•[Read the Document

Creed of Klanswomen at **myhistorylab.com**

Literary Trends

The literature of the 1920s reflects the disillusionment of the intellectuals. The wasteful horrors of the Great War and then the antics of the fundamentalists and the cruelty of the red-baiters and the Klan turned them into critics of society. Many intel-lectuals deplored the 1927 execution of Nicola Sacco and Bartolomeo Vanzetti, Italian immigrants (and anarchists) who were deprived of a fair trial in a murder case. They included the poet Edna St. Vincent Millay, the playwright Maxwell Anderson, and the novelists Upton Sinclair and John Dos Passos. After the war the poet Ezra Pound dropped his talk of an American Renaissance and wrote instead of a "botched civilization."

•◦•[Read the Document

Bartolomeo Vanzetti, Court Statement at **myhistorylab.com**

The symbol of what some called the "lost generation," in his own mind as well as to his contemporaries and to later critics, was F. Scott Fitzgerald. Born to modest wealth in St. Paul, Minnesota, in 1896, Fitzgerald attended Princeton and served in the army during the Great War. He rose to sudden fame in 1920 when he published *This Side of Paradise*, a somewhat sophomoric novel that appealed powerfully to college students and captured the fears and confusions of the lost generation. In *The Great Gatsby* (1925), a more mature work, Fitzgerald depicted a modern millionaire—coarse, unscrupulous, jaded, in love with another man's wife. Gatsby's tragedy lay in his dedication to a woman who, Fitzgerald made clear, did not merit his passion.

The tragedy of *The Great Gatsby* was related to Fitzgerald's own. Pleasure-loving and extravagant, he squandered the money earned by *This Side of Paradise*. When *The Great Gatsby* failed to sell as well, he turned to writing potboilers. "I really worked hard as hell last winter," he told the critic Edmund Wilson, "but it was all trash and it nearly broke my heart." While some of his later work, particularly *Tender Is the Night* (1934), is first-class, he descended into the despair of alcoholism and ended his days as a Hollywood scriptwriter.

Many young American writers and artists became expatriates in the 1920s. They flocked to Rome, Berlin, and especially Paris, where they could live cheaply and escape what seemed to them the "conspiracy against the individual" prevalent in their own country. Some made meager livings as journalists, translators, and editors, perhaps turning an extra dollar from time to time by selling a story or a poem to an American magazine or a painting to a tourist.

Ernest Hemingway was the most talented of the expatriates. He had served in the Italian army during the war and been grievously wounded (in spirit as well as in body). He settled in Paris in 1922 to write. His first novel, *The Sun Also Rises* (1926), portrayed the café world of the expatriate and the rootless desperation, amorality, and sense of outrage at life's meaninglessness that obsessed so many in those years. In *A Farewell to Arms* (1929) he drew on his military experiences to describe the confusion and horror of war.

Hemingway's books were best-sellers and he became a legend in his own time. Few novelists have been as capable of suggesting powerful emotions and action in so few words. Mark Twain and Stephen Crane were his models; Gertrude Stein, a writer and revolutionary genius, his teacher. But his style was his own—direct, simple, taut, sparse:

> I went out the door and down the hall to the room where Catherine was to be after the baby came. I sat in a chair there and looked at the room. I had the paper in my coat that I had bought when I went out for lunch and I read it. . . . After a while I stopped reading and turned off the light and watched it get dark outside. *(A Farewell to Arms)*

Source: Reprinted with the permission of Scribner, a Division of Simon & Schuster, Inc., from *A Farewell to Arms* by Ernest Hemingway. Copyright © 1929 by Charles Scribner's Son's; copyright renewed 1956 by Ernest Hemingway. All rights reserved.

This kind of writing, evoking rather than describing emotion, fascinated readers and inspired hundreds of imitators; it made a permanent mark on world literature. What Hemingway had to say was of less universal interest. He wrote about bullfights, hunting and fishing, and violence; while he did so with masterful penetration, these themes placed limits on his work that he never transcended. The critic Alfred Kazin summed up Hemingway in a sentence: "He brought a major art to a minor vision of life."

Edith Wharton was of the New York aristocracy. She was educated by tutors and governesses and never went to college. She traveled frequently to Europe, eventually chose to live there, and took up writing. After co-authoring a book on home decoration, she wrote novels on marriage and manners in some ways reminiscent of Henry James. In Paris at the outset of the Great War, she threw herself into war-related charities. But while the shock of the war jolted Fitzgerald and Hemingway into the vanguard of innovation, she retreated from the jangling energy of postwar life and culture. The product of her retreat, *The Age of Innocence* (1920), offered a penetrating portrait of an unsettlingly serene if vanished world. The Nation remarked that Wharton had described the wealthy of old New York "as familiarly as if she loved them and as lucidly as if she hated them."

Although neither was the equal of Hemingway, Fitzgerald, or Wharton, two other writers of the 1920s deserve mention: H. L. Mencken and Sinclair Lewis. Each reflected the distaste of intellectuals for the climate of the times. Mencken, a Baltimore newspaperman and founder of one of the great magazines of the era, the *American Mercury*, was a thoroughgoing cynic. He coined the word *booboisie* to define the complacent, middle-class majority, and he fired superbly witty broadsides at fundamentalists, prohibitionists, and "Puritans." "Puritanism," he once said, "is the haunting fear that someone, somewhere, may be happy."

But Mencken was never indifferent to the many aspects of American life that roused his contempt. Politics at once fascinated and repelled him, and he assailed the statesmen of his generation with magnificent impartiality:

> [On Coolidge]: "A cheap and trashy fellow, deficient in sense and almost devoid of any notion of honor—in brief, a dreadful little cad."

> [On Hoover]: "Lord Hoover is no more than a pious old woman, a fat Coolidge."

> Source: H. L. Mencken

Mencken's diatribes, while amusing, were not profound. In perspective he seems more a professional iconoclast than a constructive critic; like both Fitzgerald and Hemingway, he was something of a perennial adolescent. However, he consistently supported freedom of expression of every sort.

Sinclair Lewis was probably the most popular American novelist of the 1920s. Like Fitzgerald, his first major work brought him instant fame and notoriety—and for the same reason. *Main Street* (1920) portrayed the smug ignorance and bigotry of the American small town so accurately that even Lewis's victims recognized themselves; his title became a symbol for provinciality and middle-class meanness of spirit. In *Babbitt* (1922), he created what many people considered the typical businessman of the 1920s, gregarious, a "booster," blindly orthodox in his political and social opinions, a slave to every cliché, and full of loud self-confidence, but under the surface a bumbling, rather timid fellow who would have liked to be better than he was but dared not try. Lewis went on to dissect the medical profession in *Arrowsmith* (1925), religion in *Elmer Gantry* (1927), and fascism in *It Can't Happen Here* (1935).

The "New Negro"

The postwar reaction brought despair for many blacks. Aside from the barbarities of the Klan, they suffered from the postwar middle-class hostility to labor. The increasing presence of southern blacks in northern cities also caused conflict. Some 393,000 settled in New York, Pennsylvania, and Illinois in the 1920s, most of them in New York City, Philadelphia, and Chicago. The black population of New York City more than doubled between 1920 and 1930.

In earlier periods blacks in northern cities had tended to live together, but in small neighborhoods scattered over large areas. Now the tendency was toward concentration in what came to be called ghettos.

Even in small northern cities where they made up only a tiny proportion of the population, blacks were badly treated. When Robert S. and Helen M. Lynd made their classic sociological analysis of "Middletown" (Muncie, Indiana), they discovered that although black and white children attended the same schools, the churches, the larger movie houses, and other places of public accommodation were segregated. The local YMCA had a gymnasium where high school basketball was played, but the secretary refused to allow any team with a black player to use it. Even the news in Muncie was segregated. Local papers chronicled the affairs of the black community—roughly 5 percent of the population—under the heading "In Colored Circles."

Coming after the hopes inspired by wartime gains, the disappointments of the 1920s produced a new militancy among many blacks. In 1919 W. E. B. Du Bois wrote in *The Crisis*, "We are cowards and jackasses if . . . we do not marshal every ounce of our brain and brawn to fight . . . against the forces of hell in our own land." He increased his commitment to black nationalism, organizing a series of Pan African Conferences in an effort—futile, as it turned out—to create an international black movement.

Du Bois never made up his mind whether to work for integration or black separatism. Such ambivalence never troubled Marcus Garvey, a West Indian whose Universal Negro Improvement Association attracted hundreds of thousands of followers in the early 1920s. Garvey had nothing but contempt for whites, for light-skinned blacks like Du Bois, and for organizations such as the NAACP, which sought to bring whites and blacks together to fight segregation and other forms of prejudice. "Back to Africa" was his slogan; the black man must "work out his salvation in his motherland."

Garvey's message was naive, but it served to build racial pride among the masses of poor and unschooled blacks. He organized black businesses of many sorts, including a company that manufactured black dolls. He established a corps of Black Cross nurses and a Black Star Line Steamship Company to transport blacks back to Africa.

More sophisticated black leaders like Du Bois detested Garvey, whom they thought something of a charlatan. In 1923 Garvey's steamship line went into bankruptcy. He was convicted of defrauding the thousands of his supporters who had invested in its stock and was sent to prison. Nevertheless, his message, if not his methods, helped to create the "New Negro," proud of being black and prepared to resist both mistreatment and white ideas. The ghettos produced compensating advantages for blacks. One effect, not fully utilized until later, was to increase their political power by enabling them to elect representatives to state legislatures and

A painting from Jacob Lawrence's Migration Series (1940–1941).
Source: Gift of Mrs. David M. Levy. (28.1942.20). ©The Museum of Modern Art/Artists Rights Society/Art Resource, NY.

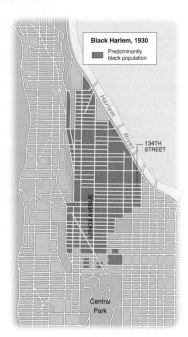

The Making of Black Harlem In 1911, African Americans lived mostly in a dozen-block region of Harlem; by 1930, they had created a predominantly black city of well over 100 city blocks.

Congress, and to exert considerable influence in closely contested elections. More immediately, city life stimulated self-confidence; despite their horrors, the ghettos offered economic opportunity, political rights, and freedom from the everyday debasements of life in the South. The ghetto was a black world where black men and women could be themselves.

Black writers, musicians, and artists found in the ghettos both an audience and the "spiritual emancipation" that unleashed their capacities. Jazz, the great popular music of the age, was largely the creation of black musicians working in New Orleans before the turn of the century. By the 1920s it had spread throughout the country and to most of the rest of the world. White musicians and white audiences took it up—in a way it became a force for racial tolerance and understanding.

Harlem, the largest black community in the world, became in the 1920s a cultural capital, center of the **Harlem Renaissance**. Black newspapers and magazines flourished along with theatrical companies and libraries. Du Bois opened *The Crisis* to

> ⦿ Watch the Video
>
> *The Harlem Renaissance* at
> myhistorylab.com

young writers and artists, and a dozen "little" magazines sprang up. Langston Hughes, one of the most talented poets of the era, described the exhilaration of his first arrival in this city within a city, a magnet for every black intellectual and artist: "Harlem! I . . . dropped my bags, took a deep breath, and felt happy again." In 1925 Zora Neale Hurston joined with Hughes to create a literary magazine, and celebrated the lives of ordinary black workers.

With some exceptions, African American writers like Hughes and Hurston did not share in the disillusionment that afflicted so many white intellectuals. The persistence of prejudice angered them and made them militant. But to be militant, one must be at some

Zora Neale Hurston, a major figure of the Harlem Renaissance, wrote eighteen novels—many of which were made into movies.

level hopeful. Sociologists and psychologists (for whom the ghettos were indispensable social laboratories) were demonstrating that environment rather than heredity was preventing black economic progress. Together with the achievements of creative blacks, which for the first time were being appreciated by large numbers of white intellectuals, these discoveries seemed to herald the eventual disappearance of racial prejudice. The black, Alain Locke wrote in *The New Negro* (1925), "lays aside the status of beneficiary and ward for that of a collaborator and participant in American civilization." Alas, as Locke and other black intellectuals were soon to discover, this prediction, like so many made in the 1920s, did not come to pass.

Economic Expansion

Despite the turmoil of the times and the dissatisfactions expressed by some of the nation's best minds, the 1920s was an exceptionally prosperous decade. Business boomed, real wages rose, unemployment declined. The United States was as rich as all Europe; perhaps 40 percent of the world's total wealth lay in American hands. Little wonder that business leaders and other conservatives described the period as a "new era."

The prosperity rested on many bases, one of which was the friendly, hands-off attitude of the federal government, which bolstered the confidence of the business community. The Federal Reserve Board kept interest rates low, a further stimulus to economic growth. The continuing mechanization and rationalization of industry provided a more fundamental stimulus to the economy. From heavy road-grading equipment and concrete mixers to devices for making cigars and glass tubes, from pneumatic tools to the dial telephone, machinery was replacing human hands at an ever more rapid rate. Industrial output almost doubled between 1921 and 1929 without any substantial increase in the industrial labor force.

Most important, American manufacturing was experiencing a remarkable improvement in efficiency. The method of breaking down the complex processes of production into many simple operations and the use of interchangeable parts were nineteenth-century innovations; in the 1920s they were adopted on an almost universal scale. The moving assembly line which carried the product to the worker, first devised by Henry Ford in his automobile plant in the decade before World War I, speeded production and reduced costs. In ten years the hourly output of Ford workers quadrupled.

The Age of the Consumer

The growing ability of manufacturers to produce goods meant that great effort had to be made to create new consumer demands. Advertising and salesmanship were raised almost to the status of fine arts. Bruce Barton, one of the advertising "geniuses" of the era, wrote a best-selling book, *The Man Nobody Knows* (1925), in which he described Jesus as the "founder of modern business," the man who "picked up twelve men from the bottom ranks . . . and forged them into an organization that conquered the world."

Producers concentrated on making their goods more attractive and on changing models frequently to entice buyers into the market. The practice of selling goods on the installment plan helped bring expensive items within the reach of the masses. Inventions and technological advances created new or improved products: radios, automobiles, electric appliances such as vacuum cleaners and refrigerators, gadgets like cigarette lighters, and new forms of entertainment like motion pictures.

Undoubtedly the automobile had the single most important impact on the nation's economy in the 1920s. Although well over a million cars a year were being regularly produced by 1916, the real expansion of the industry came after 1921. Output reached 3.6 million in 1923 and fell below that figure only twice during the remainder of the decade. By 1929, 23 million private cars clogged the highways, an average of nearly one per family.

Watch the Video
The rise and fall of the automobile economy at **myhistorylab.com**

The auto industry created companies that manufactured tires and spark plugs and other products. It triggered a gigantic road-building program: There were 387,000 miles of paved roads in the United States in 1921, and 662,000 miles in 1929. Thousands of persons found employment in filling stations, roadside stands, and other businesses catering to the motoring public. The tourism industry profited, and the shift of population from the cities to the suburbs accelerated.

The automobile made life more mobile yet also more encapsulated. It changed recreational patterns and family life. In addition, it profoundly affected the way Americans thought. It gave them a freedom never before imagined. The owner of the most rickety jalopy could travel farther, faster, and far more comfortably than a monarch of old with his pureblooded steeds and gilded coaches.

These benefits were real and priceless. Cars also became important

Would women believe the claims of cosmetics advertisements? "Kissproof" promised to make a woman's lips "pulsate with the very spirit of reckless, irrepressible youth." In a 1927 survey of housewives in Columbus, Ohio, Pond's Company found that two-thirds of the women could not even recall the company's advertisements. Younger women, however, were more impressionable. When the J. Walter Thompson advertising agency asked Vassar students to describe cosmetics, they unconsciously used the exact phrases from advertising copy—proof of its power.

symbols. They gave their owners the feeling of power and status that a horse gave to a medieval knight. According to some authorities the typical American cared more about owning an automobile than a house.

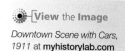

View the Image

Downtown Scene with Cars,
1911 at **myhistorylab.com**

In time there were undesirable, even dangerous results of the automotive revolution: roadside scenery disfigured by billboards, gas stations, and other enterprises aimed at satisfying the traveler's needs; horrendous traffic jams; soaring accident rates; air pollution; and the neglect of public transportation, which was an important cause of the deterioration of inner cities. All these disadvantages were noticed during the 1920s, but in the springtime of the new industry they were discounted. The automobile seemed an unalloyed blessing—part toy, part tool, part symbol of American freedom, prosperity, and individualism.

Henry Ford

The person most responsible for the growth of the automobile industry was Henry Ford, a self-taught mechanic from Greenfield, Michigan. Ford was neither a great inventor nor one of the true automobile pioneers. Ford's first brilliant insight was to "get the prices down to the buying power." Through mass production, cars could be made cheaply enough to put them within reach of the ordinary citizen. In 1908 he designed the Model T Ford, a simple, tough box on wheels. In a year he proved his point by selling 11,000 Model Ts. Relentlessly cutting costs and increasing efficiency with the assembly line system, he expanded production at an unbelievable rate. By 1925 he was turning out more than 9,000 cars a day, one approximately every ten seconds, and the price of the Model T had been reduced below $300.

Ford's second insight was the importance of high wages in stimulating output (and selling more automobiles). The assembly line simplified the laborer's task and increased the pace of work; at the same time it made each worker much more productive. Jobs became boring and fatiguing, and absenteeism and labor turnover became serious problems. To combat this difficulty, in 1914 Ford established the $5 day, an increase of about $2 over prevailing wages. The rate of turnover in his plant fell 90 percent, and although critics charged that he recaptured his additional labor costs by speeding up the line, his policy had a revolutionary effect on wage rates. Later he raised the minimum to $6 and then to $7 a day.

Ford's profits soared along with sales; since he owned the entire company, he became a billionaire. He also became an authentic folk hero: his homespun style, his dislike of bankers and sophisticated society, and his intense individualism endeared him to millions. He stood as a symbol of the wonders of the American system—he had given the nation a marvelous convenience at a low price, at the same time enriching himself and raising the living standards of his thousands of employees.

Unfortunately, Ford had the defects of his virtues in full measure. He paid high wages but refused to deal with any union and he employed spies to investigate the private lives of his workers, and gangsters and thugs to enforce plant discipline. When he discovered a worker driving any car but a Ford, he had him dismissed. So close was the supervision in the factory that workers devised the "Ford whisper," a means of talking without moving one's lips.

Success made Ford stubborn. The Model T remained essentially unchanged for nearly twenty years. Other companies, notably General Motors, were soon turning out better vehicles for very little more money. Customers, increasingly affluent and style-conscious, began to shift to Chevrolets and Chryslers. Finally, in 1927, Ford shut down all operations for eighteen months in order to retool for the Model A. His competitors rushed in during this period to fill the vacuum. Although his company continued to make a great deal of money, Ford never regained the dominant position he had held for so long.

Ford was enormously uninformed, yet—because of his success and the praise the world heaped on him—he did not hesitate to speak out on subjects far outside his area of competence, from the evils of drink and tobacco to medicine and international affairs. He developed political ambitions and published virulent anti-Semitic propaganda. He said he would not give five cents for all the art in the world.

While praising his talents as a manufacturer, historians have not dealt kindly with Ford the man, in part no doubt because he once said, "History is more or less the bunk."

The Airplane

Henry Ford was also an early manufacturer of airplanes, and while the airplane industry was not economically important in the 1920s, its development in that decade laid the basis for changes in lifestyles and attitudes at least as momentous as those produced by the automobile. The invention of the internal combustion gasoline engine, with its extremely high ratio of power to weight, made the airplane possible, which explains why the early experiments with "flying machines" took place at about the same time that the prototypes of the modern automobile were being manufactured. Wilbur and Orville Wright made their famous flight at Kitty Hawk, North Carolina, in 1903, five years before Ford produced his Model T. Another pair of brothers, Malcolm and Haimes Lockheed, built their Model G, one of the earliest commercial planes in 1913.

The great event of the decade for aviation, still an achievement that must strike awe in the hearts of reflective persons, was Charles A. Lindbergh's nonstop flight from New York to Paris in May 1927. It took more than thirty-three hours for Lindbergh's single-engine *Spirit of St. Louis* to cross the Atlantic, a formidable physical achievement for the pilot as well as an example of skill and courage. When the public learned that the intrepid "Lucky Lindy" was handsome, modest, uninterested in converting his new fame into cash, and a model of propriety (he neither drank nor smoked), his role as American hero was ensured. It was a role Lindbergh detested—one biographer has described him as "by nature solitary"—but could not avoid.

Lindbergh's flight enormously increased public interest in flying, but it was a landmark in aviation technology as well. The day of routine passenger flights was at last about to dawn. In July 1927, a mere two months after the *Spirit of St. Louis* touched down at Le Bourget Field in France, William E. Boeing of Boeing Air Transport began flying passengers and mail between San Francisco and Chicago, using the M–40, a plane of his own design and manufacture. Early in 1928 he changed the company name to United Aircraft and Transport. Two years later Boeing produced the first all-metal low-wing plane and, in 1933, the twin-engine 247, a prototype for many others.

In retrospect the postwar era seems even more a period of transition than it appeared to most people at the time. Rarely had change come so swiftly, and rarely had old and new existed side by side in such profusion. Creativity and reaction, hope and despair, freedom and repression—the modern world in all its unfathomable complexity was emerging.

Milestones

1903	Wright brothers fly at Kitty Hawk, NC	1926	Gertrude Ederle swims English Channel
1908	Henry Ford designs Model T automobile		Ernest Hemingway publishes *The Sun Also Rises*
1914	Ford establishes $5 day for autoworkers		
1919	Eighteenth Amendment outlaws alcoholic beverages (Prohibition)	1927	Charles Lindbergh flies solo across Atlantic
	Nineteenth Amendment gives women right to vote		Sacco and Vanzetti are executed
1920	Sinclair Lewis publishes *Main Street*		*The Jazz Singer*, first motion picture with sound, is released
	First commercial radio station, KDKA, Pittsburgh, begins broadcasting		Jack Dempsey loses heavyweight boxing title to Gene Tunney
1920s	Black culture flourishes in Harlem Renaissance		Babe Ruth hits sixty home runs
1921	Margaret Sanger founds American Birth Control League	1928	John B. Watson publishes *The Psychological Care of Infant and Child*
1924	Ku Klux Klan membership peaks		
1925	Scopes is convicted for teaching evolution	1929	Capone's gang kills Moran's in Valentine's Day Massacre
	F. Scott Fitzgerald publishes *The Great Gatsby*		

✔•⌐Study and Review at www.myhistorylab.com

Review Questions

1. The introduction suggests that the prohibition of alcohol encouraged people to flaunt other conventions. To what extent were the cultural shifts of the 1920s a rebellion against tradition?
2. How did traditionalists respond to these social and cultural transformations? Was the fundamental tension, as the chapter suggests, between rural and urban cultures? Or was it between classes or ethnic groups?
3. How did technological changes such as radio, the automobile, and the airplane influence culture? How did "mass culture" touch the lives of Americans? Did it improve life or diminish it?
4. How did the 1920s liberate women, African Americans, and minorities?

Key Terms

Harlem Renaissance *650*   National Origins Act *632*   Scopes trial *643*

25 From "Normalcy" to Economic Collapse: 1921–1933

((•—[Hear the Audio Chapter 25 at myhistorylab.com

Will you get a job?

IN JUNE, 2009 KYLE DALEY GRADUATED FROM UCLA WITH A 3.5 AVERAGE. He applied for 600 jobs, mostly entry-level positions in large corporations. He got two interviews but no job. He was not alone. In 2010 the Labor Department reported that nearly 11 percent of recent college graduates were without jobs, the highest rate on record. Because two-thirds had taken out student loans averaging $23,200, many considered bankruptcy.

Daley and his age cohort had grown up during the most prosperous decades the American nation had ever witnessed. But it all came crashing down in 2008. The enormous hot-air balloon that was the U.S. housing market burst. Worldwide financial markets, tethered to U.S. mortgages, fell precipitously. Major investment firms declared bankruptcy. Massive layoffs ensued. "I don't remember any time, maybe even the Great Depression, when things went down so fast," observed Paul Volker, the eighty-one-year-old former chairman of the Federal Reserve.

The Great Depression had similarly been preceded by an era of economic prosperity. In 1924 Commerce Secretary Herbert Hoover had proclaimed "a new era" in which cutthroat competition was being superseded by cooperative associations of producers. This heralded "infinite possibilities of moral progress." Such words perhaps sounded hollow, coming in the wake of a Harding administration disgraced by scandal. By 1924 Calvin Coolidge was president, to be succeeded by Hoover in 1929; both presided over a nation that basked in the dawn of a prosperous new era, though a few dark war clouds could be seen in the distance. Many Americans, giddy over their stock market winnings, placed more and more bets on Wall Street. When it all went bust in 1929, many found themselves mired in the depths of the Great Depression.

Harding and "Normalcy"

Warren G. Harding was a newspaperman by trade, publisher of the *Marion Star*, with previous political experience as a legislator and lieutenant governor in his home state, Ohio, and as a U.S. senator. No president, before or since, looked more like a statesman; few were less suited for running the country.

Harding's genial nature and lack of strong convictions made him attractive to many of the politicos after eight years of the headstrong Wilson. During the campaign he exasperated sophisticates by his ignorance and imprecision. He coined the famous vulgarism *normalcy* as a substitute for the word *normality*, and committed numerous other blunders. Senator Lodge, ordinarily a stickler for linguistic exactitude, replied acidly that he found Harding a paragon by comparison with Wilson, "a man who wrote English very well without ever saying anything." A large majority of the voters, untroubled by the candidate's lack of erudition, shared Lodge's confidence that Harding would be a vast improvement over Wilson.

Harding has often been characterized as lazy and incompetent. In fact, he was hardworking and politically shrewd; his major weaknesses were indecisiveness and an unwillingness to offend. He turned the most important government departments over to efficient administrators of impeccable reputation: Charles Evans Hughes, the secretary of state; Herbert Hoover in the Commerce Department; Andrew Mellon in the Treasury; and Henry C. Wallace in Agriculture. He kept track of what these men did but seldom initiated policy in their areas. However, Harding gave many lesser offices, and a few of major importance, to the unsavory "Ohio Gang" headed by Harry M. Daugherty, whom he made attorney general.

The president was too kindly, too well-intentioned, and too unambitious to be dishonest. He appointed corrupt officials like Daugherty, Secretary of the Interior Albert B. Fall, Director of the Mint "Ed" Scobey, and Charles R. Forbes, head of the new Veterans Bureau, out of a sense of personal obligation or because they were old friends who shared his taste for poker and liquor. Before 1921 he had enjoyed holding office. In the lonely eminence of the White House, however, he found only misery. "The White House is a prison," he complained. "I can't get away from the men who dog my footsteps. I am in jail."

"The Business of the United States is Business"

Secretary of the Treasury Mellon, multimillionaire banker and master of the aluminum industry, dominated the administration's domestic policy. Mellon set out to lower the taxes of the rich, reverse the low-tariff policies of the Wilson period, return to the laissez-faire philosophy of McKinley, and reduce the national debt by cutting expenses and administrating the government more efficiently.

In principle his program had considerable merit. Tax rates designed to check consumer spending in time of war and to raise the huge sum needed to defeat the Central Powers were undoubtedly hampering economic expansion in the early 1920s. Certain industries that had sprung up in the United States during the Great War were suffering from German and Japanese competition now that the fighting had ended. Rigid regulation necessary during a national crisis could well be dispensed with in peacetime. And efficiency and economy in government are always desirable.

Yet Mellon carried his policies to unreasonable extremes. He proposed eliminating inheritance taxes and reducing the tax on high incomes by two-thirds, but he opposed lower rates for taxpayers earning less than $66,000 a year, apparently not realizing that economic expansion required greater mass consumption as well. Freeing the rich from "oppressive" taxation, he argued, would enable them to invest

Big oil's plans to drill in the Teapot Dome oil reserves led to a major scandal in the Harding administration. (See also Re-Viewing the Past, *There Will Be Blood*, pp. 660–661.)

more in potentially productive enterprises, the success of which would create jobs for ordinary people. Mellon succeeded in balancing the budget and reducing the national debt by an average of over $500 million a year. So committed were the Republican leaders to retrenchment that they even resisted the demands of veterans, organized in the politically potent American Legion, for an "adjusted compensation" bonus.

That the business community heartily approved the policies of Harding and Coolidge is not surprising. Both presidents were uncritical advocates of the business point of view. "We want less government in business and more business in government," Harding pontificated, to which Coolidge added, "The business of the United States is business." Harding and Coolidge used their power of appointment to convert regulatory bodies like the Interstate Commerce Commission (ICC) and the Federal Reserve Board into pro-business agencies that ceased almost entirely to restrict the activities of the industries they were

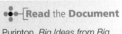

●●●[Read the Document

Purinton, *Big Ideas from Big Business* at **myhistorylab.com** supposed to be controlling. The ICC became almost the reverse of what it had been in the Progressive Era.

The Harding Scandals

At least Mellon was honest. The Ohio gang used its power in the most corrupt way imaginable. Jesse Smith, a crony of Attorney General Daugherty, was what today would be called an influence peddler. When he was exposed in 1923, he committed suicide. Charles R. Forbes of the Veterans Bureau siphoned millions of dollars appropriated for the construction of hospitals into his own pocket. When he was found out, he fled to Europe. Later he returned, stood trial, and was sentenced to two years in prison. His assistant, Charles F. Cramer, committed suicide. Daugherty himself was implicated in the fraudulent return of German assets seized by the alien property custodian to their original owners. He escaped imprisonment only by refusing to testify on the ground that he might incriminate himself.

The worst scandal involved Secretary of the Interior Albert B. Fall, a former senator. In 1921 Fall arranged with the complaisant Secretary of the Navy Edwin Denby for the transfer to the Interior Department of government oil reserves being held for the future use of the navy. He then leased these properties to private oil companies. Edward L. Doheny's Pan-American Petroleum Company got the Elk Hills reserve in California; the Teapot Dome reserve in Wyoming was turned over to Harry F. Sinclair's Mammoth Oil Company. When critics protested, Fall explained that it was necessary to develop the Elk Hills and Teapot Dome properties because adjoining private drillers were draining off the navy's oil. Nevertheless, in 1923 the Senate ordered a full-scale investigation, conducted by Senator Thomas J. Walsh of Montana. It soon came out that Doheny had "lent" Fall $100,000 in hard cash, handed over secretly in a "little black bag." Sinclair had given Fall over $300,000 in cash and negotiable securities. (For more on Doheny and Fall, see Re-Viewing the Past, *There Will Be Blood*, pp. 660–661.)

Although the three culprits in the **Teapot Dome scandal** escaped conviction on the charge of conspiring to defraud the government, Sinclair was sentenced to nine months in jail for contempt of the Senate and for tampering with a jury, and Fall was fined $100,000 and given a year in prison for accepting a bribe. In 1927 the Supreme Court revoked the leases and the two reserves were returned to the government.

●●●—Read the Document

Executive Orders and Senate Resolutions on Teapot Dome at **myhistorylab.com**

The public still knew little of the scandals when, in June 1923, Harding left Washington on a speaking tour that included a visit to Alaska. His health was poor and his spirits low, for he had begun to understand how his "Goddamn friends" had betrayed him. On the return trip from Alaska, he suffered a heart attack. He died in San Francisco on August 2.

Few presidents have been more deeply mourned by the people at the moment of their passing. Harding's kindly nature, his very ordinariness, increased his human appeal. Three million people viewed his coffin as it passed across the country. When the scandals came to light, sadness turned to scorn and contempt.

There Will Be Blood

In 2008 Daniel Day-Lewis won the Academy Award for his portrayal of Daniel Plainview in *There Will Be Blood,* a movie about wildcatting oil exploration in California in the early 1900s. Day-Lewis portrayed Plainview as a remorseless predator who lied with fluency and cheated with sincerity. He coaxed and coerced property owners into granting him oil leases on his own terms. When he didn't get what he wanted, he lashed out in violence.

Day-Lewis's Plainview fixed his coal-black eyes onto people like a fighter-pilot locking onto a target. A reviewer for the *New York Times* called Day-Lewis's performance "among the greatest I've ever seen." Day-Lewis filled Plainview "with so much rage and purpose you wait for him to blow," the reviewer added.

By the usual conventions of Hollywood, the evil Plainview would be vanquished by a white-hatted hero. But in *There Will Be Blood* no good guys ride to the rescue because there were no good guys: *Everyone* is after money.

In the absence of a conflict between good and evil, the movie turns on the question: What made Plainview so bad? Certainly, he was long-suffering. The movie begins with him in a mine shaft, hacking away at rock with a pick and scrabbling through the shards on his hands and knees, looking without success for a glint of gold or silver. When he fell down the shaft and broke his leg, he climbed out by himself. These powerfully discouraging scenes, which take up the first twenty minutes of the movie, include no dialogue whatsoever: Plainview's struggle was a solitary one.

This provides a motivational clue. Plainview hated everyone—with the exception of his son. "I see the worst in people," he declared. "I've built my hatreds up over the years, little by little." He crushed enemies not because he craved wealth but because he could not abide anyone getting the better of him. Which raises the larger question: Were the obsessions of Daniel Plainview characteristic of the industrial and financial magnates of the age?

Plainview, "born in Fond du Lac, Wisconsin," was based on California oil magnate, Edward L. Doheny, himself born in Fond du Lac. The son of a poor Irish immigrant, Doheny left home at a young age and prospected for gold and silver in New Mexico. He had little luck. His wife and children went hungry; she became an alcoholic and committed suicide. In 1891 Doheny gave up prospecting and went to Los Angeles to find a job. One day he spotted a man with a cart whose wheels were coated in tar. Doheny asked what had happened, and the man mentioned a tar pit at the corner of Patton and State Streets, near what is now Dodger Stadium.

Doheny acquired the oil rights to the area and began digging, shoveling dirt and tar into buckets and hauling it to the surface. At the depth of 155 feet, he was nearly killed by toxic fumes; then he studied a diagram of an oil rig and built a crude derrick. He used a sharpened eucalyptus tree as the drill. At 460 feet, he struck oil. Within a few years, he had built scores of derricks throughout Los Angeles. The growth of the city that became synonymous with the automobile was literally fueled by the oil that lay beneath it.

Doheny's first oil strike at Signal Hill near Los Angeles.

Edward L. Doheny, California oil magnate.

Daniel Day-Lewis as Daniel Plainview.

By 1920 southern California had become the world's leading oil-producer, and Doheny had become rich.

There Will Be Blood omitted the next stage in Doheny's life. In 1900 he went to Mexico and worked out a deal with the dictator Profirio Diaz for the oil rights to some promising regions of the undeveloped country. In 1910, Doheny hit several enormous gushers; soon his company was the largest oil producer in the world. His chief competitor in Mexico was Weetman Pearson, an English engineer and builder who had also wangled a lucrative deal out of Diaz.

Doheny was a tough and even ruthless businessman; he made many enemies. But it was not until the 1920s that he attained notoriety. He was among the oilmen who secured from Albert B. Fall, Harding's interior secretary, the right to drill in oil fields that were kept as an emergency reserve for the navy. On learning that Fall was in financial difficulties, Doheny sent his son Ned to Fall's apartment with $100,000 in cash. Fall accepted the money.

Several years later Doheny and his son were among those indicted for bribing Fall. In a Senate hearing Doheny professed his innocence. He had not bribed a government official; he had helped a friend. The amount of the gift—$100,000—was "a bagatelle to me," the equivalent of "the ordinary individual" giving $25 to a down-and-out neighbor. The statement drew gasps from the audience. Doheny, though acquitted, became the era's exemplar of greed and corruption.

There Will Be Blood ends with Plainview living alone in an enormous mansion. When an old antagonist stops by, seeking a handout, Plainview, drunk and enraged, murders him. The scene was filmed in the actual Beverly Hills mansion that Doheny had built for his son. In 1929 a deranged family friend who lived in the mansion shot and killed Ned before turning the gun on himself. It was some measure of Doheny's shattered reputation that rumors long circulated that Doheny had himself murdered both men. One recent historian has argued that Doheny was responsible for the deaths if only because his greed poisoned everything around him.

There Will Be Blood came out just before the great financial collapse of 2008–2009, when wildcatting financiers inflicted several trillion dollars' damage upon the global economy. It is tempting to see in such behavior a heart of darkness, such as the film imputed to Doheny. But we must remember that while Doheny was no paragon of propriety, he was no murderer. In painting him with the oily hues of a Daniel Plainview, Hollywood transformed the oil magnate into caricature. Indeed, Hollywood's search for box-office gushers is itself reminiscent of Day-Lewis's character. And if, like Plainview, it plays fast and loose with the literal truth, can it really be blamed?

Questions for Discussion

- Doheny pursued wealth with obsessive determination. In *Wall Street* (1987), the character Gordon Gekko declares that "Greed is good." How does greed promote economic growth? How does it become a destructive force?
- Did Doheny benefit society and, if so, how? How did he harm it?

Coolidge Prosperity

Had he lived, Harding might well have been defeated in 1924 because of the scandals. Vice President Coolidge, unconnected with the troubles and not the type to surround himself with cronies of any kind, seemed the ideal person to clean out the corrupt officials. Coolidge was a taciturn, extremely conservative New Englander with a long record in Massachusetts. He preferred to follow public opinion and hope for the best.

Coolidge defused his predecessor's scandals by replacing Harding's Attorney General Daugherty with Harlan Fiske Stone, dean of the Columbia University Law School. Soon Coolidge became the darling of the conservatives. His admiration for businessmen and his devotion to laissez-faire knew no limit. Andrew Mellon, whom he kept on as secretary of the Treasury, became his mentor in economic affairs.

Coolidge won the 1924 Republican nomination easily. The Democrats, badly split, required 103 ballots to choose a candidate. The southern wing, dry, anti-immigrant, pro-Klan, had fixed on William G. McAdoo, Wilson's secretary of the Treasury. The eastern, urban, wet element supported Governor Alfred E. Smith of New York, child of the slums, a Catholic who had compiled a distinguished record in social welfare legislation. After days of futile politicking, the party compromised on John W. Davis, a conservative corporation lawyer closely allied with the Morgan banking interests.

Dismayed by the conservatism of Coolidge and Davis, Robert M. La Follette, backed by the farm bloc, the Socialist party, the American Federation of Labor, and numbers of intellectuals, entered the race as the candidate of a new Progressive party. The Progressives adopted a neopopulist platform calling for the nationalization of railroads, the direct election of the president, the protection of labor's right to bargain collectively, and other reforms.

The situation was the opposite of 1912, when one conservative had run against two liberals and had been swamped. Coolidge received 15.7 million votes, Davis 8.4 million, La Follette 4.8 million. Conservatism was clearly the dominant mood of the country.

While Coolidge reigned, complacency was the order of the day. "Mr. Coolidge's genius for inactivity is developed to a very high point," the correspondent Walter Lippmann wrote. "It is a grim, determined, alert inactivity, which keeps Mr. Coolidge occupied constantly."[1] "The country," the president reported to Congress in 1928, "can regard the present with satisfaction, and anticipate the future with optimism."

Peace without a Sword

Presidents Harding and Coolidge handled foreign relations in much the same way they managed domestic affairs. Harding deferred to senatorial prejudice against executive domination in the area and let Secretary of State Charles Evans Hughes make policy. Coolidge adopted a similar course. In directing foreign relations, they faced the obstacle of a resurgent isolationism. The bloodiness of the Great War convinced millions that the only way to be sure it would not happen again was to "steer clear" of "entanglements." That these famous words had been used by Washington and Jefferson in vastly different contexts did not deter the isolationists of the 1920s from

---

[1]Coolidge was physically delicate, plagued by chronic stomach trouble. He required ten or eleven hours of sleep a day.

attributing to them the same authority they gave to Scripture. On the other hand, far-flung American economic interests, as well as the need for both raw materials for industry and foreign markets for America's growing surpluses of agricultural and manufactured goods, made close attention to and involvement in developments all over the world unavoidable.

Isolationist sentiments, therefore, did not deter the government from seeking to advance American interests abroad. The Open Door concept remained predominant; the State Department worked to obtain opportunities in underdeveloped countries for exporters and investors, hoping both to stimulate the American economy and to bring stability to "backward" nations. Although this policy sometimes roused local resentments because of the tendency of the United States to support entrenched elites while the mass of peasants and city workers lived in poverty, it also resulted in a further retreat from active interventionism.

The first important diplomatic event of the period revealed a great deal about American foreign policy after the Great War. During the war, Japan had greatly increased its influence in East Asia, especially in Manchuria, the northeastern province of warlord-dominated China. To maintain the Open Door in China, it would be necessary to check Japanese expansion. But there was little hope of restoring the old spheres of influence, which the mass of Chinese people bitterly resented. In addition, Japan, the United States, and Great Britain were engaged in expensive naval building programs, a competition none of them really wanted but from which all dared not withdraw unilaterally.

In November 1921, hoping to reach a general agreement with China, Japan, and the Europeans that would keep China open to the commerce of all and slow the armaments race, Secretary of State Hughes convened a conference in Washington. By the following February the Washington Conference had drafted three major treaties and a number of lesser agreements.

In the Five-Power Treaty, the United States, Great Britain, France, Japan, and Italy agreed to stop building battleships for ten years and to reduce their fleets of battleships to a fixed ratio, with Great Britain and the United States limited to 525,000 tons, Japan to 315,000 tons, and France and Italy to 175,000 tons. The new ratio was expected to produce a balance of forces in the Pacific.

The Four-Power Treaty, signed by the United States, Great Britain, Japan, and France, committed these nations to respect one another's interests in the islands of the Pacific and to confer in the event that any other country launched an attack in the area.

All the conferees signed the Nine-Power Treaty, agreeing to respect China's independence and to maintain the Open Door. On the surface, this was of monumental importance to the United States since it seemed to mean that Japan had given up its territorial ambitions on the Asian mainland and that both the Japanese and the Europeans had formally endorsed the Open Door concept.

The treaties, however, were uniformly toothless. The signers of the Four-Power Treaty agreed only to consult in case of aggression in the Pacific; they made no promises to help one another or to restrict their own freedom of action. As President Harding assured the Senate, "there [was] no commitment to armed force, no alliance, no written or moral obligation to join in defense."

The naval disarmament treaty said nothing about the number of other warships that the powers might build, about the far more important question of land and air forces, or about the underlying industrial and financial structures that controlled the ability of the nations to make war. In addition, the 5:5:3 ratio actually enabled the Japanese to dominate the western Pacific. It made the Philippine Islands indefensible and exposed Hawaii to possible attack. In a sense these American bases became hostages of Japan. Yet Congress was so unconcerned about Japanese sensibilities that it refused to grant any immigration quota to Japan under the National Origins Act of 1924, even though the formula applied to other nations would have allowed only 100 Japanese a year to enter the country. The law, Secretary Hughes warned, produced in Japan "a sense of injury and antagonism instead of friendship and cooperation."

Hughes did not think war a likely result, but Japanese resentment of "white imperialism" played into the hands of the military party in that nation. Many Japanese army and navy officers considered war with the United States inevitable.

As for the key Nine-Power Treaty, Japan did not abandon its territorial ambitions in China, and China remained so riven by conflict among the warlords and so resentful of the "imperialists" that the economic advantages of the Open Door turned out to be small indeed.

The United States entered into all these agreements without realizing their full implications and not really prepared to play an active part in East Asian affairs. The Japanese soon realized that the United States would not do much to defend its interests in China.

The Peace Movement

The Americans of the 1920s wanted peace but would neither surrender their prejudices nor build the defenses necessary to make it safe to indulge these passions.

Peace societies flourished, among them the Carnegie Endowment for International Peace, designed "to hasten the abolition of war, the foulest blot upon our civilization," and the Woodrow Wilson Foundation, aimed at helping "the liberal forces of mankind throughout the world . . . who intend to promote peace by the means of justice."

So great was the opposition to international cooperation that the United States refused to accept membership on the World Court, although this tribunal could settle disputes only when the nations involved agreed. Too many peace lovers believed that their goal could be attained simply by pointing out the moral and practical disadvantages of war.

The culmination of this illusory faith in preventing war by criticizing it came with the signing of the Kellogg-Briand Pact in 1928. The treaty was born in the fertile brain of French Foreign Minister Aristide Briand, who was eager to collect allies against possible attack by a resurgent Germany. In 1927 Briand proposed to Secretary of State Frank B. Kellogg that their countries agree never to go to war with each other. Kellogg found the idea as repugnant as any conventional alliance, but American isolationists and pacifists found the suggestion fascinating. To extricate himself from this situation, Kellogg suggested that the pact be broadened to include all nations. Now Briand was angry. Like Kellogg, he saw how meaningless such a treaty would be, especially when Kellogg insisted that it be hedged with a proviso that "every nation is free at all times . . . to defend its territory from attack and it alone is competent to decide when circumstances require war in self-defense." Nevertheless, Briand too found public pressures irresistible. In August 1928, at Paris, diplomats from fifteen nations bestowed upon one another an "international kiss," condemning "recourse to war for the solution of international controversies" and renouncing war "as an instrument of national policy." Seldom has so unrealistic a promise been made by so many intelligent people. Yet most Americans considered the Kellogg-Briand Pact a milestone in the history of civilization: The Senate, habitually so suspicious of international commitments, ratified it eighty-five to one.

The Good Neighbor Policy

The conflict between the desire to avoid foreign entanglements and the desire to advance American economic interests is well-illustrated by events in Latin America. In dealing with this part of the world, Harding and Coolidge performed neither better nor worse than Wilson had. In the face of continued radicalism and instability in Mexico, which caused Americans with interests in land and oil rights to suffer heavy losses, President Coolidge acted with forbearance. The Mexicans were able to complete their social and economic revolution in the 1920s without significant interference by the United States.

Under Coolidge's successor, Herbert Hoover, the United States began at last to treat Latin American nations as equals. Hoover reversed Wilson's policy of trying to teach them "to elect good men." The Clark Memorandum (1930), written by Undersecretary of State J. Reuben Clark, disassociated the right of intervention in Latin America from the Roosevelt Corollary. The corollary had been an improper extension of the Monroe Doctrine, Clark declared. The right of the United States to intervene depended rather on "the doctrine of self-preservation."

The distinction seemed slight to Latin Americans, but since it seemed unlikely that the existence of the United States could be threatened in the area, it was important. By 1934 the marines who had been occupying Nicaragua, Haiti, and the Dominican Republic had all been withdrawn and the United States had renounced the right to intervene in Cuban affairs. Instead of functioning as the policeman for the region, the United States would be its "**good neighbor**." Unfortunately, the United States did little to try to improve social and economic conditions in the Caribbean region, so the underlying envy and resentment of "rich Uncle Sam" did not disappear.

The Totalitarian Challenge

The futility and danger of isolationism were exposed in September 1931 when the Japanese, long dominant in Chinese Manchuria, marched their army in and converted the province into a puppet state named Manchukuo. This violated both the Kellogg-Briand and Nine-Power pacts. China, now controlled by General Chiang Kai-shek, appealed to the League of Nations and to the United States for help. Neither would intervene. When League officials asked about the possibility of American cooperation in some kind of police action, President Hoover refused to consider either economic or military reprisals.

The League sent a commission to Manchuria to investigate. Henry L. Stimson, Hoover's secretary of state, announced (the Stimson Doctrine) that the United States would never recognize the legality of seizures made in violation of American treaty rights. This served only to irritate the Japanese.

In January 1932 Japan attacked Shanghai. When the League at last officially condemned their aggressions, the Japanese withdrew from the organization and extended their control of northern China. The lesson of Manchuria was not lost on Adolf Hitler, who became chancellor of Germany on January 30, 1933.

In surveying the diplomatic events of 1920–1929, it is easy to condemn the United States and the European democracies for their unwillingness to stand up for principles, their refusal to resist when Japan and later Germany and Italy embarked

The League of Nations covenant, the Kellogg Pact, the Nine-Power Treaty—all were mere scraps of paper. They did nothing to prevent Japan's invasion of Manchuria in 1931.

on the aggressions that led to World War II. It is also proper to place some of the blame for the troubles of the era on the United States and the European democracies, which controlled much of the world's resources and were primarily interested in holding on to what they had.

War Debts and Reparations

The democracies did not take a strong stand against Japan in part because they were quarreling about other matters. Particularly divisive was the controversy over war debts—those of Germany to the Allies and those of the Allies to the United States. The United States had lent more than $10 billion to its comrades-in-arms. Since most of this money had been spent on weapons and other supplies in the United States, it might well have been considered part of America's contribution to the war effort. The public, however, demanded full repayment—with interest. "These were loans, not contributions," Secretary of the Treasury Mellon firmly declared. The total, to be repaid over a period of sixty-two years, amounted to more than $22 billion.

The Allies tried to load their obligations to the United States, along with the other costs of the war, on the backs of the Germans. They demanded that the Germans pay reparations amounting to $33 billion. If this sum were collected, they declared, they could rebuild their economies and obtain the international exchange needed to pay their debts to the United States. But Germany was reluctant even to try to pay such huge reparations, and when Germany defaulted, so did the Allies.

Everyone shared the blame: the Germans because they resorted to a runaway inflation that reduced the mark to less than one trillionth of its prewar value, at least in part in hopes of avoiding their international obligations; the Americans because they refused to recognize the connection between the tariff and the debt question; and the Allies because they made little effort to pay even a reasonable proportion of their obligations.

In 1924 an international agreement, the Dawes Plan, provided Germany with a $200 million loan designed to stabilize its currency. Germany agreed to pay about $250 million a year in reparations. In 1929 the Young Plan further scaled down the reparations bill. In practice, the Allies paid the United States about what they collected from Germany. Since Germany got the money largely from private American loans, the United States would have served itself and the rest of the world far better had it written off the war debts at the start. In any case, in the late 1920s Americans stopped lending money to Germany, the Great Depression struck, Germany defaulted on its reparations payments, and the Allies then gave up all pretense of meeting their obligations to the United States. The last token payments were made in 1933. All that remained was a heritage of mistrust and hostility.

The Election of 1928

Meanwhile, dramatic changes had occurred in the United States. The climax of Coolidge prosperity came in 1928. The president decided not to run again, and Secretary of Commerce Hoover, whom he detested, easily won the Republican nomination. Hoover was the intellectual leader, almost the philosopher, of the New Era. American capitalists, he believed, had learned to curb their selfish instincts.

Although stiff, uncommunicative, and entirely without experience in elective office, Hoover made an admirable candidate in 1928. His roots in the Midwest and West (Iowa-born, he was raised in Oregon and educated at Stanford University in California) neatly balanced his outstanding reputation among eastern business tycoons. He took a "modern" approach to both capital and labor; businessmen should cooperate with one another and with their workers too. He opposed both unionbusting and trustbusting. His

Herbert Hoover relaxes during the 1928 presidential campaign. "That man has been offering me advice for the last five years," President Coolidge said of his secretary of commerce, "all of it bad."

career as a mining engineer had given him a wide knowledge of the world, yet he had become highly critical of Europe.

The Democrats, having had their fill of factionalism in 1924, could no longer deny the nomination to Governor Al Smith. Superficially, Smith was Hoover's antithesis. Born and raised in New York's Lower East Side slums, he had been schooled in machine politics by Tammany Hall. He was a Catholic, Hoover a Quaker, a wet where Hoover supported prohibition; he dealt easily with people of every race and nationality, while Hoover had little interest in and less knowledge of African Americans and immigrants. However, like Hoover, Smith managed to combine a basic conservatism with humanitarian concern for the underprivileged. As adept in administration as Hoover, he was equally uncritical of the American capitalist system.

View the Image
A Heavy Load for Al (1928) at myhistorylab.com

In the election Hoover triumphed, 444 to 87 in the Electoral College, 21.4 million to 14 million in the popular vote. All the usually Democratic border states and even North Carolina, Florida, and Texas went to the Republicans, along with the entire West and the Northeast save for Massachusetts and Rhode Island.

After this defeat the Democratic party appeared on the verge of extinction. Nothing could have been further from the truth. The religious question and his big-city roots had hurt Smith, but the chief reason he lost was prosperity—and the good times were soon to end. Hoover's overwhelming victory also concealed a political realignment that was taking place. Working-class voters in the cities, largely Catholic and unimpressed by Coolidge prosperity, had swung heavily to the Democrats. In 1924 the twelve largest cities had been solidly Republican; in 1928 all went Democratic. In agricultural states like Iowa, Smith ran far better than Davis had in 1924, for Coolidge's vetoes of bills designed to raise farm prices had caused considerable resentment. A new coalition of urban workers and dissatisfied farmers was in the making.

Economic Problems

The American economic system of the 1920s had grave flaws. Certain industries did not share in the good times. The coal business, suffering from the competition of petroleum, entered a period of decline. Cotton and woolen textiles also lagged because of the competition of new synthetics, principally rayon. Industry began to be plagued by falling profit margins and chronic unemployment.

The movement toward consolidation in industry, somewhat checked during the latter part of the Progressive Era, resumed; by 1929, 200 corporations controlled nearly half the nation's corporate assets. General Motors, Ford, and Chrysler turned out nearly 90 percent of all American cars and trucks. Four tobacco companies produced over 90 percent of the cigarettes. One percent of all financial institutions controlled 46 percent of the nation's banking business. Most large manufacturers, aware that bad public relations resulting from the unbridled use of monopolistic power outweighed any immediate economic gain, sought stability and "fair" prices rather than the maximum profit possible at the moment. "Regulated" competition was the order of the day, oligopoly the typical situation. The trade association movement flourished; producers formed voluntary organizations to exchange information, discuss policies toward government and the public, and "administer" prices in their industry. Usually the largest corporation, such as U.S. Steel in the iron and steel business, became the "price leader," its competitors, some themselves giants, following slavishly.

The success of the trade associations depended in part on the attitude of the federal government, for such organizations might well have been attacked under the antitrust laws. Their defenders, including President Harding, argued that the associations made business more efficient and prevented violent gyrations of prices and production. Secretary of Commerce Hoover put the facilities of his department at the disposal of the associations. After Coolidge became president, the antitrust division of the Justice Department itself encouraged the trade associations to cooperate in ways that had previously been considered violations of the Sherman Act.

Even more important to the trade associations were the good times. With profits high and markets expanding, the most powerful producers could afford to share the bounty with smaller, less efficient competitors.

The weakest element in the economy was agriculture. Farm prices slumped and farmers' costs mounted. Besides having to purchase expensive machinery in order to compete, farmers were confronted by high foreign tariffs and in some cases quotas on the importation of foodstuffs. As crop yields per acre rose, chiefly because of the increased use of chemical fertilizers, agricultural prices fell further.

Despite the efforts of the farm bloc, the government did little to improve the situation. President Harding opposed direct aid to agriculture as a matter of principle. During his administration Congress strengthened the laws regulating railroad rates and grain exchanges and made it easier for farmers to borrow money, but it did nothing directly to increase agricultural income. Nor did the high tariffs on agricultural produce have much effect. Being forced to sell their surpluses abroad, farmers found that world prices depressed domestic prices despite the tariff wall.

Thus the unprecedented prosperity rested on unstable foundations. The problem was mainly one of maldistribution of resources. Productive capacity raced ahead of buying power. Too large a share of the profits was going into too few pockets. The 27,000 families with the highest annual incomes in 1929 received as much money as the 11 million with annual incomes of under $1,500, the minimum sum required at that time to maintain a family decently. High earnings and low taxes permitted huge sums to pile up in the hands of individuals who did not invest the money productively. A good deal of it went into stock market speculation, which led to the "big bull market" and eventually to the Great Depression.

The Stock Market Crash of 1929

In the spring of 1928, prices on the New York Stock Exchange, already at a historic high, began to surge. As the presidential campaign gathered momentum, the market increased its upward pace, stimulated by the candidates' efforts to outdo each other in praising the marvels of the American economic system. A few conservative brokers expressed alarm, warning that most stocks were grossly overpriced. The majority scoffed at such talk.

During the first half of 1929 stock prices climbed still higher. A mania for speculation swept the country, thousands of small investors putting their savings in common stocks. Then, in September the market wavered. Amid volatile fluctuations stock averages eased downward. Most analysts contended that the stock exchange was "digesting" previous

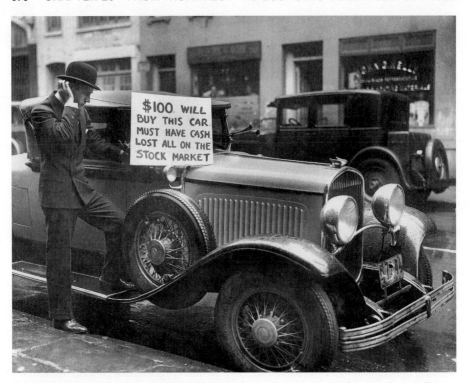

Walter Thompson saw his assets evaporate during the stock market collapse in 1929. Desperate for cash (like nearly everyone else) he offered his snappy roadster for $100.

gains. A Harvard economist expressed the prevailing view when he said that stock prices had reached a "permanently high plateau" and would soon resume their advance.

On October 24 a wave of selling sent prices spinning. Nearly 13 million shares changed hands—a record. Bankers and politicians rallied to check the decline, as they had during the Panic of 1907. But on October 29, the bottom seemed to drop out. More than 16 million shares were sold, prices plummeting. The boom was over.

Hoover and the Depression

The collapse of the stock market did not cause the Depression; stocks rallied late in the year, and business activity did not begin to decline significantly until the spring of 1930. The Great Depression was a worldwide phenomenon caused chiefly by economic imbalances resulting from the chaos of the Great War. In the United States too much wealth had fallen into too few hands, with the result that consumers were unable to buy all the goods produced. The trouble came to a head mainly because of the easy-credit policies of the Federal Reserve Board and the Mellon tax structure, which favored the rich. Its effects were so profound and prolonged because the politicians (and for that matter the professional economists) did not fully understand what was happening or what to do about it.

The chronic problem of underconsumption operated to speed the downward spiral. Unable to rid themselves of mounting inventories, manufacturers closed plants and laid off workers, thereby causing demand to shrink further. Automobile output fell from 4.5 million units in 1929 to 1.1 million in 1932. When Ford closed his Detroit plants in 1931, some 75,000 workers lost their jobs, and the decline in auto production affected a host of suppliers and middlemen as well.

The financial system cracked under the strain. More than 1,300 banks closed their doors in 1930, 3,700 more during the next two years. Each failure deprived thousands of persons of funds that might have been used to buy goods; when the Bank of the United States in New York City became insolvent in December 1930, 400,000 depositors found their savings immobilized. And of course the industrial depression worsened the depression in agriculture by further reducing the demand for American foodstuffs. Every economic indicator reflected the collapse. New investments declined from $10 billion in 1929 to $1 billion in 1932, and the national income fell from over $80 billion to under $50 billion in the same brief period. Unemployment, under 1 million at the height of the boom, rose to at least 13 million.

President Hoover was an intelligent man, experienced in business matters and knowledgeable in economics. Secretary of the Treasury Mellon believed that the economy should be allowed to slide unchecked until the cycle had found its bottom. "Let the slump liquidate itself," Mellon urged. "Liquidate labor, liquidate stocks, liquidate the farmers. . . . People will work harder, live a more moral life. Values will be adjusted, and enterprising people will pick up the wrecks from less competent people." Hoover realized that such a policy would cause unbearable hardship for millions. He rejected Mellon's advice to let the Depression run its course.

Hoover's program for ending the Depression evolved gradually. At first he called on businessmen to maintain prices and wages. The government should cut taxes in order to increase consumers' spendable income, institute public works programs to stimulate production and create jobs for the unemployed, lower interest rates to make it easier for businesses to borrow in order to expand, and make loans to banks and industrial corporations threatened with collapse and to homeowners unable to meet mortgage payments. The president also proposed measures making it easier for farmers to borrow money, and he suggested that the government should support cooperative farm marketing schemes designed to solve the problem of overproduction. He called for an expansion of state and local relief programs and urged all who could afford it to give more to charity. Above all he tried to restore public confidence: The economy was basically healthy; the Depression was only a minor downturn; prosperity was "just around the corner."

Although Hoover's plans were theoretically sound, they failed to check the economic slide, in part because of curious limitations in his conception of how they should be implemented. He placed far too much reliance on his powers of persuasion and the willingness of citizens to act in the public interest without legal compulsion. He urged manufacturers to maintain wages and keep their factories in operation, but the manufacturers soon slashed wages and curtailed output sharply. He permitted the Federal Farm Board to establish semipublic stabilization corporations with authority to buy up surplus wheat and cotton, but he refused to consider crop or acreage controls. The stabilization corporations poured out hundreds of millions of dollars without checking falling agricultural prices because farmers increased production faster than the corporations could buy up the excess for disposal abroad.

Hoover resisted proposals to shift responsibility from state and local agencies to the federal government, despite the fact—soon obvious—that they lacked the resources to cope with the emergency. By 1932 the federal government, with Hoover's approval, was spending $500 million a year on public works projects, but because of the decline in state and municipal construction, the total public outlay fell nearly $1 billion below what it had been in 1930. More serious was his refusal, on constitutional grounds, to allow federal funds to be used for the relief of individuals.

Unfortunately the Depression was drying up the sources of private charities just as the demands on these organizations were expanding. State and municipal agencies were swamped just when their capacities to tax and borrow were shrinking. By 1932 more than 40,600 Boston families were on relief (compared with 7,400 families in 1929); in Chicago 700,000 persons—40 percent of the workforce—were unemployed. Only the national government possessed the power and the credit to deal adequately with the crisis.

Yet Hoover would not act. He set up a committee to coordinate local relief activities but insisted on preserving what he called "the principles of individual and local responsibility." For the federal government to take over relief would "lead to the super-state where every man becomes the servant of the state and real liberty is lost."

Federal loans to commercial enterprises were constitutional, he believed, because the money could be put to productive use and eventually repaid. When drought destroyed the crops of farmers in the South and Southwest in 1930, the government lent them money to buy seed and even food for their livestock, but Hoover would permit no direct relief for the farmers themselves. In 1932 he approved the creation of the Reconstruction Finance Corporation (RFC) to lend money to banks, railroads, and insurance companies. The RFC represented an important extension of national authority, yet it was thoroughly in line with Hoover's philosophy. Its loans, secured by solid collateral, were commercial transactions, not gifts; the agency did almost nothing for individuals in need of relief. The same could be said of the Glass-Steagall Banking Act of 1932, which eased the tight credit situation by permitting Federal Reserve banks to accept corporate stocks and bonds as security for loans. The public grew increasingly resentful of the president's doctrinaire adherence to principle while breadlines lengthened and millions of willing workers searched fruitlessly for jobs.

As time passed and the Depression worsened, Hoover put more stress on the importance of balancing the federal budget, reasoning that since citizens had to live within their limited means in hard times, the government should set a good example. This policy was counterproductive; by reducing its expenditures the government made the Depression worse, which reduced federal revenue further. By June 1931 the budget was nearly $500 million in the red.

Hoover understood the value of pumping money into a stagnant economy. He might have made a virtue of necessity. The difficulty lay in the fact that nearly all "informed" opinion believed that a balanced budget was essential to recovery. The most prestigious economists insisted on it, and so did business leaders, labor leaders, and even most socialists.

Much of the contemporary criticism of Hoover and a good deal of that heaped on him by later historians was unfair. Yet his record as president shows that he was too rigidly wedded to a particular theory of government to cope effectively with the problems of the day. Since these problems were in a sense insoluble, flexibility and a willingness to experiment were essential to any program aimed at restoring prosperity. Hoover lacked these qualities. He was

[Watch the Video

Prosperity of the 1920s and the Great Depression at myhistorylab.com]

his own worst enemy, being too uncompromising to get on well with the politicians and too aloof to win the confidence and affection of ordinary people. He had too much faith in himself and his plans. When he failed to achieve the results he anticipated, he attracted, despite his devotion to duty and his concern for the welfare of the country, not sympathy but scorn.

The Economy Hits Bottom

During the spring of 1932, as the economy sounded the depths, thousands of Americans faced starvation. In Philadelphia during an eleven-day period when no relief funds were available, hundreds of families existed on stale bread, thin soup, and garbage. In the nation as a whole, only about one-quarter of the unemployed were receiving any public aid. Many people were evicted, and they often gathered in ramshackle communities constructed of packing boxes, rusty sheet metal, and similar refuse on swamps, garbage dumps, and other wasteland. People began to call these places "Hoovervilles."

View the Image
Depression Breadlines in New York City at myhistorylab.com

Thousands roamed the countryside begging and scavenging for food. At the same time, food prices fell so low that farmers burned corn for fuel. Iowa and Nebraska farmers organized "farm holiday" movements, refusing to ship their crops to market in protest against the thirty-one-cent-a-bushel corn and thirty-eight-cent wheat. They blocked roads and rail lines, dumped milk, overturned trucks, and established picket lines to enforce their boycott.

The national mood ranged from apathy to resentment. In 1931 federal immigration agents and local groups in the Southwest began rounding up Mexican-Americans and deporting them. Some of those returned to Mexico had entered the United States illegally; others had come in properly. Unemployed Mexicans were ejected because they might become public charges, those with jobs because they were presumably taking bread from the mouths of citizens.

In June and July 1932, 20,000 Great War veterans marched on Washington to demand immediate payment of their "adjusted compensation" bonuses. When Congress rejected their appeal, some 2,000 refused to leave, settling in a jerrybuilt camp of shacks and tents at Anacostia Flats, a swamp bordering the Potomac. President Hoover, alarmed, charged incorrectly that the **Bonus Army** was largely composed of criminals and radicals and sent troops into the Flats to disperse it with bayonets, tear gas, and tanks. The

View the Image
Burning Bonus Army Shacks, 1932 at myhistorylab.com

task was accomplished amid much confusion; fortunately no one was killed. The protest had been aimless and not entirely justified, yet the spectacle of the U.S. government chasing unarmed veterans with tanks appalled the nation.

The unprecedented severity of the Depression led some persons to favor radical economic and political changes. The disparity between the lots of the rich and the poor, always a challenge to democracy, became more striking and engendered considerable bitterness. "Unless something is done to provide employment," two labor leaders warned Hoover, "disorder . . . is sure to arise. . . . There is a growing demand that the entire business and social structure be changed because of the general dissatisfaction with the present system."

Evicted from their homes, many unemployed people gravitated to vacant industrial property, where they erected hovels from scraps of lumber, tarpaper, and cardboard. This shantytown is outside of Seattle.

The communist party gained few converts among farmers and industrial workers, but a considerable number of intellectuals, alienated by the trends of the 1920s, responded positively to the communists' emphasis on economic planning and the total mobilization of the state to achieve social goals. Even the cracker-barrel humorist Will Rogers was impressed by reports of the absence of serious unemployment in Russia. "All roads lead to Moscow," the former muckraker Lincoln Steffens wrote.

The Depression and Its Victims

Depression is a word used by economists but also by psychologists, and the depression of the 1930s had profound psychological effects on its victims as well as the obvious economic ones. Almost without exception people who lost their jobs first searched energetically for new ones, but when they remained unemployed for more than a few months they sank gradually into despair. E. Wight Bakke, a Yale sociologist who interviewed hundreds of unemployed men in the United States and England during the Depression, described the final stage of decline as "permanent readjustment," by which he meant that the long-term jobless simply gave up. The settlement house worker Lillian Wald came to a similar conclusion. Unemployed people at her famous Henry Street settlement, she noticed, had lost both "ambition and pride."

Simple discouragement alone does not explain why so many of the jobless reacted this way. People who had worked all their adult lives often became ashamed of themselves when they could not find a job. Professor Bakke reported that half the unemployed people in New Haven that he interviewed never applied for public assistance no matter how desperate their circumstances. The Depression affected the families of the jobless in many ways. It caused a dramatic drop in the birthrate, from 27.7 per thousand population in 1920 to 18.4 per thousand in the early 1930s, the lowest in American history. Sometimes it strengthened family ties. Some unemployed men spent more time with their children and helped their wives with cooking and housework. Others, however, became impatient when their children demanded attention, refused to help around the house, sulked, or took to drink.

The influence of wives in families struck by unemployment tended to increase, and in this respect women suffered less psychologically from the Depression. They were usually too busy trying to make ends meet to become apathetic. But the way they used this influence varied. Some wives were sympathetic, others scornful, when the "breadwinner" came home with empty hands. If there is any generalization about the effects of the Depression on family relations it is probably an obvious one—where relationships were close and loving they became stronger, where they were not, the results could be disastrous.

The Election of 1932

As the end of his term approached, President Hoover seemed to grow daily more petulant and pessimistic. The Depression, coming after twelve years of Republican rule, probably ensured a Democratic victory in any case, but his attitude as the election neared alienated many voters and turned defeat into rout.

Confident of victory, the Democrats chose Governor Franklin Delano Roosevelt of New York as their presidential candidate. Roosevelt owed his nomination chiefly to his success as governor. Under his administration, New York had led the nation in providing relief for the needy and had enacted an impressive program of old-age pensions, unemployment insurance, and conservation and public power projects. In 1928, while Hoover was carrying New York against Smith by a wide margin, Roosevelt won election by 25,000 votes. In 1930 he swept the state by a 700,000-vote majority, double the previous record. He also had the advantage of the Roosevelt name (he was a distant cousin of the inimitable TR), and his sunny, magnetic personality contrasted favorably with that of the glum and colorless Hoover.

Roosevelt was far from being a radical. Although he had supported the League of Nations while campaigning for the vice presidency in 1920, during the 1920s he had not seriously challenged the basic tenets of Coolidge prosperity. He never had much difficulty adjusting his views to prevailing attitudes. His life before the Depression gave little indication that he understood the aspirations of ordinary people or had any deep commitment to social reform.

Roosevelt was born to wealth and social status in Dutchess County, New York, in 1882. He was educated at the exclusive Groton School and then at Harvard. Ambition as much as the desire to render public service motivated his career in politics; even after an attack of polio in 1921 had badly crippled both his legs, he refused to abandon his

A vigorous-looking Franklin D. Roosevelt campaigns for the presidency in 1932. His vice-presidential running mate, John N. Garner, and the conveniently placed post allowed the handicapped candidate to stand when greeting voters along the way.

hopes for high office. During the 1920s he was a hardworking member of the liberal wing of his party. He supported Smith for president in 1924 and 1928.

Roosevelt was a marvelous campaigner. Like every great political leader, he took as much from the people as he gave them, understanding the causes of their confusion and sensing their needs. "I have looked into the faces of thousands of Americans," he told a friend. "They have the frightened look of lost children. . . . They are saying: 'We're caught in something we don't understand; perhaps this fellow can help us out.'"

On matters such as farm policy, the tariff, and government spending, Roosevelt equivocated, contradicted himself, or remained silent. Nevertheless Roosevelt's basic position was unmistakable. There must be a "re-appraisal of values," a "New Deal." Instead of adhering to conventional limits on the extent of federal power, the government should do whatever was necessary to protect the unfortunate and advance the public good. Lacking concrete answers, Roosevelt advocated a point of view rather than a plan: "The country needs bold, persistent experimentation. It is common sense to take a method and try it. If it fails, admit it frankly and try another. But above all, try something."

The popularity of this approach was demonstrated in November. Hoover, who had lost only eight states in 1928, won only six, all in the Northeast, in 1932. Roosevelt amassed 22.8 million votes to Hoover's 15.8 million and carried the Electoral College, 472 to 59.

●●●─Read the Document

Hoover, New York Campaign Speech at **myhistorylab.com**

During the interval between the election and Roosevelt's inauguration in March 1933, the Great Depression reached its nadir. The holdover "lame duck" Congress, last of its kind, proved incapable of effective action.[2] President Hoover, perhaps understandably, hesitated to institute changes without the cooperation of his successor. Roosevelt, for equally plausible reasons, refused to accept responsibility before assuming power officially. The nation, curiously apathetic in the face of so much suffering, drifted aimlessly, like a sailboat in a flat calm.

---

[2]The Twentieth Amendment (1933) provided for convening new Congresses in January instead of the following December. It also advanced the date of the president's inauguration from March 4 to January 20.

Milestones

1921–1922	Washington Conference tries to slow arms race	1930	Clark Memorandum renounces Roosevelt Corollary to Monroe Doctrine
1923	President Harding dies; Coolidge becomes president		Hawley-Smoot tariff raises duties on foreign manufactures
	Teapot Dome and other Harding scandals are exposed		Ten-year Dust Bowl begins in South and Midwest
1924	Dawes Plan restructures German reparations payments	1931	Japan invades Manchuria
	National Origins Act establishes immigration quotas		Hoover imposes moratorium on war debts
	Coolidge is elected president	1932	Federal troops disperse Bonus Army marchers in Washington, DC
1928	Fifteen nations sign Kellogg-Briand Pact to "outlaw" war		Reconstruction Finance Corporation (RFC) lends to banks, railroads, insurance companies
	Herbert Hoover is elected president		
1929	New York Stock Exchange crash ends big bull market; Great Depression begins		Franklin Delano Roosevelt is elected president
	Young Plan further reduces German reparations	1933	Japan withdraws from League of Nations

✓•—|Study and **Review** at www.myhistorylab.com

Review Questions

1. The introduction draws a parallel between the crash of the stock market in 1929 and the U.S. mortgage market in 2008–2009 as explanations of subsequent economic crises. What were the main differences?
2. What were the similarities in the policies of Harding, Coolidge, and Hoover? The differences?
3. What factors explained the prosperity of the 1920s? In what ways was that prosperity shaky?
4. During the 1920s and early 1930s, what role did the United States play in Latin America? In the worsening situations in Europe and Asia?
5. How did the election of 1932 constitute a political "revolution"?

Key Terms

Bonus Army   *673*

"good neighbor"   *665*

Teapot Dome scandal   *659*

26 The New Deal: 1933–1941

((•─Hear the Audio Chapter 26 at myhistorylab.com

Do you have health insurance?

IN MARCH 2010, CONGRESS NARROWLY PASSED A MAJOR HEALTH reform law. It requires most employers to provide employees with health insurance and allows parents to extend coverage of their children to age twenty-six. It also creates a fund of nearly a trillion dollars to pay for health insurance for many people not covered by employer-paid policies until 2020.

President Barack Obama compared the battle to the one waged by Franklin D. Roosevelt sixty-five years earlier over guaranteed incomes for the elderly. "When FDR proposed Social Security, he was accused of being a Socialist," Obama observed. Michelle Bachmann, a Republican congresswoman from Minnesota, opposed the health insurance proposal for that very reason: "If you look at FDR and Barack Obama, this is really the final leap to socialism."

President Franklin D. Roosevelt signed the Social Security Act in 1935, the cornerstone of his New Deal to counteract the Great Depression. Other New Deal initiatives sought to put the unemployed to work on government projects; to use federal funds to help farmers by raising the price of agricultural products; to reorganize banks, and to alter federal regulation of corporations.

These measures generated opposition. Conservatives regarded much of the New Deal as an unconstitutional infringement of private rights; populists and Marxists denounced the New Deal as a band-aid that failed to address the root causes of poverty. But times were bad. The nation was in desperate trouble. Through it all, Roosevelt won the allegiance of voters who regarded him almost as an economic savior and the New Deal as gospel.

The Hundred Days

As the date of Franklin Roosevelt's inauguration approached, the banking system completely disintegrated and a financial panic swept the land. Depositors lined up before the doors of even the soundest institutions, desperate to withdraw their savings. Hundreds of banks were forced to close. In February, to check the panic, the governor of Michigan declared a "bank holiday," shutting every bank in the state for eight days.

Maryland, Kentucky, California, and a number of other states followed suit; by inauguration day four-fifths of the states had suspended all banking operations. Other issues loomed, especially war clouds over Europe and east Asia, but few Americans could look much beyond their own immediate, and increasingly dire, economic prospects.

⦿⟩Watch the Video

FDR's Inauguration at
myhistorylab.com

Something drastic had to be done. The most conservative business leaders were as ready for government intervention as the most advanced radicals. Partisanship, while not disappearing, was for once subordinated to broad national needs. A sign of this change came in February, even before Roosevelt took office, when Congress submitted to the states the Twenty-First Amendment, putting an end to prohibition. Before the end of the year the necessary three-quarters of the states had ratified it, and the prohibition era was over.

It was unquestionably Franklin D. Roosevelt who provided the spark that reenergized the American people. His inaugural address reassured the country and at the same time stirred it to action. "The only thing we have to fear is fear itself. . . . This Nation asks for action, and action now. . . . I assume unhesitatingly the leadership of this great army of our people. . . ." Many such lines punctuated the brief address, which captured the heart of the country; almost half a million letters of congratulation poured into the White House. When Roosevelt summoned Congress into a special session on March 9, the legislators outdid one another to enact his proposals into law. In the following "hundred days" serious opposition, in the sense of an organized group committed to resisting the administration, simply did not exist.

Roosevelt had the power and the will to act but no comprehensive plan of action. He and his eager congressional collaborators proceeded in a dozen directions at once, often at cross-purposes with themselves and one another. One of the first administration measures was the Economy Act, which reduced the salaries of federal employees by 15 percent and cut various veterans' benefits. Such belt-tightening measures could only make the Depression worse. But most **New Deal** programs were designed to stimulate the economy. All in all, an impressive body of new legislation was placed on the statute books.

On March 5 Roosevelt declared a nationwide bank holiday and placed an embargo on the exportation of gold. To explain the complexities of the banking problem to the public, Roosevelt delivered the first of his "fireside chats" over a national radio network. "I want to talk for a few minutes with the people of the United States about banking," he explained. His warmth and steadiness reassured millions. A plan for

A 1933 banner celebrates the repeal of prohibition.

reopening the banks under Treasury Department licenses was devised, and soon most of them were functioning again, public confidence in their solvency restored.

In April Roosevelt took the country off the gold standard, hoping thereby to cause prices to rise. Before the session ended, Congress established the Federal Deposit Insurance Corporation (FDIC) to guarantee bank deposits. It also forced the separation of investment banking and commercial banking concerns while extending the power of the Federal Reserve Board over both types of institutions, and it created the Home Owners Loan Corporation (HOLC) to refinance mortgages and prevent foreclosures. It passed the Federal Securities Act requiring promoters to make public full financial information about new stock issues and giving the Federal Trade Commission the right to regulate such transactions.

The National Recovery Administration (NRA)

Problems of unemployment and industrial stagnation had high priority during the hundred days. Congress appropriated $500 million for relief of the needy, and it created the **Civilian Conservation Corps (CCC)** to provide jobs for men between the ages of eighteen and twenty-five in reforestation and other conservation projects. To stimulate industry, Congress passed one of its most controversial measures, the National Industrial Recovery Act (NIRA). Besides establishing the Public Works Administration with authority to spend $3.3 billion, this law permitted manufacturers to draw up industry-wide codes of "fair business practices." Under the law producers could agree to raise prices and limit production without violating the antitrust laws. The law gave workers the protection of minimum wage and maximum hours regulations and guaranteed them the right "to organize and bargain collectively through representatives of their own choosing," an immense stimulus to the union movement.

The NIRA was a variant on the idea of the corporate state. This concept envisaged a system of industry-wide organizations of Capitalists and workers (supervised by the government) that would resolve conflicts internally, thereby avoiding wasteful economic competition and dangerous social clashes. It was an outgrowth of the trade association idea, although Hoover, who had supported voluntary associations, denounced it because of its compulsory aspects. It was also similar to experiments being carried out by the fascist dictator Benito Mussolini in Italy and by the Nazis in Adolf Hitler's Germany. It did not, of course, turn America into a fascist state, but it did herald an increasing concentration of economic power in the hands of interest groups, both industrialists' organizations and labor unions.

The act created a government agency, the **National Recovery Administration (NRA)**, to supervise the drafting and operation of the business codes. Drafting posed difficult problems, first because each industry insisted on tailoring the agreements to its special needs and second because most manufacturers were unwilling to accept all the provisions of Section 7a of the law, which guaranteed workers the right to unionize and bargain collectively. Many employers were more interested in the monopolistic aspects of the act than in boosting wages and encouraging unionization. In practice, the largest manufacturers in each industry drew up the codes.

The NRA did not end the Depression. There was a brief upturn in the spring of 1933, but the expected revival of industry did not take place; in nearly every case the dominant producers in each industry used their power to raise prices and limit production rather than to hire more workers and increase output.

Beginning with the cotton textile code, however, the agreements succeeded in doing away with the centuries-old problem of child labor in industry. They established the principle of federal regulation of wages and hours and led to the organization of thousands of workers, even in industries where unions had seldom been significant. Within a year John L. Lewis's United Mine Workers expanded from 150,000 members to half a million. About 100,000 automobile workers joined unions, as did a comparable number of steelworkers.

Labor leaders used the NIRA to persuade workers that Roosevelt wanted them to join unions—which was something of an overstatement. In 1935, because the craft-oriented AFL had displayed little enthusiasm for enrolling unskilled workers on an industry-wide basis, John L. Lewis, together with officials of the garment trade unions, formed the Committee for Industrial Organization (CIO) and set out to rally workers in each of these mass-production industries into one union without regard for craft lines. Since a union containing all the workers in a factory was easier to organize and direct than separate craft unions, this was a far more effective way of unionizing factory labor. The AFL expelled these unions, however, and in 1938 the CIO became the Congress of Industrial Organizations. Soon it rivaled the AFL in size and importance.

> **View the Image**
> PWA in Action Poster at
> myhistorylab.com

The Agricultural Adjustment Administration (AAA)

Roosevelt was more concerned about the plight of the farmers than that of any other group because he believed that the nation was becoming overcommitted to industry. The Agricultural Adjustment Act of May 1933 combined compulsory restrictions on production with government payments to growers of wheat, cotton, tobacco, pork, and a few other staple crops. The object was to lift agricultural prices to "parity" with industrial prices, the ratio in most cases being based on the levels of 1909–1914, when farmers had been reasonably prosperous. In return for withdrawing part of their land from cultivation, farmers received "rental" payments from the **Agricultural Adjustment Act (AAA)**.

Since the 1933 crops were growing when the law was passed, Secretary of Agriculture Henry A. Wallace, son of Harding's secretary of agriculture and himself an experienced farmer and plant geneticist, decided to pay farmers to destroy the crops in the field. Cotton planters plowed up 10 million acres, receiving $100 million in return. Thereafter, limitation of acreage proved sufficient to raise some agricultural prices. Tobacco growers benefited, and so did those who raised corn and hogs. The price of wheat also rose, though more because of bad harvests than because of the AAA program. But dairy farmers and cattlemen were hurt by the law, as were the railroads (which had less freight to haul) and, of course, consumers. Many farmers insisted that the NRA was raising the cost of manufactured goods more than the AAA was raising the prices they received for their crops.

A far more serious weakness of the program was its effect on tenant farmers and sharecroppers, many of whom lost their livelihoods when owners took land out of production to obtain AAA payments. In addition many landowners substituted machinery for labor. In the Cotton Belt

> **Read the Document**
> An Attack on New Deal
> Farm Policies at
> myhistorylab.com

farmers purchased more than 100,000 tractors during the 1930s. Each could do the work of several tenant or sharecropping families. Yet acreage restrictions and mortgage relief helped thousands of others. The AAA was a drastic change of American policy, but foreign producers of coffee, sugar, tea, rubber, and other staples had adopted the same techniques of restricting output and subsidizing growers well before the United States did.

The Dust Bowl

A protracted drought compounded the plight of the farmers, especially in dry sections of the Midwest. During the first third of the twentieth century, midwestern farmers perfected dryland techniques. This entailed "dragging" the fields after rainfall to improve absorption, raking them repeatedly to eliminate water-devouring weeds, and plowing the soil deeply and frequently to allow rain to sink in quickly. The use of tractors, combines, plows, and trucks during the 1920s made possible this intensive working of the fields. Farmers planted the driest areas in winter wheat, which required little moisture; in Nebraska and Iowa, most farmers planted corn.

Then came the dust storms. During the winter of 1933–1934, bitter cold killed off the winter wheat and heavy storms pulverized the soil. By March 1934 driving winds whipped across the Great Plains. In April storms from the Dakotas belched great clouds of dust through Nebraska and Kansas. In May, after the fields had been plowed, more windstorms scattered the seeds and topsoil.

The summer of 1934 was dry, especially in the Dakotas and western Kansas. These farmers were accustomed to dry weather, but the topsoil had been loosened through dryland farming. Strong winds scooped up the dried-out dirt and blew it in

A huge dust cloud engulfs Dodge City, Kansas in 1935.
Source: Kansas State Historical Society.

heaving clouds throughout the plains. Dust, forced into people's lungs, induced "dust pneumonia," a respiratory ailment that sometimes proved fatal.

The winds devastated wheat and corn. Over 30 percent of the crops in much of North Dakota, South Dakota, Nebraska, Kansas, and the Oklahoma panhandle failed. Two years later, another drought produced similar results. Coming in the midst of the Great Depression, this second calamity proved more than many farmers could bear. Tens of thousands abandoned their farms.

The Tennessee Valley Authority (TVA)

Although Roosevelt could do little about the midwestern droughts, he did propose a major initiative to alter the economic infrastructure of the upper South. During the Great War the government had constructed a hydroelectric plant at Muscle Shoals, Alabama, to provide power for factories manufacturing synthetic nitrate explosives. After 1920 farm groups and public power enthusiasts, led by Senator George W. Norris of Nebraska, had blocked administration plans to turn these facilities over to private Capitalists, but their efforts to have the site operated by the government had been defeated by presidential vetoes.

During his first hundred days, Roosevelt proposed a **Tennessee Valley Authority (TVA)** to implement a broad experiment in social planning. Besides expanding the hydroelectric plants at Muscle Shoals and developing nitrate man-

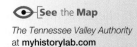

See the **Map**

The Tennessee Valley Authority
at **myhistorylab.com**

ufacturing in order to produce cheap fertilizers, he envisioned a coordinated program of soil conservation, reforestation, and industrialization.

Over the objections of private power companies, Congress passed the TVA Act in May 1933. This law created a board authorized to build dams, power plants, and transmission lines and to sell fertilizers and electricity to individuals and local communities. The board could undertake flood control, soil conservation, and reforestation projects and improve the navigation of the river. Although the TVA never became the comprehensive regional planning organization some of its sponsors had anticipated, it improved the standard of living of millions of inhabitants of the valley.

The Tennessee Valley Authority Although the Tennessee Valley Authority (TVA) never fully became the regional planning organization its sponsors had anticipated, the TVA nevertheless was able to expand the hydroelectric plants at Muscle Shoals, Alabama, and build dams, power plants, and transmission lines to service the surrounding area.

Table 26.1 First New Deal and First Hundred Days (March–June, 1933)

Legislation	Purpose
Banking Act	Provided federal loans to private bankers
Beer-Wine Revenue Act	Repealed Prohibition
Civilian Conservation Corps (CCC)	Created jobs for unemployed young men
Federal Emergency Relief Act (FERA)	Gave federal money to states and localities to provide relief of poor
Agricultural Adjustment Act (AAA)	Raised farm prices by restricting production
Tennessee Valley Authority (TVA)	Massive construction project that generated employment—and electricity—in Tennessee Valley
National Industrial Recovery Act (NIRA)	Created structure for business and labor to cooperate to make particular industries more profitable

The New Deal Spirit

By the end of the hundred days a large majority of the country labeled the New Deal a solid success. Considerable recovery had taken place, but more basic was the fact that Roosevelt had infused his administration with a spirit of bustle and optimism.

Although Roosevelt was not much of an intellectual, his openness to suggestion made him eager to draw on the ideas and energies of experts of all sorts. New Deal agencies soon teemed with college professors and young lawyers without political experience.

The New Deal lacked any consistent ideological base. Theorists never impressed Roosevelt much. His New Deal drew on the old populist tradition, as seen in its antipathy to bankers and its willingness to adopt schemes for inflating the currency; on the New Nationalism of Theodore Roosevelt, in its dislike of competition and its de-emphasis of the antitrust laws; and on the ideas of social workers trained in the Progressive Era. Techniques developed by the Wilsonians also found a place in the system: Louis D. Brandeis had considerable influence on Roosevelt's financial reforms, and New Deal labor policy was an outgrowth of the experience of the War Labor Board of 1917–1918.

Within the administrative maze that Roosevelt created, rival bureaucrats battled to enforce their views. The "spenders," led by Tugwell, clashed with those favoring strict economy, who gathered around Lewis Douglas, director of the budget. Roosevelt mediated between the factions. Washington became a battleground for dozens of special interest groups: the Farm Bureau Federation, the unions, the trade associations, and the silver miners. While the system was superior to that of Roosevelt's predecessors—who had allowed one interest, big business, to predominate—it slighted the unorganized majority. The NRA aimed frankly at raising the prices paid by consumers of manufactured goods; the AAA processing tax came ultimately from the pocketbooks of ordinary citizens.

The Unemployed

At least 9 million persons were still without work in 1934. Yet the Democrats confounded the political experts, including their own, by increasing their already large majorities in both houses of Congress in the 1934 elections. All the evidence indicates

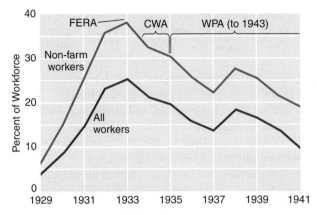

Unemployment and Federal Action, 1929–1941 Unemployment of non-farm workers reached nearly 40 percent by early 1933. The Federal Emergency Relief Act (FERA) and Civil Works Administration (CWA) (both in 1933) and the Works Progress Administration (WPA) (1935) put millions back to work.

that most of the jobless continued to support the administration. Their loyalty can best be explained by Roosevelt's unemployment policies.

In May 1933 Congress had established the Federal Emergency Relief Administration (FERA) and given it $500 million to be dispensed through state relief organizations. Roosevelt appointed Harry L. Hopkins, an eccentric but brilliant and dedicated social worker, to direct the FERA. Hopkins insisted that the unemployed needed jobs, not handouts. In November he persuaded Roosevelt to create the Civil Works Administration (CWA) and swiftly put 4 million people to work building and repairing roads and public buildings, teaching, decorating the walls of post offices with murals, and utilizing their special skills in dozens of other ways.

In May 1935 Roosevelt put Hopkins in charge of the **Works Progress Administration (WPA)**. By the time this agency was disbanded in 1943 it had found employment for 8.5 million people. Besides building public works, the WPA made important cultural contributions. It developed the Federal Theatre Project, which put actors, directors, and stagehands to work; the Federal Writers' Project, which turned out valuable guidebooks, collected local lore, and published about 1,000 books and pamphlets; and the Federal Art Project, which employed painters and sculptors. In addition, the National Youth Administration created part-time jobs for more than 2 million high school and college students.

At no time during the New Deal years did unemployment fall below 10 percent of the workforce, and in some places it was much higher. WPA did not go far enough, chiefly because Roosevelt could not escape his fear of drastically unbalancing the budget. The president also hesitated to undertake projects that might compete with private enterprises. Yet his caution did him no good politically; the business interests he sought to placate were becoming increasingly hostile to the New Deal.

Literature during the Depression

Some American novelists found Soviet communism attractive and wrote "proletarian" novels in which ordinary workers were the heroes, and stylistic niceties gave way to the rough language of the street and the factory. Most of these books are of little artistic merit, and none achieved great commercial success. The best of the Depression writers avoided the party line, although they were critical of many aspects of American life.

One was John Dos Passos, author of the trilogy *U.S.A.* (1930–1936), a massive, intricately constructed work with an anti-capitalist and deeply pessimistic point of view. It portrayed American society between 1900 and 1930 in broad perspective, interweaving the stories of five major characters and a galaxy of lesser figures.

Dos Passos's method was relentless, cold, and methodical—utterly realistic. He displayed no sympathy for his characters or their world. *U.S.A.* was a monument to the despair and anger of liberals confronted with the Depression. After the Depression, however, Dos Passos rapidly abandoned his radical views.

The novel that best portrayed the desperate plight of the millions impoverished by the Depression was John Steinbeck's *The Grapes of Wrath* (1939), which described the fate of the Joads, an Oklahoma farm family driven by drought and bad times to abandon their land and become migratory laborers in California. Steinbeck captured the patient bewilderment of the downtrodden, the brutality bred of fear that characterized their exploiters, and the furious resentments of the radicals of the 1930s. He depicted the parching blackness of the Oklahoma dust bowl, the grandeur of California, the backbreaking toil of the migrant fruit pickers, and the ultimate indignation of a people repeatedly degraded.

William Faulkner, probably the finest American novelist of the era, responded in still another way. Between 1929 and 1932, he burst into prominence with four major novels: *The Sound and the Fury, As I Lay Dying, Sanctuary,* and *Light in August.*

Faulkner was essentially a pessimist. His characters continually experience emotions too intense to be bearable, often too profound and too subtle for the natures he had given them. Nevertheless his stature was beyond question, and unlike so many other novelists of the period he maintained a high level in his later years.

Three Extremists: Long, Coughlin, and Townsend

Roosevelt's moderation and the desperation of the poor roused extremists both on the left and on the right. The most formidable was Louisiana's Senator Huey Long, the "Kingfish." Raised on a farm in northern Louisiana, Long was successively a traveling salesman, a lawyer, state railroad commissioner, governor, and, after 1930, U.S. senator. By 1933 his rule in Louisiana was absolute. Long was certainly a demagogue—yet the plight of all poor people concerned him deeply. More important, he tried to do something about it.

As a reformer, Long stood in the populist tradition; he hated bankers and "the interests." He believed that poor people, regardless of color, should have a chance to earn a decent living and get an education. His arguments were simplistic, patronizing, possibly insincere, but effective. "Don't say I'm working for niggers," he told one northern journalist. "I'm for the poor man—all poor men. Black and white, they all gotta have a chance. . . . 'Every Man a King'—that's my slogan."

Long had supported the New Deal at the start. But partly because he thought Roosevelt too conservative and partly because of his own ambition, he soon broke with the administration. While Roosevelt was probably more hostile to the big financiers than to any other interest, Long denounced him as "a phoney" and a stooge of Wall Street.

By 1935 Long's "Share Our Wealth" movement had a membership of over 4.6 million. His program called for the confiscation of family fortunes of more than $5 million and a tax of 100 percent on incomes over $1 million a year, the money to be used to buy every family a "homestead" (a house, a car, and other necessities) and provide an annual family income of $2,000 to $3,000, plus old-age pensions, educational benefits, and veterans' pensions. As the 1936 election approached, he planned to organize a third party to split the liberal vote. He assumed that the Republicans would win the election and so botch the job of fighting the Depression that he could sweep the country in 1940.

Less powerful than Long but more widely influential was Father Charles E. Coughlin, the "Radio Priest." A genial Canadian of Irish lineage, Coughlin in 1926 began broadcasting a weekly religious message over station WJR in Detroit. His mellifluous voice attracted a huge national audience, and the Depression gave him a secular cause. In 1933 he had been an eager New Dealer, but his dislike of New Deal financial policies—he believed that inflating the currency would end

●●●─┤**Read** the **Document**

Coughlin, *A Third Party (1936)* at **myhistorylab.com**

the Depression—and his need for ever more sensational ideas to hold his radio audience led him to turn against the New Deal. By 1935 he was calling Roosevelt a "great betrayer and liar."

Although Coughlin's National Union for Social Justice was especially appealing to Catholics, it attracted people of every faith, particularly in the lower-middle-class districts of the big cities. He attacked bankers, New Deal planners, Roosevelt's farm program, and the alleged sympathy of the administration for Communists and Jews, both of which Coughlin denounced in his weekly talks. His program resembled fascism more than any leftist philosophy, but he posed a threat, especially in combination with Long, to the continuation of Democratic rule.

Charles E. Coughlin, the "Radio Priest," was the father of conservative "talk radio."

Another rapidly growing movement alarmed the Democrats in 1934–1935: Dr. Francis E. Townsend's campaign for "old-age revolving pensions." Townsend, a retired California physician, had an oversimplified and therefore appealing "solution" to the nation's troubles. He advocated paying every person aged sixty years and over a pension of $200 a month, the only conditions being that the pensioners not hold jobs and that they spend the entire sum within thirty days. Their purchases, he argued, would stimulate production, thereby creating new jobs and revitalizing the economy. A stiff transactions tax, collected whenever any commodity changed hands, would pay for the program.

Economists quickly pointed out that with about 10 million persons eligible for the Townsend pensions, the cost would amount to $24 billion a year—roughly half the national income. But among the elderly the scheme proved extremely popular. Although most Townsendites were anything but radical politically, their plan, like Long's "Share Our Wealth" scheme, would have revolutionized the distribution of wealth in the country. The movement marked the emergence of a new force in American society. With medical advances lengthening the average life span, the percentage of old people in the population was rising. The breakdown of close family ties in an increasingly mobile society now caused many of these citizens to be cast adrift to live out their last years poor, sick, idle, and alone.

With the possible exception of Long, the extremists had little understanding of practical affairs. Collectively, however, they represented a threat to Roosevelt; their success helped to make the president see that he must move boldly to restore good times or face serious political trouble in 1936.

Political imperatives had much to do with Roosevelt's decisions, and the influence of Justice Brandeis and his disciples, notably Felix Frankfurter, was great. They urged Roosevelt to abandon his probusiness programs, especially the NRA, and stress restoring competition and taxing corporations more heavily. The fact that most businessmen were turning away from him encouraged the president to accept this advice; so did the Supreme Court's decision in *Schecter v. United States* (May 1935), which declared the National Industrial Recovery Act unconstitutional. (The case involved the provisions of the NRA Live Poultry Code; the Court voided the act on the grounds that Congress had delegated too much legislative power to the code authorities and that the defendants, four brothers engaged in slaughtering chickens in New York City, were not engaged in interstate commerce.)

The Second New Deal

Existing laws had failed to end the Depression. Conservatives roundly denounced Roosevelt, and extremists were luring away some of his supporters. Voters, heartened by the partial success of early New Deal measures, were clamoring for further reforms. But the Supreme Court had declared many key New Deal measures unconstitutional. For these many reasons, Roosevelt, in June 1935, launched what historians call the Second New Deal.

There followed the "second hundred days," one of the most productive periods in the history of American legislation. The National Labor Relations Act—commonly known as the **Wagner Act**—gave workers the right to bargain collectively and prohibited employers from interfering with union organizational activities in their factories. A National Labor Relations Board (NLRB) was established to supervise plant elections and designate successful unions as official bargaining agents when a majority of the workers approved.

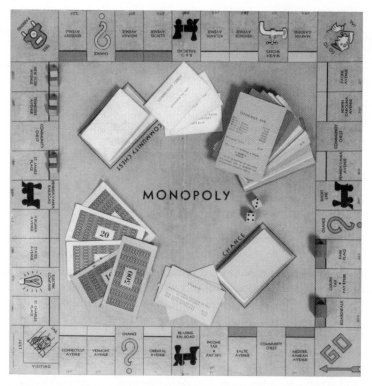

Monopoly, patented in 1935, was an instant best-seller: Players risk all their assets in an attempt to secure a real estate monopoly—and thus great wealth.

It was difficult to force some big corporations to bargain "in good faith," as the law required, but the NLRB could conduct investigations of employer practices and issue cease and desist orders when "unfair" activities came to light.

The **Social Security Act** of August 1935 set up a system of old-age insurance, financed partly by a tax on wages (paid by workers) and partly by a tax on payrolls (paid by employers). It created a state-federal system of unemployment insurance, similarly financed. Liberal critics considered this Social Security system inadequate because it did not cover agricultural workers, domestics, self-employed persons, and some other groups particularly in need of its benefits. Health insurance was not included, and because the size of pensions depended on the amount earned, the lowest-paid workers could not count on much support after reaching sixty-five. Yet the law was of major significance. Over the years the pension payments were increased and the classes of workers covered expanded.

The Rural Electrification Administration (REA), created by executive order, also began to function during this remarkable period. The REA lent money at low interest rates to utility companies and to farmer cooperatives interested in bringing electricity to rural areas. When the REA went into operation, only one farm in ten had electricity; by 1950 only one in ten did not.

Another important measure was the Wealth Tax Act of August 1935, which raised taxes on large incomes considerably. Estate and gift taxes were also increased. Stiffer

Table 26.2 Second New Deal (1935–1938)

Legislation	Purpose
Emergency Relief Appropriations Act (1935)	Created Works Progress Administration (WPA) to give jobs to blacks, white-collar workers, and even artists and writers
Rural Electrification Administration (1935)	Extended electric power lines to rural areas
Social Security Act (1935)	Devised system to provide unemployment insurance and pensions for elderly
Wagner Act (1935)	Guaranteed the rights of unions to organize and negotiate for members
Fair Labor Standards Act (1938)	Set minimum hourly wages and maximum hours of work

taxes on corporate profits reflected the Brandeis group's desire to penalize corporate giantism. Much of the opposition to other New Deal legislation arose from the fact that after these changes in the tax laws were made, the well-to-do had to bear a larger share of the cost of *all* government activities.

Herbert Hoover epitomized the attitude of conservatives when he called the New Deal "the most stupendous invasion of the whole spirit of Liberty that the nation has witnessed." Undoubtedly many opponents of the New Deal sincerely believed that it was undermining the foundations of American freedom. The cost of the New Deal also alarmed them. By 1936 some members of the administration had fallen under the influence of the British economist John Maynard Keynes, who argued that the world Depression could be conquered if governments would deliberately unbalance their budgets by reducing interest rates and taxes and by increasing expenditures to stimulate consumption and investment.

Roosevelt never accepted Keynes's theories; he conferred with the economist in 1934 but could not grasp the "rigmarole of figures" with which Keynes deluged him. Nevertheless the imperatives of the Depression forced him to spend more than the government was collecting in taxes; thus he adopted in part the Keynesian approach. Conservative businessmen considered him financially irresponsible, and the fact that deficit spending seemed to be good politics made them seethe with rage.

The Election of 1936

The election of 1936 loomed as a showdown. The GOP candidate, Governor Alfred M. Landon of Kansas, was a former follower of Theodore Roosevelt, a foe of the Ku Klux Klan in the 1920s, and a believer in government regulation of business. But he was a poor speaker and against the charm and political astuteness of Roosevelt, Landon's arguments—chiefly that he could administer the government more efficiently than the president—made little impression.

On election day the country gave the president a tremendous vote of confidence. He carried every state but Maine and Vermont. The Republicans elected only eighty-nine members of the House of Representatives and their strength in the Senate fell to sixteen, an all-time low. In dozens of city and state elections, Democratic candidates also made large gains. Both Roosevelt's personality and his program had captivated the land. He seemed irresistible, the most powerfully entrenched president in the history of the United States.

●•●⌐**Read** the **Document**

FDR, *Fireside Chat* at
myhistorylab.com

Roosevelt did not win in 1936 because of the inadequacies of his foes. Having abandoned his efforts to hold the businessmen, whom he now denounced as "economic royalists," he appealed for the votes of workers and the underprivileged. The new labor unions gratefully poured thousands of dollars into the campaign to reelect him. Black voters switched to the Democrats in record numbers. Farmers liked Roosevelt because of his evident concern for their welfare. Countless elderly persons backed Roosevelt out of gratitude for the Social Security Act.

Roosevelt Tries to Undermine the Supreme Court

On January 20, in his second inaugural address, Roosevelt spoke of the plight of millions of citizens "denied the greater part of what the very lowest standards of today call the necessities of life." A third of the nation, he added without exaggeration, was "ill-housed, ill-clad, ill-nourished." He interpreted his landslide victory as a mandate for further reforms, and with his prestige and his immense congressional majorities, nothing appeared to stand in his way. Nothing, that is, except the Supreme Court.

Throughout Roosevelt's first term the Court had stood almost immovable against increasing the scope of federal authority and broadening the general power of government, state as well as national, to cope with the exigencies of the Depression. Of the nine justices, only Louis Brandeis, Benjamin N. Cardozo, and Harlan Fiske Stone viewed the New Deal sympathetically. Four others—James C. McReynolds, Willis Van Devanter, Pierce Butler, and George Sutherland—were intransigent conservatives. Chief Justice Charles Evans Hughes and Justice Owen J. Roberts, while more open-minded, tended to side with the conservatives on many questions.

Much of the early New Deal legislation, pushed through Congress at top speed during the hundred days, had been drafted without proper regard for the Constitution. Even the liberal justices considered the National Industrial Recovery Act unconstitutional.

In 1937 all the major measures of the second hundred days appeared doomed. The Wagner Act had little chance of winning approval, experts predicted. Lawyers were advising employers to ignore the Social Security Act, so confident that the Court would declare it unconstitutional.

Faced with this situation, Roosevelt decided to ask Congress to shift the balance on the Court by increasing the number of justices, thinly disguising the purpose of his plan by making it part of a general reorganization of the judiciary. A member of the Court who reached the age of seventy would have the option of retiring at full pay. Should such a justice choose not to retire, the president was to appoint an additional justice, up to a maximum of six, to ease the burden of work for the aged jurists who remained on the bench.

Roosevelt knew that this measure would run into resistance, but he expected that the huge Democratic majorities in Congress could override any opposition and that the public would back him solidly. No astute politician had erred so badly in estimating the effects of an action since Stephen A. Douglas introduced the Kansas-Nebraska bill in 1854.

Although polls showed the public fairly evenly divided on the "court-packing" bill, the opposition was vocal and influential. To the expected denunciations of conservatives were added the complaints of liberals fearful that the principle of court packing might in the future be used to subvert civil liberties. Opposition in Congress was immediate and intense; many who had cheerfully supported every New Deal bill came out against the plan. Chief Justice Hughes released a devastating critique; even the liberal Brandeis—the oldest judge on the court—rejected the bill out of hand.

For months Roosevelt stubbornly refused to concede defeat, but in July 1937 he had to yield. Minor administrative reforms of the judiciary were enacted, but the size of the Court remained unchanged.

The struggle did result in saving the legislation of the Second New Deal. Alarmed by the threat to the Court, Justices Hughes and Roberts beat a strategic retreat on a series of specific issues. While the debate was raging in Congress, they sided with the liberals in upholding first a minimum wage law of the state of Washington that was little different from a New York act the Court had recently rejected, then the Wagner Act, and then the Social Security Act. In May Justice Van Devanter retired and Roosevelt replaced him with Senator Hugo Black of Alabama, a New Dealer. The conservative justices thereupon gave up the fight, and soon Roosevelt was able to appoint enough new judges to give the Court a large pro-New Deal majority. No further measure of significance was declared unconstitutional during his presidency. The Court fight hurt Roosevelt severely. When the president summoned a special session of Congress in November 1937 and submitted a program of "must" legislation, not one of his bills was passed.

The New Deal Winds Down

With unemployment high, wages low, and workers relatively powerless against their employers, most Americans had liked New Deal labor legislation and sympathized with the industrial unions whose growth it stimulated. The NRA, the Wagner Act, and the CIO's organization of industries like steel and automobiles changed the power structure within the economy. What amounted to a revolution in the lives of wage earners had occurred. Unionization had meant fair methods of settling disputes about work practices and a measure of job security based on seniority for tens of thousands of workers. The CIO in particular had done much to increase the influence of labor in politics and to bring blacks and other minorities into the labor movement.

In 1937 a series of "sit-down strikes" broke out, beginning at the General Motors plant in Flint, Michigan. The tolerant attitude of the Roosevelt administration ensured the strikers against government intervention. Fearful that all-out efforts to clear their plants would result in the destruction of expensive machinery, most employers capitulated to the workers' demands. All the automobile manufacturers but Henry Ford quickly came to terms with the United Automobile Workers.

The major steel companies, led by U.S. Steel, recognized the CIO and granted higher wages and a forty-hour week. The auto and steel unions alone boasted more than 725,000 members by late 1937; other CIO units conquered the rubber industry, the electrical industry, the textile industry, and many more.

These gains and the aggressive way in which the unions pursued their objectives gave many members of the middle class second thoughts concerning the justice of labor's demands. Sit-down strikes, the disregard of unions for the "rights" of nonunion workers, and the violence that accompanied some strikes seemed to many not merely unreasonable but also a threat to social order. The enthusiasm of such people for all reform cooled rapidly.

While the sit-down strikes and the Court fight were going on, the New Deal suffered another heavy blow. Business conditions had been gradually improving since 1933. Heartened by the trend, Roosevelt cut back sharply on the relief program in June 1937, with disastrous results. Between August and October the economy slipped downward like sand through a chute. Stock prices plummeted; unemployment rose by 2 million; industrial production slumped. This "Roosevelt recession" further damaged the president's reputation.

In April 1938 Roosevelt again committed himself to heavy deficit spending. At his urging Congress passed a $3.75 billion public works bill. Two major pieces of legislation were also enacted at about this time. A new AAA program set marketing quotas and acreage limitations for growers of staples like wheat, cotton, and tobacco and authorized the Commodity Credit Corporation to lend money to farmers on their surplus crops.

The second measure, the Fair Labor Standards Act, abolished child labor and established a national minimum wage of 40 cents an hour and a maximum workweek of 40 hours, with time and a half for overtime. Although the law failed to cover many of the poorest-paid types of labor, its passage meant wage increases for 750,000 workers. In later years many more classes of workers were brought within its protection, and the minimum wage was repeatedly increased.

These measures further alienated conservatives without dramatically improving economic conditions. The resistance of many Democratic members of Congress to additional economic and social "experiments" hardened. As the 1938 elections approached, Roosevelt decided to go to the voters in an effort to strengthen party discipline and reenergize the New Deal. He singled out a number of conservative Democratic senators, notably Walter F. George of Georgia, Millard F. Tydings of Maryland, and "Cotton Ed" Smith of South Carolina, and tried to "purge" them by backing other Democrats in the primaries.

The purge failed. Southern voters liked Roosevelt but resented his interference in local politics. Smith dodged the issue of liberalism by stressing the question of white supremacy. Tydings emphasized Roosevelt's "invasion" of Maryland. All three senators were easily renominated and then reelected in November. In the nation at large the Republicans made important gains for the first time since Roosevelt had taken office. The Democrats maintained nominal control of both houses of Congress, but the conservative coalition, while unable to muster the votes to do away with accomplished reforms, succeeded in blocking additional legislation.

Significance of the New Deal

After World War II broke out in 1939, the Great Depression was swept away on a wave of orders from the beleaguered European democracies. For this prosperity, Roosevelt received much undeserved credit. Despite the aid given to the jobless, the generation of workers born between 1900 and 1910 who entered the 1930s as unskilled laborers had their careers permanently stunted by the Depression. Far fewer rose to middle-class status than at any time since the 1830s and 1840s.

Roosevelt's willingness to experiment with different means of combating the Depression made sense because no one really knew what to do; however, his uncertainty about the ultimate objectives of the New Deal was counterproductive. He vacillated

To hold back immense volumes of water, the Hoover Dam, seen from above, consisted of 2.5 million cubic yards of concrete which, at the base, was thicker than two football fields set end-to-end. It was built through the New Deal.

between seeking to stimulate the economy by deficit spending and trying to balance the budget, between a narrow "America first" economic nationalism and a broad-gauged international approach, between regulating monopolies and trust-busting, and between helping the underprivileged and bolstering those already strong.

Roosevelt's fondness for establishing new agencies to deal with specific problems vastly increased the federal bureaucracy, indirectly added to the influence of lobbyists, and made it more difficult to monitor government activities. His cavalier attitude toward constitutional limitations on executive power, which he justified as being necessary in a national emergency, set in motion trends that so increased the prestige and authority of the presidency that the balance among the executive, legislative, and judicial branches was threatened.

Yet these are criticisms after the fact. Because of New Deal decisions, many formerly unregulated areas of American life became subject to federal authority: the stock exchange, agricultural prices and production, labor relations, old-age pensions, relief of the needy. By encouraging the growth of unions, the New Deal probably helped workers obtain a larger share of the profits of industry. By putting a floor under the income of many farmers, it checked the decline of agricultural living standards, though not that of the agricultural population. The Social Security program, with all its inadequacies, lessened the impact of bad times on an increasingly large proportion of the population and provided immense psychological benefits to all.

⬤▶ Watch the Video

Responding to the Great Depression: Whose New Deal? at **myhistorylab.com**

Women as New Dealers: The Network

Largely because of the influence of Eleanor Roosevelt and Molly Dewson, head of the Women's Division of the Democratic National Committee, the Roosevelt administration employed far more women in positions of importance than any earlier one. Secretary of Labor Frances Perkins, the first woman appointed to a Cabinet post, had been active in labor relations for more than twenty years, as secretary of the Consumers' League during the progressive period, as a factory inspector immediately after the war, and as chair of the New York State Industrial Commission. As secretary of labor she helped draft

New Deal labor legislation and kept Roosevelt informed on various labor problems outside the government.

Through her newspaper column "My Day" and as a speaker on public issues, Eleanor Roosevelt became a major political force, especially in the area of civil rights, where the administration needed constant prodding.

She particularly identified with efforts to obtain better treatment for blacks, in and out of government. Her best-known action occurred in 1939 after the Daughters of the American Revolution (DAR) refused to permit the use of their Washington auditorium for a concert by the black contralto Marian Anderson. Eleanor Roosevelt resigned from the DAR in protest, and after the president arranged for Anderson to sing at the Lincoln Memorial, she persuaded a small army of dignitaries to sponsor the concert. An interracial crowd of 75,000 people attended the performance. The *Chicago Defender*, an influential black newspaper, noted that the First Lady "stood like the Rock of Gibraltar against pernicious encroachments on the rights of minorities."

Blacks during the New Deal

The shift of black voters from the Republican to the Democratic party during the New Deal years was one of the most significant political turnarounds in American history. In 1932 when things were at their worst, fewer African Americans defected from the Republican party than the members of any other traditionally Republican group. Four years later, however, blacks voted for Roosevelt in overwhelming numbers.

Blacks supported the New Deal for the same reasons that whites did, but how the New Deal affected blacks in general and racial attitudes specifically are more complicated questions. Claiming that he dared not antagonize southern congressmen, whose votes he needed for his recovery programs, Roosevelt did nothing about civil rights before 1941 and relatively little thereafter. For the same reason, many southern white liberals hesitated to support racial integration for fear that other liberal causes could be injured as a result.

Many of the early New Deal programs treated blacks as second-class citizens. They were often paid at lower rates than whites under NRA codes and the early farm programs shortchanged black tenants and sharecroppers. TVA developments were rigidly segregated, and almost no blacks got jobs in TVA offices. Because the Social Security Act excluded agricultural laborers and domestic servants, it did nothing for hundreds of thousands of poor black workers or for Mexican American farmhands in the Southwest. In 1939 unemployment was twice as high among blacks as among whites, and whites' wages were double the level of blacks' wages.

The fact that members of racial minorities got less than they deserved did not keep most of them from becoming New Dealers: Half a loaf was more than any American government had given blacks since the time of Ulysses S. Grant.

In the labor movement the new CIO unions accepted black members, and this was particularly significant because these unions were organizing industries—steel, automobiles, and mining among others—that employed large numbers of blacks. Thus, while black Americans suffered horribly during the Depression, New Deal efforts to counteract its effects brought them some relief and a measure of hope. And this became

Black sharecroppers evicted from their tenant farms were photographed by Arthur Rothstein along a Missouri road in 1939. Rothstein was one of a group of outstanding photographers who created a unique "sociological and economic survey" of the nation between 1936 and 1942 under the aegis of the Farm Security Administration.

increasingly true with the passage of time. During Roosevelt's second term, blacks found far less to criticize than had been the case earlier.

A New Deal for Indians

New Deal policy toward American Indians built on earlier trends but carried them further. During the Harding and Coolidge administrations more Indian land had passed into the hands of whites, and agents of the Bureau of Indian Affairs had tried to suppress elements of Indian culture that they considered "pagan" or "lascivious." In 1924 Congress finally granted citizenship to all Indians, but it was still generally agreed by whites that Indians should be treated as wards of the state. Assimilation had failed; Indian languages and religious practices, patterns of family life, Indian arts and crafts had all resisted generations of efforts to "civilize" the tribes.

Government policy took a new direction in 1933 when President Roosevelt named John Collier commissioner of Indian affairs. In the 1920s Collier had studied the Indians of the Southwest and been appalled by what he learned. He became executive secretary of the American Indian Defense Association and, in 1925, editor of a reform-oriented magazine, *American Indian Life*. By the time he was appointed commissioner, the Depression had reduced perhaps a third of the 320,000 Indians living on reservations to penury.

Collier tried to revive the spirits of these people. He was particularly eager to encourage the revival of tribal governments that could represent the Indians in dealings with the United States government and function as community service centers.

In part because of Collier's urging, Congress passed the Indian Reorganization Act of 1934. This law did away with the Dawes Act allotment system and enabled Indians to establish tribal governments with powers like those of cities, and it encouraged Indians to return individually owned lands to tribal control. About 4 million of the 90 million acres of Indian land lost under the allotment system were returned to the tribes.

In truth the problem was more complicated than Collier had imagined. Indians who owned profitable allotments, such as those in Oklahoma who held oil and mineral rights, did not relish turning over their land to tribal control. All told, 77 of 269 tribes voted against communal holdings.

Collier resigned in 1945, and in the 1950s Congress "terminated" most government efforts aimed at preserving Indian cultures. Nevertheless, like so many of its programs, the New Deal's Indian policy was a bold effort to deal constructively with a long-standing national problem.

The Role of Roosevelt

How much of the credit for New Deal policies belongs personally to Franklin D. Roosevelt is debatable. He had little to do with many of the details and some of the broad principles behind the New Deal. His knowledge of economics was skimpy, his understanding of many social problems superficial, and his political philosophy distressingly vague. The British leader Anthony Eden described him as "a conjurer, skillfully juggling with balls of dynamite, whose nature he failed to understand."

Nevertheless, every aspect of the New Deal bears the brand of Roosevelt's remarkable personality. Roosevelt constructed the coalition that made the program possible; his humanitarianism made it a reform movement of major significance. Although

A miner greets the president. Franklin's "first-class temperament" compensated for his "second-class intellect," Justice Oliver Wendell Holmes famously observed.

considered by many a terrible administrator because he encouraged rivalry among his subordinates, assigned different agencies overlapping responsibilities, failed to discharge many incompetents, and frequently put off making difficult decisions, he was in fact one of the most effective chief executives in the nation's history.

Like Andrew Jackson, Roosevelt maximized his role as leader of all the people. His informal biweekly press conferences kept the public in touch with developments and himself in tune with popular thinking. His "fireside chats" convinced millions that he was personally interested in each citizen's life and welfare, as in a way he was. At a time when the size and complexity of the government made it impossible for any one person to direct the nation's destiny, Roosevelt managed the minor miracle of personifying that government to 130 million people.

While the New Deal was still evolving, contemporaries recognized Roosevelt's right to a place beside Washington, Jefferson, and Lincoln among the great presidents. Yet as his second term drew toward its close, some of his most important work still lay in the future.

The Triumph of Isolationism

Franklin Roosevelt was at heart an internationalist, but like most world leaders in the 1930s, he placed revival of his own country's limping economy ahead of general world recovery. In April 1933 he took the United States off the gold standard, hoping that devaluing the dollar would make it easier to sell American goods abroad. The following month the World Economic Conference met in London. Delegates from sixty-four nations sought ways to increase world trade, perhaps by a general reduction of tariffs and the stabilization of currencies. After flirting with the idea of currency stabilization, Roosevelt threw a bombshell into the conference by announcing that the United States would not return to the gold standard. His decision increased international ill feeling, and the conference collapsed.

Against this background, vital changes in American foreign policy took place. Unable to persuade the country to take positive action against aggressors, internationalists like Secretary of State Stimson had begun in 1931 to work for a discretionary arms embargo law to be applied by the president in time of war against whichever side had broken the peace. By early 1933 Stimson had obtained Hoover's backing for an embargo bill, as well as the support of President-elect Roosevelt. First the munitions manufacturers and then the isolationists pounced on it, and in the resulting debate it was amended to make the embargo apply to *all* belligerents.

Stimson's policy would have permitted arms shipments to China but not to Japan, which might have discouraged the Japanese from attacking. As amended, the embargo would have automatically applied to both sides, thus removing the United States as an influence in the conflict. Although Roosevelt accepted the change, the internationalists in Congress did not, and when they withdrew their support the measure died.

The danger of another world war mounted steadily as Germany, Italy, and Japan repeatedly resorted to force to achieve their expansionist aims. In March 1935 Hitler instituted universal military training and denounced the settlement at Versailles. In May Mussolini massed troops in Italian Somaliland, using a trivial border clash as a pretext for threatening the ancient kingdom of Ethiopia.

Congress responded by passing a series of **neutrality acts** to prevent the United States from being drawn into a wider war. The Neutrality Act of 1935 forbade the sale of munitions to all belligerents whenever the president should proclaim that a state of war existed. Americans who took passage on belligerent ships after such a proclamation had been issued would do so at their own risk. Roosevelt would have preferred a discretionary embargo or no new legislation at all, but he dared not rouse the ire of the isolationists by vetoing the bill.

In October 1935 Italy invaded Ethiopia and Roosevelt invoked the new neutrality law. Secretary of State Cordell Hull asked American exporters to support a "moral embargo" on the sale of oil and other products not covered by the act. His plea was ignored; oil shipments to Italy tripled between October and January. Italy quickly overran and annexed Ethiopia. In February 1936 Congress passed a second neutrality act forbidding all loans to belligerents.

Then, in the summer of 1936, civil war broke out in Spain. The rebels, led by the reactionary General Francisco Franco and strongly backed by Italy and Germany, sought to overthrow the somewhat leftist Spanish Republic. Here, clearly, was a clash between democracy and fascism, and the neutrality laws did not apply to civil wars. However, Roosevelt now became more fearful of involvement than some isolationists. The president believed that American interference might cause the conflict in Spain to become a global war, and he was wary of antagonizing the substantial number of American Catholics who were sympathetic to the Franco regime. At his urging Congress passed another neutrality act broadening the arms embargo to cover civil wars.

Isolationism now reached its peak. A public opinion poll revealed in March 1937 that 94 percent of the people thought American policy should be directed at keeping out of all foreign wars rather than trying to prevent wars from breaking out. In April Congress passed still another neutrality law. It continued the embargo on munitions and loans, forbade Americans to travel on belligerent ships, and gave the president discretionary authority to place the sale of other goods to belligerents on a cash-and-carry basis. This played into the hands of the aggressors. While German planes and cannons were turning the tide in Spain, the United States was denying the hard-pressed Spanish loyalists even a case of cartridges.

In January 1938 the House narrowly defeated the Ludlow amendment, which would have prohibited Congress from declaring war without the prior approval of the nation's voters.

President Roosevelt, in part because of domestic problems such as the Supreme Court packing struggle and the wave of sit-down strikes, and in part because of his own vacillation, seemed to have lost control over the formulation of American foreign policy. The American people, like wild creatures before a forest fire, were rushing in blind panic from the conflagration.

War Again in Asia and Europe

There were limits beyond which Americans would not go. In July 1937 the Japanese resumed their conquest of China, pressing ahead on a broad front. Roosevelt believed that invoking the neutrality law would only help the well-armed Japanese. Taking advantage of the fact that neither side had formally declared war, he allowed the shipment of arms and supplies to both sides.

Roosevelt came gradually to the conclusion that resisting aggression was more important than keeping out of war, but when he did, the need to keep the country united

In 1939 Hitler reviews goose-stepping troops during a celebration of his 50th birthday.

led him at times to be less than candid in his public statements. Hitler's annexation of Austria in March 1938 caused him deep concern. The Nazis' vicious anti-Semitism had caused many of Germany's 500,000 Jewish citizens to seek refuge abroad. Now 190,000 Austrian Jews were under Nazi control. When Roosevelt learned that the Germans were burning synagogues, expelling Jewish children from schools, and otherwise mistreating innocent people, he said that he "could scarcely believe that such things could occur." But public opinion opposed changing the immigration law so that more refugees could be admitted, and the president did nothing.

In September 1938 Hitler demanded that Czechoslovakia cede the German-speaking Sudetenland to the Reich. British Prime Minister Neville Chamberlain and French Premier Edouard Daladier, in a conference with Hitler at Munich, yielded to Hitler's threats and promises and persuaded the Czechs to surrender the region. Roosevelt failed again to speak out. But when the Nazis seized the rest of Czechoslovakia in March 1939, Roosevelt called for "methods short of war" to demonstrate America's determination to check the fascists.

When Hitler threatened Poland in the spring of 1939, demanding the free city of Danzig and the Polish Corridor separating East Prussia from the rest of Germany, and when Mussolini invaded Albania, Roosevelt urged Congress to repeal the 1937 neutrality act so that the United States could sell arms to Britain and France in the event of war. Congress refused.

In August 1939 Germany and the Soviet Union signed a nonaggression pact, prelude to their joint assault on Poland. On September 1 Hitler's troops invaded Poland, at last provoking Great Britain and France to declare war. Roosevelt immediately asked Congress to repeal the arms embargo. In November, in a vote that followed party lines closely, the Democratic majority pushed through a law permitting the sale of arms and other contraband on a cash-and-carry basis. Short-term loans were authorized, but American vessels were forbidden to carry any products to the belligerents. Since the Allies controlled the seas, cash-and-carry gave them a tremendous advantage.

The German attack on Poland effected a basic change in American thinking. Keeping out of the war remained an almost universal hope, but preventing a Nazi victory became the ultimate, if not always conscious, objective of many citizens. In Roosevelt's case it was perfectly conscious, although he dared not express his feelings candidly because of isolationist strength in Congress and the country. He moved slowly, responding to rather than directing the course of events.

Poland fell in less than a month; then, Hitler loosed his armored divisions. Between April 9 and June 22 he taught the world the awful meaning of **Blitzkrieg**— lightning war, spearheaded by tanks and supporting aircraft. Denmark, Norway, the Netherlands, Belgium, and France were successively overwhelmed. The British army, pinned against the sea at Dunkirk, saved itself from annihilation only by fleeing across the English Channel. After the French submitted to his harsh terms on June 22, Hitler controlled nearly all of western Europe.

Roosevelt responded to these disasters in a number of ways. In the fall of 1939, reacting to warnings from Albert Einstein and other scientists that the Germans were trying to develop an atomic bomb, he committed federal funds to a top-secret atomic bomb program, which came to be known as the **Manhattan Project**. Even as the British and French were falling back, he sold them, without legal authority, surplus government arms. When Italy entered the war against France, the president called the invasion a stab in the back. During the first five months of 1940 he asked Congress to appropriate over $4 billion for national defense. To strengthen national unity he named Henry L. Stimson secretary of war[1] and another Republican, Frank Knox, secretary of the navy.

After the fall of France, Hitler attempted to bomb and starve the British into submission. The epic air battles over England during the summer of 1940 ended in a decisive defeat for the Nazis, but the Royal Navy, which had only about 100 destroyers, could not control German submarine attacks on shipping. In this desperate hour, Prime Minister Winston Churchill, who had replaced Chamberlain in May 1940, asked Roosevelt for fifty old American destroyers to fill the gap.

Japanese Expansion, 1920–1941 The Japanese empire, which conquered Korea early in the twentieth century, seized Manchuria in 1931; Jehol, north of Beijing, in 1933; and the rest of China after 1937.

German Expansion, 1936–1939 In March 1936, Hitler's forces reoccupied the Rhineland. In 1938 Germany annexed Austria and wrested the Sudetenland from Czechoslovakia, and in 1939 occupied the remaining Czech lands.

---

[1]Stimson had held this post from 1911 to 1913 in the Taft Cabinet!

The navy had 240 destroyers in commission and more than fifty under construction. But direct loan or sale of the vessels would have violated both international and American laws. Any attempt to obtain new legislation would have roused fears that the United States was going down the path that had led it into World War I. Long delay if not outright defeat would have resulted. Roosevelt therefore arranged to "trade" the destroyers for six British naval bases in the Caribbean. In addition, Great Britain leased bases in Bermuda and Newfoundland to the United States.

The destroyers-for-bases deal was a masterful achievement. It helped save Great Britain, and at the same time it circumvented isolationist prejudices since the president could present it as a shrewd bargain that bolstered America's defenses. A string of island bastions in the Atlantic was more valuable than fifty old destroyers.

Lines were hardening throughout the world. In September 1940, despite last-ditch isolationist resistance, Congress enacted the first peacetime draft in American history. Some 1.2 million draftees were summoned for one year of service, and 800,000 reservists were called to active duty. That same month Japan signed a mutual-assistance pact with Germany and Italy. This Rome-Berlin-Tokyo coalition—the **Axis Powers**—fused the conflicts in Europe and Asia, turning the struggle into a global war.

A Third Term for FDR

In the midst of these events the 1940 presidential election took place. Roosevelt was easily renominated. Vice President Garner, who had become disenchanted with Roosevelt and the New Deal, did not seek a third term; at Roosevelt's dictation, the party chose Secretary of Agriculture Henry A. Wallace to replace him.

By using concern about the European war to justify running for a tradition-breaking third term, Roosevelt brought down on his head the hatred of conservative Republicans and the isolationists of both major parties, just when they thought they would be rid of him. The Republicans nominated the darkest of dark horses, Wendell L. Willkie of Indiana, the utility magnate who had led the fight against the TVA in 1933.

Despite his political inexperience and Wall Street connections, Willkie made an appealing candidate. He was an energetic, charming, openhearted man. His rough-hewn, rural manner (one Democrat called him "a simple, barefoot Wall Street lawyer") won him wide support in farm districts. Willkie had difficulty, however, finding issues on which to oppose Roosevelt. The New Deal reforms were too popular and too much in line with his own thinking to invite attack. He believed as strongly as the president that America could no longer ignore the Nazi threat.

In the end Willkie focused his campaign on Roosevelt's conduct of foreign relations. While rejecting the isolationist position, Willkie charged that Roosevelt intended to make the United States a participant in the war. Roosevelt retorted (disingenuously, since he knew he was not a free agent in the situation), "I have said this before, but I shall say it again and again and again: Your boys are not going to be sent into any foreign wars." In November Roosevelt carried the country handily, though by a smaller majority than in 1932 or 1936. The popular vote was 27 million to 22 million, the electoral count 449 to 82.

The Undeclared War

The election encouraged Roosevelt to act more boldly. When Prime Minister Churchill informed him that the cash-and-carry system would no longer suffice because Great Britain was rapidly exhausting its financial resources, he decided at once to provide the British with whatever they needed. Instead of proposing to lend them money, a step certain to rouse memories of the vexatious war debt controversies, he devised the lend-lease program, one of his most ingenious and imaginative creations.

First he delivered a "fireside chat" that stressed the evil intentions of the Nazis and the dangers that a German victory would create for America. Aiding Britain should be looked at simply as a form of self-defense. When the radio talk provoked a favorable public response, Roosevelt went to Congress in January 1941 with a plan calling for the expenditure of $7 billion for war materials that the president could sell, lend, lease, exchange, or transfer to any country whose defense he deemed vital to that of the United States. After two months of debate, Congress gave him what he had asked for.

Although the wording of the **Lend-Lease Act** obscured its immediate purpose, the saving of Great Britain, the president was frank in explaining his plan. He did not minimize the dangers involved, yet his mastery of practical politics was never more in evidence. To counter Irish American prejudices against the English, he pointed out that the Irish Republic would surely fall under Nazi domination if Hitler won the war. He coupled his demand for heavy military expenditures with his enunciation of the idealistic "Four Freedoms"—freedom of speech, freedom of religion, freedom from want, and freedom from fear—for which, he said, the war was being fought.

After the enactment of lend-lease, aid short of war was no longer seriously debated. The American navy began to patrol the North Atlantic, shadowing German submarines and radioing their locations to British warships and planes. In April 1941 U.S. forces occupied Greenland; in May the president declared a state of unlimited national emergency. After Hitler invaded the Soviet Union in June, Roosevelt moved slowly, for anti-Soviet feeling in the United States was intense.[2] But it was obviously to the nation's advantage to help any country that was resisting Hitler's armies. In November, $1 billion in lend-lease aid was put at the disposal of the Soviet Union.

Meanwhile, Iceland was occupied in July 1941, and the draft law was extended in August—by the margin of a single vote in the House of Representatives. In September the German submarine *U–652* fired a torpedo at the destroyer *Greer* in the North Atlantic. The *Greer*, which had provoked the attack by tracking *U–652* and flashing its position to a British plane, avoided the torpedo and dropped nineteen depth charges in an effort to sink the submarine.

Roosevelt announced that the *Greer* had been innocently "carrying mail to Iceland." He called the U-boats "the rattlesnakes of the Atlantic" and ordered the navy to "shoot on sight" any German craft in the waters south and west of Iceland and to convoy merchant vessels as far as that island. After the sinking of the destroyer *Reuben James* on October 30, Congress voted to allow the arming of American merchant ships and to permit them to carry cargoes to Allied ports. For all practical purposes, though not yet officially, the United States had gone to war.

---

[2]During the 1930s the Soviet Union took a far firmer stand against the fascists than any other power, but after joining Hitler in swallowing up Poland, it attacked and defeated Finland during the winter of 1939–1940 and annexed the Baltic states. These acts virtually destroyed the small communist movement in the United States.

Cinderella Man

As *Cinderella Man* (2005) opens, boxer James J. Braddock (Russell Crowe) lands a right-hook that sends his opponent sprawling to the canvas—a knockout. Braddock raises his hands in triumph. The crowd roars and a jazz band blares.

When Braddock arrives at his home in New Jersey, his wife, Mae (Renée Zellweger) leaps into his arms. "I'm so proud of you," she says. Three children mob their father. Later, as Braddock prepares for bed, he sets his gold watch and thick wallet onto a polished wood dresser. The year is 1928.

Abruptly, the scene dissolves. A cheap, unfinished dresser comes into focus. The watch and wallet are gone. Braddock, unshaven, looks wearily around a squalid hovel. The children, on mattresses in shadows, cough and wheeze. The year is 1933.

Braddock, like much of the nation, has fallen on hard times, his savings wiped out by the Depression. Worse, he has broken his powerful right hand and, desperate for money, resumed boxing before it healed. He tries to work at the dockyards but often there is no work to be had. The grocer refuses credit. The milkman stops deliveries. The power company shuts off the gas and electricity. His children, underfed and chilled, become sick. Braddock returns to Madison Square Garden, hat in hand, and begs for money. He also applies and receives federal assistance— welfare—at $6.40 a week. Compared to Braddock, Cinderella had it easy.

Then Braddock's agent, an unlikely fairy godmother, shows up with an extraordinary proposition. A huge, young bruiser and leading contender for the heavyweight title—"Corn" Griffin—had been scheduled to fight the next evening at Madison Square Garden. But Griffin's opponent has backed out at the last minute. Rather than cancel the fight, Madison Square Garden has offered Braddock $250 to serve as Griffin's punching bag. Desperate, Braddock accepts.

What happens the next day—June 14, 1934—is the stuff of fairy tales. Braddock borrows boxing boots and heads to Madison Square Garden. When Braddock enters the ring, his robe bears another boxer's name.

After the opening bell, Griffin, a thick-necked bull of a man, charges Braddock and pounds him mercilessly. Braddock, sustained only by raw courage—and a tough chin, sur-vives the first two rounds. Then, in the third, he surprises Griffin with a thunderous hook, knocking the giant out cold.

Because Griffin was the top contender, Braddock himself is placed on the list of contenders. He proceeds to score one upset after another until he's next in line to face Max Baer (Craig Bierko), the heavyweight champion whose fearsome right has killed two boxers. The manager of Madison Square Garden requires Braddock to sign a waiver absolving it of responsibility should Braddock also perish at Baer's hands.

On June 13, 1935, the night of the fight, as Mae goes to church to pray, reporters speculate on whether Braddock can last a single round. The betting odds against Braddock are the worst in memory. But a movie named after a fairy tale must have a happy ending, and *Cinderella Man* comes through. After fifteen harrowing rounds, Braddock wins a unani-mous decision. In 364 days, he has gone from impoverished "bum" to heavyweight champion of the world.

"This is a true story," declared director Ron Howard. Yet fairy tales, by definition, are make-believe; and Hollywood, by reputation, believes in nothing as fervently as the dollar. Thus viewers are entitled to ask: Does *Cinderella Man* tell the actual story of James J. Braddock?

The surprising answer, given the implausi-bility of the plot, is yes, up to a point. And that point begins with the Baer-Braddock fight: Madison Square Garden did not warn Braddock of the danger of fighting Baer or oblige him to sign a waiver. Also, the fight was no slugfest. The *New York Times* dubbed

Russell Crowe and Renée Zellweger embrace in *Cinderella Man*.

it "one of the worst heavyweight championship contests" in boxing history. Reporters assumed that Baer failed to take the early rounds seriously, lost others on foolish fouls, and realized too late that he was behind. Baer, too, was no unfeeling monster. Most interesting is the movie's error of omission, or, more precisely, of suppression. It makes no mention of the fact that Baer proudly trumpeted his Jewish ancestry. Baer had a large Star of David stitched onto his trunks, an image that appears in the movie once, briefly and from a distance.

Why did director Howard evade the truth about Baer? The likely answer is that Howard knew that fairy tales require villains as well as heroes. *Cinderella Man's* Braddock looms larger for slaying the Big Bad Baer.

In fact, the real enemy was the Great Depression. Braddock understood this. When asked how he managed to turn his career around, he explained, "I was fighting for milk." Damon Runyon, the writer who first called Braddock "Cinderella Man," recognized that the boxer's story took on mythic proportions because it encapsulated the aspirations of an entire nation.

But the movie misses the point that many ethnic groups had their own boxing champions. After Braddock had upset Griffin, he fought Joe Louis, the Brown Bomber. While the movie rightly shows Irish Americans praying for Braddock, it neglects the millions of African Americans who also gathered around radios, praying for Louis. Jewish fans, similarly, identified with Baer, cherishing his 1933 defeat of the German boxer, Max Schmeling, Hitler's favorite. When Braddock defeated Baer, many Jews were devastated.

Madison Square Garden, keenly aware of the ethnic appeal of boxing, worked hard to ensure that nearly every major immigrant group had someone to cheer for on fight night. Boxing promoters were among the first to learn that in sports, as in entertainment more generally, segregation did not pay.

Cinderella Man depicts, with considerable accuracy, a simple and good man's triumph over adversity. His story was, indeed, the stuff of myth. But in its earnest attempt to universalize Braddock's appeal, the movie obscures the ethnic divisions that characterized so much of American life during the first half of the twentieth century.

Question for Discussion

- Do you think the Depression encouraged solidarity among Americans of different races and ethnicities, because everyone could empathize with each other's suffering? Or did it exacerbate tensions by pitting different groups against each other in search of scarce jobs?

Milestones

1933	FDR becomes president
	Hitler is elected German chancellor
	FDR proclaims Good Neighbor Policy
	Banking Act gives FDR broad powers
	Civilian Conservation Corps (CCC) employs 250,000 young men
	Federal Emergency Relief Act (FERA) funds relief programs
	Agricultural Adjustment Act (AAA) seeks relief for farmers
	Tennessee Valley Authority (TVA) plans dams and power plants
	National Industrial Recovery Act (NIRA) establishes Public Works Administration (PWA) and National Recovery Administration (NRA)
	Banking Act establishes Federal Deposit Insurance Corporation (FDIC)
	Civil Works Administration puts 4 million to work
	Twenty-First Amendment ends prohibition
1934	Indian Reorganization Act gives tribes more autonomy
	Securities and Exchange Commission (SEC) regulates stocks and bonds
	Federal Communications Commission (FCC) regulates interstate and foreign communication
	Federal Housing Administration (FHA) gives housing loans
1935	Emergency Relief Appropriation Act creates Works Project Administration (WPA)
	Rural Electrification Administration brings electricity to farms

1935	Supreme Court rules NIRA unconstitutional in *Schechter v. United States*
	National Labor Relations Act (Wagner-Connery) encourages unionization
	Social Security Act guarantees pensions and other benefits
	Neutrality Act forbids wartime arms sales to belligerents
	Italy invades and annexes Ethiopia
	Walter Millis publishes isolationist *The Road to War: America, 1914–1917*
1936	FDR is reelected president in record landslide
	Supreme Court declares AAA unconstitutional
1937	Roosevelt tries to pack Supreme Court
	Japanese in China seize Beijing, Shanghai, Nanking
1938	Fair Labor Standards Act abolishes child labor, sets minimum wage
	House of Representatives defeats Ludlow (isolationist) Amendment
	Britain and France appease Hitler at Munich
1939	Germany invades Poland; World War II begins
1940	Hitler conquers Denmark, Norway, the Netherlands, Belgium, France
	FDR is reelected to third term
	Axis Powers sign Rome-Berlin-Tokyo pact
	Isolationists form America First Committee
1941	Lend-Lease Act helps Britain

✓•⊣Study and Review at www.myhistorylab.com

Review Questions

1. The introduction of this chapter compares the 2010 health insurance law
with that establishing Social Security
in 1935. In what ways is the comparison an apt one? How did the measures
and times differ? Was Social Security
a form of socialism?

2. Compare the First and Second New
Deals. What were the similarities and
differences?

3. What was the impact of the Great
Depression on art, literature, and popular culture? How did it affect women
and minority groups? Labor?

4. How did the New Deal expand the
role of the federal government?

5. Why did Asia and Europe slip into
war in the 1930s? How did the United
States respond during that decade
and why?

Key Terms

Agricultural Adjustment
   Act (AAA) *681*
Axis Powers *702*
Blitzkrieg *701*
Civilian Conservation
   Corps (CCC) *680*
Lend-Lease Act *703*

Manhattan Project *701*
National Recovery
   Administration
   (NRA) *680*
neutrality acts *698*
New Deal *679*
Social Security Act *689*

Tennessee Valley
   Authority (TVA) *683*
Wagner Act *688*
Works Progress
   Administration
   (WPA) *685*

27 War and Peace: 1941–1945

((•—[Hear the Audio Chapter 27 at myhistorylab.com

Does the war in Afghanistan touch your life?

ALTHOUGH ALL YOUNG AMERICAN MEN ARE REQUIRED TO REGISTER for the military draft, none has actually been drafted since the 1970s. (Registration exists in the event of a national military emergency.) In place of conscription, the Department of Defense has recruited all-volunteer military services. In times of peace, most generals prefer a volunteer army: Professional soldiers are better trained and often more attentive to orders; but in times of war, when recruiting officers struggle to fill quotas and tours-of-duty are extended, many generals call for a return to the draft.

By 2010, a heated debate among officers surfaced in the *Armed Forces Journal*. Most defended the professional army, noting that the quality of recruits was higher than in two decades. But other officers called for a return to the "citizen soldiers" envisioned by Washington and Jefferson. One reason was that wars fought by conscripts ensured that the nation as a whole engaged in the war effort. The *Seattle Times* observed that although the Iraq war had gone on far longer than World War II, "life for most Americans has clicked along without personal loss or even higher federal taxes." "Marines are at war," one general complained, "America is at the mall."

Such remarks underscored how different the current conflicts in Iraq and Afghanistan are from World War II, a monstrous global war among advanced industrial nations. Of every five American males between the ages of twenty and twenty-five, four served in World War II. At the beginning of World War II, 4 million Americans paid income tax; by its end, 43 million did so. Over 85 million Americans—half the nation's population—spent $185 billion to buy war bonds. Food and gasoline were rationed. World War II required the mobilization of the entire nation.

World War II transformed society, too. In the absence of so many young men, women assumed new roles and worked at different types of jobs. African Americans, Hispanics, American Indians, and other minorities found new opportunities even as they encountered persistent discrimination. Americans of Japanese extraction were relocated against their will to isolated camps. Technological change—culminating in the atom bomb—transformed everyone's lives. It was a war unlike any other.

The Road to Pearl Harbor

Neither the United States nor Japan wanted war. Roosevelt considered Germany by far the more dangerous enemy and was alarmed by the possibility of simultaneously fighting German armies in Europe and Japanese forces in the Pacific. In the spring of 1941 Secretary of State Cordell Hull conferred in Washington with the Japanese ambassador, Kichisaburo Nomura, in an effort to resolve their differences. Hull showed little appreciation of the political and military situation in East Asia. He demanded that Japan withdraw from China.

Japan might well have accepted limited annexations in the area in return for the removal of American trade restrictions, but Hull insisted on total withdrawal, to which even the moderates in Japan would not agree. When Hitler invaded the Soviet Union, thereby removing the threat of Russian intervention in East Asia, Japan decided to complete its conquest of China and occupy French Indochina even at the risk of war with the United States. Roosevelt retaliated in July 1941 by freezing Japanese assets in the United States and clamping an embargo on oil.

Now the ultranationalist war party in Japan assumed control. Nomura was instructed to tell Hull that Japan would refrain from further expansion if the United States and Great Britain would cut off all aid to China and lift the economic blockade. Japan promised to pull out of Indochina once "a just peace" had been established with China. When the United States rejected these demands, the Japanese prepared to attack the Dutch East Indies, British Malaya, and the Philippines. To immobilize the U.S. Pacific fleet, they planned a surprise air assault on the Hawaiian naval base at Pearl Harbor.

Japan's surprise attack on Pearl Harbor on December 7, 1941, killed more than 2,400 American sailors and soldiers and thrust the United States into World War II. President Roosevelt asked Congress for a declaration of war the next day, calling the attack "a date that will live in infamy."

An American cryptanalyst, Colonel William F. Friedman, had cracked the Japanese diplomatic code: The Japanese were making plans to attack in early December. But in the hectic rush of events, both military and civilian authorities failed to make effective use of the information collected. They expected the blow to fall somewhere in East Asia, possibly the Philippines.

The garrison at Pearl Harbor was alerted against "a surprise aggressive move in any direction." The commanders there, Admiral Husband E. Kimmel and General Walter C. Short, believing an attack impossible, took precautions only against Japanese sabotage. Thus when planes from Japanese aircraft carriers swooped down upon Pearl Harbor on the morning of December 7, they found easy targets. In less than two hours they reduced the Pacific fleet to a smoking ruin: two battleships destroyed, six others heavily battered, nearly a dozen lesser vessels put out of action. More than 150 planes were wrecked; over 2,400 soldiers and sailors were killed and 1,100 wounded.

Never had American armed forces suffered a more devastating or shameful defeat. Although the official blame was placed chiefly on Admiral Kimmel and General Short, responsibility for the disaster was widespread. Military and civilian officials in Washington had failed to pass on all that they knew to Hawaii or even to one another.

On December 8 Congress declared war on Japan. Formal war with Germany and Italy was still not inevitable—isolationists were far more ready to resist the "yellow peril" in Asia than to fight in Europe. The Axis Powers, however, honored their treaty obligations to Japan and on December 11 declared war on the United States. America was now fully engaged in another great war, World War II.

Mobilizing the Home Front

World War II placed immense strains on the American economy and produced immense results. About 15 million men and women entered the armed services; they, and in part the millions more in Allied uniforms, had to be fed, clothed, housed, and supplied with equipment ranging from typewriters and paper clips to rifles, grenades, tanks, and airplanes. Congress granted wide emergency powers to the president. However, while the Democrats retained control of both houses throughout the war, their margins were relatively narrow. A coalition of conservatives in both parties frequently prevented the president from having his way and exercised close control over expenditures.

Roosevelt was an inspiring war leader but not a very good administrator. The squabbling and waste characteristic of the early New Deal period made relatively little difference—what mattered then was raising the nation's spirits and keeping people occupied; efficiency was less than essential, however desirable. But in wartime, the nation's fate, perhaps that of the entire free world, depended on delivering weapons and supplies to the battlefronts.

Roosevelt's greatest accomplishment was his inspiring of industrialists, workers, and farmers with a sense of national purpose. In this respect his function duplicated his earlier role in fighting the Depression, and he performed it with even greater success.

The tremendous economic expansion can be seen in the official production statistics. In 1939 the United States was still mired in the Great Depression. The gross national product amounted to about $91.3 billion. In 1945, after allowing for changes in the price level, it was $166.6 billion. Manufacturing output nearly doubled and agricultural output rose

22 percent. In 1939 the United States turned out fewer than 6,000 airplanes, in 1944 more than 96,000. Shipyards produced 237,000 tons of vessels in 1939, 10 million tons in 1943.

This growth was especially notable in the South and Southwest. This region got a preponderance of the new army camps built for the war as well as a large share of the new defense plants. Southern productive capacity increased by about 50 percent, and southern per capita output, while still low, crept closer to the national average.

Wartime experience proved that the Keynesian economists were correct in saying that government spending would spark economic growth. About 8 million people were unemployed in June 1940. After Pearl Harbor, unemployment virtually disappeared, and by 1945 the civilian workforce had increased by nearly 7 million. Military mobi-

A poster encourages women to work in munitions to support the war effort.

lization had begun well before December 1941, by which time 1.6 million men were already under arms. Economic mobilization proceeded much more slowly, mainly because the president refused to centralize authority. For months after Pearl Harbor various civilian agencies squabbled with the military over everything from the allocation of scarce raw materials to the technical specifications of weapons. Roosevelt refused to settle these conflicts.

The War Economy

Yet by early 1943 the nation's economic machinery had been converted to a wartime footing and was functioning effectively. Supreme Court Justice James F. Byrnes resigned from the Court to become a sort of "economic czar." His Office of War Mobilization had complete control over priorities and prices. Rents, food prices, and wages were strictly regulated, and items in short supply were rationed to consumers. While wages and prices had soared during 1942, after April 1943 they leveled off. Thereafter the cost of living scarcely changed until controls were lifted after the war.

Wages and prices remained in fair balance. Overtime work fattened paychecks, and a new stress in labor contracts on paid vacations, premium pay for night work, and various forms of employer-subsidized health insurance were added benefits. The war effort had almost no adverse effect on the standard of living of

View the Image
Ration Stamps WWII at
myhistorylab.com

the average citizen, a vivid demonstration of the productivity of the American economy. The manufacture of automobiles ceased and pleasure driving became next to impossible because of gasoline rationing, but most civilian activities went on much as they had before Pearl Harbor. While items such as meat, sugar, and shoes were rationed, they were doled out in amounts adequate for the needs of most persons.

The federal government spent twice as much money between 1941 and 1945 as in its entire previous history. This made heavy borrowing necessary. The national debt, which stood at less than $49 billion in 1941, increased by more than that amount each year between 1942 and 1945 and totaled nearly $260 billion when the war ended. However, more than 40 percent of the total was met by taxation, a far larger proportion than in any earlier war.

This policy helped to check inflation by siphoning off money that would otherwise have competed for scarce consumer goods. Heavy excise taxes on amusements and luxuries further discouraged spending, as did the government's war bond campaigns, which persuaded patriotic citizens to lend part of their income to Uncle Sam. High taxes on incomes (up to 94 percent) and on excess profits (95 percent) convinced people that no one was profiting inordinately from the war effort.

The income tax, which had never before touched the mass of white-collar and industrial workers, was extended downward until nearly everyone had to pay it. To collect efficiently the relatively small sums paid by most persons, Congress adopted the payroll-deduction system proposed by Beardsley Ruml, chairman of the Federal Reserve Bank of New York. Employers withheld the taxes owed by workers from their paychecks and turned the money over to the government.

The steeply graduated tax rates, combined with a general increase in the income of workers and farmers, effected a substantial shift in the distribution of wealth in the United States. The poor became richer, while the rich, if not actually poorer, collected a smaller proportion of the national income. The wealthiest 1 percent of the population had received 13.4 percent of the national income in 1935 and 11.5 percent in 1941. In 1944 this group received 6.7 percent.

War and Social Change

World War II altered the patterns of American life in many ways. Never was the population more fluid. The millions who put on uniforms found themselves transported first to training camps in every section of the country and then to battlefields scattered from Europe and Africa to the far reaches of the Pacific. Burgeoning new defense plants, influenced by a government policy of locating them in "uncongested areas," drew other millions to places like Hanford, Washington, and Oak Ridge, Tennessee, where great atomic energy installations were constructed, and to the aircraft factories of California and other states. As in earlier periods the trend was from east to west and from the rural south to northern cities.

During the war the marriage rate rose steeply, from 75 per thousand adult women in 1939 to 118 in 1946. Many young couples felt the need to put down roots before the husbands went off to risk death in distant lands. The population of the United States had increased by only 3 million during the Depression decade of the 1930s; during the next *five* years it rose by 6.5 million.

Minorities in Time of War: Blacks, Hispanics, and Indians

The war affected black Americans in many ways. Several factors helped improve their lives. One was their own growing tendency to demand fair treatment. Another was the reaction of Americans to Hitler's barbaric treatment of millions of Jews, an outgrowth of his doctrine of "Aryan" superiority. These barbarities compelled millions of white citizens to reexamine their views about race. If the nation expected African Americans to risk their lives for the common good, how could it continue to treat them as second-class citizens? Black leaders pointed out the inconsistency between fighting for democracy abroad and ignoring it at home.

Blacks in the armed forces were treated more fairly than they had been in World War I. They were enlisted for the first time in the air force and the marines, and they were given more responsible positions in the army and navy. Altogether about a million served, about half of them overseas. The extensive and honorable performance of these units could not be ignored by the white majority.

However, segregation in the armed services was maintained. The navy continued to confine black and Hispanic sailors to demeaning, noncombat tasks, and black soldiers were often provided with inferior recreational facilities and otherwise mistreated in and around army camps, especially those in the South. However, economic realities operated significantly to the advantage of black civilians. More of them had been unemployed in proportion to their numbers than any other group; now the labor shortage brought employment for all. More than 5 million blacks moved from rural areas to cities between 1940 and 1945 in search of work. At least a million of them found defense jobs in the North and on the West Coast, often developing valuable skills that had been difficult for blacks to acquire before the war because of the discriminatory policies of trade unions and many employers. The black population of Los Angeles, San Francisco, Denver, Buffalo, Milwaukee, and half a dozen other large industrial cities more than doubled in that brief period. The migrants were

"above and beyond the call of duty"

DORIE MILLER
*Received the Navy Cross
at Pearl Harbor, May 27, 1942*

A poster commemorates Doris "Dorie" Miller, a mess attendant aboard the USS *West Virginia* at Pearl Harbor. Before the ship sank, Miller manned an antiaircraft machine gun and shot down several Japanese planes. He won the Navy Cross for courage, the first awarded to an African American.

mostly forced to live in urban ghettoes, but their very concentration (and the fact that outside the South blacks could vote freely) made them important politically.

However, prejudice and mistreatment of blacks did not cease. In areas around defense plants white resentment of the black "invasion" mounted. By 1943, 50,000 new blacks had crowded into Detroit. A wave of strikes disrupted production at U.S. Rubber and several former automobile plants where white workers laid down their tools to protest the hiring of blacks. In June a race riot marked by looting and bloody fighting raged for three days. By the time federal troops restored order, twenty-five blacks and nine whites had been killed. Rioting also erupted in New York and many other cities.

Watch the Video

The desegregation of the military and blacks in combat at **myhistorylab.com**

In Los Angeles the attacks were upon Hispanic residents. Wartime employment needs resulted in a reversal of the Depression policy of forcing Mexicans out of the Southwest, and many thousands flocked north in search of work. Most had to accept menial jobs. But work was plentiful, and they, as well as resident Spanish-speaking Americans, experienced rising living standards.

Blacks became increasingly embittered. Roy Wilkins, head of the NAACP, put it this way in 1942: "No Negro leader with a constituency can face his members today and ask full support for the war in the light of the atmosphere the government has created." Many black newspaper editors were so critical of the administration that conservatives demanded they be indicted for sedition.

Read the Document

Randolph, *Why Should We March* at **myhistorylab.com**

Roosevelt would have none of that, but the militants annoyed him; he felt that they should hold their demands in abeyance until the war had been won. Apparently he failed to realize the depth of black anger, and in this he was no different from the majority of whites. A revolution was in the making, yet in 1942 a poll revealed that a solid majority of whites still believed that black Americans were satisfied with their place in society. The riots of 1943 undoubtedly disabused some of them of this illusion.

Concern about national unity did lead to a reaction against the New Deal policy of encouraging Indians to preserve their ancient cultures and develop self-governing communities. There was even talk of going back to the allotment system and trying to assimilate Indians into the larger society. In fact, the war encouraged assimilation in several ways. More than 24,000 Indians served in the armed forces, an experience that brought them into contact with new people, new places, and new ideas. Many thousands more left the reservations to work in defense industries in cities all over the country.

The Treatment of German and Italian Americans

Although World War II affected the American people far more drastically than had World War I, it produced much less intolerance and fewer examples of the repression of individual freedom of opinion. People seemed able to distinguish between Italian fascism and Italian Americans and between the government of Nazi Germany and Americans of German descent in a way that had escaped their parents. The fact that few Italian Americans admired Mussolini and that nearly all German Americans were vigorously anti-Nazi helps explain this. So does the fact that both groups were well-organized and prepared to use their considerable political power if necessary to protect themselves from abuse. Nevertheless, U.S. military authorities arrested some 14,000 Germans and Italians as security risks.

Americans went to war in 1941 without illusions and without enthusiasm, determined to win but expecting only to preserve what they had. They therefore found it easier to tolerate dissent, to view the dangers they faced realistically, and to concentrate on the real foreign enemy without venting their feelings on domestic scapegoats. The nation's 100,000 conscientious objectors met with little hostility.

Internment of Japanese Americans

The relatively tolerant treatment of most Americans of German and Italian descent makes the nation's policies toward American citizens of Japanese extraction all the more difficult to comprehend. Generals on the West Coast were understandably unnerved by the Japanese attack on Pearl Harbor and warned that people of Japanese descent might engage in sabotage or espionage for Japan. "The Japanese race is an enemy race," General John L. Dewitt claimed. The 112,000 Americans of Japanese ancestry, the majority of them native-born citizens, were "potential enemies." "The very fact that no sabotage has taken place to date," Dewitt observed, "is a disturbing and confirming indication that such action will be taken." Secretary of War Stimson proposed the relocation of the West Coast people of Japanese extraction, including American citizens, to **internment camps** in Wyoming, Arizona, and other interior states.

The Japanese were properly indignant but also baffled, in some cases hurt more than angry. "We didn't feel Japanese. We felt American," one woman, the mother of three small children, recalled many years later. Some Japanese Americans challenged military authorities. Gordon Hirabayashi, an American citizen and senior at the University of Washington, refused to report for transportation to an internment camp. After being convicted and sentenced to prison, he decided to appeal. Previous Supreme Courts had ruled that the government could deprive Americans of their freedoms during war only when the "military necessity" was compelling. By the time the Supreme Court ruled on his and similar cases, the Japanese military had been thrown back in the Pacific; no

A Japanese girl in California, tagged for relocation to an internment camp, clutches her doll.

Japanese Relocation from the West Coast, 1942–1945 Japanese and Japanese Americans who lived in the West Coast Military Area were ordered to report to various "assembly centers," from which they were then deported to inland internment or isolation camps.

invasion was even conceivable. Yet the justices worried that if they declared the internment policy to be unconstitutional, they would appear, "out of step" with the nation, as Justice Felix Frankfurter put it. In June 1943, the Court upheld the conviction of Hirabayashi. Finally, in *Ex parte Endo*, it forbade the internment of loyal Japanese American citizens. Unfortunately the latter decision was not handed down until December 1944.

Women's Contributions to the War Effort

With economic activity on the rise and millions of men going off to war, a sudden need for more women workers developed. The trends of the 1920s—more women workers and more of them married—soon accelerated. By 1944, 6.5 million additional women had entered the workforce, and at the peak of war production in 1945, more than 19 million women were employed, many of them in well-paying industrial jobs. Additional thousands were serving in the armed forces: 100,000 in the Women's Auxiliary Army Corps, others in navy, marine, and air corps auxiliaries.

At first there was considerable resistance to what was happening. About one husband in three objected in principle to his wife taking a job. Many employers in so-called heavy industry and in other fields traditionally dominated by men doubted that women could handle such tasks. Unions frequently made the same point, usually without much evidence.

These male attitudes lost force in the face of the escalating demand for labor. That employers usually did not have to pay women as much as men made them attractive, as did the fact that they were not subject to the draft. A breakthrough

View the Image

Rosie the Riveter at **myhistorylab.com**

occurred when the big Detroit automobile manufacturers agreed to employ women on their wartime production lines. Soon women were working not only as riveters and cab drivers but also as welders, as machine tool operators, and in dozens of other occupations formerly the exclusive domain of men.

Women took wartime jobs for many reasons other than the obvious economic ones. Patriotism, of course, was important, but so were the excitement of entering an entirely new world, the desire for independence, even loneliness. "It's thrilling work, and exciting, and something women have never done before," one woman reported. She was talking about driving a taxi.

Black women workers had a particularly difficult time: employers often hesitating to hire them because they were black, and black men looking down on them because they were women. But the need for willing hands was infinite. Sybil Lewis of Sapula, Oklahoma, went to Los Angeles and found a job as a waitress in a black restaurant. Then she responded to a notice of a training program at Lockheed Aircraft, took the course, and became a riveter making airplane gas tanks. When an unfriendly foreman gave her a less attractive assignment, she moved on to Douglas Aircraft. By 1943 she was working as a welder in a shipyard.

Few wartime jobs were easy, and for women there were special burdens, not the least of which was the prejudice of many of the men they worked with. For married women there was housework to do after a long day. One War Manpower Commission bureaucrat figured out that Detroit defense plants were losing 100,000 woman-hours a month because of employees taking a day off to do the family laundry. Although the government made some effort to provide day-care facilities, there were never nearly enough; this was one reason why relatively few women with small children entered the labor market during the war.

Newly married wives of soldiers and sailors (known generally as "war brides") often followed their husbands to training camps, where life was often as difficult as it was around defense plants. Whatever their own behavior, war brides quickly learned that society applied a double standard to infidelity, especially when it involved a man presumably risking his life in some far-off land. There was a general relaxation of sexual inhibitions, part of a decades-long trend but accelerated by the war. So many hasty marriages, followed by long periods of separation, also brought a rise in divorces, from about 170 per thousand marriages in 1941 to 310 per thousand in 1945.

Of course "ordinary" housewives also had to deal with shortages, ration books, and other inconveniences during the war. In addition most took on other duties and bore other burdens, such as tending "victory gardens" and preserving their harvests, using crowded public transportation when there was no gas for the family car, mending and patching old clothes when new ones were unavailable, participating in salvage drives, and doing volunteer work for hospitals, the Red Cross, or various civil defense and servicemen's centers.

Allied Strategy: Europe First

Only days after Pearl Harbor, Prime Minister Churchill and his military chiefs met in Washington with Roosevelt and his advisers. In every quarter of the globe, disaster threatened. The Japanese were gobbling up East Asia. Hitler's armies, checked outside Leningrad and Moscow, were preparing for a massive attack in the direction of Stalingrad, on the

⊙ See the **Map**

World War II in Europe
at myhistorylab.com

Volga River. German divisions under General Erwin Rommel were beginning a drive across North Africa toward the Suez Canal. U-boats were taking a heavy toll in the North Atlantic. British and American leaders believed that eventually they could muster enough force to smash their enemies, but whether or not the troops already in action could hold out until this force arrived was an open question.

The decision of the strategists was to concentrate first against the Germans. Japan's conquests were in remote and, from the point of view of the **Allies**, relatively unimportant regions. If the Soviet Union surrendered, Hitler's position in Europe might prove impregnable.

American leaders wanted to attack German positions in France, at least by 1943. The Soviets, with their backs to the wall and bearing the full weight of the German war machine, heartily agreed. Churchill, however, was more concerned with protecting Britain's overseas possessions than with easing the pressure on the Soviet Union. He advocated instead air bombardment of German industry combined with an attempt to drive the Germans out of North Africa, and his argument carried the day.

During the summer of 1942 Allied planes began to bomb German cities. In a crescendo through 1943 and 1944, British and American bombers pulverized the centers of Nazi might. While air attacks did not destroy the German army's capacity to fight, they hampered war production, tangled communications, and brought the war home to

The firebombing of Hamburg (painted here by Floyd Davis, who flew with the Anglo American mission in 1943) killed 50,000 and destroyed Hamburg.

the German people. Humanitarians deplored the heavy loss of life among the civilian population, but the response of the realists was that Hitler had begun indiscriminate bombing, and victory depended on smashing the German war machine.

In November 1942 an Allied army commanded by General Dwight D. Eisenhower struck at French North Africa. After the fall of France, the Nazis had set up a puppet regime in those parts of France not occupied by their troops, with head-quarters at Vichy in central France. This collaborationist Vichy government controlled French North Africa. But the North African commandant, Admiral Jean Darlan, agreed to switch sides when Eisenhower's forces landed. After a brief show of resistance, the French surrendered.

Eisenhower now pressed forward quickly against the Germans in North Africa. In February 1943 at Kasserine Pass in the desert south of Tunis, American tanks met Rommel's Afrika Korps. The battle ended in a standoff, but with British troops closing in from their Egyptian bases to the East, the Germans were soon trapped and crushed. In May, after Rommel had been recalled to Germany, his army surrendered.

In July 1943, while air attacks on Germany continued and the Russians slowly pushed the Germans back from the gates of Stalingrad, the Allies invaded Sicily from

The Liberation of Europe After November, 1942, Allied armies pushed the German-Italian armies back on three fronts: the Soviets, from the East; and American-British armies from North Africa and then, after the Normandy invasion, from France.

Africa. In September they advanced to the Italian mainland. Mussolini had already fallen from power and his successor, Marshal Pietro Badoglio, surrendered. However, the German troops in Italy threw up an almost impregnable defense across the rugged Italian peninsula. The Anglo American army inched forward, paying heavily for every advance. Monte Cassino, halfway between Naples and Rome, did not fall until May 1944, the capital itself not until June; months of hard fighting remained before the country was cleared of Germans. The Italian campaign was an Allied disappointment even though it weakened the enemy.

Germany Overwhelmed

By the time the Allies had taken Rome, the mighty army needed to invade France had been collected in England under Eisenhower's command. On **D-Day**, June 6, 1944, the assault forces stormed ashore at five points along the coast of Normandy, supported by a great armada and thousands of planes and paratroops. Against fierce but ill-coordinated German resistance, they established a beachhead: Within a few weeks a million troops were on French soil. (See Re-Viewing the Past, *Saving Private Ryan*, pp. 722–723.)

Thereafter victory was assured, though nearly a year of hard fighting lay ahead. In August the American Third Army under General George S. Patton erupted southward into Brittany and then veered east toward Paris. Another Allied army invaded France from the Mediterranean in mid-August and advanced rapidly north. Free French troops were given the honor of liberating Paris on August 25. Belgium was cleared by British and Canadian units a few days later. By mid-September the Allies were fighting on the edge of Germany itself.

The front now stretched from the Netherlands along the borders of Belgium, Luxembourg, and France all the way to Switzerland. If the Allies had mounted a massive assault at any one point, the struggle might have been brought to a quick conclusion. Although the two armies were roughly equal in size, the Allies had complete control of the air and twenty times as many tanks as the foe. The pressure of the advancing Russians on the eastern front made it difficult for the Germans to reinforce their troops in the west. But General Eisenhower believed a concentrated attack was too risky. He prepared instead for a general advance.

While he was regrouping, the Germans on December 16 launched a counterattack, planned by Hitler himself, against the Allied center in the Ardennes Forest. The Germans hoped to break through to the Belgian port of Antwerp, thereby splitting the Allied armies in two. The plan was foolhardy and therefore unexpected, and it almost succeeded. The Germans drove a salient ("the bulge") about fifty miles into Belgium. But once the element of surprise had been overcome, their chance of breaking through to the sea was lost. Eisenhower concentrated first on preventing them from broadening the break in his lines and then on blunting the point of their advance. By late January 1945 the old line had been reestablished.

The Battle of the Bulge cost the United States 77,000 casualties and delayed Eisenhower's offensive, but it exhausted the Germans' last reserves. The Allies then pressed forward to the Rhine, winning a bridgehead on the far bank of the river on March 7. Thereafter, one German city fell almost daily. With the Soviets racing westward against crumbling resistance, the end could not be long delayed. In April, American and Soviet

Table 27.1 Turning Points of the War in Europe

Summer 1942	British bombing of German cities brings war home to Germany
November 1942	U.S./British invasion of North Africa, defeat of Rommel
February 1943	Germans turned back at Stalingrad, beginning of German retreat from Soviet Union
July 1943	U.S./British invasion of Sicily
June 1944	D-Day: U.S./British invasion of northern France
January 1945	Battle of the Bulge: Last-ditch German offensive defeated
May 8, 1945	Germany surrenders

forces made contact at the Elbe River. A few days later, with Soviet shells reducing his capital to rubble, Hitler, by then probably insane, took his own life in his Berlin air raid shelter. On May 8 Germany surrendered.

As the Americans drove swiftly forward in the late stages of the war, they began to overrun Nazi concentration camps where millions of Jews and others had been murdered. The Americans were horrified by what they discovered, but they should not have been surprised. Word of this holocaust, in which 12 million people (half of them Jews) were slaughtered, had reached the United States much earlier. At first the news had been dismissed as propaganda, then discounted as grossly exaggerated. Hitler was known to hate Jews and to have persecuted them, but that he could order the murder of millions of innocent people, even children, seemed beyond belief. By 1943, however, the truth could not be denied.

> **Watch the Video**
> *Nazi Murder Mills* at **myhistorylab.com.**
> WARNING: This clip is very graphic.

Little could be done about those already in the camps, but there were thousands of refugees in occupied Europe who might have been spirited to safety. President Roosevelt declined to make the effort; he refused to bomb the Auschwitz death camp in Poland or the rail lines used to bring victims to its gas chambers on the grounds that the destruction of German soldiers and military equipment took precedence over any other objective. Thus, when American journalists entered the camps with the advancing troops, saw the heaps of still-unburied corpses, and talked with the emaciated survivors, their reports caused a storm of protest in America.

The Naval War in the Pacific

Defeating Germany first had not meant abandoning the Pacific region entirely to the Japanese. While armies were being trained and matériel accumulated for the European struggle, much of the available American strength was diverted to maintaining vital communications in East Asia and preventing further Japanese expansion.

> **See the Map**
> *World War II in the Pacific* at **myhistorylab.com**

Saving Private Ryan

Steven Spielberg's *Saving Private Ryan* (1998), starring Tom Hanks, has been widely praised as the most realistic combat movie ever made. This judgment is based chiefly on its re-creation of the June 6, 1944, Allied assault on Omaha Beach during the invasion of Normandy. The camera focuses on Hanks, rain dripping from his helmet, huddled in a crowded landing vessel. Explosions rumble in the distance. The ship plows through heavy seas toward a blackened brow of land. Around him, men vomit. Explosions become louder and sharper. Nearby ships strike mines and blow up; others are obliterated by shellfire. Hanks's landing craft lurches to avoid the mayhem. Like hail against a tin roof, gunfire riddles the landing craft. Some of the men are hit, and the others hunch lower, still vomiting. A deafening din envelops the ship as its bow opens. A curtain of bullets cuts down the men in front. Hanks and several others leap into the sea, but the ship has stopped far short of the beach. They sink. As bullets tear through the water, ripping into those still submerged, Hanks struggles to the surface. He swims, weaponless, toward the beach.

He has crossed the threshold of hell, and over the next fifteen minutes viewers descend with him the rest of the way.

Saving Private Ryan differs from other combat films not in the graphic horror of the bloodshed, but in its randomness. The audience expects Hanks to survive the opening scenes of the movie in which he stars, and he does. But all other bets are off: a valiant exploit, a kind gesture, a handsome face—none of these influences the grim lottery of battle. A medic frenziedly works on a severely wounded man, injecting morphine, compressing arteries, and binding wounds. Then more bullets splatter his patient beyond recognition. "Why can't you bastards give us a chance?" the medic screams. That is the point: When huge armies converge, hurling high explosives and steel at each other, one's chances of survival are unaffected by ethics or aesthetics.

But having made this point with heart-pounding emphasis, the movie subverts it. Hanks, unnerved and dispirited, initially hunkers down in the relative safety of the seawall. But then he does his job, rallying his men. They blast a hole through obstacles, crawl toward the concrete fortifications above, penetrate trench defenses, blow up bunkers, and seize the hill. Many perish in the effort; Hanks, an infantry captain, is among the survivors.

Then comes a new mission that occupies the remainder of the movie. George C. Marshall, U.S. Army Chief of Staff, has learned of a Mrs. Ryan who has been notified on a single day that three of her sons were killed in action. Her fourth son, James, a private in the 101st Airborne, has just parachuted into Normandy behind German lines. Marshall orders that Private Ryan be returned to safety. This mission is given to Hanks and his platoon. They march inland, encounter snipers, ambushes, and, in the final scenes, a large detachment of German armored vehicles. But they also find Ryan (played by Matt Damon).

Along the way, the movie asks many provocative questions, such as whether war improves those who fight. "I think this is all good for me, sir," one earnest soldier confides to Hanks. "Really," Hanks says with a faint smile, "how is that?" The soldier cites Ralph Waldo Emerson: "War educates the senses. Calls into action the will. Perfects the physical constitution." "Emerson had a way of finding the bright side," Hanks deadpans. Hanks's hand twitches uncontrollably, a physical manifestation of a disordered soul. War, demonstrably, has not made men better.

Except in one way: Hanks and his men have repeatedly demonstrated a willingness to give up their lives for others. Indeed, the movie's central dilemma concerns the moral arithmetic of sacrifice. Is it right to risk eight men to save one? To send a thousand men to near certain death in an initial assault at Omaha Beach to improve the chances of

Actual photograph of American troops approach code-named Omaha Beach at Normandy.

Tom Hanks, Matt Damon, and Edward Burns in *Saving Private Ryan*.

those that follow? To make one generation endure hell so that another may have freedom? The movie provides no ready answers. But in nearly the final scene it does issue a challenge. Hanks, mortally wounded, is lying amidst the corpses of his platoon, and he beckons to Ryan, who is unhurt. "Earn this," Hanks says, vaguely gesturing to the others.

Saving Private Ryan was part of a wave of nostalgic appreciation during the 1990s for the generation that had won World War II. A spate of books, movies, and TV documentaries were other expressions of this phenomenon. On accepting the Oscar for his film, Spielberg thanked his father, a World War II vet, "for showing me that there is honor in looking back and respecting the past."

But respect for the past entails getting it right, and the movie makes some significant errors and omissions. For one, it suggests that the men huddled at the base of the seawall blew up the concrete bunkers on their own. This was not possible. In fact, commanders of destroyers took their ships close to the beaches and fired countless heavy shells into the fortifications, allowing the infantry to move up the hills.

The movie also shows the German soldiers as uniformly expert and professional. But the German army had been decimated by losses in the Soviet Union. The army manning the Normandy defenses included many units composed mostly of old men, boys, or conscripted soldiers from Poland or the Soviet Union. Many surrendered as soon as they encountered American soldiers.

Of the movie's implausible elements, the premise that the U.S. Army high command

ordered a special mission to pluck a grieving mother's son from danger was based on fact. A real Mrs. Niland received telegrams on the same day informing her that three of her sons had been killed in action. Her fourth son, "Fritz," had parachuted into Normandy with the 101st Airborne. The army did in fact snatch him from the front line and return him to safety.

The movie provides a fair rendering of many other elements of the battle: the inaccuracy of aerial bombing, which missed most of the beach fortifications; the confusion caused when hundreds of landing craft failed to reach their destination; the destruction of scores of gliders, which crashed into high hedgerows while attempting to land behind German lines.

Yet through it all, some men, like the captain portrayed by Hanks, drew heroism from some unfathomed depths of the soul. One real soldier at Omaha Beach remembered "a captain and two lieutenants who demonstrated courage beyond belief as they struggled to bring order to the chaos around them."

Saving Private Ryan is not a fully accurate representation of the attack on Omaha Beach, but it depicts—realistically and memorably— how soldiers conferred meaning on the heedless calculus of modern warfare.

Questions for Discussion
- Do generals have the right to order some men to near certain death in order to save others? To save a nation?
- Do soldiers have the right to disobey such orders? Why or why not?

Midway, a tiny Pacific island, mattered only because of its airfield. The Japanese sent a naval task force to invade the island, but in June 1942 U.S. warplanes sank several of the Japanese aircraft carriers accompanying the invasion force. With air cover gone, Japan called off the invasion. Midway marked a turning point in the war in the Pacific.

The navy's aircraft carriers had escaped destruction at Pearl Harbor, a stroke of immense good fortune because the airplane had revolutionized naval warfare. Commanders discovered that carrier-based planes were far more effective against warships than the heaviest naval artillery because of their greater range and more concentrated firepower.

This was demonstrated in May 1942 in the Battle of the Coral Sea. Having captured an empire in a few months without the loss of any warship larger than a destroyer, the Japanese believed the war already won. This led them to overextend themselves.

The Coral Sea lies northeast of Australia and south of New Guinea and the Solomon Islands. Japanese mastery of these waters would cut Australia off from Hawaii and thus from American aid. Admiral Isoroku Yamamoto had dispatched a large fleet of troopships screened by many warships to attack Port Moresby, on the southern New Guinea coast. On May 7–8 planes from the American carriers *Lexington* and *Yorktown* struck the convoy's screen, sinking a small carrier and damaging a large one. Superficially, the battle seemed a victory for the Japanese, for their planes mortally wounded the *Lexington* and sank two other ships, but the troop transports had been forced to turn back—Port Moresby was saved. Although large numbers of cruisers and destroyers took part in the action, none came within sight or gun range of an enemy ship. All the destruction was wrought by carrier aircraft.

Encouraged by the Coral Sea "victory," Yamamoto decided to force the American fleet into a showdown battle by assaulting the Midway Islands, west of Hawaii. His armada never reached its destination. Between June 4 and 7 control of the central Pacific was decided entirely by airpower. American dive bombers sent four large Japanese carriers to the bottom. About 300 Japanese planes were destroyed. The United States lost only the *Yorktown* and a destroyer. Thereafter the initiative in the Pacific war shifted to the Americans, but victory came slowly and at painful cost.

American land forces were under the command of Douglas MacArthur, a brilliant but egocentric general whose judgment was sometimes distorted by his intense concern for his own reputation. MacArthur was in command of American troops in the Philippine Islands when the Japanese struck in December 1941. After his heroic but hopeless defense of Manila and the Bataan peninsula, President Roosevelt had him evacuated by PT boat to escape capture; those under MacArthur's command endured horrific conditions as prisoners of Japan.

Thereafter MacArthur was obsessed with the idea of personally leading an American army back to the Philippines. Although many strategists believed that the islands should be bypassed in the drive on the Japanese homeland, in the end MacArthur convinced the Joint Chiefs of Staff, who determined strategy. Two separate drives were undertaken, one from New Guinea toward the Philippines under MacArthur, the other through the central Pacific toward Tokyo under Admiral Chester W. Nimitz.

Island Hopping

Before commencing this two-pronged advance, the Americans had to eject the Japanese from the Solomon Islands in order to protect Australia from a flank attack. Beginning in August 1942, a series of land, sea, and air battles raged around Guadalcanal Island in this archipelago. Once again American airpower was decisive, although the bravery and skill of the ground forces that actually won the island must not be underemphasized. American pilots, better trained and with tougher planes than the Japanese, had a relatively easier task. They inflicted losses five to six times heavier on the enemy than they sustained themselves. Japanese airpower disintegrated during the long battle, and this in turn helped the fleet to take a heavy toll on the Japanese navy. By February 1943 Guadalcanal had been secured.

In the autumn of 1943 the American drives toward Japan and the Philippines got under way at last. In the central Pacific campaign the Guadalcanal action was repeated on a smaller but equally bloody scale from Tarawa in the Gilbert Islands to

Table 27.2 Turning Points of World War II in the Pacific

December 7, 1941	Japanese sneak-attack on Pearl Harbor; United States declares war
May 1942	Japanese win Battle of the Coral Sea, but invasion of Australia foiled
June 1942	United States wins Battle of Midway; Japanese advance toward Hawaii turned back
February 1943	United States takes Guadalcanal, along the southernmost periphery of Japanese power
February 1945	United States retakes Philippines
June 1945	United States takes Okinawa, near Japanese islands
August 1945	United States drops atomic bombs on Hiroshima and Nagasaki; Japan surrenders

Kwajelein and Eniwetok in the Marshalls. The Japanese soldiers on these islands fought for every foot of ground. They almost never surrendered. But Admiral Nimitz's forces were in every case victorious. By midsummer of 1944 this arm of the American advance had taken Saipan and Guam in the Marianas. Now land-based bombers were within range of Tokyo.

Meanwhile, MacArthur was leapfrogging along the New Guinea coast toward the Philippines. In October 1944 he landed on Leyte, south of Luzon. Two great naval clashes in Philippine waters, the Battle of the Philippine Sea (June 1944) and the Battle for Leyte Gulf (October 1944), completed the destruction of Japan's sea power and reduced its air force to a band of fanatical suicide pilots called *kamikazes*, who tried to crash bomb-laden planes into American warships and airstrips. The *kamikazes* caused much damage but could not turn the tide. In February 1945 MacArthur liberated Manila.

The end was now inevitable. B-29 Superfortress bombers from the Marianas rained high explosives and firebombs on Japan. The islands of Iwo Jima and Okinawa, only a few hundred miles from Tokyo, fell to the Americans in March and June 1945. But such was the tenacity of the Japanese soldiers that it seemed possible that it would take another year of fighting and perhaps a million more American casualties to subdue the home Japanese islands.

World War II Pacific Theatre After the Battle of Midway (June, 1942), the United States began to seize one Pacific island after another, with one task force pushing west from Pearl Harbor, and another moving north from Australia.

Building the Atom Bomb

At this point came the most controversial decision of the entire war, and it was made by a newcomer on the world scene. In November 1944 Roosevelt had been elected to a fourth term, easily defeating Thomas E. Dewey. Instead of renominating Henry A. Wallace for vice president, whom conservatives considered too radical, the Democratic convention had nominated Senator Harry S Truman of Missouri, a reliable party man well-liked by professional politicians. Then, in April 1945, President Roosevelt died of a cerebral hemorrhage. Thus it was Truman who had to decide what to do when, in July 1945, American scientists placed in his hands a new and awful weapon, the atomic bomb.

After Roosevelt had responded to Albert Einstein's warning in 1939, government-sponsored atomic research had proceeded rapidly, especially after the establishment of the so-called Manhattan Project in May 1943. The manufacture of the element plutonium at Hanford, Washington, and of uranium 235 at Oak Ridge, Tennessee, continued, along with the design and construction of a transportable atomic bomb at Los Alamos, New Mexico, under the direction of J. Robert Oppenheimer. Almost $2 billion was spent before a successful bomb was exploded at Alamogordo, in the New Mexican desert, on July 16, 1945. As that first mushroom cloud formed over the desert, Oppenheimer recalled the prophetic words of the *Bhagavad Gita*: "I am become death, the shatterer of worlds."

●●●─Read the Document

Einstein, *Letter to President Roosevelt* at **myhistorylab.com**

Should a bomb with the destructive force of 20,000 tons of TNT be employed against Japan? By striking a major city, its dreadful power could be demonstrated convincingly, yet doing so would bring death to tens of thousands of Japanese civilians. Many of the scientists who had made the bomb now argued against its use. Others suggested alerting the Japanese and then staging a demonstration explosion at sea, but that idea was discarded because of concern that the bomb might fail to explode.

Truman was torn between his awareness that the bomb was "the most terrible thing ever discovered" and his hope that using it "would bring the war to an end." The bomb might cause a revolution in Japan, might lead the emperor to intervene, might even persuade the military to give up. Considering the thousands of Americans who would surely die in any conventional invasion of Japan and, on a less humane level,

Hiroshima lies in ruins, destroyed by an atomic bomb.

influenced by a desire to end the Pacific war before the Soviet Union could intervene effectively and thus claim a role in the peacemaking, the president chose to go ahead. The moral soundness of Truman's decision has been debated ever since. On August 6 the Superfortress *Enola Gay* dropped an atomic bomb on Hiroshima, killing about 78,000 persons (including twenty American prisoners of war) and injuring nearly 100,000 more out of a population of 344,000. Over 96 percent of the buildings in the city were destroyed or damaged. Three days later, while the stunned Japanese still hesitated, a second atomic bomb blasted Nagasaki. On August 15 Japan surrendered.

Thus ended the greatest war in history. Its cost was beyond calculation. No accurate count could be made even of the dead; we know only that the total was in the neighborhood of 20 million. As in World War I, American casualties—291,000 battle deaths and 671,000 wounded—were smaller than those of the other major belligerents. About 7.5 million Soviets died in battle, 3.5 million Germans, 1.2 million Japanese, and 2.2 million Chinese; Britain and France, despite much smaller populations, suffered losses almost as large as did the United States. And far more than in World War I, American resources, human and matériel, had made victory possible.

No one could account the war a benefit to humanity, but in the late summer of 1945 the future looked bright. Fascism was dead. The successful wartime diplomatic dealings of Roosevelt, Churchill, and the Soviet dictator, Joseph Stalin, encouraged many to hope that the communists were ready to cooperate in rebuilding Europe. Out of the death and destruction had come technological developments that seemed to herald a better world as well as a peaceful one. Enormous advances in the design of airplanes and the development of radar (which some authorities think was more important than any weapons system in winning the war) were about to revolutionize travel and the transportation of goods. Improvements in surgery and other medical advances gave promise of saving millions of lives, and the development of penicillin and other antibiotics, which had greatly reduced the death rate among troops, would perhaps banish all infectious diseases.

Above all, there was the power of the atom. The force that seared Hiroshima and Nagasaki could be harnessed to serve peaceful needs, the scientists promised, with results that might free humanity forever from poverty and toil. The period of reconstruction would be prolonged, but with all the great powers adhering to the new United Nations charter, drafted at San Francisco in June 1945, international cooperation could be counted on to ease the burdens of the victims of war and help the poor and underdeveloped parts of the world toward economic and political independence. Such at least was the hope of millions in the victorious summer of 1945.

Wartime Diplomacy

During the course of World War II every instrument of mass persuasion in the country had been directed toward convincing the people that the Soviets were fighting America's battle as well as their own. Even before Pearl Harbor, former Ambassador Joseph E. Davies wrote in his best-selling *Mission to Moscow* (1941) that Joseph Stalin and other communist leaders were "devoted to the cause of peace for both ideological and practical reasons."

Such views of Joseph Stalin were naive, to say the least, but the United States and the Soviet Union agreed emphatically on the need to defeat Hitler. The Soviets repeatedly expressed a willingness to cooperate with the Allies in dealing with postwar problems. The Soviet Union was one of the twenty-six signers of the Declaration of the United Nations (January 1942), in which the Allies promised to eschew territorial aggrandizement after the war, to respect the right of all peoples to determine their own form of government, to work for freer trade and international economic cooperation, and to force the disarmament of the aggressor nations.[1]

In May 1943 the Soviet Union dissolved the Comintern, its official agency for the promulgation of world revolution. The following October, during a conference in Moscow with the Allies, Soviet Foreign Minister V. M. Molotov joined in setting up a European Advisory Commission to divide Germany into occupation zones after the war. That December, at a conference held in Tehran, Iran, Roosevelt, Churchill, and Stalin discussed plans for a new league of nations. When Roosevelt described the kind of world organization he envisaged, the Soviet dictator offered a number of constructive suggestions.

Between August and October 1944, Allied representatives met at Dumbarton Oaks, outside Washington. The chief Soviet delegate, Andrei A. Gromyko, opposed limiting the use of the veto by the great powers on the future **United Nations (UN)** Security Council, but he did not take a deliberately obstructionist position. At a conference held at Yalta in the Crimea in February 1945 Stalin joined Roosevelt and Churchill in the call for a meeting in April at San Francisco to draft a charter for the UN. "We argued freely and frankly across the table," Roosevelt reported later. "But at the end, on every point, unanimous agreement was reached. I may say we achieved a unity of thought and a way of getting along together."

The UN charter drafted at the 50-nation San Francisco Conference gave each UN member a seat in the General Assembly. The locus of authority in the new organization resided in the Security Council, "the castle of the great powers." This consisted of five permanent members (the United States, the Soviet Union, Great Britain, France, and China) and six others elected for two-year terms.

The Security Council was charged with responsibility for maintaining world peace, but any great power could block UN action whenever it wished to do so. The United States insisted on this veto power as strongly as the Soviet Union did. In effect the charter paid lip service to the Wilsonian ideal of a powerful international police force, but it incorporated the limitations that Henry Cabot Lodge had proposed in his 1919 reservation to Article X of the League Covenant, which relieved the United States from the obligation of enforcing collective security without the approval of Congress.

Allied Suspicion of Stalin

Long before the war in Europe ended, however, the Allies had clashed over important policy matters. Since later world tensions developed from decisions made at this time, an understanding of the disagreements is essential for evaluating several subsequent decades.

---

[1]These were the principles first laid down in the so-called Atlantic Charter, drafted by Roosevelt and Churchill at a meeting on the USS *Augusta* off Newfoundland in August 1941.

Much depends on one's view of the postwar Soviet system. If the Soviet government under Stalin was bent on world domination, events fall readily into one pattern of interpretation. If, having endured an unprovoked assault by the Nazis, it was seeking only to protect itself against the possibility of another invasion, these events are best explained differently. Because the United States has opened nearly all its diplomatic records, we know a great deal about how American foreign policy was formulated and about the mixed motives and mistaken judgments of American leaders. This helps explain why many scholars have been critical of American policy and the "cold warriors" who made and directed it. The Soviet Union, for many years, did not let even its own historians into its archives.

It is clear, however, that the Soviets resented the British-American delay in opening up a second front. They were fighting for survival against the full power of the German armies; any American invasion of northern France, even an unsuccessful one, would have relieved some of the pressure. Roosevelt and Churchill would not move until they were ready, and Stalin had to accept their decision. At the same time, Stalin never concealed his determination to protect his country from future attack by extending its frontier after the war. He warned the Allies repeatedly that he would not tolerate any unfriendly government along the western boundary of the Soviet Union.

Most Allied leaders, including Roosevelt, admitted privately during the war that the Soviet Union would annex territory and possess preponderant power in Eastern Europe after the defeat of Germany, but they never said this publicly. They believed that the Soviets would allow free governments to be created in countries like Poland and Bulgaria.

The Polish question was a terribly difficult one. The war, after all, had been triggered by the German attack on Poland; the British in particular felt a moral obligation to restore that nation to its prewar independence. During the war a Polish government in exile was set up in London, and its leaders were determined—especially after the discovery in 1943 of the murder of some 5,000 Polish officers several years earlier at Katyn, in Russia, presumably by the Soviet secret police—to make no concessions to Soviet territorial demands. Public opinion in Poland (and indeed in all the states along Russia's western frontier) was not so much anti-Soviet as anti-Russian. Yet the Soviet Union's legitimate interests could not be ignored.

Yalta and Potsdam

Watch the Video

The Big Three Conference at Yalta at **myhistorylab.com**

At the **Yalta Conference**, Roosevelt and Churchill agreed to Soviet annexation of large sections of eastern Poland. In return they demanded that free elections be held in Poland itself. Stalin agreed, almost certainly without intending to keep his promise. The elections were never held; Poland was run by a pro-Soviet puppet regime.

Stalin apparently could not understand why the Allies were so concerned about the fate of a small country remote from their strategic spheres. That they professed to be concerned seemed to him an indication that they had some secret, devious purpose. Roosevelt, however, was worried about the political effects that Soviet control of Poland might have in the United States. Polish Americans would be furious if the United States allowed the Soviets to control their homeland.

But had Roosevelt described the difficulties to the Polish Americans and the rest of the American people more frankly, their

Churchill, Roosevelt, and Stalin meet at the Yalta, U.S.S.R., conference in February 1945. By April 1945, Roosevelt was dead.

reaction might have been less angry. In any case, when he realized that Stalin was going to act as he pleased, Roosevelt was furious. In July 1945, following the surrender of Germany, the new president, Harry Truman, met with Stalin and Churchill at Potsdam, outside Berlin.[2] At the **Potsdam Conference** they agreed to try the Nazi leaders as war criminals, made plans for exacting reparations from Germany, and confirmed the division of the country into four zones to be occupied separately by American, Soviet, British, and French troops. Berlin, deep in the Soviet zone, had itself been split into four sectors. Stalin rejected all arguments that he loosen his hold on Eastern Europe, and Truman made no concessions. But he was impressed by Stalin.

On both sides suspicions were mounting, positions hardening. Yet all the advantages seemed to be with the United States. Was this not, as Henry Luce, the publisher of *Time* had declared, "the American century," an era when American power and American ideals would shape the course of events the world over? Besides its army, navy, and air force and its immense industrial potential, alone among the nations the United States possessed the atomic bomb. When Stalin's actions made it clear that he intended to control Eastern Europe and to exert influence elsewhere in the world, most Americans expressed resentment tempered by amazement. It took time for them to realize that the war had caused a fundamental change in international politics. The United States might be the strongest country in the world, but the western European nations, victor and vanquished alike, were reduced to their own and America's surprise to the status of second-class powers. The Soviet Union, on the other hand, had gained more influence than it had held under the czars and regained the territory it had lost as a result of World War I and the communist revolution.

---

[2]Clement R. Attlee replaced Churchill during the conference after his Labour party won the British elections.

Milestones

1941	Roosevelt prohibits discrimination in defense plants (Fair Employment Practices Committee)	1943	Roosevelt, Churchill, Stalin meet at Tehran, Iran
	Japan attacks Pearl Harbor	1944	Allies invade Normandy, France (D-Day)
	Roosevelt and Churchill draft Atlantic Charter		Battle of the Bulge exhausts German reserves
1942	Executive Order 9066 sends Japanese Americans to relocation camps	1945	Big Three meet at Yalta Conference
	Japanese take Philippines		Fifty nations draft UN Charter at San Francisco
	Carrier-based planes dominate Battle of Coral Sea		Roosevelt dies; Truman becomes president
	U.S. airpower takes control of central Pacific at Battle of Midway		Germany surrenders (V-E Day)
	U.S. troops invade North Africa		United States tests atom bomb at Alamogordo, New Mexico
1943	Oppenheimer directs Manhattan Project to make atom bomb		Truman, Churchill, Stalin meet at Potsdam
	Race riots rage in Detroit and Los Angeles		United States drops atom bombs on Hiroshima and Nagasaki, Japan
	Allies invade Italy		Japan surrenders (V-J Day)

✓●—[Study and **Review** at www.myhistorylab.com

Review Questions

1. What did the U.S. government do to mobilize for war? How did the war affect women and minority groups?
2. Why did FDR order that American citizens of Japanese ancestry be placed in internment camps? What was the Supreme Court's response to the constitutionality of this decision?
3. Why, since Japan attacked first, did FDR decide to commit most American resources to defeating the Germans in Europe? What were the key phases of the war in Europe? Of the war in the Pacific?
4. What role did science and technology play in the war?
5. Should Truman have used atomic bombs against Japan? Why had American relations with the Soviet Union deteriorated by 1945?

Key Terms

Collision Courses, Abroad and at Home: 1946–1960

28

((•—⎡Hear the Audio Chapter 28 at myhistorylab.com

Do you ever drive too fast?

IN 2009 OVER 10,000 PEOPLE BETWEEN THE AGES OF SIXTEEN AND twenty-four were killed in motor vehicle accidents—the leading cause of death among young people. Each month nearly as many Americans died in car crashes as perished at the World Trade Center on September 11, 2001. American traffic fatalities totaled 34,000.

But it could have been worse—and once was. During the decade of the 1970s, a half million Americans died in traffic accidents—over 50,000 each year. Since Henry Ford first rolled out the Model-T, over three and a half million Americans have died on the nation's roads and highways. Despite the carnage, automobiles have become so much a part of American life that few can imagine living without them.

The ascendancy of the automobile over mass transit was well-established during the 1930s. But World War II put more Americans in motion than ever before. Afterwards, car ownership soared. Designers produced faster and heavier cars for "a wartime generation" that was far "bigger, taller and more active" than its predecessors. Americans hurtled along the new superhighways that the federal government built in part for military purposes.

The American nation, too, was rushing into a new era of Cold War confrontation with the Soviet Union. In both countries new weapons loomed larger, each more menacing than the last. By 1960, hundreds of millions of people could be wiped out in an instant. The Cold War between the superpowers turned hot in Korea, the Middle East, and Latin America. Real foreign spies exacerbated fears of domestic subversion.

Postwar complacency soon gave way to racial confrontation at home. African Americans who had helped defeat Nazi racism accelerated demands for fair treatment. First they challenged Jim Crow segregation in the courts. When these initiatives encountered segregationist roadblocks, they turned to nonviolent protests that they knew would likely trigger violent responses.

From 1946 through 1960, Americans lived dangerously in a postwar era of menacing uncertainty.

The Postwar Economy

Economists had feared that the flood of millions of veterans into the job market would cause serious unemployment. But the widespread craving for cars—bigger, faster, and "loaded" with features such as radios and air-conditioners—fueled the postwar economic boom. During the decade of the 1920s American factories had produced 31 million cars. In the 1950s, 58 million rolled off the assembly lines; during the 1960s, 77 million were made. The proliferation of cars contributed to the expansion of related industries, especially oil. Gasoline consumption first touched 15 billion gallons in 1931; it soared to 35 billion gallons in 1950 and to 92 billion in 1970.

Although the car industry was the leading postwar economic sector, war-weary Americans also bought new houses, washing machines, and countless other products. Unable to buy such goods during the war, they used their war-enforced savings to go on a shopping spree that kept factories operating at capacity.

In addition, the government made an unprecedented educational opportunity available to veterans. Instead of a general bonus, which would have stimulated consumption and inflation, in 1944 Congress passed the *GI Bill of Rights*, which made subsidies available to veterans so they could continue their educations, learn new trades, or start new businesses. After the war nearly 8 million veterans took advantage of the education and training grants.

Economic prosperity in the decades after World War II allowed the federal government to increase its military and economic commitments abroad without raising taxes.

Truman Becomes President

When Harry S Truman received the news of Roosevelt's death in 1945, he claimed that he felt as though "the moon, the stars, and all the planets" had suddenly fallen upon him. Although he could not have been quite as surprised as he indicated (Roosevelt was known to have been in extremely poor health), he was acutely conscious of his own limitations.

Truman was born in Missouri in 1884. He served in a World War I artillery unit, and later became a minor cog in the political machine of Democratic boss Tom Pendergast. In 1934 Truman was elected to the U.S. Senate, where he proved to be a loyal but obscure New Dealer. He first attracted national attention during World War II when his "watchdog" committee on defense spending, working with devotion and efficiency, saved the government immense sums. This led to his nomination and election as vice president.

Levittown, New York, in 1949 epitomizes the postwar housing boom.

As president, Truman sought to carry on in the Roosevelt tradition. Curiously, he was at the same time humble and cocky, even brash—both idealistic and cold-bloodedly political. He adopted liberal objectives only to pursue them sometimes by rash, even repressive means. On balance, however, he was a strong and, in many ways, successful president.

But he lost a major battle early on. In June 1947, the new Congress passed the **Taft-Hartley Act**. It outlawed the closed shop (a provision written into many labor contracts requiring new workers to join the union before they could be employed). Most important, it authorized the president to seek court injunctions to prevent strikes that, in his opinion, endangered the national interest.

Truman vetoed the bill, but Congress overrode it. The Taft-Hartley Act made the task of unionizing industries more difficult, but it did not seriously hamper existing unions.

The Containment Policy

Although he was vice president during much of World War II, Truman had been excluded from all foreign policy discussions. He was not granted full security clearance and thus knew little about the Manhattan Project. While FDR had concluded at Yalta that he could charm or otherwise personally cope with the Soviet dictator, Truman resolved to deal with Stalin firmly.

Repeatedly Stalin made it clear that he had no intention of even consulting with Western leaders about his domination of Eastern Europe, and he seemed intent on extending his power deep into war-devastated central Europe. By January 1946 Truman had decided to stop "babying" the Russians.

Truman's problem was that Stalin had far more military divisions than anyone else. Truman had swiftly responded to the postwar clamor to "bring the boys home." In the two years following the surrender of Japan, the armed forces of the United States had dwindled from 6 million to 1.5 million. Stalin, who kept domestic foes out of office by shooting them, ignored domestic pressure to demobilize the Red Army, estimated by U.S. intelligence at twice the size of the American army.

Stalin and the mighty Red Army evoked the image of Hitler's troops pouring across the north European plains. Like Hitler, Stalin was a cruel dictator who championed an ideology of world conquest. George Kennan, a scholarly foreign officer who also had served in Moscow, thought that ideology was more symptom than cause. Marxism, he wrote, provided the intellectual "fig-leaf of morality and respectability" for naked Soviet aggression. In an influential article, "The Sources of Soviet Conduct," published anonymously in the July 1947 issue of *Foreign Affairs*, Kennan argued that the instability and illegitimacy of the Soviet regime generated explosive internal pressures. These forces, vented outward, would cause the Soviet Union to

A propaganda poster enshrining Stalin proclaims that he has led his people "Forward to Communism!"

expand "constantly, wherever it is permitted to move" until it filled "every nook and cranny available to it in the basin of world power." A policy of "long-term, patient but firm and vigilant containment" was the best means of dealing with the Soviet Union.

The Atom Bomb: A "Winning" Weapon?

Although Truman authorized use of the atom bomb to force the surrender of Japan, he had hoped that a demonstration of the weapon's power also would inhibit Stalin and serve as a counterweight to the Red Army. Stalin, however, refused to be intimidated. He knew that the American atomic arsenal—slightly more than a dozen bombs in 1947—was insufficient to destroy the Soviet Union's military machine.

The atomic bomb was a doubtful deterrent for another reason. Sobering accounts of the devastation of Hiroshima and Nagasaki and the suffering of the victims of radiation poisoning left many Americans uneasy. Even Truman doubted whether the American people would again "permit" their president to use atomic weapons for aggressive purposes.

In November 1945 the United States suggested that the UN supervise all nuclear energy production, and the General Assembly created an Atomic Energy Commission to study the question. In June 1946 Commissioner Bernard Baruch offered a plan for the eventual outlawing of atomic weapons. Under this proposal UN inspectors operating without restriction anywhere in the world would ensure that no country made bombs clandestinely. When, at an unspecified date, the system was established successfully, the United States would destroy its stockpile of bombs.

Most Americans thought the Baruch plan magnanimous, and some considered it positively foolhardy, but the Soviets rejected it. They would neither permit UN inspectors in the Soviet Union nor surrender the Soviet Union's veto power over Security Council actions dealing with atomic energy. They demanded that the United States destroy its bombs at once. American leaders did not comply; they believed that the atom bomb would be, in Baruch's words, their "winning weapon" for years to come.

A Turning Point in Greece

The strategy of containment began to take shape early in 1947 as a result of a crisis in Greece. Greek communists, waging a guerrilla war against the monarchy, were receiving aid from communist Yugoslavia and Bulgaria. Great Britain had been assisting the monarchists but could no longer afford this drain on its resources. In February 1947 the British informed President Truman that they would cut off aid to Greece.

The British predicament forced American policymakers to confront the fact that their European allies had not been able to rebuild their war-weakened economies. That the Soviet Union was actually discouraging the Greek rebels out of fear of American intervention in the area the policymakers ignored.

Truman asked Congress to approve what became known as the **Truman Doctrine**. If Greece or Turkey fell to the communists, he said, all of the Middle East might be lost. To prevent this "unspeakable tragedy," he asked for $400 million in military and economic aid to Greece and Turkey. "It must be the policy of the United States to support free peoples who are resisting attempted subjugation by armed minorities or by outside pressures," he said.

●●─[Read the Document
Truman Doctrine, 1947
at myhistorylab.com

By exaggerating the consequences of inaction and by justifying his request on ideological grounds, Truman obtained his objective. The result was the establishment of a right-wing, military-dominated government in Greece. In addition, by not limiting his request to the specific problem posed by the situation in Greece, Truman caused considerable concern in many countries.

The threat to Western Europe certainly loomed large in 1947. The entire continent seemed in danger of falling into communist hands without the Soviet Union raising a finger.

The Marshall Plan and the Lesson of History

In a 1946 speech entitled "The Lesson of History," George C. Marshall, army chief of staff during World War II, reminded Americans that their isolationism had contributed to Hitler's unchecked early aggression. This time, Marshall noted, the people of the United States must be prepared to act against foreign aggressors. In 1947 Marshall was named secretary of state. He outlined an extraordinary plan by which the United States would finance the reconstruction of the European economy. "Hunger, poverty, desperation, and chaos" were the real enemies of freedom and democracy, Marshall said. The need was to restore "the confidence of the European people in the economic future of their own countries." Even the Soviet Union and Soviet-bloc nations would be eligible for American aid.

The European powers eagerly seized upon what became known as the **Marshall Plan**, a massive infusion of American aid to rebuild Europe after World War II. European leaders set up a sixteen-nation Committee for European Economic Cooperation, which soon submitted plans calling for up to $22.4 billion in American assistance.

The Soviet Union and its European satellites were tempted by the offer and sent representatives to the initial planning meetings. But Stalin grew anxious that his satellite states would be drawn into the orbit of the United States. He recalled his delegates and demanded that Soviet bloc nations do likewise. Those who hesitated were ordered to report to the Kremlin. "I went to Moscow as the Foreign Minister of an independent sovereign state," Jan Masaryk of Czechoslovakia commented bitterly. "I returned as a lackey of the Soviet government."

In February 1948 a communist coup took over the Czechoslovak government; Masaryk fell (or more likely was pushed) out a window to his death. These strong-arm tactics brought to mind the Nazi takeover of Czechoslovakia a decade earlier and helped persuade Congress to appropriate over $13 billion for the Marshall aid program. Results exceeded all expectations. By 1951 Western Europe was booming.

But Europe was now divided in two. In the West, where American-influenced governments were elected, private property was respected if often taxed heavily, and corporations gained influence and power. In the East, where the Soviet Union imposed its will and political system on client states, deep-seated resentment festered among subject peoples.

In March 1948 Great Britain, France, Belgium, the Netherlands, and Luxembourg signed an alliance aimed at social, cultural, and economic collaboration. The Western nations abandoned their understandable but counterproductive policy of crushing Germany economically. They announced plans for creating a single West German Republic with a large degree of autonomy.

In June 1948 the Soviet Union retaliated by closing off surface access to Berlin from the west. For a time it seemed that the Allies must either fight their way into the city or abandon it to the communists. Unwilling to adopt either alternative, Truman decided to fly

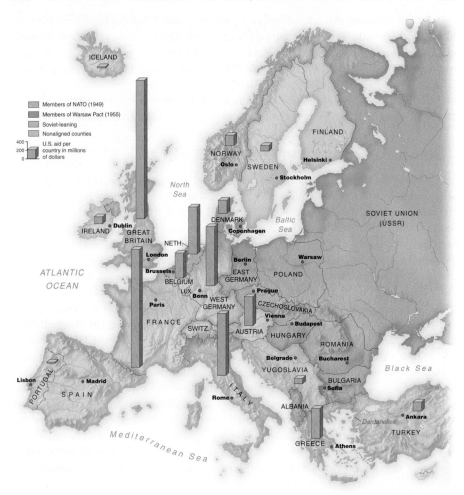

Recipients of Marshall Plan Aid, 1948–1952 Marshall Plan aid was originally offered to the Soviet Union and communist bloc states. Stalin, however, refused to accept American aid and ordered Soviet satellites to refuse, too. All did, except Yugoslavia, whose disobedience infuriated Stalin.

supplies to the capital from Frankfurt, Hannover, and Hamburg. American C-47 and C-54 transports delivered enough food, fuel, and other goods necessary to maintain more than 2 million West Berliners. The **Berlin airlift** put the Soviets in an uncomfortable position; if they were determined to keep supplies from West Berlin, they would have to start the fighting. They were not prepared to do so. In May 1949 they lifted the blockade.

American generals intensified preparation of contingency plans in the event of a Soviet attack.

The Election of 1948

In the spring of 1948 President Truman's fortunes were at low ebb. Public opinion polls suggested that a majority of the people considered him incompetent or worse. The Republicans seemed so sure to win the 1948 presidential election that many prominent

Democrats began to talk of denying Truman the nomination. Two of FDR's sons came out for General Eisenhower as the Democratic candidate. Governor Dewey, who again won the Republican nomination, ran confidently (even complacently), certain that he would carry the country.

Truman's position seemed hopeless because he had alienated both southern conservatives and northern liberals. The Southerners were particularly distressed because in 1946 the president had established a Committee on Civil Rights,

In 1948 the strongly Republican *Chicago Daily Tribune* printed its post-election headlines before all the returns were in. For Truman, it was the perfect climax to his hard-won victory.

which had recommended antilynching and antipoll tax legislation and the creation of a permanent Fair Employment Practices Commission. When the Democratic convention adopted a civil rights plank, the southern delegates walked out. Southern conservatives then founded the States' Rights ("Dixiecrat") party and nominated J. Strom Thurmond of South Carolina for president.

As for the liberals, in 1947 a group that believed Truman's containment policy a threat to world peace organized a new Progressive party and nominated former Vice President Henry A. Wallace. With two minor candidates sure to cut into the Democratic vote, the president's chances seemed minuscule.

Truman launched an aggressive whistle-stop campaign. He excoriated the "do-nothing" Republican Congress, which had rejected his program and passed the Taft-Hartley Act, and he warned labor, farmers, and consumers that if Dewey won, Republican "gluttons of privilege" would do away with all the gains of the New Deal years.

Millions were moved by Truman's arguments and by his courageous fight against great odds. The success of the Berlin airlift during the presidential campaign helped him considerably, as did disaffection among normally Republican midwestern farmers. The Progressive party fell increasingly into the hands of communist sympathizers, driving away many liberals who might otherwise have supported Wallace.

The president reinvigorated the New Deal coalition and won an amazing upset victory on election day. He collected 24.1 million votes to Dewey's 21.9 million, the two minor candidates being held to about 2.3 million. In the Electoral College his margin was a thumping 303 to 189.

Truman's victory encouraged him to press forward with what he called his **Fair Deal** program. He urged Congress to raise the minimum wage, fund an ambitious public housing program, develop a national health insurance system, and repeal the Taft-Hartley Act. However, relatively little of Truman's Fair Deal was enacted into law. Congress approved a federal housing program and measures increasing the minimum wage and Social Security benefits, but these were merely extensions of New Deal legislation.

Containing Communism Abroad

During Truman's second term the confrontation between the United States and the Soviet Union dominated the headlines. To strengthen ties with the European democracies, in April 1949 the North Atlantic Treaty was signed in Washington. The United States, Great Britain, France, Italy, Belgium, the Netherlands, Luxembourg, Denmark, Norway, Portugal, Iceland, and Canada[1] agreed "that an armed attack against one or more of them in Europe or North America shall be considered an attack against them all" and that in the event of such an attack each would take "individually and in concert with the other Parties, such action as it deems necessary, including the use of armed force." The pact established the **North Atlantic Treaty Organization (NATO)**.

In September 1949 the Soviet Union detonated an atomic bomb. When the explosion was confirmed, Truman called for rapid expansion of the American nuclear arsenal. He also asked his advisers to determine whether the United States should develop a new weapon thousands of times more destructive than atomic bombs. The "super" or hydrogen bomb would replicate the fusion process on the surface of the sun. The Atomic Energy Commission argued that there was no military use for hydrogen bombs, which would destroy hundreds of square miles as well as precipitate a dangerous arms race with the Soviet Union. The Joint Chiefs of Staff disagreed. Even if the hydrogen bomb could not be used in battle, they argued, its mere existence would intimidate enemies; and, the military men added, the Soviets would themselves build a hydrogen bomb whether or not the United States did so. (Unbeknownst to American leaders, Stalin had already ordered development of the hydrogen bomb.) On January 31, 1950, Truman publicly announced that "though none wants to use it" he had no choice but to proceed with a hydrogen bomb.

In Asia the effort to contain communism in China had failed utterly. After World War II, Nationalists under Chiang Kai-shek (sometimes spelled Jiang Jieshi) dominated the south; communists under Mao Zedong controlled much of the north. Truman tried to bring Chiang's Nationalists and Mao's communists together. He sent General Marshall to China to seek a settlement, but neither Chiang nor Mao would make significant concessions. In January 1947 Truman recalled Marshall and named him secretary of state. Soon thereafter civil war, suspended during the Japanese occupation, erupted in China.

By the end of 1949 communist armies had administered a crushing defeat to the nationalists. The remnants of Chiang Kai-shek's forces fled to the island of Formosa, now called Taiwan. Mao ruled China. The "loss" of China to communism strengthened right-wing elements in the Republican party. They charged that Truman had not backed the Nationalists strongly enough and that he had stupidly underestimated Mao's dedication to the cause of world revolution.

Containment had relied on American money, materials, and know-how, but not on American soldiers. In early 1950, Truman proposed to pare the budget by further reducing the nation's armed forces. Truman also called for a thorough review of the concept of containment. Dean Acheson, who recently had succeeded George Marshall as secretary of state, supervised the study. In March, it was submitted to the National Security Council, assigned a numerical designation (NSC-68), classified top secret, and sent to the nation's military and diplomatic leaders for review.

---

[1] In 1952, Greece and Turkey joined the alliance, and in 1954 so did West Germany.

NSC-68 called for an enormous military expansion. The Soviet Union, it declared, was engaged in a worldwide assault on freedom. Instead of relying on other nations, the United States itself must develop sufficient military forces to stop communism from spreading *anywhere in the world*. Military spending therefore had to be increased from $14 billion to nearly $50 billion. If the Soviet Union failed to keep up with the American expenditures, it would no longer pose a military threat, and if it attempted to match the high levels of American military spending, its less efficient economic system would collapse from the strain.

The document was submitted to Truman on April 7, 1950. He had planned significant cuts to the defense budget; the prospect of increasing it by 350 percent appalled him. Within a few months, however, events in Korea changed his mind.

Hot War in Korea

After World War II the province of Korea was taken from Japan and divided at 38° north latitude into the Democratic People's Republic in the north, backed by the Soviet Union, and the Republic of Korea in the south, backed by the United States and the UN. Both powers withdrew their troops from the peninsula. The Soviets left behind a well-armed local force, but the Republic of Korea's army was small and ill-trained.

⊙ See the **Map**

The Korean War, 1950–1953 at **myhistorylab.com**

America's first line of defense against communism in East Asia was to be its island bases in Japan and the Philippines. In a speech in January 1950 Acheson deliberately excluded Korea from what he described as the "defensive perimeter" of the United States in Asia. It was up to the South Koreans, backed by the UN, to protect themselves, Acheson said. This encouraged the North Koreans to attack. In June 1950, when their armored divisions, led by 150 Soviet-made tanks, rumbled across the thirty-eighth parallel, the South Koreans failed to stop them.

Truman was at his family home in Independence, Missouri, when Acheson telephoned with the news of the North Korean attack. On the flight to Washington, Truman recalled how the communists in Korea were acting "just as Hitler, Mussolini, and the Japanese had acted ten, fifteen, and twenty years earlier." "If this were allowed to go unchallenged," he concluded, "it would mean a third world war, just as similar incidents had brought on the Second World War." With the backing of the UN Security Council (but without asking Congress to declare war), he sent American planes into battle.[2] Ground troops soon followed. Truman also ordered the adoption of NSC-68 "as soon as feasible."

Nominally the Korean War was a struggle between the invaders and the United Nations. General MacArthur, placed in command, flew the blue UN flag over his headquarters, and sixteen nations supplied troops for his army. However, more than 90 percent of the forces were American. At first the North Koreans pushed them back rapidly, but in September a front was stabilized around the port of Pusan, at the southern tip of Korea. Then MacArthur executed a brilliant amphibious invasion, landing at the west coast city of Inchon, fifty miles south of the thirty-eighth parallel. Their lines of supply destroyed, the North Koreans retreated in disorder. By October the battlefront had moved north of the 1945 boundary.

---

[2]The Soviet Union, which could have vetoed this action, was at the moment boycotting the Security Council because the UN had refused to give the Mao Zedong regime China's seat on that body.

General MacArthur now proposed the conquest of North Korea, even if it meant bombing "privileged sanctuaries" on the Chinese side of the Korean border. A few of Truman's civilian advisers, the most important being George Kennan, opposed advancing into North Korea, fearing intervention not only by the Red Chinese but also by the Soviets.

Truman authorized MacArthur to advance as far as the Yalu River, the boundary between North Korea and China. It was an unfortunate decision. As the advance progressed, ominous reports came from north of the Yalu. Mao's Foreign Minister warned that the Chinese would not tolerate seeing their neighbors being "savagely invaded by imperialists." Alarmed, Truman flew to Wake Island, in the Pacific, to confer with MacArthur. The general, who had a low opinion of Asian soldiers, assured him that the

The Chinese counteroffensive of November 1950 caught the Americans by surprise and cut off many units. Here, a U.S. Marine rests during the retreat that winter.

Chinese would not dare to intervene. If they did, he added, his army would crush them easily; the war would be over by Christmas.

Seldom has a general miscalculated so badly. Ignoring intelligence reports and dividing his advancing units, he drove toward the Yalu recklessly. Suddenly, on November 26, thirty-three Chinese divisions, hidden along the interior mountains of Korea, smashed through the center of MacArthur's lines. Overnight a triumphant advance became a bloody, disorganized retreat. MacArthur now spoke of the "bottomless well of Chinese manpower" and justified his earlier confidence by claiming that he was fighting "an entirely new war."

The UN army rallied south of the thirty-eighth parallel, and MacArthur then urged that he be permitted to bomb Chinese installations north of the Yalu. He also suggested a naval blockade of the coast of China and the use of Chinese Nationalist troops. Truman rejected these proposals on the ground that they would lead to a third world war. MacArthur, who tended to ignore the larger political aspects of the conflict, attempted to rouse Congress and the public against the president by openly criticizing administration policy. Truman ordered him to be silent. When the general persisted in his criticisms, Truman fired him.

As the months passed and the casualties mounted, many citizens became disillusioned and angry. Military men backed the president almost unanimously. General Omar N. Bradley, chairman of the Joint Chiefs of Staff, said that a showdown with communist China "would involve us in the wrong war, at the wrong place, at the wrong time and with the wrong enemy." In June 1951 the communists agreed to discuss an armistice in Korea, although the negotiations dragged on interminably. The war was unresolved when Truman left office: by the time it was over, it had produced 157,000 American casualties, including 54,200 dead.

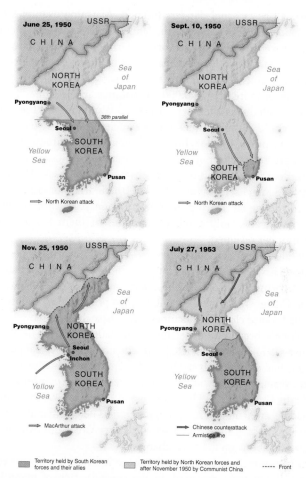

Korean War, 1950–1953 In June, North Korea nearly overran South Korea (top maps). But in September MacArthur counterattacked at Inchon and advanced far into North Korea (bottom left). The intervention of the Chinese in November led to a stalemate (bottom right).

If the Korean War persuaded Truman to adopt NSC-68, it also exposed the failings of the policy. By conceiving of communism as a monolithic force it tended to make it so, driving Red China and the Soviet Union into each other's arms. By committing American military forces to potential trouble spots throughout the world, it increased the likelihood they would prevail in none.

The Communist Issue at Home

The Korean War highlighted the paradox that, at the pinnacle of its power, the influence of the United States in world affairs was declining. Its monopoly on nuclear weapons had been lost. China had passed into the communist orbit. Elsewhere in Asia and throughout Africa, new nations, formerly colonial possessions of the Western powers, were adopting a "neutralist" position in the Cold War. Despite the billions poured into armaments and foreign aid, national security seemed far from ensured.

Internal as well as external dangers loomed. Alarming examples of communist espionage in Canada, Great Britain, and the United States convinced many citizens that clever conspirators were everywhere at work undermining American security. Both the Republicans and conservative Democratic critics of Truman's domestic policies were charging that he was "soft" on communists.

There were never more than 100,000 communists in the United States, and party membership plummeted after the start of the Cold War. However, the possibility that a handful of spies could do enormous damage fueled a kind of panic that could be used for partisan purposes. In 1947, hoping to defuse the communists-in-government issue by being more zealous in pursuit of spies than his critics, Truman established a Loyalty Review Board to check up on government employees. The program made even sympathy for a long list of vaguely defined "totalitarian" or "subversive" organizations grounds for dismissal. During the following ten years about 2,700 government workers were discharged, only a relative handful of them for legitimate reasons. A much larger number resigned.

In 1948 Whittaker Chambers, an editor of *Time* who had formerly been a communist, charged that Alger Hiss, president of the Carnegie Endowment for International Peace and a former State Department official, had been a communist in the 1930s. Hiss denied the charge and sued Chambers for libel. Chambers then produced microfilms purporting to show that Hiss had copied classified documents for dispatch to Moscow. Hiss could not be indicted for espionage because of the statute of limitations; instead he was charged with perjury. In January 1950, he was convicted and sentenced to a five-year jail term.

If a distinguished official such as Hiss had been disloyal, anything seemed possible. The case fed the fears of those who believed in the existence of a powerful communist underground in the United States. The disclosure in February 1950 that a British scientist, Klaus Fuchs, had betrayed atomic secrets to the Soviets heightened these fears, as did the arrest and conviction of his American associate, Harry Gold, and two other Americans, Julius and Ethel Rosenberg, on the same charge.

Although they were not major spies and the information they revealed was not crucial, the Rosenbergs were executed, to the consternation of many liberals in the United States and elsewhere. However, information gathered by other spies had speeded the Soviet development of nuclear weapons. This fact encouraged some Republicans to press the communists-in-government issue hard.

McCarthyism

In February 1950 an obscure senator, Joseph R. McCarthy of Wisconsin, introduced this theme in a speech to the even less well-known Ohio County Republican Women's Club of Wheeling, West Virginia. "The reason we find ourselves in a position of impotency," he stated, "is not because our only powerful potential enemy has sent men to invade our shores, but rather because of the traitorous actions of those who have been treated so well by this nation." The State Department, he added, was "infested" with communists.

•:•⎯[Read the Document

McCarthy, *Wheeling, West Virginia, Speech* at **myhistorylab.com**

McCarthy had no shred of evidence to back up these statements, as a Senate committee headed by the conservative Democrat Millard Tydings of Maryland soon demonstrated. He never exposed a single spy or secret American communist.

But because of the government loyalty program, the Hiss case, and other recent events, thousands of people were too eager to believe McCarthy to listen to reason. Within a few weeks he was the most talked of person in Congress. When McCarthy's victims indignantly denied his charges, he distracted the public with still more sensational accusations directed at other innocents. Even General Marshall, whose patriotism was beyond question, was subjected to McCarthy's abuse. The general, he said, was "steeped in falsehood," part of a "conspiracy so immense and an infamy so black as to dwarf any previous venture in the history of man."

McCarthy was totally unscrupulous and his crude tactics would have failed if the public had not been so worried about communism. The worries were caused by the reality of Soviet military power, the attack on Korea, the loss of the nuclear monopoly, and the stories about spies, some of them true.

Dwight D. Eisenhower

As the 1952 presidential election approached, Truman's popularity was again at low ebb; he chose not to seek reelection. In choosing their candidate, the Republicans passed over the twice-defeated Dewey and their most prominent leader, Senator Robert A. Taft of Ohio, an outspoken conservative, and nominated General Dwight D. Eisenhower.

Eisenhower's popularity did not grow merely out of his achievements in World War II. His genial personality and evident desire to avoid controversy proved widely appealing. In his reluctance to seek political office, Eisenhower reminded the country of George Washington, whereas his seeming ignorance of current political issues was no more a handicap to his campaign than the similar ignorance of Jackson and Grant in their times. People "liked Ike" because his management of the Allied armies suggested that he would be equally competent as head of the complex federal government. Eisenhower's campaign was also the first to use television effectively. It featured what came to be known as "spots," twenty-second tapes of candidate Eisenhower responding to questions about his opinions on issues, important and trivial. Eisenhower's promise during the campaign to go to Korea if elected to try to bring the war to an end was a political masterstroke.

Many critics lampooned Eisenhower for his banal amusements. A popular bumper sticker read: "BEN HOGAN [a famous golfer] FOR PRESIDENT. IF WE'RE GOING TO HAVE A GOLFER FOR PRESIDENT, LET'S HAVE A GOOD ONE." Others have viewed Eisenhower's passion for golf as characteristic of his presidential style: methodical, prudent, and, when in the rough, disarmingly shrewd.

The Democrats nominated Governor Adlai E. Stevenson of Illinois, whose grandfather had been vice president under Grover Cleveland. Stevenson's unpretentiousness was appealing, and his witty, urbane speeches captivated intellectuals. In retrospect, however, it is clear that he had not the remotest chance of defeating the popular Eisenhower.

The result was a Republican landslide: Eisenhower received almost 34 million votes to Stevenson's 27 million, and in the Electoral College his margin was 442 to 89.

On the surface, Eisenhower seemed the antithesis of Truman. The Republicans had charged the Democratic administration with being wasteful and extravagant, and Eisenhower planned to run his administration on sound business principles. He spoke scornfully of "creeping socialism," called for more local control of government affairs, and promised to reduce federal spending to balance the budget and cut taxes. He believed that by battling with Congress and pressure groups over the details of legislation, his immediate predecessors had sacrificed part of their status as chief representative of the American people.

Eisenhower proved to be an excellent politician. He knew how to be flexible without compromising his basic values. His "conservatism" became first "dynamic conservatism" and then "progressive moderation."

Yet his policies toward illegal Mexican immigrants and native Americans proved less than humane. In 1954 he authorized Operation Wetback, which rounded up and deported nearly a million illegal Mexican immigrants. He also sought to weaken New Deal policies that strengthened Native American tribes as political entities. Indian leaders resisted this change, and the policy ended in 1961.

The Eisenhower-Dulles Foreign Policy

The American people, troubled and uncertain over the stalemate in Korea, counted on Eisenhower to find a way to employ the nation's immense strength constructively. The new president shared the general feeling that a change of tactics in foreign affairs was needed. He counted on his secretary of state to solve the practical problems.

His choice, John Foster Dulles, was a lawyer with considerable diplomatic experience. He had been an outspoken critic of Truman's policy of containment. In a May 1952 article in *Life* entitled "A Policy of Boldness," he argued that global military containment was both expensive and ineffective. Instead of waiting for the communist powers to make a move and then "containing" them, the United States would build so many powerful nuclear weapons that the Soviet Union or communist China wouldn't dare take provocative actions. An

An eleven-megaton hyrdrogen bomb is detonated over Bikini Atoll in March 1954. One megaton had the explosive power of 1 million tons of TNT. (The bomb that had destroyed Hiroshima had the equivalent of 12,500 tons of TNT.) An earlier atom bomb test at Bikini Island prompted a French fashion designer to give the name "bikini" to his explosively provocative bathing suit.

immense arsenal of nuclear bombs, loaded on the nation's formidable fleet of bombers, would ensure a **massive retaliation** against any aggressor. Such a "new look" military would be cheaper to maintain than a large standing army, and it would prevent the United States from being caught up in "local" conflicts like the Korean War.

Korea offered the first test of his views. After Eisenhower's post-election trip to Korea failed to bring an end to the war, Dulles signaled his willingness to use tactical nuclear weapons in Korea by showily transferring nuclear warheads from the United States mainland to bomber units stationed in East Asia. Several weeks later, in July 1953, the Chinese signed an armistice that ended hostilities but left Korea divided. The administration interpreted the softening of the Chinese position as proof that the nuclear threat had worked.

Emboldened by his apparent triumph, Dulles again brandished the nation's nuclear arsenal. Chiang Kai-shek had stationed 90,000 soldiers—one-third of his army—in Quemoy and Matsu, two small islands located a few miles from mainland China. In 1954 the Chinese communists began shelling the islands, presumably in preparation to invade them. Chiang appealed for American protection, warning that loss of the islands would bring about the collapse of Nationalist China. At a press conference in 1955 Eisenhower announced his willingness to use nuclear weapons to defend the islands. The Chinese communists backed down.

Massive retaliation succeeded in reducing the defense budget by allowing Eisenhower to pare a half million men from the armed forces. On balance, however, Dulles's strategy was flawed, and many of his schemes were preposterous. Above all, massive retaliation was an extremely dangerous policy when the Soviet Union possessed nuclear weapons as powerful as those of the United States.

McCarthy Self-Destructs

Although the State Department was now controlled by Dulles, a Republican and hard-line anticommunist, Senator McCarthy refused to moderate his attacks on the department. In 1953 television newscaster Edwin R. Murrow cast doubt on McCarthy's methods; soon he and McCarthy were pummeling each other on television.

((•─ Hear the **Audio**

Joseph P. McCarthy Speech at **myhistorylab.com**

But McCarthy finally overreached himself. Early in 1954 he turned his guns on the army, accusing Pentagon officials of trying to blackmail his committee. The resulting Army-McCarthy hearings, televised before the country, and Murrow's increasingly sharp criticisms, proved the senator's undoing. When the hearings ended in June 1954 after some million words of testimony, his spell had been broken.

The Senate, with President Eisenhower (who despised McCarthy but who considered it beneath his dignity as president to "get into the gutter with that guy") applying pressure behind the scenes, at last moved to censure him in December 1954. Although he continued to issue statements and wild charges, the country no longer listened. In 1957 he died of cirrhosis of the liver.

Asian Policy after Korea

Shortly after an armistice was finally arranged in Korea in July 1953, new trouble erupted far to the south in the former French colony of Indochina. Nationalist rebels led by the communist Ho Chi Minh had been harassing the French in Vietnam, one of the three puppet kingdoms (the others were Laos and Cambodia) fashioned by France in Indochina after the defeat of the Japanese. When China recognized the rebels, who were known as the Vietminh, and supplied them with arms, President Truman countered with economic and military assistance to the French, and President Eisenhower continued and expanded this assistance.

Early in 1954 Ho Chi Minh's troops trapped and besieged a French army in the remote stronghold of Dien Bien Phu. In May the garrison surrendered. Several months later France, Great Britain, the Soviet Union, and China signed an agreement dividing Vietnam along the seventeenth parallel. France withdrew from the area. The northern sector became the Democratic Republic of Vietnam, controlled by Ho Chi Minh; the southern sector remained in the hands of the emperor, Bao Dai. An election to settle the future of all Vietnam was scheduled for 1956.

When it seemed likely that the communists would win that election, Ngo Dinh Diem, a conservative anticommunist, overthrew Bao Dai and became president of South Vietnam. The United States supplied his government liberally with aid. The planned election was never held, and Vietnam remained divided.

Dulles responded to the diplomatic setback in Vietnam by establishing the Southeast Asia Treaty Organization (SEATO), but only three Asian nations—the Philippine Republic (which was granted independence in 1947), Thailand, and Pakistan—joined this alliance.[3]

Israel and the Middle East

Truman and Eisenhower had intervened in the Far East because of a direct communist threat. But as the American love affair with cars turned into an obsession, United States policymakers became increasingly attentive to the Middle East, where seas of oil had been recently discovered. Iran, Iraq, Kuwait, and Saudi Arabia sat upon nearly 60 percent of the world's known reserves.

After World War II, Zionists, who had long sought to promote Jewish immigration to Palestine, intensified their efforts. The slaughter of six million European Jews by the Nazis strengthened Jewish claims to a homeland and intensified pressure to allow hundreds of thousands of Jewish refugees to immigrate to Palestine, which was governed by Great Britain according to a League of Nations mandate. But the influx of Jewish settlers, and their calls for creation of a Jewish state (Israel), provoked Palestinian and Arab leaders. Fighting broke out. President Truman angered Arab leaders by endorsing the partition of the region into an Israeli and a Palestinian state. In 1947, the United Nations voted for partition and on May 14, 1948, the State of Israel was established. Within hours, Truman recognized its sovereignty.

Then Arab armies from Egypt, Jordan, Iraq, Syria, and Lebanon attacked Israel. Although badly outnumbered, the Israelis were better organized and better armed than the Arabs and drove them off with relative ease. Nearly a million local Arabs were displaced, causing a desperate refugee problem in nearby countries.

President Truman had consistently placed support for Israel before other considerations in the Middle East, partly because of the conviction that survivors of the Nazi holocaust were entitled to a country of their own and partly because of the political importance of the Jewish vote in the United States. Dulles and Eisenhower tried to restore

---

[3]The other signatories were Great Britain, France, the United States, Australia, and New Zealand.

balance and mollify the Arabs by deemphasizing American support of Israel. Gas-hungry Americans could ill afford to alienate the Arab world.

In 1952 Colonel Gamal Abdel Nasser emerged as the strongman of Egypt. The United States was prepared to lend Nasser money to build a huge dam on the Nile at Aswan that would provide irrigation and electric power for much of the region. However, Eisenhower would not sell Egypt arms, but the communists would.

For this reason Nasser drifted toward the communist orbit. When Eisenhower then decided not to finance the Aswan Dam, Nasser responded by nationalizing the Suez Canal. This move galvanized the British and French. In conjunction with the French, and without consulting the United States, the British in 1956 decided to take back the canal by force. The Israelis, alarmed by repeated Arab hit-and-run raids, also attacked Egypt.

Events moved swiftly. Israeli armored columns crushed the Egyptian army in the Sinai Peninsula in a matter of days. France and Britain occupied Port Said at the northern end of the canal. Nasser sank ships to block the channel. In the UN the Soviet Union and the United States introduced resolutions calling for a cease-fire. Both were vetoed by Britain and France.

Then the Soviet Union threatened to send "volunteers" to help defend Egypt and launch atomic missiles against France and Great Britain if they did not withdraw. Eisenhower also demanded that the invaders pull out of Egypt. On November 6, only nine days after the first Israeli units had invaded Egypt, British Prime Minister Anthony Eden announced a cease-fire. Israel withdrew its troops.

The United States had won a measure of respect in the Arab countries, but at what cost? Its major allies had been humiliated. Their ill-timed attack had enabled the Soviet Union to recover much of the prestige it had lost as a result of its brutal suppression of a Hungarian revolt that had broken out a week before the Suez fiasco.

When the Soviet Union seemed likely to profit from its "defense" of Egypt in the crisis, the president announced the Eisenhower Doctrine (January 1957), which stated that the United States was "prepared to use armed force" anywhere in the Middle East against "aggression from any country controlled by international communism." In practice, the Eisenhower Doctrine amounted to little more than a restatement of the containment policy.

Eisenhower and Khrushchev

In 1956 Eisenhower was reelected, defeating Adlai Stevenson even more decisively than he had in 1952. Despite evident satisfaction with their leader, however, the American people were in a sober mood. Hopes of pushing back the Soviet Union with clever stratagems and moral fervor were fading. Although the United States detonated the first hydrogen bomb in November 1952, the Soviets followed suit within six months. The Cold War between the superpowers had become yet more chilling.

Stalin died in March 1953, and after a period of internal conflict within the Kremlin, Nikita Khrushchev emerged as the new master of the Soviet Union. Prone to violent tantrums and tearful histrionics, Khrushchev delighted in shocking people with words and gestures. In the most famous of these, he pounded his shoe on the table during a debate at the United Nations. Although a product of the Soviet system, Khrushchev recognized its deep failings and resolved to purge it of Stalinism. He released political prisoners from Stalin's gulags, or political prison camps, and told wide-eyed party functionaries that Stalin had committed monstrous crimes.

Vice President Richard M. Nixon and Soviet leader Nikita Khrushchev engage in a "kitchen debate" over the future of capitalism at a Moscow trade fair in 1959. Although the encounter did little to advance United States-Soviet relations, it established Nixon's credentials as a tough negotiator.

Eisenhower, a seasoned analyst of military capabilities, understood that Khrushchev's antics were meant to conceal the Soviet Union's many weaknesses: the bitter opposition to Soviet rule among peoples of Eastern Europe; the deficiencies of the overcentralized Soviet economy, especially in agriculture; and the bureaucratic stultification of its armed forces. Thousands of American airplanes were based in Europe, northern Africa, and Turkey, placing most Soviet targets within easy range. The United States would win (whatever that meant) any nuclear war.

But this advantage disappeared in the exhaust trail of a Soviet rocket, launched on October 4, 1957, that carried a 184-pound capsule named *Sputnik* far above the atmosphere into earth orbit. Soon, American policymakers knew, Soviet missiles capable of reaching

Table 28.1 The Cold War Escalates

Year	Event	Significance
1947	George Kennan's "Sources of Soviet Conduct"	Outlines rationale for "containment" of Soviet Union
1947	Truman Doctrine	United States supports Greece and Turkey against communist threats
1948	Marshall Plan	United States provides economic aid to Western Europe
1949	Soviet Union detonates atom bomb	Truman calls for development of hydrogen bomb
1950	North Korea invades South Korea	Truman intervenes, as does communist China
1950	NSC-68 adopted	Truman authorizes worldwide expansion of U.S. military to stop Soviet aggression anywhere
1952	United States detonates hydrogen bomb	Soviet Union follows suit, 1953
1953	NSC-68 replaced with "massive retaliation"	Dulles-Eisenhower signal willingness to start a nuclear war to defend American interests
1957	Soviet Union launches *Sputnik*	Shows Soviet capacity to hit American targets with nuclear weapons

American soil would be tipped with nuclear warheads. The nation's far-flung network of bomber defenses had become obsolete, and with it the strategy of massive retaliation.

Eisenhower refused to take chances. He secretly authorized high-altitude American planes to spy on key Soviet military installations. On May 1, 1960, high over Sverdlovsk, an industrial center deep in the Soviet Union, an American U–2 spy plane was shot down by antiaircraft fire. The pilot of the plane survived the crash, and he confessed to being a spy. His cameras contained aerial photographs of Soviet military installations. When Eisenhower assumed full responsibility for the mission, Khrushchev accused the United States of "piratical" and "cowardly" acts of aggression.

Latin America Aroused

Events in Latin America compounded Eisenhower's difficulties. During World War II the United States, needing Latin American raw materials, had supplied its southern neighbors liberally with economic aid.

But as the Cold War progressed, the United States neglected Latin America. Economic problems plagued the region, and in most nations reactionary governments reigned. Radical Latin Americans accused the United States of supporting cliques of wealthy tyrants, whereas conservatives blamed insufficient American economic aid for the plight of the poor.

Eisenhower, eager to improve relations, stepped up economic assistance. Resistance to communism nonetheless continued to receive first priority. In 1954 the government of Jacobo Arbenz Guzman in Guatemala began to import Soviet weapons. The United States promptly dispatched arms to neighboring Honduras. Within a month an army led by an exiled Guatemalan officer marched into the country from Honduras and overthrew Arbenz. Elsewhere in Latin America, Eisenhower, as Truman had before him, continued to support regimes that were kept in power by the local military.

Events in Cuba demonstrated that there was no easy solution to Latin American problems. In 1959 a revolutionary movement headed by Fidel Castro overthrew Fulgencio Batista, one of the most noxious of the Latin American dictators. Eisenhower recognized the Castro government at once, but the Cuban leader soon began to criticize the United States in highly colored speeches. Castro confiscated American property without providing adequate compensation, suppressed civil liberties, and entered into close relations with the Soviet Union. After he negotiated a trade agreement with the Soviet Union in February 1960, which enabled the Russians to obtain Cuban sugar at bargain rates, the United States retaliated by prohibiting the importation of Cuban sugar into America.

Khrushchev then announced that if the United States intervened in Cuba, he would defend the country with atomic weapons. "The Monroe Doctrine has outlived its time," Khrushchev warned. Shortly before the end of his second term, Eisenhower broke off diplomatic relations with Cuba.

Fighting the Cold War at Home

The looming Soviet threat brought the Cold War closer to the American people than ever before. Such fears provided public support for increased spending on defense. In 1955 Eisenhower worried that a Soviet nuclear attack would plunge American cities into chaos. The roads out of threatened cities "would be the breeder of a deadly congestion within hours of an attack," he noted. He therefore backed a federally-funded highway system; this would not only facilitate the evacuation of cities but would also allow the army to mobilize more rapidly. The National Interstate and Defense Highway Act of 1956 became the largest public works project in the nation's history.

The Soviet Union's success in building atomic and hydrogen bombs, and especially in launching an orbiting satellite before the United States, also prompted Eisenhower to initiate a sweeping reform of the nation's schools. "The defense of the nation depends upon the mastery of modern techniques

This interchange near Seattle was part of the interstate highway system advanced by Eisenhower to facilitate both military transports and civilian evacuations.

developed from complex scientific principles," he declared. In 1958 he signed the National Defense Education Act. It provided federal aid to promote study of science, mathematics and foreign languages in large, comprehensive (and sometimes anonymous) high schools.

"Godless" communism posed an ideological as well as military threat. In 1954 the Reverend George Docherty warned his Presbyterian congregation in Washington, DC, that "little Muscovites" in the Soviet Union were pledging allegiance to "hammer and sickle" atheism. But an "atheistic American," he intoned, was "a contradiction in terms." Later that day Eisenhower, commenting on the sermon, told a radio audience that whatever their "personal creed," Americans still "believed in a higher power." A few months later he signed a law that added the phrase "one nation under God" to the Pledge of Allegiance. The next year, Congress added "In God We Trust" to the nation's currency.

Watch the Video

Duck and Cover at myhistorylab.com

Blacks Challenge Segregation

Another front in the Cold War concerned race relations. How could African and Asian leaders be persuaded to reject communism and follow the example of the United States when American blacks were treated so poorly? American diplomats winced when the finance minister of Ghana was refused a meal at the Howard Johnson's, a chain restaurant, in Dover, Delaware. "Colored people are not allowed to eat in here," the manager explained to the African leader. Vice President Nixon declared, "In the world-wide struggle in which we are engaged, racial prejudice is a gun we point at ourselves."

But racial confrontations remained in the news. During and after World War II a demand for change had developed in the South. Its roots lay in southern industrialization, in the shift from small sharecropping holdings to large commercial farms, in the vast wartime expenditures of the federal government on aircraft factories and army bases in the region; in the impact of the GI Bill on southern colleges and universities, and in the gradual development of a southern black middle class.

Black soldiers who had served abroad demanded that they be treated with respect when they returned home. In 1947 Jackie Robinson, a black officer who had been court-martialed—and acquitted—for refusing to move to the back of a segregated military bus during World War II, was ready to integrate major league baseball. When his team— the Brooklyn Dodgers—checked into the Ben Franklin Hotel in Philadelphia, he was refused a room. A week later the Dodgers went to Pittsburgh. When he took his position at second base, the Pirates refused to come onto the field. Only under threat of forfeiting the game would they play against Robinson.

In this photo opportunity, Phillies manager Ben Chapman refused to shake Jackie Robinson's hand. Instead, he leaned toward Robinson and said quietly, "Jackie, you know, you're a good ballplayer, but you're still a nigger to me." Robinson replied by leading the Dodgers to the pennant and winning Rookie of the Year honors.

More blacks insisted on their right to vote—and many got it. In 1940 only 2 percent of African Americans in the south were registered to vote; by 1947, that had increased to 12 percent. But white resistance remained formidable. In 1946 Eugene Talmadge, behind in the polls, won his race for governor by promising that if he were elected "no Negro will vote in Georgia for four years."

The NAACP (the National Association for the Advancement of Colored People) decided that the time had come to challenge segregation in the courts. Thurgood Marshall, the organization's chief staff lawyer, went from state to state filing legal challenges to the "separate but equal" principle laid down in *Plessy v. Ferguson* in 1896 (see Chapter 20). In 1938 the Supreme Court had ordered the University of Missouri law school to admit a black student because no law school for blacks existed in the state. This decision gradually forced some southern states to admit blacks to advanced programs.

In 1953 President Eisenhower appointed California's Governor Earl Warren chief justice of the U.S. Supreme Court. Convinced that the Court must take the offensive in the cause of civil rights, Warren succeeded in welding his associates into a unit on this question. In 1954 an NAACP-sponsored case, **Brown v. Board of Education of Topeka**, came up for decision. Marshall submitted a mass of sociological evidence to show that the mere fact of segregation made equal education impossible and did serious psychological damage to both black and white children. Speaking for a unanimous Court, Warren reversed the *Plessy* decision. "In the field of public education, the doctrine of 'separate but equal' has no place," he declared. "Separate educational facilities are inherently unequal." The next year the Court ordered the states to end segregation "with all deliberate speed."

●●●—Read the Document

Brown v. Board of Education of Topeka, Kansas at **myhistorylab.com**

Flouting the Court's decision, few districts in the southern and border states integrated their schools. As late as September 1956, barely 700 of the South's 10,000 school districts had been desegregated.

Angry jeers from whites rain down on Elizabeth Eckford, one of the first black students to arrive for registration at Little Rock's Central High School in 1957. State troops turned black students away from the school until President Eisenhower overruled the state decision and called in the National Guard to enforce integration.

President Eisenhower thought equality for blacks could not be obtained by government edict. He said that the Court's ruling must be obeyed, but he did little to discourage southern resistance to desegregation.

However, in 1957 events compelled him to act. When the school board of Little Rock, Arkansas, opened Central High School to a handful of black students, the governor of the state, Orval M. Faubus, called out the National Guard to prevent them from entering the school. Unruly crowds taunted the students and their parents. Eisenhower could not ignore the direct flouting of federal authority. After the mayor of Little Rock sent him a telegram saying, in part, "situation is out of control and police cannot disperse the mob," Eisenhower dispatched 1,000 paratroopers to Little Rock and summoned 10,000 National Guardsmen to federal duty, thus removing them from Faubus's control. The black students then began to attend class. A token force of soldiers was stationed at Central High for the entire school year to protect them.

⊙ Watch the Video

How did the Civil Rights Movement change American schools? at **myhistorylab.com**

Direct Action Protests: The Montgomery Bus Boycott

While Marshall and the NAACP were dismantling the legal superstructure of segregation, its institutional foundations remained. Blacks increasingly took action on their own.

This change first came to national attention during the Eisenhower administration in the rigidly segregated city of Montgomery, Alabama. On Friday, December 1, 1955, Rosa Parks, a seamstress at the Montgomery Fair department store, boarded a bus on her way home from her job. She dutifully took a seat toward the rear as custom and law required. As white workers and shoppers filled the forward section, the driver ordered her to give up her place to a white passenger. Parks, who was also secretary of the Montgomery NAACP chapter, refused. She had decided, she later recalled, that "I would have to know once and for all what rights I had as a human being and a citizen."

She was arrested. Over the weekend, Montgomery's black leaders organized a boycott. "Don't ride the bus . . . Monday," their mimeographed notice ran. "If you work, take a cab, or share a ride, or walk." Monday dawned bitterly cold, but the boycott was a total success.

Most Montgomery blacks could not afford to miss a single day's wages, so the protracted struggle to get to work was difficult to maintain. Black-owned taxis reduced their rates sharply, and when the city declared this illegal, car pools were quickly organized. Few African Americans owned cars. Although nearly everyone who did volunteered, there were never more than 350 cars available to the more than 10,000 people who needed rides to their jobs and back every day. Nevertheless, the boycott went on.

Late in February the Montgomery authorities obtained indictments of 115 leaders of the boycott, but this move backfired because it focused national attention on the situation. A young clergyman, the Reverend Martin Luther King, Jr., was emerging as the leader of the boycott. A gifted speaker, he became an overnight celebrity. (See American Lives, "Martin Luther King, Jr.," p. 756.) Money poured in from all over the country to support the movement. The boycott lasted for over a year. Finally the Supreme Court declared the local law enforcing racial separation unconstitutional: Montgomery had to desegregate its public transportation system.

This success encouraged blacks elsewhere in the South to band together against segregation. A new organization founded in 1957, the **Southern Christian Leadership Conference (SCLC),** headed by King, moved to the forefront of the civil rights movement. Other organizations joined the struggle, notably the Congress of Racial Equality (CORE), which had been founded in 1942. The direct action movement was becoming a broad-based nationwide civil rights movement.

The Election of 1960

As the end of his momentous second term approached, Eisenhower somewhat reluctantly endorsed Vice President Richard Nixon as the Republican candidate to succeed him. Nixon had originally skyrocketed to national prominence by exploiting the public fear of communist subversion. In 1947 he was an obscure young congressman from California; in 1950 he won a seat in the Senate; two years later Eisenhower chose him as his running mate.

The Democrats nominated Senator John F. Kennedy of Massachusetts. His chief rival for the nomination, Lyndon B. Johnson of Texas, the Senate majority leader, became his running mate. Kennedy was the son of Joseph P. Kennedy, a wealthy businessman who had served as ambassador to Great Britain under Franklin Roosevelt. During World War II, Kennedy served in the Pacific, captaining a torpedo boat. When the boat was sliced in two by a Japanese destroyer, Kennedy showed personal courage in rescuing his men. Besides wealth, intelligence, good looks, and charm, Kennedy had the advantage of his Irish-Catholic ancestry, a valuable asset in heavily Catholic Massachusetts. After three terms in the House, he moved on to the Senate in 1952.

Watch the Video
Kennedy-Nixon Debate at **myhistorylab.com**

After his landslide reelection in 1958, only Kennedy's religion seemed to limit his political future. No Catholic had ever been elected president. Nevertheless, influenced by Kennedy's victories in the Wisconsin and West Virginia primaries—the latter establishing him as an effective campaigner in a predominantly Protestant region—the Democratic convention nominated him.

Kennedy had not been a particularly liberal congressman. He was not involved in the civil rights movement. He enthusiastically endorsed the Cold War and indicted the Eisenhower administration for falling behind the Soviet Union in the race to build missiles. He admitted frankly that he liked Senator Joseph McCarthy and thought that "he may have something" in his campaign against supposed communists in government. However, as a presidential candidate, he sought to appear more forward-looking. He stressed his youth and "vigor" (a favorite word) and promised to open a **New Frontier** for the country. Nixon ran on the Eisenhower record, which he promised to extend in liberal directions.

MARTIN LUTHER KING, JR.

On December 1, 1955, Rosa Parks was arrested for violating Montgomery's segregation laws. Black leaders immediately made plans to boycott the city buses the following Monday.

On Monday morning, the buses were nearly empty. That afternoon black leaders met to discuss strategy for a public meeting that evening. One minister urged that they keep their plans secret. E. D. Nixon, a railroad porter and president of the local NAACP, jumped to his feet: "How do you think you can run a bus boycott in secret?" Then he lost his temper. "You ministers have lived off these wash-women for the last hundred years and ain't never done nothing for them."

As Nixon was finishing his diatribe, the new minister in town strode into the room. Young, well-dressed Martin Luther King, Jr. was regarded as something of a dandy. Now, all eyes turned to the dapper latecomer. He called on the ministers to act in open and use their names. Someone proposed that King be named president of the protest movement. Nearly everyone agreed.

That evening, hundreds filled the largest Baptist church, with many more spilling onto the lawn and streets. A loudspeaker was set up. Inside, King outlined the situation, and then, slipping into a preaching mode, began to roll off one booming phrase after another. "And you know, my friends, there comes a time when people get tired of being trampled over by the iron feet of oppression," he said in a deep voice. By the time he finished, his words were drowned out by the stomping of feet and the roars of the crowd outside.

King's rhetorical mastery stunned nearly everyone. He was only twenty-six, and had served as a pastor for only a year.

His father had been minister of the largest Baptist church in Atlanta, and Martin's circumstances as a child had been comfortable. He briefly attended a special school run by Atlanta University, then the local public high school before going to Morehouse College in Atlanta. He eventually followed in his father's footsteps.

He attended Crozer seminary in Pennsylvania. After finishing at the top of his class, he went to Boston University, where he earned a doctorate in philosophy. He resolved to become a successful preacher in a big-city church.

In 1953 King married Coretta Scott; the next year he was appointed pastor at Dexter Avenue Baptist Church in Montgomery.

But in the first week of December, 1955, his life had taken an unexpected turn. He would be given the task of forging into a single movement the disparate elements of the black community. He would adapt the passive nonviolence tactics used by Indian nationalist Mohandas Gandhi to gain independence from Britain, and apply them to the American South. He would use the language of Christian brotherhood to reach out to whites. He would lead the movement that would change the nation.

But that was in the future. In December 1955, a convergence of fateful circumstances had pushed him into leadership of a bus boycott. Twelve years later, he would be dead, victim of an assassin's bullet.

The Rev. Martin Luther King, Jr., Coretta Scott King, and their children share a moment of calm in Montgomery, 1956. That year, while King was addressing a mass meeting, his house was bombed; Coretta and the children were unhurt.

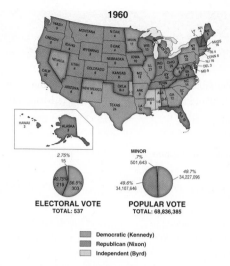

1960

2.75%
15

MINOR
.7%
501,643

40.75%
219   56.5%
303

49.7%
34,227,096

49.6%
34,107,646

ELECTORAL VOTE
TOTAL: 537

POPULAR VOTE
TOTAL: 68,836,385

▢ Democratic (Kennedy)
▢ Republican (Nixon)
▢ Independent (Byrd)

Election of 1960 Like nearly all Democrats since the Compromise of 1877, Kennedy carried most of the South. White Southerners opposed the party of Lincoln, and few black Southerners had been registered to vote.

A series of television debates between the candidates helped Kennedy by enabling him to demonstrate his maturity and mastery of the issues. Although both candidates laudably avoided it, the religious issue was important. His Catholicism helped Kennedy in eastern urban areas but injured him in many farm districts and throughout the West. Kennedy's victory, 303 to 219 in the Electoral College, was paper-thin in the popular vote, 34,227,000 to 34,109,000.

The years since the end of World War II had been dominated by the prospect of war more terrible than anyone could imagine. By the end of 1960 Eisenhower was less concerned about a communist victory than the impact of the arms race on America itself. By then defense expenditures devoured one-tenth of the nation's GNP. In his final speech as president, Eisenhower warned of the "grave implications" resulting from "the conjunction of an immense military establishment and a large arms industry." What Eisenhower called the **military-industrial complex** potentially endangered "the very structure of our society." Could the nation mount a worldwide defense of democracy without endangering that democracy at home?

Milestones

1944	Congress provides subsidies to veterans in GI Bill of Rights	1950	UN counterattack in Korea is driven back by Red Chinese army
1946	UN creates Atomic Energy Commission	1952	Dwight D. Eisenhower is elected president
1947	Taft-Hartley Act regulates unions and labor disputes	1953	John Foster Dulles institutes "New Look" nuclear-based foreign policy
	Truman announces Truman Doctrine to stop communism's spread		Korean War ends with armistice
	George Kennan ("X") urges containment policy in *Sources of Soviet Conduct*	1954	Senate holds Army–McCarthy hearings
1948	Marshall Plan provides funds to rebuild Europe		United States helps overthrow Arbenz in Guatemala
	Harry S Truman is elected president		French are defeated in Indochina after siege of Dien Bien Phu
	State of Israel is created as Jewish homeland; Arabs declare war		Supreme Court orders school desegregation in *Brown v. Board of Education of Topeka*
1948–1949	United States supplies West Berlin during Berlin airlift		Egypt nationalizes Suez Canal in Suez Crisis
1949	United States and eleven other nations form North Atlantic Treaty Organization (NATO)	1955	The Rev. Martin Luther King, Jr., leads Montgomery Bus Boycotts
	Soviet Union detonates atom bomb	1956	Eisenhower is reelected president
1950	North Korea invades South Korea	1957	M. L. King, Jr., and followers form Southern Christian Leadership Conference
	NSC-68 calls for massive military buildup		National Guard enforces desegregation of Central High School in Little Rock, Arkansas
	Alger Hiss is convicted of perjury		
	McCarran Act restricts "subversive" activity	1959	Fidel Castro overthrows Fulgencio Batista, takes power in Cuba
	Senator Joseph McCarthy charges that the State Department is riddled with communists	1960	John F. Kennedy is first Roman Catholic to be elected president

✓•⌐Study and Review at www.myhistorylab.com

Review Questions

1. The late 1940s and 1950s are often characterized as a period of complacency and consensus. Yet this chapter holds that, in foreign and domestic affairs, it was a period of "menacing uncertainty." What constituted the chief elements of menace?

2. Throughout the period from 1946 to 1960, American presidents sought to "contain" communism. How did Eisenhower's "massive retaliation" differ from Truman's worldwide "NSC-68" containment? How did *Sputnik* influence the Cold War?

3. Why did Truman intervene in Korea, and why did the war end in stalemate?

4. What was the impact of the Cold War on American society?

5. Why did the civil rights movement gain momentum after 1945? On what grounds did the Supreme Court overturn the "separate but equal" ruling in *Brown v. Board of Education* (1954)? Why did African Americans subsequently resort to "direct action" protests?

Key Terms

Berlin airlift *738*
Brown v. Board of Education of Topeka *753*
Fair Deal *739*
Marshall Plan *737*
massive retaliation *747*

military-industrial complex *757*
New Frontier *755*
North Atlantic Treaty Organization (NATO) *740*
NSC-68 *741*

Southern Christian Leadership Conference (SCLC) *755*
Taft-Hartley Act *735*
Truman Doctrine *736*

29 From Camelot to Watergate: 1961–1975

((•⃝—Hear the Audio Chapter 29 at myhistorylab.com

How do you get out of a deep hole?

On DECEMBER 2, 2009, AS POLLS REVEALED GROWING DISSATISFACTION with the wars in Iraq and Afghanistan, President Barack Obama promised to withdraw all U.S. troops from Iraq within two years. But he announced that he would send an additional 30,000 troops to Afghanistan, where the situation had deteriorated.

"I do not make this decision lightly," he said, noting that he had opposed the war in Iraq. But Afghanistan, he insisted, was different. It had been the home of the Al Qaeda terrorists who attacked on September 11, 2001. By sending more troops to Afghanistan now, Obama believed the military would defeat Al Qaeda more quickly. "There are those who suggest that Afghanistan is another Vietnam," he conceded. "I believe this argument depends on a false reading of history."

Because nothing in the past is exactly like anything else, all historical analogies are flawed. But the history of Vietnam suggests that once soldiers have fought and died for a cause, the task of getting out of a war—short of victory—is not an easy one.

Just before President John F. Kennedy sent the first American troops to Vietnam in 1961, he confided doubts to an aide: "The troops will march in; the bands will play; the crowds will cheer. . . Then we will be told we have to send more troops. It's like taking a drink. The effect wears off, and you have to take another."

By 1963, despite the infusion of some 16,000 U.S. soldiers, South Vietnam was crumbling. In 1965, with a communist takeover imminent, Lyndon Johnson, Kennedy's successor, increased U.S. troop levels to nearly a half million. Yet victory remained elusive. In 1969, his successor, Richard M. Nixon, promised to bring an honorable peace to Vietnam; but American troops remained for another four years.

The long war in Vietnam exposed deep fissures within the nation. Racial divisions widened into gaping holes. Student protests drew violent responses. Nixon's heated rhetoric and illegal campaign tactics heightened tensions. And less than a year after he resigned, communist North Vietnam completed its conquest of South Vietnam. For the United States, the war ended in failure.

Kennedy in Camelot

Having lampooned the Eisenhower administration as stodgy and unimaginative, President Kennedy made a show of his style and wit. He quoted Robert Frost and Dante. He played and replayed recordings of Winston Churchill, hoping to imprint the great orator's sonorous cadences on his own broad Bostonian vowels. At the instigation of his elegant wife, Jacqueline, Kennedy surrounded himself with the finest intellects at glittering White House galas to honor Nobel Prize winners and celebrated artists.

Kennedy's youthful senior staff boasted impressive scholarly credentials. His national security adviser, McGeorge Bundy, had been dean of the faculty at Harvard. Secretary of Defense Robert McNamara also had taught at Harvard before becoming the first nonfamily member to head the Ford Motor Company.

Kennedy's campaign slogan—"Let's get this country moving again"—was embodied in his own active life. He played rugged games of touch football with the press corps and romped with his young children in the Oval Office. In an article for *Sports Illustrated* entitled "The Soft American" published just after the election, Kennedy complained that television, movies, and a comfortable lifestyle had made too many young people flabby. His earliest presidential initiative was a physical fitness campaign in the schools.

Kennedy's image of youthful vigor was enhanced by the beauty and presence of Jacqueline, whose wide-eyed diffidence was universally admired as regal bearing. The image was enhanced by Lerner and Loewe's musical *Camelot*, which opened a few weeks before the inauguration. Its evocation of King Arthur, who sought to lead his virile young knights in challenges great and good, suggested the Kennedy White House. All Washington seemed aglow with excitement and energy.

Never, too, had the substance of an administration been so closely identified with the style of its president. But the dazzle was misleading. Although quick-witted and intelligent, Kennedy was no intellectual. Nor did the president embody physical fitness. Congenital back problems, aggravated by war injuries, forced Kennedy to use crutches or a cane in private and to take heavy doses of painkillers and amphetamines. The president's permanent "tan" did not result from outdoor exercise, as the public assumed, but from Addison's disease, an often fatal failure of the adrenal glands for which Kennedy gave himself daily injections of cortisone. Though he publicly denied it, Kennedy was chronically ill throughout his presidency.

The Cuban Crises

"The torch has been passed to a new generation of Americans," Kennedy declared in his inaugural address. Its chief task was to stop the spread of communism. While Eisenhower had relied on the nation's nuclear arsenal to intimidate the Kremlin, Kennedy proposed to challenge communist aggression whenever and wherever it occurred. A new breed of cold warrior, Kennedy called on young men and women to serve in the Peace Corps, an organization that he created to mobilize American idealism and technical skills to help developing nations. His was a call for commitment—and action.

Perhaps seduced by his own rhetoric, Kennedy blundered almost immediately. Anti-Castro exiles were eager to organize an invasion of their homeland, reasoning that the Cuban people would rise up against Castro and communism as soon as "democratic" forces provided the necessary leadership. Under Eisenhower the CIA had begun training some

2,000 Cuban exiles in Nicaragua. Kennedy was of two minds about the proposed invasion. Some in his administration opposed it strongly, but his closest advisers, including his brother Robert, urged him to give his approval. In the end he did.

The invaders, 1,400 strong, struck in April 1961. They landed at the Bay of Pigs, on Cuba's southern coast. But the Cuban people failed to flock to their lines, and soon Castro's army pinned the invaders down and forced them to surrender. Because American involvement could not be disguised, the affair exposed the United States to all the criticism that a straightforward assault would have produced, without accomplishing the overthrow of Castro. Worse, it made Kennedy appear impulsive as well as unprincipled. Castro tightened his connections with the Soviet Union.

In June, Kennedy met with Soviet Premier Khrushchev in Vienna. Furious over the invasion of Cuba, Khrushchev blustered about grabbing West Berlin. In August, he abruptly closed the border between East and West Berlin and erected the **Berlin wall**—a barrier of concrete blocks and barbed wire across the city to stop the flow of East Germans into

"Ich bin ein Berliner" (I am a Berliner), Kennedy declared from a balcony in West Berlin in June, 1961, and his words brought a roar of approval from the West Berliners. Gesturing toward the Berlin wall, he called it "the most obvious and vivid demonstration of the failures of the communist system."

the noncommunist zone. At the same time, the Soviets resumed nuclear testing. Khrushchev ordered detonation of a series of gigantic hydrogen bombs, including one with a power 3,000 times that of the bomb that had devastated Hiroshima.

Kennedy followed suit: He announced plans to build thousands of nuclear missiles, known as Minutemen, capable of hitting targets on the other side of the world. He expanded the space program, vowing that an American would land on the moon within ten years. The president called on Congress to pass a large increase in military spending.

In secret, Kennedy also resolved to destroy Castro. He ordered military leaders to plan for a full-scale invasion of Cuba. He also instructed the CIA to undertake "massive activity" against Castro's regime. The CIA devised Operation Mongoose, a plan to slip spies, saboteurs, and assassins into Cuba. Although never officially endorsed by the president, Mongoose operated under the oversight of Robert Kennedy.

In 1962 Khrushchev precipitated the most dangerous confrontation of the Cold War. To forestall the anticipated American invasion of Cuba, he moved tanks, heavy bombers, and 42,000 Soviet troops and technicians to the island. His most fateful step was to sneak several dozen guided nuclear missiles into the country and prepare them for launching. The missiles could have hit most of the eastern United States with nuclear warheads.

On October 14 American spy planes spotted the launching pads and missiles. The president faced a dreadful decision. After the **Bay of Pigs fiasco**, he could not again appear to back down to the communists. But if he invaded Cuba or bombed the Soviet bases and missile sites, Khrushchev would likely seize West Berlin or bomb U.S. missile sites in Turkey. Either action might lead to a full-scale nuclear war and millions of deaths.

On October 22 Kennedy addressed the nation on television. The Soviet buildup was "a deliberately provocative and unjustified change in the status quo." He ordered the American navy to stop and search all vessels headed for Cuba and to turn back any containing "offensive" weapons. Kennedy called on Khrushchev to dismantle the missile bases and remove from the island all weapons capable of striking the United States. Any Cuban-based nuclear attack would result, he warned, in "a full retaliatory response upon the Soviet Union."

For days, Soviet ships steamed toward Cuba and work on the missile launching pads continued. An American spy plane was shot down over Cuba. Khrushchev sent a desperate telegram, suggesting that he was near the breaking point. Robert Kennedy and others engaged in frantic negotiations through intermediaries. Then Khrushchev backed down. He recalled the ships, withdrew the missiles, and reduced his military establishment in Cuba to modest proportions. In response, Kennedy lifted the blockade. He also promised not to invade Cuba, thus ensuring Castro's survival; Kennedy further agreed to withdraw U.S. missiles from Turkey, though this latter concession was not made public at the time.

Immediately the president was hailed for his steady nerve and consummate states-manship; the Cuban missile crisis was widely regarded as his finest hour. Yet in retrospect it appears that he may have overreacted. The Soviet nuclear threat had been exaggerated. After *Sputnik*, the Soviet long-range missile program flopped, though this was not known at the time. By the summer of 1962 a "missile gap" existed, but it was overwhelmingly in favor of the United States, whose nuclear forces outnumbered those of the Soviet Union by a ratio of seventeen to one. Khrushchev's decision to put medium-range missiles in Cuba signified Soviet weakness rather than impending aggression. Both Kennedy and Khrushchev were sobered by the **Cuban missile crisis**. They signed a treaty outlawing nuclear testing in the atmosphere. But Khrushchev's bluff had been called—a public humiliation from which he never recovered. Within two years, hard-liners in the Kremlin forced him out of office. He was replaced by Leonid Brezhnev, an old-style Stalinist who inaugurated an intensive program of long-range missile development. The nuclear arms race moved to new terrain, uncertain and unimaginably dangerous.

JFK's Vietnam War

Truman's attempt to prevent Ho Chi Minh's communist insurgents from seizing Vietnam failed when the French army surrendered to Ho's troops at Dien Bien Phu in 1954. Eisenhower, equally unwilling to accept a communist victory, then supported creation of an anticommunist South Vietnam, headed by Ngo Dinh Diem, a Vietnamese nationalist who hated the communists. While the United States poured millions of dollars into strengthening Diem's South Vietnam, and especially its army, Ho Chi Minh consolidated his rule in North Vietnam. Those Viet Minh units that remained in the South—they came to be known as Vietcong—were instructed to form secret cells and bide their time. During the late 1950s they gained in strength and militancy.

In May 1959 Ho decided that the time had come to overthrow Diem. Vietcong guerril-las infiltrated thousands of villages, ambushed South Vietnamese convoys, and assassinated government officials. Soon the Vietcong controlled large sections of the countryside, some almost within sight of the capital city of Saigon.

Kennedy sharply increased the American military and economic commitment to South Vietnam. At the end of 1961 there were 3,200 American military personnel in the country; within two years, there were more than 16,000, and 120 American soldiers had been killed. Despite the expanded effort, by the summer

In the summer of 1963, Buddhist monks protested against the rule of Diem (and his brother, the Catholic archbishop of Vietnam) by setting themselves on fire.

of 1963 Diem's regime was in ruins. Unable to persuade Diem to moderate his policies, Kennedy sent word to dissident Vietnamese generals of his willingness to support them if they ousted Diem. On November 1 several of these generals surrounded the presidential palace with troops and tanks, seized Diem, and killed him. Kennedy, though appalled by Diem's death, recognized the new junta. The decision to overthrow Diem was fateful; it committed the United States to finding a solution to a worsening situation in Vietnam.

"We Shall Overcome": The Civil Rights Movement

In February 1960 four African American college students in Greensboro, North Carolina, sat down at a lunch counter at a Woolworth's store. "We do not serve Negroes," they were told. They returned with more and more demonstrators. By the end of the week over a thousand protesters descended on Woolworth's, led by a phalanx of football players from the nearby black college who cleared the way through a throng of Confederate flag-wavers.

This "sit-in" tactic was not new. But the Greensboro students sparked a national movement; students in dozens of other southern towns and cities copied their example.

●▪●[Read the Document

Charles Sherrod, *SNCC Memorandum (1961)* at myhistorylab.com

Soon more than fifty sit-ins were in progress in southern cities. By the end of 1961 over 70,000 people had participated in such demonstrations. Still another new organization, the **Student Nonviolent Coordinating Committee (SNCC)**, was founded by black college students in 1960 to provide a focus for the sit-in movement and to conduct voter registration drives in the South, actions that more than any other roused the fury of southern segregationists.

This protracted struggle eventually yielded practical and moral benefits for southern whites as well as blacks. Gradually all but the most unwavering defenders of segregation changed their attitudes. But this took time, and many blacks were unwilling to wait.

Some blacks, contemptuous of white prejudices, were urging their fellows to reject "American" society and all it stood for. In the North, black nationalism became a potent force. Elijah Muhammad, leader of the Black Muslim movement, loathed whites so intensely that he demanded that a part of the United States be set aside exclusively for blacks. He urged his followers to be industrious, thrifty, and abstemious—and to view all whites with suspicion and hatred.

"This white government has ruled us and given us plenty hell, but the time has arrived that you taste a little of your own hell," Muhammad said. He scorned Martin Luther King, Jr., and others who advocated Christian nonviolence. Another important Black Muslim, Malcolm X, put it this way in a 1960 speech: "For the white man to ask the black man if he hates him is just like the rapist asking the raped, or the wolf asking the sheep, 'Do you hate me?'"

Whites pour mustard and ketchup over black students (and one white) who were integrating a lunch-counter.

Ordinary southern blacks became increasingly impatient. In the face of brutal repression by local police, many began to question Martin Luther King's tactic of nonviolent protest. After leading a series of demonstrations in Birmingham, Alabama, in 1963, King was thrown in jail. When local white clergymen, professing themselves sympathetic to the blacks' objectives, nonetheless urged an end to "untimely" protests, which (they claimed) "incite hatred and violence," King wrote his now-famous "Letter from Birmingham Jail," which contained this moving explanation of why he and his followers were unwilling to wait any longer for justice:

Watch the Video
Civil Rights Movement at
myhistorylab.com

> [W]hen you take a cross-country drive and find it necessary to sleep night after night in the uncomfortable corners of your automobile because no motel will accept you; when you are humiliated day in and day out by nagging signs reading "white" and "colored"; when your first name becomes "nigger" and your middle name becomes "boy" . . . then you will understand why we find it so difficult to wait.

Source: Copyright 1963 Dr. Martin Luther King Jr; copyright renewed 1991 Coretta Scott King.

The brutal repression of the Birmingham demonstrations, captured in newspaper photos and on television broadcasts, brought a flood of recruits and money to the protesters' cause. Pushed by all these developments, President Kennedy reluctantly began to change his policy. His administration had from the start given lip service to desegregation and encouraged activists' efforts to register black voters in the South, but when confrontations arose the president hesitated, arguing that it was up to local officials to enforce the law. After Birmingham, however, Kennedy supported a modest civil rights bill.

When this measure ran into stiff opposition in Congress, blacks organized a demonstration in Washington, attended by 200,000 people. At this gathering, King delivered his "I Have a Dream" address, looking forward to a time when racial prejudice no longer existed and people of all religions and colors could join hands and say, "Free at last!" Kennedy sympathized with the Washington gathering but feared it would make passage of the civil rights bill more difficult. As in other areas, he was not a forceful advocate of his own proposals.

Watch the Video
Civil Rights March on Washington at
myhistorylab.com

Tragedy in Dallas: JFK Assassinated

Through it all, Kennedy retained his hold on public opinion. In the fall of 1963 most observers believed he would win a second term. Then, while visiting Dallas, Texas, on November 22, he was shot in the head by an assassin, Lee Harvey Oswald, and died almost instantly.

Kennedy's assassination precipitated an extraordinary series of events. Oswald had fired on the president with a rifle from an upper story of a warehouse. No one saw him pull the trigger. He was apprehended largely because he panicked and killed a policeman across town later in the day. He denied his guilt, but a mass of evidence connected him with the assassination of the president. Before he could be brought to trial, however, he was himself murdered by Jack Ruby, the owner of a Dallas nightclub. The incident took place in full view of television cameras, while Oswald was being transferred from one place of detention to another.

Each day brought new revelations. Oswald had defected briefly to the Soviet Union in 1959, then had returned to the United States and formed a pro-Castro organization in New Orleans. Many concluded that some nefarious conspiracy lay at the root of the tragedy. Oswald, the argument ran, was a pawn—either of communists or anticommunists—whose murder was designed to shield from exposure the masterminds who had engineered the assassination. A special commission headed by Chief Justice Earl Warren was convened to analyze the evidence. After a lengthy investigation, it concluded that Oswald had acted alone.

Instead of dampening charges of conspiracy, the report of the Warren Commission provoked new doubts. As word leaked out about the earlier CIA assassination attempts against Castro, the failure of the Warren Report even to mention Operation Mongoose made the commission suspect, all the more so since several members, including Allen Dulles, former director of the CIA, had known of the operation. While, there is little solid evidence to suggest that Oswald was part of a wider conspiracy, the decision of Dulles and other commissioners to protect CIA secrets engendered skepticism.

One measure of Kennedy's hold on the public imagination was the outpouring of grief that attended his death. Kennedy had given hope to people who had none. Young black civil rights activist Anne Moody, who later wrote *Coming of Age in Mississippi*, was working as a waitress in a segregated restaurant. "Tears were burning my cheeks," she recalled. Her boss, a Greek immigrant, gently suggested she take the rest of the day off. When she looked up, there were tears in his eyes too.

JFK and Jacqueline Kennedy ride in a motorcade with Texas Governor John Connolly and his wife in Dallas, November 22, 1963. Several minutes later, Kennedy was shot and killed; Connolly was wounded.

Lyndon Baines Johnson: The Great Society

John F. Kennedy's death made Lyndon B. Johnson president. From 1949 until his election as vice president, Johnson had been a senator from Texas and, for most of that time, Senate Democratic leader. Many people swore by him; few had the fortitude to swear at him. Above all he knew what to do with political power.

Johnson, who had consciously modeled his career after that of Franklin D. Roosevelt, considered social welfare legislation his specialty. The contrast with Kennedy could not have been sharper. Kennedy's plans for federal aid for education, urban renewal, a higher minimum wage, and medical care for the aged were blocked in Congress by Republicans and southern Democrats. But Kennedy had reacted to these defeats mildly, almost wistfully. He thought the machinery of the federal government was cumbersome and ineffective.

Johnson knew how to make it work. On becoming president, he pushed hard for Kennedy's programs. Early in his career Johnson had voted against a bill making lynching a federal crime, and he also had opposed bills outlawing state poll taxes and establishing the federal Fair Employment Practices Commission. But after he became an important figure in national affairs, he consistently championed racial equality. Bills long buried in committee sailed through Congress. Early in 1964 Kennedy's tax cut was passed. A few months later, an expanded version of another Kennedy proposal became law as the **Civil Rights Act of 1964.**

The much-strengthened Civil Rights Act outlawed discrimination by employers against blacks and also against women. It broke down legal barriers to black voting in the southern states and outlawed racial segregation of all sorts in places of public accommodation, such as movie theaters, hotels, and restaurants. In addition, unlike presidents Eisenhower and Kennedy, Johnson established agencies to enforce civil rights legislation.

Johnson's success in steering the Civil Rights Act through Congress confirmed his belief that he could be a reformer in the tradition of Franklin Roosevelt. He declared war on poverty and set out to create a **Great Society** in which poverty no longer would exist.

In 1937 Roosevelt had been accused of exaggeration for claiming that one-third of the nation was "ill-housed, ill-clad, ill-nourished." In fact Roosevelt had underestimated the extent of poverty. Wartime economic growth reduced the percentage of poor people in the country substantially, but in 1960 between 20 and 25 percent of all American families—about 40 million people—were living below the poverty line, a government standard of minimum subsistence based on income and family size.

The presence of so many poor people in an affluent society was deplorable but not difficult to explain. In any community a certain number of people cannot support themselves because of physical, mental, or emotional problems. The United States also included entire regions, the best known being Appalachia, that had been bypassed by economic development and no longer provided their inhabitants with adequate economic opportunities.

Moreover, prosperity and advancing technology had changed the definition of poverty. Telephones, radios and electric refrigerators, and other goods unimaginable to the most affluent Americans of the 1860s, were necessities a hundred years later. But as living standards rose, so did job requirements. Technology was changing the labor market. Educated workers with special skills and good verbal abilities easily found well-paid jobs. Those who had no special skills or were poorly educated went without work.

The Economic Opportunity Act of 1964 created a mixture of programs, among them a Job Corps similar to the New Deal Civilian Conservation Corps, a community

LBJ cultivated the masculine image of a Texas cowboy. Biographers have suggested that Johnson was torn between the expectations of his father, a crude local politician who flouted polite society, and those of his mother, a refined woman who insisted that her son read poetry and practice the violin. Johnson later told biographer Doris Kearns Goodwin that he persisted in Vietnam because he worried that critics would accuse him of being "an unmanly man. A man without a spine."

action program to finance local antipoverty efforts, and a system for training the unskilled unemployed and for lending money to small businesses in poor areas. The programs combined the progressive concept of government aid for those in need with the conservative idea of individual responsibility.

Buttressed by his legislative triumphs, Johnson sought election as president in his own right in 1964. He achieved this ambition in unparalleled fashion. His championing of civil rights won him the almost unanimous support of blacks; his tax policy attracted the well-to-do and the business interests; his war on poverty held the allegiance of labor and other traditionally Democratic groups. His down-home southern antecedents counterbalanced his liberalism on the race question in the eyes of many white southerners.

The Republicans played into his hands by nominating the conservative Senator Barry M. Goldwater of Arizona, whose objective in Congress had been "not to pass laws but to repeal them." As a presidential candidate he favored such laissez-faire policies

Table 29.1 Making a "Great Society"

Assisted Group	Legislation and Provisions
African Americans	Civil Rights Act (1964): Outlawed discrimination in employment, public accommodations, and federally-funded programs
	Voting Rights Act (1965): Federal registrars sent to the South
Elderly	Medicare (1965): Federally-funded medical care for elderly
Low-income people	Economic Opportunity Act (1964): Federally-funded antipoverty programs and agencies
	Medicaid (1965): Federally-funded health care for welfare recipients
	Housing and Urban Development Act: Federally-funded housing projects and rent support
Students	Elementary and Secondary Education Act (1965): Federal support for public and parochial schools for texts and materials, and for Head Start
	Higher Education Act (1965): Federally-funded loans and scholarships for college students

as cutting back on the Social Security system and doing away with the Tennessee Valley Authority. A large majority of voters found Goldwater out-of-date on economic questions and dangerously aggressive on foreign affairs.

In November, Johnson won a sweeping victory, collecting over 61 percent of the popular vote and carrying the whole country except Goldwater's Arizona and five states in the Deep South.

Quickly Johnson pressed ahead with his Great Society program. In January 1965 he proposed a compulsory hospital insurance system, known as **Medicare**, for all persons over the age of sixty-five. As amended by Congress, the Medicare Act consisted of Part A, hospital insurance for the elderly (funded by increased Social Security taxes), and a voluntary plan, Part B, covering doctors' bills (paid for in part by the government). The law also provided for grants to the states to help pay the medical expenses of poor people, even those below the age of sixty-five. This part of the system was called Medicaid. Before the passage of the Medicare Act, about half of Americans over sixty-five years old had no medical insurance.

Next, Congress passed the Elementary and Secondary Education Act in 1965, which supplied federal funds to school districts; the Higher Education Act (1965), which provided financial aid to college students; and Head Start, a program to prepare poor preschoolers for elementary school. It also provided medical examinations and nutritious meals for children.

Still another important reform was the **Voting Rights Act of 1965**, pressed through Congress by President Johnson after more brutal repressions of civil rights demonstrators in the South. This law provided for federal intervention to protect black registration and voting in six southern states. It applied to state and local as well as federal elections.

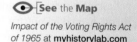

See the **Map**

Impact of the Voting Rights Act of 1965 at **myhistorylab.com**

Other laws passed at Johnson's urging in 1965 and 1966 included the creation of the National Endowment for the Arts and the National Endowment for the Humanities and measures supporting scientific research, highway safety, crime control, slum clearance, clean air, and the preservation of historic sites. Of particular significance was the Immigration Act of 1965, which did away with most provisions of the national-origin system of admitting newcomers. Instead, 290,000 persons a year were to be admitted on the basis of such priorities as job skills and need for political asylum. The law also placed a limit of 120,000 immigrants a year from countries in the Western Hemisphere. Previously, immigration from these countries had been unrestricted.

The Great Society program was one of the most remarkable outpourings of important legislation in American history. On balance, the achievements of the Great Society were far below what President Johnson had promised and his supporters had envisioned. Despite his long political experience, Johnson tried to accomplish too many things too quickly. He relied too heavily on the techniques of political manipulation. Without the crisis atmosphere that had appeared to justify hasty experimentation during the New Deal years, the public judged the results of the Great Society and the president who had shaped it skeptically.

New Racial Turmoil

One reason for skepticism was that the adoption of the Great Society coincided with increasing racial polarization. Black militancy, building steadily during World War II and the

Watch the **Video**

Malcolm X at **myhistorylab.com**

Police watch as the Watts section of Los Angeles burns during riots in August, 1965.

postwar years, burst forth in the mid-1960s. An important illustration was the response of Black Muslims to Malcolm X's 1964 decision to abandon the organization. A trip to the Middle East had exposed him to Islamic doctrines of racial equality and the brotherhood of man. In response he founded the Organization of Afro-American Unity. In 1965, while making a speech in favor of racial harmony, he was assassinated by Black Muslim fanatics.

Even Martin Luther King, Jr., the herald of nonviolent resistance, became more aggressive. "We are not asking, we are demanding the ballot," he said in January 1965. A few weeks after Malcolm's death, King led a march from Selma, Alabama, to Montgomery as part of a campaign to force Alabama authorities to allow blacks to register to vote. King chose Selma because the county in which it was located had a black majority but only 325 registered black voters. He expected the authorities to react brutally, thus attracting public sympathy for the marchers, and he was not disappointed. His marchers were assaulted by state policemen who wielded clubs and tossed canisters of tear gas.

Many African Americans lost patience with nonviolence. "The time for running has come to an end," declared Stokely Carmichael, chairman of the Student Nonviolent Coordinating Committee (SNCC). "It's time we stand up and take over." He began chanting "Black Power!" and other African-Americans chimed in. Black Power caught on swiftly among militants. This troubled white liberals, who feared that Black Power would antagonize white conservatives. They argued that since blacks made up only about 11 percent of the population, any attempt to obtain racial justice through the use of naked power was sure to fail.

•••—[Read the Document
Black Power 1967 at
myhistorylab.com

Meanwhile, black anger erupted in a series of destructive urban riots. The most important occurred in Watts, a ghetto of Los Angeles, in August 1965. A trivial incident brought thousands into the streets. The neighborhood almost literally exploded: For six days Watts was swept by fire, looting, and bloody fighting between local residents and nearly 15,000 National Guardsmen, called up to assist the police. The following two summers saw similar outbursts in scores of cities.

•••—[Read the Document
Watts Riots 1967 at
myhistorylab.com

Then, in April 1968, Martin Luther King, Jr., was murdered in Memphis, Tennessee, by a white man, James Earl Ray. Blacks in more than a hundred cities unleashed their anger in outbursts of burning and looting. The death of King appeared to destroy the hope that his peaceful appeal to reason and right could solve the problems of racism.

The most frightening aspect of the riots was their tendency to polarize society on racial lines. Whites fled to the suburbs in droves. Advocates of Black Power became more determined to separate themselves from white influence; they exasperated white supporters of school desegregation by demanding schools of their own. Extremists formed the Black Panther party and collected weapons to resist the police. "Shoot, don't loot," the radical H. Rap Brown advised all who would listen.

From the "Beat Movement" to Student Radicalism

The increased militancy of many American blacks paralleled the emergence of an increasingly strident attitude among many young people as the "conformist" decade of the 1950s gave way to the "activist" 1960s.

This common characterization, however, is overdrawn. The roots of 1960s' dissent were firmly planted in the 1950s. J. D. Salinger, perhaps the most popular writer of the decade and the particular favorite of college students—*The Catcher in the Rye* (1951) sold nearly 2 million copies—wrote about young people whose self-absorption was a product of their alienation from society. Allen Ginsberg's dark, desperate *Howl*, written in 1955, perhaps the most widely read poem of the postwar era, underscored generational differences. "I saw the best minds of my generation destroyed by madness, starving hysterical naked," the poem begins. In *On the Road* (1957), Jack Kerouac, founder of the **beat** (for "beatific") **school**, described a manic, drug-laced flight from traditional values and institutions. In *Catch-22* (1955), Joseph Heller produced a war novel at once farcical and an indignant denunciation of the stupidity and waste of warfare.

But if the "beats" were a fringe group of poets and musicians, their successors in the 1960s—generally known as hippies—could be found in large groups in every big city in the United States and Europe. They were so "turned off" by the modern world that they retreated from it, finding refuge in communes, drugs, and mystical religions. They were disgusted by the dishonesty and sordid antics of so many of the politicians, horrified by the brutality of Vietnam, appalled by racism, and contemptuous of the smugness they encountered in colleges and universities. But they rejected activism. Theirs was a world of folk songs and blaring acid rock music, of "be-ins," "love-ins," casual sex, and drugs. But the 1960s also witnessed the emergence of a new activism. Many students were frustrated by persistent racism and bigotry, but they regarded these as symptoms of a right-wing "power elite" of corporate executives and military and political leaders—a concept outlined in a book of that title by Columbia sociologist C. Wright Mills. In 1962 a

small group of students in the **Students for a Democratic Society (SDS)** put together a manifesto for action at a meeting at Port Huron, Michigan: Their main concerns were racial bigotry, the bomb, and the "disturbing paradoxes" associated with these concerns. SDS sought to wrest power from the "military-industrial" complex and institute a radical socialist government. SDS grew, powered by rising college enrollments and a seemingly unending list of local campus issues. The first great student outburst convulsed the University of California at Berkeley in the fall of 1964. Angry students, many veterans of the 1964 fight for black rights in the South, staged sit-down strikes in university buildings to protest the prohibition of political canvassing on the campus. This free speech movement

A young man perches in a tree with a guitar at Woodstock, a drug- and water-logged music festival that attracted 500,000 to rural New York in 1968.

disrupted the institution over a period of weeks. Hundreds were arrested, the state legislature threatened reprisals, the faculty became involved in the controversy, and the crisis led to the resignation of the president of the University of California, Clark Kerr.

But what transformed student activism from being a local campus irritation to a mass political movement was the decision by Lyndon Johnson to escalate the war in Vietnam.

Johnson Escalates the War

After Diem's assassination in 1963, the situation in South Vietnam worsened. One military coup followed another, and political instability aggravated military incapacity. President Johnson nevertheless felt that he had no choice but to prop up the South Vietnamese regime.

Johnson decided to punish North Vietnam directly for prosecuting the war in the South. In early 1964 he secretly ordered American warships to escort the South Vietnamese navy on commando missions far into the Gulf of Tonkin. After one such mission, American destroyers were fired on by North Vietnamese gunboats. Several nights later during a heavy storm, American ships reported that they were being fired on, though the enemy was never spotted. Using this Tonkin "incident" as pretext, Johnson demanded, and in an air of crisis obtained,

●◦●─[Read the Document

The Gulf of Tonkin Resolution Message at **myhistorylab.com**

an authorization from Congress to "repel any armed attack against the forces of the United States and to prevent further aggression." With this blank check, known as the **Gulf of Tonkin Resolution**, Johnson authorized air attacks in

From 1965 to 1968, American troops in Vietnam conducted "search and destroy" missions to shatter the insurgents. Here a soldier watches as a village is burned.

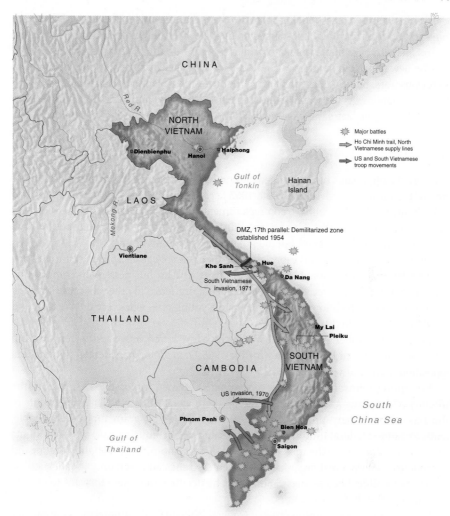

CHINA

Red R.

NORTH
VIETNAM

Dienbienphu   Haiphong
              Hanoi

Gulf of
Tonkin

Hainan
Island

Mekong R.

LAOS

Vientiane

DMZ, 17th parallel: Demilitarized zone
established 1954

Khe Sanh   Hue

South Vietnamese
invasion, 1971   Da Nang

THAILAND

My Lai
Pleiku

SOUTH
VIETNAM

CAMBODIA

US invasion, 1970

South
China Sea

Phnom Penh

Bien Hoa

Gulf of
Thailand

Saigon

✳ Major battles

➡ Ho Chi Minh trail, North
Vietnamese supply lines

➡ US and South Vietnamese
troop movements

The Vietnam War, 1961–1975 As American bombing and "search and destroy" missions spread throughout South Vietnam, North Vietnamese supply lines moved westward, into Laos and Cambodia. U.S. troops and bombers attacked there as well. This destabilized Cambodia, which fell to the brutal Khmer Rouge communists in 1975.

North Vietnam. By the summer of 1965, American bombers were conducting some 5,000 raids each month.

But the hail of bombs on North Vietnam had little effect on the struggle in the South. Worse, the Vietcong expanded the areas under their control. After a fact-finding mission in the war zone, McGeorge Bundy concluded that the prospects were grim for South Vietnam. "The energy and persistence of the Vietcong are astonishing," he reported. "They have accepted extraordinary losses and they come back for more. They show skill in their sneak attacks and ferocity when cornered." If the war was to be won, American soldiers—lots of them—would have to do much of the fighting themselves.

In July 1965 Johnson ordered the first of several huge increases in American ground forces. By the end of 1965, 184,000 Americans were in the field; a year later, 385,000; and after another year, 485,000. By the middle of 1968 the number exceeded 538,000. Each increase was met by corresponding increases from the other side. The Soviet Union and China sent no combat troops, but stepped up their aid, and thousands of North Vietnamese regulars filtered across the seventeenth parallel to fight with the Vietcong guerrillas.

The new American strategy was not to seize any particular battlefield or terrain as in all previous wars, but to kill as many of the enemy as possible through bloody "search and destroy" operations. As the scope of the action broadened, the number of American casualties rose. The United States was engaged in a full-scale war, one that Congress never declared.

The Election of 1968

Gradually the opponents of the war gained numbers and strength. They began to include some of the president's advisers. By late 1967 Secretary of Defense McNamara, who had methodically tracked kill ratios, troop replacement rates, and nearly every other conceivable statistic, concluded that "the figures didn't add up" and the war could not be won. Deeply despondent, he resigned, but did not publicly admit his doubts.

Opposition to the war was especially vehement on college campuses, some students objecting because they thought the United States had no business intervening in the Vietnam conflict, others because they feared being drafted, still others because so many students obtained educational deferments, while young men who were unable to attend college were conscripted.

Then, in November 1967, Eugene McCarthy, a low-keyed, introspective senator from Minnesota, announced his candidacy for the 1968 Democratic presidential nomination. Opposition to the war was his issue.

Preventing Johnson from being renominated seemed impossible. Aside from the difficulty of defeating a "reigning" president, there were the domestic achievements of Johnson's Great Society program: the health insurance program for retired people, greatly expanded federal funding of education and public housing, and the Civil Rights Act. Even Senator McCarthy took his chances of being nominated so lightly that he did not trouble to set up a real organization. He entered the campaign only to "alleviate . . . this sense of political helplessness." Someone, he decided, must step forward to put the Vietnam question before the voters.

Stung by the critics, Johnson ordered General William C. Westmoreland, commander of American forces in Vietnam, to reassure the American people on the course of the war. The general obligingly returned to the United States in late 1967 and told the press that he could see "some light at the end of the tunnel."

Suddenly, early in 1968, on the heels of this announcement, North Vietnamese and Vietcong forces launched a general offensive to correspond with their Lunar New Year (called Tet). Striking thirty-nine of the forty-four provincial capitals, many other towns and cities, and every American base, they caused chaos throughout South Vietnam. They held Hué, the old capital of the country, for weeks. To root insurgents out of Saigon the Americans had to level large sections of the city.

The **Tet offensive** was essentially a series of raids; the communists did not expect to hold the cities indefinitely, and they did not. Their losses were enormous. Nevertheless the psychological impact in South Vietnam and in the United States made Tet a clear victory for the communists. American pollsters reported an enormous shift of public opinion against further escalation of the fighting. When Westmoreland described Tet as a communist defeat and yet requested an additional 206,000 troops, McCarthy, who was

Table 29.2 Major Events in the Vietnam War, 1961–1968

1961	JFK dispatches thousands of U.S. military "advisers" to South Vietnam
1963	Vietnamese Buddhists rebel; United States supports overthrow of Diem
1964	LBJ obtains Gulf of Tonkin Resolution to expand war
1965	LBJ greatly increases U.S. troop levels
1968	Tet Offensive throughout South Vietnam; LBJ decides not to seek reelection; My Lai Massacre

campaigning in the New Hampshire primary, suddenly became a formidable figure. Thousands of students and other volunteers flocked to the state to ring doorbells on his behalf. On primary election day he polled 42 percent of the Democratic vote. This prompted former attorney general Robert F. Kennedy, brother of the slain president, to declare his candidacy for the Democratic nomination. Like McCarthy, Kennedy opposed Johnson's Vietnam policies but thought his chances of winning were better than McCarthy's.

Confronting this division in the ranks, President Johnson realized he could no longer hope to be an effective president. In a surprising televised announcement, he withdrew from the race. Vice President Hubert H. Humphrey then announced his candidacy, and Johnson threw the weight of his administration behind him.

Kennedy carried several primaries, including California. Immediately after his victory speech in a Los Angeles hotel, however, he was assassinated by Sirhan Sirhan, an Arab nationalist who had been incensed by Kennedy's support of Israel. In effect, Kennedy's death ensured the nomination of Humphrey.

The contest for the Republican nomination was far less dramatic, although its outcome, the nomination of Richard M. Nixon, would have been hard to predict a few years earlier. After his loss to Kennedy in 1960, Nixon ran unsuccessfully for governor of California in 1962, then moved to New York City and joined a prominent law firm. But he remained active in Republican affairs. In 1964 he had campaigned hard for Goldwater. When no other Republican developed extensive support as the 1968 election approached, Nixon entered the race, swept the primaries, and won an easy first-ballot victory at the Republican convention.

Nixon then astounded the country and dismayed liberals by choosing Governor Spiro T. Agnew of Maryland as his running mate. Agnew was a political unknown. Nixon chose him primarily to attract southern votes.

Placating the South seemed necessary because Governor George C. Wallace of Alabama was making a determined bid to win enough electoral votes for his American Independent party to prevent any candidate from obtaining a majority. Wallace was flagrantly anti-black and anti-intellectual. He denounced federal "meddling," the "coddling" of criminals, and the forced integration of schools.

This Republican strategy to win the South heightened the tension surrounding the Democratic convention, which met in Chicago in late August. Humphrey delegates controlled the convention. Several thousand activists, representing a dozen groups and advocating tactics ranging from orderly demonstrations to civil disobedience to indiscriminate violence, descended on Chicago to put pressure on the delegates to repudiate the Johnson Vietnam policy.

In the tense atmosphere that resulted, the party hierarchy overreacted. The mayor of Chicago, Richard J. Daley, whose ability to "influence" election results in a manner favorable to Democrats had often been demonstrated, ringed the convention with policemen to protect it from disruption. This was a reasonable precaution in itself. Inside the building the delegates nominated Humphrey and adopted a war plank satisfactory to Johnson. Outside, however, provoked by the abusive language and violent behavior of radical demonstrators, the police tore into the protesters, in novelist Norman Mailer's graphic phrase, "like a chain saw cutting into wood," while millions watched on television in fascinated horror.

The mayhem in Chicago seemed to benefit Nixon by strengthening the convictions of many voters that the tougher treatment of criminals and dissenters that he and Agnew were calling for was necessary. Those who were critical of the Chicago police tended to blame Humphrey, whom Mayor Daley supported.

Nixon campaigned at a deliberate, dignified pace. He made relatively few public appearances, relying instead on carefully arranged television interviews and taped commercials. He stressed firm enforcement of the law and his desire "to bring us together." As for Vietnam, he would "end the war and win the peace," by just what means he did not say. Agnew, in his blunt, coarse way, assaulted Humphrey, the Democrats, and left-wing dissident groups.

But gradually Humphrey gained ground, and on election day the popular vote was close: Nixon slightly less than 31.8 million, Humphrey nearly 31.3 million. Nixon's Electoral College margin, however, was substantial—301 to 191. The remaining 46 electoral votes went to Wallace, whose 9.9 million votes came to 13.5 percent of the total. Together, Nixon and Wallace received 57 percent of the popular vote.

Nixon as President: "Vietnamizing" the War

When he took office in January 1969, Richard Nixon projected an image of calm and deliberate statesmanship; he introduced no startling changes, proposed no important new legislation. He considered the solution of the Vietnam problem his chief task. Although he insisted during the 1968 campaign that he would end the war on "honorable" terms if elected, he suggested nothing very different from what Johnson was doing.

In office, Nixon first proposed a phased withdrawal of all non-South Vietnamese troops, to be followed by an internationally supervised election in South Vietnam. The North Vietnamese rejected this scheme and insisted that the United States withdraw its forces unconditionally. The intransigence of the North Vietnamese left the president in a difficult position. Nixon could not compel the foe to end a war it had begun against the French nearly a quarter of a century earlier, and every passing day added to the strength of antiwar sentiment, which in turn led to deeper divisions in the country. Yet Nixon could not face up to the consequences of ending the war on the communists' terms.

The president responded to the dilemma by trying to build up the South Vietnamese armed forces so that American troops could pull out without South Vietnam being overrun by the communists. He shipped so many planes to the Vietnamese that within four years they had the fourth-largest air force in the world. He also announced a series of troop cuts.

For a while, events appeared to vindicate Nixon's position. A gradual slowing of military activity in Vietnam had reduced American casualties. Troop withdrawals continued in an orderly fashion. A new lottery system for drafting men for military duty eliminated some of the inequities in the selective service law.

But the war continued. Early in 1970 reports that an American unit had massacred civilians, including dozens of women and children, in a Vietnamese hamlet known as

South Vietnamese women and children were among some 300 apparently unarmed civilians killed in the My Lai Massacre in 1968. Lieutenant William Calley was convicted of murder and sentenced to life in prison. After many appeals, he was released in 1974.

My Lai revived the controversy over the purposes of the war and its corrosive effects on those who were fighting it.

Nixon wanted to end the war but he did not want to lose it. The war's human, economic, and social costs could only vex his days and threaten his future reputation. When he reduced the level of the fighting, the communists merely waited for further reductions. When he raised it, many Americans denounced him in increasingly massive antiwar protests. If he pulled out of Vietnam and the communists won, other Americans would be outraged.

Perhaps Nixon's error lay in his unwillingness to admit his own uncertainty, something the greatest presidents—one thinks immediately of Lincoln and Franklin Roosevelt—were never afraid to do. Facing a dilemma, he tried to convince the world that he was firmly in control of events. Thus he heightened the tensions he sought to relax—in America, in Vietnam, and elsewhere.

The Cambodian "Incursion"

Late in April 1970 Nixon announced that Vietnamization was proceeding more rapidly than he had hoped, that communist power was weakening, and that within a year another 150,000 American soldiers would be extracted from Vietnam. A week later he announced that military intelligence had indicated that the enemy was consolidating its "sanctuaries" in neutral Cambodia and that he was therefore dispatching thousands of American troops to destroy these bases.

Nixon's shocking announcement triggered many campus demonstrations. One college where feeling ran high was Kent State University in Ohio. For several days students there clashed with local police; they broke windows and caused other damage to property. When the governor called out the National Guard, angry students showered the soldiers with stones. During a noontime protest on May 4 the guards-

▶ Watch the Video

Protests Against the Vietnam War at **myhistorylab.com**

men, who were poorly trained in crowd control, suddenly opened fire. Four students were killed, two of them women who were merely passing by on their way to class.

While the nation reeled from this shock, two students at Jackson State University were killed by Mississippi state policemen. A wave of student strikes followed, closing down hundreds of colleges, including many that had seen no previous unrest. Moderate students by the tens of thousands joined with the radicals.

The almost universal condemnation of the invasion and of the way it had been planned shook Nixon hard. He backtracked, pulling American ground troops out of Cambodia quickly. But he did not change his Vietnam policy, and in fact Cambodia apparently stiffened his determination. As American ground troops were withdrawn, he stepped up air attacks.

The balance of forces remained in uneasy equilibrium through 1971. But late in March 1972 the North Vietnamese again mounted a series of assaults throughout South Vietnam. Nixon responded with heavier bombing, and he ordered the approaches to Haiphong and other North Vietnamese ports sown with mines to cut off the communists' supplies.

Détente with Communism

But in the midst of these aggressive actions, Nixon and his National Security Adviser Henry Kissinger devised a bold diplomatic offensive, executed in nearly complete secrecy. Nixon and Kissinger made an effective though not always harmonious team. Abandoning a lifetime of treating communism as a single worldwide conspiracy that had to be contained at all costs, Nixon decided to deal with China and the Soviet Union as separate powers and, as he put it, to "live together and work together" with both. Nixon and Kissinger called the new policy **détente**, a French term meaning "the relaxation of tensions between governments." But détente was not an expression of friendship so much as an acknowledgment that for decades the policy of containment had driven China and the Soviet Union closer together.

First Nixon sent Kissinger secretly to China and the Soviet Union to prepare the way for summit meetings with the communist leaders. Both the Chinese and the Soviets agreed to the meetings. Then, in February 1972, Nixon and Kissinger, accompanied by a small army of reporters and television crews, flew to Beijing. After much dining, sightseeing, posing for photographers, and consultation with Chinese officials, Nixon agreed to promote economic and cultural exchanges and supported the admission of communist China to the United Nations. As a result, exports to communist China increased substantially, reaching $4 billion in 1980. Nixon's visit, ending more than twenty years of adamant American refusal to accept the reality of the Chinese revolution, marked a dramatic reversal; as such it was hailed throughout the world.

In May 1972 Nixon and Kissinger flew to Moscow. This trip also produced striking results. The mere fact that it took place while war still raged in Vietnam was remarkable. More important, however, the meeting resulted in a **Strategic Arms Limitation Treaty (SALT)**. The two powers agreed to stop making nuclear ballistic missiles and to reduce the number of antiballistic missiles in their arsenals to 200. Nixon also agreed to permit large sales of American grain to the Soviet Union.

By the summer of 1972, with the presidential election looming in the fall, Kissinger redoubled his efforts to negotiate an end to the Vietnam War. By October he and the North Vietnamese had hammered out a settlement calling for a cease-fire, the return of American prisoners of war, and the withdrawal of United States forces from Vietnam. Shortly before the presidential election Kissinger announced that peace was "at hand."

Nixon in Triumph

A few days later President Nixon was reelected, defeating the Democratic candidate, Senator George McGovern of South Dakota, in a landslide—521 electoral votes to 17. McGovern carried only Massachusetts and the District of Columbia. McGovern's campaign had been hampered by his tendency to advance poorly thought-out proposals, such as his scheme for funneling money directly to the poor, and by his rather bumbling, low-key oratorical style. The campaign marked the historical breakdown of the coalition that Franklin Roosevelt had fashioned and on which he and his Democratic successors, particularly Truman and Johnson, had ridden to power. Of that coalition, only African Americans voted solidly for McGovern.

Nixon had won over hundreds of thousands of voters who had supported Democrats in earlier elections. The "solid South" was again solid, but this time solidly Republican. Nixon's so-called southern strategy of reducing the pressure for school desegregation and otherwise restricting federal efforts on behalf of blacks had a powerful attraction to northern blue-collar workers as well.

Suddenly Nixon loomed as one of the most powerful and successful presidents in American history. His tough-minded but flexible handling of foreign policy questions, even his harsh Vietnamese policy, suggested decisiveness and self-confidence, qualities he had often seemed to lack in his earlier career. His willingness, despite his long history as a militant cold warrior, to negotiate with the communist nations indicated a new flexibility and creativity. His landslide victory appeared to demonstrate that a large majority of the people approved of his way of tackling the major problems of the times.

But Kissinger's agreement with the North Vietnamese came apart when Nguyen Van Thieu, the South Vietnamese president, refused to sign it. Thieu claimed that the agreement, by permitting communist troops to remain in the South, would ensure his ultimate defeat. To Kissinger's chagrin, Nixon sided with Thieu and resumed the bombing of North Vietnam in December 1972, this time sending the mighty B-52s directly over Hanoi and other cities. The destruction they caused was great, but their effectiveness as a means of forcing concessions from the North Vietnamese was at best debatable.

In January 1973 a settlement was finally reached. As with the October "agreement," the North Vietnamese retained control of large sections of the South, and they promised to

President and Mrs. Nixon dine with Chinese communist officials in Beijing in February 1972. Even Nixon's harshest critics conceded that his initiative in reopening United States-China relations was a diplomatic masterstroke.

release American prisoners of war within sixty days. Thieu assented this time, largely because Nixon secretly pledged that the United States would "respond with full force" if North Vietnam resumed its offensive. Within several months most prisoners of war were released, and the last American troops were pulled out of Vietnam. More than 57,000 Americans had died in the long war, and over 300,000 more had been wounded. Nearly a million communist soldiers and 185,000 South Vietnamese soldiers were reported killed.

In 1973, too, Kissinger was named secretary of state; he shared the Nobel Prize for Peace with a North Vietnamese diplomat for negotiating an end to the Vietnam War.

Domestic Policy under Nixon

When Nixon became president in 1969, the major economic problem he faced was inflation. This was caused primarily by the heavy military expenditures and easy-money policies of the Johnson administration. Nixon cut federal spending and balanced the 1969 budget, while the Federal Reserve Board forced up interest rates to slow the expansion of the money supply. When prices continued to rise, uneasiness mounted and labor unions demanded large wage increases.

In 1970 Congress passed a law giving the president power to regulate prices and wages. Nixon originally opposed this legislation, but in the summer of 1971 he changed his mind and announced a ninety-day price and wage freeze. Then he set up a pay board and a price commission with authority to limit wage and price increases when the freeze ended. These controls did not check inflation completely—and they angered union leaders, who felt that labor was being shortchanged—but they did slow the upward spiral.

In handling other domestic issues, the president was less firm. Like President Kennedy he was primarily interested in foreign affairs. He supported a bold plan for a "minimum income" for poor families, but dropped it when it alarmed his conservative supporters and got nowhere in Congress. But when a groundswell of public support for conserving natural resources and checking pollution led Congress to pass bills creating the **Environmental Protection Agency (EPA)** and the Clean Air Act of 1970, he signed them cheerfully.

After his triumphant reelection and the withdrawal of the last American troops from Vietnam, Nixon resolved to change the direction in which the nation had been moving

The Clean Air Act of 1970 mandated reductions in air pollution, arguably the most important environmental legislation passed by the United States during the twentieth century.

for decades. He announced that he intended to reduce the interference of the federal government in the affairs of individuals. People should be more self-reliant, he said, and he denounced what he called "permissiveness." Excessive concern for the interests of blacks and other minorities must end. Criminals should be punished "without pity." No person or group should be coddled by the state.

These aims brought Nixon into conflict with liberals in both parties, with the leaders of minority groups, and with those alarmed by the increasing power of the executive. The conflict came to a head over the president's anti-inflation policy. After his second inauguration he ended price and wage controls and called for voluntary "restraints." This approach did not work. Prices soared in the most rapid inflation since the Korean War. In an effort to check the rise, Nixon set a rigid limit on federal expenditures. To keep within the limit, he cut back or abolished a large number of social welfare programs and reduced federal grants in support of science and education. He even impounded (refused to spend) funds already appropriated by Congress for purposes of which he disapproved.

The impoundment created a furor on Capitol Hill, but when Congress failed to override his vetoes of bills challenging this policy, it appeared that Nixon was in total command. The White House staff, headed by H. R. Haldeman and John Ehrlichman, dominated the Washington bureaucracy. Critics began to grumble about a new "imperial presidency." No one seemed capable of checking Nixon.

The Watergate Break-In and Cover-Up

On March 19, 1973, James McCord, a former agent of both the Federal Bureau of Investigation and the Central Intelligence Agency accused of burglary, wrote a letter to the judge presiding at his trial. His act precipitated a series of disclosures that first disrupted and then destroyed the Nixon administration.

McCord had been employed during the 1972 presidential campaign as a security officer of the Committee to Re-elect the President (CREEP). At about 1 AM on June 17, 1972, he and four other men had broken into Democratic party headquarters at Watergate, a complex of apartments and offices in Washington. The burglars were members of an unofficial CREEP surveillance group known as "the plumbers." Nixon, who was compelled by a need to conceal information about his administration, had formed the group after the Pentagon Papers, a confidential report on government policy in Vietnam, had been leaked to the press. The "plumbers" had been caught rifling files and installing electronic eavesdropping devices.

Two other Republican campaign officials were soon implicated in the affair. Their arrest aroused suspicions that the Republican party was behind the break-in. Nixon denied it.

Most people evidently took the president at his word. He was far ahead in the polls and seemed so sure to win reelection that it was hard to believe he would stoop to burglary to discover what the Democrats were up to. In any case, the affair did not materially affect the election. When brought to trial early in 1973, most of the Watergate burglars pleaded guilty.

McCord, who did not, was convicted by the jury. Before Judge John J. Sirica imposed sentences on the culprits, however, McCord wrote his letter. High Republican officials had known about the burglary in advance and had paid the defendants "hush money" to keep their connection secret, McCord claimed. Perjury had been committed during the trial.

The truth of McCord's charges swiftly became apparent. The head of CREEP, Jeb Stuart Magruder, and President Nixon's lawyer, John W. Dean III, admitted their involvement. Among the disclosures that emerged over the following months were these:

- Large sums of money had been paid to the burglars at the instigation of the White House to ensure their silence.
- Agents of the Nixon administration had burglarized the office of a psychiatrist, seeking evidence against one of his patients, Daniel Ellsberg, who had been charged with leaking the Pentagon Papers to the *New York Times*. (This disclosure led to the immediate dismissal of the charges against Ellsberg.)
- CREEP officials had attempted to disrupt the campaigns of leading Democratic candidates during the 1972 primaries in a number of illegal ways.
- A number of corporations had made large contributions to the Nixon reelection campaign in violation of federal law.
- The Nixon administration had placed wiretaps on the telephones of some of its own officials as well as on those of journalists critical of its policies without first obtaining authorization from the courts.

These revelations led to the dismissal of John Dean and to the resignations of most of Nixon's closest advisers, including Haldeman, Ehrlichman, and Attorney Generals John Mitchell and Richard Kleindienst. They also raised the question of the president's personal connection with the **Watergate scandal**. This he steadfastly denied. He insisted that he would investigate the Watergate affair thoroughly and see that the guilty were punished. He refused, however, to allow investigators to examine White House documents, on grounds of executive privilege, which he continued to assert in very broad terms.

In the teeth of Nixon's denials, John Dean, testifying under oath, stated flatly and in circumstantial detail that the president had ordered him to pay the Watergate burglars to conceal White House involvement; if true, the president had been guilty of obstructing justice, a serious crime.

Dean had been a persuasive witness, but many people were reluctant to believe that a president could lie so cold-bloodedly to the entire country. Therefore, when it came out during later hearings of the Senate committee investigating the Watergate scandal that the president had systematically made secret tape recordings of White House conversations and telephone calls, the disclosure caused a sensation. It seemed obvious that these tapes would settle the question of Nixon's involvement once and for all. Again Nixon refused to allow access to the evidence.

One result of the scandals and of Nixon's attitude was a precipitous decline in his standing in public opinion polls. Calls for his resignation, even for impeachment, began to be heard. Yielding to pressure, he agreed to the appointment of an "independent" special prosecutor to investigate the Watergate affair, and he promised the appointee, Professor Archibald Cox of Harvard Law School, full cooperation.

Cox swiftly aroused the president's ire by seeking access to White House records, including the tapes. When Nixon refused to turn over the tapes, Cox obtained a subpoena from Judge Sirica ordering him to do so. The administration appealed this decision and lost in the appellate court. Then, while the case was headed for the Supreme Court, Nixon ordered the new attorney general, Elliot Richardson, to dismiss Cox. Both Richardson, who had promised the Senate during his confirmation hearings that the special prosecutor would have a free hand, and his chief assistant resigned rather than do as the president directed. The third-ranking officer of the Justice Department carried out Nixon's order.

These events of Saturday, October 20, promptly dubbed the Saturday Night Massacre, caused an outburst of public indignation. Congress was bombarded by thousands of letters and telegrams demanding the president's impeachment. The House Judiciary Committee began an investigation to see if enough evidence for impeachment existed.

Once again Nixon backed down. He agreed to turn over the tapes to Judge Sirica with the understanding that relevant materials could be presented to the grand jury investigating the Watergate affair but that nothing would be revealed to the public. He then named a new special prosecutor, Leon Jaworski, and promised him access to whatever White House documents he needed. However, it soon came out that several tapes were missing and that an important section of another had been deliberately erased.

Then Vice President Agnew was accused of income tax fraud and of having accepted bribes while serving as Baltimore county executive and governor of Maryland. To escape a jail term Agnew admitted in October that he had been guilty of tax evasion and resigned as vice president.

Acting according to the procedures for presidential and vice-presidential succession of the Twenty-Fifth Amendment, adopted in 1967, President Nixon nominated Representative Gerald R. Ford of Michigan as vice president, and he was confirmed by Congress. Ford had served continuously in Congress since 1949 and as minority leader since 1964. His positions on public issues were close to Nixon's; he was an internationalist in foreign affairs and a conservative and convinced Republican partisan on domestic issues.

The Judgment on Watergate: "Expletive Deleted"

Meanwhile, special prosecutor Jaworski continued his investigation of the Watergate scandals. In March 1974 a grand jury indicted Haldeman; Ehrlichman; former attorney general John Mitchell, who had been head of CREEP at the time of the break-in; and four other White House aides for conspiring to block the Watergate investigation. The jurors also named Nixon an "unindicted co-conspirator," Jaworski having informed them that their power to indict a president was constitutionally questionable. Judge Sirica thereupon turned over the jury's evidence against Nixon to the House Judiciary Committee.

In an effort to check the mounting criticism, late in April Nixon released edited transcripts of the tapes he had turned over to the court the previous November. In addition to much incriminating evidence, the transcripts provided the public with a fascinating and shocking view of how the president conducted himself in private. In conversations he seemed confused, indecisive, and lacking in any concern for the public interest. His repeated use of foul language, so out of keeping with his public image, offended millions. The phrase "expletive deleted," inserted in place of words considered too vulgar for publication in family newspapers, overnight became a catchword.

With the defendants in the Watergate case demanding access to tapes that they claimed would prove their innocence, Jaworski was compelled either to obtain them or to risk having the charges dismissed on the grounds that the government was withholding evidence. He therefore subpoenaed sixty-four additional tapes. Nixon refused to obey the subpoena. Swiftly the case of *United States v. Richard M. Nixon* went to the Supreme Court.

In the summer of 1974—after so many months of alarms and crises—the Watergate drama reached its climax. The Judiciary Committee, following months of study of the evidence behind closed doors, decided to conduct its deliberations in open session. While millions watched on television, thirty-eight members of the House of Representatives debated the charges and finally adopted three articles of impeachment. They charged the president with obstructing justice, misusing the powers of his office, and failing to obey the committee's subpoenas. Except in the case of the last article, many of the Republicans on the committee joined with the Democrats in voting aye, a clear indication that the full House would vote to impeach.

On the eve of the debates, the Supreme Court had ruled unanimously that the president must turn over the sixty-four subpoenaed tapes to the special prosecutor. Executive privilege had its place, the Court stated, but no person, not even a president, could "withhold evidence that is demonstrably relevant in a criminal trial."

When the subpoenaed tapes were released and transcribed, Nixon's fate was sealed. Three recorded conversations between the president and H. R. Haldeman just after the Watergate break-in proved conclusively that Nixon had tried to obstruct justice by engaging the CIA in an effort to persuade the FBI not to follow up leads in the case on the spurious grounds that national security was involved.

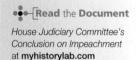

Read the Document

House Judiciary Committee's Conclusion on Impeachment at **myhistorylab.com**

When the House Judiciary Committee members read the new transcripts, all the Republican members who had voted against the impeachment articles reversed themselves. Republican leaders told the president categorically that the House would impeach him and that no more than a handful of senators would vote for acquittal.

Nixon Resigns, Ford Becomes President

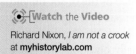

Watch the Video

Richard Nixon, I am not a crook at **myhistorylab.com**

On August 8, 1974, Nixon announced his resignation. The resignation took effect at noon on August 9, when Gerald Ford was sworn in as president. "Our long national nightmare is over," Ford declared. Within weeks of taking office, Ford pardoned Nixon for whatever crimes he had committed in office, even any, if such existed, as had yet come to light.

Whether Nixon's resignation marked the end of one era or the beginning of another is a difficult question. Like most critical moments in human history, it seems in retrospect to have been both. Nixon had extricated the United States from Vietnam—though at tremendous cost in lives and money and to little evident purpose. His détente with the Soviet Union and Red China was surely an early sign of the easing of Cold War tensions characteristic of the decades to follow. Moreover, Nixon's assault on liberals, coming just as public disillusionment with the Great Society programs was mounting, put an end to the liberal era that had begun with the reforms of the New Deal.

Milestones

1951	J. D. Salinger publishes *The Catcher in the Rye*
1955	Joseph Heller publishes *Catch*-22
	Allen Ginsberg publishes *Howl*
1957	Jack Kerouac publishes *On the Road*
1960	Black college students found Student Nonviolent Coordinating Committee (SNCC)
	John F. Kennedy elected President
1961	CIA-trained Cuban exiles launch disastrous Bay of Pigs invasion
	Soviets build Berlin wall
	John F. Kennedy founds Peace Corps
	Freedom riders integrate buses in South
1962	Soviet Premier Khrushchev precipitates Cuban missile crisis
	Students for a Democratic Society (SDS) issues Port Huron Statement
1963	United States supports coup to oust President Ngo Dinh Diem of South Vietnam
	Martin Luther King, Jr., gives "I Have a Dream" speech during March on Washington
	Lee Harvey Oswald assassinates President Kennedy; Lyndon Johnson becomes president
1964	Congress endorses escalation of Vietnam War in Gulf of Tonkin Resolution
	Lyndon Johnson is elected president, begins Great Society program
	Congress passes historic Civil Rights Act
	Free speech movement disrupts University of California at Berkeley
1965	Congress passes Immigration Act, ending national quota system
	Medicare Act pays some medical costs for senior citizens and the poor
	Congress funds education with Elementary and Secondary Education Act and Higher Education Act

1965	Black Muslim fanatics assassinate Malcolm X
1968	Communists strike all over South Vietnam in Tet Offensive
	Lyndon Johnson withdraws as candidate for reelection
	Martin Luther King, Jr., is assassinated
	Robert F. Kennedy is assassinated
	Richard Nixon is elected president
1969	Nixon announces "Vietnamization" of war
	Apollo 11 lands on the moon
1970	Nixon announces "incursion" into Cambodia
	Antiwar student protesters are killed at Kent State University and Jackson State University
	Congress passes Clean Air Act and creates Environmental Protection Agency (EPA)
1972	Nixon's "plumbers" burglarize Democratic national headquarters at Watergate complex
	Nixon and Kissinger visit China and Soviet Union
	United States and Soviet Union sign Strategic Arms Limitation Treaty (SALT)
	Nixon is reelected in landslide
1973	House Judiciary Committee begins impeachment hearings against Nixon
	Vice President Spiro Agnew resigns; Gerald Ford is appointed vice president
	Last American troops leave Vietnam
	Nixon fires Watergate special prosecutor Archibald Cox (Saturday Night Massacre)
1974	Supreme Court orders release of Nixon's White House tapes
	Nixon resigns; Gerald Ford becomes president and pardons Nixon

√•─⌐Study and Review at www.myhistorylab.com

Review Questions

1. The introduction emphasizes the difficulties JFK, LBJ, and Nixon had in getting out of the "quagmire" that was the Vietnam War. What might they have done differently? Why did they pursue the course they chose?

2. Why did the escalation of the war from 1961 to 1968 fail to produce a victory? How did Nixon change the Vietnam policies of his predecessors? Why didn't they succeed?

3. How did the war affect American society? What effect did student protests have on the war?

4. How did Johnson's Great Society differ from Franklin D. Roosevelt's New Deal? Which aspects of the Great Society proved most successful? Why did others fall short of expectations?

5. What explains the rise of Black Power during the 1960s? Why did the race riots strike just as the federal government was providing tangible assistance on matters of civil rights, racial discrimination, and poverty?

6. Why did Nixon form the "plumbers" and then obstruct justice following the Watergate break-in? Why did Ford pardon Nixon?

Key Terms

Bay of Pigs fiasco *762*
beat school *771*
Berlin wall *762*
Civil Rights Act
  of 1964 *767*
Cuban missile
  crisis *763*
détente *778*
Environmental Protection
  Agency (EPA) *780*

Great Society *767*
Gulf of Tonkin
  Resolution *772*
Medicare *769*
Strategic Arms Limitation
  Treaty (SALT) *778*
Student Nonviolent
  Coordinating
  Committee
  (SNCC) *764*

Students for a Democratic
  Society (SDS) *771*
Tet offensive *774*
United States v. Richard M.
  Nixon 784
Voting Rights Act
  of 1965 *769*
Watergate scandal *782*

Running on Empty: 1975–1991

((•—[Hear the Audio Chapter 30 at myhistorylab.com

Do you pay too much for gas?

DURING THE SUMMER OF 2008, WITH THE PRESIDENTIAL CAMPAIGN in full swing, gas prices topped $4 a gallon. Republican candidate John McCain called for laws allowing oil companies to drill for oil in U.S. coastal waters. Sarah Palin, Governor of oil-rich Alaska and McCain's running mate, put it more succinctly: "Drill, Baby, Drill!"

Senator Barack Obama had opposed offshore drilling. But as gas prices rose, his lead in the polls slipped. With the election less than two months away, Obama reversed course. Now he supported off-shore drilling. Democratic leaders in Congress, scrambling to clamber onto the offshore drilling bandwagon, pushed through a law ending the quarter-century old ban on drilling for oil in federal waters off the Atlantic and Pacific Coasts.

Then, in 2010, a British-owned oil rig forty miles off the coast of Louisiana exploded, killing eleven workers and releasing millions of barrels of crude oil into the Gulf of Mexico. The oil spill was arguably the worst environmental disaster in the nation's history.

For much of the twentieth century, the high cost and environmental risks of offshore oil drilling exceeded the projected profits of such ventures. But that changed in 1970s when the flow of crude oil to the United States and the West was cut off; the price of oil soared. Now offshore drilling made economic sense. Because most of the untapped oil lay beneath the oceans, offshore drilling platforms were built in the North Sea, off the coast of Brazil, and in the Gulf of Mexico.

For a nation dependent on the automobile, the 1970s oil shortage plunged the economy into a deep recession. Factories were closed and workers laid off. A new conservatism prevailed, part of a reaction against the costly measures of LBJ's Great Society. The need for cheap oil, moreover, pushed the United States deeper into the labyrinth of Middle Eastern politics. War would follow.

The Oil Crisis

While most Americans watched, transfixed, as the events of Watergate interred the Nixon presidency, few were aware that a battle on the other side of the world was about to transform their lives. On October 6, 1973, the eve of Yom Kippur, the Jewish Day of Atonement, Egypt and Syria attacked the state of Israel. Six years earlier Israel had trounced the

Egyptians with humiliating ease; it had then seized the Sinai peninsula and the West Bank of the Jordan River, an area including Jerusalem. But now Egypt's armored divisions roared into the Sinai and threatened to slice Israel in half; Syrian troops advanced against Israel farther north.

Israeli Prime Minister Golda Meir pleaded with President Nixon for additional arms and aircraft. The United States immediately airlifted scores of fighter planes and other desperately needed material to Israel. The Israelis recrossed the Suez Canal, cut Egyptian supply

After the Arab oil embargo, gasoline became so scarce that customers were limited to buying ten gallons at a time. This led to long lines at the pumps.

lines, and forced Egypt's president, Anwar Sadat, to capitulate. But the Arab world then aimed its biggest weapon squarely at the United States: It cut off oil shipments to the West.

Deprived of Middle Eastern oil, the American economy sputtered. The price of oil rose to $12 a barrel, up from $3. This sent prices soaring for nearly everything else. Homes were heated with oil, factories were powered by it, utility plants used it to generate electricity, and farm produce was shipped to markets on gas-fueled trucks. The Arab oil embargo pushed up gas prices; service stations intermittently ran out of gasoline; long lines formed at those that remained open.

In the spring of 1974, Henry Kissinger negotiated an agreement that required Israel's withdrawal from some territory occupied since the 1967 war; the Arab nations then lifted the oil embargo. But the principal oil exporting nations—Venezuela, Saudi Arabia, Kuwait, Iraq, and Iran—had learned a valuable lesson: If they limited production, they could drive up the price of oil. After the embargo had ended, their cartel, the **Organization of Petroleum Exporting Countries (OPEC)**, announced another price increase. Gasoline prices doubled overnight.

American automakers who had scoffed at tiny Japanese "boxes" now winced as these foreign competitors claimed the new market for small, fuel-efficient, front-wheel-drive cars. American auto companies were unable to respond to this challenge. As production costs rose, manufacturers needed to sell more of their behemoth models, loaded with expensive options such as air conditioning, power windows, and stereo systems. Because the automobile industry stimulated so many other industries—steel, vinyl, glass, rubber— the nation's manufacturing sector was soon in trouble.

Ford as President

Gerald Ford replaced Nixon as president in the summer of 1974, just as the economy was beginning to deteriorate. At first, the country greeted Ford with a collective sigh of relief. Most observers considered Ford unimaginative, certainly not brilliant. But he was hardworking, and—most important under the circumstances—his record was untouched by scandal.

Ford identified inflation as the chief economic culprit and asked patriotic citizens to signify their willingness to fight it by wearing WIN (Whip Inflation Now) buttons. Almost immediately the economy slumped. Production fell and the unemployment rate rose above 9 percent, about twice the postwar average. The president was forced to ask for tax cuts and other measures aimed at stimulating business activity. This made inflation worse and did little to promote employment.

The Fall of South Vietnam

Depressing news about the economy was compounded by disheartening events in Vietnam. In January 1975, after two years of a bloody "cease-fire", North Vietnam attacked just south of the seventeenth parallel, commencing its two-year plan to conquer South Vietnam. The South Vietnamese army retreated, then fled, and finally dissolved with a rapidity that astonished their attackers.

Ford had always supported the Vietnam War. As the military situation deteriorated, he urged Congress to pour more arms into the South to stem the North Vietnamese advance. The legislators flatly refused to do so, and on May 1, 1975, the Viet Cong and North Vietnamese entered Saigon, which they renamed Ho Chi Minh City. The long Vietnam War was finally over.

Ford versus Carter

Ford's uninspiring record on the economy and foreign policy suggested that he would be vulnerable in 1976. That year the Democrats chose Jimmy Carter, a former governor of Georgia, as their candidate.

Carter had been a naval officer and a substantial peanut farmer and warehouse owner before entering politics. He was elected governor of Georgia in 1970. While governor he won something of a reputation as a southern public official who treated black citizens fairly. Carter's political style was informal. During the campaign for delegates he turned his inexperience in national politics to advantage, emphasizing his lack of connection with the Washington establishment rather than apologizing for it. He repeatedly called attention to his integrity and deep religious faith.

Carter sought to make the election a referendum on morality. After Watergate, an atmosphere of scandal permeated Washington, and aspiring journalists and congressmen trained their sights on Kissinger, who

Georgia governor Jimmy Carter and President Gerald Ford debate in 1976. The campaign featured Carter's candor in a *Playboy* interview: "I've committed adultery in my heart many times." The headline stories often neglected the sentences that followed: "This is something that God recognizes I will do—and I have done it—and God forgives me for it."

remained secretary of state after Nixon's resignation. The most significant of the allegations was his meddling in the affairs of Chile, which in 1970 elected Salvador Allende, a Marxist, as president. After Allende's election, Kissinger called on the CIA to "destabilize" Allende's regime. In 1973, Allende was murdered in a military coup and his government toppled. Carter promised an administration of "constant decency" in contrast to Kissinger's penchant for secret diplomacy and covert skullduggery.

In the Republican primaries, Ford was challenged by Ronald Reagan, ex-governor of California, a movie actor turned politician who was the darling of the Republican right wing. Reagan was an excellent speaker, whereas Ford proved somewhat bumbling on the stump. Reagan, too, hammered away at Kissinger, citing his "immoral" détente with communist China. At Reagan's insistence, the Republican platform denounced "secret agreements, hidden from our people"—another jab at Kissinger.

Both Republican candidates gathered substantial blocs of delegates, but Ford staved off the Reagan challenge. That Ford did not win easily, possessed as he was of the advantage of incumbency, made his chances of election in November appear slim.

When the final contest began, both candidates were vague with respect to issues, a situation that hurt Carter particularly because he had made so much of honesty and straight talk. With both candidates stumbling toward the finish line, pundits predicted an extremely close contest, and they were right: Carter won, 297 electoral votes to 241, having carried most of the South, including Texas, and a few large industrial states. He also ran well in districts dominated by labor union members. The wish of the public to punish the party of Richard Nixon probably was a further reason for his victory.

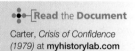

Watch the Video
Ford Presidential Campaign Ad: Feeling Good About America at **myhistorylab.com**

The Carter Presidency

Carter shone brightly in comparison with Nixon, and he seemed more forward-looking and imaginative than Ford. He tried to give a tone of democratic simplicity and moral fervor to his administration. After delivering his inaugural address he walked with his wife Rosalynn and their daughter Amy in the parade from the Capitol to the White House instead of riding in a limousine. They enrolled Amy, a fourth-grader, in a largely black Washington public school. Soon after taking office he held a "call-in"; for two hours he answered questions phoned in by people from all over the country.

Carter's actual administration of his office did not go nearly so well. He put so many Georgians in important posts that his administration took on a parochial character. The administration developed a reputation for submitting complicated proposals to Congress with great fanfare and then failing to follow up on them. Whatever matter Carter was considering at the moment seemed to absorb him totally—other urgent matters were allowed to drift.

A National Malaise

Read the Document
Carter, Crisis of Confidence (1979) at **myhistorylab.com**

To Carter, the nation's economic woes were symptomatic of a more fundamental flaw in the nation's soul. In a heralded television speech he complained that "a moral and spiritual crisis" had sapped people's energies and undermined civic pride. Critics responded that the nation needed a president rather than a preacher, and that sermons on the emptiness of consumption rang hollow to those who had lost their jobs.

The economic downturn, though triggered by the energy shortage, had more fundamental causes. In the prosperous postwar decades, many companies had grown too big and complacent, more attuned to the demands of the corporate bureaucracy than the needs of customers. Workers' boredom lowered productivity. Absenteeism at General Motors and Ford had doubled during the 1960s. On an average day in 1970, 5 percent of GM's workforce was missing without explanation, and on Mondays and Fridays 10 percent failed to show up. Two years later simmering discontents among young workers boiled over at the GM assembly division at Lordstown, Ohio. GM had installed robotic welding machines, streamlined the workforce, and accelerated the assembly line: 100 cars passed through the line each hour—40 more than under the previous system. Without authorization from the national UAW, younger workers refused to work at the faster pace, allowing many chassis to pass through untouched and throwing the factory into chaos.

Union membership slipped badly from the high point of the mid–1950s, when over one in three nonagricultural workers belonged to unions; by 1978, the proportion had declined to one in four, and by 1990, one in six. During the 1940s and 1950s, most workers voted to join a union, pay dues, and have the organization bargain for them. By 1978, however, union organizers were losing three-fourths of their campaigns to represent workers; and many workers who belonged to unions were opting to get out. Every year, 800 more union shops voted to rescind their affiliation.

The economic crisis after 1973 was unsettling because, for the first time in the nation's history, the rising tide of unemployment had failed to extinguish inflation. Millions of workers lost their jobs, yet wages and prices continued to rise. The term **stagflation** (a combination of stagnation and inflation) was coined to describe this anomaly. In 1971 an inflation rate of 5 percent had so alarmed President Nixon that he had imposed a price freeze. By 1975 inflation had soared to 11 percent and by 1979, it peaked at a whopping 13 percent; unemployment ranged from 6 to 10 percent, nearly twice the usual postwar level.

Carter had promised to fight inflation by reducing government spending and balancing the budget and to stimulate the economy by cutting taxes, policies that were very much like those of Nixon and Ford. He advanced an admirable if complicated plan for conserving energy and reducing the dependence of the United States on OPEC oil. This plan would raise the tax on

The skyrocketing price of oil caused many to champion nuclear energy. But on March 28, 1979, the failure of a cooling system caused the Three Mile Island nuclear reactor to overheat and generate radioactivity in the Harrisburg region. The reactor was shut down five days later.

gasoline and impose a new tax on "gas guzzlers," cars that got relatively few miles per gallon. But in his typical fashion he did not press hard for these measures.

The federal government made matters worse in several ways. Wages and salaries rose in response to inflation, but taxes went up more rapidly because larger dollar incomes put people in higher tax brackets. This "bracket creep" caused resentment and frustration among middle-class families. "Taxpayer revolts" erupted as many people turned against expensive government programs for aiding the poor. Federal borrowing to cover the deficit pushed up interest rates and increased the costs of all businesses that had to borrow.

Soaring mortgage rates made it difficult to sell homes. The housing slump meant unemployment for thousands of carpenters, bricklayers, and other construction workers and bankruptcy for many builders. Double-digit interest rates also hurt small businesses seeking to expand. Savings and loan institutions were especially hard-hit because they were saddled with countless mortgages made when rates were as low as 4 and 5 percent. Now they had to pay much more than that to hold deposits and offer even higher rates to attract new money.

Bad as inflation was in the mid-1970s, it got worse in 1979 when further instability in the Middle East nearly tripled the price of oil, which now reached $34 a barrel. This sent gasoline far over the $1 a gallon price barrier many had thought inconceivable. Within months Ford stock, at thirty-two in 1978, plummeted to sixteen; its credit rating with Standard and Poor's fell from AAA to an ignominious BBB. Chrysler, the third largest automaker, tottered near bankruptcy and then fell over the edge, saved in mid-fall only by a $1.2 billion federal loan guarantee. From 1978 to 1982, the jobs of one in three autoworkers were eliminated.

"Constant Decency" in Action

In contrast to the shadowy dealings of the Nixon-Kissinger years, Carter promised to conduct a foreign policy characterized by "constant decency." The defense of "basic human rights" would come before all other concerns. He then cut off aid to Chile and Argentina because of human rights violations. He also negotiated treaties with Panama that provided for the gradual transfer of the Panama Canal to that nation and guaranteed the canal's neutrality. But he said little about what was going on in a long list of other nations whose citizens' rights were being repressed.

The president also intended to carry forward the Nixon-Kissinger policy of détente, and in 1979 another Strategic Arms Limitation Treaty (SALT II) was signed with the Soviet Union. But the following winter the Soviet Union sent troops into Afghanistan to overthrow the government there. Carter denounced the invasion and warned the Soviets that he would use force if they invaded any of the countries bordering the Persian Gulf. He withdrew the SALT treaty, which he had sent to the Senate for ratification. He also refused to allow American athletes to compete in the 1980 Olympic games in Moscow.

Carter's one striking diplomatic achievement was the so-called **Camp David Accords** between Israel and Egypt. In September 1978 President Anwar Sadat of Egypt and Prime Minister Menachem Begin of Israel came to the United States at Carter's invitation to seek a peace treaty ending the state of war that had existed between their two countries for many years.

For two weeks they conferred at Camp David, the presidential retreat outside the capital, and Carter's mediation had much to do with their successful negotiations.

In the treaty Israel promised to withdraw from territory captured from Egypt during the 1967 Israeli-Egypt war. Egypt in turn recognized Israel as a nation, the first Arab country to do so. Peace ensured an uninterrupted supply of Arab oil to the United States. The Camp David Accords were the first and, as it turned out, the last significant agreement between Israel and a major Arab state.

The Iran Crisis: Origins

At this point a dramatic shift in Iran thrust Carter into the spotlight as never before. On November 4, 1979, about 400 armed Muslim militants broke into the American embassy compound in Tehran, Iran, and took everyone within the walls captive.

The seizure had roots that ran far back in Iranian history. During World War II, Great Britain, the Soviet Union, and later the United States occupied Iran and forced its pro-German shah into exile, replacing him with his twenty-two-year-old son, Muhammad Reza Pahlavi. But in the early 1950s power shifted to Prime Minister Muhammad Mossadegh, a leftist who sought to finance social reform by nationalizing the mostly American-owned Anglo-Iranian Oil Company.

In 1953, the Iranian army, backed by the CIA, arrested Mossadegh and put the young Pahlavi in power. The fall of Mossadegh ensured a steady flow of cheap oil, but it turned most Iranians against the United States and Shah Pahlavi. His unpopularity led the shah to purchase enormous amounts of American arms. Over the years Iran became the most powerful military force in the region.

The shah's rule was not one of "constant decency." His secret police, the Savak, brutally suppressed liberal opponents. At the same time, Muslim religious leaders were particularly offended by the shah's attempts to introduce Western ideas and technology into Iran. Because his American-supplied army and his American- and Israeli-trained secret police kept the shah in power, his opponents hated the United States almost as much as they hated their autocratic ruler.

Throughout 1977, riots and demonstrations convulsed Iran. When soldiers fired on protesters, the bloodshed caused more unrest, and that unrest caused even more bloodshed. Over 10,000 civilians were killed; many times that number were wounded. In 1978 the whole country seemed to rise against the shah. Finally, in January 1979, he was forced to flee. A revolutionary government headed by a religious leader, the Ayatollah Ruhollah Khomeini, assumed power. Freedom, he said, was the great enemy of Islam. He also claimed that Islam condoned terror: "Islam says: Whatever good there is exists thanks to the sword and in the shadow of the sword! . . . The sword is the key to paradise, which can be opened only for holy warriors."

Khomeini denounced the United States, the "Great Satan," whose support of the shah, he said, had caused the Iranian people untold suffering. When President Carter allowed the shah to come to the United States for medical treatment, militants in Tehran seized the American embassy.

The Iran Crisis: Carter's Dilemma

The militants announced that the Americans at the embassy would be held hostage until the United States returned the shah to Iran for trial as a traitor. They also demanded that the shah's vast wealth be confiscated and surrendered to the Iranian government. President

Carter rejected these demands. Instead Carter froze Iranian assets in the United States and banned trade with Iran until the hostages were freed.

A stalemate developed. Months passed. Even after the shah, who was terminally ill, left the United States for Panama, the Iranians remained adamant. The **Iranian hostage crisis** produced a remarkable emotional response in the United States. For the first time since the Vietnam War the entire country agreed on something.

In 1979 Islamic militants hold an American embassy worker in Tehran.

Nevertheless the hostages languished in Iran. In April 1980 Carter finally ordered a team of marine commandos flown into Iran in a desperate attempt to free the hostages. The raid was a fiasco. Several helicopters broke down when their rotors sucked desert sand into the engines. Another helicopter crashed and eight commandos were killed. The Iranians made political capital of the incident, gleefully displaying on television the wrecked aircraft and captured American equipment. The stalemate continued. When the shah died in exile in Egypt in July 1980, the Iranians made no move to release the hostages.

The Election of 1980

Despite the failure of the raid and the persistence of stagflation, Carter had more than enough delegates at the Democratic convention to win renomination on the first ballot. His Republican opponent in the campaign that followed was Ronald Reagan.

Reagan had grown up a New Deal Democrat, but during and immediately after World War II he became disillusioned with liberalism. As president of the Screen Actors Guild he attacked the influence of communists in the movie industry. After his movie career ended, Reagan did publicity for General Electric until 1960, then worked for various conservative causes. In 1966 he ran for governor of California, and struck a responsive chord by attacking the counterculture. He won the election and was easily reelected.

Both Carter and Reagan spent much of the 1980 campaign explaining why the other was unsuited to be president. Carter defended his record, though without much conviction. Reagan denounced criminals, drug addicts, and all varieties of immorality and spoke in support of patriotism, religion, family life, and other "old-fashioned" virtues. This won him the enthusiastic backing of fundamentalist religious sects and other conservative groups. He also called for increased spending on defense, and he promised to transfer some functions of the federal government to the states and to cut taxes. He insisted at the same time that the budget could be balanced and inflation sharply reduced.

On election day the voting was light, but Reagan received 8 million more votes than Carter. Dissatisfaction with the economy and the unresolved hostage crisis seem to have determined the result. The Republicans also gained control of the Senate and cut deeply into the Democratic majority in the House of Representatives.

Carter devoted his last weeks in office to the continuing hostage crisis. War had broken out between Iran and Iraq in September. The Iraqi president, Saddam Hussein, had hoped to exploit the chaos following the downfall of the shah to seize oil-rich territory in Iran. Early Iraqi victories prompted the Iranians to free the hostages in return for the release of Iranian assets that had been frozen in the United States. After 444 days in captivity, the fifty-two hostages were set free on January 20, the day Reagan was inaugurated.

Reagan as President

Reagan hoped to change the direction in which the country was moving. He demanded steep reductions in federal spending and the deficit, to be accomplished by cutting social expenditures such as welfare, food stamps and student loans, and by turning many functions of the federal government over to the states. The marketplace, not federal bureaucratic regulations, should govern most economic decisions.

He asked Congress to lower income taxes by 30 percent. When critics objected that this would increase the deficit, the president and his advisers reasoned that the tax cut would leave people with more money, which they would invest in productive ways. The new investment would generate more goods and jobs—and, ultimately, taxes for the federal government. This scheme became known as **Reaganomics**.

Helped by the votes of conservative Democrats, Reagan won congressional approval of the Budget Reconciliation Act, which reduced government expenditures on domestic programs by $39 billion.

Congress enacted most of the tax cuts the president had asked for, lowering individual income taxes by 25 percent over three years, but it resisted reducing the politically popular "entitlement" programs, such as Social Security and Medicare, which accounted for about half of the budget. Reagan himself refused to reduce the military budget to bring the government's income more nearly in line with its outlays. Instead he called for a military buildup

Ronald Reagan rides a horse—a familiar photo opportunity for presidents. (Recall the similar picture of LBJ on page 768.) But Reagan was an amiable cowboy; his smile and sense of humor were his most disarming weapons. In 1966 just after the election, when reporters asked him what sort of governor he would be, Reagan, a former actor, answered, "I don't know. I've never played a governor." Three months into his presidency, moments after he was seriously wounded in an assassination attempt, he took his wife's hand. "Honey," he said, "I forgot to duck." While being wheeled into the operating room, he quipped to the surgeons, "I hope you are all Republicans."

to ensure that the United States would prevail in any war with the Soviet Union, which he called an "evil empire." In particular, he sought to expand and improve the nation's nuclear arsenal. He made no secret of his wish to create so formidable a nuclear force that the Soviets would have to back down in any confrontation. The deficit worsened.

In Central America Reagan sought the overthrow of the left-wing government of Nicaragua and the defeat of communist rebels in El Salvador. He even used American troops to overthrow a Cuban-backed regime on the tiny Caribbean island of Grenada. When criticized for opposing leftist regimes while backing rightist dictators, Jeane Kirkpatrick, U.S. ambassador to the United Nations, explained that "rightist authoritarian regimes can be transformed peacefully into democracies, but totalitarian Marxist ones cannot."

In 1982 the continuing turmoil in the Middle East thrust the Reagan administration into a new crisis. Israel had invaded Lebanon to destroy Palestine Liberation Organization units that were staging raids on northern Israeli settlements. Israeli troops easily overran much of the country, but in the process the Lebanese government disintegrated. Reagan agreed to commit American troops to an international peacekeeping force.

Tragedy resulted in October 1983 when a fanatical Muslim crashed a truck loaded with explosives into a building housing American marines in Beirut. The building collapsed, killing 239 marines. Early the next year, Reagan removed the entire American peacekeeping force from Lebanon.

Four More Years

A sitting president with an extraordinarily high standing in public opinion polls, Reagan was nominated for a second term at the 1984 Republican convention without opposition. The Democratic nomination went to Walter Mondale of Minnesota, who had been vice president under Carter. Mondale electrified the country by choosing Representative Geraldine Ferraro of New York as his running mate. An Italian American and a Catholic, Ferraro was expected to appeal to conservative Democrats who had supported Reagan in 1980 and to win the votes of many Republican women.

Reagan began the campaign with several important advantages. He was especially popular among religious fundamentalists and other social conservatives, and these groups were increasingly vocal. Fundamentalist television preachers were almost all fervent Reaganites and the most successful of them were collecting tens of millions of dollars annually in contributions from viewers. One of these, the Reverend Jerry Falwell, founded the **Moral Majority** and set out to create a new political movement. "Americans are sick and tired of the way the amoral liberals are trying to corrupt our nation," Falwell announced in 1979.

During the first Reagan administration, the Moral Majority had become a powerful political force. Falwell denounced drugs, the "coddling" of criminals, homosexuality, communism, and abortion, all things that Reagan also disliked. Falwell also disapproved of forced busing to integrate schools. In addition, Reagan favored government aid to private schools run by church groups, something dear to the Moral Majority despite the constitutional principle of separation of church and state.

Success of the Republican "Southern Strategy" In 1968, Kevin M. Phillips, a key Nixon strategist, proposed a "southern strategy" to create an "emerging Republican majority." Many doubted that the South, which had long been opposed to the party of Lincoln, could be won over. But in presidential elections from 1968 to 1988, far more southern counties voted Republican than Democratic.

Reagan's support was also drawn from blue collar workers and white Southerners, constituencies that had been solidly Democratic during the New Deal and beyond. The president's personality was another important plus—voters continued to admire his informal yet firm style and his stress on patriotism and other "traditional" virtues.

Most polls showed Reagan far in the lead when the campaign began, and this remained true throughout the contest. Nothing Mondale or Ferraro did or said affected the president's popularity. On election day he got nearly 60 percent of the popular vote and lost only in Minnesota, Mondale's home state, and in the District of Columbia. Reagan's Electoral College margin was overwhelming, 525 to 13.

Reagan's triumph, like the two landslide victories of Dwight Eisenhower in the 1950s, was a personal one. The Republicans made only minor gains in the House of Representatives and actually lost two seats in the Senate.

"The Reagan Revolution"

Reagan's agenda for his second term closely resembled that of his first. In foreign affairs, he ran into continuing congressional resistance to his requests for military support for his anticommunist crusade. This was particularly true after Mikhail S. Gorbachev became the Soviet premier in March 1985. Gorbachev seemed far more moderate and flexible than his predecessors. He began to encourage political debate and criticism in the Soviet Union—the policy known as *glasnost* (openness)—and he sought to stimulate the stagnant Soviet economy by decentralizing administration and rewarding individual enterprise (*perestroika*).

Gorbachev also announced that he would continue to honor the unratified SALT II agreement, whereas Reagan, arguing that the Soviet Union had not respected the limits laid down in the pact, seemed bent on pushing ahead with the expansion and modernization of America's nuclear arsenal. Reagan sought funds to develop an elaborate system of missile defenses. He referred to it as the **Strategic Defense Initiative (SDI)**, although it was popularly known as Star Wars, a reference to the 1977 George Lucas film. SDI would consist of a network of computer-controlled space stations that would detect oncoming enemy missiles and destroy them with speculative high-tech weaponry.

When the president realized that the Soviets were eager for an agreement to limit nuclear weapons, he ceased referring to the Soviet Union as an "evil empire." In October 1986 he met with Gorbachev in Iceland in search of an agreement on arms control. The chief sticking point was SDI. Gorbachev proposed instead the elimination of all nuclear weapons—including SDI. Reagan, however, was determined to push Star Wars, and the summit collapsed.

Congress balked at the enormous cost of Star Wars. Expense aside, the idea of relying on the complex technology involved in controlling machines in outer space for national defense suffered a further setback in 1986, when the space shuttle *Challenger* exploded shortly after takeoff, killing its seven-member crew. This disaster temporarily put a stop to the program.

Reagan's basic domestic objectives—to reduce the scope of federal activity, particularly in the social welfare area; to lower income taxes; and to increase the strength of the armed forces—remained constant. Despite the tax cuts already made, congressional leaders of both parties agreed to the Income Tax Act of 1986, which reduced the top levy on personal incomes from 50 percent to 28 percent and the tax on corporate profits from 46 percent to 34 percent.

[●]｜Watch the Video
Ronald Reagan on the Wisdom of the Tax Cut at **myhistorylab.com**

Reagan advanced another of his objectives more gradually. This was his appointment of conservatives to federal judgeships, including Sandra Day O'Connor, the first woman named to the Supreme Court. By 1988 Reagan had appointed three Supreme Court justices and well over half the members of the federal judiciary.

The New Merger Movement

During the Reagan years, the nation began to climb out of the recession of the 1970s. Reagan's policies helped, though often in unpredictable ways. Reagan's relaxed regulation of Wall Street helped precipitate a frenzy of corporate mergers. Deregulation provided the context for the merger movement, but the person most responsible for it was Michael Milken, a shrewd stockbroker of the firm of Drexel Burnham Lambert. Milken specialized in selling "junk bonds," the debt offerings of companies whose existing debts were already high. He persuaded savings and loan associations, insurance companies, pension funds, and other big investors to buy these junk bonds, which, though risky, offered high interest rates. The success of his initial ventures prompted Milken to approach smaller companies, encourage them to borrow immense sums by floating junk bonds, and use the proceeds to acquire larger firms.

In 1985 Ronald Perelman, an aggressive entrepreneur, employed this strategy to perfection. He had recently obtained control of Pantry Pride, a supermarket chain with a net worth of about $145 million. Now he sought to acquire Revlon, a $2 billion cosmetics and health care conglomerate. With Milken's help, Pantry Pride borrowed $1.5 billion and used that capital to buy Revlon. He then paid off Pantry Pride's $1.5 billion in junk bonds ("junk" because the debt so greatly exceeded the $145 million value of Pantry Pride) by selling huge chunks of Revlon. Then he integrated the food component of Revlon into Pantry Pride.

The bond purchasers profited handsomely from the high return on the junk bonds, and Perelman made a fortune from his new food conglomerate. That same year the R. J. Reynolds Tobacco Company purchased Nabisco for $4.9 billion. Three years later this new giant, RJR Nabisco, was itself taken over by Kohlberg, Kravis, Roberts, and Company for $24.9 billion.

Workers at a Nike factory in Indonesia insert soles into sneakers.

During the frenzied decade of the 1980s, one-fifth of the *Fortune* 500 companies were taken over, merged, or forced to go private; in all, some 25,000 mergers and acquisitions were successfully undertaken; their total value was nearly a half-trillion dollars. To make their companies less tempting to cash-hungry raiders, many corporations took on whopping debts or acquired unprofitable companies. By the late 1980s, many American corporations were wallowing in red ink. Debt payments were gobbling up 50 percent of the nation's corporate pretax earnings.

●●●─┤Read the Document

Paul Craig Roberts, *The Supply-Side Revolution (1984)* at **myhistorylab.com**

"A Job for Life": Layoffs Hit Home

Most corporations coped with the debt in two ways: They sold assets, such as factories, offices, and warehouses; or they cut costs through layoffs. U.S. Steel, whose rusting mills desperately needed an infusion of capital, instead spent $5 billion to acquire Marathon Oil of Ohio; that decision meant that nearly 100,000 steelworkers lost their jobs. No firm was immune, nor any worker secure. During the 1980s, the total number of employees who worked for *Fortune* 500 companies declined by three million; nearly one-third of all positions in middle management were eliminated.

Many of the jobs went abroad, where labor costs were lower and unions nonexistent. In 1984 Nike moved sewing operations to Indonesia, where it could hire female workers for fourteen cents an hour. In 1986 the chassis for the Mustang, long a symbol of American automotive style, was built by Mazda in Hiroshima, Japan.

Towering mountains of private corporate debt nearly were overshadowed by the Everest of public debt held by the federal government itself. Reagan's insistence on a sharp cut in personal taxes and a substantial increase in military expenditures produced huge— and growing—annual federal deficits. When Reagan took office, the total federal debt was $900 million; eight years later, it exceeded $2.5 *trillion*.

Corporate Restructuring

Although few perceived it at the time, the economy was undergoing a transformation of historic dimensions. Much as the depression after 1893 had strengthened the nation's economy by wiping out thousands of inefficient steel and machinery firms, the seismic

BILL GATES

"Project Breakthrough! World's First Minicomputer Kit to Rival Commercial Models." This headline in the January 1975 issue of *Popular Electronics* triggered the neurons in Bill Gates's brain. In an instant, he perceived that the revolution had begun. Most earlier computers cost hundreds of thousands of dollars, filled room-sized air-conditioned vaults, and were found in university science centers, government agencies, and corporate headquarters. But this kit cost only $397. The computer (its name—*Altair*—came from a planet in the TV series *Star Trek*), could fit on a desktop. Gates believed that computers like this would soon be as much a part of life as telephones or automobiles. Armed with the slogan, "A computer on every desktop," Gates resolved to become the Henry Ford of the computer revolution (and to become, like Ford, immensely rich). He was twenty years old.

Gates recognized Altair's fatal flaw: It did little more than cause a few lights to blink in complex ways. It lacked internal instructions to convert electrical signals into letters and numbers. He determined to write instructions—the software—to make the personal computer useful. Gates and Paul Allen, a school friend, telephoned Ed Roberts, the president of MITS, manufacturer of the Altair. They told him they had written operating software for the machine. Roberts was skeptical. Scores of programmers had made such claims, he said, but none had actually done it. He told them to bring their software to the company headquarters in Albuquerque, New Mexico, within two months. Allen and Gates were euphoric, but not for long: They had not even begun to write a program for the Altair.

The boys had met in 1967 at Lakeside, an elite private school in Seattle, when Gates was in seventh grade, Allen in ninth. That year, the Lakeside Mothers Club had bought time on a digital training terminal that connected by phone to a company that leased a mainframe computer. Within weeks of its installation, this computer had become Gates's life. He remained in the terminal room after school and late into the evenings, breaking only for Coke and pizza. "He lived and breathed computers," a friend recalled.

Gates learned programming by writing programs and seeing what worked. His first was for playing tic-tac-toe. He also designed a program for student schedules at Lakeside. He placed "all the good girls in the school" (and very few males of any kind) in his own classes—an early manifestation of his penchant for defeating competitors by conniving to eliminate them.

Bill Gates as a young CEO at Microsoft.

Although his father was a wealthy corporate attorney and his mother a prominent socialite, Gates was preoccupied with making money. In high school he took a job tabulating automobile traffic data; this required that he count the holes in a roll of paper punched out when automobiles passed over a hose. He designed a computerized machine to count and analyze the data and he formed a company, Traf-O-Data, to build and market the device. But, Traf-O-Data failed to attract many customers—most municipalities and highway departments lost interest when they learned that the company was run by high school students.

Gates and Allen completed the program just hours before Allen boarded the plane to Albuquerque. (Allen went because he was older and presumably a more credible "corporate" spokesman.) The next morning, Allen fed long rolls of punched yellow paper tape—the software—into an Altair while company executives looked on skeptically. For fifteen minutes the machine clattered away. Misgivings mounted. Then the teletype printed the word, "READY." Allen typed, "PRINT 2 + 2." The teletype spat out "4." The program worked. Gates and Allen had a deal.

Gates dropped out of Harvard and formed a partnership with Allen. They called their company Microsoft and moved to Albuquerque. They wrote operating programs for personal computers introduced by Apple, Commodore, and Radio Shack. Soon money was pouring into Microsoft. In 1979 they moved Microsoft to Bellevue, Washington, near Seattle. Then came the blockbuster.

In 1980 IBM, the world's foremost manufacturer of mainframe computers, belatedly entered the home computer market. IBM approached Gates to write the operating software for its new, state-of-the-art personal computer. IBM intended to keep the computer's specifications secret so that other manufacturers could not copy its design, but Gates shrewdly proposed that IBM make its specifications public. Doing so would allow the IBM personal computer to become the industry standard, giving IBM the edge in developing peripherals—printers, monitors, keyboards, and various applications. IBM agreed. Now Gates's software, called Microsoft-Disk Operating System (MS-DOS), would run every IBM personal computer as well as every computer made by other companies according to the IBM specifications. In a single stroke, Gates had virtually monopolized the market for PC operating software.

Microsoft's sales jumped from $7.5 million in 1980 to $140 million in 1985. Then Microsoft moved into software applications: word processing, accounting, and games. By 1991, Gates was the wealthiest man in the world. In 1994, he and his wife established the Bill and Melinda Gates Foundation; by 2010, it had assets of over $33 billion and gave nearly $2 billion annually to charitable causes, especially education.

Questions for Discussion

- Intelligence, ambition, business sense, or all three? In what ways did Bill Gates's triumph parallel Andrew Carnegie's a century earlier?
- What was the main prerequisite for Gates's triumph?

economic upheavals after 1973 toppled many inefficient manufacturers
but created the foundations for more
efficient global conglomerates. As
weeds grew in the parking lots of the
factories of the "Rust Belt" of the
Midwest, new technology industries
sprouted in the "Silicon Valley" of
California, along Route 128 outside
of Boston, and in booming cities
such as Seattle, Washington, and
Austin, Texas.

By the end of the Reagan era,
the economy consisted of two
separate and increasingly unequal
components: a battered sector of
traditional heavy industry, characterized by declining wages and
diminishing job opportunities; and
an advancing high-tech and service sector dominated by aggressive, innovative, and individualistic
entrepreneurs. (See American Lives,
"Bill Gates," pp. 368–369.) The older
corporations that survived the
shakeout of the 1980s were leaner
and better equipped to compete in
expanding global markets.

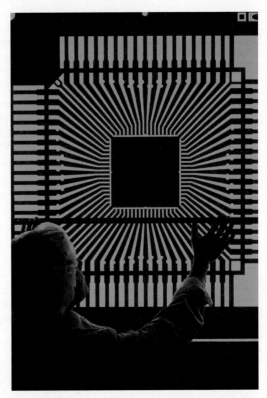

A worker studies a lighted diagram of an integrated circuit at a California computer factory.

Yet American society was becoming as fractured as the "bipolar" economy from
which it drew sustenance. The Reagan tax cuts had disproportionately benefited the
wealthy, as had the extraordinary rise of the stock market. Conversely, the economic
transformation struck low- or semiskilled wage earners hardest. At the end of Reagan's
second term the standard of living of the poorest fifth of the population (40 million
people) was 9 percent lower than it had been in 1979, while that of the wealthiest fifth
had risen about 20 percent.

Rogue Foreign Policy

Especially during his second term as president, Reagan paid little attention to the
details of administration. Thus two major initiatives unfolded of which Reagan himself
claimed little knowledge.

The first concerned Nicaragua. In 1979 leftist rebels had overthrown the dictatorial regime of Anastasio Somoza. Because the victorious Sandinista government was
supported by both Cuba and the Soviet Union, Reagan was determined to force it from
power. He backed anti-Sandinista elements in Nicaragua known as the Contras and
in 1981 persuaded Congress to provide these "freedom fighters" with arms.

But the Contras made little progress, and many Americans feared that aiding them would lead, as it had in Vietnam, to the use of American troops in the fighting.

●●●⎤Read the Document

Reagan, *Support for the Contras (1984)* at **myhistorylab.com**

In October 1984 Congress banned further military aid to the Contra rebels. Reagan then sought to persuade other countries and private American groups to help the Contras (as he put it) keep "body and soul together."

Marine Colonel Oliver North, an aide of Reagan's national security adviser, devised a scheme to indirectly funnel federal money to the Contras. He inflated the price of U.S. weapons, sold them to Iran[1], and secretly transferred the profits to the Contras. This plainly violated the congressional ban on such aid.

When North's stratagem came to light in November 1986, he was fired from his job with the security council. Reagan insisted that he knew nothing about the aid to the Contras. Critics pointed out that if he was telling the truth it was almost as bad since that meant that he had not been able to control his own administration.

Meanwhile, the Soviet invasion of Afghanistan in 1980 enraged Charles Wilson, a Democratic congressman from Texas. (Wilson, a womanizer, heavy drinker, and alleged cocaine-user, was played by Tom Hanks in the movie, *Charlie Wilson's War* [2007]). Wilson persuaded his colleagues to allocate money for the *mujahideen*, Muslim warriors who were trying to drive the Soviets out of their country. Within several years the Afghan tribes, especially Islamist radicals known as the Taliban, were covertly receiving hundreds of millions of dollars in weapons. Muslim insurgents ambushed convoys, mined roads, and engaged in various acts of terrorism. Soviet casualties increased, as did the cost of the war. Soviet generals began referring to the war in Afghanistan as "our Vietnam." In 1989 the Soviets pulled out; in 1996 the Taliban took over Afghanistan and instituted a radical Islamic state.

Assessing the Reagan Revolution

Reagan was not an able adminis-trator; the **Iran-Contra affair** and financial scandals of his administra-tion did not stick to him because he was seldom close enough to the action to get splattered by it. He articulated, simply and persuasively, a handful of concepts—chiefly the "evil" character of Soviet commu-nism, the need to get government off people's backs—and in so doing created a political climate conducive

Mujahideen in Afghanistan stand on top of a Soviet helicopter they shot down with U.S.-supplied Stinger missiles in the early 1980s.

---

[1]Earlier in the Iran-Iraq war, when Iran appeared on the verge of defeating Iraq, Reagan had provided $500 million a year in credits to allow Iraq's Saddam Hussein to buy armaments. If either Iran or Iraq won decisively, it could control the flow of Middle Eastern oil. The United States therefore preferred a stalemate.

to change. Reagan was directly responsible for neither of the great transformations of the late twentieth century—the restructuring of American corporations and the collapse of the Soviet Union. Yet his actions and, indeed, his failures to act indisputably influenced them. His decision to increase military spending and undertake the fantastically expensive SDI ("Star Wars") forced Gorbachev to seek an accommodation with the United States. Reagan's tax cuts precipitated unimaginably large federal deficits, and deregulation unloosed a sordid pack of predators who preyed on the economy. Yet the ensuing Darwinian chaos strengthened those corporations that survived and gave them the muscle to prevail in emerging global markets.

The Election of 1988

The issues that had dominated American politics for over a decade—the Soviet threat, the energy crisis, stagflation—were gone. The presidential election of 1988 initially lacked focus. The selection of Vice President George H. W. Bush as the Republican nomination was a foregone conclusion. Bush, the son of a Connecticut senator, had served as a pilot during World War II and then settled in Texas, where he worked in the family's oil business and became active in Republican politics. From 1971 to 1973 he served as ambassador to the UN and from 1976 to 1977 as director of the CIA. As Republican presidential hopeful, he trumpeted his experience as vice president.

The Democratic race was far more complicated but scarcely more inspiring. So many lackluster candidates entered the field that wits called them "the seven dwarfs." But eventually Governor Michael Dukakis of Massachusetts, stressing his record as an efficient manager, accumulated delegates steadily and won the nomination.

During the campaign, Bush attacked Dukakis as a liberal governor who had been soft on crime. Lee Atwater, campaign manager for Bush, produced and aired a television advertisement showing prisoners, many of them black, streaming through a revolving door. Dukakis's attempts to shift the focus away from crime failed. The presidential campaign became, in effect, a referendum on crime in which Dukakis failed the toughness test. Bush won 54 percent of the vote and carried the Electoral College, 426 to 112.

George H. W. Bush as President

In 1989 President Bush, having attacked Dukakis for being soft on crime, named a "drug czar" to coordinate various bureaucracies, increased federal funding of local police, and spent $2.5 billion to stop the flow of illegal drugs into the nation. Although the campaign generated plenty of arrests, drugs continued to pour in: As one dealer or trafficker was arrested, another took his place. Bush also worked to shed the tough image he had cultivated during the campaign. In his inaugural address he said that he hoped to "make kinder the face of the nation and gentler the face of the world." He also displayed a more traditional command of the workings of government and the details of current events than his predecessor. At the same time he pleased right-wing Reagan loyalists by his opposition to abortion and gun control, and by calling for a constitutional amendment prohibiting the burning of the American flag. His standing in the polls soared.

The Collapse of Communism in Eastern Europe

One important reason for this was the flood of good news from abroad. The reforms instituted in the Soviet Union by Gorbachev led to demands from its Eastern European satellites for similar liberalization. Gorbachev responded by announcing that the Soviet Union would not use force to keep communist governments in power in these nations. Swiftly the people of Poland, Hungary, Czechoslovakia, Bulgaria, Romania, East Germany, and the Baltics did away with the repressive regimes that had ruled them throughout the postwar era. Except in Romania, where the dictator Nicolae Ceausescu was executed, all these fundamental changes were carried out peacefully.

Almost overnight the international political climate changed. Soviet-style communism had been discredited. A Soviet attack anywhere was almost unthinkable. The Cold War was over.

President Bush profited from these developments immensely. He expressed moral support for the new governments but he refrained from embarrassing the Soviets. At a summit meeting in Washington in June 1990 Bush and Gorbachev signed agreements reducing American and Russian stockpiles of long-range nuclear missiles by 30 percent and eliminating chemical weapons.

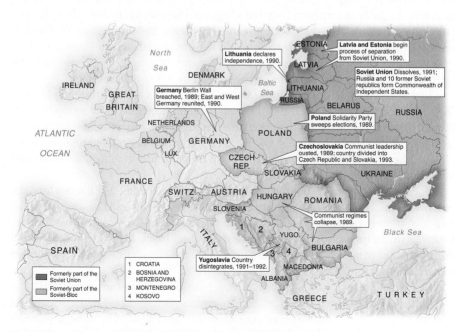

The Collapse of Communism in Eastern Europe When Gorbachev withdrew Soviet troops from Eastern Europe, the communist regimes there collapsed rapidly. The Soviet Union itself disintegrated.

In 1989 President Bush sent troops to Panama to overthrow General Manuel Noriega, who had refused to yield power when his figurehead presidential candidate lost a national election. Noriega was under indictment in the United States for drug trafficking. After temporarily seeking refuge in the Vatican embassy in Panama, he surrendered to the American forces and was taken to the United States, where he was tried, convicted, and imprisoned.

Meanwhile, in the Soviet Union, nationalist and anticommunist groups demanded more local control of their affairs. President Gorbachev, who opposed this breakup, sought compromise, backing a draft treaty that would increase local autonomy and further privatize the Soviet economy. In August, however, before this treaty could be ratified, hard-line communists attempted a coup. They arrested Gorbachev, who was vacationing in the Crimea, and ordered tanks into Moscow. But Boris Yeltsin, the anticommunist president of the Russian Republic, defied the rebels and roused the people of Moscow. The coup swiftly collapsed. Its leaders were arrested, the communist party was officially disbanded, and the Soviet Union itself was replaced by a federation of states, of which Russia, led by Yeltsin, was the most important. Gorbachev, who had begun the process of liberation, found himself without a job.

The War in the Persian Gulf

Although Reagan had provided economic assistance to Saddam Hussein of Iraq to prevent Iran from winning the Iran-Iraq war, few in the administration were enthusiastic about the Iraqi dictator. For years Saddam had been crushing the Kurds, an ethnic minority in northern Iraq that sought independence. In 1987 the U.S. State Department reported on his "widespread destruction and bulldozing of Kurdish villages." In March 1988, after Kurdish rebels had supported an Iranian advance into Iraq near Halabja, a mostly Kurdish city, Saddam's troops dropped mustard gas, sarin, and other chemical weapons on the city. Some 5,000 civilians died.

In August 1990, Saddam launched an all-out attack on Iraq's tiny neighbor to the south, the oil-rich sheikdom of Kuwait. Saddam hoped to swallow up Kuwait, thus increasing Iraq's already large oil reserves to about 25 percent of the world's total. His soldiers overran Kuwait swiftly, then systematically carried off everything of value they could bring back to Iraq. Within a week Saddam annexed Kuwait and massed troops along the border of neighboring Saudi Arabia.

The Saudis and the Kuwaitis turned to the United States and other nations for help, and it was quickly given. In a matter of days the UN applied trade sanctions against Iraq, and at the invitation of Saudi Arabia, the United States (along with Great Britain, France, Italy, Egypt, and Syria) moved troops to Saudi bases. Many Muslims opposed the presence of non-Muslim troops on Saudi soil; but the Saudi ruling family overruled them, fearing an Iraqi invasion.

By November, Bush had increased the American troops in the area from 180,000 to more than 500,000, part of a larger UN operation. On January 17, the Americans unleashed an enormous air attack, directed by General Norman Schwarzkopf. This air assault went on for nearly a month, and it reduced much of Iraq to rubble. The Iraqi forces, aside from firing a number of Scud missiles at Israel and Saudi Arabia and

Watch the Video

President Bush on the Gulf War at **myhistorylab.com**

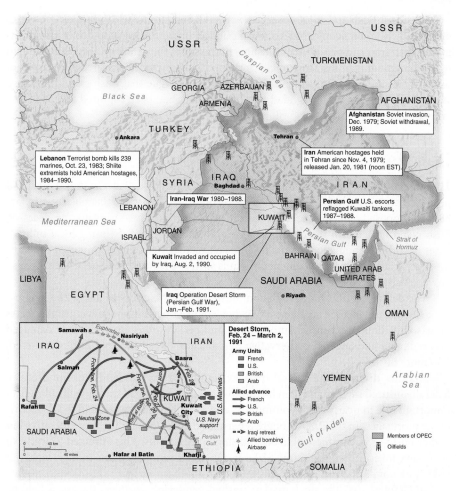

The Middle East In February 1991, combined U.S., British, French, and Arab armies drove Saddam Hussein from Kuwait and invaded Iraq.

setting fire to hundreds of Kuwaiti oil wells, simply endured the rain of destruction that fell on them daily.

On February 23 Bush issued an ultimatum to Saddam: Pull out of Kuwait or face an invasion. When Saddam ignored the deadline, UN troops (most under U.S. command) attacked. Bush called the assault "Desert Storm." Between February 24 and February 27 they retook Kuwait, killing tens of thousands of Iraqis. Some 4,000 Iraqi tanks and enormous quantities of other military equipment were destroyed.

Bush then stopped the attack, and Saddam agreed to UN terms that included paying reparations to Kuwait, allowing UN inspectors to determine whether Iraq was developing atomic and biological weapons, and agreeing to keep its airplanes out of "no-fly" zones over Kurdish territory and other strategic areas. Polls indicated that about 90 percent of the American people approved both the president's management of the **Persian Gulf War** and his overall performance as chief executive. These were the highest presidential approval ratings ever recorded.

President Bush and most observers expected Saddam to be driven from power in disgrace by his own people. Indeed, Bush publicly urged the Iraqis to do so. The Kurds in northern Iraq and pro-Iranian Muslims in the south then took up arms, but Saddam used the remnants of his army to crush them. He also refused repeatedly to carry out the terms of the peace agreement. This led critics to argue that Bush should not have stopped the fighting until Baghdad, the Iraqi capital, had been captured and Saddam's army destroyed.

Deficits

The huge cost of the Persian Gulf War exacerbated the federal deficit. Candidate Bush had promised not to raise taxes. As president he recommitted himself to that objective; in fact he even proposed reducing the tax on capital gains. But like his conservative predecessor, Bush could not control the deficit. Congress obstinately resisted closing local military bases or cutting funding for favored defense contractors. Reducing nonmilitary expenditures, especially popular entitlement programs such as Medicare and Social Security, also proved nearly impossible.

The deficit for 1992 hit $290 billion. Bush had no choice but to join with Congress in raising the top income tax rate from 28 percent to 31 percent and levying higher taxes on gasoline, liquor, expensive automobiles, and certain other luxuries. This damaged his credibility and angered conservative Republicans. "Read my lips," critics muttered, "No more Bush."

Another drain on the federal treasury resulted from the demise of hundreds of federally insured savings and loan institutions (S&Ls). S&Ls had traditionally played an important role in nearly every community, and a secure if sleepy niche in the economy: home mortgages. In the 1980s Congress permitted S&Ls to enter the more lucrative but riskier business of commercial loans and stock investments. This attracted a swarm of aggressive investors who acquired S&Ls and invested company assets in high-yield but risky junk bonds and real estate deals.

In October 1987 the stock market crashed, rendering worthless the assets held by many of the S&Ls. Hundreds were plunged into bankruptcy. In 1988 Michael Milken, the junk bond "guru," was indicted on ninety-eight charges of fraud, stock manipulation, and insider trading. He pleaded guilty, agreed to pay $1.3 billion in compensation, and was sent to jail. Drexel Burnham Lambert, his investment firm, filed for bankruptcy. The junk bond market collapsed.

Because S&L deposits were insured by the federal government, taxpayers were forced to cover the losses. The reserve fund for such purposes—$5 billion—was quickly exhausted. In 1991 Congress allocated $70 billion to close the failing S&Ls, liquidate their assets, and pay off depositors. The Justice Department charged nearly a thousand people for criminal involvement in a mess that, according to most estimates, would eventually cost taxpayers $500 billion.

During the preceding two decades, the American nation, like the automobiles that stretched for blocks in line to buy gasoline during the oil embargo, had been running on empty. The federal government was deeply in debt. Corporations had exhausted their cash reserves. Workers lived in fear of the layoff or bank foreclosure notice. Gone were the fanciful expressions of an earlier era—long and wide-bodied chassis, roaring

V-8 engines, sweeping tail fins, chromium grills like the jaws of a barracuda. Most cars had become simple boxes, trimmed with plastic, whose efficient four-cylinder engines thrummed steadily.

The nation's aspirations, like its cars, had become smaller, more sensible. Politicians muted their rhetoric, rarely issuing grandiose declarations of war against some intractable foe of humanity. Corporate executives spoke of "downsizing" firms rather than building them into empires. And the American people increasingly hunkered down in their own private spaces, which they locked up and wired with alarms.

Milestones

1973	Israel, aided by United States, defeats Egypt and Syria	1981	Iran releases U.S. hostages
1973–1974	Arabs impose oil embargo		Reagan appoints Sandra Day O'Connor to Supreme Court
1974–1976	Gerald Ford serves as president after Nixon's resignation	1981–1988	War persists between Iran and Iraq
1975	North Vietnam defeats South Vietnam; Saigon is renamed Ho Chi Minh City.	1984	Reagan is reelected president
		1985	Mikhail Gorbachev becomes premier of the Soviet Union
1976	Jimmy Carter is elected president	1986	Reagan secretly sells arms to Iran to finance Nicaraguan Contras
1978	Egypt and Israel sign Camp David Accords	1988	Republican George H. W. Bush elected president
1979	Jerry Falwell founds the Moral Majority	1989	Gorbachev allows Eastern European nations to establish independent democratic governments
	Muslim militants seize U.S. Embassy in Tehran, Iran		
	United States recognizes People's Republic of China	1990	Iraq invades Kuwait
1980	Soviet troops invade Afghanistan	1991	UN forces, led by the United States, drive Iraqi forces from Kuwait
	U.S. rescue mission in Iran fails		
	Ronald Reagan is elected president		Soviet Union is dissolved; Boris Yeltsin becomes president of Russia
1980s	Entrepreneurs' merger movement leads to huge corporate debt		

✓—[Study and Review at www.myhistorylab.com

Review Questions

1. The introduction to this chapter suggests that cheap oil and gas have long been prominent in American politics. How did the oil shortage of the 1970s affect politics? What was its impact on the economy? In what sense was "stagflation" weird?

2. Did Carter realize his hopes for a foreign policy based on "constant decency"?

3. How did Reagan contribute to corporate restructuring? What was the impact of the merger movement on the American economy generally? What new industries emerged in the late 1980s and 1990s?

4. Why did the Soviet Union collapse? What role, if any, did Reagan play in its demise?

5. Why did George H. W. Bush go to war with Iraq? Why, having defeated the Iraqi army, didn't he seize Baghdad and remove Saddam Hussein from power?

Key Terms

Camp David Accords *792*
Iran-Contra affair *803*
Iranian hostage crisis *794*

Moral Majority *796*
Organization of Petroleum Exporting Countries (OPEC) *788*
Persian Gulf War *807*

Reaganomics *795*
stagflation *791*
Strategic Defense Initiative (SDI) *798*

From Boomers to Millennials

31

Why do you go to college?

EVERY YEAR SINCE 1966, THE UCLA SCHOOL OF EDUCATION HAS surveyed nearly a quarter of a million first-year college students. The college-aged Boomers of the late 1960s were not much different from Millennials in 2009. Then as now, the great majority regarded themselves as "middle-of-the-road" in politics.

But the past forty years have witnessed a widening gulf between Boomers (born from 1946 to 1964) and Millennials (born after 1980). One example relates to life goals. According to the survey, when Boomers were in their freshman year of college, about three-fourths believed that "acquiring a meaningful philosophy of life" was "essential" or "very important." Only a third attached similar importance to "being well off financially." But forty years later the percentages had been nearly reversed. Over three-fourths of the Millennials entering college in 2009 believed that "being well off financially" was "essential" or "very important" while only a third thought it equally important to acquire "a meaningful philosophy of life." (The figures do not add up to 100 percent because respondents could give opinions for more than one statement.) Millennials are far more likely to seek wealth, while Boomers were more likely to seek "a meaningful philosophy of life."

One explanation is that Boomers came of age during a period of unprecedented economic growth. They were free to ponder the meaning of life because they rarely worried about finding a decent job. They could imagine brave new worlds of gender revolution and institutional transformation, of liberal treatment of criminals and immigrants, of a broader reform of society as a whole.

But the protracted recession after 1973 changed the way people looked at things. An infusion of new peoples, a liberalization of attitudes, and a transformation of institutions all suggested that society was becoming unhinged. A period of retrenchment was in order. Marriage and the family were to be preserved in familiar forms; tougher laws must be passed and criminals punished.

Through it all, the sphere of public life contracted; private concerns—such as making money—took precedence over grand social schemes. And public spaces receded as people retreated to their cars and homes, where they could interact with Facebook friends and virtual realities.

The New Immigration

A Pew poll in 2008 unearthed another major attitudinal difference between Boomers and Millennials. When asked whether immigrants strengthened the country with their hard work and talent, or burdened it because they took jobs, housing, and healthcare, the Boomers overwhelmingly (50 percent to 30 percent) regarded immigrants as a burden, while Millennials overwhelmingly (58 percent to 32 percent) thought immigrants strengthened the country. One reason for the attitudinal change is that a far higher proportion of Millennials are themselves immigrants or the children of immigrants.

◉ See the Map

Immigration to the U.S., 1945–1990 at **myhistorylab.com**

Since 1924, immigration to the United States had been governed by a quota system that ensured that the distribution of new immigrants mirrored the nation's existing ethnic patterns (see Chapter 24, p. 632). But the Immigration Act of 1965 eliminated the old system. It instead gave preference to immigrants with specialized job skills and education, and it allowed family members to rejoin those who had immigrated earlier. In 1986, Congress offered amnesty to illegal immigrants who had long lived in the United States and penalized employers who hired illegal immigrants in the future. Many persons legalized their status under the new law, but the influx of illegal immigrants continued. Together, these laws enabled more than 25 million to immigrate to the United States from 1970 to 2000.

Asians, many of whom possessed skills in high-tech fields, benefited most from the abandonment of the "national origins" system. Of the 9 million Asians who immigrated to the United States during these years, most were from China, South Korea, India, Pakistan, and the Philippines. Following the defeat of South Vietnam and the Khmer Rouge takeover of Cambodia, some 700,000 South Vietnamese and Cambodians received refugee status.

From 1970 to 2000 the largest number of immigrants were Latinos, sometimes called Hispanics (16 million). By 2000, the Latino population of the United States (35 million) for the first time exceeded African Americans (34 million). The overwhelming majority of these Spanish-speaking immigrants

Dolores Huerta and César Chávez, leaders of the United Farm Workers, discuss their 1968 strike of grape pickers. They are framed by photographs of Robert Kennedy, campaigning for the Democratic nomination for president, and Mohandas Gandhi, leader of the non-violent protest movement that won independence for India in 1947.

were Chicanos—Mexican Americans who settled in the Southwest. (Of the nation's 35 million Hispanics, 11 million lived in California, and nearly 7 million in Texas; over 42 percent of the population of New Mexico was Latino.) In addition,

Read the Document

LBJ Immigration Act of 1975 at **myhistorylab.com**

several million Puerto Ricans came to the mainland United States, most of whom settled in well-established Puerto Rican neighborhoods in northeastern cities. About a million Cuban immigrants arrived in Florida during these years.

But immigration was far more complex than the aggregate data suggest. Dearborn, Michigan, headquarters of the Ford Motor Company, is in many ways the prototypical American city. Yet nearly a third of its 100,000 residents are Arab-speaking immigrants from Lebanon, Iraq, Yemen, and Palestine.

About 10,000 Sudanese, refugees from a genocidal war in Africa, have flocked to Omaha, Nebraska, to work in its meatpacking plants. Nearly as many Bosnians, refugees from a civil war in the Balkans, have settled in Boise, Idaho.

In many communities, the new immigrants became a significant political force. Latinos elected Latino mayors in Los Angeles, Miami, Denver, and San Antonio. César Chávez, a pivotal figure in the history of Mexican Americans (Chicanos), succeeded in bringing tens of thousands of Mexicans into his United Farm Workers union. In a series of well-publicized strikes and boycotts, Chávez and the UFW forced wage concessions from hundreds of growers in California, Texas, and the Southwest.

But the infusion of immigrants generated concern. In 1992 Patrick Buchanan, campaigning for the Republican nomination for president, warned that the migration of "millions of illegal aliens a year" from Mexico constituted "the greatest invasion" the nation had ever witnessed. By then, about one-third of the Chicanos in the United States had arrived without valid visas, usually by slipping across the long U.S. border with Mexico. Of particular concern was the fact that the Latino poverty rate—which hovered around 10 percent—was twice the national average. In 1994 California passed Proposition 187, which made illegal immigrants ("undocumented aliens") ineligible for social services, public education, and nonemergency medical services. (The U.S. Supreme Court struck the law down as an infringement of federal powers. In 2001 the Supreme Court ruled that immigrants were entitled to all the protections the Constitution afforded citizens.)

In *Who Are We?* (2004), Harvard political scientist Samuel P. Huntington warned that the massive infusion of Latinos could "divide the United States into two peoples, two cultures, and two languages." Population projections showed that by 2050 whites might become a minority. But Huntington's dichotomy was too simple. Although immigrant groups often lived in distinct neighborhoods—Mexicans on one block and Hondurans on the next—they increasingly reached across national boundaries. Local restaurants offered wide assort-

Read the Document

Illegal Immigration Reform and Immigrant Responsibility Act of 1996 at **myhistorylab.com**

ments of ethnic fares, outdoor festivals attracted all peoples, and popular music featured a fusion of styles. Most important, immigrants increasingly ceased to think of themselves as belonging to a particular ethnic group. In 2000, nearly 7 million Americans identified themselves as "multiracial."

BARACK OBAMA

Not many thirty-three-year-olds write a memoir. But Barack Obama, who intended to write a book on race relations, instead explored the meaning of his young life.

The facts were clear enough. He was born on August 4, 1961, in Honolulu, Hawaii. His mother was Stanley (Ann) Dunham, whom a friend described as "Kansas white." His father, Barack Obama, Sr., was a Luo tribesman from Nyanza Province, Kenya, who had come to the University of Hawaii on a program to educate potential leaders of newly independent African nations. The couple had met in a Russian-language course at the university the previous year. Within a few months, Dunham was pregnant. Obama told her that he had been married in Kenya but had since divorced. Ann and Obama married in February, 1961. She was eighteen when she had Barack, Jr.

Her husband, however, had lied. Not only was he still married to a Kenyan, but he had one son by her with another on the way. In 1962, after graduating from Hawaii, he went to Harvard to pursue a graduate degree, leaving Ann and their son in Hawaii. When she went to visit him at Harvard, she brought the infant along. The trip went badly. Her husband had not told his friends about her or his wife in Kenya. Ann returned to Hawaii; it would be another ten years before she or her son saw his father again.

Ann and her son moved into her parents' two-bedroom apartment in Honolulu. She returned to college and her parents often took care of the boy, whom everyone called Barry. Several years later Ann divorced Obama—by then he had taken yet another wife—and she married an Indonesian geologist at the University of Hawaii. In 1967, Ann, her new husband and six-year-old Barry moved to the outskirts of Jakarta, Indonesia, where the family lived in a stucco house on a dirt lane. Chickens and ducks ran around the backyard and two crocodiles lived in a fenced-in pond on the property. Obama's mother had always encouraged her son to adapt to different peoples, but soon her thinking shifted. Now she realized the vast chasm separating the prospects of young people who grew up in Indonesia compared to the United States.

She enrolled in a correspondence course for elementary school children in the United States. At four each morning, she awakened Barry and together they worked through the materials. After he had completed fourth grade in Jakarta, she sent him to Honolulu to live with her parents, promising to follow within a year.

Barry's grandfather arranged for the boy to attend the elite Punahou Academy. He was one of the few African Americans in the school. When some boys teased him about living in the jungle, he invented stories about how his father was a warrior and an African prince. Obama nearly persuaded himself that this fiction was true.

When his father showed up in Honolulu for a month-long visit, Barry was appalled. What would he tell his friends? But he was also confused. His long-absent father proceeded to boss Ann and her parents

Stanley (Ann) Dunham with her son, Barack Obama, age two.

and demanded that Barry work harder in school. When Barry's teacher invited his father to give a lecture on Africa, Barry was mortified. But his father's talk was smooth and gripping. Barry's friends were impressed. His father left soon afterwards. Barry never saw him again.

As a teenager, Barry excelled at basketball; his senior year, he was on the Punahou team that won the state championship. He also wrote poetry. But he lacked motivation and managed only a B– average as a senior. He spent most of his time hanging out with slacker friends. Privately, he brooded over his father's estrangement. He coped with doubts about himself by using marijuana, booze, and cocaine. When one of his friends was busted for drug possession, Obama knew it could have been him.

His first two years at Occidental College in California were more of the same. He did little work. He was nevertheless popular with nearly everyone, navigating among different social groups with ease. "He was a hot, nice, everything-going-for-him dude," one friend recalled. "You couldn't help but like him." But issues of race weighed upon him and his black friends. After some of them teased him for using the name Barry, he began to ask people to call him Barack.

After his sophomore year, Obama transferred to Columbia University in New York. Denied campus housing as a transfer student, he lived in cheap apartments in Harlem. Then something changed. He studied, ran three miles a day, often fasted on Sundays, gave up drinking and drugs (cigarettes proved more difficult), and kept a journal to record his thoughts and poetry.

Late in the fall of his senior year, he received a phone call from Africa. His father was dead. He had been drunk and drove his car into the stump of a gum tree. Even in death, his father remained a mystery to Obama.

Obama later dreamt that he was on a long bus ride that ended up at a jail. He went in and saw his father in a cell, naked but for a cloth around his waist. As Obama entered the cell, his father teased him for being so thin. Obama embraced him and wept. His father then said that he had always loved his son.

When Obama awakened, he was crying.

Perhaps young Barack had at last reconciled with his absent father, enabling him to march toward his destiny with the singular purposefulness that became his trademark. Or perhaps he sensed that he would have to create a meaningful life through achievement of his own.

Whatever the reason, he did achieve. In 1985, after graduating from Columbia, he took a job as a community organizer in Chicago and established job training programs in schools, fought to remove asbestos in housing projects, and campaigned against drug dealers. Then he was admitted to Harvard Law School, named to the *Harvard Law Review*, and elected its president, the first black to hold this prestigious position. Afterwards he returned to Chicago to write a book; it became *Dreams from My Father* (1995), a memoir from which much of this account is taken. (The publisher has refused permission for any quotes from that book to appear in this one.) He taught constitutional law at the University of Chicago while working for a black law firm with strong connections to Chicago politics. In 1996 he ran for the Illinois state legislature and won. It was the beginning of a meteoric ascent in American politics that culminated in Obama's election as president in 2008.

Questions for Discussion
- President Barack Obama identifies himself as black. Do you agree? What is the definition of race in the contemporary United States?
- What explains Obama's transition from being an indifferent student in high school and college to a disciplined achiever?

The Emergence of Modern Feminism

"Boomers"—from the phrase "baby boom"—got that name because so many of their generation were born after World War II, when returning soldiers were reunited with their girlfriends and wives, and when ample job opportunities made it easier to raise families. Boomers' parents married earlier and had children sooner after marriage than at any other time in the twentieth century. By the late 1950s, the birthrate of the United States approached that of teeming India.

An important force in the early lives of Boomers was Dr. Benjamin Spock's *Common Sense Guide to Baby and Child Care*. First published in 1946, Spock's manual sold 24 million copies during the next quarter century. Spock's book guided young parents through the common medical crises of parenthood—ear infections, colic, chickenpox—and also counseled them on psychological issues. A mother's most important job, Spock insisted, was to shore up her children's sense of self by providing continuous support and affection. Women were naturally attuned to nurturing and childcare. Those women who entered the aggressive "men's world" of work would be at odds with their psychological inclinations.

Television picked up on this theme and hammered away at it each week in sitcoms such as Robert Young's ironically titled *Father Knows Best* (1954–1962) and Jackie Gleason's equally ironic take on working-class marriage, *The Honeymooners* (1953–1962). Repeatedly irascible or befuddled patriarchs blundered into family matters, only to be gently eased out of harm's way by their understanding and psychologically savvy wives.

But the reality of the postwar woman was more complicated. Economic expansion generated many new jobs, especially in the burgeoning corporate bureaucracies and retail stores. Women were in high demand because they would work for lower wages than men. Many took jobs, ignoring Spock and cultural conventions. In 1940, only one

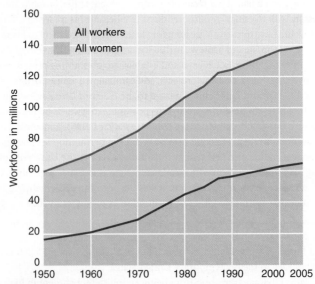

Paid Workforce, 1950–2005, by Gender The number (and percentage) of wage-earning women increased rapidly after 1960. In 1950, for example, fewer than one-third of the paid work force consisted of women; by 2006, the proportion had increased to nearly half.

in four civilian employees was female, one-third of them married. Three decades later, four in ten paid employees were women, two-thirds of them married.

Working women were acutely aware of the fact that men in similar jobs were paid more and had better opportunities for advancement. Women noticed, too, that minorities had improved their situations by fighting publicly. Increasingly activists for women's rights adopted similar strategies; they were the founders of the modern women's liberation movement.

One of its leaders was Betty Friedan, an activist journalist in the labor movement during the 1930s and 1940s who shifted to gender issues in later decades. In *The Feminine Mystique* (1963), Friedan argued that advertisers, popular magazines, and other "authorities" brainwashed women into thinking that they could thrive only at home. They were wrong, Friedan insisted. According to her survey of her classmates at Smith College, many housewives were troubled with vague but persistent feelings of anger and discomfort.

The Feminine Mystique provided what later came to be known as "consciousness raising" for thousands of women. Over a million copies were quickly sold. Friedan was deluged by hundreds of letters from women who had thought that their unease and depression despite their "happy" family life were both unique and unreasonable. Many now determined to expand their horizons by taking jobs or resuming their education.

Friedan had assumed that if able women acted with determination, employers would recognize their abilities and stop discriminating against them. As feminists were outlining plans to strengthen women's claims to fair treatment in the workplace, they won an unexpected victory. In 1964, during a debate on whether to ban racial discrimination in employment, Virginia Senator Howard Smith, seeking to scuttle the law, proposed that women also be protected from discrimination in hiring and promotion. Several congresswomen immediately endorsed the idea and proposed an amendment to that effect. This became Title VII of the Civil Rights Act of 1964.

In 1966 Friedan and other feminists founded the **National Organization for Women (NOW)**. "The time has come for a new movement toward true equality for all women in America and toward a fully equal partnership of the sexes," the leaders announced. In 1967 NOW came out for an equal rights amendment to the Constitution, for changes in the divorce laws, and for the legalization of abortion, the right of "control of one's body."

The **Equal Rights Amendment (ERA)**, which would make it unconstitutional to deny equal rights "on account of sex," had been proposed by the National Woman's party in 1923; by the late 1930s it appeared headed for adoption by Congress. But Eleanor Roosevelt and other women's groups killed the amendment, fearing it would rescind laws that protected poor women and their children. By the late 1960s, however, NOW's campaign for the ERA was yielding dividends. In 1971 the House of Representatives approved the ERA and the Senate followed the next year. By the end of 1972, twenty-two states had raced to go on record to ratify the amendment: What politician could prudently oppose equal rights for women? At the outset of 1973, only sixteen more states needed to ratify ERA before it was added to the Constitution.

View the Image

Jimmy Carter Signs the House of Representative Resolution for the Equal Rights Amendment, 1972 at **myhistorylab.com**

Feminist activists soon turned to another major goal: legalization of abortion. The Constitution made no reference to abortion. But during the nineteenth century botched surgical abortions that killed many women prompted the American Medical Association to call for the "general suppression" of the practice. By 1900, every state except Kentucky had passed antiabortion laws. Most states granted exceptions when the woman had been impregnated by rape or incest or when a doctor thought it necessary to save the woman's life. In 1967, for example, Governor Reagan of California, an opponent of abortion, signed a law allowing doctors to perform abortions if childbirth would "gravely impair the physical or mental health of the mother." The number of legal abortions in California increased from 5,018 in 1968 to more than 100,000 by 1972.

In 1970, however, feminist activists persuaded the Hawaii legislature to repeal its criminal abortion statute, the first state to do so. Later that year, another battle was waged in New York. It pitted feminists, liberals, and the medical establishment against conservatives and the Roman Catholic Church. The state assembly repealed its antiabortion law by a single vote. Feminists regarded this as a crucial but sobering victory. If a liberal state such as New York had barely mustered a majority in favor of abortion rights, how long would it take for the campaign to prevail elsewhere?

Roe v. Wade

The question soon became moot; the United States Supreme Court took the decision out of the hands of state legislatures. A key factor was a new concept in constitutional law: the "right to privacy." In the nineteenth century, the Catholic Church had persuaded many state legislatures to ban dissemination of information on contraceptives and birth control. Connecticut was one such state. But in 1961 Estelle Griswold, head of Planned Parenthood in Connecticut, opened a birth control clinic to challenge the law. In the case of *Griswold v. Connecticut*, the Supreme Court, headed by Earl Warren, struck down the Connecticut statute, contending that it violated couples' "right to privacy." While conceding that no such term appeared in the Constitution, the Court held that various other constitutional provisions—such as freedom of speech and press and prohibitions against unreasonable searches—together provided an "umbrella" of privacy-related rights. This "right to privacy" protected people from unwarranted intrusions by the state.

Then, in 1969, Norma McCorvey asked her doctor for an abortion. She was unmarried, unemployed, twenty-five years old, and pregnant. Her doctor refused. Abortion, he told her, was illegal in Texas unless performed to save the woman's life. McCorvey's lawyer encouraged her to challenge the law. She consented, using the pseudonym "Jane Roe," and her lawyer filed suit against Henry Wade, the Dallas County prosecutor.

In 1973, after McCorvey had the baby, the U.S. Supreme Court rendered a decision in *Roe v. Wade*. Rejecting any "single" theory of life, the justices maintained that a fetus did not have a "right to life" until the final three months of pregnancy, when it could likely survive without the mother. Until then, the mother's right to "privacy" took precedence. The state could not prevent a woman from having an abortion during the first six months of pregnancy. Most abortions were no longer illegal. A major goal of the feminists had been achieved almost overnight.

The *Roe v. Wade* decision resulted in a rapid expansion of abortion facilities. From 1973 to 1980, the number of abortions performed annually increased from 745,000 to 1.5 million. Abortion had become the nation's most common surgical procedure. The new feminist movement had prevailed on a number of issues that would have been unthinkable a decade earlier.

●◆●[Read the Document

Roe v. Wade (January 22, 1973) at **myhistorylab.com**

State Laws on Abortion Prior to *Roe v. Wade* (1973) Prior to *Roe v. Wade*, only Hawaii, Alaska, and New York had legalized abortion. Louisiana, Pennsylvania, and New Hampshire prohibited all abortions, while every other state allowed abortions only in cases of rape or incest or to preserve the life of the woman.

Conservative Counterattack

But the *Roe v. Wade* decision also energized a grass-roots conservative movement against abortion, often supported by the Catholic Church, the Mormons, and Protestant groups such as Falwell's Moral Majority (see Chapter 30, p. 796). The right-to-life movement endorsed the presidential campaigns of Ronald Reagan and George H. W. Bush, whose Supreme Court appointments generally favored the right-to-life position. In *Webster v. Reproductive Health Services* (1989) and *Planned Parenthood of Southeastern Pennsylvania v. Casey* (1992), the Supreme Court allowed states to impose

certain conditions, such as tests of viability and waiting periods, before abortions could be performed. But well into the twenty-first century, *Roe v. Wade* remained the law of the land.

Conservatives were more successful in contesting the ERA, which seemed headed to prompt ratification. In 1973 Phyllis Schlafly, a former vice president of the National Federation of Republican Women and publisher of a conservative newsletter, spearheaded a nationwide campaign against ratification of the ERA. She argued that it would subject young women to the military draft, deprive divorced women of alimony and child custody, and

Phyllis Schlafly drew much of her support from working-class women who were left vulnerable by the recession after 1973.

make married women legally responsible for providing 50 percent of household income. As the recession after 1973 dragged the economy down, Schlafly's words struck a responsive chord among anxious housewives and low-wage-earning women who doubted they could survive the recessionary economy on their own. The ratification campaign lost momentum and stalled, falling just three states short. By 1980, the ERA was dead.[1]

The Rise of Gay and Lesbian Rights

The rhetoric of "minority rights" and the example of activists in other movements during the 1960s encouraged gay rights activists to demand that society cease harassing and discriminating against *them*. In 1969, New York City police raided the Stonewall Inn, a popular gay bar in Greenwich Village and arrested the occupants—most of them gays—for "solicitation" of illegal sexual acts. The crowd outside threw rocks and bottles and the police were forced to retreat. The Stonewall riot lasted for several days and marked a turning point in the history of gays and lesbians. No longer would gays in Greenwich Village remain "in the closet"—hidden from view. Public advocacy of their cause strengthened it immeasurably.

●●●─[Read the Document

*The Gay Liberation Front,
Come Out (1970)* at
myhistorylab.com

Gay activists embarked on numerous campaigns to eliminate discrimination against gays. Gay psychiatrists challenged the American Psychiatric Association's longstanding judgment that homosexuality was a treatable mental illness. In 1973 the association's board of directors agreed to remove homosexuality from the standard manual of psychiatric disorders. Disgruntled traditionalists challenged the decision and forced the directors to put the matter up for a vote of the entire membership. In 1974 the members upheld the directors. The next year the American Psychological Association concurred. Homosexuality was not a mental illness.

Gay and lesbian activists also filed suits to eliminate discrimination against gays in education, housing, education, and employment. In response to such pressures, the U.S. Civil Service Commission rescinded its ban on hiring homosexuals. Now gays chose to run openly for public office. In 1977, Harvey Milk, the first openly gay man to run for office in California, was elected supervisor in San Francisco. The next year he led the fight against a California law that would fire gay teachers. Former California governor Ronald Reagan opposed the bill as a violation of human rights, as did President Jimmy Carter; the proposition was defeated by a million votes. Three weeks later Milk was assassinated; he became a martyr to the gay rights movement.

Harvey Milk was the first openly gay candidate to be elected to office in California.

---

[1]Various Supreme Court decisions, such as *Reed v. Reed* (1971), struck down laws that failed to provide "equal protection" of men and women or applied arbitrary standards in making legal distinctions between the rights of men and women.

AIDS

But by the late 1970s, as gays were openly acknowledging and celebrating their sexual identity, many were being struck down by a new disease. World health officials had spotted the outbreak of yet another viral epidemic in central Africa; but no one noticed that this virus had mutated into a more lethal strain and was spreading to Europe and North America. On June 5, 1981, the Centers for Disease Control (CDC) alerted American health officials to an outbreak of a rare bacterial infection in Los Angeles. What made the outbreak distinctive was that this particular infection had struck five healthy young men. All were homosexuals. Within months, all died.

By 1982 the CDC called this new disease **acquired immunodeficiency syndrome (AIDS)**. The CDC learned that AIDS was caused by the **human immunodeficiency virus (HIV)**, a lethal virus that destroys the body's defenses against infection. HIV spreads when an infected person's body fluids come in contact with someone else's. By the end of 1982, the CDC had documented 900 cases of AIDS; the disease was increasing exponentially. In June 1983, when the federal budget approached $1 trillion, Congress finally voted $12 million for AIDS research and treatment.

Not until 1985, when the square-jawed romantic actor Rock Hudson confirmed that he was dying of AIDS, did the subject command widespread public attention. President Reagan, an old friend of Hudson's, publicly acknowledged that the disease constituted a grave health crisis. Congress approved Reagan's call for a substantial increase in AIDS funding. But Reagan's appeal was belated and insufficient. By then, nearly 21,000 Americans had died; by 1999, the total number of AIDS-related deaths approached 400,000.

The AIDS epidemic affected public policy and private behavior. Fear of the disease, and of those who suffered from it, exacerbated many people's homophobia. But the AIDS epidemic also forced most people to confront homosexuality directly and perhaps for the first time, and thus contributed to a deeper understanding of the complexity of human nature. Gay and lesbian organizations, the vanguard in the initial war against AIDS, continued to fight for social acceptance and legal rights.

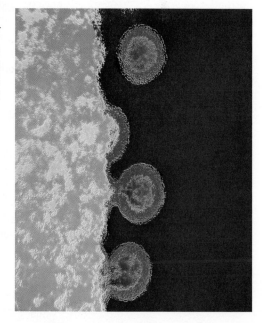

In this electron microscopic photograph, two human immunodeficiency virus (HIV) cells, in different stages of budding, are emerging from an infected T-lymphocyte human blood cell (pink). The HIV cell that has almost broken free includes RNA (green—the cell's genetic code) and it will reinfect other T-cells. T-cells are part of the body's immune system.

Publicly Gay

Although gays had always served in the military—Milk had been an officer in the navy during the Korean War—they were technically banned. In 1992 President Bill Clinton had promised to end the ban on gays and lesbians in the armed services, but when the Joint Chiefs of the armed forces and a number of important members of Congress objected, he settled for a policy known as "don't ask, don't tell," meaning that such persons would be allowed to enlist only if they did not openly proclaim their sexual preferences. In 2010 Congress voted to openly admit gays and lesbians to the armed forces.

Another long-term objective was same-sex marriage. Why, gay and lesbian couples asked, should they not be allowed to adopt children or receive the legal protections and benefits of marriage? Conservative groups argued that religious texts and moral traditions had defined marriage as heterosexual. In 2006 conservatives, backed by President

Table 31.1 Gender Activist Victories and Conservative Responses

Year	Activist Victory	Consequence	Conservative Response (after 1972)
1964	Title VII, Civil Rights Act of 1964	Prohibited employers from discriminating on account of sex; enforced by federal government	
1965	*Griswold v. Connecticut*	Supreme Court asserted a "right to privacy" to allow dissemination of information on birth control	
1972	Equal Rights Amendment (ERA) approved by Congress	Extended the equal rights protections of Fourteenth Amendment to women	Phyllis Schlafly inaugurated "Stop ERA" campaign (1973), which blocked ratification
1973	*Roe v. Wade*	Supreme Court legalized most abortions	Jerry Falwell's Moral Majority founded; helped elect Ronald Reagan president (1980); named more conservative Supreme Court justices
2000	Vermont recognized same-sex unions	Paved way for a half-dozen states to approve same-sex marriage	George W. Bush-backed proposed constitutional amendment to limit marriage to heterosexuals narrowly defeated in Senate (2006)

George W. Bush, proposed an amendment to the Constitution that would define marriage as "a union between a man and a woman." The measure fell just short of passage in the Senate.

In 2000 Vermont became the first state to recognize same-sex civil unions, providing gay and lesbian couples with some of the legal rights of marriage. In 2004 Massachusetts was the first state to recognize same-sex marriage; within the next five years, a half dozen states passed similar laws. When Washington, DC approved a same-sex marriage law, the Catholic Archdiocese of Washington, DC protested the decision by revising health care benefits of its agencies to avoid covering same-sex couples. But by 2010, according to most opinion polls, a solid majority of Americans favored same-sex marriage. And by a hefty margin, Millennials were far more likely to endorse same-sex marriage than any other age group, including Boomers.

Crime and Punishment

Civil rights protesters who intentionally violated laws rather than work within the law to change it; feminists who flouted conventional gender roles and asserted a right to abortion; gays and lesbians who claimed a right to serve openly in the military and enter into same-sex marriages—all were evidence, at least in the opinion of some, that the nation had lost its moral bearings. Such misgivings had spiked in the late 1960s, as antiwar protests closed down college campuses and race riots ravaged cities. Violent crime increased. Many called for restoration of "law and order." During the 1970s and 1980s conservative activists, borrowing strategies from activist movements on the left, succeeded in implementing many of the goals of the "law and order" movement. They elected officials who passed tougher laws, hired more police, and built additional prisons.

The shift toward capital punishment was symptomatic. No criminal had been executed since 1967. The practice simply had fallen from favor. But in response to the

Narcotics policemen in Bridgeport, Connecticut, arrest a suspect for selling crack near housing projects in 1994.

conservative demand for tough legislation against criminals, legislators rewrote capital punishment statutes in light of the *Furman* decision, depriving juries of discretion in sentencing. The Supreme Court upheld these laws and capital punishment resumed in 1976. Since then, over a thousand convicts have been executed.

Another manifestation of the crackdown on crime was the increase in the nation's prison population. In 1973 the nation's prisons—state and federal—held about 200,000 convicts. By 1990 the number of prisoners exceeded 750,000, and by 2004, 2 million. This required the construction of a 1,000-bed prison every week. In 1995, for the first time, states spent more on prisons than on higher education. By 2010, the United States incarcerated more people than any country in the world, except perhaps communist China, which did not disclose such information.

Crack and Urban Gangs

Several factors intensified the problem of violent crime, especially in the inner cities. One was a shift in drug use. During the 1960s marijuana had become commonly available, especially on college campuses; this was followed by cocaine, which was far more powerful and addictive but so expensive that few could afford it.

During the 1980s growers of coca leaves in Peru and Bolivia greatly expanded production. Drug traffickers in Colombia devised sophisticated systems to transport cocaine to the United States. The price of cocaine dropped from $120 an ounce in 1981 to $50 in 1988.

Still more important was the proliferation of a cocaine-based compound called "crack" because it crackled when smoked. Many users found that it gave an intense spasm of pleasure that overrode all other desires.

The lucrative crack trade led to bitter turf wars in the inner cities; dealers hired neighborhood youths, organized them into gangs, armed them with automatic weapons, and told them to drive competitors away. A survey of Los Angeles county in the early 1990s found that more than 150,000 young people belonged to 1,000 gangs. Violence had become a fact of life. In 1985, before crack had seized hold of the inner city, there were 147 murders in Washington, DC; in 1991, the figure skyrocketed to 482.

Black on black murder had become a significant cause of death for African Americans in their twenties. In 1988 Monsta' Kody Scott, who at age eleven pumped shotgun blasts into rival gang members, returned after prison to his Los Angeles neighborhood. He was horrified: Gangs no longer merely shot their rivals but sprayed them with automatic weapons, seventy-five rounds to a clip, or blew them away with small rockets. By 2010, 30 percent of African American men in their twenties were in prison, or on probation or parole.

Violence and Popular Culture

Conservatives—and plenty of liberals—were also dismayed by the violence of popular culture. They cited as proof the lurid violence of the movie industry, pointing out that in *Public Enemy*, reputedly the most violent film of the 1930s, and *Death Wish*, a controversial vigilante fantasy of 1974, the body count reached eight. But three movies released during the late 1980s—*Robocop, Die Hard,* and *Rambo III*—each produced a death tally of sixty or more, nearly one every two minutes. The trend culminated in *Natural Born Killers* (1994), director Oliver Stone's unimaginably violent "spoof" of media violence. Television imitated the movies as the networks crammed violent crime shows into prime time. In 1991 an exhaustive survey found that by the age of eighteen, the average viewer had witnessed some 40,000 murders on TV.

A new sound called "rap" then emerged from the ghetto. Rap consisted of unpredictably metered lyrics set against an exaggeratedly heavy downbeat. Rap performers did not play musical instruments or sing songs so much as convey, in words and gestures, an attitude of defiant, raw rage against whatever challenged their sense of manhood: other young males; women, whom they derided in coarse sexual epithets; and the police. Predictably, raps such as "Cop Killer" and "Illegal Search" contributed to the charge that rap condoned violence and crime.

The appeal of rap quickly spread beyond black audiences. When Dr. Dre (Andrew Young), founder of a gangsta rap group and head of a record firm, discovered that whites bought more rap CDs than blacks, he promoted the career of a young white rapper, Eminem. Born Marshall Bruce Mathers III, Eminem attracted attention with songs such as "Murder, Murder," "Kill You," "Drug Ballad," and "Criminal." He bashed women, gays, his wife, and nearly everyone else. His lyrics were of such surpassing offensiveness that he became an overnight celebrity and instant millionaire. His fans, whom he treated with scorn, were delighted by the universality of his contempt. The list of those suing him included his mother.

By the 1990s improvements in computer graphics led to the development of increasingly realistic—and violent—video games. "Grand Theft Auto," which by 2005 had sold over 35 million copies and generated over $2 billion, was the subject of a *60 Minutes* special. Journalist Ed Bradley described the game this way: "See a car you like? Steal it. A cop in your way? Blow him away." Bradley recounted the story of Devin Moore, an eighteen-year-old who played the game "day and night" for years. On June 7, 2003, he stole a car; when apprehended he grabbed a gun, killed three policemen, and fled in a police cruiser. When finally caught he said, "Life is like a video game. Everybody's got to die sometime."

America, it seemed, had become seemingly filled with menace. At night, few ventured downtown and many avoided public places. Car alarm systems became standard. The popular phrase—"your home is your castle"—took on an eerie reality. Americans reinforced doors with steel, nailed windows shut, and increasingly hunkered down in their own private spaces, which they locked up and wired with alarms.

From Main Street to Mall to Internet

In 1960 civil rights protesters picketed six stores in Richmond, Virginia. Within several decades, all of the stores had closed. So had most of the luncheonettes, 5 & 10 cent stores, bus stations, and community swimming pools that had been sites of civil rights protests during the late 1950s and early 1960s. Civil rights leaders targeted such facilities because they sought equal access to public spaces downtown, where community life was transacted. There people worked, bought clothing and cars, got their hair cut and cavities filled, paid taxes and filed for driver's licenses, ate meals and brokered deals, watched movies and attended ball games, and engaged in countless other activities. Thirty years later, however, many downtown business districts had been all but abandoned.

In 2007 a storm approaches the mostly abandoned main street of Robert Lee, county seat of Coke County, Texas.

Some blamed the civil rights movement itself. Inner-city protests and the deseg-regation of city schools, they said, caused many whites to flee to the suburbs. Others cited the rise in crime in the late 1960s. But "white flight" commenced in the late 1940s, long before the civil rights movement and busing disputes, before the race riots and crack infestations. Postwar federal policies played a major role in the demo-graphic upheaval that transformed the cities and gave rise to the suburbs. The G. I. Bill of 1946 offered veterans cheap home mortgages. Real estate developers bought huge tracts of land and built inexpensive houses designed especially for returning

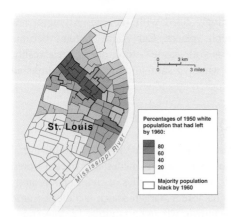

Racial Shifts in St. Louis during the 1950s During the 1950s, the white population of St. Louis declined by more than 200,000, while the black population increased by 100,000. Much of the central core was almost entirely black.

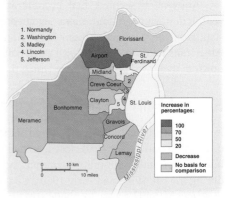

Growth of Suburban St. Louis, 1950–1960 During the 1950s, the suburban townships in St. Louis county west of the city gained nearly 300,000 people, an increase of 73 percent. More than 99 percent of the suburban residents were white.

veterans. Postwar lending policies of the Federal Housing Authority also contributed to the rise of the suburbs, chiefly by rejecting loans in older residential urban areas. Eisenhower's decision to pump money into highway construction (rather than subways and railway infrastructure) also contributed to the growth of suburbs.

Retailers followed consumers, renting space in strip malls along the busy roadways that reached out to the suburbs. Then came the shopping malls. In 1946 there were only eight shopping malls in the nation; by 1972, over 13,000. Mall managers anchored their complexes with national retailers such as Sears and JCPenney. Because such companies bought in large quantities, their stores out-priced locally owned competitors on Main Street. Main Street faded. By the 1980s, retailers such as Sam Walton took the logic of price competition several steps farther. He dispensed with the customary amenities of shopping—attractive displays, pleasant décor, professional salespeople—and built "big box" stores that were little more than shopper-accessible warehouses. Then came another shift. Early in the twenty-first century, shoppers who wearied of pushing carts through dimly lit warehouses and standing in line to pay now had an alternative: They could shop via the Internet, which by 2010 accounted for nearly 10 percent of all retail sales.

Within a half century, shopping had not only become more private, but it also was less social. Big-box stores replaced commissioned salespeople with low-paid checkers. In the past decade improvements in scanner technology allowed retailers to dispense even with checkers. And an increasing number of online consumers shop at home. Increasingly, shopping entails no social interaction whatsoever.

A similar shift from public interaction to private pursuits has characterized many other daily activities. For much of their lives, Boomers regularly visited local banks to make deposits and cash checks. But during the recession of the 1970s banks closed many branches and in subsequent decades hundreds of banks were merged. More branches were closed and tens of thousands of tellers laid off. Rather than drive to distant branches and wait in long lines, banking customers learned to use ATMs and bank online. Banking for Boomers had been a social occasion; for Millennials it became an interaction with a machine.

By the 1970s and 1980s, many service sector jobs had disappeared: milkmen who delivered fresh dairy products; door-to-door salespeople who demonstrated cosmetics, appliances, and encyclopedias; "service station" attendants who pumped gas and checked the oil; bakery owners and candy makers who sold goods they had made themselves. Then in the 1990s, person-to-person interactions in daily life occurred even less frequently. With the advent of the Internet and improved software, many people became their own travel agent, tax preparer, financial adviser, grocer, cosmetician, medical assistant, and bookseller.

From Community to Facebook

Religious institutions have long constituted the bulwark of communities, and the postwar period witnessed a remarkable expansion. By 1990, membership in all churches and synagogues surpassed 148 million, an increase of 60 million during the previous four decades. (The total population during the period increased by nearly 100 million.) With the large influx of Hispanic immigrants, membership in the Roman Catholic Church more than doubled. Membership in mainstream Protestant churches generally declined, but rose solidly in fundamentalist and evangelical churches, such as the Southern Baptist, Pentecostal, Holiness, Assemblies of God, and Church of God in Christ. The Jehovah's Witnesses and the Mormon Church grew as well. In 1990 two-thirds of all Americans reported that they belonged to a church, the highest percentage by far among the major industrial nations of the West.

But the membership numbers were misleading. Since 1970, church attendance among persons younger than sixty has declined about 20 percent. The UCLA survey cited in the introduction to this chapter found that in 1968, 9 percent of entering college freshmen said they never attended church; by 2000, that percentage had more than doubled. By the 1970s, moreover, millions of Americans went to church by turning on the TV. "Televangelists" such as Rex Humbard, Oral Roberts, Jerry Falwell, Pat Robertson, and Jim and Tammy Bakker founded their own churches and educational institutions, supported by direct appeals to viewers. A few established their own colleges, such as Falwell's Liberty University, Oral Roberts University, and Robertson's CBN University (renamed Regent University in 1990). A number of scandals involving prominent televangelists caused disillusionment and widespread defections. On the other hand, the rapid spread of cable television greatly increased the number of available channels, enabling scores of new evangelists to reach out to viewers. Community-based ministers saw congregations shrink; thousands of churches closed their doors for good. Some churches devised "healing rituals" to ease their abandonment of formerly sacred space.

Participation in team sports fell at about the same rate as church attendance. By the first decade of the twenty-first century, more young people played basketball and soccer than in the past, but far fewer played softball, baseball, football, tennis, and league bowling. The fields on which young Boomers often spent much of their lives had been sold to developers or fenced in and locked.

The lack of exercise among Millennials became a source of national concern. In 2010 Surgeon General Regina Benjamin announced that one in three American children was obese. One reason, Benjamin explained, was that youngsters between ages eight to eighteen averaged seven hours and thirty-eight minutes a day on electronic media—watching TV, talking on cell phones, playing video games, and logged into the Internet. That year, First Lady Michelle Obama inaugurated a nationwide antiobesity campaign named—appropriately—"Let's move!"

Some Millennials exercised *while* engaged with electronic media. (Multitasking became a redundant adjective for the Millennial generation.) Since 2000, membership in gyms skyrocketed. And often Millennials could be seen pounding away on treadmills or other exercise machines, staring at TV monitors or listening to music with an earpiece. Not all Millennials are sedentary; but many are nearly always plugged in.

The rise of online learning is an illustration of the transformation of social activities into solitary Internet pursuits. By 2009, over 4 million Americans enrolled in online courses, twice as many as in 2003. For many, especially full-time employees, ease of access compensated for the lack of face-to-face contact with other students. Tim Scott, a twenty-five-year-old clerk in a drugstore who enrolled in technology courses at the University of Phoenix, explained, "This is pretty much the only way I could get a college degree." Online education spread to all walks of life. Some people took courses to learn new languages and career skills, such as "Dental Anthropology," "Clown Education," or

"Golf Course Management." Others logged in to learn new hobbies, such as "building a kayak," "paragliding in the Alps," or "Salsa dancing." Employees were required to take mandatory online courses on company policies and sexual harassment. Although surveys suggest that most online learners prefer classes in which they interact with real people in a classroom, the fact was that often regular classrooms had themselves become anonymous and impersonal. As Harvard Professor Clayton Christensen observed, "Anything beyond the 10th row in a large lecture hall is distance learning."

One reason distance online education took off was that it spared commuting students the hassle of driving to college and finding parking. Such experiences underscored the extent to which cars had become the predominant mode of transportation, another shift from the earlier social context of mass transit to the mostly solitary experience of driving. Bus and train ridership was declining well before the advent of the Boomers; but the postwar population shift to the suburbs accelerated the ascendancy of cars over mass transit. As more drivers—nearly always alone—clogged the highways, traffic jams grew longer. By 2005, the average American spent thirty-eight hours a year stuck in traffic. Although many found repose within the solitary confines of a car, others coped with the loneliness of driving by chatting on their cell phones or texting friends. (A Pew poll in 2010 found that one in three texting teenagers did so while driving a car.)

The postwar suburban home itself was conceived as a private refuge from the hustle and bustle of downtown. But over time suburban homes became still more private. Newer houses were set farther back from the curb; high fences and thick hedges discouraged the over-the-barbecue conviviality of the 1950s suburbs. By the 1990s, many well-to-do people moved into privately owned "gated communities," surrounded by high fences and patrolled by private security guards. Only residents and specified guests were allowed in.

The trend toward increased privacy could be seen even within the home. Young Boomers generally ate dinner in a family dining room and played cards and board games afterwards in the living room. By the mid 1950s, television-watching had become a family affair, and a child's dreaded punishment was to be sent to his or her room after dinner. During the 1980s and 1990s, however, homes became larger and families smaller. Most Millennials had their own bedrooms. By 1975 fewer than half of Americans ate dinner with their whole family; and by 2000, that fraction had slipped to one-third. Family members instead retreated to their own rooms to watch their own television shows or log onto the Internet. (In 2010 the average number of TV sets per household—2.93— exceeded the number of *people* per household—2.88.) For Millennials, the worst punishment was to be deprived of the Internet or their Blackberries.

Millennials withdrew to the privacy of their rooms in order to socialize. David Greenfield of the Center for Internet Studies explained that the Internet was "a socially connecting device that's socially isolating at the same time." For their part, most Millennials thought the Internet improved social relations. "I've outsourced my social life exclusively to Facebook," one Millennial explained in 2009. "My time on Facebook substitutes for face time and has made my life more organized and efficient." In 2010 Facebook reported that the average college student had over 400 Facebook friends. Plenty of users greatly exceeded this average, prompting Facebook in 2008 to rule that friendship rosters would be capped at 5,000. Social connections in excess of 5,000, Facebook officials reasoned, were probably not "actual friends." While bemoaning the cutoff, Jeffrey Wolfe, a real estate broker in San Francisco with 4,447 friends, conceded that keeping up with them could be demanding: "Normally I start hitting it about 10 o'clock at night, and if I do it right, I can be done by 1 a.m."

Some worried that Millennials spent so much time attending to their own circle of Facebook friends (however great in circumference) or logging onto sites dedicated to Lady Gaga, labrador retrievers, or Legos, that they often failed to encounter people with ideas or perspectives different from their own. But others endorsed the Internet as an ideal if somewhat odd way to meet strangers and exchange opinions. *Second Life*, a virtual 3D world populated by some 18 million "residents," was among the innumerable interactive games that allowed strangers to converse and imaginatively interact. In 2009 Linden Lab, the San Francisco company behind the concept, noted that *Second Life* residents had logged over a billion hours on the site and spent a billion dollars buying unreal things (mostly clothing and cars) for their virtual personas, or avatars. One Stanford researcher explained how he had experienced "the most sexually charged non-sexual experience I've ever had" when his avatar was propositioned by another avatar in a "private room" (!).

Virtual communities possessed both the advantages and disadvantages of anonymity. "On the Internet, no one knows you're a dog," as a *New Yorker* cartoon's canine narrator remarked. A 2001 study found that half of the female Avatars in *Second Life* were actually men. Anonymity may help protect people who wish to articulate ideas and explore behaviors that might generate disapproval in "real" settings.

But the anonymity of the Internet also carries risks. Sexual predators target teen chat rooms and social-networking sites. Anonymity, too, allows people to vent frustrations, prejudices, and spite without concern for consequences. In 2006, Lori Drew, a mother in O'Fallon, Missouri, sought to teach a lesson to Megan Meier, a fourteen-year-old whom Drew believed had been spreading rumors about Drew's daughter. Drew created

In *Second Life*, a multi-player online game, these two avatars engage in virtual courtship.

a fictitious MySpace persona of a sixteen-year-old named "Josh," who friended Meier, gained her confidence, and acquired her secrets. But then "Josh" turned on Meier, advising, "The world would be a better place without you." Twenty minutes later, Meier hanged herself in her bedroom closet.

Drew was convicted of a misdemeanor for violating the terms of her MySpace agreement; but a federal judge set the ruling aside: Violation of an Internet agreement did not constitute criminal behavior. State legislatures in Missouri and California immediately passed "anti-cyberbullying" laws. In 2009 Congresswoman Linda Sanchez introduced the "Megan Meier Cyberbullying Prevention Act," but constitutional experts predicted that such laws would be struck down as infringements on free speech and privacy rights.

But what did privacy mean? During the previous four decades, Boomers and Millennials had repeatedly debated and redefined the concepts of private and public. Feminists had asserted a "right to privacy," including a right to an abortion; but the Moral Majority had insisted on the superior "right to life" of the fetus. Gays and lesbians had sought freedom from government harassment; but they also sought public acceptance through adoption of same-sex marriage laws and open acknowledgement of their service in the military. President Reagan and conservatives campaigned to "get government off our backs" and yet they expanded the government's role in prosecuting behavior deemed deviant or immoral. And if public physical spaces were disappearing, Millennials increasingly participated, often from the solitude of a bedroom or study, in a bogglingly public world of the Internet, blithely posting their innermost thoughts (and sometimes photos) on social networking sites.

Greying of the Boomers

On January 1, 2011, when the first Boomer turned sixty-five, nearly one-seventh of the American population was over sixty-five, the customary retirement age. Demographic projections indicated that by the time the Millennials reached sixty-five, one-fifth of the population would be over sixty-five.

The aging of the nation's population had serious economic implications. A substantial proportion of the nation's wealth was shifting from economically productive purposes (educating the young, building and maintaining infrastructure, and creating new businesses and technology) to the less productive task of providing health care and pensions for the elderly.

In 1980, sixty-year-old John A. Garraty, co-author of this book, completed his first twenty-six-mile marathon in New York City. He completed his last marathon when he was seventy-two.

Of particular concern was the viability of Social Security, the New Deal program that provided pensions for the elderly. In theory, workers and employers paid into the Social Security Trust Fund; when workers retired, they would draw their "savings" from the Trust Fund. But under pressure from seniors—the highest-voting proportion of the population—Congress increased old-age benefits. As of 2010, the Social Security Trust Fund had $2 trillion in assets, but the projected cost of Social Security by 2050 exceeded $7 trillion. The difference would have to be covered by the contributions made by working Millennials, many of whom worried that the fund would be gone by the time they retired. A 2009 poll by the American Association of Retired Persons (AARP) found that only 31 percent of Americans between the ages of eighteen and thirty-nine believe that Social Security will be available to them on retirement.

Medical advances during the late twentieth century led to an increase in the life span: An American born in 1900 could expect to live to be fifty, while one born in 2000 was projected to live to seventy-seven. But this good news further complicated the transition from Boomers to Millennials.

Compounding the difficulty were attitudinal differences between the generations, such as those cited elsewhere in this chapter. The 2008 Pew poll also found that 75 percent of Millennials had profiles on a social networking site, compared to 30 percent of Boomers; that 38 percent of Millennials had a tattoo, compared to 15 percent of Boomers; and that 23 percent of Millennials had body piercings other than an ear lobe, compared to fewer than 1 percent of Boomers. How Millennials will treat aging Boomers is anyone's guess.

Milestones

1946	Dr. Benjamin Spock publishes *Common Sense Guide to Baby and Child Care*	1969	Stonewall riots mark public assertion of rights of homosexuals
1947	Construction begins on Levittown, New York, first tract-house suburb	1973	Supreme Court legalizes abortion in *Roe v. Wade*
1960	FDA approves sale of birth control pills	1979	Jerry Falwell founds the Moral Majority
1963	Betty Friedan publishes *The Feminine Mystique*	1982	Center for Disease Control identifies new disease, AIDS
1965	Congress passes Immigration Act that ends "national origins" quotas	1989	Supreme Court limits abortion rights in *Webster v. Reproductive Health Services*
	Supreme Court affirms "right to privacy" in *Griswold v. Connecticut*	2000	Vermont recognies same-sex unions
	César Chávez organizes boycott to support grape pickers	2010	Michelle Obama introduces anti-obesity campaign

✓●─|Study and **Review** at www.myhistorylab.com

Review Questions

1. The introduction to this chapter argues that young Boomers were more inclined to look for a "meaningful philosophy of life," while young Millennials were more interested in being "well-off financially." Do you agree? What evidence from the chapter supports your position? What refutes it?

2. What accounted for the emergence of modern feminism in the 1960s? Did it succeed in changing gender roles and if so, how? What explained the emergence of gay and lesbian activism?

3. What were the main components of the conservative movement after 1970? How did it influence culture and society?

4. How did the cultural shift from "downtown" to the suburbs change society more generally? In what sense has life become more or less "private"?

Key Terms

acquired immunodeficiency syndrome (AIDS)   *821*

Equal Rights Amendment (ERA)   *817*

human immunodeficiency virus (HIV)   *821*

National Organization for Women (NOW)   *817*

32 Shocks and Responses: 1992–Present

((•—|Hear the Audio Chapter 32 at myhistorylab.com

What will happen to you?

"THOSE WHO FAIL TO LEARN FROM THE PAST ARE DOOMED TO REPEAT it"—This cliché, a favorite of history teachers, contains some truth. The book you are reading, for example, provides some solid guidance: Governments that ignore the wishes of the people probably won't long endure; wars are easier to start than to stop; and investments that seem to be "too good to be true" probably are. But apart from such common-sense observations, history provides few clues about the future.

The first decade of the twenty-first century proves this point emphatically. In 2000 Americans were mostly optimistic, and for good reason. After the dissolution of the Soviet Union in 1991, a new era of peace was dawning. Successive American presidents reduced the nation's armed forces by nearly a million men and women; defense spending (as a proportion of the GNP) was nearly cut in half. Three decades of deficits had come to an end: In 2000 the U.S. Treasury operated at a $250 billion *surplus*. The Congressional Budget Office projected a $4 *trillion* federal surplus for the coming decade.

It didn't happen. The terrorist attack of September 11, 2001 shattered hopes for peace. Within two years, American soldiers were fighting fierce battles in Afghanistan and Iraq. By the end of the decade, over 5,000 U.S. servicemen and women would be dead.

By then, too, an economic earthquake had nearly toppled the nation's major financial institutions. By late 2008 political and economic leaders were spending trillions to prop up banks, investment houses, and insurance firms that "were too big to fail." The federal deficit for the decade approached $4 *trillion*.

More bad news was to come. In early 2010 an oil rig owned by British Petroleum blew up, killing eleven and releasing millions of barrels of oil into the Gulf of Mexico. President Obama called it the nation's worst environmental disaster ever.

By then, *Time* magazine had already pronounced these years "The Decade from Hell." But no one had any inkling of this in 1992.

A New Face: Bill Clinton

William (Bill) Clinton was born William Jefferson Blythe IV, but his father died in a car accident before he was born. Though his stepfather was an abusive alcoholic, at age fifteen Bill legally took his stepfather's name. He graduated from Georgetown, won a Rhodes scholarship to study at Oxford University, and graduated from Yale Law School. He returned to Arkansas and was soon elected state attorney general.

In 1977 Clinton and his wife, Hillary Rodham, joined with James McDougal, a banker, to secure a loan to build vacation homes in the Ozarks. But the development, which they named Whitewater, eventually became insolvent. McDougal illegally covered the debts with a loan from a savings and loan company he had acquired. In 1989 the savings and loan failed, costing the federal government $60 million to reimburse depositors. In 1992 federal investigators claimed that the Clintons had been "potential beneficiaries" of McDougal's illegal activities.

By this time Clinton, now governor of Arkansas, was campaigning in the New Hampshire primary for the Democratic nomination for president. Few voters could make much sense of the financial mess known as the "Whitewater scandal," nor did they have much opportunity to do so: Another, far more explosive story threatened to sink the Clinton campaign. It came out that Clinton had for many years engaged in an extramarital affair with one Gennifer Flowers; Clinton's standing in the polls tumbled.

> **Watch the Video**
> *Bill Clinton Sells Himself to America: Presidential Campaign Ad, 1992* at **myhistorylab.com**

Hillary Rodham Clinton appeared with her husband on CBS's *60 Minutes* to address the allegations. Bill Clinton indignantly denied Flowers's statements but then issued an earnest if ambiguous appeal for forgiveness. "I have acknowledged causing pain in my marriage," he said. "I think most Americans will know what we're saying; they'll get it." Clinton was right, early evidence of his ability to address the American people directly, but on his own—carefully worded—terms. He finished second in New Hampshire, captured most of the remaining primaries, and won the Democratic nomination with ease. His choice of running mate—Senator Al Gore of Tennessee, a Vietnam veteran, family man, and environmentalist— helped the ticket considerably.

Young Bill Clinton (left) shakes hands with President John F. Kennedy. "The torch has been passed to a new generation of Americans," Kennedy had declared in his inaugural. "Ask not what your country can do for you—ask what you can do for your country," JFK added. Thirty years later, Clinton's inaugural echoed Kennedy's: "Today, a generation raised in the shadows of the Cold War assumes new responsibilities," Clinton declared. "I challenge a new generation of young Americans to a season of service."

The Election of 1992

While Clinton tiptoed through a minefield of personal scandals, President George (Herbert Walker) Bush rested secure in the belief that, after crushing Saddam Hussein and the Iraqi army in the Gulf War, the 1992 election campaign would be little more than a victory lap. But he encountered unexpectedly stiff opposition within the Republican party. Patrick Buchanan, an outspoken conservative, did well enough to alarm White House strategists. Then Ross Perot, a billionaire Texan, announced his independent candidacy. His platform had both conservative and liberal planks. He would avoid raising taxes, and cut government spending by "getting rid of waste." He also supported gun control, backed a woman's right to an abortion, and called for an all-out effort to "restructure" the health care system.

Polls quickly revealed that Perot was popular in California, Texas, and other key states that Bush was counting on winning easily. At the Republican convention in August, Bush was nominated without opposition.

On election day, more than 100 million citizens voted. About 44 million voted for Clinton, 38 million for Bush, and 20 million for Perot. Clinton was elected with 370 electoral votes to Bush's 168. Perot did not win any electoral votes.

A New Start: Clinton as President

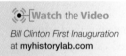

Watch the Video

Bill Clinton First Inauguration at **myhistorylab.com**

Clinton first used his executive authority to strengthen the Supreme Court majority in favor of upholding the landmark case of *Roe v. Wade.* The majority included three conservative justices who had been appointed by Reagan and Bush. Clinton appointed Ruth Bader Ginsberg, a judge known to believe that abortion was constitutional. Clinton indicated that he would veto any bill limiting abortion rights.

The first major test of the president's will came when he submitted his first budget to Congress. He hoped to reduce the deficit by roughly $500 billion in five years, half by spending cuts, half by new taxes. The proposal for a tax increase raised a storm of protest. Even so, the final bill passed by the narrowest of margins. Clinton rightly claimed a victory.

He then turned to his long-awaited proposal to reform the nation's expensive and incomplete health insurance system. A committee headed by his wife had been working for months with no indication that a plan acceptable to the medical profession,

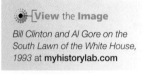

View the Image

Bill Clinton and Al Gore on the South Lawn of the White House, 1993 at **myhistorylab.com**

the health insurance industry, and ordinary citizens was likely to come from its deliberations. The plan that finally emerged seemed even more complicated and possibly more costly than the existing system. It never came to a vote in Congress.

Emergence of the Republican Majority

The Whitewater scandal, which Clinton had managed to brush aside during the campaign, gnawed at his presidency. Public pressure forced Attorney General Janet Reno to appoint a special prosecutor. She named Kenneth W. Starr, a Republican lawyer, to investigate Whitewater and other alleged misdeeds of the Clintons.

More troubles followed. Paula Corbin Jones, a State of Arkansas employee, charged that Clinton, while governor, had invited her to his hotel room and asked her to engage in oral sex. Clinton's attorney denied the accusation and sought to have the case dismissed on the grounds that a president could not be sued while in office. The case commenced a tortuous route through the courts.

Eager to take advantage of Clinton's troubles, Republicans looked to the 1994 congressional elections. Led by Congressman Newt Gingrich of Georgia, they offered voters an ambitious program to stimulate the economy by reducing both the federal debt and the federal income tax. Federally administered welfare programs were to be replaced by block grants to the states. Many measures protecting the environment, such as those making businesses responsible for cleaning up their waste, were to be repealed.

On election day, the Republicans gained control of both houses of Congress. Under the firm direction of Gingrich, now Speaker, the House approved nearly all of the provisions of this **Contract with America**. This appalled Clinton, who vetoed the 1995 budget drafted by the Republicans. When neither side agreed to a compromise, the government for a time ran out of money and shut down all but essential services.

The Election of 1996

The public tended to blame Congress, and particularly Speaker Gingrich, for the shutdown. The president's approval rating rose. But the main issue of the day was the economy, and the upturn during and after 1991 benefited Clinton enormously. By the fall of 1996, unemployment had fallen well below 6 percent, and inflation below 3 percent. Clinton was renominated for a second term without opposition.

A number of Republicans competed in the presidential primaries, but after a slow start Bob Dole of Kansas, the Senate majority leader, won the nomination. His main proposal was a steep reduction of the deficit and a 15-percent income tax cut. Pressed to explain how this could be done without drastic cuts in popular social programs, especially Social Security and Medicare, he gave a distressingly vague reply.

On election day Clinton won an impressive victory, sweeping the Northeast, all the Midwest except Indiana, the upper Mississippi Valley, and the Far West. He divided the South with Dole, who carried a band of states running north from Texas. Clinton's Electoral College margin was substantial, 379 to 159. The Republicans, however, retained control of both houses of Congress.

Clinton Impeached

Although President Clinton steadfastly denied allegations of womanizing, in January 1998 a judge ordered him to testify in Paula Corbin Jones's lawsuit against him. Jones, who sought to strengthen her suit by showing that Clinton had a history of propositioning women, also subpoenaed a former White House intern. Her name was Monica Lewinsky.

Lewinsky and Clinton were separately asked if they had had an affair, and each denied the charge. When word of their alleged relationship was leaked to the press, Clinton declared in a TV news conference, "I did not have sexual relations with that woman, Miss Lewinsky."

Unbeknown to the Clintons, however, Lewinsky had been confiding to Linda Tripp, a former White House employee, and Tripp had secretly tape-recorded some twenty hours of their conversations. Tripp turned these tapes over to special prosecutor Starr, whose investigations of the Clintons' roles in the Whitewater scandal had broadened into a more general inquiry. In the tapes Lewinsky provided intimate details of repeated sexual encounters with the president. Clinton and Lewinsky appeared to have lied under oath. Starr threatened to indict Lewinsky for perjury. In return for immunity from prosecution, she admitted that she had engaged in sexual relations with the president and that he and his aides had encouraged her to give misleading testimony in the Jones case.

When called in August to testify on videotape before the Starr grand jury, Clinton conceded that he had engaged in "inappropriate intimate contact" with Lewinsky. But he insisted, "I have not had sex with her as I defined it." When pressed to supply his own definition, he responded with legalistic obfuscation: "My understanding of this definition is it covers contact by the person being deposed with the enumerated areas, if the contact is done with an intent to arouse or gratify." Because Clinton had not intended to arouse or gratify Lewinsky, he had not "had sex" with her. He allowed that this definition was "rather strange."

●●●–[Read the Document

Bill Clinton, Answers to the
Articles of Impeachment at
myhistorylab.com

Clinton's testimony infuriated Starr, who made public Lewinsky's humiliatingly detailed testimony and announced that Clinton's deceptive testimony warranted consideration by the House of Representatives for impeachment.

But throughout Clinton's legal battles, opinion polls indicated that two in three Americans approved of his performance as president. Buoyed by the vibrant economy, most Americans blamed the scandal on the intrusive Starr nearly as much as the evasive Clinton. The November election proved disastrous for the Republicans, who nearly lost their majority in the House.

Clinton's troubles, however, were by no means over. Republican leaders in the House impeached Clinton on the grounds that he had committed perjury and had

A seemingly anonymous well-wisher from the crowd greets President Bill Clinton. When Clinton was later investigated for having an affair with Monica Lewinsky, a former White House intern, this photograph of the two surfaced. Clinton's lack of discretion struck many as self-destructive.

obstructed justice by inducing Lewinsky and others to give false testimony in the Jones case. The vote closely followed party lines.

The impeachment trial in the Senate began in January 1999. Chief Justice William Rehnquist presided. The Republicans numbered fifty-five, enough to control the proceedings but twelve short of the two-thirds necessary to convict the president and remove him from office. Democrats, while publicly critical of Clinton's behavior, maintained that his indiscretions did not constitute "high crimes and misdemeanors" as specified in the Constitution for removal from office. They prevailed. The article accusing Clinton of perjury was defeated by a vote of fifty-five to forty-five; on the article alleging obstruction of justice, the vote was fifty to fifty. Clinton remained president.

Clinton's Legacy

One reason why Clinton survived was the health of the economy. Few wanted to rock the ship of state when it was stuffed with cash. Until the final months, the Clinton years coincided with the longest economic boom in the nation's history. Clinton deserves considerable credit for the remarkable prosperity of the era. His reducing the federal deficit drove interest rates down, spurring investment and economic growth. By August 1998 unemployment had fallen to 4.5 percent, the lowest level since the 1960s; inflation had eased to a minuscule 1 percent, the lowest level since the 1950s. In 1998 the federal government operated at its first surplus since 1969. In the 2000 fiscal year, the surplus hit $237 billion.

Clinton also supported globalization of the economy. He successfully promoted the **North American Free Trade Agreement (NAFTA)** to reduce tariff barriers; Congress approved NAFTA in 1993. But the new global economy harmed many. Some union leaders bitterly asked how their members could compete against convict labor in China or sweatshop workers in Indonesia or Malaysia. Others complained that the emphasis on worldwide economic growth was generating an environmental calamity. International protests against the World Trade Organization culminated in the disruption of its 2000 meeting in Seattle, when thousands of protesters went on a rampage, setting fires and looting stores.

Clinton's record in foreign affairs was mixed. In 1993 he failed in an effort to assemble an international force to prevent "ethnic cleansing" by Serbian troops against Muslims in Bosnia, formerly part of Yugoslavia. In 1999 critics predicted another debacle when Clinton proposed a NATO effort to prevent General Slobodan Milosevic of Yugoslavia from crushing the predominantly Muslim province of Kosovo, which was attempting to secede. But after several months of intense NATO bombing of Serbia, Milosevic withdrew from Kosovo. Within a year, he was forced out of office and into prison, awaiting trial for war crimes before a UN tribunal.

Clinton labored, as had his predecessors in the White House, to broker peace between Israel and the Palestinians; like his predecessors, he failed. In 1993 Yitzhak Rabin, Israeli prime minister, and Yassir Arafat, leader of the Palestine Liberation Organization, signed an agreement preparing for a Palestinian state. But extremists on both sides shattered the fragile accord. In 1995 Rabin was assassinated by a Jewish zealot. Palestinians, enraged by the construction of Israeli settlements in Palestinian territory, stepped up their campaign of suicide bombings. Israel retaliated with tank and helicopter attacks on suspected terrorist strongholds. The negotiations collapsed. Arafat unleashed a new wave of uprisings, and hardliners, headed by Ariel Sharon, took charge of Israel. Violence intensified on both sides.

Whatever the successes and shortcomings of his administration, the Clinton presidency will always be linked to his relationship with a White House intern and the impeachment proceedings that ensued. Though by no means the first president to stray from matrimonial propriety, Clinton's behavior, in an era when the media thrived on scandal, was symptomatic of an almost willful self-destructiveness.

The Economic Boom and the Internet

A significant part of the prosperity of the 1990s came from new technologies such as cellular phones and genetic engineering. But the most important was the development of a revolutionary form of communication: the Internet.

In the early 1990s, Tim Berners-Lee, a British physicist working at a research institute in Switzerland, devised the software that became the grammar—the "protocols"—of the Internet "language." With this language, the Internet became the World Wide Web (WWW), a conduit for a stream of electronic impulses flowing among hundreds of millions of computers.

The number of Web sites increased exponentially. In 1995 Bill Gates's Microsoft entered the picture with its Windows operating system, which made the computer easy to use. It created a Web browser—Microsoft Internet Explorer—and embedded its software in the Windows 95 bundle.

"Venture capitalists," independent investors seeking to fund emerging "tech" companies, sensed a glittering new economic frontier somewhere down the Internet super-highway, and they poured billions into start-up dot-coms. In 1999 some 200 Internet companies "went public," selling shares in the major stock exchanges. They raised $20 billion easily. In the spring of 2000, with the stock market still surging, a selling wave hit the tech stocks and spilled over to other companies. Stock prices plummeted. In all, some $2 trillion in stock funds disappeared. As the 2000 election approached, many feared that the economy was nearing a recession.

The 2000 Election: George W. Bush Wins by One Vote

During the 2000 campaign, Vice President Al Gore secured the Democratic nomination and chose as running mate Senator Joseph Lieberman of Connecticut, an observant Jew and outspoken critic of Clinton during the impeachment proceedings.

The leading contender was George W. Bush, son of former President Bush. Like his father, Bush graduated from Yale and worked in the family oil business. He headed a group that bought the Texas Rangers baseball team. Although some doubted Bush's abilities, his visible success with the Rangers catapulted him into Texas politics. An effective and personable campaigner, he was elected governor in 1994. Six years later he defeated Senator John McCain of Arizona in a battle for the Republican nomination for president. Bush selected as running mate Dick Cheney, who had served as defense secretary in his father's administration.

The main issue was what to do with the federal surplus, which by some projections would soon exceed $1 trillion. Bush called for a substantial tax cut; Gore wanted to increase spending on education and shore up the Social Security system.

Gore, though knowledgeable, seemed stiff, and he occasionally indulged in self-serving bombast, as when he claimed to have "invented" the Internet. Bush's principal offense was against the English language. "Rarely is the question asked," he once declaimed, "Is our children learning?" His poetic flights of fancy did not stay long aloft, as when he evoked American aspirations for "wings to take dream" and endorsed economic growth to "make the pie higher." However exaggerated or garbled their messages, the candidates spent a record $1 billion getting it to the voters.

Having been inundated with advertisements, many on election night breathed a sigh of relief that the election was finally over. They were wrong. By midnight it appeared that Bush had 246 electoral votes, and Gore, 267, with 270 necessary to win; but Florida, with 25 electoral votes, had not been decided. As returns trickled in, the television networks reversed themselves and declared Florida—and the election—"too close to call." Bush's lead there was 1,784 out of nearly 6 million cast.

After a machine recount, Bush's margin in Florida was reduced to several hundred votes, with Democrats complaining that a punch-card ballot used in some communities was confusing, depriving Gore of thousands of votes; worse, the machines routinely failed to count incompletely punched ballots. Gore's lawyers demanded that the ballots in several predominantly Democratic counties be counted by hand. Republicans countered that Democrats had no right to change voting procedures after the election. They demanded that the hand recounts cease.

The entire election ended up in the courts. On December 12, more than a month after the election, the Supreme Court ruled by a five to four vote that the selective hand recounts violated the Constitution's guarantee of equal protection. Bush's victory stood.

Nationwide, Gore received 51 million votes, Bush, 50.5 million.

The New Terrorism

After the fall of the Soviet Union, American military might seemed unassailable. Military dictators who had been kept afloat by the Soviets or the Americans—and often from both simultaneously—now were obliged to seek the support of the people they had long ruled. This further destabilized the Middle East. The military leaders of Egypt and hereditary rulers of Saudi Arabia, for example, sought to retain the support of Islamic clerics while refraining from accepting an Islamic theocracy—direct rule by Islamic rulers. Arab leaders cultivated popular support by denouncing Israel, which refused to return land seized in the 1967 war. Insofar as Israel relied ultimately on American support, Arab rage was increasingly directed at the United States.

During these years, Islamist terrorists emerged throughout the Middle East, usually in response to the repression of radical Islamic clerics. In 1998 a new figure surfaced from among such groups: Osama bin Laden, son of a Saudi oil billionaire. In 1998, bin Laden published a *fatwa*—a religious edict—to Islamic peoples throughout the world: "To kill Americans and their allies, both civil and military, is an individual duty of every Muslim who is able . . ." By now, bin Laden was protected by an extremist Islamic group, the Taliban, that ruled Afghanistan. (The United States had provided military assistance to the Taliban in its ultimately successful campaign to drive the Soviet Union out of the country a decade earlier. See Chapter 30.) Six months later, bin Laden's terrorist organization—al-Qaeda—had planned and ordered the bombings of the U.S. embassies in Nairobi and Dar es Salaam in Africa, which killed hundreds of people.

September 11, 2001

At 8:40 on the morning of September 11, 2001, Madeline Amy Sweeney, an attendant on American Airlines Flight 11, placed a cell phone call from the galley of the plane to her supervisor in Boston. In a whisper, she said that four Arab men had slashed the throats of two attendants, forced their way into the cockpit, and taken over the plane. She gave him their seat numbers so that their identities could be determined from the passenger log. The supervisor asked if she knew where the plane was headed. She looked out the window and noted that it was descending rapidly. "I see water and buildings." The water was the Hudson River, and the buildings were the skyscrapers of lower Manhattan, foremost among them the 110-story twin towers of the World Trade Center.

The hijackers pushed the throttle to full, and the Boeing 767 was traveling at 500 miles per hour at 8:46 when it slammed into the ninety-sixth floor of the north tower. A fireball, fed by 10,000 gallons of jet fuel, instantly engulfed eight or nine stories.

Fifteen minutes later a second airliner came into view over Manhattan harbor, banked sharply, and plowed into the eightieth floor of the south tower. New York mayor Rudolph Giuliani, who had raced to the scene, asked Fire Chief Peter Ganci, "What should I communicate to people?" "Tell them to get in the stairways," Ganci replied. "I think we can save everyone below the fire." The World Trade Center employed 50,000. As thousands fled the buildings, hundreds of firefighters, Ganci among them, charged up the stairs to rescue those who were trapped.

At 9:30 the White House received word that another hijacked airliner was barreling toward Washington, DC. Secret Service agents rushed Vice President Cheney to an emergency command bunker far below the White House. At 9:35 the airliner plunged into the Pentagon and burst into flames. Cheney telephoned President Bush, who was in Sarasota, Florida. The nation was under attack. Bush authorized the Air Force to shoot down any other hijacked airliners. A few minutes later a fourth hijacked airliner crashed into a field in Pennsylvania after passengers had declared their intention— again by cell phone—to retake the plane.

While television viewers absorbed these shocks, they watched as the upper floors of the World Trade Center towers blackened, like charred matches. At 9:59, the south tower collapsed, followed by the north tower a half hour later, pulverizing millions of tons of concrete and glass and enveloping lower Manhattan in choking dust. Nearly three thousand lay dead in the mountain of rubble, including Chief Ganci and 350 firemen; several hundred more perished at the Pentagon and in the crash of the airliner in Pennsylvania.

Teams of four or five Arabic-speaking men had hijacked each of the planes. Several of the hijackers were quickly linked to the al-Qaeda terrorist network run by bin Laden, who had previously been indicted (but not captured) for the 1998 bombing of U.S. embassies in East Africa and the 2000 attack on the USS *Cole*. Bin Laden operated with impunity in Afghanistan.

A second jetliner approaches the south tower of the World Trade Center on September 11, 2001. The north tower had already been hit and was engulfed in flames and smoke.

That evening President Bush addressed the nation. He spoke simply and with force. "We will find these people," he said of the terrorists. "They will pay." Any government harboring the terrorists—an obvious reference to the Taliban—would be held equally responsible for the attack.

●●●─Read the Document

George W. Bush, Address to Congress (September 20, 2001) at **myhistorylab.com**

Several weeks later, Bush declared that bin Laden would be taken "dead or alive." The president also offered a $25 million reward for his death or capture, an evocation of swift frontier justice that suited the national mood. Within the United States, thousands of Arabs were rounded up and detained; those with visa and immigration violations were imprisoned.

Then more trouble arrived at the capital, this time in the mail. Several letters addressed to government officials included threatening messages and a white powder consisting of billions of anthrax spores, which could prove fatal if touched or inhaled. Thousands of government employees took antibiotics as a precaution, but some spores had seeped out of the envelopes and killed five postal workers and mail recipients.

Bush responded to these multiple threats by creating a Cabinet position, the Office of Homeland Security, and naming Pennsylvania Governor Tom Ridge to direct it. Repeatedly Ridge issued vague warnings of imminent terrorist attacks. How exactly Americans were to protect themselves, he did not say.

America Fights Back: War in Afghanistan

Bush had declared a **war on terror**, a war unlike any other the nation had fought. Al-Qaeda had secret terrorist cells in many countries. Bin Laden was ensconced in remote Afghanistan, protected by thousands of Taliban soldiers who had inflicted heavy losses on Soviet invaders in the 1980s. The source of the anthrax letters proved even more problematic, because the spores resembled a strain developed in American military laboratories.

Bush's challenge was all the greater because of his own stated opposition to ill-defined and far-flung military operations. He had chastised the Clinton-Gore administration for "extending our troops all around the world." He underscored his reticence for such ventures by naming Colin Powell secretary of state. Powell, who had been sobered by his experiences in Vietnam, maintained that U.S. troops should only be deployed when their political objective was clear, military advantage overwhelming, and means of disengaging secure. This became known as the Powell doctrine, and Bush had endorsed it during the campaign. But the proposed war against terror adhered to none of its precepts. Now such scruples did not matter; the president had little choice but to fight.

Powell urged European, Asian, and even Islamic states to crack down on terrorist cells in their countries and to provide assistance in the U.S. military campaign against the Taliban; he also persuaded anti-Taliban factions within Afghanistan to join forces to topple the regime. On September 20 Bush ordered the Taliban to surrender bin Laden and top al-Qaeda leaders; when the Taliban refused, Bush unleashed missiles and warplanes against Taliban installations and defenses.

For several weeks, Taliban soldiers cowered in bunkers as bombs thudded nearby; but they defended their positions when anti-Taliban forces attacked. Then small teams of elite American soldiers, armed with hand-held computers and satellite-linked navigational devices, joined with anti-Taliban contingents, marking Taliban positions with laser spotters and communicating with high-altitude bombers. These planes, circling at 30,000 feet, dropped electronically guided bombs on Taliban troops with uncanny (but not infallible) accuracy. Within weeks the Taliban were driven from power. Only one American soldier was killed by hostile fire. The United States had won the first battles in the war against terror.

The Second Iraq War

In January 2002, after the Taliban had been crushed, President Bush declared that he would not "wait on events while dangers gather." The United States would take "preemptive actions"—war—against regimes that threatened it. He identified Iran, North Korea, and Iraq as an **axis of evil** that warranted scrutiny. Immediately after September 11, he secretly initiated plans to attack Iraq, ruled by Saddam Hussein.

Secretary of State Powell advised Bush not to attack Iraq. If Saddam were driven from power, Powell warned, Bush would become "the proud owner of 25 million people—you'll own it all." Vice President Cheney, Defense Secretary Donald Rumsfeld, and others in the administration insisted that the Iraqis would welcome liberation and embrace democracy.

In September, Bush sought congressional support for an attack on Iraq. "The Iraqi regime possesses chemical and biological weapons," he declared, adding that Saddam also sought nuclear weapons. Congress voted overwhelmingly for the war appropriation.

Bush then called on the United Nations to join the United States. That Saddam had used chemical weapons during the Iran-Iraq war and also against the Kurds was beyond dispute; but following Saddam's defeat in 1991, UN inspectors had destroyed thousands of tons of Iraqi chemical weapons. They doubted that more such weapons had been stockpiled. Bush saw this as proof that Saddam had hoodwinked the inspectors. When the Security Council delayed taking action, Bush formed a coalition to oust Saddam. The United States was joined by Great Britain, Italy, Spain, and a few other countries.

On March 20, 2003, American missiles and bombs pounded Saddam's defenses. The "Shock and Awe" campaign to liberate Iraq had begun. Two armored columns roared across the Kuwaiti border into Iraq, passing burned-out Iraqi tanks from the first Gulf War. British forces moved along the coast toward the oil port of Basra. Television reporters, perched atop Humvees and armored personnel carriers, provided live coverage. The first night, American units advanced halfway to Baghdad.

On April 4, the U.S. Army seized the Baghdad International Airport. The next morning, some 800 American soldiers in tanks and armored vehicles blasted their way into downtown Baghdad. While some Iraqis poured into the streets

"Mission Accomplished" proclaimed the banner on the USS *Abraham Lincoln*, where on May 1, 2004, President George W. Bush declared, "Major combat operations in Iraq have ended." But the war continued for years.

to celebrate, others looted offices, museums, stores, and hospitals. Saddam disappeared and his government evaporated. By mid-April, the Pentagon declared that major combat operations had come to an end.

But Iraq was in chaos. There were too few U.S. troops to preserve order. Islamist radicals, enraged by the American occupation, joined with Saddam's supporters in ambushing occupation forces. The insurgents rammed trucks filled with explosives into police stations, wired cell phones to artillery shells, and detonated them as Americans approached. Others sabotaged oil pipelines and power generators.

2004: Bush Wins a Second Term

The war became the main issue of the presidential campaign. In December 2003 American soldiers captured Saddam, hiding in an underground bunker. Bush's approval rating soared.

By January, however, Senator John Kerry, a Democratic senator from Massachusetts, was gaining in the polls. The son of a diplomat and a graduate of Yale, Kerry appeared accomplished and steady. He had commanded a patrol boat during the Vietnam War and was decorated for courage under fire. In April, he won the Democratic nomination. He chose Senator John Edwards of North Carolina, a wealthy trial lawyer, as his running mate.

In Iraq, the situation deteriorated further. In April the *60 Minutes* news program revealed that American captors had tortured Iraqi captives in the Abu Ghraib prison. Photographs of American soldiers, including women, taunting naked Muslim men fueled the insurgency. Casualties mounted. The cost of the occupation spiraled upward. Worse, American forces failed to find any Iraqi weapons of mass destruction.

At the Democratic convention in July, Kerry emphasized his military service in Vietnam. He criticized Bush for attacking Iraq before capturing Osama bin Laden, who remained at large. He also chided the president for initiating war with insufficient international support, and not sending enough troops to preserve order and rebuild Iraq.

Bush mobilized conservatives and religious fundamentalists by proposing a constitutional amendment that would define marriage as the union between a man and a woman. Kerry endorsed gay rights but endlessly qualified earlier statements in support of same-sex marriage.

Republicans also portrayed Kerry as opportunistic. If Kerry and Edwards thought the war was a mistake, why did they vote for the original war resolution in the Senate? During a debate with Bush, Kerry conceded that he had "made a mistake" in explaining his position on Iraq. "But the president made a mistake in invading Iraq. Which is worse?"

The election, one of the most divisive in recent decades, brought 12 million more voters to the polls than in 2000. Kerry received 57 million votes, 3 million more than Ronald Reagan in his 1984 landslide. But Bush got over 60 million, a record. He also prevailed in the Electoral College, 286 to 252.

Crime: Good News and Bad

The crime wave of the 1980s subsided during the 1990s. By 2009, the homicide rate nationwide was 40 percent below 1991. In many big cities the decline was astonishing. In 1990, for example, 5,641 felonies were committed in New York City's twenty-fourth precinct, near Central Park; in 2009 the number of felonies there had declined to 987.

But if urban crime was down, violence repeatedly jolted the nation. On April 20, 1999, two teenagers wearing trench coats and armed with automatic weapons went on a rampage at Columbine High School in Littleton, Colorado. Before shooting themselves to death, they killed twelve students and a teacher and wounded more than thirty. On October 2, 2006, a thirty-two-year-old truck driver took a dozen Amish schoolgirls hostage and shot and killed six of them. A week earlier, in two separate incidents, a gunman took six girls hostage at Platte Canyon High School at Bailey, Colorado, and shot and killed one; and a fifteen-year-old student at Weston High School in Cazenovia, Wisconsin, shot and killed his principal.

Perhaps inspired by these attacks, a deranged student at Virginia Tech in February 2007 bought a .22 caliber Walther P22 pistol on the Internet. The next month he bought a Glock 19 rapid-fire semiautomatic pistol and acquired ammunition from online vendors and from Wal-Mart and Dick's Sporting Goods. On April 16 he went to another dorm and shot and killed a female student and the resident advisor. After reloading, he entered Norris Hall, an engineering building, chained all three entry doors closed, climbed the stairs to the second floor, and walked up and down the hallway, taking aim at students and teachers and shooting them. Then he put a pistol to his head and committed suicide. The shooting spree at Norris lasted less than ten minutes: He shot over sixty people, killing thirty-three.

The massacre at Virginia Tech was the worst mass killing in recent American history. But each year, about 14,000 Americans are killed with guns. The spate of shootings reignited a heated debate. Proponents of gun control deplored the easy access to such lethal weapons. The National Rifle Association and other defenders of the right to bear arms, affirmed by the Second Amendment to the Constitution, blamed criminals for the mayhem. They insisted that law-abiding citizens needed guns to defend themselves from such evildoers. In 2010 the Supreme Court struck down municipal laws banning handguns in Chicago and the District of Columbia (*McDonald v. Chicago*).

Hurricane Katrina

The Bush presidency was largely shadowed by two events over which he initially had little control: the terrorist attack of September 11, 2001, and Hurricane Katrina, which swept across Florida and into the warm waters of the Gulf Coast in August 2005. On the morning of August 28, the National Weather Service released so dire a warning about Katrina—"devastating damage," "most of the area will be uninhabitable for weeks"—that some broadcasters refused to read it, thinking it might be a hoax. State and federal officials ordered mandatory evacuation of the Louisiana coastline.

Millions fled in their cars, clogging the highways. But of the half million residents of New Orleans, 100,000 remained, many of them poor African Americans who lacked access to automobiles. As rain started to fall that evening, some 10,000 took refuge in the New Orleans Superdome stadium.

Early the next morning Katrina crashed ashore. Within minutes, it destroyed nearly every building in Plaquemines Parish. Winds approaching 150 miles per hour ripped two holes in the Superdome. By afternoon, the hurricane had moved north, dumping more water along the way, swelling the rivers, streams, and canals that emptied into the Gulf. Within hours, rising waters spilled over the banks and collapsed canals. Then the levees at Lake Pontchartrain broke.

Downtown New Orleans after Hurricane Katrina.

By that evening, much of New Orleans was underwater. Some 25,000 people crowded into the Superdome. Food and water grew scarce. Fights broke out. When officials locked the Superdome's doors, the thousands left outside went to the nearby Convention Center, surged past security guards, and took possession of the complex.

Over the next three days, the situation worsened. Over a million people had been displaced from their homes. In the heat and humidity, dead bodies, sewage, rotting food and plants, and factory effluents combined to form a fetid and toxic inland sea. The Convention Center, which now housed 20,000, descended into anarchy. There were reports of rape and murder. Throughout the storm-devastated region, looting became widespread; public order collapsed.

"Mr. President, we need your help," declared Louisiana Governor Kathleen Blanco. But TV crews arrived on the scene long before assistance from the Federal Emergency and Management Agency (FEMA). Television viewers were outraged to see footage of the dead floating in pools of filth or abandoned in wheelchairs.

Yet Michael Chertoff, secretary of Homeland Security (which oversaw FEMA), expressed satisfaction with its efforts. "Considering the dire circumstances that we have in New Orleans, virtually a city that has been destroyed—things are going relatively well," he declared. By then, more than 1,300 were dead.

Many shared in the blame. For decades, engineers had warned that the levees and canals in New Orleans could fail, but little was done to strengthen them. Environmentalists had complained of the overdevelopment and erosion of the coastal marshes and wetlands whose vegetation sponged up excess water, but their warnings, too, had been mostly ignored. Officials in New Orleans had neglected to devise an evacuation plan for those without cars; worse, one-sixth of the police force abandoned the city before the storm struck. In Washington, FEMA director Michael Brown was so worried about making a mistake that he failed to do much at all—the worse mistake possible. Bush erred in publicly complimenting the beleaguered FEMA director: "Brownie, you're doing a heck of a job," a statement so obviously at variance with public perception that it became an instant joke. Within a week Brown was demoted; soon afterward he resigned.

Katrina was not the worst natural disaster in the nation's history. In 1900 a hurricane destroyed Galveston, then the largest city in Texas, killing 10,000. In 1906 an earthquake hit San Francisco, ignited hundreds of fires that burned 500 blocks of the city, and killed 700—a larger proportion of the population than perished in Katrina. But apart from Katrina's terrible human toll, the hurricane pointed up the nation's vulnerability. If Homeland Security could not get buses or water to New Orleans in a timely fashion, how could it protect the nation from determined terrorists or respond effectively should they mount another attack?

Iraq Insurgency and Bush's "Surge"

Bush faltered during Katrina partly because he was distracted by Iraq. Insurgents blew up police stations and marketplaces; saboteurs destroyed power facilities and cut oil pipelines; and rival religious sects, tribes, warlords, and criminal gangs pushed the country toward anarchy.

While coalition forces attempted to halt the violence, political officials laid the foundations for a new Iraqi government. On June 28, 2004, the coalition transferred nominal authority to an Iraqi Governing Council whose chief task was to organize the

In 2006 an Iraqi tribunal convicted Saddam Hussein of murdering his own people and sentenced him to death by hanging. What might have been a defining moment in the emergence of a new Iraq was marred when he was rushed to the gallows and taunted by his executioners.

election of a National Assembly to draft a constitution. On January 30, 2005, nearly 8 million Iraqis went to the polls, almost two-thirds of the eligible voters.

The election, though fraught with irregularities, offered a glimpse of the democratic Iraq that Bush hoped would initiate a broader transformation of the Middle East. But the election also underscored the divisions within Iraq. In the north, the Kurdish majority won most of the seats, but Kurdish leaders sought to form their own state and secede. In the south, the Shiites forged strong ties to the radical Islamic clerics who ruled Iran. The Sunnis dominated the region around Baghdad. Post-Saddam Iraq was on the verge of fracturing into separate nations.

Complicating matters further was the decision by terrorists to wreck the new government by driving a deeper wedge between Sunnis and Shiites. On February 22, 2006, insurgents blew up the golden dome of the Askariya Mosque in Sammara, a Shiite shrine. Enraged Shiites attacked Sunni mosques and clerics, triggering an endless cycle of reprisals. Some Iraqi military and police officers formed extralegal death squads to eliminate Sunni leaders and terrorize their followers. Sunni militias responded in kind.

In the fall of 2006, an Iraqi tribunal convicted Saddam of killing 148 Shiites, the first of several planned trials to chronicle his regime's genocide. But on December 30, 2006, the Iraqi government dispatched Saddam to the gallows. Instead of marking the triumph of law over tyranny, the executioners resembled the Shiite death squads: Hangmen taunted Saddam and chanted the name of Muqtada Al Sadr, a Shiite cleric whose militias caused much of the chaos.

Attacks on security forces and civilians intensified and casualties mounted. As the 2006 U.S. congressional elections approached, the war was costing $2 billion a week; the annual U.S. deficit soared to a half trillion dollars. Democrats, most of whom had voted for the war, increasingly withdrew their support. Some Republicans, too, defected from the president's position.

THREE HEROES

On March 20, 2003, American, British, and NATO forces commenced the assault to drive Saddam Hussein from power. It marked the beginning of the second Gulf War, also known as "Operation Iraqi Freedom." Saddam was swiftly driven from power, but by March 20, 2010, the seventh anniversary of the war, Americans were still fighting in Iraq and Afghanistan. By then, over 5,000 United States service personnel had died, including over 100 women; over 25,000 had been wounded. The following soldiers are a random sample of that group, chosen because they died on the March 20 anniversary of the onset of the war.

Francisco ("Paquito") Martinez, 20

"Paquito" Martinez was born on December 16, 1984, in San Juan, Puerto Rico. He was the son of Francisco Martinez, an army soldier and air force airman, and Carmen R. Hernandez. In 2000 Paquito moved to Ft. Worth, Texas, where he joined his father, "Paco," and his stepmother Maria. His father worked as a computer software engineer. Paquito enjoyed skateboarding, drawing, poetry and Web design. An "army brat," he vowed never to follow his father into military service. But several months after graduating from Eastern Hills High School in 2002, "Paquito" enlisted. He thought he might eventually go into computer-based graphic design.

Francisco G. Martinez.

In 2003 he was stationed in Korea. The next year he was sent to Iraq. He soon had doubts about the war. "I will serve myself, my family, my friends, and my loved ones," he blogged. "I won't serve my country, nor will I serve its leaders."

Later that year he completed a video entitled "Peacefull." Grass sways before a distant hill. In editing the video, Martinez drained it of color. The text is sparse:

> take this time to breathe
> open your mind
> feel your worries flow free

Then a monarch butterfly, in dazzling yellows and orange, wafts across the scene.

> life is what you make of it

On March 20, 2005, while on patrol in Tamin, Iraq, a sniper shot Martinez in the hip, severing an artery; despite trauma surgery, he died within an hour.

Curtis E. Glawson Jr., 24

Curtis E. Glawson was born on June 10, 1982, in Detroit, Michigan. His parents—Yolanda and Curtis Sr.—were both career soldiers. As a child Curtis traveled with his parents from one base to another in Germany, New Mexico, Georgia, and Alabama. He learned to adapt to different people and cultures and made friends quickly; his smile was electric.

Glawson was fast and agile and he excelled in sports. When not engaged in football, baseball, basketball and running, he enjoyed sports-related video games. He was a passionate fan of all Detroit (and Michigan) sports teams. Friends called him Mr. ESPN.

Curtis E. Glawson Jr.

In 2000 Glawson graduated from Daleville high school in Alabama, near Fort Rucker. He immediately enlisted in the army. That fall he was sent to Fort Jackson, South Carolina, where he received advanced training in mechanics. Certified as a light truck mechanic, he was subsequently stationed in Afghanistan, Uzbekistan, and Korea.

In Korea, he met Hyunjung Jang; the couple married at the United States embassy in Seoul in September, 2005.

In February, 2007 he was sent to Baghdad in Iraq. Once, when his unit made a wrong turn, they encountered a group of preteens armed with AK-47 automatic weapons. Although he grew increasingly nervous about his missions, he relished his work. When his mother urged him to beg off dangerous assignments, he replied, "No, momma, I can't do that. I have a job to do."

On the morning of March 20, 2007, Glawson was sent to retrieve a truck that broke down in the outskirts of Baghdad. He went out, fixed it, and brought it back to the motor pool. Later that afternoon, his platoon sergeant asked if Curtis could rescue another disabled vehicle in a dangerous sector. "I'm good to go, sergeant," Glawson replied. "Are you sure?" the officer asked, looking him in the eye. "Always ready, sergeant," Glawson replied.

That journey proved to be his last. As the road wound toward the dusty hills outside Baghdad, an **improvised explosive device (IED)** blew up his vehicle. Glawson was killed instantly. He wanted to be remembered as a loving son, husband, brother, friend, and dedicated soldier.

Daniel J. Geary, 22

Daniel Geary was born on September 12, 1986, the son of Michael Geary, machine foreman, and Agnes Geary, machine operator, in Rome, New York. Daniel was the fourth of seven children. When he was eight, he smelled smoke and pulled his four-year-old sister from a room that was engulfed in flames.

As a teenager, Geary enjoyed paintball, working on his Chrysler Sebring, and bowling. At sixteen, he bowled his first perfect game. He attended Rome Free Academy, a public high school, but dropped out a few weeks before graduation. For a time, he was

Daniel J. Geary.

unsure of what to do with his life. He landed a job at the Turning Stone Casino in Rome, owned by the Oneida Indians. Several months later, however, he resolved to get his diploma. "I was never more proud of him," his mother recalled. In 2006 he returned to school, joined the officer training program, and decided on a career in the military. In June, shortly before receiving his diploma, he enlisted in the Marines and soon subscribed to its motto wholeheartedly: *semper fidelis* (always faithful).

In September, Geary reported to Camp Lejeune, North Carolina, where he met his fiancée. In November, 2008, after a tour of duty on a ship in the Indian Ocean, he was sent to Kandahar, Afghanistan. He was impressed by the mountains that towered above ancient valleys. "Other than people trying to shoot me and blow me up," he told his mother, "you can't believe how beautiful it is over here."

On March 19, 2009, he was part of a team of Marines that caught an enemy bomber near a police station. The next day the team returned to the station to encourage the local police to work harder to capture insurgents. While the others were meeting inside, Geary stood guard, manning a machine gun in a Humvee. Then a car with police markings came through the gate, approached the Humvee and blew up, killing Geary instantly.

Question for Discussion

■ These three soldiers are among the millions who contributed to the American destiny but whose names so often are missing from historical accounts. What other unsung heroes are missing from this book?

When the midterm votes were counted, the Republicans were decisively defeated. Democrats now controlled Congress—and the budget. Several days after the election Bush dismissed Defense Secretary Rumsfeld, acknowledging voter "displeasure with the lack of progress in Iraq." But the president vowed to remain. "America's going to stand with you," Bush promised Iraqi leaders.

Democrats named Nancy Pelosi Speaker of the House of Representatives, the first woman to hold that position. Insofar as the speaker follows the vice president in chain of succession, Pelosi became the highest-ranking woman ever to hold office in the United States. In January 2007, when Bush called for a modest increase in troop levels in Iraq, Pelosi and some prominent Democrats opposed the measure. The Democratic leadership in Congress voted to reduce funding for the war, actions Bush vetoed.

In January, 2007 Bush named General David Petraeus to command a "**surge**" in American troop levels in Iraq. The troops were to remove insurgents from a region, establish military control over it, and build stronger ties with the Iraqi people. Initially, Petraeus made little progress. The losses among American military personnel mounted (see American Lives, "Three Heroes," pp. 850–851). Petraeus shifted more military tasks to the Iraqis and reduced operations that would likely lead to high civilian casualties. He also worked to bring former Sunni leaders into the Iraqi government. By the spring of 2008, the violence in Iraq had declined; the "surge" appeared to be working.

2008: McCain v. Obama

By the spring of 2008 John McCain, a Republican senator from Arizona, was far ahead in the race for the Republican nomination. McCain had piloted a navy fighter-bomber during the Vietnam war. After his plane was shot down over North Vietnam, he was held as a prisoner-of-war for six years; occasionally he was tortured. Now seventy-one, McCain if elected would be the oldest person to serve as a first-term president. Although McCain's positions were similar to those of Bush, McCain had often criticized the president and described himself as a "maverick."

Watch the Video

The Historical Significance of the 2008 Presidential Election at **myhistorylab.com**

True to his own label, he surprised pundits by naming Sarah Palin, the little-known governor of Alaska, as running mate. Her youth (forty-four) counterbalanced McCain's age. Palin also exhibited a down-to-earth feistiness. She was a new type of feminist: a former beauty queen who hunted and fished; an ardent defender of traditional family values who pursued an extravagantly ambitious career.

Among Democrats, Hillary Clinton, now a senator from New York, emerged as frontrunner. But she was soon eclipsed by Barack Obama, a first-term senator from Illinois (see Chapter 31, American Lives, "Barack Obama"). Clinton had voted for the war in Iraq while Obama opposed it; otherwise they agreed on most issues. Obama won the Democratic nomination and named Joe Biden, a senator from Delaware, as his running-mate.

During the general election McCain pointed out that Obama had failed to serve even a single full term as U.S. senator: Obama, he claimed, was unqualified for the presidency. But McCain's choice of Palin deprived McCain of his strongest issue. Palin had served as governor for only two and a half years; before that she was mayor of tiny Wasilla, Alaska. When critics questioned her experience in foreign affairs, her breezy reply—"You can actually see Russia from land here in Alaska"—cast doubt on McCain's judgment.

Obama criticized the Republican administration for waging war against Iraq, thereby diverting resources that might have crushed the main 9/11 culprits: the

Taliban in Afghanistan and Osama bin Laden, who remained at large. Obama proposed moving troops from Iraq to Afghanistan. He also advocated a major expansion of federally backed health care. McCain sought to send more troops to Iraq: The "war on terror" did not allow retreats. He also criticized Obama's health-care proposal as a major step toward socialized medicine.

As the campaign was heating up, a tremor rocked the foundations of the global economic system. Alarming financial news pushed the campaign out of the headlines.

Republican candidates John McCain and Sarah Palin campaign at Franklin & Marshall University in 2008.

Financial Meltdown

The fault lines of the 2008–2009 crisis extended to the 1990s. At that time the economy appeared to have recovered from the recession that began in 1973. But while the stock market soared, wages lagged far behind. By 2005, for the first time since the Great Depression, the American people spent more than they earned. Mostly they bought houses. But how, without savings, could they afford down payments? Politicians, bankers, and financial "wizards" had devised several solutions. In 2002 President George W. Bush declared that the government should "encourage folks to own their own home." Homeowners, he believed, were more responsible citizens than renters. Leaders in both parties advocated easier lending requirements and prodded the huge federally owned mortgage companies to issue more mortgages. Private mortgage companies followed suit. They reasoned that as house prices increased, the ability of homeowners to repay loans mattered less: A repossessed house could be sold for more than the original mortgage loan.

Granted easier credit, millions of Americans for the first time bought homes. In 1994, 64 percent of U.S. families owned homes; by 2004, the percentage had increased to

Table 32.1 Causes of the 2008–2009 Financial Crisis

Consumers exhaust savings to buy houses
The president and Congress call on federally owned mortgage companies to relax lending requirements
Global investment bankers devise complicated bundles of mortgages and market them globally
Credit-rating agencies grade these mortgage investments as solid and AIG insures them
Lending banks issue mortgages greatly in excess of available reserves
Millions of homeowners fall into debt and cannot make mortgage payments
Collapse of mortgage investments brings down investment banks
Capital evaporates, leading to layoffs and threatening a second Great Depression

69 percent, the highest ever. Housing prices soared. Many homeowners bought bigger ones—"McMansions," in the slang of the day.

Soon banks and mortgage companies had exhausted their capital. Large international investment banks such as Goldman Sachs, Lehman Brothers, and Bear Stearns more than filled the void. They bought tens of thousands of mortgages from the original banks and lending institutions. Lending banks used this revenue to loan out more mortgages— thereby generating more profits (and bonuses). International investment firms chopped up the mortgages like sausages, clumped them into complicated investment bundles, and sold the bundles to investors worldwide. Credit-rating companies, such as Moody's and Standard and Poor's, pronounced the bundles to be sound investments. And many investors bought insurance from the American Insurance Group (AIG) to protect them if the bundles somehow went bad. AIG, perceiving little risk, failed to set aside much money to cover potential losses.

By late 2008, however, millions of homeowners were swamped with bills they could not pay. Total household debt in the United States exceeded $14.5 *trillion*—twenty times more than in 1974. Nearly 10 percent of all American mortgages were delinquent or in foreclosure. Goldman Sachs quietly placed bets that the mortgage bundles it had mass-marketed would lose their value!

Investors suddenly caught on and dumped their mortgage bundles. Panic selling hit financial markets worldwide. Almost overnight, Bear Stearns collapsed and Lehman Brothers went bankrupt. The Dow Jones Industrial Average plunged from over 14,000 to under 9,000; stocks lost $8 trillion. Pension funds, corporate reserves, and personal accounts for retirement and college education lost one-third of their value. AIG, swamped with claims, neared bankruptcy. Its failure would take down many of the world's major banks and investment firms.

Nearly all banks and investment houses ran low on capital; many struggled to stave off bankruptcy. Few could make new loans. But most businesses, hospitals, schools, state and municipal governments relied on short-term loans, which were repaid as revenues came in. In the absence of these customary loans, few employers could pay bills or cover payrolls. A global calamity loomed.

In the final months of 2008, Bush and his chief financial advisers raced to avert catastrophe. Ben Bernanke, head of the Federal Reserve and a scholar of the Great Depression, pleaded with Congress to authorize over $700 billion to buy up the "toxic" mortgage bundles, an indirect way of preserving the banks and global investment firms that had issued them. He also proposed to pump hundreds of billions directly into Goldman Sachs, AIG, and scores of other investment banks. Such companies, he warned, were "too big to fail." Congress seethed at using taxpayers' money to bail out avaricious corporate executives; but political leaders could not risk a second Great Depression.

"Yes We Can": Obama Elected President

The economic crisis caught nearly everyone by surprise. Much of the blame fell on Republicans, whose support for deregulation of financial markets dated from the Reagan era. McCain was especially hurt by the economic meltdown. On September 15, 2008, the day after Lehman Brothers declared bankruptcy, McCain downplayed the crisis, claiming "The fundamentals of our economy are strong." Within a few hours, the stock market fell 500 points. He appeared to be out of touch.

Obama's oft-repeated (albeit vague) insistence on change now acquired new meaning. When confronted with "impossible odds," he insisted, "Americans have responded with a simple creed: Yes we can." The nation was ready for change. On election day, Obama won by over 8 million votes; his victory in the Electoral College was by a 365 to 173 margin.

▶ Watch the Video

The Connection Between Obama & Lincoln at **myhistorylab.com**

Obama's victory stunned foreigners. Nelson Mandela, the black leader of the movement that toppled white rule in South Africa, claimed that Obama's election inspired everyone who wanted "to change the world for a better place." Gordon Brown, prime minister of Great Britain, called Obama's election "a moment that will live in history as long as history books are written."

Obama as President

Only a few weeks after Obama, his wife Michelle, and their two daughters had moved into the White House, he was awarded the Nobel Prize "for his extraordinary efforts to strengthen international diplomacy and cooperation between peoples." Abashed at receiving an award in the expectation that he would earn it, Obama gave the $1.4 million prize to charity. Nevertheless, Obama's intentions of changing the course of American foreign policy were evident. He closed CIA-run secret prisons and banned torture and other means of coercion during interrogation of suspected terrorists. He named Hillary Clinton secretary of state and promised to work more closely with the international community.

In Iraq, Obama proceeded cautiously. He asked Robert Gates, secretary of defense under Bush, to remain in that capacity in his administration. He also announced a plan to withdraw most American troops from Iraq by the fall of 2010.

During his first months as president, however, Obama was mostly absorbed in the financial crisis. Despite repeated promises of change, he retained many of Bush's chief financial advisers; nearly all were Wall Street insiders. Critics grumbled that it made little sense to ask those who had broken the economy to put it back together. But Obama had little choice. No one else understood the complicated mathematical models on which modern trading was based; unfortunately, few Wall Street executives understood them either. Macroeconomics, some economists maintained, had become an elaborate exercise in chaos theory.

By late March 2009 the Dow Jones had fallen below 6,600, down from 14,000 seventeen months earlier. Chrysler declared bankruptcy, followed by General Motors several months later. Huge layoffs ensued. Unemployment rose steadily, surpassing

President-elect Barack Obama, his daughters, and wife, Michelle, celebrate his victory in November, 2008.

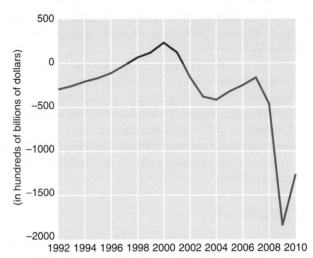

Annual Federal Deficit (and Surplus), 1992–2010 After years of deficits, the federal government operated at a $250 billion surplus in 2000. But the war on terror after 9/11 resulted in massive deficits, which were exacerbated by the financial meltdown after 2008.

10 percent for the first time in several decades. Obama pumped another $700 billion into the struggling economy.

Then word leaked out that hundreds of millions of dollars had been paid in bonuses to executives of Goldman Sachs, AIG, and many of the big banks that had been saved by federal bailouts. Obama railed against their ill-timed greed and slapped the companies with nuisance taxes, but he could do little else. He needed the big financial institutions to help jolt the economy back to life.

By the fall of 2009, the strategy appeared to be working. Employment increased and the stock market rose. Some banks repaid their government loans. Talk of economic collapse abated, partly because predictions varied widely. Some economists insisted that once the stimulus money had been exhausted, employment, wages, and prices would again fall and the nation would slip into a recession—or worse. Others pointed to the projected $1.8 trillion deficit for 2009 and predicted rampant inflation. Insofar as no one had forecast the financial meltdown of 2008–2009, most political leaders discounted *all* economic predictions and simply hoped for the best.

Health Care Reform

By 2009 nearly everyone agreed that medical costs had spun out of control. In 1990, per capital medical expenditures were $3,000; by 2009, they exceeded $8,000. That year, though nearly 18 percent of the nation's gross domestic product went for medical care, some 46 million Americans lacked any coverage whatsoever. When struck by serious illness, they were denied treatment or were hit with staggering bills. More than half of the nation's personal bankruptcies were precipitated by illness.

Obama's goal was twofold: to provide health care to Americans who lacked it and to reduce health care costs. Some advocated a government-run system, such as Franklin Roosevelt had done with old age pensions through Social Security. Many European governments operated health care systems along similar lines. But opposition

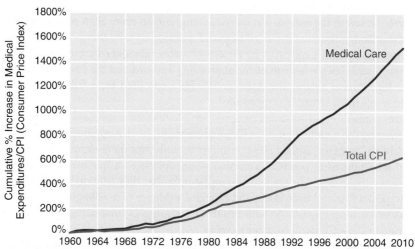

Price Increases - CPI vs. Medical Care (Cumulative % Increase)

The Increasing Cost of Health Care, 1960–2008 (% increase) By the 1990s, health care cost increases greatly exceeded the increase in the Consumer Price Index.

to socialized medicine in the United States was intense. Polls showed that few Americans wanted their doctors to be employees of the federal government.

Supported by Democratic leaders in Congress, Obama proposed a system that combined private and public health insurance. Elderly and poor Americans would continue to be covered by the government; private insurers would continue to insure millions of Americans, but they could not kick people out of their systems when they became ill; companies with more than fifty employees would be required to provide health care insurance for employees and their families or else face stiff penalties; most other persons would be eligible for publicly supported health insurance.

Republicans almost uniformly denounced the plan; they insisted that Americans did not want the federal government to control health care. Republicans instead recommended tax incentives or state initiatives to encourage private employers to broaden coverage. Republicans added that the federal government, with a looming annual deficit of $1.8 trillion, would be hard-pressed to pay for Medicare in the future; to embark on a major new commitment was madness.

The Democrats, despite strong majorities in both houses of Congress, were themselves divided on Obama's plan. The final compromise provided for his reform to be phased in over ten years at a cost of $1 trillion, and coverage would not be universal: By 2019, 24 million people would still lack health insurance, about a third of them illegal immigrants.

In March 2010, Congress approved the measure—the vote in the House was 220 to 207. No Republican voted for the bill. Obama had nevertheless engineered the first major health care reform since 1965, when President Lyndon Johnson signed Medicare into law.

Immigration Reform

Buoyed by this success, Obama turned to immigration. Early in his presidency, he strengthened border security to cut down on illegal immigration from Mexico, an action that angered Mexican leaders (see the introduction to Chapter 11, p. 299).

Yet illegal immigration persisted. In 2010 Arizona governor Jan Brewer, complaining that "the majority of illegal trespassers" were "bringing drugs in," signed the toughest immigration law in the nation. It required immigrants to carry alien registration forms at all times and authorized police to stop and question anyone they suspected of being an illegal immigrant. Legislators in dozens of states introduced similar bills. Obama denounced such laws as a form of racial profiling and ordered the Justice Department to take legal action against the Arizona bill. He also called for a federal initiative to prevent states from acting "irresponsibly."

Obama also steered toward a compromise. He rejected state plans for rounding up and deporting the nation's 11 million illegal immigrants; he also opposed liberal proposals to declare an "amnesty" against illegal immigrants and grant them immediate citizenship. Instead he proposed a "practical, common-sense" solution—a "pathway to citizenship." Illegal immigrants would be granted citizenship only after they admitted they had broken the law, paid a fine and back taxes, and provided evidence of a willingness to assimilate, such as by learning English. As with health care reform, Obama outlined few specifics, preferring to allow Congress to shape the plan.

Republicans bristled; without more effective policing of the border, Obama's "reform" would encourage more illegal immigrants to pour into the country. Many complained that Obama was courting Hispanic voters just a few months ahead of the 2010 congressional elections. The prospects for quick passage of comprehensive immigration reform seemed poor.

Environmental Concerns and Disaster in the Gulf

During his first weeks in office, Obama had pledged a "new era of global cooperation on climate change." Nearly everyone assumed that he intended to push for ratification of the 1997 agreement, signed by more than 130 nations at Kyoto, Japan, to reduce emissions of carbon dioxide and other atmospheric pollutants. The Senate had opposed the Kyoto accords because developing nations—including China, the worst air polluter in the world—were exempted from its costly provisions. President Clinton never submitted the treaty for ratification. In 2001, President George W. Bush withdrew the United States from subsequent negotiations. But in 2006 the mayors of over 200 U.S. cities, struggling with smog and air pollution, signed a Climate Protection Agreement pledging to meet the Kyoto targets for greenhouse gas reductions by 2012. But if Obama intended to move in the direction of the Kyoto agreements, the economic crisis of 2008–2009 changed his mind. With the nation's economy in recession, Obama thought it unwise to impose new environmental restrictions. In late 2009 he quietly withdrew support for an international arrangement on atmospheric pollutants.

By then, political economic realities had already caused Obama to backtrack on another environmental issue. Originally an opponent of oil drilling off the Atlantic coast, he changed his position during the 2008 presidential campaign: The nation needed cheap oil and gasoline (see introduction, Chapter 30, p. 787). On April 21, 2010, disaster struck in the Gulf of Mexico. Workers aboard a British Petroleum (BP) oil platform forty-one miles off the coast of Louisiana were drilling for oil at a depth of 5,000 feet. The drill hit a pocket of methane gas under high pressure; it shot upward through the drilling pipe and exploded, blasting eleven workers from the platform and engulfing it in flames. Oil gushed from the damaged pipe, an upsetting image captured by underwater cameras

A brown pelican surveys the ecological damage caused by the BP oil spill in the Gulf of Mexico in 2010.

and transmitted by streaming video on the Web. The world watched in horror as BP's repeated attempts to cap the well failed; weeks passed as hundreds of millions of gallons of oil spewed into the Gulf, fouling marshes and beaches, killing fish, birds, and aquatic life. Obama called it the "worst environmental disaster America has faced."

Pressure built on him to "do something." Exactly what was unclear. "He can't put on scuba gear and go down and stop this well," observed New York City mayor Michael Bloomberg, a Republican. Obama forced BP to set aside $20 billion to cover damage claims and sacked the director of the Minerals Management Service for failing to adequately inspect the off-shore platforms. He also declared a six-month moratorium on deepwater drilling, pending the inspection of existing platforms.

Opponents of the moratorium included both of Louisiana's senators and its governor, Bobby Jindal, who noted that the oil industry accounted for 17 percent of Louisiana's jobs and much of the state's revenue. Such opposition underscored the dilemma confronting a nation whose thirst for cheap oil was unquenchable. The exhaustion of oil reserves beneath the earth's landmass necessitated offshore drilling; but the environmental risks of deep-sea drilling were all too apparent.

Obama resurrected his campaign goal of promoting alternative sources of energy, such as solar and wind power. But such solutions seemed to lie far in the future. Whether the disaster in the Gulf of Mexico would reinvigorate the environmental movement remained to be seen.

Afghanistan, Again

The economic crisis and the environmental calamity in the Gulf of Mexico notwithstanding, Afghanistan loomed as the dominant issue for Obama's presidency. Few could have imagined such a development in December 2001, when the war in Afghanistan appeared to be over. The Taliban had been driven from power; most of

An Army helicopter arrives to evaluate soldiers wounded after their armored vehicle hit an improvised explosive device (IED) in the Tangi Valley in Afghanistan.

its leaders had been killed or captured or they had fled to Pakistan. Bush shifted his attention to driving Saddam Hussein from power in Iraq; a United Nations commission was given the task of building a new Afghan government.

In late 2001, the commission summoned Afghan leaders who eventually chose Hamid Karzai as interim leader of the nation. Karzai had helped channel American aid to the Taliban when it was fighting the Soviet Union; he later became a staunch opponent of the Taliban and worked with Americans to forge a coalition in opposition to it. As interim leader, Karzai relied on United Nations troops—one-half of them provided by the United States—to enforce the new government's authority.

For a time it appeared that a new Afghanistan was emerging. Hundreds of schools, hospitals, and roads were built; women were granted new rights. In 2004 Karzai defeated twenty-two opponents to become the first democratically elected president of the Islamic Republic of Afghanistan.

But much of the progress was illusory. Karzai's government was weak and riddled with corruption. In the southern sections of Afghanistan, Islamic radicals resurfaced and the former Taliban slipped back into the country, calling on Muslims to fight "infidel" troops. In the north, tribal leaders jockeyed to expand their power. Nearly everywhere, criminal militias vied for control of the lucrative opium trade.

The election scheduled for the fall of 2009 made matters worse. The first round was marred by voting fraud, which UN observers confirmed. During the final campaign the chief opposition candidate withdrew, charging Karzai's government with rigging the outcome. Karzai "won" by default. Enemies of Karzai's regime exploited the controversy.

By late 2009 Obama, who had opposed the "surge" in Iraq, sent another 30,000 troops to Afghanistan. American forces increasingly relied on drones—unmanned planes—to drop guided bombs on suspected enemies in Afghanistan and Pakistan. When the bombs missed the targets and killed civilians, riots ensued and UN casualties mounted.

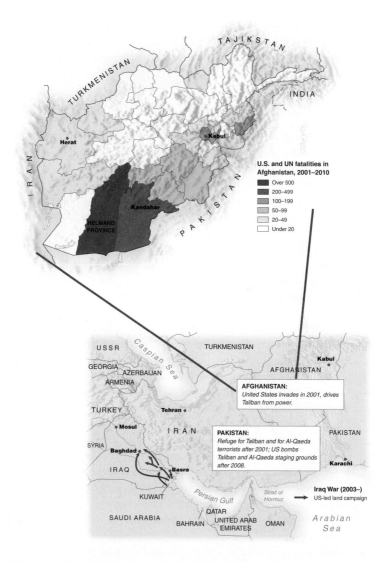

War in Iraq and Afghanistan, 2001–Present Since 2003, the United States has fought two major wars in Central Asia: in Afghanistan, first to drive the Taliban from power and later to suppress an insurgency; and in Iraq, first to crush Saddam Hussein and later to install a democratic government. In Afghanistan, American losses have been heaviest in the southern provinces bordering Pakistan.

For some time, General Stanley McChrystal, commander of the United Nations troops, had chafed at rules of engagement designed to limit civilian casualties. Obama's administration, McChrystal's aides complained to reporters for *Rolling Stone*, was weak and ineffective. The article appeared in June 2010, the month with the heaviest losses of the war. Obama sacked McChrystal for insubordination, replacing him with David Petraeus, architect of the "surge" in Iraq. "We have arrived at a critical point," Petraeus declared on July 4, 2010. "We are in this to win."

A month later secret government documents, leaked to the press, revealed that while Pakistan had pledged to support the war on terror, its intelligence service helped the Taliban plan attacks on American soldiers. Insurgents in Iraq and Afghanistan persisted in blowing up crowded marketplaces, mosques, and government offices. Prospects for victory in the region remained bleak; no one could even imagine what it would look like.

The Persistent Past and Imponderable Future

But the previous eighteen years had shown that human events rarely unfold in predictable ways. The 9/11 terrorist attack, the subsequent wars in Iraq and Afghanistan, the near-collapse of the economy in 2008–2009, Hurricane Katrina, and the massive oil spill in the Gulf of Mexico all shocked the American people. And the surprises were not all bad. No one in 1992 could have predicted that the tidal wave of crime would recede the following decade. For that matter, the relative absence of racial references during the 2008 campaign that resulted in the election of the nation's first African American president would have been unimaginable decades earlier.

But if the past does not enable us to predict the future, what do we ever "learn" from history? Consider an analogy with seismology, the study of earthquakes. Seismologists cannot predict exactly when and where any earthquake will strike, but their study of the underlying forces—the shift and collision of tectonic plates—helps explain the phenomenon. Historians similarly cannot predict the future course of human events. But the study of history can provide insights on the underlying forces that generate historical change. No one predicted, for example, that a particular deep-sea oil well would explode and release millions of barrels of oil into the Gulf of Mexico in the summer of 2010; but the American nation's voracious thirst for oil—a result of many developments during the previous century—led to the demand for the exploitation of deep-water oil resources. Similarly, in the first decades of the twenty-first century Americans fought and died in Iraq and Afghanistan because of a wide variety of historical forces, ranging from a commitment to democratic values and human rights to a demand for cheap Middle Eastern oil. History does not predict the future, which emerges through the convergence of infinite actions and reactions. But history can help reveal the various forces that are heaving beneath the surface of time.

This book was conceived as a reminder that the past is never truly past. It radiates through time. It touches our lives, just as what we do today will influence the future. By connecting to the past, we better understand ourselves and perhaps gain an inkling of what will become of us.

Milestones

1992	Democrat Bill Clinton is elected president
1993	Ruth Bader Ginsberg becomes second woman justice of the Supreme Court
1994	Republicans win control of both houses of Congress
	Congress defeats Clinton's health care reform plan
1996	Democrat Bill Clinton is reelected president; Republicans retain control of Congress
	Measure revamping federal welfare system is passed by Congress and signed by President Clinton
1998	The House of Representatives impeaches Clinton
1999	Clinton acquitted by Senate, Clinton remains in office
	NATO troops, including Americans, are sent to Kosovo to stop Serbian "ethnic cleansing"
	Gun violence in schools escalates; twelve die at Columbine High School in Colorado
2000	Republican George W. Bush is elected president when Supreme Court halts Florida recounts
2001	Terrorists hijack airliners and fly them into the twin towers of the World Trade Center in New York and the Pentagon, killing 3,000
	United States drives Taliban from power in Afghanistan

2002	President Bush prepares for war as he accuses Saddam Hussein of Iraq of developing weapons of mass destruction
2003	United States and United Kingdom attack and defeat Iraq and capture Saddam Hussein
2004	Republican George W. Bush is reelected president
2005	Hurricane Katrina devastates New Orleans and Gulf Coast region
2007	Democrat Nancy Pelosi becomes first woman Speaker of the House
2008	Deranged student kills thirty-three at Virginia Tech
	Democrat Barack Obama is first African American to be elected president
	Collapse of U.S. mortgage markets triggers global financial crisis
2009	Obama implements troop surge in Afghanistan
2010	Congress approves health care bill
	BP-owned rig explodes, killing eleven and spewing oil into the Gulf of Mexico
	Arizona passes law to crack down on illegal immigrants; national debate ensues
	Republicans take control of House of Representatives

✓●─[Study and **Review** at **www.myhistorylab.com**

Review Questions

1. The introduction divides this chapter into two different narrative arcs: the first one—from 1992 to 2001—is mostly positive; the second, from 9/11 through 2010, is said to constitute—as *Time* magazine put it—"The Decade from Hell." What were the "positive" aspects of the period from 1992 to 2001? The "negative" components of the subsequent one? How is this characterization too simple?

2. Bill Clinton was hardly the first president to commit adultery. Why did his indiscretions lead to charges that resulted in an impeachment proceeding? Did his actions constitute "high crimes and misdemeanors"? What were the major achievements of the Clinton presidency?

3. The section of this chapter on the disputed 2000 presidential election is subtitled: "George W. Bush Wins by One Vote." What does that mean? Why did Bush win the election?

4. Why did Islamist terrorists attack on 9/11? Why did George W. Bush go to war against Afghanistan shortly afterwards? Why did he then invade Iraq? What issues in Iraq made it difficult to withdraw United States troops?

5. Hurricane Katrina was a natural disaster. To what extent, however, did human actions—and inactions—aggravate the calamity?

6. Why did global financial markets nearly collapse from 2008–2009? What caused the financial meltdown? What impact did it have on Americans?

7. What factors contributed to Barack Obama being elected president? What were the major elements of his health care reform act and how did he get it through Congress?

8. Why did Obama send American troops back into Afghanistan?

Key Terms

axis of evil *844*

Contract with America *837*

improvised explosive device (IED) *851*

North American Free Trade Agreement (NAFTA) *839*

"surge" *852*

war on terror *843*

APPENDIX: The Declaration of Independence

In Congress, July 4, 1776

The Unanimous Declaration of the Thirteen United States of America,

When, in the course of human events, it becomes necessary for one people to dissolve the political bonds which have connected them with another, and to assume, among the powers of the earth, the separate and equal station to which the laws of nature and of nature's God entitle them, a decent respect to the opinions of mankind requires that they should declare the causes which impel them to the separation.

We hold these truths to be self-evident: That all men are created equal; that they are endowed by their Creator with certain unalienable rights; that among these are life, liberty, and the pursuit of happiness; that, to secure these rights, governments are instituted among men, deriving their just powers from the consent of the governed; that whenever any form of government becomes destructive of these ends, it is the right of the people to alter or to abolish it, and to institute new government, laying its foundation on such principles, and organizing its powers in such form, as to them shall seem most likely to effect their safety and happiness. Prudence, indeed, will dictate that governments long established should not be changed for light and transient causes; and accordingly all experience hath shown that mankind are more disposed to suffer, while evils are sufferable, than to right themselves by abolishing the forms to which they are accustomed. But when a long train of abuses and usurpations, pursuing invariably the same object, evinces a design to reduce them under absolute despotism, it is their right, it is their duty, to throw off such government, and to provide new guards for their future security. Such has been the patient sufferance of these colonies; and such is now the necessity which constrains them to alter their former systems of government. The history of the present King of Great Britain is a history of repeated injuries and usurpations, all having in direct object the establishment of an absolute tyranny over these states. To prove this, let facts be submitted to a candid world.

He has refused his assent to laws, the most wholesome and necessary for the public good.

He has forbidden his governors to pass laws of immediate and pressing importance, unless suspended in their operation till his assent should be obtained; and, when so suspended, he has utterly neglected to attend to them.

He has refused to pass other laws for the accommodation of large districts of people, unless those people would relinquish the right of representation in the legislature, a right inestimable to them, and formidable to tyrants only.

He has called together legislative bodies at places unusual, uncomfortable, and distant from the depository of their public records, for the sole purpose of fatiguing them into compliance with his measures.

He has dissolved representative houses repeatedly, for opposing, with manly firmness, his invasions on the rights of the people.

He has refused for a long time, after such dissolutions, to cause others to be elected; whereby the legislative powers, incapable of annihilation, have returned to the people at large for their exercise; the state remaining, in the mean time, exposed to all the dangers of invasions from without and convulsions within.

He has endeavored to prevent the population of these states; for that purpose obstructing the laws for naturalization of foreigners; refusing to pass others to encourage their migration hither, and raising the conditions of new appropriations of lands.

He has obstructed the administration of justice, by refusing his assent to laws for establishing judiciary powers.

He has made judges dependent on his will alone, for the tenure of their offices, and the amount and payment of their salaries.

He has erected a multitude of new offices, and sent hither swarms of officers to harass our people and eat out their substance.

He has kept among us, in times of peace, standing armies, without the consent of our legislatures.

He has affected to render the military independent of, and superior to, the civil power.

He has combined with others to subject us to a jurisdiction foreign to our constitution, and unacknowledged by our laws, giving his assent to their acts of pretended legislation:

For quartering large bodies of armed troops among us;

For protecting them, by a mock trial, from punishment for any murder which they should commit on the inhabitants of these states;

For cutting off our trade with all parts of the world;

For imposing taxes on us without our consent;

For depriving us, in many cases, of the benefits of trial by jury;

For transporting us beyond seas, to be tried for pretended offenses;

For abolishing the free system of English laws in a neighboring province, establishing therein an arbitrary government, and enlarging its boundaries, so as to render it at once an example and fit instrument for introducing the same absolute rule into these colonies;

For taking away our charters, abolishing our most valuable laws, and altering fundamentally the forms of our governments;

For suspending our own legislatures, and declaring themselves invested with power to legislate for us in all cases whatsoever.

He has abdicated government here, by declaring us out of his protection and waging war against us.

He has plundered our seas, ravaged our coasts, burned our towns, and destroyed the lives of our people.

He is at this time transporting large armies of foreign mercenaries to complete the works of death, desolation, and tyranny already begun with circumstances of cruelty and perfidy scarcely paralleled in the most barbarous ages, and totally unworthy the head of a civilized nation.

He has constrained our fellow-citizens, taken captive on the high seas, to bear arms against their country, to become the executioners of their friends and brethren, or to fall themselves by their hands.

He has excited domestic insurrection among us, and has endeavored to bring on the inhabitants of our frontiers the merciless Indian savages, whose known rule of warfare is an undistinguished destruction of all ages, sexes, and conditions.

In every stage of these oppressions we have petitioned for redress in the most humble terms; our repeated petitions have been answered only by repeated injury. A prince, whose character is thus marked by every act which may define a tyrant, is unfit to be the ruler of a free people.

Nor have we been wanting in our attentions to our British brethren. We have warned them, from time to time, of attempts by their legislature to extend an unwarrantable jurisdiction over us. We have reminded them of the circumstances of our emigration and settlement here. We have appealed to their native justice and magnanimity; and we have conjured them, by the ties of our common kindred, to disavow these usurpations, which would inevitably interrupt our connections and correspondence. They, too, have been deaf to the voice of justice and of consanguinity. We must, therefore, acquiesce in the necessity which denounces our separation, and hold them, as we hold the rest of mankind, enemies in war, in peace friends.

We, therefore, the representatives of the United States of America, in General Congress assembled, appealing to the Supreme Judge of the world for the rectitude of our intentions, do, in the name and by the authority of the good people of these colonies, solemnly publish and declare, that these United Colonies are, and of right ought to be, FREE AND INDEPENDENT STATES; that they are absolved from all allegiance to the British crown, and that all political connection between them and the state of Great Britain is, and ought to be, totally dissolved; and that, as free and independent states, they have full power to levy war, conclude peace, contract alliances, establish commerce, and do all other acts and things which independent states may of right do. And for the support of this declaration, with a firm reliance on the protection of Divine Providence, we mutually pledge to each other our lives, our fortunes, and our sacred honor.

John Hancock

New Hampshire
Josiah Bartlett
William Whipple
Matthew Thornton

Massachusetts
John Adams
Samuel Adams
Robert Treat Paine
Elbridge Gerry

New York
William Floyd
Philip Livingston
Francis Lewis
Lewis Morris

Rhode Island
Stephen Hopkins
William Ellery

New Jersey
Richard Stockton
John Witherspoon
Francis Hopkinson
John Hart
Abraham Clark

Pennsylvania
Robert Morris
Benjamin Rush
Benjamin Franklin
John Morton
George Clymer
James Smith
George Taylor
James Wilson
George Ross

Delaware
Caeser Rodney
George Read
Thomas McKean

Maryland
Samuel Chase
William Paca
Thomas Stone
Charles Carroll
of Carrollton

North Carolina
William Hooper
Joseph Hewes
John Penn

Virginia
George Wythe
Richard Henry Lee
Thomas Jefferson
Benjamin Harrison
Thomas Nelson, Jr.
Francis Lightfoot Lee
Carter Braxton

South Carolina
Edward Rutledge
Thomas Heyward, Jr.
Thomas Lynch, Jr.
Arthur Middleton

Connecticut
Roger Sherman
Samuel Huntington
William Williams
Oliver Wolcott

Georgia
Button Gwinnett
Lyman Hall
George Walton

Preamble

We the People of the United States, in Order to form a more perfect Union, establish Justice, insure domestic Tranquility, provide for the common defence, promote the general Welfare, and secure the Blessings of Liberty to ourselves and our Posterity, do ordain and establish this Constitution for the United States of America.

Article I

Section 1

All legislative Powers herein granted shall be vested in a Congress of the United States, which shall consist of a Senate and House of Representatives.

Section 2

The House of Representatives shall be composed of Members chosen every second Year by the People of the several States, and the Electors in each State shall have the Qualifications requisite for Electors of the most numerous Branch of the State Legislature.

No Person shall be a Representative who shall not have attained to the Age of twenty five Years, and been seven Years a Citizen of the United States, and who shall not, when elected, be an inhabitant of that State in which he shall be chosen.

Representatives and direct Taxes shall be apportioned among the several States which may be included within this Union, according to their respective Numbers, *which shall be determined by adding to the whole Number of free Persons, including those bound to Service for a Term of Years, and excluding Indians not taxed, three fifths of all other Persons.* The actual Enumeration shall be made within three Years after the first Meeting of the Congress of the United States, and within every subsequent Term of ten Years, in such Manner as they shall by Law direct. The Number of Representatives shall not exceed one for every thirty Thousand, but each State shall have at Least one Representative; *and until such enumeration shall be made, the State of New Hampshire shall be entitled to chuse three, Massachusetts eight, Rhode-Island and Providence Plantations one, Connecticut five, New York six, New Jersey four, Pennsylvania eight, Delaware one, Maryland six, Virginia ten, North Carolina five, South Carolina five, and Georgia three.*

When vacancies happen in the Representation from any State, the Executive Authority thereof shall issue Writs of Election to fill such Vacancies.

The House of Representatives shall chuse their Speaker and other Officers; and shall have the sole Power of Impeachment.

---

*Passages no longer in effect are printed in italic type.

Section 3

The Senate of the United States shall be composed of two Senators from each State, *chosen by the Legislature thereof*, for six Years; and each Senator shall have one Vote.

Immediately after they shall be assembled in Consequence of the first Election, they shall be divided as equally as may be into three Classes. The Seats of the Senators of the first Class shall be vacated at the Expiration of the second Year, of the second Class at the Expiration of the fourth Year, and of the third Class at the Expiration of the sixth Year so that one third may be chosen every second Year; and if Vacancies happen by Resignation, or otherwise, during the Recess of the Legislature of any state, the Executive thereof may make temporary Appointments until the next Meeting of the Legislature, which shall then fill such Vacancies.

No Person shall be a Senator who shall not have attained to the Age of thirty Years, and been nine Years a Citizen of the United States, and who shall not, when elected, be an Inhabitant of that State for which he shall be chosen.

The Vice President of the United States shall be President of the Senate, but shall have no Vote, unless they be equally divided.

The Senate shall chuse their other Officers, and also a President *pro tempore*, in the Absence of the Vice President, or when he shall exercise the Office of President of the United States.

The Senate shall have the sole Power to try all Impeachments. When sitting for that Purpose, they shall be on Oath or Affirmation. When the President of the United States is tried the Chief Justice shall preside: And no Person shall be convicted without the Concurrence of two thirds of the Members present.

Judgment in Cases of Impeachment shall not extend further than to removal from Office, and disqualification to hold and enjoy any Office of honor, Trust or Profit under the United States: but the Party convicted shall nevertheless be liable and subject to Indictment, Trial, Judgment and Punishment, according to Law.

Section 4

The Times, Places and Manner of holding Elections for Senators and Representatives, shall be prescribed in each State by the Legislature thereof; but the Congress may at any time by Law make or alter such Regulations, except as to the Places of chusing Senators.

The Congress shall assemble at least once in every Year, *and such Meeting shall be on the first Monday in December, unless they shall by Law appoint a different Day.*

Section 5

Each House shall be the Judge of the Elections, Returns and Qualifications of its own Members, and a Majority of each shall constitute a Quorum to do Business; but a smaller Number may adjourn from day to day, and may be authorized to compel the Attendance of absent Members, in such Manner, and under such Penalties as each House may provide.

Each House may determine the Rules of its Proceedings, punish its Members for disorderly Behaviour, and, with the Concurrence of two thirds, expel a Member.

Each House shall keep a Journal of its Proceedings, and from time to time publish the same, excepting such Parts as may in their Judgment require Secrecy; and the Yeas and Nays of the Members of either House on any question shall, at the Desire of one fifth of those Present, be entered on the Journal.

Neither House, during the Session of Congress, shall, without the Consent of the other, adjourn for more than three days, nor to any other Place than that in which the two Houses shall be sitting.

Section 6

The Senators and Representatives shall receive a Compensation for their Services, to be ascertained by Law, and paid out of the Treasury of the United States. They shall in all Cases, except Treason, Felony and Breach of the Peace, be privileged from Arrest during their Attendance at the Session of their respective Houses, and in going to and returning from the same; and for any Speech or Debate in either House, they shall not be questioned in any other Place.

No Senator or Representative shall, during the Time for which he was elected, be appointed to any civil Office under the Authority of the United States, which shall have been created, or the Emoluments whereof shall have been encreased during such time, and no Person holding any Office under the United States, shall be a Member of either House during his Continuance in Office.

Section 7

All Bills for raising Revenue shall originate in the House of Representatives; but the Senate may propose or concur with Amendments as on other Bills.

Every Bill which shall have passed the House of Representatives and the Senate, shall, before it become a Law, be presented to the President of the United States; If he approve he shall sign it, but if not he shall return it, with his Objections to the House in which it shall have originated, who shall enter the Objections at large on their Journal, and proceed to reconsider it. If after such Reconsideration two thirds of that House shall agree to pass the Bill, it shall be sent, together with the Objections, to the other House, by which it shall likewise be reconsidered, and if approved by two thirds of that House, it shall become a Law. But in all such Cases the Votes of both Houses shall be determined by yeas and Nays, and the Names of the Persons voting for and against the Bill shall be entered on the Journal of each House respectively. If any Bill shall not be returned by the President within ten Days (Sundays excepted) after it shall have been presented to him, the Same shall be a Law, in like Manner as if he had signed it, unless the Congress by their Adjournment prevent its Return, in which Case it shall not be a Law.

Every Order, Resolution, or Vote to which the Concurrence of the Senate and House of Representatives may be necessary (except on a question of Adjournment) shall be presented to the President of the United States; and before the Same shall take Effect, shall be approved by him, or being disapproved by him, shall be repassed by two thirds of the Senate and House of Representatives, according to the Rules and Limitations prescribed in the Case of a Bill.

Section 8

The Congress shall have Power To lay and collect Taxes, Duties, Imposts and Excises, to pay the Debts and provide for the common Defence and general Welfare of the United States; but all Duties, Imposts and Excises shall be uniform throughout the United States;

To borrow Money on the credit of the United States;

To regulate Commerce with foreign Nations, and among the several States, and with the Indian Tribes;

To establish an uniform Rule of Naturalization, and uniform Laws on the subject of Bankruptcies throughout the United States;

To coin Money, regulate the Value thereof, and of foreign Coin, and fix the Standard of Weights and Measures;

To provide for the Punishment of counterfeiting the Securities and current Coin of the United States;

To establish Post Offices and post Roads;

To promote the Progress of Science and useful Arts, by securing for limited Times to Authors and Inventors the exclusive Right to their respective Writings and Discoveries;

To constitute Tribunals inferior to the supreme Court;

To define and punish Piracies and Felonies committed on the high Seas, and Offences against the Law of Nations;

To declare War, grant Letters of Marque and Reprisal, and make Rules concerning Captures on Land and Water;

To raise and support Armies, but no Appropriation of Money to that Use shall be for a longer Term than two Years;

To provide and maintain a Navy;

To make Rules for the Government and Regulation of the land and naval Forces;

To provide for calling forth the Militia to execute the Laws of the Union, suppress Insurrections and repel Invasions;

To provide for organizing, arming, and disciplining, the Militia, and for governing such Part of them as may be employed in the Service of the United States, reserving to the States respectively, the Appointment of the Officers, and the Authority of training the Militia according to the discipline prescribed by Congress;

To exercise exclusive Legislation in all Cases whatsoever, over such District (not exceeding ten Miles square) as may, by Cession of particular States, and the Acceptance of Congress, become the Seat of the Government of the United States, and to exercise like Authority over all Places purchased by the Consent of the Legislature of the State in which the Same shall be, for the Erection of Forts, Magazines, Arsenals, dock-Yards, and other needful Buildings;—And

To make all Laws which shall be necessary and proper for carrying into Execution the foregoing Powers, and all other Powers vested by this Constitution in the Government of the United States, or in any Department of Officer thereof.

Section 9

The Migration or Importation of such Persons as any of the States now existing shall think proper to admit, shall not be prohibited by the Congress prior to the Year one thousand eight hundred and eight, but a Tax or duty may be imposed on such Importation, not exceeding ten dollars for each Person.

The Privilege of the Writ of Habeas Corpus shall not be suspended, unless when in Cases of Rebellion or Invasion the public Safety may require it.

No Bill of Attainder or ex post facto Law shall be passed.

No Capitation, or other direct, Tax shall be laid, unless in Proportion to the Census or Enumeration herein before directed to be taken.

No Tax or Duty shall be laid on Articles exported from any State.

No Preference shall be given by any Regulation of Commerce or Revenue to the Ports of one State over those of another: nor shall Vessels bound to, or from, one State, be obliged to enter, clear, or pay Duties in another.

No Money shall be drawn from the Treasury, but in Consequence of Appropriations made by Law; and a regular Statement and Account of the Receipts and Expenditures of all public Money shall be published from time to time.

No Title of Nobility shall be granted by the United States: And no Person holding any Office of Profit or Trust under them, shall, without the Consent of the Congress, accept of any present, Emolument, Office, or Title, of any kind whatever, from any King, Prince, or foreign State.

Section 10

No State shall enter into any Treaty, Alliance, or Confederation; grant Letters of Marque and Reprisal; coin Money; emit Bills of Credit; make any Thing but gold and silver Coin a Tender in Payment of Debts; pass any Bill of Attainder, ex post facto Law, or Law impairing the obligation of Contracts, or grant any Title of Nobility.

No State shall, without the Consent of the Congress, lay any Imposts or Duties on Imports or Exports, except what may be absolutely necessary for executing its inspection Laws: and the net Produce of all Duties and Imposts, laid by any State on Imports or Exports, shall be for the Use of the Treasury of the United States; and all such Laws shall be subject to the Revision and Controul of the Congress.

No State shall, without the Consent of Congress, lay any Duty of Tonnage, keep Troops, or Ships of War in time of Peace, enter into any Agreement or Compact with another State, or with a foreign Power, or engage in War, unless actually invaded, or in such imminent Danger as will not admit of delay.

Article II

Section 1

The executive Power shall be vested in a President of the United States of America. He shall hold his Office during the Term of four Years, and, together with the Vice President, chosen for the same Term, be elected, as follows:

Each State shall appoint, in such Manner as the Legislature thereof may direct, a Number of Electors, equal to the whole Number of Senators and Representatives to which the State may be entitled in the Congress: but no Senator or Representative, or Person holding an Office of Trust or Profit under the United States, shall be appointed an Elector.

The Electors shall meet in their respective States, and vote by Ballot for two Persons, of whom one at least shall not be an Inhabitant of the same State with themselves. And they shall make a List of all the Persons voted for, and of the Number of Votes for each; which List they shall sign and certify, and transmit sealed to the Seat of the Government of the United States, directed to the President of the Senate. The President of the Senate shall, in the Presence of the Senate and House of Representatives, open all the Certificates, and the Votes shall then be counted. The Person having the greatest Number of Votes shall be the President, if such Number be a Majority of the whole number of Electors appointed; and if there be more than one who have such Majority, and have an equal Number of Votes, then the House of Representatives shall immediately chuse by Ballot one of them for President; and if no Person have a Majority, then from the five highest on the List the said House shall in like Manner chuse the President. But in chusing the President, the Votes shall be taken by States, the Representation from each State having one Vote; A quorum for this Purpose shall consist of a Member or Members from two thirds of the States, and a Majority of all the States shall be necessary to a Choice. In every Case, after the Choice of the President, the Person having the greatest Number of Votes of the Electors shall be the Vice President. But if there should remain two or more who have equal Votes, the Senate shall chuse from them by Ballot the Vice President.

The Congress may determine the time of chusing the Electors, and the Day on which they shall give their Votes; which Day shall be the same throughout the United States.

No person except a natural born Citizen, *or a Citizen of the United States, at the time of the Adoption of this Constitution,* shall be eligible to the Office of

President; neither shall any Person be eligible to that Office who shall not have attained to the Age of thirty five Years, and been fourteen Years a Resident within the United States.

In Case of the Removal of the President from Office, or of his Death, Resignation, or Inability to discharge the Powers and Duties of the said Office, the Same shall devolve on the Vice President, and the Congress may by Law provide for the Case of Removal, Death, Resignation or Inability, both of the President and Vice President, declaring what Officer shall then act as President, and such Officer shall act accordingly, until the Disability be removed, or a President shall be elected.

The President shall, at stated Times, receive for his Services, a Compensation, which shall neither be encreased nor diminished during the Period for which he shall have been elected, and he shall not receive within that period any other Emolument from the United States, or any of them.

Before he enter on the Execution of his Office, he shall take the following Oath or Affirmation:—"I do solemnly swear (or affirm) that I will faithfully execute the Office of President of the United States, and will to the best of my Ability, preserve, protect and defend the Constitution of the United States."

Section 2

The President shall be Commander in Chief of the Army and Navy of the United States, and of the Militia of the several States, when called into the actual Service of the United States; he may require the Opinion, in writing, of the principal Officer in each of the executive Departments, upon any Subject relating to the Duties of their respective Offices, and he shall have Power to grant Reprieves and Pardons for Offences against the United States, except in Cases of Impeachment.

He shall have Power, by and with the Advice and Consent of the Senate, to make Treaties, provided two thirds of the Senators present concur; and he shall nominate, and by and with the Advice and Consent of the Senate, shall appoint Ambassadors, other public Ministers and Consuls, Judges of the supreme Court, and all other Officers of the United States, whose Appointments are not herein otherwise provided for, and which shall be established by Law: but the Congress may by Law vest the Appointment of such inferior Officers, as they think proper in the President alone, in the Courts of Law, or in the Heads of Departments.

The President shall have Power to fill up all Vacancies that may happen during the Recess of the Senate, by granting Commissions which shall expire at the End of their next Session.

Section 3

He shall from time to time give to the Congress Information of the State of the Union, and recommend to their Consideration such Measures as he shall judge necessary and expedient; he may, on extraordinary Occasions, convene both Houses, or either of them, and in Case of disagreement between them, with Respect to the Time of Adjournment, he may adjourn them to such Time as he shall think proper; he shall receive Ambassadors and other public Ministers; he shall take Care that the Laws be faithfully executed, and shall Commission all the officers of the United States.

Section 4

The President, Vice President and all civil Officers of the United States, shall be removed from Office on Impeachment for, and Conviction of, Treason, Bribery or other high Crimes and Misdemeanors.

Article III

Section 1

The judicial Power of the United States, shall be vested in one supreme Court, and in such inferior Courts as the Congress may from time to time ordain and establish. The Judges, both of the supreme and inferior Courts, shall hold their offices during good Behaviour, and shall, at stated Times, receive for their Services, a Compensation, which shall not be diminished during their Continuance in Office.

Section 2

The judicial Power shall extend to all Cases, in Law and Equity, arising under this Constitution, the Laws of the United States, and Treaties made, or which shall be made, under their Authority;—to all Cases affecting Ambassadors, other public Ministers and Consuls;—to all Cases of admiralty and maritime Jurisdiction;—to Controversies to which the United States shall be a Party;—to Controversies between two or more States;— *between a State and Citizens of another State;*—between Citizens of different States;— between Citizens of the same State claiming Lands under Grants of different States, and between a State, or the Citizens thereof, and foreign States, Citizens or Subjects.

In all Cases affecting Ambassadors, other public Ministers and Consuls, and those in which a State shall be Party, the supreme Court shall have original Jurisdiction. In all the other Cases before mentioned, the supreme Court shall have appellate Jurisdiction, both as to Law and Fact, with such Exceptions, and under such Regulations as the Congress shall make.

The Trial of all Crimes, except in Cases of Impeachment, shall be by Jury; and such Trial shall be held in the State where the said Crimes shall have been committed, but when not committed within any State, the Trial shall be at such Place or Places as the Congress may by Law have directed.

Section 3

Treason against the United States, shall consist only in levying War against them, or in adhering to their Enemies, giving them Aid and Comfort. No person shall be convicted of Treason unless on the Testimony of two Witnesses to the same overt Act, or on Confession in open Court.

The Congress shall have Power to declare the Punishment of Treason, but no Attainder of Treason shall work Corruption of Blood, or Forfeiture except during the Life of the Person attainted.

Article IV

Section 1

Full Faith and Credit shall be given in each State to the public Acts, Records, and judicial Proceedings of every other State. And the Congress may by general Laws prescribe the Manner in which such Acts, Records and Proceedings shall be proved, and the Effect thereof.

Section 2

The Citizens of each State shall be entitled to all Privileges and Immunities of Citizens in the several States.

A Person charged in any State with Treason, Felony, or other Crime, who shall flee from Justice, and be found in another State, shall on Demand of the executive

Authority of the State from which he fled, be delivered up, to be removed to the State having Jurisdiction of the Crime.

No Person held to Service or Labour in one State, under the Laws thereof, escaping into another, shall, in Consequence of any Law or Regulation therein, be discharged from such Service or Labour, but shall be delivered up on Claim of the Party to whom such Service or Labour may be due.

Section 3

New States may be admitted by the Congress into this Union; but no new State shall be formed or erected within the Jurisdiction of any other State; nor any State be formed by the Junction of two or more States, or Parts of States, without the Consent of the Legislatures of the States concerned as well as of the Congress.

The Congress shall have Power to dispose of and make all needful Rules and Regulations respecting the Territory or other Property belonging to the United States; and nothing in this Constitution shall be so construed as to Prejudice any Claims of the United States, or of any particular States.

Section 4

The United States shall guarantee to every State in this Union a Republican Form of Government, and shall protect each of them against Invasion; and on Application of the Legislature, or of the Executive (when the Legislature cannot be convened) against domestic violence.

Article V

The Congress, whenever two thirds of both Houses shall deem it necessary, shall propose Amendments to this Constitution, or, on the Application of the Legislatures of two thirds of the several States, shall call a Convention for proposing Amendments, which, in either Case, shall be valid to all Intents and Purposes, as Part of this Constitution, when ratified by the Legislatures of three fourths of the several States, or by Conventions in three fourths thereof, as the one or the other Mode of Ratification may be proposed by the Congress; Provided *that no Amendment which may be made prior to the Year One thousand eight hundred and eight shall in any Manner affect the first and fourth Clauses in the Ninth Section of the first Article;* and that no State, without its Consent, shall be deprived of its equal Suffrage in the Senate.

Article VI

All Debts contracted and Engagements entered into, before the Adoption of this Constitution, shall be as valid against the United States under this Constitution, as under the Confederation.

This Constitution, and Laws of the United States which shall be made in Pursuance thereof; and all Treaties made, or which shall be made, under the Authority of the United States, shall be the supreme Law of the Land; and the Judges in every State shall be bound thereby, any Thing in the Constitution or Laws of any State to the Contrary notwithstanding.

The Senators and Representatives before mentioned, and the Members of the several State Legislatures, and all executive and Judicial Officers, both of the United States and of the several States, shall be bound by Oath or Affirmation, to support this Constitution; but no religious Test shall ever be required as a Qualification to any Office of public Trust under the United States.

Article VII

The Ratification of the Conventions of nine States, shall be sufficient for the Establishment of this Constitution between the States so ratifying the Same.

Done in Convention by the Unanimous Consent of the States present the Seventeenth Day of September in the Year of our Lord one thousand seven hundred and Eighty seven and of the Independence of the United States of America the Twelfth[†] IN WITNESS whereof We have hereunto subscribed our Names,

George Washington
President and Deputy from Virginia

Delaware
George Read
Gunning Bedford, Jr.
John Dickinson
Richard Bassett
Jacob Broom

Maryland
James McHenry
Daniel of St. Thomas
Jenifer
Daniel Carroll

Virginia
John Blair
James Madison, Jr.

North Carolina
William Blount
Richard Dobbs Spraight
Hugh Williamson

South Carolina
John Rutledge
Charles Cotesworth
Pinckney
Charles Pinckney
Pierce Butler

Georgia
William Paterson
William Few
Abraham Baldwin

New Hampshire
John Langdon
Nicholas Gilman

Massachusetts
Nathaniel Gorham
Rufus King

Connecticut
William Samuel Johnson
Roger Sherman

New York
Alexander Hamilton

New Jersey
William Livingston
David Brearley
Jonathan Dayton

Pennsylvania
Benjamin Franklin
Thomas Mifflin
Robert Morris
George Clymer
Thomas FitzSimons
Jared Ingersoll
James Wilson
Gouverneur Morris

[†]The Constitution was submitted on September 17, 1787, by the Constitutional Convention, was ratified by the Convention of several states at various dates up to May 29, 1790, and became effective on March 4, 1789.

Amendments to the Constitution

Amendment I

Congress shall make no law respecting an establishment of religion, or prohibiting the free exercise thereof; or abridging the freedom of speech, or of the press; or the right of the people peaceably to assemble, and to petition the Government for a redress of grievances.

Amendment II

A well regulated Militia being necessary to the security of a free State, the right of the people to keep and bear Arms, shall not be infringed.

Amendment III

No Soldier shall, in time of peace be quartered in any house, without the consent of the Owner, nor in time of war, but in a manner to be prescribed by law.

Amendment IV

The right of the people to be secure in their persons, houses, papers, and effects, against unreasonable searches and seizures, shall not be violated, and no Warrants shall issue, but upon probable cause, supported by Oath or affirmation, and particularly describing the place to be searched, and the persons or things to be seized.

Amendment V

No person shall be held to answer for a capital, or otherwise infamous crime, unless on a presentment or indictment of a Grand Jury, except in cases arising in the land or naval forces, or in the Militia, when in actual service in time of War or public danger; nor shall any person be subject for the same offense to be twice put in jeopardy of life or limb; nor shall be compelled in any criminal case to be a witness against himself, nor be deprived of life, liberty, or property, without due process of law; nor shall private property be taken for public use, without just compensation.

Amendment VI

In all criminal prosecutions, the accused shall enjoy the right to a speedy and public trial, by an impartial jury of the State and district wherein the crime shall have been committed, which district shall have been previously ascertained by law, and to be informed of the nature and cause of the accusation; to be confronted with the witnesses against him; to have compulsory process for obtaining witnesses in his favor, and to have the Assistance of Counsel for his defence.

Amendment VII

In Suits at common law, where the value in controversy shall exceed twenty dollars, the right of trial by jury shall be preserved, and no fact tried by a jury, shall be otherwise re-examined in any Court of the United States, than according to the rules of the common law.

Amendment VIII

Excessive bail shall not be required, nor excessive fines imposed, nor cruel and unusual punishments inflicted.

Amendment IX

The enumeration in the Constitution, of certain rights, shall not be construed to deny or disparage others retained by the people.

Amendment X*

The powers not delegated to the United States by the Constitution, nor prohibited by it to the States, are reserved to the States respectively, or to the people.

Amendment XI

[Adopted 1798]

The Judicial power of the United States shall not be construed to extend to any suit in law or equity, commenced or prosecuted against one of the United States by Citizens of another State, or by Citizens or Subjects of any Foreign State.

Amendment XII

[Adopted 1804]

The Electors shall meet in their respective states, and vote by ballot for President and Vice President, one of whom, at least, shall not be an inhabitant of the same state with themselves; they shall name in their ballots the person voted for as President, and in distinct ballots the person voted for as Vice President, and they shall make distinct lists of all persons voted for as President, and of all persons voted for as Vice President, and of the number of votes for each, which lists they shall sign and certify, and transmit sealed to the seat of the government of the United States, directed to the President of the Senate;—The President of the Senate shall, in the presence of the Senate and House of Representatives, open all the certificates and the votes shall then be counted;—The person having the greatest number of votes for President, shall be the President, if such number be a majority of the whole number of Electors appointed; and if no person have such majority, then from the persons having the highest numbers not exceeding three

---

*The first ten amendments (the Bill of Rights) were ratified and their adoption was certified on December 15, 1791.

on the list of those voted for as President, the House of Representatives shall choose immediately, by ballot, the President. But in choosing the President, the votes shall be taken by states, the representation from each state having one vote; a quorum for this purpose shall consist of a member or members from two-thirds of the states, and a majority of all the states shall be necessary to a choice. And if the House of Representatives shall not choose a President whenever the right of choice shall devolve upon them, before *the fourth day of March* next following, then the Vice President shall act as President, as in the case of the death or other constitutional disability of the President.—The person having the greatest number of votes as Vice President, shall be the Vice President, if such number be a majority of the whole number of Electors appointed, and if no person have a majority, then from the two highest numbers on the list, the Senate shall choose the Vice President; a quorum for the purpose shall consist of two-thirds of the whole number of Senators, and a majority of the whole number shall be necessary to a choice. But no person constitutionally ineligible to the office of President shall be eligible to that of Vice President of the United States.

Amendment XIII

[Adopted 1865]

Section 1

Neither slavery nor involuntary servitude, except as a punishment for crime whereof the party shall have been duly convicted, shall exist within the United States, or any place subject to their jurisdiction.

Section 2

Congress shall have power to enforce this article by appropriate legislation.

Amendment XIV

[Adopted 1868]

Section 1

All persons born or naturalized in the United States, and subject to the jurisdiction thereof, are citizens of the United States and of the State wherein they reside. No State shall make or enforce any law which shall abridge the privileges or immunities of citizens of the United States; nor shall any State deprive any person of life, liberty, or property, without due process of law; nor deny to any person within its jurisdiction the equal protection of the laws.

Section 2

Representatives shall be apportioned among the several States according to their respective numbers, counting the whole number of persons in each State, excluding Indians not taxed. But when the right to vote at any election for the choice of electors for President and Vice President of the United States, Representatives in Congress, the Executive and Judicial officers of a State, or the members of the Legislature thereof, is denied to any of the male inhabitants of such State, being twenty-one years of age, and citizens of the United States, or in any way abridged, except for participation in rebellion, or other crime, the basis of representation therein shall be reduced in the proportion which the number of such male citizens shall bear to the whole number of male citizens twenty-one years of age in such State.

Section 3

No person shall be a Senator or Representative in Congress, or elector of President and Vice President, or hold any office, civil or military, under the United States, or under any State, who, having previously taken an oath, as a member of Congress, or as an officer of the United States, or as a member of any State legislature, or as an executive or judicial officer of any State, to support the Constitution of the United States, shall have engaged in insurrection or rebellion against the same, or given aid or comfort to the enemies thereof. But Congress may by a vote of two-thirds of each House, remove such disability.

Section 4

The validity of the public debt of the United States, authorized by law, including debts incurred for payment of pensions and bounties for services in suppressing insurrection or rebellion, shall not be questioned. But neither the United States nor any State shall assume or pay any debt or obligation incurred in aid of insurrection or rebellion against the United States, or any claim for the loss or emancipation of any slave; but all such debts, obligations and claims shall be held illegal and void.

Section 5

The Congress shall have power to enforce, by appropriate legislation, the provisions of this article.

Amendment XV

[Adopted 1870]

Section 1

The right of citizens of the United States to vote shall not be denied or abridged by the United States or by any State on account of race, color, or previous condition of servitude.

Section 2

The Congress shall have power to enforce this article by appropriate legislation.

Amendment XVI

[Adopted 1913]

The Congress shall have power to lay and collect taxes on incomes, from whatever source derived, without apportionment among the several States, and without regard to any census or enumeration.

Amendment XVII

[Adopted 1913]

The Senate of the United States shall be composed of two Senators from each State, elected by the people thereof, for six years; and each Senator shall have one vote. The electors in each State shall have the qualifications requisite for electors of the most numerous branch of the State legislatures.

When vacancies happen in the representation of any State in the Senate, the executive authority of such State shall issue writs of election to fill such vacancies: *Provided,*

That the legislature of any State may empower the executive thereof to make temporary appointments until the people fill the vacancies by election as the legislature may direct.

This amendment shall not be so construed as to affect the election or term of any Senator chosen before it becomes valid as part of the Constitution.

Amendment XVIII

[Adopted 1919, repealed 1933]

Section 1

After one year from the ratification of this article the manufacture, sale, or transportation of intoxicating liquors within, the importation thereof into, or the exportation thereof from the United States and all territory subject to the jurisdiction thereof for beverage purposes is hereby prohibited.

Section 2

The Congress and the several States shall have concurrent power to enforce this article by appropriate legislation.

Section 3

This article shall be inoperative unless it shall have been ratified as an amendment to the Constitution by the legislatures of the several States, as provided in the Constitution, within seven years from the date of the submission hereof to the States by the Congress.

Amendment XIX

[Adopted 1920]

The right of citizens of the United States to vote shall not be denied or abridged by the United States or by any State on account of sex.

Congress shall have power to enforce this article by appropriate legislation.

Amendment XX

[Adopted 1933]

Section 1

The terms of the President and Vice President shall end at noon on the 20th day of January, and the terms of Senators and Representatives at noon on the 3d day of January, of the years in which such terms would have ended if this article had not been ratified and the terms of their successors shall then begin.

Section 2

The Congress shall assemble at least once in every year, and such meeting shall begin at noon on the 3d day of January, unless they shall by law appoint a different day.

Section 3

If, at the time fixed for the beginning of the term of the President, the President elect shall have died, the Vice President elect shall become President. If a President shall not have been chosen before the time fixed for the beginning of his term, or if the President elect shall have failed to qualify, then the Vice President elect shall act as President until a President shall have qualified; and the Congress may by law provide for the case wherein neither a President elect nor a Vice President elect shall have qualified, declaring who shall then act as President, or the manner in which one who is to act shall be selected, and such person shall act accordingly until a President or Vice President shall have qualified.

Section 4

The Congress may by law provide for the case of the death of any of the persons from whom the House of Representatives may choose a President whenever the right of choice shall have devolved upon them, and for the case of the death of any of the persons from whom the Senate may choose a Vice President whenever the right of choice shall have devolved upon them.

Section 5

Sections 1 and 2 shall take effect on the 15th day of October following the ratification of this article.

Section 6

This article shall be inoperative unless it shall have been ratified as an amendment to the Constitution by the legislatures of three fourths of the several States within seven years from the date of its submission.

Amendment XXI

[Adopted 1933]

Section 1

The eighteenth article of amendment to the Constitution of the United States is hereby repealed.

Section 2

The transportation or importation into any State, Territory, or possession of the United States for delivery or use therein of intoxicating liquors in violation of the laws thereof, is hereby prohibited.

Section 3

This article shall be inoperative unless it shall have been ratified as an amendment to the Constitution by conventions in the several States, as provided in the Constitution, within seven years from the date of the submission hereof to the States by the Congress.

Amendment XXII

[Adopted 1951]

Section 1

No person shall be elected to the office of the President more than twice, and no person who has held the office of President, or acted as President, for more than two years of a term to which some other person was elected President shall be elected to the office of the President more than once. But this Article shall not apply to any person holding the office of President when this Article was proposed by the Congress, and shall not prevent any person who may be holding the office of President, or acting as President, during the term within which this Article becomes operative from holding the office of President or acting as President during the remainder of such term.

Section 2

This article shall be inoperative unless it shall have been ratified as an amendment to the Constitution by the legislatures of three-fourths of the several States within seven years from the date of its submission to the States by the Congress.

Amendment XXIII

[Adopted 1961]

Section 1

The District constituting the seat of Government of the United States shall appoint in such manner as the Congress shall direct:

A number of electors of President and Vice President equal to the whole number of Senators and Representatives in Congress to which the District would be entitled if it were a State, but in no event more than the least populous State; they shall be in addition to those appointed by the States, but they shall be considered, for the purposes of the election of President and Vice President, to be electors appointed by a State; and they shall meet in the District and perform such duties as provided by the twelfth article of amendment.

Section 2

The Congress shall have power to enforce this article by appropriate legislation.

Amendment XXIV

[Adopted 1964]

Section 1

The right of citizens of the United States to vote in any primary or other election for President or Vice President, for electors for President or Vice President, or for Senator or Representative in Congress, shall not be denied or abridged by the United States or any state by reason of failure to pay any poll tax or other tax.

Section 2

The Congress shall have the power to enforce this article by appropriate legislation.

Amendment XXV

[Adopted 1967]

Section 1

In case of the removal of the President from office or his death or resignation, the Vice President shall become President.

Section 2

Whenever there is a vacancy in the office of the Vice President, the President shall nominate a Vice President who shall take the office upon confirmation by a majority vote of both houses of Congress.

Section 3

Whenever the President transmits to the President pro tempore of the Senate and the Speaker of the House of Representatives his written declaration that he is unable to discharge the powers and duties of his office, and until he transmits to them a written declaration to the contrary, such powers and duties shall be discharged by the Vice President as Acting President.

Section 4

Whenever the Vice President and a majority of either the principal officers of the executive departments or of such other body as Congress may by law provide, transmit to the President pro tempore of the Senate and the Speaker of the House of Representatives their written declaration that the President is unable to discharge the powers and duties of his office, the Vice President shall immediately assume the powers and duties of the office as Acting President.

Thereafter, when the President transmits to the President pro tempore of the Senate and the Speaker of the House of Representatives his written declaration that no inability exists, he shall resume the powers and duties of his office unless the Vice President and a majority of either the principal officers of the executive department or of such other body as Congress may by law provide, transmit within four days to the President pro tempore of the Senate and the Speaker of the House of Representatives their written declaration that the President is unable to discharge the powers and duties of his office. Thereupon Congress shall decide the issue, assembling within 48 hours for that purpose if not in session. If the Congress, within 21 days after receipt of the latter written declaration, or, if Congress is not in session, within 21 days after Congress is required to assemble, determines by two-thirds vote of both houses that the President is unable to discharge the powers and duties of his office, the Vice President shall continue to discharge the same as Acting President; otherwise, the President shall resume the powers and duties of his office.

Amendment XXVI

[Adopted 1971]

Section 1

The right of citizens of the United States, who are 18 years of age or older, to vote shall not be denied or abridged by the United States or any state on account of age.

Section 2

The Congress shall have the power to enforce this article by appropriate legislation.

Amendment XXVII

[Adopted 1992]

No law, varying the compensation for the services of the Senators and Representatives shall take effect, until an election of Representatives shall have intervened.

Glossary

abolitionism (p. 282) Worldwide movement to end slavery. In the United States the term chiefly applies to the antebellum reformers whose cause culminated in the Civil War.

acquired immunodeficiency syndrome (AIDS) (p. 821) A deadly, and very often sexually transmitted disease that emerged in the 1980s and that at first spread chiefly among injection drug users and gay male populations, but soon affected all communities. The disease is a complex of deadly pathologies resulting from infection with the **human immunodeficiency virus (HIV)**. By 2000, AIDS deaths in the United States had surpassed 40,000.

Agricultural Adjustment Act (AAA) (p. 681) New Deal legislation that raised farm prices by restricting output of staple crops. It restricted production and paid subsidies to growers; declared unconstitutional in 1936.

Albany Plan (p. 87) A proposal, drafted in Albany, New York, in 1754 by Benjamin Franklin of Pennsylvania, for a "plan of union" for the collective defense of the British colonies. Because it held the potential for unifying the colonies against its rule, the British government never adopted the plan.

Alien and Sedition Acts (p. 167) Four laws passed by the Federalist-dominated Congress in 1798 directed against sympathizers to the **French Revolution**—chiefly Thomas Jefferson and his **Republican party**. The laws, which stifled dissent and made it more difficult for immigrants to gain citizenship, had lapsed by 1802.

Allied Powers (p. 603) The military alliance during World War I, chiefly consisting of Britain, France, Russia, and Italy, that opposed the **Central Powers**, chiefly Germany, Austria-Hungary, and Turkey.

Allies (p. 718) In the context of United States history, a term that refers to the nations that opposed the **Axis Powers**, chiefly Nazi Germany, Italy, and Japan, during World War II. The Allies included Britain, France (except during the Nazi occupation, 1940–1944), the Soviet Union (1941–1945), the United States (1941–1945), and China.

American Colonization Society (p. 235) An organization, founded in 1816, that proposed to solve the "Negro problem" by transporting freed slaves from the United States to Africa. Although the society purchased land in Africa (Liberia), few African Americans chose to resettle there.

American Federation of Labor (AFL) (p. 472) A union, formed in 1886, that organized skilled workers along craft lines. It focused on workplace issues rather than political or social reform.

American System (p. 216) Kentucky Senator Henry Clay's plan for national economic development; it included protective tariffs, a national bank, and federal subsidies for railroad and canal construction.

Anaconda Plan (p. 381) General Winfield Scott's strategy for defeating the Confederacy; its central elements included a naval blockade and seizure of the Mississippi River valley.

Antifederalists (p. 152) Critics of the Constitution who initially opposed its ratification. By the late 1790s, they generally endorsed states' rights and sought limitations on federal power.

antinomianism (p. 35) A religious doctrine that affirmed that individuals who possessed saving grace were exempt from the rules of good behavior and from the laws of the community. In puritan New England, such beliefs were generally regarded as heresy.

Arminianism (p. 30) A religious doctrine that held that good works and faith could lead to salvation. In puritan New England, this was regarded as heresy akin to Catholicism because it implied that God's will was contingent on the acts of man.

Articles of Confederation (p. 130) The charter establishing the first government of the United States, ratified in 1781. The Articles placed the coercive powers to tax and regulate trade within the individual state governments; the national government, widely criticized for being weak, was superseded by the government established by the Constitution of the United States, effective in 1789.

Ashcan School (p. 545) Artists in the early twentieth century who used as their subject matter the things and people found in city streets and slums. Ashcan artists often supported progressive political and social reform.

Atlanta Compromise (p. 529) A social policy, propounded by black leader Booker T. Washington in 1895, advocating that blacks concentrate on learning useful skills rather than agitate over segregation, disfranchisement, and discrimination. In Washington's view, black self-help and self-improvement was the surest way to economic advancement.

axis of evil (p. 844) A pejorative phrase, coined by President George W. Bush in 2002, referring to states that supported terrorism and sought weapons of mass destruction. He specifically identified Iraq, Iran, and North Korea.

Axis Powers (p. 702) A term for the alliance between Nazi Germany and Italy after 1936 and, after 1940, Japan.

Bacon's Rebellion (p. 59) An armed uprising in 1676, led by Nathaniel Bacon, against Virginia governor Sir William Berkeley. Initially the rebels attacked Indian settlements but later moved against Berkeley's political faction and burned Jamestown, capital of the colony. After Bacon's death that year, the rebellion collapsed.

Bank of the United States (p. 157) Established as a joint public and private venture in 1791 at the behest of Secretary of Treasury Alexander Hamilton, the Bank of the United States served as a depository of government funds, collected and expended government revenue, and issued notes to serve as a national medium of exchange. The bank's charter expired in 1811. A Second Bank of the United States was chartered in 1816.

Bank war (p. 253) The political dispute over whether to renew the charter of the Second Bank of the United States. In 1832, Congress voted to recharter the bank but President Andrew Jackson vetoed the measure and the charter expired in 1836. He argued that the Bank was unconstitutional, a dangerous monopoly, and vulnerable to control by foreign investors.

Bay of Pigs fiasco (p. 762) A military debacle in April 1961, during an American-organized effort to invade Cuba and drive Fidel Castro, the communist ruler, from power. The invasion force of some 1,500 Cuban exiles was routed at the Bay of Pigs, a major embarrassment for President John F. Kennedy.

beat school (p. 771) Also known as "beats," "beatniks," or the "beat generation"—nonconformists in the late 1950s who rejected conventional dress and sexual standards and cultivated avant-garde literature and music.

Berlin airlift (p. 738) U.S. effort to deliver supplies including 2 million tons of food and coal by air to West Berlin in 1948–1949 in response to the Soviet blockade of the city.

Berlin wall (p. 762) Erected by East Germany in 1961 and torn down by a Dutch company in 1989, the wall isolated West Berlin from the surrounding areas in communist controlled East Berlin and East Germany.

Bill of Rights (p. 155) The first ten amendments to the United States Constitution (adopted in 1791); they protected individual liberties and states' rights against the power of the national government.

Black Codes (p. 409) Special laws passed by southern state and municipal governments after the Civil War that denied free blacks many rights of citizenship.

Bland-Allison Silver Purchase Act (p. 534) An 1878 compromise law that that provided for the limited coinage of silver.

***Blitzkrieg* (p. 701)** A German tactic in World War II, translated as "lightning war," involving the coordinated attack of air and armored firepower.

Bonus Army (p. 673) A gathering of 20,000 Great War veterans in Washington, DC in June

1932, to demand immediate payment of their "adjusted compensation" bonuses voted by Congress in 1924. Congress rejected their demands, and President Hoover ordered U.S. troops to drive them from the capital.

Boston Massacre (p. 106) A violent confrontation between British troops and a Boston mob on March 5, 1770; the soldiers opened fire and killed five, an incident that inflamed sentiment against the British.

***Brown v. Board of Education of Topeka* (p. 753)** The 1954 Supreme Court decision that held that racially segregated education, which prevailed in much of the South, was unconstitutional. The ruling overturned the doctrine of "separate but equal" that had provided the legal justification for racial segregation ever since the 1896 *Plessy v. Ferguson* Supreme Court decision.

Camp David Accords (p. 792) A 1978 peace treaty between Egypt and Israel, mediated by President Jimmy Carter, signed at Camp David, a presidential retreat near Washington, DC.

carpetbaggers (p. 419) A pejorative term for Northerners who went to the South after the Civil War to exploit the new political power of freed blacks and the disenfranchisement of former Confederates.

Central Powers (p. 603) Germany and its World War I allies—Austria-Hungary, Turkey, and Bulgaria.

Chinese Exclusion Act (p. 434) A law passed by Congress in 1882 that prohibited Chinese immigration to the United States; it was overturned in 1943.

Civil Rights Act of 1964 (p. 767) Legislation outlawing discrimination in public accommodations and employment on the basis of race, skin color, sex, religion, or national origin.

civil rights cases (p. 526) A group of cases in 1883 in which the U.S. Supreme Court declared unconstitutional the Civil Rights Act of 1875, which had prohibited racial discrimination in hotels, theaters, and other privately owned facilities. The Court ruled that the **Fourteenth Amendment** barred state governments from discriminating on the basis of race but did not prevent private individuals, businesses, or organizations from doing so.

Civilian Conservation Corps (CCC) (p. 680) A **New Deal** program to provide government jobs in reforestation, flood control, and other conservation projects to young men between ages eighteen and twenty-five.

Clayton Antitrust Act (p. 566) Legislation that strengthened antitrust laws. Passed in 1914, it outlawed interlocking directorates, exempted labor unions from antitrust laws, and limited the use of injunctions in labor disputes.

Coercive Acts (p. 108) A series of laws passed by Parliament in 1774 to punish Boston and Massachusetts for the destruction of tea during the "Boston Tea Party." Many colonists, who regarded these and similar laws as "intolerable," moved closer toward war.

Columbian Exchange (p. 23) The transfer of plants, animals, and diseases from Europe, Africa, and Asia to and from the Americas after Columbus's fateful voyage in 1492.

***Common Sense* (p. 117)** An influential tract, published by Thomas Paine in January 1776, calling for American independence from Great Britain and establishment of a republican government.

Compromise of 1850 (p. 318) Several laws that together sought to settle several outstanding issues involving slavery. They banned the slave trade, but not slavery in Washington, DC; admitted California as a free state; applied popular sovereignty to the remaining Mexican Cession territory; settled the Texas-New Mexico boundary dispute; and passed a more stringent **Fugitive Slave Act**.

Compromise of 1877 (p. 429) A brokered arrangement whereby Republican and Democratic leaders agreed to settle the disputed 1876 presidential election. Democrats allowed returns that ensured the election of Republican Rutherford B. Hayes; and Republicans agreed to withdraw federal troops from the South, ensuring an end to Reconstruction.

Comstock Lode (p. 441) The first major vein of silver ore in the United States, discovered in the late 1850s, near Virginia City, Nevada.

***conquistadores* (p. 17)** The Spanish term for "conquerors," specifically the explorers, adventurers, and soldiers who crushed the native peoples of the Americas.

Conservation (p. 561) The efficient management and use of natural resources, such as forests, grasslands, and rivers; it represents a "middle-of-the-road" policy as opposed to the uncontrolled exploitation of such resources or the preservation those resources from any human exploiters.

Continental army (p. 115) The regular or professional army authorized by the **Second Continental Congress**, mostly under the command of General George Washington during the Revolutionary War.

Contract with America (p. 837) A pledge, signed by many Republicans running for Congress in 1994, to support conservative reforms limiting federal power and expenditures. Championed by House Speaker Newt Gingrich, it contributed to a Republican electoral victory; but opposition by President William Clinton, a Democrat, prevented passage of much of the contract's legislative agenda.

Copperheads (p. 382) Term that initially applied to northern Democrats who resisted Republican war measures and advocated negotiation with the Confederacy. Later in the Civil War, the term became tantamount to an accusation of treason against the Union.

Crittenden Compromise (p. 373) Legislation proposed by Kentucky Senator John Crittenden during the Secession Crisis in 1860–1861. It called for a constitutional amendment recognizing slavery in all territory south of 36°30' (the "Missouri Compromise line") and an ironclad amendment guaranteeing slavery in slave states. President-elect Lincoln and the Republicans rejected the proposals.

crop-lien system (p. 423) A system of agriculture in which local landowners and merchants loaned money to farm workers in return for a portion of the harvest of cash crops. By forcing farmers to plant cash crops, the system discouraged diversified agriculture in the South.

Cuban missile crisis (p. 763) The showdown between the United States and the Soviet Union during October 1962, after the Soviet Union had sneaked medium-range nuclear missiles into communist Cuba. After President John F. Kennedy publicly demanded their removal and ordered the blockade of Cuba, Soviet leader Nikita Khrushchev agreed to do so, averting a nuclear war.

Cult of True Womanhood (p. 274) An ideal of middle-class womanhood in the early nineteenth century that asserted that women were naturally pious, pure, and submissive; exemplars of Christian precepts; and best-suited to supervise the moral development of the family.

D-Day (p. 720) June 6, 1944, the day Allied troops crossed the English Channel, landed on the coast of Normandy, and opened a second front in Western Europe during World War II. The "D" stands for "disembarkation"—to leave a ship and go ashore.

***Dartmouth College v. Woodward* (p. 243)** The 1819 Supreme Court case that held that a state charter—in this case, to Dartmouth College—was a contract and that contracts could not be canceled or altered without the consent of both parties, a ruling that strengthened corporations and encouraged investment.

Dawes Severalty Act of 1887 (p. 439) An 1887 law terminating tribal ownership of land and allotting some parcels of land to individual Indians with the remainder of the land left open for white settlement. It included provisions for Indian education and eventual citizenship. The law led to corruption, exploitation, and the weakening of Indian tribal culture. It was reversed in 1934.

détente (p. 778) A French term, meaning the relaxation of tensions, applied to an easing of Cold War antagonisms during the 1970s. Under President Richard Nixon and foreign affairs adviser Henry Kissinger, détente was a strategy to allow the United States to weaken the bonds between the Soviet Union and communist China.

dollar diplomacy (p. 597) A policy of President William Taft to promote American economic penetration to underdeveloped nations, especially in Latin America; it sought to strengthen American influence without requiring the presence of U.S. troops.

Dred Scott decision (p. 360) The 1857 Supreme Court ruling that held that blacks were not citizens and could not sue in a federal court, and, most important, that Congress had exceeded its constitutional authority in banning slavery from the territories. By declaring the Missouri

Compromise unconstitutional, and making future compromises even more difficult, the decision pushed the nation closer to civil war.

Electoral College (p. 150) An assembly of delegates representing each of the states who choose the president of the United States. This mechanism, established by the U.S. Constitution, was regarded as less volatile than allowing voters to elect the president directly.

Emancipation Proclamation (p. 390) A decree by President Abraham Lincoln that freed all slaves in Confederate states that remained in active rebellion on January 1, 1863, when the proclamation went into effect.

Embargo Act (p. 188) A law passed by Congress in 1807 prohibiting all American exports. President Thomas Jefferson, who proposed the law, sought to pressure Britain and France—then at war with each other—into recognizing neutral rights.

***encomienda* system (p. 18)** A feudal labor arrangement, imposed in the Spanish colonies of the Americas, by which Spanish settlers were granted a certain number of Indian subjects who were obliged to pay tribute in goods and labor.

Enlightenment (p. 88) An intellectual movement of the eighteenth century that celebrated human reason and scientific advances and expressed doubts about the truth claims of sacred texts.

Environmental Protection Agency (EPA) (p. 780) A federal agency created in 1970 to oversee environmental monitoring and cleanup programs.

Equal Rights Amendment (ERA) (p. 817) A proposed amendment to the U.S. Constitution to outlaw discrimination on the basis of sex. Although first proposed in 1923, the amendment was not passed by Congress until 1972; but the ratification movement fell short and the ERA was not added to the Constitution.

Era of Good Feelings (p. 210) A period from 1817 to 1823 in which the disappearance of the **Federalists** enabled the Republicans to govern in a spirit of seemingly nonpartisan harmony.

Espionage Act (p. 614) A law passed in 1917 that made it a crime to obstruct the nation's effort to win World War I.

Fair Deal (p. 739) President Harry Truman's 1949 program for expanded economic opportunity and civil rights.

Farewell Address (p. 165) President Washington's influential 1796 speech in which he deplored the rise of political factions and warned against "permanent alliances" with foreign nations.

Federal Reserve Act (p. 566) A 1913 law establishing a Federal Reserve Board, which controlled the rediscount rate and thus the money supply; this helped regularize the national banking system.

***Federalist Papers* (p. 153)** A series of essays, chiefly written by Alexander Hamilton, James Madison, and John Jay, explaining and defending the national government proposed by the Constitutional Convention of 1787.

Federalists (p. 152) Advocates of a strong national government; they supported ratification of the Constitution and subsequently supported measures to expand federal revenues and functions.

Fifteenth Amendment (p. 419) An amendment (1870), championed by the Republican party, that sought to guarantee the vote to blacks in the South following the Civil War.

First Continental Congress (p. 109) An assembly comprised of delegates from twelve colonies that met in Philadelphia in 1774. It denied Parliament's authority to legislate for the colonies, adopted the Declaration of Rights and Grievances, created a Continental Association to enforce a boycott of British imports, and endorsed a call to take up arms against Britain.

Force Acts (p. 424) Three laws passed by the Republican-dominated Congress in 1870–1871 to protect black voters in the South. The laws placed state elections under federal jurisdiction and imposed fines and imprisonment on those guilty of interfering with any citizen exercising his right to vote.

Fourteen Points (p. 620) A comprehensive plan, proposed by President Woodrow Wilson in January 1918, to negotiate an end to World War I. It called for freedom of the seas, free trade, arms reduction, national self-determination and an end to colonial rule and secret diplomacy.

Fourteenth Amendment (p. 415) An amendment, passed by Congress in 1866 and ratified in 1868, that prohibited states from depriving citizens of the due process or the equal protection of the laws. Although the amendment was a response to discriminatory laws against blacks in the South, it figured prominently in the expansion of individual rights and liberties during the last half of the twentieth century.

Free Soil party (p. 315) A party that emerged in the 1840s in opposition to the expansion of slavery into the territories. Formally organized in 1848, it nominated Martin Van Buren for president. In 1856, Free Soil party members joined with former **Whigs** and other disaffected voters to form the **Republican party**.

Freedmen's Bureau (p. 414) A federal refugee agency to aid former slaves and destitute whites after the Civil War. It provided them food, clothing, and other necessities as well as helped them find work and set up schools.

French and Indian War (p. 92) Fourth in the series of great wars between Britain and France, this conflict (1754–1763) had its focal point in North America and pitted the French and their Indian allies against the British and their Indian allies. Known in Europe as the **Seven Years' War**, this struggle drove the French government from much of North America.

French Revolution (p. 159) The massive and violent social and political upheaval commencing in 1789 that ended the French monarchy, established a republic, expropriated the land and property of the Catholic Church, and culminated in a bloody reign of terror.

Fugitive Slave Act (p. 318) Initially, a 1793 law to encourage the return of runaway slaves; this law was amended, as part of the **Compromise of 1850**, so as to authorize federal commissioners to compel citizens to assist in the return of runaway (fugitive) slaves. The law offended Northerners and its nonenforcement offended Southerners.

Gibbons v. Ogden **(p. 244)** Supreme Court ruling (1824) that held that no state could pass laws affecting interstate trade, thereby ensuring the federal government's supremacy in interstate commerce.

Glorious Revolution (p. 66) The peaceful accession of William II, a Protestant, and Queen Mary to the British throne in 1688, ending the Catholic rule of James II. Many colonists rebelled against governors who had been appointed by James II and demanded greater political rights.

gold rush (p. 313) Term for the gold-mining boom in the U.S. western territories in the late 1840s and 1850s.

"good neighbor" (p. 665) President Herbert Hoover's policy to promote better relations between the United States and nations in the Western Hemisphere; it declared America's intention to disclaim the right to intervention pronounced in the **Platt Amendment** and the **Roosevelt Corollary**.

Great Awakening (p. 85) A widespread evangelical revival movement of the 1740s and 1750s, sparked by the tour of the English evangelical minister George Whitefield. The Awakening spread religious fervor but weakened the authority of established churches.

Great Compromise (p. 150) Resolved the differences between the New Jersey and Virginia delegations to the Constitutional Convention by providing for a bicameral legislature: the Senate, with equal representation for each state, and the House of Representatives, apportioned by population.

Great Society (p. 767) The sweeping legislative agenda of President Lyndon Johnson; it sought to end poverty, promote civil rights, and improve housing, health care, and education. The program was criticized as costly and ineffective.

greenbacks (p. 382) Paper currency issued by the Union government during the Civil War, resulting in inflation. Whether to continue the issue of greenbacks became a key political issue in the decades after the Civil War.

Gulf of Tonkin Resolution (p. 772) Congressional action, undertaken at President Johnson's request, giving the President the authority to deploy U.S. troops to repel aggression in Southeast Asia. This provided congressional sanction for the escalation of the Vietnam war.

Half-Way Covenant (p. 65) A modification of puritan practice, adopted by many Congregational churches during the 1650s and afterwards, that allowed baptized puritans who had not experienced saving grace to acquire partial church membership and receive sacraments.

Harlem Renaissance (p. 650) A modern artistic and literary movement that celebrated African American life and culture in early twentieth-century Harlem, New York. Among its key figures were Langston Hughes, Richard Wright, and Zora Neale Hurston (literature); Duke Ellington (music); Jacob Lawrence (painting); and Aaron Douglas (sculpture).

Hartford Convention (p. 203) A gathering of New England **Federalists** from December 1814 through January 1815 to channel opposition to Thomas Jefferson and the **War of 1812**. Some participants may have regarded the meeting as preparatory to a secession movement by the New England colonies.

headright (p. 54) A system of land distribution, adopted first in Virginia and later in Maryland, that granted colonists fifty acres for themselves and another fifty for each "head" (or person) they brought with them to the colony. This system was often used in conjunction with indentured servitude to build large plantations and supply them with labor.

Hepburn Act (p. 560) Federal legislation, passed in 1906, that gave the Interstate Commerce Commission sufficient power to inspect railroad companies' records, set maximum rates, and outlaw free passes.

Homestead Act (1862) (p. 396) Federal law granting 160 acres of public land in the West to any settler who would farm and improve it within five years of the grant; it encouraged migration into the Great Plains.

human immunodeficiency virus (HIV) (p. 821) A virus, usually spread through sexual contact, that attacks the immune system, sometimes fatally. HIV, which causes **acquired immunodeficiency syndrome (AIDS)**, first appeared in the United States in the 1980s.

impressment (p. 187) The policy whereby Britain forced people to serve in its navy. The impressment of sailors—even American citizens—on neutral vessels during the Napoleonic Wars outraged Americans and was a major cause of the **War of 1812**.

improvised explosive device (IED) (p. 851) Also known as "roadside bombs," IEDs are homemade bombs that usually consist of captured artillery shells that are wired to a detonator. Either they are exploded remotely or by suicide bombers. IEDs

accounted for over a third of the casualties sustained by American and United Nations forces in the Iraq and Afghanistan wars.

indentured servants (p. 55) Individuals working under a form of contract labor that provided them with free passage to America in return for a promise to work for a fixed period, usually seven years. Indentured servitude was the primary labor system in the Chesapeake colonies for most of the seventeenth century.

Industrial Workers of the World (IWW) (p. 546) A militant labor organization, founded in 1905 and inspired by European anarchists, that advocated "abolition of the wage system" and called for a single union of all workers, regardless of trade or skill level; it was repressed during and after World War I.

internment camps (p. 715) Detainment centers, mostly located in western states, that held approximately 110,000 Japanese aliens and American citizens of Japanese origin during World War II.

Interstate Commerce Act (p. 468) Federal law establishing the Interstate Commerce Commission in 1887, the nation's first regulatory agency.

Iran-Contra affair (p. 803) Scandal involving high officials in the Reagan administration accused of funding the Contra rebels in Nicaragua in violation of 1984 Congressional laws explicitly prohibiting such aid. The Contra funding came from the secret sale of arms to Iran.

Iranian hostage crisis (p. 794) Protracted crisis that began in 1979 when Islamic militants seized the American embassy in Tehran, Iran, and held scores of its employees hostage. The militants had been enraged by American support for the deposed Shah of Iran. The crisis, which lasted over a year, contributed to President Jimmy Carter's defeat in his reelection campaign in 1980.

isolationism (p. 575) A national policy that eschews foreign alliances, such as was propounded by George Washington in his "**Farewell Address**." Isolationism was also embraced by part of the **Monroe Doctrine** of 1823 and after the First World War, when the United States refused to join the **League of Nations** and sought to distance itself during the 1930s from the rumblings of another world war. Isolationism ended as national policy when Japan attacked Pearl Harbor on December 7, 1941.

Jacksonian democracy (p. 248) A political doctrine, chiefly associated with Andrew Jackson, that proclaimed the equality of all adult white males—the common man—and disapproved of anything that smacked of special privilege, such as chartered banks.

Jay's Treaty (p. 164) Named after John Jay, the American negotiator, and ratified in 1795, this treaty eased tensions with Great Britain. By its provisions Britain agreed to evacuate forts on the United States' side of the Great Lakes and submit questions of neutral rights to arbitrators.

joint-stock companies (p. 25) Businesses in which investors pooled capital for specific purposes, such as conducting trade and founding colonies. Examples include the English joint-stock companies that founded the Virginia, Plymouth, and Massachusetts Bay colonies.

judicial review (p. 150) A crucial concept that empowered the Supreme Court to invalidate acts of Congress. Although not explicitly propounded in the U.S. Constitution, Chief Justice John Marshall affirmed in *Marbury v. Madison* (1803) that the right of judicial review was implicit in the Constitution's status as "the supreme Law of the Land."

Kansas-Nebraska Act (p. 354) A compromise law in 1854 that superseded the **Missouri Compromise** and left it to voters in Kansas and Nebraska to determine whether they would be slave or free states. The law exacerbated sectional tensions when voters came to blows over the question of slavery in Kansas.

Kentucky and Virginia Resolves (p. 168) Political declarations in favor of states' rights, written by Thomas Jefferson and James Madison, in opposition to the federal **Alien and Sedition Acts**. These resolutions, passed by the Kentucky and Virginia legislatures in 1798, maintained that states could nullify federal legislation they regarded as unconstitutional.

Knights of Labor (p. 471) A national labor organization, formed in 1869 and headed by Uriah Stephens and Terence Powderly, that promoted union solidarity, political reform, and sociability among members. Its advocacy of the eight-hour day led to violent strikes in 1886 and the organization's subsequent decline.

Know-Nothing party (p. 355) A nativist, anti-immigrant and anti-Catholic party that emerged in response to the flood of Catholic immigrants from Ireland and Germany in the 1840s. The party achieved mostly local successes in the Northeast port cities; but in 1856 former President Millard Fillmore, whose Whig party had dissolved, accepted the nomination of southern Know-Nothings but carried only Maryland, a failure that contributed to the movement's decline.

Ku Klux Klan (p. 424) Founded as a social club in 1866 by a handful of former Confederate soldiers in Tennessee, it became a vigilante group that used violence and intimidation to drive African Americans out of politics. The movement declined in the late 1870s but resurfaced in the 1920s as a political organization that opposed all groups—immigrant, religious, and racial—that challenged Protestant white hegemony.

laissez-faire (p. 462) A French term—literally, "to let alone"—used in economic contexts to signify the absence of governmental interference in or regulation of economic matters.

League of Nations (p. 623) A worldwide assembly of nations, proposed by President Woodrow Wilson, that was included in the Treaty of Versailles ending World War I. The refusal of the United States to join the League limited its effectiveness.

Lecompton constitution (p. 362) A proslavery constitution, drafted in 1857 by delegates for Kansas territory, elected under questionable circumstances, seeking admission to the United States. It was rejected by two territorial governors, supported by President Buchanan, and decisively defeated by Congress.

Leisler's Rebellion (p. 73) An uprising in 1689, led by Jacob Leisler, that wrested control of New York's government following the abdication of King James II. The rebellion ended when Leisler was arrested and executed in 1690.

Lend-Lease Act (p. 703) A military aid measure, proposed by President Franklin D. Roosevelt in 1941 and adopted by Congress, empowering the president to sell, lend, lease, or transfer $7 billion of war material to any country whose defense he declared as vital to that of the United States.

Lewis and Clark expedition (p. 184) An exploration of the Louisiana Territory and the region stretching to the Pacific, commissioned by President Jefferson. Commanded by Meriwether Lewis and William Clark, the enterprise (1804–1806) brought back a wealth of information about the region.

Louisiana Purchase (p. 177) An 1803 agreement whereby the United States purchased France's North American Empire, the vast region drained by the Mississippi and Missouri Rivers, for $15 million; it doubled the size of the nation.

Loyalists (p. 120) Sometimes called Tories, the term for American colonists who refused to take up arms against England in the 1770s.

lyceums (p. 294) Locally sponsored public lectures, often featuring writers, that were popular in the nineteenth century.

Manhattan Project (p. 701) The code name for the extensive United States military project, established in 1942, to produce fissionable uranium and plutonium, and to design and build an atomic bomb. Costing nearly $2 billion, the effort culminated in the destruction of Hiroshima and Nagasaki in August 1945.

manifest destiny (p. 303) Originating in the 1840s, a term that referred to support of the expansion of the United States through the acquisition of Texas, Oregon, and parts of Mexico. The term was also used in the 1890s in reference to the conquest of foreign lands not meant to be incorporated into the United States.

Marbury v. Madison **(p. 176)** An 1803 Supreme Court ruling that declared the Judiciary Act of 1789 unconstitutional and established the precedent for judicial review of federal laws.

Marshall Plan (p. 737) A proposal, propounded in 1947 by Secretary of State George Marshall, to use American aid to rebuild the war-torn economies of European nations. Adopted by Congress in 1948 as the European Recovery Program, it pumped some $13 billion into Europe during the next five years.

massive retaliation (p. 747) The "New Look" military policy of the Dwight D. Eisenhower and Secretary of State John Foster Dulles relying on nuclear weapons to inhibit communist aggression during the 1950s.

Mayflower Compact (p. 31) An agreement, signed aboard the *Mayflower* among the Pilgrims en route to Plymouth Plantation (1620), to establish a body politic and to obey the rules of the governors they chose.

McCulloch v. Maryland **(p. 243)** An 1819 Supreme Court ruling that state governments could not tax a federal agency—in this case the second Bank of the United States—for "the power to tax involves the power to destroy." The decision affirmed the doctrine of the implied powers of the federal government.

Medicare (p. 769) A social welfare measure, enacted in 1965, providing hospitalization insurance for people over sixty-five and a voluntary plan to cover doctor bills paid in part by the federal government.

mercantilism (p. 81) A loose system of economic organization designed, through a favorable balance of trade, to guarantee the prosperity of the British empire. Mercantilists advocated possession of colonies as places where the mother country could acquire raw materials not available at home.

Mexican War (p. 308) Fought between the United States and Mexico from May 1846 to February 1848, the Mexican War greatly added to the national domain of the United States; see also **Treaty of Guadalupe Hidalgo**.

military-industrial complex (p. 757) A term, popularized by President Dwight D. Eisenhower in his 1961 farewell address, for the concert of interests among the U.S. military and its chief corporate contractors.

Missouri Compromise (p. 218) A legislative deal, brokered in 1820, that preserved the balance of slave and free states in the Union by admitting Missouri as a slave state and Maine as a free state; it also banned slavery from that part of the Louisiana Territory north of 36°30'.

Monroe Doctrine (p. 207) A foreign policy edict, propounded by President James Monroe in 1823, declaring that the American continents were no longer open to European colonization or exploitation and that the United States would not interfere in the internal affairs of European nations.

Moral Majority (p. 796) A term associated with the organization by that name, founded in 1979 by the Reverend Jerry Falwell to combat "amoral liberals," drug abuse, "coddling" of criminals, homosexuality, communism, and abortion.

muckraker (p. 545) A term for progressive investigative journalists who exposed the seamy side of American life at the turn of the twentieth century by "raking up the muck."

mugwumps (p. 524) A group of eastern Republicans, disgusted with corruption in the party, who campaigned for the Democrats in the 1884 elections. These anticorruption reformers were conservative on the money question and government regulation.

National American Woman Suffrage Association (NAWSA) (p. 554) An organization, founded in 1890, that united the National Woman Suffrage Association, headed by Elizabeth Cady Stanton and Susan B. Anthony, and the American Woman Suffrage Association, headed by Lucy Stone. After ratification of the Nineteenth Amendment granting women the vote in 1920, the NAWSA became the League of Women Voters.

National Association for the Advancement of Colored People (NAACP) (p. 571) A national interracial organization, founded in 1909, that promoted the rights of African Americans. Initially it fought against lynching, but from 1955 through 1977, under the leadership of Roy Wilkins, it launched the campaign that overturned legalized segregation and it backed civil rights legislation. The NAACP remains the nation's largest African American organization.

National Grange of the Patrons of Husbandry (p. 467) A farmers' organization, founded in 1867 by Oliver H. Kelley, that initially provided social and cultural benefits but then supported legislation, known as the Granger laws, providing for railroad regulation.

National Organization for Women (NOW) (p. 817) An organization, founded in 1966 by Betty Friedan and other feminists, to promote equal rights for women, changes in divorce laws, and legalization of abortion.

National Origins Act (p. 632) A federal law, passed in 1929 that curtailed immigration, especially from southern and eastern Europe and Asia.

National Recovery Administration (NRA) (p. 680) A **New Deal** agency, established in 1933, to promote economic recovery, that promulgated industry-wide codes to control production, prices, and wages.

nationalism (p. 135) An affinity for a particular nation; in particular, a sense of national consciousness and loyalty that promotes the interests and attributes of that nation over all others.

nativism (p. 486) A fear or hatred of immigrants, ethnic minorities, or alien political movements.

Navigation Acts (p. 82) Seventeenth-century Parliamentary statutes to control trade within the British empire so as to benefit Britain and promote its administration of the colonies.

Neolithic revolution (p. 4) The transition from a hunter-gather economy to one mostly based on the cultivation of crops.

neutrality acts (p. 698) Legislation affirming nonbelligerency in the event of war. In relation to American history, such legislation was passed in 1794 to preclude American entanglement in the Napoleonic Wars; similar laws were passed just before and after World War I, especially during the 1930s.

New Deal (p. 679) A broad program of legislation proposed by President Franklin D. Roosevelt to promote recovery from the Great Depression and provide relief for those in distress.

New Freedom (p. 564) Democratic candidate Woodrow Wilson's term in the 1912 presidential campaign for a proposed policy that would restore competition by breaking up the trusts and punishing corporations that violated rules of business conduct.

New Frontier (p. 755) President John F. Kennedy's term for a revitalized national agenda, particularly in relation to foreign policy and space exploration.

new immigration (p. 485) Reference to the influx of immigrants to the United States during the late nineteenth and early twentieth century predominantly from southern and eastern Europe.

New Jersey Plan (p. 148) The proposal to the Constitutional Convention of 1787 by New Jersey delegate William Paterson to create a federal legislature in which each state was represented equally. The concept became embodied in the United States Constitution through the Senate, in which each state has two representatives, though this was counterbalanced by the House of Representatives, in which each state's representation is proportional to its population.

New Nationalism (p. 563) Progressive candidate Theodore Roosevelt's term in the 1912 presidential election for an expansion of federal power to regulate big business and enact legislation to promote social justice.

Niagara movement (p. 570) A response by W. E. B. Du Bois and other blacks, following a meeting in Niagara Falls in 1905, in opposition to Booker T. Washington's advocacy of black accommodation to white prejudice; these leaders drafted a political program to achieve equal opportunity, equal justice, and an end to segregation that led to the founding of the **National Association for the Advancement of Colored People (NAACP)**.

North American Free Trade Agreement (NAFTA) (p. 839) A 1993 accord signed by Canada, Mexico, and the United States to reduce and eventually eliminate barriers to trade, including tariffs, among the signatories.

North Atlantic Treaty Organization (NATO) (p. 740) A military mutual-defense pact, formed in 1948, by the United States, Canada, and ten European nations, including Great Britain, France, and West Germany; the Soviet Union countered with the formation of the Warsaw Pact among communist regimes in Eastern Europe.

Northwest Ordinance (p. 137) A 1787 measure of the Continental Congress, passed according to the **Articles of Confederation**, to provide for governance of the region north of the Ohio River and the eventual admission of up to five territories—ultimately the states of Ohio, Indiana, Illinois, Michigan, and Wisconsin. The ordinance also prohibited slavery in the region and reserved lands for Indians.

NSC-68 (p. 741) A secret policy statement, proposed by the National Security Council in 1950, calling for a large, ongoing military commitment to contain Soviet communism; it was accepted by President Harry Truman after the North Korean invasion of South Korea.

nullification (p. 261) A doctrine, forcefully articulated by John C. Calhoun in 1828, asserting that a state could invalidate, within its own boundaries, federal legislation the state regarded as unconstitutional.

Open Door policy (p. 593) A policy, propounded by Secretary of State John Hay in 1899, affirming the territorial integrity of China and a policy of free trade.

Organization of Petroleum Exporting Countries (OPEC) (p. 788) A cartel of oil-producing nations in Asia, Africa, and Latin America that gained substantial power over the world economy in the mid- to late-1970s.

Ostend Manifesto (p. 351) A confidential 1854 dispatch to the U.S. State Department from American diplomats meeting in Ostend, Belgium, suggesting that the United States would be justified in seizing Cuba if Spain refused to sell it to the United States. When word of the document was leaked, Northerners seethed at this "slaveholders' plot" to extend slavery.

Paleolithic revolution (p. 1) Period 750,000 years ago when humans devised simple stone tools, inaugurating life based on hunting and gathering.

Pendleton Act (p. 523) An 1883 law bringing civil service reform to federal employment; it classified many government jobs and required competitive exams for these positions.

People's (Populist) party (p. 531) The People's party of America was an important "third party," founded in 1891, that sought to unite various disaffected groups, especially farmers. The party nominated James B. Weaver for president in 1892 and in 1896 joined with the Democratic party in support of William Jennings Bryan for president.

Persian Gulf War (p. 807) The 1991 war following Iraq's takeover of Kuwait; the United States and a coalition of allies defeated the army of Iraqi leader Saddam Hussein but failed to drive him from power.

Platt Amendment (p. 589) A law, passed in 1901 and superseding the **Teller Amendment**, which stipulated the conditions for the withdrawal of

American forces from Cuba; it also transferred ownership of the naval base at Guantanamo Bay to the United States.

***Plessy v. Ferguson* (p. 526)** Supreme Court ruling (1896) that held that racial segregation of public accommodations did not infringe on the "equal protection" clause of the Constitution; this "separate but equal" doctrine was overturned by *Brown v. Board of Education* in 1954.

popular sovereignty (p. 314) The principle of allowing people to make political decisions by majority vote. As applied to American history, the term generally refers to the 1848 proposal of Michigan Senator Lewis Cass to allow settlers to determine the status of slavery in the territories.

Potsdam Conference (p. 731) A wartime conference (April 1945) held in occupied Germany where Allied leaders divided Germany and Berlin into four occupation zones, agreed to try Nazi leaders as war criminals, and planned the exacting of reparations from Germany.

pragmatism (p. 513) A philosophical system, chiefly associated with William James, that deemphasized abstraction and assessed ideas and cultural practices based on their practical effects; it helped inspire political and social reform during the late nineteenth century.

predestination (p. 30) The Calvinist belief, accepted by New England puritans, that God had determined who would receive eternal grace at the dawn of time; nothing people did during their lifetime could alter their prospects of salvation.

Progressivism (p. 543) A cluster of movements for various forms of social change—some of them contradictory—during the early twentieth century; progressives generally opposed corruption and inefficiency in government, monopoly power among corporations, and wayward behavior among immigrants and others.

Protestant Reformation (p. 24) A religious movement of the sixteenth century initially focused on eliminating corruption in the Catholic Church; but under the influence of theologians Martin Luther and John Calvin, it indicted Catholic theology and gave rise to various denominations that advanced alternative interpretations.

puritans (p. 30) A term, initially derisive, referring to English religious dissenters who believed that the religious practices and administration of the Church of England too closely resembled those of the Catholic Church; many migrated to Massachusetts Bay after 1630 to establish a religious commonwealth based on the principles of John Calvin and others.

Quakers (p. 39) Adherents of a religious organization founded in England in the 1640s who believed that the Holy Spirit lived in all people; they embraced pacifism and religious tolerance, and rejected formal theology. In the decades after 1670, thousands of Quakers emigrated to New Jersey and Pennsylvania.

Radical Republicans (p. 382, 412) A faction within the Republican party, headed by Thaddeus Stevens and Benjamin Wade, that insisted on black suffrage and federal protection of the civil rights of blacks. After 1867, the Radical Republicans achieved a working majority in Congress and passed legislation promoting Reconstruction.

Reaganomics (p. 795) A label pinned on President Ronald Reagan's policies of tax cuts, social welfare cuts, and increased military spending; it generated huge federal deficits, but also promoted the reorganization of large corporations.

"reconcentration" camps (p. 580) A term that referred to the Spanish refugee camps into which Cuban farmers were herded in 1896 to prevent them from providing assistance to rebels fighting for Cuban independence from Spain.

"red scare" (p. 628) Public hysteria over Bolshevik influence in the United States after World War I; it led to the arrest or deportation of thousands of radicals, labor activists, and ethnic leaders.

Republican party (p. 356) One of the original two political parties, sometimes called "Democratic Republican," it was organized by James Madison and Thomas Jefferson and generally stood for states' rights, an agrarian economy and the interests of farmers and planters over those of financial and commercial groups, who generally supported the **Federalist** party; both of the original parties faded in the 1820s. A new Republican party emerged in the 1850s in opposition to the extension of slavery in the territories. It also adopted most of the old Whig party's economic program. The party nominated John C. Fremont for president in 1856 and Abraham Lincoln in 1860.

romanticism (p. 288) A loosely defined aesthetic movement originating in the late eighteenth century and flowering during the early nineteenth century; it encompassed literature, philosophy, arts, and music and enshrined feeling and intuition over reason.

Sanitary Commission (p. 398) A private and voluntary medical organization, founded in May 1861, that sought to improve the physical and mental well-being of Union soldiers during the Civil War.

scalawags (p. 419) White southern Republicans—mainly small landowning farmers and well-off merchants and planters—who cooperated with the congressionally imposed Reconstruction governments set up in the South following the Civil War.

Scopes trial (p. 643) Also called the "Monkey Trial," it was a celebrated 1924 contest that pitted Darwinian evolutionists against fundamentalist "Creationists." John T. Scopes, a teacher charged with defying Tennessee law by teaching evolution, was found guilty and fined $100.

Second Continental Congress (p. 114) A gathering of American Patriots in May 1775 that organized the **Continental army**, requisitioned soldiers and supplies, and commissioned George Washington to lead it.

Second Great Awakening (p. 275) A wave of religious enthusiasm, commencing in the 1790s and lasting for decades, that stressed the mercy, love, and benevolence of God and emphasized that all people could, through faith and effort, achieve salvation.

second party system (p. 263) A term for the political contention between the Democratic party, as rejuvenated by Andrew Jackson in 1828, and the **Whigs**, who emerged in response to Jackson.

Sedition Act (p. 614) Federal legislation, first passed in 1798 and expired in 1801, that placed limits on freedom of speech during wartime. Another such act was passed in 1918 and led to the imprisonment of Socialist Eugene V. Debs and others during World War I.

Seneca Falls Convention (p. 287) A meeting, held at Seneca Falls, New York in 1848, that affirmed that "all men and women are created equal" and sought the franchise (vote) for women.

settlement houses (p. 495) Community centers, founded by reformers such as Jane Addams and Lillian Wald beginning in the 1880s, that were located in poor urban districts of major cities; the centers sought to Americanize immigrant families and provide them with social services and a political voice.

Seven Years' War (p. 93) The global conflict, sometimes known as the **French and Indian War**, that lasted from 1756 to 1763 and pitted France and its allies against Britain and its allies. Britain ultimately prevailed, forcing France to surrender its claims to Canada and all territory east of the Mississippi River.

Shakers (p. 277) A religious commune founded by Ann Lee in England that came to America in 1774. Shakers practiced celibacy, believed that God was both Mother and Father, and held property in common.

sharecropping (p. 422) A type of agriculture, frequently practiced in the South during and after Reconstruction, in which landowners provided land, tools, housing, and seed to a farmer who provided his labor; the resulting crop was divided between them (i.e., shared).

Shays's rebellion (p. 145) An armed rebellion of western Massachusetts farmers in 1786 to prevent state courts from foreclosing on debtors. Nationalists saw such unrest as proof of the inadequacy of the federal government under the **Articles of Confederation**.

Sherman Antitrust Act (p. 469) A federal law, passed in 1890, that outlawed monopolistic organizations that functioned to restrain trade.

Sherman Silver Purchase Act (p. 534) An 1890 law that obliged the federal government to buy and coin silver, thereby counteracting the deflationary tendencies of the economy at the time; its repeal in 1894, following the Depression of 1893, caused a political uproar.

social Darwinism (p. 464) A belief that Charles Darwin's theory of the evolution of species also applied to social and economic institutions an practices: The "fittest" enterprises or individuals prevailed, while those that were defective naturally faded away; society thus progressed most surely when competition was unrestricted by government.

Social Gospel (p. 495) A doctrine preached by many urban Protestant ministers during the early

1900s that focused on improving living conditions for the city's poor rather than on saving souls; proponents advocated civil service reform, child labor laws, government regulation of big business, and a graduated income tax.

Social Security Act (p. 689) A component of Franklin Roosevelt's **New Deal**, it established in 1935 a system of old-age, unemployment, and survivors' insurance funded by wage and payroll taxes.

Southern Christian Leadership Conference (SCLC) (p. 755) A civil rights organization, founded in 1957 by Martin Luther King, Jr. and his followers, that espoused Christian nonviolence but organized mass protests to challenge segregation and discrimination; it played a major role in support of the **Civil Rights Act of 1964** and the **Voting Rights Act of 1965**.

Specie Circular (p. 262) An edict, issued by President Andrew Jackson in 1836, obliging purchasers of public land to do so with gold coins rather than the paper currency issued by state banks; it caused the speculative boom in real estate to collapse and exacerbated a financial panic the following year.

spoils system (p. 252) A term, usually derisive, whereby newly elected office-holders appoint loyal members of their own party to public office.

Square Deal (p. 559) The phrase, initially employed by President Theodore Roosevelt in 1904, to describe an arbitrated settlement between workers and an employer, but more generally employed as a goal to promote fair business practices and to punish "bad" corporations that used their economic clout unfairly.

stagflation (p. 791) A term coined in the 1970s to describe the period's economic downturn and simultaneous deflation in prices.

Stamp Act Congress (p. 101) A meeting in New York City of delegates of most of the colonial assemblies in America to protest the Stamp Act, a revenue measure passed by Parliament in 1765; it was a precursor to the Continental Congress.

Strategic Arms Limitation Treaty (SALT) (p. 778) A treaty, signed by the United States and the Soviet Union in 1972, restricting the testing and deployment of nuclear ballistic missiles, the first of several such treaties.

Strategic Defense Initiative (SDI) (p. 798) The concept of a space-based missile defense system—popularly known as "Star Wars," after the movie by that name—proposed by President Ronald Reagan in 1983. Controversial and costly, the concept was never fully realized.

Student Nonviolent Coordinating Committee (SNCC) (p. 764) A civil rights organization, founded in 1960, that drew heavily on younger activists and college students. After 1965, under the leadership of Stokely Carmichael and then H. Rap Brown, the group advocated "Black Power."

Students for a Democratic Society (SDS) (p. 771) An organization created by leftist college students in the early 1960s; it organized protests against racial bigotry, corporate exploitation of workers, and, especially after 1965, the Vietnam war.

"surge" (p. 852) The sudden increase in troop strength that appeared to have been used successfully against the Iraq insurgency in 2007. President Barack Obama similarly adopted a surge in 2009 to stabilize a deteriorating situation in Afghanistan.

Taft-Hartley Act (p. 735) A 1947 federal law that outlawed the closed shop and secondary boycotts and obliged union leaders to sign affidavits declaring that they were not communists.

Tariff of Abominations (p. 193) An exceptionally high tariff, passed in 1828, that provoked Vice President John C. Calhoun to write the "South Carolina Exposition and Protest"—a defense of the doctrine of **nullification**.

Teapot Dome scandal (p. 659) A scandal during the administration of Warren Harding in which the Secretary of the Interior, Albert Fall, accepted bribes from oil companies that then leased the Teapot Dome federal oil reserve in Wyoming.

Teller Amendment (p. 582) A rider to the 1898 war resolution with Spain whereby Congress pledged that it did not intend to annex Cuba and that it would recognize Cuban independence from Spain.

temperance movement (p. 281) A reform movement of the nineteenth and early twentieth centuries in which women and ministers played a major role and that advocated moderation in the use of alcoholic beverages, or, preferably, abstinence. The major organizations included the American Temperance Society, the Washingtonian movement, and the Women's Christian Temperance Union (WCTU).

Ten Percent Plan (p. 411) A measure drafted by President Abraham Lincoln in 1863 to readmit states that had seceded once 10 percent of their prewar voters swore allegiance to the Union and adopted state constitutions outlawing slavery.

tenement (p. 489) Four- to six-story residential apartment house, once common in New York and certain other cities, built on a tiny lot with little regard for adequate ventilation or light.

Tennessee Valley Authority (TVA) (p. 683) A **New Deal** agency that built and operated dams and power plants on the Tennessee River; it also promoted flood control, soil conservation, and reforestation.

Tet offensive (p. 774) A wide-ranging offensive, launched by North Vietnamese and Vietcong troops throughout South Vietnam in February 1968. It failed to cause the South Vietnamese government to collapse, but persuaded many Americans that the war was not winnable. President Lyndon B. Johnson announced his decision not to run for reelection several months later.

Thirteenth Amendment (p. 413) Passed in 1865, this amendment declared an end to slavery and negated the Three-fifths Clause in the Constitution, thereby increasing the representation of the southern states in Congress.

Three-Fifths Compromise (p. 149) The provision in the Constitution that defined slaves, for purposes of representation in the House of Representatives and state tax payments, not as full persons, but as constituting only three-fifths of a person.

Trail of Tears (p. 259) The name for the 1838 forced removal of Cherokee and other Indians from Georgia and the western Appalachians to Indian Territory in Oklahoma and nearby regions.

transcendentalism (p. 288) A diverse and loosely defined philosophy that promoted a mystical, intuitive way of looking at life that subordinated facts to feelings. Transcendentalists argued that humans could transcend reason and intellectual capacities by having faith in themselves and in the fundamental benevolence of the universe. They were complete individualists.

Transcontinental Treaty (p. 207) Also called the Adams-Onís Treaty. Ratified in 1821, it acquired Florida and stretched the western boundary of the Louisiana Territory to the Oregon coast.

Treaty of Guadalupe Hidalgo (p. 312) Signed in 1848, this treaty ended the **Mexican War**, forcing that nation to relinquish all of the land north of the Rio Grande and Gila Rivers, including what would eventually become California, in return for monetary compensations.

Treaty of Tordesillas (p. 17) Negotiated by the pope in 1494, this treaty resolved the territorial claims of Spain and Portugal; in the Western Hemisphere Portugal was granted Brazil, while Spain was granted nearly all of the remaining lands.

triangular trade (p. 69) An oversimplified term for the trade among England, its colonies in the Americas, and slave markets in Africa and the Caribbean.

Truman Doctrine (p. 736) A foreign policy, articulated by President Harry Truman in 1947, that provided financial aid to Greek and Turkish governments then under threat by communists rebels.

underground railroad (p. 348) A support system established by antislavery groups in the upper South and the North to help fugitive slaves who had escaped from the South to make their way to Canada.

Underwood Tariff (p. 566) A 1913 reform law that lowered tariff rates and levied the first regular federal income tax.

United Nations (UN) (p. 729) An international organization, founded in 1945, that sought to promote discussion and negotiation and thereby avoid war; it was joined by nearly all nations.

United States v. Richard M. Nixon (p. 784) A Supreme Court ruling (1974) that obliged President Richard Nixon to turn over to the Watergate special prosecutor sixty-four White House audiotapes; these helped prove that Nixon had known about the cover-up of the Watergate burglary.

utopian (p. 278) Any of countless schemes to create a perfect society.

Virginia Plan (p. 148) An initiative, proposed by James Madison of Virginia, calling on the

Constitutional Convention to declare that seats in the federal legislature would be proportionate to a state's population, a concept that caused smaller states to propose a New Jersey plan in which each state would have the same number of representatives. The controversy was resolved in the Great Compromise.

Voting Rights Act of 1965 (p. 769) Federal legislation that empowered federal registrars to intervene when southern states and municipalities refused to let African Americans register to vote.

Wade-Davis bill (p. 412) An 1864 alternative to Lincoln's "**Ten Percent Plan**," this measure required a majority of voters in a southern state to take a loyalty oath in order to begin the process of Reconstruction and guarantee black equality. It also required the repudiation of the Confederate debt. The president exercised a pocket veto, and it never became law.

Wagner Act (p. 688) Officially the National Labor Relations Act and sometimes called Labor's Magna Carta, it gave workers the right to organize and bargain collectively. It also created the National Labor Relations Board to supervise union elections and stop unfair labor practices by employers.

War Hawks (p. 196) Young congressional leaders who in 1811 and 1812 called for war against Great Britain as the only way to defend the national honor.

War Industries Board (WIB) (p. 612) A federal agency, established during World War I, that reorganized industry for maximum efficiency and productivity.

War of 1812 (p. 197) A war fought by the United States and Britain from 1812 to 1815 over British restrictions on American shipping.

war on terror (p. 843) Initially, a worldwide campaign to catch and prosecute those guilty of the September 11, 2001, attacks; as terrorist attacks spread throughout the world, the war became defined far more broadly.

Watergate scandal (p. 782) A complex scandal involving attempts to cover up illegal actions taken by administration officials and leading to the resignation of President Richard Nixon in 1974.

Webster-Ashburton Treaty (p. 301) A treaty between the United States and Britain, signed in 1842, that settled the controversy of the Maine-Canada boundary. The treaty allowed Canada to build a military road from Halifax to Quebec while the United States got most of the disputed territory.

Whigs (p. 264) Originally a reference to British politicians who sought to exclude the Catholic Duke of York from succession to the throne in the 1760s; in the United States after the 1830s, it referred to a political party that opposed the Jacksonian Democrats and favored a strong role for the national government, especially in promoting economic growth.

Whiskey Rebellion (p. 162) A violent protest by western Pennsylvania farmers who refused to pay the whiskey tax proposed by Alexander Hamilton. In 1794, the rebels threatened to destroy Pittsburgh; by the time the Union army had arrived, the rebels had dispersed.

Wilmot Proviso (p. 314) A proposed amendment to an 1846 appropriations bill that banned slavery from any territory the United States might acquire from Spain. It never passed Congress, but generated a great debate on the authority of the federal government to ban slavery from the territories.

woman suffrage (p. 553) The right of women to vote, ensured by the passage and ratification of the Nineteenth Amendment (1920).

Works Progress Administration (WPA) (p. 685) A **New Deal** agency, established in 1935 and run by Harry Hopkins, that spent $11 billion on federal works projects and provided employment for 8.5 million persons.

XYZ Affair (p. 167) A political furor caused by French diplomats who in 1797 demanded a bribe before they would enter into negotiations with their American counterparts; some **Federalists**, furious over this assault on national honor, called for war.

Yalta Conference (p. 730) A wartime conference (February 1945) held in the Russian Crimea, where the **Allies**—Franklin Roosevelt, Winston Churchill (Britain), and Josef Stalin (Soviet Union)—agreed to final plans for the defeat and joint occupation of Germany; it also provided for free elections in Poland, but such elections were never held.

Young America movement (p. 351) The confident enthusiasm, infused with a belief in the nation's "**manifest destiny**," that spread rapidly during the 1850s.

Credits

PROLOGUE 3 Peter Menzel/Photo Researchers, Inc. 5 (left) From Doebley, *J. Plant Cell*, 2005 Nov; 17(11): 2859-72. Courtesy of John Doebley/University of Wisconsin. 5 (right) Waltraund Schneider-Schuetz/Bildarchiv Preussischer Kulturbesitz/Art Resource, NY. 8 Cahokia Mounds State Historic Site, painting by Lloyd K. Townsend. 11 The Granger Collection, New York.

CHAPTER 1 19 Archivo Fotographico Oronoz, Madrid. 21 and 22 (loading horses) Courtesy of The Bancroft Library. University of California, Berkeley. 22–23 All other images © Photos.com. 27 George Gower (1540–96), *Elizabeth I, Armada Portrait*, c.1588 (oil on panel), Gower, George (1540-96) (attr. to)/Woburn Abbey, Bedfordshire, UK/The Bridgeman Art Library. 29 Portrait of Pocahontas, Daughter of Powatan Chief (detail), National Portrait Gallery, Smithsonian Institution/Art Resource, New York. 32 Ernst Wrba/Alamy Images. 41 Benjamin West, *William Penn's Treaty with the Indians* (detail), 1771–1772. Courtesy of the Pennsylvania Academy of the Fine Arts, Philadelphia. Gift of Mrs. Sarah Harrison (The Joseph Harrison, Jr. Collection) (1878.1.10). 43 (left) Samson Productions Pty. Ltd. 43 (right) © Ocean/CORBIS All Rights Reserved. 45 (left) Chas Howson © The British Museum. 45 (right) Oneida Indian Nation.

CHAPTER 2 50 Kevin Moloney/The New York Times/Redux. 56 (top) Werner Forman Archive/Art Resource, N.Y. 56 (bottom) Saul Loeb/AFP Photo/Newscom. 58 Erich Lessing/Art Resource, NY. 62 Abby Aldrich Rockefeller Folk Art Museum, The Colonial Williamsburg Foundation, Williamsburg, VA. 64 The Freake-Gibbs Painter, active 1670. *David, Joanna, and Abigail Mason*, c. 1670, Fine Arts Museum of San Francisco. Gift of Mr. and Mrs. John D. Rockefeller 3rd., 1979.7.3. 67 Museum Purchase, 1978. Peabody Essex Museum, Salem, Massachusetts. 70 *Portrait of an Unidentified Woman* (Formerly Edward Hyde, Viscount Cornbury), 18th century. Collection of The New-York Historical Society, 1952.80. 75 20th Century Fox/Barry Welcher/Album/Newscom.

CHAPTER 3 82 John Greenwood, American, 1727–1792; *Sea Captains Carousing in Surinam*, c. 1752–58; oil on bed ticking; 37 3/4 x 75 in. (95.9 × 190.5 cm); St. Louis Art Museum, Museum Purchase 256:1948. 85 John Wallaston, *Portrait of George Whitefield*, c. 1742. National Portrait Gallery, London. 88 Sonderegger Christof/SuperStock, Inc. 92 *George Washington as Colonel of the Virginia Regiment*, 1772, by Charles Wilson Peale, Washington-Curtis-Lee Collection, Washington and Lee University, Lexington, VA. 97 Getty Images, Inc. – Liaison. 101 The Granger Collection. 105 Courtesy of the Massachusetts Historical Society, Boston. 107 Courtesy of the Library of Congress.

CHAPTER 4 114 Concord Museum, Concord, MA www.concordmuseum.org. 115 Winthrop Chandler, American, *The Battle of Bunker Hill* (detail), c. 1776–1777. Oil on panel, 88.58 × 136.21 cm (34-⅞ × 53-⅝") Museum of Fine Arts, Boston. Gift of Mr. and Mrs. Gardner Richardson, 1982.281. Photograph © 2002 Museum of Fine Arts, Boston. All rights reserved. 122 (top) Emanuel Leutze, *Washington Crossing the Delaware*, 1851 Image © The Metropolitan Museum of Art, New York/Art Resource, NY. 122 (bottom) Getty Images Inc. - Hulton Archive Photos. 128 The Granger Collection, New York. 135 *Abigail Adams*. ca. 1795, Artist Unidentified, H: 30-¼" × W 26-½", N0150.1955. Fenimore Art Museum, Cooperstown, NY. Photograph by Richard Walker. 137 Alex Maclean/Landslides Aerial Photography. 139 (left) William Ranney, *The Battle of Cowpens*. Oil on canvas. Photo by Sam Holland. Courtesy South Carolina State House. 139 (right) Photofest.

CHAPTER 5 145 North Wind Picture Archives. 146 The Granger Collection, New York. 154 North Wind Picture Archives. 155 National Portrait Gallery, Smithsonian Institution/Art Resource, New York. 156 Courtesy of the Library of Congress. 160 Raphaelle Peale, portrait of Absolom Jones, Delaware Art Museum/Gift of Absolom Jones School, The Bridgeman Art Library. 167 CORBIS-NY.

Index

Note: Italicized letters *f*, *m*, and *n* following page numbers indicate figures (photos, illustrations, and graphs), maps, and footnotes, respectively.

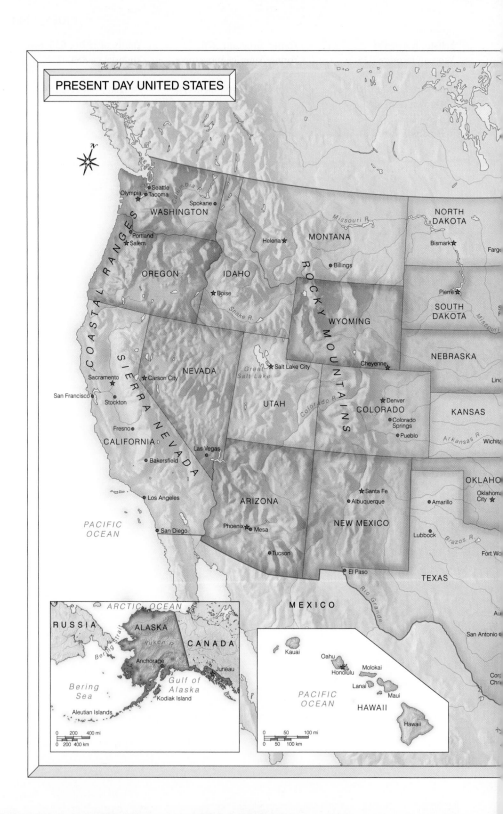

PRESENT DAY UNITED STATES

N

WASHINGTON
Olympia • Seattle
★ • Tacoma
Spokane •

• Portland
★ Salem

OREGON

IDAHO
★ Boise

Snake R.

COASTAL RANGES

SIERRA NEVADA

Sacramento ★
• Carson City
San Francisco •
• Stockton

NEVADA

Fresno •

CALIFORNIA

• Bakersfield

Las Vegas ★

• Los Angeles

• San Diego

PACIFIC
OCEAN

MONTANA
Helena ★

• Billings

Missouri R.

ROCKY MOUNTAINS

WYOMING

Great
Salt Lake
★ Salt Lake City

UTAH

Colorado R.

ARIZONA

Phoenix ★ • Mesa

• Tucson

• El Paso

NORTH
DAKOTA
Bismark ★   Farg

SOUTH
DAKOTA
Pierre ★
                            Missouri R.

Cheyenne
★

NEBRASKA

Linc

★ Denver
COLORADO
• Colorado
  Springs
• Pueblo

KANSAS

Arkansas R.   Wichita

★ Santa Fe
• Albuquerque

NEW MEXICO

Lubbock •

OKLAHO
Oklahoma
City ★

• Amarillo

Brazos R.

Fort Wo

TEXAS

Au

San Antonio •

Corp
Chri

Rio Grande

MEXICO

ALASKA inset

ARCTIC OCEAN

RUSSIA   ALASKA

Bering Strait   CANADA

Yukon R.

Anchorage •

Bering
Sea
                    Gulf of
                    Alaska
                    • Kodiak Island
Aleutian Islands

Juneau •

0   200   400 mi
0   200 400 km

HAWAII inset

Kauai

Oahu
Honolulu ★   Molokai

Lanai   Maui

PACIFIC
OCEAN   HAWAII

Hawaii

0   50   100 mi
0   50 100 km

CANADA

200 mi
400 mi
0 200 400 km

MINNESOTA

Lake Superior

St. Paul ★
Minneapolis ●

WISCONSIN

Madison ★

Milwaukee ●

Lake Michigan

MICHIGAN

Grand
Rapids ●
Lansing ★

Detroit ●

Lake Huron

Lake Ontario

St. Lawrence R.

VERMONT

Montpelier ★

NEW YORK

Albany ★
Syracuse ●

Buffalo ●

Lake Erie

MAINE

Augusta ★

Portland ●

Concord ★

NEW
HAMPSHIRE

Boston ★
Providence ●
Hartford ★

MASSACHUSETTS

RHODE ISLAND
CONNECTICUT

IOWA

Davenport ●

Des Moines ●

Omaha ●

ILLINOIS

Peoria ●

Springfield ★

Chicago ●

Gary ●

INDIANA

Indianapolis ★

OHIO

Toledo ●

Cleveland ●

Columbus ★

Cincinnati ●

WEST
VIRGINIA

Charleston ★

PENNSYLVANIA

Harrisburg ★
Pittsburgh ●
Philadelphia ★

Newark ●
New York City ★
Trenton ★

Baltimore ●
Dover ★
Annapolis ★
Washington D.C. ✿

NEW JERSEY

DELAWARE

MARYLAND

Mississippi R.

Topeka ★

Kansas
City ●

Jefferson
City ★

St. Louis ●

MISSOURI

Louisville ●
Frankfort ★
Lexington ●

KENTUCKY

Ohio R.

Richmond ★

Norfolk ●
Newport News ●

VIRGINIA

A P P A L A C H I A N   M T S.

Tennessee R.

Raleigh ★

NORTH
CAROLINA

Tulsa ●

ARKANSAS

Little
Rock ★

Memphis ●

Nashville ★
Knoxville ●

TENNESSEE

Chattanooga ●
Huntsville ●

Charlotte ●

Columbia ★

SOUTH
CAROLINA

Charleston ●

ATLANTIC
OCEAN

Red R.

Dallas ●

MISSISSIPPI

Jackson ★

Shreveport ●

LOUISIANA

ALABAMA

Birmingham ●

Columbus ●

Montgomery ★

Atlanta ★

GEORGIA

Savannah ●

Mobile ●

Tallahassee ★

FLORIDA

Jacksonville ●

Baton
Rouge ★

Houston ●

New Orleans ●

Brazos R.

Gulf of
Mexico

St. Petersburg ●
Tampa ●

Orlando ●

Fort Lauderdale ●
Miami ●

Lake
Okeechobee

BAHAMAS

Key West ●

Straits of Florida

CUBA

ATLANTIC OCEAN

San Juan ★

Bayamon ●
Carolina ●

Isla de
Culebra

PUERTO RICO

Ponce ●

Isla de
Vieques

Caribbean
Sea

0   40 mi
0 20 40 km

— National boundary
— State boundary
✿ National capital
★ State capital
● Other city

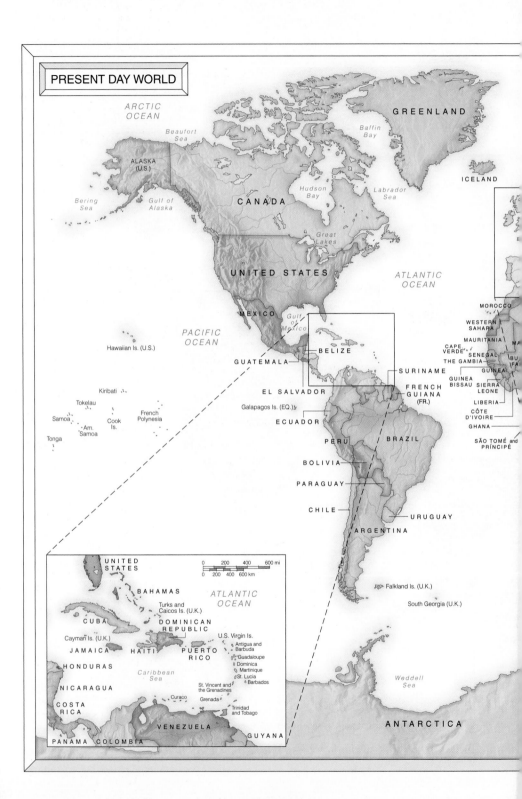

PRESENT DAY WORLD

ARCTIC OCEAN

GREENLAND

Beaufort Sea

Baffin Bay

ALASKA (U.S.)

ICELAND

Bering Sea

Gulf of Alaska

Hudson Bay

Labrador Sea

CANADA

Great Lakes

ATLANTIC OCEAN

MOROCCO

UNITED STATES

WESTERN SAHARA

MEXICO

Gulf of Mexico

MAURITANIA

PACIFIC OCEAN

CAPE VERDE

SENEGAL

THE GAMBIA

BU FA

Hawaiian Is. (U.S.)

BELIZE

SURINAME

GUINEA BISSAU

GUINEA

SIERRA LEONE

GUATEMALA

FRENCH GUIANA (FR.)

LIBERIA

Kiribati

CÔTE D'IVOIRE

Tokelau

EL SALVADOR

French Polynesia

Galapagos Is. (EQ.)

GHANA

Samoa

Cook Is.

ECUADOR

SÃO TOMÉ AND PRÍNCIPE

Am. Samoa

Tonga

PERU

BRAZIL

BOLIVIA

PARAGUAY

CHILE

URUGUAY

ARGENTINA

Falkland Is. (U.K.)

South Georgia (U.K.)

Weddell Sea

ANTARCTICA

UNITED STATES

| 0 | 200 | 400 | 600 mi |
| 0 | 200 | 400 | 600 km |

BAHAMAS

ATLANTIC OCEAN

Turks and Caicos Is. (U.K.)

CUBA

DOMINICAN REPUBLIC

Cayman Is. (U.K.)

U.S. Virgin Is.

JAMAICA

HAITI

PUERTO RICO

Antigua and Barbuda

Guadaloupe

Dominica

HONDURAS

Caribbean Sea

Martinique

St. Lucia

Barbados

NICARAGUA

St. Vincent and the Grenadines

COSTA RICA

Curaço

Grenada

Trinidad and Tobago

VENEZUELA

PANAMA

COLOMBIA

GUYANA

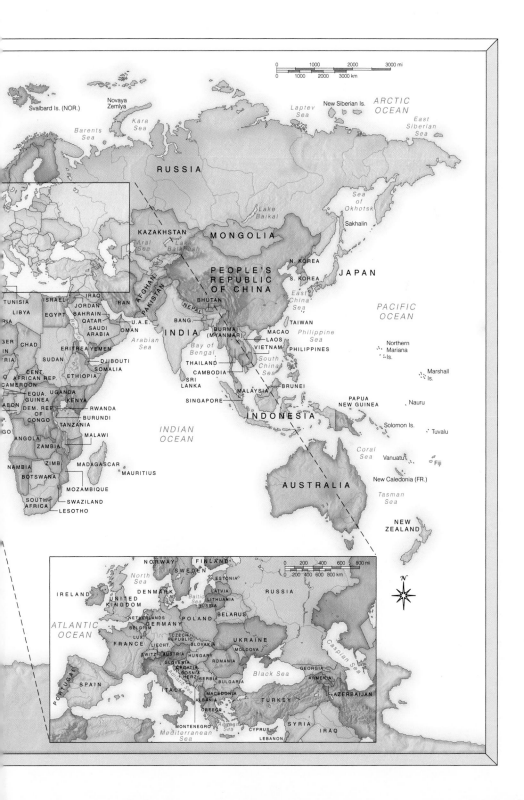

0   1000   2000   3000 mi
0 1000 2000 3000 km

ARCTIC
OCEAN

Svalbard Is. (NOR.)
Novaya
Zemlya
Kara
Sea
Barents
Sea
Laptev
Sea
New Siberian Is.
East
Siberian
Sea

RUSSIA

Sea
of
Okhotsk
Lake
Baikal
Sakhalin

KAZAKHSTAN
Aral
Sea
Lake
Balkhash
MONGOLIA

N. KOREA
S. KOREA
JAPAN

PEOPLE'S
REPUBLIC
OF CHINA

East
China
Sea

PACIFIC
OCEAN

TUNISIA
LIBYA
ISRAEL
IRAQ
JORDAN
IRAN
AFGHAN.
PAKISTAN
NEPAL
BHUTAN
EGYPT
BAHRAIN
QATAR
SAUDI
ARABIA
U.A.E.
OMAN
BANG.
BURMA
(MYANMAR)
TAIWAN
MACAO
Philippine
Sea
Northern
Mariana
Is.

CHAD
ERITREA
YEMEN
Arabian
Sea
INDIA
LAOS
VIETNAM
PHILIPPINES
Marshall
Is.

SUDAN
DJIBOUTI
SOMALIA
Bay of
Bengal
THAILAND
South
China
Sea

CENT.
AFRICAN REP.
CAMEROON
ETHIOPIA
CAMBODIA
SRI
LANKA

EQUA.
GUINEA
UGANDA
KENYA
RWANDA
MALAYSIA
BRUNEI

DEM. REP.
OF
CONGO
BURUNDI
TANZANIA
SINGAPORE
PAPUA
NEW GUINEA
Nauru

ANGOLA
ZAMBIA
MALAWI
INDONESIA
Solomon Is.
Tuvalu

INDIAN
OCEAN

NAMBIA
ZIMB.
BOTSWANA
MADAGASCAR
MAURITIUS
Coral
Sea
Vanuatu
Fiji

MOZAMBIQUE
New Caledonia (FR.)

SOUTH
AFRICA
SWAZILAND
LESOTHO
AUSTRALIA
Tasman
Sea

NEW
ZEALAND

NORWAY
FINLAND
North
Sea
SWEDEN
ESTONIA
LATVIA
RUSSIA

IRELAND
DENMARK
LITHUANIA
Baltic
Sea
RUSSIA
BELARUS

UNITED
KINGDOM
NETHERLANDS
GERMANY
POLAND
UKRAINE

ATLANTIC
OCEAN
BELGIUM
LUX.
LIECHT.
CZECH
REPUBLIC
SLOVAKIA
MOLDOVA

FRANCE
SWITZ.
AUSTRIA
HUNGARY
ROMANIA

SLOVENIA
CROATIA
GEORGIA
ARMENIA

BOSNIA
HERZ.
SERBIA
BULGARIA
Black Sea
Caspian
Sea

SPAIN
PORTUGAL
ITALY
MACEDONIA
ALBANIA
GREECE
TURKEY
AZERBAIJAN

MONTENEGRO
Aegean
Sea
CYPRUS
SYRIA
IRAQ

Mediterranean
Sea
LEBANON

0   200   400   600   800 mi
0 200 400 600 800 km

N